W9-ANF-441

Racial & Ethnic Relations in America

Second Edition

Racial & Ethnic Relations in America

Second Edition

Volume 2

Editors

Kibibi Mack-Shelton, PhD
Michael Shally-Jensen, PhD

SALEM PRESS

A Division of EBSCO Information Services
Ipswich, Massachusetts

GREY HOUSE PUBLISHING

Copyright ©2017, by Salem Press, A Division of EBSCO Information Services, Inc., and Grey House Publishing, Inc.

All rights reserved. No part of this work may be used or reproduced in any manner whatsoever or transmitted in any form or by any means, electronic or mechanical, including photocopy, recording, or any information storage and retrieval system, without written permission from the copyright owner. For permissions requests, contact proprietarypublishing@ebsco.com.

∞ The paper used in these volumes conforms to the American National Standard for Permanence of Paper for Printed Library Materials, Z39.48 1992 (R2009).

Publisher's Cataloging-In-Publication Data
(Prepared by The Donohue Group, Inc.)

Names: Mack-Williams, Kibibi, 1955- editor. | Shally-Jensen, Michael, editor.
Title: Racial & ethnic relations in America / editors, Kibibi Mack-Shelton, PhD, Michael Shally-Jensen, PhD.
Other Titles: Racial and ethnic relations in America
Description: Second edition. | Ipswich, Massachusetts : Salem Press, a division of EBSCO Information Services; [Amenia, New York] : Grey House Publishing, [2017] | First edition published in 2000. | Includes bibliographical references and index.
Identifiers: ISBN 978-1-68217-315-2 (set) | ISBN 978-1-68217-317-6 (v. 1) | ISBN 978-1-68217-318-3 (v. 2) | ISBN 978-1-68217-319-0 (v. 3)
Subjects: LCSH: North America—Ethnic relations—Encyclopedias. | North America—Race relations—Encyclopedias. | Minorities—North America—Encyclopedias.
Classification: LCC E49.R33 2017 | DDC 305.8/0097—dc23

PRINTED IN THE UNITED STATES OF AMERICA

CONTENTS

Volume 2

COMPLETE LIST OF CONTENTS

Volume 1

Volume 2

Volume 3

E

ETHNIC HERITAGE REVIVAL

Beginning in the 1960s, a resurgence of interest in ethnic identity, ancestry, and cultural heritage occurred among many Americans who were of European descent. Among the manifestations of this revival was a renewed interest in ethnic literature, music, art, folklore, and cuisine. Ethnic festivals, genealogical pursuits, and travel to ancestral homelands all signaled an increased awareness of ethnic identity. Although some people saw this as an indication of the persistence of ethnicity as a powerful element of individual self-identity, others pointed out the limitations to the revival. A minority of ethnic groups were actually involved in revival activities, and a revitalization of ethnic communities and institutions did not occur. Ancestral language loyalty similarly declined. People picked and chose the cultural values from their heritage to embrace, in general, selecting those that did not conflict with mainstream American values. Finally, intermarriage rates grew dramatically, complicating the ethnic identities of families. Nevertheless, for those involved in the ethnic revival, it marked an important way in which assimilated European Americans could continue to maintain a nostalgic attachment to the folkways and mores of their ancestors. Even today, there continue to be annual celebrations and marches devoted to particular ethnic minority communities and their contribution to American society.

——*Peter Kivisto*

Mid-Autumn Festival at the Botanical Garden, Montreal. By Tango7174.

ETHNIC IDENTITIES OF WOMEN

Ethnic identity is often omitted from studies of women and women's issues in the United States and Canada. History, however, shows that women have not always identified themselves as members of one particular group. Ethnicity has played a large role in women's social and political activities, in their economic activities, and in their domestic household activities. Ethnic group identification has been found to divide and bring women together depending on the issues and environment. The status of women and their activities

457

on behalf of women can effectively be understood within the context of the general social and political history of which they are a part, especially their cultural and ethnic backgrounds. Ethnic identity for women is their individual identity; the part that is female cannot be separated from women's ethnicity.

RESURGENCE OF ETHNICITY

Ethnicity is a complex concept based roughly on common or shared cultural properties, such as language, descent, and religion. Ethnic identity requires defining oneself according to notions of shared culture and focusing on the cultural uniqueness of a particular group. Various interpretations exist of why ethnicity persists and why it slowly diminishes. Until the ethnic violence shook Eastern Europe and Africa in the late 1980s and early 1990s, ethnicity was held by many theorists to be slowly disappearing with modernization and technological advancement. This view was held especially in modern countries such as the United States and Canada. Thus arose the problem of whether to place one's loyalty with one's ethnic group or with one's nation-state. Women faced the additional option of placing their sense of womanhood over loyalty to the ethnic group or nation-state. Since ethnicity became recognized as a factor in US and Canadian societies, theorists found that it develops for self-interested reasons, such as gaining some type of economically based rewards from the political system. The basis for this position is that in competitive societies, one of the best ways to compete successfully is to organize. Organizing around ethnic groups can be effective. The tremendous increase in immigrants to the United States and Canada, many of whom were more resistant to change and assimilation than were earlier immigrants, also led to a renewed focus on ethnicity.

ETHNIC V. GENDER IDENTITY

When women organize along gender lines, it is often within the context of the cultural and political conditions in which they live. Gender, social class membership, age, and other criteria can vary from ethnic group to ethnic group. One group may fit well into modern Western society, whereas another ethnic group living in the same society will experience adjustment problems. Some ethnic groups may refuse attempts at adjustment to modernism and hold to traditionalism. This variance means that ethnicity can be a problem for women because,

often, traditional cultural values of an ethnic group that define roles for women can conflict with overall societal values. In other situations, traditional values of an ethnic group can be advantageous to women dealing with real and perceived threats and roadblocks in contemporary US or Canadian society. An increase in women's awareness of their ethnicity occurred alongside increased attention to women's issues. The result has been renewed recognition of an interwoven relationship, with both positive and negative characteristics between ethnic identity and women's issues.

To place a priority on women's issues as one form of identity while minimizing another form of identity, such as ethnicity, results in incomplete analysis. Prior to the post-World War II period, ethnicity was largely associated with immigrants and any group unidentifiable as Northern European or British. The dawning of the twentieth century, for example, found women and African Americans without the right to vote, but the status of African American women was misinterpreted by white women in several of the political organizations to which they belonged. African American women were not regarded as true woman suffragists by white-dominated organizations because they practiced political action on the basis of race and gender rather than gender alone. Separation in American society of women's issues and ethnicity created gender divisions of labor and assigned particular significance regarding race and ethnicity to occupational and socioeconomic standing that was typically less favorable. For example, ethnic groups were among the lower working class, whereas members of the dominant nonethnic society occupied the upper and more desirable classes. Hence, studies of race and ethnicity often leave out issues specific to women, and studies of women deemphasize race and ethnicity. It is apparent that ethnicity and women's issues coalesce at some points. For example, it can be claimed that women and racial minorities occupy subordinate places in society; both are underrepresented in high-level occupations, and both earn lower average incomes than white men.

Inserting women's issues into the rubric of ethnic group membership is difficult in nationalistic societies such as the United States and Canada, where being American or Canadian involves a mix of several ethnic groups. There is also a tendency in these societies to be secular, while a large percentage of ethnic groups have strong religious bases. For example, an Italian American woman may encounter a conflict between Catholicism and her position on abortion. Ethnicity often infers linkages to a homeland far from US and Canadian societies. In this instance, native cultural practices may persist within Western modernization through the maintenance of cultural enclaves such as Chinatown, Little Italy, and Germantown. Women who maintain close links to their respective ethnic groups often live in two different worlds. The preservation of access to membership in the group, such as knowledge of rituals and traditions, is an important function of any ethnic group, and anyone involved in these groups must know them.

WOMEN AS CULTURE CARRIERS

One of the key means of controlling ethnic group membership is through socialization of the young. One significant role for women is guiding the young into adulthood. This is especially the case in groups in which religion is a major factor in the community. As carriers of culture, women are crucial to communities. In the course of her work on the life histories of Italian American families in Northern California, Micaela di Leonardo introduced the idea of the "work of kinship," defined as the conception, maintenance, and ritual celebration of cross household kin ties, including visits, letters, telephone calls, presents, and cards to kin; the organization of holiday gatherings; the creation and maintenance of quasi-kin relations; the decision to neglect or to intensify particular ties; the mental work of reflection about all these activities; and the creation and communication of altering images of family and kin in relation to the images of others, both folk and mass media. She found that over time, women developed greater knowledge of their husbands' kin than their husbands had.

On the basis of Leonardo's review of other research, kin-work is not nearly as much an ethnic, racial, or class phenomenon as it is a gender phenomenon. She found gender-based division of labor across ethnic, racial, and class groups. To the degree that the daily behavioral expression of community membership is embedded in how one eats, dresses, and uses household space and is woven through activities that span a lifetime (for example, family-based celebrations such as family reunions), women's kin-work translates also as culture work. This critical women's role partly explains why women take on such importance in defining the ethnic community and what it stands for. Women are valuable

community possessions as the principal vehicle for transmitting values from one generation to another. Many ethnic communities regard women as particularly vulnerable to defilement and exploitation by negative outside forces, and many see women as being especially susceptible to assimilation and influence by outsiders. This is one cause of the oppression ethnic women often feel. For example, an ethnic family may feel particularly threatened when a female relative leaves the house in nontraditional clothing.

Additionally, the historically symbolic role of women in the politics of cultural relations has shaped cultural expressions. As women have played important roles in the family and ethnic community through their activities as wives, mothers, and homemakers, they have also played important roles in intercultural relations through other women-based roles as teachers, missionaries, and social workers. For example, women in the Northeast region of the United States went to the Southern and Western United States to teach, civilize, Americanize, and ultimately culturally transform ethnic-based Latino, African American, American Indian, and European settler communities of the nineteenth century into culturally assimilated members of the nation.

Interpreters of women's relationships within ethnic groups have a difficult task because men tend to construct ethnic identity. Women and men come together in the family structure when competing identities, such as between male and female, could lead to disagreements. In such situations, preference usually goes to the ethnic affiliations of the male partner. Because ethnic groups often identify with physical markers, such as clothing, hairstyles, or body alterations, individuals can be identified with regard to both gender and ethnicity in the way they dress. In the area of dress and style, women and men are treated differently. For example, women are encouraged to wear traditional types of dress, whereas men can easily move from one type of dress (Western) to another (traditional).

GENDER AND RACE

Gender and ethnic terms can influence the construction of each other. "Ethnic" does not have to mean race, and race is only a partial basis for determining ethnic identity. Race is one way in which gender and ethnicity merge when women use racial metaphors to illustrate real and perceived discrimination against women. For women, especially feminists, the gendered construction of racism serves as an excellent vehicle for faulting a male system in which women are oppressed. The experiences of European immigrant women, especially Italians and Jews, illustrate that numerous examples of discrimination can be drawn from other ethnic groups. Despite this, race is usually treated as a secondary factor in social organization, and ethnicity is a distant third factor. Much of the feminists' perspective and activity has focused on the sexist behavior of men rather than on the positives and negatives of ethnic identification.

Part of the answer to the construction of whiteness can be traced to the cultural symbolism of European women that is rooted in a system based on good and bad, or Madonna and Magdalena symbolism. Interpretations that began to appear at the end of the eighteenth century identified particular personality traits with particular classes or races of women. Leonore Davidoff argued that the material division of household tasks in the nineteenth century caused good and bad aspects of women to be linked to socially distinct groups of women. The mistress no longer did heavy labor; all dirty, arduous physical labor was now performed by the domestic, whose stigmatizing labor accorded with her inferior character and her working-class status. Good women were wives, mothers, and spinsters, and bad women were prostitutes, laborers, and single mothers. The dual symbolism of good/bad was usually connected with race and class, but it could be used to chastise any woman moving out of her assigned place.

Women active in women's issues who are members of ethnic minorities experience conditions that are distinct from those of white feminists. The development of ethnic minority feminism and the relationships among minority feminists, white feminists, and feminists of other racial and ethnic groups are shaped by experiences in their respective communities. Unlike their white counterparts, minority women (or ethnic groups in general) face a different type of division in their construction of identity. Because of the emphasis on traditions in many ethnic groups in America, they are usually divided along lines of obedience versus independence, collective (or familial) versus individual interest, and self-control versus self-expression or spontaneity. These divisions are more complex and difficult to deal with than the good versus bad division.

African American, Asian American, and Latina female activists are aware that social inequality for women of color is two-sided. On one side, the struggle is to gain equality in male-dominated ethnic enclaves or communities; on the other side, the struggle is for equality for women in society as a whole. Among minority women, women's issues involve more than gender because, as minority women, they are affected by both ethnic identification and nationalist ideology in their everyday lives. Minority women's emphasis on ethnic pride and difficulties within a white-dominated society has provided significant political direction to the movement in addressing women's issues within ethnic communities.

WOMEN'S MOVEMENT AND ETHNICITY

Ethnicity creates important economic, ideological, and experiential divisions among women. These lead to differences in perception of identity and its place in society for women while at the same time, the communality of womanhood may cut across ethnic lines and provide the conditions for shared understanding. Women developed concepts around women's issues that fostered unity. One example of this is the concept of sisterhood; it has been an important unifying force in the contemporary women's movement and one with the ability to overcome ethnic differences. By stressing the similarities of women's secondary social and economic positions in all societies and in the family, the sisterhood concept is useful in the movement against sexism. Yet, sisterhood has engaged only a small segment of the female population in the United States. African American, American Indian, and Latina women are seldom involved in feminist activities. In Canada, various feminist and other women's organizations have cooperated on specific projects even though they have had different ideological perspectives. For example, an active feminist group may have interest in a child care and education project, which puts them in working contact with more moderate women's groups advancing the same issues. On the intellectual level, socialist feminist theory finds the concept of sisterhood to be apolitical and lacking in class analysis. The problem has to do with perceptions that the women's movement is an upper- and middle-class movement. Supporters of sisterhood stress the sense of being part of a collective movement toward a fairer and more equal society. Regardless of these varying positions, sisterhood has shown an ability to unify women beyond ethnic identifications.

The women's movements in the United States and Canada arose within nationalist and cultural movements. In the United States, for example, the experience white women gained from participating in the civil rights movement gave them the opportunity to become involved with civil rights groups in which the decision making was shared by men and women alike. During the later part of the movement (after 1965), African American men began to exercise more control in organizations, such as the Student Nonviolent Coordinating Committee (SNCC) and the Southern Christian Leadership Conferences (SCLC); they effectively isolated the women, especially the white women. Many of the original organizers of women's groups were women who gained their experience in the civil rights struggle in the South. A similar situation occurred with respect to the woman suffrage movement and other political activities for women's rights in pre-1919 United States, in which many of the politically active white women evolved out of antislavery groups. In the United States, the ethnic division appeared along racial lines.

In Canada, some ethnic tensions were clearly present in the woman suffrage movement. For example, in 1906, non-British suffragists rejected the tactics of the British suffragists as being "unwomanly." The year 1902 witnessed a conflict over ideological differences in New Brunswick between the Women's Enfranchisement Association and the Saint John Local Council of Women. Ethnic differences created a threat to cooperation among women. After 1896, substantial numbers of immigrants who were not Anglo-Saxon pushed antiethnic feelings to higher levels. The Anglo-Saxon membership of the majority of Canadian women's reform organizations did not include women of other ethnic groups. The women in these organizations identified, and consequently organized, with their own cultural or ethnic groups. For example, African Canadian women in Montreal began to meet in 1900, which constituted the first organized black women's group in that city. Canadian women's labor groups organized along Finnish, Jewish, and Ukrainian lines.

The US and Canadian examples of cooperation, conflict, and exclusion illustrate the greater degree of ethnic divisions within the Canadian women's movement as compared with that in the United States.

They also illustrate how women's individual identity *as* women—subjected to societal elements that affect them both as women and as members of particular religious, ethnic, or other cultural groups—can create a dilemma. It appears that when women organized from the nineteenth century to the present, they did so within the context of their contemporary cultural and political conditions.

Language is another factor affecting the acculturation and political participation of women on a nonethnic basis. Language barriers limit the extent to which women from some ethnic groups can express themselves. These barriers in turn limit their accessibility to different types of information and to women's groups that may be working on issues that positively affect them. An example of this problem can be drawn from the situation in the United States in which Chicanas often organized in isolation from mainstream feminist groups because of language differences. Language is a major problem, but cultural interpretations of womanhood also play a role in the cooperative political participation among these groups. For Europeans, the ethnic factors that brought a particular group together actually eased the task of and facilitated the process of assimilation.

ETHNICITY IN CANADA

Because of significant differences between US and Canadian experiences with women and ethnic identity, the Canadian situation merits particular attention. One of the major turning points for women in Canada occurred during World War I, with the achievement of woman suffrage. Another turning point occurred during World War II, when large numbers of married women entered the labor force. For Canadian women, ethnicity created numerous inequities. Industrial development in the late 1800s was predicated on cheap labor; thousands of immigrants, especially those from non-English-speaking countries, paid a high price for their entry into Canada by being channeled into low-paying and unsafe working conditions.

Early demographics found that Canadians of British origin decreased from 60 percent of the population in 1871 to 55 percent in 1921, and those of French origin from 31 percent to 28 percent. In terms of gender, when men began heading to the prairies and the Northwest Territories seeking economic opportunities between 1851 and 1891, women of marriageable age outnumbered men in the same age range in the original British North American provinces. Conversely, the 1881 and 1891 censuses revealed that men significantly outnumbered women in Manitoba and British Columbia. In either case, women faced a certain amount of isolation, but more so in the new settlements. Many women dealt with their isolation through maintaining links with friends and family left behind and by creating new links with women in their new communities. This proved to be much easier with those of the same ethnic origin.

In the early years of Canadian development, women supported the preservation of ethnic cultures. A negative aspect of these women's work involved certain restrictions they erected to prevent those who did not conform or belong to their ethnic group. Similar to particular circumstances in the United States, these women touted the superiority of their culture over other cultures. Mixed-blood women were also subjected to discrimination from English-speaking settlers in the West.

Ethnic organizing in Canada continued through the 1920s and 1930s. The organizational strategy of Jewish women, mainly of Western European origins, who worked together to form the National Council of Jewish Women, is illustrative of ethnic activity among women. Through vehicles such as fundraising and volunteer work, this council supported schools, orphanages, and summer camps and cared for senior citizens. This also illustrates that, like women in the United States, they were responsible for ethnic culture well into the future. By the 1970s, some feminists, including Jewish feminists, fought to remain within the religious community while working for change from within. Work remains for Canadian women in dealing with ethnic, cultural, and gender biases.

Organizing around ethnic identity, aboriginal women initiated social and political activities. These women redefined themselves in a way that incorporated their traditions. Iroquois women accepted that Indian women were originally active participants in policy-making decisions and should therefore assume that role in contemporary Canada. The main conflict has been between traditional means of policymaking and modern/Western methods. To take the Western route is to deny the cultural roots of the group in favor of what appears to be acceptance of white government. Without giving up their ethnic identification, Indian women formed socially and politically

active groups that existed in many instances outside the cultural confines of their ethnic group and inside the Western political arena. Multiethnic cooperation also existed, as exemplified by the Ontario Native Women's Association, founded in 1972, which includes mixed-blood Indian women. Indian women also organized to deal with serious social problems, such as alcoholism and an educational system that does not include Indian traditions in its curriculum.

ETHNIC BOUNDARIES AND ETHNIC IDENTITY
This discussion has illustrated both the loose and tight boundaries of ethnicity and how these boundaries can be manipulated for political purposes. Ethnic boundaries can also be manipulated for personal purposes because, unlike territorial boundaries, they are social. They do not isolate groups entirely from one another; rather, there is a continuous flow of interaction and sometimes people across them. For example, Shirlee Taylor Haizlip told how, prior to the civil rights movement of the 1960s, her mother, one of several children of mixed racial descent, was the only one to retain her African American identity. Since the movement, more individuals have accepted their ethnic heritage. It appears that maintaining an ethnic identity is not incompatible with simultaneous identification with a nationalist group, such as Canada and the United States.

Ethnic identity has been identified as an important part of women and women's issues. Women are found to transcend their ethnicity at critical junctures and to organize into collectives. Although some problems exist between women of different ethnic groups, there are also instances in which women cooperate strictly along gender lines. One highly visible problem is the persistence of tradition among some ethnic groups. Tradition may dictate that women are forbidden to organize or devote much time to anything other than advancing the culture by nurturing and socializing the children. It is becoming difficult, however, to remain rooted in any ethnic tradition in the United States and Canada, primarily because of communication technologies and frequent encounters among group members in the marketplace. In addition, women in these countries have historically shown that they are more likely than their male counterparts to bridge the ethnic gap and work together. This is one indication that ethnicity and women's issues are not incompatible. In fact, a primary concern for both minorities and women is pay equality. A study by the American Association of University Women (AAUW) found that women in general earn significantly less than white men, and the differences are most glaring among ethnic minorities. For example, white women earn 78 percent of what white men earn, while Hispanic women earn only 53 percent of what white men do (and 89 percent of what Hispanic men do). The difference is equally glaring when comparing African American women with white men.

——Gregory Freeland

BIBLIOGRAPHY AND FURTHER READING

Brown, Nadia E., and Sarah Allen Gershon, eds. *Distinct Identities: Minority Women in US Politics.* New York: Routledge, 2016. Print.

Driedger, Leo, ed. *Multi-ethnic Canada: Identities and Inequalities.* Toronto: Oxford UP, 1996. Print.

Epp, Marlene, and Franca Iocovetta, eds. *Sisters or Strangers: Immigrant, Ethnic, and Racialized Women in Canadian History.* Toronto: U of Toronto P, 2016. Print.

Haizlip, Shirlee Taylor. *The Sweeter the Juice.* New York: Simon, 1994. Print.

"How Does Race Affect the Gender Wage Gap?" AAUW. Amer. Assoc. of Univ. Women, 3 Apr. 2014. Web. 30 Apr. 2015.

Waters, Mary C. *Ethnic Options: Choosing Identities in America.* Berkeley: U of California P, 1990. Print.

Winters, Loretta I., Herman L. DeBose, eds. *New Faces in a Changing America: Multiracial Identity in the 21st Century.* Thousand Oaks: Sage, 2003. Print.

ETHNIC IDENTITY: CHOICE AND DEVELOPMENT

The United States is not a static society in which ethnic identities remain the same. Some ethnic groups and some people within certain ethnic groups have opted for new ethnic classifications. Some people receive new ethnic labels regardless of whether they want them. There are two reason for this relabeling. First, the United States and similar pluralistic countries such as Canada have increased their populations by accepting immigrants from a vast variety of cultures and nations. As these immigrants succeeded financially, politically, and socially in the receiving country, their cultures were changed or they attempted to change their group or personal cultures. Cultural change meant ethnic identity changes. Second, the mythology regarding the characteristics of a stereotypical American persuaded many immigrants to opt for cultural characteristics that reflected this myth. The myth was largely formed about English-oriented cultural traits or what is colloquially called Anglo culture. Immigrants have perceived that there are advantages to being as American or Anglo as culturally possible. This is called the Anglo-conformity model, in which people and groups are subtly encouraged to accept these characteristics if they want economic, social, and political success. Two groups from two different racial identifications are examples of these options for ethnic identity.

The massive waves of Irish immigrants to the United States in the nineteenth century resulted in widespread discrimination against them. However, the Irish had several advantages: They were needed for manual labor; they were Catholic but had a strong sense of separation of church and state; and they formed influential institutions, such as political organizations, that helped make them social powers in the larger society. They were also white. Increasingly, the Irish in the United States married non-Irish, so that by the 1960s, more than half of Irish American men married women from other ethnic groups. By the 1990s, it was difficult for census workers to determine who could be categorized as Irish because so many Irish Americans considered themselves to be fully American and to have the same cultural characteristics as English Americans. They had risen socioeconomically from what had been termed "shanty Irish" to "lace-curtain Irish" seeking social acceptance, and then to Americans whose original characteristics had been superseded by conforming to Anglo models. They had opted for a differing ethnic identity.

A second example of ethnic options is taken by many Afro-Caribbean immigrants to the United States. Those from English-speaking nations often conform culturally to the American myth of the United States being a land of unusual opportunity if one is educated properly and willing to work diligently. These immigrants may perceive African Americans as rejecting this opportunity and may attempt to distance themselves from black Americans and not want to be perceived as being similar to them. They may even reject the idea of race, claiming that national ethnic characteristics are a person's identity rather than physical traits associated with race. Black Caribbean immigrants interpret this distance as an advantage to them. They do not always choose to associate with the oppressed history of African Americans, their culture, or their racial self-identification. Instead, they opt to identify as Jamaican Americans or Bahamian Americans or others who share English or Anglo values and who expect to succeed in the receiving country without being racially stereotyped. Afro-Caribbeans have often achieved a higher social status than African Americans with educational levels and family income levels surpassing those of African Americans in many cities. By distinguishing their ethnicities from the African American ethnicity, they may negotiate better social statuses in a white-dominated society.

——*William Osborne and Max Orezzoli*

Bibliography and Further Reading

Citrin, Jack, and David O. Sears. *American Identity and the Politics of Multiculturalism.* New York: Cambridge UP, 2014. Print.

Roediger, David R. *Working toward Whiteness: How America's Immigrants Became White; The Strange Journey from Ellis Island to the Suburbs.* New York: Basic, 2005. Print.

Shaw-Taylor, Yoku, and Steven A. Tuch, eds. *The Other African Americans: Contemporary African and Caribbean Families in the United States.* Lanham: Rowman, 2007. Print.

Spickard, Paul, and W. Jeffrey Burroughs, eds. *We Are a People: Narrative and Multiplicity in Constructing Ethnic Identity.* Philadelphia: Temple UP, 2000. Print.

Soong, Miri. *Choosing Ethnic Identities.* Malden: Blackwell, 2003. Print.

Waters, Mary C. *Ethnic Options: Choosing Identities in America.* Berkeley: U of California P, 1990. Print.

Ethnic studies programs

Ethnic studies programs are courses of study devoted to the history and culture of various ethnic groups. They are valuable for members of the ethnic group that is being studied and also for members of other ethnic or racial groups. Members of groups that are the focus of ethnic studies programs develop a sense of belonging from learning about their group's cultural history. They also develop a sense of pride and self-esteem from learning about the contributions that members of their group have made to society. When people study the achievements and histories of groups other than their own, they develop an appreciation of the contributions that all groups have made to the development of the United States and Canada. By helping students understand that every group has made its contribution to American history, ethnic studies programs can help eliminate prejudices and racial conflicts.

History

The first fully developed ethnic studies programs were black studies programs that American colleges and universities began to offer in the late 1960s and early 1970s. The first college to offer black studies courses was Merritt Junior College in Oakland, California. Courses were set up after Huey P. Newton and other members of the Black Panther Party, who were students at the college, agitated for their establishment. The first fully developed program in black studies was offered by San Francisco State University very soon after a coalition of African American students took over campus buildings in 1967 and demanded, among other things, a black studies program, dormitories for black students, and admission policies that included an affirmative action philosophy.

After the takeover of San Francisco State University, black student groups all across the United States staged demonstrations and takeovers, including a particularly hostile one at Columbia University, demanding black studies programs and other concessions that would recognize the special culture of African Americans. Larger universities such as Harvard developed black studies majors that generally included courses dealing with the history and cultures of Africa and the African American experience, including African American history, African American literature, and sociological, psychological, and economic issues related to African Americans. Even colleges and universities that could not offer fully developed black studies programs attempted to accommodate African American students by offering courses in African American history and African American literature. Enrollment in these courses was not confined to African American students. Students of other races were very interested in finding out about the African American experience.

In the early 1970s, other ethnic groups, influenced generally by certain social trends of the 1960s, the civil rights movement, the women's movement, and various student uprisings, began to demand recognition of their cultural values and of their members' contributions to the American experience. Such organizations as the American Indian Movement agitated for Native American control of their children's education and for an opportunity for young Native Americans to study their culture. When federal legislation established tribal colleges on many Indian reservations in the 1970s and early 1980s, Native American studies became the topic of some of the courses taught at these colleges. All aspects of Native American culture, including history, literature, art, music, and spiritual beliefs, were part of the curriculum. In addition to the tribal colleges, other colleges and universities, particularly those situated in states with large numbers of Native Americans, began to offer courses that explored Native American history and culture.

In the 1970s, universities, particularly in California and Texas, where there are large numbers of Mexican immigrants and Mexican Americans, began to offer courses in Chicano (Mexican American) studies, usually concentrating on Mexican American history and literature. Many universities also began offering courses in Asian American history and literature.

Women's studies programs center around the issue of gender rather than ethnicity, so they cannot be truly classified as ethnic studies programs. However, some researchers have suggested that women constitute a special cultural group. Many of the women's studies programs in the 1970s were modeled on ethnic studies programs and shared similar goals of promoting understanding and increasing self-respect. Feminists believed that such programs would enhance young women's self-esteem and feelings of self-worth and that women would derive more respect from society if their contributions became well known. Women's studies programs had curriculum elements similar to those found in ethnic studies programs—history, literature, psychology, sociology, and economic issues related to women.

By the late 1980s, the number of ethnic studies courses offered by American colleges and universities had dropped since their peak in the late 1970s. Most major colleges and universities still offered many courses that related to the experiences of most major ethnic groups, particularly history and literature courses; however, these courses no longer were designed to teach members of ethnic groups about their own culture and history (the original reason given for black studies courses) but rather to acquaint the general student body with the history and culture of the ethnic group under study.

IMPACT ON AMERICAN CULTURE

By the early 1980s, the United States was no longer regarded as a "melting pot" in which members of various cultural groups would assimilate and adopt the values and customs of the Euro-American majority. Instead, the nation was viewed as a culture more appropriately described by terms such as "salad bowl" or "stew pot" in that members of diverse cultural groups maintained many aspects of their culture and lived for the most part in harmony with members of the majority culture. All Americans were expected to attempt to understand and respect the contributions that members of other ethnic and racial groups had made to develop, support, and sustain the nation. Ethnic studies courses contributed to these changes in the philosophical basis of American society.

Ethnic studies programs not only affected those who took these courses in colleges and universities but also changed the curriculum offered to public school students. Public schools, in the late 1970s and 1980s, began to accept the philosophical tenets of ethnic studies programs: that members of all ethnic groups should be exposed to their own history and heritage and that the history and heritage of all ethnic groups is that of the United States. Additionally, these beliefs suggested that every American needs to know and understand the history and heritage of all groups so that all citizens will have a complete understanding of the nation's culture and history.

Multiculturalism became an essential part of the curricula of public schools. By the end of the twentieth century, public school curricula all across the United States had incorporated multicultural elements. For example, literature courses used anthologies that contained writers who spoke in many different voices, not just Euro-American male writers. History courses attempted to chronicle the contributions of all of the nation's people, not just its white majority.

ADVANTAGES AND CONCERNS

In addition to teaching ethnic and racial minorities about their cultural heritage, these programs often make minority students feel more comfortable on college and university campuses because they increase the likelihood that administrators, professors, and other students will respect their ethnic roots. The programs can serve to ease tensions on campuses as they contribute to overall understandings of various groups' contributions to society.

Some scholars express concern about ethnic studies programs because they believe these programs contribute to a fragmentation of certain disciplines. For example, some feel that the study of US history is too fragmented when divided into African American, Asian American, Native American, and Latino history. Other scholars have expressed

concern that ethnic studies textbooks attempt to rewrite history, giving certain ethnic groups a predominant role in particular historical or cultural events, when, in fact, the group played only a minor role. In highlighting the contributions of all ethnic groups, these scholars argue, historical facts should not be negated or distorted.

In the 1990s the field was impacted by newer approaches, such as postmodern philosophical thinking as applied to ethnic studies issues and debates. Something of a split began to emerge between the "old guard" of the discipline and the new generation. The National Association of Ethnic Studies, founded in 1972, continued to represent most scholars and to evolve with the field. Nevertheless, in 2011 a new professional group was founded, the Critical Ethnic Studies Association, to represent the interests of those looking for intersections with other disciplines and a more critical approach generally.

——*Annita Marie Ward, updated by Michael Shally-Jensen*

BIBLIOGRAPHY AND FURTHER READING

Banks, James A. *Teaching Strategies for Ethnic Studies,* 7th ed. Boston: Allyn and Bacon, 2003. Print.

Critical Ethnic Studies Editorial Collective, ed. *Critical Ethnic Studies: A Reader.* Durham: Duke UP, 2016. Print.

Sandoval, Denise M., et al., eds. *"White" Washing American Education: The New Culture Wars in Ethnic Studies.* Santa Barbara: Praeger, 2016. Print.

Yang, Philip Q. *Ethnic Studies: Issues and Approaches.* New York: State UP of New York, 2000. Print.

ETHNICITY AND ETHNIC GROUPS

Despite the considerable amount of attention devoted to the subject, scholars have not reached a consensus on the precise meaning of ethnicity. Since ethnicity is such a complex concept, many scholars have chosen to identify ethnic groups as those groups characterized by some of the following fourteen features: common geographic origins; migratory status; race; language or dialect; religious faith or faiths; ties that transcend kinship, neighborhood, and

community boundaries; shared traditions, values, and symbols; literature, folklore, and music; food preferences; settlement and employment patterns; special interests in regard to politics; institutions that specifically serve and maintain the group; an internal sense of distinctiveness; and an external perception of distinctiveness.

Sociologist Milton Yinger defines an ethnic group as one whose members are thought by themselves and others to have a common origin and who share a common culture that is transmitted through shared activities that reinforce the group's distinctiveness. The term "ethnic group" has been used by social scientists in two different ways. Some definitions of ethnic groups are broad and include both physical (racial) and cultural characteristics. Others are narrower and rely solely on cultural or nationality characteristics. Sociologist Joe R. Feagin emphasizes that ancestry, whether real or mythical, is a very important dimension of ethnic group identity.

Sociologist William Yancey and his associates argue that ethnic groups have been produced by structural conditions which are linked to the changing technology of production and transportation. Structural conditions including common occupational patterns, residential stability, concentration, and dependence on common institutions and services reinforce kinship and friendship networks. According to Yancey, common cultural heritage is not a prerequisite dimension of ethnicity. Ethnicity is a manifestation of the way populations are organized in terms of interaction patterns, institutions, values, attitudes, lifestyle, and consciousness of kind.

NEW DEFINITIONS

A new consciousness is emerging concerning the meaning of ethnicity. Ethnic groups are joining together into larger ethnic groupings. The adoption of a panethnic identity is common among Asian Americans, American Indians, and Hispanics. Sociologist Felix Padilla writes about the development of a Latino collective identity among Mexican Americans and Puerto Ricans. Ethnicity and one's ethnic identity are becoming matters of choice, especially for white Americans of European descent. Most people have multiple layers of ethnic identity because of generations of interethnic marriages; these layers can be added to or subtracted from one's current identity. Sociologists Richard Alba and Mary Waters acknowledge that people often know their ancestors are from a variety of ethnic groups but for one reason or another identify with only some of them (or none of them). Often people identify with those with whom they have the least connection.

Sociologist Robert Blauner, in his influential book *Black Lives, White Lives* (1989), addresses the confusion that is often produced in the American consciousness by the concepts of race and ethnicity. Blauner argues that the imagery of race tends to be more powerful than the imagery of ethnicity and therefore often overshadows it. The reason for this is that race—although generally viewed by scientists and social scientists as a social construct rather than a scientific reality—is associated with biological and scientific imagery, whereas ethnicity is associated with cultural imagery. Other important concepts, such as class and religion, are also overwhelmed by the powerful social meanings of race. The confounding of race and ethnicity is a daily occurrence in American society. Blauner holds that African Americans represent both a racial and an ethnic group and argues that when blacks assert their ethnicity, whites perceive it instead as an assertion of racial identity. He postulates that part of the American heritage of racism has been to deny the ethnicity or cultural heritage of African Americans.

HISTORY AND INTERRELATIONS OF ETHNIC GROUPS

In his book *Ethnic America* (1981), economist Thomas Sowell argues that the experiences of white ethnic groups and racial minorities have been different in degree rather than in kind. Historian Ronald Takaki, however, in his book *From Different Shores* (1987), challenges Sowell's assumption. Takaki emphasizes the facts that only blacks were enslaved, only American Indians were placed on reservations, only Japanese Americans were placed in concentration camps, and only the Chinese were excluded from naturalized citizenship. To understand fully the experiences and histories of ethnic groups one must acknowledge the role of economic and governmental contexts within which particular ethnic groups have immigrated and adjusted. The time of immigration and the resources brought by the immigrants have affected not only their economic and political success but also their social class position in the United States.

In his book *Race and Ethnic Relations* (1994), sociologist Martin N. Marger describes the American ethnic hierarchy as consisting of three parts. The top third consists primarily of white Protestants from various ethnic backgrounds. The middle third consists of Catholics from various ethnic backgrounds, Jews, and many Asians. The bottom third consists of blacks, Hispanics, American Indians, and some Asians. The most important aspect of this ethnic hierarchy is the gap between those groups in the bottom third of the hierarchy and the other two segments.

DIRECTIONS

Around the time of World War II and soon thereafter, the expectation was that ethnic Americans would assimilate and their sense of ethnicity would gradually disappear. This assumption was known as the melting pot theory. During the 1950s, 1960s, and 1970s, however, sociologist Nathan Glazer and political scientist Daniel Patrick Moynihan (among others) questioned the viability of the melting pot theory. Glazer, Moynihan, and others suggested that the United States was leaning more in the direction of cultural pluralism.

In the 1980s and early 1990s, the debate about the melting pot versus cultural pluralism, according to Alba, no longer dominated discussions of ethnicity, especially concerning white European ethnic groups. Alba argues that ethnicity is not less embedded in the structure of American society but rather that ethnic distinctions are undergoing change. He believes that ethnic distinctions based on European ancestry are dissolving, while a new ethnic group is forming based on ancestry from anywhere on the European continent.

Such ideas seemed less viable as the twenty-first century began to unfold. Immigration to Europe from the Middle East and elsewhere sparked a resurgent nationalism, at least among activist political parties and groups, in countries such as France, Hungary, the Netherlands, Denmark, and Britain. Some even started to question the viability of the European Union (EU), as local identities reasserted themselves. In the United States, the presidency of Barack Obama failed to deliver the "post-racial" society that some had expected. By the end of Obama's second term, a white nationalist identity had pushed out the prevailing multicultural order and succeeded in electing an anti-immigrant nativist, Donald Trump, to replace Obama. Ethnicity, that is, seemed to be playing out in terms of a "white" versus "them" (black, brown, other) dynamic.

——*William L. Smith, updated by Michael Shally-Jensen*

BIBLIOGRAPHY AND FURTHER READING

Alba, Richard D. *Ethnic Identity: The Transformation of White America.* New Haven: Yale UP, 1990. Print.

Bayor, Ronald H., ed. *The Oxford Handbook of American Immigration and Ethnicity.* New York: Oxford UP, 2013-2016. Database.

Krysan, Maria, and Amanda E. Lewis, eds. *The Changing Terrain of Race and Ethnicity.* New York: Russell Sage, 2004. Print.

McDonald, Jason. *American Ethnic History: Themes and Perspectives.* New Brunswick: Rutgers UP, 2007. Print.

Rees, Richard W. *Shades of Difference: A History of Ethnicity in America.* Lanham: Rowman and Littlefield, 2007. Print.

Treitler, Vilna Bashi. *The Ethnic Project: Transforming Racial Fiction into Ethnic Factions.* Stanford: Stanford UP, 2013. Print.

ETHNOCENTRISM IN AMERICAN HISTORY

Ethnocentrism involves judging the worth of the attributes, beliefs, or customs of another people or culture by the standards of one's own culture. William G. Sumner, in his 1906 book *Folkways*, described ethnocentrism as the attitude that "one's own group is the center of everything, and all others are scaled and rated with reference to it." Ethnocentrism contrasts with relativism, which means viewing each culture on its own terms. Ethnocentrism thrives on a sense of cultural or racial superiority to more "primitive" peoples or cultures. It implies that one's customs and way of life are the correct and appropriate ones. Ethnocentrism is generally associated with a superficial knowledge of the other culture in question. When coupled with a relationship of unequal power, it may lead to persecution or subjugation of the less powerful group. Ethnocentrism is also intimately connected to moral sensibilities. For example, British colonial governors ended the traditional Indian practice of *suttee* , or the burning of a widow along with her deceased husband. To the British, the practice was barbaric. To Indians, it was the accepted way of maintaining the sanctity of the marital bond after the death of the husband. This is but one illustration of the complex moral dilemmas that often accompany ethnocentrism: The choice between tolerance of an arrangement that one finds morally offensive and denial of the right of each society to organize its affairs as it wishes.

——Aristide Sechandice

ETHNOCIDE

The prefix "ethno" commonly refers to a group of people united by common cultural characteristics, but it can also refer to the culture itself. Therefore, the term "ethnocide" means either the killing of people in an ethnic group or the destruction of the group's way of life. Many American historians use the latter definition to describe brutal attempts to destroy, for example, Native American culture. Young American Indians in the nineteenth century were sent to boarding schools (such as the famous Carlisle Indian School in Pennsylvania) far away from their parents with the goal of forced assimilation into Anglo-Protestant ways.

In other contexts, "ethnocide" signifies one ethnic group killing members of another group, often with the goal of "ethnic cleansing." In this sense, the term "ethnocide" is almost synonymous with "genocide," except that the latter usually suggests a systematic and well-organized extermination, as occurred during the Holocaust of World War II, when Nazis exterminated approximately six million Jews. In many places, diverse ethnic groups manage to coexist peacefully with one another, but ethnic rivalries frequently produce violence when two or more groups compete with each other in conditions of perceived scarcity. Fear of the "other" and a desire for revenge often create a cycle of ethnocide.

——Thomas T. Lewis

ETHNOGENESIS THEORY

Ethnogenesis theory is a perspective used in the study of ethnic differentiation in American society. The perspective has been employed by author and researcher Andrew Greeley as an alternative to the most common considerations of ethnic differences.

Although analyses of assimilation, or the "melting pot," in American society vary, most assume that progress toward a common culture is inevitable. Pervasive throughout American society, the assimilation picture is entrenched in consciousness and established as the "official" view. The elimination of diversity, accomplished through common schools, mass media, social and political norms, and intermarriage, propels society toward a state of similarity in which differentiation occurs only by social class. However, this perspective contains limitations concerning the complexity of ethnicity that affect research findings and therefore frustrate the formulation of hypotheses.

Acculturation, or change in customs and beliefs resulting from living within a dominant society with different cultural traditions, also leaves unanswered questions. As a model, it fails to explain questions regarding the United States' capacity to cope with complex racial, religious, geographic, and social differentiation.

In *Ethnicity in the United States* (1974), Andrew Greeley proposes the ethnogenesis theory as an alternative and complementary perspective that focuses on the creation of an ethnic group or the study of its genesis, free of the belief that it must eventually disappear. By stressing the complex interaction between heritage, culture, and identification, Greeley develops a model whereby American ethnic groups may be "dynamic and flexible institutions for becoming a part of society." Greeley's model indicates that in situations in which the host country and the immigrants may have common ground to begin with, immigrants and the host become more alike. Certain immigrant traits persist, and some become even become more distinctive. Challenged by American society, however, the ethnic groups develop cultural systems different from those of their immigrant predecessors and more in common with the common culture.

Although essentially an extension of the assimilation and acculturation perspectives, the ethnogenesis model requires an enormous amount of research to collect data from the past that could facilitate the projection of trends. The natural history of ethnic groups affords an explanation of the cultural diversity that exists among them. Useful information includes knowledge of the land of origin, the strata or stratum of society from which the society migrated, under what circumstances the migration occurred, and the areas of the country in which the immigrants tended to settle. Information concerning cultural characteristics in early or late years of ethnic group history as well as family structure and childhood socialization also indicates the future social reality of an immigrant population in the United States.

Ethnogenesis theory suggests that American ethnic differentiation follows the collectivities of common origin that are tolerated and encouraged by the larger society; it also promotes the study of the genesis and history of ethnic groups as dynamic, growing mechanisms.

—Mary Hurd

BIBLIOGRAPHY AND FURTHER READING

Cipolla, Craig N. *Becoming Brothertown: Native American Ethnogenesis and Endurance in the Modern World.* Tucson: U of Arizona P, 2013. Print.

Fennell, Christopher C. *Crossroads and Cosmologies: Diasporas and Ethnogenesis in the New World.* Gainesville: UP of Florida, 2007. Print.

Greeley, Andrew M. *Ethnicity, Denomination and Inequality.* Beverly Hills: Sage, 1976. Print.

Greeley, Andrew M. *Ethnicity in the United States: A Preliminary Reconaissance.* New York: Wiley, 1974. Print.

Hill, Jonathan D., ed. *History, Power, and Identity: Ethnogenesis in the Americas, 1492–1992.* Iowa City: U of Iowa P, 1996. Print.

Yang, Philip Q. *Ethnic Studies: Issues and Approaches.* Albany: State U of New York P, 2000. Print.

ETHNOVIOLENCE

Ethnoviolence, as defined by sociologists Fred Pincus and Howard Ehrlich, has several characteristics, including motivation by prejudice and intent to impart psychological or physical damage to others *because* they are members of an ethnic group (that is, a group defined on the basis of race, nationality/national origin, sexual orientation, or religion). The forms that ethnoviolence takes include verbal abuse (such as racial slurs), harassment, property damage, and assault. Victims of ethnoviolence report greater psychological harm than do victims of similar crimes that are not ethnicity-based. Moreover, the effects of ethnoviolence may spread to other, nonvictimized group members, causing fear, distrust, or anger.

Many communities now track "hate crimes," a process hampered by greater nonreporting rates for ethnoviolence than for other, similar crimes. In the 1990s, rates of ethnoviolence in the United States were rising, however; one national organization reported a 24 percent rise in a single year, 1992. Some analysts attributed this rise to escalating prejudicial views, engendered by competition for dwindling resources, political manipulation or advances in telecommunications (such as the Internet) that allow unprecedented dissemination of prejudiced views. Others ascribed the growth to an overall increase in societal violence. Anthropologist Thomas Eriksen suggests that ethnicity need not breed ethnoviolence, but states that policies seeking unity through "color-blindness" are prone to failure—the stresses of transcending ethnic identity prove too great. However, policies that view ethnicity as difference without hierarchy show promise, allowing the benefits of ethnic identity while blunting intergroup fear, exclusion, and violence.

—James B. Epps

EURO-AMERICAN

Euro-American (or European American) is a panethnic identity that includes Americans of European ancestry (English, German, Irish, Italian, Polish, and so on), ranging from descendants of the earliest colonizers to recent immigrants. As Richard Alba observed in *Ethnic Identity: The Transformation of White America* (1990), the emergence of a Euro-American group has been shaped by the decline of individual European ethnic affiliations, the creation of a common historical narrative of immigration, struggle, and mobility, and the increasing Euro-American reaction to political challenges from peoples of color and post-1965 immigrants.

As a group label, "Euro-American" is problematic in that it is less widely used than other panethnic identities (including Asian American, Hispanic, and Native American). Dominant identities tend to be "hidden" in intergroup interactions, and the lack of awareness or use of the Euro-American label reflects the dominant status of the group in the United States. This process is compounded by the existence of competing labels for Euro-Americans: White, Caucasian, and Anglo-American— the latter term reflecting the historical dominance of British Americans within the group. The future role of Euro-American group identity will be determined by both the political and social strategies of the group itself, and the external and structural forces that mold all panethnic identities.

——*Ashley W. Doane, Jr.*

The New York City Metropolitan Area is home to the largest European population in the United States. By Dschwen.

EUROCENTRISM

The term "Eurocentrism" most often refers to an inordinate emphasis on the cultural achievements of peoples of European ancestry. It is used especially in reference to an educational curriculum that tends to disregard or minimize other traditions. As the United States has become more diverse, educators have increasingly attempted to promote a multicultural perspective that encompasses non-European cultures and considers the accomplishments of African Americans, Asian Americans, Latinos, and Native American peoples. Some African American scholars have proposed that Eurocentrism should be replaced by an Afrocentric curriculum, at least for black students. Most educators, however, prefer to encourage pluralism rather than any one particularism.

Some critics of the European tradition use the term "Eurocentrism" in a politicized way to refer to an ideology of white supremacy, as reflected in exploitative practices such as imperialism and slavery. These critics charge that the "Eurocentric paradigm" is founded on greed and racial domination. Admirers of the European tradition respond that Europeans are not more ethnocentric than other peoples and that Europeans have made worthwhile contributions, such as the Scientific Revolution and the Enlightenment. Egyptian economist Samir Amin argues in *L'eurocentrisme* (1988; *Eurocentrism*, 2010) that the modernization that began in Europe during the Renaissance provides a model for all countries of the world.

——*Thomas T. Lewis*

EUROPEAN IMMIGRATION TO CANADA: 1867–PRESENT

Canada became a nation on July 1, 1867. At that time, the ethnic composition of the new country was largely homogeneous: The majority of citizens were of British (English, Scottish, Welsh, and Irish) or French origin, the latter almost entirely centered in the province of Quebec. Immigration policy in the early years of Canadian history reflected the country's British roots. The immigration policy between 1867 and 1896, however, also largely proved a failure. A depression discouraged immigrants from making the voyage to the new nation. Many of the immigrants who did arrive (almost exclusively from the British Isles and Northern Europe) simply used Canada as a stopping-off point before moving to the United States. In several years during the 1870s and 1880s, Canada barely managed to maintain its population, let alone increase it.

Immigration was important to Canada. Immigrants were needed in order to populate the western plains acquired in 1870. Britain was the preferred source of immigrants; many, however, came from urban areas and proved completely unsuitable for harsh rural conditions. The Canadian government had no choice but to begin to expand the definition of those deemed suitable for immigration to Canada.

German-speaking Mennonites from Russia were encouraged to come to Canada; they settled in the province of Manitoba in the 1870s. Icelanders arrived in western Canada in the same decade. Even though these various groups challenged previous definitions of suitable immigrants, they were allowed in because of their competency as farmers.

THE IMMIGRATION BOOM, 1896–1914

The real boom in immigration to Canada, a period that reflected a changed perception of the ideal immigrant, occurred between 1896 and 1914. In 1896, Wilfrid Laurier and his Liberal Party were voted into office. Laurier's government, especially Minister of the Interior Clifford Sifton, was determined to fill western Canada with immigrants. Sifton and his ministry created an immigration policy that reflected Canada's need: European newcomers had to be farmers. For the first time, Canada began to seek immigrants from eastern Europe. Ukrainians, for example, who had experience farming in conditions much like those of Canada's west, began to arrive in large numbers.

At the same time that Sifton had in mind an ideal immigrant, he also had a vision of those who were unsuitable for Canada. This category included urban dwellers, industrial workers, southern Europeans, Asians, and African Americans. The last two groups were excluded—the Chinese formally through a head tax and then the 1923 Chinese Exclusion Act, and blacks informally through efforts by immigration agents, specifically because it was believed that they could never be assimilated into the mainstream of Canadian society. Sifton's opposition to industrial workers created tension with business interests, especially the railway, who wanted laborers to work in mines, in logging camps, and on the rail lines. These groups did everything they could to bring in such workers.

Other Canadians began to worry that too many non-British immigrants were flocking to Canada from Europe. These attitudes escalated as immigration to Canada rose in the first decade of the new century. After Sifton resigned in 1905, his successor attempted to steer Canadian immigration policy back toward its original British emphasis. This policy failed, as record numbers of non-British immigrants arrived in Canada just before World War I. Because these European newcomers settled largely in the west, a new multiethnic society arose in that region. With the beginning of World War I in August of 1914, all immigration to Canada effectively ended.

RETRACTION, EXPANSION, AND RETRACTION, 1919–45

Canada's immigration policy in the immediate aftermath of World War I was strongly influenced by the war. Large numbers of immigrants had arrived from Germany and Austria-Hungary, nations that had become Canada's enemies during the war. The presence of what many called "enemy aliens" during the war caused people to openly question the continuation of the prewar immigration policy after the war ended. Immigration from "enemy alien" countries was banned into the 1920s. The policy changed again in the mid-1920s because of the lobbying effort of business interests. Companies such as the railways needed cheap labor; immigration was the best source of this. In 1925, the Railways Agreement was signed. This new policy allowed railway companies to recruit and bring immigrants to Canada specifically to work on the lines.

Despite widespread opposition, large numbers of nonpreferred European immigrants such as Ukrainians entered Canada in the last half of the 1920s. The policy changed again in the 1930s because of the Great Depression. With so many Canadians out of work, immigration and immigrants became a natural target of those affected by the economic collapse. The Railways Agreement was canceled, and once again, all immigration came to a virtual end. Many newly arrived immigrants were also deported in the 1930s. Among those prevented from entering Canada during the 1930s were Jewish immigrants from Europe attempting to escape Nazi persecution.

POSTWAR IMMIGRATION BOOM, 1945–68

The initial postwar years saw large numbers of European immigrants arrive in Canada. First were the "war brides," women whom Canadian soldiers had met and married while fighting overseas during World War II. "Displaced persons" were another large group of European immigrants who left the devastation of their home countries and came to Canada. Collectively, Canadian immigration between 1945 and 1955 reached record levels. Of all immigrants to Canada since 1867, 30 percent arrived during this period. Overall during this period, immigrants continued to come from traditional sources. In 1956-1957, a year with a particularly large number of immigrants, 40 percent came from the United Kingdom. As Canada's economy slowed in the late 1950s, politicians began to talk about restricting immigration. Many Canadians favored such restrictions because of the increased difficulty in finding work. The economic downturn, however, slowed the growth of Canada by immigration. Between the opening years of the 1950s and the early years of the 1970s, between 25 percent and 33 percent of immigrants to Canada returned home or moved to the United States. For many immigrants, the reality of Canada did not match the perception.

IMMIGRATION SINCE 1968

Beginning in the 1960s and increasing in the 1970s, the ethnic and racial composition of immigrants to Canada changed dramatically. The shift in origin of immigrants began in the early 1960s, and then escalated under the Liberal governments of Lester B. Pearson and, after 1968, Pierre Trudeau. The government instituted a more impartial immigration system that eliminated traditional preferences given to immigrants from Europe. The Department of Manpower and Immigration was created in 1966 in an increased effort by the federal government to tie together Canada's economic and immigration policy. The numbers demonstrate a dramatic shift in the origins of immigrants to Canada. As late as 1966, 87 percent of those who came to Canada were of European origin. By 1970, fully half of newcomers came from new parts of the world including Hong Kong, the Caribbean, India, the Philippines, and Indochina. In 1968, eight of the top ten countries that supplied immigrants to Canada were European. By 1984, only two European countries, Britain and Poland remained in the top ten, and only Britain cracked the top five at fifth. Once again immigration was in the process of remaking Canada. In the early twenty-first century, most immigrants to Canada came from Asian countries. In 2013, more than thirty-four thousand immigrants came from China, the most of any country. China was followed by India, the Philippines, Pakistan, and Iran.

——*Steven Hewitt*

BIBLIOGRAPHY AND FURTHER READING

Cohen, Rina, and Guida Man. *Engendering Transnational Voices: Studies in Family, Work, and Identity.* Waterloo: Wilfrid Laurier UP, 2015. Print.

Cook, Ramsay, and Robert Craig Brown. *Canada, 1896–1921: A Nation Transformed.* Toronto: McClelland, 1991. Print.

Fleras, Augie. *Immigration Canada: Evolving Realities and Emerging Challenges in a Postnational World.* Vancouver: UBC, 2015. Print.

Iacovetta, Franca. *Such Hardworking People: Italian Immigrants in Postwar Toronto.* Montreal: McGill-Queen's UP, 1992. Print.

Palmer, Howard. *Patterns of Prejudice: A History of Nativism in Alberta.* Toronto: McClelland, 1982. Print.

EUROPEAN IMMIGRATION TO THE UNITED STATES: 1790–1892

In 1790, the initial United States census was conducted and Congress passed the first uniform naturalization law. For the next 102 years, more than 90 percent of the immigrants came from Germany, Great Britain, Ireland, and Scandinavia (old immigrants). In 1892, for the first time, more arrivals were from Eastern and Southern Europe (new immigrants) than from Northern Europe. That same year, Ellis Island replaced the Castle Garden as the major receiving center for immigrants landing in New York when the federal government took control of the process. From 1821 to 1892, approximately 4.5 million German Protestants, Catholics, and Jews; 3.5 million Irish Catholics; 2.7 million British Protestants; and 1 million Scandinavian Protestants emigrated, with more than two-thirds coming to the United States. The Irish gravitated toward unskilled labor in the Eastern cities; the English, Welsh, and Scots often found work as skilled laborers in this same region. Germans tended to find positions as skilled craftspeople or in the trades in both Eastern and Midwestern cities. Many Germans, Scandinavians, and Dutch became farmers in the Midwest.

RELATIONS WITH THE DOMINANT CULTURE

At the onset of large-scale immigration, the descendants of the early colonists, who were mostly Protestants of English and Scotch-Irish descent, dominated the United States in numbers and control over society. They resented and discriminated against the new arrivals for a variety of reasons. As a group, they were generally satisfied with their lives in the United States and had established an "American culture" separate from that of Europe. A new wave of Europeans could disrupt this. Consequently, many Americans became nativists, hoping to prevent what they viewed as an immigrant "takeover" of the nation. The hierarchical structure of Catholicism, which they considered at odds with the tenets of democracy, negatively affected the large Irish and German Catholic population. Jews

MILESTONES OF EUROPEAN IMMIGRATION TO THE UNITED STATES, 1790–1892

Year	Event
1790	First US census reveals that 60.9 percent of the population is of English ancestry, 9.7 Scotch-Irish, 8.7 German, and 8.3 Scottish. This clearly indicates Euro-American dominance in the new nation. Congress passes legislation stating that any free white person who has lived in the country for two years can become a citizen.
1798	The Federalist leadership passes the Alien Act, the first attempt to impede immigrant assimilation.
1815	Napoleonic Wars end, allowing for greater emigration from Europe.
1820s	Innovations in manufacturing technology and the legalization of corporations help start the Industrial Revolution in the United States, which becomes a major draw for impoverished immigrants.
1840s	The Potato Famine drives 2 million people from Ireland.
1851–1854	First great peak in immigration occurs; 1.5 million people per year arrive in the United States.
1861–1865	Civil War curtails immigration.
1866–1873	Second immigration peak occurs; 1 million people arrive annually.
1870s	Immigration from eastern and southern Europe begins.
1881	Congress takes action to restrict immigration, ending the Open Door era.
1891	Congress establishes an agency for immigration control under the auspices of the Treasury Department, thus initiating full-scale federal control.
1892	The number of immigrants from eastern and southern Europe surpasses that of arrivals from northwestern and central Europe. This, and the opening of the Ellis Island immigration facility, mark a new era in immigration history.

were still blamed for the death of Christ, and many people overestimated their influence in the financial world. Although American Protestants increasingly embraced temperance and prohibition of alcoholic beverages, many Irish and German immigrants saw spirits as a part of their culture. Irish, Welsh, and English laborers often believed that organized labor was the key to better pay and working conditions; however, many native stock Americans felt that labor unions were in opposition to American individualism and free labor capitalism. Germans and Scandinavians, who desired to maintain Old World languages and traditions, were chastised for being un-American. All of these factors were responsible for divisions between colonial stock Americans and the immigrants.

RELATIONS AMONG OLD IMMIGRANTS
Despite commonalties of the ethnic experience, the old immigrants never viewed themselves as a unified group. Conflict between the groups was more apparent than cooperation. These differences often had European roots that combined with American circumstances.

Religious differences continued to separate people in the United States as they had in Europe. Almost all the British, Scandinavians, and Dutch were Protestants, as were half of the Germans. Like their American counterparts, the British Protestants were at odds with Irish Catholics. The religious differences in the German states were also brought to the United States. Germans viewed themselves as German Protestants, German Catholics, or German Jews rather than as a single culture.

Political issues also divided the old immigrants. Catholics and urban laborers, especially the Irish, gravitated toward the more open Democratic Party. Protestant skilled workers and midwestern farmers believed that the Whigs, and later the Republicans, reflected their interests of upward socioeconomic mobility and conservative social values. Catholics and the less conservative German Protestants objected to any laws restricting alcohol. Conversely, many English, Welsh, and German Pietist Protestant immigrants abstained from liquor and favored its prohibition. In regard to slavery, unskilled Irish laborers feared that emancipation could bring about competition with African Americans for low-paying jobs; English, Welsh, and German skilled workers and tradespeople believed that the extension of slavery would damage the free-labor, capitalist economy.

THE ASSIMILATION PROCESS

The Americanization process for the older group of immigrants was hastened because all ethnic groups began to enjoy increased social and economic mobility by the latter part of the nineteenth century and because the arrival of the new immigrants lifted them to a higher level of social status.

The various ethnic groups achieved social and economic mobility differently. The English, Welsh, and Scots often moved from their skilled labor positions to become bosses, supervisors, and managers in corporate America. They used the school systems to educate their children, who moved into professional positions. Many descendants of the Welsh and English immigrants became teachers and administrators in elementary and secondary education systems, giving those groups a tremendous impact upon education in the United States.

Working from positions as unskilled laborers, the Irish moved through the corporate ranks. Politics was also a means of Irish mobility. Colonial stock Americans found local politics disdainful; however, the Irish recognized an opportunity to gain political power in the growing urban areas. By the late 1800s, many Eastern cities were under the control of political machines dominated by the Irish. Although colonial stock and other old immigrants criticized boss politics, the machines served the rapidly expanding urban-ethnic community at a time when official government agencies were lacking. The Irish were also able to gain mobility through their leadership in the Roman Catholic Church. The Church became a major force in American life with the arrival of numerous Catholic immigrants. The Irish Church hierarchy was instrumental in sponsoring a vast educational network that educated all Catholics from elementary school through the university.

Germans and Scandinavians were perhaps less inclined to use higher education as a means of mobility. However, as the United States rapidly expanded, the services of German tradespeople and farmers were all the more needed. This, in turn, brought about a growth in German businesses and farms, resulting in the upward mobility of ship owners and workers alike. German Jews, many of whom began as peddlers and small shopkeepers, were able to expand their businesses to meet the increasing consumer demand. This economic success combined with a strong emphasis upon education was responsible for a remarkable degree of socioeconomic mobility for German Jews.

The arrival of ten million Eastern and Southern Europeans resulted in a higher socioeconomic status for the old immigrants. The new arrivals provided a large labor pool to fill unskilled positions. The old immigrants could move into the more lucrative skilled and management jobs or expand their businesses to serve the growing population. Also, many of the values of the Northern European immigrants were more identifiable as American ideals. To both colonial stock and old immigrants, the new immigrants appeared to be considerably different. Consequently, the colonial stock found the old immigrants more acceptable.

By the mid-twentieth century, the descendants of the old immigrants were less commonly viewed as distinct ethnic groups. The British found their heritage largely assimilated into the larger American culture, and Germans' ethnic identification diminished during the two world wars. Certain groups, such as the Welsh and Scandinavians, still maintain ethnic institutions. However, these institutions are intended more to preserve the vestiges of the cultures than to help immigrants deal with challenges in the United States. To most observers, the descendants of the old immigrants are firmly entrenched in mainstream American culture.

——*Paul J. Zbiek*

BIBLIOGRAPHY AND FURTHER READING

Berthoff, Rowland. *British Immigrants in Industrial America, 1790–1950.* Cambridge: Harvard UP, 1953. Print.

Handlin, Oscar. *The Uprooted: The Epic Story of the Great Migrations That Made the American People,* 2d ed. Boston: Little, 1990. Print.

Higham, John. *Strangers in the Land: Patterns of American Nativism, 1860-1925.* New Brunswick: Rutgers UP, 1969. Print.

Hirota, Hidetaka. *Expelling the Poor: Atlantic Seaboard States and the Nineteenth-Century Origins of American Immigration Policy.* New York: Oxford UP, 2017. Print.

Sherling, Rankin. *The Invisible Irish.* Montreal: McGill-Queens UP, 2016. Print.

Thernstrom, Stephan. *Harvard Encyclopedia of American Ethnic Groups,* 2d ed. Cambridge: Belknap P of Harvard U, 1980. Print.

EUROPEAN IMMIGRATION TO THE UNITED STATES: 1892–1943

In 1808, the US government purchased Ellis Island from the state of New York for ten thousand dollars. The new federal property, located in New York Harbor about one mile from the southern tip of Manhattan Island, served first as a fort and later as an arsenal. Until 1882, the state of New York had guided the influx of immigration from the old Castle Garden station at the tip of Manhattan. The opening of Ellis Island on January 1, 1892, as the first federal immigration station symbolized a new era for the United States as well as the beginning of the end of free immigration to the New World.

Congress had begun the selective process of excluding undesirable elements among those emigrating to the United States with the passage of the federal Immigration Act in 1882. That measure was designed to prevent the immigration of persons who had criminal records and those who were mentally incompetent or indigent. That same year, Congress also passed the Chinese Exclusion Act (later extended to all Asians), barring an entire nationality from entry as racially undesirable for a period of ten years. In 1904 the act's provisions were extended indefinitely, to be repealed only in 1943.

IMMIGRATION PATTERNS SHIFT

Most immigrants before the 1890s had come from northern and western Europe. In the 1880s a fundamental change occurred. In addition to the traditional immigrants, who shared common language patterns with persons already in the United States, people from Mediterranean and Slavic countries began to arrive in increasing numbers. One may measure the change more dramatically by comparing two peak years in US immigration. In 1882, 87 percent of the 788,000 immigrants came from northern and western Europe. In 1907, only 19.3 percent were from northern and western Europe, while 80.7 percent came from southern and eastern Europe.

A great impetus to immigration was the transportation revolution engendered by the steamship. In 1856, more than 96 percent of US immigrants came aboard sailing ships, on trips that took between one and three months. By 1873, the same percentage came by steamships, which took only ten days. The new steamships were specifically designed for passengers, and while still subject to overcrowding and epidemics, they were a major improvement over the sailing ships. Steamship companies competed for immigrant business and maintained offices in Europe. The Hamburg-Amerika line, for example, had thirty-two hundred US agencies throughout Europe. More than half of the immigrants in 1901 came with prepaid tickets supplied by relatives in the United States.

As the older agricultural economy of Europe was replaced by an industrial one, many former farmers moved to European cities in search of employment; often unsuccessful in that search, they were easily persuaded to try the New World, where jobs were said to be plentiful. The same railroad-building process that opened the American West to the immigrant made it easier and cheaper for the Europeans to reach their coastal areas and embark for the United States.

Most of the emigration from southern Europe was occasioned by economic distress. Southern Italy's agriculture was severely affected by competition from Florida in oranges and lemons, as well as by a French tariff against Italian wines. The Italian emigration began with 12,000 in 1880 and reached a peak of nearly 300,000 in 1914. After immigration restriction laws took full effect, Italian immigration fell to 6,203 in 1925.

From Russia and the Slavic areas, emigration was also caused by political and religious problems. Jews fled in reaction to the riots set off by the assassination of Czar Alexander II in 1882, the pogroms of 1881–82 and 1891, and the 1905-1906 massacres of thousands of Jews. Jewish immigration to the United States began with 5,000 in 1880 and reached a peak of 258,000 in 1907. Some two million Roman Catholic Poles also arrived between 1890 and 1914. In 1925, however, the Immigration Service recorded only 5,341 entrants from Poland and 3,121 from Russia and the Baltic States.

Nativist Fears

Two issues caused the greatest concern to American nativists in the 1890s: the tendency of the new immigrants to congregate in the cities, and the fact that they spoke seemingly unassimilable languages. One of the first articulate spokesmen against unrestricted immigration, the Reverend Dr. Josiah Strong, was alarmed by the concentration of foreign peoples in cities. Strong's famous book, *Our Country*, published in 1885, clearly stated what many other US citizens feared: that the new influx of immigrants would create permanent slums and perpetuate poverty.

The urban nature of the settlement was unavoidable. US agriculture was suffering from the same shocks that had disrupted European agriculture, and the populist movement in the country made clear that the myth of utopia in the western United States was no longer believable. Most of the new immigrants were attracted by the pull of US industry and opportunity, and they came to the United States with the express purpose of settling in a city. In addition, new industrial technology had reduced the demand for skilled labor, while the need for unskilled and cheap factory help increased. To add to the social clash between the new and old immigrants, the arrival of a new labor force in great numbers probably allowed some older laborers to move up to more important supervisory and executive positions.

Many new immigrants did not share the optimism and enthusiasm of established Americans. Some tended to be pessimistic and resigned, distrustful of change, and unfamiliar with democratic government after having lived in autocratic situations. At the height of the new immigration occurred the Panic of 1893, followed by a depression that lasted until 1897, which seemed to confirm the fears of persons already settled in the United States that the country and the system were failing. The new immigration, however, was but one of the major social, cultural, and economic changes taking place in the turbulent United States of the 1890s.

In 1907, Congress created the Dillingham Commission to investigate the problems of immigration. Many of the commission's findings reflected the fears of citizens concerning the new immigration and led to the passage of restrictive legislation in the 1920s. Unrestricted immigration ended with the passage of the National Origins Act of 1924, which restricted immigrants in any year to 154,277. Each country's quota could be no more than 2 percent of the number of its natives counted in the 1890 census, a year in which few born in southern and eastern Europe were part of the US population.

When Ellis Island closed as a reception center in 1943, few immigrants still arrived by ship, and the Immigration Service could handle all arrivals at Manhattan's docks. When the Atlantic reopened after World War II, planes began to replace ships as vehicles of immigration, and there was no need for Ellis Island. By that time, much of the fear of the "new" immigration had evaporated. Italian, Slavs, and Jews had not remained in permanent slums, mired in perpetual poverty, as Strong had feared, and their descendants had fought side by side with US soldiers of British and German ancestry against the Nazis and the Japanese.

In the 1940s, there was much criticism of the rigidity of the immigration restriction legislation that hampered attempts to deal with the problems of refugees. Not until 1965, however, would the rigid quota system established in 1924 be replaced with a more flexible system. When that reform opened the door to increased entry by Asians and Latin Americans, complaints about the new "new immigrants" began to echo nineteenth century uneasiness about the former "new immigrants."

———*Richard H. Collin, updated by Milton Berman*

BIBLIOGRAPHY AND FURTHER READING

Bayor, Ronald H. *Encountering Ellis Island.* Baltimore: Johns Hopkins UP, 2014. Print.

Daniels, Roger. *Coming to America: A History of Immigration and Ethnicity in American Life,* 2d ed. New York: Perennial, 2002. Print.

Handlin, Oscar. *The Uprooted.* 2nd ed. Boston: Little, 1990. Print.

Higham, John. *Strangers in the Land: Patterns of American Nativism, 1860–1925.* New Brunswick: Rutgers UP, 1955. Print.

Reimers, David M. *Still the Golden Door: The Third World Comes to America,* 2d ed. New York: Columbia UP, 1992. Print.

EX PARTE CROW DOG

Crow Dog, a well-known Lakotan, killed Spotted Tail, another popular tribal leader, at the Rosebud Agency in Dakota Territory in 1883. Crow Dog was arrested, removed from the reservation, and tried in the territorial court of Dakota, where he was convicted and sentenced to death. In killing Spotted Tail, Crow Dog admitted he had broken Lakota law, but he maintained he should be punished according to Lakota customs, not by United States law. Under tribal law, Crow Dog would be shunned by his own family and would become responsible for care and protection of Spotted Tail's family.

The US Supreme Court sided with Crow Dog and declared the United States had no jurisdiction over the crime of one Indian against another on Indian land. Because Congress provided no federal jurisdiction over Indian crimes on reservations, even a murderer could not be punished. Therefore, Crow Dog returned to his people.

The victim, Chief Spotted Tail (Sinté Gleška). By C. M. Bell ; Print by Barry, D. F. (David Frances), 1854-1934.

This decision proved to be a major step in relations between Native Americans and the US government, in that it encouraged Congress to enact legislation to give federal jurisdiction over Indians in certain legal matters. One key piece of legislation, the Major Crimes Act (1885), directed federal courts to assume jurisdiction over seven crimes committed on Indian land: murder, manslaughter, rape, assault with intent to kill, arson, burglary, and larceny.

——*Carole A. Barrett*

EXTERNAL COLONIALISM

External colonialism is the classical form of colonialism, describing the processes that occurred during European imperialist expansion, which began during the late fifteenth century and extended well into the nineteenth. External colonialism is the process of global imperialism that involved the political and economic control of less powerful societies by more powerful societies to acquire and exploit land, labor, and natural resources for geopolitical and economic interests. The relative power of nations reflects a disparity in levels of politico-military dominance and economic resources.

Because external colonialism was a worldwide process of empire building, it commonly involved the remote control of distant, less powerful nations by powerful nations. Colonizers were typically European imperialist powers that industrialized first, while the colonized tended to be strategic territories in the path of colonial expansion. Because religious zeal commonly accompanied and justified colonization in the form of missionary expansion, the cross and the sword were typically two sides of the same colonialist coin. Five fundamental conditions were intertwined in this process of external colonialism: forced entry into a distant territory, political subjugation of the colonized people, economic exploitation of labor and natural resources, cultural alteration or annihilation of colonized peoples' ways of life, and racial ideologies justifying inferiority and colonization.

——*Michael P. Perez*

F

FAIR EMPLOYMENT PRACTICES COMMITTEE (FEPC)

In the spring of 1941, as the United States prepared to enter World War II, African American leaders pressured the administration of Franklin D. Roosevelt to eliminate segregation in the armed forces and discriminatory hiring practices in the booming war industries. A. Philip Randolph, president of the Brotherhood of Sleeping Car Porters, the largest black labor union, threatened a massive march on Washington, DC, by a hundred thousand demonstrators under the banner Democracy Not Hypocrisy—Jobs Not Alms. Roosevelt, hoping to avoid an embarrassing racial protest that might divide the Democratic Party and his administration at a time when he needed unity for his war-preparedness program, moved to head off the March on Washington movement by meeting with Randolph and Walter White, president of the National Association for the Advancement of Colored People (NAACP). On June 25, 1941, a week before the planned march, Roosevelt issued Executive Order 8802. It prohibited discrimination by employers, unions, and government agencies involved in defense work on the basis of race, creed, color, or national origin but made no mention of desegregating the armed forces. Roosevelt established the Fair Employment Practices Committee (FEPC) to investigate complaints and redress grievances stemming from the order. Randolph and White accepted the compromise arrangement and called off the march.

Although African Americans hailed the FEPC as the greatest step forward in race relations since the Civil War, Roosevelt initially gave the agency little

An FEPC press conference, c. 1942. By United States Office of War Information.

authority. Underfunded and understaffed, the FEPC at first could do little more than conduct investigations into complaints received and make recommendations, relying on the powers of publicity and persuasion to achieve change. In mid-1943, however, amid mounting concern that manpower shortages were hurting the war effort, Roosevelt beefed up the agency by giving it the authority to conduct hearings, make findings, issue directives to war industries, and make recommendations to the War Manpower Commission to curb discrimination.

The FEPC had a mixed record of accomplishment in eliminating racial discrimination in the war industries and government agencies. It resolved less than half of the eight thousand complaints received, and employers and unions often ignored its compliance orders with impunity. Although African American employment in the war industries increased from 3 percent in 1942 to 8 percent in 1945 and the federal government more than tripled its number of black employees, such changes had more to do with wartime labor shortages than FEPC actions. Nevertheless, the FEPC scored some significant successes. In 1944, federal troops broke up a strike by white Philadelphia transit workers and enforced an FEPC directive that blacks be upgraded to positions as streetcar operators. At war's end, despite the FEPC's shortcomings, African American leaders and white liberals hoped to transform the committee into a permanent agency. In 1946, however, southern Democrats in the Senate filibustered a bill to extend the FEPC and killed the agency. Although several northern states passed their own Fair Employment Practices acts, the Senate

again blocked bills to create a permanent FEPC in 1950 and 1952. Not until the Civil Rights Act of 1964 did the federal government establish another agency devoted to eliminating racial discrimination in employment practices.

——*Richard V. Damms*

BIBLIOGRAPHY AND FURTHER READING

Cletus, Daniel. *Chicano Workers and the Politics of Fairness: The FEPC in the Southwest, 1941-1945.* Austin: U of Texas P, 1991. Print.

Lucander, David. *Winning the War for Democracy: The March on Washington Movement, 1941-1946.* Urbana: U of Illinois P, 2014.

FAIR HOUSING ACT

The Civil Rights Act of 1866 provided that all citizens should have the same rights "to inherit, purchase, lease, sell, hold, and convey real and personal property," but the law was never enforced. Instead, such federal agencies as the Farmers Home Administration, the Federal Housing Administration, and the Veterans Administration financially supported segregated housing until 1962, when

Sign with American flag "We want white tenants in our white community," directly opposite the Sojourner Truth homes, a new US federal housing project in Detroit, Michigan. A riot was caused by white neighbors' attempts to prevent African American tenants from moving in. By Arthur S. Siegel.

President John F. Kennedy issued Executive Order 11063 to stop the practice.

California passed a general nondiscrimination law in 1959 and an explicit fair housing law in 1963. In 1964, voters enacted Proposition 14, an initiative to repeal the 1963 statute and the applicability of the 1959 law to housing. When a landlord in Santa Ana refused to rent to an African American in 1963, the latter sued, thus challenging Proposition 14. The California Supreme Court, which heard the case in 1966, ruled that Proposition 14 was contrary to the Fourteenth Amendment to the US Constitution, because it was not neutral on the matter of housing discrimination; instead, based on the context in which it was adopted, Proposition 14 served to legitimate and promote discrimination. On appeal, the US Supreme Court let the California Supreme Court decision stand in *Reitman v. Mulkey* (1967).

JOHNSON'S EFFORTS

President Lyndon B. Johnson had hoped to include housing discrimination as a provision in the comprehensive Civil Rights Act of 1964, but he demurred when southern senators threatened to block the nomination of Robert Weaver as the first African American cabinet appointee. After 1964, southern members of Congress were adamantly opposed to any expansion of civil rights. Although Johnson urged passage of a federal law against housing discrimination in requests to Congress in 1966 and 1967, there was no mention of the idea during his State of the Union address in 1968. Liberal members of Congress pressed the issue regardless, and southern senators responded by threatening a filibuster. This threat emboldened Senators Edward W. Brooke and Walter F. Mondale, a moderate Republican and a liberal Democrat, respectively, to cosponsor fair housing legislation, but they needed the support of conservative midwestern Republicans to break a filibuster. Illinois Republican senator Everett Dirksen arranged a compromise whereby housing discrimination would be declared illegal, but federal enforcement power would be minimal.

In the wake of *Reitman v. Mulkey*, the assassination of Martin Luther King, Jr., on April 4, 1968, and subsequent urban riots, Congress established fair housing as a national priority on April 10 by adopting Titles VIII and IX of the Civil Rights Act of 1968, also known as the Fair Housing Act or Open Housing Act. Signed by Johnson on the following day, the law originally prohibited discrimination in housing on the basis of race, color, religion, or national origin. In 1974, an amendment expanded the coverage to include sex (gender) discrimination; in 1988, the law was extended to protect persons with disabilities and families with children younger than eighteen years of age.

Title VIII prohibits discrimination in the sale or rental of dwellings, in the financing of housing, in advertising, in the use of a multiple listing service, and in practices that "otherwise make unavailable or deny" housing, a phrase that some courts have interpreted to outlaw exclusionary zoning, mortgage redlining, and racial steering . Blockbusting, the practice of inducing a white homeowner to sell to a minority buyer in order to frighten others on the block to sell their houses at a loss, is also prohibited. It is not necessary to show intent in order to prove discrimination; policies, practices, and procedures that have the effect of excluding minorities, women, handicapped persons, and children are illegal, unless otherwise deemed reasonable. Title VIII, as amended in 1988, covers persons who believe that they are adversely affected by a discriminatory policy, practice, or procedure, even before they incur damages.

The law applies to about 80 percent of all housing in the United States. One exception to the statute is a single-family house sold or rented without the use of a broker and without discriminatory advertising, when the owner owns no more than three such houses and sells only one house in a two-year period. Neither does the statute apply to a four-unit dwelling if the owner lives in one of the units, the so-called Mrs.-Murphy's-rooming-house exception. Dwellings owned by private clubs or religious organizations that rent to their own members on a noncommercial basis are also exempt.

ENFORCEMENT

Enforcement of the statute was left to the secretary of the Department of Housing and Urban Development (HUD). Complaints originally had to be filed within 180 days of the offending act, but in 1988, this period was amended to one year. HUD has estimated that there are about two million instances of housing discrimination each year, although formal complaints have averaged only forty thousand per year. The US attorney general can bring a civil suit against a flagrant violator of the law.

According to the law, HUD automatically refers complaints to local agencies that administer "substantially equivalent" fair housing laws. HUD can act if the local agencies fail to do so, but initially was expected only to use conference, conciliation, and persuasion to bring about voluntary compliance. The Fair Housing Amendments Act of 1988 authorized an administrative law tribunal to hear cases that cannot be settled by persuasion. The administrative law judges have the power to issue cease and desist orders to offending parties.

HUD has used "testers" to show discrimination. For example, a team of blacks and whites might arrange to have an African American apply for a rental; if turned down, the black tester would contact a white tester to ascertain whether the landlord were willing to rent to a white instead. That testers have standing to sue was established by the US Supreme Court in *Havens v. Coleman* (1982).

Under the administrative law procedure, penalties are up to $10,000 for the first offense, $25,000 for the second offense, and $50,000 for each offense thereafter. Attorneys' fees and court costs can be recovered by the prevailing party. In 1988, civil penalties in a suit filed by the US attorney general were established as up to $50,000 for the first offense and $100,000 for each offense thereafter.

Title IX of the law prohibits intimidation or attempted injury of anyone filing a housing discrimination complaint. A violator can be assessed a criminal penalty of $1,000 and/or sentenced to one year in jail. If a complainant is actually injured, the penalty can increase to $10,000 and/or ten years of imprisonment. If a complainant is killed, the penalty is life imprisonment.

Under the laws of some states, a complainant filing with a state agency must waive the right to pursue a remedy under federal law. In 1965, a couple sought to purchase a home in a St. Louis suburban housing development, only to be told by the realtor that the home was not available because one of the spouses was African American. Invoking the Civil Rights Act of 1866, the couple sued the real estate developer, and the case went to the Supreme Court. In *Jones v. Alfred H. Mayer Company* (1968), the Court decided that the Civil Rights Act of 1866 did permit a remedy against housing discrimination by private parties.

The effect of the 1968 Fair Housing Act, however, has been minimal. Without a larger supply of affordable housing, many African Americans in particular have nowhere to move in order to enjoy integrated housing. Federal subsidies for low-cost housing, under such legislation as the Housing and Urban Development Act of 1968 and the Housing and Community Development Act of 1974, have declined significantly since the 1980s. Conscientious private developers are confronted with the text of a law that aims to provide integrated housing but proscribes achieving integration by establishing quotas to ensure a mixed racial composition among those who seek to buy or rent dwelling units.

——*Michael Haas*

BIBLIOGRAPHY AND FURTHER READING

Metcalf, George R. *Fair Housing Comes of Age.* New York: Greenwood, 1988. Print.

Schwemm, Robert G., ed. *The Fair Housing Act after Twenty Years.* New Haven: Yale Law School, 1989. Print.

Silverman, Robert Mark. *Fair and Affordable Housing in the US.* Leiden: Brill, 2011. Print.

FASCISM IN CANADA

In Canada, as in several other countries in the world, fascism was largely a phenomenon of the economically destitute 1930s. Fascist organizations appeared and gained limited support, which quickly waned once World War II had begun. The main areas of fascist support in Canada during the 1930s were in the provinces of Quebec, Ontario, Manitoba, and Saskatchewan. Underlying its limited popularity was its message of anti-Semitism, anticommunism, and nationalism. Because of these sentiments, even those who did not belong to a fascist organization and would never have considered joining found fascism less of a threat to Canadian values and society than communism. Anti-Semitic feeling was widespread in Canada during the 1930s.

Fascism among French Canadians was centered in the province of Quebec and was strongly anti-Semitic in character. The leader of the Quebec movement was the charismatic Adrien Arcand. His organization, the National Social Christian Movement, was the most successful fascist movement in Canada during this period, although it still remained outside the mainstream of French Canadian society. Its anti-Semitic and anticommunist values, however, were shared by many in the province.

Fascism also had supporters among Germans and Italians who had emigrated to Canada but still remained unassimilated into Canadian society. Levels of support were never high in either the German or Italian communities, and the movements were dependent on support from Germany and Italy. In the 1920s, Italian consulates in Canada began a campaign promoting fascism. In 1934, the Deutscherbund Canada was created by German diplomats in an effort to disseminate the Nazi message among German-speaking citizens; it would eventually have two thousand members. Once the war began, however, it was suppressed, and in 1940, several hundred German and Italian fascists were arrested and interned for the duration of World War II.

In English-speaking Canada, support for fascism was centered in the cities of Toronto and Winnipeg. In the former, several small fascist organizations, motivated chiefly by anti-Semitism, formed. In 1933, an anti-Semitic display led to a violent clash between Toronto Jews and fascists. In Manitoba, a region of Canada with a history of hostility toward non-British immigrants, the Canadian Nationalist Party formed under the leadership of William Whittaker. Anti-Semitism and anticommunism were important themes in Whittaker's party, which had a swastika surrounded by the Canadian maple leaf as its symbol. Again, however, support for this organization was marginal.

In 1938, to widespread publicity, Arcand and a fascist leader from Ontario announced the merging of their parties into a single body, the National Unity Party, with the motto "Canada for Canadians" and Arcand as leader. A few days later, Nazi Germany absorbed Austria. By the end of the 1930s, with Canadians increasingly alarmed at the prospects of war with fascist Germany, support for fascism dropped. Once the war began, fascist organizations were outlawed, and in 1940, leaders such as Arcand found themselves arrested and interned by the Canadian government.

——*Steven Hewitt*

FEDERAL RIOT

A riot at Saint Mary's Church in Philadelphia on February 10, 1799, was the direct result of the passage of the Alien and Sedition Acts of 1798. These four laws—the Naturalization Act, the Alien Act, the Alien Enemies Act, and the Sedition Act—had been passed in June and July and sought collectively to limit the rights of immigrants and to silence criticism of the new US government. Two main political factions dominated at the time, the conservative Federalists and the Jeffersonian Republicans. Federalists were mainly the wealthy and established, and Catholics as well as Protestants were among this group. Saint Mary's Church, considered one of the most venerable and well-respected Catholic congregations in the United States, counted many of these Federalists among its members and included both established Anglo-Americans and Irish Americans. Republicans were made up largely of immigrants, including many new Irish immigrants, and these less affluent and newer Americans felt the impact of the Alien and Sedition Acts most sharply. They circulated petitions protesting the acts and gathered signatures throughout Philadelphia without incident. They intended to present the petitions to Congress.

Four of these immigrant Republicans—James Reynolds, Samuel Cummings, Robert Moore, and William Duane—posted fliers protesting the Alien and Sedition Acts at Saint Mary's, again requesting signatures from the Irish members of the congregation. Following the February 10, 1799, Sunday service at Saint Mary's, a violent confrontation took place between these men and members of the congregation. The four were tried on February 21, 1799, for causing the riot. Saint Mary's Father Leonard Neale, who had accused the men, strongly condemned the actions of the Republicans, while Father Matthew Carr testified that it was a long-honored tradition in Ireland to post notices and seek support for petitions following church services. The jury delivered a verdict of "not guilty" to the charge of causing a riot.

The riot signified a turning point in the early history of intergroup relations in the United States. Although the short-range effect of this conflict was to weaken the Federalist hold within Saint Mary's congregation, the "Irish riot" became a symbol of conflict between an established, dominant group and an incoming immigrant population. Such conflicts would characterize much of US history.

——*Kathleen Schongar*

BIBLIOGRAPHY AND FURTHER READING

McGee, Thomas D'Arcy. *A History of the Irish Settlers in North America from the Earliest Period to the Census of 1850.* Boston: American Celt, 1851. Print.

Schwartz, Michael. *The Persistent Prejudice: Anti-Catholicism in America.* Huntington: Our Sunday Visitor, 1984. Print.

Wood, John. *The Suppressed History of the Administration of John Adams, from 1797 to 1801.* Philadelphia: Walker, 1846. Print.

FEDERALLY RECOGNIZED TRIBES

The term "federally recognized tribe" is a US government designation for an American Indian tribe that has official relations with the United States. These relations have been established in various ways through the years—through treaties (treaty making ended in the late nineteenth century), executive orders, court decrees, and acts of Congress, and through meeting the requirements set forth by the Federal Acknowledgment Program. Federal recognition is both a political and economic issue, as recognized tribes are eligible for federal services that unrecognized tribes cannot receive, such as education, housing, and health benefits.

The Federal Acknowledgment Program (a Bureau of Indian Affairs program) was created in 1978. The Federal Acknowledgment Program established criteria and procedures through which unrecognized tribes could attempt to attain recognized status. The creation of a federal recognition process was hailed a victory by some American Indians, but others countered that the requirements are unnecessarily complex, even unfulfillable. Among the criteria is proof of continuous existence as a tribe; the tribe also must have a governing body, be governed by a constitution or similar document, and have membership criteria and a roll of current members.

In the 1950s a government policy known as termination successfully urged many tribes to disband, becoming no longer recognized and thus no longer eligible for government benefits. Subsequently, some terminated tribes attempted to regain recognized tribal status; the regaining of tribal status by the Menominees in 1973 was the first major success. As of early 2015, there were 566 federally recognized tribes. Some of these groups are very small; for example, there are some two hundred Alaskan village groups.

——*McCrea Adams*

Vanessa Paukeigope Jennings, Kiowa Regalia Maker. By Tom Pich.

BIBLIOGRAPHY AND FURTHER READING

Miller, Mark Edwin. *Claiming Tribal Identity: The Five Tribes and the Politics of Federal Recognition.* Norman: U of Oklahoma P, 2013. Print.

Pevar, Stephen. *The Rights of Indians and Tribes.* New York: Oxford UP, 2012. Print.

Wilkins, David E., and Heidi Kiiwetinepinesiik Stark. *American Indian Politics and the American Political System.* 3rd ed. Lanham: Rowman, 2011. Print.

FEMA RESPONSE TO HURRICANE KATRINA: AN OVERVIEW

More than a year before Hurricane Katrina hit New Orleans in August 2005, the Federal Emergency Management Agency (FEMA) estimated that one-third to one-half of the population of New Orleans would not be able to evacuate the city in time if a Category 3 hurricane hit the city. FEMA planned to institute several sweeping changes in their current aid and disaster relief programs based on their findings.

Nevertheless, when a scenario similar to the one predicted occurred, FEMA seemed to be unprepared. Many people have claimed that, despite FEMA's lack of preparedness, the poor response to Hurricane Katrina represented a failing in all levels of the government, rather than a single agency, and that lack of communication between different agencies caused the ultimate breakdown in relief efforts. The result was the costliest natural disaster in US history.

Many people accused FEMA Director Michael Brown of having insufficient experience in disaster management, but President George W. Bush attracted significant ire, as well, based on what many perceived as a flippant and opportunistic attitude toward the disaster. He was roundly mocked for a comment made during a press conference, saying that Brown—who Bush referred to as "Brownie"—was "doing a heck of a job." Many people pointed out that, despite significant warning of an impending hurricane, FEMA had not made plans for how to evacuate people, reinforce the levees, or ship supplies to survivors. New Orleans has a large population of low-income people without access to cars, who were unable to evacuate on their own. Thus, what seemed to be a slow reaction to the disaster looked to many people like class and race discrimination.

Hurricane Katrina was the first major disaster—natural or man-made—that fell under the jurisdiction of the Department of Homeland Security (DHS). After the lack of adequate response to Hurricane Katrina, many people questioned the efficacy of DHS and wondered how it would respond to an unannounced attack, when it was clear that it was incapable of managing a predicted disaster such as Hurricane Katrina. In the fallout after Katrina, FEMA was scrutinized by the media and the public, and many found fault with its handling of prior disasters. For example, it was discovered that, after Hurricane Frances, which hit Florida in 2004, FEMA paid $31 million to residents of Miami-Dade County, which was one of the few areas of Florida that had not been hit by the storm.

HISTORY

Despite FEMA's fairly narrow aim, once it became part of DHS in 2003, 75 percent of its budget was dedicated to anti-terrorism, according to the Government Accountability Office (GAO). Many have criticized this reallocation as incompatible with FEMA's mission, though some critics have said that natural disasters require the same skills and the same actions as terrorist attacks or any other disaster, and thus the placement of FEMA under the DHS umbrella was appropriate.

In July 2004, FEMA conducted an exercise to determine the effect that a Category 3 hurricane, with 120-mile-per-hour winds, would have on New Orleans. The exercise, called Hurricane Pam, was remarkably prescient, predicting that water from Lake Pontchartrain would overwhelm the levees, flooding much of the city and damaging 87 percent of the city's homes. FEMA also predicted that about half of the New Orleans population would evacuate prior to the flooding. The results of the Hurricane Pam exercise showed that a comprehensive plan would have to be instituted to avoid the predicted outcome. At that time, director Michael Brown noted the importance of planning in Louisiana and said "Over the next sixty days, we will polish the action plans developed during the Hurricane Pam exercise."

More than a year later, on August 29, 2005, Hurricane Katrina struck Louisiana. The storm had already hit Florida but had since moved back out into the Gulf of Mexico and gained strength, becoming a Category 4 storm. The 145-mile-per-hour winds and 28-foot waves overwhelmed the 17.5-foot New Orleans levees, flooding parts of the city almost immediately. About five hours after this first strike, Brown sent a request to DHS Director Michael Chertoff for 1,000 additional aid workers over the next two days, followed by 2,000 more in the following week. The memo, which eventually was leaked to the Associated Press, seemed to illustrate that Brown had underestimated the severity of the disaster.

Displaced New Orleans residents were housed in the city's football stadium called the Superdome for three days before buses arrived to take them to Houston. Additionally, there were thousands of people who had sought refuge in the New Orleans Convention Center, which Brown claimed not to know about until September 1, three days after the storm hit. He later admitted FEMA had known about the Convention Center evacuees on August 31 but was unable to take action until the following day.

In response to the agency's slow reaction time, DHS Director Michael Chertoff announced that the monetary aid delivery process would be streamlined, in order to prevent further delays. Thus, rather than the standard procedure of sending a FEMA official personally assess the damage at each home, the agency allowed people to apply for aid over the phone or online. To further circumvent the logistical problems inherent in distributing large quantities of cash or checks, FEMA and the Red Cross distributed thousands of debit cards valued at $2,000 to victims of the disaster. Nevertheless, the monetary distribution proved to be more difficult to manage than anyone had anticipated. Despite instructions that the debit cards only be used for necessities, such as food and clothing, in September 2005 it was reported that many of the victims who had received government-funded debit cards were using them to buy luxury items.

After distributing more than 10,000 debit cards, with a total value of $20.6 million, FEMA discontinued the program but did not recall the cards that had already been distributed. It also eventually became clear that much of $1.46 billion distributed was given to people and families who either were not affected by the hurricane or had already received their share of the aid. In one New Orleans–area parish, FEMA distributed money to 224,008 applicants, despite there only being about 182,120 households in the parish; this resulted in an apparent overpayment of $83.8 million. In parts of Mississippi, more than 2,000 families that were not displaced by the storm managed to collect funds from FEMA. Inland towns in Louisiana, far from the damage of the hurricane, received upwards of $1.6 million dollars for its residents. Following these revelations, DHS created the Office for Hurricane Katrina Oversight, which was charged with auditing FEMA-distributed funds.

Shortly after the debit card program was discontinued, Brown stepped down from his position at FEMA, and the agency began instead to deposit money directly in victims' bank accounts. Brown was mocked in the media even following his dismissal; many outlets pointed out that Brown's most significant management experience prior to working at FEMA was supervising horse-show judges and that he had only gotten the job at FEMA because the former director had been a friend of his.

Many people have argued that the blame heaped on FEMA is unfair, since there were numerous failings by numerous parties during the disaster. Amtrak officials have claimed that they contacted local authorities to offer free space on a train, with

room for several hundred people, which left New Orleans several hours before the hurricane hit, but were turned down. New Orleans Mayor Ray Nagin denies this offer was ever extended, but there were also reports of unused school buses, abandoned in parking lots, which some say could have been used to evacuate residents. The Red Cross was repeatedly denied access to the city by state officials, first on Thursday, September 1, and then again on the following day, despite possessing adequate supplies and workers to provide necessary aid. Louisiana officials claimed they needed twenty-four hours to set up escorts for the Red Cross workers, but once that time had elapsed, they had already begun evacuating residents. President Bush eventually sent 11,000 active duty troops to help in the relief effort, but not until five days after the hurricane hit, by which point 21,000 National Guard troops were already in place.

FEMA/HURRICANE KATRINA TODAY

According to documents released in December 2005, FEMA officials realized early on that their response was lacking and that their emergency supplies were inadequate. The documents, consisting of correspondence between several FEMA officials and the governors of Mississippi and Louisiana, showed that FEMA realized as early as September 1 that its shipments of water and ice were vastly insufficient. The spokesperson for FEMA admitted that the agency's technology and logistics were insufficient, and Homeland Security Director Michael Chertoff emphasized that updating and repairing the agency would be one of his priorities. In April 2006, the DHS inspector general said that most of the criticism leveled at FEMA for the mismanaged response to Katrina is warranted and made nearly forty suggestions for improving both FEMA and DHS.

In April 2006, President Bush asked Congress to approve an additional $2.2 billion—to come from FEMA's disaster relief fund—to continue the repairs on New Orleans levees. In June 2006, with the next hurricane season looming, DHS declared that New Orleans was not prepared for another disaster.

As of 2007, FEMA was still distributing funds to displaced residents of Louisiana and Mississippi. Despite the overpayments that FEMA made to many families, much of the money allocated for Katrina relief (about $5.1 billion in Louisiana alone) had not found its way into the hands of displaced persons, many of whom were facing eviction, unemployment, and massive reconstruction costs. In January 2007, Louisiana officials appealed to FEMA to distribute the remainder of the money allotted to them, which amounted to about $3 billion.

In late 2008, FEMA stated in a press release that funding to Louisiana for Hurricanes Katrina and Rita totaling $13.7 billion had been spent on relief to individuals, public entities, and for mitigation of hazards. $2.04 billion was spent in 2008 alone. At the height of the disaster about 92,000 families were housed in temporary housing trailers or mobile homes. At the end of 2008, about 26,000 remained in temporary housing. At the same time, reports surfaced of additional problems and needed improvements for one $849 million Katrina relief program. The program was designed to help Louisiana landlords rebuild. These landlords had been unable to access loans to because of the 2008 financial crisis and government bureaucracy. The program, called the Louisiana Small Rental Program, was supposed to result in the restoration of 18,000 rental properties but had only let 433 grants by year end 2008. The goal of the program changes was to reduce bureaucracy by giving money directly to landlords though some government agencies feared yet again duplication of another relief program.

These essays and any opinions, information or representations contained therein are the creation of the particular author and do not necessarily reflect the opinion of EBSCO Information Services.

———*Alex K. Rich and Marlanda English*

BIBLIOGRAPHY AND FURTHER READING

Birkland, Thomas A. *Lessons of Disaster: Policy Change after Catastrophic Events.* Washington, DC: Georgetown UP, 2006. Print.

Childs, John Brown, ed. *Hurricane Katrina: Response and Responsibilities.* Santa Cruz: New Pacific, 2005. Print.

Dyson, Michael Eric. *Come Hell or High Water: Hurricane Katrina and the Color of Disaster.* New York: Basic Civitas, 2006. Print.

Farber, Daniel A., and Jim Chen. *Disasters and the Law: Katrina and Beyond.* New York: Aspen, 2006. Print.

Lindell, Michael K., Carla Prater, and Ronald W. Perry. *Introduction to Emergency Management.* Hoboken: Wiley, 2007. Print.

Mann, Eric. *Katrina's Legacy: White Racism and Black Reconstruction in New Orleans and the Gulf Coast.* Los Angeles: Frontlines, 2006. Print.

Reed, Betsy, ed. *Unnatural Disaster: The Nation on Hurricane Katrina.* New York: Nation, 2006. Print.

FERGUSON UNREST

On August 9, 2014, Michael Brown and his friend, Dorian Johnson, stopped at Ferguson Market and Liquor in Ferguson, Missouri. Surveillance footage from the store's security system shows Brown stealing cigars and intimidating the store clerk. At 11:54 a.m., Brown and Johnson left the store, and police were notified of the robbery and given a description of the suspect. At 12:01 p.m., police officer Darren Wilson encountered Brown and Johnson walking down the middle of Canfield Drive. Wilson ordered the pair to move onto the sidewalk. Brown and Johnson ignored Wilson's order and continued walking down the middle of the street.

At that point, Wilson realized that Brown matched the description of the suspect in the robbery, and he stopped his vehicle near Brown and Johnson. Reports about the events that followed vary. Brown allegedly reached into Wilson's vehicle and hit Wilson in the face, and the two struggled over Wilson's firearm. During the struggle, Wilson fired two shots, one of which hit Brown. Brown then ran, and Wilson reportedly called for backup and pursued Brown on foot. Wilson and some witnesses stated that Brown then turned and charged at him; other eyewitness testimony stated that Brown turned toward Wilson and put his hands up in the air. Either way, Wilson fired at Brown several more times, and Brown died at the scene. Multiple autopsies of Brown's body indicated that he had at least six bullet wounds.

AFTERMATH OF THE SHOOTING

A wave of riots, protests, and demonstrations erupted in Ferguson after the shooting. Some groups rallied around Brown and his family, arguing that Brown had

Tear gas. By Loavesofbread (Own work).

tried to surrender and that Wilson had used excessive force against him. Others threw their support behind Wilson, arguing that Brown had assaulted the officer and that Wilson had acted in self-defense.

On August 10, a candlelight vigil to mourn Brown turned violent. Some members of the crowd became rowdy and confronted police. Others began looting businesses and vandalizing vehicles. A convenience store was lit on fire. Police officers in riot gear responded to the chaos, which continued into the early morning hours of August 11.

Rioting and protests continued in the following days, and police began to use more forceful methods to disperse crowds, including firing bean bags and rubber bullets at protesters and setting off tear gas. The rallying cry often heard during the protests was "Hands up, don't shoot," the implication being that Brown had been trying to surrender when he was shot.

A week after the shooting, the riots and demonstrations, which seemed to grow worse overnight, prompted Missouri governor Jay Nixon to declare a state of emergency in Ferguson and impose a curfew between midnight and 5 a.m. When violent clashes between police and protesters continued, Nixon called in the National Guard to help control the situation. Demonstrations and rallies, some violent and some peaceful, continued through September, October, and November.

GRAND JURY DECISION

Following the shooting, a grand jury was selected to determine whether enough evidence existed for an indictment against Wilson, or to charge him with a crime in connection with the shooting. Over a period of three months, the grand jury listened to testimony from medical examiners, police officers (including

Wilson), and eyewitnesses. On November 24, the grand jury decided not to indict Wilson. Based on the evidence presented, the jury members believed that Wilson had acted in self-defense when he fired at Brown.

The grand jury's decision sparked another wave of protests in Ferguson and increased the momentum of activists such as those in the Black Lives Matter movement. Rioters set fire to at least twelve buildings and one vehicle. Angry protesters hurled objects at police and members of the National Guard, who tried to use tear gas and smoke to disperse unruly crowds.

NATIONWIDE UNREST

Protests and demonstrations were not confined to Ferguson, however. In cities across the United States, from Los Angeles to New York, people protested the grand jury's decision in the streets. Many have suggested that the problems in Ferguson are indicative of much larger issues, including racial and ethnic discrimination, civil rights abuses, and militarization of police forces. Both the Federal Bureau of Investigation and the Justice Department launched investigations to determine whether discrimination, misuse of force, or civil rights abuses occurred in Ferguson.

The unrest in Ferguson also contributed to a growing distrust of police. In Brooklyn, New York, a gunman referenced Brown's shooting death on social media before exacting "revenge" on law enforcement by shooting two New York City police officers on December 20, 2014. Both officers, Wenjian Liu and Rafael Ramos, died as a result of their injuries.

In March 2015, the Justice Department concluded its investigation, determining that Ferguson's criminal justice system was so fraught with constitutional violations and had such an ingrained culture of racism that it needed to be entirely rethought and reworked. Not long after these findings were publicized, Thomas Jackson, Ferguson's police chief, resigned from his position. On the anniversary of Brown's death in August of that year, several nights of protest occurred once more on the streets of Ferguson, resulting in several arrests. Later that year, the Justice Department released yet another report that criticized the police response to the initial unrest in Ferguson as inadequate and ineffective due to a lack of understanding about community views of law enforcement.

Throughout 2015 and into 2016, the issues of police brutality and racism brought forth by the shooting of Brown continued to remain areas of concern and spark further protest as more shootings of African Americans by white police officers occurred.

——*Lindsay Rohland*

BIBLIOGRAPHY AND FURTHER READING

Bello, Marisol, and Yamichie Alcindor. "Police in Ferguson Ignite Debate About Military Tactics." *USA Today*, 19 Aug. 2014, www.usatoday.com/story/news/nation/2014/08/14/ferguson-militarized-police/14064675/. Accessed 18 Oct. 2016.

Buchanan, Larry, et al. "What Happened in Ferguson?" *New York Times*, 25 Nov. 2014, www.nytimes.com/interactive/2014/08/13/us/ferguson-missouri-town-under-siege-after-police-shooting.html. Accessed 18 Oct. 2016.

Celona, Larry, et al. "Gunman Executes 2 NYPD Cops in Garner 'Revenge.'" *New York Post*, 20 Dec. 2014, nypost.com/2014/12/20/2-nypd-cops-shot-execution-style-in-brooklyn/. Accessed 18 Oct. 2016.

Eckholm, Erik. "Witnesses Told Grand Jury That Michael Brown Charged at Darren Wilson, Prosecutor Says." *New York Times*, 24 Nov. 2014, www.nytimes.com/2014/11/25/us/witnesses-told-grand-jury-that-michael-brown-charged-at-darren-wilson-prosecutor-says.html?_r=1. Accessed 18 Oct. 2016.

Ellis, Ralph, Jason Hanna, and Shimon Prokupecz. "Missouri Governor Imposes Curfew in Ferguson, Declares Emergency." *CNN*, 16 Aug. 2014, www.cnn.com/2014/08/16/us/missouri-teen-shooting/. Accessed 18 Oct. 2016.

"Ferguson State of Emergency Ends after Week of Michael Brown Protests." *Guardian*, 14 Aug. 2015, www.theguardian.com/us-news/2015/aug/14/ferguson-state-of-emergency-ends-michael-brown. Accessed 18 Oct. 2016.

"Ferguson Unrest: From Shooting to Nationwide Protests." *BBC News*, 26 Nov. 2014, www.bbc.com/news/world-us-canada-30193354. Accessed 18 Oct. 2016.

Kesling, Ben, and Dan Frosch. "Justice Department Faults Police Response to Ferguson Unrest." *Wall Street Journal*, 3 Sept. 2015, www.wsj.com/articles/justice-department-faults-police-response-to-ferguson-unrest-1441300481. Accessed 18 Oct. 2016.

Mejia, Paula. "Altercation Between Michael Brown and Darren Wilson Unfolded in 90 Seconds: Report." *Newsweek*, 15 Nov. 2014, www.newsweek. com/altercation-between-michael-brown-and-officer-darren-wilson-unfolded-90-284728. Accessed 18 Oct. 2016.

"What Happened in Ferguson?" *New York Times*, 10 Aug. 2015, www.nytimes.com/interactive/2014/08/13/us/ferguson-missouri-town-under-siege-after-police-shooting.html. Accessed 18 Oct. 2016.

FIFTEEN PRINCIPLES

In 1983, in the midst of federal constitutional negotiations, the province of Quebec established a legal framework to guide its relationships with the Inuit and Indian residents of Quebec. Known as the Fifteen Principles, the policy statement affirmed that the province of Quebec accepted native claims to self-determination with respect to culture, education, language, and economic development. It further acknowledged that Inuit and Indian residents are entitled to certain aboriginal rights and land claims (left to be determined by future negotiations). Finally, the Fifteen Principles recognized that those aboriginal rights applied equally to men and women.

The Fifteen Principles were adopted, in large part, to bolster the claim by the ruling Parti Québécois that Quebec is a distinct and sovereign nation either within or apart from Canada. If this was to be the case, Quebec could not argue, as it had previously, that the federal government bore sole responsibility for native residents living within the borders of Quebec. In fact, it was Quebec's earlier insistence that the federal government must absorb all the costs of native administration that led to the 1939 Supreme Court decision that for legal purposes Inuit were to be regarded as Indians as specified in the British North America Act

of 1867. By adopting the Fifteen Principles, Quebec attempted to place itself on equal footing with the Canadian government.

——*Pamela R. Stern*

BIBLIOGRAPHY AND FURTHER READING

Barrett, Carole A. *American Indian History*. Pasadena: Salem, 2003. *eBook Collection (EBSCOhost)*. Web. 23 Apr. 2015.

Boldt, Menno. *Surviving as Indians: The Challenge of Self-Government*. Toronto: U of Toronto P, 1993. *eBook Collection (EBSCOhost)*. Web. 23 Apr. 2015.

Fraser, Graham, and Ivon Owen. *René Lévesque & the Parti Québécois in Power*. Montreal: MQUP, 2001. Print.

Lindau, Juan David, and Curtis Cook. *Aboriginal Rights and Self-Government: The Canadian and Mexican Experience in North America*. Montreal: MQUP, 2000. *eBook Collection (EBSCOhost)*. Web. 23 Apr. 2015.

Maurais, Jacques. *Quebec's Aboriginal Languages: History, Planning, and Development*. Clevedon: Multilingual Matters, 1996. *eBook Collection (EBSCOhost)*. Web. 23 Apr. 2015.

FIFTEENTH AMENDMENT

The purpose of the Fifteenth amendment was to extend the franchise to the African American men who had been freed from slavery as a result of the Civil War. At the time, women were not regarded as citizens and were therefore not covered by the measure. The amendment marked a continuation of the program of the Republican Party to provide political rights for black men after the defeat of the Confederacy. The Thirteenth Amendment had

ended slavery, and the Fourteenth Amendment had provided civil rights to all citizens born or naturalized in the United States. These amendments, however, had not ensured that black men could vote throughout the United States. To accomplish that end, the Republicans in Congress, in a lame-duck Congress that met in early 1869, decided that ensuring the right to vote would both carry on the moral impetus of Reconstruction (1863-1877) and

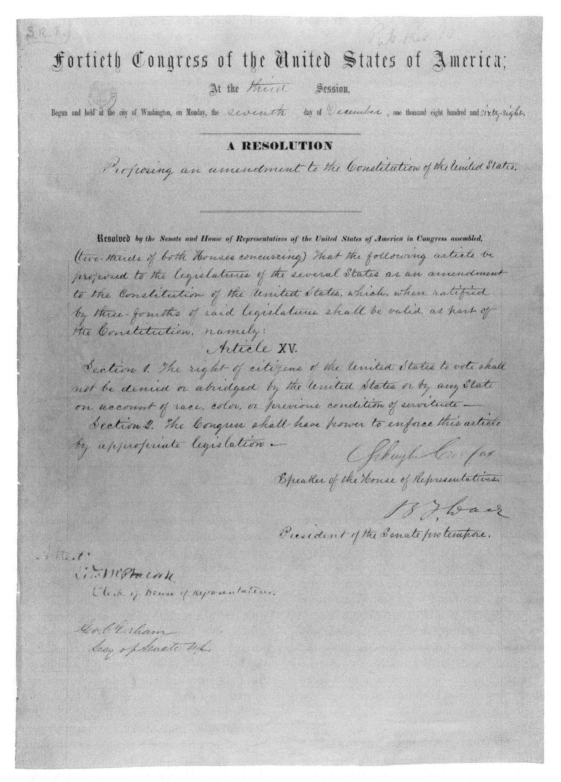

The Fifteenth Amendment in the National Archives. By National Archives of the United States.

act to offset any political comeback of the antiblack Democratic Party.

A constitutional amendment would have the additional benefit, as the Republicans saw it, of providing a clear legal basis for enforcement of voting rights in the South. In its language, the amendment did not ensure that blacks could hold public positions nor did it rule out such barriers to voting as literacy tests or property requirements. Nonetheless, it represented a clear forward step for African Americans and offered the promise of greater participation in elections and the operations of government.

The ratification process broke down along the existing party alignments of the Reconstruction era. Republicans favored the measure and Democrats resisted it in the state legislatures that addressed ratification. It required vigorous campaigning, especially in such key states as Ohio, to achieve approval from the requisite number of states by March, 1870.

Despite its place in the US Constitution, the Fifteenth Amendment did not prevent southerners from excluding African Americans from the political process at the end of the nineteenth century. With a political stalemate between Republicans and Democrats in Washington, enforcement of the amendment proved difficult. Federal courts did not encourage a broad interpretation of the amendment. In 1889-1890, the Republicans endeavored to strengthen federal legislation to ensure fair elections in the South, but Democrats defeated their efforts. When the Democrats regained control of the White House and both branches of Congress in 1893-1895, they repealed the existing legislation that gave the government authority over elections. As a result, discriminatory practices kept African Americans from voting in many parts of the South for three-quarters of a century.

In the middle of the twentieth century with the rise of the Civil Rights movement, efforts resumed to revive the Fifteenth Amendment. The Voting Rights Act of 1965 enabled blacks to enter the political process in large numbers and, in so doing, to redeem the unfulfilled promise that the framers of the Fifteenth Amendment had originally envisioned. However, it was the expansion of civil rights under the Fourteenth Amendment that had, and continues to have, the greater impact.

——*Lewis L. Gould*

FILIPINO AMERICANS AND RACE RELATIONS

The term "Filipino" refers to someone who comes from the Philippines, or whose ancestors are from the Philippines, a nation consisting of a cluster of islands located across the China Sea from mainland Southeast Asia. The Philippines has close ties to the United States because it was a US possession or territory from 1898 to 1946. The United States established English as the language of instruction in high schools and colleges in the Philippines, and Filipinos have long been familiar with American movies and other media. Filipinos began settling in North America soon after the Philippines became part of the United States, and the numbers of Filipino Americans began to increase greatly in the late 1960s.

HISTORY OF FILIPINO AMERICAN SETTLEMENT
Filipino settlement in North America falls into three major periods. The first period, from 1906 to the beginning of World War II in 1941, resulted from the US demand for cheap agricultural labor. Sugar plantations dominated the economy of Hawaii early in the twentieth century, and plantation owners were interested in finding hardworking field hands who would work for low wages. The Hawaii Sugar Planters Association began recruiting in the Philippines, and by 1946, the association had brought more than a quarter of a million Filipinos to Hawaii. California, which also had a need for seasonal agricultural workers, was the home of more than thirty-one thousand of the forty-six thousand Filipinos living on the mainland in 1940. Filipino Americans continue to make up part of the migrant farm labor force of California and other western states, but the numbers of migrant Filipino workers are steadily decreasing.

The second migration period began in 1946, when the Philippines became politically independent of the United States. Large US military bases had been established in the Philippines, and many of the Filipinos admitted to the United States were women married to American servicemen. At the same time, Filipinos who had become naturalized American citizens after the war were able to petition to have family members enter the United States. Because of these two factors, most immigrants in this period came as a result of marriage or family connections.

The United States maintained military bases in the Philippines until 1991, so Filipinos who married US military personnel continued to arrive in the United States. Another form of migration through marriage is the phenomenon of mail-order brides, women who meet and marry American men through correspondence. In the 1990s, approximately nineteen thousand mail-order brides were leaving the Philippines each year to join husbands and fiancés abroad, with the United States as the primary destination. In 1997, social scientist Concepcion

Quarters for Filipino workers at a salmon cannery in Nushagak, Alaska in 1917. John Nathan Cobb.

Montoya identified Filipina mail-order brides, who often establish social networks among themselves, as a rapidly emerging American community.

The third migration period began in 1965, when the United States passed a new immigration law that ended the discrimination against Asians present in all previous immigration laws. The result was a rapid growth in the Asian American population in general and in the Filipino American population in particular. The number of Filipinos living in the United States grew by roughly 100 percent in each ten-year period from 1960 to 1990: from 176,000 in the census of 1960 to 343,000 in that of 1970, to 775,000 in 1980, to more than 1,400,000 in the 1990 census.

The third period of Filipino immigration differs greatly from the earlier periods. Although immigrants before 1965 were mostly laborers from the rural Philippines, immigrants after 1965 tended to be highly educated professionals (such as doctors, nurses, teachers, and engineers), and they often came from cities. Migration to the United States became a goal for many Filipino professionals because economic opportunities were much greater in the United States. During the 1970s, one out of every five graduates of nursing schools in the Philippines left for the United States, and

the majority of those nurses did not return to the Philippines. This may have created "brain drain" problems for the Philippines, because it lost many of its medical professionals, executives, and technicians to the United States, but this migration has been a benefit to the American economy. Filipino doctors and nurses are on the staff of many US hospitals, and teachers from the Philippines are employed in many US schools.

FILIPINOS IN AMERICAN SOCIETY

By 2010, about 3.4 million people in the United States identified themselves as Filipino Americans. Nearly two-thirds of these Filipino Americans lived in California, and almost another third of the members of this group lived in Hawaii. The Seattle area is also home to a fairly large number of Filipinos, as is the Las Vegas area.

Most Filipino Americans are immigrants. In 1990, of all Filipinos in the United States, 64 percent were foreign-born and almost one-third had arrived during the previous decade. Numbers of foreign-born Filipinos increased even more during the 1990s. From 1990 to March 1997, according to US Census Bureau estimates, the number of foreign-born Filipino Americans grew from 913,723 to 1,132,000. By the time of the 2010 census, that trend seemed firmly in place, with nearly sixty-nine percent having been born outside the United States.

Women outnumber men among foreign-born Filipinos, largely because marriage to US citizens has continued to be a major source of migration from the Philippines. In 1990, women made up 57 percent of all foreign-born Filipino Americans and almost 60 percent of foreign-born Filipino Americans who had arrived during the 1980s. In the 2000s and 2010s, women still made up a majority of US Filipino residents, many of them employed in the domestic service industry.

The fact that professionals, especially medical professionals, have been such a large part of the third wave of immigrants has meant that many Filipino Americans hold middle-class jobs. A majority of employed Filipinos in the United States (55 percent) held white-collar jobs in 1990, but in later decades that number was rivaled by those working in the service industries. Almost one out of every four employed Filipino Americans over the age of sixteen worked in health services. By contrast, fewer than one out of every ten employed Americans of all backgrounds worked in hospitals or in health-related jobs in that year.

The professional specialization of so many Filipino Americans tends to make them a relatively prosperous group. The median household income of Filipino Americans in 2010 was $75,000, compared with $66,000 among Americans in general. Further, although 10 percent of all American families lived below the poverty level, only slightly more than 5 percent of Filipino families in the United States lived in poverty.

Many Filipino Americans, especially the early agricultural laborers in California, experienced discrimination. However, contemporary Filipinos usually report relatively few problems in their relations with members of other racial and ethnic groups. Familiarity with the English language and with mainstream American culture, high levels of marriage with white and black Americans, and a concentration in skilled occupations and white-collar professions tend to help Filipino Americans in interethnic relations.

One reflection of the high degree of integration of Filipino Americans into American society is the high percentage of foreign-born Filipino Americans who take on US citizenship. More than one-fourth of the Filipinos who arrived in the United States during the 1980s had been naturalized as citizens by 1990. More than 80 percent of those who had arrived before 1980 had become citizens. By contrast, fewer than 15 percent of all people who had immigrated to the United States in the 1980s had become citizens, and only 61 percent of foreign-born people who had immigrated before 1980 had become citizens.

——*Carl L. Bankston III*

Bibliography and Further Reading

Cherry, Stephen M. *Faith, Family, and Filipino American Community Life.* New Brunswick: Rutgers UP, 2014. Print.

Jamero, Peter. *Vanishing Filipino Americans: The Bridge Generation.* Lanham: UP of America, 2011. Print.

Okamura, Jonathan Y. *Imagining the Filipino Diaspora: Transnational Relations, Identities, and Communities.* New York: Routledge, 2011. Print.

Zhao, Xiaojian, and Edward J. W. Park, eds. *Asian Americans: An Encyclopedia of Social, Cultural, Economic, and Political History.* Santa Barbara: ABC-CLIO, 2013. Print.

Filipino Veterans' movement

In 1941, after the beginning of World War II, United States president Franklin D. Roosevelt signed an order to bring draftees and volunteers in the Philippines, then under US rule, into the US Army. The order promised full veterans' benefits to all Filipinos who served. In 1942, the US Congress promised American citizenship to all Filipino soldiers who wanted to apply after the war. However, in 1946, when the war was over, the US Congress voted to deny both veterans' benefits and citizenship to Filipino veterans of the US military.

In 1997, Congress began to consider a Filipino veterans' equity bill. Of the 240,000 Filipinos who served in the US military, 70,000 were still alive and about half of the survivors were living in the United States. These former soldiers organized demonstrations in cities around the United States, especially

Los Angeles and Washington, DC, during 1997 and 1998 to urge passage of the equity bill.

In 2009, as part of the American Recovery and Reinvestment Act, all Filipino veterans of World War II were offered a one-time payment of $15,000 for US citizens and $9000 for noncitizens. Many Filipino veterans were dissatisfied with this gesture, and there were enough complaints of claims being unfairly rejected that the US government formed a committee to look into these problems and work for greater transparency in the process. A bill called the Filipino Veterans Equity Act, assuring citizenship for any Filipino citizen who has completed an enlistment in the US armed forces, has been introduced multiple times by members of both parties since 1993, but has died in committee on every occasion.

——*Carl L. Bankston III*

FINANCIAL CRISIS OF 2008 AND COMMUNITIES OF COLOR

While the full history of the financial crisis of 2008 and its aftermath is still being written, one of the underappreciated aspects of the lead-up to and the fallout from that crisis is the deleterious impact of pre-crisis practices–and their consequences–on communities of color, most notably the African American middle class. The crisis was a product of many forces, including risky lending together with hyper-inflated speculation and experimentation in financial instruments tied to that risky lending. The foreclosure wave that followed this mortgage frenzy has led to the loss of $9 trillion in wealth from American households, as many homeowners, whether they faced foreclosure or not, saw what is, for many, their most significant asset—the value of their home—depreciate in value considerably. African Americans were affected dramatically, having lost roughly 50 percent of their wealth due to lending practices and the unemployment that followed the crisis. One of the reasons for this is that, as the following discussion shows, African American borrowers were far more likely than white borrowers to find themselves in *subprime loans*, or loans with higher interest rates and poorer terms, generally, compared to conventional loans. The more likely they were to be steered into subprime loans, the more likely such borrowers were to face foreclosure. Moreover, since subprime loans were concentrated in communities of color, the harmful effects of the foreclosure of these loans has fallen more squarely on these same communities.

REDLINING AND SUBPRIME LENDING
The roots of these effects on communities of color can be found in the original practice of "redlining."

Redlining is a practice, often encouraged by federal government actors who indicated in which neighborhoods they would insure mortgages, whereby lenders draw red lines around those neighborhoods having a greater concentration of borrowers of color. As a joint report from the US Department of Housing & Urban Development (HUD) and the US Treasury Department found, this legacy of discrimination meant that in many communities of color, when subprime mortgage lenders sought communities in which to market and sell their loans, these same communities were those ripe for subprime practices because more traditional lenders had less of a history of lending to those communities. As a result, when subprime lending came on the scene in the late 1990s, financial institutions marketing and packaging such loans found themselves looking to lend in these communities. The practice of redlining thus turned into "reverse redlining": targeting communities of color for loans on unfair terms, as opposed to excluding such communities from traditional lending.

While bringing mortgage products to communities historically excluded from such lending might be seen as cause for celebration, this positive view changes when one considers that many of these borrowers received loan terms that were more onerous than white borrowers of similar credit risk, with predictable results. While significant gains were made in homeownership rates in communities of color in the early 2000s, much of this expansion was fueled by subprime loans. As analysis of lending practices conducted on behalf of the Federal Reserve showed, in 2005 alone, the height of the subprime mortgage frenzy, while only 20 percent of all mortgages issued in that year had subprime features, more than half of the mortgages made to African American families, and 40 percent of mortgages made to Latino families, were subprime in nature. The history of lending discrimination in these communities meant there was pent up demand for home loans, fewer traditional lending options, and fewer channels that could offer sensible, informed counsel and advice.

Analysis in the joint HUD-Treasury report that looked at lending in the early days of the subprime mortgage market's expansion showed that, in 1998, 39 percent of residents of upper-income African American neighborhoods used subprime products to refinance their existing mortgages, compared to just 6 percent of residents of upper-income white neighborhoods. In an even starker contrast, residents of *low-income* white neighborhoods refinanced their homes with subprime products only 18 percent of the time. Thus, in 1998, even before the subprime mortgage market became overheated, upper-income residents of African American neighborhoods were twice as likely as residents of low-income white neighborhoods to utilize subprime refinance products.

Additional lending data, from 2006, reveals similar discrepancies in subprime lending based on race. Roughly 54 percent of home purchase loans made to African Americans in that year had subprime features, compared to only 18 percent of the loans made to non-Hispanic whites. Even controlling for some borrower and lender characteristics, including income, 30 percent of loans made to African American borrowers still had subprime features, compared to 18 percent for whites. Thus, African American borrowers of similar economic profile to their white counterparts still took out subprime loans at nearly twice the rate as whites. Controlling for those same features, Latino borrowers were saddled with subprime loans 24 percent of the time, a nearly 50 percent higher subprime rate as compared to whites. Looking at the refinancing of mortgages, and controlling for many borrower characteristics, subprime refinance loans were extended to blacks 33 percent of the time and to non-Hispanic whites 26 percent of the time in that year—an unexplained difference of 7.3 percent—and Latinos received subprime refinance loans 29.7 percent of the time.

Even within subprime lending there are racial and ethnic disparities in pricing and subprime terms. The Center for Responsible Lending (CRL) studied Housing Mortgage Disclosure Act (HMDA) data from 2004 relating to subprime lending in that year. Controlling for borrower variables, the CRL found that African Americans and Latinos were more likely to have higher priced subprime loans and features, such as prepayment penalties, than similarly situated white borrowers. The researchers found that "Latinos and African Americans were 28 percent and 37 percent more likely, respectively, to receive a higher-rate subprime loan than whites." With fixed-rate home purchase loans carrying prepayment penalties, African Americans were 31 percent more likely than whites to have higher interest rates on their loans, and 34 percent more likely to have higher interest rates in their refinance loans. For Latinos, the figures are even more striking: for fixed-rate home purchase loans carrying a prepayment penalty, Latino borrowers were 45 percent more likely to receive a loan with a higher interest rate than white borrowers; with fixed-rate loans without a prepayment penalty, Latino borrowers were 142 percent more likely to have a higher interest rate than similarly situated white borrowers.

For lending in 2007, analysis of HMDA data actually reveals some improvements in subprime lending to African Americans and Latinos, which was probably a product of more than a hundred subprime mortgage lenders going out of business in that year; in fact, 169 institutions that reported making home loans in 2006 ceased operations in 2007. A review of the data on the lending patterns of these institutions in terms of their lending to different communities when they were in business, and comparing that lending to industry averages at the time, reveals striking discrepancies. These failed institutions originated subprime loans to blacks 74 percent of the time and to Latinos 63 percent of the time, compared to the industry average of 50 percent and 37 percent, respectively, for all lenders. Thus, the riskiest lenders were those that were more likely to offer subprime loans to African Americans and Latinos.

RISK, FRAUD, AND DISCRIMINATION

While it might be simple to blame borrowers taking out subprime loans for the financial crisis that followed the origination of these loans, the evidence related to the causes of the fallout of the subprime market is that the problem in that market was not risky borrowers but predatory loans. The Center for Community Capital at the University of North Carolina compared the performance of risky subprime loans with loans where strong underwriting guidelines were used, even if the loans were made to borrowers with similar economic profiles. For loans made in 2004, the subprime loans were four times more likely to enter into default than the more stable loan products; in 2006, they were 3.3 times as likely. In other words, "risky" borrowers were not the problem; risky loans were.

Indeed, according to FBI estimates, roughly 80 percent of losses due to mortgage fraud were caused by misconduct by banks and mortgage brokers, not the actions of borrowers. As revealed through an investigation conducted by the US Senate, at least one internal study by the now defunct lender, Washington Mutual, found that in just one of its offices, in Montebello, California, 83 percent of the mortgages originated in that office involved some form of fraud on the part of bank officials.

But it was not simply fraud that resulted in the rampant abusive lending practices in communities of color; it was discrimination as well. As reported in the *New York Times*, affidavits uncovered in a lawsuit filed under the Fair Housing Act, a US law that prohibits race-based discrimination in lending, former employees of the bank Wells Fargo, an aggressive subprime lender facing civil suits and federal investigations, alleged that "[t]he prevailing attitude" in the bank "was that African-American customers weren't savvy enough to know they were getting a bad loan, so we would have a better chance of convincing them to apply for a high-cost, subprime loan." In litigation over allegations of discriminatory lending by Wells Fargo, another bank employee explained that "[i]t was generally assumed that African-American customers were less sophisticated and intelligent and could be manipulated more easily into a subprime loan with expensive terms than white customers."

This sort of targeting of communities of color, particularly middle income communities, for subprime loans is evident from research done on the focus of subprime lending. One study, performed by *The New York Times* on lending patterns in the New York City concluded as follows: "[T]he hardest blows" from subprime lending "rain down on the backbone of minority neighborhoods: the black middle class." Indeed, that study found that in New York City, black households making more than $68,000 a year were

almost five times as likely to hold high-interest subprime mortgages as were whites of similar—and even lower—incomes.

Taking a national perspective, and looking at foreclosure rates by state in the height of the foreclosure crisis—late 2010—and combining such rates with a number of factors—namely the percentage of economic inequality in a state, the median income of the African American community in a state, and the percentage of the African American community in a particular state—yields a striking picture that supports the idea that that the African-American middle class was targeted for subprime loans (see Table 1).

This data analysis is consistent with the findings of a report issued by the National Community Reinvestment Coalition, which described the effects of a legacy of discrimination in communities of color as including being the locus of "disproportionately high numbers of subprime loans" and "historically lower homeownership rates." This was a product of the bank redlining outlined above. "[W]hen financial institutions rapidly expanded their lending to minority households," the researchers would find, "it was associated with the use of high-cost, or otherwise unfair and abusive products." That "high density of subprime loans" meant a higher incidence of foreclosures as well as declining property values and increased crime.

TABLE 1. TARGETING THE BLACK MIDDLE CLASS

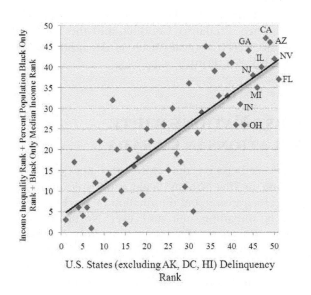

U.S. States (excluding AK, DC, HI) Delinquency Rank

Furthermore, as Table 1 suggests, the targeting of African Americans for subprime loans would appear to be more prevalent in larger and wealthier African American communities. Indeed, the correlation between borrower median income and the size of the African American population with foreclosure rates in a state suggests just that: the larger the African American middle class in a state, and the wealthier it was, the more likely that subprime lending was more prevalent in that state (hence the higher foreclosure rates, because foreclosures are more prevalent with subprime loans). It is not surprise, then, that the foreclosure tsunami that followed the financial crisis of 2008 had devastating effects on communities of color, particularly those targeted for subprime loans during the lead up to the crisis.

——*Ray Brescia*

BIBLIOGRAPHY AND FURTHER READING

Avery, Robert B., et al. *Higher-Priced Home Lending and the 2005 HMDA Data.* Federal Reserve Bulletin. Washington, DC: Federal Reserve, 2006.

Barr, Michael S. "Credit Where It Counts: The Community Reinvestment Act and Its Critics." New York University Law Review 80 (2005): 513. Print.

Bocian, Debbie Gruenstein, et al. *Unfair Lending: The Effect of Race and Ethnicity on the Price of Subprime Mortgages.* Durham: Center for Responsible Lending, 2006. PDF file.

Brecia, Raymond H. "The Cost of Inequality: Social Distance, Predatory Conduct, and the Financial Crisis." *NYU Annual Survey of American Law* 66 (2010): 241. Print.

Carr, James H., et al. *State of Black Housing in America.* Lanham: National Association of Real Estate Brokers, 2013. PDF file.

Ding, Lei, et al. "Risky Borrowers or Risky Mortgages Disaggregating Effects Using Propensity Score Models." *Journal of Real Estate Research* 33 (2011): 245.

Engel, Kathleen C., and Patricia A. McCoy. "The CRA Implications of Predatory Lending." *Fordham Urban Law Journal* 29 (2002): 1571.

Federal Bureau of Investigations. U.S. Department of Justice, Financial Crimes Report to the Public. Washington, DC: FBI/DOJ, 2005. PDF file.

Gordon, Adam. "The Creation of Homeownership: How New Deal Changes in Banking Regulation Simultaneously Made Homeownership Accessible to Whites and Out of Reach for Blacks." *Yale Law Journal* 115 (2005): 186. Print.

Immergluck, Dan. *Credit to the Community: Community Reinvestment and Fair Lending Policy in the United States.* New York: Routledge, 2004. Print.

Jayasundera, Tamara, et al. *Foreclosure in the Nation's Capital: How Unfair and Reckless Lending Undermines Homeownership.* Washington, DC: National Community Reinvestment Coalition, 2010. PDF file.

Kiff, John, and Paul Mills. *Money for Nothing and Checks for Free: Recent Developments in U.S. Subprime Mortgage Markets.* Washington, DC: International Monetary Fund, 2007. PDF file.

U.S. Department of Housing and Urban Development and U.S. Department of Treasury. *Curbing Predatory Home Mortgage Lending: A Joint Report.* Washington, DC, 2000. PDF file.

FIRST NATIONS-WHITE RELATIONS IN CANADA

Relations between the whites and aboriginals in Canada, or First Nations, began with exploration followed by invasion and domination by the European powers spreading into and over North America during the sixteenth and seventeenth centuries. British and French competing interests and colonialization, piqued by growing trade economies and political conflicts, decimated and divided the native nations and peoples along the Saint Lawrence waterway and the Great Lakes. Larger confederacies that were effectively destroyed include the Haudenosaunee, known as the Six Nations Iroquois Confederacy, and the Wyandot-Huron alliances. The Mohawk at Kahnesatake were particularly targeted, but they and other Iroquoian peoples, have survived as a people and a nation into modern times.

Eric Wolf in *Europe and the People Without History* (1982) describes some of these processes from the world-systems analysis perspective, including the European Canadian expansion into and incorporation of Indian lands through the fur trade and the incursion's effects on First Nations across the northern woodlands and plains and in the northern tundra and arctic regions. Small wars and internecine fighting characterized much of the Indian-white relations extending from the Great Lakes region to the western seaboard; generally peaceful negotiations were followed by large land transfers first to the incursive colonial power of England and then to the Canadian commonwealth. Major wars connected to the formation and expansion of the United States from the eastern colonies across the Great Lakes region had generally devastating effects on native peoples and their nations. Colonial powers and the Americans forced First Nation peoples into alignments with warring governments and then punished those native Canadians connected with the other side, typically not recognizing earlier treaties and agreements. The British and Americans, after forcing the French out, rarely observed treaty agreements with those First Nations who sided with them, instead whittling away at their lands and sometimes relocating them to frontier areas and usually into further conflicts.

CULTURAL GENOCIDE

These wars and a series of intertribal conflicts led to the First Nation peoples involved being stereotyped as "savage" and "uncivilized." These same labels were applied to those native peoples resisting the European Canadian expansion and conquest of western and northern frontiers, pitting white settlers against Indians in struggles over land and trade. In the 1700s and 1800s, European Canadians employed coercive assimilation practices. They forced Indian children into residential boarding schools that attempted to eliminate native cultures and replace them with "civilized" white lifestyles. This attempt to destroy native families and their historical and cultural legacies exacerbated tensions between Indians and whites. Most of these practices continued well into the 1950s and 1960s. In 1867, the British North America Act established the dominion of Canada and formalized the development of "reserves" based on diminished land claims and treaty provisions. Despite the establishment of reserves and attempts to

Chief Anotklosh of the Taku Tribe. By William Howard Case (1868–1920.)

eliminate Indian culture, Canadian governance was often less harsh than that of the United States. For example, after the 1876 fight over the taking of the Black Hills in direct violation of an 1868 treaty and reservation boundaries, Sitting Bull fled to Canada, where he lived for five years with many Hunkpapa Lakota (Sioux). Also, northern Canadian native peoples such as the Inuit and Cree did not suffer the full effects of the reserve system until the twentieth century.

The policies of coercive assimilation, cultural genocide, boarding schools, relocation, land takings, and sociopolitical erosion of rights did not completely destroy the native peoples of Canada, although many of these groups have undergone intense social change. These patterns are especially evident in the development of the Métis, a mixture of French and Indian peoples, usually Ojibwa or Cree, in the provinces of Manitoba and Saskatchewan down into the Dakotas and Minnesota in the United States. In the late 1800's, Métis leader Louis Riel, Jr., led uprisings in protest of the mistreatment of Métis, the

MILESTONES IN INDIAN-WHITE RELATIONS IN CANADA

Year	Event
1600's	Europeans make contact with First Nation peoples along the eastern seaboard and the St. Lawrence waterway.
1700's	British and French establish towns, colonies, and trade networks in the new land, creating multiple treaties with First Nation peoples and beginning their incursion into and taking of native peoples' land.
1763	Royal Proclamation (of Indian Country) establishes First Nation peoples as treaty-making entities with which the English crown may negotiate regarding land and trade.
1794	John Jay's Treaty (between the United States and Great Britain) completely omits mention of First Nation peoples, disregarding the Royal Proclamation of 1763.
1849	Residential boarding schools for First Nation children are established across Canada, creating a pattern of coercive assimilation and extreme discrimination against aboriginal cultures that lasts until the 1960's.
1850's	Great Lakes Ojibwa and other treaties and unilateral agreements establish physical distinctions between First Nation territories and European Canadian settlements.
1867	British North America Act (which established the Dominion of Canada) creates a singular nation without formal recognition of First Nation treaty provisions.
1880's	Attempts by the Métis to defend their rights lead to armed conflict with Canadian government forces.
1885	Louis Riel, Jr., returns to Canada after living in exile, leads a failed Métis rebellion over cultural rights and land claims, and is hanged for treason.
1900's	Series of laws, edicts, and "agreements" passed unilaterally by Canada cause erosion of cultural and sovereignty rights for First Nations and establish reserves.
1970's	James Bay and Northern Quebec Agreement, bolstered by the Meech Lake Accord, take away indigenous peoples' lands for development purposes.
1980's	Increasingly better organized indigenous peoples make claims to the United Nations about ongoing discrimination and establish the Assembly of the First Nations.
1990	In Oka, a conflict between European Canadians and Mohawks over ancient lands related to Kahnesatake leads to armed conflict with Canadian military forces and increased discrimination.
1997	Oral tradition as a basis for land claims is recognized by the Canadian Supreme Court.
1998	The Canadian government issues a Statement of Reconciliation, a formal apology to the First Nations.
2007	Indian Residential Schools Settlement Agreement provides compensation to former students and promises to chronicle the true experiences of residential school survivors
2008	Prime minister of Canada offers a formal apology to all former students of residential schools
2015	First Nations' genocide publicly acknowledged by Quebec premier

government's nonrecognition of mixed-bloods and their French language, and discriminatory practices against Cree, Ojibwa, and other native languages and cultures. The Riel-led and similar uprisings were termed rebellions and put down by the federal and local military, leading to many indiscriminate killings. Riel was hanged for treason in 1885, as were four other native leaders. The Canadian government's suppression of the Métis, who represented an early mixing of European and indigenous cultures, marks the government's division of racial identities into two definite categories: white and Indian.

FURTHER DETERIORATION OF RELATIONS

Indian-white relations continued to deteriorate in the first half of the twentieth century because unilateral government edicts, laws, and agreements eroded cultural and political sovereignty of native peoples. In tandem with existing negative stereotypes and active social discrimination, whites in the dominant culture ignored or repressed Indians on reserves and discriminated against urban Indians as racial minorities. These attitudinal practices, with Canadian government support, spread throughout Canada.

Boarding school policies, land-reduction strategies, and government-appointed "tribal councils" generally had negative effects and demoralized First Nation peoples, sometimes leading to friction with whites living nearby. Criminal justice systems began to target Indians more actively in the 1900s. Gradually, indigenous groups began to organize and protest against the injustices. Developments in the United States, including the Civil Rights movement of the 1960s, crossed the border into Canada, resulting in the polarization of native Canadians and European Canadians. Those sympathetic to the native peoples' causes found themselves labeled "Indian lovers" and the targets of criticism.

CONFLICTS AND PROGRESS

In the 1970s, provincial governments fought the First Nations in courts of law. The James Bay I and II coalitions of government and private power companies were formed to take away vast land tracts from Cree and Inuit peoples under the Northern Quebec Agreement. In the 1980's, First Nation members protested this and other governmental acts, stressing issues of sovereignty and self-determination, at meetings of the United Nations in Geneva and later in New York. Many European Canadians supported the

First Nations' efforts. In response, the Assembly of First Nations was formed to provide aboriginal peoples with access to legal and constitutional resources.

Some towns made up primarily of European Canadians resented the sovereignty of First Nation peoples. In 1990, a crisis developed between the Mohawk community, descendants of the Kahnesatake, at Oka in Quebec and the neighboring European Canadians. The town wanted to build a golf course on an area called "the Pines," but the Mohawks considered this area to be treaty land containing sacred burial sites. The Mohawk Warrior Society resisted the taking of the land, and armed forces were called in to "put down" Mohawk resistance without review of the legal grounds for either side's argument. After a long siege, the military prevailed, leading to court trials for Indian resisters. However, because of First Nations representation and public support for the Mohawks, positive dialogues grew out of this confrontation.

In December, 1997, in *Delgamuukw v. British Columbia* , the House of Delgamuukw, speaking on behalf of fifty-one hereditary First Nation chiefs, won an important court victory that recognized the oral tradition as a valid historical source for land claims and cultural authenticity. Also, in 1998, the Canada government extended a formal apology in its Statement of Reconciliation to the First Nations. This official recognition, the first of its kind in Canada, presents a potential for healing and building healthier Indian-white relations in future generations.

—*James V. Fenelon*

BIBLIOGRAPHY AND FURTHER READING

Barman, Jean. "Schooled for Inequality: The Education of British Columbia Aboriginal Children." *Schooling in Transition: Readings in Canadian History of Education* (2012): 255–76. Print.

"First Nations." *AADNC*. Government of Canada, 7 Apr. 2015. Web. 5 June 2015.

"First Nations People in Canada." *AANDC*. Government of Canada, 13 Mar. 2014. Web. 5 June 2015.

MacDonald, David B., and Graham Hudson. "The Genocide Question and Indian Residential Schools in Canada." *Canadian J of Political Science* 45.2 (2012): 427–49. Print.

Muckle, Robert J. *The First Nations of British Columbia: An Anthropological Overview.* Vancouver: U of British Columbia, 2014. Print.

FISHER V. UNIVERSITY OF TEXAS

In 2008, Abagail Fisher and Rachel Michalewicz were denied entry to the University of Texas at Austin. They filed a lawsuit against UT claiming racial discrimination against them because they were white. (Michalewicz dropped out of the lawsuit in 2011.) In 1997, the state legislature had passed a law that everyone who graduated in the top ten percent of their high school class was automatically admitted to main campus of the UT system, UT Austin. This was in response to affirmative action admissions policies having been ruled unconstitutional by the courts. It did increase the number of minority students due to a high number of essentially segregated school systems in Texas. The university asserted that having a diverse student body was beneficial to all students, and therefore, as allowed by state law, used race as one factor in the system used to fill any remaining seats. When the law was passed, it was assumed that about twenty-five percent of the incoming class would be from this pool. However, in 2008, a larger than average number of students accepted automatic admission to UT Austin, which meant that only about nineteen percent of incoming freshmen would not be among those accepted by the university under the ten percent rule.

The formula for the vacant seats was a blend of academic and non-academic criteria. Fisher, in her suit, claimed that she had been denied admittance because she was white. Fisher was in the top twelve percent of her high school class. She had a good SAT score, although not outstandingly high as compared to those who were admitted to UT that year. Her lawyers, supplied by a conservative public policy organization, argued that she would have been admitted if race were not considered, and in addition race should never be a factor in admission's decisions. They could demonstrate that some non-white applicants with weaker academic records did get into UT Austin. However, they could not demonstrate that if Fisher were not white, she would have been admitted.

UT Austin argued the having an inclusive student body was not just about giving minority students opportunities, but about white students benefiting from interaction with non-white students. (The guiding court ruling at that time, *Gruttre v. Bollinger* did allow race to be a secondary consideration, to meet a socially beneficial goal.) UT also showed that under their formula Fisher would not have been admitted if she had not been white. UT could not document exactly how many students were admitted because of race, although it was believed to be relatively few in number, nor could the university document what gains had been achieved because these additional minority students were on campus.

FISHER I – PROCESS AND RULING

Having filed suit in West Texas US District Court, and both sides using argument previously mentioned, the ruling, in 2009, was that UT had acted correctly in developing its policy and its implementation. This was appealed to the Fifth Circuit Court of Appeals, where the three judge panel unanimously also ruled in UT's favor. Thus, in 2012, it was before the Supreme Court. As with many Supreme Court cases, the arguments presented before the court went far beyond the relief sought by the plaintiff. In a 7 to 1 ruling, on June 24, 2013, nine months after initially hearing the case, the justices supported the idea that considerations of race could be legal, if necessary to meet beneficial goals. As a part of this ruling, the majority stated that the Appeals Court had not used "strict scrutiny" to determine if UT's admission program met the previous criteria for a "narrowly tailored" affirmative action program. Thus, the case was once again before the Fifth Circuit.

FISHER II – PROCESS AND FINAL RULING

After studying whether or not UT Austin's admission program followed the new Supreme Court guidelines, by a 2-1 vote the Appeals Court continued to support UT's assertion that it had acted properly. This ruling, in July, 2014, was appealed by Fisher's attorneys to the full circuit, which voted not to rehear the case. Thus, in June, 2015, the Supreme Court agreed to once again take the case, with arguments scheduled for December. At the hearing, UT's attorneys seemed to take a much greater onslaught than did Fisher's. It seemed to most observers that UT's position was not going to be upheld. However, in its 4-3 decision, the Supreme Court ruled in favor of UT with Justice Kennedy writing the majority opinion, the first time he had supported affirmative action. While cautioning the university to continually "assess whether changing demographics have undermined the need for a race-conscious policy," the justices ruled that Fisher had not proven any of the four major points her attorneys raised. These were that: adequate diversity was already present without this policy; enough progress had been made in recent classes; the race factor was such a small part of the admissions process, it could be dropped; and there were other ways to increase diversity without using the current system. Having found none of these convincing and having the Fifth Circuit's finding that UT's policy was stringent, and narrowly defined, the majority rejected the plaintiff's appeal.

The dissenters variously claimed that the university did not have a clear need for more diversity, and the basic position that any use of race is improper. However, the majority thought that the additional benefits from considering race in just this one part of the admission's program, to meet the university's goal of a diverse student body, allowed UT's system to be constitutional. ·

———*Donald A. Watt*

BIBLIOGRAPHY AND FURTHER READING

Barnes, Robert. "Supreme Court upholds University of Texas Affirmative-Action Admissions." *The Washington Post*. Washington: The Washington Post, 2016. Web. 8 February 2017.

Epps, Garrett. "Is Affirmative Action Finished?" *The Atlantic*. Washington: Atlantic Media Company, 2015. Web. 8 February 2017.

Goldstein, Tom, Amy Howe, et al. "Fisher v. University of Texas at Austin." *SCOTUSblog*. Washington: SCOTUSblog, 2017. Web. 8 February 2017.

Liptak, Adam. "Supreme Court Upholds Affirmative Action Program at University of Texas." *The New York Times*. New York: The New York Times Company, 2016. Web. 8 February 2017.

Santoro, Thomas and Stephen Kent Wirth. "Fisher v. University of Texas at Austin (11-345)." *LII Supreme Court Bulletin*. Ithaca NY: Legal Information Institute, Cornell University Law School, 2017. Web. 8 February 2017.

FISH-INS

During the 1960s, American Indians in the Pacific Northwest began to stage fish-ins to protest restrictions on their fishing rights, especially within the states of Washington, Oregon, and Idaho. In turn, sports fishers' groups, commercial fishing operations, and canneries pressured the state governments to get American Indians off the rivers. Controversies over fishing rights stemmed from treaties negotiated with various Pacific Northwest tribes in 1854 and 1855. In those treaties, tribes gave up claim to vast areas of land but specifically preserved fishing rights along waterways ceded to the federal government. Those treaties guaranteed to Indians "the right of taking fish, at all usual and accustomed grounds and stations . . . in common with all citizens of the Territory."

Almost from the start, the states ignored the treaty provisions, and by the 1930s, the states openly restricted Indian subsistence and commercial fishing. Some tribes challenged the states; however, they had no legal success. During the next two decades, state restrictions increased, particularly in the state of Washington, and although some cases went to court, restrictions on Indian fishing were upheld.

In the 1960s, Indian nations began to push for economic development, and tribes began to demand their treaty rights. In the Pacific Northwest, the tribes openly challenged the states' ability to exert regulatory authority over matters negotiated in treaties between the federal government and tribal nations. The state of Washington responded by issuing a series of orders forbidding Indian fishing, and in 1964, Washington set aside the treaty guarantees.

Indians from various affected tribes attempted to channel their energies in a unified front and formed the Survival of American Indians Association in 1964. This organization began a series of actions designed to assert their rights. One important strategy was to engage in night fishing in restricted areas. Washington aggressively policed night fishing, and it confiscated boats, nets, and motors, rammed fishing boats, and prosecuted lawbreakers.

The most dramatic and effective protests sponsored by the Indian association were fish-ins. These were highly publicized events, well attended by

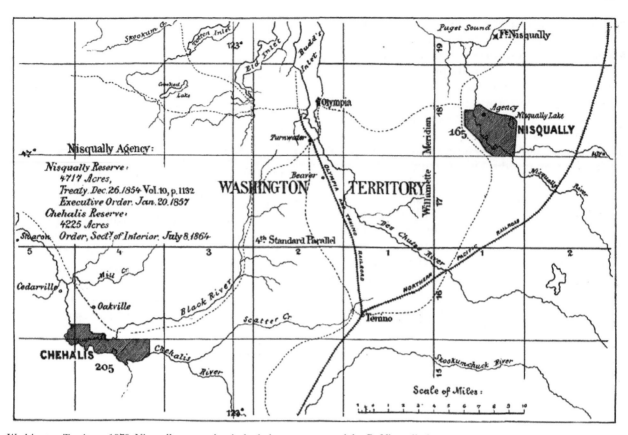

Washington Territory, 1879; Nisqually reservation is shaded area on upper right. By Nisqually Agency.

media, in which Indian people, including many women and children, would assert their treaty rights and fish, despite state restrictions. The state response was aggressive: Often large numbers of game wardens and police swarmed over the protesters and made many arrests. The media documented these incidents, and the fish-ins attracted national attention and even celebrity participants, including actors and entertainers such as Marlon Brando, Jane Fonda, and Dick Gregory. As more Indians were arrested, various church organizations, the American Civil Liberties Union, and prominent lawyers began to provide legal assistance, and this, in turn, increased media coverage.

In 1970, the federal government brought suit to ensure that the states honored the treaties and allowed American Indians a fair harvest of fish. US District Court judge George Boldt sent shockwaves through the Pacific Northwest when he ruled in favor of Indian fishing rights in *United States v. Washington* (1974) and determined that the treaties entitled the Indians to half the fish passing through the waters.

This decision was challenged but remained in force and ultimately allowed many tribes to develop successful economic ventures such as canneries, fish hatcheries, and aquaculture programs. The fish-ins also produced a number of Indian activists who went on to participate in the early years of the American Indian Movement, including Dino Butler, Sid Mills, Janet McCloud, Joseph Stuntz Killsright, and Leonard Peltier.

On April 2, 2014, Governor Jay Inslee of Washington state signed state House Bill 2080, which makes it possible for previous convictions for certain tribal fishing activities to be vacated. The law went into effect on June 12, 2014.

—*Carole A. Barrett*

BIBLIOGRAPHY AND FURTHER READING

Parham, Vera. "'It Was a Spearhead of Change': The Fish-Ins of the Pacific Northwest and the Boldt Decision, Shifting Native American Protest Identities in the 1960s and 1970s." *Native Studies Rev.* 22.1/2 (2013): 1–26. Web. 16 Apr. 2015.

Shreve, Bradley Glenn. *Red Power Rising: The National Indian Youth Council and the Origins of Native Activism.* Norman: U of Oklahoma P, 2011. Print.

FOREIGN PROFESSIONALS IN THE UNITED STATES

Since the beginning of the twentieth century, US immigration legislation has been largely influenced by the nation's need for labor. Although earlier laws typically involved unskilled workers, legislation in the 1990's began to focus on the admittance of foreign professionals. Those who advocate increasing the number of specialty visas are primarily in, but not limited to, the health care and high-tech fields. They argue that not enough qualified people are available in the United States. To support their position, they cite the shortage in medical personnel, claiming that many rural and inner-city health-care systems would have collapsed had it not been for foreign medical professionals who filled these positions. Proponents also say that US-born professionals do not work as hard and are much more expensive than foreign professionals. Opponents counter that many qualified individuals are available, but companies prefer to terminate middle-aged, more expensive employees and hire foreign professionals. In addition, opponents say that these companies are creating sweatshops by not providing foreign professionals with the proper wages and benefits.

Proponents argue that by hiring foreign professionals, businesses become more competitive, have greater flexibility in reducing or augmenting the size of the workforce, and benefit from the best foreign talent; this increased competitiveness results in additional jobs and a stronger US economy. For example, at Sun Microsystems (acquired by Oracle in 2010), more than half of its twenty thousand employees worked on technology developed by foreign professionals who first entered on temporary visas.

To hire a foreign professional, organizations are required to demonstrate to the US Department of Labor that the foreigner being hired is not taking a job that could be filled by an American citizen. Managers are highly critical of this procedure because it not only decreases organizational efficiency but also makes the US Department of Labor the personnel manager of an organization. Another option that has been suggested is to tax organizations that use foreign professionals; however, organizations have been critical of this idea because it negatively affects efficiency and profits.

Two other issues—education and the phenomenon called "brain drain"—also come to the forefront in discussions concerning foreign professionals. As long as US companies and facilities are able to hire foreign professionals cheaply, the American educational system will not develop adequate training facilities in those areas, making the United States dependent on overseas talent. In addition, the recruiting of highly educated or skilled professionals from other countries by US companies produces a phenomenon called brain drain—a situation in which a country loses its best and brightest to another country that can offer these people better economic opportunities. No country can truly afford such a loss of educated talent, despite often receiving much-needed remittances that such professionals send to their family members, and many set up barriers to leaving. This could result in a diminished ability to recruit foreign professionals.

Some scholars have begun reframing "brain drain" as "brain gain," shifting the emphasis to the country of relocation rather than the loss by the home country. Those countries that gain more professional than they lose would be characterized as experiencing "brain gain." And, in fact, there is a school of thought that brain drain does not cause detrimental outcomes, such as poor health in health-care professionals' home countries, since many of the negative conditions attributed to the emigration of professionals are actually the result of several, often-unrelated factors. Some also argue that the home country may regain better-skilled workers at a later point in a phenomenon known as "brain circulation."

——*Arthur W. Helweg*

BIBLIOGRAPHY AND FURTHER READING

Becker, Sascha O., and Tito Boeri. *Brain Drain and Brain Gain: The Global Competition to Attract High-Skilled Migrants.* Oxford: Oxford UP, 2012. Print.

Giovanetti, Tom. "Solving the H1B Visa Impasse." *Congress Blog.* Capitol Hill Pub. Corp., 3 Dec. 2014. Web. 27 Apr. 2015.

Miller, Paul W., and Barry R. Chiswick. *Handbook of the Economics of International Migration.* Amsterdam: North Holland, 2014. Print.

Ritzer, George, and Paul Dean. "Global Flows of People: Migration, Human Trafficking, and Tourism." *Globalization: A Basic Text.* Chichester: Wiley Blackwell, 2014. 263–93. Print.

Saunders, Bradley, and Michael Nieto. "Opportunities and Challenges for Organisations and Highly Skilled Migrant Professionals." *Global Talent Management: Challenges, Strategies, And Opportunities.* Ed. Akram Al Ariss. Cham: Springer, 2014. 107–19. Print.

"Understanding H-1B Requirements." *US Citizenship and Immigration Services.* US Dept. of Homeland Security, n.d. Web. 27 Apr. 2015.

FOURTEENTH AMENDMENT

A definition of citizenship designed for former slaves, the Fourteenth Amendment provides protection against state violations of civil rights that has become crucial to all citizens of the United States.

The Fourteenth Amendment to the US Constitution, ratified by Congress in 1868, was part of the plan for Reconstruction following the Civil War (1861-1865) and was formulated by the Republican majority in the Thirty-ninth Congress. Before Congress met in December, 1865, President Andrew Johnson had authorized the restoration of white self-government in the former Confederate states, and the congressmen and senators from those states waited in Washington to be seated in Congress. The abolition of slavery had destroyed the old compromise under which five slaves counted as three free persons in apportioning representation in the House and the electoral college, and the Republicans wanted to make sure that the South did not add to its numbers in the House and thus profit from rebellion.

Between December, 1865, and May, 1866, the Republicans attempted to hammer out a program that would accomplish their purposes in the South, unite members of their party in Congress, and appeal to northern voters. Given the diversity of opinion within the party, this undertaking proved to be difficult. Radical Republicans wanted African American suffrage, permanent political proscription, and confiscation of the property of ex-Confederates. Some

maintained they were authorized in these actions by the Thirteenth Amendment, which, they believed, gave Congress the power to abolish the "vestiges of slavery." Moderate Republicans, on the other hand,

Senator Jacob M. Howard of Michigan, author of the Citizenship Clause. Mathew Brady.

feared political repercussions from African American suffrage, as such a requirement would result in beginning the Reconstruction process over again. Many moderates also believed that an additional amendment to the Constitution was needed to provide precise authority for Congress to enact civil rights legislation.

From deliberations of the joint committee and debate on the floor of the House came the Fourteenth Amendment. Many Republicans believed that the proposal was in the nature of a peace treaty, although this view was not explicitly stated. If the South accepted the amendment, the southern states were to be readmitted and their senators and representatives seated in Congress; in other words, Reconstruction would end. Republicans presented a united front during the final vote as a matter of party policy. Because the amendment was an obvious compromise between radicals and moderates, it was too strong for some and too weak for others.

The Amendment

The Fourteenth Amendment became the most important addition to the Constitution since the Bill of Rights had been adopted in 1791. It contains five sections:

Section 1, the first constitutional definition of citizenship, states that all persons born or naturalized in the United States are citizens of the United States and of the state in which they reside. It includes limits on the power of states, by providing that no state may abridge the privileges and immunities of citizens, deprive any person of life, liberty, or property without due process of law, or deny to any person within its jurisdiction the equal protection of law. This section was intended to guarantee African Americans the rights of citizenship, although the amendment's framers did not define exactly which rights were included. Nor did they define "state action" to specify whether the term meant only official acts of state government or the actions of individuals functioning privately with state approval.

The courts later interpreted the due process clause to extend the rights of the accused listed in the Bill of Rights, which had applied only to the federal government, to the states. They expanded the notion of equal protection to include other categories, such as sex and disability, as well as race. They also interpreted the word "person" to include corporations

as legal persons; under this interpretation, corporations found protection from much state regulation.

Section 2 gives a new formula of representation in place of the old three-fifths compromise of the Constitution, under which five slaves were counted as equal to three free persons in determining a state's representation in the House of Representatives and the electoral college. All persons in a state were to be counted for representation, but if a state should disfranchise any of its adult male citizens, except for participation in rebellion or any other crime, the basis of its representation would be reduced proportionately. While not guaranteeing suffrage to African Americans, this provision threatened the South with a loss of representation should black males be denied the vote.

Section 3 declares that no person who has ever taken an oath to support the Constitution (which included all who had been in the military service or held state or national office before 1860) and has then participated in the rebellion can be a senator or representative or hold any civil or military office, national or state. This disability could be removed only by a two-thirds vote of both houses of Congress. This section took away the pardoning power of the president, which congressional Republicans believed Andrew Johnson used too generously.

Section 4 validates the debt of the United States, voids all debts incurred to support rebellion, and invalidates all claims for compensation for emancipated slaves.

Section 5 gives Congress authority to pass legislation to enforce the provisions of the Fourteenth Amendment.

The correspondence and speeches of those who framed the Fourteenth Amendment do not support any theories of economic conspiracy or ulterior motives. The framers desired to protect the former slaves and boost Republicanism in the South by barring old Confederates from returning to Congress and the electoral college with increased voting strength. They hoped to do this without threatening the federal system or unduly upsetting the relationship between the central government and the states. At the same time, Republicans wanted to unify their party and project a popular issue for the approaching electoral contest against Andrew Johnson.

——William J. Cooper, Jr., updated by Mary Welek Atwell

BIBLIOGRAPHY AND FURTHER READING

Araiza, William D. *Enforcing the Equal Protection Clause: Congressional Power, Judicial Doctrine, and Constitutional Law.* New York: New York UP, 2015. Print.

Epps, Garrett. *Democracy Reborn: The Fourteenth Amendment and the Fight for Equal Rights in Post–Civil War America.* New York: Holt, 2006. Print.

Lively, Donald E. *The Constitution and Race.* New York: Praeger, 1992. Print.

Rutherglen, George. *Civil Rights in the Shadow of Slavery: The Constitution, Common Law, and the Civil Rights Act of 1866.* New York: Oxford UP, 2013. Print.

FRANCOPHONE

The term "francophone" is of relatively recent coinage. Its first attested use was in 1949 in French. Its literal meaning is "one who speaks French." In this original use, francophone referred both to native speakers of French and to others who had learned to speak French fluently. Canada has officially been a bilingual country since the British North America Act of 1867 created Canada as an independent country, and as of the 2011 census, about 80 percent of Canadians considered either English or French to be their native language. By the 1960's, both native speakers of French and English in Canada began to use the terms "francophone" and "anglophone" to identify respectively native speakers of French and English. This modern usage of these words was important because it demonstrated to Canadians that their commitment to Canada was perfectly compatible with their love of their ethnic and linguistic heritages in a multicultural and bilingualbilingual country. Federal laws that recognized French and English as the official languages of Canada both in theory and in daily practice helped to preserve and protect linguistic diversity and equality in such a diverse country as Canada.

Haiti, Switzerland, Belgium, Luxembourg, the United States, and former French colonies in the Caribbean, Africa, and Asia are home to francophone populations as well. In fact, as of 2015, French was the official language of more than two dozen countries worldwide, according to the government of France.

———*Edmund J. Campion*

BIBLIOGRAPHY AND FURTHER READING

Beauclair, Marie. *The Francophone World: Cultural Issues and Perspectives.* New York: Lang, 2003. Print.

Corcoran, Patrick. *The Cambridge Introduction to Francophone Literature.* Cambridge: Cambridge UP, 2007. Print.

"French and the Francophonie in Canada." *Statistics Canada.* Govt. of Canada, 14 Jan. 2014. Web. 8 Apr. 2015.

Gafaïti, Hafid, Patricia M. E. Lorcin, and David G. Troyansky, eds. *Transnational Spaces and Identities in the Francophone World.* Lincoln: U of Nebraska, 2009. Print.

"Linguistic Characteristics of Canadians." *Statistics Canada.* Govt. of Canada, 14 Jan. 2014. Web. 8 Apr. 2015.

"The Status of French in the World." *France Diplomatie.* French Ministry of Foreign Affairs and International Development, 2015. Web. 8 Apr. 2015.

FRANK LYNCHING

In 1913, Leo Frank, a Jew born in Texas in 1884, was the superintendent of a pencil factory in Atlanta, Georgia. When one of his employees, a thirteen-year-old gentile girl named Mary Phagan, was murdered, Frank was accused of the crime. Credible evidence pointed to an African American janitor, Jim Conley, as the likely killer, but anti-Semitic passions outweighed the racial tensions of the time. Frank was tried, convicted, and given the death penalty. Newspapers and politicians used strident anti-Jewish stereotyping and

Leo Frank in a portrait photograph. By Bain News Service.

bigotry to arouse public opinion against Frank. When Georgia governor John M. Slaton became doubtful about the verdict, he commuted Frank's sentence to life in prison. Outraged at Slaton's action, a group of armed men attacked the executive mansion. On August 16, 1915, a mob stormed the prison where Frank was being held and rushed him away to exact their own vengeance. A few hours later, on August 17, 1915, Frank was lynched. In 1984, Frank received a posthumous pardon from the state of Georgia. His well-publicized lynching was one of the most sensational and controversial examples of mob lawlessness and anti-Semitism during the early years of the twentieth century.

——*Lewis L. Gould*

BIBLIOGRAPHY AND FURTHER READING

Alphin, Elaine Marie. *An Unspeakable Crime: The Prosecution and Persecution of Leo Frank.* Minneapolis: Carolrhoda, 2010. Print.

Berger, Paul. "Leo Frank Case Stirs Debate 100 Years after Jewish Lynch Victim's Conviction." *Forward.* Forward Assoc., 19 Aug. 2013. Web. 24 Apr. 2015.

Oney, Steve. *And the Dead Shall Rise: The Murder of Mary Phagan and the Lynching of Leo Frank.* New York: Pantheon, 2003. Print.

Oney, Steve. "The People v. Leo Frank." *Atlanta* Sept. 2013: 32–36. Print.

Zola, Gary Phillip, and Marc Dollinger, eds. *American Jewish History: A Primary Source Reader.* Waltham: Brandeis UP, 2014. Print.

FREE AFRICAN SOCIETY

Both the origins of the Free African Society and the long-term repercussions of its founding form an essential part of the religious history of African Americans. The original organization itself was of short duration. About seven years after it was organized in 1787, it disappeared as a formal body. In its immediate wake, however, closely related institutions emerged that tried to take over its proclaimed mission.

Generally speaking, prior to the 1790s people of African slave origins who managed to obtain their individual freedom had only one option if they wished to practice Christianity: association, as subordinate parishioners, in an existing white-run church. Several churches in the American colonies before independence, including the Quakers and Methodists, had tried to identify their religious cause with that of the black victims of slavery.

RICHARD ALLEN

Richard Allen, born in 1760 as a slave whose family belonged to Pennsylvania's then attorney general, Benjamin Chew, was destined to become one of the earliest religious leaders of the black segment of the American Methodist Church. As a youth, Allen gained extensive experience with Methodist teachings after his family was separated on the auction block in Dover, Delaware. Allen was encouraged by his second owner, Master Stokeley, to espouse the religious teachings of the itinerant American

Methodist preacher Freeborn Garrettson. Allen's conversion to Methodism was rewarded when Stokeley freed him at age twenty to follow the calling of religion. His freedom came just as the Revolutionary War ended.

For six years, Allen worked under the influence of Methodist evangelist Benjamin Abbott and the Reverend (later Bishop) Richard Whatcoat, with whom he traveled on an extensive preaching circuit. Allen's writings refer to Whatcoat as his "father in Israel." With Whatcoat's encouragement, Allen accepted an invitation from the Methodist elder in Philadelphia to return to his birthplace to become a preacher. At that time, Philadelphia's religious environment seemed to be dominated by the Episcopal Church. This church had been active since 1758 in extending its ministry to African Americans. It was St. George's Methodist Episcopal Church, however, that, in the 1780s, had drawn the largest number of former slaves to its rolls. Once the circumstances of African Americans' second-class status became clear to Allen, he decided that his leadership mission should be specifically dedicated to the needs of his people. Within a short time, he joined another African American, Absalom Jones, in founding what was originally intended to be more of a secular movement than a formal denominational movement: the Free African Society.

ABSALOM JONES

Absalom Jones was older than Allen and had a different set of life experiences. Born a slave in Delaware in 1746, Jones served for more than twenty years in his master's store in Philadelphia. He earned enough money to purchase his wife's freedom, to build his own home, and finally, in 1784, to purchase his own freedom. He continued to work for his former master for wages and bought and managed two houses for additional income. His success earned for him great respect among other free African Americans and opened the way for him to serve as lay leader representing the African American membership of St. George's Methodist Episcopal Church.

Traditional accounts of Jones's role in the founding of the Free African Society assert that, when Jones refused to comply with the announcement of St. George's sexton that African American parishioners should give up their usual seats among the white congregation and move to the upper

gallery, he was supported by Richard Allen, in particular. The two then agreed that the only way African Americans could worship in an environment that responded to their social, as well as religious, needs would be to found an all-black congregation. Some sources suggest that Jones's reaction to the reseating order was the crowning blow, and that Allen previously had tried to organize several fellow black parishioners, including Doras Giddings, William White, and Jones, to support his idea of a separate congregation, only to have the idea rejected by the church elders.

ORGANIZATION GOALS

Whatever the specific stimulus for Allen's and Jones's actions in 1787, they announced publicly that their newly declared movement would not only serve the black community's religious needs as a nondenominational congregation but also function as a benevolent mutual aid organization. The latter goal involved plans to collect funds (through membership fees) to assist the sick, orphans, and widows in the African American community. Other secular social assistance aims included enforcement of a code of temperance, propriety, and fidelity in marriage. It is significant that a number of the early members of the Free African Society came to it from the rolls of other Protestant churches, not only St. George's Methodist Episcopal congregation.

The dual nature of the organization's goals soon led to divisions in the politics of leadership. Apparently, it was Allen who wanted to use the breakaway from St. George's as a first step in founding a specifically black Methodist church. Others wished to emphasize the Free African Society's nondenominational character and pursue mainly social and moral aid services. Within two years, therefore, Allen resigned his membership, going on to found, in July 1794, the Bethel African Methodist Episcopal Church. Although this move clearly marked the beginnings of a specifically African American church with a defined denominational status, Allen's efforts for many years continued to be directed at social and economic self-help projects for African Americans, irrespective of their formal religious orientation.

By 1804, Allen was involved in founding a group whose name reflected its basic social reform goals: the Society of Free People of Color for Promoting the Instruction and School Education of Children of African Descent. Another of Allen's efforts came in 1830, when Allen, then seventy years of age, involved his church in the Free Produce Society in Philadelphia. This group raised money to buy goods grown only by nonslave labor to redistribute to poor African Americans. It also tried to organize active boycotts against the marketing and purchase of goods produced by slave-owning farmers, thus providing an early model for the grassroots organizations aimed at social and political goals that would become familiar to African Americans in the mid-twentieth century.

The Free African Society passed through several short but key stages both before and after Richard Allen's decision to remove himself from active membership. One focal point was the group's early association with the prominent medical doctor and philanthropist Benjamin Rush. Rush helped the Free African Society to draft a document involving articles of faith that were meant to be general enough to include the essential religious principles of any Christian church. When the organization adopted these tenets, in 1791, its status as a religious congregation generally was recognized by members and outsiders alike. More and more, its close relationship with the Episcopal Church (first demonstrated by its "friendly adoption" by the Reverend Joseph Pilmore and the white membership of St. Paul's Church in Philadelphia) determined its future denominational status. After 1795, the Free African Society per

se had been superseded by a new church built by a committee sparked by Absalom Jones: the African Methodist Episcopal Church. This fact did not, however, prevent those who had been associated with the Free African Society's origins from integrating its strong social and moral reform program with the religious principles that marked the emergence of the first all-black Christian congregations in the United States by the end of the 1790s.

——*Byron D. Cannon*

BIBLIOGRAPHY AND FURTHER READING

George, Carol V. R. *Segregated Sabbaths: Richard Allen and the Emergence of Independent Black Churches, 1760–1840.* New York: Oxford UP, 1973. Print.

Glaude, Eddie S., Jr. *African American Religion: A Very Short Introduction.* New York: Oxford UP, 2014. Print.

Mwadilitu, Mwalimi I. *Richard Allen: The First Exemplar of African American Education.* New York: ECA Assoc., 1985. Print.

Newman, Richard S. *Freedom's Prophet: Bishop Richard Allen, the AME Church, and the Black Founding Fathers.* New York: New York UP, 2008. Print.

Thomas, Rondda Robinson. *Claiming Exodus: A Cultural History of Afro-American Identity, 1774–1903.* Waco: Baylor UP, 2013. Print.

FREE BLACKS

In 1860, an estimated 500,000 free people of African ancestry resided in the United States; of these, approximately half lived in the slaveholding South. Most of these free blacks were former slaves who had purchased their freedom or were freed in their masters' wills, but a significant minority were freeborn. Their experiences varied by region; those in the northern states, although limited in economic opportunity, enjoyed greater political and social freedom than their counterparts in the South, where demand for black labor was greater but free blacks were regarded with suspicion. The majority of free blacks lived in extreme poverty; however, a small but significant number achieved modest prosperity and a few attained substantial

wealth, in some instances purchasing plantations and becoming slaveholders.

Free African Americans of the antebellum period exerted profound influence upon black society in the post-slavery United States. The abolitionist rhetoric of former slaves such as Frederick Douglass and Samuel Ringgold Ward influenced later generations of black activists, and the activities of free southern blacks set precedents for race relations and relations among African Americans after emancipation. The political and legal restrictions placed on free blacks by fearful southern whites in the antebellum period provided a blueprint for racial oppression in the South during the era of segregation.

——*Michael H. Burchett*

BIBLIOGRAPHY AND FURTHER READING

Callaway, Shelby. "Free Blacks in Antebellum America." *African Americans in the Nineteenth Century: People and Perspectives.* Ed. Dixie Ray Haggard. Santa Barbara: ABC-CLIO, 2010. 17–32. Print.

Copeland, David. *The Antebellum Era: Primary Documents on Events from 1820 to 1860.* Westport: Greenwood, 2003. Print.

King, Stewart R. *Encyclopedia of Free Blacks and People of Color in the Americas.* New York: Facts On File, 2012. Print.

FREEDMEN'S BUREAU

On March 3, 1865, Congress created the Freedmen's Bureau, a temporary agency within the War Department. The bureau, also known as the United States Bureau of Refugees, Freedmen, and Abandoned Lands, was administered by General Oliver Otis Howard from 1865 until it was dismantled by Congress in 1872. The primary objective of the Freedmen's Bureau was to help newly freed African Americans to function as free men, women, and children. In order to achieve this goal, the bureau was expected to assume responsibility for all matters related to the newly freed slaves in the Southern states.

The bureau's mission was an enormous undertaking because of limited resources, political conflicts over Reconstruction policies, and a hostile environment. The work of the bureau was performed by General Howard and a network of assistant commissioners in various states, largely in the South. The Freedmen's Bureau attempted to address many of the needs of the newly freed African Americans, including labor relations, education, landownership, medical care, food distribution, family reunification, legal protection, and legal services within the African American community.

LABOR AND EDUCATION

In the area of labor relations, the Freedmen's Bureau dealt with labor-related issues such as transporting and relocating refugees and the newly freed persons for employment, contract and wage disputes, and harsh legislation enacted by some states. Concerning the last issue, many Southern states had passed laws, called black codes, that required adult freed men and women to have lawful employment or a business. Otherwise, they would be fined and jailed for vagrancy, and sheriffs would hire them out to anyone who would pay their fine. Given the scarcity of jobs, this policy resulted in former slave owners maintaining rigid control over newly freed African Americans. Another discriminatory law gave the former owners of orphaned African Americans the right to hire them as apprentices rather than placing them with their relatives. Again, this law resulted in the continuation of free labor for many white Southerners. The Freedmen's Bureau has been criticized for the failure of its agents to negotiate labor contracts in the interest of the newly freed. The bureau was frequently accused of protecting the rights of the white Southern planters instead.

Obtaining an education was extremely important to the newly freed African Americans. They knew that learning to read and write would enable them to enter into contracts and establish businesses, and would aid them in legal matters. The Freedmen's Bureau provided some support, by providing teachers, schools, and books and by coordinating volunteers. The bureau also made a contribution to the founding of African American colleges and universities. Southern opposition to educating African Americans was a result of the white Southerners' fear that education would make African Americans too independent and unwilling to work under the terms established by their former owners. Therefore, Southerners instituted control over the educational administration and classrooms and the entire system. White Southern planters used various methods to exert control: frequent changes in administrative personnel, the use of racial stereotypes regarding the intellectual inferiority of African Americans, and educational policy decision making based on paternalism and self-interest. Consequently, educational opportunities were significantly restricted for African American youth.

PROPERTY AND OTHER RIGHTS

The newly freed African Americans were eager to acquire property. They demonstrated their interest in owning their own land as individuals and formed associations to purchase large tracts of land. Their sense of family and community was the basis for their strong desire to own land. The Freedmen's Bureau was initially authorized to distribute land that had been confiscated from Southern plantation owners during the Civil War. The Freedmen's Bureau also attempted to provide for the social welfare of the freed persons. The agency was noted for rationing food to refugees and former slaves; it assisted families in reuniting with members who had been sold or separated in other ways during slavery.

Protecting the rights of the former slaves was a major task of the Freedmen's Bureau. Republicans believed that African Americans should have the same rights as white Americans. However, many Southern states enacted black codes that severely restricted the civil rights of the freed men, women, and children. These laws, exacting social and economic control over African Americans, represented a new form of slavery. When state legislation prohibited African Americans' equal rights, the bureau attempted to invoke the Civil Rights Act of 1866, which offered African Americans the same legal protections and rights as whites to testify in courts, to own property, to enforce legal contracts, and to sue. The bureau found it extremely difficult to enforce the Civil Rights Act and to prosecute state officials who enforced laws that were discriminatory against African Americans. A shortage of agents and a reluctance among bureau commissioners to challenge local officials contributed to the agency's limited success in enforcing the Civil Rights Act. Finally, the Freedmen's Bureau also established tribunals to address minor legal disputes of African Americans within their own communities. In many instances, freed slaves were able to resolve their own problems. When they could not, they presented their legal concerns to bureau agents.

The task assigned to the Freedmen's Bureau was monumental. The responsibilities of the bureau significantly exceeded the resources and authority granted to it by Congress. The bureau's ability to perform its varied tasks also was impeded by personnel shortages. The Reconstruction policies of President Andrew Johnson represented another major challenge to the bureau, as they were not always supportive of the bureau's mandate and objectives. Myriad problems associated with the bureau meant that the newly freed men, women, and children were not able to receive the goods and services necessary to gain economic independence. Consequently, they developed extensive self-help networks to address their needs.

Congress dismantled the bureau in July 1872.

——*K. Sue Jewell*

BIBLIOGRAPHY AND FURTHER READING

Crouch, Barry A. *The Freedmen's Bureau and Black Texans*. Austin: U of Texas P, 1982. Print.

Farmer-Kaiser, Mary. *Freedwomen and the Freedmen's Bureau: Race, Gender, and Public Policy in the Age of Emancipation*. New York: Fordham UP, 2010. Print.

Magdol, Edward. *A Right to the Land: Essays on the Freedmen's Community*. Westport: Greenwood, 1977. Print.

Nieman, Donald G., ed. *The Freedmen's Bureau and Black Freedom*. New York: Garland, 1994. Print.

FREEDOM RIDERS

Freedom Riders were civil rights activists who traveled on interstate bus lines in 1961 in order to promote enforcement of a 1960 Supreme Court ruling that prohibited racial segregation in facilities that served interstate travelers. James Farmer, the national director of the Congress of Racial Equality (CORE), modeled the protest after a similar effort that the organization had undertaken in 1947. Like their predecessors in 1947, the Freedom Riders were both African Americans and whites committed to a nonviolent approach to achieving the goal of a racially integrated United States.

The first group of Freedom Riders, seven African Americans and six whites, met in Washington, DC, for training sessions on May 1, 1961. They left the nation's capital three days later, traveling south on two different bus lines. The Freedom Riders met with little resistance until they arrived in Rock Hill, South Carolina. When

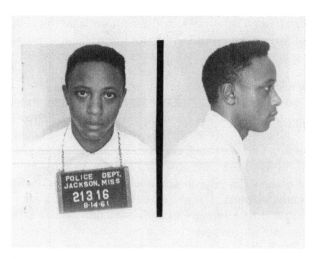

George Raymond Jr. was a CORE activist arrested in the Trailways bus terminal in Jackson, Mississippi on August 14, 1961. By Mississippi State.

John Lewis, an African American seminary student, and Albert Bigelow, a white retired naval officer, attempted to enter the white waiting room in the bus station, a group of white youths beat them. This incident foreshadowed the violence that the Freedom Riders would meet later on their journey through the American South. Outside Anniston, Alabama, on May 14, a mob firebombed the bus on which the Freedom Riders were traveling and attacked the passengers as they hurried off the burning wreckage. That same day, another contingent of Freedom Riders suffered beatings at the bus station in Birmingham, Alabama. Because of the violence, the bus drivers refused to carry the Freedom Riders any farther, and the protest ended with a plane flight to New Orleans, Louisiana.

The premature end of the first Freedom Ride did not mark the end of the effort, which had captured the attention of the nation and placed pressure on the administration of President John F. Kennedy to enforce the Supreme Court ruling. A second group

of Freedom Riders, eight African Americans and two whites, set forth from Nashville, Tennessee, just days after the first ride had ended. After a great deal of difficulty, most of this group reached Montgomery, Alabama, where they met with a second group of eleven activists who had arrived to join the protest. Angry white segregationists confronted the Freedom Riders, and the scene at Montgomery degenerated into a riot during which several Freedom Riders were badly injured. Despite this incident, supporters of civil rights throughout the nation volunteered to continue the protests. Biracial Freedom Rides continued throughout the summer of 1961, with hundreds of riders jailed in southern states for violating local ordinances. The continuing crisis prompted the Interstate Commerce Commission to issue regulations, in September 1961, enforcing the Supreme Court ruling regarding segregation in interstate travel facilities.

The biracial nature of the Freedom Rides revealed that Americans from diverse backgrounds were willing to risk their safety, even their lives, to secure the civil rights of African Americans. The violence surrounding the Freedom Rides also proved that southerners committed to perpetuating racial segregation would attack white civil rights activists with as much abandon as they did the African American protesters.

——*Thomas Clarkin*

BIBLIOGRAPHY AND FURTHER READING

Catsam, Derek. *Freedom's Main Line: The Journey of Reconciliation and the Freedom Rides.* Lexington: UP of Kentucky, 2009. Print.

"CORE Volunteers Put Their Lives on the Road." *CORE: Congress of Racial Equality.* CORE, n.d. Web. 13 Apr. 2015.

Silver, Carol Ruth. *Freedom Rider Diary: Smuggled Notes from Parchman Prison.* Jackson: UP of Mississippi, 2014. Print.

FREEDOM SUMMER

The Freedom Summer convinced many black SNCC workers that nonviolence and cooperation with whites were not succeeding and that more radical measures were necessary.

In 1964, the Council of Federated Organizations (COFO), comprising mostly volunteers from the

Student Nonviolent Coordinating Committee (SNCC), launched a black voter registration campaign in Mississippi. Leaders sought to expose the ways that whites denied blacks the right to vote and to prod the federal government into enforcing the voting rights of black Americans. The struggle would also encourage the emergence of black community leaders.

In June, the first of nearly nine hundred white student volunteers, mainly from northeastern schools, arrived in Mississippi. White and black volunteers operated about fifty Freedom Schools and about the same number of community centers.

Local white reaction was swift and violent. Even before the project started, three civil rights workers were murdered. Throughout the summer, white segregationists burned churches, shot at volunteers, and

bombed homes and civil rights headquarters. The violence had the opposite effect of what whites had intended; it galvanized national opinion that the racial situation in Mississippi and the South had to change. At the same time, continued violence contributed to growing rifts within the Civil Rights movement. The Freedom Summer convinced many black SNCC workers that nonviolence and cooperation with whites were not succeeding and that more radical measures were necessary.

——*Robert E. McFarland*

Free-Soil Party

As the Whig Party disintegrated, the Free-Soil Party was one of the factions that filled the political vacuum; in time Free-Soil Party members helped to form the Republican Party. In 1846, Representative David

Wilmot introduced a measure to prohibit slavery in territories obtained as a result of the Mexican-American War, and almost immediately the political parties divided on the matter. Uniting with the

In this 1850 political cartoon, the artist attacks abolitionist, Free Soil, and other sectionalist interests of 1850 as dangers to the Union. By James S. Baillie.

Liberty Party and antislavery Whigs, the antislavery "barnburners" formed the Free-Soil Party, which nominated Martin Van Buren for the presidency in 1848. He did not obtain a single electoral vote, but he won 291,000 popular votes in the North and Midwest. The election was won by Zachary Taylor, a hero of the Mexican-American War who refused to state his political positions.

The Free-Soilers next formed the "Free Democracy of the United States," which held a convention in 1852 during which it nominated John Hale for the presidency on the platform of "Free Soil, Free Speech, Free Labor, and Free Men." The Democratic nominee, Franklin Pierce, who favored the Compromise of 1850, won the election.

The nation seemed to want compromise and avoidance of war. This time the Free-Soil candidate received only 156,000 presidential votes, and the party seemed to have lost influence.

Even so, the antislavery forces recovered, as antagonisms between the sections intensified. Eventually, violence erupted in Kansas, as the two groups contested for control of the territory. In July, 1854, antislavery elements came together to form the Republican Party. Free-Soilers filtered into the Republican ranks and were very much in evidence at the party's 1856 convention, which nominated John C. Frémont for the presidency. With this, the Free-Soil Party dissolved.

——*Robert Sobel*

BIBLIOGRAPHY AND FURTHER READING

Cumbler, John T. *From Abolition to Rights for All: The Making of a Reform Community in the Nineteenth Century.* Philadelphia: U of Pennsylvania P, 2008. Print.

Earle, Jonathan Halperin. *Jacksonian Antislavery and the Politics of Free Soil, 1824-1854.* Chapel Hill: U of North Carolina P, 2004. Digital file.

Green, Donald J. "Antebellum Third Parties: Liberty, Free Soil, American (Know-Nothings), Constitutional Union." *Third-Party Matters : Politics, Presidents, and Third Parties in American History.* Santa Barbara: Praeger, 2010. 5–26. Digital file.

FRENCH CANADIAN WOMEN

French Canadians, also known as Québécois, reside mostly in the Canadian province of Quebec and in the northeastern and midwestern United States. (Another, much smaller French-speaking group known as the Acadians resides primarily in the Canadian Maritimes.) As a group, French is the primary language of the French Canadians and Catholicism their dominant religion. According to the 2011 census, French Canadians constituted 5,065,700 (about one-sixth) of Canada's total population of 32,852,320. Québécois feminists are concerned with such women's issues as rape, physical harassment, abortion rights, gender equity, political representation, family issues, and women's health.

While Québécois feminists and other feminists share much in common, national concerns also help shape Québécois feminist views, particularly the struggle for autonomy for the French-speaking people of Canada. The Quebec Act of 1774 allowed French Canadians to retain their own language, religion, and civil law, but the Meech Lake Accord that would have provided constitutional protection for French language and culture was defeated in 1990. This defeat led to the Charlottetown Accord in 1992, which would have extended constitutional recognition of Quebec's "distinct society" but which was also defeated. A resolution granting Quebec full independence was defeated in 1980, another in 1995.

Several prominent feminist organizations have formed in French Canada, such as the Fédération des Femmes du Québec (FFQ). The FFQ withdrew from the National Action Committee on the Status of Women (NAC), the principal Canadian women's umbrella organization, in the early 1980's but reaffiliated with NAC in the mid-1980's after a constitutional controversy had subsided. The FFQ withdrew from the NAC again in 1989, triggered by opposition from the Front de Libération des Femmes (FLF). The FLF is a vehicle for the radical Front de Libération du Québec (FLQ), which was established in 1963. Both groups share a basic commitment to an independent socialist Quebec and remain separate from groups that do not support the same objectives. Thus, the FLF has organized its own protests against Canada's abortion policies, deliberately excluding anglophone feminists in Quebec and elsewhere in Canada.

Although Franco-American groups in the United States are decidedly less separatist than their Canadian counterparts, they nevertheless promote Franco-American interests based on the belief that Franco-Americans are a distinct minority group. Like their sister organizations in Canada, Franco-American women's groups in the United States have sought solidarity with American Indian groups. Other Franco-Americans compare their struggle to that of African American women and display political characteristics not unlike those found among black separatists in the United States.

——*Samory Rashid*

BIBLIOGRAPHY AND FURTHER READING

Dumont-Johnson, Micheline, Nicole Kennedy, and Sarah Swartz. *Feminism à la Québécoise.* Ottawa: Feminist History Soc., 2012. Print.

Eichler, Margarit, and Marie Lavigne. "Women's Movement." *Canadian Encyclopedia.* Historica Canada, 4 Mar. 2015. Web. 8 Apr. 2015.

"Immigration and Ethnocultural Diversity in Canada." *Statistics Canada.* Govt. of Canada, 14 Jan. 2014. Web. 8 Apr. 2015.

Matthews Green, Mary Jean. *Women and Narrative Identity: Rewriting the Quebec National Text.* Montreal: McGill-Queen's UP, 2001. Print.

Minahan, James. "Québécois." *Ethnic Groups of the Americas: An Encyclopedia* Santa Barbara: ABC-CLIO, 2013. 309–11. Print.

FRENCH CANADIANS

The very motto of Quebec, *Je me souviens* ("I remember"), clearly indicates that the distant past continues to have a profound influence on current events in the province. French Canadians refer to the British victory over French forces in 1759 as the Conquest of Canada, whereas English Canadians speak of the Seven Years' War. The decisive battle in this war took place on the Fields (or Plains) of Abraham in Quebec City in 1759, and this area has been preserved by the Quebec government as a reminder of English efforts to destroy French culture in Canada. French Canadians firmly believe that England strove to impose an alien culture on them, and they have not forgotten this perceived lack of respect for their cultural values.

EARLY CONFLICTS

In the years immediately after Canada became an English colony, successive English governments attempted to reduce French influence in Canada. Thousands of French-speaking Acadians were expelled from Nova Scotia. English-speaking Canadians came to dominate economic and political life in Quebec.

French-speaking Canadians were largely restricted to manual labor and farming. Although the French Rebellion of 1837 against the English government of Canada failed, it did create cultural unity among Catholic French Canadians against Protestant

Habitants by Cornelius Krieghoff (1852). Cornelius Krieghoff.

English Canadians. While Canada remained under the direct rule of England, social peace in Canada was impossible because of the extreme antagonism between the two major ethnic groups of Canada. During the American Civil War, the English government aided the Confederacy and President Abraham Lincoln had to use considerable diplomatic skill in order to prevent a declaration of war against England. As the American Civil War ended, the English government concluded that it was in England's self-interest to transform Canada from a colony into a new form of government. Quebec, Ontario, New Brunswick, and Nova Scotia agreed to join together, and the British North America Act of 1867 created the Dominion of Canada. When John A. Macdonald became the first prime minister of Canada on July 1, 1867, English and French Canadians hoped that this political unity would unite the new country socially.

FROM THE CONFEDERATION OF 1867 TO WORLD WAR I

With the creation of the Canadian Confederation in 1867, French Canadians were optimistic because the British North America Act of 1867 guaranteed linguistic and religious rights for all Canadians. The new Canadian government included Catholics and Protestants and English Canadians and French Canadians. The first Canadian prime minister, Macdonald, was a Protestant from Ontario, and his chief political adviser was George Étienne Cartier, a Catholic French Canadian from Quebec. Macdonald's sensitivity to the aspirations of French Canadians boded well for the unity of this new country, but after Cartier's death in 1873, the influence of French Canadian Catholics diminished in Canadian national politics. With the exception of the fifteen years between 1896 and 1911 when Wilfrid Laurier was prime minister, between 1867 and the election of Louis St. Laurent in 1948, all Canadian prime ministers were English-speaking Protestants. French Canadian Catholics felt excluded from high political offices. Laurier and his supporters in Quebec wanted to create an independent Canada with no interference from Britain, but Robert Borden, who served as the Conservative prime minister from 1911 to 1920, and English-speaking Canadians affirmed that it was Canada's duty to fight in World War I

because the British government had asked Canada and other members of the British Empire to do so. French Canadians and their leader Laurier argued that this war did not concern Canada. Borden alienated French Canadians when he questioned their patriotism because they opposed military conscription during World War I. The imposition of conscription provoked anticonscription riots in Quebec City between March 29 and April 2, 1918. Calm was restored only when Catholic bishops in Quebec and Laurier persuaded French Canadians to return to their homes because they could do nothing to change the attitudes of antagonistic English Canadians, who did not respect their culture and religion. At that time, the profound influence of the Catholic Church in Quebec served to discourage the desire for separatism in that province.

FROM WORLD WAR I TO THE 1960'S

Borden's insensitivity and the comment by his minister of justice, Arthur Meighen, that French Canadians were "a backward people" because of their opposition to military conscription transformed Quebec from a province that had elected both Conservative and Liberal members of parliament into a province that sent almost exclusively Liberal members of parliament to Ottawa for the next four decades.

In the 1921 general election, for example, the Liberals won all sixty-five seats in Quebec. William Lyon Mackenzie King, who served as prime minister from 1921 to 1930 and then from 1935 to 1948, and his successor Louis St. Laurent made a determined effort to include French Canadians at the highest levels of the Canadian government, but when the Conservative leader John Diefenbaker became prime minister in 1957, he appointed almost no French Canadians to important government positions. Once again, French Canadians had been snubbed by their national leaders and made to feel like second-class citizens. By the 1960's, the social and political influence of the Catholic Church in Quebec began to wane, although most French Canadians remained practicing Catholics. Catholic bishops in Quebec no longer had the ability to dissuade French Canadians from expressing both their profound alienation from the rest of Canada and their desire to separate from Canada.

MILESTONES IN FRENCH CANADIAN HISTORY

Year	Event	Impact
1759	Battle of Quebec	The British victory over French forces in the battle in Quebec City ends French control of Canada.
1837	French Rebellion	The brutal suppression of this French Canadian rebellion against English Canada demonstrates to French Canadians that the English will not respect their social values.
1867	British North America Act	This English law creates Canada as an independent country within the British Empire and establishes French and English as the official languages of Canada.
1896	Election of Wilfrid Laurier as prime minister of Canada	Laurier becomes the first French Canadian to serve as prime minister of Canada.
1918	Anti-conscription riots in Quebec City	Five days of rioting by French Canadians enraged by the imposition of conscription for a war that in the minds of French Canadians concerns European and not Canadian interests.
1948	Election of Louis St. Laurent as prime minister of Canada	This election indicates to French Canadians that the legendary Laurier is not the only one of them who can lead Canada.
1965	Canadian Maple Leaf flag instated	Removes British symbolism from the Canadian flag.
1976	The Parti Québécois takes power in Quebec	This separatist party wins political control in Quebec under René Lévesque.
1980	Defeat of the first separatist referendum in Quebec	The defeat of this referendum in Quebec permits the continued unity of Canada.
1982	Canadian Charter of Rights and Freedoms	Reaffirms the equality between English and French as the official languages of Canada.
1995	Defeat of the second separatist referendum in Quebec	The defeat of this referendum in Quebec permits the continued unity of Canada.

THE 1960'S AND SUBSEQUENT DECADES

Diefenbaker was succeeded as prime minister in 1963 by Lester Pearson, a distinguished Canadian diplomat and Nobel Prize laureate. Pearson understood the profound alienation of French Canadians. He undertook two specific measures to reestablish social unity in Canada. Until 1965, the Canadian flag had contained a British Union Jack, a symbol that French Canadians associated with the Conquest of Canada and efforts by English Canadians to suppress French culture in Canada. In late 1964, Parliament approved Pearson's proposal for a new red-and-white maple leaf flag. Red and white have traditionally been the colors of Canada; the maple trees grow in many regions of Canada; and the maple leaf symbolizes Canada.

This new flag was psychologically very important for Canadian unity because it contained purely Canadian images and included no reference to the earlier French and British domination of Canada. Pearson also appointed a Royal Commission on Bilingualism and Biculturalism, which affirmed in its 1967 report both the equality between French and English as the official languages of Canada and the need for mutual respect and understanding between the two major cultural groups of Canada. His efforts to unify Canada were continued by Pierre Trudeau, who served as prime minister from 1968 to 1979 and then from 1980 to 1984.

The kidnapping in October, 1970, in Montreal of a British trade commissioner named James Cross and the kidnapping and murder soon thereafter of Quebec minister of labor Pierre Laporte provoked a major political crisis. Daniel Johnson, who was then the premier of Quebec, felt that he had no choice but to ask Prime Minister Trudeau to invoke the War Measures Act to restore peace to Quebec. Trudeau sent Canadian soldiers to Quebec to assist local police officers in their search for the hostages. Cross was released unharmed, but the terrorists murdered Laporte. The decision of Prime Minister Trudeau to send soldiers to Quebec to restore order reminded separatists that English Canadians had used military force on several occasions since the Conquest of Canada to impose their will on Quebec.

In 1976, a separatist party called the Parti Québécois won the Quebec provincial elections and René Lévesque became the premier of Quebec. He wanted Quebec to separate from Canada. In a referendum held in 1980, the province soundly rejected by 59 percent to 41 percent the proposal for Quebec to separate from Canada. Fifteen years later, a similar referendum was held in Quebec and it also was defeated, although by a much closer margin than in 1980. Although the separatist movement remains strong in Quebec, it is not clear what the future holds for the multicultural and bilingual country named Canada.

—*Edmund J. Campion*

BIBLIOGRAPHY AND FURTHER READING

Berry, J. W., and J. A. Laponce, eds. *Ethnicity and Culture in Canada: The Research Landscape.* Toronto: U of Toronto P, 1994. Print.

Bothwell, Robert, Ian Drummond, and John English. *Canada since 1945: Power, Politics, and Provincialism.* Rev. ed. Toronto: U of Toronto P, 1989. Print.

Durflinger, Serge. "French Canada and Recruitment during the First World War." *Canadian War Museum–Musée Canadien de la Guerre.* Canadian Museum of History, n.d. Web. 8 Apr. 2015.

Jones, Richard. "French Canadian Nationalism." *Canadian Encyclopedia.* Historica Canada, 4 Mar. 2015. Web. 8 Apr. 2015.

Minahan, James. "Québécois." *Ethnic Groups of the Americas: An Encyclopedia* Santa Barbara: ABC-CLIO, 2013. 309–11. Print.

Woodcock, George. *The Canadians.* Cambridge: Harvard UP, 1979. Print.

FRIENDS OF THE INDIAN

Friends of the Indian organizations were formed in the last two decades of the nineteenth century by mainly eastern Christian humanitarians who were determined to influence federal American Indian policy. Members of these organizations were convinced of the superiority of Christian civilization and were determined to do away with Indianness and tribal traditions; their goal was to turn individual Indians into patriotic Americans.

The Friends of the Indian groups supported the allotment system in order to break up tribal land ownership and force individual ownership; they sought to end tribal jurisdiction and to bring Indians as individual citizens before the law. They supported vocational education for Indian children, particularly boarding schools, and they were generally intolerant of Indian culture or spiritual expression and worked to outlaw Sun Dances, vision questing, giveaways, plural marriages, and so on. These well-intentioned Christian men and women sought to influence and direct Indian policy by engaging in intense lobbying efforts with federal officials and by educating the general public through newsletters, pamphlets, and speakers. These reformers and their supporters were convinced of the righteousness of their cause and greatly affected federal Indian policy well into the twentieth century.

Beginning in 1883 these groups came together annually for the Lake Mohonk Conference of the Friends of the Indian in New Paltz, New York, to coordinate their efforts. General harmony and a good working relationship existed among the various groups because they shared a common religious outlook that they were doing God's will by guiding Indians from savagery to civilization. The most significant and far-reaching areas affected by these organizations were the federal Indian education system and the General Allotment Act (Dawes Severalty Act) of 1887. One of the most prominent groups, the Indian Rights Association, continues to exist; however, it now supports tribalism and tribal self-determination.

——*Carole A. Barrett*

BIBLIOGRAPHY AND FURTHER READING

Berkhofer, Robert F., Jr. *The White Man's Indian: Images of the American Indian from Columbus to the Present*. New York: Vintage, 1979. Print.

Block, Michael D. "Lake Mohonk Conference." *Encyclopedia of Native American History*. Vol. 2. Ed. Peter C. Mancall. New York: Facts On File, 2011. Digital file.

"Friends of the Indian." *The West*. The West Film Project and WETA, 2001. Web. 24 Apr. 2015.

Prucha, Francis Paul. *Americanizing the American Indians: Writings by the "Friends of the Indian," 1880-1900*. Lincoln: U of Nebraska P, 1978. Print.

FRUSTRATION-AGGRESSION THEORY

From the beginning of recorded history, one can trace the theme that people often become aggressive when prevented from reaching some very basic goals—having food, feeling a reasonable degree of personal safety, having the chance to better themselves, and so on. Many people have been hurt because they were responsible for blocking the goals of others, thereby creating frustration. They have been victims of "instrumental aggression"—aggression that is primarily directed at attaining a goal rather than hurting another. Even more people, however, have been hurt as innocent victims of frustrated individuals purposely venting their rage on whatever nearby group or individual was easy to identify and was relatively powerless. This is known as "hostile aggression," and it is carried out to make the aggressor feel better.

FREUD'S IDEAS

The seeds of a modern frustration-aggression theory can be found in the writings of Sigmund Freud, the father of psychoanalysis. He stated that aggression is an inherent characteristic of people and that they often use "displacement," an ego defense mechanism, to redirect aggression from its appropriate target to a more easily available and safer one. Freud stated that much of what people do is motivated by "unconscious" forces. By unconscious, he meant forces of which people are largely unaware but that are nevertheless active in their minds. This concept of unconscious motivation is key to the process of scapegoating. If people realized consciously that they were blaming innocent individuals for their problems, rational thought would stop them from doing so. Unconscious direction of behavior, however, bypasses such rationality.

American theorists expanded on Freud's ideas about frustration and aggression. John Dollard and his colleagues authored the now classic *Frustration and Aggression* (1939), which proposed that frustration always leads to aggression and that aggression is always preceded by frustration. The basic proposal was ultimately too simplistic, but the book motivated many researchers to examine and challenge parts of it. Leonard Berkowitz, for example, provided support for the commonsense notions that aggression may be generated by circumstances other than frustration and that frustration may produce responses other than aggression. He also documented what he termed the "trigger effect," the ability of something in the environment to set off aggression under conditions of high frustration.

SCAPEGOATING AND RACISM

When the cause of frustration is something that cannot be attacked, such as poor economic conditions, or when the cause is too dangerous to attack (for example, a powerful dictator), innocent victims often become scapegoats of hostile "displaced aggression." For the displacement of aggression to be comforting to a frustrated individual, several conditions must be satisfied. First, since displacement is carried out as a substitute for aggression against the causes of frustration that cannot directly be attacked, a good scapegoat must be a manageable target. Attacking a person, or a few people, is far more manageable than attacking the government or an environmental condition such as a drought.

Second, a satisfying scapegoat must be relatively harmless compared with other possible targets and with the real cause of the frustration. Third, a scapegoat must be readily identifiable and easy to locate. Often a group (such as an ethnic or religious group) is an easy source of such individual scapegoats. A group contains many victims, some of whom are almost always present when needed, and the fact that it may also be easily identified and used by others gives social support for displacing aggression. Others may target the scapegoat for different reasons, but such differences are immaterial. That people can agree on their hatred is sufficient. This fact illuminates the connections between frustration, aggression, and racial prejudice.

FORMATION OF PREJUDICE
Historical precedent can greatly enhance the utility of a group used as a scapegoat. African Americans were the first victims of institutionalized racial prejudice in the United States. Very early in the nation's history, they became an ideal scapegoat group; because they were slaves, they were helpless to defend themselves against unjust blame, and because of their appearance, most were subject to easy identification.

Prejudice against many peoples can be explained by many of the factors that still contribute to prejudice against blacks. Immigrants have often been the targets of displaced aggression. Even those who speak English are, for a time, easily identifiable by accented speech, differences in preferred dress, and different customs. Those immigrants speaking different languages are easier to spot, and those with different features and skin color easier still. Identifiability as a factor leading to scapegoating was used in a malicious, yet clever, way by Adolf Hitler in the 1930s and 1940s. German Jews had assimilated to a greater degree than Jewish people in many other countries and were thus not always identifiable by dress or behavior, much less appearance, so Hitler demanded that they identify themselves and their businesses by symbols (for example, a yellow star) worn on clothing or the word "Jew" displayed on properties. Hitler

and his advisers well understood scapegoating, and they used it to deflect aggression away from themselves and toward a common "enemy." Historically, many politicians in the United States have done the same in an equally vile way, using Chinese, African Americans, or Hispanics, for example, as easily identified targets for hatred. Communists, intellectuals, and homosexuals have also been targets, but they have had to be somehow specially identified. Such scapegoating still occurs, but it generally takes more subtle and covert forms than it did in the past.

The long-honored view that racism can be caused by the formation of negative attitudes (prejudices) that lead to limiting behavior (discrimination) is also compatible with the frustration-aggression theory. "Aggression," as the theory uses it, can be at any level—intellectual, emotional, or behavioral. A frustrated individual who uses blacks as a scapegoat may believe that they are inferior people, may hate them, and may discriminate against them at every opportunity. Such a person holds the prejudice that is often hypothesized to underlie racism and to facilitate scapegoating.

STEREOTYPING
The view that stereotypes encourage racism and scapegoating is also compatible with the frustration-aggression theory. Often a group chosen as a scapegoat is far more variable than the frustrated individual recognizes. By accurate perception, a person would recognize that only some (if any) of the group members "deserve" the hostility directed at them. Widely held stereotypes simplify the process of scapegoating. If all black people are lazy, for example, and all Jewish people are money-hungry, the frustrated individual can simply hate them all without giving the matter further thought.

THE AUTHORITARIAN PERSONALITY
Even the most individualistic theory about scapegoating and racism, that of the authoritarian personality, meshes well with the frustration-aggression theory. An authoritarian personality, as first characterized in the 1950s, is a personality type characterized by a number of qualities that fall only a bit short of ones needed for classification as mentally ill. The person designated "high authoritarian" by a score on the F-scale devised by Theodor Adorno and the other authors of *The Authoritarian Personality* (1950) displays several qualities—conventionalism, authoritarian aggression, superstition and stereotypy, and

projectivity—that directly predispose him or her to scapegoating as well as most of the behaviors inherent in the several other theories of racism. High authoritarians have developed their personalities over a lifetime and are not likely to change spontaneously or to be changed by others' efforts. Because of their typically rigid behaviors, they face many frustrations and are especially likely to find reasons other than their own shortcomings for their problems. High authoritarians' aggressiveness under frustrating conditions is a prototype for the frustration-aggression hypothesis.

——*Harry A. Tiemann, Jr.*

BIBLIOGRAPHY AND FURTHER READING

Chadee, Derek, ed. *Theories in Social Psychology.* Malden: Wiley, 2011. Print.

Churchman, David. *Why We Fight: The Origins, Nature, and Management of Human Conflict.* 2nd ed. Lanham: Rowman, 2013. Print.

Houghton, David Patrick. *Political Psychology: Situations, Individuals, and Cases.* 2nd ed. New York: Routledge, 2015. Print.

Kecmanovic, Dusan. *The Mass Psychology of Ethnonationalism.* New York: Springer, 1996. Print.

FUGITIVE SLAVE LAWS

Although the US Constitution provided for the return of fugitive slaves across state borders, it did not specify the mechanism by which this would be accomplished. Congress therefore enacted the Fugitive Slave Law of 1793, by which slaves could be seized by masters or agents crossing state lines. State officials were made responsible for the enforcement of the federal law. For the slaves, the law embodied no protection of *habeas corpus* , trial by jury, or right to testify in their own behalf. In response, many northern states passed laws granting slaves personal liberties.

The Fugitive Slave Law of 1850 made the federal government responsible for returning slaves to their owners. Interference with the law became a felony. Again, the alleged fugitive was denied personal rights. Furthermore, since commissioners received a higher fee for delivering a slave than for rejecting a claim, the law resulted in the confiscation of free people. The law's constitutionality was upheld in 1859 in *Ableman v. Booth* . Northern furor over the law and increasing abolitionist sentiment helped bring the country closer to the brink of war.

——*Mary E. Virginia*

BIBLIOGRAPHY AND FURTHER READING

Murphy, Angela F. *The Jerry Rescue: The Fugitive Slave Law, Northern Rights, and the American Sectional Crisis.* New York: Oxford UP, 2015. Print.

Smith, David G. *On the Edge of Freedom: The Fugitive Slave Issue in South Central Pennsylvania, 1829–1870.* New York: Fordham UP, 2013. Print.

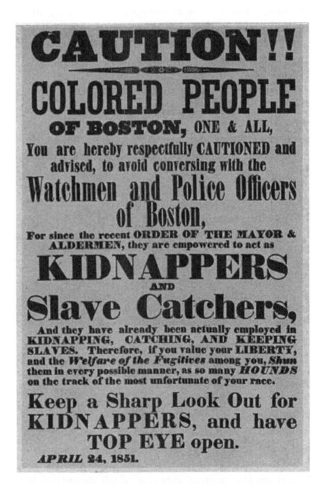

Massachusetts had abolished slavery in 1783, but the Fugitive Slave Law of 1850 required government officials to assist slavecatchers in capturing fugitives within the state.

FULLILOVE V. KLUTZNICK

In *Fullilove v. Klutznick*, the Supreme Court on July 2, 1980, ruled that setting aside a percentage of federal contracts for minority business enterprises was constitutional as long as it was intended to remedy demonstrated discrimination.

In passing the Public Works Employment Act of 1977, Congress required 10 percent of local public works contracts to be "set aside"for minority businesses—businesses with at least 50 percent ownership or 51 percent stockholding by African Americans, Spanish-speaking people, Asian Americans, American Indians, Eskimos, or Aleuts. Nonminority prime contractors were required, in subcontracting to minority businesses, to provide guidance and technical assistance in making bids, to lower or waive bonding requirements, and to assist minority businesses in obtaining working capital from financial institutions and government agencies.

Shortly after Juanita Krebs, US secretary of commerce, issued administrative guidelines for bidding under the new law, several potential project grantees (H. Earl Fullilove and trustees of the New York Building and Construction Industry Board of Urban Affairs Fund, two general contractor associations, and a firm engaged in heating, ventilation, and air conditioning work) filed suit against Krebs, the city and state of New York, the New York Board of Higher Education, and the Health and Hospitals Corporation for a temporary restraining order to block implementation of the law. After they lost the case in the district court (in December, 1977) and on appeal (in 1978), they took the case to the Supreme Court. When the case was decided, Philip Klutznick was US secretary of commerce. Chief Justice Warren Burger wrote the majority opinion; three justices provided concurring majority opinions, and two wrote dissents.

The Court answered the argument that government should act in a color-blind manner by noting that Congress had the power to spend money for the general welfare and thus to design a remedy for minority businesses. The argument that nonminority businesses were deprived of equal access to contracts was rejected: a 10 percent set-aside rate was considered light in view of the larger percentage of minorities. The Court responded to the argument that the definition of "minority" was underinclusive and should have added other groups by noting that such a definition was entirely up to Congress. The argument that the "minority" definition was overinclusive and might favor minority businesses unqualified to do the technical work was refuted by a reference to the statutory provisions that only bona fide minorities were covered by the law and that a waiver from the set-aside could be issued if no minority business was able to do the work.

The Supreme Court thus held that a numerical goal could be designed as a remedy for a statistically demonstrated inequality for minorities, with provisions tailored to removing specific, documented barriers to the success of minorities. Plans failing these tests have been consistently rejected by the Court, as in *Richmond v. J. A. Croson Company* (1989).

——*Michael Haas*

FUSION MOVEMENT

Beginning in 1890, leaders of the Populist, or People's, Party courted black votes in an effort to vote Democratic "redeemers" (southern whites who had regained control of local governments after Reconstruction had ended in the 1870s) out of office in the southern states. The appeal was based on the mutual interest of all downtrodden farmers, whatever their race. Fusionists argued that black farmers shared the same economic problems as white ones and that the Republican Party only wanted to help the white business community. State organizations elected black delegates to their councils and gave them a voice in the party organization. Party rallies and speeches were attended by both races, although seating was segregated. Black Populist clubs served to indoctrinate members in party principles and to encourage speakers and leaders. Sometimes deals were made with Republican bosses to deliver black votes.

Fusion was never accepted by all white Populists. In the 1894 election, the party was divided between fusionists and antifusionists led by Tom Watson of Georgia. Watson believed that fusion would taint the party by association with the party of Abraham Lincoln (the Republicans). In any case, fusion was never a formal platform but a series of local agreements that led to success at the polls across the South. The demise of fusion and the Populist Party came in the presidential election of 1896.

——*Robert E. McFarland*

BIBLIOGRAPHY AND FURTHER READING

Alexander, Shawn Leigh. *An Army of Lions: The Civil Rights Struggle Before the NAACP.* Philadelphia: U of Pennsylvania P, 2012. Print.

Beeby, James M., ed. *Populism in the South Revisited: New Interpretations and New Departures.* Jackson: U of Mississippi P, 2012. Print.

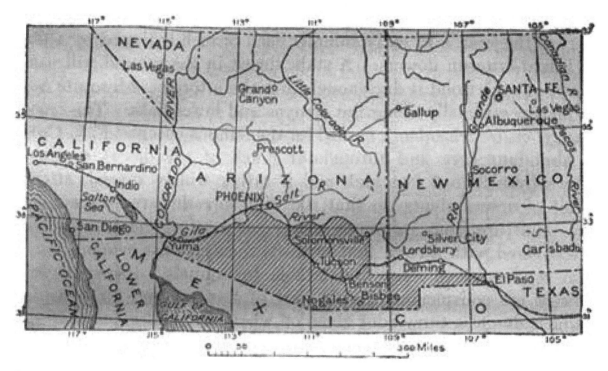

Gadsden Purchase.

G

GADSDEN PURCHASE

On behalf of President James Buchanan, Gadsden negotiated America's purchase of 45,535 square miles of territory from Mexico for the payment of fifteen million dollars (reduced later to ten million).

James Gadsden was a South Carolina railroad promoter turned diplomat. On behalf of President James Buchanan, he negotiated America's purchase of 45,535 square miles of territory from Mexico for the payment of fifteen million dollars (reduced later to ten million). A block of land nearly the size of New York State, the Gadsden Purchase lies south of the Gila River, forming part of present-day Arizona and New Mexico. The treaty embodying the purchase was signed on December 30, 1853, and ratified on June 29, 1854, settling boundary questions between the United States and Mexico left unresolved by the Treaty of Guadalupe Hidalgo at the end of the Mexican-American War in 1848.

The purchase was prompted by American politicians eager to build a transcontinental railroad through the Southwest. Neither the Mexican nor American government consulted with the Tohono O'odhams (Papagos) and Chiricahua Apaches who lived in the area, and these Indians subsequently ignored boundaries that were not their own.

——*Clifton K. Yearley*

GENDERED RACISM

Social psychologist Philomena Essed coined the term "gendered racism" to refer to the way that sexism and racism interact to subordinate minority-group women. Scholars sometimes refer to minority women as a "double minority" because they are affected by cultural definitions of gender that vary by race or ethnicity. Whites historically have defined African American women, for example, as "Aunt Jemima," the overweight, subservient maid or housekeeper; or as a sexual object, to be used by men and then discarded; or as "beasts of burden." These negative images, like ones for other minority women, can be traced to the historical exploitative relationship not only between whites and minority groups but also between men and women. Gendered racism has implications for minority women by restricting their access to education, limiting their occupational options, restricting their income to minimum or below-minimum wages, and making it difficult for minority families to escape poverty. Consequently, minority women lag behind white women and men of all racial and ethnic groups in terms of political, economic, cultural, and social positions.

——*Cheryl D. Childers*

GENERAL ALLOTMENT ACT

When the General Allotment Act became law on February 8, 1887, proponents hailed it as the Indian Emancipation Act and Secretary of the Interior L. Q. C. Lamar called it "the most important measure of legislation ever enacted in this country affecting our Indian affairs."

The law dealt primarily with Native American ownership of land. It authorized the president of the United States, through the Office of Indian Affairs in the Department of the Interior, to allot the lands on reservations to individual Native Americans, so that they would hold the land in severalty instead of the tribe's owning the land communally. Each head of a household would receive a quarter-section of land (160 acres); single persons over eighteen years of age and orphans would receive 80 acres; and other persons, 40 acres. (In 1891, an amendment to the law equalized the allotments to provide 80 acres for each individual, regardless of age or family status.) The United States government would hold the allotments in trust for twenty-five years, during which time a Native American could not sell or otherwise dispose of his or her land. At the end of that period, he or she would receive full title to it. After the process of dividing up the reservation land for allotments, the federal government could sell the surplus land (often a considerable portion of the reservation) to willing purchasers (most of whom would be Euro-Americans). The money from such sales would go to a fund to benefit Native American education.

The Dawes Act also provided for Native American citizenship. Native Americans who received allotments in severalty or who took up residence apart from their tribe and adopted what Euro-Americans considered civilized ways became citizens of the United States and subject to the laws of the state or territory in which they lived. In 1924, Congress passed the Indian Citizenship Act, granting full citizenship to nearly all Native Americans who were not already citizens, and measures in the late 1940's extended such status to Arizona and New Mexico Native Americans whom the 1924 law had missed.

SUPPORT FOR THE ACT

Two groups of Euro-Americans especially welcomed the Dawes Act. Land-hungry settlers who had long cast covetous eyes on the reservation lands—which, to Euro-American thinking, were going to waste because of the lack of productive agricultural practices by Native Americans, whom they considered to be hunters and gatherers—were now able to acquire the lands left over from the allotment process. No doubt, the less scrupulous among the settlers also looked forward to the day when individual Native Americans would receive full title to their land and

be able to sell, lease, or otherwise dispose of it. Then pressure, legitimate or not, would likely induce the new owner to part with the acreage.

A second group of Euro-Americans, however, was more influential in securing passage of the Dawes Act. These were the humanitarian reformers of the day, who considered private ownership of land in severalty, US citizenship, education, and consistent codification of laws to be indispensable means for the acculturation of the Native Americans and their eventual assimilation into the mainstream of US society. As ministers from the several Christian denominations, educators, civil servants, politicians, and even a few military personnel, these philanthropists exerted a clout beyond their numbers. Calling themselves the Friends of the Indian, these reformers had been meeting annually since 1869 at the Catskills resort of Lake Mohonk to discuss ways to bring the tribal peoples to what the conveners deemed to be civilization.

Federal politicians had long considered private ownership of land essential to the civilizing process. Thomas Jefferson and the like-minded policymakers of his time had strongly advocated it, and in 1838 the Commissioner of Indian Affairs gave voice to a widespread view when he said, "Unless some system is marked out by which there shall be a separate allotment of land to each individual . . . you will look in vain for any general casting off of savagism. Common property and civilization cannot co-exist."

REFORM EFFORTS

It was not until the post-Civil War years, when increasing Euro-American pressures on the Native Americans created crisis after crisis, that humanitarians and philanthropists began a concerted drive for "Indian reform." Land in severalty would be the most important factor in breaking up tribalism. The reform groups that were organized—the Board of Indian Commissioners (1869), the Women's National Indian Association (1879), the Indian Rights Association (1882), the Lake Mohonk Conference of Friends of the Indian (1883), and the National Indian Defense Association (1885), to name the most important—all strongly espoused allotment in severalty. Nor were they satisfied with the piecemeal legislation that affected one tribe at a time; the panacea they sought was a general allotment law. Although supporters argued over the speed of implementing allotment, such proponents as Carl Schurz, Herbert

Welsh, and the Reverend Lyman Abbott fought energetically for such legislation. They finally won to their cause Senator Henry L. Dawes, chairman of the Senate Committee on Indian Affairs, who successfully shepherded through Congress the measure that bears his name.

Only a few Euro-American voices cried out against the proposal. Congressman Russell Errett of Pennsylvania and a few others protested that the bill was a thinly disguised means of getting at the valuable tribal lands. Senator Henry M. Teller of Colorado argued that the Native Americans did not want to own land in severalty and were not prepared to assume the responsibilities that went with private property and citizenship. He denied the contention of the reformers that private ownership of land would lead to civilization. Albert Meacham, editor of *The Council Fire*, maintained that there was little enthusiasm for severalty among traditionalist Native Americans, and anthropologist Lewis Henry Morgan thought that allotment would result in massive poverty. Presbyterian missionaries apparently were disunited on the subject of allotment, and their views fell by the wayside as the juggernaut of reform forged ahead.

Native American response to allotment has largely gone unrecorded. The Cherokee, Creek, Chickasaw, Choctaw, Seminole, Sac, Fox, and a few other tribes in Indian Territory, as well as the Seneca in New York, contended that they already mostly owned land individually and won exclusion from the act's operation. By 1906, however, Congress extended allotment to them as well. Most of the complaints came after the act's passage, when Native Americans lost land and found farming difficult under its provisions.

"February 8, 1887," one optimistic spokesman of the Board of Indian Commissioners commented, "may be called the Indian emancipation day." Although much sincere Christian goodwill motivated

passage of the Dawes Act, it turned out to be a disaster for Native Americans. In 1891, Congress allowed Native Americans to lease their allotments if they were not able to farm for themselves.

The allotments and the leasing moved faster and with less careful discrimination than Dawes and other promoters had intended. Instead of being a measure that turned Native Americans into self-supporting farmers, the act, through the rapid alienation of the Native Americans' lands, meant the loss of the land base on which the tribal peoples' hope for future prosperity depended. Tribal peoples held claim to about 150 million acres of land in 1887. The Dawes Act eventually diverted two-thirds of that acreage out of Native American ownership, down to about 48 million acres by 1934. Not until that year, with the passage of the Indian Reorganization Act (the Wheeler-Howard Act, also known as the Indian New Deal), did the federal government repeal the Dawes Act and encourage communal forms of ownership again, but by that time much of the former reservation land was gone as surplus sales, leases, or sales by the individual allottees.

———*Francis P. Prucha, updated by Thomas L. Altherr*

BIBLIOGRAPHY AND FURTHER READING

Black, Jason Edward. *American Indians and the Rhetoric of Removal and Allotment.* Jackson: UP of Mississippi, 2015. Print.

Greenwald, Emily. *Reconfiguring the Reservation: The Nez Perces, Jicarella Apaches, and the Dawes Act.* Albuquerque: U of New Mexico P, 2002. Print.

Hoxie, Frederick E. *A Final Promise: The Campaign to Assimilate the Indians, 1880-1920.* Lincoln: U of Nebraska P, 1984. Print.

Washburn, Wilcomb E. *The Assault on Indian Tribalism: The General Allotment Law (Dawes Act) of 1887.* Philadelphia: J. B. Lippincott, 1975. Print.

GENETIC BASIS FOR RACE

It is obvious that humans vary tremendously in physical appearance. Other biological features such as blood type and enzyme production are equally diverse. Many people, if asked, would probably claim that these differences are profound and consistent

enough to allow for categorizing humans into various distinct racial categories. A "race" might be defined as an isolated population within a species that has little or no gene flow with other members of that species. After a substantial period of time,

¹34

which will furnish information in regard to Indian affairs to those who need it.

Col. R. H. Pratt was asked to follow Dr. Frissell.

Col. R. H. Pratt.—I want especially to endorse what the good Bishop said in his classical paper this morning. It went right to the root of the matter. The conditions in New York are not exceptional. I also endorse the Commissioner's short-hair order. It is good because it disturbs old savage conditions. A celebrated American writer makes one of his characters say,

"The great American idee
Is to make a man a man
And then to let him be."

In dealing with the Indian the eternal thing with us is his property. Property is the stumbling block all the time, and I am glad to see any steps taken to get it out of the way. The Indian's property and our greed for it stands in the way of the Indian's progress. If we can make the Indian a man and get him to the point where he has ability to take care of himself and then let him alone, there will be no trouble.

Segregating any class or race of people apart from the rest of the people kills the progress of the segregated people or makes their growth very slow. Association of races and classes is necessary in order to destroy racism and classism. Almost all the humanitarian and Government contrivances for the Indian within my knowledge are segregating in their influences and practically accomplish only segregation.

We have brought into our national life nearly forty times as many negroes as there are Indians in the United States. They are not altogether citizen and equal yet, but they are with us and of us; distributed among us, coming in contact with us constantly, they have lost their many languages and their old life, and have accepted our language and our life and become a valuable part of our industrial forces. The Indian, on the contrary, through our contrivances and control, has been held away from association with us, with all his affairs entirely under our control. We constantly treat him as an alien, and even in his education and industrial training we alienize him from all association and competition in our schools and industries. The system has been successful in making him the most un-American and foreign to our affairs of any of our peoples. Ten millions of negroes are all English speaking and have been made citizens. Two hundred and fifty thousand Indians, one fortieth as many, are yet largely speaking their own languages and living their own old life.

Long experience proves that it is just as easy to give the Indian the English language and our American industries, Yankee shrewdness and the push-and-go of our people, as it is to give it to any other man of any race. The only condition necessary to the ac-

·:)190⁰

'PROCEEDINGS

OF THE

TWENTIETH ANNUAL MEETING

OF THE

Lake Mohonk Conference

OF

FRIENDS OF THE INDIAN

1902

Reported and edited by Isabel C. Barrows

published by
THE LAKE MOHONK CONFERENCE
1903

1902 use of the word "racism". By Isabel C. Barrows.

this subgroup may take on numerous physical characteristics that are slightly different from the others of the species.

Although there might be some human populations that could called races, the way that the term is commonly used is simply not scientifically justifiable and has little value. In short, for all practical purposes, "races" do not exist as a natural biological category in the way that "species" do. The "races" of human beings are all of the same species and, biologically, are essentially identical. To be sure, as many people can personally attest, races do exist as social categories (discrimination being just one manifestation). However, these social categories are no more real or natural than any other arbitrary cultural construct (such as having to wear ties to work in an office).

HISTORICAL RACIAL TYPOLOGIES AND EXPLANATIONS

The most common way of dividing the world racially has been the tripartite "white" (Caucasian), "black" (Negroid), and "Asian" (Mongoloid), using the vernacular and pseudoscientific terms respectively. Since the days of naturalist Charles Darwin, who developed the theory of evolution, natural selection has often been the primary explanatory device to account for the great physical diversity seen in the world's people. For example, the tall and thin East African Dinka have bodies that radiate heat, an obvious advantage in a equatorial environment. People living in the Andes or near the Arctic Circle are short and squat for the opposite reason: Their bodies have less surface area to radiate heat, a useful trait for living in the extreme cold. However, such explanations are not completely compelling, as not everyone living in a warm climate is lean and tall, nor are all peoples in cold climates fat and small. Likewise, consider skin pigmentation as an adaption to varying exposures to sunlight. Although darker skins are believed to protect against sunburn, and white skin allows for easier absorption of necessary ultraviolet light in places with long winters, some of the darkest-skinned people in the world are the Tasmanians, who lived in an area receiving only moderate sunlight. Attributes such as eye color and hair color and texture seem to have no genetic adaptive advantage whatsoever.

RACIAL CRITERIA, AND SOME "NEW" RACES

If adaptive or environmental explanations of racial variation are lacking, so are the definitions of race. There are thousands of ways to define a race. In recent times in Western countries, skin color has been the primary way to classify people; however, this has not always been the case, nor is this the only characteristic that can be used to separate people. For example, if classification were made by the epicanthic fold (which covers the inner edge of the eyes and is typically found among people in East Asian countries), Japanese, Chinese, Koreans, and the Kung San of Africa would fall into the same "race." The emperor of Japan and South African leader Nelson Mandela share this feature. If blood typology were used, hundreds of different races could be constructed. For instance, Scots, central Africans, and Australian aboriginals could be placed together in the same biological (racial) category, because about 75 percent of their populations have O-type blood. Using the presence or absence of the sickle-shaped red blood cell, most Africans and African Americans would be placed in the same race along with Greeks and Italians. If dentition were used, East Asians, Native Americans, and Swedes could form a race, as they all share incisors (eyeteeth) that are "scooped out" in the back.

PROBLEMS WITH DEFINITIONS

Inherent in every definition of race are at least four major problems involving clines, covariation, randomness, and arbitrary or self-definitions. Although clines, or gradations, of skin color and other traits exist, people do not fall into clear-cut, distinct categories. Even if skin color, the most common measure, is used as the primary racial criteria, no clear or natural separations exist between peoples. There are groups of light-skinned blacks and populations of swarthy whites; people exist in every skin shade from light to dark.

Traits do not covary. If races were indeed real categories, different features should vary together. For example, all members of a particular race (white, black, or Asian) should have the same hair texture, facial features, blood type, eye and hair color, and other inheritable characteristics. However, among the world's peoples are populations of blond-haired "black" Australian aboriginals, "white" people who typically have flat "Asian" noses, and "Asians" with kinky hair. The features used to classify people according to "race" do not always occur as sets, which would be the case if true biological categories existed. In addition, biological anthropologists have long known that, using measurements of almost any physical criteria, just as much random variation exists within a so-called racial category as between "races." This calls into question the notion of race as a useful, or even valid, category.

Racial designations—especially legal ones—are basically arbitrary. One Jewish grandparent was enough to make an individual a Jew in Nazi Germany. In many southern states in the United States, if a person had any black ancestors, according to the one-drop rule, that individual was black, regardless of appearance. In the 1990s, because of increasing diversity and interracial marriage in the American population, the question of racial designations became more complex. What should a person with a "white" grandfather, "black" grandmother, and Asian mother be called? Often, this is something that people decide for themselves. Golfing superstar Tiger Woods, for example, says that when filling out forms, he checks every racial category that applies to make certain all of his ancestries are represented. The US government is also aware of the arbitrariness of the racial and ethnic categories it uses to classify people, including those used in the census. For example, in 1997, federal agencies debated whether native Hawaiians, when filling out census questionnaires, should remain grouped with Asians and Pacific Islanders or be placed in the category with Alaskans and Native Americans. The decision was tabled, and no change regarding Hawaiians was incorporated into the year 2000 census.

Between 50,000 and 100,000 pairs of genes are required to make a human being, and perhaps 75 percent of these are the same for everyone in the world. Only a small fraction of these genes—perhaps less than a dozen pairs—might account for skin pigmentation. The genes of white and black Americans are probably about 99.9 percent alike. There is simply no way to put five million Americans into three, six, or even a hundred racial categories that makes biological sense or has any scientific validity.

——*James Stanlaw*

BIBLIOGRAPHY AND FURTHER READING

Cohen, Mark Nathan. "Culture, Not Race, Explains Human Diversity." *Chronicle of Higher Education* 17 Apr. 1998. Print.

Diamond, Jared. *The Third Chimpanzee: The Evolution and Future of the Human Animal.* New York: Harper, 1992. Print.

Gould, Stephen Jay. *The Mismeasure of Man.* Rev. and expanded ed. New York: Norton, 1996. Print.

Jacoby, Russell, and Naomi Glauberman. *The Bell Curve Debate.* New York: Random, 1995. Print.

THE BELL CURVE DEBATE: RACE, INTELLIGENCE, AND GENES

One of the most controversial books of the mid-1990's was *The Bell Curve: Intelligence and Class Structure in American Life,* by psychologist Richard Herrnstein and political scientist Charles Murry. In some eight hundred pages of dense text, charts, and graphs, Herrnstein and Murry argue that in a democracy, the more intelligent people will rise above their socioeconomic class, thus leaving the lower classes, on the average, to consist of members who are less gifted intellectually. Though couched in rather careful language, they also claim that differences in intelligence quotient (IQ) between populations are mostly due to genetics. That is, while acknowledging that any particular person from group A may or may not be more intelligent than some particular person from group B, in terms of averages, group A and group B may show striking discrepancies in IQ scores. To put it bluntly, distinct races—because of their genetic makeups—demonstrate differences in intelligence.

The two topics of *The Bell Curve*—intelligence and race—are among the most controversial in American public discourse. Murry and Herrnstein's book immediately caught the attention of the popular media (appearing, for example, on the covers of *Newsweek, The New Republic,* and *The New York Times Book Review*). In the presidential elections of 1990 and 1994, welfare reform, teen pregnancy, and chronic unemployment were some of the most widely discussed social problems brought up by the campaigns, and in many ways *The Bell Curve* focused on these concerns. However compelling the arguments in this book may appear at first glance, many technical flaws exist in the data analysis. However, more important are the two premises on which the book is based: General human intelligence can be measured by a single numerical factor such as IQ, and humans can be categorized as belonging to racial categories, forming distinct and separate genetic groupings. The first claim is doubtful, with ambiguous support at best; but the second is simply wrong.

——*James Stanlaw*

GENOCIDE OF AMERICAN INDIANS

The European discovery of the New World had devastating consequences for the native population. Within a century of Christopher Columbus's landing in 1492, the number of people living in the Americas had declined from 25 million to 1 million. Whole societies in Mexico and South America died within weeks of initial contact with Spanish explorers and adventurers. The major cause of the devastation was disease. Native Americans had lived in total isolation from the rest of the world since first arriving in the New World from Central Asia around 20,000 BCE; hence, they had escaped the devastating epidemics

A mass grave being dug for frozen bodies from the 1890 Wounded Knee Massacre, in which the US Army killed 150 Lakota people, marking the end of the American Indian Wars. By Northwestern Photo Co.

and diseases, such as smallpox and the plague, that had afflicted the rest of humankind for generations. Such diseases normally required human carriers to pass them on to others, and such conditions did not exist in the New World until after 1492.

DEADLY CONTACT

Columbus and his crew made four separate voyages to the New World between 1492 and 1510, and on each of those voyages sailors brought new diseases with them. Even the common flu had devastating consequences for Native American babies and children. Other people of the world had built up immunities to these killers, but Native Americans had none, so they died in massive numbers. In the 1500s, most of the dying took place from Mexico south, since the Spanish appeared to be uninterested in colonizing North America. Only after the English settled

Jamestown in 1607–8 and Plymouth in Massachusetts in 1620 did the epidemics affect Native Americans in that region.

The first major tribe to be exterminated in North America was the Massachusetts of New England, whose population died out completely between 1619 and 1633 from a smallpox epidemic. Yet other things besides disease were killing Native Americans. Most Europeans believed that the people they came across in their explorations were not human at all, but instead savage, inferior beings who had no law and order, no cities, no wealth, and no idea of God or progress. When they died from "white man's diseases," this offered further proof of the weakness and helplessness of the population. Europeans soon turned to Africa for their supply of slave laborers; Africans, who had had a much longer history of contact with other peoples of the world, had built up

NATIVE AMERICAN TRIBES THAT HAVE BEEN COMPLETELY EXTERMINATED

Tribe	Region Inhabited	Years Exterminated	By Whom/What
Calusa	Florida	1513–30	Spanish/war
Massachusetts	New England	1617–33	Smallpox
Powhatan	Virginia	1637–1705	English/war
Narraganset	Rhode Island	1675–76	English/war
Susquehannock	New York	1675–1763	Disease/war
Chitimacha	Louisiana	1706–17	French/war
Natchez	Mississippi	1716–31	French/war
Chinook	Columbia River region	1782–1853	Smallpox
Yavapai	Arizona	1873–1905	Tuberculosis

immunities to the killing diseases. Native Americans were not so lucky.

CONFLICT OVER LAND

As time passed, immunities were built up by native peoples, and fewer tribes were extinguished by diseases. Warfare, however, continued to take its toll. Thousands of Native Americans died defending their homelands from American settlers in the aftermath of the War for Independence. Native Americans were not made citizens by the Constitution of 1787 but were legally defined as residents of foreign nations living in the United States. Wars and conflicts over territory devastated many tribes by 1830. In that year, president Andrew Jackson and Congress adopted a program, the Indian Removal Act , that they hoped would put an end to wars with the Native Americans. Under this new act, the American government would trade land west of the Mississippi River for land owned by the tribes in the east. Land in the west, acquired from France in 1803 as part of the Louisiana Purchase, was deemed unsuitable for farming by Europeans. Native Americans, on the other hand, would be able to survive on the Great Plains, called the "Great American Desert" by most whites, by hunting buffalo and other game.

Congress authorized the president to exchange land beginning in 1831. Three years later, a permanent Indian Country was created in the West and settlement by whites was declared illegal. By 1840, Indian Removal was complete, though it took the Black Hawk War in Illinois, the Seminole Wars in Florida, and the terrible march forcing the Cherokee from Georgia to the Indian Territory, to complete the process. At least three thousand Native American women and children died at the hands of the US Army on the Cherokee Trail of Tears. Indian Removal meant death and disaster for many eastern tribes.

Conflict was reduced by the program only until whites began moving into the West in the 1860s. During the Civil War (1861–65), several Indian Wars were fought in Minnesota and Iowa, and the infamous Chivington Massacre took place in Colorado in 1864. In this incident, 450 Native Americans were slaughtered without warning in a predawn raid by the Colorado militia. To prevent massacres in the West, Congress enacted a "reservation policy," setting aside several million acres of western lands for "permanent" Indian settlement. The Army had the job of keeping the tribes on their reservations. Frequent wars resulted as Great Plains tribes attempted to leave their reservations to hunt buffalo (bison) and the army drove them back.

Problems increased with the coming of railroads. The first transcontinental railroad began carrying passengers in 1869. Huge buffalo herds presented the railroads with a major problem, however, because they took hours and sometimes days to cross the tracks. To keep trains running on time, railroads hired hunters to kill the buffalo. By the late 1880s, they had nearly accomplished their goal of killing off all the herds. Buffalo had once numbered 100 million, but by 1888, there were fewer than 1,000. With the destruction of the buffalo came the end of the Native American way of life. The final war was fought in 1890 in the Black Hills of South Dakota on the Pine Ridge Reservation. An Indian holy man claimed that the whites would disappear and the buffalo would return if Native Americans danced a Ghost Dance . Magical shirts were given to the dancers that were supposed to protect them from white men's bullets. When the white Indian agent asked Washington for help to put down the Ghost Dancers, the Army responded by killing hundreds of the Native Americans, whose magical shirts did not work.

Native Americans did not become American citizens until 1924 and were required to live on reservations. Not until 1934 was self-government granted to the tribes, and by that time the reservations had become the poorest communities in the entire United States. It is only in recent decades, with the rise in Indian activism and legislation protecting Indian civil and tribal rights, that Native Americans have begun to recover.

——*Leslie V. Tischauser*

BIBLIOGRAPHY AND FURTHER READING

Anderson, Gary Clayton. *Ethnic Cleansing and the Indian.* Norman: U of Oklahoma P, 2014. Print.

Carpenter, Roger M. *Times Are Altered with Us: American Indians from First Contact to the New Republic.* Malden: Wiley Blackwell, 2015. Print.

Madley, Benjamin. *An American Genocide.* New Haven: Yale UP, 2016. Print.

Woolford, Andrew John, Jeff Benvenuto, and Alexander Laban Hinton. *Colonial Genocide in Indigenous North America.* Durham: Duke UP, 2014. Print.

GENOCIDE: CULTURAL

Cultural genocide is the deliberate and systematic destruction of a culture. It is not ethical to destroy the culture of another group of human beings or change it without their consent. Each culture should be judged by its own standards of excellence and morality, unless its cultural practices threaten to harm others physically or mentally.

The Canadian government outlawed many indigenous customs of the Kwakwaka'wakw (sometimes called Kwakiutl) people of Canada's Northwest Coast in an effort to convert them to a more Euro-Canadian lifestyle. The Kwakwaka'wakw were renowned for a unique custom that they called the potlatch. Kwakwaka'wakw chiefs competed with one another for status and power through this custom. It involved accumulating vast wealth in the form of artistic items known as "coppers," blankets, and food. After accumulating a fortune, a chief would invite his rival and the rival's followers to a feast. During this feast, the host would wine and dine all of his guests lavishly. Dancers would entertain them. At a prearranged time, the host would conspicuously destroy the valuable coppers and other treasures to demonstrate that he could afford to do so. He would challenge his guest to top this feat or accept inferior status. Upon leaving the feast, guests were given many blankets and food to take home with them. The Canadian government viewed this practice as a wanton and savage destruction of valuable property and a waste of labor, so they outlawed the potlatch.

Anthropologists have argued that, in addition to serving the overt function of leveling individuals, the potlatch served a covert or hidden function by redistributing wealth from areas that had accumulated a surplus to areas that had experienced shortages during bad years. The destruction of this and other pivotal institutions caused the Kwakwaka'wakw culture to collapse, leaving in its wake a vacuum that was soon filled by alcoholism, dysfunctional families, and other social problems.

Another example of cultural genocide comes from Africa. In 1884, at the Berlin Conference, European powers unilaterally carved up the African continent into territories that they claimed for themselves. Africans were not invited to this meeting. These European powers pledged to support the "civilizing" of Africans by Christian missionaries, which was "calculated to educate the natives and to teach them to understand and appreciate the benefits of civilization." The missionaries immediately declared traditional religions "devil worship." They collected all indigenous statues, relics, and artifacts and destroyed them. They fought to outlaw clitoridectomy, polygyny, and other native customs that they found "repugnant." These acts led to a clash of cultures and to an identity crisis for many Africans.

The classic example of cultural genocide in North America grew out of slavery . Plantation owners feared that allowing African slaves to speak their own languages, use African names to identify themselves, or practice African culture would encourage slave revolts. Consequently, every effort was made to stamp out African culture in the United States. The people survived, but much of their culture was destroyed. Today, African Americans are culturally more like other Americans than they are like Africans, despite strong physical similarities and a common ancestry.

The assumption that one's own culture is better for others than theirs is constitutes the ultimate cultural arrogance. It assumes that one's own culture is superior and that one has the right to impose one's values on others. This imposition is unfair and unethical. Cultures, like individuals, have a right to life unless their customs threaten the lives of others.

——*Dallas L. Browne*

BIBLIOGRAPHY AND FURTHER READING

Davidson, Lawrence. *Cultural Genocide*. New Brunswick: Rugters UP, 2012. Print.

Moses, A. Dirk, ed. *Empire, Colony, Genocide: Conquest, Occupation, and Subaltern Resistance in World History*. New York: Berghahn, 2008. Print.

Woolford, Andrew, Jeff Benvenuto, and Alexander Laban Hinton, eds. *Colonial Genocide in Indigenous North America*. Durham: Duke UP, 2014. Print.

GENOCIDE: PHYSICAL

Physical genocide is the deliberate and systematic attempt to annihilate an entire human population. Perpetrators of this practice direct their actions against groups that differ from their own in religious belief, race, ethnic affiliation, nationality, or sexual orientation. Often the extermination of a human group is prompted when the entire group is attributed with some presumed guilt that is associated with a small segment of that group or their ancestors.

HITLER AND THE JEWS
Brutal massacres of entire Jewish populations were ordered by Adolf Hitler as his "final solution" to the "Jewish question" in Germany and throughout Europe. Hitler argued that many of Germany's problems stemmed from the fact that Jews formed a separate, degenerate race. To Hitler, each race inherited certain qualities through its blood and genes; the Aryans were thus a naturally superior race, while Jews were sinister and devious. Hitler accused the Jews of secretly forming an "international Jewish conspiracy" aimed at dominating the globe economically and politically by cheating everyone else. He argued that because Jews were a lower and undesirable form of life, the only real

solution to the "Jewish question" was total extermination. As a result, he ordered the extermination of more than six million Jews. Hitler's Nazi Party used the Holocaust to cover up its theft of Jewish families' valuable art treasures, life savings, and property. The Nazi Party used the term *Judenrein*, meaning to clean an area of Jews, as a euphemism for genocide. Hitler applied the same flawed reasoning to Gypsies, the mentally disabled, and homosexuals. All were to be exterminated because they were considered inherently inferior and unworthy of life.

OTHER HISTORICAL EXAMPLES
History provides numerous examples of genocide. When the Australian government wanted land on the island of Tasmania, the native population refused to sell it or give it away. Ultimately, the Tasmanians' water supply was poisoned. Every native Tasmanian perished, and settlers from Australia subsequently claimed the land.

Turkey offers another example of this crime against humanity. Sultan Abdul Hamid II encouraged Kurdish depredations against Armenian villages. By 1894, these actions had grown into full-scale war, and the Turkish army assisted in the massacre of Armenians. Initially, an estimated 200,000 Armenians were killed. During World War I, the Turks sided with Germany, but the Armenians sided with Russia and Britain. As a result, the Turks viewed them as subversives. To secure its border with Russia, Turkey forcibly removed millions of Armenians and forced them to march south without adequate food or shelter. Armenians claim that the result was a holocaust and that more than one million Armenians died in Turkey in 1915. The Turks took more than 90 percent of the Armenians' land. The Turkish government has never admitted guilt for these events and has claimed that Armenians killed an equal number of Turks during World War I.

The Nobel Prize-winning physicist William Shockley proposed a theory of "dysergenics" that states that African Americans are biologically inferior to whites. Shockley proposed making America more competitive globally by the forced sterilization of all African Americans living in the United States. Within one generation, there would be no race problem because the black race would die out. Shockley was barred from speaking in Britain by authorities who considered his theory outrageous. World history is replete with examples of human willingness to violate moral and ethical codes, yet genocide constitutes the gravest violation of ethical principles on record.

——*Dallas L. Browne*

BIBLIOGRAPHY AND FURTHER READING

Bauman, Zygmunt. *Modernity and the Holocaust.* Ithaca: Cornell UP, 1989. Print.

Chalk, Frank, and Kurt Jonassohn. *The History and Sociology of Genocide.* New Haven: Yale UP, 1990. Print.

Shurkin, Joel N. *Broken Genius: The Rise and Fall of William Shockley.* New York: Macmillan, 2006. Print.

GENTLEMEN'S AGREEMENT

The first Japanese immigrants who arrived in California in 1871 were mostly middle-class young men seeking opportunities to study or improve their economic status. By 1880, there were 148 resident Japanese. Their numbers increased to 1,360 in 1891, including 281 laborers and 172 farmers. A treaty between the United States and Japan in 1894 ensured mutual free entry although allowing limitations on immigration based on domestic interests. By 1900, the number of Japanese recorded in the US census had increased to 24,326. They arrived at ports on the Pacific coast and settled primarily in the Pacific states and British Columbia.

An increase in the demand for Hawaiian sugar in turn increased the demand for plantation labor, especially Japanese labor. An era of government-contract labor began in 1884, ending only with the US annexation of Hawaii in 1898. Sixty thousand Japanese in the islands then became eligible to enter the United States without passports. Between 1899 and 1906, it is estimated that between forty thousand and fifty-seven thousand Japanese moved to the United States via Hawaii, Canada, and Mexico.

TENSIONS DEVELOP

On the Pacific coast, tensions developed between Asians and other Californians. Although the Japanese immigrant workforce was initially welcomed, antagonism increased as it began to compete with US labor. The emerging trade-union movement advocated a restriction of immigration. An earlier campaign against the Chinese had culminated in the 1882 Chinese Exclusion Act, which suspended immigration of Chinese laborers to the United States for ten years. This act constituted the first US law barring immigration based on race or nationality. A similar campaign was instigated against the Japanese. On March 1, 1905, both houses of the California State legislature voted to urge California's congressional delegation in Washington, D.C., to pursue the limitation of Japanese immigrants. At a meeting in San Francisco on May 7, delegates from sixty-seven organizations launched the Japanese and Korean Exclusion League, known also as the Asiatic Exclusion League.

President Theodore Roosevelt, who was involved in the peace negotiations between Japan and Russia, observed the developing situation in California. George Kennan, who was covering the Russo-Japanese

War, wrote to the president: "It isn't the exclusion of a few emigrants that hurts here . . . it's the putting of Japanese below Hungarians, Italians, Syrians, Polish Jews, and degraded nondescripts from all parts of Europe and Western Asia. No proud, high spirited and victorious people will submit to such a classification as that, especially when it is made with insulting reference to personal character and habits."

Roosevelt agreed, saying he was mortified that people in the United States should insult the Japanese. He continued to play a pivotal role in resolving the Japanese-Russian differences at the Portsmouth Peace Conference.

Anti-Japanese feeling waned until April, 1906. Following the San Francisco earthquake, an outbreak of crime occurred, including many cases of assault against Japanese. There was also an organized boycott of Japanese restaurants. The Japanese viewed these acts as especially reprehensible. Their government and Red Cross had contributed more relief for San Francisco than all other foreign nations combined.

Tension escalated. The Asiatic Exclusion League, whose membership was estimated to be 78,500 in California, together with San Francisco's mayor, pressured the San Francisco school board to segregate Japanese schoolchildren. On October 11, 1906, the board passed its resolution. A protest filed by the Japanese consul was denied. Japan protested that the act violated most-favored-nation treatment. Ambassador Luke E. Wright, in Tokyo, reported Japan's extremely negative feelings about the matter to Secretary of State Elihu Root. This crisis in Japanese American relations brought the countries to the brink of war. On October 25, Japan's ambassador, Shuzo Aoki, met with Root to seek a solution. President Roosevelt, who recognized the justification of the Japanese protest based on the 1894 treaty, on October 26 sent his secretary of commerce and labor to San Francisco to investigate the matter.

In his message to Congress on December 4, President Roosevelt paid tribute to Japan and strongly repudiated San Francisco for its anti-Japanese acts. He encouraged Congress to pass an act that would allow naturalization of the Japanese in the United States. Roosevelt's statements and request pleased Japan but aroused further resentment on the Pacific coast. During the previous twelve months, more than seventeen thousand Japanese had entered the mainland United States, two-thirds coming by

way of Hawaii. Roosevelt recognized that the basic cause of the unrest in California—the increasing inflow of Japanese laborers—could be resolved only by checking immigration.

US AND JAPAN NEGOTIATE

Negotiations with Japan to limit the entry of Japanese laborers began in late December, 1906. Three issues were involved: the rescinding of the segregation order by the San Francisco school board, the withholding of passports to the mainland United States by the Japanese government, and the closing of immigration channels through Hawaii, Canada, and Mexico by federal legislation. The Hawaiian issue, which related to an earlier Gentlemen's Agreement of 1900, was the first resolved through the diplomacy of Japan's foreign minister, Tadasu Hayashi, ambassadors Wright and Aoki, and Secretary of State Root.

Before Japan would agree to discuss immigration to the mainland, it was necessary for the segregation order to be withdrawn. In February, 1907, the president invited San Francisco's entire board of education, the mayor, and a city superintendent of schools to Washington, D.C., to confer on the segregation issue and other problems related to Japan. On February 18, a pending immigration bill was amended to prevent Japanese laborers from entering the United States via Hawaii, Mexico, or Canada. Assured that immigration of Japanese laborers would be stopped, the school board rescinded their segregation order on March 13. An executive order issued by the president on March 14 put into effect the restrictions on passports. Subsequently, the Japanese government agreed to conclude the Gentlemen's Agreement. In January, 1908, Foreign Minister Hayashi agreed to the terms of immigration discussed in December, 1907. On March 9, Secretary of State Root instructed Ambassador Wright to thank Japan, thus concluding the negotiations begun in December, 1906.

As reported by the commissioner general of immigration in 1908, the Japanese government would issue passports for travel to the continental United States only to nonlaborers, laborers who were former residents of the United States, parents, wives, or children of residents, and "settled agriculturalists." A final provision prevented secondary immigration into the United States by way of Hawaii, Mexico, or Canada.

When the Gentlemen's Agreement of 1907 cut off new supplies of Japanese labor, Filipinos were recruited to take their place, both in Hawaii and in California, as well as in the Alaskan fishing industry. As US nationals, Filipinos could not be prevented from migrating to the United States.

——*Susan E. Hamilton*

BIBLIOGRAPHY AND FURTHER READING

Raymond A. Esthus's *Theodore Roosevelt and Japan* (Seattle: University of Washington Press, 1967) provides a detailed examination of Roosevelt's relationship with Japan. Akemi Kikumura's *Issei Pioneers: Hawaii and the Mainland, 1885 to 1924* (Los Angeles: Japanese American National Museum, 1992) is a brief but well-researched text, with photographs that accompanied the premiere exhibit of the Japanese American National Museum. The US Department of State's *Report of the Hon. Roland S. Morris on Japanese Immigration and Alleged Discriminatory Legislation Against Japanese Residents in the United States* (1921; reprint, New York: Arno Press, 1978) collects correspondence regarding the Gentlemen's Agreement.

GERMAN AMERICANS

The first German colony was established in Germantown, Pennsylvania, in 1683 by Mennonites, an Anabaptist sect. (The Amish later separated from the Mennonites.) However, individual Germans were already present in the English colonies and in the Dutch colony of New Amsterdam. The Hutterites, another Anabaptist sect, came to America in 1874, settling in South Dakota. Although pacifists, they were subjected to conscription during World War I. Most of the community migrated to Canada, but many later returned. Two Hutterites who were sentenced for refusing conscription died from maltreatment.

Methodism developed a following among German Americans in the nineteenth century, and although the Methodist Church began phasing out the German branch in 1924, some congregations of the German Methodist Church persisted throughout the twentieth century. Germans also set up Baptist and Presbyterian churches. By 1890, nearly half of German Americans were Roman Catholic. Catholics and Lutherans did not mix much, which tended to divide German American political influence. The German and Irish wings of the American Catholic Church experienced some conflict in the 1880s and 1890s, and before World War I, German, Irish, and Polish congregations attended separate Catholic churches. Similarly, German and Scandinavian congregations often established separate Lutheran churches, and German American and Eastern European Jews generally formed separate worship groups, although the Eastern European Jews commonly spoke Yiddish, which is more than 80 percent German. German American Jews maintained cultural ties with Germany until the Nazi period.

RELATIONS WITH AMERICAN INDIANS

The Germans seemed to have less trouble with American Indians than other settlers in the eighteenth century, and in Texas, where thriving German settlements were established in the 1830s and 1840s, the Meusenbach-Comanche Treaty of 1847, negotiated between John Meusenbach and Comanche leaders Buffalo Hump, Santana, and Old Owl, was never broken by either side.

Two German travelers and a German American made significant contributions to American Indian ethnology. Alexander Philipp Maximilian, Prince of Wied-Neuwied, visited the United States in 1832 and produced a comprehensive study of the Mandan tribe, which later became extinct. Friedrich Gerstäcker, who visited the United States from 1837 to 1843 and again in 1849 and 1867, created a detailed ethnography of American Indian culture. German American Gustavus Sohon, born in Prussia, served in the US Army as a surveyor in the Northwest. There he became familiar with several American Indian tribes along the Columbia River and made numerous sketches of their lives, which are a valuable part of the anthropological record.

GERMAN AMERICANS AND SLAVERY

Various German American groups spoke out against slavery in the United States. The Mennonites of Germantown, Pennsylvania, made the first protest in 1688. The Salzburger Protestant colony of Ebenezer in Georgia, founded in 1734, also opposed slavery.

The failed Revolution of 1848, during which reactionary authorities in Berlin and Vienna suppressed attempts at constitutional reform, resulted in thousands of liberal intellectuals migrating to the United States. These new immigrants, who were particularly active in establishing newspapers, had a major impact on the cultural life of German American communities. The Forty-eighters, as they were known, were strongly opposed to slavery, and under their influence, a strong alliance formed between abolitionist forces and the German press in the United States.

Among the Forty-eighters was Mathilde Franziska Anneke-Giesler, an early champion of women's rights who came to the United States in 1850. Although she wrote almost exclusively in German, she was in close contact with suffragists Susan B. Anthony and Elizabeth Cady Stanton and often lectured in English. Antagonism to her feminist and antislavery attitudes caused her to go to England in 1860, where she lectured against slavery, returning to the United States in 1865.

In 1854, Germans meeting in San Antonio, Texas, declared their opposition to slavery, and German Americans fought on the North's side during the Civil War. In a battle with Confederate soldiers, one German American guard of sixty-five men lost twenty-seven people and had nine of its wounded murdered by opposition forces.

RELATIONS WITH ANGLO-SAXON SOCIETY

In the early nineteenth century, the German community in New York was significant enough to be courted by both political parties. A German Democratic Party organization was created in 1834, and eventually a German language newspaper was established to reflect the party's platform.

The years before the Civil War saw the rise of nativism, and anti-Catholicism was rampant. In 1855, murderous rioters in Louisville, Kentucky, attacked German Americans because many of them were Catholic and foreign-born and tended to be politically radical. The German Americans' opposition to slavery also created hostility in several regions.

German Americans experienced some friction with Anglo-Saxon Protestants of a puritanical bent, who disdained frivolity, especially on Sunday, and disliked some German customs associated with Christmas because they appeared to be pagan in origin. This immigrant group also clashed with the growing temperance movement in the nineteenth and twentieth centuries. The breweries founded by Germans in cities such as Cincinnati, Ohio; Milwaukee, Wisconsin; and St. Louis, Missouri, contributed to the economic development of these cities, and German Americans largely controlled the American brewing industry. German Americans in Texas kept that state from becoming a dry state until national Prohibition went into effect. One of the major purposes of the German American Alliance was to oppose prohibition. The German American Alliance (Deutsch-Amerikanische Nationalbund) was formed in 1901 as a national, sectarian, politically nonpartisan German American organization. It reached a membership of three million by 1916 to become the largest ethnic organization in US history. Congress abrogated the organization's charter in 1918.

Germans were also active in the labor movement that began after the Civil War and in radical politics, which caused some conflict with the dominant society.

WORLD WAR I

The United States' entry into World War I unleashed a tremendous irrational hostility toward anything German, including music—not just folk or popular music but classical music and opera. German Americans were harassed and subjected to physical assault, vandalism, and even murder. This hysteria existed even in areas where German Americans constituted more than one-third of the population or even a majority.

Laws in various states forbade teaching German in schools and speaking German in public, and thousands were convicted. Such laws were declared unconstitutional by the US Supreme Court in 1923. Anti-German attitudes lingered for a few years after the war and accelerated Anglicization of churches, social organizations, and newspapers.

World War II

In 1936, the Deutschamerikanische Volksbund, the German American Bund, replaced an earlier organization intended to represent the Nazi Party in the United States. The membership was believed to be only sixty-five hundred, and 40 percent were not actually of German stock, but the organization's posturing, arrogance, and hostility in effect mobilized public opinion against the Nazis and complicated diplomatic relations between the United States and Germany. The Steuben Society, the most prestigious German American organization, and other German organizations felt it necessary to repudiate the Bund, and German American antifascist organizations were formed.

After World War II, German American ethnic identity became increasingly tenuous as the population moved to the suburbs, and changes in recreational tastes weakened ties to German culture. Postwar German immigrants were less inclined to take part in German cultural organizations.

In 1948, the Russian blockade of the land routes to West Berlin made that city, and by extension West Germany, a symbol of freedom and democracy, giving Americans a more positive attitude toward Germany. West Germany became a military ally, and during the second half of the century, became increasingly integrated into the Pan-European identity of the European Union. Similarly, German Americans came to identify more with the broader European American culture.

——*William L. Reinshagen*

Bibliography and Further Reading

Franck, Irene M. *The German American Heritage.* New York: Facts on File, 1988. Print.

Lich, Glen E., and Dona B. Reeves, ed. *German Culture in Texas.* Boston: Twayne, 1980.

Kazal, Russell Andrew. *Becoming Old Stock: The Paradox of German-American Identity.* Princeton: Princeton UP, 2004. Print.

Llau, Alfred. *Deutschland: United States of America, 1683–1983.* Bielefeld: Univers-Verlag, 1983. Print.

Ripley, LaVern. *The German-Americans.* Boston: Twayne, 1976. Print.

Ghost Dance religion

The Ghost Dance religious movement began in 1890 as a result of the visions of the Northern Paiute leader called Wovoka, or Jack Wilson, who was based in Nevada. Wovoka began delivering a series of prophetic messages that described a future which would see the restoration of Native Americans to their lives as they had been before contact with the European American settlers and the destruction or removal of the settlers through an apocalypse, though Wovoka encouraged pacifism. The movement's practice was based around a circle dance and other meditative ceremonies meant to purify the spirit in preparation for the new world rather than any active resistance against white settlers. The belief spread quickly through various tribal groups in the western United States, with some embracing the movement fully and others co-opting certain elements with their own beliefs.

The Ghost Dance movement was typically viewed with suspicion by white settlers and the US government, who saw it as a potential source of unrest and rebellion. The Bureau of Indian Affairs (BIA) banned practice of the Ghost Dance, and fear of the movement's influence was deeply implicated in the massacre at Wounded Knee in Pine Ridge, South Dakota, in December 1890, in which three hundred Lakota Sioux were killed.

Included among the visions of Wovoka were such basic ideas as the resurrection of tribal members who had died, the restoration of game animals, a flood which would destroy only the white settlers, the necessity and importance of the performance of a dance ritual (the Ghost Dance itself), and a coming era which would be free of suffering and disease. Of these major ideas, the primary focus seemed to be on resurrection and the restoration of important elements of the old ways, as well as the performance of the dance itself. Related developments of the Ghost Dance movement were certain ethical precepts and, at least among the Sioux, the

SUPPLEMENT TO HARPER WEEKLY, DECEMBER 6, 1890.

THE GHOST DANCE BY THE OGALLALA SIOUX AT PINE RIDGE AGENCY, DAKOTA—Drawn by Frederic Remington from Sketches taken on the Spot.—[See Page 947.]

The Ghost Dance by the Oglala Lakota at Pine Ridge. Illustration by Frederic Remington, 1890.

creation and wearing of distinctive "ghost shirts," which identified adherents to the movement and were used in the performance of the ritual dancing itself. Some of the movement's elements, such as the belief in a single god, were influenced by Christianity.

As predicted dates for the cosmic events described by Wovoka came and passed, the initial fervor of the Ghost Dance and Wovoka's teachings in general began to dissipate. The Wounded Knee Massacre also suppressed the spread of the religion. Among some tribes, however, the focus shifted from apocalyptic expectations of events to a longer-term stress on daily ethics. In short, the movement became partially institutionalized, which is not uncommon for religious groups whose roots lie in visionary experiences.

——*Daniel L. Smith-Christopher*

BIBLIOGRAPHY AND FURTHER READING

Hittman, Michael, and Don Lynch. *Wovoka and the Ghost Dance*. Lincoln: U of Nebraska P, 1998. Print.

Smoak, Gregory E. *Ghost Dances and Identity: Prophetic Religion and American Indian Ethnogenesis in the Nineteenth Century*. Berkeley: U of California P, 2008.

Vander, Judith. *Shoshone Ghost Dance Religion: Poetry, Songs, and Great Basin Context*. Urbana: U of Illinois P, 1997. Print.

GLASS CEILING

After the Equal Employment Opportunity Commission (EEOC) was established in 1964 and additional legislation was passed in the 1970's by the US government that made discrimination in employment illegal, more members of minority groups were hired by corporations. Although these people had good jobs, many of them soon discovered that they could rise to a certain level within the corporate structure and no further. Certain barriers, which became collectively known as the glass ceiling, prevented their further advancement, particularly in the business world. These obstacles result from bias or prejudice on the part of employers and from institutional racism and sexism; they are difficult to detect and even harder to eliminate. Tolerance of the glass ceiling often exists in companies that try to appear nondiscriminatory by opening jobs to a few token minorities and women as a means of avoiding lawsuits and criticism. Some observers have countered that standards for measuring corporate compliance with fair hiring practices fail to take into account that it takes roughly twenty-five years or more to rise to top management levels. Nevertheless, the continued existence of the glass ceiling prevents many female and minority employees from reaching top management positions even though they seem qualified for such promotions.

GLOBALIZATION'S IMPACT ON US RACIAL/ETHNIC DEMOGRAPHICS

Globalization is the market-driven integration of world economies and cultures into international systems of production, distribution, and consumption. Theoretically, specialization of economic assets and resources and the free flow of goods and services enhances industrial efficiency and consumer choice, which leads to the natural decline of uncompetitive industries and the success of those that can better compete in the global marketplace. Increased reinvestment of profits benefits employment across the board, regardless of ethnicity and race. It moves jobs into more productive industries and raises the demand for labor, which also entails preparing low-skilled workers for higher skilled blue-collar opportunities through education and training. Over the medium to long-term, competition for jobs among different ethnic and racial groups should be minimal and largely nonoverlapping.

Problems for ethnic and racial groups occur when theory meets reality. Globalization entails steady but modest industrial change over the long term, but the movement of labor to more efficient businesses is a short to medium-term necessity. As inefficient businesses shed jobs, many of which are in minority-intensive manufacturing and agricultural sectors, education, training, and employment cannot keep pace. Also, the measured but ongoing shift from manufacturing to service industries, which is a common characteristic of fully industrialized economies, promotes the growth and creation of white-collar service-sector jobs at the expense of blue-collar workers. Immigrants and first-generation residents from Southeast Asia and Latin America, and to a lesser extent Africa and Eastern Europe, find themselves working two or three part-time jobs to feed their families. This may skew unemployment figures by the overreporting of job seekers who are gainfully employed and squeeze African-Americans employed in part-time service jobs out of the labor pool.

Prospects for college-educated white-collar workers are much better, with the US continuing its long-established pattern of job creation in service industries. Due to frequent white-collar service-sector labor shortages, federal and state governments promote the immigration of white-collar professionals to fill jobs in key industries, such as engineering, information technology, the physical and biological sciences, and medicine. College-educated immigrants from Canada, East Asia, India, Australia, the Middle East, Western Europe, and India encounter a welcoming American labor market. The influx of white-collar professionals does not directly affect ethnic and racial minorities, but it does solidify income gaps between high-skilled professionals and low-skilled blue-collar workers and indirectly affects socioeconomic mobility. Nonetheless, it does not appear to depress real (adjusted for inflation) wages among low to semi-skilled ethnic and racial groups.

Reduced socioeconomic mobility and the desire for higher wages and job security have promoted increases in college enrollments among high-skilled blue-collar minorities and ethnic groups, and also low-income Caucasians. This trend has not alleviated short to medium-term job dislocations. Instead, it has reinforced an oversupply of college graduates, many of whom are underemployed or unemployed. It has also contributed to labor shortages among high-skilled blue-collar workers in industries such as the construction and building trades. These and other industries have begun to absorb college graduates eager for work and willing to learn trades that at least provide a secure income. The effect on low-skilled jobs among African-American, Southeast Asian, and Hispanic workers has been variable, but those taking part-time or full-time jobs at lower wages have usually found consistent, albeit less rewarding, work.

Economic theory predicts that the distribution of labor will eventually reach a "natural" equilibrium that best suits the associated distribution of skills and that wages will adjust accordingly. At this point, it is difficult to predict how long this will take and how closely reality and theory will overlap, but globalization does drive developed economies in that direction.

—Tomislav Han

BIBLIOGRAPHY AND FURTHER READING

Barlow, Andrew L. *Between Fear and Hope: Globalization and Race in the United States.* New York: Rowman & Littlefield, 2003.

Mobasher, Mohsen and Mahmoud Sadri, eds. *Migration, Globalization, and Ethnic Relations: An Interdisciplinary Approach.* New York: Pearson, 2003.

Ritzer, George and Paul Dean. *Globalization: A Basic Text.* Hoboken, NJ: Wiley-Blackwell, 2015.

GOETZ INCIDENT

On December 22, 1984, an unidentified white man, later dubbed the Subway Vigilante, drew a pistol and shot four black youths who surrounded him and asked him for money on a New York subway. The shooter then fled. On December 31, 1984, Bernhard Goetz, age thirty-seven, surrendered to police. Goetz was arraigned January 3, 1985, and indicted January 25.

Goetz gained support among conservative white Americans when it emerged that the young men were known offenders armed with sharpened screwdrivers, that Goetz had been a victim of a mugging in which charges were dropped, and that his request for a gun permit had been denied despite a job-related need to carry cash on the subway.

After a charge of attempted murder was dropped, Goetz went to trial April 27, 1987, on a variety of lesser charges. On June 16, 1987, he was convicted of a single charge, a misdemeanor weapons charge, and on October 19, 1987, he was sentenced to six months in jail and five years' probation. One of the injured youths remained seriously disabled. Many blacks and some whites felt Goetz's acts were excessive, despite his fear of victimization.

The case raised serious issues about urban racial conflict, gun control, citizen safety, and

self-defense. Some label his actions self-defense; others call Goetz a trigger-happy racist, noting that the fourth boy was shot twice in the back as he turned away from Goetz. The undisputed facts are that Goetz bought the gun legally in Florida, took it illegally to New York where gun laws are stricter, and then carried it illegally on the subway. The case further illustrates the deep gulf that divides the races in urban America. Since 1984 several other court cases, including the Rodney King and O. J. Simpson cases as well as the racially charged Ferguson, Missouri, incidents and the Trayvon Martin/George Zimmerman case, have made it clear that racial conflicts remain.

—Tom Cook

BIBLIOGRAPHY AND FURTHER READING

Dershowitz, Alan M. *America on Trial: Inside the Legal Battles that Transformed Our Nation.* New York: Warner Books, 2004. Print.

Fletcher, George P. *A Crime of Self-Defense: Bernhard Goetz and the Law on Trial.* Chicago: U of Chicago P, 1990. Print.

GRAHAM V. RICHARDSON

In *Graham v. Richardson*, the US Supreme Court declared alienage, like race, a "suspect classification" under the Fourteenth Amendment, thus subjecting state classifications based on alienage to strict scrutiny, under which states must promote a compelling government interest.

Carmen Richardson, a Mexican citizen, was lawfully admitted to the United States in 1956. From that time, she resided continuously in Arizona, where she became permanently disabled. When she applied to the state for welfare benefits, she was denied them because she had not met Arizona's requirement that welfare beneficiaries who are not US citizens must have resided in the state for fifteen years. Richardson brought a class action on behalf of other similarly situated individuals against the Arizona commissioner of public welfare, claiming that the residency requirement violated their right to equal protection under the Fourteenth Amendment. She won her case in federal court, and the state appealed to the Supreme Court, claiming that limited public resources justified states favoring their own residents over aliens.

On June 14, 1971, the Supreme Court unanimously upheld the lower court's decision. The Court agreed with the finding that residency requirements such as that at issue in *Graham v. Richardson* violate the Fourteenth Amendment's equal protection clause and that government classifications based on alienage, like those based on race, can be upheld only if they are closely related to a compelling state interest. Arizona's interest in husbanding its financial resources was clearly not compelling enough. In addition, the Court provided an alternative ground for striking down the Arizona statute: Because the Constitution empowers the federal government to control the conditions under which aliens reside in the United States, state laws addressing the same concerns were preempted because of the supremacy clause (Article VI of the Constitution).

The Court subsequently created a series of exceptions to *Graham*. In *Sugarman v. Dougall* (1973), for example, the Court indicated that states could bar aliens from certain posts in government. In *Foley v. Connelie* (1978), it employed only ordinary scrutiny (requiring the state to meet a much lower burden of proof) in upholding a New York statute barring aliens from becoming state troopers. Subsequent Supreme Court cases followed the political job function argument of *Foley* to uphold state laws barring aliens from employment as public school teachers (*Ambach v. Norwick*, 1979) and as deputy probation officers (*Cabell v. Chavez-Salido*, 1982). In the seminal case *Plyler v. Doe* (1982), although the Court voted 5 to 4 to invalidate a Texas law withholding public education from children of aliens who had migrated to the United States outside legal channels, it lowered the burden of proof to that of intermediate scrutiny. Thus a different standard of proof was made to apply in cases involving so-called illegal aliens from that which applied to those concerning lawful resident aliens. Unlike discriminatory racial classifications, which are inherently suspect, alienage has proven to be a more protean concept.

——Lisa Paddock

GRANDFATHER CLAUSES

After the Civil War (1861-1865), the Fifteenth Amendment to the US Constitution guaranteed the voting rights of people of color in southern states. It expressly stated that the right to vote could not be "denied or abridged . . . on account of race, color, or previous condition of servitude." During the period of Reconstruction (1863-1877), the military administration in charge of the former Confederate states enforced this prescription. When Reconstruction ended, and the civil authority of these states replaced the federal military administration, white southerners devised various methods of circumventing the Fifteenth Amendment. One of these methods was the grandfather clause.

Grandfather clauses based eligibility to vote on the capacity of one's grandfather to vote. Of course, the grandfathers of the vast majority of African Americans in the South had been slaves and therefore had never been allowed to vote. Seven southern states incorporated such a clause into their state constitutions.

Along with poll taxes, literacy tests, and other so-called Jim Crow measures, grandfather clauses effectively prohibited African Americans from voting for several decades. In 1915, the US Supreme Court declared the grandfather clause to be an unconstitutional qualification for voting.

——*Aristide Sechandice*

GREAT MIGRATION

The Great Migration, a demographic shift of African Americans from southern states to midwestern and northeastern states, occurred roughly between 1910 and 1930. Because migration figures are based on the US census, which is conducted every tenth year, the dating of migration events is imprecise. The data indicate only that this migration took place sometime between 1910 and 1930, but other historical evidence suggests that it began sometime during World War I (between 1914 and 1918) and ended around the onset of the Great Depression in 1929.

During the Great Migration, the industrial northern and midwestern states of New York, Illinois, Pennsylvania, Ohio, and Michigan experienced the greatest net migration of African Americans. The greatest net loss of African American population was from the southern, agricultural states of Georgia, South Carolina, Virginia, Alabama, and Mississippi. As they moved from one region to another, most of the migrants also moved from rural areas to urban areas. Between 1910 and 1920, the African American population of Detroit grew from 5,000 to 40,800; that of Cleveland from 8,400 to 34,400; that of Chicago from 44,000 to 109,400; and that of New York from 91,700 to 152,400. The transition from rural to urban locales was accompanied by a transition from employment in agriculture to employment in industrial or service occupations for increasing numbers of African Americans.

REASONS FOR LEAVING

The reasons that African Americans did not leave the South in large numbers until fifty years after the end of the Civil War have been the subject of debate among social scientists and historians. Both social and economic factors were involved. After the Civil War, owners of plantations and farms in the South imposed new ways of controlling labor that were almost as restrictive as slavery had been. As sharecroppers, former slaves and their descendants were allowed to farm land belonging to the property owner in return for part of the harvest. These arrangements usually left the sharecroppers perpetually indebted to the landowners, so that they were financially obligated to stay on the land although legally they were free to leave. In addition, many African Americans who were born during the period of slavery were accustomed or resigned to their inferior social and economic positions and were reluctant to seek change. According to W. E. B. Du Bois, a leading African American intellectual of the period, African Americans who came of age around 1910 were the first generation for whom slavery was a distant memory. Jim Crow laws that formalized segregation and discrimination and racial violence that included lynchings motivated many in this new generation of African Americans to seek better conditions in the North.

Because the vast majority of African Americans in the South worked in agriculture, particularly in the production of cotton, several bad crop years and a boll weevil infestation in the mid-1910's contributed to the decision on the part of some to migrate when they did. The increase in out-migration was greatest in the areas that experienced the greatest crop failures.

Changing conditions in the North also played an important role in the timing of the Great Migration. Prior to World War I, immigration from Europe had supplied the labor needs of northern industry, and African Americans in northern cities usually could find work only as servants, porters, janitors, or waiters. Most industries hired African Americans only during strikes, as a way to exert pressure on Euro-American workers. Restrictions imposed during World War I reduced the number of European immigrants entering the United States by more than 90 percent, from 1.2 million in 1914 to 110,000 in 1918. This reduction in the available labor force took place just as the war increased demand for industrial production. Northern factories, mills, and workshops that previously had disdained African American workers were

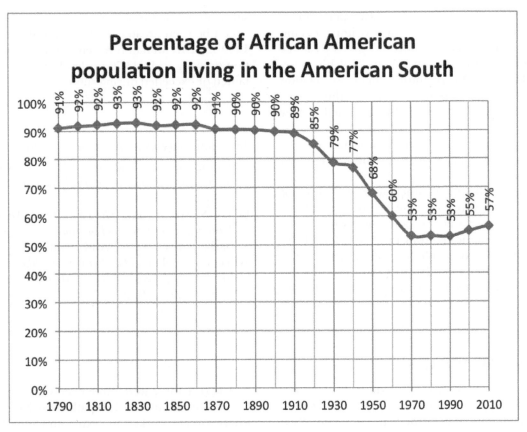

Percentage of African American population living in the American South

Graph showing the percentage of the African-American population living in the American South, 1790-2010. By Jajhill.

forced actively to recruit them, offering wages that were often twice what African Americans could earn in the South, plus inducements such as free rooms and train fare. Northward migration was encouraged by news of opportunities spread not only by personal letters home from new arrivals but also by advertisements and articles in newspapers such as the *Chicago Defender*, published by Robert Abbott, an African American editor. In some industries, managers attempted to foster racial division among their workers by encouraging segregated labor unions. The strategy was effective, and workplace competition sometimes contributed to antagonism and racial violence.

FORMING OF COMMUNITIES

African Americans in northern cities established their own communities, including the Manhattan neighborhood of Harlem. Although it was primarily occupied by wealthy European Americans at the beginning of the twentieth century, African Americans had been in Harlem since Dutch colonial times. Philip A. Payton, Jr., was among several African American business people who saw an opportunity when a housing glut in Harlem coincided with an influx of African Americans. He leased apartment buildings and rented the apartments to African American tenants, antagonizing some of the wealthy Euro-American residents. Harlem was soon an almost exclusively African American enclave.

Harlem became not only a home for African American workers but also a center of intellectual, cultural, and political development. The Harlem Renaissance, fostered by such African American intellectuals as Du Bois and the poet Langston Hughes, was embraced by white liberals as an alternative to bourgeois American culture. Harlem also became known for African American performing arts, which attracted many white visitors seeking entertainment. Jamaican-born Marcus Garvey arrived in 1916 to establish a branch of his newly formed Universal Negro Improvement Association (UNIA), which was intended to unite all the "Negro peoples of the world." The UNIA flourished in New York and other northern cities during the 1920's. Garvey encouraged African Americans to take pride in their heritage and to establish their own businesses.

The Great Migration ended with the onset of the Great Depression. Because of poverty and the fierce competition with Euro-Americans for scarce jobs, African Americans from the South found the North to be a less desirable destination. During the 1930's, net migration of African Americans from the South was diminished by about one-half, to 347,500. The Great Migration set the stage, however, for

subsequent migrations of African Americans that would be even greater in absolute numbers. By the 1940's, the trend had reversed again, with net migration growing to 1,244,700, a level that would be sustained or exceeded during subsequent decades.

——*James Hayes-Bohanan*

BIBLIOGRAPHY AND FURTHER READING

Lemann, Nicholas. *The Promised Land: The Great Black Migration and How It Changed America.* New York: Knopf, 1991. Print.

Reich, Steven A., ed. *The Great Black Migration: A Historical Encyclopedia of the American Mosaic.* Santa Barbara: Greenwood, 2014. Print.

Wilkerson, Isabel. *The Warmth of Other Suns: The Epic Story of America's Great Migration.* New York: Vintage, 2011. Print.

GREEK AMERICANS

The US Census counts approximately 1.3 million Americans as having Greek ancestry. Greek American identity first formed in the Great Wave of Greek immigration between 1890 to 1924. An average of 11,000 Greeks arrived annually during these years. Greeks from nations other than Greece – most notably the Ottoman Empire, Balkan countries, Egypt, and Cyprus – added to the total. All told, more than 500,000 Greeks, mostly male, arrived in the United States before the door of immigration shut in 1924.

Between 1924 and the end of World War II, Greek inward migration averaged one thousand per year. After 1945 immigration recommenced under provisions for "displaced persons." In twenty years of postwar migration, 5,000 Greeks arrived annually, on average. This flow doubled in the late 1960s and continued through the 1970s, when political upheaval in Greece and Cyprus combined with changes in the US immigration laws that made it easier for relatives of Greek Americans to immigrate.

Perhaps half of Greek migrants in the early twentieth century worked for a finite period and then returning to Greece. Those who remained often paid for relatives or potential brides to join them. Once

in America, there were three main working paths for Greek immigrants. The first path was to New England, where Greeks worked in textile and shoe factories. The foremost mill town was Lowell, Massachusetts, but by 1910, sizable Greek communities could also be found in New Hampshire, Connecticut, and elsewhere in Massachusetts. There were counterparts in the factory towns of Ohio, Pennsylvania, and upstate New York.

A second path lead West. The Greek consul general estimated in 1907 that there were between thirty and forty thousand Greek laborers in the American West. These workers, often lured by an unscrupulous "padrone," or labor agent, could find employment in mines and smelters, particularly in Colorado and Utah, and on railroad gangs, most often in California. In 1910, 40 percent of all Greek Americans, could be found west of the Mississippi. This number decreased after the peak of railroad track expansion in 1916.

The third path of Greek immigrants was to the big cities of the East Coast and Midwest. In the 1910s, Greeks could be found in most industrialized towns and cities, but New York and Chicago became the preeminent Greek American cities. By the 1920s each city could count upwards of 50,000 Greeks. Chicago's Greek American community, concentrated around Halsted Street, became both the largest and most concentrated "Greektown" in America. The greatest number of Greek Americans, however, lived in and around New York City.

Though many Greeks found work in meatpacking plants, mines, steel mills, and factories, it was in their entrepreneurial capacity that Greek immigrants made their most distinguishing mark on American society. Greek immigrants often started in menial jobs and then moved on to a small but self-owned business. Greek American businesses were concentrated in produce, flowers, sweets, hatters, shoeshine parlors, and, most notably and enduring, restaurants. In 1920 Greeks owned 3,000 restaurants in Chicago, 35 percent of the city's total. Today, there are over 3,000 restaurants that categorize themselves as Greek and there are perhaps 15,000 Greek-American owned restaurants.

Often within a generation, Greek Americans moved into the American middle class, and educational levels increased. Economically, very few other ethnic groups have done as well as Greek Americans. Median household income is 30 percent higher for Greek Americans than for non-Greeks ($78,500 versus $60,700)—a percentage that has remained consistent since 1970. On the other end of the spectrum, just nine percent of Greek households are beneath the poverty line, significantly less than the national average of 15 percent. Thirty-nine percent of Greek American adults have a four-year college degree, compared with 28 percent of all Americans.

In terms of religion, although there are a very small number of Jewish and Muslim Greek Americans, most Greek Americans identify, at least for cultural and historic reasons, with the Greek Orthodox Church based in Istanbul. There are roughly 500,000 Greek Orthodox adherents in America, of whom just 110,000 attend church regularly. Roughly 20 percent of Greek Orthodox in America are converts through marriage.

New York State has the largest population of Greek Americans, with 163,300. California is second with 139,100. New Hampshire, with 20,400 Greeks, has the highest concentration of Greeks, 1.55 percent of the population, which is three times the national average. After New Hampshire, the states with the greatest concentration of Greek Americans are Massachusetts (85,600 Greeks, 1.3 percent of the population) and Connecticut (32,000, 0.9 percent). The least Greek states are North and South Dakota, Mississippi, Louisiana, Arkansas, and Kansas, which collectively have fewer than 18,000 Greek Americans.

Since their arrival in the United States, the perception of "the Greek American" has shifted from Greek to American. That is, over the course of the twentieth century, the perception of Greek Americans has gone from "oriental" (i.e., eastern) and "swarthy" to European and white. The stereotype of the Greek American—based on labor, entrepreneurship, food, and family—went from one that threatened "American" values to representing them.

Since 1980, there has been very little Greek immigration to America. Fewer than 2,000 have arrived annually, with an unknown and perhaps greater number leaving. With an improved economic and political situation in Greece, fewer Greeks wanted to emigrate—and those who do generally find it easier to get visas to Canada or Australia. Since Greece's economic collapse in 2010, large numbers of Greeks have begun to emigrate, but these migrants generally move to other countries in the European Union.

The Greek arrivals of the early twentieth century had to stand together because many did not speak English and all were looked upon with prejudice (as was the case with most foreign immigrants). Today, Greek American is an ethnicity of choice more than an immigrant's story. The percentage of Greek Americans who are foreign-born (13 percent and declining) is lower than the American average. The future of Greek America, as opposed to simply Americans of Greek decent, will ultimately be determined by cultural and demographic trends. Indeed, despite a low birth rate, the end of immigration, less strong ties to the church, and a decline in Greek speakers, the number of self-identifying Greek Americans has continued to rise. Intermarriage has played a significant role in the perpetuation of the Greek American community. How strongly this identity will continue in future generations—and in what forms Greek American identity will be expressed—remains open questions.

——Peter Moskos

BIBLIOGRAPHY AND FURTHER READING

Chicago Daily Journal, "Review of the Greeks of Chicago" by Andrew J. Vlachos. December 31, 1926. Web. 10 March 2017

Fairchild, Henry Pratt. *Greek Immigration to the United States.* New Haven: Yale UP, 1911. Print.

Grammich, Clifford, et al. *2010 U.S. Religion Census: Religious Congregations & Membership Study. Association of Statisticians of American Religious Bodies.* Hartford: Institute for Religious Research, 2012. Print.

Moskos, Peter, and Charles C. Moskos. *Greek Americans: Struggle and Success,* 3rd ed. New Brunswick: Transaction Publishers, 2013. Print.

Saloutos, Theodore. *They Remember America.* Berkeley: U of California P, 1956. Print.

Saloutos, Theodore. "Causes and Patterns of Greek Emigration to the United States." *Perspectives in American History* 7, 1973: 397–437.

US Census. American Community Survey, 2006–10 and 2009–11. Washington, DC: US Census. Web. 9 March 2017.

Zotos, Stephanos. *Hellenic Presence in America.* Wheaton: Pilgrimage, 1976. Print.

GREEN V. COUNTY SCHOOL BOARD OF NEW KENT COUNTY

In the wake of the Supreme Court's 1954 decision in *Brown v. Board of Education* that outlawed school segregation, few southern school boards took action to integrate their schools. Finally, in the mid-1960's, under the threat of federal fund cutoffs and adverse court decisions, most southern school boards made some effort to integrate their schools. Many such school boards did so by adopting an assignment system whereby students were permitted to choose which school they wished to attend. Most such freedom-of-choice plans resulted in little racial integration. Black students typically chose to attend traditionally black schools, whereas white students chose to attend traditionally white schools. As a result, schools remained racially segregated in many southern school districts following the introduction of free-choice plans.

One school district that adopted a free-choice plan during the 1960's was the school district in New Kent County, Virginia. New Kent County is a rural county; its student population was about half black and half white, with blacks and whites scattered throughout the county. Prior to 1965, the schools in New Kent County had been completely segregated, with all the black students attending the county's one black school and all the white students attending the county's one white school. In 1965, the school board adopted a free-choice plan whereby every student was permitted to choose between the two schools. As a result of the free choice, all the white students chose to remain in the white school and 85 percent of the black students chose to remain in the black school.

A group of black parents, with the assistance of the National Association for the Advancement of Colored People (NAACP) Legal Defense and Educational Fund, filed a lawsuit challenging this free-choice plan. These parents contended that the plan was deficient because it did not effectively dismantle the old dual school system. The Supreme Court, faced with thirteen years of southern school board recalcitrance on school desegregation, agreed that the school board's free-choice plan did not satisfy constitutional standards and announced that the school board had an affirmative duty to devise a desegregation plan that actually resulted in substantial pupil mixing. This decision, the Supreme Court's most important school desegregation decision since the 1954 *Brown* decision, helped transform school desegregation law by forcing school boards to devise assignment plans that resulted in greater integration. In the wake of the *Green* decision, lower courts throughout the South required school boards to take additional action to integrate their schools.

——*Davison M. Douglas*

GREENSBORO SIT-INS

The next day, the students returned along with twenty-six more students. By the end of the week, more than three hundred black students were involved in nonviolent demonstrations in downtown Greensboro.

The white community at first refused to make any change in the status quo, but in April, white leaders offered a plan for partial desegregation. The student leadership, the Student Executive Committee for Justice, rejected this offer as a blatant attempt at tokenism. Greensboro officials then tried arrests, sending forty-five demonstrators to jail on trespassing charges. The protesters responded with a boycott, which cut profits for retail businesspeople by one-third. Finally, six months after the protest began, the white community gave up and desegregated downtown businesses.

The sit-in at Woolworth's launched a region-wide campaign and marked the beginning of the student phase of the Civil Rights movement, led by a new organization called the Student Nonviolent Coordinating Committee (SNCC). By August of 1961, more than seventy thousand blacks and whites had taken part in similar protests and more than three thousand had been arrested.

The February One monument and sculpture stands on North Carolina Agricultural and Technical State University's campus and is dedicated to the actions taken by the Greensboro Four that helped spark the Civil Rights Movement in the South. By Cewatkin.

——*Robert E. McFarland*

GRIFFIN V. BRECKENRIDGE

Griffin v. Breckenridge, decided June 7, 1971, extended federal civil rights guarantees of equal protection of the law to the protection of personal rights. On July 2, 1966, a group of African Americans who were suspected of being civil rights workers were halted on a Mississippi highway near the Alabama border by Lavon and Calvin Breckenridge, who purposely blocked the road with their car. The Breckenridges forced the African Americans from their vehicle and then subjected them to intimidation by firearms. They were clubbed about their heads, beaten with pipes and other weapons, and repeatedly threatened with death. Although terrorized and seriously injured, the African Americans (who included Griffin) survived. They subsequently filed a suit for damages, charging that they had been assaulted for the purpose of preventing them and "other Negro-Americans" from enjoying the equal rights, privileges, and immunities of citizens of the state of Mississippi and of the United States, including the rights to free speech, assembly, association, and movement, and the right not to be enslaved.

A federal district court dismissed the complaint by relying on a previous US Supreme Court decision, *Collins v. Hardyman* (1951), which in order to avoid difficult constitutional issues had held that federal law extended only to "conspiracies" condoned or perpetrated by states. That is, the Court tried to avoid opening questions involving congressional power or the content of state as distinct from national citizenship, or interfering in local matters such as assault and battery cases or similar illegalities that clearly fell under local jurisdiction.

The *Collins* case, however, had been decided a decade before the nationwide civil rights movement of the 1960s, a period marked by the enactment of a new series of federal civil rights laws as well as by attentive regard by the US Supreme Court of Chief Justice Warren Burger to cases involving civil rights violations. The Burger court heard the *Griffin* case on appeal.

The Supreme Court's unanimous decision in *Griffin* was delivered by Justice Potter Stewart on June 7, 1971. The Court broadly interpreted the federal statute under which Griffin brought damages, Title 42 of the US Code, section 1985. Section 1985 stipulated that if two or more persons conspired or went in

disguise on public highways with the intent to deprive any person or any class of persons of equal protection of the laws or of equal privileges and immunities under the laws, a conspiracy existed and damages could be brought. The Court waived consideration of whether the *Collins* case had been correctly decided. Instead, reviewing previous civil rights legislation, starting in 1866, the justices determined that the language of the federal statute clearly indicated that state action was not required to invoke federal protection of constitutionally guaranteed personal rights from impairment by personal conspiracies. *Griffin* effectively extended federal safeguards of civil rights to reach private conspiracies under the Thirteenth Amendment as well as under congressional powers to protect the right of interstate travel.

——*Clifton K. Yearley*

GRIGGS V. DUKE POWER COMPANY

The Supreme Court's 1971 decision in *Griggs v. Duke Power Company* established the "adverse impact" test for discrimination so that an unequal statistical pattern could be used as *prima facie* evidence.

The Civil Rights Act of 1964, Title VII, prohibited workplace segregation. Shortly after the law took effect in mid-1965, Duke Power Company in North Carolina rescinded its policy of restricting black workers to its labor department, so in principle they could transfer to other departments. Nevertheless, according to a company policy, begun in 1955, all employees but those in Duke's labor department had to have a high school diploma. Therefore, all those applying for a transfer from the labor department in 1965 needed a diploma. For those lacking a high school diploma (African Americans were far less likely to have completed twelve grades than white Americans in that part of North Carolina), an alternative was to score at the national median on two standardized aptitude tests.

Willie Griggs and coworkers in the labor department at the company's Dan River steam-generating plant filed a class-action charge with the Equal Employment Opportunity Commission (EEOC), which ruled in favor of Griggs. When the company refused to conciliate the case, Griggs and his coworkers filed suit in district court. The court held

that a claim of prior inequities was beyond the scope of Title VII and that the requirements for a high school diploma or a passing score on standardized tests were not intentionally discriminatory.

The district court's decision was overruled by the Supreme Court. Chief Justice Warren E. Burger delivered a unanimous Supreme Court opinion (8 to 0), setting forth the adverse impact test. According to this principle, if statistics show that a job requirement screens out one race, the employer must prove that the requirement is relevant to the performance of the job. Since the percentage of black high school graduates and percentages of African Americans who passed the two tests were substantially below percentages for white Americans, Duke Power had to prove that the jobs sought by Griggs and his coworkers required completing high school or having a level of intelligence at the national median. Since the company advanced no such evidence, the Court ruled that Title VII discrimination had occurred and decreed that "any tests used must measure the person for the job and not the person in the abstract."

The decision had an extremely broad impact: it called into question all lists of qualifications for every job in the United States. Employers were called upon to review job qualifications and to recalibrate job duties to job qualifications or risk successful discrimination suits.

In the 1980s the Supreme Court began to chip away at the *Griggs* ruling. In *Wards Cove Packing Company v. Atonio* (1989), the Court shifted the burden of proof so that those filing suit must prove that specific job requirements alone cause statistical disparities. Congress responded by passing the Civil Rights Act of 1991, codifying the original *Griggs* ruling into law.

———*Michael Haas*

BIBLIOGRAPHY AND FURTHER READING

Belton, Robert. *The Crusade for Equality in the Workplace: The Griggs v. Duke Power Story.* Lawrence: UP of Kansas, 2014. Print.

Smith, Robert Samuel. *Race, Labor, and Civil Rights: Griggs vs. Duke Power and the Struggle for Equal Employment Opportunity.* Baton Rouge: Louisiana State UP, 2008. Print.

GROVEY V. TOWNSEND

One of the most successful devices in eliminating black voters in the South was the white primary. Since the Democratic Party dominated the solid South, whoever won the Democratic primary went on to win the general election. If blacks could not participate in the primaries, they were denied any real choice in selecting public officials.

In *Newberry v. United States* (1921), the US Supreme Court held that primary elections were not constitutionally protected. Although the *Newberry* case took place in Michigan and involved the issue of vote fraud rather than racial discrimination, the South immediately took advantage of the ruling. In 1924 the Texas legislature passed a law that barred blacks from participation in that state's primary elections. Three years later, a unanimous Supreme Court struck down the Texas law in *Nixon v. Herndon* (1927), finding the actions of the Texas legislature a clear violation of the equal protection clause of the Fourteenth Amendment.

The Texas legislature then passed a law authorizing the executive committees of the political parties to determine eligibility for voting in primary elections. As expected, the executive committee of the Texas Democratic Party excluded blacks from the primary. In *Nixon v. Condon* (1932), in a 5-4 decision,

the US Supreme Court ruled that the executive committee had acted as the agent of the state. As such, the attempt to bar black participation in the primary still violated the equal protection clause.

Texas succeeded on its third attempt to ban black voting. Immediately after the *Condon* decision, the Texas Democratic Party convention, without any authorization from the legislature, adopted a resolution restricting party membership to whites. R. R. Grovey, a black resident of Houston, brought suit against the county clerk who refused to give him a primary ballot. On April 1, 1935, a unanimous US Supreme Court upheld the actions of the state party convention. According to the Court, there was no violation of the equal protection clause because there was no state action involved. The Democratic Party was a voluntary association of individuals who acted in their private capacity to exclude blacks from primary elections.

In 1941 the US Supreme Court reversed *Newberry* in *United States v. Classic* (1941). The *Classic* decision brought primary elections under constitutional protection for the first time. *Classic* also paved the way for *Smith v. Allwright* (1944), the Supreme Court case banning white primaries.

———*Darryl Paulson*

GUADALUPE HIDALGO TREATY

The Mexican-American War and the treaty that ended it were largely the result of manifest destiny, the theory used to justify American acquisition of

both Indian and Mexican territory. President James K. Polk, a leading advocate of manifest destiny, was the most important figure in the Mexican-American

A section of the original treaty.

administration's desire to annex New Mexico and California. The United States was pressing claims against Mexico, and the Texas boundary dispute was becoming more critical. After fighting broke out in the disputed area along the Rio Grande, the United States declared war. Attempts to negotiate peace before and during the war were unsuccessful. Mexico saw no advantage in it, and the United States hoped to occupy more territory.

As a result of its military success, the United States was able to make acquisition of New Mexico and California a condition of peace. Polk chose Nicholas P. Trist as peace commissioner in April, 1847, and gave him a draft of a treaty which called for the cession of Alta and Baja California and New Mexico, the right of transit across the Isthmus of Tehuantepec, the Rio Grande as the Texas border, and a payment to Mexico of $15 million plus the assumption of claims of United States citizens against Mexico.

Opposition quickly developed in both Mexico and the United States to the proposed treaty. Mexico did not want an imposed peace, and the United States envisioned better terms. When Trist negotiated a peace unacceptable to Polk, the president recalled Trist. Trist remained in Mexico, however, and finally negotiated a modified treaty that Mexico accepted because of financial problems and fear of additional losses if war continued. The possibility of a successful revolution in Mexico added urgency to the peace process.

The United States dropped its demand for transit across the isthmus and agreed to stop Indian raids across the border. The treaty was signed on February 2, 1848, in Guadalupe Hidalgo, and ratification was exchanged on May 30, 1848, in Mexico City.

Although Articles IX and X guaranteed the political and property rights of Mexican citizens and Indians in the territory transferred to the United States, the Indians of California did not receive citizenship, nor were their property rights protected. As

War and the peace negotiations that followed. In Mexico, chronic instability caused by the struggle between the various political parties and leaders made waging war and negotiating peace difficult and made preserving the peace impossible.

Tension between the United States and Mexico had been increasing in the years preceding the war. Mexico was aware of, and feared, the Polk a result of violence and other factors such as disease, the Indian population declined by 100,000 within two decades. In New Mexico Territory the Indians were placed under federal protection and denied citizenship, but they did not lose their lands. Citizenship was granted to the Indians in 1869, and reservations were later created.

——*Robert D. Talbott*

BIBLIOGRAPHY AND FURTHER READING

Foley, Neil. *Mexicans in the Making of America.* Cambridge: Harvard UP, 2014. Print.

Sadaña-Portillo, María Josefina. *Indian Given: Racial Geographies across Mexico and the United States.* Durham: Duke UP, 2016. Print.

Van Wagenen, Michael. *Remembering the Forgotten War: The Enduring Legacies of the US/Mexican War.* Amherst: U of Massachusetts P, 2012. Print.

GUINN V. UNITED STATES

Though the Fifteenth Amendment supposedly prohibited racial discrimination in voting, during the late nineteenth and early twentieth centuries southern and border states found ways to prevent African Americans from voting in significant numbers. One method was the literacy test. One potential drawback to this practice, however, was that such a test would also prevent poorly educated whites from voting. A number of states solved this problem by adopting grandfather clauses, provisions that allowed anyone registered before a certain date or anyone descended from such a person to vote regardless of literacy. Since the date selected was usually set at a point when there would have been few black voters (1866 was popular), very few blacks would qualify. Thus a measure that was nonracial on the surface was decidedly discriminatory in its effects.

Many grandfather laws had only temporary application, and most southern states moved away from them in the early twentieth century. In 1910, however, Oklahoma enacted a literacy test requirement with a permanent grandfather clause. The measure threatened not only black voting rights but also the position of the state's Republican Party. Fearing the loss of several thousand black votes, the US attorney brought suit under the Reconstruction-era Enforcement Acts and won a conviction against state officials who were trying to enforce the literacy test.

The state appealed the case to the US Supreme Court, attracting the attention of the National Association for the Advancement of Colored People (NAACP), which was just beginning to use litigation as a strategy for combating racial discrimination. Moorfield Story of the NAACP filed a brief in support of the government. In a unanimous decision, the Court upheld the convictions and ruled that the grandfather clause was a clear attempt to thwart the Fifteenth Amendment's ban on racial discrimination in voting.

The decision had relatively little immediate impact: Only one other state still had a grandfather clause at the time, and the Court carefully avoided declaring literacy tests themselves discriminatory. Nevertheless, the decision was not without its significance. Not only did it mark a modest revival of the Fifteenth Amendment, but it also encouraged the NAACP to continue its strategy of using litigation to put the Constitution on the side of racial equality.

——*William C. Lowe*

GULLAH

The Gullahs came to North America in the first decades of the nineteenth century as slaves, originally from Angola (hence the name). Gullah is also a creole form of English that derives from the sea islands of Georgia and South Carolina. Gullah, once similar to the language spoken on slave plantations in the South, is very different from other African American dialects of English. The Gullah dialect combines elements of English vocabulary with grammar and punctuation elements of several West

African languages such as Ewe, Mandinka, Igbo, Twi, and Yoruba.

Gullah traditions, myths, and language stayed longer with the Coastal Carolina Gullahs because of the isolation and self-sufficiency they experienced on the sea islands. As with many minority languages around the world, television, education, and increased social contact have all undermined the Gullah language and culture. Many Gullah speakers use various African American English dialects in dealing with nonislanders, though Gullah remains the language of home, family, and community. Gullah has affected culture and language beyond the Carolina sea islands with words such as goober (peanuts), gumbo, and yam. The Gullah dialect and culture were spread to mainstream America through the tales of Uncle Remus and Bre'r Rabbit.

——*Jason Pasch*

BIBLIOGRAPHY AND FURTHER READING

Cross, Wilbur. *Gullah Culture in America*. Westport: Praeger, 2008. Print.

Morgan, Philip D., and Georgia Humanities Council. *African American Life in the Georgia Lowcountry : The Atlantic World and the Gullah Geechee*. Athens: U of Georgia P, 2010. Print.

H

HAITIANS AND HAITIAN REFUGEES

During the 1980's and early 1990's, many Haitians seeking asylum in the United States were intercepted at sea and forced to return to Haiti. This treatment contrasts with that of Cuban asylum seekers, who have generally received a generous welcome to US shores as legitimate refugees (although the law covering Cubans was changed in 2017). The US government's differential treatment of Cubans fleeing the Marxist-dominated Castro government and of Haitians fleeing a very poor country governed, often, by right-wing repressive leaders caused many to question US refugee policy. In addition, Haitians speak Creole and are black, leading some to suggest latent racist motivations for the US government's actions.

THE HAITIAN IMMIGRATION EXPERIENCE

Haitians, like citizens of most Caribbean countries, have for many decades participated in labor-based migration throughout the Caribbean region, including to the United States. Haiti's economy is among the poorest in the Western Hemisphere, providing a significant reason for migration. However, authoritarian regimes also contributed to migration, as some people fled political repression. In the 1950's and 1960's, skilled Haitian professionals legally entered the United States and Canada as permanent or temporary immigrants. Although many left Haiti in part because of political repression, they were treated as routine immigrants rather than refugees. Legal immigration continued throughout the 1970's and 1980's, but larger numbers of much poorer people also began to leave Haiti by boat.

For many years, Haiti was governed by the authoritarian regimes of François "Papa Doc" Duvalier and his son, Jean-Claude "Baby Doc" Duvalier, who finally fled the country in 1986. A series of repressive regimes continued to rule the country until Haiti's first democratically elected government, that of Jean-Bertrand Aristide, was established in 1990, but this government was overthrown by a military coup in 1991 and had to be reinstalled by the international community in 1994, after three years of devastating economic sanctions imposed by the United Nations that, coupled with domestic political repression, precipitated large flows of refugees. The refugee flows slowed once the military regime gave up power, the U.N. peacekeeping forces were deployed, the Aristide government was reestablished, and the economic sanctions were removed.

Thousands of Haitians have immigrated to the United States since the early 1970's. Many thousands more were deported because they were judged to be lacking legitimate asylum claims. Those who managed to stay in the United States concentrated around already existing Haitian communities in Florida, especially in the Miami area, and in New York City, where several hundred thousand Haitians make their home. Lacking significant public assistance, the Haitians who settled in the United States during the 1970's and 1980's were obliged to rely on aid from charitable organizations and the already established local Haitian communities.

REACTIONS TO THE IMMIGRANTS

Reactions to the Haitian migration varied considerably. Generally, the earlier and more skilled migration out of Haiti was uncontroversial. As larger numbers of poorer Haitians, especially the "boat people," sought entry into the United States, however, concern about the economic implications of these undocumented migrants arose. Local politicians, especially in southern Florida, under pressure from their constituents, including elite members of the Cuban exile group, along with others concerned about the potentially disruptive Haitian flow, put

Most Haitian refugees were interned in a tent camp on a disused air terminal at Guantanamo. .

pressure on Congress and successive presidents to deter the Haitian migration.

However, steps by the federal government to staunch the Haitian migratory flows eventually prompted political opposition by second-generation Cubans, voluntary agencies, human rights groups, and the Congressional Black Caucus. Many of these groups charged that the discriminatory treatment of Haitians was based at least in part on race. Efforts to detain Haitians in the United States were successfully challenged in court, and advocates for Haitians won a number of court-related victories to ensure fairer treatment for Haitian asylum seekers. The interdiction programs instituted by President Ronald Reagan, however, continued under the presidencies of George H. W. Bush and Bill Clinton. Only with the return of democracy to Haiti in 1994 did the migration pressures from Haiti to the United States ease.

Even following the 2010 earthquake that laid waste to much of Haiti, the levels of migration did not return to the high of the early 1990s, but public concern for Haiti and its inhabitants rose. The administration of President Barack Obama extended temporary protected status to an estimated 58,000 Haitians then living in the United States or who came within a year of the earthquake. Starting in early 2015, the families of Haitian American citizens and permanent residents were allowed expedited entry and work permitting.

FUTURE PROSPECTS

The return of stability to the Haitian political system and the application of considerable international economic assistance holds out hope that Haiti will benefit from economic development, thus encouraging investment at home and further reducing pressures for migration abroad. The steady economic recovery in the United States after the 2008 recession and the reduction in illegal and undocumented migration from Haiti helped to reduce the controversy surrounding Haitian migration.

——*Robert F. Gorman*

BIBLIOGRAPHY AND FURTHER READING

Masud-Piloto, Felix R. *From Welcomed Exiles to Illegal Immigrants.* Lanham: Rowman, 1996. Print.

Portes, Alejandro, and Rubén G. Rumbaut. *Immigrant America: A Portrait,* 4th ed. Berkeley: U of California P, 2014. Print.

Rey, Terry, and Alex Stepnick. *Crossing the Water and Keeping the Faith: Haitian Religion in Miami.* New York: New York UP, 2013. Print.

Zephir, Flore. *The Haitian Americans.* Westport: Greenwood, 2004. Print.

HANSEN EFFECT

Hansen reported that the first generation of immigrants, often finding it difficult to learn English and seek gainful employment, remained oriented to the home country. The first generation tended to observe customs of the home country in matters of dress, food, language spoken at home, recreation, and cultural values.

The second generation, whether born in the United States or brought to the new country at a very early age, attended school with nonimmigrant children and attempted to assimilate because of peer pressure, which often ridiculed old-fashioned habits and values. The second generation, thus, rejected an identification with the parents' home country in order to be accepted and prosper in the new country.

The third generation, in contrast, has been eager to rediscover the traditions of the root cultures from which they came. Cultural pride, in short, emerged as the third generation's reaction to the efforts of the second generation to neglect its origins and cultural heritage.

The Hansen effect was postulated primarily with reference to European Americans, however. The culture of African Americans was thoroughly suppressed, and the various generations of Asian Americans and Hispanic Americans have tended to retain the values of their ancestors.

——*Michael Haas*

HARLEM RENAISSANCE

In the years after World War I, the population of the New York City neighborhood of Harlem was almost entirely black; the area constituted the largest center of urban African Americans anywhere. Blacks poured into Harlem from all over the United States and the Caribbean, a migration at once optimistic and confident. During the 1920's and well into the 1930's, Harlem produced a cultural richness that made it a mecca for New Yorkers of all colors and creeds.

Writers and musicians were the heart of the Harlem Renaissance, helping to make Harlem a social and cultural magnet. Poets such as Claude McKay, Langston Hughes, and Countée Cullen were some of Harlem's brightest stars. They fostered an ethnic pride that strongly influenced later African American writers.

Jamaican-born but having moved to the United States in 1912, Claude McKay glorified blackness. His fame rests on poems such as those that appeared in the first American collection of his work, *Harlem Shadows*, published in 1922. Although he published three novels, some short stories, and an autobiography, McKay's best works remain his poems, which celebrate the Harlem proletariat and call for racial militancy. McKay's poems savor blackness in the midst of white hostility. His most famous poem, "If

"An' the stars began to fall."

By Douglas

"An' the stars began to fall." by Aaron Douglas. By Barahona003.

We Must Die," is often cited for its militant spirit. In it, McKay calls on black Americans to resist oppression even to the death if necessary.

Perhaps the most popular writer of the Harlem Renaissance was Langston Hughes, whose poems and prose focus on the triumphs of the "little people" over adversity, the masses struggling to keep their American Dream alive. His characters suffer defeat and humiliation, but they are survivors. In works such as "The Weary Blues," "Let America Be America Again," and "Dreams," Hughes proclaims the desire and the need to save democracy for all Americans. He evokes universal values, not only black ones.

Like McKay and Hughes, Countée Cullen published poems in his youth, and by the early 1920's, his poetry was highly popular. In 1925, he published his first collection of verse, *Color*, which revealed a strong sense of racial pride. His anthologies *Caroling*

Dusk, Copper Sun, and *The Ballad of the Brown Girl: An Old Ballad Retold* were published in 1927, but in these works Cullen generally reduced his references to race. *Copper Sun,* for example, included only seven "race" poems, a fact that disappointed many readers.

Unlike McKay and Hughes, Cullen saw color in mostly negative terms, as in "The Shroud of Color," which focuses on the burden of being black. Cullen implies that the black is an alien in America, an exile from the African homeland. He portrays the price of being black and striving for full human rights as a crushing weight. With the publication of *The Black Christ, and Other Poems* in 1929, Cullen clearly moved away from race, presenting himself as a poet, not a black poet. It was his protest poems, however, that earned Cullen lasting fame.

African American music was also being accepted and promoted in the American culture at large by the 1920's. Jazz came of age, helped in large measure by white bandleader Paul Whiteman's introduction of classical jazz to New York in 1924. Yet it was mainly black bandleaders such as Fletcher "Smack" Henderson, Duke Ellington, and Louis Armstrong who popularized jazz in and beyond Harlem. Jazz dates from the post-Civil War era, when it was created out of a mixture of the blues, work songs, and spirituals. In the early 1900's, New Orleans musicians were the first to employ jazz's characteristic improvisation. Henderson, Ellington, and Armstrong brought the style—with modifications—to New York's nightclubs, where both white and black patrons embraced it ardently. Ironically, the first major showplace for these bandleaders was the Cotton Club, which admitted only white audiences.

The growth of jazz was aided by the rise of the recording industry, which brought the music to parts of the United States where live performances were not possible or rare. Some critics, many of them black intellectuals, considered jazz unrefined, too raw, and even denigrating to the African American image. Jazz became a craze, however; it was unstoppable. On March 12, 1926, Harlem's Savoy Ballroom opened, an architectural and musical phenomenon. Its sheer size and elegant furnishings awed patrons and made it a showplace for music and dancing. Henderson's orchestra performed there regularly, luring patrons with performer-audience interaction. Henderson has often been called the "father of swing," although he was strongly influenced by the young solo trumpeter

Louis Armstrong. The Savoy was open to people of all classes and colors.

Music was a serious business there; in addition to the Henderson and Ellington ensembles, the bands of Benny Goodman, Tommy Dorsey, Count Basie, and Louis Armstrong were frequent performers. The Savoy gave opportunities to many musical talents, including such future singing greats as Bessie Smith and Ella Fitzgerald. Duke Ellington expanded the boundaries of jazz as a composer and orchestrator. He was the master of form, a great synthesizer of jazz elements. His band developed a unique collaboration among leader, soloist, and group. Himself a fine pianist, Ellington refined jazz without taking away its spontaneity. Louis Armstrong made his impact primarily as a solo artist. As early as 1923, he was noted for his stylish playing as a solo trumpeter in the King Oliver Creole Jazz Band, and he played with the Fletcher Henderson Orchestra in 1924. Armstrong had an intuitive genius that transformed the sound of jazz. He became a popular singer as well, with records selling in the millions. These artists and many others contributed much to the enrichment of black self-awareness and self-confidence.

The 1930's, however, brought the Harlem Renaissance to a halt. The Great Depression hit Harlem hard. African American financial institutions failed, taking with them not only monetary savings but also many symbols of black aspiration. Yet the Harlem Renaissance continued until the riot of March 19, 1935. Responding to rumors of the death by beating of a black youth at the hands of police, thousands of Harlem citizens went on a rampage, destroying not only millions of dollars worth of property but also hopes and dreams.

The Harlem Renaissance gave rise to the "New Negro," proud of black culture yet determined to participate fully in American life. With Harlem in vogue during the 1920's, white people flocked to the neighborhood's nightclubs and theaters, attracted by its exotic and lively culture. Many African Americans experienced a new self-consciousness and awareness. Black folktales and music were "discovered" and revitalized, serving as therapy for both white and black.

Harlem's artists—who included sculptors, painters, and dancers as well as writers and musicians—were very image-conscious. They promoted and advanced black talent, searching for black identity and a place within American society. They projected a black image that was respectable and strong, with character triumphing over race. Yet blacks were proud of their distinctive characteristics, too, and did not want to reject their past, although cultural integrity and commercial success were sometimes in conflict.

White America courted and cultivated Harlem's subculture. White patrons gave encouragement and funding to black talent, sometimes serving as guides and judges as well, and provided scholarships, grants, and outlets for black artists, particularly for writers. This dependency of black artists had the potential to subvert black sensibilities and interests, for some patrons had their own agendas. Major publishing companies accepted and sought out black talent. None of the black writers' works became best sellers, but they sold enough copies to warrant continued support by white publishers and critics. Although discrimination in the publishing industry was not entirely eliminated, post-1920's black writers found more doors open to them than had earlier generations.

Whether later African American writers admired or rejected the works of the Harlem Renaissance, they could not ignore those works. Such writers as Zora Neale Hurston, Richard Wright, and James Baldwin carved out careers that were different from and yet built on those of the giants of the 1920's. Reacting to their predecessors, writers of the new generation were stimulated to examine life for African Americans as it was and as it could be.

The Harlem Renaissance reached beyond the borders of the United States. Peter Abrahams, a black South African writer, first read American black literature in a library in Johannesburg. He was enthralled by the poems, stories, and essays he found, and they had a great influence on his life, as he later noted: "I became a nationalist, a colour nationalist, through the writings of men and women who lived a world away from me. To them I owe a great debt for crystallizing my vague yearnings to write and for showing me the long dream was attainable." Abrahams spoke for many African and Caribbean blacks who were eager to know that white people did not have a monopoly on the writing of real literature.

Black music influenced American culture even more strongly than did black literature. Black music—spirituals, ragtime, and particularly jazz—intrigued white arrangers and composers. White pioneers in jazz such as Bix Beiderbecke, Jack Teagarden, Gene

Krupa, and Benny Goodman studied jazz intently, often spending long hours in cabarets listening to black masters. At first merely imitative, these white musicians would go on to rival their teachers and then to dominate commercial jazz.

European musicians also became enamored of jazz. Among them, the composers Darius Milhaud and Kurt Weill helped pioneer continental classical jazz. (A wave of enthusiasm for Ellington and Armstrong's "hot" jazz swept Europe later.) Referring to classical jazz, Leopold Stokowski said of the black musicians of the United States, "They are causing new blood to flow in the veins of music...they are path finders into new realms." This tribute was seconded by such great composers as Maurice Ravel and Igor Stravinsky, who acknowledged the strong links between jazz and much other modern music.

Jazz helped to interpret the spirit of the times, bringing joy and vigor to the post-World War I world. Along with it came popular dances such as the turkey trot, the black bottom, and the Lindy. Talented black dancers and singers enabled this music to conquer a broad public and to be recognized as art. Although older than jazz, blues music was mostly a fad among white composers and audiences. The blues became a craze in 1920s Harlem, however, as an expression of black lives. Much of the popularity stemmed from the work of singers such as Bessie Smith and, earlier, Ma Rainey. Blues songs mingled hope and realism with a weary determination; they were songs of the black masses struggling to be accepted for who they were.

Langston Hughes saw the blues as distinctly black, helping to free blacks from American standardization. Many of his poems, such as "The Weary Blues," reflect the influence of the blues and use the music's structures, themes, and imagery. Later writers such as Ralph Ellison and James Baldwin used the blues both to express sadness and as a source of strength. As alternating expressions of despair and hope, blues songs were also sometimes used to protest societal conditions.

Although it produced important works of literature, music, and art, the Harlem Renaissance proved above all to be important for the race-consciousness it fostered, the new sense that black people had a rich culture. To a degree, however, the Harlem Renaissance left a paradoxical gift: the lesson of its failures. Writers such as Countée Cullen and Claude

McKay were not as innovative or as fresh as they could have been; they were tied too closely to white norms of art and culture to be true innovators. Heavily dependent on white patrons for approval, many black artists lacked a truly personal vision.

The Harlem Renaissance died in the mid-1930s, mortally wounded by both the Depression and the disillusionment of black artists who failed to find a common ideology to bind them together. Still, the Harlem Renaissance served as a symbol and a reference point. It was a stepping-stone for black writers and artists who followed, more sophisticated and cynical but proclaiming loudly and clearly that blacks must be free to be themselves.

——S. Carol Berg

BIBLIOGRAPHY AND FURTHER READING

Bontemps, Arna. *The Harlem Renaissance Remembered.* New York: Dodd, 1972. An excellent set of essays on leading figures of the Harlem Renaissance. Chapter 2 is particularly useful as an overview. Includes notes, Bibliography and Further Reading, and index.

Butcher, Margaret J. *The Negro in American Culture.* 2d ed. New York: Knopf, 1972. A cultural history of blacks throughout American history. Traces folk and formal contributions of blacks to American culture as a whole in historical sequence. Includes index.

Davis, Arthur P. *From the Dark Tower: Afro-American Writers 1900 to 1960.* Washington, D.C.: Howard UP, 1974. Divided into two long sections: "The New Negro Renaissance" (1900-1940) and "In the Mainstream" (1940-1960). Quotes extensively from writers' works and provides biographical details and selective Bibliography and Further Reading for each author. Includes index.

Floyd, Samuel A. *Black Music in the Harlem Renaissance.* New York: Greenwood, 1990. Excellent collection of essays covering varied types of music and major black musicians. One essay discusses activities in England associated with the Harlem Renaissance. Includes a list of major composers and their works, illustrations, Bibliography and Further Reading, and index.

Fullinwider, S. P. *The Mind and Mood of Black America.* Homewood: Dorsey, 1969. Study covering the period of the 1880's to the 1960's examines black myths and the Harlem Renaissance revolt against these myths. Discusses several key figures of the Harlem Renaissance. Includes brief Bibliography and Further Reading and index.

Huggins, Nathan Irvin. *Harlem Renaissance.* New York: Oxford UP, 1971. An analysis of several black artists and their works within the context of American cultural history. Questions and challenges the quality of African American artistic expressions. Includes photographs, notes, chapter bibliographies, and extensive index.

Krasner, David. *A Beautiful Pageant: African American Theatre, Drama, and Performance in the Harlem Renaissance, 1910-1927.* New York: Palgrave, 2002. Covers a period that begins somewhat earlier than that often delineated for the Harlem Renaissance and focuses on an art form—theater—that is sometimes neglected in discussions of this period. Includes illustrations and index.

Lewis, David Levering. *When Harlem Was in Vogue.* 1981. Reprint. New York: Penguin, 1997. An intellectual and social history covering many aspects of 1920's Harlem. Focuses primarily on written works and musical events. Lavishly illustrated. Includes chapter bibliographies and index.

Shaw, Arnold. *Black Popular Music in America.* New York: Schirmer Books, 1986. A chronological study of black popular music from spirituals to funk. Notes the debt of American popular music to black artists and songwriters and includes a "White Synthesis" in each chapter. Includes illustrations, chapter bibliographies and discographies, and index.

Watson, Steven. *The Harlem Renaissance: Hub of African-American Culture, 1920-1930.* New York: Pantheon Books, 1995. Highly illustrated volume features many examples of the art, poetry, and prose produced by the Harlem Renaissance and discusses the cultural, economic, and political forces that converged to produce this period in African American life. Includes chronology, Bibliography and Further Reading, and index.

Wintz, Cary D. *Black Culture and the Harlem Renaissance.* 1988. Reprint. College Station: Texas A&M P, 1997. Examines the Harlem Renaissance as a social and intellectual movement within the framework of African American social and intellectual history. Relates the Harlem Renaissance to earlier black literature and its new urban setting and ties black writers to the larger literary community. Includes figures and tables, chapter bibliographies, and index.

HARLINS, LATASHA, MURDER

After a dispute over a $1.79 bottle of orange juice, fifteen-year-old Latasha Harlins was shot and killed at the Empire Liquor Market Deli in South Central Los Angeles on March 16, 1991. A security camera recorded the African American teenager being shot in the back of the head by the market owner. The merchant, Soon Ja Du, a forty-nine-year-old Korean woman, was charged with murder. Because the shooting occurred only thirteen days after African American Rodney King was beaten by Los Angeles police, it aggravated racial and ethnic tensions in Los Angeles.

At the court proceedings, Judge Joyce Karlin lectured African Americans and reportedly told Harlan's grandmother that the murder would not have occurred if her granddaughter had not gone into Ja Du's store. On March 26, 1991, Ja Du was found guilty of voluntary manslaughter, but Judge Karlan granted the defendant probation. This decision angered African Americans in Los Angeles and made Korean businesses primary targets for theft and vandalism by African Americans. In addition, the decision escalated the number of conflicts between African American and Asian youth in Los Angeles. Bitter feelings generated by the Harlins and Rodney King verdicts were unleashed during the Los Angeles riots of 1992.

——*Alvin K. Benson*

BIBLIOGRAPHY AND FURTHER READING

Jennings, James, ed. *Blacks, Latinos, and Asians in Urban America.* Westport: Praeger, 1994. Print.

Stevenson, Brenda E. *The Contested Murder of Latasha Harlins: Justice, Gender, and the Origins of the LA Riots.* New York: Oxford UP, 2013. Print.

HARPER V. VIRGINIA BOARD OF ELECTIONS

The Supreme Court's March 24, 1966, decision in *Harper v. Virginia Board of Elections* eliminated the use of poll taxes in state and local elections. Poll taxes, or the payment of a fee in order to vote, were widely used in Southern states as a means to restrict the electorate, and in particular black voters. Because poll taxes led to corruption—as candidates and political organizations would pay the taxes of their supporters—and because there were more effective ways of eliminating black voters, many Southern states started to repeal their poll taxes. Opposition to the poll tax was led by the National Committee to Abolish the Poll Tax and the National Association for the Advancement of Colored People (NAACP). On five occasions the House of Representatives passed legislation to ban the tax, but Southern senators filibustered, blocking passage in the Senate. In 1964, the Twenty-fourth Amendment to the Constitution was ratified, eliminating the use of poll taxes in federal elections. Five states—Alabama, Arkansas, Mississippi, Texas, and Virginia—continued to use poll taxes in state and local elections. Arkansas dropped its poll tax in 1964 after the passage of the Twenty-fourth Amendment.

In 1965 the US House of Representatives passed a poll tax ban in state elections as part of the Voting Rights Act of 1965. The Senate failed to support the ban, however, and the final version of the Voting Rights Act merely stated that the poll tax "denied or abridged" the constitutional right to vote.

Blacks in Virginia brought suit against that state's $1.50 annual poll tax as a requirement for voting in state and local elections. The US district court, citing the 1937 case *Breedlove v. Suttles*, dismissed the claim. In *Breedlove*, the US Supreme Court had held that, except where constrained by the Constitution, the states may impose whatever conditions on suffrage that they deem appropriate. On appeal, a 6–3 majority in the Supreme Court overruled *Breedlove* and held that the payment of a fee in order to vote violated the Constitution.

Interestingly, although the plaintiffs were African American, the ruling was based on economic discrimination rather than racial discrimination. "To introduce wealth or payment of a fee as a measure of a voter's qualifications," wrote Justice William O. Douglas in the majority opinion, "is to introduce a capricious or irrelevant factor." In the view of the Court's majority, voter qualifications had no relationship to wealth. The three dissenters believed that a "fairly applied" poll tax could be a reasonable basis for the right to vote. The *Harper* decision actually had little direct impact. Since only four states used poll taxes as a condition for voting at the time of the *Harper* decision, the ban on poll taxes barely generated a ripple on the surface of American politics.

——*Darryl Paulson*

HATE CRIME STATISTICS ACT

The Hate Crime Statistics Act (HCSA) was passed into law on April 23, 1990, and reauthorized on September 13, 1994. It required the US attorney general to collect data annually on crimes that "manifest evidence of prejudice based on race, gender and gender identity, religion, disability, sexual orientation, or ethnicity." Subsequently, the attorney general assigned the task of data collection to the Federal Bureau of Investigation (FBI).

The data enable the government and other agencies to conduct accurate research and perform statistical analysis on these types of crimes. Until passage of this law, there was no way to identify crimes that were committed as a result of hate. This was a concern both in the law enforcement community and among civil rights organizations that represented affected constituencies.

The FBI wanted to make sure that the various police agencies across the nation used sufficiently objective criteria, as described in a set of guidelines that the FBI distributed, to assess hate accurately as a motivation for a particular offense. Most jurisdictions found it necessary to create legislation to address hate crimes to facilitate the counting of these offenses. These cases were eventually litigated to the Supreme Court on First Amendment issues. The cases of *R.A.V. v. City of St. Paul* (1992) and *Wisconsin v. Mitchell* (1993) settled the constitutional questions surrounding this act and related local and state legislation.

The Hate Crime Statistics Act was expanded in 1994 to include hate crimes directed against people with disabilities. It was further amended in 2009 after the Matthew Shepard and James Byrd, Jr., Hate Crime Prevention Act was passed. The changes recognized crimes based on gender or gender identity and specified coverage of crimes committed by or against juveniles.

——*Michael L. Barrett*

BIBLIOGRAPHY AND FURTHER READING

"FBI Hate Crime Statistics." *Partners Against Hate.* Leadership Conference on Civil Rights Education Fund, 2003. Web. 24 Apr. 2015.

"Hate Crime." *Bureau of Justice Statistics.* Office of Justice Programs, 8 July 2014. Web. 24 Apr. 2015.

"Hate Crime Legislation." *Leadership Conference.* Leadership Conference on Civil and Human Rights, Leadership Conference Education Fund, 2015. Web. 24 Apr. 2015.

"Hate Crime Statistics Act." *FBI.* Dept. of Justice, 2010. Web. 24 Apr. 2015.

"Hate Crimes Timeline." *Human Rights Campaign.* Human Rights Campaign, 2015. Web. 24 Apr. 2015.

HATE CRIMES AND RACIAL RELATIONS

In 1984, Alan Berg, a Jewish talk radio show host on a Denver radio station, was fatally shot on his way home by several members of a neo-Nazi hate group. In 1986, a mob white teenagers attacked three black men in Howard Beach, New York, simply because the victims were black. Both these actions were hate crimes, defined by the Federal Bureau of Investigation as "a criminal offense committed against a person or property motivated in whole or in part by the offender's bias against a race, religion, disability, sexual orientation, ethnicity, gender, or gender identity."

Hate crimes are typically excessively brutal, and quite often they are carried out in a random fashion against strangers, as with the incidents involving the Howard Beach black men. Authors Jack Levin and Jack McDevitt have given several explanations as to why these crimes occur: the perpetrator's negative and stereotypic view of other people, the possibility that bigotry is becoming more widely tolerated, the resentment that one group feels toward another because it has been left out of the mainstream of society, a perpetrator's desire for the thrill of the action, a perpetrator's reaction to a perceived or imagined injury such as the loss of a job promotion or a benefit, and, finally, a perpetrator's wish to rid the world of evil. According to the FBI, the rate of reported hate crimes in the United States peaked in 2001, but in 2015, 5,818 hate crimes were reported, 340 more than 2014. Race continues to be the primary bias motive for hate crimes.

FEDERAL LAWS AGAINST HATE CRIMES

There are a number of different types of laws that victims of hate crimes can use against perpetrators. Most states have enacted laws to deal specifically with these types of crimes. Several statutes also address these crimes on a federal level. There are federal laws prohibiting conspiracies against the rights of citizens, prohibiting a deprivation of rights under color of law, and prohibiting damage to religious property and obstruction of persons in the free exercise of their religious beliefs. In addition, there are federal statutes that prohibit forcible interference with civil rights and willful interference with civil rights under the fair housing laws. These federal statutes have rarely been applied to hate crimes for several reasons. First, if a president does not emphasize civil rights, the attorney general in that administration will not be likely to prosecute these crimes. Second, since most of these statutes require that the victim be engaged in an activity involving a federally protected right, such as buying a house or eating in a restaurant, they do not apply to many victims. Third, the remedies under the federal statutes are limited.

Nonetheless, over the years, the federal government has expanded protections for victims of hate crimes. This includes the 2009 Matthew Shepard and James Byrd, Jr. Hate Crimes Prevention Act, which expanded prosecutable hate crimes to areas such as gender, sexual orientation, and disability.

STATE LAWS PROHIBITING EXPRESSIVE CONDUCT

On June 21, 1990, two young white men burned a cross on the property of a black family in St. Paul, Minnesota. One of the men, designated by his initials, R.A.V., because he was only seventeen at the time, was charged in accordance with a new city "bias-motivated" disorderly conduct ordinance which read, "Whoever places on public or private property, a symbol, appellation, characterization, or graffiti, including, but not limited to, a burning cross or Nazi swastika, which one knows or has reasonable grounds to know arouses anger, alarm or resentment in others on the basis of race, color, creed, religion, or gender, commits disorderly conduct and shall be guilty of a misdemeanor." R.A.V. could have been charged with simple trespass, disorderly conduct, breach of the peace, or even a more severe crime such as terroristic threats. Instead, in what was to become a test case of the statute and others similar to it, the prosecutor decided to invoke this law, which punished the expression of a viewpoint.

R.A.V.'s attorney, Edward J. Cleary, decided to challenge the constitutionality of the law under the First Amendment to the Constitution. A Minnesota district court agreed that the ordinance was unconstitutional. The prosecutor decided to appeal the decision to the Minnesota Supreme Court. This court overturned the lower court ruling. R.A.V. appealed to the Supreme Court of the United States for a review of the case. On June 22, 1992, the Court issued a unanimous opinion in *R.A.V. v. City of St. Paul* declaring that the ordinance was unconstitutional. Five of the justices held that the ordinance was unconstitutional because it prohibited the expression of subject matter protected by the First Amendment. Four of the justices said that the ordinance was overbroad in that it included in its proscriptions expression which was protected by the First Amendment. The entire Court thought that the city had other means by which to prosecute R.A.V. Thus, the Court concluded that, offensive as the action in which R.A.V. had engaged

was, the action was protected under the Constitution to the extent that it was expressive conduct.

STATE HATE LAWS PROHIBITING CONDUCT

In 1991, a nineteen-year-old black man, Todd Mitchell, and his friends came out of a theater showing the film *Mississippi Burning* so enraged that, upon seeing a fourteen-year-old white youth (Gregory Riddick) on the street, they assaulted him. Coming out of the theater, Mitchell said to others in his group, "Do you all feel hyped up to move on some white people?" Then, when Mitchell saw Riddick walking by, he added, "There goes a white boy—go get him." The group kicked and beat the boy for five minutes. Riddick remained in a coma for four days before he returned to consciousness with probably permanent brain damage. Mitchell was convicted of aggravated battery, normally punishable by a maximum sentence of two years. Because the jury found that the crime was motivated by racial animus, however, the sentence was increased to seven years in accordance with a state statute that read, "If a person commits the crime of aggravated battery and intentionally selects the victim 'in whole or in part because of the actor's belief or perception regarding the race, religion, color, disability, sexual orientation or ancestry of that person,' the maximum sentence may be increased by not more than five years."

Within hours after the Supreme Court announced its opinion in *R.A.V.*, the Wisconsin Supreme Court struck down this law as unconstitutional. The state appealed the decision to the Supreme Court of the United States, and on June 11, 1993, in a unanimous opinion less than half the length of *R.A.V.*, the Supreme Court reversed the decision and held that "enhancement" laws such as this which punish hate-motivated conduct are constitutional. The Court, in *Wisconsin v. Mitchell*, distinguished this case from *R.A.V.* by stating that *R.A.V.* dealt with expression and this case with conduct. The Court went on to state that with criminal acts, the more purposeful the conduct, the more severe is the punishment. Thus, when a defendant's beliefs add to a crime and motivate the defendant into action, the motive behind the conduct is relevant to the sentencing and punishment. Second, the Court stated that these enhancement laws are similar in aim to civil antidiscrimination laws and that they are justified because the conduct involved inflicts greater individual and societal harm than do other crimes. Some commentators, such as Edward J. Cleary, who argued *R.A.V.* before the Supreme Court, viewed *Mitchell* with alarm and sensed that these enhancement statutes come dangerously close to punishing a person's thoughts and thereby infringing upon First Amendment rights. He questioned why those who attack a person of another race should, because they hate that race and express it, be subject to stricter laws than those who attack in silence. By upholding the enhancement laws, Cleary suggested, the Supreme Court blurred the lines between speech and action. Others believe that, because of the Court's emphasis on the analogy between these enhancement-type laws and antidiscrimination laws, these laws are constitutional. In sum, if a statute infringes upon expression, as in *R.A.V.*, it will be held unconstitutional; if a statute prohibits conduct, it will be upheld.

As of 2015, forty-five states had adopted some form of law to deter hate crimes. These laws, if they pass constitutional scrutiny, are not without practical problems. First, in many instances (as was the case in *R.A.V.*), prosecutors may wait to find the perfect case to fit the statute. The usefulness of the statute is thereby limited. Second, if there is a successful prosecution under the statute, there may be problems in carrying out a severe punishment. Most hate crime offenders are under age twenty-one and do not have prior criminal records. Jails are overcrowded, and it seldom makes sense to jail the entire group involved in the crime. If only leaders are jailed, there is ample evidence that prison will make them worse.

———*Jennifer Eastman*

BIBLIOGRAPHY AND FURTHER READING

Cleary, Edward J. *Beyond the Burning Cross: The First Amendment and the Landmark R.A.V. Case.* New York: Random, 1994. Print.

Haiman, Franklyn S. *"Speech Acts" and the First Amendment.* Carbondale: Southern Illinois UP, 1993. Print.

Hall, Nathan. *The Routledge International Handbook on Hate Crime.* London: Routledge, 2015. Print.

Kelly, Robert J., ed. *Bias Crime: American Law Enforcement and Legal Responses.* Chicago: U of Illinois P, 1993. Print.

Levin, Jack and McDevitt, Jack. *Hate Crimes: The Rising Tide of Bigotry and Bloodshed.* New York: Plenum, 1993. Print

Lewis, Clara S. *Tough on Hate? The Cultural Politics of Hate Crimes.* New Brunswick: Rutgers UP, 2014. Print.

Shah, Robina, and Paul Giannasi, eds. *Tackling Disability Discrimination and Disability Hate Crime: A Multidisciplinary Guide.* Philadelphia: Jessica Kingsley, 2015. Print.

HATE SPEECH

Generally, hate speech refers to speech that impugns an individual or group based on race, ethnicity, religion, gender, or sexual orientation or uses epithets and pejorative language. The definition of speech for this purpose includes symbols that may represent a particular viewpoint, as the Supreme Court ruled in *Tinker v. Des Moines Independent Community School District* (1969). Jokes, innuendo, playacting, street jargon or slang terminology, and nonverbal communication employed in relaying messages may also be considered hate speech. One discussion that frequently arises is the dividing line between speech and conduct. It is difficult to distinguish between speech and conduct because human activity generally contains both.

The issue is not necessarily whether the speech offends someone but rather the original intent of the speech. If the speech is presenting ideas, it can be said to be linked to thought or theory. As stated by Justice Oliver Wendell Holmes in *Abrams v. United States* in 1919, "The best test of truth is the power of the thought to get itself accepted in the competition of the market, and that truth is the only ground upon which their wishes can safely be carried out." This "marketplace of ideas" concept has remained important in the free speech debate since 1919. The core question is what counts as an idea, that is, whether ideas include emotional outbursts that have no basis in truth or sense or only speech asserting intellectual concepts.

The humanistic perspective suggests that identifiable insults should be subject to quick condemnation and that the values of social order and decency supersede or restrict the rights of free speech granted by the First Amendment. Unfortunately, it is not that easy to separate hate speech from other forms of speech; the gray areas far outnumber those that are crystal clear.

THE FIRST AMENDMENT

Ultimately any attempt to regulate speech will lead to a legal challenge and then to a rigorous evaluation by the US Supreme Court of the hate speech regulation based on First Amendment principles. For most of the twentieth century, the Court was increasingly protective of all speech regardless of the crudeness of its content. As stated by former Supreme Court justice Hugo L. Black, "Freedom of speech is indivisible; unless we protect it for all, we will have it for none."

Since its 1964 decision in *New York Times Company v. Sullivan*, the Supreme Court has upheld a legal doctrine known as affirmative First Amendment theory. This theory states that speech is protected against any restraint or sanction, and it regards any infringement on speech with intense suspicion. This theory has six provisions— neutrality, emotion, symbolism, harm, causation, and precision of speech—that govern whether speech should be controlled.

Neutrality, the heart of affirmative First Amendment theory, states that the government cannot restrict speech simply because it disagrees with the message; it must remain neutral. Also of importance is the concept that there is no such thing as a false idea, regardless of how noxious an opinion may seem. The next provision is emotion. Speech not only is intellectual in scope but also can contain passionate portions that could seem vulgar to some. The mere presence of passion or vulgarity in speech does not mean that it has to be controlled. The third provision is symbolism. Speech is not only words but also anything that is equally vivid, including objects, figures, characters, pictures, and numerous other nonverbal communication devices. The fourth provision concerns harm. Speech may be controlled if it causes physical or relational harm. The fifth provision is causation. Speech does not need to be controlled unless the harm it will cause presents a clear and present danger, that is, if the speech is directed toward inciting or producing imminent lawless action and is likely to incite or produce such action. The last provision, precision, dictates that speech, if it meets the above harm and causation tests, may only be controlled by legislation that is exactly worded so that potential speakers will know the exact boundaries of prohibited speech.

HATE SPEECH LAWS

In the public environment, hate speech can be controlled only in limited circumstances. It can be controlled when it is presented to people in a location where they cannot escape its message. The captive audience doctrine allows speech to be restricted in certain environments: residential units, workplaces, and certain educational locales. This doctrine applies only to places where people are required to be or where they perform necessary life tasks; in the workplace, it would apply to the common office/ production areas, the lunchrooms, restrooms, and the access and egress points. It would not apply to the offices of individuals or the lockers of production workers. On a college campus, it would apply in the dormitories, bath areas, food service areas, classrooms, and public office areas. It would not apply to the auditorium, the open grounds of the campus, or a faculty office. Many colleges have tried unsuccessfully to restrict hate speech on the entire campus through conduct codes.

Hate speech can also be sanctioned when it contains "fighting words." This principle identifies as unprotected those words that originate in a face-to-face confrontation and are so inflammatory that they would be likely to produce a violent response from the average person. Legislatures must produce laws that specifically describe particular circumstances that would meet the criteria for this doctrine. The Ohio Revised Code, 2917.01, requires that a person "knowingly engage in conduct designed to urge or incite another to commit an offense of violence, under circumstances where such conduct creates a clear and present danger that an offense of violence will result, or such conduct proximately results in an offense of violence." The Supreme Court approved of this exception in the case of *Chaplinsky v. New Hampshire* in 1941. It remains part of most criminal codes as an arrestable offense.

Hate speech can be punished when it is evidence of illegal discriminatory conduct. People who are responsible under one of the many laws or provisions that regulate discriminatory activity—fair housing law, employment law, sexual harassment law, and hate crime law, to name a few—may have their speech used as evidence of discriminatory tendencies in the pursuance of civil, criminal, or administrative relief. This exception was clearly illustrated by the Supreme Court in the 1993 case of *Wisconsin v. Mitchell*. Todd Mitchell, after watching *Mississippi Burning* (the 1988 film dealing with desegregation in the South), walked out onto the street with his friends. Mitchell, an African American, was in a highly emotional state. He saw a white man walking on the sidewalk and, while shouting racial epithets at the man, urged his friends to attack him. He was convicted under a Wisconsin statute that added to the sentence for a crime when it contained a hate component. This type of sentence enhancement has become part of most states' hate-crime legislation. It was upheld by the Supreme Court because Mitchell's hate speech displayed beliefs that motivated him to action, or conduct, not mere expression. The case thus differed from statutes that punish just the speech component—for example, placing a burning cross on a lawn, as in *R.A.V. v. City of St. Paul* (1992).

In April of 2014 Senator Edward J. Markey sponsored a bill that called for the examination of hate crimes and hate speech on the Internet, television, and radio. The bill would study the role of telecommunications in encouraging hate crimes, but it did not gain traction in the House.

——*Michael L. Barrett*

BIBLIOGRAPHY AND FURTHER READING

Dees, Morris. *Gathering Storm*. New York: Harper, 1996. Print.

Herz, Michael, and Peter Molnar. *The Content and Context of Hate Speech: Rethinking Regulation and Responses*. New York: Cambridge UP, 2012. Print.

Lewis, Anthony. *Make No Law: The Sullivan Case and the First Amendment*. New York: Random, 1991. Print.

Smith, Paul, and Robert Allen Warrior. *Like a Hurricane*. New York: New Press, 1996. Print.

Walker, Samuel. *Hate Speech: The History of an American Controversy*. Lincoln: U of Nebraska P, 1994. Print.

HAWAIIAN AND PACIFIC ISLANDER AMERICANS

Hawaiian Americans are individuals with Hawaiian ancestry who are American citizens. Pacific Islander Americans are American Samoans, Guamanians, and people of the Northern Mariana Islands and Pacific atolls who reside on their islands, in Hawaii, or on the mainland United States. Pre-1980 census publications did not differentiate Pacific Islander groups except for Hawaiians. In addition, Native Hawaiians and Pacific Islanders were considered to be included in the "Asian" racial category until the 2000 census, making accurate statistics difficult to obtain. The same year, the census added the ability to select multiple races and ethnicities, and the Native Hawaiian and Pacific Islander (NHPI) group was found to be the most likely to report multiple races. 56 percent of NHPI Americans identified as mixed-race in 2010. Despite the separation of Asian Americans and NHPI Americans in the census, they are often grouped together informally, and resources for or about Asian Americans and Asian American issues may still include NHPI people as well.

Pacific Islanders sometimes move to the mainland United States because of the mainland's better economic prospects and educational opportunities. Generally, they adapt more easily to suburban and rural areas than to large urban areas.

GUAM AND THE NORTHERN MARIANA ISLANDS
The territory of Guam and the US commonwealth of the Northern Mariana Islands are believed to have been inhabited as early as 2,000 BCE by ancient Chamorros of Mayo-Polynesian descent. Colonized by Spanish missionaries in 1668, Guam was annexed by the United States in 1898 and ceded to the United States in 1919. Guam was occupied by the Japanese during World War II and retaken by the United States in 1944. In 1950, Guam's inhabitants were given US citizenship. When the 1962 Naval

Clearing Act allowed other ethnic groups to make Guam their home, Filipinos, Caucasians, Japanese, Chinese, Indians, and Pacific Islanders moved there, joining the Carolinians and Chamorros. The 2010 census recorded a population that was 37.3 percent Chamorro, 26.3 percent Filipino, and 7.1 percent Caucasian, with the remaining group mostly made up of East Asian people and other Pacific Islanders. Ninety percent are Roman Catholics. Guam is a self-governing, organized unincorporated territory with policy relations between Guam and the United States under the jurisdiction of the US Department of the Interior. A 1972 US law gave Guam one nonvoting delegate to the US House of Representatives. Guam remains a cosmopolitan community retaining customs and traditions from many cultures and has a flourishing tourist industry.

Saipan, Tinian, and Rota, the principal islands of the Mariana Islands, have a long history of foreign occupation, by the Spanish from 1521 to 1899, the Germans from 1899 to 1914, and the Japanese from 1914 to 1944. From 1947 to 1978, the area was recognized as a trust territory of the United Nations with the United States as the administering authority. In 1978, the islands became self-governing in political union with the United States. When the United Nations Trusteeship Council concluded that the United States had discharged its obligations to the Mariana Islands, the United States conferred citizenship upon individuals who met the necessary qualifications. The Security Council of the United Nations voted to dissolve the trusteeship in 1990.

AMERICAN SAMOA

The Samoans' heritage is Polynesian. European visitors, traders, and missionaries arrived in the eighteenth century. In 1872, Pago Pago harbor was ceded to the United States as a naval station. An 1899 treaty between Britain, Germany, and the United States made Samoa neutral, but when kingship was abolished the following year, the Samoan islands east of 171 degrees were given to the United States. American Samoa remains an unincorporated territory administered by the United States Department of the Interior. The 57,366 people (as of 1995), who live mostly on Tutuila, are American nationals. Although unable to vote in federal elections, American Samoans can freely enter the United States and, after fulfilling the residency requirements, can

become citizens. Their language is Samoan but many speak English.

In 2010, it was estimated that there were over 180,000 people of partial or full Samoan descent in the United States, living mainly in California, Washington, and Hawaii. This makes them the second largest Pacific Islander group in the United States, after Native Hawaiians. In Hawaii, they have experienced cultural discrimination before a public housing eviction board and have been called a stigmatized ethnic group.

HAWAII

It is estimated that the final migration of Hawaiians from Polynesia occurred about 750 CE Hawaii's early social system consisted of the *ali'i* (nobility), who imposed hierarchical control over the *maka'ainana* (commoners), whose labor supported a population that, by the mid-1700s, had increased to at least three hundred thousand. England's Captain James Cook, who reached Kauai in 1778, named Hawaii the Sandwich Islands. King Kamehameha I first unified the islands of Maui, Oahu, Hawaii, Lanai, and Molokai under a single political regime in 1795. Kauai and Niihau joined the union in 1810. The first Congregationalist missionaries arrived from New England in 1820, followed by European and American merchants and Yankee traders. With Western contact came diseases for which the Hawaiians had no immunity or treatment. By 1853, the native population had fallen to seventy-one thousand.

Chinese, Japanese, and Portuguese immigrants arrived to provide labor for the sugar plantations. Workers coming from Korea, Puerto Rico, Europe, Scandinavia, Russia, Micronesia, Polynesia, and the Philippines considered themselves temporary immigrants. By 1890, Hawaii was a multiethnic society in which non-Hawaiians made up most of the population. Hawaii's independence was recognized by the United States from 1826 until 1893, when American and European sugar plantation owners, descendants of missionaries, and financiers deposed the Hawaiian monarchy, established a provisional government, and proclaimed Hawaii a protectorate of the United States. Annexed by Congress in 1898, Hawaii became a US territory in 1900 and the fiftieth state in 1959.

During the 1970s, a Hawaiian rights and sovereignty movement emerged. Viewed, at first, as a radical grassroots minority, the movement gained momentum after a series of demonstrations and acts of civil disobedience. In 1977, representatives from many organizations and individual Hawaiians met in Puwalu sessions to discuss Hawaiian issues. State Supreme Court justice William Richardson advised Hawaiians to use the courts to redress grievances, challenge laws, and assert gathering, access, and water rights. A constitutional convention, primarily concerned by the state's improper use of lands ceded to the United States after annexation and transferred to the state in 1959, reviewed and revised the functions and responsibilities of Hawaii's government in 1978. The following year, the legislature created the Office of Hawaiian Affairs (OHA) to provide and coordinate programs, advocate for Hawaiians, and serve as a receptacle for reparations. Throughout the succeeding ten years, sovereignty groups strongly criticized OHA. In 1993, the US Congress officially acknowledged and apologized for the actions a hundred years earlier (US Public Law 103-150). That same year, the sovereignty groups Ka Laahui and Hui Na'auao were awarded education grants, and Governor John Waihee formed the Hawaiian Sovereignty Advisory Commission, which was renamed in 1996 to Ha Hawaii. The most radical sovereignty group, the Oahana Council, declared independence from the United States in January, 1994. In 1997, a number of workshops were conducted by *kupuna* (elders) who emphasized unity among the various factions. When Governor Benjamin Cayetano resolved in his 1998 state-of-the-state address "to advance a plan for Hawaiian sovereignty," he echoed the words of former governor Waihee. Waihee had also ventured his concern that while establishing self-determination, Hawaiians would tear apart the "multicultural fabric" of contemporary Hawaiian society.

Even seeking greater self-governance within the bounds of Hawaii's status as a US state has proved challenging for Native Hawaiians. One issue that has faced them in this area is that they have not been officially recognized as an indigenous group of the United States and thus have not been covered by the same laws that afford a degree of autonomy, among other benefits, to American Indians and Alaska Natives. A bill intended to address this, the Native Hawaiian Government Reorganization Act of 2009, was passed by the House of Representatives, but died in the Senate.

Hawaii's population, which had doubled after the islands gained statehood, fell in the 1990s, partly because of the slow growth that resulted from an economic recession and the vast reduction of the military presence on the islands. Between 1990 and 1995, the state experienced a net loss of 376,752 residents to domestic migration, partly because of the high cost of living, which in 1994 was 35 percent to 39 percent greater than the average US large city, while the median income was only about 10 percent higher.

Hawaiians living on the mainland remain connected with their heritage and values through social, university, and cultural associations that promote cultural events and regularly publish newsletters. Hula halaus exist in many states, and Hawaii's music industry brings musicians to the mainland for live performances. Local Hawaiian newspapers are available on the Internet.

As of the 2010 census, there were approximately 518,000 people in the United States who identified as Native Hawaiian, in part or in full.

Most Pacific Islanders reside in the western states. The Pacific Islanders' Cultural Association, founded in 1995, is an umbrella organization whose aim is to meet the common needs of all Pacific Islanders living in Northern California.

——*Susan E. Hamilton*

BIBLIOGRAPHY AND FURTHER READING

Chi, Sang, and Emily Moberg Robinson, eds. *Voices of the Asian American and Pacific Islander Experience.* Santa Barbara: ABC-CLIO, 2012. Print.

Haas, Michael. *Institutional Racism: The Case of Hawaii.* Westport: Praeger, 1992. Print.

Museus, Samuel D., Dina C. Maramba, and Robert T. Teranishi, eds. *The Misrepresented Minority: New Insights on Asian Americans and Pacific Islanders, and the Implications for Higher Education.* Sterling: Stylus, 2013. Print.

Yoo, David K., and Eiichiro Azuma, eds. *The Oxford Handbook of Asian American History.* New York: Oxford, 2014. Print.

Zhao, Xiaojian, and Edward J. W. Park, eds. *Asian Americans: An Encyclopedia of Social, Cultural, Economic, and Political History.* Santa Barbara: Greenwood, 2013. Print.

HAWKINS MURDER

Yusef (also spelled Yusuf) Hawkins, a sixteen-year-old African American, was confronted and killed by a group of Italian American young men in the predominantly white Bensonhurst section of Brooklyn, New York, on August 23, 1989. The murder was racially motivated and served as a sign of the deep-seated animosities and racial divisions that existed in New York City at the time.

Hawkins and three African American friends had traveled to Bensonhurst from their home in East New York to look at a used car for sale. They were confronted by a group of white youths with baseball bats led by Keith Mondello, Joseph Fama, and others. Hawkins was trapped by the group when four shots from a .32-caliber automatic pistol were fired. Hawkins was hit once in the hand and twice in the chest and died shortly after.

The Reverend Al Sharpton leading the first protest march over the death of Yusef Hawkins in Bensonhurst, 1989. By christian razukas from Honolulu, Hawaii.

Police reported that the white youths mistakenly believed that Hawkins and his companions were friends of a white neighborhood girl, Gina Feliciano. Feliciano, who once dated Mondello, had reportedly begun a series of friendships with African American and Hispanic men. The night that Hawkins was killed, Mondello was reportedly told either by Feliciano or someone else that a group of her black and Hispanic friends would arrive with bats to beat up him and his friends.

Eight men were charged in the attack. The eighteen-year-old Fama was the only one convicted of second-degree murder and sentenced to the maximum sentence on June 11, 1990. The nineteen-year-old Mondello was convicted of riot, unlawful imprisonment, discrimination, menacing, and criminal possession of a weapon and sentenced on June 11, 1990, to five and one-third to sixteen years in prison.

Joseph Serrano, John Vento, and Pasquale Raucci were convicted on lesser charges. Three others were acquitted of all charges.

The fact that Mondello was acquitted of the major charges of murder and manslaughter, along with pent up tension over other mob killings of African Americans in New York City, led to a series of protests from the African American community. Most notably, the Reverend Al Sharpton led a protest march over the issue.

——*Erica Childs*

BIBLIOGRAPHY AND FURTHER READING

Chancer, Lynn S. *High-Profile Crimes*. Chicago: U of Chicago P, 2005. Print.

DeSantis, John. *For the Color of His Skin: The Murder of Yusuf Hawkins and the Trial of Bensonhurst*. New York: Pharos, 1991. Print.

HEAD START

Head Start is a US government program established in 1965 to improve the potential for children in disadvantaged households to escape poverty and succeed later in life. The program provides early education and nutritional programs to children between the ages of three and five years old. It is targeted primarily at low-income households and children with disabilities.

In addition to the main program, the Early Head Start program targets pregnant women and infants and toddlers, and the Migrant Head Start program helps migrant workers. All the Head Start programs serve a disproportionately large number of minority children and involve federal grants to local service providers.

The programs are founded on the reasoning that early intervention is the most effective way to ensure a person's long-term success. Investment in nutrition and education during a child's early years is thought to create a solid foundation for later learning and development. Such investment would therefore reduce the need for more costly and controversial programs at later stages, such as youth counseling, welfare, drug rehabilitation, or incarceration.

Such investment is also seen as a means for increasing minority enrollment in college that is more politically acceptable than alternatives such as affirmative action. The programs are therefore highly popular with the public and politicians of both the Democratic and Republican Parties. Nevertheless, formal long-term evaluations of Head Start programs have raised questions about their actual effectiveness.

——*Steve D. Boilard*

First Lady Lady Bird Johnson visits a Head Start class in 1966. By White House Photograph Office, Robert L. Knudsen.

BIBLIOGRAPHY AND FURTHER READING

McNamee, Gillian Dowley. *The High-Performing Preschool: Story Acting in Head Start Classrooms.* Chicago: U of Chicago P, 2015. Print.

National Head Start Association. NHSA, 2015. Web. 30 Apr. 2015.

Sanders, Crystal. *A Chance for Change: Head Start and Mississippi's Black Freedom Struggle.* Chapel Hill: U of North Carolina P, 2016. Print.

HEALTH CARE AND RACIAL/ ETHNIC RELATIONS

The passage of the Affordable Care Act (ACA) under the Obama administration in 2010, and the Trump administration's promise to repeal and replace ACA in 2017, have helped to highlight the challenges of living in a diverse society in which health disparities along racial/ethnic lines, as well as class lines, continue to exist. Generally speaking, the attention to and understanding of issues relating to race, gender, and religion, among others, have increased exponentially in recent decades. The current social context is also marked by the dominance of race in general, and black-white relations in particular, as the dividing construct in intergroup relations in the United States.

However, intergroup relations in the United States are marked by a range of complexities and contradictions. Although considerable progress has been made since the 1950s, prejudice, discrimination, and inequality persist and are widespread. In addition, increasing ethnic, racial, and religious diversity further complicate the situation, as new conflicts emerge between the majority and new entrants and among different minority groups. In considering the possible linkages between public policies designed to erode racial inequalities and improve intergroup relations, one may observe that intergroup relations both influence and are influenced by public policy approaches to racial inequality.

LIFE EXPECTANCY AT BIRTH, BLACKS AND WHITES, IN YEARS

Year of Birth	Black Men	Black Women	White Men	White Women
1970	60.0	68.3	68.0	75.6
1980	63.8	72.5	70.7	78.1
1990	64.5	73.6	72.7	79.4
2000	68.2	75.1	74.7	79.9
2010 (projection)	70.2	77.2	75.7	80.8

Source: US Bureau of the Census. "Expectation of Life at Birth, and Projections: 2008."
The 2012 Statistical Abstract. Washington: US GPO, 2012.

Against this background, it is not surprising that issues and policies related to the health of Americans are being discussed in the context of interracial and interethnic relations. When the authors of the US Department of Health and Human Services' 1990 report *Healthy People 2000* outlined its framework, they recognized that a healthier America would depend substantially on the nation's ability to improve and sustain the health promotion, disease prevention, and general health care of at-risk groups within the general population. The 2000 report *Healthy People 2010* had similar objective, specifically the goal of "eliminating health disparities." The 2010 report *Healthy People 2020* expanded the goal further, "to achieve health equity … and improve the health of all groups." Progress has been made, but the goal of equitable health care has been elusive.

MINORITY HEALTH ISSUES

The government report *One America in the Twenty-first Century: Forging a New Future* (2009) notes that gaps in longevity and health care access for minorities and people of color are well documented. The report also noted that the continuing gap in health care access undermines the vision of one America. The authors proclaimed that "America should not be a society where babies of different racial backgrounds have significantly different life expectancies. If our Nation is committed to the proposition that all people are created equal, our most basic indicators of life and health should reflect this principle."

In an earlier report of the president's Advisory Commission on Consumer Protection and Quality in the Health Care Industry, *Quality First: Better Health Care for All Americans* (1998), the fundamental basis for developing a national policy on health care is articulated in the statement of purpose. This statement declares that the "purpose of the health care system must be to continuously reduce the impact and burden of illness, injury, and disability and to improve the health and functioning of the people of the United States."

However, statistics show that disparities in health care and delivery continue to exist and even to grow in certain areas. The Henry J. Kaiser Family Foundation 2010 report "Health Reform and Communities of Color: Implications fro Racial and Ethnic Health Disparities," notes that "Although people of color represent one-third of the US population, they comprise more than half of the uninsured."

In discussing the issues of race and health, *One America in the Twenty-First Century: Forging a New Future* makes conclusions about three critical areas in health care in the context of race. The report identifies structural inequities, discrimination by providers, and the cultural competency of providers as key factors that contribute to continuing inequity in health care delivery.

Structural inequities are difficulties in accessing the health care system that stem from disparities in employment, income, and wealth. The statistics show that, on average, people of color receive medical treatment less frequently and in later stages of disease than whites. Such inequities in access affect rates of sickness, disease, suffering, life expectancy, and mortality among racial groups. Furthermore, studies indicate that racial disparities in health and health care are interrelated and sustained in various socio-economic groups.

Racial issues may also affect relationships between health care providers and patients of color and the quality of the care delivered. The health care establishment is disproportionately white. Health care providers, like everyone else, can be affected by racial stereotypes and may lack the language and intercultural skills to serve patients of color fully. Furthermore, providers may, intentionally or unintentionally, discriminate against patients on the basis of stereotypes. Such discrimination can result in differences in care such as inadequate, denied, or delayed medical treatment, unnecessarily prescribed treatment, or cursory care.

In addition to structural inequities and provider discrimination, racial disparities in health care access may be affected by differences in language or culture between the provider and patient. Providers need to be culturally competent in order to deliver effective medical care to people from different cultural backgrounds. Often, these cultural differences undermine the necessary cooperation between providers and clients, which in turn results in less effective medical services.

RECOMMENDATIONS FOR CHANGE

In the late 1990s, President Bill Clinton announced efforts to eliminate long-standing racial disparities in infant mortality, cancer screening and management, heart disease, AIDS, and immunizations by the year 2010. The authors of *One America in the Twenty-First Century: Forging a New Future* outlined a range of additional steps to eliminate disparities in other key areas of health care and access. These recommendations included continued advocacy for broad-based expansions in health-insurance coverage; continued advocacy of increased health care access for underserved groups; increased funding for existing programs targeted to underserved and minority populations; enhanced financial and regulatory mechanisms to promote culturally competent care; and increased emphasis on the importance of cultural competence to institutions training health care providers.

Winborne and Cohen (1998) observed that "advocates of race consciousness in public policy believe that race functions so powerfully in American society that to ignore it is to perpetuate institutionalized inequalities and marginalization of certain groups."

Furthermore, they concluded that "race-cognizant public policies may be seen as improving race relations by fostering equality and recognition of marginalized groups, despite causing backlash against groups benefitting from them." In the light of the evidence, it is clear that in order to accomplish the statement of purpose articulated in *Quality First: Better Health Care for All Americans*, it would be necessary to design and implement policies that serve to erode racial inequalities and improve intergroup relations. One of the primary objectives of the Affordable Care Act, signed by President Barack Obama in 2010, has been to close the gap in health care disparity between whites and people of color. For example one of the provisions expands Medicare benefits to individuals who are below 133 percent of the federal poverty level (FPL). As of 2010, 60 percent of uninsured nonelderly Americans fit into this category. Another provision allows for affordable care for those who are either not granted insurance through an employer or cannot afford their employer's plan; this provision applies to those whose incomes fall between 133 and 400 percent of the FPL. Eighty percent of Hispanics, blacks, American Indians, and Alaskan natives fit into these parameters. Thus, the Affordable Care Act, as long as it remains in place, offers hope that the racial and ethnic health care gaps in the United States might be closed.

——*Yonette F. Thomas*

BIBLIOGRAPHY AND FURTHER READING

"Health Reform and Communities of Color: Implications for Racial and Ethnic Health Disparities." Henry J. Kaiser Family Foundation, Sept. 2010. PDF file.

Hoberman, John M. *Black and Blue: The Origins and Consequences of Medical Racism.* Berkeley: U of California P, 2012. Print.

Matthew, Dayna Bowen. *Just Medicine: A Cure for Racial Inequality in American Health Care.* New York: New York UP, 2015. Print.

President's Initiative on Race. *One America in the Twenty-first Century: Forging a New Future,* rpt. ed. edited by Steven F. Lawson. New Haven: Yale UP, 2009. Print.

Thompson, Tamara. *The Affordable Care Act.* Farmington Hills: Greenhaven, 2015. Print.

US Advisory Commission on Consumer Protection and Quality in the Health Care Industry. *Quality First: Better Health Care for All Americans.* Washington: GPO, 1998. Print.

US National Center for Health Statistics. *Healthy People 2010.* Hyattsville: US Dept. of Health and Human Services, Centers for Disease Control and Prevention, Natl. Center for Health Statistics, 2012. Print.

Winborne, Wayne, and Renae Cohen. *Intergroup Relations in the United States: Research Perspectives.* Bloomsburg: Haddon, 1998. Print.

HEART OF ATLANTA MOTEL V. UNITED STATES

After the Civil War, Congress passed the Thirteenth, Fourteenth, and Fifteenth Amendments in order to establish legal and political rights for the newly freed slaves. The Fourteenth Amendment, in part, was designed to protect black citizens from discrimination by state and local governments in the South. It did not address the issue of private discrimination against blacks in hotels, restaurants, and theaters. Was discrimination by private individuals therefore legal? The US Congress addressed this question when it passed the Civil Rights Act of 1875. This law made it illegal to discriminate against individuals in public accommodations. In 1883 the US Supreme Court declared the Civil Rights Act of 1875 to be unconstitutional. According to the Court, the Fourteenth Amendment only protected against state discrimination and not discrimination by private individuals in their private businesses.

Almost a century later, the US Congress addressed this issue again. Congressional hearings were held concerning the difficulty African Americans faced in using public accommodations. According to the hearings, blacks traveling from Washington, D.C., to New Orleans, Louisiana, in 1963 would find that the average distance between hotel and motel accommodations available to them was 174 miles. As a result of the hearings, Congress incorporated a public accommodations section as part of the Civil Rights Act of 1964. The public accommodations section prevented discrimination in hotels, motels, restaurants, theaters, sports arenas, and other public facilities. Congress based its authority to regulate public accommodations on the "commerce clause"of the Constitution, which grants Congress the authority to "regulate Commerce with foreign Nations, and among the several States."

The *Heart of Atlanta* case involves the immediate challenge to the constitutionality of the public accommodations section of the Civil Rights Act of 1964. The Heart of Atlanta Motel, a local operation, refused to serve African Americans. As a local motel, it argued that its not serving blacks had no impact on interstate commerce. Attorneys for the US government argued that interstate commerce was affected by the motel's policy because three-quarters of its clientele came from outside the state. In upholding the public accommodations section of the Civil Rights Act of 1964, a unanimous Supreme Court argued that it made no difference that the motel was a local operation. If interstate commerce is affected at all, "it does not matter how local the operation which applies the squeeze." A companion case, *Katzenbach v. McClung* (1964), involving a small, local restaurant in Birmingham, Alabama, which refused sit-down service to blacks, reached a similar conclusion. Although the Court was unanimous in upholding the public accommodations section of the Civil Rights Act of 1964, the justices did not all concur on the reasoning. A majority of the justices upheld the law on the basis of the commerce clause, but Justice William Douglas wanted to base the decision on the equal protection clause of the Fourteenth Amendment.

——*Darryl Paulson*

BIBLIOGRAPHY AND FURTHER READING

Cortner, Richard C. *Civil Rights and Public Accommodation: The Heart of Atlanta Motel and McClung Cases.* Lawrence: UP of Kansas, 2001. Print.

Irons, Peter, and Stephanie Guitton, eds. *May It Please the Court: 23 Live Recordings of Landmark Cases as Argued before the Supreme Court.* New York: New P, 1993. Audio recording (cassette/CD).

HINDU HOLIDAYS AND FESTIVALS

Hindu holidays and festivals either commemorate certain mythical events or call attention to seasonal changes and their significance for spiritual and social life. While many of them are observed with religious rituals, some are purely secular in nature. Since Hinduism is India's common cultural as well as religious heritage, non-Hindus also participate in many of the celebrations. Because most holidays follow the lunar cycle, the date of the annual occurrence of these holidays and festivals varies. However, a few of them follow the solar calendar and are celebrated on a relatively fixed date every year. Not all the holidays and festivals are celebrated with equal enthusiasm throughout India and some are exclusive to specific states or regions. Below is a description of the major Hindu holidays and festivals and their significance, listed sequentially according to their occurrence during the year.

MAKARA SANKRANTI

Makara or *Makar* is the Indian name for the zodiacal sign Capricorn and *Sankranti* means transition. It is not only the first major festival of the year observed throughout India, but also arguably the most important one. The festival signifies the point of the sun's transition to Capricorn, which begins with the winter solstice. *Makara Sankranti* is one of the few holidays celebrated on a fixed date according to the solar calendar and it falls on January 14 or January 15 if the year is a leap year. However, the normal date will shift to January 15 starting in 2019 due to a change in the Hindu calendar that adjusts the date periodically according it its own calculation of the position of the sun. The northward movement of the sun (*uttarayana*) after the winter solstice signals a season of hope, peace, and auspiciousness, while the southward movement of the sun (*dakshinayana*) that starts with the summer solstice is the beginning of darkness and sorrow. *Makara Sankranti* is also a harvest festival that celebrates the end of the northeast monsoon season and the completion of all harvest activities. Although the festival is celebrated all over India, it is known under different names in different regions. For instance, in Tamil Nadu it is known as *Pongal* while in Kerala it is celebrated as *Makara Vilakku* and in Gujarat and Rajastan as *Uttarayan.* The Sikhs also celebrate the festival, but under the name *Maghi.*

VASANT PANCHAMI

Literally meaning the fifth day (*panchami*) of the spring season (*vasanth),* it celebrates the arrival of spring. Since the day falls on the 5th day of the waxing moon in the lunar month of Magh, the date varies each year, but it falls in January or February. It is also a religious festival dedicated to Saraswati, the goddess of wisdom and learning. Children are often initiated into learning on this day by teaching them to write letters of the alphabet. Because it is an auspicious day, some seek to enter into important commitments, such as marriages that day. Signifying the season of spring when flowers bloom, people wear yellow as they participate in celebrations. Because it occurs in the spring, the festival is also a celebration of romantic love. Sikhs also celebrate this festival.

MAHA SHIVARATRI

The name of the festival means the great night of Shiva, one of the Hindu Trinity (the other two being Brahma and Vishnu), and it is a major festival devoted to the worship of Lord Shiva. Although the date changes from year to year, following the lunar cycle, it is usually celebrated toward the end of February or early March (14th night of the new moon in the month of *Phalgum*). Many legends exist to explain the reason of the celebration. Some believe it was the wedding night of Shiva and his consort Parvati, while others believe that it was the night of the great creative dance, represented by the famous bronze sculpture *Shivathandavam,* by which Shiva brought the universe into existence. The creative power of Shiva is also represented by *lingam,* a phallic-shaped stone that symbolizes fertility, which priests bathe with milk, honey, butter, and water. Devotees spend the day and night of the festival in fasting and prayer.

HOLI

Popularly called the festival of colors, *Holi* is perhaps the best known Hindu festival. It is the culminating celebration of the spring season and it occurs forty days after *Vasanth Panchami,* the first spring festival. The date falls on the full moon of Phalgum that occurs late February or early March. Holi is most popular in North India. Although it has become a thoroughly secular holiday in modern times, the myth behind it has a religious significance. Holi is short form for the name Holika, the evil sister of the mythical demon king Hiranyakashipu, who tried to burn to death Prahalada, Hiranyakashipu's god-fearing son. As it happened, Prahalada escaped from the fire unharmed and Holika, who got trapped in the fire, burned to death. To commemorate this event, the Holi celebration begins with a bonfire on the night before the day of the festival. Holi is also a commemoration of another mythical story in which it described how Lord Krishna turned dark blue from being poisoned by Puthana, a female demon. Because of his dark skin color which resulted from being poisoned, Krishna was worried that he would not be able to marry a fair-skinned girl. As advised by his mother Devaki, Krishna approached Radha, a fair-skinned girl and applied colors to her face. This playful act of coloring Radha's face ventually led to their marriage to each other. The custom of throwing colored powder on anyone who is seen outdoors during Holi celebrations is a reminder of this mythical event. Holi thus signifies the overcoming of evil and bad luck and urges everyone to leave the troubles of the past behind, forgive and forget all offenses, and begin a new life.

NAVARATRI

The word means nine nights, and it is celebrated both in the spring and in the fall. The spring *Navaratri* is called *Chaitra* or *Vasant Navaratri* that occurs during the lunar month of *Chaitra* (March –April) and *Sharad Navaratri*, the more popular one, is celebrated during the lunar month of *Ashwin* (September – October). Celebrations are held for nine nights, exalting the power of the divine as a woman and mother most popularly represented in the form of goddess *Durga*, who destroyed demon *Mahishaswara* in a mythical battle that lasted nine days. The tenth day of the festivities is called *Dussehra*, a day when people take out the image of goddess Durga in procession. This is also the day when Lord Rama's killing of the evil king Ravana is commemorated, symbolizing the victory of good over evil.

DIWALI (DEEPAWALI)

Diwali is the short form for *Deepavali* or array of lights. As the name indicates, it is a festival of lights and it is held during the lunar month of *Kartika* (October – November), although it may sometimes begin in September. It is an official holiday in India. Lamps are lit throughout the night, welcoming the return of Lord Rama and his wife Sita who spent 14 years in exile before defeating the evil king Ravana. It is also a celebration of the victory of good over evil and of light over darkness. People celebrate the holiday differently in different regions of India, but being a religious holiday, the celebrations involve praying, exchange of gifts, and traditional dances. Diwali is celebrated also by Jains and Buddhists.

———*Mathew Kanjrathinkal*

BIBLIOGRAPHY AND FURTHER READING

"List of Festivals." *Hindu Online* web site: http://hinduonline.co/HinduCulture/ListOfFestivals.html

Mukundcharandas, Sadhu. *Hindu Festivals: Origins, Sentiments and Rituals.* Amdavad: Swaminarayan Aksharpith, 2010. Print.

Sivananda, Swami. *Hindu Festivals and Fasts.* Shivanandanagar: Divine Life Society, 2000. Print.

Rai, Bahadur Balakrishna Gupte. *Hindu Holidays and Ceremonials with Dissertations on Origins, Foklore and Symbol.* Calcutta: Thacker Spink, 1916. Print.

HIP HOP CULTURE

Around the late 1960s and early 70s, many black communities across the nation, were seeing an influx of drugs into their neighborhoods and were experiencing rising levels of gang violence. Many young black people within these communities were either immersed in the violence, involved with drugs in some capacity, or were taking jobs with a vocational focus that would soon be rendered obsolete. In short, these primarily black communities were suffering and people in these neighborhoods felt despair and hopelessness. In the midst of this extreme struggle, a cultural revolution began to form re-focusing the energy of many community members in a positive way. This revolution would go on to be known

Phase 2 is an influential graffiti artist who began painting in the 1970s. By MikaV (Own work).

world-wide as hip hop culture, and would have significant influence on black cultural identity, music, dance, and fashion for years to come.

By the late 1970s in areas known to be gang territories in the Bronx, block parties began to spring up. These parties included a variety of artistic expressions, such as DJ battles where pre-recorded music was played for the audience by Disc Jockeys. Street dancers known as "b-boys" and "b-girls" would perform in a variety of dance styles, including breakdancing. Men and women would paint, primarily using brightly colored spray paint, words or pictures on public buildings. People would rap or rhyme over beats or samples from R&B music, a practice known as "MCing," which stands for Master of Ceremonies. Most of these artists engaged in a form of battling, or competing against one another in their chosen form of expression. For many, these artistic battles took the

place of the gang violence so deeply entrenched in some of these communities.

This hip hop culture existed for five years, from around 1974-1979, before it began to spread to other communities and gain recognition as a legitimate genre of popular music. This local ethos that served as a cultural identity for primarily black communities became a world-wide phenomenon. The oppression felt by many inner-city youth had generated a recognized, valued art form that evolved into a multi-billion dollar industry. Hip hop culture began as a way for black communities to take back and transform their racial identity. A community that had once been known for gang violence and drugs was now recognized as one of the leading contributors to influences on music, spoken word expressions, styles of dance, and clothing styles.

——*Amber R. Dickinson*

BIBLIOGRAPHY AND FURTHER READING

Clay, Andreana. "Keepin' It Real: Black Youth, Hip-Hop Culture, and Black

Identity." *American Behavioral Scientist*, vol. 46, no. 10, 1 June 2003, pp. 1346–Web, 17 Feb. 2017.

Garofoli, Wendy, and Rokafella. *Breakdancing (snap)*. New York: Capstone, 2007. Print.

Price, Emmett G. *Hip Hop Culture*. Santa Barbara: ABC-CLIO, 2006. Print.

Schloss, Joseph G. *Foundation: B-Boys, B-Girls, and Hip-Hop Culture in New York*.

New York: Oxford UP, 2009. Print.

HIRABAYASHI V. UNITED STATES

In 1942, Gordon Kiyoshi Hirabayashi, an American citizen of Japanese ancestry, was arrested for violating the curfew set by General John L. DeWitt on the West Coast and subsequently failing to report to a designated Civil Control Station for assignment to a "relocation center"(internment camp). The military acted under the authority of Executive Order 9066, issued on February 19, 1942, by President Franklin D. Roosevelt. This order authorized the secretary of war and appropriate military commanders to establish military areas from which any or all persons might be excluded. The president issued this order solely on his authority as commander in chief of the Army and Navy. After Hirabayashi was found guilty of violating the curfew and failing to report to the Civil Control Station, he appealed to the US Supreme Court.

In 1943, the US Supreme Court ruled 9 to 0 in favor of the United States and upheld the military's right to authorize a curfew. The majority opinion was written by Chief Justice Harlan Stone, who emphasized the grave character of the national emergency that had confronted the nation in 1942 and the possible disloyalty of portions of the Japanese American minority. He further noted that "in time of war residents having ethnic affiliations with an invading enemy may be a greater source of danger than those of a different ancestry." The Court, he thought, ought not to challenge the conclusion of the military authorities that the federal power be interpreted as broadly as possible. While there was some question of the constitutionality of the military order under the Fifth Amendment, Justice Stone denied that the curfew was unconstitutional because the amendment contained no equal protection clause.

Interestingly, though the Court was unanimous in its holding, there were three separate concurring opinions, by Justices Frank Murphy, William O. Douglas, and Wiley Rutledge. Justice Murphy made it clear that he found restrictions upon minority rights on the basis of race odious even in wartime: "Distinctions based on color and ancestry are utterly inconsistent with our traditions and our ideals." He believed that the curfew order bore "a melancholy resemblance to the treatment accorded to members of the Jewish race in Germany and other parts of Europe." He nevertheless justified the order, constitutionally, because of the "critical military situation" on the West Coast.

While the Court upheld the act of Congress of March 21, 1942, authorizing the curfew, it seems clear that at least some of the justices were quite uncomfortable with the relocation program. Therein is the legacy of this case: Why did the justices not offer a decision on the Japanese Relocation Program? It seems evident that a majority of the justices were extremely reluctant to interfere with the program, primarily because they were unwilling to dispute the judgment of the president and military commanders as to what was necessary to win the war. Therefore, it was easier for them to determine only that the curfew order was constitutional and lay within the combined congressional and presidential powers.

——*Kevin F. Sims*

BIBLIOGRAPHY AND FURTHER READING

Hirabayashi, Gordon K., with J.A. and L.R. Hirabayashi. *A Principled Stand: The Story of Hirabayashi v. United States*. Seattle: U of Washington P, 2013. Print.

Hispanic v. Latino

The group of United States residents who have a common connection to the Spanish language are termed Hispanics, while Americans of Latin American descent are termed Latinos. Thus, in essence, Hispanic denotes language, and Latino denotes geography. There is a great degree of overlap between the two groups, and often the terms Hispanic and Latino are used interchangeably. However, Californians, most New Yorkers, and Chicagoans favor Latino, while many Texans and almost everyone in Florida prefer Hispanic. The main distinguishing factor is that the appellation "Hispanic" is typically associated with affluence, whereas "Latino" is associated with a struggle for social and economic justice. Based on this diversity, Mexican Americans, who live primarily in the Southwest, and Puerto Ricans, who live mainly in the Northeast, often call themselves Latino, while Cuban Americans, who are concentrated in Florida, tend to prefer being called Hispanic.

The US Bureau of the Census uses the term "Hispanic" to denote people of Spanish/Hispanic origin. According to its classification system, a person of Hispanic origin may be of any race. In the 1990 census, people could self-identify as belonging to one of the Hispanic subgroups: Mexican, Puerto Rican, Cuban, or Other Spanish/Hispanic. Those in the "Other" category could write in their subgroup. For the 2000 and 2010 censuses, respondents were asked to select from five racial categories—White, African American or black, American Indian or Native Alaskan, Asian, and Native Hawaiian or other Pacific Islander—and also check "Hispanic or Latino."

Hispanic/Latino discrimination

Suzanne Wintner and Joanna Almeida

Hispanics/Latinos are currently the largest racial/ethnic minority group in the United States (US), and represented 17.6 percent of the population in 2015. According to US Census projections, by 2060 Hispanics/Latinos are expected to comprise nearly 30 percent of the US population. The Office of Management and Budget defines Hispanic or Latino as "a person of Cuban, Mexican, Puerto Rican, South or Central American, or other Spanish culture or origin regardless of race." Despite the common ethic designation, Hispanics/Latinos in the US are heterogeneous in terms of their migratory patterns, phenotypes, sociopolitical histories and socioeconomic position within the US), which complicates the notion that they can be considered one monolithic social group. Nonetheless, US Hispanics/Latinos have some degree of shared experiences, including exposure to discrimination.

While there are many definitions, the *Collins Dictionary of Sociology* defines discrimination as "the process by which members of a socially defined group are treated differently (especially unfairly) because of their membership of that group." Discrimination can occur at multiple levels (e.g. individual, institutional) and in many domains (e.g. criminal justice system, labor market, housing, health care, education). In contrast to the large body of literature on discrimination among African Americans, research on discrimination among Hispanics/Latinos is in the incipient stages, despite the large and growing population of Hispanics/Latinos in the US Extant studies of discrimination among Hispanics/Latinos have yielded discrepant findings. For example, a study conducted in 2015 in four major US metropolitan areas where large populations of Hispanics/Latinos reside found a 79.5 percent prevalence of lifetime discrimination. In 2003 and 2013, two studies that used similar versions of the Everyday Discrimination Scale among nationally representative samples of Hispanics/Latinos reported lifetime rates of 30 percent and 68.4 percent. Some of the variation in prevalence rates may be due to different measurement methods across studies. However, the higher rates observed more recently might reflect the fact that discrimination in the form of anti-immigrant policies was sanctioned in many states across the US in the decade after 2003, and as such discrimination was more proximate in Hispanics/Latinos' everyday life in 2013-2015 than it was in 2003.

Consistent across studies is the finding that Cubans in the US report lower levels of discrimination relative to other Hispanic/Latino groups, and younger Hispanics/Latinos report more discrimination than older Hispanics/Latinos in the United States. While findings have been mixed with regard to gender differences in discrimination among Hispanics/Latinos, younger age and greater exposure to the U.S., as measured by nativity status, generation status, acculturation, English language ability and age of arrival to the U.S., have almost uniformly been associated with greater discrimination. The question of whether there are differences in discrimination among Hispanics/Latinos in the US by country of origin remains unclear. Results of the two aforementioned nationally representative studies of Hispanics/Latinos conducted in 2003 and 2013 both suggest that Puerto Ricans report higher rates of discrimination compared to Hispanics/Latinos from other countries. As US citizens, Puerto Ricans are not formally subject to certain types of state-sanctioned discrimination (e.g. immigration policy) on the basis of immigration or documentation status that Hispanics/Latinos of other national origins are. However, the fact that Puerto Ricans more often have darker skin, coupled with research suggesting that darker-skinned Hispanics/Latinos are more likely to experience discrimination, lends credence to the idea that Puerto Ricans on the mainland US may in fact be impacted by other forms of discrimination.

Although the literature is inconclusive with regard to which sociodemographic groups of Hispanics/Latinos in the US are more likely to experience discrimination, the adverse effects of discrimination (at multiple levels and across domains) on a wide range of social, economic and health indicators is clear. Research has demonstrated that discrimination limits Hispanics/Latinos' access to job opportunities, career advancement and income earnings. In school settings, discrimination is associated with poor psychosocial and academic outcomes among Hispanics/Latinos. Furthermore, discrimination has an adverse impact on health, mental health and engagement in risk behaviors among Hispanic/Latino adults and adolescents. Taken together, the body of empirical evidence overwhelmingly suggests that discrimination is detrimental to Hispanics/Latinos in myriad aspects of life.

This article has briefly summarized the phenomenon of discrimination among Hispanics/Latinos in the US Although much remains to be learned about discrimination among Hispanics/Latinos, it is clear that discrimination plays an important role in shaping the trajectories of and life chances for this large and growing segment of the US population. In light of this country's shifting demographics and changing political landscape, both of which can rouse prejudicial beliefs and discriminatory practices, there has never been a more important time to focus our attention towards understanding and eliminating discrimination among Hispanics/Latinos in the United States.

——*Alvin K. Benson*

BIBLIOGRAPHY AND FURTHER READING

Almeida, J., K.B. Biello, F. Pedraza, S. Wintner, and E. Viruell-Fuentes. "The association between anti-immigrant policies and perceived discrimination among Latinos in the US: A multilevel analysis." *Social Science & Medicine-Population Health* 2, 2016: 897-903. Web. 12 March 2017.

Araújo, B., and L. Borrell. "Understanding the link between discrimination, mental health outcomes, and life chances among Latinos." *Hispanic Journal of Behavioral Sciences,* 28(2), 2006: 245-266. Web. 10 March 2017.

Arellano-Morales, L., et al. "Prevalence and correlates of perceived ethnic discrimination in the Hispanic Community Health Study/Study of Latinos Sociocultural Ancillary Study." *Journal of Latina/o Psychology* 3(3), 2015: 160-176. Web. 10 March 2017.

Cook, B., M. Alegría, J. Lin, and J. Guo. "Pathways and correlates connecting Latinos' mental health with exposure to the United States." *American Journal of Public Health* 99(12), 2009: 2247-2254. Web. 12 March 2017.

Finch, B., B. Kolody, and W. Vega. "Perceived discrimination and depression among Mexican-origin adults in California." *The Journal of Health and Social Behavior* 41(3), 2000: 295-313. Print.

Gee, G., and C. Ford. "Structural racism and health inequities: Old issues, new directions." *Du Bois Review-Social Science Research on Race* 8(1), n.d.: 115-132. Web. 17 March 2017.

Huynh, V.W., and A.J. Fuligni. "Discrimination Hurts: The academic, psychological, and physical well-being of adolescents." *Journal of Research on Adolescence* 20(4), 2010: 916-941. Web. 15 March 2017.

Lee, D.L., and S. Ahn. "Discrimination against Latina/os: A Meta-analysis of individual-level resources and outcomes." *Counseling Psychologist 40*(1), 2012: 28-65. Print.

Molina, K., and Y. Simon. "Everyday discrimination and chronic health conditions among Latinos: the moderating role of socioeconomic position." *Journal of Behavioral Medicine* 37(5), 2014: 868-880. Web. 15 March 2017.

Otiniano Verissimo, A.D., G.C. Gee, C.L. Ford, and M.Y. Yaguchi. "Racial discrimination, gender discrimination, and substance abuse among Latina/os nationwide." *Cultural Diversity and Ethnic Minority Psychology 20*(1), 2014: 43-51. Web. 10 March 2017.

Perez, D.J., L. Fortuna, and M. Alegria. "Prevalence and correlates of everyday discrimination among US Latinos." *Journal of Community Psychology 36*(4), 2008. 421-433. Web. 11 March 2017.

United States Census Bureau. "Hispanic Origin." Web. 6 March, 2017.

HMONG AMERICANS

The Hmong (pronounced "mong") people have a long history of escaping adversity. For centuries the Hmong were an ethnic group persecuted in China. In the early nineteenth century, they moved to Burma (Myanmar), Thailand, Vietnam, and Laos. In Laos, the Hmong settled in the isolated highlands. During the political turmoil in the 1950's and 1960's, many Hmong fought for the anticommunist army under General Vang Pao. The US Central Intelligence Agency (CIA) secretly ran and financed this Vietnam War effort in which Laotian men served in rescue missions and guerrilla operations. When the Communists took power in Laos in 1975 and the United States withdrew, there were reprisals against the Hmong. To escape persecution, many Hmong fled to United Nations refugee camps in Thailand. In Ban Vinai and other refugee camps, Hmong families waited to establish political refugee status so that they could emigrate to the United States.

REFUGEES ON THE MOVE
The first Hmong refugees arrived in the United States in 1976, assisted by world relief organizations and local organizations such as churches. Between 1976 and 1991, an estimated 100,000 Hmong came to the United States. Because of their high birthrate, the population increased substantially. The Hmong dispersed throughout the United States, settling wherever sponsors could be found. The Hmong later followed a secondary migration pattern within the United States, moving to concentrations in California, Minnesota, Montana, Wisconsin, Colorado, Washington, North Carolina, and Rhode Island. Areas of second settlement were selected based on climate, cheap housing, job availability, state welfare programs, and family unification. As of the early 2010s, Fresno County, California, has the largest settlement, followed by the Minneapolis-St. Paul metropolitan area. The reception the Hmong have received varies from hearty welcomes to ethnic antagonism on the part of some Americans who were ignorant of Hmong bravery and sacrifices in the Vietnam War and who do not grasp the difficulty of Hmong adjustment to life in the United States.

CULTURE SHOCK
Three branches of the Hmong came to the United States: the Blue Hmong, the White Hmong, and the Striped Hmong. They spoke different dialects and wore distinct traditional clothing but shared many cultural traditions that made it difficult to adjust to life in a modern society. Most refugees had never experienced indoor plumbing, electricity, or automobiles. For many Hmong, their only work experience before coming to the United States was as soldiers and as farmers. The traditional crops of rice and corn were raised on fields so steep that sometimes farmers tethered themselves to a stump to keep from falling off their fields. For the Hmong who tried farming in the United States, adjustment was difficult. Their slash-and-burn method of clearing land was not permitted. They were unfamiliar with pesticides and chemical fertilizers. Refugees worked as migrant farmworkers and in many low-paid urban positions that did not require English proficiency. The unemployment rate was very high for many Hmong communities. In 1990, over two-thirds of the Fresno Hmong depended on welfare and refugee assistance.

Hmong Americans at a community recycling event in Saint Paul. By RamseyCountyMN.

By 2010, nearly one quarter remained below the poverty line.

Education was another area of difficult cultural adaptation. In the 1990's, many Hmong children struggled in US schools. Many attended English-as-a-second-language classes, and many were placed in a vocational track. Hmong children often had low scores on standardized tests of vocabulary and reading comprehension. When large numbers of Hmong children entered certain school systems in the late 1970's and 1980's, administrators and teachers were completely unprepared. Learning English proved difficult, especially for the older Hmong who had never attended school in Laos. Special training programs first taught Hmong language literacy, then English. By 2010, about 13 percent had earned a bachelor's degree, compared to over 18 percent for all Americans.

Hmong beliefs about religion and medicine are very different from common attitudes in the United States. Traditional Hmong religion is a form of animism, a belief that spirits dwell in all things, including the earth, the sky, and animals. Hmong attempted to placate these spirits in religious rituals that often included animal sacrifice. In medical ceremonies, a shaman or healer tried to locate and bring back the patient's runaway soul. Many bereaved Hmong refused autopsies, believing they interfered with reincarnation.

Hmong family traditions often put them at odds with US culture. The Laotian practice was to arrange marriages, usually interclan agreements in which a bride price was paid. Women married as teenagers, then derived their status from being a wife and mother of many children. Marriage by capture was part of Hmong tradition but led to US criminal charges of kidnapping and rape. Divorce was discouraged but possible in Laos, and children could be kept by the husband's family. Such practices conflict with many US laws and folkways.

Other conflicts arose over US laws that the Hmong did not understand. Carrying concealed weapons was common in Laos but led to arrest in the United States. Zoning laws stipulating where to build a house or plant a field were unfamiliar to the Hmong. Disputes arose over Hmong poaching in wildlife refuges.

Culture shock seems to have taken a toll on the Hmong. In the 1970's and early 1980's, many apparently healthy Hmong men died in their sleep in what was labeled Sudden Unexplained Death Syndrome. Possible explanations were depression, "survivor guilt," and the stress of a new environment in which the men lacked control of their lives. The peak years for the syndrome were 1981 and 1982.

STRENGTHS OF THE HMONG

Not all aspects of Hmong tradition handicapped their adjustment to life in the United States. Some members possessed fine-motor skills honed in their intricate needlework. Without sewing machines or patterns, Hmong women embroidered and appliquéd to produce marketable products that also preserve their cultural memories. Flower cloths are square designs with symmetrical patterns. Story cloths are sewn pictures depicting past events, including war brutality and refugee camp life. Hmong developed memorization skills as part of their oral tradition of elaborate folktales. Hmong women were credited with admirable parenting skills, especially in their sensitivity to their children's needs. The fierce independence and will to survive exhibited by many Hmong were also assets in their transition.

The Hmong eventually began to adjust to the new culture in which they found themselves, especially the younger generation. Hmong youth typically adopted American ways, wearing Western dress and enjoying rock music and video games. The group showed resilience in adapting traditions to changed circumstances. The Hmong devised a custom of group support as clans formed mutual-aid societies and political organizations; by 2000, there were at least forty-five such groups listed by the Southeast Asia Resource Action Center (SEARAC). A number also began to attain higher levels of education, with more than 60 percent holding high school diplomas and 36 percent attending college, according to a 2013 SEARAC fact sheet.

——*Nancy Conn Terjesen*

BIBLIOGRAPHY AND FURTHER READING

Faderman, Lillian, and Ghia Xiong. *I Begin My Life All Over: The Hmong and the American Immigrant Experience*. Boston: Beacon, 1998. Print.

Fadiman, Anne. *The Spirit Catches You and You Fall Down: A Hmong Child, Her American Doctors, and the Collision of Two Cultures*. 1997. New York: Farrar, 2012. Print.

Grigoleit, Grit. "Hmong Americans." *Multicultural America: An Encyclopedia*. Vol. 1. Ed. Carlos E. Cortés. Thousand Oaks: Sage, 2013. 1097–99. Print.

Huping Ling and Allan W. Austin, eds. *Asian American History and Culture: An Encyclopedia*. New York: Routledge, 2015. Print.

Lan Cao, and Himilce Novas. *Everything You Need to Know about Asian American History*. Rev. ed. New York: Penguin, 2004. Print.

Lee, Erika. *The Making of Asian Americans*. New York: Simon and Schuster, 2015. Print.

Southeast Asia Resource Action Center. "Increase Access to Education." N.p.: Southeast Asia Resource Action Center, Feb. 2013. PDF file.

HOLOCAUST

The Holocaust was Nazi Germany's planned total destruction of the Jewish people and the actual murder of nearly six million of them. That genocidal campaign—the most systematic, bureaucratic, and unrelenting the world has seen—also destroyed millions of non-Jewish civilians. They included Gypsies (Roma and Sinti), Slavs, Jehovah's Witnesses, Freemasons, homosexuals, the intellectually disabled, the physically handicapped, and the insane. The Nazis believed that their threat to the Third

Reich approached, though it could never equal, the one posed by Jews.

In German, this unprecedented destruction process became known euphemistically as *die Endlösung*—the Final Solution. The Hebrew word *Shoah,* which means catastrophe, is also used to name it, but the term "Holocaust" most commonly signifies the event. That word has biblical roots. In the Septuagint, a Greek translation of the Hebrew Bible, the Hebrew word *olah* is translated as *holokauston.* In context, *olah* means that which is offered up. It refers to a sacrifice, often specifically to "an offering made by fire unto the Lord." Such connotations make "Holocaust" a problematic term for the devastation it names. The word's religious implications seem inappropriate, even repulsive, to many people, including many Jews. Still, Holocaust remains the term that is most widely used.

Nazi Germany's system of concentration camps, ghettos, murder squadrons, and killing centers took more than twelve million defenseless human lives. Between five million and six million of them were Jewish, including approximately one million children under fifteen. Although not every Nazi victim was Jewish, the Nazi intent was to rid Europe, if not the world, of Jews. Hitler went far in meeting that goal. Although Europe's Jews resisted the onslaught as best they could, by the end of World War II two-thirds of European Jews—and about one-third of Jews worldwide—were dead. The vast majority of the Jewish victims came from Eastern Europe. More than half of them were from Poland; there, the German annihilation effort was 90 percent successful. At Auschwitz alone—located in Poland, the largest of the Nazi killing centers—more than one million Jews were gassed.

How did the Holocaust happen and why? Those questions are both historical and ethical. Their implications are huge. As Elie Wiesel , Jewish survivor of Auschwitz and winner of the 1986 Nobel Peace Prize, has said of Birkenau, the major killing area at Auschwitz: "Traditional ideas and acquired values, philosophical systems and social theories—all must be revised in the shadow of Birkenau."

Further controversy regarding the Holocaust erupted in 2015 when Israel's prime minister, Benjamin Netanyahu, made statements suggesting that the idea of the genocide of the European Jews had not actually been Hitler's. Netanyahu claimed

that the grand mufti of Jerusalem, Haj Amin al-Husseini, had suggested the plan to Hitler during a meeting in 1941 as a means of avoiding large amounts of expelled Jews from relocating to Palestine. Holocaust victims, historians, and commentators widely criticized Netanyahu's statements for the lack of historical evidence and the detraction from Hitler's responsibility for the crime against humanity.

HISTORY

Adolf Hitler became chancellor of Germany on January 30, 1933. He soon consolidated his power through tyranny and terror. Within six months, the Nazis stood as the only legal political power in Germany, Hitler's decrees were law, basic civil rights had been suspended, and thousands of the Third Reich's political opponents had been imprisoned.

Emphasizing the superiority of the German people, Nazi ideology was anti-Semitic and racist to the core. The Nazis affirmed that German racial purity must be maintained. Building on precedents long established by Christianity's animosity toward Jews, the Nazis went further and vilified Jews as the most dangerous threat to that goal. Nazi ideology defined Jewish identity in biological and racial terms.

German law established detailed conditions to define full and partial Jews. To cite three examples, if one had three Jewish grandparents, that condition was sufficient to make one fully Jewish. If one had only two Jewish grandparents and neither practiced Judaism nor had a Jewish spouse, however, then one was a *Mischlinge* (mongrel) first-class. A person with only a single Jewish grandparent would be a *Mischlinge* second-class. The identity of one's grandparents was determined, paradoxically, not by blood but by their membership in the Jewish religious community. Once these Nazi classifications were in effect, the identity they conferred was irreversible.

Defining Jewish identity was crucial for identifying the population targeted by the Nazis' anti-Semitic policies. Those policies focused first on segregating Jews, making their lives intolerable, and forcing them to leave Germany. Between 1933 and the outbreak of World War II in September 1939, hundreds of decrees, such as the Nuremberg Laws of September 1935, deprived the Third Reich's Jews of basic civil rights. When Jews tried to emigrate from German territory, however, they found few havens. In general, doors around the world, including those in the

United States, were opened reluctantly, if at all, for Jewish refugees from Hitler's Germany.

World War II began with Germany's invasion of Poland on September 1, 1939. With the notable exception of its failure to subdue England by air power, the German war machine had things largely its own way until it experienced reversals at El Alamein and Stalingrad in 1942. By the end of that year, four million Jews had already been murdered.

As Hitler's forces advanced on all fronts, huge numbers of Jews, far exceeding the six hundred thousand who lived in Germany when Hitler took control, came under Nazi domination. For a year after the war began, Nazi planning had still aimed to enforce massive Jewish resettlement, but there were no satisfactory ways to fulfill that intention.

THE KILLING BEGINS

In the spring of 1941, as plans were laid for the invasion of the Soviet Union, Hitler decided that special mobile killing units—*Einsatzgruppen*—would follow the German army, round up Jews, and kill them. A second prong of attack in Germany's war against the Jews became operational as well. Instead of moving killers toward their victims, it would bring victims to their killers.

Utilizing a former Austrian military barracks near the Polish town of Okwicim, the Germans made their concentration camp of Auschwitz operational in June 1940, when 728 Polish prisoners were transferred there. By the summer of 1941, the original camp (Auschwitz I) had been supplemented by a much larger camp at nearby Birkenau (Auschwitz II). Within the next year—along with five other sites in occupied Poland (Chelmno, Belzec, Sobibor, Treblinka, and Majdanek)—Auschwitz-Birkenau became a full-fledged killing center. Auschwitz employed fast-working hydrogen cyanide gas, which suppliers offered in the form of a deodorized pesticide known as Zyklon B. In 1943 new crematoria became available for corpse disposal. When Schutzstaffel (SS) leader Heinrich Himmler ordered an end to the systematic killing at Auschwitz in late 1944, his reasoning was not based entirely on the fact that Soviet troops were nearby. For all practical purposes, he could argue, the Final Solution had eliminated Europe's "Jewish problem."

At the same time, with the Allied forces encroaching further into German territory, German forces had begun evacuating many of these camps and forcing prisoners to march away from enemy advancements. Hundreds of thousands died in the process. In January of the following year, Soviet forces liberated Auschwitz. By the beginning of May, Hitler had committed suicide and Germany had officially surrendered.

Nazi war criminals, including high-ranking officials, were brought before a court. Thirteen trials, known as the Nuremberg Trials, were conducted between 1945 and 1949 in an attempt to bring justice in the face of such crimes against humanity. New laws and procedures had to be created to govern these unprecedented international trials. Over the next several decades, the German government, as well as others, made efforts to supply restitution funds for the survivors, who had suffered torture, property loss, and displacement. The United Nations General Assembly designated January 27 as International Holocaust Remembrance Day. As the years have continued to pass and fewer survivors remain alive, organizations and museums, such as the United States Holocaust Memorial Museum, have continued to dedicate resources to study and education regarding the genocide.

ETHICAL PROBLEMS AND MORAL CHALLENGES

The most crucial moral problem posed by the Holocaust is that no moral, social, religious, or political constraints were sufficient to stop Nazi Germany from unleashing the Final Solution. Only when military force crushed the Third Reich did the genocide end.

David Rousset, a French writer who endured German concentration camps, understated the case when he said simply, "The existence of the camps is a warning."

The Holocaust warns about the depth of racism's evil. If one takes seriously the idea that one race endangers the well-being of another, the only way to remove that menace completely is to do away, once and for all, with everyone and everything that embodies that race. If most forms of racism shy away from such extreme measures, Nazi Germany's anti-Semitism did not. The Nazis saw what they took to be a practical problem: the need to eliminate "racially inferior" people. Then they moved to solve it.

Consequently, the Holocaust did not result from unplanned, random violence. It was instead a state-sponsored program of population elimination made possible by modern technology and political organization. As Nazi Germany became a genocidal state, its anti-Semitic racism required a destruction process that needed and got the cooperation of every sector of German society. The killers and those who aided and abetted them directly—or indirectly as bystanders—were civilized people from a society that was scientifically advanced, technologically competent, culturally sophisticated, and efficiently organized. These people were, as Holocaust scholar Michael Berenbaum has noted, "both ordinary and extraordinary, a cross section of the men and women of Germany, its allies, and their collaborators as well as the best and the brightest."

Teachers and writers helped to till the soil in which Hitler's virulent anti-Semitism took root; their students and readers reaped the wasteful harvest. Lawyers drafted and judges enforced the laws that isolated Jews and set them up for the kill. Government and church personnel provided birth records to document who was Jewish and who was not. Other workers entered such information into state-of-the-art data-processing machines. University administrators curtailed admissions for Jewish students and dismissed Jewish faculty members. Bureaucrats in the finance ministry confiscated Jewish wealth and property. Postal officials delivered mail about definition and expropriation, denaturalization and deportation. Driven by their biomedical visions, physicians were among the first to experiment with the gassing of *lebensunwertes Leben* (lives unworthy of life). Scientists performed research and tested their racial theories on those branded subhuman or nonhuman by German science. Business executives found that Nazi concentration camps could provide cheap labor; they worked people to death, turning the Nazi motto, *Arbeit macht frei* (work makes one free), into a mocking truth. Stockholders made profits from firms that supplied Zyklon B to gas people and from companies that built crematoria to burn the corpses. Radio performers were joined by artists such as the gifted film director Leni Riefenstahl to broadcast and screen the polished propaganda that made Hitler's policies persuasive to so many. Engineers drove the trains that transported Jews to death, while other officials took charge of the billing arrangements for this service. Factory workers modified trucks so that they became deadly gas vans; city policemen became

members of squadrons that made the murder of Jews their specialty. As the list went on and on, so did the racially motivated destruction of the European Jews.

Short of Germany's military defeat by the Allies, no other constraints—moral, social, religious, or political—were sufficient to stop the Final Solution. Accordingly, a second Holocaust warning is the challenge that no one should take human rights for granted. Hans Maier, born on October 31, 1912, as the only child of a Catholic mother and a Jewish father, considered himself an Austrian, not least because his father's family had lived in Austria since the seventeenth century. Hans Maier, however, lived in the twentieth century, and so it was that in the autumn of 1935 he studied a newspaper in a Viennese coffeehouse. The Nuremberg Laws had just been passed in Nazi Germany. Maier's reading made him see that, even if he did not think of himself as Jewish, the Nazis' definitions meant that in their view he was Jewish. By identifying him as a Jew, Maier would write later on, Nazi power made him "a dead man on leave, someone to be murdered, who only by chance was not yet where he properly belonged."

When Nazi Germany occupied Austria in March 1938, Maier drew his conclusions. He fled his native land for Belgium and joined the Resistance after Belgium was swept into the Third Reich in 1940. Arrested by Nazi police in 1943, Maier was sent to Auschwitz and then to Bergen-Belsen, where he was liberated in 1945. Eventually taking the name Jean Améry, by which he is remembered, this philosopher waited twenty years before breaking his silence about the Holocaust. When Améry did decide to write, the result was a series of essays about his experience. In English, they appear in a volume entitled *At the Mind's Limits: Contemplations by a Survivor on Auschwitz and Its Realities.* "Every morning when I get up," he tells his reader, "I can read the Auschwitz number on my forearm. . . . Every day anew I lose my trust in the world. . . . Declarations of human rights, democratic constitutions, the free world and the free press, nothing," he went on to say, "can lull me into the slumber of security from which I awoke in 1935."

In *The Cunning of History: The Holocaust and the American Future*, Richard L. Rubenstein echoes Améry's understanding. "Does not the Holocaust demonstrate," he suggests, "that there are absolutely no limits to the degradation and assault the managers and technicians of violence can inflict upon men and women who lack the power of effective resistance?" Rubenstein believes that "the dreadful history of Europe's Jews had demonstrated that *rights do not belong to men by nature.*" If Rubenstein is correct, then, practically speaking, people can expect to enjoy basic rights such as those proclaimed by the Declaration of Independence—life, liberty, and the pursuit of happiness—only within a political community that honors and defends those rights successfully.

——*John K. Roth*

BIBLIOGRAPHY AND FURTHER READING

Améry, Jean. *At the Mind's Limits: Contemplations by a Survivor on Auschwitz and Its Realities.* Trans. Sidney Rosenfeld and Stella P. Rosenfeld. Bloomington: Indiana UP, 1980. Print.

Berenbaum, Michael. *The World Must Know: The History of the Holocaust as Told in the United States Holocaust Memorial Museum.* Boston: Little, 1993. Print.

Browning, Christopher R. *Ordinary Men: Reserve Police Battalion 101 and the Final Solution in Poland.* New York: HarperCollins, 1992. Print.

Carol, Carol, and John K. Roth, eds. *Different Voices: Women and the Holocaust.* New York: Paragon, 1993. Print.

Gutman, Israel, et al., eds. *Encyclopedia of the Holocaust.* 4 vols. New York: Macmillan, 1990. Print.

Haas, Peter J. *Morality After Auschwitz: The Radical Challenge of the Nazi Ethic.* Philadelphia: Fortress, 1988. Print.

Hallie, Philip P. *Lest Innocent Blood Be Shed: The Story of the Village of Le Chambon and How Goodness Happened There.* New York: Harper, 1979. Print.

Hayes, Peter, ed. *How Was It Possible? A Holocaust Reader.* Lincoln: U of Nebraska P, 2015. Print.

Hilberg, Raul. *The Destruction of the European Jews.* Rev. ed. New York: Holmes, 1985. Print.

Lifton, Robert Jay. *The Nazi Doctors: Medical Killing and the Psychology of Genocide.* New York: Basic, 1986. Print.

Rubenstein, Richard L. *The Cunning of History: The Holocaust and the American Future.* New York: Harper, 1987. Print.

Rubenstein, Richard L., and John K. Roth. *Approaches to Auschwitz: The Holocaust and Its Legacy.* Atlanta: John Knox, 1987. Print.

Rudoren, Jodi. "Netanyahu Denounced for Saying Palestinian Inspired Holocaust." *New York Times.* New York Times, 21 Oct. 2015. Web. 3 Nov. 2015.

Sereny, Gitta. *Into That Darkness: An Examination of Conscience.* New York: Vintage, 1983. Print.

Wachsmann, Nikolaus. *KL: A History of the Nazi Concentration Camps.* New York: Farrar, 2015. Print.

Wiesel, Elie. *Night.* New York: Bantam, 1982. Print.

HOLOCAUST DENIAL

Holocaust denial is the assertion, despite documented evidence to the contrary, that the systematic Nazi extermination of an estimated five million to six million Jews between 1933 and 1945 did not occur. It was begun by Nazi commandants, who, near the end of World War II, destroyed concentration camp records and other evidence of mass destruction and carried out the orders of Reichsführer Heinrich Himmler that no prisoner should survive. After the war, many leaders of the Schutzstaffel (SS, a special Nazi military unit) fled the country and began the publication of denial materials.

The origins of Holocaust denial are in the works of European and American historical revisionists designed to absolve Germany of its role in World War I. However, one of the earliest apologists for the Nazi regime was Paul Rassinier, a French prisoner confined to Buchenwald in 1943, who claimed that there were no gas chambers in Nazi concentration camps. Despite the fact that gas chambers had been implemented in Poland and not in Buchenwald, Rassinier asserted his personal experience as proof. Rassinier's *Crossing the Line* (1948) and *The Holocaust Story and the Lie of Ulysses* (1950) maintain that the atrocities that were committed by the Germans have been greatly exaggerated and that the inmates who ran the camps, not the Germans, were the perpetrators of these atrocities.

The works of Rassinier, republished in 1977 by Noontide Press as *Debunking the Genocide Myth*, were translated by Henry Barnes of Smith College, the first American historian to pursue Holocaust denial. Barnes had denounced the United States' foreign policy during World War I, but with his discovery of Rassinier, he began to argue that the atrocity stories had been exaggerated and eventually came to insist that they had been fabricated. Barnes raised doubts about the existence of gas chambers as a means of extermination by contending that gas chambers were a postwar invention. Barnes learned of American revisionist David Leslie Hoggan, whose dissertation at Harvard University maintained that Great Britain was responsible for World War II and depicted Adolf Hitler as a victim of the Allies. Through Barnes's help, Hoggan's book *The Forced War* (1961) became a Nazi apologia.

Holocaust denial assumed a more scholarly character with the advent of Austin J. App, professor at the University of Scranton, who sought through demographic studies to prove that the estimates of Jewish victims had been inflated. App's position, that no Jews were gassed in German camps and the small number who had "disappeared" was exaggerated to victimize Germany, became a central tenet of Holocaust denial. In 1976, Arthur P. Butz, a professor at Northwestern University, published *The Hoax of the Twentieth Century*, which denies that huge numbers of gassings and cremations could have occurred given the technological limitations of the equipment used.

In 1978, the beliefs supporting Holocaust denial were incorporated in a Los Angeles-based organization, the Institute for Historical Review (IHR), funded by Willis Carto. The IHR, which makes use of Carto's periodical publication and his book publication company, Noontide Press, also published, until 2002, the *Journal of Historical Review*. The Southern Poverty Law center lists the IHR as a hate group.

——*Mary Hurd*

BIBLIOGRAPHY AND FURTHER READING

Green, Emma. "The World Is Full of Holocaust Deniers." *Atlantic*. Atlantic Monthly, 14 May 2014. Web. 1 Apr. 2015.

Kollerstrom, Nicholas. *Breaking the Spell: The Holocaust; Myth & Reality*. Washington, DC: TBR, 2014. Print.

Lang, Berel. "Six Questions on (or about) Holocaust Denial." *History and Theory: Studies in the Philosophy of History* 49.2 (2010): 157–68. Print.

Lewy, Guenter. *Outlawing Genocide Denial: The Dilemmas of Official Historical Truth*. Salt Lake City: U of Utah P, 2014. Print.

Wistrich, Robert S., ed. *Holocaust Denial: The Politics of Perfidy*. Boston: de Gruyter, 2012. Print.

HOMELESSNESS AND RACIAL/ ETHNIC RELATIONS

In the 1980s, when many housing and social-service programs lost their federal funding, the homeless population in the United States rose to an estimated 500,000 on any given night, or a total of 1.2 million throughout the year. Included among this number were men, women, and children of all racial and ethnic backgrounds; urban and rural workers; displaced and deinstitutionalized persons; alcoholics, drug addicts, AIDS victims, and the mentally ill; physically abused mothers and their children; sexually abused teenagers and preadolescents; neglected elderly people; and migrants, refugees, and veterans.

Like other social problems, the problem of homelessness has historically been framed by the way in which specific societal groups and class interests have defined the social issue in the first place. Generally, public policies in the United States regarding homelessness, the homeless, and the shortage of low-income or subsidized housing are influenced by and inseparable from local and national politics. Moreover, economic crises and considerations, grounded in the ideological perspectives of laissez-faire, free-market capitalism and liberal social reformism, are also at work. At the same time, while most people do not blame individual homeless people per se for their predicament, they still support a public-policy ideology that essentially does nothing to alter the victimizing conditions of homelessness.

In part, this has to do with a legacy of viewing homeless people primarily as middle-aged men and elderly eccentric "shopping-bag ladies" rather than primarily as children, mothers, and families. When most people think about the homeless, rarely do images come to mind of teenage runaways, lacking marketable skills and financial resources, selling their bodies to the highest urban bidders. Typically, people do not think about homeless children, most of them abused or neglected, sleeping in abandoned buildings without heat, electricity, and running water. Most people do not think about homeless mothers who believe that it is better to exchange sexual services for shelter than to avail themselves of shelter opportunities and risk losing their children to foster care or an adoption agency.

As a group of people, today's homeless may be thought of as a new subclass of people at the bottom of the stratification and class system. Although they are most obvious in urban areas, camping near downtown shelters or requesting aid at freeway off-ramps, there is also a less obvious group, the hidden homeless.

Far away from the more conspicuous sights of the urban homeless, on the rural roads of the corporate agri-economy of the United States, thousands are doing their best to stay out of the way of local citizens and police, who may arrest and charge them for criminal trespassing, squatting, panhandling, or littering. In more than a few cases, these homeless persons have been arrested for merely trying to feed themselves. In the sparsely populated regions of the Midwest and the South, bankrupted and marginal farmers have been forced off their land, joining the ranks of other migrant workers in search of unskilled work. Crisscrossing the country, these members of a new migrant class, with and without their families, spend varying periods of time traveling the state highways and byways. If they are fortunate, they sleep in cars and trucks; if they are not, they sleep at rest stops or all-night truck stops, in plowed fields, or on the side of the road.

In many more communities, including medium-sized cities as well as urbanized metropolitan areas, a sizable majority of the homeless population remain, if not hidden, at least relatively invisible. Most of the urban homeless populations are warehoused out of sight in abandoned armories, terminals, or motels. In part, this situation is a result of governmental assistance and programs; it is also a result, in part, of the private efforts of concerned citizens and groups, especially of church-related assistance.

PROGRAMS AND POLICIES

Temporary or emergency assistance is available through bureaucracies that operate at all levels of government. At the same time, public and private armories and shelters—some for whole families, some for couples only, some for single women, and some for battered women and their infants—protect these homeless groups from physical elements, at least during the night. There are also various secular and religious efforts to provide the homeless, the hungry, and the nearly destitute with day shelters, soup kitchens, clothes closets, and food pantries. A few notable private nonprofit secular programs, out of literally hundreds of programs nationwide, are the Atlanta Day Shelter for Women and Children; Pathways, in Birmingham, Alabama, also dedicated to homeless women and children; and the Drop Inn Center, Cincinnati's largest homeless shelter.

Despite these programs and other services, such as city policies that require the police to pick up homeless individuals and drive them to one of the nearby community shelters on nights when the temperature drops below zero, hundreds of Americans still freeze to death every winter. As for the homeless of communities that do not or cannot provide forms of social welfare, most do not quickly perish. Even in the most caring and compassionate urban communities, where people do not necessarily look away as they step over or around homeless persons, after a while even those unfortunate souls who can be found sleeping in doorways, in metal trash receptacles, and in homemade cardboard shelters become invisible.

When one examines the growing percent of the population living below the poverty line in the United States, which rose from a twenty-plus-year low of 11.3 percent in 2000 to a high of 15.1 percent in 2010—a year that saw an estimated homeless population of 640,466 people per night—one finds that more and more people have not only slipped down the socioeconomic ladder but also become part of a permanent group of have-nots. These people, many of whom have become members of the new homeless groups consisting of women and children, can therefore be regarded as marginal victims of a changing global political economy that has reduced the size of the unskilled and semiskilled industrial workforce in North America. These fundamental changes in the domestic economy must be reflected in the development of social housing for the nonaffluent. Until the United States adopts a public policy grounded in both a commitment to social and economic justice and a recognition of the need for the development of an alternative approach to homelessness and inexpensive housing, the delivery of adequate and permanent housing for all persons living in the United States will remain a utopian dream of the thousands of homeless advocates and volunteers found nationwide.

————*Gregg Barak*

BIBLIOGRAPHY AND FURTHER READING

Barak, Gregg. *Gimme Shelter: A Social History of Homelessness in Contemporary America*. New York: Praeger, 1991. Print.

Chen, Daphne. "Federal Policy Changes Contribute to Rise in Local Homeless Population." *Homelessness in Berkeley*. Daily Californian, 7 Aug. 2013. Web. 17 June 2015.

Golden, Stephanie. *The Women Outside: Meanings and Myths of Homelessness*. Berkeley: U of California P, 1992. Print.

Henry, Meghan, et al. *The 2014 Annual Homeless Assessment Report (AHAR) to Congress*. Washington: Dept. of Housing and Urban Development, 2014. *HUD Exchange*. Web. 17 June 2015.

Polakow, Valerie. *Lives on the Edge: Single Mothers and Their Children in the Other America*. Chicago: U of Chicago P, 1993. Print.

Rossi, Peter H. *Down and Out in America: The Origins of Homelessness*. Chicago: U of Chicago P, 1989. Print.

Snow, David A., and Leon Anderson. *Down on Their Luck: A Study of Homeless Street People*. Berkeley: U of California P, 1993. Print.

HORTON INCIDENT

Willie Horton, an African American man and convicted rapist and murderer, was the subject of an advertisement produced during the 1988 US presidential election campaign in support of George H. W. Bush's bid for the presidency. The advertisement is now widely regarded as a significant example of the "politics of hate" that became prevalent in political campaigning in the late 1980s and 1990s.

The thirty-second ad, which ran for twenty-eight days on cable television, was primarily used to argue that Michael Dukakis, the governor of Massachusetts and Bush's Democratic opponent in the race for president, was soft on crime. It did so by stating that Bush "support[ed] the death penalty for first-degree murder" and that Dukakis not only opposed the death penalty but also allowed first-degree murderers to have weekend passes from prison. As evidence, the ad showed a police photograph of a glaring Horton and announced that "Horton murdered a boy in a robbery, stabbing him nineteen times." The announcer continued by explaining that "despite the life sentence, Horton received ten weekend passes from prison. Horton fled, kidnapping a young couple, stabbing the man and repeatedly raping his girlfriend." While the announcer spoke, the words "kidnapping," "stabbing," and "raping" flashed on the screen. Over a final photo of Dukakis, the voiceover said, "Weekend prison passes. Dukakis on crime."

The advertisement, although not officially produced by the Bush campaign for reelection, was made by the National Security Political Action Committee (NSPAC), a political action committee that strongly supported Bush's bid for the presidency. The advertisement was widely criticized in the mass media as racist. According to one media critic, for example, the Horton advertisement was evidence of the use of the black man as a "racialized-sexualized threat to white women and white social order generally" (John Fiske's *Media Matters*, 1994). Although the script of the advertisement never mentioned race, the visual image clearly identified Horton as a menacing black man and implied, to many, that his victims were white. Despite the charges of racism in the media, Bush denied that the advertisement was racist.

————*Susan Mackey-Kallis*

BIBLIOGRAPHY AND FURTHER READING

Anderson, David C. *Crime and the Politics of Hysteria: How the Willie Horton Story Changed American Justice*. New York: Random House, 1995. Print.

Danielson, Chris. *The Color of Politics: Racism in the American Political Arena Today*. Santa Barbara: Praeger, 2013. Print.

HOUSING AND RACE RELATIONS

African Americans, historically the largest US ethnic or racial minority, have been a predominantly metropolitan-area population. As of the 2010 census, about 51 percent resided in suburbs of large metropolitan areas. In contrast, 41 percent of the white population is metropolitan, and 78 percent was suburban. In part, this reflects the historically greater degree of home ownership by whites as compared to blacks, a majority of whom have rented their homes..

The African American population has been predominantly southern; 57 percent of the African American population lived in the South in 2010. Many American blacks lived in the Northeast, slightly fewer in the Midwest, and very few in the West, with the exception of California. Whites, on the other hand, were rather evenly distributed, making up approximately 60 to 90 percent of the residents in each state in 2010. The metropolitan area with the largest African American population was New York City, with more than three million, followed by Atlanta, Georgia; Chicago, Illinois; and Washington, DC.

Hispanics, many of whom are recent immigrants, were concentrated primarily in California, New York, Florida, Texas, Illinois, and Arizona, as of 2010. Ten large metropolitan areas were home to more than half the nation's Latinos, predominantly Mexican immigrants or people of Mexican ancestry. Florida's Latino population is largely Cuban American. Puerto Ricans make up the majority of Hispanics in New York State, although Spanish-speaking immigrants from other parts of the Caribbean, such as the Dominican Republic, represent a sizable contingent.

A majority of Hispanics were metropolitan area residents. The metropolitan area with the greatest Latino population was the Los Angeles-Anaheim-Riverside area of California, which contained one-fifth of the US Hispanic population. The majority of Hispanics in the New York metropolitan area are Central and South American and Puerto Rican. Nearly 60 percent of Hispanics lived in metropolitan suburbs.

Asian Americans encompass both descendants of nineteenth- and early-twentieth-century immigrants (primarily Japanese and Chinese) as well as newcomers from nations that, until the late twentieth century, were not represented among the Asian American population (including Vietnamese, Asian Indians, and Southeast Asians). This minority includes Pacific Islanders (mostly Native Hawaiians) and Samoan and Guamanian immigrants. In 2010, 54 percent of Asian Americans were large-metropolitan-area residents, with 62 percent being suburban. Most were residents of California, New York, or Texas.

CAUSES OF RESIDENTIAL SEGREGATION

Waves of African American migrants have left the South since the early 1900's. Following World War II, a massive migration of blacks to the industrial centers of the Northeast, Midwest, and West resulted from the industrialization of southern agriculture, which displaced many tenant farmers and sharecroppers. Also, black veterans returning to the United States after World War II, having visited other areas of the country while in the military, were attracted to the job opportunities in northern factories. Consequently, in several of these cities, the numbers of African Americans doubled between 1950 and 1970.

Many strategies have been employed by whites to discourage newcomers of color from moving into white residential areas, contributing to the maintenance of residential racial segregation. History records instances of violence and other acts of intimidation in order to discourage perceived intrusions into white neighborhoods. Restrictive covenants added to property deeds were employed in order to prevent the sale of housing to minorities. In some cohesive communities, researchers have found sales and rentals of residences conducted by means of informal communications in order to avoid the use of public advertising that might result in minority applicants. Slum clearance and public housing construction in the inner city have contributed to a concentration of minority residences. Following World War II, suburbanization, stimulated by the construction of housing developments, federally guaranteed mortgages for veterans, and new highways, contributed to white flight from cities, further segregating minorities. Court-mandated school busing and black migration to cities contributed to white flight as well. Banks in many areas adopted the practice of "redlining," which resulted in the denial of mortgage loans to prospective buyers of homes in designated areas, usually racially transitional ones. Though illegal, the practice intensified the black concentration in central city areas.

Although some have suggested that African American preferences are the root cause of residential segregation, survey evidence has repeatedly indicated a preference for racially mixed neighborhoods on the part of blacks. Similar studies among whites indicate increased tolerance by whites of black residents living in their neighborhoods so long as they represent a numerical minority.

Social scientists have offered a variety of perspectives explaining the reasons for the persistence of residential segregation. Some theorists hold that the welfare system dulls incentives for minorities and the poor in general. The supposed predictability in subsistence provided by a monthly welfare check results in laziness and a lessened ambition to improve one's lot in life. Life becomes stagnant, as do the segregated neighborhoods in which these people reside.

The "culture of poverty" view, exemplified by the writings of anthropologist Oscar Lewis, holds that poverty conditions result in a general perspective that includes psychological depression and a view of life devoid of any hope of ever extricating oneself from one's predicament. A fatalism and the feeling that any efforts to improve one's life are doomed to failure result in a cycle of poverty that continues from generation to generation.

The institutional racism perspective attributes segregation to factors inherent in the institutions serving the poor in the inner city. Deteriorating, aging schools with inexperienced teachers lacking insight into ghetto life, a political institution concerned with servicing other populations in the society that are more likely to vote, an urban economy that no longer provides a living wage as low-paying service employment has replaced manufacturing jobs, and increased unemployment as jobs migrate to the suburbs have left the black population behind as society has changed.

Sociologist William Julius Wilson holds the view that the upward social mobility experienced by middle-class blacks as a consequence of the civil rights revolution resulted in community leaders moving out of ghetto neighborhoods. This development, coupled with changes in the economy that reduced employment opportunities in the central cities, leaves the poor who have not benefited from civil rights advances behind in increasingly deteriorating areas abandoned by many community businesses. The result is a racially homogeneous neighborhood characterized by crime, drug use, out-of-wedlock births, and other conditions characteristic of the underclass syndrome.

PATTERNS OF RESIDENTIAL SEGREGATION

The ethnic segregation experienced by the European immigrants of the late nineteenth and early twentieth centuries was a transient phenomenon. Financial limitations and the psychological comfort of familiar cultural surroundings resulted in formation of an ethnic ghetto in the central city. With cultural assimilation attained through education and upward social mobility, later generations attained "respectable" middle-class occupations.

Research by Nancy Denton and Douglas Massey in the late 1980s on ethnic and racial minorities indicated that this scenario has not occurred for all groups. Unlike advances made by African Americans in education and the workplace, residential segregation appeared to be a relatively permanent condition of life for a large majority of blacks. This was true across social class lines. Tract data from US censuses were used in calculating an index of dissimilarity, a statistical indicator of the proportion of the minority population that would have to move its census tract residence in order for proportional residential "evenness" or integration to occur. The researchers used data from sixty metropolitan areas that contained the largest populations of blacks, Latinos (termed Hispanics), and Asians.

Denton and Massey's findings indicated that for the twenty metropolitan areas containing the largest black populations, residential segregation from whites was high regardless of black social class. Social class was measured using income, education, and occupational status, each of which was examined independently. Segregation indexes declined for blacks of higher social class but remained high. Cleveland, Detroit, and Chicago exhibited the highest degree of black/white residential segregation; Washington, D.C., and San Francisco, the lowest. The authors pointed out that unlike earlier European immigrants who lived in relatively heterogeneous neighborhoods, an overwhelming majority of blacks live in racially homogeneous neighborhoods. This segregation has been relatively impervious to advances in social mobility and has not been transitory. Federal efforts such as the Fair Housing Act of 1968, an outgrowth of the urban disorders of the 1960's, have had little impact on this phenomenon.

Significantly smaller proportions of blacks than Hispanics and Asians lived in suburbs. Data indicated that suburban blacks received somewhat higher incomes than those residing in the inner city. The degree of residential racial segregation experienced by African Americans across class lines indicated that a high proportion of the black middle class in the suburbs lived under segregated conditions, as did their urban counterparts.

For Hispanics, in contrast to blacks, the index of dissimilarity was moderate, even for those in the lowest categories of social class. For US-born Hispanics, descendants of immigrants (for research purposes, Puerto Ricans are treated as immigrants, although they are US citizens), the segregation index declined with upward social mobility. For Latinos, in fact, increased education resulted in sharp declines in segregation, indicating a general acceptance by non-Hispanic whites of middle-class Latinos as neighbors. This decline was particularly true in Miami, where the Latino population is predominantly Cuban American and white, and in Los Angeles, where the great majority of Latinos are of Mexican ancestry. This was less the case in New York City and Newark, New Jersey, where the majority of Hispanics are of Puerto Rican descent. This Hispanic population was more segregated from whites than from blacks. Puerto Ricans are the only one of the three Hispanic populations with significant, readily-identifiable African ancestry; this may indicate that they are experiencing color prejudice, consistent with the findings for African Americans.

Federal housing studies of the residential accommodations of blacks and Latinos produced findings consistent with those groups' lower socioeconomic status. In contrast with medians for the total US population, these minorities inhabited smaller living quarters, shared fewer square feet per person, were less likely to have air conditioning, lived in homes that were more likely to be older, and lived in areas with streets or roads that were more likely to be in need of repair. Respondents from both minorities rated their neighborhoods lower as environments in which to live.

Asian Americans (including Pacific Islanders), although racially distinct from whites, experienced reduced segregation with attainment of higher class status. Middle-class Asian Americans appeared to be undergoing a minority immigration experience not unlike that of the European immigrants who arrived near the beginning of the twentieth century, although they did not seem to be forming ethnic enclaves to the same extent as the European immigrants did. Most lived in ethnically heterogeneous neighborhoods. In general, the dominant white population did not appear to object to sharing communities with upwardly mobile Asian Americans.

CONSEQUENCES OF RESIDENTIAL SEGREGATION

In addition to exacerbating such urban ghetto problems as poor schools, crime, and illegal drug use, residential segregation serves to limit communication between groups and, thus, precludes cooperation between populations in solving common problems. Separation promotes distrust, feelings of hostility, and occasionally open conflict. African Americans are segregated not only from whites but also from Asian Americans and most Hispanic Americans. For African Americans, attainment of higher education and other criteria of middle-class status do not readily translate into either acceptance as neighbors by the dominant whites or attendance at newly built, quality suburban schools by their children. Furthermore, homogeneous black neighborhoods are often perceived by political and economic powers as areas that can be sacrificed when new roads are to be built or when undesirable municipal facilities are to be erected. In addition, the ability of relatively few blacks to attain the American Dream divides the dominant whites from the largest US racial or ethnic minority and breeds continual intergroup tensions.

AMERICAN INDIAN POPULATION

As of the 2010 US census, about 22 percent of American Indians, or Native Americans, and Alaska Natives lived on reservations; however, there is substantial movement by Indians to and from reservations. American Indians do not make up a sufficiently large population to establish enclaves equivalent to the ethnic communities of other minorities, so most urban Indians have resided in heterogeneous working-class neighborhoods. Movement to the city is ordinarily for economic reasons. Returning to the reservation is often caused by loss of employment or to secure health care from the Bureau of Indian Affairs' Indian Health Service. According to the 2013 American Community Survey, roughly 29 percent of American Indians and Alaska Natives were living in poverty, 8.5 percent were unemployed, and 42 percent were not in the labor force; just over half lived in owner-occupied housing as opposed to rental units. For many, reservation life involves overcrowded conditions, substandard housing, and lack of adequate sanitation. Government housing and mortgage programs administered by some of the individual tribes have made it easier for new home building and home improvements, and income from gaming (gambling) has promised to do more, but many American Indians are simply too poor to consider new housing, even with the help of these agencies.

——*Edward V. Mednick*

BIBLIOGRAPHY AND FURTHER READING

Denton, Nancy, and Douglas Massey. "Residential Segregation of Blacks, Hispanics, and Asians by Socioeconomic Status and Generation." *Social Science Quarterly* 69.4 (1988): 797. Print.

Brooks, Richard Rexford Wayne, and Carol M. Rose. *Saving the Neighborhood: Racially Restrictive Covenants, Law, and Social Norms.* Cambridge: Harvard UP, 2013. Print.

Brown, Adrienne, and Valerie Smith, eds. *Race and Real Estate.* New York: Oxford UP, 2016. Print.

Frey, William H. *Melting Pot Cities and Suburbs: Racial and Ethnic Change in Metro America in the 2000s.* Washington: Metropolitan Policy Program, Brookings Institution, May 2011. PDF file.

Frey, William H. *The New Metro Minority Map: Regional Shifts in Hispanics, Asians, and Blacks from Census 2010.*v Washington: Metropolitan Policy Program, Brookings Institution, Aug. 2011. PDF file.

Jonas, Andrew E. G., Mary E. Thomas, and Eugene McCann. *Urban Geography: A Critical Introduction.* Chichester: Wiley, 2015. Print.

Taylor, Dorceta. "The Rise of Racially Restrictive Covenants: Guarding against Infiltration." *Toxic Communities: Environmental Racism, Industrial Pollution, and Residential Mobility.* New York: New York UP, 2014. 192–227. Print.

HUMAN RIGHTS ACT

Canada's Bill C-25, the Human Rights Act—first read in the House of Commons November 29, 1976, and first read in the Senate June 6, 1977—received the Royal Assent July 14, 1977, and was proclaimed to be in force August 10, 1977. The act was revised and expanded in 1985 to provide for those with physical disabilities and to clarify issues involving sexual harassment, the elderly, and women on maternity leave.

PROVISIONS OF THE ACT

The Canadian Human Rights Act extends the laws that proscribe discrimination and that protect the privacy of individuals. The law is premised on the notion that every person should have an opportunity equal to that of other persons to make for himself or herself the life that he or she is able and wishes to have, consistent with his or her duties and obligations as a member of society, without being hindered in or prevented from doing so by discriminatory practices based on race, national or ethnic origin, color, religion, age, sex, marital status, or conviction for an offense for which a pardon has been granted. The privacy of individuals, and their right of access to records containing personal information concerning them for any purpose, including the purpose of ensuring accuracy and completeness, should be protected to the greatest extent consistent with the public interest.

Part 1 of the Canadian Human Rights Act defines discrimination as the denial of goods, services, facilities, or accommodations customarily available to the general public. In employment, it is discriminatory to refuse to employ, to refuse to continue to employ, or to differentiate adversely in the course of employment. Part 1, Section 11, requires that equal wages be paid to men and women for equal work value, based on skill, effort, and responsibility.

Part 2 of the act created the Canadian Human Rights Commission to administer the Canadian

Human Rights Act and to ensure that the principles of equal opportunity and nondiscrimination are followed within the areas of federal jurisdiction. This commission is composed of two full-time and six part-time commissioners. The commission is authorized to investigate complaints of discrimination in employment and in the provision of services, and complaints alleging inequities in pay between men and women based on equal work. The commission monitors annual reports filed by federally regulated employers under the Employment Equity Act, and programs, policies, and legislation affecting women, aboriginal peoples, visible minorities, and persons with disabilities, to ensure that their human rights are protected. It also develops and conducts information programs to promote public understanding of the Canadian Human Rights Act and the commission's activities.

Part 3 of the Canadian Human Rights Act explains the procedures to be used when a complaint is filed with the Canadian Human Rights Commission. Upon receipt of a complaint, the commission first determines whether or not its agency is the correct one to handle the complaint. The complaint is either accepted for investigation by the commission or sent to another federal agency for appropriate action. If the commission accepts the complaint for investigation, every effort is made to reach an early settlement between the two parties. If the complaint cannot be settled, the commission prepares an investigative report requesting the appointment of a conciliator to arbitrate the dispute.

If conciliation cannot be reached, the case is returned to the commission for a decision either to dismiss the case or to refer it to a human rights tribunal. A tribunal hearing results in a written decision, binding on all parties. Tribunal decisions may be appealed to a review tribunal or to the federal courts. In some discrimination cases, Canada's Supreme Court makes the final decision. Remedies for complainants include reinstatement and/or compensation for lost wages, letters of apology, or the issuance of antiharassment policy by an employer. The Canadian Human Rights Act provides for fines of up to fifty thousand dollars for threatening, intimidating, or discriminating against an individual who has filed a complaint, or for hampering the investigation process.

ADMINISTRATIVE STRUCTURE

The act authorized the Canadian Human Rights Commission to create an administrative structure to administer the Human Rights Act. By 1994, the Canadian Human Rights Commission had delegated to the Office of the Secretary General of the Human Rights Commission the authority to oversee staff at headquarters and regional offices that investigate discrimination complaints throughout the country, except those dealing with employment and pay equity.

The secretary general's office provides support to the Canadian Human Rights Commission and its seven specialized branch agencies: the Legal Services Branch, which represents the commission before tribunals, review tribunals, and the courts; the Anti-Discrimination Programs Branch, which handles all complaints filed with the commission, except employment and pay equity complaints; the Employment and Pay Equity Branch, which advises the Human Rights Commission on employment and pay equity matters, offers educational programs to employers and community groups, and investigates and conciliates equal pay complaints; the Policy and Planning Branch, which monitors and researches domestic and international human rights issues of interest to the commission; the Communications Branch, which explains the role and activities of the commission, discourages discriminatory practices, and fosters public understanding of the act; the Corporate Services Branch, which provides headquarters and regional operations with support services; and the Personnel Services Branch, which provides headquarters and regional operations with support services in pay, benefits, staffing, resource planning, and health and safety.

COMPLAINTS AND RECOMMENDATIONS

Between 1985 and 1994, the Canadian Human Rights Commission received 464,535 inquiries. Actual complaints filed between 1991 and 1994 totaled 4,852, including all referrals to alternate redress. For the years 1991 to 1994, based on the number of discrimination complaints filed, the types of complaints were ranked in the following order: disability, sex, national or ethnic origin, race or color, family or marital status, age, religion, and discrimination after being pardoned. In the same years, the ranking order of methods of disposition of complaints was dismissal, settlement approved by all parties and the commission, sent to conciliation, no further proceedings, and early resolution.

The 1995 Canadian Human Rights Commission's annual report recommended the following changes: that amendments to the Canadian Human Rights Act be adopted to prohibit discrimination based on sexual orientation, to protect the human rights of Canada's aboriginal population, and to allow anyone present in Canada, not just those lawfully present, the right to file a discrimination complaint; that the commission report directly to Parliament instead of the Department of Justice and the Treasury Board; that a permanent appeals tribunal be established to replace the existing system of ad hoc tribunals and review tribunals; that a mandatory retirement age be considered a discriminatory action; and that employers under federal jurisdiction be required to take the initiative in eliminating sex-based inequities from their compensation systems. These recommendations would enable the Canadian Human Rights Act to

provide the same protection against discrimination currently institutionalized in the Canadian Charter of Rights and Freedoms, international practice, and provincial legislation.

——*William A. Paquette*

BIBLIOGRAPHY AND FURTHER READING

Acts of the Parliament of Canada. Vol. 2. Ottawa: Queen's Printer, 1976–77. Print.

Canadian Human Rights Commission. *Annual Report, 1994.* Ottawa: Minister of Supply and Service Canada, 1995. Print.

Eliadis, F. Pearl. *Speaking Out on Human Rights: Debating Canada's Human Rights System.* Montreal: MQUP, 2014. *eBook Collection (EBSCOhost).* Web. 24 Apr. 2015.

House of Commons Debates, Official Report. Vol. 3. Ottawa: Queen's Printer, 1976–77. Print.

Revised Statutes of Canada, 1985. Vol. 5. Ottawa: Queen's Printer, 1985. Print.

HURRICANE KATRINA AND FEMA'S RESPONSE

More than a year before Hurricane Katrina hit New Orleans in August 2005, the Federal Emergency Management Agency (FEMA) estimated that one-third to one-half of the population of New Orleans would not be able to evacuate the city in time if a Category 3 hurricane hit the city. FEMA planned to institute several sweeping changes in their current aid and disaster relief programs based on their findings. Nevertheless, when a scenario similar to the one predicted occurred, FEMA seemed to be unprepared. Many people have claimed that, despite FEMA's lack of preparedness, the poor response to Hurricane Katrina represented a failing in all levels of the government, rather than a single agency, and that lack of communication between different agencies caused the ultimate breakdown in relief efforts. The result was the costliest natural disaster in US history.

Many people accused FEMA Director Michael Brown of having insufficient experience in disaster management, but President George W. Bush attracted significant ire, as well, based on what many perceived as a flippant and opportunistic attitude toward the

disaster. He was roundly mocked for a comment made during a press conference, saying that Brown—who Bush referred to as "Brownie"—was "doing a heck of a job." Many people pointed out that, despite significant warning of an impending hurricane, FEMA had not made plans for how to evacuate people, reinforce the levees, or ship supplies to survivors. New Orleans has a large population of low-income people without access to cars, who were unable to evacuate on their own. Thus, what seemed to be a slow reaction to the disaster looked to many people like class and race discrimination.

Hurricane Katrina was the first major disaster—natural or man-made—that fell under the jurisdiction of the Department of Homeland Security (DHS). After the lack of adequate response to Hurricane Katrina, many people questioned the efficacy of DHS and wondered how it would respond to an unannounced attack, when it was clear that it was incapable of managing a predicted disaster such as Hurricane Katrina. In the fallout after Katrina, FEMA was scrutinized by the media and the public, and many found fault with its handling of prior disasters. For example, it was discovered that, after Hurricane Frances, which hit Florida in 2004, FEMA paid $31 million to residents of Miami-Dade County, which was one of the few areas of Florida that had not been hit by the storm.

HISTORY

Despite FEMA's fairly narrow aim, once it became part of DHS in 2003, 75 percent of its budget was dedicated to anti-terrorism, according to the Government Accountability Office (GAO). Many have criticized this reallocation as incompatible with FEMA's mission, though some critics have said that natural disasters require the same skills and the same actions as terrorist attacks or any other disaster, and thus the placement of FEMA under the DHS umbrella was appropriate.

In July 2004, FEMA conducted an exercise to determine the effect that a Category 3 hurricane, with 120-mile-per-hour winds, would have on New Orleans. The exercise, called Hurricane Pam, was remarkably prescient, predicting that water from Lake Pontchartrain would overwhelm the levees, flooding much of the city and damaging 87 percent of the city's homes. FEMA also predicted that about half of the New Orleans population would evacuate prior to the flooding. The results of the Hurricane Pam exercise showed that a comprehensive plan would have to be instituted to avoid the predicted outcome. At that time, director Michael Brown noted the importance of planning in Louisiana and said "Over the next sixty days, we will polish the action plans developed during the Hurricane Pam exercise."

More than a year later, on August 29, 2005, Hurricane Katrina struck Louisiana. The storm had already hit Florida but had since moved back out into the Gulf of Mexico and gained strength, becoming a Category 4 storm. The 145-mile-per-hour winds and 28-foot waves overwhelmed the 17.5-foot New Orleans levees, flooding parts of the city almost immediately. About five hours after this first strike, Brown sent a request to DHS Director Michael Chertoff for 1,000 additional aid workers over the next two days, followed by 2,000 more in the following week. The memo, which eventually was leaked to the Associated Press, seemed to illustrate that Brown had underestimated the severity of the disaster.

Displaced New Orleans residents were housed in the city's football stadium called the Superdome for three days before buses arrived to take them to Houston. Additionally, there were thousands of people who had sought refuge in the New Orleans Convention Center, which Brown claimed not to know about until September 1, three days after the storm hit. He later admitted FEMA had known about the Convention Center evacuees on August 31 but was unable to take action until the following day.

In response to the agency's slow reaction time, DHS Director Michael Chertoff announced that the monetary aid delivery process would be streamlined, in order to prevent further delays. Thus, rather than the standard procedure of sending a FEMA official personally assess the damage at each home, the agency allowed people to apply for aid over the phone or online. To further circumvent the logistical problems inherent in distributing large quantities of cash or checks, FEMA and the Red Cross distributed thousands of debit cards valued at $2,000 to victims of the disaster. Nevertheless, the monetary distribution proved to be more difficult to manage than anyone had anticipated. Despite instructions that the debit cards only be used for necessities, such as food and clothing, in September 2005 it was reported that many of the victims who had received government-funded debit cards were using them to buy luxury items.

After distributing more than 10,000 debit cards, with a total value of $20.6 million, FEMA discontinued the program but did not recall the cards that had already been distributed. It also eventually became clear that much of $1.46 billion distributed was given to people and families who either were not affected by the hurricane or had already received their share of the aid. In one New Orleans–area parish, FEMA distributed money to 224,008 applicants, despite there only being about 182,120 households in the parish; this resulted in an apparent overpayment of $83.8 million. In parts of Mississippi, more than 2,000 families that were not displaced by the storm managed to collect funds from FEMA. Inland towns in Louisiana, far from the damage of the hurricane, received upwards of $1.6 million dollars for its residents. Following these revelations, DHS created the Office for Hurricane Katrina Oversight, which was charged with auditing FEMA-distributed funds.

Shortly after the debit card program was discontinued, Brown stepped down from his position at FEMA, and the agency began instead to deposit money directly in victims' bank accounts. Brown was mocked in the media even following his dismissal; many outlets pointed out that Brown's most significant management experience prior to working at FEMA was supervising horse-show judges and that he had only gotten the job at FEMA because the former director had been a friend of his.

Many people have argued that the blame heaped on FEMA is unfair, since there were numerous failings by numerous parties during the disaster. Amtrak officials have claimed that they contacted local authorities to offer free space on a train, with room for several hundred people, which left New Orleans several hours before the hurricane hit, but were turned down. New Orleans Mayor Ray Nagin denies this offer was ever extended, but there were also reports of unused school buses, abandoned in parking lots, which some say could have been used to evacuate residents. The Red Cross was repeatedly denied access to the city by state officials, first on Thursday, September 1, and then again on the following day, despite possessing adequate supplies and workers to provide necessary aid. Louisiana officials claimed they needed twenty-four hours to set up escorts for the Red Cross workers, but once that time had elapsed, they had already begun evacuating residents. President Bush eventually sent 11,000 active duty troops to help in the relief effort, but not until five days after the hurricane hit, by which point 21,000 National Guard troops were already in place.

FEMA/HURRICANE KATRINA TODAY

According to documents released in December 2005, FEMA officials realized early on that their response was lacking and that their emergency supplies were inadequate. The documents, consisting of correspondence between several FEMA officials and the governors of Mississippi and Louisiana, showed that FEMA realized as early as September 1 that its shipments of water and ice were vastly insufficient. The spokesperson for FEMA admitted that the agency's technology and logistics were insufficient, and Homeland Security Director Michael Chertoff emphasized that updating and repairing the agency would be one of his priorities. In April 2006, the DHS inspector general said that most of the criticism leveled at FEMA

for the mismanaged response to Katrina is warranted and made nearly forty suggestions for improving both FEMA and DHS.

In April 2006, President Bush asked Congress to approve an additional $2.2 billion—to come from FEMA's disaster relief fund—to continue the repairs on New Orleans levees. In June 2006, with the next hurricane season looming, DHS declared that New Orleans was not prepared for another disaster.

As of 2007, FEMA was still distributing funds to displaced residents of Louisiana and Mississippi. Despite the overpayments that FEMA made to many families, much of the money allocated for Katrina relief (about $5.1 billion in Louisiana alone) had not found its way into the hands of displaced persons, many of whom were facing eviction, unemployment, and massive reconstruction costs. In January 2007, Louisiana officials appealed to FEMA to distribute the remainder of the money allotted to them, which amounted to about $3 billion.

In late 2008, FEMA stated in a press release that funding to Louisiana for Hurricanes Katrina and Rita totaling $13.7 billion had been spent on relief to individuals, public entities, and for mitigation of hazards. $2.04 billion was spent in 2008 alone. At the height of the disaster about 92,000 families were housed in temporary housing trailers or mobile homes. At the end of 2008, about 26,000 remained in temporary housing. At the same time, reports surfaced of additional problems and needed improvements for one $849 million Katrina relief program. The program was designed to help Louisiana landlords rebuild. These landlords had been unable to access loans to because of the 2008 financial crisis and government bureaucracy. The program, called the Louisiana Small Rental Program, was supposed to result in the restoration of 18,000 rental properties but had only let 433 grants by year end 2008. The goal of the program changes was to reduce bureaucracy by giving money directly to landlords though some government agencies feared yet again duplication of another relief program.

——*Alex K. Rich and Marlanda English*

BIBLIOGRAPHY AND FURTHER READING

Birkland, Thomas A. *Lessons of Disaster: Policy Change after Catastrophic Events.* Washington, DC: Georgetown UP, 2006. Print.

Childs, John Brown, ed. *Hurricane Katrina: Response and Responsibilities.* Santa Cruz: New Pacific, 2005. Print.

Dyson, Michael Eric. *Come Hell or High Water: Hurricane Katrina and the Color of Disaster.* New York: Basic Civitas, 2006. Print.

Farber, Daniel A., and Jim Chen. *Disasters and the Law: Katrina and Beyond.* New York: Aspen, 2006. Print.

Lindell, Michael K., Carla Prater, and Ronald W. Perry. *Introduction to Emergency Management.* Hoboken: Wiley, 2007. Print.

Mann, Eric. *Katrina's Legacy: White Racism and Black Reconstruction in New Orleans and the Gulf Coast.* Los Angeles: Frontlines, 2006. Print.

Reed, Betsy, ed. *Unnatural Disaster: The Nation on Hurricane Katrina.* New York: Nation, 2006. Print.

HYMIETOWN STATEMENT

In January of 1984, the Reverend Jesse Jackson labeled Jews as "Hymies" and referred to New York City as "Hymietown." These comments were made in the presence of black journalists following Jackson's presidential election campaign. One of the journalists, Milton Coleman, relayed Jackson's comments to his associates at *The Washington Post.* The remarks were printed weeks later, buried deep within a broader article discussing Jackson's attitudes on foreign policy, particularly Israeli-Palestinian conflict in the Middle East. Initially, neither the article nor Jackson's slurs garnered much attention. However, on February 18 of that year, *The Washington Post* ran an editorial denouncing Jackson's comments, thus triggering national media attention.

Jackson first denied making the remarks and claimed that Jews were conspiring to defeat his campaign. He later acknowledged making the comments and apologized, asking a group of national Jewish leaders for forgiveness in a Manchester, New Hampshire, synagogue shortly before the state's election primary. Jackson then publicly questioned whether this isolated incident should dismantle the progress made in Jewish–African American relations. He argued that the remarks did not reflect his basic attitudes toward Jews or Israel, and continued to invite Jews to join his Rainbow Coalition, an organization comprising oppressed groups.

——*Scott A. Melzer*

BIBLIOGRAPHY AND FURTHER READING

Dinnerstein, Leonard. *Antisemitism in America.* New York: Oxford UP, 1995. Print.

Hirschorn, Michael W. "Jesse and the Jews." *Harvard Crimson.* Harvard Crimson, 5 Mar. 1984. Web. 30 Apr. 2015.

"Rev. Jesse Jackson on Principles & Values." *On the Issues.* OnTheIssues.org, 5 Jul. 2014. Web. 30 Apr. 2015.

Sabato, Larry J. "Jesse Jackson's 'Hymietown' Remark—1984." *Feeding Frenzy.* Washington Post, 1998. Web. 30 Apr. 2015.

Tapper, Jake. "Don't Ask, Don't Tell." *Salon.* Salon Media Group, 16 Aug. 2000. Web. 30 Apr. 2015.

HYPERSEGREGATION

The term "hypersegregation" refers to the excessive physical and social separation of a class, ethnic, or racial group by forcing the group, usually through institutional arrangements, to reside in a limited area or neighborhood with low-quality educational facilities and few economic opportunities.

According to sociologists Norman A. Anderson and Cheryl Armstead, many minority group members, especially African Americans and Latinos who live in large metropolitan areas in the United States, experience hypersegregation. This phenomenon creates a state of extreme isolation from resources that allow people to improve their social and economic well-being. The isolation also diminishes people's ability to obtain adequate health care and thus negatively affects their health.

Hypersegregation is the result of a number of factors, one of the most prominent being pervasive

Sign for "colored" waiting room at a Greyhound bus terminal in Rome, Georgia, 1943. By Esther Bubley.

how likely minority and majority group members are to come in contact with one another; *clustering*, or whether minority neighborhoods are distributed throughout the city or grouped together in one large ghetto; *centralization*, or how many minority group members reside in urban centers rather than more affluent suburbs; and *concentration*, or the physical space occupied per minority group member. Low degrees of evenness and exposure and high degrees of clustering, centralization, and concentration are all indicators of segregation. Hypersegregation, according to Massey and Denton, is when several of these dimensions occur at once.

——*Gwenelle S. O'Neal*

BIBLIOGRAPHY AND FURTHER READING

Denton, Nancy A. "Segregation and Discrimination in Housing." *A Right to Housing: Foundation for a New Social Agenda*. Ed. Rachel G. Bratt, Michael E. Stone, and Chester Hartman. Philadelphia: Temple UP, 2006. 61–81. Print.

Massey, Douglas S., and Nancy A. Denton. "Hypersegregation in US Metropolitan Areas: Black and Hispanic Segregation along Five Dimensions." *Demography* 26.3 (1989): 373–91. Print.

Oliver, J. Eric. *The Paradoxes of Integration: Race, Neighborhood, and Civic Life in Multiethnic America*. Chicago: U of Chicago P, 2010. Print.

Wilkes, Rima, and John Iceland. "Hypersegregation in the Twenty-First Century." *Demography* 41.1 (2004): 23–36. Print.

housing discrimination against low-income minority group members. Noted sociologist William J. Wilson has shown that low-income people of color are more likely to live in impoverished residential areas than are low-income white Americans.

In 1989, sociologists Douglas Massey and Nancy Denton established five dimensions of segregation: *evenness*, or how well the percentage of minority group members in residential areas reflects their percentage of the city's population; *exposure*, or

HYPODESCENT

The rule of hypodescent is a social mechanism that determines racial group membership of the offspring of interracial unions between European Americans and Americans of color. It defines this membership based exclusively on the background of color (including Native American, Asian American, Pacific Islander American, Latino, and African American).

The dominant European Americans began enforcing rules of hypodescent beginning in the late 1600s in order to draw social distinctions between themselves and the subordinate groups of color.

However, the rule of hypodescent has historically been such an accepted part of the American fabric that its oppressive origins have often been obscured. The rule was implemented primarily in the area of interracial sexual relations, more specifically interracial marriages, in order to preserve white racial "purity." However, it has also helped maintain white racial privilege by supporting other legal and informal barriers to racial equality in most aspects of social life. These barriers have existed in public facilities and various areas of the public sphere (political, economic, educational), as well as the private sphere (residential, associational, interpersonal). At the turn of the twentieth century, these restrictions reached extreme proportions with the institutionalization of Jim Crow segregation.

The rule of hypodescent has been applied to differing degrees to the first-generation offspring of European Americans and Americans of color. In regard to later generations of individuals whose lineage has included a background of color along with European ancestry, however, the rule has been more flexible. These individuals have not invariably been designated exclusively, or even partially, as members of that group of color if the background is less than one-fourth of their lineage. Furthermore, self-identification with that background has been more a matter of choice.

This flexibility has not been extended to individuals of African American and European American descent. The first-generation offspring of interracial relationships between African Americans and European Americans, as well as later generations of individuals whose lineage has included African American and European American ancestry, have experienced the most restrictive rule of hypodescent: the one-drop rule. This mechanism designates as black everyone with any amount of African American ancestry ("one drop of blood"). It precludes any notion of choice in self-identification and ensures that all future offspring with African American ancestry are socially designated as black. Furthermore, the one-drop rule is unique to the United States and is specifically applied to Americans of African descent. It emerged in the late seventeenth and early eighteenth centuries as a means of increasing the number of slaves. The one-drop rule also exempted white landowners (particularly slaveholders) from the legal obligation of passing on inheritance and other benefits of paternity to their multiracial offspring.

American attitudes toward the offspring of unions between African Americans and other groups of color (for example, Native Americans) have varied. More often than not, these individuals have been subject to the one-drop rule. Greater ambivalence has been displayed toward offspring whose ancestry has combined other backgrounds of color (for example, Mexican American/Asian American or Native American/Mexican American), partly because these other groups of color occupy a more ambiguous position in the racial hierarchy than that of African Americans. Also, membership in these groups—except perhaps in the case of Native Americans—has been less clearly defined in US law. Consequently, the racial subordination of Americans of color by European Americans, while similarly oppressive, has not been exactly the same. This makes it more difficult to assess intergroup relations among groups of color in terms of the rule of hypodescent.

In the 1960s and 1970s, the United States generally repudiated notions of racial "purity" that had supported the ideology of white supremacy. Many European Americans, nevertheless, continued to maintain notions of white racial exclusivity and privilege originating in the rule of hypodescent. Alternately, the rule of hypodescent paradoxically has had some unintended consequences. Its purpose was to draw boundaries solidifying subordinated racial identity and excluding Americans of color from having contact with European Americans as equals. However, it has also legitimated and forged group identity, which in turn has formed the basis for mass mobilization and collective action among groups of color in the struggle against racial inequality. These dynamics have thus helped reinforce, even if unintentionally, the notion that European Americans (and whiteness) and Americans of color are categories of experience that are mutually exclusive, if not hierarchical, and that have an objective and independent existence of their own.

—G. Reginald Daniel

BIBLIOGRAPHY AND FURTHER READING

Brown, Kevin D. "The Rise and Fall of the One-Drop Rule: How the Importance of Color Came to Eclipse Race." *Color Matters: Skin Tone Bias and the Myth of a Post-Racial America*. Ed. Kimberly Jade Norwood. New York: Routledge, 2014. 44–94. Print.

Davis, F. James. *Who Is Black? One Nation's Definition*. 10th anniv. ed. University Park: Pennsylvania State UP, 2001. Print.

Dawkins, Marcia Alesan. *Clearly Invisible: Racial Passing and the Color of Cultural Identity*. Waco: Baylor UP, 2012. Print.

Lee, Jennifer, and Frank D. Bean. *The Diversity Paradox: Immigration and the Color Line in 21st Century America*. New York: Sage, 2010. Print.

Murji, Karim, and John Solomos, eds. *Theories of Race and Ethnicity: Contemporary Debates and Perspectives.* Cambridge: Cambridge UP, 2015. Print.

Sweet, Frank W. *Legal History of the Color Line: The Notion of Invisible Blackness.* Palm Coast: Backintyme, 2005. Print.

HYPOGAMY

The marriage of a woman to a man in a lower social stratum is designated "hypogamy." In an article entitled "Intermarriage and the Social Structure" (*Psychiatry*, 1941), sociologist Robert Merton described interracial marriage involving a black husband and a white wife as—given the racial hierarchy in the United States—hypogamous. Because marriages typically consist of persons within a given group (endogamy), marriage outside a given group (exogamy) calls for theoretical explanation. Hypogamy also contradicts the traditional cross-cultural patterns of homogamy (marriage consisting of persons who share similarities) and its frequent alternative, hypergamy (marriage of women upward). Anthropologists argue that hypergamy is a cultural universal because men have typically been the breadwinners and women tend to seek as much prestige and financial support for themselves and their children as possible. In general, occupation has been the route to upward social mobility for men. Hypergamy, in a sexist society that deters women from entering many occupations, is one avenue to higher status.

Merton hypothesized that hypogamy occurs because white women of lower economic background trade their higher racial rank for the relatively elevated economic station of a (racially) lower-ranked African American man. Research has shown, however, that many biracial couples manifest educational and economic homogamy and marry for the same reasons that endogamous couples do.

——*Gil Richard Musolf*

I

IDENTIFICATION ASSIMILATION

"Identification assimilation" is the fourth of sociologist Milton Gordon's seven stages of assimilation of minority groups into a host society. At this stage, members of a minority group, usually newly arrived immigrants, develop a sense of peoplehood based exclusively on the host society, acquiring the memories, sentiments, and attitudes of people of the dominant culture. Assimilation of immigrants into American society provides a good example. Although racial, ethnic, and religious identity may or may not change, assimilating groups, when they reach this stage, identify themselves exclusively with the members of the host society.

The speed and number of generations required for identification assimilation vary among different racial and ethnic groups, depending upon their socioeconomic status, rate of interracial or interethnic marriage, and degree of prejudice and discrimination against them. First-generation immigrants, usually foreign-born, have difficulties achieving this stage because of cultural differences, lack of integration with mainstream Americans at the primary level of socialization, and prejudice and discrimination. Most subgroups of European Americans, descendants of immigrants between the post-colonial period and the early 1900s, have achieved identification assimilation regardless of their ethnic background. However, numerous barriers—economic, cultural, and educational, among others—have prevented some members of other racial and ethnic groups, such as African, Asian, Hispanic, and Native Americans, from achieving the same degree of identification assimilation as European Americans.

——*Hisako Matsuo*

IDEOLOGICAL RACISM

Ideological racism is a system of beliefs in or assertions of the genetic and/or cultural inferiority of dominated racial groups. Incorporated into eugenics theories, into social scientist Daniel Patrick Moynihan's notion of "cultural deficiency" in *The Negro Family: The Case for National Action* (1965), into appeals to the Bible by some Christian fundamentalists, and into racist stereotypes held by Americans in general, ideological racism sustains white Americans' certainty that their advantages and unequal share of resources have been achieved meritoriously, thereby legitimizing both their privileges and the deprivations suffered by minorities. Ideological racism functions to blame the victims for their misery and to shunt attention away from the social circumstances of both the well-off and the impoverished that reproduce their respective superior and inferior social statuses. For example, Moynihan's report counseled "benign neglect" rather than governmental action to assist African Americans. Europeans conceptualized race as an ideology to justify colonization. They conquered, enslaved, and committed genocide remorselessly, believing non-Europeans were inferiors or members of subhuman species. Almost all scientists today discredit ideological racism and affirm the equal humanity of all racial and ethnic groups.

——*Gil Richard Musolf*

IMMIGRANT ADVANTAGE

The term "immigrant advantage" is used by sociologists to refer to a set of distinctions between minority groups that reside within a society and those peoples who immigrate to these societies voluntarily from other nations. Resident minority groups are often "marginalized," living on the fringe of society, often in poverty, lacking education, occupational skills, political power, or the means to integrate into the mainstream. These marginalized groups, like the immigrants, are frequently composed of ethnic and racial minorities.

However, compared with marginalized groups, immigrants have numerous advantages and often become successful, productive members of a society. One of the primary advantages is that immigrants *choose* to move to a new country and are therefore motivated to succeed. Another advantage is that they often have the resources needed to relocate to a new country; the immigration services work hard at keeping out low-skilled, and less educated immigrants. A third advantage is that immigrants tend to believe in the "great melting pot" ideal and want to join the mainstream society and learn the new language. To become citizens of the United States, for example, immigrants must speak, read, and write English and pass an exam on US history and government. Therefore, although immigrants may start on the lowest rungs of the economic ladder, they often move up quickly, unlike marginalized resident minorities.

——*Rochelle L. Dalla*

IMMIGRANT BASHING

Since the dawn of history most societies have demonstrated hostility toward "the other." The Ancient Greeks for instance, labelled anyone of a different ethnic group with the pejorative "barbarian." This hostility toward the unknown or foreign often manifested itself in genocide or enslavement. As populations boomed and nation-states composed of multiple ethnicities and cultures began to emerge in the eighteenth and nineteenth centuries, hostility toward immigrants became an ever more common and complex phenomenon.

In the United States for instance, few ethnic groups were spared hostility or attack. As each new wave of immigrants entered the country, immigrant bashing, as it came to be known, was employed by those groups that had come earlier and had managed to establish and acculturate themselves. Those considered new were viewed as "un-American." These individuals and groups were often characterized as criminals, as spreading disease, and as a burden to greater society.

When the Irish began to immigrate to the United States in the nineteenth century, they were famously depicted as being violent and alcoholic. These xenophobic stereotypes were spread by regular people fearful of foreigners who did not seem like them, and even by public officials hoping to use anti-immigrant sentiment to garner votes. This mix of casual and official immigrant bashing resulted in widespread discrimination of Irish immigrants, often barred from jobs and housing solely on the basis of their ethnicity. For decades the Irish were depicted as little more than animals, and were not considered to be of the same race by many native white Americans. The fact that most Irish were Catholic only exacerbated ethnic hatred. These biases continued well into the twentieth century.

German immigrants to the United States came to be the focus of immigrant bashing at the turn of the century, as German beer-hall culture found itself at odds with the growing prohibition movement. With the outbreak of World War I, attacks on Americans of German decent and recent arrivals from Germany became part government policy, as German immigrants were often suspected of being secret agents working on behalf of the German war effort. Germans were depicted as bloodthirsty monsters or traitors, lurking in the shadows. Former president Theodore Roosevelt even went so far as to denounce German "hyphenated Americanism" declaring duel loyalties to be tantamount to treason.

A more recent example is that of Japanese immigrant bashing. Although Japanese immigrants to the United States had been discriminated against

Mexican immigrants march for more rights in Northern California's largest city, San Jose (2006). By z2amiller.

since the nineteenth century, a new wave of Japanese bashing erupted in 1941 after forces of the Japanese Imperial Navy attacked the American base at Pearl Harbor. As had been the case with the Irish and Germans, the Japanese came to be depicted as monsters, and discrimination became part of official government policy. Despite the fact that the United States was at war with Germany, Italy, and Japan, it was only immigrants from Japan, and Japanese Americans, who were subject to internment in American prisoner camps. Millions of ordinary Japanese Americans were forced to leave their homes and businesses and live in prisoner camps for the duration of the war. Hostility against the Japanese flared again in the 1970s and 1980s as a downturn in the American economy, most notably in the American auto industry, led to a renewed wave of bigotry and xenophobia.

Today, immigrant bashing continues to be an issue in the United States. Mexican arrivals are often characterized as entering the country illegally, and as a drain on local and federal resources once arrived. Muslim immigrants, often trying to escape instability and war at home, are most often depicted as terrorists, come to do harm. As in centuries past, bigotry informs policy, and under President Donald Trump, several major actions have been taken seemingly informed by ethnic and racial stereotype, including the government's Muslim travel ban and the building of a wall on the country's southern border. Immigrant bashing of these groups continues to rise and incidents of violence and discrimination have been reported across the country.

——*K.P. Dawes*

BIBLIOGRAPHY AND FURTHER READING

Behdad, Ali. *A Forgetful Nation: On Immigration and Cultural Identity in the United States.* Durham: Duke UP, 2005. Print.

Chen, Amy, and Ying Chang. *The Chinatown Files.* New York: Filmmaker's Library, 2001. Documentary/DVD.

Knobel, Dale T. *America for Americans: The Nativist Movement in the United States.* New York: Twayne, 1996. Print.

Lerner, Jesse, Scott Sterling, and the University of Southern California Center for Visual Anthropology. *Immigrant Bashing on the Border.* New York: Filmmaker's Library, 2005. Documentary/DVD.

Madison, Nathan Vernon. *Anti-Foreign Imagery in American Pulps and Comics, 1920-1960.* Jefferson: McFarland, 2013. Print.

IMMIGRANT WOMEN

Since the seventeenth century, women have journeyed alone or as members of families to North America. Coming first from England, Africa, Ireland, northern and western Europe, in the nineteenth century they immigrated from southern and eastern Europe and from China and Japan. The major source of immigration shifted in the twentieth century from Europe to Latin America and Asia.

HISTORY

In early colonial America, women arrived from England as wives or were imported as purchased wives. Many came as indentured servants who were bought and sold like slaves; they endured physical and sexual abuse. Some were transported as convicts. Female slaves were brought from Africa. Throughout the eighteenth century, although female immigrants experienced extreme job discrimination, they worked in a variety of trades.

Between 1820 and 1880, many women settled in the rural Midwest, where life on the prairies was lonely and harsh. In urban areas, the most commonly available work for young single women was domestic service, although as the century progressed they began to find employment in factories. Married women often preferred to undertake piecework at home or to take in boarders. Compared to men, there was a high proportion of destitute immigrant women. In towns and cities, women joined the developing union movement and began to speak out against intolerable working conditions. Their first strike was organized in 1825, when the United Tailoresses of New York demanded higher wages. Women labored as domestic servants, teachers, and factory workers,

half of whom were employed in textile mills. Leonora Barry, an Irish immigrant, commented on the largest problem for female workers: "Through long years of endurance they have acquired, as a sort of second nature, the habit of submission and acceptance without question of any terms offered them."

From 1880 to 1920, arrivals from Europe substantially increased. For women, positions as domestic servants continued to be most easily secured. In 1900, when white-collar jobs became available to women, Irish women worked in Canada and the United States as office workers, shop clerks, or teachers. Chinese and Japanese women immigrated to Hawaii, the continental United States, and Canada. As the number of Asian immigrants on the Pacific Coast increased, an exclusionary movement developed. The 1882 Chinese Exclusion Act abruptly curtailed Chinese immigration; it would not be repealed until 1943. The 1907 Gentlemen's Agreement strictly limited Japanese immigration. It did not exclude family members of residents, however, and therefore many Japanese women immigrated to the United States as "picture brides." In 1917, the ban on Chinese immigrants was extended to all Asian countries.

THE EARLY TWENTIETH CENTURY

In the twentieth century, many female immigrants continued to live under grim circumstances. Entering the labor force at an unprecedented rate, they faced discrimination and grueling conditions. Urban domestic service was managed by a network of unregulated and exploitative city agencies. Rents were frequently inflated. The Chicago Immigrant Protective League was founded in 1907 to help foreign-born arrivals find work, housing, and education. In New York City, new immigrants found work in sweatshops, in which conditions ranged from unhealthy to dangerous and in the garment industry. In the winter of 1909, some women organized and voted to strike. As a result, membership increased in the International Ladies' Garment Workers' Union. Demands were won in more than three hundred shops, and some women succeeded in becoming union officials. Yet, improved factory conditions were not sufficient to prevent a number of fires, including one in 1911 at the Triangle Shirtwaist Company that killed 146 people, mostly women. That same year, social scientist Francis Kellor described immigrants as "the poorest protected of all humanity in this country . . . even worse than children."

Immigration during the first decade of the twentieth century exceeded by thirty-five million the total of any previous decade. Nativistic sentiment prompted Congress to enact new restrictions on immigration, including a literacy test (1917), a quota system (1921, 1924, and 1927), and the extension of deportation criteria. The Great Depression provoked further exclusion, so that total immigration for the decade of the 1930's was lower than at any previous point since the 1820's.

POST-WORLD WAR II

During World War II (1939-1945), Issei (first-generation Japanese immigrants) were interned with their families in camps by the US government. Following the war, the War Brides Act (1945) allowed Chinese, Japanese, and European women to enter the United States as wives of servicemen. Similarly, in the 1960's and 1970's, such marriages were common throughout Southeast Asia. In 1962, the Migration and Refugee Assistance Act was passed to help Cubans resettle in the United States. By 1965, the major source of immigration had shifted from Europe to Latin America and Asia. The Immigration Law of 1965, which amended the Immigration and Naturalization Act of 1952, abandoned national origins quotas and introduced preference categories. After 1976, no country could send more than 20,000 people in any year to the United States, which resulted in a higher proportion of blue-collar immigration. The 1980 Refugee Act was introduced to deal with the refugees from Indochina who were admitted following the end of hostilities in Vietnam in 1975. In the 1970's, a "mail-order bride" industry developed that enabled women from the Philippines, Thailand, and Eastern Europe to immigrate to the United States.

In 1991, procedural guidelines for immigration screening were developed by the United Nations High Commissioner for Refugees. Canada developed gender-sensitive rules to make it easier for women to pass through the screening process. In 1992, in order to manage the immigration of refugees more strictly, Canada introduced new restrictive laws.

By the start of the 21st century, women were as likely as men to immigrate to the United States. Developing nations, such as Mexico and the Philippines, became the primary source of immigration. Mexico provided the largest number of immigrants, including numerous undocumented women. As more American women sought employment out of the home, Central American women, migrating in order to gain economic and social security, filled the need for domestic help in cities. Concern surfaced regarding immigrant beneficiaries of two welfare programs in the United States: Temporary Assistance for Needy Families (TANF) and Supplemental Security Income (SSI). In 2007, 32.7 percent of the immigrant population were on public assistance, compared with 19.4 percent of non-immigrants. Eighteen percent of immigrants were living below the poverty line, compared with 12.6 percent of non-immigrants. In 2010, 55 percent of all people obtaining a green card were women. Women comprised 47 percent of all refugee arrivals and 53 percent of all people who naturalized to become a citizen.

When women depart from their own cultures, they may lose their customary support systems. They have often left patriarchal and hierarchical traditions. In the United States, they enter a more egalitarian world with a more open sexuality. Gender and family roles can be thrown into disequilibrium. Domestic violence against women immigrants has increased, and there has been a higher incidence of depression and substance abuse among these women. Often eager to take advantage of opportunities, immigrant women are more willing than men to accept any job that is offered. Women from different immigrant groups face many of the same issues, but how they cope with these issues varies from one culture to another.

——*Susan E. Hamilton*

BIBLIOGRAPHY AND FURTHER READING

Bayor, Ronald H., ed. *The Oxford Handbook of American Immigration and Ethnicity.* New York: Oxford UP, 2016. Print.

Brettell, Caroline. *Gender and Migration.* Malden: Polity, 2016. Print.

Hondagneu-Sotelo, Pierette, ed. *Gender and US Immigration: Contemporary Trends.* Berkeley: U of California P, 2003. Print.

O'Leary, Anna Ochoa. *Undocumented Immigrants in the United States: An Encyclopedia of Their Experience.* Santa Barbara: Greenwood, 2014. Print.

Pearce, Susan C., Elizabeth J. Clifford, and Reena Tandon. *Immigration and Women: Understanding the American Experience.* New York: New York UP, 2011. Print.

IMMIGRANTS IN THE MILITARY

IMMIGRATION "CRISIS"

In 1965, the US Congress passed an immigration act that did away with the European bias of the nation's immigration policy and made family reunification, rather than national origin, the primary qualification for admission. At first, it was thought that the Immigration and Nationality Act of 1965 would not greatly expand immigration. However, legal immigration increased from about 330,000 per year in the early 1960s to more than 1 million since the 1990s. Illegal immigration, particularly from Mexico, also increased during this time period. As a result, a backlash against immigration developed among some segments of the American population.

A NEW IMMIGRANT POPULATION

According to estimates of the US Census, the legal immigrant population in 1997 contained 25.8 million people. Immigrants, then, made up nearly one out of every ten people in the United States by the end of the 1990s. These were mostly relatively new immigrants: More than 80 percent had arrived since 1970 and more than 60 percent had arrived since 1980. In addition to these legal immigrants, approximately 300,000 to 400,000 illegal, or unauthorized, immigrants entered the United States each year. Although many of these unauthorized immigrants were in the United States only for seasonal or other temporary employment, it was estimated that the unauthorized immigrant population of the United States was about 4 million people in the 1990s. By 2010, that number had reached 10.8 million, according to the Department of Homeland Security. Thirty-nine percent of that population had arrived between 2000 and 2010. The bulk of the unauthorized arrivals—62 percent—were from Mexico (but often having originated from countries in Central or South America).

Heavy immigration from Latin America and Asia, combined with comparatively large family sizes among Latin Americans and Asians, have changed the racial and ethnic makeup of the United States. For most of US history, the overwhelming majority of Americans were white Europeans, with a large minority of African Americans. The new immigrants and their children, however, have brought a new cultural and racial diversity to the United States. According to projections of the US Census, the white non-Hispanic component of the population could be expected to decline from 62 percent to 43 percent from the year 2014 to 2060. Black non-Hispanic Americans are expected to increase only slightly during this period, from 13.2 percent to 14.3 percent. Asians, who made up less than 1 percent of the US population in 1970, had increased to more than 5 percent by 2014. By 2060, it is predicted that 9 percent of all Americans will be Asian. Hispanics, who were less than 5 percent of the US population in 1970, grew to 9 percent in 1990; and by 2014 that number was 17.4. Thus, by the year 2060, if ethnic trends in immigration and fertility continue as expected, more than one out of every four Americans would be Hispanic.

Although many Americans are not cognizant of the statistical data on immigration or of scientific projections of population trends, they have become aware that large numbers of immigrants, both legal and illegal, have entered the country over the past few decades. They have also become aware of the cultural changes brought about by immigration. In southern Florida, Texas, California, and many other

FOREIGN-BORN POPULATION AND PERCENTAGE OF TOTAL POPULATION, FOR THE UNITED STATES: 1970–2010

Years of Entry	Number (in millions)	Percentage of Total Population
1970	9.6	4.7
1980	14.1	6.2
1990	19.8	7.9
2000	31.1	11.1
2010	40.0	12.9

Source: US Census Bureau, Census of Population, 1850 to 2000, and the American Community Survey, 2010. PDF file.

parts of the country, English-speaking Americans have heard languages they do not themselves speak or understand and have come into contact with cultures unfamiliar to them. Thus, both concern over the amount of immigration and reactions to cultural changes have fueled the perception of an immigration crisis. With the nation as a whole having become increasingly polarized politically in recent years, the urgency of the crisis often depends on where one stands on the political spectrum. Conservatives generally claim that the crisis is serious and needs to be addressed immediately using harsh measures. Liberals, on the other hand, argue that the "crisis" is overblown and that immigrants, lawful or otherwise, contribute significantly to the US economy and its ongoing growth.

ECONOMIC CONCERNS OVER IMMIGRATION

Many of those who feel that the flow of immigrants into the United States constitutes a crisis maintain that immigration poses serious economic problems. Immigrants, they argue, compete for jobs with people already living in the United States. Under US immigration policy, there are two primary reasons that people from other countries can receive an immigrant visa that gives them permission to settle in the United States. The first reason concerns family: People who have family members who are citizens of or residents in the United States are given priority in the granting of immigrant visas. The second reason concerns employment: People with special professional abilities or workers arriving to take jobs for which Americans are in short supply are eligible for visas.

Roy Beck, an advocate of limiting immigration, has argued that those who receive permission to immigrate for purposes of employment do so at the expense of employees already in the United States. He points out that immigration lawyers, who help people find ways to enter the United States, frequently work for businesses that wish to employ foreign labor. These lawyers, according to Beck, help employers draw up job descriptions that make it appear that no qualified American workers are available so that the employers can import cheaper foreign workers.

George Borjas, an economist specializing in immigration issues, maintains that high levels of immigration pose a problem for low-income American workers. Borjas has observed that most immigrants enter the United States to join family members, and these immigrants tend to have few job skills and little educational background. Therefore, immigrants are more likely than other people to rely on public assistance, making them a financial burden, and they competed for jobs with low-skilled, low-income natives. Borjas estimates that immigration has been the source of about one-third of a decline in the wages of less-educated American workers in the late twentieth and early 21st century.

CULTURAL CONCERNS OVER IMMIGRATION

Some of those alarmed over the influx of immigrants see it as a cultural crisis. They have claimed that immigrants are arriving in such large numbers, with cultures that are so foreign to the existing culture of the United States, that they cannot be assimilated readily into American culture.

PROJECTED CHANGES IN THE ETHNIC AND RACIAL COMPOSITION OF THE UNITED STATES, 2000-2050

(Percentage of total US population)				
Year	White, non-Hispanic	Black, non-Hispanic	Asian & Pacific Islander	Hispanic
2000	71.8	12.2	3.9	11.4
2005	69.9	12.4	4.4	12.6
2010	68.0	12.6	4.8	13.8
2015	66.1	12.7	5.3	15.1
2020	64.3	12.9	5.7	16.3
2025	62.4	13.0	6.2	17.6
2030	60.5	13.1	6.6	18.9
2035	58.6	13.2	7.1	20.3
2040	56.7	13.3	7.5	21.7
2045	54.7	13.5	7.9	23.1
2050	52.8	13.6	8.2	24.5

Source: US Bureau of the Census. *Current Population Reports,* Series P25-1130, "Population Projections of the United States by Age, Sex, Race, and Hispanic Origin, 1995 to 2050." March 1997. Washington: US GPO.

Journalist Peter Brimelow has written that immigration poses a crisis for American political culture. The arrival of masses of immigrants who do not speak English, according to Brimelow and others, threaten the position of English as a language understood everywhere around the country. Moreover, cultural critics of immigration have argued that newly arrived Mexicans, Dominicans, and Chinese often identify with their own cultural backgrounds rather than with mainstream "American" culture. Therefore, critics such as Brimelow claim that immigration endangers national unity.

Some of those who believe that massive immigration could create a crisis for US political culture argue that immigration is especially dangerous for African Americans. They point out that African Americans are likely to be replaced as the nation's largest minority and that this will likely decrease this group's political power. Many opponents of immigration also maintain that new immigrants would have little commitment to overcoming the racial inequality created by the United States' history of slavery and discrimination.

RESPONSES TO CLAIMS OF CRISIS

Although no one denies that immigration increased greatly in the past several decades, many political figures and scholars question whether this should be seen as an immigration "crisis." Economist Julian Simon has argued that immigrants are frequently energetic and industrious and can create, not simply compete for, jobs. The economy of southern Florida, for example, boomed as a result of the activities of Cuban immigrants. Many supporters of immigration maintain that immigration is an economic blessing, since immigrants often perform work in areas that are experiencing labor shortages.

A number of observers believe that the influx of immigrants pose no threat to American culture. They point out that American culture has changed continually throughout its history. Moreover, the sociologist Alejándro Portes and other scholars have cited evidence that the children of immigrants overwhelmingly become fluent in English and are often weaker in their parents' languages than they are in English.

——Carl L.Bankston III, updated by Michael Shally-Jensen

BIBLIOGRAPHY AND FURTHER READING

Anderson, Stuart. *Immigration.* Santa Barbara: Greenwood, 2010. Digital file.

Beck, Roy. *The Case against Immigration.* New York: Norton, 1996. Print.

Borjas, George. *Immigration Economics.* Cambridge: Harvard UP, 2014. Print.

Brimelow, Peter. *Alien Nation: Common Sense about America's Immigration Disaster.* New York: Random, 1995. Print.

Bulmer, Martin, and John Solomos. *Multiculturalism, Social Cohesion and Immigration.* New York: Routledge, 2015. Print.

Haugen, David M., Susan Musser, and Kacy Lovelace. *Immigration.* Detroit: Greenhaven, 2009. Print.

Portes, Alejándro, and Rubén G. Rumbaut. *Immigrant America: A Portrait,* 4th ed. Berkeley: U of California P, 2014. Print.

Simon, Julian L. *The Economic Consequences of Immigration,* 2d ed. Ann Arbor: U of Michigan P, 1999. Print.

Todd, Carissa. *Immigration Policy: Political Influences, Challenges, and Economic Impact.* Hauppauge: Nova, 2014. Digital file.

IMMIGRATION ACT OF 1917

Public concern over immigration prompted the US Congress to establish a Joint Commission on Immigration in 1907. The commission consisted of three members of the Senate, three members of the House of Representatives, and three other appointees. In 1911, the Dillingham Commission, named after the legislation's author and the commission's chairman, Senator William P. Dillingham of Vermont, issued a forty-two-volume report that advocated the restriction of immigration. It stated that recent immigrants from southern and eastern Europe were more likely to be unskilled, unsettled, and generally less desirable than the northern and western European immigrants who had arrived previously. Experts later disputed these conclusions, but the report was used to justify the new restrictions that Congress continued to write into law in the comprehensive Immigration Act of 1917.

A number of different ways to restrict immigration were suggested by the commission. They included instituting a literacy test, excluding unskilled laborers, increasing the amount of money that immigrants were required to have in their possession, and increasing the head tax. The commission also advocated the principle of racial quotas.

Major attention was directed toward the literacy test. Congress had introduced prior bills requiring literacy tests for immigrants. In 1897, such a bill was vetoed by President Grover Cleveland, who said that immigration restrictions were unnecessary. The House voted to override the president's veto on March 3, 195 to 37. The Senate referred the veto message and bill to the Committee on Immigration. When the bill resurfaced at the Sixty-second Congress, it was the Senate that voted to override President William Howard Taft's veto on February 18, 1913, while the House voted to sustain it on February 19. During the Sixty-third Congress (1914-1917), the House voted to sustain the veto of President Woodrow Wilson.

At the second session of the Sixty-fourth Congress, a bill was introduced "to regulate the immigrating of aliens to, and the residence of aliens in, the United States." Again, Wilson vetoed the bill. On February 1, 1917, the House voted to override the president's veto, 287 to 106, and the Senate voted similarly on February 5, 1917, 62 to 19. The veto was overridden, and the bill became Public Law 301. The act excluded from entry "all aliens over sixteen years of age, physically capable of reading, who can not read the English language, or some other language or dialect, including Hebrew or Yiddish." Other major recommendations made by the Dillingham Commission six years earlier were passed. The head tax was increased, and vagrants, alcoholics, advocates of violent revolutions, and "psychopathic inferiors" all were barred. A further provision created an Asiatic Barred Zone in the southwest Pacific, which succeeded in excluding most Asian immigrants who were not already excluded by the Chinese Exclusion Act and the Gentlemen's Agreement.

——Susan E. Hamilton

Immigrants arriving at Ellis Island, 1902.

BIBLIOGRAPHY AND FURTHER READING

American Immigration Policy (Port Washington, N.Y.: Kennikat Press, 1969), edited by William S. Bernard, includes the text of the 1917 Immigration Act. Ellis Cose's *A Nation of Strangers* (New York: William Morrow, 1992) presents an overview of immigration, from colonial settlement to World War I. Part 2 of Roger Daniels's *Coming to America: A History of Immigration and Ethnicity in American*

Life (New York: HarperCollins, 1990) concentrates on immigration from 1820 to 1924. Elizabeth J. Harper's *Immigration Laws of the United States* (3d ed., Indianapolis: Bobbs-Merrill, 1975) discusses immigration history and trends. Walter Nugent's *Crossings: The Great Transatlantic Migrations, 1870-1914* (Bloomington: Indiana University Press, 1992) is a thorough treatise accompanied by maps, tables, and photographs.

IMMIGRATION ACT OF 1924

There was no clearly defined official US policy toward immigration until the late nineteenth century. The United States was still a relatively young country, and there was a need for settlers in the West and for workers to build industry. Chinese immigrants flowed into California in 1849 and the early 1850's, searching for fortune and staying as laborers who worked the mines and helped to build the transcontinental railroad.

The earliest immigration restriction focused on Asians. In 1875, the federal government restricted the number of Chinese and Japanese coming into the country. The push for restriction of Asian immigrants was led by US workers. After the depression of 1877, Denis Kearney, an Irish-born labor organizer, helped found the Workingman's Trade and Labor Union of San Francisco, an anti-Chinese and anticapitalist group. Kearney and others believed that lower-paid Chinese workers took jobs away from white workers, and they agitated for expulsion of the Chinese and legal restrictions on future immigrants. Their efforts were successful in 1882, when the Chinese Exclusion Act was passed. The act exempted teachers, students, merchants, and pleasure travelers, and remained in effect until 1943. With the act of 1882, the federal government had, for the first time, placed restrictions on the immigration of persons from a specific country. More specific policy toward European immigration began in the 1880's. In 1882, the federal government excluded convicts, paupers, and mentally impaired persons. Organized labor's efforts also were successful in 1882, with the prohibition of employers' recruiting workers in Europe and paying their passage to the United States.

RESTRICTIVE CHANGES

Federal law became more aggressive by the early twentieth century, with the passage of the Act of 1903, which excluded epileptics, beggars, and anarchists. In 1907, the United States Immigration Commission was formed. This group, also known as the Dillingham Commission, published a forty-two-volume survey of the impact of immigration on American life and called for a literacy test and further immigration restriction. Although several presidential vetoes had prevented a literacy requirement, in 1917, the US Congress overrode President Woodrow Wilson's veto and passed a law requiring a literacy test for newcomers. The test was designed to reduce the number of immigrants, particularly those from southeastern Europe, where the literacy rate was low.

The marked change in official policy and in the view of a majority of people in the United States was caused by several factors. A strong nativist movement had begun after World War I with such groups as the American Protective Association, an organization that began in the Midwest in the 1880's and focused on prejudice against aliens and Catholics. Senator

Henry Cabot Lodge organized the Immigration Restriction League in Boston, indicating the addition of US leaders and intellectuals to the restriction movement. The war had brought the United States into position as a major world power, with a resultant view that the United States should be a nation of conformity. Political and economic problems in Europe, including the war and a postwar economic depression, had led to fear of too many immigrants fleeing Europe. Changes in the US economy reduced the need for manual labor, thus creating a fear of lack of job security.

The push for restriction coincided with the most intensive era of immigration in United States history. From the late 1880's until the 1920's, the nation experienced wave after wave of immigration, with millions of persons coming into the country each decade. The growth of new physical and social sciences that emphasized heredity as a factor in intelligence led many people to believe that persons such as Slavs or Italians were less intelligent than western Europeans such as the Norwegians or the English. The belief in genetic inferiority gave credence to the immigration restriction movement and helped sway the government.

At the same time that millions of newcomers were entering the United States, a spirit of reform, the Progressive Era, had grown throughout the country. Americans who saw themselves as progressive and forward-looking pushed for change in politics, society, and education, particularly in the crowded urban areas of the Northeast. Europeans had emigrated in large numbers to the cities, and newer groups, such as Italians and Poles, were seen by many progressive-minded reformers as the root of urban problems. Thus it was with the help of progressive leaders that a push was made at the federal level to restrict the number of immigrants.

QUOTA SYSTEM

In 1921, Congress passed a temporary measure that was the first US law specifically restricting European immigration. The act established a quota system that held the number of immigrants to 3 percent of each admissible nationality living in the United States in 1910. Quotas were established for persons from Europe, Asia, Africa, Australia, and New Zealand. Although only a temporary measure, the Immigration Act of 1921 marked the beginning of a permanent policy of restricting European immigration. It began a bitter three-year controversy that led to the Immigration Act of 1924.

The United States Congress amended the 1921 act with a more restrictive permanent measure in May of 1924, the Johnson-Reid Act. This act, which became known as the National Origins Act, took effect on July 1, 1924. It limited the annual immigration to the United States to 2 percent of a country's population in the US as of the census of 1890. With the large numbers of northern and western Europeans who had immigrated to the country throughout the nation's history, the act effectively restricted southern and eastern European immigrants to approximately 12 percent of the total immigrant population. Asian immigration was completely prohibited, but there was no restriction on immigration from independent nations of the Western Hemisphere.

The new law also changed the processing system for aliens by moving the immigration inspection process to US consulates in foreign countries and requiring immigrants to obtain visas in the native country before emigrating to the United States. The number of visas was held to 10 percent in each country per month and thus reduced the number of people arriving at Ellis Island, leading to the eventual closing of the facility.

The Immigration Act of 1924 reflects a change in the controversy that occurred in the three-year period after the act of 1921. By 1924, the major factor in immigration restriction was racial prejudice. By using the US Census of 1890 as the basis for

quotas, the government in effect sharply reduced the number of southern and eastern Europeans, who had not begun to arrive in large numbers until after that census year. The passage of the act codified an official policy of preventing further changes in the ethnic composition of US society, and it was to remain in effect until passage of the Immigration and Nationality Act of 1965.

——*Judith Boyce DeMark*

BIBLIOGRAPHY AND FURTHER READING

August C. Bolino's *The Ellis Island Source Book* (Washington, D.C.: Kensington Historical Press, 1985) includes a history of Ellis Island and immigration restriction. Thomas J. Curran's *Xenophobia and Immigration, 1820-1930* (Boston: Twayne, 1975) provides a basic overview of the reasons for immigration restriction throughout US history. Robert A. Divine's *American Immigration Policy, 1924-1952* (New Haven, Conn.: Yale University Press, 1957; reprint, New York: Da Capo Press, 1972) is a comprehensive treatment of the history of immigration restriction from the 1924 act through the mid-1950's. Maxine S. Seller's "Historical Perspectives on American Immigration Policy: Case Studies and Current Implications," in *US Immigration Policy* (Durham, N.C.: Duke University Press, 1984), edited by Richard R. Hofstetter, contains a chronology of the series of events leading up to the Immigration Act of 1924, with a discussion of how those events relate to recent immigration history.

IMMIGRATION ACT OF 1943

The passage by Congress of the Immigration Act of 1943, also known as the Magnuson Act, and President Franklin D. Roosevelt's signing it into law ended the era of legal exclusion of Chinese immigrants to the United States and began an era during which sizable numbers of Chinese and other Asian immigrants came to the country. It helped bring about significant changes in race relations in the United States.

The first wave of Chinese immigrants came from the Pearl River delta region in southern China. They

began coming to California in 1848 during the gold rush and continued to come to the western states as miners, railroad builders, farmers, fishermen, and factory workers. Most were men. Many came as contract laborers and intended to return to China. Anti-Chinese feelings, begun during the gold rush and expressed in mob actions and local discriminatory laws, culminated in the Chinese Exclusion Act of 1882, barring the immigration of Chinese laborers for ten years. The act was renewed in 1892, applied to Hawaii when those islands were annexed by the

United States in 1898, and made permanent in 1904. Another bill, passed in 1924, made Asians ineligible for US citizenship and disallowed Chinese wives of US citizens to immigrate to the United States. As a result, the Chinese population in the United States declined from a peak of 107,475 in 1880 to 77,504 in 1940.

The passage of the Magnuson Act of 1943, which repealed the Chinese Exclusion Act of 1882, inaugurated profound changes in the status of ethnic Chinese who were citizens or residents of the United States. It made Chinese immigrants, many of whom had lived in the United States for years, eligible for citizenship. It also allotted a minuscule quota of 105 Chinese persons per year who could enter the United States as immigrants. The 1943 bill was a result of recognition of China's growing international status after 1928 under the Nationalist government and growing US sympathy for China's heroic resistance to Japanese aggression after 1937. It also was intended to counter Japanese wartime propaganda aimed at discrediting the United States among Asians by portraying it as a racist nation.

POST-WORLD WAR II CHANGES

World War II was a turning point for Chinese-US relations. After Japan's attack on Pearl Harbor in December, 1941, China and the United States became allies against the Axis powers. Madame Chiang Kai-shek, wife of China's wartime leader, won widespread respect and sympathy for China during her visit to the United States; she was the second female foreign leader to address a joint session of Congress. In 1943, the United States and Great Britain also signed new equal treaties with China that ended a century of international inequality for China. These events and the contributions of Chinese Americans in the war favorably affected the position and status of Chinese Americans. The 1943 act also opened the door for other legislation that allowed more Chinese to immigrate to the United States. In the long run, these laws had a major impact on the formation of Chinese families in the United States.

The War Brides Act of 1945, for example, permitted foreign-born wives of US soldiers to enter the United States and become naturalized. Approximately six thousand Chinese women entered the United States during the next several years as wives of US servicemen. An amendment to

this act, passed in 1946, put the Chinese wives and children of US citizens outside the quota, resulting in the reunion of many separated families and allowing ten thousand Chinese, mostly wives, and also children of US citizens of Chinese ethnicity, to enter the country during the next eight years. The Displaced Persons Act of 1948 granted permanent resident status, and eventually the right of citizenship, to 3,465 Chinese students, scholars, and others stranded in the United States by the widespread civil war that erupted between the Chinese Nationalists and Communists after the end of World War II. The Refugee Relief Act of 1953 allowed an additional 2,777 refugees to remain in the United States after the civil war ended in a Communist victory and the establishment of the People's Republic of China. Some Chinese students from the Republic of China on Taiwan, who came to study in the United States after 1950 and found employment and sponsors after the end of their studies, were also permitted to remain and were eligible for naturalization.

The four immigration acts passed between 1943 and 1953 can be viewed as a result of the alliance between the United States and the Republic of China in World War II and US involvement in the Chinese civil war that followed. In a wider context, they were also the result of changing views on race and race relations that World War II and related events brought about. Finally, they heralded the Immigration and Nationality Act of 1965, which revolutionized US immigration policy in ending racial quotas. Its most dramatic consequence was the significant increase of Asian immigrants in general, and Chinese immigrants in particular, into the United States.

The new immigrants changed the makeup of Chinese American society and caused a change in the way the Chinese were perceived by the majority groups in the United States. Whereas most of the earlier immigrants tended to live in ghettoized Chinatowns, were poorly educated, and overwhelmingly worked in low-status jobs as laundrymen, miners, or railroad workers, the new immigrants were highly educated, cosmopolitan, and professional. They came from the middle class, traced their roots to all parts of China, had little difficulty acculturating and assimilating into the academic and professional milieu of peoples of European ethnicity in the

United States, and tended not to live in Chinatowns. The latter group was mainly responsible for revolutionizing the way Chinese Americans were perceived in the United States.

——*Jiu-Hwa Lo Upshur*

BIBLIOGRAPHY AND FURTHER READING

Entry Denied: Exclusion and the Chinese Community in America, 1882-1943 (Philadelphia: Temple University Press, 1991), edited by Sucheng Chan, contains articles from nine scholars on different facets of the era. Fred W. Riggs's *Pressure on Congress: A Study of the Repeal of Chinese Exclusion* (1950; reprint, Westport, Conn.: Greenwood Press, 1972) gives a detailed account of the reasons for the repeal. Betty Lee Sung's *Mountain of Gold: The Story of the Chinese in America* (New York: I Company, 1967) is a good overview of Chinese immigration.

IMMIGRATION ACT OF 1990

The US Immigration Act of 1990 was passed in response to a widespread belief among legislators and the general public that many of the economic and social ills of the United States were caused by large populations of poor, non-English-speaking immigrants and in response to a growing need for skilled workers in technical fields in an increasingly international marketplace. The act, one of a number of immigration laws passed since the Immigration Act of 1891, set numerical limits for immigrants to the United States and established a system of preferences to determine which of the many applicants for admission should be accepted. Under the terms of the 1990 act, only 675,000 immigrants, not including political refugees, were to be admitted to the United States each year. These immigrants were eligible for preferential admission consideration if they fell into one of three groups: immigrants who had family members already legally in the country; employment-based immigrants who were able to prove that they had exceptional ability in certain professions with a high demand; and those from designated underrepresented nations, who were labeled "diversity immigrants."

Because the new law nearly tripled the annual allotment of employment-based immigrants from 54,000 to 140,000, business and industry leaders heralded their increased opportunity to compete internationally for experienced and talented engineers, technicians, and multinational executives. Others believed that the preference for certain kinds of workers masked a preference for whites over nonwhites, and wealthier immigrants over poorer. Divisions over the law between racial and political groups intensified when successful lobbying led to refinements in the law making it easier for fashion models and musicians, especially from Europe, to gain visas, while efforts to gain admittance for more women fleeing genital mutilation in African and Arabic nations failed.

The act made it easier for certain people—contract workers, musicians and other artists, researchers and educators participating in exchange programs—to perform skilled work in the United States on a temporary basis, with no intention of seeking citizenship. At the same time, the new law made it more difficult for unskilled workers, such as domestic workers and laborers, to obtain immigrant visas.

Finally, the Immigration Act of 1990 attempted to correct criticism of the 1986 Immigration Reform and Control Act by increasing that act's antidiscrimination provisions and increasing the penalties for discrimination. In a significant change in US immigration law, the act revised the reasons a person might be refused immigrant status or be deported. After 1952, for example, Communists were denied permission to enter the country on nonimmigrant work visas and were subject to deportment if identified, and potential political refugees from nations friendly to the United States were turned away as a matter of foreign policy. Under the new law, a wider range of political and ideological beliefs became acceptable.

——*Cynthia A. Bily*

IMMIGRATION AND CUSTOMS ENFORCEMENT (ICE)

With the creation of the Department of Homeland Security, in 2003, parts of the law enforcement divisions of the former Immigration and Naturalization Service (INS) and US Customs Service were combined into a new agency, Immigration and Customs Enforcement (ICE). This created the second largest federal law enforcement agency, with only the FBI having more agents. However, the sections of the previous immigration and customs services that dealt with activities at the actual borders were not included in ICE. ICE has responsibility only for enforcing the laws regarding people and actions within the United States, not the actual crossing of the border by people or goods (which belongs to US Customs and Border Protection).

One of the two major divisions within ICE is Enforcement and Removal Operations (ERO). For most people this is the most visible aspect of ICE's work. It is authorized to "identify, arrest, and remove aliens" who have entered the country illegally or aliens who are a threat to public safety. Historically, ICE has focused on criminals and fugitives from other nations. The millions of undocumented immigrants, who have come to the United States for economic reasons, have been a secondary concern for ERO. Among this group, undocumented immigrants who have arrived most recently are the priority for detention and deportation.

The other major division is the Homeland Security Investigations (HSI). This portion of the agency focuses on organized crime and terrorist organizations. HSI is more focused on smuggling operations,

HSI special agents preparing for an enforcement action.

including the creation of fraudulent documents used in smuggling attempts. It also investigates groups that organize the movement of undocumented immigrants into the United States. Cybercrimes and threats from outside the United States are also part of HSI's responsibilities.

——*Donald A. Watt*

BIBLIOGRAPHY AND FURTHER READING

Immigration and Customs Enforcement. "US Immigration and Customs Enforcement." *Department of Homeland Security.* Washington: Department of Homeland Security, 2017. Web. 30 January 2017.

IMMIGRATION AND EMIGRATION

Migration refers to the movement of people from one place to another. *Migration* can be internal (within a country) or international, and both types can have significant impacts. *Immigration* (the movement into a new country) and *emigration* (movement from a country) are forms of international migration. The term "net migration rate" is a way to measure the impact of migration on the population and refers to the difference between the rate of immigration and the rate of emigration. It is expressed as the number of people per one thousand who enter or leave an area during one year. Migration may have a number of important effects, such as relieving population pressure in crowded areas, spreading culture from one area to another, and bringing groups into contact—and possible conflict. More recently, return migration has become the focus of studies about immigrants that venture abroad but return home, indicating that the process of migration is dynamic and not simply a one-time movement in one direction.

Sociologists study the experiences of immigrants in relation to prejudice, discrimination, social stratification and mobility within their adopted country. They explore the various experiences of immigrants of differing ethnicities and races; such studies have revealed much about the nature of prejudice and about the disparity between the ideology and the reality of American life. A look at various aspects of immigration allows an examination of these processes at work in the history of the United States. In the period of immigration to the United States, beginning in the sixteenth century (if one excludes the first immigration, the prehistoric migration of the ancestors of Native American, and the forced migration of African slaves), most immigrants have come for the following reasons: to escape persecution, to seek economic opportunities, and to obtain freedoms available in the United States. While early studies of immigration often focused on individual reasons for migration and the separate forces that pulled them toward the United States, others, such as David M. Reimers's *Still the Golden Door* (1985), emphasize structural forces—economic and political—that have influenced population movements. Mark Wyman's *Round-Trip to America, The Immigrants Return to Europe, 1880-1930* (1993) also suggests that workers have migrated throughout Europe since the Middle Ages and then to America, seeking temporary work before returning home. Some transatlantic immigrants came to the United States without the intention to remain permanently, with more than 60% of Italians returning home.

IMMIGRATION PATTERNS
Many studies of immigration to the United States identify two massive waves of immigration between 1820 and 1914. The first decades of the nineteenth century brought increasing numbers of immigrants; 151,000 arrived in the 1820s, nearly 600,000 in the 1830s, more than 1 million in the 1840s, and 2.3 million in the 1850s. Many were Irish Catholics escaping political persecution and famine and Germans fleeing political upheavals. These "old immigrants" came to cities on the East Coast; some moved inland to the farmlands of the Great Plains.

"New immigrants" were those from eastern and southern Europe who arrived between the 1880s and World War I. This second period of immigration far surpassed the earlier waves in numbers, rising from 788,000 in 1872 to 1,285,000 in 1907. By 1914 nearly 15 million immigrants had arrived in the United States, many from Austria-Hungary, Italy, Russia, Greece, Romania, and Turkey. The federal Dillingham Commission (1907) regarded this group as poor, unskilled, and mostly male, and its report reinforced prejudices about eastern and southern Europeans. It concluded that these immigrants would be more difficult to assimilate into American society. As the children or grandchildren of immigrants adapted to American culture, the concept of American society as a "melting pot" into which many nationalities merged into one, has been replaced by the reality that many immigrants adapted to rather than assimilated into American society, retaining cultural norms and traditions of their homelands.

Often invisible in early immigration studies were the numbers of Africans and Latin Americans who had not come voluntarily to the United States. Africans were forcibly brought to the United States as slaves. Many Mexicans did not technically immigrate but were absorbed into the United States when lands from Texas to California were conquered in the Mexican-American War (1846–48). These groups needed to adapt to a new nation and a new culture, as did European immigrants, but they faced both discrimination and a lack of understanding about their circumstances. Asian immigrants formed another group that was long invisible in immigration histories. Chinese men were imported as cheap labor to build the railroads in the mid-1800s, and they were expected to leave when their job was done. Many Japanese, Filipino, and Korean immigrants came first to Hawaii as agricultural laborers, and some moved on to California before the United States barred Chinese immigration entirely and forced Japan to halt emigration.

REASONS FOR MIGRATION
Some structural reasons for immigration and emigration have not changed greatly over the last three hundred years. Many individuals have come to North America to escape religious or political persecution. Early refugees in this category included the English Pilgrims and French Huguenots. Later

religious groups came from Norway, Holland, and Russia, among them Jews and Mennonites. From the early nineteenth century to the present, immigrants have come because of economic changes in their native lands and opportunities in the United States. The enclosure movement in England and Western Europe, which began in the 1700s, forced many peasants off the land. They sought new land in America. Factories brought ruin to skilled artisans, who came to the United States hoping to open workshops. Many also came to escape political turmoil. Revolutions in 1830 and 1848 in Europe led refugees to seek safety in the United States. Twentieth-century upheavals such as World War II, the Cuban Revolution, repression in Southeast Asia, and civil wars in Lebanon and El Salvador brought more refugees to the United States. The flow of refugees has continued into the twenty-first century with wars and conflict in African nations, including Sudan, Ethiopia and Somalia and in the Middle East.

IMMIGRANTS AND US-BORN AMERICANS

Immigrants and refugees have not settled equally in all regions of the United States, although by the early twenty-first century immigrant communities have sprung up in Minneapolis, New England, Georgia and throughout the Pacific Northwest. Large immigrant communities in California, New York, and Florida have led to the need for government services in many languages. Students in schools speak Vietnamese, Spanish, Korean, Ethiopian, Haitian, and a number of Chinese dialects. Many require courses in English as a second language. Courts need to provide translators, and social service agencies struggle to communicate with many immigrant groups.

Some Americans have responded to foreigners with resentment for both economic and security reasons. Some states and localities have passed laws declaring English to be the only official language, although there are no federal language requirements. Sociologists studying immigration, however, have found that the large number of immigrants has led to a gradual shift in the population of the United States and its culture. Television stations around the country broadcast programs in many languages. Spanish-speaking markets in particular represent many new business opportunities, and large American companies offer advertisements in Spanish. Confusing the issue even more is the

presence of undocumented immigrants who either enter the country by surreptitiously crossing the border or overstaying their tourist or student visas. A major change in attitudes about immigration came with the destruction of the World Trade Center and attack on the Pentagon on September 11, 2001 by terrorists, mostly from Saudi Arabia

Americans have been proud of their heritage of immigration yet ambivalent about immigrant groups who have come to the United States. Federal legislation has expressed the varying reactions of Americans toward immigrants and immigration over time. Before 1820, there were no laws requiring passenger lists of arrivals in the United States. Immigrants brought skills and talents that were needed by the new country, and they were welcomed. Non-British immigrants in the early nineteenth century, however, did experience discrimination. Irish Catholics and German immigrants, whose religion or language was different from that of the majority, faced ridicule and were stereotyped as drunkards or dullards. Asian and Mexican immigrants also faced racial prejudice.

Despite mixed reaction to foreigners, the first federal immigration law was not passed until 1875. In that year prostitutes and convicts were prohibited from entering as immigrants. Additional exclusions for lunatics and idiots were added later.

By the 1880s, increasing immigration from areas outside northern Europe, the closing of the frontier, and increasing urbanization led to attempts to control immigration. Some Americans claimed that southern and eastern Europeans were replacing American stock and that immigration produced a declining birthrate among Americans. Others were more worried about Asian immigrants. The Chinese Exclusion Act of 1882 specifically denied entry to Chinese immigrants, while the Forant Act (1885) made it unlawful for employers to import aliens to perform labor in the United States. This law was aimed at large companies who were importing eastern Europeans to fill low-wage jobs instead of hiring American labor, and it reflected suspicion that immigration caused wages to decline. The Immigration Act of 1917 barred Asians not by nationality, but by excluding geographically any immigrants from East or South Asia.

Immigration to the United States was regulated for most of the twentieth century by the Immigration Act of 1924, which reflected the nation's desire to encourage European immigration and discourage

623

non-Western immigrants. This law established a series of quotas for immigrants from all countries except the Western Hemisphere. Larger quotas were assigned to countries whose citizens were more traditionally identified with the American population. The Immigration and Nationality Act of 1952 tightened the quota system.

IMMIGRATION REFORM

A significant change in United States policy toward immigration came with the Immigration and Nationality Act of 1965. This law removed strict quotas and Asian exclusion. Instead, it created preferences for persons with certain skills and gave priority to people with immediate family in the United States. The consequences of this legislation led to greater changes in immigration than were anticipated. By 1974, for example, foreign-born physicians made up 20 percent of all medical doctors in the United States. The "brain drain" from developing countries continued, as scientists, engineers, and scholars sought better conditions and higher salaries in the United States. The law also brought increasing non-European immigration, as family members petitioned to bring relatives from Asia, Africa, and Latin America.

The increasing number of undocumented immigrants in the United States has led to calls for policing the US border with Mexico and for physical barriers, including high walls and increased penalties for employers of undocumented immigrants. Undocumented immigrants have been accused of stealing jobs from United States citizens, draining social services, and changing the very nature of American society. In 1986 the Immigration Reform and Control Act attempted to resolve these issues for many of these immigrants. Those who could show permanent residency in the United States since 1982 could become legal residents. Employers who hired undocumented immigrants were to be fined, and additional funds were appropriated for stronger immigration enforcement.

Immigration reforms have continued, showing the changing response of American society over time. The Kennedy-Donnelly Act of 1988 permitted a lottery to provide visas for permanent resident status, and the 1990 Immigration Act raised annual immigration ceilings and ended restrictions on homosexuals, communists, and people with acquired immune deficiency syndrome (AIDS); it also granted safe haven status for Salvadorans. This law was not without opposition from those who feared that disease or undesirable ideas would be spread by immigrants.

Refugees have become an increasingly important part of population movements. Emigration from countries experiencing conflict increased in the twentieth and twenty-first centuries, and the United States has traditionally thought of itself as a nation receptive to the oppressed. The need to resettle large numbers of eastern European refugees after World War II was recognized by the Refugee Relief Act of 1953. In the 1980s the church-sponsored sanctuary movement broke immigration laws by providing asylum for Salvadorans who feared deportation by immigration authorities enforcing strict refugee policies. The impact of immigration on American society has continued to challenge cherished concepts and ideologies and to highlight prejudices. The idea of the United States as an open door, a place where people from all lands can find a haven, is still shared by many. Since the 1980s, however, this ideal has faced considerable challenges. The large numbers of Central Americans, Asians, and Haitians seeking asylum in the United States has led to tighter controls at borders and interdiction on the high seas. Americans, more fearful of terrorism than economic challenges, increasingly want restrictions on foreigners entering the country as the traditional stance of welcome is replaced by fear and anger.

While recent scholarship has stressed structural rather than personal reasons for population movements and has challenged the concept of the melting pot, American society has continued to mold immigrants from many nations. At the same time, American society has changed as a result of this immigration. This tension between sharing American values of freedom and potential for success and the fear of foreigners destroying traditional American culture is the continuing challenge of immigration in American history.

——*James A. Baer*

BIBLIOGRAPHY AND FURTHER READING

Bourke, Dale Hanson. *Immigration: Tough Questions, Direct Answers.* Downers Grove: InterVarsity P, 2014. Print.

Barkan, Elliot R.,Hasia Diner, Alan Kraut. *From Arrival to Incorporation: Migrants to the US in a Global Era,* New York: New York University Press, 2008.Print.

Chomsky, Aviva. *Undocumented: How Immigration Became Illegal.* Boston: Beacon, 2014. Print.

Daniels, Roger. *Coming to America: A History of Immigration and Ethnicity in American Life.* New York: HarperCollins, 1990. Print.

Glazer, Nathan, and Daniel Patrick Moynihan. *Beyond the Melting Pot.* Cambridge: MIT P, 1963. Print.

Jones, Maldwyn Allen. *American Immigration.* 2nd ed. Chicago: U of Chicago P, 1992. Print.

Reimers, David M. *Still the Golden Door: The Third World Comes to America.* 2nd ed. New York: Columbia UP, 1992. Print.

Sowell, Thomas, Migration and Cultures: A Worldview, Basic Books, New York: Basic Books, 1997. Print

Wyman, Mark, *Round-Trip to America, The Immigrants Return to Europe, 1880-1930,* Ithaca, NY: Cornell University Press, 1993. Print

Yans-McLaughlin, Virginia, ed. *Immigration Reconsidered.* New York: Oxford UP, 1990. Print.

IMMIGRATION AND NATIONALITY ACT OF 1952

In the early 1950's, as it had periodically throughout the twentieth century, immigration again became the subject of intense national debate, and a movement arose to reform immigration law. At the time, there were more than two hundred federal laws dealing with immigration, with little coordination among them.

REFORM EFFORTS

The movement toward immigration reform actually began in 1947, with a US Senate committee investigation on immigration laws, resulting in a voluminous report in 1950 and a proposed bill. The ensuing debate was divided between a group who wanted to abandon the quota system and increase the numbers of immigrants admitted, and those who hoped to shape immigration law to enforce the status quo. Leaders of the latter camp were the architects of the Immigration and Nationality Act of 1952: Patrick McCarran, senator from Nevada, Francis Walter, congressman from Pennsylvania, and Richard Arens, staff director of the Senate Subcommittee to Investigate Immigration and Naturalization. McCarran was the author of the Internal Security Act of 1951, which provided for registration of communist organizations and the internment of communists during national emergencies; Walter was an immigration specialist who had backed legislation to admit Europeans from camps for displaced persons; Arens had been staff director for the House Committee on Un-American Activities. Each looked upon immigration control as an extension of his work to defend the United States against foreign and domestic enemies.

McCarran was most outspoken in defending the concept of restrictions on the basis of national origin, stating in the Senate that

There are hard-core indigestible blocs who have not become integrated into the American way of life, but who, on the contrary, are its deadly enemy.... this Nation is the last hope of western civilization; and if this oasis of the world shall be overrun, perverted, contaminated, or destroyed, then the last flickering light of humanity will be extinguished.

Arens branded critics of the proposed act as either communists, misguided liberals enraptured by communist propaganda, apologists for specific immigrant groups, or "professional vote solicitors who fawn on nationality groups, appealing to them not as Americans but as hyphenated Americans." Among the bill's critics, however, were Harry S Truman, the US president in 1952, and Hubert H. Humphrey, senator from Minnesota and future Democratic presidential nominee. One liberal senator, Herbert Lehman, attacked the national origins provisions of the existing immigration code as a racist measure that smacked of the ethnic purity policies of the recently defeated German Nazis. Truman vetoed the bill, but his veto was overridden, 278 to 113 in the House, and 57 to 26 in the Senate.

In several areas, the 1952 law made no significant changes: Quotas for European immigrants were little changed, no quotas were instituted for immigrants from North and South American countries, and the issue of illegal immigration was given scant attention. There were significant changes in some areas, however: reversal of the ban on Asian immigration, extension of naturalization to persons regardless of race or sex, and the first provision for refugees as a special class of immigrants.

PROVISIONS

The Asiatic Barred Zone that had been established in 1917 was eliminated by providing for twenty-five hundred entries from the area—a minuscule number for the region, but the first recognition of Asian immigration rights in decades. This small concession for Asians was offset partially by the fact that anyone whose ancestry was at least half Asian would be counted under the quota for the Asian country of ancestry, even if the person was a resident of another country. This provision, which was unlike the system of counting quotas for European countries, was specifically and openly designed to prevent Asians living in North and South American countries, which had no quota restrictions, from flooding into the United States.

The Immigration and Nationality Act of 1952, or McCarran-Walter Act, also ensured for the first time that the "right of a person to become a naturalized citizen of the United States shall not be denied or abridged because of race or sex." The provision of not denying citizenship based on sex addressed the issue of women who had lost their US citizenship by marrying foreign men of certain categories; men who had married women from those categories had never lost their citizenship.

The issue of refugees was a new concern resulting from World War II. More than seven million persons had lost their homelands in the aftermath of the war, as a result of the conquering and reorganization of countries primarily in Eastern Europe. The 1952 act did not present a comprehensive solution to the problem of refugees but did give the attorney general special power, subject to congressional overview, to admit refugees into the United States under a special status. Although this was expected to be a seldom-used provision of the law, regular upheavals throughout the world later made it an important avenue of immigration into the United States.

Finally, the Immigration and Nationality Act also included stringent security procedures designed to prevent communist subversives from infiltrating the United States through immigration. Some of these harsh measures were specifically mentioned by Truman in his veto message, but the anticommunist Cold War climate made such measures hard to defeat.

Over the objections of Congress, President Truman appointed a special commission to examine immigration in September, 1952. After hearings in several cities, it issued the report *Whom Shall We Welcome?*, which was critical of the McCarran-Walter Act. Some liberal Democrats attempted to make the 1952 presidential election a forum on immigration policy, but without success. Dwight D. Eisenhower, the victorious Republican nominee for president, made few specific statements on immigration policy during the campaign. After his election, however, he proposed a special provision for allowing almost a quarter of a million refugees from communism to immigrate to the United States over a two-year period, couching his proposal in terms of humanitarianism and foreign policy. The resulting Refugee Relief Act of 1953 allowed the admission of 214,000 refugees, but only if they had assurance of jobs and housing or were close relatives of US citizens and could pass extensive screening procedures designed to deter subversives. Several similar exceptions in the following years managed to undercut the McCarran-Walter Act, which its many critics had been unable to overturn outright.

——*Irene Struthers*

BIBLIOGRAPHY AND FURTHER READING

Marius A. Dimmitt's *The Enactment of the McCarran-Walter Act of 1952* (Lawrence: University Press of Kansas, 1971) is a dissertation giving a complete discussion of the 1952 immigration bill. Michael C. LeMay *From Open Door to Dutch Door: An Analysis of US Immigration Policy Since 1820* (New York: Praeger, 1987) is a comprehensive overview of the forces behind and results of changing US immigration policy; chapter 5 opens with a discussion of the Immigration Act of 1952.

IMMIGRATION AND NATIONALITY ACT OF 1965

The Immigration and Nationality Act of 1952 codified legislation that had developed haphazardly over the past century. Although it liberalized some areas, it was discriminatory in that quotas were allotted according to national origins. This resulted in western and northern European nations receiving no less than 85 percent of the total allotment. The Immigration and Nationality Act of 1965 allowed non-Europeans to enter the United States on an equal basis with Europeans. Before the 1965 legislation, US immigration policies favored northern and western Europeans.

REFORM BEGINS

With the election of John F. Kennedy in 1960, circumstances for meaningful immigration reform came into being: Kennedy believed that immigration was a source of national strength, the Civil Rights movement had promoted an ideology to eliminate racist policies, and the US position during the Cold War necessitated that immigration policies be just. Thus, Kennedy had Abba Schwartz, an expert on refugee and immigration matters, develop a plan to revise immigration policy.

In July of 1963, Kennedy sent his proposal for immigration reform to Congress. His recommendations had three major provisions: the quota system should be phased out over a five-year period; no natives of any one country should receive more than 10 percent of the newly authorized quota numbers; and a seven-person immigration board should be set up to advise the president. Kennedy also advocated that family reunification remain a priority; the Asiatic Barred Zone be eliminated; and nonquota status be granted to residents of Jamaica and Trinidad and Tobago, as it was to other Western Hemisphere residents. Last, the preference structure was to be altered to liberalize requirements for skilled people.

After the assassination of President Kennedy, President Lyndon B. Johnson took up the cause of immigration. Although immigration was not a major issue during the 1964 campaign, both sides had courted diverse ethnic communities, whose will now had to be considered. The Democratic Party's landslide victory gave Johnson a strong mandate for his Great Society programs, of which immigration

reform was a component. Secretary of State Dean Rusk argued the need for immigration reform to bolster US foreign policy. Rusk, Attorney General Robert F. Kennedy, and others criticized the current system for being discriminatory and argued that the proposed changes would be economically advantageous to the United States. Senator Edward "Ted" Kennedy held hearings and concluded that "all recognized the unworkability of the national origins quota system."

Outside Congress, ethnic, voluntary, and religious organizations lobbied and provided testimony before Congress. They echoed the administration's arguments about discrimination. A few Southerners in Congress argued that the national origins concept was not discriminatory—it was a mirror reflecting the US population, so those who would best assimilate into US society would enter. However, the focus of the congressional debate was on how to alter the national origins system, not on whether it should be changed. The most disputed provisions concerned whether emphasis should be on needed skills, family reunification, or limits set on Western Hemisphere immigration. Family unification prevailed.

PROVISIONS

The new law replaced the national origins system with hemispheric caps, 170,000 from the Old World and 120,000 from the New. Spouses, unmarried minor children, and parents of US citizens were exempt from numerical quotas. Preferences were granted first to unmarried adult children of US citizens (20 percent); next, to spouses and unmarried adult children of permanent resident aliens (20 percent). Professionals, scientists, and artists of exceptional ability were awarded third preference (10 percent) but required certification from the US Department of Labor. Married children of US citizens had fourth preference (10 percent). Next were those brothers and sisters of US citizens who were older than twenty-one years of age (24 percent), followed by skilled and unskilled workers in occupations for which labor was in short supply (10 percent). Refugees from communist or communist-dominated countries or the Middle East were seventh (6 percent). Nonpreference status was assigned to anyone not eligible under any of the above categories; there have been more preference applicants than can be accommodated, so nonpreference status has not been used.

The law had unexpected consequences. The framers of the legislation expected that the Old World slots would be filled by Europeans. They assumed that family reunification would favor Europeans, because they dominated the US population. However, those from Europe who wanted to come were in the lower preference categories, while well-trained Asians had been coming to the United States since 1943 and were well qualified for preference positions. Once they, or anyone else, became a permanent resident, a whole group of people became eligible to enter the country under the third preference category. After a five-year wait—the residential requirement for citizenship—more persons became eligible under the second preference category. As a result, many immigrants were directly or indirectly responsible for twenty-five to fifty new immigrants.

The law set forth a global ceiling of 290,000, but actual totals ranged from 398,089 in 1977 to 904,292 in 1993. Refugees and those exempt from numerical limitations were the two major categories that caused these variations. The refugee count had varied according to situations such as that of the "boat people" from Cuba in 1981. In 1991, refugees and asylees totaled 139,079; in 1993, they totaled 127,343. Persons in nonpreference categories increased from 113,083 in 1976 to 255,059 in 1993. Total immigration for 1991 was 827,167 and for 1993 was 904,292—well above the global ceiling.

The Immigration and Nationality Act of 1965 enabled some of the most able medical, scientific, engineering, skilled, and other professional talent to enter the United States. The medical profession illustrates this trend. In the ten years after the enactment of the 1965 act, seventy-five thousand foreign physicians entered the United States. By 1974, immigrant physicians made up one-fifth of the total number of physicians and one-third of the interns and residents in the United States. Each immigrant doctor represented more than a million dollars in education costs. In addition, they often took positions in the inner-city and rural areas, which prevented the collapse of the delivery of medical services to those locations.

——*Arthur W. Helweg*

BIBLIOGRAPHY AND FURTHER READING

Roger Daniels's *Coming to America: A History of Immigration and Ethnicity in American Life* (New York: HarperCollins, 1990) analyzes the causes and consequences of the Immigration and Nationality Act of 1965. *Clamor at the Gates: The New American Immigration* (San Francisco: ICS Press, 1985), edited by Nathan Glazer, contains a superb evaluation of the "new immigration" that resulted from the Immigration and Nationality Act of 1965. David M. Reimers's *Still the Golden Door: The Third World Comes to America* (2d ed., New York: Columbia University Press, 1992), provides a detailed study of the passage of the Immigration and Nationality Act of 1965.

IMMIGRATION AND NATURALIZATION SERVICE (INS)

The INS, which existed between 1933 and 2003, when it was replaced by Immigration and Customs Enforcement (ICE), had jurisdiction over immigrants in the United States. The US attorney general is charged with administering and enforcing all laws relating to aliens' immigration and naturalization. During the time of the INS, the attorney general delegated most such duties to the agency—as he or she does now to ICE. The INS had jurisdiction over aliens in the United States, handling visa petitions, adjusting people's status (as from nonimmigrant to immigrant), granting citizenship, and dealing with deportations and exclusions.

The commissioner of the INS was appointed by the president, normally on the recommendation of the attorney general, with the consent of the Senate. INS headquarters were located in Washington, D.C. The headquarters handled administrative matters and general policymaking almost exclusively. Directly under the headquarters were four INS regional offices. The basic function of the regional offices was fiscal management to assist INS field offices in their areas. Under the four regional offices were thirty-six district offices worldwide and twenty border patrol sectors throughout the United States. The district office was the basic operating unit of the INS. Each district director had authority and responsibility to

grant or deny various applications or petitions submitted to the service, to initiate investigations and deportations, and to issue orders to show cause or warrants of arrest in deportation proceedings. Many of the same functions are now carried out by ICE.

——*Wei Luo*

IMMIGRATION LAW IN CANADA

Until the mid-twentieth century, Canada traditionally restricted immigration to northern and western Europeans. After World War II, Canada's economy boomed, and the business lobby exerted pressure to open immigration channels. Starting in the 1950s, Canada needed immigrants in order to have sufficient people to maintain its economy. On the other hand, there was a desire to maintain the predominance of northern and western Europeans in the population.

The Immigration Act of 1952 had contributed to European domination in the Canadian population by giving the minister of immigration and immigration officials wide discretionary powers to open and close off immigration to any group. However, in the 1950s, many Third World countries gained independence, and Canada had to consider their growing importance as trading partners and their influence in the United Nations. Thus, Canada started by assigning small quotas to Asian Commonwealth partners. When the expected inflow from northern and western Europe did not materialize, Canada set up offices in Italy, which started the large Italian influx that climbed into the hundreds of thousands. By the mid-1960s, Italians were the dominant laborers in Canada's construction industry.

CHANGING POLICIES

The need for laborers and the refugee issue challenged Canadian immigration policy and the Canadian policy on refugees. The change started in 1956, when Hungarian refugees, following the communist takeover in Hungary, poured into Australia. By sending teams to refugee settlements and setting aside established procedures, Canada successfully resettled thirty-seven thousand Hungarians in Canada. In the early 1960s, the Canadian market for laborers began to shrink, and active immigration

"The same act which Excludes Orientals Should Open Wide the Portals of British Columbia to White Immigrations." Cartoon by N.H. Hawkins, Saturday Sunset. (1907)

Exclusionist cartoon in Saturday Sunset magazine by N. H. Hawkins, Vancouver, 24 August 1907. By N H Hawkins.

work fell by 50 percent. De facto segregation existed during this period: Immigration offices were established in Europe and North America, but only two in Asia.

In the 1960s, illegal entrants became a problem. The numerous illegals caused the creation of a government commission to review all aspects of immigration. The White Paper on Immigration released in 1966 called for a complete and final overhaul of Canadian immigration policy. This policy should be free of discrimination based on race or ethnicity. The White Paper of Canada on immigration also advocated the right of Canadian citizens to sponsor immediate relatives, if their educational and occupational standards met those of regular immigrants.

When the report came up for discussion in parliamentary committee, ethnic communities exhibited surprising strength. By 1970, they represented one-third of Canada's population and had become a "third force" in Canadian politics. They were confident, had economic affluence, and demanded a new deal for themselves, which included a society that demanded less conformity to the Anglo culture and a more pluralistic focus. One response to these demands, in the later 1960s, was the development and implementation of an equitable immigration system based on domestic economic requirements and on prospects for short-term and long-term integration. From 1967 to the mid-1970's, the key immigration issues for Canada were refugees (Czechoslovakian, Ugandan, Asian, and Chilean) and illegal immigration.

REPORT ON IMMIGRATION

In 1972, Robert Andras, who was to be the chief architect of the Immigration Act of 1976, became minister of manpower and immigration. Andras not only revitalized his department but also energetically worked for immigration reform. In September, 1973, he initiated a major review of immigration and population policies, which resulted in the publication of a green paper on the subject. Because there was a lack of scholars and scholarship on the subject, the document was a disappointing, overcautious, and inadequate. Consequently, a Special Joint Committee of the Senate and House of Commons was appointed in March of 1975. The committee held fifty public hearings, heard four hundred witnesses, and received fourteen hundred briefs. The report it presented to Parliament in November, 1975, was warmly received, and sixty of its sixty-five recommendations were accepted. Its principal recommendation was that Canada continue to be a country of immigration, for demographic, economic, family, and humanitarian reasons. The report argued that a new immigration act should contain a clear and formal statement of principal objectives concerning admission, nondiscrimination, sponsorship of relatives, refugees, and classes of persons prohibited. Operational details should be specified in the regulations.

The report communicated that immigration should be a central variable in Canada's population policy to forestall the decline of Canada's population, especially of francophones. In relation to population policy, immigration should be linked to population growth and economic conditions. However, the policy and target figures should be determined and presented for parliamentary scrutiny after consulting with the provinces. Other recommendations were that the point system be retained but modified to encourage settlement in underdeveloped areas, and that more staff be hired and better enforcement procedures be instituted.

IMMIGRATION ACT OF 1976

These recommendations were incorporated into the Immigration Act of 1976, which had its first reading on November 22, 1976 (hence that year has become linked with the name of the act), received royal assent on August 5, 1977, and became law on April 10, 1978. The act contained constructive provisions and was politically sensitive and forward-looking. It made a positive contribution to the Canadian public image in the area of immigration management. Its most significant provisions were included in a clear statement of the basic principles of Canadian immigration policy, as recommended by the Special Joint Committee—the first time that had been attempted in Canadian immigration law.

The act created a new system of planning and managing Canadian immigration. It sought to involve the provinces in immigration planning and decision making, as well as to open the process to parliamentary and public discussion. The act established three classes of immigrants: family, refugee, and others selected on the basis of the point system. Ministerial discretion was reduced in areas of exclusion, control, and enforcement. Other provisions dealt with refugees, revising the point system and ensuring that actual immigrant landings were consistent with announced immigration levels.

The Immigration Act of 1976 was praised as a responsible and forward-looking piece of legislation. In some respects, the act proved worthy of that praise. In 1979, Canada's commitment to easing the distress of refugees, displaced persons, and the persecuted was seriously challenged by the "boat people" of Southeast Asia. There was a great outpouring of public concern for the situation. The government dispatched immigration officials to the refugee camps and, by the end of 1980, admitted more than sixty thousand ethnic Vietnamese, Cambodians, Laotians, and Chinese from Southeast Asia—the highest per capita "boat people" resettlement program of any nation. One group that has become highly visible is entrepreneurs, who, with an investment of $250,000, can immigrate to Canada. Chinese immigrants from Hong Kong have been particularly noticeable in this category.

All did not go as expected, however. Sympathy for those entering Canada and then claiming refugee status waned, because undocumented immigration continued to be a major problem. The law resulted in a backlog of refugee-status-determination cases. The provinces, except for Quebec and Ontario, did not cooperate in setting up population guidelines. The potentially valuable Demographic Policy Steering Group and Demographic Policy Secretariat disappeared, and federal government efforts to develop a population policy were initially stalled. There has been a long-term trend of fertility falling in the industrialized world, especially in Canada, and rising in the nonindustrialized countries. Thus, by the mid-1980s, Canada had to develop a population policy for falling birth rates and emigration to the United States; it had to use immigration as a vital part of its population policy. Because western and northern European countries were no longer significant sources of immigration, Canada turned to Asia a means of maintaining a sufficient population level. The Immigration Act of 1976 provided the framework for Canada to adapt to changing circumstances and to exhibit humanitarian behavior by providing refuge to the dispossessed in the world.

IMMIGRATION AND REFUGEE PROTECTION ACT
In 2002, the Immigration Act of 1976 was replaced by the Immigration and Refugee Protection Act. Among other provisions, this law created four classes of immigrants: to family class, refugee class, and other, it added economic class, designed to admit highly educated and employable immigrants likely to make positive contributions to the Canadian economy.

Between 1989 and 2013, the number of permanent residents admitted to Canada has fluctuated between about 174,000 (1998) and 280,000 (2010), with nearly 259,000 admitted in 2013. According to the *Globe and Mail*, the Conservative Canadian government plans to increase immigration levels as it heads into the 2015 election year. Citizenship and Immigration Minister Chris Alexander said, "Canada aims to welcome as many as 285,000 new permanent residents in the next year." Nearly 65 percent of all admissions to Canada were projected to be economic immigrants looking for better employment and an improved financial position.

——*Arthur W. Helweg*

BIBLIOGRAPHY AND FURTHER READING
Friesen, Joe. "Canada to Open the Door Wider to 'Higher Calibre' Immigrants." *Globe and Mail.* Globe and Mail, 31 Oct. 2014. Web. 30 Apr. 2015.

Hawkins, Freda. *Canada and Immigration: Public Policy and Public Concern.* 2nd ed. Kingston: McGill-Queen UP, 1988. Print.

Omidvar, Ratna. "Changing the Rules on Immigration Changes Canada's Narrative." *Globe and Mail.* Globe and Mail, 13 Feb. 2015. Web. 30 Apr. 2015.

Palmer, Howard, ed. *Immigration and the Rise of Multiculturalism.* Vancouver: Copp Clark, 1975. Print.

Whitaker, Reginald. *Double Standard: The Secret History of Canadian Immigration.* Toronto: Lester, 1987. Print.

IMMIGRATION REFORM AND CONTROL ACT OF 1986

The Immigration Reform and Control Act (IRCA) was signed into law by President Ronald Reagan on November 6, 1986. The act amended the Immigration and Nationality Act of 1965 and was based in part on the findings and recommendations of the Select Commission on Immigration and Refugee Policy (1978–81). In its 1981 report to Congress, this commission had proposed that the United States continue to accept large numbers of immigrants and enact a program of amnesty for undocumented workers already in the United States. To deter migration of illegal immigrants to the United States, the commission also proposed to make the employment of undocumented workers a punishable offense.

DEVELOPMENT OF THE BILL

These proposals were incorporated into the Simpson-Mazzoli bill, a first version of which was introduced in 1982. In the five years between its introduction and its enactment, the bill ran into opposition from a variety of quarters. Agricultural interests, especially growers of perishable commodities, were concerned that the proposed employer sanctions would jeopardize their labor supply. Mexican American advocacy groups also opposed employer sanctions, while organized labor and restrictionists who were concerned about the massive influx of foreign workers favored employer sanctions. Many liberals and humanitarians supported the notion of legalizing the status of undocumented immigrants and expressed concerns over potential discrimination against them.

In the 1980s, the bill repeatedly was pronounced dead only to be revived again as various lawmakers, notably Representatives Leon Panetta, Charles Schumer, and Peter Rodino, introduced compromises and amendments to respond to their constituencies or to overcome opposition by congressional factions. Differences also developed between the House Democratic leadership and the Republican White House over funding the legalization program. On October 15, 1986, the House at last approved the bill, by a vote of 238 to 173; the Senate approved the bill on October 17, by a vote of 63 to 24.

PROVISIONS

The major components of the Immigration Reform and Control Act provided for the control of illegal immigration (Title I), the legalization of undocumented immigrants (Title II), and the reform of legal immigration (Title III). Other sections of the act provided for reports to Congress (Title IV), state assistance for the incarceration costs of illegal immigrants and certain Cuban nationals (Title V), the creation of a commission for the study of international migration and cooperative economic development (Title VI), and federal responsibility for deportable and excludable immigrants convicted of crimes (Title VII).

A major objective of the IRCA, the control of illegal immigration, was to be achieved by imposing sanctions on employers. The IRCA made it unlawful for any person knowingly to hire, recruit, or refer for a fee any immigrant not authorized to work in the United States. Before hiring new employees, employers would be required to examine certain specified documents to verify a job applicant's identity and authority to work.

The act established civil and criminal penalties, and employers could be fined up to two thousand dollars per unauthorized immigrant, even for a first offense. Employers who demonstrated a pattern of knowingly hiring undocumented immigrants could face felony penalties of up to six months' imprisonment and/or a three-thousand-dollar fine per violation. Employers also were required to keep appropriate records. Failure to do so could result in a civil fine of up to one thousand dollars. In order to allow time for a public education campaign to become effective, penalties against employers for hiring undocumented immigrants were not phased in until June, 1987.

The second major objective of the IRCA, the legalization of undocumented immigrants, was to be realized by granting temporary residence status to immigrants who had entered the United States illegally prior to January 1, 1982, and who had resided in the United States continuously since then. They could be granted permanent residence status after eighteen months if they could demonstrate a minimal understanding of English and some knowledge of the history and government of the United States. After a five-year period of permanent residence, they would become eligible for citizenship.

The act also permitted the attorney general to grant legal status to undocumented immigrants who could show that they had entered the United States prior to January, 1972, and lived in the country since then. Newly legalized immigrants were barred from most forms of public assistance for five years, although exceptions could be made for emergency medical care, aid to the blind or disabled, or other assistance deemed to be in the interest of public health.

To assure passage of the bill, support of the growers in the West and Southwest was essential. After protracted negotiations, the growers succeeded in getting the kind of legislation that assured them of a continued supply of temporary agricultural workers. The new program differed from earlier bracero programs by providing for the legalization of special agricultural workers who could work anywhere and who could become eligible for permanent resident status or for citizenship. The IRCA granted temporary residence status to undocumented immigrants who had performed field labor in perishable agricultural commodities in the United States for at least ninety days during the twelve-month period ending May 1, 1986, as well as to persons who could demonstrate to the Immigration and Naturalization Service that they had performed appropriate agricultural field labor for ninety days in three successive previous years while residing in the United States for six months in each year.

The act also revised and expanded an existing temporary foreign worker program known as H-2. In case of a shortage of seasonal farmworkers, employers could apply to the secretary of labor no more than sixty days in advance of needing workers. The employer also was required to try to recruit domestic workers for the jobs. H-2 also provided that during fiscal years 1990-1993, additional special agricultural workers could be admitted to temporary residence status as "replenishment workers." Their admission was contingent upon certification of the need for such workers by the secretaries of labor and of agriculture. Replenishment workers who performed ninety days of field work in perishable agricultural commodities in each of the first three years would be eligible for permanent resident status. They were, however, disqualified from public assistance. In order to become eligible for citizenship, they would have to perform seasonal agricultural services for ninety days during five separate years.

The IRCA also provided permanent resident status for a hundred thousand specified Cubans and Haitians who entered the United States prior to January 1, 1982. The law increased quotas from former colonies and dependencies from five hundred to six thousand and provided for the admission of five thousand immigrants annually for two years, to be chosen from nationals of thirty-six countries with low rates of immigration. Altogether, the Immigration Reform and Control Act led to the legalization of the status of three million undocumented immigrants; however, IRCA was not as successful in curbing illegal immigration as had been anticipated.

Mindful of the potential for discrimination, Congress established an Office of Special Counsel in the Department of Justice to investigate and prosecute charges of discrimination connected with unlawful immigration practices. The act also required states to verify the status of noncitizens applying for public aid and provided that states be reimbursed for the implementation costs of this provision. To reimburse states for the public assistance, health, and education costs resulting from legalizing undocumented immigrants, the act provided for the appropriation of one billion dollars in each of the four fiscal years following its enactment.

——*Helmut J. Schmeller*

BIBLIOGRAPHY AND FURTHER READING

Cohen, Steve, Ed Mynott, and Beth Humphries. *From Immigration Controls to Welfare Controls.* Hoboken: Routledge, 2014. Print.

Fuchs, Lawrence H. *The American Kaleidoscope: Race, Ethnicity, and the Civic Culture.* Hanover: UP of New England, 1990. Print.

Newton, Lina. *Illegal, Alien, or Immigrant: The Politics of Immigration Reform.* New York: New York UP, 2008. Print.

Zolberg, Aristide R. "Reforming the Back Door: The Immigration Reform and Control Act of 1986 in Historical Perspective." *Immigration Reconsidered: History, Sociology, and Politics.* Ed. Virginia Yans-McLaughlin. New York: Oxford UP, 1990. Print.

IMMIGRATION RESTRICTIONS: AN OVERVIEW

Immigration refers to the movement of persons from one nation or region to another with the purpose of seeking permanent residence. Immigrants leave their countries of origin for a variety of reasons, including employment opportunities, economic or social conditions, military conflict, and political turmoil.

Historically, nations have imposed restrictions on immigration based on xenophobia—the fear of alien or "other" cultures—or to protect political, economic, or ethnic dominance. Modern restrictions place more emphasis on the economic and social effects of immigration. According to the United Nations' "International Migration 2013" report, 3.2 percent (232 million) of the world's population was living outside their native country in 2013. Of this number, one-third migrated from a developing nation to a developed one. The United Nations estimated that 214 million no longer live in their country of origin.

In recent years, the United States Congress has debated immigration reform largely due to concerns about illegal immigration, predominantly from Mexico, El Salvador, Guatemala, and Honduras. The case of immigration reform in the United States is unique, in that immigration played a major role in the settlement of the country, and its cultural, social, and economic effects are evident throughout the country's history and its present population.

HISTORY

With the exception of American Indians, all persons living in the United States are descended from immigrants or slaves who came to the country during the last four hundred years. In the late seventeenth century, foreign-born persons constituted 75 percent of the American population.

Initially, the US government encouraged open immigration in the interest of settling as much territory as possible. Following the Civil War, however, states began to pass their own immigration statutes. The United States Supreme Court determined that immigration came under federal jurisdiction in 1875, and Congress established the Immigration Service in 1891.

Most early immigration laws were instituted in order to control the composition of the US population. In 1790, Congress passed the Naturalization Act, which effectively limited immigration to persons of European and Caucasian descent. In 1882, Congress passed the Chinese Exclusion Act, which made immigration from China illegal. This law was repealed by the 1943 passage of the Magnuson Act. There were some who also proposed restrictions against people from particular European nations, including Ireland, Italy, and Poland.

In addition to ethnicity, the US government was also concerned with the moral composition of the population. Between 1872 and 1890, Congress passed laws restricting the immigration of, among other groups, prostitutes, criminals, individuals with mental illness, and financially unstable persons. In the late nineteenth century, the government became concerned about the potential for foreign laborers to negatively affect employment or payment rates for native laborers. Laws passed in 1885 and 1887 were among the first to restrict immigration based on economic concerns. Labor issues remain a major part of the modern immigration debate.

From 1900 to 1921, Congress established a "quota system," which granted permission to a set number of individuals from each ethnic group to immigrate. Certain ethnic groups, including people from most Asian nations, were excluded entirely. The number of immigrants from each ethnic group was determined according to the census. The government also developed provisions intended to promote the immigration of certain types of laborers whose skills were lacking in the existing population.

In 1924, as concerns about border security increased, Congress established the first office of border control to monitor immigration from Canada and Mexico. Immigration rates dropped substantially between 1925 and 1945, especially during the Great Depression (1929–1940). In 1948, Congress made temporary revisions to immigration policy to allow people left homeless by World War II to come to the United States.

In 1952, Congress passed the McCarran-Walter Immigration and Nationality Act, which formally repealed any remaining restrictions based on ethnicity and opened immigration to people from any nation. Reflecting recent political developments, the government began to restrict immigration based on political ideology: Those with alleged ties to communist organizations were actively prevented from entering the United States.

In 1965, Congress abandoned the quota system and based immigration acceptance on the relative "need" of each applicant. Under the new system, a certain number of people were allowed entrance for labor, family unification, and political asylum. The new system greatly restricted immigration from Mexico and Central and South America and led to an increase in illegal immigration.

During the 1980s, illegal immigration and border security became the chief issues in the immigration debate. In 1986, Congress granted additional powers to law enforcement agencies to allow for the punishment of persons who aided or facilitated illegal immigration.

In 1990, Congress made it illegal for the US government to deny entrance into the United States based on political beliefs, ideologies, or associations. At the same time, Congress voted to allow a 40 percent increase in the number of immigrants lawfully permitted per year. In 1996, Congress addressed illegal immigration from Latin America with laws that doubled the number of border control agencies, added fences in areas with heavy traffic, and increased penalties for harboring or aiding illegal immigrants.

IMMIGRATION RESTRICTIONS TODAY

The modern immigration debate in the United States focuses primarily on illegal immigration. In the early 2000s, a committee within the House of Representatives formulated a new immigration bill, H.R. 4437 (Sensenbrenner/King Border Protection, Antiterrorism and Illegal Immigration Control Act of 2005). The bill proposed to construct nearly 700 miles of fencing along the southwest border of the United States and to classify illegal immigrants as "aggravated felons," thus allowing for additional legal penalties against migrants and those who aid or harbor them.

A US Senate committee formulated a competing legislative proposal, S. 2611, the Comprehensive Immigration Reform Act (CIRA). The Senate version provided for additional funding for border security and would have established a method for tracking illegal immigrants. CIRA would also have allowed thousands of illegal immigrants currently residing in the United States to seek permanent residency.

Members of Congress were scheduled to debate the alternative proposals in June 2006, but debate was postponed to allow additional time for independent research sessions and to hear testimony from experts regarding specific portions of both bills. The proposal of the House legislation, which was more stringent, was partially responsible for the mass immigrant rights protests that occurred throughout the country during the first half of 2006. In the end, S. 2611 passed by a 62–36 vote, and H.R. 4437 passed

by a vote of 239–182. Neither bill was enacted into law, however, as both failed to pass conference committee. With the end of the 2007 legislative session both bills died.

The 2007 legislative session saw another attempt at CIRA in the form of S. 1348, which, among other provisions, would have provided a path to legal citizenship for many illegal immigrants in the United States and would have provided funding for border patrol agents and the construction of 300 miles of vehicle barriers. The bill was troubled from the beginning, undergoing a series of amendments. On June 28, 2007, the majority of the Senate voted to block the bill, officially quashing it before it even received an up-or-down vote.

In 2001, the Development, Relief and Education for Alien Minors Act (DREAM Act) was first introduced to Congress. The DREAM Act is an American legislative proposal that would grant residency to immigrants based on certain conditions, such as good moral standing, those with a high school diploma or college degree, and immigrants who arrived illegally in the United States as minors. The bill, however, was replaced with other more limited versions, such as the Student Adjustment Act of 2001. The DREAM Act was reintroduced in 2009, but it failed to pass by a mere five votes. The DREAM Act has yet to pass on a national level, but as of 2016, fifteen states had passed legislation conferring benefits and privileges to certain illegal immigrants that are determined at the state level, such as reduced tuition for in-state universities.

The issue of immigration made national news on April 23, 2010, when Arizona governor Jan Brewer signed into law a state immigration act known as Arizona SB 1070 or the Support Our Law Enforcement and Safe Neighborhoods Act. The legislation caused widespread controversy because it required legal aliens to carry registration documents on their person at all times while allowing police to investigate and search anyone they deem with "reasonable suspicion" to be an illegal alien, which critics argued would lead to widespread racial profiling in the state. Demonstrations and boycotts occurred as a result of the bill being signed by Brewer. Several lawsuits were also filed, including one by the United States Department of Justice. As a result of the Justice Department's action, a temporary injunction was put on the law, preventing its most controversial elements from taking effect. In response, Governor Brewer filed a countersuit criticizing the lack of federal assistance with immigration issues in Arizona. In June 2012, the Supreme Court issued a ruling in *Arizona v. United States* that struck down several provisions of the Arizona law under the Supremacy Clause of the US Constitution but allowed the requirement to verify the citizenship of all detained person to stand.

In 2012, the administration of President Barack Obama instituted the Deferred Action for Childhood Arrivals (DACA) policy as an executive action, allowing those who had entered the country illegally prior to their sixteenth birthdays to gain a two-year work permit and exemption from deportation. However, DACA does not provide a path to citizenship, as the DREAM Act would. In 2014, President Obama issued an executive action called the Deferred Action for Parents of Americans and Lawful Permanent Residents (DAPA), which would have allowed approximately five million undocumented immigrants who are the parents of US citizens or permanent residents to apply for a program that would have protected them from deportation and allowed them to work legally in the United States. In June 2016, the US Supreme Court announced it had deadlocked on *United States v. Texas No. 15-674* in a 4–4 tie, thereby allowing an appeals court ruling that blocked DAPA to stand.

Supporters of stricter immigration restrictions cite labor, economy, national security, and terrorism as chief issues. However, a clear link between immigration levels and crime rates or terrorism has not been established. In addition, recent research suggests that higher rates of immigration are not linked to increased unemployment among native workers.

Public opinion polls conducted by the Gallup Organization, the Pew Hispanic Center, the Center for Immigration Studies, and other polling organizations indicate that the majority of Americans favor immigration reform. There appears to be little consensus, however, on the manner in which the government should formulate and implement reforms.

The administration of US president Barack Obama has deported more illegal immigrants than any other presidential administration since 1925 (when official records started being kept). However,

in 2015, net migration from Mexico was in the negative, as more people left the United States for Mexico than came into the country from Mexico. This issue of immigration has been a contentious one in the 2016 presidential race, and candidates have wide-ranging opinions about policy. Donald Trump, the Republican presidential nominee, repeatedly called for the completion of the border wall between the United States and Mexico, while the Democratic candidate, Hillary Clinton, affirmed her general support for Obama's policies. A 2016 report by the Center for Migration Studies reported that there were an estimated 10.9 million illegal immigrants living the United States in 2014, the lowest since 2003, and that the total undocumented immigration population in the United States declined every year between 2008 and 2014.

Nevertheless, Obama's successor, Donald Trump, rode to the White House in the 2016 election on a campaign of strong anti-immigration pledges. In one of his first acts in office, in early 2017, Trump imposed a temporary ban on immigration from seven Muslim-majority countries in the Middle East—but the order was stopped by a federal district court. Shortly thereafter, Trump introduced a similar executive order that was somewhat more cautiously worded. This time, several state attorneys general stood together in saying that they would oppose implementation of the ban.

——*Micah L. Issitt and Andrew Walter*

BIBLIOGRAPHY AND FURTHER READING

Borjas, George J. *Heaven's Door: Immigration Policy and the American Economy.* Princeton: Princeton UP, 2001. Print.

Daniels, Robert. *Guarding the Golden Door: American Immigrants and Immigration Policy Since 1882.* New York: Hill & Wang, 2004. Print.

DeSipio, Louis, and Rodolfo O. De la Garza. *US Immigration in the Twenty-First Century: Making Americans, Remaking America.* Boulder: Westview, 2015. Print.

Ngai, Mae M. *Impossible Subjects: Illegal Aliens and the Making of Modern America.* Princeton: Princeton UP, 2004. Print.

Schueths, April M., and Jodie Michelle Lawston. *Living Together, Living Apart: Mixed-Status Families and Us Immigration Policy.* Seattle: U of Washington P, 2015. Print.

IMMIGRATION'S POSITIVE IMPACT ON US SOCIETY

The United States is home to approximately 40 million foreign-born Americans, which accounts for 13 percent of the population. Such a large immigrant pool has a considerable effect on economy, society, and culture. The nature of that effect has been the cause of ongoing debate, pitting those who view immigration as necessary and beneficial against those who see it as socioeconomically suspect. Both sides have marshalled empirical evidence to support their claims, yet relevant data can be scarce. Still, what is available often contradicts the conclusions advanced by critics.

Believing that immigration has disruptive economic consequences, critics cite evidence of competition between native and foreign-born workers, crowding-out of American low-skilled and semi-skilled jobs, suppression of wages, and depletion of social services. However, much of the evidence points in the opposite direction. Researchers have found that immigrant and native-born labor is complementary rather than overlapping. Immigrants can take credit for net job creation, both as employees and entrepreneurs, and for the repatriation of American corporations from abroad.

Immigrants increase consumer demand and consumption through purchases of American goods and services. By stimulating corporate investment, wages, and job creation, the net contribution to economic growth is positive, particularly over the medium to long term. Expanded inventories spur growth throughout the supply chain. In turn, this "knock-on effect" leads to an increase in the Gross Domestic Product (GDP) and federal tax revenues. Greater federal revenues enhance the government's capacity to meet its social-service obligations, invest in public-sector projects, and create jobs.

Opponents argue that immigrants are a net drain on social services, such as health care, education, public housing, welfare, and pensions, but recent studies suggest that documented aliens (legal immigrants) pay more into these programs than they deplete. This may even be true for undocumented aliens (illegal immigrants), though relevant data are scant. The Social Security Administration Actuary has stated that undocumented aliens pay roughly $12 billion per annum and have paid a total of $300 billion into the Social Security Trust Fund, or close to 10 percent of the total. They also pay income, sales, and property taxes plus taxes on certain goods, such as fuel, alcohol, tobacco products, and medical goods and services, contributing about $12 billion to state and local tax revenues.

Critics also believe that immigration causes an increase in crime rates, though recent studies undermine such claims. Available data suggest that both rural and urban communities with comparatively higher rates of immigration are safer than those that have experienced a negligible influx. Specifically, murders and other serious crimes among African-Americans, Latinos, and Caucasians seem to have decreased as a result of higher immigrant populations. Although more research is needed to corroborate initial conclusions, it is safe to say that claims about high crime rates and related assumptions about cultural tendencies are questionable at best.

Disagreements about the socioeconomic effects of immigration flourish unabated, but not all aspects of immigration are so hotly contested. For instance, sizable majorities of native-born Americans agree that immigrants have made positive contributions to American culture. They have embraced an array of immigrant traditions, which have become an indelible part of the country's cultural heritage. Whether through food, art, music, literature, sports, television, clothing, or architecture, the influence of immigrant cultures has been celebrated for generations. The mixture of native and immigrant cultural characteristics has been so pervasive that separating the two would be impossible.

——*Tomislav Han*

BIBLIOGRAPHY AND FURTHER READING

Berger, David. *American Immigration: A Very Short History.* New York, NY: Oxford University Press, 2011.

Borjas, George J. *We Wanted Workers: Unraveling the Immigration Narrative.* (New York, NY: W.W. Norton, 2016.

Daniels, Roger. *Coming to America: A History of Immigration and Ethnicity in American Life.* New York, NY: Harper Perennial, 2002.

Wong, Tom K. *The Politics of Immigration: Partisanship, Demographic Change, and American National Identity.* New York, NY: Oxford University Press, 2016.

INCORPORATION

Incorporation is the process whereby social groups, classes, and individuals are integrated into a larger social entity. This is achieved either through the extension of rights and the subsequent exacting of obligations, as in "citizenship communities," or through mechanisms such as social mobility, inter-marriage, and urban desegregation. Like social closure, incorporation implies marginalized groups, elite mass relations, and co-optation. The term has been widely employed in discussions about the allegedly revolutionary role of the proletariat, whose historical mission is said to have been frustrated by the incorporation of this class through the welfare state, political representation, and home ownership.

However, the term has expanded to include racial, ethnic, gender, and religious groups.

For racial and ethnic groups, incorporation can be seen as a form of assimilation. For ethnic groups to achieve rights, they not only have to acquire citizenship but also must relinquish parts of their ethnic culture to be included in mainstream society. Incorporation can also be seen as forms of social and political movement, in which ethnic minority groups collectively pressure the larger society to accept and include their ethnic groups in the mainstream society.

——*Mary Yu Danico*

INDENTURED SERVITUDE

Indentured servitude is a labor relationship in which the laborer contracts to work exclusively for a single employer for a fixed period of time. Although this contract, or indenture, represents a free act of the contracting parties, it legally binds the laborer to the employer during the term fixed by the agreement. Indentured servitude initially played an important role in inducing settlement of the original American colonies. In its most common form, the employer paid the passage of a laborer to the New World, a sum that was beyond the means of ordinary laborers in Europe. In return, the laborer would agree to work for an extended period, usually seven years, in the colonies. At the end of the period of indenture, the servant would acquire land and perhaps an amount of money for fulfilling the terms of the contract, thus becoming free and independent again.

The system of indentured servitude paved the way for the establishment of slavery in North America. The first African Americans to arrive in today's mainland United States, in 1619, came as indentured servants. The expansive need for labor generated by the size of the colonies and the labor-intensive cultivation of such cash crops as tobacco was too great, however, to be met exclusively by indentured servitude. As a result, Africans were captured and imported into the colonies.

——*Aristide Sechandice*

An indentured servant's contract. The original uploader was Greensburger at English Wikipedia.

INDIAN

In its use to refer to the native peoples of the Americas, the term "Indian" is based on a historical error. In the late fifteenth century, there was some disagreement over the size of the earth, although it had been accurately determined by the ancient Greeks many centuries earlier. Christopher Columbus and explorers who followed him believed the earth's circumference to be roughly half what we know it to be today.

The purpose of the early explorations of the Americas was to find a pathway to India by sailing west instead of east from Europe, primarily to avoid trouble with the Muslim nations that controlled the territory between Europe and India. Apparently, Columbus thought he had reached India when he landed on the island of Hispaniola (today occupied by Haiti and the Dominican Republic), named the area the West Indies, and referred to the natives as *indios* (Spanish for Indians).

While the later British and French explorers who landed in North America did not believe that Massachusetts and Quebec were India, the term was still used, translated into the appropriate languages. The term is still in wide use, essentially because no better collective term has been widely accepted. Some native people find the term "Indian" deeply offensive, whereas others find it and "American Indian" acceptable

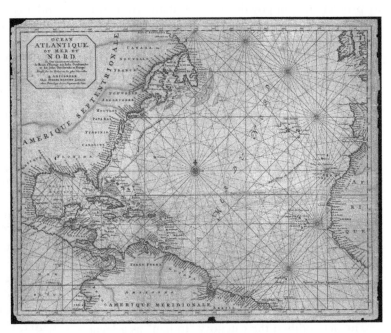

1693 nautical chart of the Atlantic Ocean marked with "Route de Europe aux Indes Occidentales" or "West Indies". By http://www.geographicus.com/mm5/cartographers/mortierpierre.txt.

and even preferable to such well-intentioned revisions as "Native American" or the less widely used "Amerind." The most accurate—and most widely accepted—way to identify a person or tradition is simply to refer to the specific tribe or group to which the person or tradition belongs.

——*Marc Goldstein*

INDIAN ACT OF 1876

The Indian Act of 1876, the Canadian parliament's first major piece of legislation setting forth the federal government's role and responsibilities with respect to the Indians, continued nearly all of the policies established during British colonial rule. As with the British policy, the dual features of the legislation were the protection of the Indians and their eventual assimilation into Canadian society. Ironically, these goals worked at cross purposes. Paternalistic efforts to protect the Indians emphasized the distinctions between Indians and

Euro-Canadians and therefore actually discouraged assimilation. This legislation first applied only to Canadians of Indian descent. It was later extended to include the Inuit as well.

The act established a series of reserved lands, which were to be laboratories for training the Indians in the ways of white people, and established elected band councils whose powers were minimal. The reserves, administered by a government agent, were exempt from taxation, and those living on a reserve had access to food and supplies in the form of disaster rations. While the reserves were intended to protect the supposedly naïve Indians from the unscrupulous practices of outsiders, they isolated Indians from most Euro-Canadians and subjected them to the sometimes unscrupulous practices of the all-powerful Indian agents. These agents had control over social, political, and economic activities on the reserves. They also had the ability to withhold rations from those who did not adhere to their dictatorial policies.

Numerous abuses occurred. For several decades Indians on the prairies were forbidden to leave their reserve without a pass from the agent. They were further prohibited from staying overnight on a reserve other than their own, and in many cases non-Indians (including non-Status Indians) were forbidden to reside on reserves. Subsequent amendments to the Indian Act banned native religious activities such as the Sun Dance and potlatch and made it illegal for Indians to solicit contributions in order to pursue land claims.

The act codified the category "Indian" as a legal rather than racial or cultural designation and gave the government the legal power to determine who qualified as an Indian. It further provided for the enfranchisement of individuals, wherein a man could surrender Indian status for himself, his wife, and his children in exchange for Canadian citizenship and a plot of land. Women who married non-Indians, including non-status Indians, lost their own Indian status and benefits. Their children were also precluded from claiming Indian status. Non-Indian

women who married Status Indians became Status Indians themselves. Enfranchisement could also be imposed upon Indians who earned a college degree or entered a profession such as minister, teacher, lawyer, or doctor. Though amended many times, the Indian Act was not significantly revised until 1951.

BIBLIOGRAPHY AND FURTHER READING

Binnema, Ted. "Protecting Indian Lands by Defining Indian: 1850–76." *Jour. of Canadian Studies* 48.2 (2014): 5–39. *Academic Search Complete.* Web. 29 Apr. 2015.

Borrows, John. *Canada's Indigenous Constitution.* Toronto: U of Toronto P, 2010. *eBook Collection (EBSCOhost).* Web. 29 Apr. 2015.

Flanagan, Thomas, Christopher Alcantara, and André Le Dressay. *Beyond the Indian Act: Restoring Aboriginal Property Rights.* Montréal: MQUP, 2010. *eBook Collection (EBSCOhost).* Web. 29 Apr. 2015.

Fullerton-Owl, David. "Titanic Canada: The Indian Act, 1876." *Windspeaker* 24.11 (2007): 13. *Academic Search Complete.* Web. 29 Apr. 2015.

Manzano-Munguía, Maria C. "Indian Policy and Legislation: Aboriginal Identity Survival in Canada." *Studies in Ethnicity & Nationalism* 11.3 (2011): 404–426. *Academic Search Complete.* Web. 29 Apr. 2015.

Wakeham, Pauline, and Jennifer Henderson. *Reconciling Canada: Critical Perspectives on the Culture of Redress.* Toronto: U of Toronto P, 2013. *eBook Collection (EBSCOhost).* Web. 29 Apr. 2015.

INDIAN ACT OF 1951

Although the Indian Act of 1951 was the first comprehensive revision of Canada's 1876 Indian Act, it did little to undo the paternalism of its predecessor. Like the previous law, it gave nearly absolute control of Indian activities to the Department of Indian Affairs and Northern Development (DIAND). This included the development of Indian lands and resources as well as oversight of band councils. The new act also retained the enfranchisement provisions of the earlier legislation, including those that denied Indian status to women who married non-Indians. In a well-known sex discrimination suit brought by Jeannette Lavell, an Ojibwa who was

denied Indian status as a result of her marriage, the Supreme Court in 1973 upheld those provisions of the act. A Maliceet woman, Sandra Lovelace, took a similar case before the United Nations in 1981. Although Canada was found to have violated international human rights covenants, the enfranchisement provisions of the Indian Act were not repealed until 1985.

The new act did, however, repeal the most blatant discrimination inherent in the Indian Act of 1876. It no longer prohibited Indian religious ceremonies, political fund-raising, or consumption of alcohol off reserve lands. Later amendments permitted the consumption of alcohol on reserves and gave Indians the right to vote in Canadian elections.

The 1951 act continued a number of benefits of the earlier legislation, including the exemption of Indian lands from property and estate taxes and exemption of income earned on reserves from taxation. Although these provisions have protected Indian property from seizure, they have also hindered economic development on the reserves. Because Indians have been unable to mortgage their lands, it has often been difficult for them to raise capital for development projects.

Despite the restrictions imposed by the 1951 Indian Act, natives have fought efforts to discard it altogether. Fearing that the federal government would abandon its responsibilities to native welfare, many natives fought the 1969 white paper proposal to repeal the Indian Act. The Indian Act was rewritten in 1985, but other than the repeal of enfranchisement provisions, it remained virtually unchanged.

INDIAN ACT OF 1985

Because of the confusion created by a diversity of local laws in different provinces under the federal government in Canada, legislators have created certain acts that cannot vary according to locality. Such is the case of the Indian Act of 1985. In effect a compendium of earlier acts (of 1927 and 1951), it also added new laws more in keeping with contemporary conditions.

The main divisions of the act provide for the designation of reserves (land vested in Her Majesty's Crown, but "reserved for Indian use"), establishment of band councils and election of band leaders, and a comprehensive Indian Register. By the act, the sole authority of the band council to assign possession of specific reserve lands to individuals is recognized for the first time. This right of possession must be recognized by the Superintendent General of Indian Affairs, who issues a Certificate of Possession. Possessors may transfer their land rights, but only to other members within their band, or back to the band council itself.

Provisions respecting the security of reserves against government expropriation ended misunderstandings that had developed over many years. With the right of security went defined areas of band responsibility (to maintain roads, bridges, and so on) which, if unfulfilled, could lead to government charges against band councils. Common responsibility between councils and government for revenues accruing to bands (through royalties or sale of Indian produced goods) is spelled out, including the government right to use such funds to assure proper sanitary facilities and disease control.

One use of government funds on reserves reflects benevolent subsidies under the 1985 act. Schools are to be provided to all bands on an equal basis, and attendance up to a minimum age is required of all Indian children. Provisions for tax-exempt status (lands, personal property, or salaries earned in reserve areas) and taxable income earned from contacts beyond the reserves are meant to protect both Indian and government interests.

The act contains brief mention of individual rights. There is a right of testamentary wills for family security. Otherwise, where individual Indian rights might be jeopardized owing to band council inaction, government intervention is allowed (mainly to aid orphans or the mentally handicapped).

——Byron D. Cannon

BIBLIOGRAPHY AND FURTHER READING

Flanagan, Thomas, Christopher Alcantara, and André Le Dressay. *Beyond the Indian Act: Restoring Aboriginal Property Rights.* Montréal: MQUP, 2010. *eBook Collection (EBSCOhost).* Web. 29 Apr. 2015.

Jay, Makarenko. "The Indian Act: Historical Overview." *Maple Leaf Web* 13 Mar. 2009: NewsBank. Web. 29 Apr. 2015.

Manzano-Munguía, Maria C. "Indian Policy and Legislation: Aboriginal Identity Survival in Canada." *Studies in Ethnicity & Nationalism* 11.3 (2011): 404–426. *Academic Search Complete.* Web. 29 Apr. 2015.

Peach, Ian. "Section 15 of the Canadian Charter of Rights and Freedoms and the Future of Federal Regulation of Indian Status." *U of British Columbia Law Rev.* 45.1 (2012): 103. Print.

Sanderson, Douglas. "Overlapping Consensus, Legislative Reform, and the Indian Act." *Queen's Law Journal* 2 (2014): 511. Print.

INDIAN AMERICANS

Emigration from South Asia has been a dominant behavioral pattern since the Indus Valley civilization (2500–1700 BCE). The impact of merchants and Buddhist missionaries from India is evident today in Central and East Asia, where Indian mythology, dance, and theater have had lasting effects. Movement from western India to Africa dates back to the second century CE Small-scale movement changed to mass emigration as Indians provided cheap labor for British colonies, many becoming indentured servants. The result was a diaspora of nine million Indians scattered throughout the British Empire but concentrated in places with labor-intensive economies, especially plantation systems, such as Mauritius, Fiji, Trinidad, and East Africa. Wide-scale migration to the United States, Australia, and Canada developed in the 1960s, largely because changes in immigration regulations removed existing racial barriers. The oil-rich Middle East has become a focus for South Asian immigration since 1970.

COMING TO AMERICA

Initially, Asian Indians came to the United States as sea captains and traders in the 1790s, actively pursuing trade between India and North America. A very few came as indentured laborers. By 1900, the nation was home to about two thousand Indians, including about five hundred merchants, several dozen religious teachers, and some medical professionals. Six thousand Indians entered the United States through the West Coast between 1907 and 1917, but another three thousand were barred entry. Many of these immigrants came from Canada, where they had faced hostilities, only to meet with the same sort of treatment in the United States. Most immigrants from India during this period originated from Punjab and were adherents of the Sikh faith.

As Indian immigration increased, anti-Asian violence on the West Coast began to target Indians. Discriminatory laws were passed, prohibiting them from owning land and being eligible for US citizenship. In fact, the Immigration Act of 1917 is sometimes referred to as the Indian Exclusion Act. The hostile environment, along with the Great Depression of the 1930s, resulted in several thousand immigrants returning to India. Therefore, in 1940, only 2,405 Asian Indians were living in the United States, mostly around Yuba City, California.

After World War II, new legislation gave Asian Indians the rights to become citizens and own land and established a quota of 100 immigrants per year, allowing for family reunification. Between 1948 and 1965, 6,474 Asian Indians entered the United States as immigrants. The Immigration and Nationality Act of 1965 removed the national origins clause in US immigration legislation and gave preference to highly educated and skilled individuals. India had a ready pool of such talent, and the mass movement from India to the United States began. Sixty-seven percent of the foreign-born Indians in the United States have advanced degrees, as opposed to only 25 percent of the American-born. In addition, Indian Americans are highly represented in the managerial and sales/technical/clerical workers and have low representation in the service, blue-collar categories.

The post-1965 immigrants fall into three categories: initial immigrants, second-wave immigrants, and sponsored immigrants. The initial immigrants, who came soon after restrictions were lifted in 1965, are mainly very highly educated men—doctors, scientists, and academics—who migrated for better educational and professional opportunities. By the 1990s, most of these immigrants, now middle-aged, were earning more than $100,000 annually. Their wives typically had little more than a high school education and did not work outside the home, and their children were in their late teens or early twenties. This first wave of immigrants were concerned about retirement and their children. The second-wave immigrants, who came in the 1970s, were also highly educated professionals. However, these professionals tended to be couples, both of whom worked. Their children were mostly college-bound teenagers, and one of their main concerns was getting their children through college. The third group of immigrants were those individuals sponsored by established family members. They generally were less well educated and more likely to be running small businesses such as motels, grocery stores, gas stations, and other ventures. Their concerns were to establish themselves in a successful business.

PROFILE

The Asian Indian population in the United States—which consisted of about 7,000 people in 1970—grew to close to one million by the late 1990s, making them the fourth-largest immigrant group. This group reached 815,447 in 1990, a 111 percent rise since 1980, when they numbered 387,000. The percentage of foreign-born was up from 70 percent in 1980 to 75 percent in 1990. By 2000 their number was about 2.8 million, and by 2013, according to the US Census Bureau, the population of Indian Americans had added almost another half million people, reaching a total of 3.2 million.

The community is, on the average, getting younger; the median age dropped from thirty years in 1980 to twenty-eight years in 1990. It has stayed roughly the same through the mid-2010s. However, over the same period, the size of the elderly population increased. The gender balance has become more equitable as well: In 1966, women made up 34 percent of the population; by the mid 1990s, they accounted for more than 50 percent. In 2014, the mean family income of Indian Americans reached $101,591, the highest of any ethnic group.

The post-1965 immigrants flocked to the major metropolitan areas, where their skills were most marketable. By the early 21st century, over three-quarters of the Indian population lived in eight major industrial-urban states: California, New York, New Jersey, Texas, Illinois, Florida, Virginia, and Pennsylvania. However, the Asian Indians in the United States generally do not live in concentrated areas but are dispersed throughout the city. The vast majority speak English and are familiar with American ways, so they do not need to rely on their compatriots for help. In addition, because many of them are professionals, they are affluent enough to live where they choose.

The educational attainment of the Indian population is very high: As of 2010, 71 percent of those age twenty-five or older have a bachelor's degree or higher (compared with a national average of 28 percent), and Indians form sizable proportions of the student bodies at the elite colleges in the United States.

The Indian population uses lobbying and campaign contributions to promote its special interests, which range from revisions of immigration policy to efforts to advancing Indian-owned businesses and maintaining good relations with the natal country.

One of the best-known areas of South Asian entrepreneurial behavior is the hotel and motel business. Hindus from the Gujarat region in India, most with the surname of Patel, began arriving in California in the late 1940s. They bought dilapidated hotels and motels in deteriorating neighborhoods and, with cheap family labor, turned the businesses into profitable enterprises. In the mid-1980s, the newsstand business in New York City was dominated by Indian and Pakistani immigrants, who controlled 70 percent of the kiosks. However, ten years later, the Indians and Pakistanis were being replaced by immigrants from the Middle East. South Asians have also been prominently involved in gift shops, the garment industry, and small businesses generally. They have also, since the late 1990s, been very prominent in the high-tech industry in Silicon Valley, frequently filling top engineering and senior management positions.

India has benefited tremendously from emigration to the United States. Remittances, sent by immigrants to remaining family, have made a variety of areas in India relatively prosperous. Large amounts of capital from abroad have been invested in high technology, and new ideas from the United States and elsewhere are also evident. Beginning in the mid-1990s, many Asian Indians returned from abroad to set up industries or work for international companies establishing a presence in India. The bicultural knowledge and skills of these returnees have contributed to Bangalore's becoming the Silicon Valley of India. However, the impact is not limited to Bangalore; it can be seen in Mumbai, Kolkata, and Delhi as well as other municipalities.

——*Arthur W. Helweg*

BIBLIOGRAPHY AND FURTHER READING

Chakravorty, Sanjoy, et al. *The Other One Percent: Indians in America*. New York: Oxford UP, 2017. Print.

Dingra, Pawan. *Life behind the Lobby: Indian American Motel Owners and the American Dream*. Stanford: Stanford UP, 2012. Print.

Helweg, Arthur W. *Immigrants in a Not-So-Strange Land: Indian American Immigrants in the Global Age*. Belmont: Wadsworth, 2004. Print.

Rangaswamy, Padma. *Indian Americans*. New York: Chelsea House, 2007. Print.

INDIAN APPROPRIATION ACT

In 1871, Congress voted to end treaty making with Native American peoples. Since the origins of the republic, the US government had dealt with tribes by recognizing each one as an independent nation living within the United States. Hence, ambassadors were sent out from Washington, D.C., to negotiate treaties, and each agreement had to be ratified by two-thirds of the Senate, as provided in the Constitution. Chief Justice John Marshall, in *Worcester v. Georgia* (1832), had determined that this process had to be followed because each tribe was self-governing and sovereign in its own territory.

The change took place because many people in the United States came to believe that the Native American nations no longer acted like sovereign states. They were too weak, post-Civil War whites believed, and many had become dependent on the federal government for their existence. Members of Congress expressed that view in a series of discussions on American Indian policy in 1870-1871. In the House of Representatives, a sense had also arisen that the House was being ignored in the development of Indian policy. The only way the House could influence Native American relations was by renouncing the treaty concept. The attack on treaty making gained strength during the debate over the money to be appropriated for the United States Board of Indian Commissioners. This agency had been created in 1869 to oversee money authorized to be spent on Indian programs.

END OF TREATY MAKING PROPOSED

The commissioners' first report suggested major changes in Indian policy. It called for ending the treaty system and dealing with "uncivilized" native peoples as "wards of the government." Board chair Felix R. Brunot echoed the views of many US citizens when he declared that it was absurd to treat "a few thousand savages" as if they were equal with the people and government of the United States. President Ulysses S. Grant supported that view, as did his commissioner of Indian affairs, Ely S. Parker, a member of the Seneca nation. Parker believed that it was a cruel farce to deal with the tribes as equals; in his view, most were "helpless and ignorant wards" of the federal government.

The resentment of members of the House of Representatives at their exclusion from Indian policymaking became apparent during debates over treaties negotiated in 1868 and 1869. A May, 1868, agreement with the Osage Nation in Kansas had ceded eight million acres of land to the government. The land then would be sold to a railroad company for twenty cents per acre. The House voted unanimously to recommend that the Senate not ratify the treaty because the land transfer had taken place outside the traditional methods of selling public property. The Senate responded to the House plea by rejecting the treaty. Later, however, the land was sold to the railroad company with the approval of the House.

The House took up the issue of treaty making again in 1869 during a violent debate over the Indian appropriation for 1870. It provided money for food, clothes, and education for tribe members living on reservations. The House refused to accept an increase in funds voted by the Senate. Representatives also began to question whether native peoples were capable of signing official treaties with the United States. Most members attacked the traditional system, although three congressmen spoke in favor of the treaty process. Representative William Windom of Minnesota argued that changing the process would be a breach of faith with the tribes. Revoking the process would create great confusion among Native Americans and add to their distrust of the US government.

Representative John J. Logan, Republican of Illinois, responded for the majority, however, by declaring that "the idea of this Government making treaties with bands of wild and roving Indians is simply preposterous and ridiculous." Amid loud cheers and laughter, Logan attacked the character of native peoples and suggested that they were an inferior race that should not be treated as equal in status to the people of the United States. The House refused to approve the appropriation, and the Senate refused to compromise; therefore, no Indian appropriation bill passed Congress in 1869.

In the debate over the 1871 appropriation, both sides raised the same arguments. In the Senate, supporters of the treaty system argued that any change would severely injure any goodwill native peoples still held toward the US government system. Senator Richard Yates reiterated the antitreaty sentiment, declaring that the tribes were not civilized and that making treaties with them had been a mistake. The Senate, however, passed an appropriation bill and sent it to the House. While the debate took place, many tribes were waiting for the money due to them under treaties negotiated in 1868 and 1869. Unless Congress agreed to an appropriation bill, they would receive nothing. In a compromise arranged between the two legislative branches, a sum of two million dollars was appropriated to pay off prior obligations. Debate over the appropriation for the next year bogged down in the House, however.

The Board of Indian Commissioners helped the House position by calling for an end to treaty making and for abrogating all existing agreements. Only Representative Eugene M. Wilson of Minnesota spoke in favor of continuing the historic policy. If Native Americans were not protected by treaties, they would be cheated out of their lands by white speculators and end up with nothing, he argued. Debate in the Senate and the House seemed far more concerned with constitutional technicalities than with the welfare of native peoples. Once more, no bill seemed possible. On the last day of the session, President Grant urged a compromise, or, he warned, a war with the tribes was sure to break out. Under this threat, Congress agreed to put aside its differences temporarily and passed a bill.

THE ACT IS CREATED

When the new Congress opened on January 4, 1871, Representative Henry Dawes of Massachusetts led the call for change. Dawes, who in 1887 would author a major bill in the Senate drastically changing policy toward native peoples, called for a quick program of assimilation in this earlier debate. If natives were to become Americanized—a policy he supported—they should be treated as individuals rather than as members of foreign nations. Native peoples were not and never had been equal to the United States. The House passed a bill denouncing "so-called treaties."

In the Senate, an amendment to delete the words "so-called" before "treaties" led to a vigorous debate. Senator William Morris Stewart of Nevada objected to the amendment. "The whole Indian policy of feeding drunken, worthless, vagabond Indians, giving them money to squander... has been a growing disgrace to our country for years." Treaties with "irresponsible tribes" were no treaties at all. Only a few senators agreed with this amendment, however, and "so-called" was eliminated. This angered the House, which refused to accept the Senate version.

Many congressmen and senators were tired of the endless debate and seemed willing to compromise. A conference committee of senators and representatives agreed that past treaties would be accepted or the integrity of the United States would be compromised. It agreed that no more treaties should be negotiated with Native Americans, however. Most conferees agreed that the tribes remaining hardly seemed like legitimate nations, as they were too small, weak, and miserable. The final compromise asserted the validity of prior agreements but provided that in the future, "no Indian nation or tribe within the territory of the United States shall be acknowledged or recognized as an independent nation, tribe, or power with whom the United States may contract by treaty." Both the Senate and the House accepted the compromise, and President Grant signed it into law on March 3, 1871. Treaties would no longer be negotiated with Native American peoples. Native Americans would, instead, become "wards of the state."

——Leslie V. Tischauser

BIBLIOGRAPHY AND FURTHER READING

Fay G. Cohen's *Treaties on Trial: The Continuing Controversy over Northwest Indian Fishing Rights* (Seattle: University of Washington Press, 1986) shows the continuing importance of treaties and the bitterness still evoked by pre-1871 agreements. Dorothy V. Jones's *License for Empire: Colonialism by Treaty in Early America* (Chicago: University of Chicago Press, 1982) discusses abuses of the treaty system and how native peoples failed to understand the process. Francis Paul Prucha's *American Indian Treaties: The History of a Political Anomaly* (Berkeley: University of California Press, 1994) gives the full story of the treaty-making process and its end.

INDIAN CHILD WELFARE ACT

The Indian Child Welfare Act (ICWA), passed into law in 1978, establishes minimum federal standards for the removal of American Indian children from their families and the placement of these children in foster or adoptive homes. In essence, the act restricts the placement of American Indian children in non-American Indian homes and gives jurisdiction to tribal courts in deciding matters of child welfare involving adoptive or foster placement. The law removes state jurisdiction in most American Indian child welfare cases, even when problems occur off the reservation.

The law affirms the continued existence and the integrity of American Indian tribes and was specifically designed to end discriminatory practices of state and county welfare agencies which disregarded Indian extended family arrangements and placed large numbers of American Indian children in non-American Indian homes. Senate hearings conducted in 1974 documented evidence that as many as 25 percent of American Indian children were being systematically removed from their natural families. This in turn was causing the breakup of American Indian families and a high degree of social disruption in American Indian communities.

The law provides that when foster care or adoption is necessary, the child's extended family has first priority to assume custody. If no extended family member is available, a member of the child's tribe or an American Indian from another tribe has priority over non-Indians.

The US Supreme Court ruled in *Adoptive Couple v. Baby Girl* (2013) that ICWA does not cover cases in which a biological parent abandons an American Indian child before birth and does not have custody.

——*Carole A. Barrett*

BIBLIOGRAPHY AND FURTHER READING

Fletcher, Matthew L.M., et al., eds. *Facing the Future: The Indian Child Welfare Act at 30*. East Lansing: Michigan State UP, 2009. Print.

Jones, B.J., et al. *The Indian Child Welfare Act Handbook*. Chicago: Amer. Bar Assoc., 2008. Print.

INDIAN CITIZENSHIP ACT

The Indian Citizenship Act conferred US citizenship on all American Indians born within the territorial limits of the United States, permitting dual US and tribal citizenship, but did little to secure or improve American Indians' rights.

American Indians hold a unique position in US society and law, so the acquisition of citizenship took special congressional action. Several factors made citizenship difficult to obtain. As long as Indians were members of tribes or nations which negotiated treaties with the United States government as independent political units, they could not be considered American citizens. Two significant rulings made it clear that a specific act of Congress would eventually be required to grant Indians citizenship. An 1870 Senate committee on the judiciary ruled that tribal Indians were not granted citizenship under the Fourteenth Amendment (1868), which gave citizenship to recently emancipated slaves, because Indians were not subject to the jurisdiction of the United States. In 1884, in *Elk v. Wilkins*, an American Indian who had severed tribal relations and lived among white people was ruled ineligible to be a United States citizen because he had been born a tribal member.

By the 1880s many in the United States sought to end tribal sovereignty, to individualize Indians, and to make them citizens. The General Allotment Act (1887) therefore carried provisions for citizenship as a reward for adopting "the habits of civilized life." In 1901 a congressional act granted every Indian in Oklahoma Territory citizenship, and by 1917, through a variety of federal statutes, more than two-thirds of all American Indians were United States citizens. It was World War I that reopened the debate about citizenship for all Indians.

American Indians actively supported the war effort through increased food production and contributions to the Red Cross. Most dramatically, six thousand to ten thousand Indians, many of whom were not citizens, enlisted for military service. In return, through the act of November 6, 1919, Congress provided any Indian who received an honorable discharge from military service during World War I the right to apply for citizenship with no restriction on the right to tribal property. Still, by 1920, 125,000 Indians were not citizens, so in 1923 a citizenship bill for all Indians was introduced in Congress. Political maneuverings began at once.

Many mainstream Americans favored citizenship as a way to sever the legal relationship between Indian tribes and the federal government. Full-bloods in many tribes were fearful that citizenship would end tribal sovereignty, bring them under state jurisdiction, and ultimately destroy tribal values. These conflicting views led to a compromise. In January, 1924, Congressman Homer P. Snyder of New York introduced House Resolution 6355, authorizing the secretary of the interior to grant citizenship to all Indians yet stating that "the granting of such citizenship shall not in any manner impair or otherwise affect the right of any Indian to tribal or other property." The American Indian Citizenship Act, signed into law on June 2, 1924, by President Calvin Coolidge, made American Indians both citizens of the United States and persons with tribal relations. Ultimately citizenship changed little for American Indians; the Bureau of Indian Affairs continued to treat them as wards of the government and to administer affairs for American Indian citizens, and many American Indians were denied the right to vote until the 1960s.

BIBLIOGRAPHY AND FURTHER READING

Davies, Wade, and Richmond L. Clow. *American Indian Sovereignty and Law.* Lanham: Scarecrow, 2009. Print.

Pevar, Stephen L. *The Rights of Indians and Tribes.* Oxford: Oxford UP, 2012. Print.

INDIAN CLAIMS COMMISSION

The Indian Claims Commission was established by act of Congress in 1946. Its mandate was to review all pending territorial claims by native peoples within the forty-eight contiguous states and, where these were found to be valid, to retire them through payment of appropriate compensation.

Although the life of the commission was originally expected to be ten years, the sheer volume of the cases it encountered caused its duration to be repeatedly extended. When it was finally suspended on September 30, 1978, the ICC still had a docket of sixty-eight cases remaining to be heard (these were reassigned to the US Court of Claims). In the interim, it had considered several hundred separate claims which, in aggregate, led it to reach some rather striking conclusions in its final report.

As Russel Barsh summarized the ICC's general findings, "about half a country was purchased by treaty or agreement at an average price of less than a dollar an acre; another third of a[billion] acres, mainly in the west, were confiscated without compensation; another two-thirds of a[billion] acres were claimed by the United States without presence of a unilateral action extinguishing title."

Since the ICC was specifically precluded under its authorizing legislation from effecting transfers of land title where none had previously occurred, the clear implication of the last finding was that legal ownership of the land in question remained vested in American Indians. In effect, then, the United States was engaged in the illegal occupation of approximately one-third of its claimed "domestic" territoriality. There was, however, little the ICC could do to rectify the situation, even if it had been so inclined, because its authorizing legislation also prevented it from actually restoring property to its rightful owners.

——*Ward Churchill*

INDIAN EDUCATION ACTS

The Indian Education Act of 1972, Public Law 92-318, was an attempt to remedy some of the problems in Indian education identified in the National Study of American Indian Education (carried out from 1967 to 1971) and in the hearings of the Special Senate Subcommittee on Indian Education that summarized its findings in 1969 under the title *Indian Education: A National Tragedy, a National Challenge* (also known as the Kennedy Report). Both studies found that Indian people wanted a better education for their children, wanted schools to pay more attention to Indian heritage, and wanted more to say in how their children's schools were run.

The 1972 act pertained to public schools on and off reservations and provided supplemental funding for schools with ten or more Indian students in order to meet their special needs. All public schools with Indian students could get this funding and were required to involve Indian parents and communities in designing the supplemental programs. Grant money was also provided.

Part A of the act required parental and community participation in impact-aid programs (programs that provided federal money to local school districts to make up for tax-exempt federal lands such as Indian reservations). Part B authorized a series of grant programs to stress culturally relevant and bilingual curriculum materials. Part C provided money for adult-education projects. Part D established an Office of Indian Education within the US Office of Education (now the Department of Education). Part E provided funds for training teachers for Bureau of Indian Affairs (BIA) schools, with preference to be given to Indians. The act also established the National Advisory Council on Indian Education.

The Indian Education Amendments of 1978 (P.L. 95-561) established standards for BIA schools, institutionalized BIA school boards, required formula funding of BIA schools, and provided for increased Indian involvement in the spending of impact-aid funds.

——*Jon Reyhner*

BIBLIOGRAPHY AND FURTHER READING

Glenn, Charles L. *American Indian/First Nations Schooling: From the Colonial Period to the Present.* New York: Palgrave Macmillan, 2011. Print.

Samson, Derek C. *Education Issues for American Indians and Alaska Natives.* New York: Nova Science Publishers, 2011. Print.

INDIAN GAMING REGULATORY ACT

The Indian Gaming Regulatory Act (IGRA), signed into law on October 17, 1988, by President George H. W. Bush, represents an amalgamation of ideas presented in various bills introduced in Congress from 1983 through 1987 and provides a system to permit and regulate gaming on American Indian lands.

The IGRA divides gaming into three classes. Class I gaming includes social games of minimal value, as well as traditional games played as a part of tribal ceremonies or celebrations. Class I gaming is exclusively regulated by the tribes. Class II gaming includes bingo, and if played within the same location, pull tabs, lotto, tip jars, instant bingo, games similar to bingo, and certain card games. A tribe may engage in Class II games if the state in which the tribe is located permits such gaming for any purpose by any person, organization, or entity. Class III gaming includes all forms of gaming other than Class I or II, for example, banking card games like blackjack, baccarat and chemin de fer, slot machines, craps, pari-mutuel horse racing, and dog racing. Class III gaming is prohibited unless authorized by a tribal-state compact.

In addition to classifying games, the IGRA established a three-member National Indian Gaming Commission within the Department of the Interior. The commission chairman is appointed by the president of the United States with Senate approval; the other two members are appointed by the secretary of the interior. At least two members must be enrolled members of an American Indian tribe. The commission has the power to approve all tribal gaming ordinances and resolutions, shut down gaming activities, levy and collect fines, and approve gaming management contracts for Class II and Class III gaming. The commission has broad power to monitor Class II gaming by inspecting gaming permits, conducting background investigations of personnel, and inspecting and auditing books and records. Regulation and jurisdiction of Class III gaming are more complicated. Class III gaming is lawful when it is authorized by a tribal ordinance, approved by the

Sandia Casino, owned by the Sandia Pueblo of New Mexico. By Cathy from USA.

chairman of the commission, located in a state that permits such gaming (whether for charitable, commercial, or government purposes), and conducted in compliance with a tribal-state compact that is approved by the secretary of the interior.

A tribe seeking to conduct Class III gaming must request that the state in which its lands are located negotiate a tribal-state compact governing the conduct of gaming activities. The compact may include provisions concerning the application of tribal or state criminal and civil laws directly related to gaming, the allocation of jurisdiction between the state and tribe, state assessments to defray the costs of regulation, standards for operation and maintenance of the gaming facility, and other subjects related to the gaming activity. The state is not authorized to impose a tax or assessment upon a tribe unless the tribe agrees. The state cannot refuse to negotiate a compact based on its inability to impose a tax, fee, or other assessment.

The question of gaming on American Indian reservations is one that involves both sovereignty and economic issues for tribes and states alike. The IGRA grants United States district courts jurisdiction over actions by tribes. Reasons for such action include failure of a state to negotiate with a tribe seeking to enter a compact; failure of the state to negotiate in

good faith; or any violation of the tribal-state compact. The IGRA provides that a federal district court may order a tribe and state to reach a compact if the state fails to meet its burden of proving that it negotiated in good faith. If no compact is forthcoming, a court may appoint a mediator to recommend a compact. In March, 1996, the United States Supreme Court ruled in *Seminole Tribe of Indians v. Florida* that Congress cannot force states into federal court to settle disputes over gambling on reservations. Federal law, through the IGRA, still permits tribes to seek help from the secretary of the interior when state officials balk at tribal plans for gaming operations.

The IGRA requires that all gaming facilities be tribally owned and that revenue from gaming operations be directed for specific tribal programs, such as education, elderly programs, or housing. Restriction of gaming to tribal governments ensures that American Indian gaming remains a government function rather than a personal endeavor.

Controversy

The most controversial aspect of the IGRA involves the tribal-state compact required for Class III gaming. Tribal sovereignty is diminished by the IGRA, because it forces states and tribes into an agreement. Most laws recognize that tribes have a government-to-government relationship with the federal government and are not under state jurisdiction unless there is prior agreement (as Public Law 280 states). Nevertheless, the IGRA specifically requires negotiations between tribes and states.

States have objected to tribal-state compacting on the grounds that it violates their sovereignty under the Eleventh Amendment of the Constitution, which protects states from being sued in federal court against their will. In a 1996 Supreme Court decision, it was ruled that Congress cannot attempt to resolve stalled negotiations between states and tribes over on-reservation gambling by making states and their officials targets of federal lawsuits. The Eleventh Amendment rights of states were upheld.

The IGRA has been embraced by many tribes in the United States as a way to bolster reservation economies. Some of the most poverty-stricken areas in the United States are American Indian reservations, and gaming revenues give tribes income to reinvest in other business ventures. However, the compacting process can result in conflict of interest for some states that rely heavily on gaming revenues. In addition, the issue of untaxed revenues resulting from American Indian gaming operations is a factor in establishing compacts, and states in need of such revenue cannot act dispassionately with tribes when they negotiate those compacts. Gaming on American Indian reservations is fraught with issues of competing interests for both tribes and states.

——*Carole A. Barrett*

BIBLIOGRAPHY AND FURTHER READING

Davies, Wade, and Richmond L. Clow. *American Indian Sovereignty and Law.* Lanham: Scarecrow, 2009. Print.

Pevar, Stephen L. *The Rights of Indians and Tribes.* Oxford: Oxford UP, 2012. Print.

INDIAN NEW DEAL

The Indian New Deal refers to John Collier's innovative years as director of the US Bureau of Indian Affairs (1933–1945). Collier was an energetic and humane visionary who sought to revolutionize federal Indian policy. The keystone of New Deal Indian reform was the Indian Reorganization Act, which ended allotment, organized tribal self-government, established revolving loan programs for tribes, and provided a mechanism for tribes to buy back lost lands. Collier also targeted Indian education and health for improvement. Day schools began to replace boarding schools, and preventive health programs reduced the incidence of certain diseases. Religious freedoms also were extended to Indian people during this time, and bans on the practice of traditional ceremonies were lifted.

Possibly the most lasting achievements in the New Deal era lay in the area of economic development. Tribes were aided in developing resources, preserving the reservation land base, and participating in a variety of public programs available to other Americans. Increasingly, Collier's revolutionary ideas were attacked, in part, because they encouraged Indian traditions and respect for Indian culture rather than assimilation of Indian people into mainstream American life. Collier resigned in 1945 amid increasing criticism, but he left a definite mark on federal Indian policy.

——*Carole A. Barrett*

INDIAN OFFENSES

Courts of Indian Offenses were created by the Bureau of Indian Affairs in 1883. The judges of these courts were Indian men appointed by the federal agent on each reservation, and they heard only cases involving certain cultural practices, termed "Indian offenses," which were banned on the reservations. All decisions of the court were subject to the approval of the Indian agent.

Essentially, the Indian offenses were a list of common traditional practices that the government determined were "demoralizing and barbarous" and therefore should be discontinued so that Indians could become more assimilated into mainstream American culture and values. The list of Indian offenses included prohibitions against dancing, plural marriages, feasts, giveaways, and destroying the property of the dead (a funerary custom among some tribes). Additionally, and most devastating to many Indian people, traditional religious practices including sun dances, sweat-lodge ceremonies, vision quests, and shamanism were strictly prohibited in the hope that Indian people would be more likely to convert to Christianity. In short, Indian offenses were an extensive body of religious and cultural practices that the federal government banned because they were deemed disruptive to the smooth functioning of reservations. When living within the reservation context, Indian people were not granted constitutional protections.

—*Carole A. Barrett*

INDIAN PREFERENCE

Title VII of the United States Civil Rights Act of 1964 prohibits employment discrimination on the basis of race, sex, national origin, color, or religion. However, this provision does not apply to Indians uniformly. During the period of reforms in the John Collier era, often referred to as the Indian New Deal (1933–1945), Indian preference in employment was instituted first in the Bureau of Indian Affairs and eventually in other federal agencies, such as the Public Health Service, which work closely with Indian people. Later, tribal governments, tribal colleges, and other Indian organizations were able to invoke Indian preference in making hiring decisions.

Commonly tribes develop criteria that give first preference to members of their own tribe, next preference to an American Indian from any tribe, and last preference to a non-Indian. When Title VII provisions are dropped, there is no uniform protection against employment discrimination. Indian preference was permitted as a way to increase the numbers of Indian people working within agencies and organizations that deal primarily with American Indian populations. It was also viewed as a way to increase the number of Indian people in the workforce significantly and so address the chronic issue of Indian unemployment.

—*Carole A. Barrett*

INDIAN REMOVAL ACT

The federal policy of Indian removal, formalized by the Indian Removal Act of 1830, was advocated by humanitarian reformers seeking to protect Indians from white encroachment, by white settlers who coveted Indian lands, and by state and federal officials who were challenging the vaguely defined constitutional status of Indians living within states' borders. Removal was accomplished by President Andrew Jackson, who was seeking to meliorate conflicts between states and the federal government over issues of state sovereignty.

By the 1820's, efforts to assimilate Indians through education and Christianization appeared unacceptably slow to land-hungry settlers and state officials. Because of disease, wars, treaties, illegal encroachments, and land speculations, most regions of the eastern United States already had been virtually cleared of Indians. Several tribes remained, however, including the Five Civilized Tribes—Cherokee, Creek, Choctaw, Chickasaw, and Seminole—of the South and the Iroquois of the North.

With the Louisiana Purchase of 1803 providing a vast new tract of land, President Thomas Jefferson suggested removal—the exchange of eastern for western lands—as a humanitarian measure designed to protect Indians from demoralization and corruption attending their contact with whites. After President James Monroe in 1824 recommended to Congress that all Indians be moved west of the Mississippi, some tribes and groups of individuals accepted subsequent congressional offers for relocation. Others, notably the Five Civilized Tribes, refused to vacate their ancestral lands.

When Andrew Jackson assumed the presidency in 1828, Georgia was exerting force on the federal government to meet the terms of an 1802 agreement by which Georgia had ceded claims to western lands in exchange for federal promises to extinguish Indian land claims within Georgia. The ineluctable spread of cotton agriculture and the discovery of gold on Cherokee lands in 1829 intensified Georgia's impatience. Accordingly, in

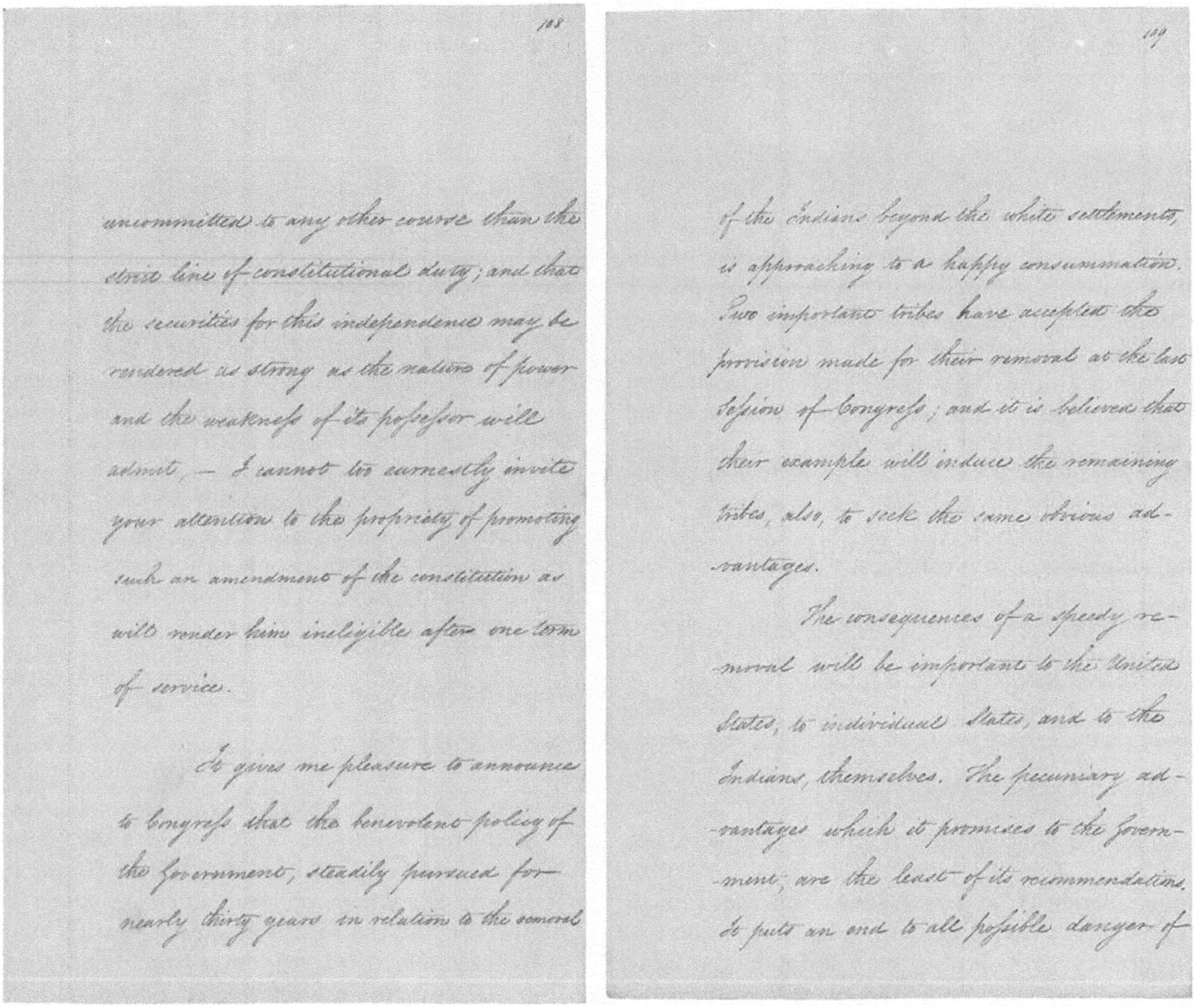

108

uncommitted to any other course than the strict line of constitutional duty; and that the securities for this independence may be rendered as strong as the nature of power and the weakness of its possessor will admit. — I cannot too earnestly invite your attention to the propriety of promoting such an amendment of the constitution as will render him ineligible after one term of service.

It gives me pleasure to announce to Congress that the benevolent policy of the Government, steadily pursued for nearly thirty years in relation to the removal

109

of the Indians beyond the white settlements, is approaching to a happy consummation. Two important tribes have accepted the provision made for their removal at the last session of Congress; and it is believed that their example will induce the remaining tribes, also, to seek the same obvious advantages.

The consequences of a speedy removal will be important to the United States, to individual States, and to the Indians, themselves. The pecuniary advantages which it promises to the Government, are the least of its recommendations. It puts an end to all possible danger of

Andrew Jackson's December 1830 message to Congress, justifying the relocation of southeastern Native American tribes allowed by the Indian Removal Act. By Andrew Jackson.

1828 and 1829, Georgia enacted laws nullifying Cherokee land claims and extended state law over the Cherokee nation. The Cherokee, in turn, lodged a congressional protest. Jackson, however, sympathized with Georgia and in 1830 secured passage of the Indian Removal Act, providing for the removal of all eastern Indians to lands west of the Mississippi. Furthermore, in 1831 and 1832, he refused to enforce Supreme Court decisions promising Cherokee federal protection.

Theoretically, removal was to have been voluntarily negotiated between the United States government and Indian tribes. Those Indians choosing to remain in the east as individuals were offered allotments of land and the right to become United States citizens. In practice, however, those who remained were victimized by land speculators and squatters, while those who rejected removal or allotment were moved westward involuntarily. The plight of the Cherokee, as they embarked on a forced march known as the Trail of Tears, symbolized the inexorable and historical dispossession of American Indians facilitated by the Indian Removal Act.

—*Mary E. Virginia*

Indian Reorganization Act

The Great Depression caused considerable rethinking about whether the United States was progressing toward a future of wealth and plenty. Some people, including Franklin D. Roosevelt's commissioner of Indian affairs John Collier, in their doubts looked to the close-knit, nonmaterialistic world of the American Indians for an alternative to what they saw was wrong with modern society. Through the Indian Reorganization Act (IRA) of 1934, Collier sought to preserve Indian cultures and to implement the recommendations of the 1928 Meriam Report, which was very critical of how the Bureau of Indian Affairs (BIA) had dealt with Indians.

Collier's original version of the Indian Reorganization Act (IRA) was rewritten and toned down in the legislative process, but the act was still radical for the time. The IRA ended further allotment of Indian lands and provided for Indian religious freedom, a measure of tribal self-government, a revolving loan fund for economic development, and Indian preference in hiring within the BIA. Collier hoped to revitalize Indian tribes, but many legislators, while voting in favor of the IRA in the fervor of the first years of Roosevelt's "New Deal," did not really support Collier's goal.

Through 1935, 172 tribes and communities held referendums and agreed to come under the Indian Reorganization Act; another 63 refused. Most tribes were deeply suspicious of any government efforts no matter how beneficial the government said they were. Some tribes were influenced by missionaries and Christianized Indians who saw Collier's admiration of Indian traditional religions as anti-Christian and antiprogressive.

While Collier's efforts received a setback during the termination period after World War II, the IRA continued to provide a legal framework for tribal governments, whose powers greatly expanded when the federal termination policies of the 1950's and 1960's gave way to self-determination policies in the 1970's and 1980's.

The Johnson-O'Malley (JOM, 1934) Act authorized the secretary of the interior to enter into contracts with states to pay them for providing services to Indians, including the education of Indians in public schools. Since 1891, the BIA had dealt with each school district individually. Putting Indian children in public schools was problematic. Rural teachers tended to conform to local prejudices against Indians. In addition, public schools in the 1930's were in financial crisis because of the Depression and were dropping health, physical education, shop, and other courses that Collier and others thought were basic for Indian students.

Originally, JOM funding went into the general operating fund of the school districts and could be used to support the education of non-Indian students (as pointed out by a study, *An Even Chance*, done by the National Association for the Advancement of Colored People in 1971). Such reports led to JOM funding being targeted for special programs that required Indian parent committee approval and that were only for Indian students.

—*Jon Rehyner*

Indian Rights Association (IRA)

The Indian Rights Association was founded in Philadelphia in 1882 by Henry Panacoast and Herbert Welsh, and it became the most important of the humanitarian groups which formed in the last two decades of the nineteenth century to seek the assimilation of Indians into mainstream American society. Welsh and Panacoast viewed the federal reservation system as a cultural and economic failure and asserted that reservations were obstacles to the civilization of Indians.

The Indian Rights Association diligently pursued its agenda to break up tribalism and bring Christian civilization to Indians by pressing for abolition of the reservation system through allotment of tribal lands, by supporting industrial education for Indians in order to encourage self-sufficiency, and by pressing for immediate citizenship for Indians so they would come under constitutional and state laws. The organization's political goals were inextricably bound to a belief in the superiority of Christian civilization. In

1886 Welsh asserted that the organization was doing God's will by guiding Indians "from the night of barbarism into the dawn of civilization."

The Indian Rights Association was successful because it was well organized and had dedicated members who pushed its agenda. The association hired a lobbyist in order to exert constant pressure on congressional committees, legislators, and Indian affairs officials. The organization also influenced public opinion by publishing pamphlets, news articles, and speeches that advanced its views. The association got much public and congressional support for its programs because it regularly sent representatives into Indian country to gather facts that gave such programs credibility. Additionally, the organization mirrored American society of the day by combining religious sentiment with patriotism in its proposals for reforming Indian policy. The association's goal was to acculturate and assimilate Indians fully into American society, and it viewed Indian culture and traditions as being un-American and pagan.

The Indian Rights Association declined in power and influence after Welsh resigned as secretary in 1902 and as federal Indian policy gradually began to support tribalism in the 1920s. The association continues to exist, although it now supports Indian self-determination and Indian groups seeking federal recognition.

——*Carole A. Barrett*

BIBLIOGRAPHY AND FURTHER READING

Hagan, William T. *The Indian Rights Association: The Herbert Welsh Years, 1882–1904.* Tuscon: U of Arizona P, 1985. Print.

Harjo, Suzan Shown. *Nation to Nation: Treaties between the United States and American Indian Nations.* Washington, DC: Natl. Museum of the Amer. Indian, Smithsonian Books, 2014. Print.

INDIAN TERRITORY

Terms such as "Indian country" and "Indian territory" had different meanings at different times in the history of relations between the United States and various Indian nations. The concept of a defined Indian territory developed alongside the policy of Indian removal—removing eastern tribes to lands west of the Mississippi River—created by the administration of Andrew Jackson in the late 1820s and early 1830s. It was first proposed as a large area west of the Mississippi that would include present-day Kansas and Oklahoma as well as parts of Nebraska, Colorado, and Wyoming. The land area considered Indian Territory soon shrank, however, as the government gave large parts of it away to white settlers, until it assumed the size it maintained until Oklahoma became a state in 1907. It is this area, essentially modern-day Oklahoma, that is most often meant by Indian Territory.

INDIAN REMOVAL

In 1828, President Jackson recommended Indian removal legislation to Congress, and the Indian Removal Act was passed May 28, 1830. The Choctaws were the first tribe to cede their homeland and consent to removal to Indian Territory. The main body of the tribe moved between 1830 and 1833. The Creeks were moved second, as a military measure. In 1836, 2,495 Creeks were transported to Indian Territory and left to live or die without clothes, weapons, or cooking utensils. The Chickasaw removal proceeded without resistance during the winter of 1837–38. They paid the Choctaws for the right to settle on Choctaw land. The Cherokees were divided over the question of removal, but those who were against it outnumbered those in favor of removal, who became known as the Treaty Party. Although the Treaty Party's first negotiated treaty was rejected by the Cherokee council, in December 1835 members of the Treaty Party drafted the Treaty of New Echota, which called for voluntary removal of all Cherokees by 1838. Once the treaty deadline passed, the main tribe was forcibly removed during the bitter winter of 1838–39. So many died on what the Cherokees called the Trail of Tears that they finally agreed to manage their own removal. The Seminoles resisted removal, were hunted down by the army and navy, and were taken to Indian Territory in chains. In 1856, the United States purchased land from the Creeks for the Seminoles and provided school funds. The Cherokees, Choctaws, and Chickasaws established governments, school systems, and churches as quickly as possible. The Creeks did also, but more slowly. The Seminoles took steps to develop a government and a school system, but progress was interrupted by the US Civil War.

The Osages received a large tract along the border of southern Kansas. The Quapaws were removed from Arkansas and acquired a small reservation northeast of the Cherokees. The Senecas and the Shawnees were also moved into Indian Territory. By the end of the 1830s the Indians owned land in Nebraska, a solid block of reservations along the eastern and most of the southern boundary of Kansas, and all of Oklahoma except the panhandle. This whole region was known as Indian Territory, although a territorial government was never established. Also seeking refuge in Indian Territory were bands of Shawnee, Delaware (Lenni Lenapes), and fragments of other tribes from the Old Northwest. Around 1839, more Shawnees and Delawares and some Kickapoos fled Texas and came to Indian Territory. In 1846, a peace treaty was made with the Caddos, the Tonkawas, and the Penateka (or Southern) Comanches; two reservations in Indian Territory were set aside for them in 1854. When the Kansas-Nebraska Act (1854) created Kansas and Nebraska, the Indians were moved southward and the term Indian Territory became restricted to Oklahoma.

The Civil War created great divisions among and within the tribes in Indian Territory. In 1866, the Five Civilized Tribes signed treaties, forced on them by the United States government for having allied with the Confederacy, that relinquished a large part of their western land, thus dividing Indian Territory into two parts. The eastern half belonged to the Five Civilized Tribes, and the remainder became part of the Oklahoma Territory. This western land was to be used as homes for western tribes to be settled on reservations as part of the consolidation policy. In 1907, the remaining Indian Territory, along with Oklahoma Territory, became the new state of Oklahoma.

——*Lynn M. Mason*

BIBLIOGRAPHY AND FURTHER READING

Blackman, Jon S. *Oklahoma's Indian New Deal.* Norman: U of Oklahoma P, 2013. Print.

Hoxie, Frederick E., ed. *The Oxford Handbook of American Indian History.* New York: Oxford UP, 2016. Print.

Oskison, John M., and Lionel Larré. *Tales of the Old Indian Territory and Essays on the Indian Condition.* Lincoln: U of Nebraska P, 2012. Print.

Parins, James W., and Daniel F. Littlefield. *Encyclopedia of American Indian Removal.* Santa Barbara: Greenwood, 2011. Print.

INDIAN-WHITE RELATIONS IN CANADA

Relations between the whites and aboriginals in Canada, or First Nations, began with exploration followed by invasion and domination by the European powers spreading into and over North America during the sixteenth and seventeenth centuries. British and French competing interests and colonialization, piqued by growing trade economies and political conflicts, decimated and divided the native nations and peoples along the Saint Lawrence waterway and the Great Lakes. Larger confederacies that were effectively destroyed include the Haudenosaunee, known as the Six Nations Iroquois Confederacy, and the Wyandot-Huron alliances. The Mohawk at Kahnesatake were particularly targeted,

but they and other Iroquoian peoples, have survived as a people and a nation into modern times.

Eric Wolf in *Europe and the People Without History* (1982) describes some of these processes from the world-systems analysis perspective, including the European Canadian expansion into and incorporation of Indian lands through the fur trade and the incursion's effects on First Nations across the northern woodlands and plains and in the northern tundra and arctic regions. Small wars and internecine fighting characterized much of the Indian-white relations extending from the Great Lakes region to the western seaboard; generally peaceful negotiations were followed by large land transfers first to the incursive

Louis Riel in 1884. By Photographer: I. Bennetto & Co. (Israel Bennetto, 1860-1946[2]) (possibly) Engraver: Octave-Henri Julien (1852-1908).

colonial power of England and then to the Canadian commonwealth. Major wars connected to the formation and expansion of the United States from the eastern colonies across the Great Lakes region had generally devastating effects on native peoples and their nations. Colonial powers and the Americans forced First Nation peoples into alignments with warring governments and then punished those native Canadians connected with the other side, typically not recognizing earlier treaties and agreements. The British and Americans, after forcing the French out, rarely observed treaty agreements with those First Nations who sided with them, instead whittling away at their lands and sometimes relocating them to frontier areas and usually into further conflicts.

CULTURAL GENOCIDE

These wars and a series of intertribal conflicts led to the First Nation peoples involved being stereotyped as "savage" and "uncivilized." These same labels were applied to those native peoples resisting the European Canadian expansion and conquest of western and northern frontiers, pitting white settlers against Indians in struggles over land and trade. In the 1700's and 1800's, European Canadians employed coercive assimilation practices. They forced Indian children into residential boarding schools that attempted to eliminate native cultures and replace them with "civilized" white lifestyles. This attempt to destroy native families and their historical and cultural legacies exacerbated tensions between Indians and whites. Most of these practices continued well into the 1950's and 1960's. In 1867, the British North America Act established the dominion of Canada and formalized the development of "reserves" based on diminished land claims and treaty provisions. Despite the establishment of reserves and attempts to eliminate Indian culture, Canadian governance was often less harsh than that of the United States. For example, after the 1876 fight over the taking of the Black Hills in direct violation of an 1868 treaty and reservation boundaries, Sitting Bull fled to Canada, where he lived for five years with many Hunkpapa Lakota (Sioux). Also, northern Canadian native peoples such as the Inuit and Cree did not suffer the full effects of the reserve system until the twentieth century.

The policies of coercive assimilation, cultural genocide, boarding schools, relocation, land takings, and sociopolitical erosion of rights did not completely destroy the native peoples of Canada, although many of these groups have undergone intense social change. These patterns are especially evident in the development of the Métis, a mixture of French and Indian peoples, usually Ojibwa or Cree, in the provinces of Manitoba and Saskatchewan down into the Dakotas and Minnesota in the United States. In the late 1800's, Métis leader Louis Riel, Jr., led uprisings in protest of the mistreatment of Métis, the government's nonrecognition of mixed-bloods and their French language, and discriminatory practices against Cree, Ojibwa, and other native languages and cultures. The Riel-led and similar uprisings were termed rebellions and put down by the federal and local military, leading to many indiscriminate killings. Riel was hanged for treason in 1885, as were four other native leaders. The Canadian government's suppression of the Métis, who represented an early mixing of European and indigenous cultures, marks the government's

MILESTONES IN INDIAN-WHITE RELATIONS IN CANADA

Year	Event
1600's	Europeans make contact with First Nation peoples along the eastern seaboard and the St. Lawrence waterway.
1700's	British and French establish towns, colonies, and trade networks in the new land, creating multiple treaties with First Nation peoples and beginning their incursion into and taking of native peoples' land.
1763	Royal Proclamation (of Indian Country) establishes First Nation peoples as treaty-making entities with which the English crown may negotiate regarding land and trade.
1794	John Jay's Treaty (between the United States and Great Britain) completely omits mention of First Nation peoples, disregarding the Royal Proclamation of 1763.
1849	Residential boarding schools for First Nation children are established across Canada, creating a pattern of coercive assimilation and extreme discrimination against aboriginal cultures that lasts until the 1960's.
1850's	Great Lakes Ojibwa and other treaties and unilateral agreements establish physical distinctions between First Nation territories and European Canadian settlements.
1867	British North America Act (which established the Dominion of Canada) creates a singular nation without formal recognition of First Nation treaty provisions.
1880's	Attempts by the Métis to defend their rights lead to armed conflict with Canadian government forces.
1885	Louis Riel, Jr., returns to Canada after living in exile, leads a failed Métis rebellion over cultural rights and land claims, and is hanged for treason.
1900's	Series of laws, edicts, and "agreements" passed unilaterally by Canada cause erosion of cultural and sovereignty rights for First Nations and establish reserves.
1970's	James Bay and Northern Quebec Agreement, bolstered by the Meech Lake Accord, take away indigenous peoples' lands for development purposes.
1980's	Increasingly better organized indigenous peoples make claims to the United Nations about ongoing discrimination and establish the Assembly of the First Nations.
1990	In Oka, a conflict between European Canadians and Mohawks over ancient lands related to Kahnesatake leads to armed conflict with Canadian military forces and increased discrimination.
1997	Oral tradition as a basis for land claims is recognized by the Canadian Supreme Court.
1998	The Canadian government issues a Statement of Reconciliation, a formal apology to the First Nations.

division of racial identities into two definite categories: white and Indian.

FURTHER DETERIORATION OF RELATIONS

Indian-white relations continued to deteriorate in the first half of the twentieth century because unilateral government edicts, laws, and agreements eroded cultural and political sovereignty of native peoples. In tandem with existing negative stereotypes and active social discrimination, whites in the dominant culture ignored or repressed Indians on reserves and discriminated against urban Indians as racial minorities. These attitudinal practices, with Canadian government support, spread throughout Canada.

Boarding school policies, land-reduction strategies, and government-appointed "tribal councils" generally had negative effects and demoralized First Nation peoples, sometimes leading to friction with whites living nearby. Criminal justice systems began to target Indians more actively in the 1900's. Gradually, indigenous groups began to organize and protest against the injustices. Developments in the United States, including the Civil Rights movement of the 1960's, crossed the border into Canada, resulting in the polarization of native Canadians and European Canadians. Those sympathetic to the native peoples' causes found themselves labeled "Indian lovers" and the targets of criticism.

CONFLICTS AND PROGRESS

In the 1970's, provincial governments fought the First Nations in courts of law. The James Bay I and II coalitions of government and private power companies were formed to take away vast land tracts from Cree and Inuit peoples under the Northern Quebec Agreement. In the 1980's, First Nation members protested this and other governmental acts, stressing issues of sovereignty and self-determination, at meetings of the United Nations in Geneva and later in New York. Many European Canadians supported the First Nations' efforts. In response, the Assembly of First Nations was formed to provide aboriginal peoples with access to legal and constitutional resources.

Some towns made up primarily of European Canadians resented the sovereignty of First Nation peoples. In 1990, a crisis developed between the Mohawk community, descendants of the Kahnesatake, at Oka in Quebec and the neighboring European Canadians. The town wanted to build a golf course on an area called "the Pines," but the Mohawks considered this area to be treaty land containing sacred burial sites. The Mohawk Warrior Society resisted the taking of the land, and armed forces were called in to "put down" Mohawk resistance without review of the legal grounds for either side's argument. After a long siege, the military prevailed, leading to court trials for Indian resisters. However, because of First Nations representation and public support for the Mohawks, positive dialogues grew out of this confrontation.

In December, 1997, in *Delgamuukw v. British Columbia*, the House of Delgamuukw, speaking on behalf of fifty-one hereditary First Nation chiefs, won an important court victory that recognized the oral tradition as a valid historical source for land claims and cultural authenticity. Also, in 1998, the Canada government extended a formal apology in its Statement of Reconciliation to the First Nations. This official recognition, the first of its kind in Canada, presents a potential for healing and building healthier Indian-white relations in future generations.

——*James V. Fenelon*

BIBLIOGRAPHY AND FURTHER READING

Excellent sources describing interactions between First Nation peoples and European Canadians are Eric Wolf's *Europe and the People Without History* (Berkeley: University of California Press, 1982); *Justice for Natives: Search for Common Ground*, edited by Andrea Morrison (Montreal: McGill-Queen's University Press, 1997); Olive Dickason's *Canada's First Nations: A History of Founding Peoples from Earliest Times* (Norman: University of Oklahoma Press, 1992); and J. R. Miller's *Skyscrapers Hide the Heavens: A History of Indian-White Relations in Canada* (Toronto: University of Toronto Press, 1989).

INDIAN-WHITE RELATIONS IN THE UNITED STATES

The landmark Indian Reorganization Act of 1934, which remained the legislative model for relations between the US government and Indian tribes until the mid-1950s, was based on a massive 1928 report entitled *The Problem of Indian Administration* (also called the Meriam Report). This report had been requested by Secretary of the Interior Hubert Work. It was intended to reexamine the effects of the General Allotment Act of 1887. Briefly stated, the 1887 act had provided for allotment to each Indian family a specific plot of land within their tribe's "traditional" holdings. Under this law, after titles had been held for twenty-five years, families would gain full property rights, including the right to sell their land. Any tribal land that was left after plot allotment to families was to be sold to the government for homesteading. It is estimated that, when the Indian Reorganization Act came into effect in 1934, Indians held legal rights to only one-third of the land they had before the General Allotment Act. This fact, coupled with a number of other critical factors pointed out in the Meriam Report (including inferior conditions in the areas of health care and education), led to the policy changes embodied in 1934's Indian Reorganization Act. Most of the responsibility for implementing these changes rested with President Franklin D. Roosevelt's appointee to the post of commissioner of Indian affairs, John Collier.

INDIAN REORGANIZATION ACT

In addition to slowing the loss of Indian lands, the 1934 act brought a new philosophy to the Bureau of Indian Affairs (BIA). It proclaimed a need to reverse a long-standing policy of forced assimilation of Indians into "mainstream" America and to build stronger bases for the retention of local Indian cultures. In Collier's words, it aimed at "both the economic and spiritual rehabilitation of the Indian race."

In the first domain, plans were laid to appropriate funds to buy back for the tribes Indian land that had been lost since 1887. The BIA also initiated a program to spread knowledge of land and timber conservation technology to receptive tribes and began steps to provide local development loans. Although the deepening of the Great Depression soon made special appropriations impossible, much surplus government land that had not gone to homesteading was returned. In its bid to encourage a greater sense of local tribal identity, the 1934 act also offered aid for drawing up and implementing tribal constitutions as the basis for their own local government.

WORLD WAR II

In the period between 1934 and the next major redefinition of BIA policy in 1953, many domestic policy factors intervened to affect what Roosevelt's policymakers had seen as the long-term goals of the BIA. The greatest single factor affecting tens of thousands of Indian lives during the decade of the 1940s, however, was initially set in play by forces far beyond the reservations: This factor was military service in the US forces during

WORLD WAR II

More than twenty-five thousand Indians served between 1941 and 1945. Many thousands more left reservations to work in war-related industrial factories. Indian women were also welcomed as volunteers in the army nurses' corps and the Red Cross.

Whatever their experiences in the ranks of the armed forces, still strictly segregated along racial lines, clear problems confronted thousands of returning Indian veterans at the end of the war. Part of the dilemma stemmed from continuing economic underdevelopment on the reservations they left. Equally debilitating, thousands of returning American Indian veterans felt alienated from their own people after experiencing life off the reservation.

Problems such as these impelled US lawmakers to consider once again whether assimilation, rather than "protected separation," was the best policy to pursue in Indian affairs. Parties supporting the former, including outspoken conservative Republican Senator Arthur Watkins from Utah, introduced what became, in House Concurrent Resolution Number 108, the policy of "termination and relocation."

TERMINATION ACT OF 1953

When HCR 108 became law in mid-1953, it pledged "to make Indians . . . subject to the same laws and entitled to the same privileges and responsibilities as . . . other citizens . . . and to end their status as wards of the United States." Even as HCR 108 was about to become law, a number of Indian spokesmen for the first tribes scheduled for termination (which meant stopping various forms of federal government "protective" intervention in their affairs) openly questioned Senator Watkins's claims that, since there were multiple sources to develop potential wealth on their reservations, the tribes should be able to "go it better alone."

Menominee leader Gordon Keshena was not alone in expressing worries that, if BIA supervision over local Indian affairs ended, the tribes' lack of experience would produce deterioration of many Indian material interests. Some congressional supporters of the general principles behind HCR 108 also admitted that the government might find itself spending large amounts of money trying to prepare the weakest and poorest Indian groups to know what forms of local autonomy might suit them best.

In fact, just as local termination bills began to appear in 1954, President Dwight D. Eisenhower seemed prepared to increase budgetary allocations to encourage the establishment of new industries in or near tribal areas. For example, by 1956, $300,000 of tribal funds formerly held in trust were earmarked to induce industrial plant owners to locate on the fringes of Navajo territory. Two companies constructed factories, one manufacturing baby furniture, the other making electronic equipment, near Flagstaff, Arizona.

In 1957 the Indian Vocational Training Act was intended to provide job skills to Indian applicants to make them attractive to potential employers, even if such jobs meant relocating off reservations. More than a hundred different occupations were included in the curriculum of free schools located in twenty-six states. This ambitious program continued to expand even as economic recession worsened in 1956 and 1957. Indian policy makers seemed convinced that the overall objectives of the 1953 termination laws would be best served if Indians who could not expect to gain employment on economically backward reservations relocated in off-reservation towns. Ideally, such a movement of families would also ease pressures on the limited economic means of their respective homelands.

RELOCATION

A separate budget for relocation came by the mid-1950s, to avoid negative consequences for Indians who left the reservations without adequate security. Statistics showed that, of the nearly 100,000 Indians who left reservations between 1945 to 1958, some 75,000 had relocated without federal assistance, sometimes causing familial disasters. Thus, job training and relocation funds expended in 1957 doubled in one year, reaching $3.5 million. In the same year, 7,000 Indians moved from their reservations. Controversy soon developed over shortcomings in the relocation program.

Realistic prospects for employment fell short of demands; moreover, job layoffs left many Indians "stranded" and unemployed in unsympathetic white-dominated environments. At the same time, there were very high dropout rates in BIA-sponsored vocational schools. Nurse's aide programs for women registered the lowest percentage of dropouts (21 percent), while rates for less challenging factory-type programs for men were very high (a 50 percent dropout rate for sawmill workers and a rate as high as 62 percent among furniture factory trainees).

As the 1960s approached, critics of the effects of termination and relocation, including Sophie Aberle, formerly responsible for the United Pueblos Agency, warned Indian Commissioner Glenn Emmons of trouble ahead. Emmons tried to defend his office by reiterating a philosophy that was not accepted by all—that whatever successes were occurring usually stemmed from individual initiative, whereas groups that fell back on the security of "communal lifestyle" tended to accept status quo conditions. Emmons cited gains that were not so easily measured in paychecks, such as advances in tribal health programs and in education. The number of Indians going beyond high school by this date (the 1958–59 school year) showed an increase of more than 65 percent in only three years.

TOWARD SELF-DETERMINATION: 1960S AND 1970S

Despite the fact that the Eisenhower administration's last BIA budget (for fiscal year 1960) was the largest ever ($115,467,000), it was during the 1960 presidential campaign that controversy over Indian policy began to come to public attention. Party platform committees actually heard testimony from tribal leaders such as Frank George, a Nez Percé who asked not for abandonment of termination but for improvement in its procedures for aiding needy tribes. Other claims, such as the Miccosukee Seminole demand for all of Florida to reconstitute their sovereignty, received less sympathy. The new tide that was coming was best expressed by La Verne Madigan of the Association on American Indian Affairs, who stated that Indians should have the right to choose freely between assimilation and "life in cultural communities of their own people."

In general, the Kennedy-Johnson Democratic years (1960–68) witnessed a continuation of termination actions despite the views of Lyndon B. Johnson's interior secretary, Stewart Udall. It was Udall's insistence that the BIA should do more to secure better conditions of relocation that led to the replacement of Commissioner Philleo Nash by Wisconsin Oneida Indian Robert Bennett in 1966. Under Bennett's influence, the president began, in the troubled political climate of 1967, to declare the nation's need to end the termination policy. Soon thereafter, Johnson urged passage of the American Indian Civil Rights Act (1968).

The 1970s, under Presidents Richard M. Nixon, Gerald Ford, and Jimmy Carter, brought what has been described as the "self-determination" policy, emphasizing the development of tribal resources on restored reservations. Perhaps the most dramatic example of reversal of what many perceived to be the harmful effects of termination occurred in 1973, when the Menominee tribe was told that (as the tribe had requested) its twenty-year experience of termination was over and that its entire reservation was to be restored to it as "unencumbered Menominee property." Yet despite pronouncements of "better intentions" coming from Washington and the BIA, the cumulative effects of decades of misunderstanding were not to be dispelled easily. In the same year that the Menominees regained tribal control over their own destiny, a breakdown in relations between federal troops and Lakota Indians during a seventy-one-day siege on the Pine Ridge Reservation ended in an assault that the Lakotas call "Wounded Knee II." Similar confrontations with threats of violence came in different regions, pressing government authorities to review its Indian policy yet again.

In May, 1977, the congressional American Indian Policy Review Commission, which included five Indian members for the first time, made more than two hundred recommendations, most of which aimed at confirming all tribes' power to enact laws within the confines of their own reservations. On the heels of this symbol of intended reform, the US Congress passed the 1978 American Indian Religious Freedom Act, which guaranteed freedom for tribes to practice their own traditional religions. This act ended the mixed legacy of several centuries of insistence that missionary conversion and education following Christian principles were vital aspects of Indian-white relations in the United States.

1980S AND 1990S

During the Republican presidencies of Ronald Reagan and George Bush (1980–92), budgetary cuts seriously affected the continuity of existing programs of assistance to Indian tribes. In 1981 alone, one-half of the prior budget for health services was cut, while funding for Indian higher education was reduced from $282 million to $200 million. By the mid-1980s, the education budget had been cut further, to $169 million.

Despite alarming cutbacks in BIA funding and looming questions of Indian demands for restoration of their sovereignty, the Bush administration made one major contribution by enacting the Native American Languages Act, which allowed tribal use of (formerly banned) traditional languages in BIA schools.

The issue of Indian land claims was prominent throughout the 1980s and early 1990s. In 1980, the US Supreme Court (in *United States v. Sioux Nation*) upheld a $122 million judgment against the United States for having taken the Black Hills from the Sioux illegally. In 1986, a federal court awarded each member of the White Earth Chippewa group compensation for land lost under the 1887 General Allotment Act. A significant piece of legislation regarding land claims was the 1982 Indian Claims Limitation Act, which limited the time period during which land claims could be filed against the US government.

The issue of Indian sovereignty and the related issue of gambling on Indian lands created considerable controversy among Indians and non-Indians in the early 1990s. The 1988 Indian Gaming Regulatory Act legalized certain types of gambling on reservations, and the vast amounts of income that could be generated appealed to many tribes struggling with widespread poverty. Gambling engendered protests by some non-Indians, however, and created tribal divisions that occasionally turned violent; in 1990, violence between gambling and antigambling contingents on the St. Regis Mohawk reservation caused state and federal authorities to intervene. An important court decision involving another aspect of sovereignty was handed down in 1990: The US Supreme Court decided in *Duro v. Reina* that tribes do not have criminal jurisdiction over non-Indians living on reservation lands.

In 1992, a number of American Indian groups protested the celebrations planned for the five-hundredth anniversary of Christopher Columbus's arrival in the Americas. Two events in 1994 symbolized both an increasing respect for and the continuing problems of American Indians. The first facility of the National Museum of the American Indian, a new part of the Smithsonian Institution, opened in New York (funding had been approved by Congress in 1989). On the other hand, the National Congress of American Indians and the National Black Caucus announced an alliance, stating that American Indians and African Americans continued to face similar forces of political and economic oppression.

Recent Controversies

In recent decades, American Indian groups have successfully raised the issue of Native American mascots in sports, questioning the virtue of using stereotypical depictions of Indians as team symbols and causing numerous teams, from high schools to professional sports organizations, to swap their mascots for something less offensive.

Another issue is crime on reservations and jurisdictional questions regarding law enforcement. A high incidence of rape is of particular concern. Serious crimes on reservations are generally permitted to be investigated by the F.B.I., but reporting statistics reveal a low rate of response relative to the level of crime. A 2010 law now allows tribal courts to impose sentences of up to three years on offenders, and a 2012 measure lays out plans for increased cooperation between federal agencies and tribal courts in the prosecution of criminals.

A confrontation between the federal government and Native residents of the Standing Rock Indian Reservation in North Dakota occurred in 2016. Residents, primarily from the Sioux nation, objected to the construction of the Dakota Access Pipeline, an oil conduit, because it infringed on their water rights by risking pollution of a lake used by the residents as their water supply. Protestors managed to stop construction of the pipeline after a summer of demonstrations and occupation of the site. But with a change in US presidential administrations in 2017, construction resumed under the incoming president, Donald Trump. Protesters were forced to leave the site, although some of them reassembled in Washington, DC, to continue their resistance.

——*Byron D. Cannon, updated by Michael Shally-Jensen*

BIBLIOGRAPHY AND FURTHER READING
Fixico, Donald L. *Call for Change: The Medicine Way of American Indian History, Ethos, and Reality.* Lincoln: U of Nebraska P, 2013. Print.

King, Thomas. *The Inconvenient Indian: A Curious Account of Native People in North America.* Minneapolis: U of Minnesota P, 2013. Print.

Miller, J.R. *Skyscrapers Hide the Heavens: A History of Indian-White Relations in Canada,* 3d ed. Toronto: U of Toronto P, 2000. Print.

Nichols, Roger L. *American Indians in US History.* Norman: U of Oklahoma P, 2014. Print.

Nichols, Roger L., ed. *The American Indian: Past and Present.* U of Oklahoma P, 2014. Print.

Pevar, Stephen. *The Rights of Indians and Tribes.* New York: Oxford UP, 2012. Print.

Reyhner, Jon, and Jeanne Eder. *American Indian Education: A History.* Norman: U of Oklahoma P, 2015. Print.

INDIGENOUS SUPERORDINATION

Indigenous superordination refers to a particular type of intergroup relations whereby a "native" dominant group within a geographical area subordinates incoming immigrant groups. This process results in a particular form of stratification within the society in which the resident dominant group enjoys a disproportionate share of the resources, prestige, and power. This differential can be manifest in economic, political, or cultural realms, interactively. The power relationship is then justified by a system of beliefs that rationalizes the superiority of the indigenous group in relation to the incoming groups and that often scapegoats the immigrants by placing blame on them as the cause of various societal problems. This type of superordinate-subordinate group relationship is less overtly conflictual than migrant superordination. An example of indigenous superordination is found in the United States, where most voluntary immigrants occupy lower levels of the stratification system.

——*M. Bahati Kuumba*

INDIVIDUAL RACISM

Activists Stokely Carmichael and Charles V. Hamilton, in *Black Power: The Politics of Liberation in America* (1967), defined individual racism as "individual whites acting against individual blacks." Sociologist Fred L. Pincus, in an article published in *American Behavioral Scientist* (1996), entitled "Discrimination Comes in Many Forms," renamed and expanded Carmichael and Hamilton's concept as *individual discrimination*, which he defined as "the behavior of individual members of one race/ethnic/gender group that is intended to have a differential and/or harmful effect on the members of another race/ethnic/gender group." Individual racism is distinguished from institutional racism, which is, according to Pincus, the intentional harm of minority groups by institutional practices such as the enactment of Jim Crow laws and the internment of Japanese Americans during World War II. Individual racism is here specified as actions by members of a dominant group that are intended to harm members of other racial and ethnic groups.

A range of individual racism prevails in American society, from intolerance to hate crimes. Included are incidents such as not hiring minority members in one's place of business, scapegoating minority groups for economic problems, stereotyping that leads to anti-Semitic and nativist prejudice and de facto residential segregation, and hurling racist insults and slurs. This last problem, known as hate speech, erupted on many college campuses in the late 1980s and early 1990s. Universities enacted hate-speech codes to protect minorities, but such codes were later found unconstitutional. Violent hate crimes include intimidation, harassment, assaults, beatings, church and synagogue burnings and bombings, cross burnings, destruction of personal property, lynchings, police brutality, and even an instance of white soldiers hunting African Americans as prey in 1995 at Fort Bragg, North Carolina. Police brutality, if isolated within a department, is an example of individual racism. However, if it is widespread with lax norms and *unenforced* formal sanctions against it, then, according to Pincus, it is an institutional harm. In the late 1990s, a flare-up of church burnings, reminiscent of those in the 1960s, terrorized the rural South. According to the Southern Poverty Law Center's Klanwatch Project, white supremacist hate groups—skinheads and those adhering to movements and groups such as Christian Identity, White Aryan Resistance, Aryan Nations, the Ku Klux Klan, and militias of various types—remain strong; some, such as the militias, have been on the rise. Many sociologists argue that an increase in acts of individual racism stems from the growing racial diversity of American society and the intensifying competition for scarce resources, such as jobs, in a global economy. With frustration escalating from mounting class stratification, individual racism is a classic example of scapegoating, that is, displacing one's anger at the economy onto minority groups.

Social scientist Gunnar Myrdal, in *An American Dilemma* (1944), argued that a moral dilemma, or contradiction, flourishes in American society between the American creed (freedom, equality of opportunity, and justice) and discrimination. Inequality is maintained through a vicious cycle whereby dominated groups are despised, engendering discrimination. Discrimination, whether individual or institutional, perpetuates minority groups' inferior social circumstances and engenders ideologies and stereotypes that blame minority groups for their deprivation and justify dominant group advantages. Thus, individual and institutional racism are inextricably intertwined.

——*Gil Richard Musolf*

BIBLIOGRAPHY AND FURTHER READING

Bonilla-Silva, Eduardo. *Racism without Racists: Color-Blind Racism and the Persistence of Racial Inequality in America.* Lanham: Rowman, 2014. Print.

Gerstenfeld, Phyllis B. *Hate Crimes: Causes, Controls, and Controversies.* Thousand Oaks: SAGE, 2013. Print.

Ioanide, Paula. *The Emotional Politics of Racism: How Feelings Trump Facts in an Era of Colorblindness.* Stanford: Stanford UP, 2015. Print.

Jones, James M., John F. Dovidio, and Deborah L. Vietze. *The Psychology of Diversity: Beyond Prejudice and Racism.* Hoboken: Wiley, 2014. Print.

Whitlock, Kay, and Michael Bronski. *Considering Hate: Violence, Goodness, and Justice in American Culture and Politics.* Boston: Beacon, 2015. Print.

INEQUALITY

Inequality is the unequal distribution of resources, opportunities, and rewards within society. In the United States, resources such as money, power, prestige, educational degrees, access to private clubs, political offices, and housing have been unequally distributed in a manner that has excluded racial and ethnic minorities.

Two early contributors to discussions concerning inequality were Karl Marx and Friedrich Engels. Marx and Engels, in *The Communist Manifesto* (1848), argued two views, known as the Marxist models, that the most important source of inequality relates to the control or ownership of the means of production, meaning the materials, tools, resources, and organizations by which society produces and distributes goods and services. The bourgeoisie, the owners of the means of production, are in a position to exploit and coerce the proletariat, or working class, thus enabling them to claim the greatest proportion of economic resources. Max Weber, in *Economy and Society* (1921), disagreed with Marx, arguing that stratification is multidimensional and involves economics, prestige, and power. Economic inequality is based on ownership or control of property, wealth, and income. Inequality in terms of prestige is based on the amount of esteem or respect given to an individual by others. Inequality of power is based on the differing impact individuals have on the societal decision-making process. Those with more power are better able to protect their interests and achieve their goals than the less powerful.

Kingsley Davis and Wilbert Moore, in their article "Some Principles of Stratification" (*American Sociological Review*, 1945), argued that inequality is necessary, contending that some positions are of greater importance than others to the well-being of society. If all individuals received equal shares of societal resources regardless of their position, there would be no motivation for an individual to undergo the rigorous training necessary to fill the important positions. Inequality rewards the most qualified individuals, encouraging them to take important positions in society and work to the best of their ability. Therefore, Davis and Moore assert that society would not be able to motivate people to work hard and achieve without unequal reward systems.

In the United States, the constitutional basis for many court cases challenging inequality in terms of opportunities, resources, or treatment by the government, its agents, or private citizens is the Fourteenth Amendment. This amendment, in conjunction with court rulings, declares that states cannot make laws that abridge the privileges of citizens; deprive any person of life, liberty, or property without due process of law; deny any citizen the equal protection of the laws; or deny any citizen the right to vote. As a result, by defining equal treatment, the Fourteenth Amendment and court rulings since the ratification of the amendment have defined inequality as the unequal treatment of people based on race, color, ethnic background, sexual orientation, religion, sex, or previous condition of servitude.

——*Ione Y. DeOllos*

BIBLIOGRAPHY AND FURTHER READING

Bartels, Larry M. *Unequal Democracy: The Political Economy of the New Gilded Age,* 2d ed. Princeton: Princeton UP, 2016. Print.

Galbraith, James K. *Inequality: What Everyone Needs to Know.* New York: Oxford UP, 2016. Print.

Stiglitz, Joseph. *The Price of Inequality: How Today's Divided Society Endangers Our Future.* New York: Norton, 2012. Print.

INITIATIVE ON RACE

On June 14, 1997, President Bill Clinton unveiled the Initiative on Race in his "One America" speech, delivered at the University of California at San Diego's commencement ceremony. The Initiative on Race promoted a national dialogue on race relations in the United States. This dialogue was to take place largely through open meetings around the country and was designed to produce a plan to calm racial tensions and promote economic opportunities for all Americans.

By executive order, Clinton created an Advisory Board of seven individuals representing diverse perspectives on the race issue: historian John Hope Franklin (chair); Linda Chavez-Thompson, executive vice president of the AFL-CIO; the Reverend Susan Johnson Cook; former New Jersey governor Thomas Kean; Los Angeles attorney Angela Oh; Robert Thomas, chief executive officer of Nissan, USA; and former Mississippi governor William Winter. The board was charged with promoting a constructive national dialogue to confront and work through concerns on race, increasing understanding of both the history and course of the country with respect to race relations, encouraging community leaders across the nation to develop initiatives to soothe racial tensions, and producing solutions to racial problems.

In his speech, President Clinton called race relations the nation's "greatest challenge" and "greatest opportunity." He spoke of the United States' complicated history of race relations, which has been marked by both progress and division. The challenge, he said, was to "break down the barriers in our lives, our minds and our hearts." For this to happen, the country had to engage in "a candid conversation on the state of race relations today." Clinton promised to help lead the American people "in a great and unprecedented conversation about race." In addition to the dialogue on race, Clinton's speech focused on expanding opportunities to all people—which included using affirmative action "in the right way" and ensuring educational opportunities—and demanding that each individual as well as the justice system take responsibility for respecting the rights of all citizens and enforcing each person's civil rights. Clinton also called on the advisory board to examine problem areas of "substantial impact," including education, economic opportunity, housing, health care, and administration of justice.

The Initiative on Race was not meant to seek a quick or easy fix. The multicultural democracy envisioned by President Clinton would require commitments from government, businesses, communities, and individuals. In his speech, Clinton suggested that the ultimate solution must come from the human spirit.

The board, which succeeded in assembling various "best practices" for advancing the national dialogue on race and for helping communities to address racial divides, was disbanded in September 1998.

——Robert P. Watson and Claudia A. Pavone Watson

INSTITUTIONAL RACISM

Racial discrimination, in the most general sense, is the denial of equal opportunities and rights to groups on the basis of race or ethnicity. The study of institutional racism (sometimes called institutional discrimination), rather than looking at individual attitudes as an explanation for racial inequality, focuses on the way society itself is structured or organized. Sociologist Joe R. Feagin distinguishes among four types of discrimination, and he includes two types of institutional racism in his typology: "direct institutionalized [institutional] discrimination" and "indirect institutionalized discrimination." An example of the former, which was documented by Diana Pearce in a 1976 study in Detroit, is the practice by real estate companies of "steering" African Americans away from homes in white areas. This direct form of institutional discrimination is the easiest to identify, understand, and (given the will) eradicate. Most sociologists, however, use the term "institutional racism" to refer to the second type noted by Feagin, indirect discrimination.

The term was coined in 1967 by African American civil rights activist Stokely Carmichael (Kwame Toure) and Charles V. Hamilton. Toure and Hamilton were attempting to shift attention away from individual, overt, and direct forms of racial discrimination as the principal explanation for the persistence of racial inequality.

From the perspective of sociologists studying unintentional and indirect forms of institutional racism, consequences are the most important indicator of discrimination. If the results or consequences of a policy or practice are unequal along racial lines, then indirect institutional racism is thought to exist. As sociologist Jerome Skolnick avers, "a society in which most of the good jobs are held by one race, and the dirty jobs are held by people of another color, is a society in which racism is institutionalized no matter what the beliefs of its members are."

STATISTICAL EVIDENCE

In the 2010s, statistical evidence of racism could be found in every institutional area. In 2014, white men, for example, constituted 31 percent of the population of the United States and yet held 65 percent of all elected offices. Approximately 13 percent of the nation's population is African American, but almost 40 percent of all prison inmates were African American in 2009. The dropout rate for Hispanics in education was more than twice that of whites in 2014—11 percent compared to 5 percent. The infant mortality rate for whites in 2013 was 5.1 per 1,000 live births, but for Native Americans it was 8.1 and for African Americans it was 11.3 per 1,000. The maternal mortality rate in 2013 for whites was 12.1 deaths per 100,000 live births, whereas for black women the rate was 40.4. The number of children and youth living in poverty in 2015 was in the 30 percentile range for

African American, Latino, and American Indian kids, whereas for whites it was 12 percent. The median household income for African Americans and Native Americans in 2014 was $36,544 and $38,540, respectively, compared to $59,698 for whites. These inequities strongly suggested the existence of institutional racism, which persists. (The fact that Asian Americans fared better statistically than most other groups must be qualified by the realization that poverty and other negative demographic characteristics do affect selected groups *within* the Asian American population.)

The fact that African Americans do not own businesses proportional to their percentage of the population demonstrates another important element of institutional racism: the interrelatedness of institutions. A society's institutions are interrelated in ways such that exclusion from one frequently means exclusion from all. Harold M. Baron has called this phenomenon the "web" of urban racism—or what others have called the "network" of racism. Black and Hispanic enterprise in the United States has been burdened by discrimination in education and the job market and by discriminatory banking practices that make it difficult for members of these communities to secure loans to start businesses.

RESEARCH AND REMEDIAL EFFORTS

The study of institutional racism also places considerable importance on the deep historical roots and lasting effects of direct racial discrimination. The effects of earlier practices, policies, and laws that were designed purposely to exclude and harm particular groups have continued to be felt even after most of them were eliminated by legislative and other measures. The cumulative effect of this discrimination left African Americans and other racial and ethnic minorities—notably Mexican Americans/Chicanos, American Indians, and Puerto Ricans—at a competitive disadvantage with majority group members in virtually every institutional area.

Knowledge gained from the study of institutional racism is applied in a number of ways in attempts to counter institutional racism. Among the many approaches are civil rights legislation; executive orders, such as those for affirmative action; and changes in the criteria used by admissions offices in higher education.

COLLEGE ADMISSIONS

Historically, college admissions officers have relied on so-called objective criteria in their decisions. The most important of these criteria have been class rank, grade point average, scores on the Scholastic Aptitude Test (SAT), participation in extracurricular activities, and the quality of the high school attended by applicants. While it was not necessarily the intent of colleges to discriminate against members of minority groups, reliance on these criteria, in effect, did so. Minority-group applicants, for example, are disproportionately poorer than majority-group applicants. As a consequence, they are more likely to have attended poorly funded schools that offer fewer extracurricular activities and that generally provide a lower-quality education. Minority students also are more likely to have to work and to care for siblings, which in turn affects their academic performance and limits their participation in extracurricular activities.

Because of studies of institutional racism, universities and colleges were able to see how their admissions policies were discriminating against members of certain groups. In the 1960s, most of these institutions adjusted their admissions processes, including the criteria used to determine admissibility and predict academic potential, to take into account the disadvantaged positions in which members of minority groups find themselves. Instead of automatically penalizing students for not participating in extracurricular activities, for example, admissions officers obtained information from applicants and high school guidance counselors on the activities available in the school and on applicants' responsibilities, including work, which may have made it difficult for them to participate in school-sponsored programs. Admissions officers also began to consider possible biases in standardized tests and accorded test scores less weight in their decision to admit or not to admit a student.

HIRING PRACTICES

Affirmative action programs are principally intended to be remedies for institutional discrimination. Affirmative action requires race consciousness rather than "color blindness," because (as studies of institutional racism have shown) society is structured in such a way that race-neutral or color-blind policies exclude members of minority groups. In the area of employment, for example, affirmative action programs were created to increase the pool of qualified minority candidates and to eliminate discriminatory practices from the selection process. Approaches include advertising positions in places where potential candidates from minority groups can be reached more effectively.

A long-standing and common recruitment practice has been to hire new workers through personal connections. Because of prior racial discrimination, however, the people doing the hiring were disproportionately white, and their connections tended to be white as well. Hence, African Americans and members of other minority groups often were excluded. Affirmative action programs have sought to eliminate this practice, which, even if its practitioners did not intend it to be, is discriminatory. Advertising positions widely, even nationally when possible, has been one remedy prescribed.

A seemingly innocuous practice used by some police agencies provides another example of institutional racism. Many police forces maintained a minimum height requirement, which placed Latinos, Asians, and women at a disadvantage. Because members of these groups generally tend to be shorter than white or black males, this requirement reduced significantly the pool of qualified applicants from these groups. Although the height requirement seemed to be neutral, or nondiscriminatory, it in fact discriminated against particular groups; intent is not necessary for a requirement to be discriminatory. In many instances, such discriminatory job requirements have been eliminated or modified.

In yet another example, seniority systems, established to provide job security for longtime employees, discriminate against minority group members. African Americans are adversely affected in disproportionate numbers by this practice because, as a group, they were denied job opportunities on the basis of race until court decisions and legislative initiatives made it illegal to discriminate on this basis. Being the most recently hired employees, they would be the first fired when layoffs became necessary. While seniority systems may not have been established to discriminate intentionally against members of certain groups, they did so nevertheless. As a consequence, the courts in a number of instances have ordered employers to cease the practice.

The Civil Rights Act of 1991, signed into law by President George H.W. Bush, was drafted partly in response to a number of Supreme Court decisions that, in effect, required plaintiffs in discrimination suits to prove intent on the part of the defendant, usually an employer. The bill stipulates that once the plaintiff is able to show that an employer's practice adversely affects a particular group, then the burden falls on the employer to "demonstrate that the challenged practice is job related for the position in question and consistent with business necessity." The bill is consistent with an approach designed to counter institutional discrimination. A practice is deemed discriminatory if it has a disparate impact on any group, irrespective of intent.

Between the election of President Ronald Reagan in 1980 and the passage of this bill, the tendency had been to place the burden of proof increasingly on plaintiffs in discrimination cases. In other words, a plaintiff had to prove that an employer intended to discriminate against him or her—a very difficult, often impossible, task. This approach of the 1980s was a departure from the approach that began in the 1960s, based on countering institutional discrimination. The Civil Rights Bill of 1991 returned, although in a somewhat weakened fashion, to the earlier approach intended to counter institutional racism.

CONTEXT

Prior to the 1920s, few sociologists studied race relations. When they did, beginning with the work of such sociologists as Edward Ross, Lester Ward, and William Sumner, the tendency was to view discrimination as conscious acts performed by prejudiced individuals; this view continued to dominate until the 1960s. The assumption inherent in this "prejudice causes discrimination" model, as noted by Joe Feagin and Clairece Feagin, is that the way to eradicate racial discrimination is to eliminate racial prejudice. It was believed that, with time, this would happen. Racial discrimination was seen as an aberration, inconsistent with American ideals of equality and justice. Swedish sociologist Gunnar Myrdal captured this belief well in the title of his classic and influential work on discrimination in the United States, *An American Dilemma: The Negro Problem and Modern Democracy* (1944).

Beginning with the pioneering work on immigration by American sociologist Robert Ezra Park in the first half of the twentieth century, immigration scholars as a rule predicted the eventual assimilation of various ethnic groups. While most conceded that the situation of African Americans was unique in some respects, their assimilation into American society was also predicted. Along with this, it was thought, would come the diminution and eventual elimination of racial prejudice. Milton Gordon, in the 1960s, developed a more sophisticated theory of assimilation, in which he distinguished between cultural and structural assimilation. Structural assimilation refers to the ability of members of a minority group to participate in such societal groups and institutions as businesses, government, and private clubs; Gordon pointed out that cultural assimilation does not assure equal opportunities in these areas.

In the 1950s and 1960s, the Civil Rights movement made great strides in attaining legal equality for African Americans and other minorities. Robert Blauner observed that initially the Civil Rights movement adopted the view that African Americans, if guaranteed legal equality, would be able to assimilate into American society. In time, however, it became increasingly apparent to civil rights activists as well as to many scholars that racist ideologies and prejudiced attitudes were not the "essence" of racism. Rather, racism was inherent in society's institutions. This realization quickly led to a fundamental change in the study of race relations, a change spurred by the cultural climate of social unrest and protest during the 1960s. The Black Power movement of the 1960s called attention to how little the status of African Americans had changed or promised to change despite progressive civil rights legislation and a reduction in racial prejudice. This relatively new way of analyzing racial stratification shifted the focus from individual expressions of racism to the manner in which society itself was structured and operated to favor some groups over others. The Black Lives Matter movement of the 2010s picked up this thread, specifically with respect to bias—often deadly bias—in law enforcement.

——*Héctor L. Delgado*

BIBLIOGRAPHY AND FURTHER READING

Aviles de Bradley, Ann M. *From Charity to Equity: Race, Homelessness, and Urban Schools*. New York: Teachers College P, 2015. Print.

Barr, Donald A. *Health Disparities in the United States,* 2d ed. Baltimore: Johns Hopkins UP, 2014. Print.

Feagin, Joe R. *Racist America: Roots, Current Realities, and Future Reparations,* 3d ed. New York: Routledge, 2014. Print.

Fredrickson, George M. *Racism: A Short Story.* Princeton: Princeton UP, 2015. Print.

Hoberman, John M. *Black and Blue: The Origins and Consequences of Medical Racism.* Berkeley: U of California P, 2012. Print.

Provine, Doris Marie. *Unequal Under Law: Race in the War on Drugs.* Chicago: University of Chicago Press, 2007. Print.

Satter, Beryl. *Family Properties: Race, Real Estate, and the Exploitation of Black Urban America.* New York: Metropolitan Books, 2009. Print.

Ward, James D., and Mario Antonio Rivera. *Institutional Racism, Organizations and Public Policy.* New York: Lang, 2014. Print.

INTEGRATION

A racially integrated society would be one in which African Americans and other racial or ethnic groups could participate in all aspects of national life without being handicapped by their color. In such a society, there should be no neighborhood where an African American could not reside simply because of being black; no hotel, restaurant, or other public facility that an African American could not use on equal terms with whites; no school that an African American child could not attend because of being black; no kind of vocational training, university education, or line of work from which an African American would be barred because of being black; and no public office for which an African American could not contend. In an integrated society, whites would see African Americans not as pariahs but as fellow Americans, fellow veterans, coworkers, and neighbors. This goal of a racially integrated society, despite much progress, is only half achieved; the role that public policy should play in creating a more racially integrated society remains a matter of lively debate.

Those who discuss the ethics of integration are dealing with the ethics of public policy rather than (as is the case, to some extent, with prejudice and racism) the morality of private behavior. The promotion of racial integration has been seen by its proponents as essential to the realization of an important value in public policy ethics: that of equality under the law regardless of race or color. This principle was publicly recognized in the United States by the Fourteenth Amendment to the Constitution (ratified in 1868), which mandated that every state guarantee its citizens the equal protection of the laws. Nevertheless, de facto segregation reigned for nearly three-quarters of a century before significant steps were taken to break down racial barriers.

MILESTONES IN INTEGRATION: 1945 TO 1968

Signposts of progress during these years (which witnessed the flowering of the Civil Rights movement) included the gradual desegregation of the American military, which began with President Harry S Truman's Executive Order 9981 in 1948; the Supreme Court decision of 1954, that struck down the constitutionality of segregated schools; the admission of African Americans into southern state universities; the Civil Rights Act of 1964, which established the right of equal access to public accommodations and banned discrimination in employment; the Voting Rights Act of 1965; the Supreme Court decision of 1967 that overturned state laws against black-white intermarriage; and the federal Fair Housing Act of 1968. By 1990, many of these changes had achieved general acceptance; efforts to integrate employment, schools, and housing, however, continued to arouse controversy.

THE AFFIRMATIVE ACTION CONTROVERSY

By the late 1970's, affirmative action, in which the presence or absence of a fixed percentage of African Americans in a business, government department, or university is used to determine whether that institution discriminates, had become the chief tool by which the federal government tried to open up opportunities for African Americans. In 1975, in the book *Affirmative Discrimination,* the white sociologist Nathan Glazer condemned the application of this policy in both private businesses and government employment. Glazer argued that affirmative action undermines respect for merit and encourages ethnic and racial divisiveness; unlike many liberals, he denied that the underrepresentation of African Americans in a particular job or profession is necessarily evidence of discrimination. In the 1990's African American conservatives asserted that affirmative action stigmatizes as inferior those African Americans who do gain entrance to prestigious universities or get good jobs. Yet other thinkers— white as well as African American—argue that many employers would hire no African Americans at all if they were not prodded to do so by the existence of a numerical goal.

RACIAL INTEGRATION OF ELEMENTARY AND SECONDARY SCHOOLS

In *Brown v. Board of Education*, in 1954, the Supreme Court declared that officially enforced school segregation by race (then found mostly in the southern states) violated the Fourteenth Amendment to the Constitution. In a 1968 decision, the Supreme Court exerted pressure on southern school boards to end segregation more quickly; in a 1971 decision, *Swann v. Charlotte-Mecklenburg Board of Education*, the Court held that school busing—the transportation of children out of their neighborhoods for schooling— might be an appropriate tool for achieving desegregation.

In the 1960's, the question arose of what to do about the de facto racial segregation of the schools, based on neighborhood racial patterns rather than on the law, found in many northern cities. In 1973, the Supreme Court ordered, for the first time, a northern school district (Denver, Colorado) to institute a desegregation plan. In 1974, however, the Court, in a sudden shift (in the decision *Milliken v. Bradley*) banned busing for integration purposes across city-suburban boundaries. In general, the Court has ordered steps toward ending de facto segregation only when evidence exists that local authorities have deliberately rigged school district boundaries to keep the races apart.

Ever since 1954, people have argued about how necessary integration of the races in the classroom is to providing equal educational opportunities for African American children. In the 1980's, some African American thinkers, such as Thomas Sowell and Robert Woodson, had their doubts. Woodson argued that a neighborhood school, even if it is

exclusively African American, can become a valuable focus of neighborhood pride for low-income city dwellers; Sowell pointed nostalgically to a high-quality African American secondary school of the pre-1954 era of segregation, Dunbar High School in Washington, D.C. (Critics stress how atypical Dunbar was.)

Integrationist scholars, however, argue that forcible exclusion from the company of white schoolchildren stigmatizes and psychically wounds African American children. The African American journalist Carl Rowan thinks that such exclusion is psychically wounding even if it results from white flight to the suburbs rather than government edict. White liberal political scientist Gary Orfield suggests that racial integration of the schools is necessary if African American children are to have greater access to information about jobs and other opportunities; white liberal education writer Jonathan Kozol contends, like many African American thinkers, that all African American public schools are more likely than integrated ones to be starved of money by legislatures that are beholden to white-majority electorates.

Although the compulsory busing of children into schools predominantly of the other race may be necessary to achieve racial integration in some cases, it does severely limit the rights of parents, thereby causing some resentment. However, the rights of parents over their children are, as the African American philosopher Bernard R. Boxill points out, by no means absolute. There is a societal interest in promoting interracial harmony, Boxill suggests, that perhaps should be allowed to prevail over the wish of bigoted white parents to preserve their children from all contact with African American children, and perhaps even over the wishes of parents who simply wish to spare their children the additional time spent traveling to and from home. Rejecting the notion (found in the writings of African American conservative Glenn Loury) of an unresolvable tension between integrationist goals and individual rights, Boxill also argues that government can use inducements as well as penalties to promote integration, in education and in other areas.

To promote integration of the schools while keeping busing to a minimum, some local school authorities have instituted so-called magnet schools. By placing elementary and secondary schools with above-average endowment in facilities and curricula in the middle of African American neighborhoods, authorities have sometimes persuaded, rather than forced, white parents to accept racial integration of the schools. Yet because funds are limited, the number of magnet schools that can be established is also limited; inevitably, some African American schoolchildren have often remained in primarily minority schools.

HOUSING INTEGRATION

By 1990, neither the federal Fair Housing Act of 1968 nor the many state and local laws banning discrimination in the sale or rental of housing had solved the problem of racially segregated neighborhoods. One troublesome issue that arises with respect to housing integration is the tension between individual rights and the goal of keeping a neighborhood integrated over time. Many whites are reluctant to live in a neighborhood or an apartment complex when the percentage of African American residents exceeds a certain number. To prevent wholesale evacuation by whites, so-called benign quotas have been introduced limiting the African American influx in the interest of stable integration. Benign quotas have been used by real estate agents in the Chicago suburb of Oak Park and by the management of the Starrett City apartment complex in New York City; in the latter case, the constitutionality of benign quotas was challenged in the 1980's.

Another difficult question is whether poor as well as middle- or upper-income African Americans should be given the chance to live in the prosperous and mostly white suburbs. White suburbanites who might tolerate the occasional prosperous African American homeowner as a neighbor might also oppose the building of public housing projects in suburbia; yet it is the poorer African American who might benefit most from the greater employment opportunities found in the suburbs. In Chicago, the Gautreaux program attempted to circumvent

the problem by settling small numbers of carefully selected poor African American families in prosperous white suburbs.

Nathan Glazer, in a 1993 magazine essay, argued that only an extremely intrusive government could make racially integrated neighborhoods remain racially integrated over time. Bernard Boxill contends, however, that not every action that is beyond the penalties of law is necessarily moral, and that government, if it cannot force whites to stay in integrated neighborhoods, can at least offer inducements for them to do so.

——*Paul D. Mageli*

BIBLIOGRAPHY AND FURTHER READING

Useful studies of integration can be found in Bernard R. Boxill's *Blacks and Social Justice* (Totowa, N.J.: Rowman & Allanheld, 1984); Gertrude Ezorsky's *Racism and Justice: The Case for Affirmative Action* (Ithaca, N.Y.: Cornell University Press, 1991); Nathan Glazer's *Affirmative Discrimination: Ethnic Inequality and Public Policy* (New York: Basic Books, 1975); Andrew Hacker's *Two Nations: Black and White, Separate, Hostile, Unequal* (New York: Charles Scribner's Sons, 1992); Jonathan Kozol's *Savage Inequalities: Children in America's Schools* (New York: Crown, 1991); Glenn C. Loury's “Matters of Color—Blacks and the Constitutional Order,” in *Slavery and Its Consequences: The Constitution, Equality, and Race,* edited by Robert A. Goldwin and Art Kaufman (Washington, D.C.: American Enterprise Institute Press, 1988); Douglas S. Massey and Nancy A. Denton's *American Apartheid: Segregation and the Making of the Underclass* (Cambridge, Mass.: Harvard University Press, 1993); and Harvey Molotch's *Managed Integration: Dilemmas of Doing Good in the City* (Berkeley: University of California Press, 1972).

INTELLIGENCE AND RACE

Observed differences in mean IQ levels, as measured by intelligence tests or scholastic aptitude/achievements, for racial/ethnic groups have generated prolonged and intense controversy on whether intelligence is determined by environment or genetics. The fact that human DNA is nearly identical across racial and ethnic groups argues against race-based genetic differences. Consequences of the position taken on this issue are enormous for social policy, education, and overall race relations.

Contemporary debate on the relationship between intelligence and race can be traced to the nineteenth-century eugenics movement initiated by Francis Galton, Charles Darwin's half-cousin. Eugenics is a science that aims to improve the hereditary characteristics of a race or breed, usually through selective mating. Galton proposed eugenics as a means of promoting the chances of "superior" races to prevail over the rapid growth of "inferior" races. In *Hereditary Genius* (1869), Galton concluded that mental traits were as inheritable as physical features. Galton's colleague, Karl Pearson, the founder of the Pearson statistical correlation, shared his anxiety about a dysgenic trend, one that favored the "weaker races," which were reproducing at a higher rate than the "mentally better stock."

Galton's efforts to measure intelligence using the speed and accuracy of mental processes as criteria led to attempts to create mental tests. The term "mental test" itself was coined in 1890 by British scientist James McKeen Cattell.

TEST DEVELOPMENT

During this time, French psychologist Alfred Binet was conducting experiments on his two daughters to develop an accurate method of measuring intelligence. Binet's major concern was not eugenics but helping schoolteachers distinguish the "malicious" (students who lacked motivation) from the "stupid" (students who lacked the intellectual capacity to succeed). In 1904, Binet created a scale known as the Binet-Simon scale and advocated that all students be tested with it to separate the "malicious" from the "stupid."

At the start of the twentieth century, several US psychologists, including Edward L. Thorndike, Naomi Norsworthy, Henry Goddard, and Lewis Terman, all believers in eugenics, were also developing methods to test intelligence. The first version of the Stanford-Binet Intelligence Test, which improved on the Binet-Simon Scale, was produced by Terman at Stanford University in 1916. The notion of intelligence quotient, or IQ—mental age divided by the chronological age of the person tested and multiplied by 100— was introduced by Wilhelm Stern, making it possible to compare people's performances. Finding that the average IQ of children from upper-class families was

107 and that of working-class children was only 93, Terman concluded that the difference was genetic, not an outcome of home environment. He questioned the utility of education to help lower-class children become "intelligent voters or capable citizens."

During World War I, Terman convinced the United States army to use psychological testing to assess the mental fitness of soldiers. Because many of the 1.7 million men who were tested were not proficient in English or hailed from impoverished backgrounds, their test scores were depressed, leading the researchers to conclude that immigrants from the non-English-speaking world and lower-class Americans were genetically inferior. This conclusion influenced immigration policy, helping spread the view that immigrants who were not white Anglo-Saxon Protestants were harming American culture.

In 1939, David Wechsler developed a new IQ test, the Wechsler-Bellevue test. It was very similar to the Stanford-Binet; however, it measured not only verbal skills but also performance skills. In 1955, it was renamed the Wechsler Adult Intelligence Scale (WAIS). Modifications were added later to create the Wechsler Intelligence Scale for Children (WISC) and the Wechsler Preschool and Primary Scale Intelligence (WPPSI). By the end of the twentieth century, hundreds of other tests, including tests designed to measure scholastic aptitude and achievement, had been created and used, highlighting the United States' fascination with intelligence.

CHALLENGES TO IQ TESTING

Objections to intelligence testing were first raised as early as 1913 by J. E. Wallace Wallin, a clinical psychologist from Iowa who noticed that children judged to be morons (a term coined by Goddard to refer to someone with an IQ below a certain level) were sometimes unfairly institutionalized. Robert M. Yerks, a psychologist from Harvard University, also warned about the dangers of untrained examiners clinically diagnosing people. In response, the American Psychological Association, at its 1915 meeting, passed a resolution discouraging unqualified individuals from administering psychological testing.

Widespread criticism of psychological testing arose in the 1960s in response to two conclusions that had been reached by most psychologists: Blacks as a group consistently scored fifteen points lower than

AVERAGE ACT AND SAT TEST SCORES BY RACIAL/ETHNIC GROUP

	ACT (2012)	SAT (2012) Verbal	SAT (2012) Math
American Indian	18.4	482	489
Asian American	23.6	518	595
Black	17.0	428	428
Mexican American	—	448	465
Puerto Rican	—	452	452
Other Hispanic	18.7	447	461
White	22.1	527	536

Note: The ACT is scored on a scale from 1 to 36; the SAT is scored on a scale from 200 to 800.

Source: Data are from Scott Jaschik, "SAT Scores Drop Again" (25 Sept. 2012) and "ACT Scores Are Flat" (22 Aug. 2012), *Inside Higher Ed* (web).

whites on standardized IQ tests, and blacks did better or at least as well as whites on test items involving simple tasks and rote memorization. These conclusions reinforced prevalent negative stereotypes of African Americans, providing justification for continued discrimination against them in education and jobs. As criticism of intelligence testing became louder, the validity of the tests was challenged in court. Civil rights activists protested against placing children in special education programs based on IQ tests. Charges of racism and examiner bias were made in professional circles as well as in the media. An avalanche of books, articles, and dissertations were produced, mostly challenging the black inferiority thesis.

RACIAL/ETHNIC DIFFERENCES AND IQ

Few contest the fact that a definite difference exists between blacks and whites in the United States in mean scores on IQ tests. Most people also acknowledge that regardless of race, class differences exist in mean IQ scores: Upper-class whites perform better than lower-class whites. What is contentious is the interpretation of these observed differences, that is, whether they stem from the genetic make-ups of different groups or are determined by environmental factors.

The controversy was sharpened by an article published by Arthur Jensen, an educational psychologist, in the *Harvard Educational Review* in 1969. This article held that inherited factors largely accounted for individual differences in human intelligence. Jensen asserted that educational programs designed to raise the IQs of African American children were largely ineffective, because of African Americans' genetic limitations. Although he did not deny the influence of environmental factors, he claimed that they were merely "threshold variables."

Two other prominent psychologists who have for decades defended the hereditarian thesis are Hans Eysenck, a British psychologist, and Richard Herrnstein, a psychologist from Harvard University. Eysenck supported Jensen's position and distinguished between two main types of intellectual abilities: abstract reasoning ability, on which IQ is based, and associative learning ability, which involves memory and rote learning. In his estimation, large racial and social class differences exist in abstract reasoning, although virtually no such differences are found in associative learning.

Herrnstein has also long maintained that genetics is a significant factor in IQ differences between racial and ethnic groups. His definitive statement, coauthored by Charles Murray, is *The Bell Curve: Intelligence and Class Structure in American Life* (1994). Herrnstein and Murray insist that race and IQ are genetically linked. Problems of the poor—unemployment, crime, poverty, and the like—are to be blamed, at least in part, on low IQ. Herrnstein and Murray are pessimistic in their assessment of programs designed to raise people's intellectual abilities. Evoking Galton's fears of a dysgenic trend, the authors believe that the United States is irrevocably turning into a caste society, stratified by IQ differences.

Critics of *The Bell Curve* question the findings of this book on several grounds: Data collected in this book are unreliable; available data do not support the thesis that intelligence is unequally distributed among various races; its authors reach conclusions that are far beyond what the data warrant; and, finally, even if genetics is a factor in intelligence, by the authors' own admission, it accounts for no more than 5 percent to 10 percent of the variance, far from what is needed to justify their fatalistic view on social stratification.

WHAT IS INTELLIGENCE?

The difficulties in resolving the IQ controversy are many: There is no reliable method of isolating the influence of environmental variables from genetics in measuring intelligence, and the concepts used—intelligence, race, and ethnicity in particular—are not precisely definable.

Perhaps the most difficult problem is determining what constitutes intelligence. Intelligence is generally understood as a concept, rather than an objective entity, that is constructed to account for certain cognitive abilities. Intelligence tests are designed to identify and measure cognitive abilities, using quantitative methods based on some theoretical conception of intelligence. Existing intelligence tests measure such abilities as the ability to master common information (such as how many days there are in a year), verbal comprehension (such as what "serendipity" means), knowledge of culturally/legally acceptable ways to deal with problems (such as what one would do if one were the first person in a movie theater to notice smoke and fire), basic mathematical ability (such as the abilities to add, subtract, and multiply), the ability to reason abstractly, the ability to compare and contrast different objects or ideas, the ability to recall information, the ability to manipulate situations mentally, the ability to analyze and solve practical problems, the ability to distinguish what is essential from what is merely accidental, and the ability to learn a new task.

Considerable discussion exists on whether human intelligence is a unitary idea or whether there are several kinds of intelligence. In 1904, British psychologist Charles Spearman proposed that intelligence is made up of two parts: general intelligence (g) and the specific ability measured by particular test items (s). In 1941, R. B. Cattell distinguished between fluid (Gf) and crystallized (Gc) intelligences. Going beyond Cattell, some have recognized the need to consider intelligence as comprising several types, some of which are not measured by available IQ tests. Psychologist Howard Gardner has identified many types and forms of intelligence other than cognitive. Studies also show that intelligence is not fixed but remains changeable over time, depending on new opportunities and experiences. For example, one study found that the IQs of African American college students rise significantly higher as a result of their receiving a college education.

CULTURAL AND OTHER BIASES

It has been pointed out that IQ tests measure, more than anything else, knowledge of white middle-class culture. Researchers have noted that subcultural differences play a decisive role in the ways in which people grasp and process information, their learning styles, and their attitudes toward test taking. Not all groups are equally familiar with the content of the test items presented to them; words are not univocal across subcultures. Researcher Janet E. Helms has suggested that socioeconomic status, culture, and race may influence a person's performance on the Wechsler Adult Intelligence Scale-Revised (WAIS-R). For example, persons from lower socioeconomic classes may not establish a trusting relationship with the examiner, and individual characteristics of the examiner and their biases in interpretation of ambiguous answers may affect test scores. African Americans score lower when tested by whites than when tested by blacks, a fact that was known as early as 1936 but ignored until the 1960s. Also, people with limited vocabulary may not understand the instructions given and the explanations offered in response to their questions.

IMPACT ON SOCIAL POLICY

Intelligence testing has become an incendiary issue because of its linkages with a variety of other historically sensitive issues, including a belief in the superiority of the Anglo-Saxon race, eugenics movements, black slavery, discriminatory immigration policies, and efforts to remedy past injustices. Some observers have pointed out that the intense interest in IQ today parallels its ideological beginnings toward the end of the nineteenth century.

In the nineteenth century, when industrialization was in full swing, the pressures of the marketplace demanded greater social equality and inclusion of all social strata in the social processes. Eugenics and social Darwinism arose as reactionary movements to oppose programs and policies designed to open up greater opportunity to the poor and the working classes.

The second half of the twentieth century saw a social revolution that in many ways paralleled the Industrial Revolution. In the United States, disadvantaged people demanded fundamental changes in social institutions and the abolition of racist policies. Following the civil rights victories of the 1960s, social and educational affirmative action programs were put in place to remedy the effects of past discrimination. The 1980s and 1990s witnessed the rise of a reactionary movement that resulted in the gradual dismantling of many of these programs, and debate about them has continued into the twenty-first century.

That debate seems to have reached a dead end for three major reasons: (1) the notion of race has become quite fuzzy; (2) there is widespread and growing recognition that intelligence assumes many forms and these cannot be limited to what is measured by traditional IQ tests or scholastic tests; (3) the value of the standardized scholastic tests such as American College Testing (ACT) and Scholastic Aptitude Test (SAT) have become dubious as they are being discontinued for college admission purposes.

Due to the peculiar manner in which the United States evolved as a nation through the experiences of slavery, colonial expansion, and immigration from nearly every region of the world, the so-called races have been intermingling in this country for centuries to such an extent that the traditional construct of race based on biological characteristics is no longer meaningful. Research has shown that most whites and blacks in the United States are interracial or even multiracial due to generations of racial mixing. Many Americans find it difficult to categorize themselves as belonging to a single race and an increasing number of people prefer to identify themselves as multiracial, a category that is now officially recognized by the US Census Bureau.

Although race as a construct still has social significance—meaning that members of society still act on it—biologically race is a bankrupt notion. To use a famous example, the former President Barack Obama was socially defined as a black man although biologically he was 50 percent white and 50 percent black or perhaps even multiracial. The "black or white" categorization of people in such cases conceals the fuzzy biological reality, making it impossible to meaningfully link intelligence to race. Racial self-identification, the only method by which a person's race is now determined, is certainly unreliable. For instance, many Arabs who used to identify themselves as white prior to September 11, 2001, no longer do so. Biologically, human beings belong to a single species (*Homo sapiens*) and the notion of race is a concept in continuous flux, with no fixed meaning. Because the attempts to classify human beings into distinct races based on physical features have failed, anthropologists have altogether abandoned the notion of race, except as a social category (i.e., something defined by society).

The notion of intelligence is also equally fuzzy. Numerous attempts have been made to define intelligence, with little consensus. The notion that intelligence manifests itself in multiple forms has gained ground in recent years, forcing people to reject narrow definitions based on what is measured by IQ tests or scholastic tests. Howard Gardner's notion of multiple intelligences, which goes beyond the traditional focus on linguistic and logico-mathematical aptitudes, recognizes many other abilities such as the ability for music as well as bodily-kinesthetic, interpersonal, and intra-personal abilities. It has gained some traction in advancing new ways of thinking about intelligence. Even so, it is difficult to enumerate all the forms that intelligence can take, making the concept nebulous. Obviously, it is impossible to measure multiple intelligences, using a single test or any number of tests. It would be equally difficult to isolate these abilities from their social and cultural contexts because what is valued and adaptive in one culture may not be so in another culture.

Broadening the concept of intelligence to include adaptive abilities required for success at a given task in a given social and cultural context has given rise to other constructs such as emotional intelligence, cultural intelligence, and spiritual intelligence. The concept of emotional intelligence (EI), first proposed by psychologists John D. Mayer and Peter Salovey in 1990 and elaborated by Daniel Goleman later, has attracted considerable attention in recent years. Emotional intelligence refers to people's problem-solving abilities in relation to emotions – abilities to recognize, understand, and manage emotions. First identified by P. Christopher Earley and Soon Ang as a distinct form of intelligence, the core of cultural intelligence (CQ) includes motivational, cognitive, and behavioral dimensions which make a person effective in collaborating with others from different cultures.

Such a broadening of the concept of intelligence makes it totally unrelated to anything that can be called race. In other words, the new thinking about intelligence has not only broadened the concept of intelligence, but also distanced it from the racial thinking of the early intelligence theorists.

Consensus seems to be emerging that intelligence testing serves no helpful purpose today and because it contributes to stratification based on race, gender, culture, and socio-economic status, many argue that it should be discontinued as a tool to diagnose even learning disabilities. For instance, students with language difficulties are disadvantaged by standardized scholastic testing. Recognizing the cultural and socio-economic biases associated with intelligence testing and standardized scholastic testing, increasingly more colleges and universities are dropping the use of SAT or ACT scores in college admission decisions.

The cultural contexts from which intelligence cannot be isolated make it nearly impossible to have a universal definition of intelligence, let alone the possibility of designing culture-free tests to measure this elusive concept. If one were to ultimately settle for the notion that a person's intelligence is the degree to which he or she possesses the necessary adaptive abilities and skills to be effective in a given sociocultural milieu, the development of such abilities depend on multiple social, economic, cultural, and environmental factors and there is no evidence to demonstrate that it is linked to race in a biological sense.

——*Mathew J. Kanjirathinkal*

Bibliography and Further Reading

Ang, Soon and Linn Van Dyne (Eds.). 2015. *Cultural Intelligence: Theory, Measurement and Applications*. London and New York: Routledge. Print.

Ceci, Stephen, and Wendy M. Williams. "Darwin 200: Should Scientists Study Race and IQ? Yes: The Scientific Truth Must Be Pursued." *Nature*. 12 Feb. 2009: 788–89. Print.

Crowne, Kerri Anne. 2013. "Cultural exposure, emotional intelligence, and cultural intelligence: An exploratory study." *International Journal of Cross Cultural Management* 13(1) 5–22. Print.

Daley, Christine E., and Anthony J. Onwuegbuzie. "Race and Intelligence." *The Cambridge Handbook of Intelligence*. Ed. Robert J. Sternberg and Scott Barry Kaufman. New York: Cambridge UP, 2011. 293–306. Print.

Flyn, James. *Race, IQ, and Jensen*. London: Routledge, 1980. Print.

Helms, Janet E. "The Triple Quandary of Race, Culture, and Social Class in Standardized Cognitive Ability Testing." *Contemporary Intellectual Assessment: Theories, Tests, and Issues*. Ed. Dawn P. Flanagan et al. New York: Guilford, 1997. Print.

Herrnstein, Richard, and Charles Murray. *The Bell Curve: Intelligence and Class Structure in American Life*. New York: Free, 1994. Print.

Jacoby, Russell, and Naomi Galuberman, eds. *The Bell Curve Debate: History, Documents, Opinions*. New York: Random, 1997. Print.

Jensen, Arthur R. "How Much Can We Boost IQ and Scholastic Achievement?" *Environment, Heredity, and Intelligence*. Cambridge: Harvard Educational Review, 1969. Print.

Kaufman, James C. 2015. "Why Creativity Isn't in IQ Tests, Why it Matters, and Why it Won't Change Anytime Soon Probably." *Journal of Intelligence*, 3, 59-72. Print.

Mayer, John D., David R., and Caruso and Peter Salovey. 2016. "The Ability Model of Emotional Intelligence: Principles and Updates." *Emotion Review*, Volume 8 (4) 290-300. Print.

Richardson, Ken. 2002. "What IQ Tests Test." *Theory and Psychology* 12 (3) 283-314. Print.

Rose, Steven. "Darwin 200: Should Scientists Study Race and IQ? No: Science and Society Do Not Benefit." *Nature*. 12 Feb. 2009: 786–88. Print.

Schaler, Jefrey A. 2006. *Howard Gardner Under Fire: The Rebel Psychologist Faces His Critics*. Chicago: Open Court Publishing. Print.

INTERNAL COLONIALISM

Some observers believe that certain subordinate ethnic and racial groups are colonies within their own countries, controlled by the dominant ethnic group. The applicability of this concept is disputed by other observers, who point out difficulties in the analogy between external and internal colonialism.

EXTERNAL COLONIALISM

A nation can establish an external colony by imposing control over a territory located beyond its existing borders. To maintain control, the colonial power must send civilian and military personnel to live in the country. Military personnel are sent to keep order, that is, to suppress any opposition to the colonial power, which displaces the former indigenous power structure. Civilian personnel are sent to maintain control through economic, political, and social means.

Economic control is maintained by such methods as restricting licenses to operate local businesses, imposing heavy taxes, buying out local businesses and property, importing workers from other countries, paying lower wages to the subordinate group for the same work performed by members of the dominant ethnic group, setting up absentee landlords, turning areas into ghettos, and banning local businesses. The colonial power's objective is to dominate the market so that the colonized people will lack economic autonomy, become economically marginalized, and can be exploited in order to enrich the colonizers. Money can then flow from the dominated peoples to the rulers.

Political control is maintained by arresting independent leaders, banning opposition groups, locating pliable local leaders who will carry out the colonial agenda, and restricting civil liberties. The aim of the colonial power is to dominate the political system so that the colonized people lack any ability to influence public policy. Compliance can then result from a belief that resistance is useless.

Social control is maintained by banning the local language, controlling the educational system and the media, geographically displacing the subordinate ethnic group, moving in settlers from the home country of the colonial power, and ridiculing the supposed backwardness of the subordinate ethnic group. The aim of the colonial power is to dominate society to the extent that the colonized people believe in their own inferiority. The ruling group can then break the spirit of the subordinate population.

One example of external colonialism occurred a century ago, when the United States attempted to seize control of the Philippine Islands by suppressing an armed independence struggle in 1901. US military personnel arrived first, followed by bureaucrats, educators, media, traders, and others, who established themselves as colonists. This classical form of external colonialism ended in 1946, when the Philippines became an independent country and US bureaucrats withdrew. US armed forces, however, remained in the Philippines for more than four decades after 1946 on bases that were transferred to Philippine sovereignty.

AMERICAN INDIANS AS COLONIZED PEOPLE

In external colonialism, a dominant and powerful country goes overseas to take over a country that is weak and can be dominated. However, the same methods can be used inside a country: A dominant ethnic group can act as a colonial power in subordinating a weaker ethnic group inside the same country.

For many centuries, the natives of North and South America lived in isolation from the rest of the world. When Europeans set foot in the Western Hemisphere with the intent of occupying the land, conflict between the two groups was inevitable. The history of the European conquest of the Americas began as a form of external colonialism. When the countries of North and South America became independent, internal colonialism existed because the population that was of European origin continued to hold a dominant position over the indigenous population and imposed economic, political, and social control.

Today, American Indians in the United States can live on reservations, that is, plots of land in which they alone are permitted to reside. Although tribal authorities are allowed to make some decisions on behalf of the reservation population, ultimate political authority is held by the US Department of the Interior's Bureau of Indian Affairs (BIA). American Indians can develop their own sources of income, but the BIA runs reservation schools in a manner quite similar to the educational systems that operate in colonies.

Many examples of internal colonialism abound outside the United States. In the seventeenth century, after suppressing an Irish rebellion, Henry VIII of England encouraged British settlers to move to Ulster, in the northern part of Ireland; the result was a colonization of Ireland. Later in the same century, Dutch settlers arrived to establish colonial enclaves amid the indigenous peoples of South Africa; however, when apartheid was adopted in 1948, it was the Africans who were forcibly relocated into enclaves. After the United States gained control of the Philippines from Spain in 1901, the indigenous peoples of Mindanao Island and the Sulu archipelago refused to recognize the authority of the new colonial power, so the US authorities encouraged Filipinos to move to Mindanao in the role of internal colonists.

AFRICAN AMERICANS AS COLONIZED PEOPLE

Some observers claim that a form of internal colonialism involving African Americans exists in the United States. They believe that African Americans who live primarily in segregated housing and territorial enclaves have been treated as colonial subjects. For example, businesses in these enclaves tend not to be run by African Americans. As further evidence, they cite how African Americans, for more than three centuries, were denied positions of political authority, rendering them politically dependent. The dominant white population made sure that the Africans lost their own culture and, during the era of slavery, would not have an opportunity to acquire American culture.

Robert Blauner's *Racial Oppression in America* (1972) is one of the most famous statements of the thesis that African Americans have been internally colonized. Economically, African Americans have worked for white Americans in low-paying jobs. Until the 1960s, blacks rarely held executive positions in government. Indeed, the practice among whites was to deal with captive leaders in the African American community, that is, blacks who represented the interests of whites more than the needs of blacks. Moreover, blacks lost African culture and have been excluded from the mainstream of American culture. Advocates of the concept of internal colonialism argue that these facts establish the existence of a separate caste status for African Americans, who

are forced to confront a split labor market in which they are the lowest-paid workers, are harassed by police, ignored by politicians, and subjected to inferior schooling so that they will not acquire the skills needed for upward mobility.

Critics of the concept of internal colonialism point out several reasons why they believe that the concept of internal colonialism does not fit the situation of African Americans. Whites and blacks can be found in all classes: Some African Americans are economically much better off than the average white American. Also, African Americans are not confined to a specific bounded territory but live in many neighborhoods. Similarly, African Americans have been elected mayors of most larger American cities, so they are hardly politically impotent. Finally, African Americans have developed their own distinctive culture within the United States, and most Americans are well acquainted with the African American entertainers and other cultural leaders. Marxists argue that the real divisions in society are not between racial groups but rather between social classes.

IMPACT ON PUBLIC POLICY

When members of an ethnic or racial group believe that they are being colonized, at least four courses of action are open to them. One is to assimilate into the dominant culture, thereby ending discriminatory treatment. European ethnic groups in the United States, many of which initially formed enclaves such as Little Italies, have generally been successful in becoming part of the mainstream.

A second course is to leave the country to escape persecution. In the early part of the twentieth century, Turkey instituted massacres of Armenians, many of whom chose to emigrate to the United States. Chinese left Indonesia and Malaysia in the 1960s for similar reasons.

A third course is to protest unequal treatment with the aim of reversing an ethnic group's colonial status. The American Civil Rights movement of the 1960s agitated successfully for the passage of legislation to outlaw discrimination on the basis of race and sex, though enforcement of the legislation has not eliminated discrimination.

The fourth alternative is nationalism and the establishment of a separate country. However, the weaker ethnic group can expect to lose if it engages in a war of independence unless it can find an ally abroad.

In 1971, for example, the peoples of East Pakistan believed that they were being exploited and badly governed by authorities in West Pakistan. After a war successfully waged with the help of India, East Pakistan was recognized as the new nation of Bangladesh. Similarly, some of the Moros of Mindanao and the Sulu archipelago have continued to agitate for an independent state consisting of the territories of the former Sultanate of Sulu. Within the United States, some members of the African American liberation movement of the 1960s, inspired by the agenda in Stokely Carmichael and Charles V. Hamilton's *Black Power* (1967), urged the United Nations to hold plebiscites in the "black colonies of America." An echo of this form of action can be seen in the Black Lives Matter movement.

——*Michael Haas*

BIBLIOGRAPHY AND FURTHER READING

Allen, Robert L. "Reassessing the Internal (Neo) Colonialism Theory." Black Scholar 35.1 (2005): 2–11. Print.

Benjamin, Russell, and Gregory O. Hall, eds. *Eternal Colonialism.* Lanham: UP of America, 2010. Print.

Byrd, Jodi A. *The Transit of Empire: Indigenous Critics of Colonialism.* Minneapolis: U of Minnesota P, 2011. Print.

Chávez, John R. "Aliens in Their Native Lands: The Persistence of Internal Colonial Theory." *Journal of World History* 22.4 (2011): 785–809. Print.

Takaki, Ronald, ed. *From Different Shores: Perspectives on Race and Ethnicity in America,* 2d ed. New York: Oxford UP, 1994. Print.

INTERNALIZED RACISM

A foundational principle in sociology is that the self is socially constructed through the role-taking aspect of socialization, whereby we see ourselves from the perspectives of significant others and the general perspective of our culture. Other people and the media provide a looking glass, supplying us with reflected appraisals of the self and racial or ethnic groups in the United States. Because racist stereotypes prevail in American culture, it is possible for some minority members to internalize them and to denigrate themselves by thinking about, feeling toward, and treating themselves in the same way members of the dominant culture may. However, a caveat is warranted here, as minority members are not passive victims of oppression; if a minority individual has a favorable self-feeling through, for example, internalizing a positive racial or ethnic group identity from significant others and his or her primary groups, then the ability to resist racist evaluations is greatly enhanced. Individuals are also able to interpret situations reflectively, enabling some minority members to realize that many dominant-group representations of their groups and cultural heritages are stereotypical and ideological. Nevertheless, an individual can succumb to the enormous influence that a media-saturated culture exerts on the construction of his or her identity.

Internalized racism has been poignantly illustrated in such portraits as African American writer Jean Toomer's book *Cane* (1923) and African American novelist Toni Morrison's *The Bluest Eye* (1970). The latter novel tells the story of Pecola Breedlove, an adolescent African American girl tormented by her internalization of the white standards of beauty as symbolized by blue eyes. Social psychologist Kurt Lewin researched the phenomenon of group self-hatred. Another social psychologist, Kenneth Clark, documented the prevalence of internalized racism, providing persuasive testimony to the US Supreme Court in *Brown v. Board of Education* (1954) that segregated schools taught black children that they were inferior, engendering emotional devastation and psychological harm. Along similar lines, social theorist Bell Hooks, in *Black Looks: Race and Representation* (1992), describes internalized racism as a "colonization of the mind."

In the United States, the Declaration of Independence declares that those who rule must have the "consent of the governed." If minority members believe that their status in society is a result of *natural* inequality in a system of fair play, meritocracy, or equality of opportunity, then their internalized racism manufactures the consent needed to be governed although oppressed. Internalizing a view of innate inferiority dissuades minorities from seeking redress for their grievances, encouraging instead accommodation, acquiescence, and resignation. Nevertheless, many minority individuals have resisted white supremacy, developing a consciousness of social injustice, igniting a movement for civil rights, and, occasionally, sparking violent protest (expressed in the slogan "No justice, no peace!"). Over the years, African Americans have forged positive self and group identities as "New Negroes" of the 1920's Harlem Renaissance and have transformed their identity from Negro to black, epitomized by the 1960's, "Black is beautiful" movement. Native Americans have acted similarly through such activities as a revival of tribal consciousness and of pow-wows, the rise of the American Indian Movement (AIM), and the concept of Red Power. Many Mexican Americans have responded similarly by adopting "Chicano" as a term of group pride and, particularly in the past, Chicanismo as a counterideology and by forming the political party La Raza Unida.

——*Gil Richard Musolf*

BIBLIOGRAPHY AND FURTHER READING

Hooks, Bell. *Rock My Soul: Black People and Self-esteem.* New York: Atria, 2003. Print.

Patterson, James T. *Brown V. Board of Education: A Civil Rights Milestone and Its Troubled Legacy.* New York: Oxford UP, 2001. Print.

Quintana, Stephen. *Mexican American Children's Ethnic Pride and Internalized Racism.* East Lansing: Julian Sasmora Research Inst., 1999. Print.

Samuels, Robert. *Writing Prejudices: The Psychoanalysis and Pedagogy of Discrimination from Shakespeare to Toni Morrison.* Albany: U of New York P, 2001. Print.

INTERNATIONAL INDIAN TREATY COUNCIL

The International Indian Treaty Council was founded during a conference convened on the Standing Rock Reservation (North Dakota) during July 1974. Its initial mandate, conveyed by the Lakota elders, was to "take the 1868 Fort Laramie Treaty and place it before the community of nations." American Indian Movement (AIM) leader Russell Means, asked to assume responsibility for IITC, accepted by agreeing to serve as "Permanent Trustee." Jimmie Durham, a Cherokee AIM member, became IITC's founding director.

By 1975, Means and Durham had established an office in New York and expanded the mission of the "international diplomatic arm of AIM" to include advocacy of the rights of all indigenous peoples, worldwide. Durham then set about organizing the first major forum on indigenous rights in the history of the United Nations.

This resulted in the "Indian Summer in Geneva," an assembly of delegates from ninety-eight indigenous nations throughout the Western Hemisphere at the Palace of Nations in Geneva, Switzerland, during July 1977. As the coordinating entity, IITC became the first indigenous nongovernmental organization (NGO; Type-II, Consultative) ever recognized by the United Nations.

The assembly stimulated the United Nations to establish a formal body, the Working Group on Indigenous Populations, under its Economic and Social Council (ECOSOC) for purposes of receiving annual reports on the grievances of the world's native peoples. The Working Group's broader charge was to make the studies necessary to prepare a Draft Declaration on the Rights of Indigenous Peoples by 1992 (later extended to 1994) for ratification by the UN General Assembly as international law.

With this established, Durham resigned in 1981 to pursue a career as an artist. He was replaced by Russell Means's younger brother, Bill, who proved a far less appropriate director. Almost immediately, the younger Means initiated a policy of aligning IITC with a range of leftist governments, many of them oppressing indigenous peoples within their borders. The result was a steady erosion of constituent support for IITC.

By 1986, disputes over IITC's support of Nicaragua's Sandinista regime in its drive to subordinate the Miskito, Sumu, and Rama peoples of the country's Atlantic coast led to a purge. "Indigenists," such as Harvard-trained Shawnee attorney Glenn Morris, were summarily expelled from IITC. The

Lakota elders' original mandate was negated, Russell Means displaced from his permanent trusteeship, and IITC structurally separated from AIM by its incorporation under US law.

Thereafter, although Bill Means continued to speak of "representing more than a hundred indigenous nations," IITC's isolation and decline accelerated. By the early 1990s, it was increasingly encumbered by the fund-raising requirements of supporting its staff. Fortunately, many of the peoples whose rights it had once championed had by then learned to represent themselves internationally.

——*Ward Churchill*

BIBLIOGRAPHY AND FURTHER READING

Cobb, Daniel M., ed. *Say We Are Nations: Documents of Politics and Protest in Indigenous America since 1887.* Chapel Hill: U of North Carolina P, 2015. Print.

Harjo, Suzan Shown, ed. *Nation to Nation: Treaties Between the United States and American Indian Nations.* Washington, DC: Nat. Mus. of American Indian, 2014. Print.

Johansen, Bruce E. "International Indian Treaty Council. (IITC)." *Encyclopedia of the American Indian Movement.* Santa Barbara: Greenwood, 2013. 155–156. Print.

Trask, Mililani, and Elvira Pulitano. *Indigenous Rights in the Age of the UN Declaration.* Cambridge: Cambridge UP, 2012. Print.

INTERRACIAL AND INTERETHNIC FRIENDSHIP

Since the 1950s, legislation such as the Civil Rights Act of 1964 and the Voting Rights Act of 1965 has helped to reduce discrimination against racial and ethnic groups. Similarly, the US Supreme Court's 1954 decision in *Brown v. Board of Education* began the movement to desegregate public schools and, as a result, did much to break down personal barriers between blacks, whites, Latinos, Asian Americans, and other groups. As a result of such factors, contact across group lines in American schools, colleges, workplaces, neighborhoods, and social gatherings has increased, but these situations do not often lead to increased acceptance and the growth of friendships across racial and ethnic boundaries. According to numerous sources, including S. Dale McLemore's *Racial and Ethnic Relations in America* (1998) and Joseph F. Healey's *Race, Ethnicity, Gender, and Class* (1998), interracial and interethnic friendships in the 1990s and before remained relatively infrequent. That is not surprising given the centuries of racism and prejudice, as well as the differences in socioeconomic status, places of residence, and levels of education, that continue to exist between groups. Moreover, the slowly changing norms concerning issues of race and ethnicity also discourage the growth of interracial and interethnic friendships. Despite significant legal and political efforts to control them, racial stereotyping and prejudice remain powerful social forces. Whereas interactions with members of the same racial or ethnic group promote social stability, interactions with members of different racial or ethnic groups mark social change and instability, which can be seen as threatening to a group's sense of security. By the 2000s and, especially, the 2010s, however, the picture had begun to change, as not only interracial friendships became much more common (particularly on college campuses and in cities) but the very concept of separate races interacting was questioned, in part because so many individuals increasingly identified as belonging to "more than one race."

INTERGROUP CONTACT

Though statistics regarding the incidence of interracial and interethnic friendships are substantially harder to find than are corresponding statistics regarding intermarriage, there is a body of research within the social sciences that addresses the issue of interracial/interethnic friendships. Sociologist Gordon Allport's contact hypothesis is applicable to the study of these friendships. The contact hypothesis proposes that when social, political, and economic barriers to integration and equality disappear, the social distance between racial groups should also decrease. Social distance can be defined as the degree of intimacy to which an individual is willing

681

to admit persons of other groups, ranging from inter-marriage to complete segregation.

A variety of social settings in which interracial and interethnic contact leads to friendships have been studied, but the majority of research has focused on desegregated schools. Since *Brown v. Board of Education*, the desegregation of schools has facilitated the interaction of students, teachers, and parents from different racial and ethnic groups. Yet when it comes to friendship, or social interaction outside the school context, the majority of the research has found that students prefer members of their own racial and ethnic group as friends, although the frequency of these friendships differs depending on what racial and ethnic groups are involved. For example, studies such as Nathan Glazer and Daniel P. Moynihan's *Beyond the Melting Pot* (1970) and Richard Alba's *Ethnicity and Race in the USA* (1988) have found that social distance between white ethnic groups is being reduced by interethnic friendships and inter-marriage. Similarity in attitudes, values, behaviors, and socioeconomic status are often the basis of inter-personal attraction, with race an important factor in the choice of friends. Therefore, it is understandable why interethnic friendships, especially between white European Americans, would be more common than interracial friendships.

Racial stereotypes and societal norms act as bar-riers to the formation of interracial friendships. One study has found that students often cite the tendency of members of other groups to segregate themselves and the perception that they lack common ground upon which to build a friendship as reasons why they do not have friends from other racial or ethnic groups. Other studies have also found that some school practices, such as tracking, contribute to the low number of interracial friendships; tracking, for example, may tend to segregate African Americans and other minorities into classrooms devoted to lower academic tracks. Another barrier to the forma-tion of interracial and interethnic friendships is the perception of negative family attitudes toward these friendships.

Among adults, research has tended to focus on the effects of residential desegregation on inter-racial contact and friendships. Douglas Massey and Nancy Denton's *American Apartheid* (1993) explored the issue of residential segregation and found that racial groups remain virtually segregated, even when

they are of the same social class. Among adults, there-fore, interracial friendships remain infrequent, both because of a lack of opportunities to interact and because of prejudices and stereotypes. One study by James E. Rosenbaum et al. found that when low-income blacks moved to middle-class white suburbs as part of a housing voucher program, considerable racial integration was achieved, including a substan-tial number of individual friendships.

ASIAN AMERICANS, HISPANIC AMERICANS, AND AFRICAN AMERICANS

Rates of interracial and interethnic friendships vary depending on the groups involved. According to sources such as S. Dale McLemore's *Racial and Ethnic Relations in America* (1998) and Joseph F. Healey's *Race, Ethnicity, Gender, and Class* (1998), Asian Americans in the twentieth century experi-enced considerable assimilation in the areas of pri-mary relations such as friendships and marriage, especially with white European Americans. That pic-ture remains largely true today. Overall the extent of intimate contact between Hispanic Americans and whites is higher than for African Americans, yet lower than for Asian Americans and whites, according to Healey. For example, according to McLemore, Mexican Americans decreasingly have only Mexican friends over the passage of time. This generational trend is more pronounced among those living in desegregated neighborhoods and among those of higher income, suggesting that if Mexican Americans continue to live, work, and send their children to school in desegregated areas, the number of friend-ships with non-Hispanics will continue to increase. Similarly, Clara Rodriguez's *Puerto Ricans: Born in the USA* (1991) found that rates of interracial contact increase for Hispanic Americans of the more affluent social classes who live in the cities and for the pre-sumably more Americanized younger generations.

According to the majority of research, including McLemore's *Racial and Ethnic Relations in America* and Healey's *Race, Ethnicity, Gender, and Class*, friend-ships between African Americans and whites are the least frequent. These two groups remain virtually separated in their personal relationships everywhere but in the schools. Even in school, the proportion of African American/white friendships remains low. According to research, it is common for black stu-dents to remain virtually segregated within primary and secondary school systems, and black college students are increasingly forming their own sororities, fraternities, and student organizations. The low level of interracial contact between African Americans and whites is further evidenced in the low rates of intermarriage between the two groups. Therefore, McLemore, for example, concludes that the level of primary assimilation of African Americans, as evidenced in the low number of interracial friendships and marriage, is low compared to that of other racial and ethnic groups.

IMPROVING INTERGROUP FRIENDSHIPS

One of the most commonly proposed methods of improving intergroup relations is for people to establish communication, get to know one another, and participate in group activities together. This process enables individuals to judge members of a different race or ethnicity on the basis of their individual characteristics rather than their group membership. It is often maintained that such transformations are most likely to occur if the individuals involved are of equal socioeconomic status, if they are given the chance to work cooperatively together, if their interaction is supported by those in authority, and if there is a high level of intimacy. Often, intergroup contacts that occur under different circumstances do not alter prejudices and rarely result in the formation of friendships, because they simply mirror the power differentials and inequalities of the larger society. Other factors that have been shown to influence the outcome of contacts between members of different racial and ethnic groups include minimal competition, voluntary interaction, and similarities in beliefs and values.

Schools can encourage intergroup contact by offering noncompetitive, supportive environments where different racial and ethnic groups can interact and work cooperatively. Proposed methods of accomplishing this include the implementation of small-group learning teams and interracial extracurricular activities. Moreover, positive effects on the development of interracial friendships have been observed when school officials and teachers have implemented programs that reduce status differences between students of different racial and ethnic groups.

——*Erica Childs*

BIBLIOGRAPHY AND FURTHER READING

Allport, Gordon. *The Nature of Prejudice*. Garden City: Doubleday, 1958. Print.

Gordon, Milton. *Assimilation in American Life*. New York: Oxford UP, 1964. Print.

Hallinan, Maureen T., and Ruy A. Teixeira. "Opportunities and Constraints: Black-White Differences in the Formation of Interracial Friendships." *Child Development* 58 (1987). Print.

Hallinan, Maureen T., and Richard A. Williams. "Interracial Friendship Choices in Secondary Schools." *American Sociological Review* 54 (1989). Print.

Hallinan, Maureen T. and Richard A. Williams. "The Stability of Students' Interracial Friendships." *American Sociological Review* 52 (1987). Print.

Healey, Joseph F. *Race, Ethnicity, Gender, and Class: The Sociology of Group Conflict and Change*. Thousand Oaks: Pine Forge, 1998. Print.

Massey, Douglas, and Nancy Denton. *American Apartheid*. Cambridge: Harvard UP, 1993. Print.

McLemore, S. Dale. *Racial and Ethnic Relations in America*, 5th ed. Boston: Allyn, 1998. Print.

INTERRACIAL AND INTERETHNIC MARRIAGE

In the United States, racial and ethnic groups have tended to marry within their own group. Throughout US history, there have been laws against various types of interracial and interethnic marriage; such laws were usually directed at African Americans, Native Americans, and Asian Americans. For example, in the early twentieth century, Chinese and Japanese immigrants were denied "white" status, which meant, among other things, that they were subject to restrictions on their right to marry outside their own groups. Since the institution of slavery, interracial relations between African Americans and whites have

Robert De Niro and his wife Grace Hightower are a prominent interracial couple, shown here at the 2012 Tribeca Film Festival. By David Shankbone (Own work).

been closely monitored and restricted. Up until 1966, seventeen states still had formal prohibitions against one or more forms of interracial marriage, and forty states at one time had laws prohibiting blacks from marrying whites. On June 12, 1967, the US Supreme Court rendered a decision in *Loving v. Virginia* that overturned the sixteen existing state antimiscegenation statutes.

INTERMARRIAGE RATES

Rates of intermarriage thus differ depending on the racial or ethnic groups involved. According to numerous studies, interethnic marriages, especially between European Americans, are fairly common. Richard Alba and Nancy Foner (2015) have concluded that among white ethnic groups there has been a steady increase in interethnic marriage—both in the United States and in Western Europe. (For example, only 20 percent of Italian American men born after World War II were married to Italian American women.) Similarly, in an early study Nathan Glazer and Daniel P. Moynihan's *Beyond the Melting Pot* (1970) analyzed ethnic groups in New York City and found that distinctions between white ethnic groups were being reduced by intermarriage. Despite this increase in interethnic marriages, these

two studies both found that individuals are still somewhat more likely to choose mates from their own ethnic group than from another. In 2012, the US Census Bureau reported that interracial or interethnic opposite-sex married couples grew by 29 percent between the years 2000 and 2010.

Interethnic marriage, though, is different from interracial marriage. People are often willing to cross ethnic boundaries to marry, but there is a much greater resistance to crossing racial boundaries. In addition, there are disparities between rates of intermarriage for the various racial groups. Hispanic Americans are an interesting example, since this group can be classed as both an ethnic minority group and a racial minority group. Marriages between Hispanic Americans and whites account for only 2.6 percent of all US marriages, according to 1996 US Census Bureau data; however, this represents a substantial increase from 1970, when the rate was closer to 1 percent. (As noted above, the increase in interethnic married couples was even more significant in the United States between 2000 and 2010.) Some researchers, such as Clara Rodriguez (2000), have found that rates of intermarriage increase for Hispanic Americans of the more affluent social classes who live in the cities and for the presumably more Americanized younger generations.

Asian Americans have higher rates of intermarriage than African Americans and Hispanic Americans, according to scholars Sharon Lee and Keiko Yamanaka, who found the outmarriage rate for Chinese Americans to be 15 percent and for Japanese Americans 34 percent. However, not all Asian American groups have high rates of intermarriage. Robert Jiobu's *Ethnicity and Assimilation* (1988) found that Vietnamese Americans have very low rates of intermarriage.

African Americans have the lowest rates of intermarriage among all racial groups. According to the US Census Bureau, in 1995, black-white marriages accounted for less than 1 percent of all US marriages. Black males have traditionally outmarried at higher rates than black women. This is consistent with a 1990 study by Tucker and Mitchell-Kernan, which found that 3.6 percent of all married black men are married to white women, while only 1.2 percent of married black women are married to white men. Yet, according to the 2010 US Census, the number of black-white married couples increased to almost 12 percent that year. This is in keeping with other studies that show the same trend.

INTERMARRIAGE AND PREJUDICE

Despite the increasing occurrence of intermarriage, there is still prejudice against these unions, especially marriages between blacks and whites. This disapproval is communicated through formal channels such as social institutions as well as via informal channels such as families and friends. Other forms of opposition that the interracial couple may face come from outside the family. According to Rosenblatt et al., the refusal to accept or acknowledge interracial marriages occurs in a variety of ways, such as not selling a house or not renting a hotel room to an interracial couple. Other typical examples are restaurant hostesses asking one member of an interracial couple if it is "one for dinner" or supermarket cashiers trying to separate their food items in line at the grocery store, which are both refusals to acknowledge that the two are a couple. Religious reasons are also widely used, with Christian groups distributing information over the Internet that "interracial marriages are not biblical" or preachers interpreting the scriptures as explicitly opposing interracial marriages. Interracial couples have also cited police harassment, getting "pulled over" a disproportionate number of times when together, and being told that the white woman

fits the description of a kidnap victim. Often, whites who intermarry are marginalized and stereotyped in much the same way as minorities, with the assumption that they have pathological problems or are "white trash." The general trend, however, is toward an increasingly multiracial society, as more and more individuals identify as belonging to more than one race and marry partners who similarly cannot be classified as belonging to one race or another.

——*Erica Childs*

BIBLIOGRAPHY AND FURTHER READING

Alba, Richard, and Nancy Foner. *Strangers No More: Immigration and the Challenges of Integration in North American and Western Europe.* Princeton: Princeton UP, 2015. Print.

Frey, William H. *Diversity Explosion: How New Racial Demographics Are Remaking America.* Washington, DC: Brookings Institution, 2015. Print.

Rodriguez, Clara E. *Changing Race: Latinos, the Census, and the History of Ethnicity in the United States.* New York: New York UP, 2000. Print.

Rosenblatt, Paul, Terri A. Karis, and Richard D. Powell. *Multiracial Couples: Black and White Voices.* Thousand Oaks: Sage, 1995. Print.

US Census. "2010 Census Shows Interracial and Interethnic Married Couples Grew by 28 Percent Over Decade." *US Census.* US Department of Commerce, 25 Apr. 2012. Web. 5 June 2015.

Yancy, George A., and Richard Lewis Jr. *Interracial Families: Current Concepts and Controversies.* New York: Routledge, 2009. Print.

IRANIAN AMERICANS

In early 2017, as one of the first acts of his presidency, Donald J. Trump signed a ban on immigration from seven Muslim-majority countries, including Iran. The concern of the administration was that, without such a ban, terrorists intending to do harm to the United States could slip into the country—even though stringent immigrant vetting procedures were already in place and even though no one in the United States had ever been killed by any "jihadist" from Iran or, for that matter, most of the other countries named in the ban. Furthermore, Trump stated that he

intended to increase sanctions against Iran because leaders in that country had tested a middle-range missile, although the test did not violate an agreement reached between the two countries the previous year regarding nuclear technology. The heightened sense of alarm communicated by the Trump administration was owing to little more than a longstanding distrust of the Islamic Republic of Iran's theocratic government, and, it seems, of most Muslims, among many right-leaning Americans who voted for Trump. That distrust first arose in the wake of the 1979

Iranian Revolution, it continued to be fueled during the period following the 9/11 attacks (even though no Iranians were involved) and the US-led war in Iraq, and it persisted into the years of the Obama administration, which sought limited engagement with the Iranian regime even as it hoped to support antigovernment forces in Iran. This long and complicated history has affected Iranian Americans and the way in which they are perceived in the United States.

REVOLUTION, REACTION, AND REVISION

The trauma of the 1979 Iranian Revolution and subsequent terror and economic deterioration, combined with the long Iran-Iraq war (1980-1988), resulted in widespread dispersions of Iranians outside their homeland. It is estimated that between 500,000 and 1 million Iranian Americans now live in the United States, many of them having taken refuge here during the 1980s. (Some estimates range as high as 2 million.) The majority of Iranian immigrants live in suburban areas such as Los Angeles, Washington, DC, and New York's Long Island, and hold middle-class jobs.

Since the Iranian Revolution and the taking of the US embassy, images of Iranians as unpredictable and wild anti-American fanatics and terrorists have dominated the minds of the American public, according to sociologist Ali Akbar Mahdi of Ohio Wesleyan University in a 1997 issue of *The Iranian*. For example, when the federal building in Oklahoma City was bombed on April 19, 1995, at first many Americans believed that Middle Eastern terrorists were responsible. Those fears were confirmed with the 9/11 attacks, although, again, no Iranians were involved. Living in such a negative environment is a difficult but conscious choice for most first-generation Iranian immigrants. Second-generation Iranians also suffer from the negative images associated with the national origins of their parents, as do, in many cases, third-generation Iranians.

Mahdi wrote that the presence of many Iranian immigrants in Western countries is partially due to the conversion of Iran into an Islamic theocracy after the revolution. Most Iranian immigrants are secular people who do not want to mix religion with politics and education. He said that most Iranian immigrants in the United States consist of middle- and upper-class people who are highly educated and have a better-than-average standard of living. Many of those who

came from more modest backgrounds have secured middle-class positions for themselves through education, dedication, and hard work. By 2011, according to the American Community Survey, 58 percent held bachelor's degrees. A 2013 survey by Public Affairs Alliance of Iranian Americans found that 54 percent had annual household incomes of $60,000 or more, while 32 percent reported income of $100,000 or more.

RELATIONS WITH OTHER GROUPS/ COMMUNITIES

Iranians who came to the United States before the hostage crisis received a generally positive reception. However, after that crisis and the ongoing rise of Islamic fundamentalism in the Middle East, the American perception of Iran changed from a country of peace to a country of turmoil and unpredictability. The US State Department has labeled the Iranian government a "rogue state." The unfavorable portrayal of Iranians (and other Muslims) in the US media helps breed prejudice and discrimination, placing a strain on Iranian Americans. Some researchers accuse American political, religious, and cultural leaders of using xenophobia and unfounded fears to gain popularity. They say that while the United States prides itself on its sociocultural diversity, it simultaneously denounces cultures it cannot understand.

A survey of 157 Iranian Americans conducted by Laleh Khalili, a graduate student at Columbia University (*The Iranian Times*, April, 1998), showed that although 37 percent of respondents select mostly other Iranian Americans as friends, 63 percent do not. Khalili found that those who prefer friends who are not Iranian Americans associate with members of other transnational communities rather than typical white Americans. The most frequently mentioned areas of origin are Southeast Asia, the Middle East, and Latin America. "A shared knowledge of what crossing borders entails and a similarity in sociopolitical (if not always cultural) backgrounds provide a context in which the Iranian in the United States can operate comfortably," Khalili said.

Iranian American writer Michael C. Walker has written, "We must proactively teach antidiscrimination in our schools and our communities. It must explore the world's diverse cultures, religions, and ethnicities. Such education should especially concentrate on nations like Iran where America's hatred and misunderstanding is prismed and clearly focused" (*The Iranian*, Feb. 26, 1998).

Following the 2017 Trump "Muslim ban," as it is widely termed, Arash Saedinia, an Iranian American English professor and rights activist, participated in demonstrations at Los Angeles International Airport, observing that "We saw black, brown and white people, young and old, hijabs and yarmulkes. The crowd was as diverse as this city" (quoted in Hayoun, 2017).

Another demonstration participant noted that Trump reminded him of the former hardliner Iranian president, Mahmoud Ahmadinejad (ruled 2005-2013). "The campaign that Trump ran was word-by-word copied from Ahmadinejad," he said, adding that Ahmadinejad also ran on a populist platform and ignored many of Iran's deeper traditions of humanism and understanding.

——Marian Wynne Haber, updated by Michael Shally-Jensen

BIBLIOGRAPHY AND FURTHER READING

Ansari, Maboud. *The Iranian Americans: A Popular Social History of a New American Ethnic Group.* Lewiston: E. Mellen, 2013. Print.

Hayoun, Massoud. "Immigration Ban: Hope Trumps Fear for many Iranian Americans." *AlJazeera*, 30 January 2017. Web. February 4, 2017.

Khalili, Laleh. "Mixing Memory and Desire: Iranians in the United States." *Iranian*. Abadan, 13 May 1998. Web. 4 June 2015.

Mahdi, Ali Akbar. "The Second Generation Iranians: Questions and Concerns." *Iranian*. Abadan, Feb./Mar. 1997. Web. 4 June 2015.

Marvasti, Amir B., and Karyn D. McKinney. *Middle Eastern Lives in America.* Lanham: Rowman and Littlefield, 2004. Print.

Shavarini, Mitra K. *Desert Roots: Journey of an Iranian Immigrant Family.* El Paso: LFB Scholarly Pub., 2012. Print.

Tehranian, John. *Whitewashed: America's Invisible Middle Eastern Minority.* New York: New York UP, 2009. Print.

Wagenknecht, Maria D. *Constructing Identity in Iranian-American Self-Narrative.* New York: Palgrave Macmillan, 2015. Print.

Walker, Michael C. "Understanding Iranians? Not a Bad Idea." *Iranian*. Abadan, 26 Feb. 1998. Web. 4 June 2015.

IRISH AMERICAN STEREOTYPES

Between 1820 and 1920, approximately five million people emigrated from Ireland to the United States. Most of these immigrants were Irish Catholic farmers who were living in abject poverty in an Ireland dominated politically and economically by England. Until the late nineteenth century, Irish Catholics were not allowed to own farms in Ireland, and during the Irish Potato Famine of 1845-1849, more than five hundred thousand Irish farmers were evicted from their farms. The only real choice for these displaced people was to leave Ireland for the United States; however, they were not well received by white Protestants, who then completely controlled the nation's politics, business, and society. These Irish Catholic immigrants were viewed as a threat for several reasons. Many first-generation Irish immigrants spoke only Gaelic, and they became manual laborers who worked for low wages,

creating competition for jobs. The new immigrants built their own Catholic churches and schools and made it very clear that they would not tolerate in the United States the religious discrimination that they and their ancestors had experienced in Ireland.

As early as the 1840's, extremely offensive representations of Irish immigrants began to appear in American newspapers and magazines. The magazine *Harper's Monthly* published numerous drawings in which Irish Americans were depicted as apelike creatures with whom normal Americans would not want to associate. The same magazine printed in its April 6, 1867, issue a drawing by Thomas Nast entitled "The Day We Celebrate." Nast suggested that Irish Americans celebrated St. Patrick's Day by becoming drunk and then attacking police officers. Such stereotypical images of Irish immigrants as violent drunkards appeared in numerous magazines throughout the last six decades of the nineteenth century. Frequently, racist cartoons would simultaneously criticize Irish and Jewish immigrants. The fact that overt discrimination was directed against Jews and Irish Catholics at the same time may well explain why Jewish American and Irish American immigrants came to realize that they had a good deal in common.

Other cartoons ridiculed Irish Americans because of their religious beliefs. Throughout the nineteenth century, the Bible was taught in many American public schools, but the translation used was the King James version, the official translation of Protestant churches. In the 1840's, many Catholic leaders asked school boards to allow Catholic pupils to receive religious instruction based on the Douay translation, which was the approved Catholic version. Numerous anti-catholicism cartoons in the 1840's and 1850's suggested that Catholics were opposed to the reading of the Bible; however, nothing could be further from the truth.

Although disparaging representations of Irish Americans continued to be published in US magazines, most people came to realize that these stereotypical images distorted the truth and revealed more about the prejudices of those creating the images than about Irish Americans whom they attempted to ridicule.

——*Edmund J. Campion*

BIBLIOGRAPHY AND FURTHER READING

Barton, Ruth, ed. *Screening Irish-America: Representing Irish-America in Film and Television*. Portland: Irish Academic P, 2009. Print.

Kibler, M. Alison. *Censoring Racial Ridicule: Irish, Jewish, and African American Struggles over Race and Representation, 1890-1930*. Chapel Hill: U of North Carolina P, 2015. Print.

Mooney, Jennifer. *Irish Stereotypes in Vaudeville, 1865-1905*. New York: Palgrave Macmillan, 2015. Print.

IRISH AMERICANS

The Irish have been a vital component of American life since the days of colonialism. The early Irish immigrants were mainly Presbyterian Protestants from Ulster, Ireland. Although some belonged to the Church of Ireland, most came in search of financial gains. The majority of the Ulster-born Irish were tenant farmers or skilled artisans of modest means. The Irish who would follow in the famine years would be vastly different in their beliefs, their financial status, and their social standing. Each new wave of Irish immigrants would add something to the fabric of American life.

Irish immigrants in Kansas City, Missouri, c. 1909. Family photo scanned by User: Jeanne boleyn).

THE "FAMINE IRISH"

Whereas the earliest Irish immigrants had come to the United States to better themselves, the "famine Irish" sought simple survival in an often hostile land. The Penal Laws in Ireland had long put native Irish Catholics at a serious disadvantage in their homeland. Irish farmers were uneducated, poor, and dependent upon their rocky plots of land for subsistence. Families were large. The lifestyle was one of intense social interaction. They had little, but they shared what they had and celebrated their beliefs with tradition, song, dance, and religious ritual. They were dependent upon the potato crop as their sole food source.

MILESTONES IN IRISH AMERICAN HISTORY

Year	Event	Impact
1776	Signing of the Declaration of Independence by Charles Carroll	Unites Irish Catholics and Anglo-Saxon Protestants in seeking freedom from Britain.
1818	Employment of three thousand Irish to dig the Erie Canal continues.	Increases trade; encourages westward expansion.
1844	Nativist riots in Philadelphia	Heighten anti-Catholic sentiment, social concerns.
1845-1849	Great Irish Famine	Sets off mass immigration of poor Irish to the United States that changes American cities.
1854	Formation of Know-Nothing Party	Advocates restrictions on immigration and seeks to protect Nativist interests.
1859	Discovery of silver in Comstock, Nevada	Creates financial boom that increases westward expansion and business.
1863	Draft riots in New York and other large cities	Impair race relations; create fear among Irish that newly freed blacks will take their jobs.
1869	Completion of the transcontinental railroad	Unites country by rail; further promotes westward expansion and land development.
1875	Elevation of Archbishop John McCloskey to cardinal	Becomes first American cardinal in the Roman Catholic Church.
1911	Triangle Factory fire in New York City	Exposes plight of the working poor; spawns labor laws and social reform.
1928	Defeat of Catholic Alfred E. Smith in presidential election	Spawns fear of possible Papal influence on American politics and anti-Catholic sentiment.
1960	Election to presidency of Catholic John F. Kennedy	Becomes first Irish Catholic president.

When blight struck the potato crop between the years 1845 and 1854, the poor had nowhere to turn. Some had compassionate landlords. However, when Parliament passed the Poor Law Extension Act of 1847, landlords became responsible for the cost of care of their tenantry. Even well-meaning landowners could not cover such expense. Evictions became the rule. The poor then had the option of going to disease-infested workhouses or starving on the road in search of food and shelter. They fled their native land strictly for survival.

Between 1840 and 1860, more than 1.5 million Irish came to the shores of the United States. They settled in cities, concentrating in certain neighborhoods. A large contingent settled in New Orleans. Most of those who fled the Irish potato famine stayed in eastern cities such as New York or Boston simply because they had no money and no marketable skills to move on. Some would move toward Chicago or join the movement westward in search of employment. Most of the famine Irish were poor and Catholic. They represented the first large wave of non-Anglo-Saxon immigrants in the history of the nation.

The Irish immigrants were uneducated, Catholic, and considered uncultured by the social elite in the United States. Many were unaccompanied women, a fact that set the Irish apart from previous immigrant groups. The young Irish girls took positions as domestic servants in the homes of the wealthy. They worked to save enough to rescue more relations in Ireland from starvation. These women and the unskilled Irish men who sought to make a living digging ditches or building canals or bridges were scorned by the nativists. However, from the lowest levels of society, these Irish American began to build their version of the American Dream.

RELIGION

The Irish Catholic poor, social by nature and custom and isolated by their religious beliefs, built their own comfortable enclaves within the cities where they settled. Irish neighborhoods in New York, Boston, Chicago, and elsewhere developed into parishes. The Catholic parishes evolved into social and educational centers within the communities. As the Irish developed a reputation for hard drinking and fighting, it was the parish priest who often served as counselor and role model. The Church cared for the immigrants' spiritual, social, educational, medical, and emotional needs. As the number of immigrants increased, parishes and religious orders built schools, hospitals, and orphanages to meet the needs of the communities.

POLITICS AND SOCIAL REFORMS

As the growing numbers of Irish immigrants began to frighten the white Anglo-Saxon Protestants already established in the cities and to threaten the status quo, the children of the famine generation began to see the possibilities that existed for them by virtue of their numbers and their ambition. Politics was a natural extension of the parish culture. Precinct by precinct, the Irish began to embrace the US political system as a tool for personal advancement and a mechanism for social change.

One individual who came up from the streets of New York was young Alfred E. "Al" Smith. Raised on the streets of Brooklyn as the Brooklyn Bridge was being built, he took advantage of the political patronage in Tammany Hall to gain a foothold in politics. Under the tutelage of Charles Murphy and Jimmy Walker, Smith rose up through the political ranks in New York and eventually became the governor of New York State. Similar political machines evolved in Kansas City and Chicago, as politicians sought to serve their constituencies. Smith initiated social reforms, including child labor laws, and improved safety requirements to protect workers. Elsewhere in the nation, labor unions were gaining support.

With many successes to his credit in New York, Smith ran unsuccessfully for president in 1928. Many people still distrusted the Irish, and the nativists and many non-Catholics feared papal interference in US politics should Smith be elected. The first Irish Catholic to claim the office of the president of the United States would be another descendant from Irish peasant stock, John F. Kennedy, in 1960. Kennedy would stand as a symbol of the Irish American dream brought to fruition.

APPRECIATION OF TRADITIONS

By the late twentieth century, Irish Americans no longer bore the stigma of most negative stereotypes. The Irish generally assimilated into US society, often intermarrying with persons of other ethnicities, yet there continued to be a lingering appreciation of Irish history and traditions, with a renewed interested in traditional Irish music and dance that became a part of American popular culture, transcending ethnic origins and religious beliefs.

——*Kathleen Schongar*

BIBLIOGRAPHY AND FURTHER READING

Byron, Reginald. *Irish America.* New York: Oxford UP, 1999. Print.

Golway, Terry. *The Irish in America.* Ed. Michael Coffrey. New York: Hyperion, 1997. Print.

Gleason, David T., ed. *The Irish in the Atlantic World.* Columbia: U of South Carolina P, 2010. Print.

Griffin, William D. *A Portrait of the Irish in America.* New York: Scribner's, 1981. Print.

Ignatiev, Noel. *How the Irish became White.* New York: Routledge, 1995. Print.

IRISH CATHOLIC "RACE"

The English used notions of a "savage race" in colonialized Ireland to justify systems that dominated and oppressed the Irish long before the American colonies existed. These systems, which codified Irish Catholics by religion and placed them on the bottom of cultural hierarchies. Labels were given substance by combining religious identity with "race." The English also used immigrant groups of English and Scots for social control, according to scholar Roy Forester, in *Oxford Illustrated History of Ireland* (1989). Successive generations of English who were born in Ireland identified themselves as Irish Protestants rather than as English. Scottish people were brought to northern Ireland to serve as buffer groups against Irish kingdoms. These peoples—the Protestant Irish and Scotch-Irish—began identifying themselves as superior to the Irish Catholic "race."

These hierarchies were transferred to North America along with the waves of immigrants; however, cultural and "race" demarcations lost their sharpness in the new land. The Scotch-Irish, as they had in Ireland, acted as buffers in the American colonies until the American Revolution caused distinctions to largely disappear within southern racial slavery hierarchies. Later immigration by Irish Catholics, especially during the 1850's potato famine, in the end contributed more to the enlargement of the "white race" than to the creation of another ethnicity, according to Noel Ignatiev, in *How the Irish Became White* (1995). In the nineteenth century, Irish Catholics faced heavy discrimination, and through this process, a notion of an Irish Catholic "race" developed among other Americans.

——*James V. Fenelon*

IRISH–AFRICAN AMERICAN
RELATIONS

Conflict has existed between Irish Americans and African Americans since the first great waves of Irish immigration in the 1840s. Before the Civil War, Irish Catholics were confronted with harsh discrimination by Anglo-Protestant Americans. When dangerous work needed to be done, many employers opted to hire cheap Irish labor instead of using slaves, preferring to risk the life of an Irishman over one of their slaves, the latter being valuable property. Struggling to survive at the bottom of the economic ladder, the Irish feared that if slaves were set free, they would face even more competition for scarce jobs. Many also believed that they should focus their energies on improving their own plight before expending any of their resources helping African Americans. Irish Americans' concern for their own survival and their view of blacks as competition worked to sour relations between the two struggling groups.

During the Civil War, Irish Americans, who were loyal to the Union generally, had no interest in fighting a war to free the slaves. During the war, when disproportionate numbers of poor Irish were drafted to serve in the Union forces, riots broke out in cities throughout the North. On July 11, 1863,

antidraft rioting broke out in New York City, lasting until July 15. Irish Americans, who viewed the conflict as a rich man's war fought by the poor, took out their anger at abolitionists and African Americans by burning, looting, and beating any blacks in their path. New York militia were called out to stop the rioting.

After the Civil War, the economic struggle between African Americans and Irish Americans continued. Irish Americans and other white immigrants took jobs in the booming industrial sector, and African Americans found themselves once again relegated to southern fields. Many African Americans, seeing immigrants usurp jobs they felt rightly belonged to them, began to engage in nativist rhetoric. Many African Americans vociferously supported the anti-immigration legislation of the 1920's.

As Irish Americans gained greater political and economic power in the twentieth century, they continued to do so at the expense of African Americans. Although literacy tests and structural racism denied the majority of African Americans the vote until the Voting Rights Act of 1965, the Irish used their access to the ballot to gain control of local political machines and city halls. As they lost their brogues and became established in the mainstream of white America, the Irish used their political influence to monopolize civil service positions while excluding blacks and new immigrants.

By the end of the twentieth century, Irish Americans exceeded the national average in education and income, and the poverty rate among African American households was lower than it had ever been. Although by then one-third of African Americans could be considered middle class, there were three times more poor blacks than white Americans.

——*Kathleen Odell Korgen*

BIBLIOGRAPHY AND FURTHER READING

Duffy, Jennifer Nugent. *Who's Your Paddy? Racial Expectations and the Struggle for Irish American Identity.* New York: New York UP, 2014. Print.

Ignatiev, Noel. *How the Irish became White.* New York: Routledge, 1995. Print.

IRREDENTISM

Irredentism is a political policy or guideline aimed at uniting irredentas—groups of people ethnically or historically related to one political system but under the control of a different polity—within ethnically or historically related territories. The word *irredenta* is Italian for "unredeemed" and was used by Italian patriots in the nineteenth and twentieth centuries who sought to liberate all Italian-speaking lands from foreign control. The hopes of these patriots, or irredentists, were basically fulfilled with the Treaty of Versailles that ended World War I. Modern examples of irredentist movements include Bosnian War, Kurdish nationalism, and according to some, the Russian annexation of Crimea.

In US politics, irredentist policies have come in many forms and guises. It is possible to view programs of racial or ethnic segregation as having irredentist intents. For example, African Americans could be restricted to a particular geographic area to keep intact an Irish American neighborhood. Another way that irredentism influences US politics is through the drawing of boundaries for electoral districts. Since 1812, political parties have redrawn electoral districts to favor representation of one group over another. This gerrymandering, though ruled unconstitutional by the US Supreme Court in 1964, has been justified as a means of giving minority groups better political representation. It can also been seen in relation to American Indian relocation and subsequent land-claims suits and in US–Mexico border issues.

——*Paul J. Chara, Jr.*

ISLAMOPHOBIA

Islamophobia, or the fear and or hatred of people of Islamic faith or culture, first emerged in the twentieth century as more and more Muslims immigrated to the United States and Europe, but became especially prevalent with the rise of Islamic terrorism following the attacks of September 11, 2001. Although the vast majority of Muslims do not engage in terrorist activity, many non-Muslims have come to equate violence with Islam. This bigoted stereotype is built out of several inaccurate beliefs, including the idea that Islam is a monolithic bloc, that its core values are somehow different from those of Judaism or Christianity, and that it represents a violent political ideology, waging a war on women and the West in particular. Many of these ideas are born out of a basic ignorance of Islam as a religion and Islamic cultures in general.

For instance, in the United States, Muslims are usually depicted as bearded Middle Easterners, when in fact the majority of Muslims in the world hail from Southeast Asia. Nonetheless, both in the political and media realms Muslims are regularly depicted as fundamentalists and violent extremists who are driven by religious zeal to commit crimes against Jews and Christians. Muslims are also often falsely associated with all acts of mass violence, including domestic terrorism and mass shootings, despite the fact that Muslims have been responsible for only a small fraction of such attacks, and out of those only a handful have been classified as acts of terror. Yet, negative stereotypes and fears of Islam continue to dominate and many groups and organizations have been founded since 2001 to combat negative depictions of Muslims. However, despite these efforts, Islamophobia continues to be a major challenge for Western nations and the United States in particular, where the 2016 presidential victory of Donald Trump was partly fueled by anti-Islamic sentiment.

——*K.P. Dawes*

Bibliography and Further Reading

ABC News Productions. *Should Americans Fear Islam? A Town Hall Meeting.* New York: Films Media Group, 2012. Streaming video.

Bryfonski, Dedria. *Islamophobia.* Farmington: Greenhaven/Cengage, 2012. Print.

Kumar, Deepa. *Islamophobia and the Politics of Empire.* Chicago: Harmarket Books, 2012. Print.

Israeli Americans

Constituting only about 1 percent of the US immigrant population, Israeli immigrants often perceive themselves to be sojourners, temporary residents of the host country. They maintain social, cultural, and economic ties to their country of origin, even while living abroad. Some retain dual citizenship. With the aid of technology and the global economy, their lifestyles seem to fit the new trend of transnationalism (allegiances and orientations that go beyond the boundaries of a single nation). Rather than forsake their homelands and become completely assimilated, new immigrants actively participate in both social worlds.

Rates of Immigration

Israeli immigration rates vary depending on how the term "Israeli" is defined and whether only legal immigrants are counted. According to the US Census Bureau, as of 2009 approximately 139,000 people of Israeli ancestry lived in the United States. Most were settled in metropolitan areas, especially New York City and Los Angeles. Certain immigration trends are evident. First, the number of legal Israeli immigrants entering the United States has gradually increased since 1948. For example, data from the US Immigration and Naturalization Service indicate that the numbers increased from about 1,000 to 2,000 per year between 1967 and 1976 and from 3,000 to 4,000 per year from 1976 to 1986. Second, Israeli immigration was especially pronounced during the 1970s, especially after 1975, when, as 1990 census figures reveal, rates of Israelis traveling to Los Angeles alone more than doubled from 8 percent (1970–1974) to 17 percent (1975–1979). Some have suggested the growth was due in part to increases following war, in this case, the 1973 Yom Kippur War. Third, in response to changing Israeli policy toward emigrants and economic conditions in Israel, the number of Israelis returning to Israel rose during the 1980s. According to estimates by the American-Israeli Cooperative Enterprise, the number of those immigrating from the United States to Israel peaked at 3,806 in 1983. It tapered off in subsequent years and decades, climbing again to 3,300 in 2008.

According to the *2012 Yearbook of Immigration Statistics* published by the Department of Homeland Security, the number of Israelis who became naturalized American citizens each year from 2003 to 2012 fluctuated between a low of 2,036 (2003) and a high of 3,410 (2009). In 2012 the number of Israelis granted US citizenship was 2,859.

Motives for Emigration

In contrast to previous Jewish immigrants, contemporary Israelis are not "pushed" to emigrate to the United States because of persecution or extreme economic hardship. Rather, the decision to emigrate is primarily motivated by "pull" factors. Many Israelis cite personal development, particularly greater educational and economic opportunity, as most important. They seek professional advancement, as well as a higher income and standard of living. Others desire to reunite with family members already in the United States or leave to fulfill a personal need for adventure and escape from the limited confines, both geographically and socially, of Israel. Some engage in chain migration, being assisted by Israelis who have already made the trip. Travel, especially among those completing required military service, often leads to extended stays.

Certain features of Israeli society may be "push" factors: high inflation, bureaucratic red tape, burdensome taxes, housing shortages, the difficulty in developing capitalistic enterprises, and government regulations that intrude into personal life. As part of a country prone to societal violence and war, Israelis may mention the need to escape the siege mentality and the tensions permeating society, as well as reserve army duty. Interethnic tensions motivate some to flee from perceived discrimination waged by upper-class Ashkenazim against those of lower status.

RELATIONS WITH THE AMERICAN JEWISH COMMUNITY

Israelis were not initially welcomed with open arms by the American Jewish community. Relations between the two groups have been strained because of historical and cultural factors. Historically, the creation of the State of Israel in 1948 realized the Zionist dream of a Jewish homeland. To emigrate to Israel, or to make *Aliyah* ("ascent"), was a firm demonstration of loyalty to the Zionist cause. To immigrate from Israel and return to the Jewish diaspora, however, has pejoratively been referred to as *Yerida* ("descent"). Hence, *Olim*, "those who go up" to Israel, are admired, in contrast to *Yordim*, "those who go down," who are disparaged for emigrating. Israeli Americans accept this stigmatized identity, often expressing guilt and shame for leaving.

In classifying Israeli immigrants as *Yordim*, American Jews were following the lead of Israelis. In 1976, Prime Minister Yitzhak Rabin himself referred to *Yordim* as "the leftovers of weaklings." Israeli emigration, coupled with rising Arab birthrates, is perceived as a threat to the future of the Jewish homeland. Israeli Americans, on the other hand, are often alienated from American Jews, who, in their minds, have offered only monetary contributions, rather than real sacrifice, for Israel. American Jews sometime condemn *Yordim*, yet many would never consider emigrating to Israel themselves.

Culturally, a gap exists between Israeli Americans and American Jews. They eat distinct foods and have different lifestyles, political ideologies, and entertainment preferences. Their language also differs; Israelis speak Hebrew as their primary language. Many Israeli Americans also follow the culture of their country of origin, be it Yemenite, Ethiopian, or Russian. An improved relationship between Israeli Americans and American Jews has been prompted by shifts in official Israeli policy toward *Yordim* enacted during the mid-1980s. In an effort to promote the return of Israeli Americans, the Israeli government softened its position regarding emigration and offered enticements such as employment, housing assistance, and travel loans. At the same time, a number of American Jewish organizations initiated outreach programs for Israeli Americans. Previously, such organizations provided little, if any, assistance in an effort to discourage Israelis from staying in America.

THE SOJOURNER MENTALITY AND SELF-IDENTITY

Stemming from the negative stereotype of *Yordim*, Israeli Americans label themselves sojourners, insisting, in the face of perhaps contrary evidence, that their stay in the United States is temporary. Lower-status Israelis frequently become settlers, integrating into the host country. Higher-status Israelis often become permanent sojourners; they intend to return to Israel but have no serious plans to do so. As permanent sojourners, they practiced what Natan Uriely, in a 1994 article in *International Society*, has termed rhetorical ethnicity. Their identity is rooted in their ethnicity, and they have a strong symbolic commitment to Israel. This is evident in their repeatedly expressed desire to go home. Israelis resist identifying themselves as Americans or Israeli Americans, preferring an Israeli identity. Many never fully assimilate.

SOCIAL LIFE IN THE UNITED STATES

Israelis tend to socialize with each other, often in ethnic nightclubs, at communal singing sessions, or at ethnic celebrations such as Israeli Independence Day. A few belong to ethnic organizations such as Tzofim, an Israeli group similar to the Boy Scouts. Some form ethnic subgroups based on their country of origin. Friends frequently substitute for family and are invited to holiday observances or children's bar/bat mitzvahs. Many Israelis consider themselves to be secular Jews, linking religious observance with being Israeli rather than Jewish. However, many do participate in religious activities in the United States, by joining synagogues at a slightly higher rate than American Jews, providing their children with religious educations, and engaging in religious rituals to a greater extent in the United States than in Israel. Some of the Sephardim have found the orthodox Hasidic movement appealing. Perhaps this increased religiosity is a reaction to the transition from being a religious majority in Israel to being a religious minority in the United States.

——Rosann Bar

BIBLIOGRAPHY AND FURTHER READING

Ari, Lilach Lev. "Israelis in the United States." *Wiley-Blackwell Encyclopedia of Race, Ethnicity and Nationalism.* Ed. John Stone, et al. Malden: Wiley-Blackwell, 2015. Online Resource. Web 5 Feb. 2017.

Lederhendler, Eli. *American Jewry: A New History.* Cambridge: Cambridge UP, 2017. Print.

Shokeid, Moshe. *Children of Circumstances: Israeli Immigrants in New York.* New York: Cornell UP, 1988. Print.

ITALIAN AMERICAN STEREOTYPES

The two major stereotypes regarding Italian Americans are that this group is inextricably linked to the Mafia and that Italians are fun-loving buffoons. The Mafia stereotype involves a belief that Italian Americans developed and control organized crime in the United States, which is a by-product of the Mafia, a criminal organization in Sicily, and that a significant percentage of Italian Americans are involved in organized crime. The buffoon stereotype involves the belief that Italian Americans are not achievement-oriented but simply fun-loving, easygoing individuals. Sociological investigation demonstrates that neither image of Italian Americans is accurate.

Major studies of organized crime such as *The Mythology of Crime and Criminal Justice* (2004), by Victor E. Kappeler, and Gary W. Potter, *On the Take: From Petty Crooks to Presidents* (1988), by William Chambliss, and *Organized Crime in America* (1967), by Gus Tyler, show that organized crime in the United States was not developed by any one ethnic group and that its roots lie deep within the nation's culture. These works show that the high demand for illicit drugs, sex, and gambling (and the desire for profit) are largely responsible for the creation of organized crime groups. Books such as *The City and the Syndicate: Organizing Crime in Philadelphia* (1985), by Gary W. Potter and Philip Jenkins, *The Mafia Mystique* (1975), by Dwight Smith, and *Blood of My Blood: The Dilemma of the Italian Americans* (2000), by Richard Gambino, make clear that there is no evidence supporting the belief that organized crime in the United

States is an offshoot of the Mafia in Sicily. Moreover, studies, such as *Organized Crime* (2012), by Howard Abadinsky, *Disorganized Crime* (1985), by Peter Reuter, and *The Politics of Corruption: Organized Crime in an American City* (1970), by John Gardiner, found that no ethnic group exercises control over organized crime activities such as gambling and the drug trade. Furthermore, the article "America's Most Tolerated Intolerance: Bigotry Against Italian Americans," in *The Italian American Review* (Spring/Summer, 1997), by Richard Gambino, points out that only a fraction of 1 percent of all Italian Americans participate in organized crime. The research does not provide support for the Mafia stereotype of Italian Americans. Still, images of gangsters in suits and fedoras and large, hairy, men with gold chains remain entrenched in the public conscious as stock characters of organized crime and Italian American culture.

In rebuttal of the buffoon stereotype, US census data and books such as *Italian Americans into the Twilight of Ethnicity* (1985), by Richard Alba, and *Italian Americans* (1970), by Joseph Lopreato, provide data demonstrating that since the 1960s, Italian Americans have experienced high levels of occupational and educational achievements. Moreover, starting in the 1960s, the average household income of Italian Americans has been well above the US average. Since the 1970s, the percentage of Italian Americans who have graduated from college has been well above the national average. These statistics also counter the related stereotypes that Italian

American men are violent and uneducated and that Italian American women are overweight and spend most of their time cooking pasta and other "Italian" foods or are elderly grandmothers.

Although a very small number of Italian Americans are involved in organized crime, these represent a minority of Italian Americans. Although some Italian Americans may very well be fun-loving, they show as wide a range of personality types as any group of people and no predilection toward any one trait. The negative images of Italian Americans created by these stereotypes have greatly distorted reality concerning this ethnic group. These stereotypes are often reinforced by media portrayals of Italian American characters, especially popular depictions of organized crime as seen in the film *The Godfather* and the television series *The Sopranos*. The association is so well known that mobster imagery is often used in advertising for stereotypically Italian American products

such as pasta sauce and pizza, while gangster themes used in advertising for other products often take on an Italian American connotation, whether intended or not.

——*Louis Gesualdi*

BIBLIOGRAPHY AND FURTHER READING

Cinotto, Simon, ed. *Making Italian America: Consumer Culture and the Production of Ethnic Identities.* New York: Fordham UP, 2014. Print.

Connell, William J., and Fred Gardaphé, eds. *Anti-Italianism: Essays on Prejudice.* New York: Palgrave Macmillan, 2010. Print.

Ferraro, Thomas J. *Feeling Italian: The Art of Ethnicity.* New York: New York UP, 2005. Print.

Kappeler, Victor E., and Gary W. Potter. *The Mythology of Crime and Criminal Justice,* 4th ed. Long Grove: Waveland, 2004. Print.

ITALIAN AMERICANS

Italy sent few immigrants to the United States before the Civil War (1861–65). The 1850 census, the first to record ethnic group populations, listed only 3,645 Italian Americans, and these individuals were primarily skilled artisans, merchants, musicians, actors, and entrepreneurs. However, these numbers do not reflect their overall significance. Albeit sponsored by Spain, England, and France, Italian explorers helped chart the European pathway to the Americas. After Christopher Columbus navigated the Atlantic in 1492, several of his countrymen continued his pursuits. Giovanni Caboto, often referred to as John Cabot in popular history textbooks, obtained financial backing from England's King Henry VII and organized a successful expedition to the New England coast in 1497. Amerigo Vespucci helped popularize interest in America following the publication of two pamphlets highlighting the potential rewards available to new settlers on the eastern seaboard. Giovanni da Verrazano was the first European to enter New York Harbor in the early sixteenth century.

Although numerous adventurers from other countries also facilitated European migration to America, the efforts of several Italians were crucial for the

success of many early colonial enterprises. Catholic missionaries helped carve out the French empire in the Mississippi Valley. Artisans developed glassware and silk industries in Jamestown, Virginia. Thomas Jefferson recruited Italian masons to help construct his home at Monticello and enlisted the aid of several musicians to form the United States Marine Corps Band. Italians also helped design and decorate the interior of the early White House, and Italian opera emerged as one of the most popular forms of entertainment among the upper classes in antebellum America. Although there were few Italian Americans in the nation, they had made a significant cultural impact.

THE GREAT WAVE

From 1880 to 1920, more than four million Italians entered the United States. Approximately 80 percent were men, and because 97 percent initially passed through New York City, the bulk of the Italian American community settled in major eastern cities such as Philadelphia, Boston, and New York; however, a large community also emerged in Chicago. Following the unification of Italy in the 1860s, southern Italians soon began to feel alienated from and experienced widespread disillusionment with northern leadership. Absentee landlords systematically exploited the peasants, and agricultural policies produced massive hunger among sharecroppers and tenant farmers. Others succumbed to outbreaks of malaria. Northern politicians enacted oppressive conscription laws forcing southerners to serve seven-year terms in the military. As Italy quickly evolved into a two-tiered system in which southerners were excluded from all facets of decision making, a large number of Italians voted with their feet and abandoned their traditional attachment to their villages, emigrating to the United States. Most Italians did not initially intend to remain in the United States. Estimates vary, but between 30 percent and 50 percent returned to the homeland. Strong familial ties and attachments to ancestral villages caused many to return despite the fact that few earned enough to reverse their impoverished status.

The majority of Italian Americans became manual laborers. Ethnic labor contractors, or *padroni*, persuaded many to emigrate from Italy by promising them unlimited economic opportunities upon arrival in North America. The *padroni* secured employment for émigrés and arranged the financing for the transatlantic voyage. Italians helped build railroads and the New York City subway system. Others toiled in dangerous and precarious conditions in factories; several became miners. Some were able to procure opportunities in agricultural communities, but the majority of Italian Americans remained locked in ethnic urban enclaves and were subjected to the outburst of nativist xenophobic practices that accompanied the great wave of migration.

ASSIMILATION AND NATIVISM

Racial and ethnic relations in the United States have adhered to a complex hierarchical pecking order. Generally, each wave of immigrants has encountered a number of discriminatory practices designed to eradicate all remnants of ethnic identity. Because the dominant culture reflected a solid Anglo-Saxon bias following the Civil War (1861–5), new groups from southeastern Europe were expected to embrace assimilationist policies and Americanize. Reformers demonstrated little sympathy for immigrant culture and introduced a variety of measures to diminish and weaken traditional ethnic ways.

Italian American children were extremely susceptible to Anglo-Saxon assimilationists. They were forced into a form of cultural tug-of-war. Required either to abandon their native culture or to face social ostracization and the loss of economic opportunity, the second generation began to embrace Anglo-Saxon culture. This caused considerable psychological problems. For example, Italian American children were expected to find work and contribute to the household economy. This, however, resulted in a premature departure from school. If a child decided to stay in school and pursue a profession, that child risked the wrath of his or her family. Because most Italian Americans considered the family to be sacred, young Italian Americans faced a classic dilemma. As a result, rates of socioeconomic mobility were quite low among the first few generations.

Other forms of nativism also surfaced. Public schools insisted that children speak only English, and officials often shortened and Americanized Italian family names. Some families experienced violence when they attempted to move outside the ethnic enclave. Many people were subjected to racial remarks such as *dago*, *wop*, and *guinea*. Although studies have shown that the rates of alcoholism and mental illness were lower compared with those of other groups, the suicide rate among Italian Americans tripled during the great wave of migration.

Perhaps the greatest example of nativist xenophobic pressure occurred in the 1920s during the trial of two Italian anarchists, Nicola Sacco and Bartolomeo Vanzetti. Nativist sentiment, spurred by fears of communism, had been growing in the United States when Sacco and Vanzetti were arrested under questionable circumstances for murder and robbery in Massachusetts. Both men were judged as violent revolutionaries and subversive ethnic agents rather than on the merits of their case. Although their guilt remains debatable, both men were executed in 1927.

ORGANIZED CRIME

The average Italian American suffered from the negative impression created by a select minority of Italians who attempted to construct vast empires in organized crime. As congressional committees cracked down on criminals, some Americans concluded that all Italian Americans were associated with a nationwide crime syndicate commonly referred to as La Cosa Nostra or the Mafia. These rumors

MILESTONES IN ITALIAN AMERICAN HISTORY

Year	Event	Impact
1492	Columbus travels to the Americas	Facilitates widespread European expansion in North America.
1497	Cabot explores eastern coast of Canada	Helps promote a prosperous growing British fishing industry.
1653	Italian Jesuits publish a brief history of New France	Challenges the pervasive myth surrounding the lack of civilization among Canada's Native Americans.
1770s	Political philosopher Fillipo Mazzei works with Thomas Jefferson	Italian ideas are incorporated into the US Declaration of Independence.
1891	Eleven acquitted Italians are lynched in New Orleans	Reveals victimization of Italian immigrants during the great wave of immigration.
1920s	Rudolph Valentino becomes Hollywood's leading male sex symbol	Reveals the vital role of Italian Americans in the emergence of the US film industry.
1921–24	Passage of restrictive immigration quotas in the United States	Leads to the rise of vibrant Italian communities in Montreal, Toronto, and Vancouver, Canada.
1927	Anarchists Nicola Sacco and Bartolomeo Vanzetti are executed	Demonstrates how Italians were sometimes punished for radical political beliefs.
1941	New York Yankee Joe DiMaggio establishes a major league record by hitting in fifty-six consecutive games	Indicates Italian American influence on American sports.
1965	Poet John Robert Columbo publishes "Oh Canada"	Emphasizes that despite Canada's ethnic diversity, the country's culture primarily reflects a blending of English, French, and British influences.
1970	Lee Iacocca named president of Ford Motor Company	Illustrates that many Italians attained prominent positions in US business and industry.
1972	Francis Ford Coppola's film, *The Godfather*, wins the Academy Award for best film	Reveals how many Americans associate Italians with organized crime.
1982	Mario Cuomo elected governor of New York	Becomes first Italian to serve as head of a state government.
1991	National Canadian census reveals that less than 3 percent of the population is Italian	Demonstrates that Italians primarily emigrated to either the United States or South America.

received considerable credibility in 1963 when career criminal Joseph Valachi broke a code of silence and exposed his associates. As a result, the nation became obsessed with the Mafia. References to the Mafia in *The New York Times* increased from 2 in 1962 to 359 in 1969. Mario Puzo's novel *The Godfather* (1969) was made into an Academy Award-winning film, but his violent portrayal of Italian criminals negatively affected many law-abiding Italian Americans. Other gangsters such as John Gotti acquired national fame in the 1980s, and once again Italian Americans were found guilty by association. Numerous popular authors flooded the market with books detailing how murder was used to settle disputes between Italians. Despite the fact that only a select few were involved in criminal activity, all Italian Americans were described as being sympathetic toward the Mafia.

FAMOUS ITALIANS

Not all Italian Americans were unskilled workers or common criminals. Many achieved considerable success in their fields. Joe DiMaggio established a major league baseball record for hitting in fifty-six consecutive games. Heavyweight boxer Rocky Marciano defeated several notable champions, including Joe Louis, Ezzard Charles, and Jersey Joe Wolcott, and retired as an undefeated champion. Frank Capra emerged as one of the nation's finest filmmakers, and his 1946 film, *It's a Wonderful Life,* is considered one of the country's classic movies. Singer Frank Sinatra, who was often unjustly accused of being in the Mafia,

entertained generations of Americans with his swagger and ballads. Politician Fiorello La Guardia served as a congressman, New York City mayor, and United Nations relief official. Poet and publisher Lawrence Ferlinghetti provided much-needed support for and helped solidify the Beat generation's place in American literature. Geraldine Ferraro was the first woman to become a vice presidential candidate in 1984. Pop singer Madonna (Ciccone) evolved into a cultural icon in the 1980s. Martin Scorsese is one of the premier filmmakers of recent decades. Countless others also achieved prominent status in American life, thus proving that despite being victimized by ethnic stereotyping, Italian Americans have risen to the highest pinnacles of success in the United States.

——*Robert D. Ubriaco, Jr.*

BIBLIOGRAPHY AND FURTHER READING

Albright, Carol Bonomo, and Joanna Clapps Herman, eds. *Wild Dreams: The Best of Italian Americana.* New York: Fordham UP, 2008. Print.

Gambino, Richard. *Blood of My Blood: The Dilemma of the Italian Americans,* 2d ed. New York: Guernica, 1996. Print.

Iorizzo, Luciano J., and Salvatore Mondello. *The Italian Americans,* 3d ed. Youngstown: Cambria, 2006. Print.

PBS/WETA. *The Italian Americans.* Wash., DC: PBS/WETA, 2015. Documentary/DVD.

Belafonte in John Murray Anderson's Almanac on Broadway, photographed by Carl Van Vechten, 1954. Carl Van Vechten.

J

JAMAICAN AMERICANS

The movement of Jamaicans to the United States began in the early twentieth century and increased greatly after the 1965 relaxation of immigration restrictions. Jamaican immigrants clustered in metropolitan areas along the Eastern seaboard and in California, where many attained success as leaders in politics, religion, education, and business.

The Caribbean island of Jamaica was colonized by Spaniards in the sixteenth century. After most of the Arawak Indians died, the Spanish brought African slaves to work their sugar plantations. The British acquired Jamaica in 1670 and continued the practice of slavery. West Indian slavery did not encourage passivity, nor did it damage slaves' self-confidence to the extent that United States slavery did. Jamaican slavery ended in 1838, a generation before slavery's demise in the southern United States. Jamaica gained national independence in 1962.

Centuries of slavery left the island with a majority black population (many of whom were very poor), a smaller mixed-race segment, and a small, prosperous white population. Jamaica, unlike the United States, never developed Jim Crow laws, rigid color castes, or a tradition of lynching. Race is not a pressing issue in Jamaica, where blacks occupy positions at all levels of society. Jamaican immigrants to the United States, most of whom are of African ancestry, often experience shock upon entering a society with a powerful white majority and a long history of blatant and rigid color prejudice and discrimination. They develop various strategies to deal with racism, such as confrontation, resignation, and development of heightened race consciousness.

IMMIGRATION
Immigration from Jamaica to the United States occurred throughout the twentieth and into the twenty-first centuries. Many propertied and educated Jamaicans had established themselves in New York City by the 1920s. Other Jamaicans entered the country as temporary migrant farmworkers under special visas. During the World War II labor shortage, Jamaicans were encouraged to work on farms and in factories in the United States. The 1952 Immigration and Nationality Act reduced West Indian immigration; however, Jamaican immigration surged following passage of the Immigration and Nationality Act of 1965 , which opened admission to nonwhite immigrants from Asia, Latin America, and the Caribbean. Jamaican newcomers settled mostly in the metropolitan areas of New York City and Miami. By 1990, 435,024 Jamaicans lived in the United States, about 80 percent of whom were foreign-born. The leading states of residence were New York, Florida, California, New Jersey, and Connecticut, according to 1990 US census figures. As of 2013, according to the US Census Bureau, over 1 million people of Jamaican descent lived in the United States. According to the *2012 Yearbook of Immigration Statistics* published by the Department of Homeland Security, the number of Jamaicans who became naturalized American citizens each year from 2003 to 2012 fluctuated between a low of 11,218 (2003) and a high of 21,324 (2008). In 2012 the number of Jamaicans granted US citizenship was 15,531.

EDUCATION, BUSINESS, AND LEADERSHIP
Jamaicans arriving in the first decades of the twentieth century became black community leaders in the areas of business, politics, and the arts. In New York City, many were business owners and professionals. Some, such as Marcus Garvey, became government, civil rights, or labor union leaders. Others, including Claude McKay, a prominent writer who helped found the Harlem Renaissance of the 1920s, became cultural leaders.

The 1965 immigration act established a preference for skilled migrants. Accordingly, Jamaican immigrants in the latter part of the twentieth century tended to be well educated. The departure of many technical, managerial, and professional workers badly needed for the island's economic development has produced a "brain drain" in Jamaica. The value Jamaican immigrants place on education is reflected in the school performance of Jamaican American youth. Ruben Rumbaut's 1992 survey found that the children of Jamaican immigrants tended to have high grade-point averages and to score high on standardized reading and math tests. The children reported spending a large amount of time doing homework (versus watching television) and had very high educational aspirations.

COMPARISONS WITH US BLACKS

Economic motivation underlies much Jamaican migration, and some transplanted islanders become business owners. Social scientists vary in their interpretations of West Indian entrepreneurship. Some, such as Thomas Sowell and Daniel Patrick Moynihan, credit West Indians with habits of thrift and hard work that cause them to be more successful economically than US-born blacks. Others, including Reynolds Farley and Stephen Steinberg, argue that Jamaican immigrants constitute a select group, skilled and highly motivated before they leave the island. Farley and Steinberg also argue that the differences in economic success between immigrant and US-born blacks have been exaggerated. Farley cites statistics showing that while West Indians are more often self-employed than US-born blacks, the self-employment rate for whites is much larger than for either nonwhite group. Statistics for unemployment and income also place Jamaican Americans well below whites. Most Jamaican Americans are not self-employed. Many obtain advanced education and become lawyers, doctors, and teachers; others work in construction. Women have high labor force participation and many work in domestic service and nursing.

QUESTIONS OF IDENTITY

As Jamaican Americans attempt to arrive at a sense of racial or ethnic identity, they encounter opposing forces. On one hand, they tend to retain their ethnic identity, thinking of themselves as Jamaican Americans, because of the constant influx of new immigrants who revitalize distinct cultural elements of folklore, food preferences, religion, and speech. This separateness is enforced by the attitudes of African Americans, who sometimes resent the islanders because of their foreignness, their entrepreneurial success, and because some white employers apparently prefer foreign-born workers. On the other hand, Jamaican Americans may adopt an assimilated label, calling themselves black or African American, prompted by daily experiences with racism. Because of the conflicting pressures of living in the United States, second-generation islanders sometimes vacillate, at times identifying with African Americans and other times attempting to distance themselves from them.

——*Nancy Conn Terjesen*

BIBLIOGRAPHY AND FURTHER READING

Bishop, Jacqueline. *My Mother Who Is Me: Life Stories from Jamaican Women in New York*. Trenton: Africa World P, 2006. Print.

Griffith, David. *American Guestworkers: Jamaicans and Mexicans in the US Labor Market*. University Park: Pennsylvania State UP, 2006. Print.

Gunst, Laurie. *Born fi' Dead: A Journey through the Jamaican Posse Underworld*. New York: H. Holt, 1995. Print.

Portes, Alejandro, ed. *The New Second Generation*. New York: Russell Sage Foundation, 1996. Print.

Vickerman, Milton. *Crosscurrents: West Indian Immigrants and Race*. New York: Oxford UP, 1998. Print.

JAPAN BASHING

Japan bashing, or extremely negative criticism of Japan and its people, occurred a number of times in the nineteenth and twentieth centuries, often creating problems for Japanese Americans. In the late nineteenth and early twentieth century, dislike for the Japanese eventually led to anti-Japanese land

and immigration laws on the West Coast. During World War II, the Japanese were vilified as purveyors of international destruction. This distrust, combined with other factors, resulted in Japanese Americans being confined to internment camps for most of the war. In the 1970s and 1980s, in response to higher gasoline prices, Americans began to buy fuel-efficient compact cars made in Japan, causing a decline in the demand for large American cars and a subsequent decline in the US automobile industry. Many autoworkers lost their jobs, and resentment against the Japanese grew. In 1982, two Detroit men, one of whom was a laid-off autoworker, bludgeoned to death Vincent Chin, a Chinese American whom they mistakenly believed was Japanese.

In the latter part of the 1980s and early 1990s, when the Japanese economy was very strong, many US politicians and journalists accused the Japanese government of being protectionist and unfairly excluding American-made goods. They suggested that the Japanese lacked creativity and had gained its economic success by producing cheap copies of American products or slight improvements on American ideas. They claimed that Japan had an unfair advantage regarding production standards because its people sacrificed their personal lives and health to keep the nation's economy strong. The Japanese school system was said to place so much pressure on children that they regularly committed suicide over their failure to succeed.

In fact, *karoshi* (death from overwork) was confirmed in only a few cases in Japan, and the suicide rate among people aged fifteen to twenty-four had been lower in Japan than in the United States since 1981. However, all of the accusations, subtle and not so subtle, hurled against the Japanese by American politicians and journalists negatively affected many Japanese Americans. Many other Americans seemed to believe that Japanese Americans shared the negative characteristics that politicians and journalists accused the Japanese of having.

——*Annita Marie Ward*

BIBLIOGRAPHY AND FURTHER READING

Fiset, Louis, and Gail M. Nomura. *Nikkei in the Pacific Northwest: Japanese Americans and Japanese Canadians in the Twentieth Century.* Seattle: Center for the Study of the Pacific Northwest, U of Washington P, 2005. Print.

Hatamiya, Leslie T. *Righting a Wrong: Japanese Americans and the Passage of the Civil Liberties Act of 1988.* Stanford: Stanford UP, 1994. Print.

Howard, John. *Concentration Camps on the Home Front: Japanese Americans in the House of Jim Crow.* Chicago: U of Chicago P, 2008. Print.

Petersen, William. *Japanese Americans: Oppression and Success.* New York: Random, 1971. Print.

Wukovits, John F. *Internment of Japanese Americans.* Detroit: Lucent, 2013. Print.

JAPANESE AMERICAN INTERNMENT

Historically in the continental United States there were severe restrictions on Japanese immigration and naturalization, and in 1941 there were only about 40,000 foreign-born Japanese people (Issei) plus about 87,000 American-born citizens (Nisei). Many were tenant farmers under West Coast state and local restrictions on land ownership, housing, employment, and education; Japanese Americans were a semisegregated community.

EVACUATION

Following the December, 1941, Japanese attack on Pearl Harbor, the Federal Bureau of Investigation arrested 2,192 Japanese security risks, followed by

German and Italian counterparts. False reports of Japanese American espionage at Pearl Harbor, Japanese victories in the Pacific, and radio and press rumors combined to create unfounded fears that traitors and saboteurs might assist a Japanese invasion of the West Coast. On February 14, 1942, Lieutenant General John DeWitt, with War Department encouragement, and misrepresenting rumors as security threats, recommended removing persons of the Japanese "enemy race," including American citizens, from his West Coast command area. The Justice Department acquiesced, and on February 19, 1942, President Franklin D. Roosevelt signed Executive Order 9066, authorizing the army to create restricted

Families of Japanese ancestry being removed from Los Angeles, California during World War II. By Clem Albers, Photographer (NARA record: 8452194) (U.S. National Archives and Records Administration).

zones excluding "any or all persons." On March 21, 1942, Congressional Law 503 provided criminal penalties for noncompliance.

INTERNMENT

DeWitt put more than 100,000 West Coast Japanese Americans under curfew, exclusion, removal, collection, and evacuation orders, which resulted in permanent job and property losses. Their ten relocation camps in the Western United States were isolated, barren, crowded, and crude, with barbed-wire fences and armed guards. Liberals and conservatives alike

generally seemed to approve this mass imprisonment, conspicuously limited to the Japanese race. Internees who hoped that compliance would demonstrate their loyalty to the United States became demoralized by camp conditions and popular hostility.

In 1943, Japanese American soldiers changed the situation. Aside from their Pacific theater intelligence service, Nisei already in uniform plus volunteers from the internment camps formed the 100th Infantry Battalion and the 442d Regimental Combat Team. Their European combat and casualty records earned public respect for the Nisei soldiers and a more positive policy for the internees. By early 1944, 15,000 Nisei civilians were on restricted camp leave; finally, on December 17, 1944, the West Coast exclusion order was lifted.

Following Japan's surrender on September 2, 1945, detention and exclusion were phased out; the last camp closed March 20, 1946. The 1948 Evacuation Claims Act offered meager compensations—about $340 per case—for those renouncing all other claims against the government.

COURT CASES

Four significant wartime appeals by Nisei reached the US Supreme Court. On June 21, 1943, in *Hirabayashi v. United States* and *Yasui v. United States*, the Court upheld convictions for curfew violations, ruling the curfews constitutional and the emergency real, and found that Japanese Americans "may be a greater source of danger than those of a different ancestry." The Court held that winning the war must prevail over judicial review, implicitly reversing *Ex parte Milligan* (1866). On December 18, 1944, the Court granted *habeas corpus* in *Ex parte Endo*, ruling that Congress had not authorized long-term detention for a "concededly loyal" American citizen; the Court avoided broader questions of internment. On the same day, however, in *Korematsu v. United States*, the Court upheld Korematsu's conviction, on the *Hirabayashi* precedent. Although three dissenting justices argued that the exclusion order was part of a detention process, that Korematsu's offense of being in his own home was not normally a criminal act, and that only his race made it a crime under the exclusion orders, the Court majority upheld the government's wartime powers.

REDRESS

America's postwar generation developed different priorities. The Civil Rights movement and Vietnam War protests emphasized racial justice and deemphasized "national security." In 1980 Congress established the Commission on Wartime Relocation and Internment of Civilians to review facts and recommend remedies. Their 1982 report, *Personal Justice Denied*, exposed General DeWitt's misrepresentations, finding that "not a single documented act of espionage, sabotage or fifth column activity was committed by an American citizen of Japanese ancestry," that Executive Order 9066 resulted from "race prejudice, war hysteria and a failure of political leadership," and that "a grave injustice was done," deserving compensation. Of the Supreme Court, the report contended that "the decision in *Korematsu* lies overruled in the court of history."

The commission's work enabled Yasui, Hirabayashi, and Korematsu to file motions to vacate their convictions in the original courts on writ of *coram nobis*, alleging prosecutorial misrepresentation and impropriety. Yasui died while his case was in progress. On April 19, 1984, US district court judge Marilyn Patel granted Korematsu's petition, acknowledging the 1944 Supreme Court decision as "the law of this case" but terming it an anachronism, "now recognized as having very limited application." On this precedent, Hirabayashi's convictions were overturned in 1987.

In 1988, a congressional act signed by President Ronald Reagan accepted the findings of the 1980 commission, provided $1.2 billion in redress for 60,000 internees, and added, "for these fundamental violations of the basic civil liberties and constitutional rights of these citizens of Japanese ancestry, the Congress apologizes on behalf of the Nation." The history of Japanese American internment illustrates both the difficulty of limiting emergency powers during a popular war and the abuses caused by failing to do so.

——*K. Fred Gillum*

BIBLIOGRAPHY AND FURTHER READING

Bannai, Lorainne K. *Enduring Conviction: Fred Korematsu and His Quest for Justice.* Seattle: U of Washington P, 2015. Print.

Daniels, Roger. *Prisoners without Trial: Japanese Americans in World War II.* New York: Hill and Wang, 2004. Print.

Irons, Peter. *Justice at War: The Story of Japanese American Internment Cases.* Berkeley: U of California P, 1993. Print.

Reeves, Richard. *Infamy: The Shocking Story of the Japanese American Internment in World War II.* New York: Holt, 2015. Print.

Robinson, Greg. *A Tragedy of Democracy: Japanese Confinement in North America.* New York: Columbia UP, 2009. Print.

Yamaguchi, Precious. *Experiences of Japanese American Women during and after World War II.* Lanham: Lexington Books, 2014. Print.

JAPANESE AMERICANS

In the 1890s, a few of the Japanese who had moved to Hawaii in the 1880s migrated to California, but large-scale Japanese immigration did not take place until 1900. From 1900 to 1910, more than 100,000 Japanese moved to the West Coast, first and primarily to California but eventually as far north as Vancouver, British Columbia. By 1930, about 275,000 people living in the United States were of Japanese origin or descent. By the end of the twentieth century, this number had reached about 1.8 million.

EARLY REACTION TO JAPANESE IMMIGRATION

In 1882, Congress passed the Chinese Exclusion Act, primarily at the insistence of Californians who claimed that the Chinese could not be assimilated into American culture. Many Californians, therefore, were outraged when after Chinese immigration was virtually stopped by the 1882 act, Japanese immigration began. These citizens simply could see no difference between Chinese and Japanese immigrants, although, in fact, the Japanese, who had been carefully screened by the Japanese government, were generally better educated than the earlier Chinese immigrants.

Soon after 1900, politicians and journalists agitated to stop Japanese immigration, speaking of the "yellow peril." They maintained that the Japanese could not be assimilated into American culture and represented an outside group that would attempt to control the United States. In 1905, the public schools of San Francisco banned Japanese children from attending school with white children, causing the Japanese government to become very angry. The issue of San Francisco's school segregation was resolved in 1908 when President Theodore Roosevelt signed a Gentlemen's Agreement with the Japanese government, requiring that it not issue any more visas for workers to come to the United States. The San Francisco school board then allowed Japanese children to attend school with whites.

California and other states continued to harass Japanese immigrants. In 1913, California passed the Alien Land Act, which stipulated that Asians who were ineligible for citizenship could not own land. This meant that the Japanese immigrants, who were mostly agricultural workers, could work only as tenant farmers and could not own the land on which they worked.

Miscegenation laws, making marriages between people of different races illegal, were also enforced against the early Japanese immigrants, most of whom were men. Unable to find wives in the United States, these men turned to matchmakers in Japan. Often the immigrants would marry brides whom they had seen, before the wedding, only in a photograph. White Californians were angered by the Japanese practice of marrying "picture brides." They pointed to this behavior as further evidence that the Japanese could not be assimilated into American culture.

JAPANESE AMERICANS DURING WORLD WAR II

By the start of World War II, two generations of Japanese Americans (Issei, or first-generation Japanese Americans, and Nisei, second-generation Japanese Americans) lived in the United States and Canada. In 1942, members of the American and Canadian governments felt that the Japanese Americans posed a threat to security. Therefore, on February 19, 1942, President Franklin D. Roosevelt issued Executive Order 9066, requiring people of Japanese origin or descent living in the western part of the United States (California, Oregon, Washington, and the southern part of Arizona) to be placed in internment camps; this order affected more than 100,000 people. The Japanese Americans were given very little time to gather their property or to take care of businesses before they were interned. Property that actually belonged to Nisei (who were American citizens) was seized. Areas such as Japantown (Nihonmachi) in the Fillmore district of San Francisco and Little Tokyo in Los Angeles became nearly deserted. What is more, within twenty-four hours of the bombing of Pearl Harbor, the United States government detained one thousand Japanese American community leaders and teachers.

In Canada, the 1942 War Measures Act placed Japanese aliens and Japanese Canadians in camps and required them to pay for their housing. Those who objected to having to live in these camps were placed in prisoner-of-war camps along with captured German soldiers in northern Ontario. In the United States, various court cases were brought to challenge the government's treatment of Japanese Americans, but this treatment was deemed to be legal in decisions such as *Korematsu v. United States*

MILESTONES IN JAPANESE AMERICAN HISTORY

Year	Event
Late 1860s	Japanese agricultural workers move to Hawaii to work on plantations.
1900–10	More than 100,000 Japanese immigrants, primarily male, come to the United States, settling mainly in California.
1905	Public schools in California require Japanese children to attend classes that are separate from those for other children.
1908	In Gentleman's Agreement between the United States and Japan, Japan agrees to restrict immigration to the United States. San Francisco schools integrate Japanese children with other children.
1912	Mayor of Tokyo gives more than 3,000 Japanese cherry trees to the United States as a gesture of friendship.
1913	California passes the Alien Land Act, which precludes most Asians, including Japanese immigrants, from owning land.
1942	Executive Order 9066 requires people of Japanese origin or descent living in the western United States to be placed in internment camps.
1943	The 42nd Regimental Combat Team, composed totally of Japanese Americans, is formed. This 30,000-soldier unit becomes the most decorated unit in US military history.
1943	Supreme Court decision in *Hirabayashi v. United States* upholds the right of the United States government to place Japanese Americans in internment camps, suggests that Japanese had brought the situation on themselves by not assimilating quickly into the mainstream culture
1943–75	About 67,000 Japanese women enter the United States as brides of American servicemen.
1945	Japanese aliens and Japanese Americans are allowed to leave internment camps.
1952	Immigration and Nationality Act (McGarran-Walter Act) permits Japanese immigrants to become US citizens.
1956	By popular vote, California repeals the Alien Land Act, making it possible for people born in Japan to own land in California.
1967	Japanese Americans living in the Fillmore District of San Francisco organize a Cherry Blossom Festival, which becomes an annual event.
1988	Congress passes the Civil Liberties Act, apologizing for internment of Japanese Americans and agreeing to pay reparations of $20,000 to each eligible person.
1990	President George H. W. Bush begins the reparations process.
1992	Japanese American National Museum established in Los Angeles.
2016	President Barack Obama visits Hiroshima in Japan (May), and Prime Minister Shinzo Abe visits Pearl Harbor in the United States (December).

(1944) and *Hirabayashi v. United States* (1943). In the decision handed down in *Hirabayashi*, the Court suggested that because Japanese Americans had chosen to live together as a group and had not assimilated well into the mainstream culture, the US government was justified in being suspicious of them.

In January, 1945, Japanese aliens and Japanese Americans were allowed to leave the camps. Unable to live in the western United States, these people and their families settled in the East. Soon after the United States released the detainees from camps, the Canadians followed suit.

JAPANESE AMERICANS AFTER WORLD WAR II

For a variety of reasons, life for Japanese Americans improved after World War II. The bravery of the Nisei soldiers during World War II had impressed upon many other Americans how loyal Japanese Americans actually were. Having seen firsthand the racial hatred practiced by the Nazis, Americans and Canadians did not want this sort of prejudice practiced in their home countries. Finally, much of the original prejudice and hatred against the Japanese and Asians as a whole stemmed from white Americans' fears of economic competition. The strength of the postwar US economy lessened these fears and created advancement possibilities for many racial and ethnic groups.

In 1952, with the passage of the Immigration and Nationality Act (also known as the McCarran-Walter Act), it became possible for Japanese immigrants to become naturalized citizens. Although many Japanese citizens had entered the United States as wives of US servicemen under the 1945 War Brides Act, many more entered under the 1952 act. From 1947 through 1975, 67,000 Japanese women entered as wives of US servicemen, thus, becoming Japanese Americans. These new Japanese Americans encountered a very different United States from the one experienced by earlier immigrants. After 1952, it was much less likely that Japanese Americans would isolate themselves in areas where only people of Japanese heritage lived. In 1956, California, by popular vote, largely through a campaign orchestrated by Japanese American Sei Fujii, repealed its Alien Land Law, making it possible for people born in Japan to own land in California.

JAPANESE AMERICANS IN LATER DECADES

In the latter part of the twentieth century, Americans became interested in all things Japanese. Japanese influences could be found in American music, fashion, architecture, philosophy, and religion. Japanese Americans were able to lead the way in introducing other ethnic and racial groups to Japanese culture and philosophy. In the 1960s, recognizing that expressions of cultural heritage were becoming popular, the Japanese Americans in the Fillmore district of San Francisco organized the first annual San Francisco Cherry Blossom Festival to share Japanese philosophy and culture associated with the cherry blossom with other Americans. Other cities such as Seattle, Washington, also organized cherry blossom festivals. One of the better-known festivals is the National Cherry Blossom Festival, held in Washington, DC, each spring to celebrate the donation of more than three thousand Japanese cherry trees to the American people by the mayor of Tokyo in 1912.

Led by Japanese American citizens' groups, Japanese Americans for many decades attempted to obtain justice from the US government for its treatment of them during World War II. Finally, in 1988, Congress passed the Civil Liberties Act. The American government acknowledged that an injustice had been done, apologized for that injustice, and agreed to pay reparations of twenty thousand dollars to each eligible Japanese American. In 1990, President George H. W. Bush began the reparations process.

Another highlight for Japanese Americans and for Japanese-US relations came in 2016, when US president Barack Obama visited Hiroshima, site of one of the two US nuclear detonations in Japan near the end of World War II. Later that same year, Japanese prime minister Shinzo Abe visited Pearl Harbor in Hawaii, where Japanese military forces bombed the US Pacific Fleet, causing the United States to enter the war.

——*Annita Marie Ward*

BIBLIOGRAPHY AND FURTHER READING

Hoobler, Dorothy, Thomas Hoobler, and George Takei. *The Japanese American Family Album*. New York: Oxford UP, 1996. Print.

Iida, Deborah. *Middle Son.* Chapel Hill: Algonquin, 1996. Print.

Kitano, Dorothy. *The Japanese Americans.* New York: Chelsea House, 1987. Print.

Peoples of North America. Long, Robert Emmett, ed. *The Reference Shelf: Immigration.* New York: Wilson, 1996. Print.

Reeves, Richard. *Infamy: The Shocking Story of the Japanese American Internment in World War II.* New York: Holt, 2015. Print.

Yoo, David. *Growing Up Nisei: Race, Generation, and Culture among Japanese Americans in California, 1924-49.* Urbana: U of Illinois P, 2000. Print.

JEWISH AMERICAN OUTMARRIAGE

The striking increase in the number of marriages between Jews and non-Jews since 1970 has worried some American Jews of a conservative or traditionalist orientation. However, outmarriage is not a new phenomenon for Jews. In the colonial and early national period of US history, the number of Jews in the population was small, immigrants were mostly men, and Jews were widely dispersed across the countryside. Jewish men therefore found it hard to find prospective brides within the Jewish population, and in 1840, when about fifteen thousand Jews were in the United States, the estimated rate of outmarriage was 28 percent.

The rate dropped significantly when the American Jewish community began to grow rapidly, as first German Jews and then Eastern European Jews arrived in substantial numbers. By 1900, approximately one million Jews lived in the United States, most in cities with extensive communal organizations, which made Jewish marriage partners easier to find. Increasing anti-Semitism from 1890 to 1940 made Jews less acceptable to Gentiles as marriage partners. In the years from 1890 to 1920, only 2 percent of Jews were involved in outmarriage; the rate increased slowly to about 6 percent in the 1950s.

A tremendous increase in outmarriage occurred during the 1960s. Although less than 10 percent of all American Jews were outmarried in 1971, a National Jewish Population Survey that year revealed that in the previous decade, more than 30 percent of new marriages were outmarriages. Jewish economic success after World War II, as well as the increasing number of young Jews who attended prestigious colleges, made it more likely that Jews would meet attractive non-Jews socially. Economic and social success, as well as the postwar decline in anti-Semitism, made Jews more attractive marriage partners.

Particularly worrying to Jews was the belief, held by most demographers, that the American Jewish birthrate had fallen below replacement level. If not enough children were born to keep the population level and one-third or more of those born left the community, a steady decline in numbers seemed inevitable. Pessimists foresaw the total disappearance of Jewish Americans. Others were more optimistic, claiming that because about one-third of non-Jewish spouses converted to Judaism and raised their children as Jews, the situation was not a disaster.

Faced with this problem, the more liberal branches of Judaism began to promote conversion to Judaism of non-Jewish marriage partners. The Reform movement established an outreach commission to support the conversion program. The Conservative movement did not engage in outreach but did urge rabbis to encourage conversion of marriage partners. Although the Orthodox rabbis accepted conversion in principle, they did not believe Reform and Conservative rabbis were competent to carry out this procedure and would not accept their converts, raising the possibility of a split within Judaism.

Rather than converts, Reform and Conservative groups began to speak of "Jews by Choice," a term that in a sense fit all Jews in the United States where religious liberty and individual freedom gave all persons the right to decide their own religious affiliation.

——*Milton Berman*

BIBLIOGRAPHY AND FURTHER READING

Carlisle, Rodney P. *The Jewish Americans.* New York : Facts On File, 2011. Print.

Fishman, Sylvia Barack. *Double or Nothing? Jewish Families and Mixed Marriage.* Lebanon: UP of New England, 2005. Print.

Fishman, Sylvia Barack. *Jewish Life and American Culture*. Albany: State U of New York P, 2000. Print.

Goldberg, J. J. *The Jewish Americans*. New York: Mallard, 1992. Print.

Thompson, Jennifer A. *Jewish on Their Own Terms: How Intermarried Couples Are Changing American Judaism*. Piscataway: Rutgers UP, 2014. Print.

Wenger, Beth S. *The Jewish Americans: Three Centuries of Jewish Voices in America*. New York: Doubleday, 2007. Print.

JEWISH AMERICANS

In 1654, twenty-three Jewish refugees, who had fled Brazil when it was retaken by the Portuguese from the Dutch, arrived in New Amsterdam seeking asylum. They were not welcomed by Governor Peter Stuyvesant, who put them in jail and requested permission from the Dutch West India Company to ban all Jews from the colony. The company, which had several substantial Jewish shareholders, refused, and Stuyvesant had to permit the newcomers to remain. Despite facing prejudice, the Jews were able to worship undisturbed. The congregation grew slowly after the British conquered the colony in 1664 and renamed it New York. Other small Jewish settlements emerged in the port cities of Newport, Philadelphia, Charleston, and Savannah. Most newcomers were descendants of Spanish and Portuguese Jews who used Sephardic rituals in their synagogues and spoke a dialect of Spanish in their homes.

By 1776, the Jewish population in the British mainland colonies reached between 1,500 and 2,500. The Jews were accepted by their neighbors and could practice their religion unmolested, but they occasionally faced overt prejudice and legal disabilities. Jews could be, but were not always, barred from voting in colonial elections or holding political office because they were unable to take required oaths as a Christian. Jewish merchants and craftspeople participated fully in the commercial life of Newport, Rhode Island. However, even after the London Parliament passed a naturalization act providing special oaths for Jews in the American colonies, Rhode Island courts refused to naturalize Jews, claiming this would violate the purpose for which the colony was founded.

The state and federal constitutions established after the American Revolution shifted Jewish-Gentile relations from sometimes uneasy toleration toward civil and political equality. The US Constitution and Bill of Rights provided federal protection for freedom of conscience, and the new state constitutions began to remove test oaths and disestablish religion. The movement was steady if uneven. Rhode Island did not grant Jews the right to vote or hold office until 1842; North Carolina did not do so until 1868.

GERMAN JEWS

Until significant numbers of Jews from German-speaking areas of Europe arrived in the United States in the 1840s, the Jewish population remained small. In 1840, probably fewer than 15,000 Jews were in the United States; when Jewish immigration from Slavic lands began to increase in 1880, there were an estimated 250,000. Unlike their Sephardic predecessors, these Jews used Ashkenazic rituals and many spoke Yiddish. The vast majority of migrants were young men and women reacting to economic and political changes that worsened the position of Jews in their home countries.

The German Jewish immigrants flourished in the New World and greatly valued the political and economic freedoms they enjoyed in the United States. As the nation expanded, the young men moved west, some beginning as peddlers serving the scattered farmsteads, then opening mercantile establishments in the towns; a few very successful merchants established major department stores in the new cities. Their services were appreciated by their fellow townspeople; the first settlers in a town often became respected political and social leaders. In the early years of this migration, a small, thinly scattered Jewish population made finding Jewish marriage partners difficult, and a significant percentage married Gentiles. As they became economically successful, they founded families and brought young relatives to join them. Increased population meant Jews could create their own communal organizations, first a synagogue and a cemetery, then clubs that eased social isolation, and also philanthropic organizations to care for the poor and the elderly. Often unable to observe the Sabbath as commanded by orthodox Jewish law, they were particularly receptive to the relaxed requirements of the Reform movement, designed to modernize Judaism, that had already begun in Germany.

During the nineteenth century, a number of anti-Semitic incidents occurred in the United States. Civil War general Ulysses S. Grant issued an order calling for the expulsion of all Jews from his army department on December 17, 1862, after hearing that some were trading with the enemy. President Abraham Lincoln reversed the order shortly thereafter. When financially successful German Jews began to arrive in resorts that had been the preserve of the highest-ranking social groups of the United States, they experienced prejudice and discrimination. Famous resorts near New York such as Saratoga, Newport, and Long Branch began to turn away Jews, even wealthy New York City investment bankers. Lesser hotels began to use code words such as "restricted clientele" or "discriminating families only" in their advertisements.

EASTERN EUROPEAN JEWS

Between 1881 and 1924, approximately 2.5 million Jews, about one-third of the Jewish population of Eastern Europe, left their homelands; nearly 2 million came to the United States. The modernization of agriculture in Eastern Europe had eliminated many of the petty merchant and artisan occupations on which Jews depended. The major reason for the timing and scale of the migration, however, was the impact of government-sponsored anti-Semitism, especially the pogroms (anti-Jewish massacres) encouraged by the Russian government after the assassination of Czar Alexander II in 1881. Unlike the German Jews who had preceded them, these Jews concentrated in major cities, especially on the East Coast. Unlike other European groups of the period, few would return to their countries of origin. Theirs was a migration of families, with an almost even sex ratio. Lacking financial resources, they crowded into the poorest sections of the cities.

The German Jews did not welcome them. Class and cultural arrogance, anxiety that they would be burdened by masses of poor, and fear that the huge influx would exacerbate the already increasing anti-Semitism in the United States led to negative reactions toward the newcomers. Only slowly did the prosperous German Jews overcome their dislike and provide philanthropic support for those needing help. Not until the lynching of murder defendant Leo Frank in Georgia in 1913, amid violent anti-Jewish attacks, did they organize the Anti-Defamation League to combat anti-Semitism

The reaction of the non-Jewish community was even more negative. Old-line Yankees viewed the Jewish areas of cities as a foreign intrusion corrupting the fabric of American society. Psychologists, using intelligence tests to rank ethnic groups, placed these Jews at the bottom, calling them genetically defective and ineducable. Immigration restrictionists claimed the Eastern European Jews proved the need to close the United States to new immigrants.

ANTI-JEWISH PREJUDICE AND DISCRIMINATION

Dislike and fear of the newly arriving Jews helped spur the drive to restrict immigration, which took the form of legislation in 1924. It also provoked an outburst of overt prejudice and discrimination in the years from 1920 to 1940. As the children of the massive Eastern European Jewish immigration began to enter colleges and professional schools, they faced direct discrimination. Columbia College established quotas limiting admission of Jewish candidates, and other prestigious colleges and medical schools followed its example during the 1920s. Economic opportunities narrowed as few manufacturing companies, corporate law firms, major banks and insurance companies, or government bureaucracies such as the State Department were willing to employ Jews. Restrictive covenants, which barred homeowners from selling their houses to Jewish Americans or members of other "undesirable" groups, proliferated.

In 1922, Henry Ford began to publish a seven-year-long series of anti-Jewish articles in his newspaper, *The Dearborn Independent*, propagating older European stereotypes of Jews as both international bankers conspiring to control the country and communist conspirators determined to undermine capitalism. In the 1930s, the rise of Adolf Hitler inspired right-wing orators to preach ideological anti-Semitism. They defended Hitler, blaming Jews for the Great Depression and the international crises in Europe. More than one hundred anti-Semitic organizations appeared across the nation. In New York City, the Christian Front held street-corner rallies

MILESTONES IN JEWISH AMERICAN HISTORY

Year	Event
1654	Arrival of twenty-three Jews, the first in North America, in New Amsterdam
1820–80	Major years of German Jewish immigration
1880–1924	Major years of Eastern European Jewish immigration
1881–83	Pogroms (anti-Jewish riots) in Russia after the assassination of Alexander II
1892	Foundation of American Jewish Historical Society
1906	American Jewish Committee founded to aid Jews abroad
1913	Leo Frank is lynched; raises fears of persecution in Jewish community
1913	Anti-Defamation League of B'nai B'rith founded to combat prejudice
1922	Henry Ford begins publishing anti-Semitic propaganda in his newspaper
1924	Restrictive immigration law passes, ending large-scale immigration
1933	Adolf Hitler elected chancellor of Germany
1939	United Jewish Appeal organized to coordinate relief for Hitler's victims
1939–45	Holocaust kills about six million Jews
1948	Israel proclaims independence
1974	Anti-Semitic slurs made during Jesse Jackson's presidential campaign worry Jews
1991	Conflict erupts between Jews and blacks in Crown Heights in Brooklyn

that often ended in fistfights between adherents of the movement and Jewish passersby.

The reluctance to respond effectively to the plight of German Jews in the 1930s reflected the impact of prejudice against Jews. No agency enforced immigration restriction rules more rigidly than the United States consular service in Germany, which insisted on absolute proof of the ability of prospective immigrants to be self-supporting. As a result, despite the desperate need of German Jews to escape, between 1933 to 1940 some 30 percent of the visas available for Germans were never issued.

POST-WORLD WAR II
American revulsion at the sight of photographs of Hitler's death camps changed attitudes toward Jews. Overt anti-Semitism was no longer acceptable, and relations of Jews with other ethnic groups eased. When the courts refused to enforce restrictive covenants, the movement of Jews out of cities and into suburbs increased. Restrictions on college entry and job opportunities began to disappear. New York City home offices of major insurance companies, embarrassed by the revelation that they did not employ any Jewish stenographers in a city with a huge Jewish population, hastened to change their practices. The founding of the State of Israel and its survival under attack increased Jewish pride and improved American perceptions of Jews; they now appeared a normal ethnic group, not greatly different in its support of Old World nationalism from American Poles or Irish Americans.

Although pre-World War II anti-Semitism had surfaced predominantly among members of the Right, during the radical upheaval of the 1960s, Jews began to experience overt expressions of prejudice from members of the Left. Support of Israel when it was attacked by its Arab neighbors was a rallying point for all branches of the Jewish community. To Jewish ears, advocacy of Palestinian rights by radicals too often sounded like attacks on Jews, rather than simply criticisms of Israeli policy.

Even more disturbing was the open expression of anti-Jewish prejudices by African Americans. The long-term alliance of the two groups in the fight for civil rights seemed a thing of the past. Verbal attacks by Louis Farrakhan and his Nation of Islam followers and the slur against New York Jews uttered by Jesse Jackson in his 1984 presidential campaign were particularly worrisome because African Americans seemed the only major group believing it acceptable to express such prejudices publicly. Verbal and physical violence against Jewish shopkeepers in Harlem and the riots in Brooklyn's Crown Heights neighborhood intensified the feelings of antagonism between blacks and Jews.

Greater acceptance by other Americans helped raise the rate of outmarriage by Jews to more than 30 percent, which, combined with a birthrate that dropped below replacement level, led to fears that the American Jewish population would decline and ultimately disappear. Others were more optimistic, believing that many of the children of outmarriages would remain Jews. Immigration from Israel and the Soviet Union increased the Jewish community. Estimates in 2007 indicated that the Jewish American population was stable at almost 6 million people.

——*Milton Berman*

BIBLIOGRAPHY AND FURTHER READING

Birmingham, Stephen. *"Our Crowd": The Great Jewish Families of New York*, new ed. Syracuse: Syracuse UP, 1996. Print.

Cohen, Naomi Werner. *Encounter with Emancipation: The German Jews in the United States, 1830–1914*. Philadelphia: Jewish Pub. Soc. of America, 1984. Print.

Gerber, David, ed. *Anti-Semitism in American History*. Urbana: U of Illinois P, 1986. Print.

Howe, Irving. *World of Our Fathers,* 30 anv. ed. New York: New York UP, 2005. Print.

Rader, Jacob Marcus. *The Colonial American Jew, 1492–1776.* 3 vols. Detroit: Wayne State UP, 1950–70. Print.

Sachar, Howard M. *A History of the Jews in America.* New York: Knopf, 1992. Print.

JEWISH AMERICANS AS A MIDDLEMAN MINORITY

A middleman minority—or more simply a middle minority—is a distinctive racial or ethnic group occupying an intermediate position in the class structure between the higher and lower strata in the population (which may include other minorities). Middle minorities tend to be positioned in a special economic niche, often marginal but nonetheless of value to those in statuses above and below them. They are placed broadly within the middle class but fall into two subtypes: the small-scale shopkeepers and businesspeople who arrived poor and worked their way up and the middle-class businesspeople and professionals who were already established in their chosen lines of work before arriving in the new country.

TWO TYPES

Small-scale shopkeepers and businesspeople and independent professionals of modest practice can be considered "middle" in a limited occupational sense. These immigrants generally arrive without much wealth and little capital; shopkeepers often rely on family members for low-cost labor. In a relatively open class structure where racial and ethnic discrimination by the majority group can be restrained, these minorities can often improve their financial status— if not in a generation, then in two or three. Basically, they serve their urban neighborhoods, which are made up of predominantly working-class and lower-middle-class populations, including their own and other minority communities.

The second type of middle minority consists of those groups who were already established in middle-class businesses and professions before leaving, as emigrants or refugees, the country of origin. Although they often start by serving their own ethnic community, after a period of transition and possibly downward mobility, they can enter horizontally into the mainstream market or state economy, and they may eventually regain their original status positions. By playing a part in the larger world of corporate business, the professions, and government, they can come to exercise a considerable degree of power within private and public institutions. Although this path of mobility is also open to the other type of middle minority, their transition is usually more difficult.

The two types of middle minorities and combined versions of them are found around the world. In the United States, middle minorities include the Chinese American community in San Francisco, the Korean Americans in Los Angeles, the Cuban Americans in Miami, and the Dominican Americans in New York. Other middle minorities include the Lebanese in certain African cities, the ethnic Chinese in Southeast Asia, and the Japanese in Brazil. Although these groups are called "middle" minorities, these communities generally contain a fair proportion of the near poor and the poverty-stricken.

DISCRIMINATION

Although one might expect that the buffer of class and in-group cultural solidarity would provide protection at least against the more extreme forms of racism, discrimination certainly affects middle minorities. In tightly knit urban neighborhoods, shopkeepers and small-business owners are vulnerable to severe outgroup hostility, especially from other minorities whose anger and frustration, far from being directed toward the dominant power structure, is diverted toward the middle minorities, whom they see and deal with every day. Economic downturns and political crises that render governments unstable can provoke severe discrimination against the second type of middle minority, their power and influence notwithstanding.

AMERICAN JEWS

American Jews, often described as a middle minority, fit this model, albeit with great variation. The American Jewish experience is vastly different from that of the court Jews of eighteenth century Western Europe or that of the Jewish middlemen and small traders, barred from landholding and many strategic occupations, in Eastern Europe. The more than 5 million American Jews are highly urbanized and overwhelmingly middle-class (although some pockets of

Jewish poverty exist). However, like so many other minority populations, they are quite diverse—in religion from Orthodox to Conservative to Reform to secular, in status from lower-middle-class to upper-middle-class. In addition, they are highly assimilated structurally and culturally with a high degree of outmarriage yet still strongly attached to a variously defined "Jewish cultural heritage." Nonetheless, generalization is possible.

The German Jews who arrived in the United States in the mid-nineteenth century exemplified a variation on the theme of the middle minority: They started as itinerant peddlers and owners of small dry-goods stores and moved on and up to managerial positions in large-scale retailers and mass communication and entertainment companies and became doctors and lawyers. However, as they improved their financial status, they became integrated into the economy and the urban-suburban social structure; they were no longer in a separate economic niche or necessarily in a localized community.

The millions of Eastern European Jews, many of them working-class and impoverished, who came between the 1880s and World War I to labor in the workshops of the garment industry and to establish their small shops in the heart of the cities, exemplified the first stage of the first type of middle minority. Their children pursued higher education, many entering the professions, and the Eastern European Jews, like the German Jews before them, gradually became integrated into the central economy and the urban-suburban secular culture. Despite residual anti-Semitism (for the most part confined to the societal fringe groups but still at work in some sectors of employment, housing, and social club life), American Jews, in their class status, their mobility patterns, and their diverse religiosity and ethnic subculture, seem distant from the conventional middleman model, particularly as expressed in Europe and Asia, because there is as much variation as commonality.

——*Richard Robbins*

BIBLIOGRAPHY AND FURTHER READING

Carlisle, Rodney P. *The Jewish Americans*. New York: Facts On File, 2011. Print.

Fishman, Sylvia Barack. *Jewish Life and American Culture*. Albany: State U of New York P, 2000. Print.

Goldberg, J. J. *The Jewish Americans*. New York: Mallard, 1992. Print.

Mendelsohn, Adam. *The Rag Race: How Jews Sewed Their Way to Success in America and the British Empire*. New York: New York UP, 2015. Print.

Wenger, Beth S. *The Jewish Americans: Three Centuries of Jewish Voices in America*. New York: Doubleday, 2007. Print.

JEWISH CANADIANS

Jews first arrived in Canada after the British conquest in 1763 and by 1768 had consecrated their first synagogue in Montreal. The Jewish population was small until persecution of Jews in the Russian empire during the 1880s and the early 1900s intensified, creating a surge of refugees. From approximately 2,500 in the early 1880s, the Jewish population in Canada rose to 16,000 by 1900; the census of 1921 counted 126,000. Few Jews were permitted to enter in the 1920s and 1930s.

The 1991 federal census counted 365,315 Jews, 1.3 percent of the Canadian population of 27 million. More than 95 percent of the Jewish population lived in urban areas; three-fourths were concentrated in two cities, 163,000 in Toronto and 101,000 in Montreal. In 2011, the Jewish population in Canada was 391,665, accounting for 1.2 percent of Canada's overall population.

ANTI-SEMITISM

Jews were not welcomed by either French-or English-speaking Canadians. Jews were barred from entering Canada while it was part of the French empire. The British granted Jews equal civil and political rights with other Canadian subjects in 1832. Although Canada encouraged immigration between 1880 and 1914, attempts by Jewish organizations to settle Jewish refugees on farms in the Canadian prairie provinces received little support and sometimes open opposition from government officials.

By the 1920s, young Canadian-born Jewish men and women applying for admission to colleges and universities faced both overt and covert barriers. McGill University, particularly attractive because it taught in English, secretly began to require higher grades from Jewish candidates than from other applicants, thereby successfully reducing the percentage of Jewish students from 25 percent to 12 percent. L'Université de Montréal was less successful in maintaining secrecy. French nationalists openly questioned the presence of Jews, who were less than 5 percent of the student body. The agitation spurred the 1929 undergraduate student association to petition the administration for the expulsion of all persons of Jewish origin. In the summer of 1934, interns at the university-affiliated Notre-Dame Hospital went on strike over the admission of a Jewish intern, who was consequently forced to resign.

Canada began to restrict all immigration in the 1920s, and with the coming of the Great Depression, the barriers to entry became almost impenetrable. Jewish community organizations desperately petitioned the Canadian government to grant exceptions for refugees from Nazi Germany but failed to convince any officials. The manuscripts left by the director of the immigration office reveal him as totally contemptuous of Jews, devising bureaucratic tactics to prevent any from entering Canada. Appeals to accept refugee Jewish children—whose parents were inadmissible—were rejected on the grounds that it was bad policy to break up families. The director's policies were approved by the prime minister and supported by public opinion throughout the country. The French Quebec press and political leaders were especially vigorous in opposing admission of any more Jews. Although the government claimed in 1943 that it had admitted 39,000 immigrants since 1933, most of them refugees, the total actually included 4,500 German civilians who had been interned in Great Britain and 25,000 Axis prisoners of war. Fewer than 5,000 Jews managed to enter Canada in the entire 1933–45 period.

POST-WORLD WAR II

During the first years after the war, the Canadian government policy, supported by public opinion, was no more generous than before in accepting Jewish survivors of the Holocaust. Finally, in 1948, the government reversed its position on immigration and began to accept new immigrants; it also removed the barriers to Jewish immigration. Changing attitudes, as Canadians began to celebrate their multicultural diversity, eased relations between Jews and their fellow Canadians, one consequence of which was an increase in marriages between Jews and non-Jews, which made some Jewish community leaders worry about the future survival of Jews in Canada.

Relations between Jews and the Quebec separatists have been strained. English-speaking Jews have overwhelmingly supported the federalists in the various referendums on independence from Canada, leading to open expressions of hostility on the part of the separatists. The premier of Quebec blamed the narrow defeat of the October 1995, referendum on the "ethnic vote," which Jews understood included them, and promised that Québécois would take their revenge in their own country. Anxiety about the future led many Jews to move from Montreal to Toronto and the cities of western Canada. Montreal's Jewish population stagnated as immigrants (including a significant group of French-speaking Jews driven out of Arab lands in North Africa) barely replaced the young men and women who had left.

All signs of anti-Semitism have not disappeared. Instances of vandalism against synagogues and cemeteries occasionally occur. A constant irritant to Jewish Canadians is the presence of people who deny that the Holocaust ever happened. That assertion also includes the accusation that Jews control the media, using it to convince the public of a falsehood, thus conspiring to manipulate public opinion and use the government for group advantage. Yet most Jewish leaders view the position of Jews in Canada as eminently satisfactory.

——*Milton Berman*

BIBLIOGRAPHY AND FURTHER READING

Arbella, Irving, and Harold Troper. *None Is Too Many: Canada and the Jews of Europe, 1933–1948*. Toronto: Lester, 1982. Print.

Davies, Alan, ed. *Anti-Semitism in Canada: History and Interpretation*. Waterloo: Wilfrid Laurier UP, 1992. Print.

Elazar, Daniel J., and Harold M. Waller. *Maintaining Consensus: The Canadian Jewish Polity in the Postwar World*. Lanham: UP of America, 1990. Print.

Rosenberg, Stuart E. The Jewish Community in Canada—Volume I: A History. Toronto: McClelland, 1970. Print.

Weinfeld, J., W. Shaffir, and I. Cotler. *The Canadian Jewish Mosaic*. New York: Wiley, 1981. Print.

JEWISH DEFENSE LEAGUE (JDL)

The Jewish Defense League (JDL) was founded in 1968 by thirty young Jews who believed that the position of Jews in the United States was deteriorating and who also felt that the activities of established Jewish organizations did not meet the present needs of Jews. They argued that such organizations as B'nai B'rith, the American Jewish Committee, and the American Jewish Congress no longer served the interests of Jewish Americans because they focused too heavily on non-Jewish causes such as civil rights. The founders feared that overt expressions of black anti-Semitism and the increasing impact of street crime against Jews indicated that the United States was experiencing something similar to the Nazi street violence that had prepared the way for the Holocaust. Using the slogan "Never Again," the members of the JDL looked for ways to alert the world to what they perceived as a marked deterioration everywhere in the quality of Jewish life. Meir Kahane, an Orthodox rabbi, soon emerged as the leader of the JDL.

In 1969, the JDL attracted national attention by dramatizing the plight of Soviet Jewry in demonstrations before the Soviet mission to the United Nations and at other Soviet agencies in the New York City area. Their forceful picketing of the Soviet airline at John F. Kennedy Airport disrupted air travel between the United States and the Soviet Union. The JDL believed that agitating against American-Soviet sport and cultural exchanges and trying to disrupt trade between the two countries would embarrass the Soviet government and convince it to improve the position of Jews in the Soviet Union as well as end the ban on emigration from the country by Jews.

The JDL turned its attention to Israel in 1971 and began to urge American Jews to emigrate to Israel. Only by doing so, they argued, could American Jews recapture their religious zeal and offer effective resistance to anti-Semitism. There they could join with the Israelis in defending the land from attacks by the Palestinians. As Kahane studied the situation in Israel, he became convinced that the only solution to the problem was for Israel to expel all Arabs from the country. He explained his reasoning in his 1981 book, *They Must Go*. Shortly after publishing his book, Kahane moved to Israel with his family, founded the KACH political party, and was elected to the Knesset, the Israeli parliament, in 1984.

The high point in JDL membership was in 1972, when its membership reached fifteen thousand people. However, the shift in the JDL's focus from the United States to Israeli politics, the increasing rigidity of its ideology, and accusations that the JDL had gone beyond militancy to illegal use of force, including bombings, disillusioned many of its members. Their numbers declined markedly. Kahane remained popular, and his speeches drew crowds and press coverage, but after he was assassinated in New York City in 1990, the JDL ceased to exert much influence on Jewish life in the United States.

——*Milton Berman*

BIBLIOGRAPHY AND FURTHER READING

Altschiller, Donald. "Jewish Defense League." *Conspiracy Theories in American History: An Encyclopedia.* Ed. Peter Knight. Santa Barbara: ABC-CLIO, 2003. 371–73. Print.

Weisheit, Ralph A., and Frank Morn. *Pursuing Justice: Traditional and Contemporary Issues in Our Communities and the World.* 2nd ed. New York: Routledge, 2015. Print.

Zola, Gary Phillip, and Marc Dollinger. *American Jewish History: A Primary Source Reader.* Lebanon: Brandeis UP, 2014. Print.

JEWISH ETHNICITY

Jews trace a four-thousand-year history to a common origin in the biblical characters of Abraham and Sarah of Ur (Southeastern Iraq). Eventually twelve tribes settled the land of Israel. Modern Jews are descendants of the southern tribe, Judah, which maintained Jerusalem, the temple, and the kingship of David. From their beginnings, Jews were a diverse group. They have often existed as "alien residents" among other peoples, which has made them targets for exploitation, attack, and expulsion. Their ancient language of Hebrew became their common religious language. Monotheism, circumcision of males, and concern about social justice all have long traditions in Jewish history. Because of their preservation of the Torah (Bible) and their study and practice of its ethical and religious laws, Jews have been called "the people of the Book." Because both Christianity and Islam credit Judaism for their beginnings, early Jewish history continues to be known throughout the world.

The question of who is a Jew is variously answered. The traditional *halacha* (*rabbinic* religious rulings) upheld by Orthodox and Conservative branches is that a Jew is born from a Jewish mother (matrilineal descent) or has undergone a conversion that includes religious instruction, immersion in water, and, for men, circumcision. The liberal Reform movement ruled that patrilineal descent would be accepted if the child was raised as a Jew. These differences in rulings create problems for marriages between Jews. The *bar/bat mitzvah* remains an affirming religious ceremony for adolescents in all branches of Judaism.

Jews in the United States are drawn from many countries to which their ancestors were dispersed after the Romans' conquest of Israel in 70 C.E. The main subgroups are Ashkenazic (Polish, German, Russian, and other Eastern European), Sephardic (Spanish and Portuguese), and Mizrahi (Middle Eastern). There are other smaller groups as well, such as the North African Maghrebi Jews and the Beta Israel of Ethiopia. Secular Jews maintain social, cultural, and national connections but not religious involvement with the Jewish community.

Like Irish, Greek, and Italian immigrants, Jews in the United States were initially defined as "non-white." However, by the 1950s, Ashkenazi Jews, most of whom were more or less visually indistinguishable from other European Americans, were viewed as religious rather than racial or ethnic in their differences from the European American mainstream.

Indeed, much of what distinguishes Jews has religious roots: the weekly Sabbath from sundown Friday to sundown Saturday; holidays such as Yom Kippur, Rosh Hashanah, Sukkot, Hanukkah, Purim, and Pesach (Passover); keeping *kosher* (observing dietary restrictions which forbid the eating of pork and certain kinds of seafood, among other things); males wearing *kippah* (skullcaps); and foods such as *matzah* and *halah*. However, many secular Jews continue to observe these traditions, in much the same way that a nonreligious American with a Christian background might continue to celebrate Christmas and Easter. Like some other religious minority groups, Jews maintain religious day schools and advanced religious educational institutions. *Jews by Choice* (1991), by Brenda Forster and Joseph Tabachnik, contains detailed descriptions of the religious and ethnic aspects that are part of Jewish culture.

Jewish Americans share concerns that include maintaining Jewish identity, opposing anti-Semitism, maintaining "separation of church and state," remembering the Holocaust, and handling intermarriage or outmarriage. According to 2013 data from the Pew Research Center, 58 percent of American Jews marry non-Jews, with the number rising to 71 percent when Orthodox Jews are excluded. More traditional Jewish people tend to consider this a problem which may lead to a dilution of Jewish identity, though other communities are more accepting of the practice. In addition, the percentage of self-identified Jewish Americans who consider themselves culturally rather than religiously Jewish is growing. In 2013, 22 percent of American Jews did not consider themselves religious; this group included just 7 percent of Jewish Americans born before 1927, but 32 percent of those born after 1980. This has also caused concern in more religious Jewish communities, but rather than being a specifically Jewish problem, it reflects an overall trend; the percentages of nonreligious persons by age group in the general population are about the same. Despite these changes, 94 percent of Jewish Americans say that they are proud to be Jewish, and 67 percent claim a strong sense of belonging to the Jewish people.

—*Brenda Forster*

BIBLIOGRAPHY AND FURTHER READING

Pew Research Center. *A Portrait of Jewish Americans: Findings from a Pew Research Center Survey of US Jews.* Washington, DC: Author, 2013. Print.

Raphael, Marc Lee, ed. *The Columbia History of Jews and Judaism in America.* New York: Columbia UP, 2008. Print.

Schwarz, Sidney. *Jewish Megatrends: Charting the Course of the American Jewish Future.* Woodstock: Jewish Lights, 2013. Print.

Zola, Gary Phillip, and Marc Dollinger, eds. *American Jewish History: A Primary Source Reader.* Lebanon: Brandeis UP, 2014. Print.

JEWISH FEDERATIONS OF NORTH AMERICA

The Jewish Federations of North American (JFNA) is a Jewish American organization whose purpose is to raise funds and to unite and support Jewish communities around the world. It also supports other charitable causes in various communities. Formerly known as the United Jewish Communities (UJC), the group was formed through the combination of the United Jewish Appeal (UJA), Council of Jewish Federations (CJF), and the United Israel Appeal (UIA), which each pursued similar goals. It collectively represents 151 Jewish Federation social organizations as well as more than three hundred networked communities. As of 2015 JFNA raised over $3 billion each year and distributed the funds to various social and educational causes, ranking it among the largest charities in North America.

The UJA was formally born in 1939, resulting from a union of the United Palestine Appeal, the American Jewish Joint Distribution Committee, and the National Refugee Service. At first, the groups did not trust one another, and the Council of Jewish Federations served as mediator. *A History of the United Jewish Appeal 1939–1982* (1982), by Marc Lee Raphael, states that the catalyst for its formation occurred in Germany on November 10, 1938, *Kristallnacht* , when Germans rioted against Jews and many Jewish businesses were vandalized. Despite the atrocities of the Holocaust, American Jews remained fragmented. It was the Six-Day War in 1967, a triumphant victory for the Israelis, that served to solidify the organization's credibility and reliability.

In *Living UJA History* (1997), Irving Bernstein states that Henry Montor, the UJA's first executive vice president, established a union of disparate groups to support the organization. His initiatives strengthened the participation not only of religious Jews but also of less religious Jews, Christians, and women. Most of this work is carried on by local federations. A large percentage of the funds raised are donated to hospitals, clinics, community centers, universities, and museums.

In 1999 the UIA, UJA, and CJF agreed to merge into a unified national organization, originally known as the United Jewish Communities (UJC). In 2009 the group officially changed its name to the Jewish Federations of North America.

——*Jonathan Kahane*

JEWISH HOLIDAYS AND CELEBRATIONS

As with all religions that have adherents spread around the world, Judaism has regional variations in the celebration, or observance, of holy days or religious holidays/festivals. As a more secular community than in most other nations, many American Jews focus on the familial celebrations of Passover, Chanukah, and, to a lesser extent, the communal observances of Rosh Hashanah and Yom Kippur. However, individuals who are often referred to as "observant Jews" celebrate/observe many additional special days.

Historically, within the American Jewish community, there were three divisions: Reform, Conservative, and Orthodox (in order of theologically most liberal to most conservative). As the Jewish population moved from the cities on the east coast of the United States into other areas of the country, the Reform branch of Judaism became the most numerous, being less strict in its religious observances (which differed from the Christian religious celebrations of the majority of the population). This enabled the Jews to blend more fully into the larger community. Theologically, this was justified by an understanding that in reading the scriptures and histories of the Jewish people, it was obvious that Judaism evolved over the centuries, including holy days to commemorate special events. Thus, for most Jews in the United States, observing/not observing specific days on the calendar, and how these were observed, became much more a personal/congregational decision. As the Jewish calendar is a lunar calendar, the dates for the holy days are always the same on it, but vary on the solar calendar used by society in general. (For many holy days on the Jewish calendar, there is more than one way in which the Hebrew name is transliterated

A man in a tallit blows the shofar for Yom Kippur. By Library of Congress Prints and Photographs Division Washington, D.C. 20540 USA (the Matson Collection, ca.).

into English. Thus, the names used in this essay may not be the same as used in other works on the topic.)

719

FOUR MAJOR HOLIDAYS

Passover is the holiday with the greatest religious significance of those widely celebrated by American Jews. It is of such significance worldwide that all formal liturgies, for any occasion, make reference to the Hebrew migration from Egypt to the Promised Land (Israel). The Jewish calendar has been set so that Passover always follows the first day of spring. Passover being the 15th of Nissan, which is the time of the first full moon of the season. A seven- or eight-day holiday (depending upon various traditions) centers around the home; it includes a special family meal (Seder) on the first evening. A traditional Seder includes four cups of wine, vegetables dipped in salt water, matzah (dry unleavened flat bread), bitter herbs, and other items such as hard boiled eggs. During this period, there are dietary restrictions beyond the normal kosher rules, to commemorate the fact that the Jewish people did not have time for normal meals during the Exodus.

Chanukah (Hanukkah) is also known as the Festival of Lights. It began in the second century B.C.E. with Jewish forces taking back the Temple from the Seleucid Empire. The Temple was re-consecrated and a small amount of oil miraculously burnt for eight days until a new supply arrived. In homes, one candle, mounted in a menorah (candelabrum), is lit each evening during the festival, which begins on Kislev 25th. While lighting a menorah was brought to North America from Europe, Chanukah's proximity to Christmas, and the societal emphasis on Christmas gifts, seems to have resulted in the new North American tradition of giving gifts to children on each of the eight nights. (In the United States, the push for, and acceptance of, public menorahs began in the second half of the twentieth century.) Unlike some Jewish observances, there are no special food prohibitions during this festival. However, there are special foods that are associated with Chanukah, including fried foods like latkes (potato pancakes).

On the calendar, Rosh Hashanah and Yom Kippur are related in that both commemorate the beginning of a new year, although they have different emphases. Even though the month in which Passover is celebrated is considered the first month of the calendar, it is not the beginning of the new year. Rosh Hashanah, the first day of Tishri, in September or October, is the day on which the year changes. (Rosh Hashanah in the Gregorian calendar 2018 will begin year 5779 in the Jewish calendar.) This is a day for communal celebration in the synagogue. It includes reflecting on the past as well as planning (making resolutions) for the new year.

Yom Kippur is on the tenth of Tishri. Unlike the Rosh Hashanah celebration, Yom Kippur is known in English as the Day of Atonement. This is the most important day of communal worship in the synagogue, and the day with the largest attendance. It is a day when Jews are to fast as a symbol of their repentance, seeking divine reconciliation. All restrictions of the Sabbath are also observed, with additional ones such as not wearing leather shoes. Children, and those whose health would be put at risk by fasting, are exempt from the obligation. Yom Kippur is the day on which the liturgy in the synagogue takes its highest form, in all branches of Judaism. The focus is on seeking forgiveness for the community's sins of the past year. The element of the service that the general population in the United States knows best is the blowing of the ram's horn to end the traditional service.

OTHER HOLIDAYS

There are many other days on the calendar that may be celebrated/observed, among which are the following:

Sukot – Five days after Yom Kippur, the Festival of Booths, which is a remembrance of the wandering in the wilderness during the exodus. Some build temporary shelters in their yards, sleeping and eating in them for two to seven days. This is more commonly done outside the US.

Shemini Atzeret/Simkhat Torah – Two festivals that fall on the same day, the day after the end of Sukot. Shemini Atzeret represents divine grace, with the people invited to stay an additional day in the presence of the divine. Simkhat Torah is the day when the last verses of the Torah (the Jewish holy book, consisting of the biblical books Genesis through Deuteronomy) are read in the synagogue and then the readings start all over with the first verses.

Purim – This is derived from the events in the book of Esther, which was set in the time of the Achaemenid Persian Empire, where a plan to kill all the Jews was foiled. It is a time of great celebration and falls one month prior to Passover.

Yom Ha Atxmant – This holiday is a celebration of the independence of the modern state of Israel in

1948. The date of 5 Iyar falls in the period of April/May. The original date aligned with May 14, 1948.

Shavu'ot – Fifty days after Passover, this holy day commemorates the law (Torah) being received on Mt. Sinai, as well as the beginning of the harvest in ancient Israel. Theologically, Passover and Shavu'ot are connected in that the first represents freedom from physical oppression while the second represents freedom from spiritual ignorance and immorality.

Tisha B'Av – This is a day of fasting, during which the people are called to remember the destruction of the First and Second Temples and, by extension, other tragedies that Jewish people have experienced. It falls in the July/August time period (Av 9th).

——Donald A. Watt

BIBLIOGRAPHY AND FURTHER READING

Jewish Virtual Library. "Jewish Holidays." *Jewish Virtual Library: A Project of AICE*. Chevy Chase: American-Israeli Cooperative Enterprise, 2017. Web. 15 March 2017.

Ohtzky, Rabbi Kerry M. and Rabbi Daniel Judson. *Jewish Holidays: A Brief Introduction for Christians.* Woodstock: Jewish Lights Publishing, 2006. Print.

Pogrebin, Abigail and A.J. Jacobs. *My Jewish Year: 18 Holidays, One Wondering Jew.* Bedford: Fig Tree Books LLC, 2017. Print.

Rich, Tracey R. "A Gentile's Guide to the Jewish Holidays." *Judaism 101*. Tracey R. Rich, 2004-2011. Web. 15 March 2017.

Waskow, Rabbi Arthur O. *Seasons of Our Joy: A Modern Guide to the Jewish Holidays*. Philadelphia: Jewish Publication Society, 2012. Print.

JEWISH STEREOTYPES

Jewish stereotypes include negative and positive images that are based on perceived physical traits and cultural patterns. In the late 1800s, cartoons depicted Jewish Americans as having big noses. Jewish Americans have also been portrayed as clannish people who have undue influence and power in politics and in the world of finance. Other stereotypes involve the image of the Jewish American Princess (JAP), a spoiled, privileged young woman, or the Jewish mother, an interfering mother who makes her children feel guilty. More favorable stereotypes portray Jewish Americans as industrious people who are good financial providers and value education for themselves and their children.

Clannishness is the outgrowth of being part of a minority, feeling left out, or not belonging and sometimes feeling inferior. According to Sidney J. Jacobs and Betty J. Jacobs's *Clues About Jews for People Who Aren't* (1985), minority members often seek a sense of belonging and comfort by forming groups with similar people. Clannishness may be the price Jews and other minority groups pay to retain distinctive cultural and religious practices. Jews may interact closely with each other partly because they have been barred from joining the greater society by restrictive housing clauses, university quotas limiting the number of Jews admitted, country clubs that refused to accept Jews, and discrimination that kept them out of top executive jobs.

Several stereotypes of Jews involve finance. Some of the earliest Jewish immigrants in the United States as well as the Eastern European Jews were peddlers and shopkeepers, and perhaps because of non-Jewish resentment of this role, Jews have been accused of being crafty, devious merchants. An old European stereotype saw Jews as international bankers trying to control the financial world; this image was accepted by many Americans, some of whom still believe that Jews control the US banking industry. More recently, the stereotype has been extended to the claim that Jewish people control the media and Hollywood. The belief that a secret Jewish conspiracy has undue influence over the world's power structures can be a dangerous one; the *Protocols of the Elders of Zion* , an early-twentieth-century text making such a claim, was widely used as anti-Semitic propaganda, including by the Nazis.

The Jewish American Princess (JAP) stereotype depicts a spoiled, hedonistic, self-centered young American Jewish woman who has been pampered and overindulged by her wealthy parents. This exaggerated and offensive portrayal may reflect non-Jewish jealousy of some Jewish Americans' socioeconomic success. Because the term "JAP" is part of the

American vocabulary, many people who use the term may be unaware of its offensive nature. (The term is, however, also sometimes used by Jewish people themselves.)

The Jewish mother stereotype portrays a woman who invokes guilt in her children. This stereotype often goes hand-in-hand with a portrayal of Jewish men as "mama's boys" who are insufficiently masculine due to the influence of this overbearing female figure. Jewish American writers such as Philip Roth and Woody Allen have used this stereotype in their writing for dramatic or humorous effect. Such use of racial and ethnic stereotypes by members of the minority group has been criticized as promoting prejudice but also defended as the minority member's right to create an in-joke. The question of whether it is acceptable for Jews to invoke Jewish stereotypes aside, the "Jewish mother" stereotype has also been criticized within the Jewish community for its perceived sexism. There are, however, less gendered stereotypes that are frequently embraced by Jewish writers in a self-deprecating manner, such as the idea that Jewish people are particularly neurotic or that they love to argue.

To promote better relations between Jews and non-Jews and to attempt to eliminate stereotypes, Jewish religious congregations sometimes hold interfaith activities and worship services. Rabbis and board members frequently serve on citywide boards and committees. Jews play an active role in such organizations as the National Conference of Christians and Jews (now known as the National Congress for Community and Justice), formed in 1927 to combat racism, bias, and bigotry in the United States.

——*Marian Wynne Haber*

BIBLIOGRAPHY AND FURTHER READING

Abrams, Nathan. *The New Jew in Film: Exploring Jewishness and Judaism in Contemporary Cinema.* New Brunswick: Rutgers UP, 2012. Print.

Epstein, Lawrence J. *American Jewish Films: The Search for Identity.* Jefferson: McFarland, 2013. Print.

Ferrari, Chiara Francesca. *Since When Is Fran Drescher Jewish? Dubbing Stereotypes in The Nanny, The Simpsons, and The Sopranos.* Austin: U of Texas P, 2010. Print.

Wisse, Ruth. *No Joke: Making Jewish Humor.* Princeton: Princeton UP, 2013. Print.

JEWISH WOMEN

Between 1654 and 1920, five thousand Jews migrated from Spain, Portugal, and Brazil to North America and settled in New York, Newport, Savannah, Philadelphia, Charleston, and Richmond. By the 1870s, another fifty thousand Jews had arrived from Ireland, Austria, Bohemia, Hungary, and Germany and settled into trade and commerce activities, moving up to banking and department stores. In the late nineteenth and early twentieth centuries, a Jewish immigration of more than two million came from Russia, Galicia, Romania, and Hungary. Perhaps some of these Jews had migrated to Canada and, like other immigrants, quickly left for the United States. These Eastern European Jews were lower middle class, and they and their descendants made the greatest impact of all the Jews in the United States. By 1971, two-fifths of the nearly six million Jews lived in and around New York City. Some had moved to Boston, Philadelphia, Baltimore, and Chicago.

HISTORY

Jewish immigrants brought with them traditions of family and family work groups. Consequently, women made up 43.4 percent of all Jews between 1899 and 1910. They were concentrated in the clothing, metalworking, woodworking, building, textile, and tobacco industries; the majority found work in the needle trades. By 1890, 60 percent of employed Jews worked in the garment industry, and by 1939, the percentage was even higher.

Initially, working conditions were poor. Families labored in tiny shops, in factories, and in home sweatshops for long hours and low wages. Because there was no public assistance, every Jewish community helped the immigrants. In 1893, the National Council of Jewish Women was organized to serve as a bridge to a new life for the immigrants.

Many Jews became involved in the labor movement and, in 1900, helped to found the International

Ladies' Garment Workers' Union (ILGWU). The union movement helped the Jews improve their labor conditions. With the availability of educational and business opportunities, Eastern European Jews made economic and social advances quickly because they wanted to "Americanize" their children by having them learn the language and customs of the new country.

CHANGE IN LIFESTYLE

Second in importance to learning the English language was wearing fashionable clothing. Dress was seen as a major symbol of assimilation. Jewish women embraced American lifestyles and American clothing with a high level of enthusiasm. Their dominant role in the garment industry and needle trades gave them ample exposure to the latest clothing trends and a heightened fashion-consciousness. Growing up in a religious culture that used clothing as symbolic wares to give meaning to their lives, Jewish women honored their religious holidays with new articles of dress. In America, this meant, among other things, replacing huge, out-of-style country boots with thin-soled, high-heeled American shoes. The acculturation process also included wearing a corset to emphasize a small waist and rounded hips.

Part of the Americanizing process resulted in the establishment of the Jewish Theological Seminary of America (JTSA) in New York City to train Conservative rabbis. Conservatism provided a compromise between Reform Judaism and Jewish Orthodoxy because it preached American values while retaining most Orthodox traditions. Through their religious institutions, Jewish women began making strides. Historically, the Talmud, consisting of the Jewish laws, was studied only by men. Conservative and Reform Jews ordained male and female rabbis, but their Talmud study remained in the rabbinical schools. Orthodox Jews did not ordain women, but Talmud study for women became more available. For centuries, women were given little access to the Torah and the Jewish laws, but increased exposure excited the women and gave them greater respect for the development of Jewish laws. The Drisha Institute, a school of Jewish studies for women, was established in New York City.

This type of intellectual awakening was a reflection of women's advances in secular education. In the 1970s, they began to investigate the role of women in Jewish history and society. Holocaust survivors wrote with a feminist consciousness. Others wrote about spirituality, lesbianism, sociology, religious life, theology, history, and biblical scholarship; these subjects reflected the religious and feminist impulses of Jewish women.

Advances in secular education and in feminism reflected a revolution in the lifestyle of Jewish women. Prior to 1970, they were likely to obtain a college education first and marry slightly later than the general population. They had three or four children and remained home to raise them, returning to the labor market only after all their children were well into adolescence. This probably resulted in the even higher educational level and resourcefulness of Jewish children, which has been attributed to the fact that many Jewish mothers devote comparatively more time to playing, reading, and talking with their children than do women in the general population.

A national Jewish population study in the early 1990s found that two-thirds of Jewish women age twenty-five to forty-five had college degrees, as opposed to less than one-fifth of the general population. However, the 1990s also saw a change in the Jewish family. Marriage and family formation were postponed by more Jews until they were into their thirties and forties. The Jewish family consisted of one or two children. This shrinkage in family size was a result of family planning and the parents' placing more emphasis on careers and social lives, among other factors. Studies indicate that the majority of mothers with children under six years old worked outside the home for pay. Although the divorce rate among Jews increased, it was lower than among families in general.

The revolution in the lifestyle of Jewish women reflected that of middle-class American women of all stripes. They were getting married later, having children later, and working throughout their offspring's preschool years. Because of the higher divorce rate, they encountered special problems, such as alcoholism and family violence, and had needs such as high-quality infant and toddler day care and after-school programs. The Jewish family became a microcosm of the general population. Its demands for communal support reflected the same calls throughout American society.

——*Bill Manikas*

BIBLIOGRAPHY AND FURTHER READING

Fuchs, Ilan. *Jewish Women's Torah Study: Orthodox Religious Education and Modernity.* New York: Routledge, 2014. Print.

Hirsch, Luise. *From the Shtetl to the Lecture Hall: Jewish Women and Cultural Exchange.* Lanham: UP of America, 2013. Print.

Kaplan, Marion A., and Deborah Dash Moore, eds. *Gender and Jewish History.* Bloomington: Indiana UP, 2011. Print.

Klapper, Melissa R. *Ballots, Babies, and Banners of Peace: American Jewish Women's Activism, 1890–1940.* New York: New York UP, 2013. Print.

JEWISH-AFRICAN AMERICAN RELATIONS

Although the leaders of the African American and Jewish communities enjoyed undeniably good relations in the thirty years after World War II, their friendship was not the historical norm. The periods before and after these years of closeness and cooperation were marked by ambivalence. The relationship between the two communities has varied across time, depending upon economic developments, geographical proximity, and the presence of other ethnic groups.

EARLY US HISTORY

Although both Africans and Jews came to North America early, their interaction was very limited. Most of the Africans were slaves on plantations; however, almost no Jews owned slaves or had reason to interact with them. Minimal contact began in the mid-nineteenth century in southern and border-state towns that had a population of freed slaves and a scattering of Jews from Central Europe. The Jews, many of whom opposed slavery, were among the few merchants willing to trade with the former slaves. Both groups shared a sense of being outsiders, a strong attachment to the Hebrew Bible and its message of freedom for the slaves, and support for Abraham Lincoln and the liberal Republican Party during the Civil War (1861–1865).

TURN OF THE CENTURY

Large-scale Jewish immigration, largely from Eastern Europe, did not start until the mid-1880s. They came to the United States to escape legal discrimination, religious persecution, pogroms, and dire poverty. Very few of them had experienced any contact with blacks; however, they firmly believed in equality and the rights of the workers, the oppressed, and the poor. Therefore, they were sympathetic to the plight of the African Americans, many of whom had moved from the rural South to northern cities in which Jews lived to escape problems very similar to those from which the Jews had fled.

DEPRESSION AND WORLD WAR II

During the Great Depression of the 1930s, the Jewish and African American communities came into contact in large industrial cities, but relations were mixed. Both groups shared poverty, persecution and liberal Democratic affiliation. However, as some of the Jews began to prosper, conflict ensued. Many Jews went into business for themselves, partly because of prejudice against them in the workforce. Because they had limited resources, they opened small stores and later bought small apartment buildings in their urban neighborhoods. Normal shopkeeper-customer and landlord-tenant conflicts developed with African American neighbors, intensified by the racial and ethnic differences.

During World War II, the events in Germany provided a common enemy for Jews and African Americans, but that did not eliminate problems. Nazism was not a salient issue for most African Americans. One of the serious rifts between the two groups involved a charismatic member of the Nation of Islam, Sufi Abdul Hamid, who built a reputation for himself partly by insulting Jews and their religion.

POST-WORLD WAR II

World War II and its aftermath provided opportunities for both groups. African Americans, still fleeing the South, moved into the neighborhoods evacuated by Jews. A decline in public anti-Semitism, combined with higher education, allowed Jews to move from blue-collar to white-collar jobs and to escape the inner-city ghettos. Many Jews who went to college were exposed to and apparently moved by the plight of African Americans.

Early in the twentieth century, Jews had formed a number of organizations, such as the Anti-Defamation League, to protect their rights. Several Jews worked with African American leaders to help them bolster parallel institutions to protect black people's rights, including the National Association for the Advancement of Colored People (NAACP), which had a significant Jewish presence both in funding and in legal staffing.

These civil rights organizations grew in number and in strength, especially after the sit-ins in the South during the early 1960s. The NAACP Legal Defense and Educational Fund, later headed by Jack Greenberg, took the lead in prosecuting the civil rights cases that broke down the legal support for segregation. In the most famous case, *Brown v. Board of Education* (1954), a number of Jewish defense organizations acted as supporting counsel and argued, along with Thurgood Marshall, before the US Supreme Court against the segregation laws. It was this cooperation at the top that led to the golden age of Jewish-African American relations.

Cooperation and support by Jews pervaded the Civil Rights movement. Jews offered much stronger support for racial equality than did other white Americans. Jews constituted more than one-third of all the northern Freedom Riders who went to the South to help organize and register African American citizens to vote. The 1964 murder of three civil rights activists—Michael Schwerner and Andrew Goodman, who were Jewish, and James Chaney, an African American—was one of the defining moments of the Civil Rights movement.

THE MID-1960S AND BLACK POWER

The bond between the Jews and African Americans began to unglue with the increasingly antiwhite and anti-Semitic rhetoric of young black radicals such as Stokely Carmichael (later Kwame Toure) of the Student Nonviolent Coordinating Committee. Leaders of the nascent Black Power movement wanted complete control over their destiny; they wanted to run their own organizations and to live by their own cultural standards, not those of white

Europeans. The role of Jews in these movements, therefore, began to diminish.

As the Black Power movement grew, several radical African Americans started attacking Israel, hastening the departure of most Jews. Many young secular Jews grew up with a strong affinity for civil rights but were ambivalent or had weak feelings toward Israel. However, because of the shrill anti-Israel rhetoric and the threat to Israel's existence in 1967 by numerically larger Arab forces, American Jews started to become more supportive of the Israelis. As the younger generation of Jews left the Civil Rights movement in response to the rise of black power, they turned their attention to issues involving Israeli and Russian Jews, and their sense of themselves as an ethnic group increased.

Although Carmichael was critical of the Jewish people, civil rights activist Martin Luther King, Jr., had many friends among Jewish leaders. King was a hero not just to African Americans but also to Jews, in part because of his intolerance for anti-Semitism and his support for Israel. King's death accelerated the split between African Americans and Jews. In the riots following his assassination, a disproportionate amount of loss was sustained by Jewish shopkeepers and landlords who had stayed in the ghetto because they could not afford to relocate. The remaining Jews left quickly.

At the end of the 1960s, a series of hostile confrontations occurred, many in New York, where unionized Jewish teachers battled local African American leaders. Disputes also arose over a proposed housing project in a middle-class Jewish neighborhood and among white-collar municipal employees over jobs and promotions. After the 1970s, many of these inner-city conflicts subsided as Jews moved to the suburbs. For example, in the Los Angeles riots of 1992, friction arose between African Americans and Koreans, not Jews. In other cities, conflicts involved African Americans and Latinos rather than Jews.

LATER DECADES

Although friction between the two groups was more limited, it did not disappear. Black leader Jesse Jackson angered Jews during his 1984 bid for the presidency by referring to New York as "Hymietown" ("hymie" is a derogatory term used to describe Jews) and courting Arab leader Yasser Arafat. On college campuses, a conflict of opinion arose over affirmative action. Jews, who had suffered from quotas that limited their enrollment in higher education, tended to oppose affirmative action, although perhaps less strongly than many white Americans. In 1991, in the racially mixed community of Crown Heights, Brooklyn, a car driven by a Hasidic Jew hit and killed an African American boy and injured his companion. In the rioting that followed, a Hasidic Jew was killed.

An ongoing source of tension in the 1980s and 1990s was Louis Farrakhan, a dynamic and media-sensitive member of the Nation of Islam with a passionate hatred of Jews and Judaism, which he called a "gutter religion." For many Jews, he was the devil incarnate; for many African Americans, he was an articulate spokesperson for black self-determinism and for self-respect and dignity.

The ties between the two groups were never completely severed, however. Both groups tended to be liberal and Democratic, so they had a common political predisposition. They typically lived in the same metropolitan areas and had a partial common history. Nonetheless, at the end of the twentieth century, their political interests diverged. African Americans were mainly focused on the large numbers of blacks in what seemed like a permanent American

underclass; many Jews were worried about overseas Jews and their declining numbers due to widespread intermarriage and low birthrates. To many African Americans, Jews were just "white folks"; to many Jews, African Americans were ungrateful for the help that Jews had given in the past.

——*Alan M. Fisher*

BIBLIOGRAPHY AND FURTHER READING

"Black-Jewish Relations." *From Swastika to Jim Crow.* PBS, WGBH, n.d. Web. 24 Apr. 2015.

Brackman, Harold. "Black-Jewish Relations at a Crossroads." *Jerusalem Post.* JPost, 16 May 2013. Web. 24 Apr. 2015.

Diner, Hasia R. *In the Almost Promised Land: American Jews and Blacks, 1919-1935.* Baltimore: Johns Hopkins UP, 1997. Print.

Friedman, Murray. *What Went Wrong: The Creation and Collapse of the Black-Jewish Alliance.* New York: Free, 1995. Print.

Greenberg, Cheryl Lynn. *Troubling the Waters: Black-Jewish Relations in the American Century.* Princeton: Princeton UP, 2010. Print.

JEWISH-MUSLIM RELATIONS

Although most Americans think about Jewish-Muslim relations in the United States in terms of Jewish American and Arab American relations, Arab Americans are no longer the majority of Muslims in the United States. Thus, while conflicting views regarding Israel, Palestinians, and the Middle East is a major concern, it is not the only one. For most Jews and Muslims living in the United States a more pressing concern has become domestic movements directed against these religious minorities.

A 2016 Pew research Center study placed the number of Muslims in the United States at about 3.3 million, which would be 1 percent of the nation's population. This clearly made it the third largest religious group in the United States. The same study found that there were about 5.7 million American Jews, which is 1.8 percent of the population. Mainly due to immigration, with the birth rate playing a smaller role, it was anticipated that by 2035 the Jewish population would decrease slightly, but that the

Muslim population would grow fast enough that the total number of Muslims would surpass that of Jews in the United States. Conversions were not projected to be an important factor in the change in the number for both faiths. The Muslim community has historically had a much larger number of converts, but, in the United States, about the same number convert to Islam as leave the faith.

DEMOGRAPHICS

Although records indicate that some of the slaves brought to the United States in the seventeenth century were Muslims, because they were slaves they were not allowed to openly practice their faith; most, at least outwardly, became Christians. After the end of the slave trade, it was decades before any Muslims immigrated to the United States. The first were Arab immigrants, who arrived between 1900 and World War II, and most of these, in fact, were Christians from Syria and Lebanon. Most had little formal education and were predominantly illiterate. Their success in running small family businesses, mostly in poor neighborhoods, made it possible for their children to become well-educated and enter the professions or obtain high-level, white-collar jobs. Following World War II and especially after 1965, when quota restrictions were lifted, Muslim immigration increased significantly and became more diverse. These newer Arab immigrants were more affluent, better educated, largely Muslim professionals and businesspeople. (Arab Americans trace their origins to the twenty-one countries of the Arab League, established on March 22, 1945: Algeria, Bahrain, Djibouti, Egypt, Iraq, Jordan, Kuwait, Lebanon, Libya, Mauritania, Morocco, Oman, Palestine, Qatar, Saudi Arabia, Somalia, Sudan, Syria, Tunisia, United Arab Emirates, and Yemen.) Immigrants from other regions included more from the lower part of the economic spectrum.

Less than half of the Muslims in the United States (as of 2011) were born in the US (37 percent), or lived in the United States prior to 1980 (8 percent), according to Pew Research Center study. Contrary to the situation forty years earlier when virtually all Muslims were Arab-Americans, by 2011 only 26 percent of Muslim Americans were ethnically Arab. This was matched by Muslims from South Asia, which included a large number from Pakistan (9 percent), the largest nationality of the immigrants prior to coming to the United States. In 2015, Muslims comprised about 10 percent of legal immigrants, with a much smaller number of undocumented immigrants. Of the 63 percent of American Muslims who immigrated to the United States, about 81 percent had become citizens, as of 2011. The majority of Muslims in the United States have, and do, live in urban areas. In terms of how they viewed themselves racially, 30 percent of Muslim Americans said white, 23 percent black, 21 percent Asian, 6 percent Hispanic, and 19 percent other.

Jews have been in North America for about four hundred years. The earliest immigrants were Sephardic Jews coming to New York in the 1600s. The 1800s saw the arrival of Ashkenazic Jews from Germany and the surrounding areas. They often worked as merchants and soon became prosperous. In the late 1800s, Eastern European Jews, many of them lacking resources, migrated in great numbers to the United States, often settling in cities. These late arrivals faced prejudice from both non-Jewish Americans and the earlier German Jews. After World War II and the Holocaust, anti-Semitism diminished greatly, and all Jewish groups found greater acceptance in the United States. Most Jews came to the United States from Europe to escape religious persecution and poverty. In recent years, immigration has not played as major a role for the Jewish community as for the Muslim community. As of 2013, only 14 percent of Jews in America were foreign born, most of them from Europe (including Russia). Since early in their history in the United States, Jewish Americans have primarily lived in urban areas. By individual self-reporting to Pew Research, 94 percent of the Jewish Americans were white, 2 percent black, 3 percent Hispanic, and 2 percent other.

Jewish Americans have a higher rate of college graduation than do Muslim Americans, 58 percent to 15 percent. More foreign-born Muslims (18 percent) are college graduates than native born (12 percent). In 2016, Muslim Americans fairly closely reflected the national household income of the general population, except at the extremes, where 6 percent fewer reported incomes above $75,000 (22 percent versus 28 percent) and 9 percent more reported incomes below $30,000 (45 percent versus 36 percent). Jewish Americans (2013) had a much higher income level than average, with 56 percent having incomes above $75,000 versus 29 percent for the general population in the same survey. In the low-income category, 20 percent of Jewish American households had incomes less than $30,000, while 36 percent of the general population were at the same level.

RELATIONS

With the Muslim population in the United States initially predominately Arab, early relations between the two groups reflected the history of Jewish-Muslim relations in the Middle East. However, prior to 1948, the number of Muslims was relatively small, as, again, most of the early Arab immigrants were Christians. Thus, conflicts between Jews and Muslims in the United States were no different than conflict that arose between any number of ethnic groups within the US With the creation of the state of Israel, tensions grew between Arab Americans and Jewish Americans. The fact that the US government supported Israel was generally reflected in domestic policy. However, changes came about after President

Jimmy Carter worked with Israeli and Egyptian leaders to obtain peace between the two nations, and a pledge that Israel would negotiate with the Palestinians. Although support for the Jewish community remained the norm, it was less automatic after the Camp David Accords (1978) than before.

In addition to conflict over the state of Israel, or the Palestinian people, there is a basic religious disagreement as well. Islam, as the newer religion, has always claimed that it replaced Judaism (and Christianity) as the legitimate religion worshipping the God who has been made known through the Bible and the Qur'an. While this has been an issue causing division for ultra-orthodox members of each faith, it has not generally been the issue driving division within the United States.

Thus, in the 1980s Jewish Muslim relations in the United States started moving in a positive direction. Several groups organized for discussion on issues which had divided them, while others actually planned possible joint business ventures for when peace was achieved among all nations in the region. Thus, ironically, the conflicts in the Middle East brought Arab Americans and Jewish Americans closer. Efforts to improve intergroup relations have centered on events not in the United States but in the Middle East, where Israel and many members of the Arab League had been at war or in conflict since the establishment of the Arab League in 1945 and of the state of Israel in 1948. This improvement in Arab American–Jewish American relations created new dialogues between Jewish Americans and other Muslim group as well.

Not all groups, Muslim or Jewish, supported this improvement in relations. A big impediment to improving relations has been conservative and orthodox newspapers published exclusively for either Muslims (often Arabs) or Jews. Their biases and prejudices—and sometimes blatant hatred—can stand in the way of improving intergroup relations. The papers have reflected the hardline fundamentalist branches of both faiths. Those most willing to talk about peace and justice have been the more liberal Jews (Reform and secular Jews) and progressive Muslims.

In the early 1990s, there was widespread Jewish American support for causes such as supporting the Bosnian Muslims who were facing possible genocide from Serbian forces. However, broad Jewish support for Muslim causes faltered with the 9/11 events and the terrorist group al Qaeda's diatribes against Jews and "Crusaders." Thus relations between Jewish Americans and Muslim Americans worsened due to outside influences, rather than to any new domestic differences.

Just as events surrounding Israel and its neighbors presented opportunities for closer Muslim Jewish relations in the United States, 9/11 and its aftermath have presented new opportunities for developing mutual trust. Immediately after 9/11, several prominent Muslim and Jewish leaders wrote a joint public letter condemning the attack. Historically, there had been many Jewish organizations that focused on community outreach and education. After 9/11, the number of mosques having similar outreach increased dramatically, enabling better relations with non-Muslims. However, the area in which Muslims and Jews have become most united in the U.S has been in denouncing attacks on each other. For example, the American Jewish Committee has on a number of occasions denounced attacks, or proposed legislation, which targeted Muslims. Similarly, the Council on American-Islamic Relations, which often gets strongly criticized for support of Palestinian groups, has issued statements condemning vandalism of synagogues. Regarding the major international issue that has tended to divide Jews and Muslims, within the Muslim American community, in 2011, almost the same percentage of Muslims believe that Israel and Palestine can peacefully co-exist as did members of the Jewish American community in 2013 (62 percent of Muslims, 61 percent of Jews).

Thus, while the dominant factor in Jewish-Muslim relations is external to the United States, there are some individuals, and groups, within the nation having the goal of separation. Historically, the right-wing Jewish Defense League (JDL) and Jewish Defense Organization (JDO) have been the leading voices of separation—and the antithesis of those seeking better relations. The JDL and the JDO are pathologically anti-Arab/anti-Muslim. The JDL, founded by the late Meir Kahane, was involved not only in defamation of Arab-Americans but also in the destruction of Arab American property and even murder, including the killing of the Arab-American leader Alex Odeh.

Similarly, within the Islamic community, there are individuals and groups that have been just as rabidly anti-Jewish, and often anti many other things. However, because the US tends to support Israel and because of the 9/11 attacks, these individuals and groups have not been as visible as the JDL. In recent years, most of these individuals/groups have claimed to be allied with al Qaeda or ISIS (Islamic State), whether or not there was any real connection between the Americans and these foreign organizations. Those which have become known were small local, or regional, organizations promoting anti-American goals as much as anti-Jewish goals.

ORGANIZATIONS WORKING FOR TOGETHERNESS

On the national level, few organizations have been as active and effective in bringing Muslims and Jews together as the New Jewish Agenda (NJA). Founded in the late 1970s, at its height it had twenty-eight chapters, most of which were in large urban areas where Jewish Americans and Arab Americans live and work. NJA was started by Jews who felt that conservatives had dominated Jewish life in the United States and who yearned to create a strong progressive voice in the Jewish community. One of its major goals has been to have ongoing Jewish-Arab dialogues on crucial matters of mutual concern within the United States and in the Middle East, especially resolution of the Israeli-Palestinian question.

American Arab and Jewish Friends (AAJF) was founded in 1981 by George Bashara (an Arab American) and Arnold Michlin (a Jewish American) in metropolitan Detroit. It is a program of the Greater Detroit Interfaith Round Table of the National Conference for Community and Justice (formerly known as the National Conference of Christians and Jews). The AAJF's purpose is to improve understanding and friendship between the Arab and Jewish communities by coming together informally through luncheons, dinners, forums, and its sponsorship of an annual essay scholarship contest for graduating seniors in area high schools. The essays, which describe innovative and meaningful approaches toward the realization of the AAJF goal, are the joint effort of two students, one Jewish and one Arab American.

The Seeds of Peace summer camp was started in the early 1990 to bring together more than 160 teenagers from the Middle East—Palestinian Arabs and Jewish Israelis as well as American Jewish and Arab

youngsters—for a month long experience. Supported by donations, the young people learn about their counterparts, and discuss issues of importance. Similarly, at the college level, there is the Center for Muslim-Jewish Engagement. This was founded in Los Angeles by departments within Hebrew Union College, the Omar Ibn Al-Khattab Foundation, and the University of Southern California. Its goal has been to seek "solutions for the complicated issues that surround Muslim-Jewish relations."

Another step toward unity has been the Muslim-Jewish Advisory Council, formed in November 2016 by the American Jewish Committee and the Islamic Society of North America. This was formed in response to an increase in hate crimes (toward a broad range of targets, not just Jewish or Muslim) in the United States. The organization seeks not only to change negative stereotypes of members of both religions, but to work positively to demonstrate the contributions made by Jews and Muslims to American society.

The US Council of Muslim Organizations and the Conference of Presidents of Major American Jewish Organizations have both been active in supporting community outreach by their member organizations. The threats, and actions, by ultra-right wing nationalistic Americans toward various minority groups, including Jews and Muslims, has brought these groups, and communities, together in seeking to end the violence and threats. Thus, in recent years the more unified position of Jewish and Muslim Americans has not been the result of any major reconciliation, but rather of unity against a common foe.

——*Donald A. Watt and R. M. Frumkin*

BIBLIOGRAPHY AND FURTHER READING

AJC "Muslim-Jewish Relations." *AJC Global Jewish Advocacy.* New York: American Jewish Committee, 2017. Web. 16 March 2017.

Gopin, Marc. *Bridges across an Impossible Divide: The Inner Lives of Arab and Jewish Peacemakers.* New York: Oxford UP, 2012. Print.

Haddad, Yvonne Yazbeck. *Becoming American?: The Forging of Arab and Muslim Identity in Pluralistic America.* Waco TX: Baylor University Press, 2012. Print.

Levy, Mordecai. *By Any Means Necessary.* New York: Jewish Defense Organization, 1998. Print.

Marger, Martin. *Race and Ethnic Relations: American and Global Perspectives*. Stamford: Cengage, 2015. Print.

McCarus, Ernest, ed. *The Development of Arab-American Identity*. Ann Arbor: U of Michigan P, 1994. Print.

Murphy, Caryle. "There's Mideast Peace in the Wilds of Maine." *Washington Post* 16 Aug. 1997. Print.

Pew Research Center. "Muslim Americans: No Signs of Growth in Alienation or Support for Extremism." *Pew Research Center: U.S. Politics & Policy*. Washington: Pew Research Center, 2011. Web. 16 March 2017.

Pew Research Center. "A Portrait of Jewish Americans." *Pew Research Center: U.S. Politics & Policy*. Washington: Pew Research Center, 2011. Web. 16 March 2017.

JIM CROW LAWS

The precise origins of the term "Jim Crow" are unknown. It may have first appeared in 1832, in a minstrel play by Thomas D. "Big Daddy" Rice. The play contained a song about a slave titled "Jim Crow." The expression was used commonly beginning in the 1890's. In 1904, the *Dictionary of American English* listed the term "Jim Crow law" for the first time.

Jim Crow laws had predecessors in the so-called black codes, passed in many southern states after the Civil War (1861-1865) to limit the freedom of African Americans and assure a continuous labor supply for the southern plantation economy. Radical Reconstruction, which placed most parts of the South under military government, put an end to this. Even after the official end of Reconstruction in 1877, race relations in the South remained in a state of flux.

THE JIM CROW ERA

Jim Crow laws emerged during the 1880's and 1890's as conflict over political control in the South between different parties and between factions within parties intensified. Disfranchisement of African Americans and the segregation of whites and blacks were intended to assure the permanent subjugation of the latter and the prevention of future biracial political movements which could challenge white rule in the South. Domestic politics do not bear the sole responsibility, however: Jim Crow laws emerged at a time when the United States acquired colonies in the Pacific and the Caribbean and in the process subjugated the indigenous populations of those areas. Race theories used to justify American imperialism did not substantially differ from the white supremacy rhetoric of southern politicians.

The first Jim Crow law was passed by the state of Florida in 1887, followed by Mississippi in 1888, Texas in 1889, Louisiana in 1890, Alabama, Arkansas, Georgia, and Tennessee in 1891, and Kentucky in 1892. North Carolina passed a Jim Crow law in 1898, South Carolina in 1899, and Virginia in 1900. Statutes requiring racial segregation had been quite common in northern states before the Civil War, but only in the post-Reconstruction South did racial segregation develop into a pervasive system regulating the separation of white and black in all walks of life. Jim Crow laws segregated public carriers, restaurants, telephone booths, residential areas, workplaces, public parks, and other recreational spaces. Mobile, Alabama, passed a special curfew law for African Americans in 1909. In Florida, the law required separate textbooks, which had to be separately stored. The city of New Orleans segregated white and black prostitutes in separate districts. Many states outlawed interracial marriages. Jim Crow laws were not even limited to life: Cemeteries, undertakers, and medical school cadavers were all subjects of segregation under the laws.

These laws, however, represented only symptoms of larger and even more pervasive patterns of discrimination and racial oppression. White vigilante groups, such as the Ku Klux Klan, often enforced their own brand of racial justice through violent means, frequently with the quiet consent and even cooperation of law enforcement officers. In addition, contract labor laws and corrupt law enforcement and prison officials created a system of peonage, which kept large numbers of African Americans in the turpentine and cotton belts in debt slavery.

US SUPREME COURT

In the process of legally entrenching racial segregation through so-called Jim Crow laws, the US Supreme Court served as a willing handmaiden. In the 1883 *Civil Rights* cases, the Supreme Court ruled that segregation in privately owned railroads, theaters, hotels, restaurants, and similar places comprised private acts of discrimination and as such did not fall under the Fourteenth Amendment. In the 1896 case of *Plessy v. Ferguson*, concerning the constitutionality of a Louisiana Jim Crow law, the Supreme Court redefined segregation from a matter of private prejudice into a mandate of state law. In *Plessy v. Ferguson*, the Supreme Court approved of segregation as long as facilities were "separate but equal." In the 1930's and 1940's, the Supreme Court began to strike down segregation. Eventually, on May 17, 1954, the Supreme Court, in the landmark decision in *Brown v. Board of Education*, declared that separate facilities by their very nature were unequal, thereby reversing previous decisions.

JIM CROW IN THE TWENTY-FIRST CENTURY

Despite the progressive measures of the late twentieth century, there are some who believe that a racial caste system is alive and well in the United States of the twenty-first century. Issues cited as evidence include racial profiling, instances of police brutality against African Americans and other minorities of color, and the seemingly mass incarceration of African Americans in the country's prisons. In 2010, former litigator Michelle Alexander published a book titled *The New Jim Crow: Mass Incarceration in the Age of Colorblindness* focusing specifically on the idea that the criminal justice system targets African Americans, offering statistics that convey the reality

of the number of African Americans criminalized and kept behind bars. In general, she claims that African Americans remain in a subordinate state, albeit one slightly different from that of their ancestors. Alexander emphasizes that there are actually a greater number of African Americans in prisons or on probation and parole than were enslaved in 1850. Such arguments have sparked several debates, especially following Barack Obama's election as president in 2008.

——*Thomas Winter, updated by William V. Moore*

BIBLIOGRAPHY AND FURTHER READING

Higginbotham, F. Michael. *Ghosts of Jim Crow: Ending Racism in Post-Racial America.* New York: New York UP, 2013. Print.

Litwack, Leon. *Trouble in Mind: Black Southerners in the Age of Jim Crow.* New York: Knopf, 1998. Print.

Rasmussen, R. Kent. *Farewell to Jim Crow: The Rise and Fall of Segregation in America.* New York: Facts on File, 1997. Print.

Schuessler, Jennifer. "Drug Policy as Race Policy: Best Seller Galvanizes the Debate." *New York Times.* New York Times, 6 Mar. 2012. Web. 4 Feb. 2015.

Williamson, Joel. *The Crucible of Race: Black-White Relations in the American South Since Emancipation.* New York: Oxford UP, 1984. Print.

Woodward, C. Vann. *The Strange Career of Jim Crow.* 3rd ed. New York: Oxford UP, 1974. Print.

JOB CORPS AND RACIAL RELATIONS

The Job Corps is a United States government agency that provides job training, education, health care, and personal counseling for disadvantaged youth, many of whom come from racial and ethnic minority groups. The corps was established by the Economic Opportunity Act of 1964 as part of President Lyndon B. Johnson's War on Poverty program. From 1973 to 1982, the program was funded under the Comprehensive Employment and Training Act, but since then it has operated with open-ended annual funding under the Job Training Partnership Act. The Job Corps organization provides its services at 125 residential centers located across the United States and Puerto Rico.

By the mid-1990s, the Job Corps housed, educated, and trained approximately 62,000 young men and women between the ages of sixteen and twenty-two. Training lasts from six to twenty-four months, and most of the residential centers serve people from a particular state or region and design their programs to meet job needs in that locality. By training together in the Job Corps programs, youth of different races and ethnic backgrounds learn how to cooperate and work together. As of 2013 about 75 percent of the young people who completed the program each year found a job, returned to school, or joined the armed forces.

——*Alvin K. Benson*

JOHN BROWN'S RAID

John Brown's abortive raid on the federal arsenal at Harpers Ferry, Virginia (now West Virginia), on October 16–18, 1859, stands out as a critical episode in the spiraling sequence of events that led Northerners and Southerners into the Civil War in 1861. Brown, long a militant abolitionist, emigrated to Kansas Territory in 1855 with five of his sons to participate in the struggle between proslavery and Free State forces for control of the territory. Their insurrection was in the same spirit as earlier violence perpetrated by abolitionist, Free State militias such as the Border Ruffians following election of a proslavery, territorial legislature in 1854. With a small band of Free State men, Brown helped initiate civil war in Kansas by murdering five allegedly pro-slavery settlers along Pottawatomie Creek, in May 1856. Historians would later dub this era "Bleeding Kansas."

BROWN'S PLAN

Brown's experience in the Kansas civil war convinced him that a conspiracy existed to seize the national territories for slavery. Having long since lost faith in combating slavery by peaceful means, Brown vowed to strike a violent blow at the heart of slavery. An intense Calvinist, Brown had come to believe that he was God's personal instrument to eradicate the inhuman institution. As early as 1857, he had decided to seize a mountain fortress in Virginia with a small guerrilla force and incite a bloody slave rebellion that would overthrow the slave powers throughout the South.

To that end, Brown sought funds and arms from abolitionists in the North. Under the guise of seeking money to continue the Free State fight in Kansas, Brown secured the friendship and financial aid of the Massachusetts State Kansas Committee—a group dedicated to helping the Free-Soil forces in Kansas and elsewhere. The resolute and persuasive Brown won the support of six prominent antislavery figures, who agreed to form a secret Committee of Six to advise him and raise money for his still-secret mission. The Secret Six consisted of a well-educated group of dedicated abolitionists and reformers: Franklin B. Sanborn, a young Concord schoolteacher and secretary of the Massachusetts State

Kansas Committee; Thomas Wentworth Higginson, a "disunion abolitionist" and outspoken Unitarian minister; Theodore Parker, a controversial theologian-preacher; Samuel Gridley Howe, a prominent physician and educator; George Luther Stearns, a prosperous merchant and chairman of the Massachusetts State Kansas Committee; and Gerrit Smith, a wealthy New York landowner and reformer.

Throughout the remainder of 1857, the indefatigable Brown trained a small group of adventurers and militant abolitionists in preparation for his mission. In May, 1858, Brown moved on to Chatham, Canada, holding a secret "Constitutional Convention" attended by thirty-four African Americans and twelve whites. There, he outlined his plans to invade Virginia, liberate and arm the slaves, defeat any military force brought against them, organize the African Americans into a government, and force the southern states to concede emancipation. Under Brown's leadership, the convention approved a constitution for a new state once the slaves were freed and elected Brown commander in chief with John Kagi, his chief lieutenant, as secretary of war.

Brown's proposed invasion was delayed in 1858, when a disgruntled follower partially betrayed the plans to several prominent politicians. The exposé so frightened the Secret Six that they urged Brown

An illustration of Brown trying to persuade abolitionist Frederick Douglass to join him in the raid on Harpers Ferry. Douglass refused. By Jacob Lawrence, 1917-2000, Artist (NARA record: 1981548) (US National Archives and Records Administration).

to return to Kansas and create a diversionary operation until rumors of the Virginia plan dissipated. Brown also agreed not to inform the Secret Six of the details of his plans, so that they could not be held responsible in case the invasion failed. In December, 1858, Brown conducted the diversion as planned, by leading a raid into Missouri, liberating eleven slaves, and escorting them to Canada. He then began final preparations for the invasion of Virginia.

THE RAID

Harpers Ferry, situated at the confluence of the Potomac and Shenandoah Rivers in northern Virginia, was the initial target in Brown's plan, because he needed weapons from the federal arsenal there to arm the liberated slaves. Brown and three of his men arrived at Harpers Ferry on July 3, 1859, and set up headquarters at the Kennedy farm, seven miles east of Harpers Ferry in Maryland. The rest of Brown's twenty-one young recruits (sixteen whites and five African Americans) slowly trickled in. On the night of October 16, 1859, after several months of refining his plans, Brown led eighteen of his followers in an assault on the arsenal and rifle works at Harpers Ferry. They quickly captured the arsenal, the armory, and a nearby rifle works, and then seized hostages from the townspeople and surrounding countryside.

Fearing a slave insurrection, the armed townspeople gathered in the streets, and church bells tolled the alarm over the countryside. Brown stood his ground, anxiously waiting for the slaves from the countryside to rally to his cause. By 11:00 a.m. the next day, Brown's men—holed up in the small fire-enginehouse of the armory—engaged in a pitched battle with the assembled townspeople, farmers, and militia. By dawn the following morning, a company of horse Marines under the command of Colonel Robert E. Lee took up positions in front of the armory. When Brown refused Lee's summons to surrender unconditionally, the Marines stormed the armory, wounded Brown, and routed his followers. Seventeen people died in the raid; ten of the dead, including two of Brown's sons, were raiders. Five raiders were captured, two were taken prisoner several days later, but five escaped without a trace.

THE CONSEQUENCES

Governor Henry A. Wise of Virginia decided that Brown and his coconspirators should be tried in Virginia rather than by federal authorities, even though their attack had been against federal property. Brown and the captured raiders stood trial at Charles Town, Virginia; on October 31, the jury found them guilty of inciting a slave rebellion, murder, and treason against the state of Virginia. After the trial, in a final attempt to save his life, Brown's lawyers collected affidavits from many of his friends and relatives alleging that Brown suffered from hereditary insanity and monomania. Brown rejected his defense, claiming that he was sane. He knew that he could better serve the abolitionist cause as a martyr, a sentiment shared by Northern abolitionists. Governor Wise agreed that Brown was sane, and on December 2, 1859, John Brown was hanged at Charles Town. Six of his fellow conspirators met a similar fate.

Brown's raid intensified the sectional bitterness that led to the Civil War. Although the vast majority of Northerners condemned the incident as the work of a fanatic, the outraged South, racked by rumors of a slave insurrection, suspected all Northerners of abetting Brown's crime. Republican denials of any link with Brown were of little avail. Northern abolitionists, including the Secret Six, who had been cleared of complicity, gathered by the hundreds throughout the North to honor and acclaim Brown's martyrdom. The South was in no mood to distinguish between the Northern Republicans who wanted to contain slavery and the small group of abolitionists who sought to destroy the institution. The South withdrew even further into a defense of its institution, stifled internal criticism, and intensified its hatred and suspicion of the "Black Republican" Party. In 1861, Northerners marched to war to the tune of "John Brown's Body"—fulfilling Brown's prophecy that "the crimes of this guilty land will never be purged away; but with Blood."

——*Terry L. Seip, updated by Richard Whitworth*

BIBLIOGRAPHY AND FURTHER READING

Boyer, Richard O. *The Legend of John Brown: A Biography and a History.* New York: Knopf, 1972. Print.

Horwitz, Tony. *Midnight Rising: John Brown and the Raid That Sparked the Civil War.* New York: Holt, 2011. Print.

Oates, Stephen B. *Our Fiery Trial: Abraham Lincoln, John Brown, and the Civil War Era.* Amherst: U of Massachusetts P, 1979. Print.

Oates, Stephen B. *To Purge This Land with Blood: A Biography of John Brown.* 2nd ed. Amherst: U of Massachusetts P, 1984. Print.

Quarles, Benjamin. *Blacks on John Brown.* Urbana: U of Illinois P, 1972. Print.

Renehan, Edward J. *The Secret Six: The True Tale of the Men Who Conspired with John Brown.* New York: Crown, 1995. Print.

Jones Act of 1917

On December 10, 1898, the Treaty of Paris between Spain and the United States ended the Spanish-American War and set forth terms that became effective April 11, 1900. The agreement transferred the control of Puerto Rico to the United States, thereby legitimizing the occupation of the island and its satellites by US forces. One of the provisions of the Treaty of Paris was as follows: "The civil rights and the political status of the native inhabitants of the territories hereby ceded to the United States shall be determined by the Congress." The natives of Puerto Rico, no longer subjects of the Spanish crown, now found themselves without any citizenship recognized under international law or US domestic law.

The Organic Act of 1900 (known as the Foraker Act, after its sponsor) established a political entity called the People of Porto Rico (Puerto Rico), but there was no mention of US citizenship for those born on the island, only that they would be "held to be citizens of Porto Rico, and as such entitled to the protection of the United States." Puerto Ricans were now stateless, essentially confined to their island because of the difficulty of traveling without a passport. The US Supreme Court, in cases such as *Downes v. Bidwell* (1901), confirmed that Puerto Rico was merely a possession of the United States, not an incorporated territory, to be disposed of by the US Congress.

The Citizenship Debate

The reelection of William McKinley to the US presidency in 1900 favored US imperial expansion. Nevertheless, the debate as to whether racially, culturally, and linguistically distinct peoples brought under US control should be granted US citizenship and, if so, with what rights, continued intermittently between 1900 and 1916. In that year, the Philippines, also seized by the United States from Spain in the war, was promised independence by the

Organic Act of the Philippine Islands (also known as the Jones Act). The Organic Act of 1917 (the Jones Act of 1917) did not similarly grant independence to Puerto Rico, but it did confer US citizenship collectively on the natives of the island. Although the Jones Act changed the status of Puerto Ricans from that of US nationals—noncitizens, but owing allegiance to and subject to the protection of the United States—the granting of citizenship did not give the islanders the right to vote in US federal elections because the territory fell short of statehood. In *Balzac v. Porto Rico* (1922), the Supreme Court ruled that as citizens of an unincorporated territory, the islanders enjoyed only fundamental provisions in the Bill of Rights of the US Constitution, not procedural or remedial rights such as the guarantee of trial by jury.

The extent to which Puerto Ricans participated in the debate relating to their prospective status between 1900 and 1917 remains a matter of conjecture. For one thing, the spokesmen of the Puerto Rican community—such as Resident Commissioner Luís Muñoz Rivera and the Puerto Rican House of Delegates (the local legislature)—were ambivalent and contradictory on the subject. For another, much of the evidence placed before the Congress about the Puerto Ricans' preferences during the drawn-out debate was impressionistic and anecdotal rather than objective.

Accordingly, while some US legislators talked of the yearnings, longings, and aspirations of Puerto Ricans to citizenship, critics claim that citizenship was pressed on the islanders. It is also charged that the expediency of acquiring additional recruits for military service only weeks before President Woodrow Wilson sought a declaration of war on Germany on April 4, 1917, was not absent from congressional thinking. Whatever the truth, making Puerto Ricans native US citizens and the

establishment of a seemingly permanent political link between the United States and Puerto Rico by the Jones Act of 1917 contrasted with the creation of an articulately temporary relationship between Washington, D.C., and the Philippines. In fact, the defining of the latter's status under the 1916 Jones Act catalyzed the following year's Jones Act relating to Puerto Rico. The racist comments peppering the congressional debates were infinitely harsher as they related to Filipinos, partly because of their spirited resistance to US occupation, than in regard to Puerto Ricans, who were much more receptive to occupation. Some legislators even produced statistics to "prove" that a high percentage of the islanders were white in order to justify their being granted US citizenship.

THE ACT
The final version of the Jones bill, introduced in the House on January 20, 1916, was only slightly different from Congressman Jones's earlier versions. The only noteworthy change was that Puerto Ricans residing on the island were allowed one year, instead of six months, to reject US citizenship if they desired. The House passed the bill by voice vote on May 23, 1916; the Senate approved it on February 20, 1917; and the House-Senate Conference Committee followed suit on February 24, 1917. President Wilson, a Democrat, signed it into law on March 2, 1917. Only 288 Puerto Ricans legally declined to accept US citizenship within the statutory period, thereby losing their right to hold or run for any public office on the island. Because the Jones Act had established five different categories in determining the status of different individuals, there was great confusion as to who qualified for citizenship. The US Congress subsequently passed several additional laws in the interest of administrative simplification.

In 1952, the US Territory of Puerto Rico became the Commonwealth of Puerto Rico, known in

Spanish as a "free associated state." As such, Puerto Rico elected a nonvoting representative to the US Congress but cast no vote in presidential, congressional, or senatorial elections. While islanders paid no federal taxes, the aid Puerto Rico received from Washington was less than it would have received had it been a state.

On November 14, 1993, a nonbinding referendum, which President Bill Clinton nevertheless pledged to respect, was held regarding the island's future status. Puerto Ricans who opted for continued commonwealth status cast 48.4 percent of the votes; statehood received 46.2 percent; and 4.4 percent of the 2.1 million ballots cast favored independence. The spread between the first two options had narrowed drastically since an earlier referendum in 1967. The issue of Puerto Rico's status—and thus the nature of the citizenship of the islanders—was far from over. It now was up to Puerto Ricans themselves, increasingly aware of their Latino roots, to decide their own political future.

——*Peter B. Heller*

BIBLIOGRAPHY AND FURTHER READING
Jose A. Cabranes's *Citizenship and the American Empire: Notes on the Legislative History of the United States Citizenship of Puerto Ricans* (New Haven, Conn.: Yale University Press, 1979) is a well-annotated, objective account of how Congress decided that the people of a colonial territory should be made US citizens. Kenneth L. Karst's *Belonging to America: Equal Citizenship and the Constitution* (New Haven, Conn.: Yale University Press, 1989) argues that equal citizenship for cultural minorities who have experienced exclusion, forced conformity, and subordination under the influence of US nativism has become more topical over the years.

JONES V. ALFRED H. MAYER COMPANY

Reversing many precedents, the Supreme Court held in this 1968 decision that the Civil Rights Act of 1866 prohibited both private and state-backed discrimination and that the Thirteenth Amendment authorized

Congress to prohibit private acts of discrimination as "the badges of slavery."

Joseph Lee Jones, alleging that a real estate company had refused to sell him a house because he was African

American, sought relief in a federal district court. Since the case appeared before the passage of the Civil Rights Act of 1968, Jones and his lawyer relied primarily on a provision of the 1866 Civil Rights Act that gave all citizens the same rights as white citizens in property transactions. Both the district court and the court of appeals dismissed the complaint based on the established view that the 1866 law applied only to state action and did not address private acts of discrimination. The US Supreme Court, however, accepted the case for review.

All the precedents of the Supreme Court supported the conclusions of the lower courts. In the *Civil Rights* cases (1883) the Court had ruled that the Thirteenth Amendment allowed Congress to abolish "all badges and incidents of slavery," but the Court had narrowly interpreted these badges or incidents as not applying to private acts of discrimination. In *Hodges v. United States* (1906) the Court held that Congress might prohibit only private actions that marked "a state of entire subjection of one person to the will of another," and even in *Shelley v. Kraemer* (1948) the Court recognized the right of individuals to make racially restrictive covenants.

In *Jones*, however, the Court surprised observers by voting 7 to 2 to overturn its precedents. Writing for the majority, Justice Potter Stewart asserted that Congress under the Thirteenth Amendment possessed the power "to determine what are the badges and incidents of slavery, and the authority to translate that determination into effective legislation." In addition, the majority reinterpreted the 1866 law so that it proscribed both governmental and private discrimination in property transactions—an interpretation that is questioned by many authorities.

Justice John M. Harlan wrote a dissenting opinion which argued that the majority probably was wrong in its interpretation of the 1866 law. Harlan also wrote that the passage of the Fair Housing Act of 1968 eliminated the need to render this decision that relied on such questionable history.

Since the *Jones* decision was based on the Thirteenth rather than the Fourteenth Amendment, it was important in diluting the Court's traditional distinction between state and private action, and it appeared to grant Congress almost unlimited power to outlaw private racial discrimination. *Jones* became a precedent for new applications of the almost forgotten post-Civil War statutes in cases such as *Griffin v. Breckenridge* (1971) and *Runyon v. McCrary* (1976). In the quarter-century after *Jones*, however, the Congress did not pass any major legislation based upon the authority of the Thirteenth Amendment.

——*Thomas T. Lewis*

BIBLIOGRAPHY AND FURTHER READING

"Jones v. Alfred H. Mayer Co." *Legal Information Institute.* Cornell U Law School, n.d. Web. 27 Apr. 2015.

"Jones v. Mayer." *Oyez.* Oyez, IIT Chicago-Kent College of Law, 2014. Web. 27 Apr. 2015.

JUDAISM AND ETHNIC RELATIONS

Judaism has a complex history of development that has been traced as far back as the twentieth century b.c.e. Most scholars agree, however, that modern Judaism is rooted either in the Haskala (the Enlightenment) of the Ashkenazic Jews of eastern and central Europe in the eighteenth century c.e. or, somewhat earlier, in the acculturation of the Sephardic Jews in Italy and western Europe. These two branches of diaspora Jews, with some minor doctrinal differences, held firmly to the traditional beliefs of Judaism and the basic authority of the Talmud, the collection of rabbinical writings making up the religious and civil codes of Jewry.

While monotheism, messianism, and other fundamental tenets of their faith remained intact, adherents of Judaism gradually broke with the passivity that had marked Jewry throughout the Middle Ages, rejecting its self-perception as a people patiently awaiting redemption from their suffering in exile among the Gentiles, who persecuted them for their beliefs or, worse, expelled or destroyed them in pogroms (anti-Jewish massacres).

While the insularity that marked Jewish communities in the diaspora never completely vanished, from the end of the eighteenth century on there was a greater trend toward cultural assimilation, especially in North America and industrialized Europe.

By the nineteenth century, in most European nations emancipated Jews could study at universities and enter such professions as medicine and law, long prohibited to them. It was a considerable step forward: Through much of their history, in their dealings with Christians, European Jews had been limited to such activities as itinerant trading and usury (money lending).

DISCRIMINATION

Discrimination against Jews in the diaspora has continued despite the fact that in most industrialized nations its legal sanctions have been removed for almost two centuries. This discrimination partly results from the fact that residual discrimination against ethnic minorities tends to outlive legalized or institutionalized discrimination, even when there are statutory safeguards against it. Anti-Jewish discrimination is compounded by the fact that it has evolved from both anti-Judaism and anti-Semitism, which are not precisely the same thing, though the distinction between them is largely moot.

Anti-Judaism first arose in antiquity, in both polytheistic paganism and Pauline Christology. According to many scholars, the earliest Christians, themselves Semites, had to compete with Jews in efforts to win new converts to their separatist faith. At the time, the Hebrews were militant and zealous proselytizers who dared to defy even the Romans, as their unyielding mass suicide at Masada in 73 c.e. testifies.

In the diaspora, at least in the medieval Christian world, the Jews carried the stigma of being "Christ killers" and a reputation for theological intractability for not accepting Jesus as the true messiah. Their ethnocentrism led to terrible suspicions—that, for example, they desecrated the host, sacrificed Christian children (the notorious "blood libel"), and brought on the Black Death (1348–50) by poisoning wells—but the persecutions largely remained religiously based. Some Jews, notably moneylenders, were despised for other reasons, but the official sanctions against them were usually imposed on more theological than ethnic grounds. In some Islamic areas, notably in Spain, the Sephardic Jews, considered "people of the book," were often treated much better, and some even rose to great political prominence. It was there, under the Arab sponsorship of arts and letters, that they produced the Golden Age of Hebrew Literature (c. 1000–1150 c.e.).

The persecution of Jews until the time of the Enlightenment was partly prompted by their insularity. For their distinct self-identity, they were forced to pay a terrible price. By the end of the sixteenth century, in most European cities, they were required to live in their own quarter, or ghetto, under all sorts of legal restrictions and prohibitions. They were at times expelled from some countries, including England.

JUDAISM IN THE TWENTIETH CENTURY

Even in the United States, with its fundamental doctrine of religious freedom, Jews did not escape a more insidious sort of persecution based on ethnic prejudices rather than strong religious convictions. Jews were often accused of being clannish, secretive, miserly, aggressive, and, at times, un-American. Among other important Americans, industrialist Henry Ford was rabidly anti-Semitic. He used the newspaper he controlled, *The Dearborn Independent*, to spread the idea that there was an international Jewish conspiracy dedicated to overthrowing legitimate governments by fostering atheism and anarchy. It was to counter such libels that the ecumenical National Conference of Christians and Jews was founded in 1928.

In Europe, particularly in post-World War I Germany, the Jews were subjected to an increasingly virulent persecution that would reach its full horror under the regime of Adolf Hitler. Many disillusioned Jews had already turned to Zionism, believing that their only hope lay in the creation of a nation of their own in Palestine, their ancestral home. Some Jews did place their hopes on radical sociopolitical change, including socialism and communism, but most rejected the atheism at the core of Marxism. Modern Zionism was actually a rekindling of beliefs that had been suppressed in the Enlightenment and Emancipation, centering on the idea that someday, under the providential guidance of Jehovah, the Jews would return from exile, restored to their rightful nation-home. It would take its vigorous secular and militant "back to Jerusalem" form after the Holocaust, resulting in the creation of the state of Israel, but it was advocated decades earlier, even in the United States, where the new Zionism was espoused by the Reconstructionist followers of Mordecai Menahem Kaplan (1881–1983) as early as the 1920s.

Zionism in Europe was even more trenchant. By the end of the nineteenth century, liberal Jews who had sought an end to Jewish-Christian conflict had their hopes dashed in eastern Europe, especially Russia, where the Orthodox Church aided and abetted the pogroms and disseminated the spurious *Protocols of the Elders of Zion* , one source of the Jewish conspiracy theory that poisoned the minds of many non-Jews. Despairing of ever reconciling their Jewish culture to the non-Jewish religions and cultures of their host nations, Jews in eastern Europe either hunkered down in their segregated tradition, emigrated, or sought solutions in Zionism. Zionism also attracted radical antireligious Jews and socialistic Jews whose Zionism was purely secular in vision.

The plight of nonemigrating European Jews was gravely intensified with the rise of Adolf Hitler in Germany and his racist theories of Aryan supremacy. While most European Christians stood by silently and watched without protest, Hitler vilified the Jews. They were an easy scapegoat, especially in the romantic anti-intellectualism that characterized the Nazi vision of the world. When he came to power, Hitler began a systematic campaign of persecution that, during World War II, culminated in the "final solution"—the genocidal extermination of Jews. Jews were rounded up throughout the conquered nations of Europe and North Africa and sent to extermination camps, where more than six million were put to death.

The Holocaust severely reduced the number of Jews in Europe, which, until the war, had been the center of Jewish culture and tradition in the diaspora. In effect, it severed the ties of many emigrant Jews to their past, obliterating such important Jewish cultural enclaves as the Warsaw ghetto. It also resulted in a major demographic shift, moving the centers of contemporary Judaism away from Europe to the United States and Israel.

AFTERMATH OF THE HOLOCAUST

In the Holocaust the Jews experienced the greatest single calamity in their history, surpassing even their loss of sovereignty over Palestine with the Roman destruction of Jerusalem in 70 C.E. The Nazi efforts to exterminate the Jews resulted in three major

changes: the destruction of whole communities of diaspora Jews in Europe and North Africa, the disappearance of millennial Jewish settlements in Islamic countries in the Middle East, and the "ingathering" of exiled Jews in the nation-state of Israel.

Although Israel was created in 1948 as a secular democracy, it fostered pride in Jews throughout the world, particularly in its succession of victories over the Islamic nations that had vowed to drive the Jews out of the Holy Land. Many liberal Jews who had neglected or even rejected their heritage before the Holocaust made a new commitment to it in the post-World War II years. They also won the sympathy of many Christians, who were shocked by the horror and dehumanizing impact of the Nazi policy. As Stephen Sharot notes in *Judaism: A Sociology* (1976), in the postwar "Western Diaspora there was a sharp decline of overt anti-Semitism and all forms of discrimination." Cultural and religious insularity, where it persists in the West, reflects choice rather than compulsion. The vestiges of anti-Semitism in the West are largely found in such settings as private clubs, where membership may exclude religious, ethnic, or racial minorities.

——*John W. Fiero*

BIBLIOGRAPHY AND FURTHER READING

Lederhendler, Eli, ed. *Ethnicity and Beyond: Theories and Dilemmas of Jewish Group Demarcation.* New York: Oxford UP, 2011. Print.

Rabinovitch, Simon. *Jews & Diaspora Nationalism: Writings on Jewish Peoplehood in Europe and the United States.* Lebanon: Brandeis UP, 2012. Print.

Reinharz, Shulamit, and Sergio DellaPergola, eds. *Jewish Intermarriage Around the World.* New Brunswick: Transaction, 2009. Print.

Sharot, Stephen. *Comparative Perspectives on Judaisms and Jewish Identities.* Detroit: Wayne State UP. Print.

Silver, M. M. *Louis Marshall and the Rise of Jewish Ethnicity in America.* Syracuse: Syracuse UP, 2013. Print.

Zeitlin, Irving M. *Jews: The Making of a Diaspora People.* Malden: Polity, 2012. Print.

JURY NULLIFICATION

Under the US system of justice, three questions must be answered before a person can be convicted of a crime: What are the facts, what was the defendant's moral intent, and what is the law? The jury decides the first two under definitions of the law which are presented to it by the judge. "Jury nullification" takes place when the jury ignores (or nullifies) the law and acquits the defendant in spite of the judge's instructions. Under the constitutional provision forbidding "double jeopardy," the defendant cannot be tried again.

Historically, before juries could exercise this power, two great issues had to be settled. The first was whether judges have the power to punish jurors for bringing in the "wrong" verdict. A precedent was established in England in 1670, in what is generally referred to as Bushel's case. Bushel was one of twelve jurors who refused to convict William Penn (later to become governor of the American colony of Pennsylvania) of fomenting a riot. Penn had been preaching a Quaker sermon in public at a time when the Quakers were being persecuted. After the jurors refused to change their verdict, the judge fined them forty marks apiece. They refused to pay and were committed to Newgate Prison. Eventually they were released on bail, and when England's high court finally decided the case a year later, it was held that no jury can be punished for its verdict.

The second issue was whether juries could return "general verdicts" or only "special verdicts." A special verdict results when the jury is only allowed to answer specific questions of fact. A general verdict determines whether the accused is guilty or innocent. To render a general verdict, juries must judge the application of the facts to the law. The move from special to general verdicts was largely the result of unpopular prosecutions brought against printers by royal governors in the eighteenth century. At the trial of John Peter Zenger for seditious libel, Zenger's attorney argued that the jury had the power to decide whether Zenger was truly guilty of seditious libel. The prosecution argued that the jury could decide only whether Zenger had published the articles at issue in the case. Zenger was acquitted when the jury brought in the general verdict of "not guilty."

It is the general verdict that allows jury nullification. Juries may decide to disobey the judge's instructions if they believe either that the law is unjust or that the defendant's act was admirable or justified in some way. Prosecutors have no recourse, because acquittal is final in the American judicial system. During the nineteenth century, there was a substantial free jury movement in the United States, led by the radical American essayist Lysander Spooner. Although the movement subsided, many still argue that judges should inform jurors that they may "nullify" the law if they think it unjust. Regardless of whether juries are formally notified of this power, there are undoubtedly cases in which nullification takes place. For example, it is sometimes suggested that African American jurors are prone to acquit African American defendants, particularly on less serious charges, because they believe that there is considerable official harassment of blacks. It is difficult to tell with any certainty how common this practice may be.

——*Robert Jacobs*

JURY SELECTION

Before the Civil War (1861-1865), Massachusetts was the only state that permitted nonwhites to serve on juries. After the war, most southern states enacted legislation that effectively barred African Americans and other minorities from jury service, irrespective of the protections of the Fourteenth Amendment. Northern states tended to produce largely the same outcome mostly through the use of an exclusive *venire* (jury pool) process, whereby "prominent" citizens (which effectively left out minorities) filled out the rolls not allowing for equal protection under the law.

The exclusionary laws typical in the southern states were struck down when the US Congress criminalized racism in jury selection in 1875. However, Congress left the exclusionary *venire* procedures common in the North unaddressed. These procedures soon became quite prevalent in the South as well.

New Reforms

Although nonexclusionary *voir dire* (selection to sit on a jury) became the standard guideline by the middle of the twentieth century, major changes were not initiated until the 1960's, when the United States Fifth Circuit Court began overturning convictions and indictments within its jurisdiction (mostly southern states) on the basis of exclusionary selection. Although the US Supreme Court ruled in *Swain v. Alabama* (1965) that constitutional requirements were satisfied as long as minorities were on the *venire* and part of the grand jury that brought down an indictment, it was not until the Jury Selection and Service Act (1968) that Congress outlawed "blue ribbon" juries in federal courts. Consequently, the *venire* process had to be more open. In *Taylor v. Louisiana* (1975) the Supreme Court extended this requirement to the state and local courts.

Nevertheless, exclusion persisted through use of the peremptory challenge in petit (trial) jury *voir dire*—whereby attorneys have the right to strike potential jurors without stating any reason. Such screening of potential grand jurors is less prevalent. In *Batson v. Kentucky* (1986), the Supreme Court curtailed unrestricted use of peremptory challenge in petit juries by allowing judges to inquire as to the rationale for and to limit strikes (dismissals) of potential jurors when there appeared to be a pattern of exclusion. However, it is difficult to determine motivation definitively unless the prosecutor is unusually inept or unusually honest. The fact that more minorities have had adverse contacts with the criminal justice system can be used as a rationale for exclusion.

Consequently, some experts argued that "affirmative action" is necessary to guarantee representative juries. Others criticized this idea, saying that affirmative action in jury selection would translate into imposing quotas of minorities on juries, and some local jurisdictions did impose quotas on jury selection. However, in *Holland v. Illinois* (1990), the Supreme Court held that as long as the *venire* provided an appropriate cross section of the community, *voir dire* did not have to produce representative results because the Constitution merely guarantees equality of opportunity, not necessarily representativeness.

Jury Nullification

The most potentially problematic issue in the late twentieth century involved the Fully Informed Jury Association (FIJA) and related initiatives. FIJA proponents tend to be opposed to governmental authority in that they try to encourage potential jurors—especially those who may be judging antigovernment activists—to ignore the facts and/or the law in order to acquit. This "jury nullification," about which the government has no legal appeal (unless there is evidence of something like jury tampering), may contribute to even greater use of "scientific" jury selection. This innovation uses social research and psychological studies to profile and include or exclude (through peremptory challenge) jurors who may be more or less favorable to the case presented.

The jury nullification notions of the FIJA appear to be shared by some minority activists, who argue that members of their communities on juries judging their peers have a duty to vote for acquittal in almost all instances in order to redress the social injustices visited upon their community by the majority. Although this might accomplish nothing more than "hung" (unable to decide) juries—which permit the government to retry the cases—if minority members on subsequent juries act the same way, government efforts to convict members of the minority will be stymied. If such postures become widespread, racially based peremptory challenges might become acceptable with the rationale that these minorities have an antigovernment bias such that they cannot meet the requirement of impartiality.

——*Scott Magnuson-Martinson*

Bibliography and Further Reading

Furkurai, Hiroshi. *Race in the Jury Box.* Albany: State U of New York P, 2003. Print.

Papachristou, Alexander, ed. *Blind Goddess: A Reader on Race and Justice.* New York: New Press, 2011. Print.

Rothwax, Harold. *Guilty: The Collapse of Criminal Justice.* New York: Random, 1996. Print.

K

KANSAS-NEBRASKA ACT

Senator Stephen A. Douglas, chairman of the Committee on Territories, introduced legislation to organize the land west of Missouri and Iowa as the Nebraska Territory. New settlements in the region and the potential for a transcontinental rail route prompted Douglas's action. It soon became apparent to Douglas that obtaining support from the South required two major revisions. First, the region was split into the Kansas and Nebraska territories. Second, the bill called for repeal of that part of the Missouri Compromise of 1820 which prohibited slavery north of 36° 30' latitude. Rather, settlers in each territory would vote to accept or prohibit slavery.

Douglas viewed slavery from economic rather than moral grounds, reasoning that its unprofitability in northern climates would be its demise. Douglas's concessions to slave states reflected both the desire to get on with nation building and the necessity of obtaining Southern support for his presidential ambitions. The act, which became law May 30, 1854, widened the growing rift between North and South and encouraged the formation of the Republican Party.

——*John A. Sondey*

BIBLIOGRAPHY AND FURTHER READING

Earle, Jonathan, and Diane Mutti Burke, eds. *Bleeding Kansas, Bleeding Missouri: The Long Civil War on the Border.* Lawrence: UP of Kansas, 2013. Print.

Epps, Kristin. *Slavery on the Periphery: The Kansas-Missouri Border in the Antebellum and Civil War Eras.* Athens: U of Georgia P, 2016. Print.

KEELER COMMISSION

The intent of federal Indian policy from 1953 to 1962 was to dissolve government obligations and responsibilities toward Native Americans in order to bring about assimilation. This disastrous program was called "termination." It undermined tribal governments and resources, eroded ethnic identities, and impoverished groups such as the Klamath of Oregon and Menominee of Wisconsin. By the end of the decade, so much criticism had been generated by these developments that a new political consciousness concerning Indian problems began to emerge.

John F. Kennedy, elected president in 1960, affirmed that Indian land would be protected, that self-determination would be promoted, and that steps would be taken to avoid undermining the cultural heritage of any group. Secretary of the Interior Stewart Udall appointed a special task force on Indian affairs in February of 1961 with an eye toward reorganizing the Bureau of Indian Affairs (BIA) in order to carry out this mandate.

William Wayne Keeler, a top-level executive with Phillips Petroleum Company and principal chief of the Cherokee Nation, was appointed chairman of the task force. Other members included Philleo Nash, an anthropologist and former lieutenant governor of Wisconsin who had participated in the Menominee termination plans; James Officer, a University of Arizona anthropologist; William Zimmerman, Jr., assistant commissioner of the BIA from 1933 to 1950; and consultant John Crow. After hearings and field trips to western reservations, the commission filed its seventy-seven-page report on July 10, 1961. Nash also included a summary of the report in the *Annual Report of the Commissioner of Indian Affairs* for 1961.

The commission's main finding was that future BIA policy should emphasize development rather than termination. Recommendations included the attraction of industries to reservations, along with job training and placement services. Loan programs were encouraged, rapid settlement of Indian Claims Commission cases was urged, and increased efforts to educate the general public about Indian culture were promoted. The report also stressed the need for Indian participation in government programs.

In the 1960s, Congress granted authorization for Indian loans, tribal resources increased, and development of reservation resources replaced the focus on assimilating Indians through relocation to the cities. The Keeler Commission played a small but noticeable role in the shift away from the termination policy.

——Gary A. Olson

Keetoowah Society

The Keetoowah Society was founded by two white clergymen in 1859 in an effort to advance the interests of full-blooded Cherokee. The men were abolitionists, and their goal, ostensibly, was to organize Cherokee opposition to slavery. Members of the order were full-bloods, and some called themselves "Pin Indians," wearing crossed pins on their left lapels. The Keetoowah Society evolved from simple support of abolition to a group whose purpose was the protection of Cherokee interests. Society goals were taken from the ancient Anti-Kutani, designed to oppose adoption of European American ways. "Pin Indians" were Christians who wished to syncretize their religion with ancient tribal rites.

The Keetoowah Society was popular and at one time had a membership of more than two thousand men. It was fiercely loyal to the Union during the Civil War (1861–1865). That fact threatened the Confederacy, which impressed society members into military service. Stories abound of men who were forced to serve the South and deserted at the first opportunity.

Following the Civil War, the Keetoowah Society remained active in Cherokee political and social life. It opposed the Dawes Commission and the Dawes General Allotment Act in the 1890s, insisting on the observance of treaty obligations, a guarantee of self-government, and freedom from territorial organization. When the Cherokee delegation reached agreement with the Dawes Commission in 1900, the full-blood Keetoowah Society urged its members to boycott the agreement. In 1906, the Dawes Commission agreement prevailed. The society then functioned as a political party (the Union Party) and fraternal lodge, the only fraternal lodge in the United States whose principal emblem is the United States flag.

——David N. Mielke

Bibliography and Further Reading

McLoughlin, William Gerald. *Cherokees and Christianity, 1794–1870: Essays on Acculturation and Cultural Persistence.* Athens: U of Georgia P, 2009.

Minges, Patrick N. *Slavery in the Cherokee Nation: The Keetoowah Society and the Defining of a People, 1855–1867.* New York: Routledge, 2003. Print.

Keyes v. Denver School District No. 1

Decided June 21, 1973, this ruling outlawed de facto desegregation and expanded prohibitions on segregation. *Brown v. Board of Education* (1954) invalidated laws that required or permitted segregated black and white schools. Nevertheless, many school districts remained segregated, in part because of de facto segregation (segregation "in fact" rather than de jure, or "by law"). Wilfred Keyes did not want his daughter, Christi Keyes, to attend any kind of segregated school in Denver. In 1970, when a newly elected school board rescinded a desegregation plan adopted by the previous board in 1969, he brought a class-action suit.

In 1970, the district court ordered Park Hill schools desegregated after hearing evidence that the school board deliberately segregated its schools through school site selection, excessive use of mobile classroom units, gerrymandered attendance zones, student transportation routes, a restrictive transfer policy, and segregated faculty assignment to schools. Keyes was also successful before the court in arguing that inner-city schools, with substantial black and Hispanic student populations, should also be desegregated, but Denver prevailed on appeal in 1971, arguing that the large percentages of black and Hispanic students in these schools resulted from a "neighborhood school" policy.

Justice William J. Brennan delivered the opinion of the US Supreme Court. Six justices joined Brennan, one justice affirmed the decision in part and dissented in part, and the remaining justice dissented. The Supreme Court ruled that since intentional segregation was proved in one part of the city, there was a presumption of intentional discrimination in the other case. The burden of proof thus shifted to the school board to prove that the intentional segregation of one section of the district was isolated, separate, and unrelated to the pattern of pupil assignment to the "core city schools."

When the case was sent back to the district court in 1973, Denver was determined to have practiced unlawful segregation in both areas of the city, and the school board was required to desegregate. When the school board failed to design an adequate plan to desegregate by 1974, the court drew up a plan of its own.

The effect of *Keyes* was to open all northern school districts to the possibility of desegregation lawsuits. Eventually almost every city of at least moderate size then grappled with desegregation plans, voluntary or court ordered. The lone exception is the statewide school district of Hawaii, which has never been desegregated despite the existence of schools situated to serve certain geographic areas where only persons of Hawaiian ancestry by law can reside.

——*Michael Haas*

KING ASSASSINATION

For more than a decade, Martin Luther King, Jr., led the Southern Christian Leadership Conference (SCLC) and was, for many people, the quintessential symbol and spokesman for nonviolence. By the spring of 1968, however, King had lost some of his mystique, as the relatively simpler issues of voting rights and access to public facilities were superseded by more costly and divisive social and economic problems, accompanied by the deepening US involvement in the Vietnam War.

King had lost his close alliance with President Lyndon B. Johnson because of his opposition to the president's Vietnam policy. King also faced challenges from younger, more militant African American leaders, for whom King's philosophy of passive resistance seemed too slow.

On the evening of April 4, King walked onto the balcony of his Memphis motel and was struck down by a bullet, fired from a building across the street. He died almost instantly. Initial attempts to identify and apprehend the killer failed, and while fires and riots raged in several cities in protest of King's death, an intensive search began, spreading eventually to Canada and Great Britain. On June 8, British immigration officials arrested an escaped US convict traveling under the name of Roman George Sneyd and returned him to the United States to stand trial for the murder of King. The prisoner, whose real name was James Earl Ray, pleaded guilty to the charge in March, 1969, and was sentenced to ninety-nine years in prison. Later, Ray changed his position, claimed innocence, and wrote a book entitled *Who Killed Martin Luther King?* (1992), with a foreword by the Reverend Jesse Jackson that cautiously endorsed Ray's conspiracy argument.

The immediate aftermath of King's death was marked by serious urban rioting in several cities, and somewhat later, by the granting of a substantial number of the strikers' demands in Memphis. More difficult to appraise is the place that his martyrdom earned for him and for his ideas in the Civil Rights movement. At a time when his influence was threatened by men such as H. Rap Brown and Huey P. Newton, King was killed in a way that served to restore his prestige among many African Americans. Under the leadership of King's longtime assistant Ralph David Abernathy, the SCLC continued to play a leading role in the Civil Rights movement after King's death. On the other hand, some African Americans, finding in King's death a confirmation of the futility of passive resistance, turned instead to more militant tactics.

In death, King remained an inspiring symbol, even a martyr, to many people who supported his causes. The SCLC, which King helped to found and which he led for eleven years as its president, continued under presidents Ralph Abernathy and Joseph E. Lowery to keep the vision of a nonviolent society central to their organizational and personal goals.

——*Courtney B. Ross, updated by Thomas R. Peake*

BIBLIOGRAPHY AND FURTHER READING

Lane, Mark, and Dick Gregory. *Murder in Memphis: The FBI and the Assassination of Martin Luther King.* New York: Thunder's Mouth, 1993. Print.

Pepper, William F. *An Act of State: The Execution of Martin Luther King.* New York: Verso, 2003. Print.

Posner, Gerald L. *Killing the Dream: James Earl Ray and the Assassination of Martin Luther King, Jr.* New York: Random House, 1998. Print.

Sides, Hampton. *Hellhound on His Trail: The Stalking of Martin Luther King, Jr., and the International Hunt for His Assassin.* New York: Doubleday, 2010. Print.

Smiley, Tavis. *Death of a King: The Real Story of Dr. Martin Luther King Jr.'s Final Year.* New York: Little, Brown, 2014. Print.

KING CASE

Following a high-speed chase along a Los Angeles highway that ended just after midnight on March 3, 1991, California Highway Patrol officers Timothy and Melanie Singer stopped driver Rodney Glen King and his two passengers, Bryant Allen and Freddie Helms, for questioning. More than twenty Los Angeles Police Department (LAPD) officers soon arrived on the scene in Los Angeles' Lake View Terrace neighborhood. Police sergeant Stacey Koon, assisted by officers Theodore Briseno, Laurence Powell, and Timothy Wind, took over the investigation. The police quickly subdued and handcuffed Allen and Helms without incident. Their encounter with King, however, caused a controversy with far-reaching legal and social consequences.

KING'S ARREST
According to the four white police officers who arrested King, a black man, King refused at first to leave the car and then resisted arrest with such vigor that the officers considered it necessary to apply two jolts from a Taser electric stun gun, fifty-six blows from aluminum batons, and six kicks (primarily from Briseno) to subdue King before they successfully handcuffed and cordcuffed King to restrain his arms and legs. The event probably would have gone unnoticed had not George Holliday, an amateur cameraman who witnessed the incident, videotaped

the arrest and sold the tape to a local television station news program. The videotape became the crucial piece of evidence that the state of California used to charge the four LAPD arresting officers with criminal assault and that a federal grand jury subsequently used to charge the officers with civil rights violations.

Broadcast of Holliday's tape on national news programs elicited several responses from the LAPD. On March 6, 1991, the LAPD released King from custody and admitted that officers failed to prove that King had resisted arrest. On March 7, Los Angeles Police Chief Daryl Gates announced that he would investigate King's arrest and, if the investigation warranted it, would pursue criminal assault charges against the arresting officers. On March 14, a Los Angeles County grand jury indicted Sergeant Koon and officers Briseno, Powell, and Wind for criminal assault, and they subsequently pleaded not guilty.

INVESTIGATION OF POLICE BRUTALITY
Overwhelming public sympathy for King following the national broadcast of Holliday's videotape prompted Los Angeles Mayor Thomas Bradley to investigate charges that instances of police brutality motivated by racism were commonplace during LAPD arrest operations. On April 1, 1991, Mayor Bradley appointed a nonpartisan commission,

headed by Warren Christopher (who had formerly served as President Jimmy Carter's deputy secretary of state), to study the LAPD's past record of complaints regarding police misconduct. On April 2, Mayor Bradley called on Police Chief Gates, who had served on the LAPD since 1949 and had been police chief since 1978, to resign. In May, the LAPD suspended Sergeant Koon and officers Briseno and Powell without pay and dismissed officer Wind, a rookie without tenure, pending the outcome of their criminal trial. King then filed a civil rights lawsuit against the city of Los Angeles.

Several significant developments occurred as the officers awaited trial. On July 9, 1991, the Christopher Commission released the results of its investigation and its recommendations to the five-member Los Angeles Police Commission. The Police Commission employed the police chief and was responsible for the management of the LAPD. The Christopher Commission found that the LAPD, composed of 67.8 percent white officers in 1991, suffered from a "siege mentality" in a city where 63 percent of the population were people of color. The commission also found that a small but significant proportion of officers repeatedly used excessive force when making arrests and that the LAPD did not punish those officers when citizens filed complaints. Finally, the commission recommended measures to exert more control over the LAPD's operations, including limiting the police chief's tenure to a five-year term, renewable by the Police Commission for one additional term only. After the release of the Christopher Commission report, Police Chief Gates announced his retirement, effective April, 1992 (which he later amended to July, 1992). On July 23, 1991, a California court of appeal granted the police defendants' request for a change of venue for the upcoming criminal trial.

THE STATE OF CALIFORNIA COURT TRIAL
The trial of the four officers began on March 4, 1992, in the new venue—the primarily white community of Simi Valley in Ventura County. The jury who heard the state of California's case against the four officers consisted of ten whites, one Latino, and one Asian. The officers' defense lawyers presented Holliday's videotape broken down into a series of individual still pictures. They asked the jury to judge whether excessive force—that is, force that

was not warranted by King's "aggressive" actions—was employed at any single moment during the arrest. Referring often to the "thin blue line" that protected society from the "likes of Rodney King," the defense built a case that justified the police officers' actions. King's lawyer, Steven Lerman, a personal injury specialist, advised King not to testify at the trial out of concern that King's "confused and frightened" state of mind since the beating might impair his memory of events and discredit his testimony. The Simi Valley jury acquitted the four officers of all charges of criminal assault, with the exception of one count against officer Powell on which the jury was deadlocked.

The acquittal of the four police officers on April 29, 1992, ignited widespread and destructive riots led by poor and angry black Angelenos. The riots affected areas throughout Los Angeles but particularly devastated parts of impoverished South Central Los Angeles. Fifty-three people died during the riots, which raged until May 2, and more than one billion dollars' worth of property was damaged. There had long been friction between Los Angeles' neighboring Korean and black communities, and the Korean American community bore the brunt of the rioters' destructive attacks.

THE FEDERAL COURT CIVIL RIGHTS TRIAL
On August 5, 1992, a federal grand jury indicted the four officers for violating King's civil rights. The grand jury charged Sergeant Koon with violating the Fourteenth Amendment, which obligated Koon, as the officer in charge of the arrest, to protect King while he was in police custody. Officers Briseno, Powell, and Wind were charged with violating the Fourth Amendment in using more force than necessary, and using that excessive force willfully, when they arrested King. King testified during the federal trial. On April 17, 1993, a jury of nine whites, two blacks, and one Latino found Koon and Powell guilty and Briseno and Wind not guilty. On August 4, 1993, Koon and Powell were sentenced to two-and-one-half-year prison terms. In May, 1994, a Los Angeles jury awarded King $3.8 million in compensatory damages in his civil rights lawsuit against the city, but on June 1, 1994, the jury denied King's request for additional punitive damages.

The Rodney King beating case would be recalled in the 2010s as the Black Lives Matter movement got under way in reaction to police brutality and murder cases involving unarmed black citizens who found themselves questioned by or otherwise running afoul of law enforcement officials (most of whom were white).

——*Karen Garner*

BIBLIOGRAPHY AND FURTHER READING

Cannon, Lou. *Official Negligence: How Rodney King and the Riots Changed Los Angeles and the LAPD*. New York: Times Books, 1997. Print.

Gooding-Williams, Robert, ed. *Reading Rodney King/ Reading Urban Uprising*. New York: Routledge, 1993. Print.

Jacobs, Ronald N. *Race, Media, and the Crisis of Civil Society: from Watts to Rodney King*. New York: Cambridge UP, 2000. Print.

Metcalf, Josephine, and Carina Spaulding, eds. *African American Culture and Society after Rodney King*. Burlington: Ashgate, 2015. Print.

Owens, Tom, and Rod Browning. *Lying Eyes: The Truth Behind the Corruption and Brutality of the LAPD and the Beating of Rodney King*. New York: Thunder's Mouth, 1994. Print.

KNOW-NOTHING PARTY

The Know-Nothing Party was a political organization that prospered in the United States between 1852 and 1856. During that period, the antiforeign and anti-Catholic feelings of Americans concerned about the large numbers of immigrants arriving in the United States, especially from Ireland, led to the creation of political organizations grounded in prejudice. The secret Order of the Star-Spangled Banner, informally known as the Know-Nothings because "I know nothing" was the response of members queried regarding the organization, emerged as the most prominent of the nativist organizations. The Know-Nothings eventually dropped their secrecy to become a force in US politics. Under a new name, the American Party, the Know-Nothings surprised the nation with electoral victories in 1854 and 1855. The new party successfully shifted attention away from the issue of slavery in many parts of the country by playing on unrealistic fears of foreign and papal plots to control the United States. The American Party platform called for reforming immigration laws by limiting the number of immigrants and extending the time requirement for naturalization. Former president Millard Fillmore, the American Party candidate for president in 1856, received 21 percent of the popular vote but carried only the state of Maryland. Unable to emerge as a dominant force in national politics, the American Party split into factions over the issue of slavery.

——*Donald C. Simmons, Jr.*

Citizen Know Nothing, image of the Know Nothing party's nativist ideal. By Sarony & Co., lithographer.

KOMAGATA MARU INCIDENT

At the beginning of the twentieth century, the Sikhs (a religious community who originate in South Asia) became the targets of resentment, discrimination, and violence in Canada's British Columbia. In response to the anti-Sikh sentiment, in 1908 the Canadian government passed two orders-in-council specifically designed to stop East Indian immigration. The first raised the amount an immigrant had to have in his or her possession from twenty-five dollars to two hundred dollars. The second prohibited entry unless the person came directly from his or her country of birth or citizenship by continuous voyage; there were no direct or continuous voyage sea routes from India to Canada. Only East Indians were subject to these restrictions.

To enter Canada, a group chartered the Japanese ship *Komagata Maru* and made a continuous voyage from Calcutta to Vancouver with 346 Sikhs and 30 East Indians aboard. Even though the passengers satisfied all the immigration requirements, only a few, who were returnees, were allowed to disembark. After two months of negotiations, anti-Sikh demonstrations, and violence, the ship and her passengers were forced to leave. The incident had lasting influence on Sikhs in Canada and the Canadian government's legacy of racial and ethnic discrimination.

——*Arthur W. Helweg*

BIBLIOGRAPHY AND FURTHER READING

Hickman, Pamela M. *The Komagata Maru and Canada's Anti-Indian Immigration Policies in the Twentieth Century.* Toronto: Lorimer, 2014. Print.

Kazimi, Ali. *Undesirables: White Canada and the Komagata Maru: An Illustrated History.* Vancouver: Douglas, 2012. Print.

Nguyen, Kevin. "The Komagata Maru Incident as a Violation of Human Rights." *OHRC.* Ontario Human Rights Commission, n.d. Web. 27 Apr. 2015.

"Remembering the Komagata Maru." *Citizenship and Immigration Canada.* Gov. of Canada, 10 Nov. 2014. Web. 27 Apr. 2015.

Rode, Ajmer, and Jarnail Singh. *The Journey with Endless Eye: Stories of the Komagata Maru Incident.* Victoria: Ekstasis, 2014. Print.

KOREAN AMERICANS

Koreans first began settling in the United States in the 1950s, when American servicemen serving in Korea returned home with brides and war orphans. Korean migration to the United States continued at very low levels, however, until the US Congress changed immigration laws in 1965, giving Asians the same opportunity as Europeans to settle in the United States. This triggered an almost immediate increase in Korean immigrants: Although only 10,179 Koreans immigrated from 1961 to 1965, the number jumped to 25,618 in the next half-decade, from 1966 to 1970. As more Koreans made their homes in the United States, more followed. During the period from 1986 to 1990, 172,851 Koreans immigrated. By 2010, according to that year's census, over 1,700,000 Americans identified as wholly or partly Korean.

After the 1965 change in immigration law, Korean immigrants were not only more numerous but also more likely to come as entire family groups. With large numbers of Koreans in the United States, they began to form Korean American communities instead of settling as isolated individuals. Korean businesses and Korean churches began to appear in American cities and suburbs.

California is home to the largest portion of Koreans in the United States—30 percent of the total Korean population as of 2010. California is followed by New York, which was home to 9 percent of Korean Americans in 2010. New Jersey, Texas, and Virginia also had large Korean populations.

KOREAN BUSINESSES

As new immigrants, Koreans often have few job opportunities in the United States. However, Koreans do have a strong tradition of helping one another, and this has contributed to the growth of Korean-owned businesses in the United States. In the rotating credit system known as the *kye*, groups of Koreans pool money to make interest-free loans to group members.

Changes in the US economy also encouraged the development of Korean businesses. During the 1970s and 1980s, as poverty became increasingly concentrated in American inner-city areas, many small business owners began closing or selling stores in these areas. New Korean immigrants, who had limited English-language abilities and few contacts to find jobs in established US corporations, moved into ownership of small businesses. As of 2007, there were nearly two hundred thousand Korean-owned businesses in the United States, mainly in the sectors of retail and repair, maintenance, personal, and laundry services.

Korean businesses have become the basis for many local and national Korean organizations. The Korean American Grocers' Association is one of the most important of the national business-based organizations, with local groups in most areas that have substantial Korean populations. The Korean Dry Cleaning and Laundry Association is another national Korean American organization based on small-business ownership.

The Korean pattern of employment has had consequences for the relations between Korean Americans and members of other groups. Koreans are often highly dependent on one another for financial and social support, sometimes creating the impression that they isolate themselves from the rest of American society. They tend not to live in the inner-city neighborhoods where they own their businesses, leading to cultural misunderstandings and conflicts between Korean business owners and their customers, many of whom are African American.

KOREAN CHURCHES
Although Korean culture is traditionally Confucian and Buddhist, numerous Christian congregations, mostly Protestant, exist in South Korea. It is estimated that about 70 percent of Korean Americans are Christians and that the overwhelming majority of them are members of Korean churches. By the 1990s, there were more than two thousand Korean churches in the United States. Churches have become social centers for many Korean Americans, places where they can come together with others who speak their language and share their culture.

Korean American churches are places of worship, but they fulfill many other needs as well. Church members provide one another with information on available employment and housing. Language classes at churches teach English to new immigrants and Korean to US-born children. The churches help to pass Korean culture on to children who may never have visited the home country of their parents.

KOREANS AND AMERICAN SOCIETY
Many Korean American business owners do not pass on their businesses to their US-born children. Instead, these children are typically encouraged to achieve high educational levels and obtain professional jobs in US corporations. Over time, then, the distinctive employment patterns of Korean Americans are likely to disappear. Korean Americans have also shown increasing rates of marriage with members of other racial and ethnic groups, although as of 2010, the proportion of Korean Americans identifying as one or more other ethnic groups as well was still less than one quarter.

——*Carl L. Bankston III*

BIBLIOGRAPHY AND FURTHER READING
Abelmann, Nancy, and John Lie. *Blue Dreams: Korean Americans and the Los Angeles Riots.* Cambridge: Harvard UP, 1995. Print.

Hurh, Won Moo. *The Korean Americans.* Westport: Greenwood, 1998. Print.

Min, Pyong Gap. *Caught in the Middle: Korean Merchants in America's Multiethnic Cities.* Berkeley: U of California P, 1996. Print.

Min, Pyong Gap, ed. *Koreans in North America: Their Experiences in the Twenty-First Century.* Lanham: Lexington, 2013. Print.

Park, Kyeyoung. *The Korean American Dream: Immigrants and Small Business in New York City.* Ithaca: Cornell UP, 1997. Print.

Takaki, Ronald. *From the Land of Morning Calm: The Koreans in America.* New York: Chelsea, 1994. Print.

Yoo, Grace J., and Barbara W. Kim. *Caring Across Generations: The Linked Lives of Korean American Families.* New York: New York UP, 2014. Print.

Young, Jacob Yongseok. *Korean, Asian, or American? The Identity, Ethnicity, and Autobiography of Second-Generation Korean American Christians.* Lanham: UP of America, 2012. Print.

Korean-African American Relations

Ownership of a small business is the most common job for people of Korean ancestry in the United States. Assisted by rotating credit associations (organizations that Koreans form to grant each other interest-free business loans requiring little collateral), Korean Americans have specialized in self-employment in small stores. The majority of Korean businesses in the United States are located in California and New York. In 2007, according to the US Bureau of the Census, 41.7 percent of all Korean businesses were in California and 12.4 percent were in New York or New Jersey. Within these states, they were concentrated in the Los Angeles-Long Beach area and in New York City (primarily Queens).

Korean businesses are most often located in central areas of cities. During the 1970s and 1980s, owners of inner-city businesses began to leave, and Koreans, having access to business loans from their rotating loan associations but few job opportunities in established American businesses, began buying small urban shops. Although their businesses were in the city, the Koreans tended to settle in the suburbs. The people who do live in central urban areas and make up the majority of the customers in Korean businesses are African Americans. Korean shop owners are often looked upon by their inner-city customers as exploiters who come into neighborhoods to make a profit on the people and then take the money elsewhere. These customers complain about high prices, poor merchandise, and discourteous treatment. As new arrivals to the United States, Korean merchants sometimes have trouble with English and do not communicate well with those who come into their shops.

Korean businesspeople tend to hire other Koreans to work in their shops. Most of these shops are family enterprises, so family members frequently provide labor. As a result, Koreans not only live outside the communities where their stores are located but also hire few people who live in those communities. African Americans complain that Korean merchants do not hire black employees, do not buy from black suppliers of goods, and do not invest in the black neighborhoods in which they have located their businesses.

Although African American shoppers frequently view Koreans as outsiders and exploiters, the Koreans sometimes look with suspicion on those living in the neighborhoods where their businesses are located. Having little understanding of the history of US racial inequality, Korean business owners may see low-income urban residents as irresponsible and untrustworthy. The high crime rates in these neighborhoods can lead them to see all members of the communities, even the most honest, as potential shoplifters or robbers.

Mistrust and Culture Clash

The cultural gap between African Americans and the Korean Americans who often own stores in black neighborhoods has resulted in a number of well-publicized clashes. In the spring of 1990, African Americans in Brooklyn began a nine-month boycott of Korean stores after a Korean greengrocer allegedly harassed an African American shopper. In 1992, trouble flared up again in the same neighborhood when an African American customer in a Korean grocery was allegedly harassed and struck by the owner and an employee. During 1995, an African American man was arrested while attempting to burn down a Korean-owned store, and both white and Korean store owners in Harlem received racial threats.

California, home to the nation's greatest number of Korean businesses, has seen some of the most serious conflicts between Koreans and African Americans. In April of 1992, a judge gave a sentence of probation to a Korean shopkeeper convicted in the shooting death of a fifteen-year-old African American girl, Latasha Harlins. Two weeks after that, on April 29, riots broke out in South Central Los Angeles after the acquittal of police officers who had been video-taped beating an African American motorist, Rodney King. Although none of the police officers was Korean, Korean groceries and liquor stores in South Central Los Angeles became targets of the riots. The riots destroyed more than one thousand Korean businesses and an estimated twenty-three hundred Korean-owned businesses were looted.

Korean shop owners began leaving South Central Los Angeles in the years after the riots. Those who remained became even more wary of the local population than they were previously.

Efforts at Improving Relations
Korean and African American leaders have made efforts to improve relations between the two groups. In the days following the riots in Los Angeles, some African American and Korean leaders formed the Black-Korean Alliance to improve communication and find common ground. In New York, the Korean-American Grocer's Association has tried to find ways of bringing African Americans and Koreans together. These have included sending African American community leaders on tours of South Korea and providing African American students with scholarships to Korean universities.

It may be difficult to resolve the problems between Korean merchants and their African American customers as long as American central cities continue to be places of concentrated unemployment and poverty. Investment in low-income communities and the creation of economic opportunities for their residents are probably necessary in order to overcome

the suspicion and resentment between members of these two minority groups.

——*Carl L. Bankston III*

Bibliography and Further Reading
Foner, Nancy. *One Out of Three: Immigrant New York in the 21st Century.* New York: Columbia UP, 2013. Print.

Kim, Kwang Chung, ed. *Koreans in the Hood: Conflict with African Americans.* Baltimore: Johns Hopkins UP, 1999. Print.

Min, Pyong Gap, ed. *Koreans in North America: Their Twenty-First Century Experiences.* Lanham: Lexington, 2013. Print.

Olson, James S., and Heather Olson Beal. "Asian Americans in the Modern World." *The Ethnic Dimension in American History.* 4th ed. Malden: Wiley, 2010. 282–97. Print.

"Survey of Business Owners—Asian-Owned Firms: 2007." *United States Census Bureau.* United States Census Bureau, 2007. Web. 12 May. 2015.

Korematsu v. United States

In *Korematsu v. United States*, the Supreme Court refused to rule in favor of the privacy rights of an American citizen of Japanese ancestry who was detained in a relocation camp during World War II. In 1942, American military authorities arrested Fred Toyosaburo Korematsu, an American citizen of Japanese ancestry, for remaining in San Leandro, California, a restricted region, in violation of a military order. The military acted under authority of President Franklin Roosevelt's Executive Order 9066, which authorized the secretary of war and appropriate military commanders to establish military areas from which persons might be excluded. The president issued this order on his authority as commander in chief of the army and navy. After being found guilty of violating the military order, Korematsu appealed his case to the US Supreme Court.

On December 18, 1944, the US Supreme Court ruled 6 to 3 in favor of the United States and in support of Korematsu's arrest. The majority opinion, written by Justice Hugo L. Black, sustained

Korematsu's removal because "the properly constituted military authorities" feared an invasion of the West Coast and had decided that military urgency required the removal of persons of Japanese origin from the area. Black admitted that the exclusion order worked hardship on the Japanese American population, "but hardships are a part of war and war is an aggregation of hardships." Furthermore, Black reasoned, the exclusion program did not constitute racial discrimination as such; Korematsu had not been excluded because of his race but because of the requirements of national security. As to the question of loyalty, Black stated that there was insufficient time to separate the loyal from the disloyal Japanese. The only recourse, then, was for the military leaders to take such action as they deemed necessary to protect the country and its citizens from possible aggression. The section of Black's opinion that has most often been cited, however, states that "all legal restrictions which curtail the civil rights of a single racial group are immediately suspect" and must be given "the most rigid scrutiny."

Three justices differed from the majority and registered vigorous dissents. Justice Owen J. Roberts objected on the grounds of both loyalty and race. This was a "case of convicting a citizen as punishment for not submitting to imprisonment in a concentration camp, solely because of his ancestry," without evidence concerning his loyalty to the United States. Justice Frank Murphy was equally adamant in his dissent. He denounced the removal of Japanese citizens as "one of the most sweeping and complete deprivations of constitutional rights in the history of this nation in the absence of martial law." He concluded that the exclusion program itself "goes over the 'very brink of constitutional power' and falls into the very ugly abyss of racism."

The importance of *Korematsu v. United States* lies in the difficulty that the Court had in determining the dividing line between the constitutional rights of the citizen and the nation's power to defend itself. In this case, the Court did not rule on the constitutionality of the internment of someone on the basis of race, only that the presidential executive order and the subsequent military orders were deemed necessary for the defense of the nation and its citizens. While it took the United States more than forty years officially to rectify and repudiate the internment of Japanese Americans (reparations payments were authorized by Congress in 1988), many commentators have long believed that the United States acted improperly and in violation of the civil rights of American citizens by its use of the internment camp program.

——*Kevin F. Sims*

Bibliography and Further Reading

Bannai, Lorainne K. *Enduring Conviction: Fred Korematsu and His Quest for Justice.* Seattle: U of Washington P, 2015. Print.

Daniels, Roger. *The Japanese American Cases: The Rule of Law in a Time of War.* Lawrence: UP of Kansas, 2013. Print.

Tushnet, Mark, ed. *I Dissent: Great Opposing Opinions in Landmark Supreme Court Cases.* Boston: Beacon, 2008. Print.

Ku Klux Klan

With the end of the Civil War and the emancipation of African American slaves in the South, tension arose between old-order Southern whites and Radical Republicans devoted to a strict plan of Reconstruction that required Southern states to repeal their black codes and guarantee voting and other civil rights to African Americans. Federal instruments for ensuring African American rights included the Freedmen's Bureau and the Union Leagues. In reaction to the activities of these organizations, white supremacist organizations sprouted in the years immediately following the Civil War: the Knights of the White Camelia, the White League, the Invisible Circle, the Pale Faces, and the Ku Klux Klan (KKK).

Beginnings

The last of these would eventually lend its name to a confederation of such organizations, but in 1866 it was born in Pulaski, Tennessee, as a fraternal order for white, male, Anglo-Saxon Protestants joined by their opposition to Radical Reconstructionism and an agenda to promote white, Southern dominance. This incarnation of the Klan established many of the strange rituals and violent activities for which the KKK became known throughout its history. They named the South the "invisible empire," with "realms" consisting of the Southern states. A "grand dragon" headed each realm, and the entire "empire" was led by Grand Wizard General Nathan B. Forrest. Positions of leadership were dubbed "giant," "cyclops," "geni," "hydra," "goblin." The white robes and pointed cowls stem from this era; these were donned in the belief that African Americans were superstitious and would be intimidated by the menacing, ghostlike appearance of their oppressors, who thus also maintained anonymity while conducting their activities.

Soon the Klan was perpetrating acts of violence, including whippings, house-burnings, kidnappings, and lynchings. As the violence escalated, Forrest disbanded the Klan in 1869, and on May 31, 1870, and April 20, 1871, Congress passed the Ku Klux Klan Acts, or Force Acts, designed to break up the white supremacist groups.

SECOND RISE OF THE KLAN

The next rise of the Klan presaged the period of the Red Scare (1919–20) and the Immigration Act of 1921, the first such legislation in the United States to establish immigration quotas on the basis of national origin. In November 1915, on Stone Mountain, Georgia, a second Ku Klux Klan was founded by preacher William J. Simmons, proclaiming it a "high-class, mystic, social, patriotic" society devoted to defending womanhood, white Protestant values, and "native-born, white, gentile Americans." Such an image of the Klan was perpetrated by the popular 1915 film *The Birth of a Nation*, in which a lustful African American is shown attempting to attack a white woman, and the Klan, in robes and cowls, rides to the rescue.

The new Klan cloaked itself as a patriotic organization devoted to preserving traditional American values against enemies in the nation's midst. An upsurge of nationalist fervor swelled the ranks of the Klan, this time far beyond the borders of the South. This second Klan adopted the rituals and regalia of its predecessor as well as the same antiblack ideology, to which it added anti-Catholic, anti-Semitic, anti-immigrant, anti-birth control, anti-Darwinist, and anti-Prohibition stances. Promoted by ad-man Edward Y. Clarke, its membership reached approximately one hundred thousand by 1921 and over the next five years, by some estimates, grew to five million, including even members of Congress.

The second Klan perpetrated more than five hundred hangings and burnings of African Americans. In 1924, forty thousand Klansmen marched down Pennsylvania Avenue in Washington, DC, sending a message to the federal government that there should be a white, Protestant United States. Finally, the Klan's growing wave of violence alienated many of its members, whose numbers dropped to about thirty thousand by 1930.

Klan activities increased again prior to World War II, and membership rose toward the one hundred thousand mark, but in 1944 Congress assessed the organization more than a half million dollars in back taxes, and the Klan dissolved itself to escape. Two years later, however, Atlanta physician Samuel Green united smaller Klan groups into the Association of Georgia Klans and was soon joined by other reincarnations, such as the Federated Ku Klux Klans, the Original Southern Klans, and the Knights of the Ku Klux Klan. These groups revived the agenda of previous Klans and were responsible for hundreds of criminal acts. Of equal concern was the Klan's political influence; a governor of Texas was elected with the support of the Klan, as was a senator from Maine. Even a Supreme Court justice, Hugo L. Black, revealed in 1937 that he had been a member of the Ku Klux Klan.

CHALLENGES

In the 1940s, many states passed laws that revoked Klan charters, and many southern communities issued regulations against masks. The US Justice Department placed the Klan on its list of subversive elements, and in 1952 the Federal Bureau of Investigation used the Lindbergh law (one of the 1934 Crime Control Acts) against the Klan. Another direct challenge to the principles of the KKK came in the 1960s with the advent of the Civil Rights movement and civil rights legislation. Martin Luther King Jr. prophesied early in the decade that it would be a "season of suffering." On September 15, 1963, a Klan bomb tore apart the Sixteenth Street Baptist Church in Birmingham, Alabama, killing four young children. Despite the outrage of much of the nation, the violence continued, led by members of the Klan who made a mockery of the courts and the laws that they had broken. Less than a year after the bombing, three civil rights workers were killed in Mississippi, including one African American and two whites from the North involved in voter registration. This infamous event was later documented in the motion picture *Mississippi Burning*. Viola Lee Liuzzo was killed for driving freedom marchers from site to site. Such acts prompted President Lyndon B. Johnson, in a televised speech in March 1965, to denounce the Klan as he announced the arrest of four Klansmen for murder.

After the conviction of many of its members in the 1960s, the organization became somewhat dormant, and its roster of members reflected low numbers. Still, as it had in previous periods of dormancy, the Klan refused to die. Busing for integration of public schools in the 1970s engendered Klan opposition in the South and the North. In 1979, in Greensboro, North Carolina, Klan members killed several members of the Communist Party in a daylight battle on an open street. Klan members have patrolled the Mexican border, armed with weapons and citizen-band radios, trying to send illegal aliens back to Mexico. The Klan has been active in suburban California, at times driving out African Americans who attempted to move there. On the Gulf Coast, many boats flew the infamous AKIA flag, an acronym for "A Klansman I Am," a motto that dates back to the 1920s. Klan members tried to discourage or run out Vietnamese fishers. Klan leaders active since 1970 include James Venable, for whom the Klan became little more than a hobby, and Bill Wilkinson, a former disciple of David Duke. Robert Shelton, long a grand dragon, helped elect two Alabama governors. Duke, a Klan leader until the late 1980s, decided to run for political office and was elected a congressman from Louisiana despite his well-publicized past associations; in 1991, he ran for governor, almost winning. In the 1980s the Klan stepped up its anti-Semitic activities, planning multiple bombings in Nashville. Klan leaders in the 1990s trained their members and their children for what they believed was an imminent race war, learning survival skills and weaponry at remote camps throughout the country.

A major blow was struck against the Klan by the Klanwatch Project of the Southern Poverty Law Center, in Montgomery, Alabama, when, in 1984, attorney Morris Dees began pressing civil suits against several Klan members, effectively removing their personal assets, funds received from members, and even buildings owned by the Klan.

According to the Southern Poverty Law Center, by 2015 the Klan, identified primarily as a hate group, had divided into several different, disorganized, and even clashing chapters. Estimating the total number of members within these chapters to be between five and eight thousand, the Anti-Defamation League cites illegal immigration and same-sex marriage as two major contemporary issues taken up by the Klan groups. Despite the rise of the Internet, Klan groups have not been able to successfully utilize this forum to increase their ranks. After a white police officer killed an unarmed black man in Ferguson, Missouri, in 2014, inciting mass protest, the Traditionalist American Knights of the KKK issued fliers threatening to take action against the protesters if they caused any harm to peaceful citizens of the neighborhood. On the fiftieth anniversary of the civil rights march in Selma, Alabama, a number of Klan members left fliers on doorsteps throughout the city denouncing the words of King as well as immigration. In June of that year, following the racially charged deaths of nine African Americans during a shooting at their church in Charleston, South Carolina, the local chapter of the Klan got support from the South Carolina government to hold a rally in support of continuing to display the controversial Confederate flag in that state.

BIBLIOGRAPHY AND FURTHER READING

"About the Ku Klux Klan." *ADL*. Anti-Defamation League, n.d. Web. 8 July 2015.

Bridges, Tyler. *The Rise of David Duke*. Jackson: UP of Mississippi, 1994. Print.

Chalmers, David Mark. *Hooded Americanism: The History of the Ku Klux Klan*. New York: Watts, 1981. Print.

Ezekiel, Raphael. *The Racist Mind: Portraits of American Neo-Nazis and Klansmen*. New York: Viking, 1995. Print.

Gass, Nick. On 'Bloody Sunday' Anniversary, KKK Leaves Fliers in Selma." *POLITICO*. POLITICO, 9 Mar. 2015. Web. 8 July 2015.

Stanton, Bill. *Klanwatch: Bringing the Ku Klux Klan to Justice*. New York: Weidenfeld, 1991. Print.

Wade, Wyn Draig. *The Fiery Cross: The Ku Klux Klan in America*. New York: Simon, 1987. Print.

Workneh, Lilly. "KKK Threatens 'Lethal Force' against Ferguson Protestors and Appears on TV To Explain Why." *Huffington Post*. HuffingtonPost.com, 14 Nov. 2014. Web. 8 July 2015.

KU KLUX KLAN ACTS

Also known as the Enforcement Acts, or Force Acts, these three laws were enacted by the US Congress in response to the terrorist activities of the Ku Klux Klan and other groups committed to white supremacy in the South during the era of Reconstruction, immediately following the Confederate defeat at the end of the Civil War. The first act, passed in May 1870, made night riding (the practice of riding on horseback at night and committing various acts of intimidation and harassment) a federal felony and reaffirmed the rights of African Americans provided for in the Fourteenth and Fifteenth Amendments. Congress passed a second act in February 1871, which provided for election supervisors to ensure against fraud and racial discrimination. Two months later, Congress approved a third statute aimed specifically at the activities of the Ku Klux Klan. This law made it a federal offense to violate anyone's voting rights. In addition, it allowed the president to proclaim areas in which state governments failed to curb domestic violence to be in "rebellion" and authorized the use of military force and the suspension of the writ of *habeas corpus* to end rebellions. In October 1871, President Ulysses S. Grant used the law to declare nine counties in South Carolina to be in rebellion. These laws proved effective in suppressing white supremacy organizations.

——*Thomas Clarkin*

BIBLIOGRAPHY AND FURTHER READING

Alexander, Shawn Leigh. *Reconstruction Violence and the Ku Klux Klan Hearings.* Boston: Bedford, 2015. Print.

Langguth, A. J. *After Lincoln: How the North Won the Civil War and Lost the Peace.* New York: Simon, 2014. Print.

Newton, Michael. *White Robes and Burning Crosses: A History of the Ku Klux Klan from 1866.* Jefferson: McFarland, 2014. Print.

Williams, Lou Falkner. *The Great South Carolina Ku Klux Klan Trials, 1871–1872.* Athens: U of Georgia P, 1996. Print.

L

LABOR MOVEMENT AND RACE RELATIONS

An unusually diverse mix of racial and ethnic groups have formed and replenished the labor force of the United States since the Reconstruction era following the Civil War. Emancipated slaves and their descendants rapidly expanded the American labor ranks, with many entering agricultural and industrial production in both the North and the South. In a similar manner, immigration began to alter the appearance and form of American labor. In the late nineteenth century, the United States opened its doors to foreign migrants, in large part because the nation's rapidly expanding economy needed labor. Between 1880 and 1924, more than twenty-five million immigrants (primarily from Asia and Europe) poured into the country to join people of other nationalities working in factories and industries. Through their collective labor as workers, their actions as union members, and their varied responses to exploitation and insecurity, this varied ethnic mix was a crucial element in shaping the American economy and labor force through the twentieth century.

Such heterogeneity has had both negative and positive consequences for the American labor movement as a whole. It has produced interethnic and interracial conflict among working people; such conflict has often been purposefully exacerbated by employers to lessen the threat of worker solidarity. Yet this heterogeneity has also fostered strong ethnic identification and has been utilized toward worker mobilization for protection and advancement. Both tendencies can be seen within some of the key labor organizations that emerged during the United States' two "labor eras" (the 1880s and the 1930s) and in minority and immigrant labor activity in later decades.

KNIGHTS OF LABOR

The Noble Order of the Knights of Labor (KOL) was initially organized in Philadelphia in 1869; however, the period of its most successful accomplishment did not come until the 1880s. Led by Terence Powderly, a machinist from Scranton, Pennsylvania, the KOL aimed to unite all those who worked (except for liquor dealers, lawyers, gamblers, and bankers) into one huge union that would produce and distribute goods on a cooperative basis.

Recognizing the need for a broad-based labor solidarity to achieve this goal, the Knights of Labor opened its membership to men and women of all ethnic and racial groups. Powderly traveled the country gathering all those who advocated equal pay for equal work and the abolition of child labor. This recruitment campaign was quite successful, and more than thirty cooperative enterprises were established with membership that spanned national and racial boundaries. At its peak, the Knights of Labor included about seventy thousand black members and thousands of Asian and European laborers.

The results of such multiethnic labor solidarity can be seen in the strike against the Missouri Pacific Railroad in 1885. Through work stoppages and interruptions, certain unions affiliated with the Knights of Labor forced railroad mogul Jay Gould to restore wages he had cut the previous year and to rehire hundreds of fired union members. This victory so raised the KOL's standing that membership grew from about one hundred thousand to more than seven hundred thousand within a year.

AMERICAN FEDERATION OF LABOR

The American Federation of Labor (AFL), formed in Philadelphia in 1886, was a very different organization. Its members were not individual workers but rather craft unions encompassing laborers from specific trades. Regular dues from these members provided the federation with money to fund strikes and to hire full-time organizers and labor-dispute negotiators.

Although the AFL provided these supportive labor services, it did so for a narrow spectrum of workers. The way in which AFL leader Samuel Gompers structured the organization made it racially and ethnically divisive and restrictive. In his recruitment campaigns, Gompers made membership appeals only to the elite males of the working class, the skilled workers. Few minority group members fit this description; even those who did were excluded from membership. Gompers's position was that allowing members of various ethnic and immigrant groups (especially African Americans) to join the federation would embroil the organization in the controversial issue of race in the labor movement; he wished to avoid ethnic entanglements at all costs. Believing that the AFL had more "imperative" and "concrete" matters on which to focus, he closed the ranks of the AFL to minority workers. By the early 1920s, the AFL was the dominant workers' organization in the United States, but fewer than 10 percent of the nation's wage earners were organized into unions eligible for AFL membership.

THE TWENTIETH CENTURY

Evidence of the ways in which racial diversity can be utilized both to help and to hinder the labor movement is not restricted to the nineteenth century. Similar examples can be found in the second wave of labor organization that hit the United States in the 1930s.

The American Federation of Labor had survived into this decade despite the continuance of its strategies of labor elitism and racial division. The descendants of the craft union leaders who had come together in the federation of the 1880s sought to retain the legacy of their power and standing as the "aristocracy of labor." They continued to deny membership to unskilled or semiskilled immigrant labor from the mass-production industries; they also prohibited other leaders from organizing these workers in new unions.

AFL leaders doubted the ability of immigrant groups to provide valuable support for the labor movement. Racist and nativist ideologies led many to see these groups not as a possibly valuable coalition in the advancement of labor policies but as individual nationalities whose differences were potentially subversive to the labor movement. As a source of cheap labor, immigrant groups emerged as second only to capitalists themselves as organizers' and native workers' enemies.

Debate over this issue culminated between 1935 and 1938, when John L. Lewis and seven other AFL leaders broke from the Federation to form the Congress of Industrial Organizations (CIO). They asserted that the same defensive mindset that manifested itself within the AFL in exclusionary impulses could also impart great cohesion toward resistance to employers. To this extent, the CIO was organized to solidify those workers whom the AFL ignored or overlooked: the semiskilled and unskilled immigrant and minority ranks. Altogether, more than 1.8 million workers were organized by the CIO, and they proved to be a valuable tool toward labor advancement.

The CIO utilized its large membership (and the ethnic and ideological solidarity it often represented) to challenge repressive labor practices in the steel and automobile industries. In these challenges, the tool of the CIO was the sit-down strike: Instead of walking off the job and picketing, workers went to their posts in the plants and stayed there, making it difficult for others to replace them. In 1937, successful sit-down strikes against General Motors, Chrysler, and US Steel won the CIO recognition as the bargaining agent for workers previously thought unorganizable.

The eventual merger of the AFL and the CIO in 1955 was of great interest to minority labor. CIO leader Walter Reuther and AFL leader George Meany worked declarations of opposition to racial discrimination into the new organization's merger agreement and subsequent constitution. Members of both organizations hailed these statements, but they still waited anxiously to see if the words would be backed by actions. These members would be both pleased and disappointed. The AFL-CIO won respect in the black community early in its career when its executive council called on President Dwight D. Eisenhower to comply with the US Supreme Court's 1954 decision on school desegregation and deny school-construction funds to any state that defied the ruling. Yet it also antagonized the black community by remaining aloof during the great Montgomery bus boycott of 1955 and 1956.

The 1950s were charged with racial strife, and racial tensions often exacerbated difficulties in labor organization and negotiation. Specifically, most AFL-CIO union leaders feared regional political and economic repercussions and avoided adopting a stand clearly in favor of egalitarian racial principles. The ultimate result was the alienation of black workers from the AFL-CIO. Indeed, the National Association for the Advancement of Colored People (NAACP) issued a report in 1959 announcing that the AFL-CIO had not achieved its merger goals, having failed to unify racial and labor issues.

AFRICAN AMERICANS

Even before the CIO's split from the AFL, A. Philip Randolph had welded a powerful union from the many African Americans who worked on the nation's passenger railroads. Randolph's organization, the Brotherhood of Sleeping Car Porters, won significant concessions from the Pullman Company in the 1930s and later provided a solid base from which black labor could challenge discrimination on a variety of fronts. In 1941, Randolph organized a march on Washington to protest discrimination in the defense industry; he canceled the march when President Franklin D. Roosevelt agreed to issue an executive order forbidding employment discrimination by defense contractors. Further pressure by Randolph and the union helped prompt President Harry S Truman to end segregation in the armed forces in 1948. After the AFL-CIO merger in 1955, Randolph became the only black member of the union's executive council.

The 1960s and 1970s saw more African American and Mexican American laborers attempt to assert their political, economic, and social identities. During these decades, a movement was begun to unify labor and civil rights issues and to extend that cause through the nation. Such a movement began locally, however, with significant labor strikes among black sanitation workers in Memphis, Tennessee, and black hospital workers in Charleston, South Carolina.

The strikes at Memphis and Charleston were among previously unorganized, heavily exploited, poverty-level workers who desired safer working conditions, better pay, and job security. Both strikes were bitterly opposed by the power structure in the communities involved, yet both were supported by top civil rights leaders, including Ralph Abernathy and

Coretta Scott King. The strikes also won the support of powerful unions, including the United AutoWorkers' Union, the United Steelworkers of America, the United Rubber Workers, and the Tobacco Workers' International Union. Further, the black community at large bolstered the strikers through marches, mass meetings, boycotts, and financial aid. Despite their overall success, both strikes received only limited support from white workers.

LATINOS

This struggle for black equality was paralleled by the rising aspirations of Hispanic Americans, including Cubans, Puerto Ricans, and Mexicans. Although these groups were linked by similar ethnic roots and by a common language and religious heritage, their labor experiences differed. Mexican American laborers, in particular, advanced under the leadership of César Chávez, the son of migrant farm workers. In the early 1960s, pressure from Chávez and other activists helped force the end of the Bracero program, a government-sponsored importation of Mexican laborers that had undercut the agricultural labor market since the early part of World War II. In 1965, Chávez's leadership launched the Delano Grape Strike, which brought national attention to the plight of migrant farm workers; he subsequently became head of the newly formed United Farm Workers. Chávez continued to use strikes and national boycotts against fruit- and vegetable-raising agribusinesses to win concessions from California grape growers. Yet as important as the victories of the United Farm Workers were, in both an economic and a cultural sense, the union, in an increasingly urbanized nation, could not become a major organizational base among the primarily rural Mexican American population as a whole.

ASIAN AMERICANS

In recent decades, Hispanic and black workers have continued their struggle for labor and ethnic recognition and have been joined in this effort by other minority labor groups. One of the most active since the early 1990s has been the Asian Pacific American Labor Alliance (APALA), founded in 1992 to address the needs of the Asian and Pacific Island American labor community. APALA's commitment to labor includes the empowerment of all Asian Pacific workers through unionization on a national level and the provision of national support for individual, local unionization efforts. The organization actively promotes the formation of AFL-CIO legislation to create jobs, ensure national health insurance, and reform labor law. It also supports national governmental action to prevent workplace discrimination against immigrant laborers and to prosecute perpetrators of racially motivated crimes.

These efforts of the Asian Pacific American Labor Alliance are certainly not the final word on the relevance of racial and ethnic diversity to the labor movement. Their successes have not resolved the debate about the role of immigrant and minority workers in American labor, but they have ensured the continuance of discussion. Indeed, many of the same issues that have captured the attention of American labor organizers since the late nineteenth century continue to spark debate: the means to secure just and equitable treatment, higher wages, and other improvements in working conditions. Unlike in earlier eras, however, since the 1980s labor organizations have been challenged by both business and government to an unprecedented degree, leaving many organizations severely depleted in membership.

——*Thomas J. Edward Walker and Cynthia Gwynne Yaudes*

BIBLIOGRAPHY AND FURTHER READING

Alimahomed-Wilson, Jake. *Solidarity Forever? Race, Gender, and Unionism in the Ports of Southern California.* Lanham: Lexington Books, 2016. Print.

Asher, Robert, and Charles Stephenson, eds. *Labor Divided: Race and Ethnicity in United States Labor Struggles, 1835–1960.* Albany: State U of New York P, 1990. Print.

Kent, Ronald C., et al., eds. *Culture, Gender, Race and US Labor History.* Westport: Greenwood, 1993. Print.

Pozzetta, George E., ed. *Unions and Immigrants: Organization and Struggle.* New York: Garland, 1991. Print.

Zieger, Robert H. *For Jobs and Freedom: Race and Labor since 1865.* Lexington: UP of Kentucky, 2014. Print.

LATINOS: AN OVERVIEW

The Latino minority, also often referred to as the Hispanic American sector of United States society, continues to increase in proportion to the total population with each succeeding decade. The US Census Bureau defines "Hispanic or Latino" as a person of any race whose cultural background or place of origin is a Spanish-speaking country (primarily those of Latin America); other sources define the term to include people from a Brazilian (Portuguese-speaking) background, and some people make distinctions between the terms "Hispanic" and "Latino," but this article will use the Census definition. In 2013, The US Census Bureau estimated that nearly 52 million (16.6 percent) of residents of the United States were Hispanic or Latino. Almost two-thirds of those were Mexican Americans. Included in these numbers are recent immigrants, those who have arrived from Latin American nations both legally and illegally, and US citizens whose families have been residents of the United States for many generations. The combination of this group's high birthrate coupled with the constant influx of immigrants into the United States has led to the prediction that by the year 2040 the Latino population will approach 95 million, representing 25 percent of the total US population.

NATIONALISM

The Latino population described above is far from a homogeneous cultural group. Its members can be characterized better by their diversity than by their similarity. Strong nationalistic identification with their countries or regions of origin serves to divide Mexican Americans from Cuban Americans from Puerto Ricans—and a host of other nationals—and to militate against their acting in concert politically, economically, or socially. For example, the large Cuban American colony in greater Miami, Florida, tends to be highly conservative politically, while the Puerto Ricans of New York state and the Mexican Americans of California generally are Democratic or liberal in political affiliation.

RACE AND ETHNICITY

Members of the Latino community run the gamut of virtually every racial and ethnic group found in the world. The initial voyages of exploration and discovery of the Western Hemisphere by Europeans from Spain, England, Portugal, France, and the Netherlands led quickly to a racial amalgamation of these primarily Caucasian peoples with the bronze-skinned indigenous peoples mistakenly called "Indians" (under the false belief that they occupied the Asian continent). This admixture of races resulted in what came to be referred to in Spanish America as mestizos, soon to become the predominant racial entity throughout much of Central and South America, as well as what would ultimately become the US Southwest.

When the European settlers in Mexico, Central America, and South America found that they could not successfully exploit the indigenous peoples in mining and agriculture, they turned to the importation of Africans, initially as indentured servants but ultimately as slaves. England, France, Portugal, Spain, and the Netherlands entered into an extensive and lucrative transshipment of Africans to the Western Hemisphere, where they were sold as labor for the mining of precious metals and the manufacture of sugar, cotton, rice, and a wide variety of other marketable crops.

Owners of black slaves bred their human chattels with other slaves as part of the existing economic system, and soon blacks—now typed as mulattoes, quadroons, octoroons, and other racial mixtures—became part of a gene pool already containing a mixture of Caucasian and American Indian strains. In the course of the centuries that followed, Asians joined the heterogeneous racial population that spread throughout the Western Hemisphere. Chinese settled in substantial numbers along the borders of Mexico's northernmost states. Faced with persecution by warring factions during Mexico's Revolution of 1910, they migrated to the United States in large numbers.

RELIGION

When Europeans landed in what became Mexico in the sixteenth century, they encountered a highly civilized society that was in many ways more advanced than that of Europe at the time. Spaniards, however, did not perceive or value the cultural sophistication of the newly discovered civilization—considering it their responsibility, rather, to replace what they perceived as a heretic religion (in which the Aztec emperor was revered as a demigod) with Catholicism. The Europeans therefore adopted a program of ruthless destruction of what they considered idolatry. Similarly, in other parts of the continent, Portuguese, French, and English forced their own brands of Christianity on the natives whom they conquered and exploited. In the initial four centuries following the opening of the hemisphere, Catholicism and Protestantism became the dominant religions throughout North, Central, and South America.

Nevertheless, some indigenous peoples attempted to retain their identification with their old gods. Often this took the form of hiding their ancient sacred images behind the altars of European places of worship. Today, in more tolerant times, native and European religions are often practiced side by side, venerating gods and saints together, although by different names, as can be seen in contemporary Guatemala.

African slaves, seized and transported from their native lands to the Western Hemisphere, often brought their native religions with them, a source of comfort and hope under truly trying conditions. These African religions, sometimes modified by exposure to Christian sects, have open, active communicants in countries such as Haiti, Cuba, the Dominican Republic, and Brazil. Immigrants to the United States from these nations often bring these ancestral religious practices with them. These religious societies play an active role in the daily lives of their followers in the United States.

LANGUAGE

Most second- and third-generation Latinos in the United States have a good command of English. Newcomers, however—like most immigrants from non-English-speaking nations—often lack basic English-language skills, severely limiting their ability to progress economically, politically, and socially. In a few areas, there are neighborhoods large and insular enough in their organization, and where Spanish is so widely spoken among commercial establishments, that English is unnecessary to carry on daily activities. Opportunities exist in most areas, however, for newcomers to acquire the basic English skills necessary to move into the mainstream of US culture. Nevertheless, some immigrants from isolated communities in Latin America, often still committed to tribal mores and language, find it difficult to blend into the larger culture. Some do not even speak Spanish, but depend on native dialects such as Mayan, Quechua, or Nahuatl for communication. Lacking either English or Spanish, quite often these small, essentially tribal, groups are subject to exploitation by unscrupulous business interests and often are forced to work for miserably low wages and threatened with being turned in to US immigration authorities if they seek redress under the law.

MEXICO
Mexico leads all other nations both in the number of foreign-born living in the United States and in the quantity of new Mexican immigrants arriving each year. With a population of over 120 million, Mexico cannot provide enough jobs for those entering its workforce every year. This pool of surplus labor, combined with the availability of unskilled or entry-level jobs in the United States, has accounted for Mexico's primary position in terms of immigrant influx. There were an estimated 33 million Mexican Americans as of 2013.

Included in this wave of new arrivals are members of Mexico's Indian communities, who speak a variety of tribal tongues as their first language. Primarily from rural areas and with a minimum of education, they are subject to economic exploitation to a greater degree than are other immigrants.

Mexicans have lived in areas of what is now the United States since before they were incorporated into the Union. Texas, New Mexico, Arizona, and California were under the Mexican flag until the Mexican-American War of 1846–1848. The Treaty of Guadalupe Hidalgo signed in 1848 between the two countries ceded this territory to the United States for $15 million—a cheap price for the Americans.

PUERTO RICO
The United States defeated Spain in a brief war in 1898. In the ensuing Treaty of Paris, Spain gave up Puerto Rico, the Philippine Islands, and Guam to the victorious Americans. The United States also reluctantly agreed to the island of Cuba's independence under that treaty. However, the Americans retained sovereignty over Puerto Rico, viewing it as critical to US defenses in the event of an attack

from the Caribbean. In 1953, Puerto Rico achieved Commonwealth status, becoming a self-governing territory.

Following World War II, thousands of Puerto Ricans moved to the continental United States. In the immediate postwar period, airplane fares to the mainland sold for as little as seventy-five dollars. Because they are by law US citizens, Puerto Rican immigrants are required only to demonstrate proof of birth in Puerto Rico before entering the continental United States. They now make up the second-largest Hispanic American community, numbering about 4.9 million in 2013.

CUBA
The takeover in 1959 of the island of Cuba by Fidel Castro and his supporters resulted in a mass exodus of much of the country's upper-class and middle-class professional and business interests, who did not agree with the imposition of what eventually became a socialist, Communist-supported regime. Numbering close to one million, most of these refugees established themselves initially in the greater Miami area. In the spring of 1980, the Mariel boatlift brought a second wave of refugees, numbering perhaps one hundred thousand, to the United States with the permission of both the Castro regime and the administration of President Jimmy Carter. The Cuban American community, numbering about 1.9 million in 2013 and still centered in southern Florida, developed into a powerful economic and political force.

CENTRAL AMERICA
Throughout the 1970s and 1980s, the countries of El Salvador, Guatemala, and Nicaragua were plagued by civil wars. As a consequence of those unsettled political times, between one million and one and a half million Central American refugees entered the United States. Nicaraguans had easy access, since the United States compared the leftist government of Daniel Ortega to Castro's regime in Cuba. US supporters of Salvadoran and Guatemalan refugees insisted on the same opportunity for victims of political oppression in those countries as well; this was known as the Sanctuary movement.

Most of these three groups have continued to remain in this country through one form of amnesty

LATIN AMERICAN MIGRATION TO THE UNITED STATES

Year	Event	Impact
1910–1920	Mexican Revolution	Ten years of political and economic chaos force a quarter million Mexicans to resettle north of the US-Mexico border.
1942–1964	Bracero program	Wartime labor shortages create a need for farmworkers that is filled by a Mexican and US program that brings Mexicans to the United States to work the fields. The program establishes a pattern of migration of farmworkers.
1945–1950	Puerto Rican immigration	Following World War II, seventy-five-dollar economy air flights permit thousands of Puerto Ricans to resettle in the New York area. Since Puerto Ricans are US citizens, no official entry papers are required.
1957–1960	Cuban Revolution	The takeover by the leftist Fidel Castro sends more than one million Cuban businesspeople and professionals to Miami.
1980–1990	Central American conflicts	Civil wars in El Salvador, Nicaragua, and Guatemala send more than one million political and economic refugees north, mostly to California and the East Coast.
1981–1990s	Mexican economic crises	The continuing erratic behavior of the Mexican economy, in addition to the inability of the country to provide employment for those entering the workforce each year, sends a constant wave of Mexican immigrants north to find work.

or another, concentrating in California, Florida, and communities on the Eastern seaboard.

DOMINICAN REPUBLIC

As has been the case with so many of the small Caribbean island nations, the Dominican Republic cannot furnish enough job opportunities for all its citizens. Depending primarily on the export of sugar, some mining, and the attraction of cruise ships to its ports, this country, which shares the island of Hispaniola with Haiti, exports a substantial number of its working-class citizenry as well.

Many Dominican immigrants seeking illegal entry into the United States have used Puerto Rico as a staging area. False documents are obtained to establish a Puerto Rican identity. Most Dominicans have gravitated to the New York area after arriving in the United States. The little island nation ranked fourteenth in recent figures on immigration to the United States.

OTHER LATIN AMERICANS

The balance of the Latin American countries have contributed immigrants as well, although generally as smaller percentages of their total populations. For example, the drug trade and the resulting political unrest has caused Bolivians, Peruvians, and Colombians to seek asylum in the United States, which continues to represent a beacon of hope to citizens of those countries where political disorder or economic deprivation threaten the lives of their citizens.

DIVERSITY V. UNITY

Despite the formidable growth of the Latino element in US society, its diversity has prevented this group from reaching its potential as a unitary political force. Instead, the members of each particular ethnicity have shown a preference to confine their organizational efforts to members of their own particular community—to establish themselves as Mexican American, Cuban American, or Puerto Rican political associations, with membership confined to their own ethnic group. Nevertheless, should there come a time when diverse organizations such as these come to realize the potential strength that their combined numbers represent, the fast-growing Latino contingent could become a major factor in determining the course of the future of the United States. In the interim, the Latino sons of immigrants have followed the paths of other racial and ethnic minorities in US society in past decades. Many, showing a high degree of individual initiative, have worked their way into positions of greater responsibility in business and the professions.

——*Carl Henry Marcoux*

BIBLIOGRAPHY AND FURTHER READING

Carr, Raymond. *Puerto Rico: A Colonial Experiment.* New York: Vantage, 1984. Print.

Fox, Geoffrey. *Hispanic Nation.* Secaucus: Carol Pub. Group, 1996. Print.

Hansen, Niles. *The Border Economy.* Austin: U of Texas P, 1981. Press. Levine, Robert. *Race and Ethnic Relations in Latin America and the Caribbean.* Metuchen: Scarecrow P, 1980. Print.

Malavé, Idelisse, and Esti Giordani. *Latino Stats: American Hispanics by the Numbers.* New York: New P, 2015. Print.

Mora, G. Cristina. *Making Hispanics: How Activists, Bureaucrats, and Media Constructed a New American.* Chicago: U of Chicago P, 2014. Print.

LATINOS: EMPLOYMENT

Latino Americans were the fastest-growing minority group in the United States during the last quarter of the twentieth century. In 1980, they made up 6.5 percent of the civilian population, and by 1996, they had increased to 10.6 percent. The Bureau of the Census indicated that this group reached 16 percent in 2010. Empirical research on their employment situation has lagged behind such rapid changes, and it is difficult to discern patterns and trends when the available statistical information is not broken down into national-origin subgroups.

HISTORICAL BACKGROUND

In the late nineteenth century and early twentieth century, Mexican laborers (mainly displaced peasants) began to cross the border into the American Southwest to find work. Throughout the twentieth century, US immigration policy alternatively encouraged and restricted the entry of Mexicans, but the net result has been essentially a steady stream of immigrants. Their numbers, along with the descendants of earlier Mexican immigrants, have made Mexicans the largest subgroup of Latinos in the United States.

During World War I, Puerto Ricans were granted citizenship to ease US labor shortages. By 1920, nearly 12,000 Puerto Ricans had left their home for the United States, settling mostly in New York City and finding employment mainly in manufacturing and services. Their numbers have grown, making them the second largest Latino subgroup.

Cubans constitute the third most numerous subgroup. From 1959, the year when Fidel Castro assumed power following the Cuban Revolution, to 1990, the Cuban population in the United States—which had previously numbered only about 30,000—grew to 1,044,000 people.

THE LATINO AMERICAN LABOR FORCE

The Latino American share in the civilian labor force was 5.7 percent of the total in 1980, but it had almost doubled by 1996, to 9.6 percent. As of 2013, 16 percent of the labor force was Hispanic.

In the 1980s and 1990s, the labor force participation rates (that is, the percentage of persons who are employed) for the Latino population age sixteen and older approximated those of the non-Latino white population in the same age group (66.5 percent for

Latinos and 67.2 percent for non-Latino whites in 1996). However, the rate for Latino men (79.6 percent) was higher than that for non-Latino white men (75.8 percent) in the same year, while Latinas had a lower rate (53.4 percent) than non-Latino white women (59.1 percent).

The occupational distribution of the Latino population reflects both the traditional background of the subgroups and the economic changes of later decades. According to the *Statistical Abstract*, in 1996, Mexicans were mostly operators, fabricators, and laborers (24.5 percent); they also had the highest percentage of workers in farming, forestry, and fishing among all the other subgroups (8.4 percent). Cubans had the highest proportion in managerial and professional occupations (21.7 percent) as well as in technical, sales, and administrative support positions (32.7 percent). The advances made by Puerto Ricans were evidenced by the fact that their concentration in the latter positions (32.1 percent) and in managerial and professional occupations (19 percent) closely approximated those of the Cubans. However, this advance may be more apparent than real because of changes in the occupational structure that have reduced the availability of lower-level, high-paying blue-collar occupations in favor of low-paying white-collar occupations.

COMPARISON WITH NON-LATINO WHITES

A comparison of the occupational distribution of Latinos with that of non-Latino whites reveals that the former are concentrated in lower-level occupations and that white men are concentrated in managerial and professional occupations. In the late 1980s, Mexican American men were concentrated in skilled and semiskilled blue-collar jobs, although they were advancing to better jobs; Puerto Rican men were in service and lower-level white-collar jobs. Latinas were more likely than white or black women to be semiskilled manual workers.

Regarding the evolution of Latino earnings and incomes, Gregory DeFreitas reports that in 1949, US-born men of Mexican and Puerto Rican ancestry had incomes that were 55 percent and 76 percent, respectively, of the white non-Latino level. During the 1960s, both groups improved relative to whites; but in the 1970s, the Puerto Ricans experienced a decline and the Mexicans remained at the

same level. Latinos generally suffered decreases in income during the 1970s. Median Latino incomes declined in absolute and relative terms after the 1970s. By 1987, Latino income was still almost 9 percent lower in real terms than it had been in 1973 and, when compared with the income of non-Latino whites, even lower than it had been fifteen years earlier.

According to the *Statistical Abstract*, the median income of Latino households, at constant 1995 dollars, was $25,278 in 1980; it rose later to $26,037 in 1990 but fell to $22,860 in 1995. It was 64 percent of the white non-Latino median income, which in 1995 was $35,766, and practically equal to that of blacks, which stood that year at $22,393.

Since the 1950s, Latinos have made progress in occupational mobility and earning levels, especially during periods of economic expansion. Cuban Americans are nearly equal with non-Latino whites in educational and economic achievement; Mexican Americans and Puerto Ricans, however, are still the most disadvantaged.

UNEMPLOYMENT

Unemployment has been a long-term problem for Latinos. Their actual unemployment rates reflect structural factors such as business-cycle fluctuations, industrial restructuring, and changes in demand as well as individual characteristics such as educational level and previous work experience. As indicated in the *Statistical Abstract* (1997), in 1980, the total unemployment rate was 7.1 percent, while it was 10.1 percent for Latinos. By 1992, these rates had risen to 7.5 and 11.6 percent, respectively. In 1996, both had decreased; the total rate stood at 5.4 percent and the Latino rate at 8.9 percent.

The rates, however, vary among the national-origin subgroups. Cuban Americans' unemployment rates have been almost as low as those of non-Latino whites, largely because of their above-average educational levels and accumulated work experience. By contrast, Mexican Americans and Puerto Ricans have generally experienced above-average unemployment. Puerto Ricans' unemployment rates are usually twice as high as those of Cuban Americans. Some scholars claim that Puerto Ricans' history of "circular migration" (their frequent returns to the island) tends to destabilize their employment.

FACTORS THAT INFLUENCE THE LATINO LABOR MARKET

Education is one of the main factors that affect the labor market situation for Latinos. DeFreitas, after analyzing the trends in earnings of Latinos and non-Latinos from 1949 to 1979, found that those Latinos who were better educated were able to approximate the earnings of non-Latino whites in the 1960s.

Limited English ability is another relevant factor. Several empirical studies carried out in the 1980s found that language limitations could account for up to one-third of wage differentials between Latino and non-Latino white men. Other research has established that Puerto Rican and Cuban American men, who are concentrated in urban areas, tend to have lower participation rates in the labor force than men from the same national-origin subgroups with better English language skills. Mexican Americans, who are mainly operators, fabricators, laborers, and agricultural workers, have higher participation rates because those occupations do not require a good command of English.

Empirical studies have tried to establish the extent of discrimination suffered by Latinos in the labor market. According to the findings of a major study undertaken by the General Accounting Office (1990) to evaluate the effects of the Immigration Reform and Control Act of 1986, discrimination in hiring is practiced against "foreign-looking" or "foreign-sounding" applicants. In particular, an audit carried out as part of the study found that Hispanic job seekers were more likely than similarly qualified Anglos to be unfavorably treated and less likely to receive interviews and job offers. Consequently, discrimination could partially account for the higher Latino unemployment rates.

Self-employment may be a way to escape unemployment, low wages, and obstacles to promotion. However, capital is required to start a business, and many poorer Latinos find it difficult to accumulate savings and are not likely to receive loans from credit institutions. Cuban Americans, who have a higher status background, have opened many small businesses, creating an "ethnic enclave" of Latino businesses in Miami. The benefits of this type of social and economic arrangement have been highly debated. Some contend that it is an avenue of economic mobility for new immigrants; others argue that it may hinder their assimilation into the larger society. However, given the small proportion of self-employed Latinos and the level of their earnings, it is not likely that this type of employment will soon become a prevalent means to reduce inequality for Latinos in the labor market.

—————*Graciela Bardallo-Vivero*

BIBLIOGRAPHY AND FURTHER READING

Allegro, Linda, and Andrew Grant Wood. *Latin American Migrations to the US Heartland: Changing Social Landscapes in Middle America.* Urbana: U of Illinois P, 2013. Digital file.

Blancero, Donna, and Robert G. DelCamp. *Hispanics at Work: A Collection of Research, Theory, and Application.* Hauppauge: Nova, 2012. Print.

DeFreitas, Gregory. *Inequality at Work: Hispanics in the US Labor Force.* New York: Oxford UP, 1991. Print.

Kanellos, Nicolás, ed. *The Hispanic American Almanac.* New York: Gale, 1997. Knouse, Stephen B., P. Rosenfeld, and A. L. Culbertson, ed. *Hispanics in the Workplace.* Newbury Park: Sage, 1992. Print.

LATINOS: FAMILIES AND SOCIALIZATION

The implications of family and socialization among Latinos is especially significant to racial and ethnic relations in the United States because Latinos are the fastest-growing populations in the nation. The group known as Latinos encompasses numerous subgroups traceable to various regions of the Americas and the Caribbean and a wide range of socioeconomic, cultural, and national backgrounds. Generalizations about such a diverse group therefore will not apply to many groups and individuals who are Latinos. Nonetheless, some common family characteristics and socialization patterns exist among the major Latino groups in the United States: Mexicans, Puerto Ricans, and Cubans. These patterns of commonality are a result of similar historical experiences and colonial conditions, cultural continuity, proximity to or contact with their homelands, and exposure to discrimination. Therefore, although the first Mexicans became Americans through annexation of northern Mexico, Puerto Ricans through their commonwealth status and political territorial relationship with the United States, and Cubans through their arrival as refugees, each group had to survive and adapt to a dramatically different social, cultural, political, and economic context in the United States. These historical conditions generated common family characteristics and socialization patterns.

FAMILY CHARACTERISTICS

Although Latino families are in flux, continuing to adapt, families in the major Latino groups can be characterized in terms of familism, extended kin structures, myths of machismo, and biculturalism. "Familism" refers to the priority placed on the family as opposed to individual interests. Family unity is believed to be central to life among many Latino families. In addition to this emphasis on family solidarity, sociologist Maxine Baca Zinn identifies other dimensions of familism among Mexican families regarding family size (demographic familism), multigenerational households (structural familism), and interaction in kinship networks (behavioral familism). These additional dimensions of familism explain the prevalence of extended kin structures among Latino families, which often provide emotional and financial support. Extended family formations also extend to nonrelatives or fictive-kin. The *compadrazgo* system, for example, establishes relations between parents and godparents or coparents, further locating the Latino family within a larger network of support and reciprocity. In addition, *respeto* (respect and support for elders) remains a viable value within the extended family structure. This is an important indicator of multigenerational relations, which is central to the extended family structure.

Extended family structures are also central to generating economic resources among Cubans, in spite of blocked financial opportunities within mainstream markets of the United States. Using these extended family structures, Cuban exiles in the early 1960s generated funds for investment within ethnic enclaves. In this way, kinship relations extended to the communal level, creating ethnic communities and generating upward mobility.

Although popular notions describe Latino families as the epitome of patriarchy, authoritarianism, and machismo, more recent research suggests that Latino families are no more patriarchal than mainstream American families. In fact, Latino families continue to move toward egalitarian familial relations as Latinas continue to achieve higher familial status from their labor force participation and control of the household. Sociologist and legal scholar Alfredo Mirande dispels many myths of Latino masculinity by showing some aspects of Latino male sensitivity, emotional expression, and egalitarian family relations between Chicanos and Chicanas.

Although Latino families in the United States maintain cultural continuity, they undergo a hybridization process, incorporating new cultural forms into their traditional culture to adapt to changing social conditions. Therefore, Latino families are neither equivalent to mainstream American families nor replicas of traditional families in their homelands. For example, Puerto Rican studies professor Hector Carrasquillo describes the innovative strategy of fusing mainland US values and the English language with traditional Puerto Rican culture and the Spanish language. A similar process of hybridization also seems evident among Chicanos in the Southwest.

SOCIALIZATION AND PSYCHOLOGICAL WELL-BEING

The complex history of racial and ethnic relations that shaped Latino family characteristics can affect socialization and individual well-being. Social work professors Andres G. Gil and William A. Vega noted the important role of the family in buffering stress associated with immigrant adaptation among Cuban and Nicaraguan families. They showed that low family cohesion was related to parent-child conflicts and poor adolescent self-esteem in the context of acculturation pressures.

Social scientists Kathleen Ethier and Kay Deaux explored the experiences of Hispanic students at two predominantly white Ivy League universities and analyzed the relationships between strength of cultural background, ethnic identification, self-esteem, and perceptions of threat to Hispanic identity within dominant Euro-American institutions. Based on interviews, the researchers found that the majority of

Hispanic students felt their ethnic identity, derived from their family socialization, was an important dimension of the self. Strength of ethnic identification was found to buffer perceived threats and to increase collective self-esteem among Hispanic students.

Exploring extended family systems, self-esteem, and support for Hispanic elderly, social work professor Juan J. Paz showed that family support is a major source of positive self-esteem for the elderly. Hispanic elders tend to hold a collective self-identity embedded in the family, and therefore, emotional and social support from the family has positive social psychological outcomes. On the other hand, researchers Robert Strom, Lydia P. Buki, and Shirley K. Strom revealed higher levels of frustration among Spanish-speaking grandparents with the English-speaking younger generations than among bilingual grandparents. This implies that cultural and language departure create negative well-being among the Mexican American elderly.

——*Michael P. Perez*

BIBLIOGRAPHY AND FURTHER READING

Ethier, Kathleen, and Kay Deaux. "Hispanics in Ivy: Assessing Identity and Perceived Threat." *Sex Roles* 22.7–8 (1990): 427–40. Print.

Gil, Andres G., and William A. Vega. "Two Different Worlds: Acculturation Stress and Adaptation among Cuban and Nicaraguan Families." *Journal of Social and Personal Relationships* 13.3 (1996): 435–56. Print.

Mirande, Alfredo. *Hombres y Machos: Masculinity and Latino Culture*. Boulder: Westview, 1997. Print.

Strom, Robert, Lydia P. Buki, and Shirley K. Strom. "Intergenerational Perceptions of English Speaking and Spanish Speaking Mexican-American Grandparents." *International Journal of Aging and Human Development* 45.1 (1997): 1–21. Print.

Taylor, Ronald L., ed. *Minority Families in America: A Multicultural Perspective*. 2nd ed. Upper Saddle River: Prentice, 1998. Print.

Zentella, Ana Celia. *Building on Strength: Language and Literacy in Latino Families*. New York: Teachers College P, 2005. Print.

LATINOS: FILM

Latinos portrayed in early films were predominantly Mexicans or Mexican Americans, given the vast number of Westerns produced by the American film industry. Puerto Ricans, as an ethnic group, began to appear in later decades, generally in an urban setting.

ETHNOCENTRISM IN AMERICAN FILM
The target audience of the filmmakers in the first half of the twentieth century was predominantly white, Anglo-Saxon, and US-born. Racial prejudice was the norm; nonwhites were not allowed to participate in film production and were unwelcome in motion picture theaters.

Western genre films were set in the Southwest, which is made up of the states ceded by Mexico in the Treaty of Guadalupe Hidalgo (1848). The narrative formula of nineteenth century dime novels was adapted to the screen with only minor variations. The Mexican-US conflict was presented as a conflict of cultures based on stereotypes. The Anglo (non-Hispanic) society values of thrift, hard work, and democracy were contrasted with the laziness, backwardness, and despotic power structures of Mexican society. In these films, the moral superiority of the Americans justified their overcoming the more primitive Hispanic society in their western expansion.

Some scholars distinguish the following types of Latino characters in early American films: the main male type is the greedy Mexican bandit, or greaser. The second type is the bumbling buffoon, usually an inept sidekick. Greasers or buffoons belong to the lower classes; not so the third type, the aristocratic caballero, a kind of Latino Robin Hood in colonial California, exemplified by Zorro, the Cisco Kid, and don Arturo Bodega. In the early 1930s, a fourth type appeared: the greaser gangster, who was a coward and a traitor. The fifth type is the Latin lover, a modern version of Don Juan.

Latinas had much more restricted roles: They existed in relationship to an Anglo hero. The usual types were the sexy cantina girl; the self-sacrificing, faithful señorita; and the vamp or seductress.

THE 1930S

The heightened concern with social conditions brought about by the Great Depression was reflected in Hollywood's "social problem" films. The crude ethnic stereotypes of early films began to give way to stronger and more psychologically complex characters. The formula for these films was that sometimes American social institutions experienced problems that needed to be corrected by limited social change; therefore, the oppressed had to be patient and have faith that in the end justice would prevail.

The first Hispanic social problem film, *Bordertown* (1935), ends with the disillusioned Chicano protagonist returning to his barrio home, a suggestion that acceptance of the status quo is the right moral choice. However, the two best social problem films about Latinos, which were independently produced, *The Lawless* (1950) and *Salt of the Earth* (1954), portrayed Mexicans as real people who fought for their rights. Two important "historical message" films were *Juárez* (1939) and *Viva Zapata!* (1952), in which Mexican characters and Mexican history were treated much better than usual.

WORLD WAR II

The Good Neighbor policy practiced by the United States toward Latin America during World War II as a way of securing alliances against Nazism resulted in two Disney animated films: *Saludos Amigos* (1943) and *The Three Caballeros* (1945), as well as a series of escapist Latin musicals, designed to improve hemispheric relations.

Some Latino actors were able to use stereotypical Hispanic roles, which were first played by American actors, as an effective vehicle to stardom. One of these actors was Lupe Vélez, the typical "Mexican Spitfire"; another was Leo Carrillo, who played gangsters and border bandits. When the star system began to dominate Hollywood, light-skinned Hispanic actors had to choose between being typecast in negative ethnic roles or anglicizing their names and their images to "reposition" themselves. Margarita Carmen Cansino became Rita Hayworth, and Raquel Tejada became Raquel Welch.

THE 1960S AND BEYOND

In the 1960s, the liberalization of sexual mores, the emergence of the civil rights movement, and a growing Hispanic filmgoing audience profoundly affected the film industry. The classical Hispanic stereotypes were intensified by the explicit sex and violence of the new Westerns. Hollywood created new stereotypes such as the Hispanic avenger and youthful Hispanic gang member. Notable examples of the gang theme are *West Side Story* (1961) and *The Young Savages* (1961); *Boulevard Nights* (1979) and *Colors* (1988) treat the topic with more realism. Films of this genre usually presented Puerto Rican main characters as gang members involved in violent acts, thus reinforcing the notion that all Hispanics are law breakers.

In the 1970s and 1980s, two parallel phenomena fundamentally altered the position of Hispanics in the film industry. Members of the Chicano movement, determined to present their own view of the Chicano experience, began independently to produce and direct documentaries and docudramas, and later, feature films, some of which were aired on television and some supported and distributed by Hollywood. Outstanding examples are *Alambrista!* (1977, Robert M. Young), *The Ballad of Gregorio Cortez* (1982, Moctesuma Esparza and Robert M. Young), *Seguín* (1981, Jesús Salvador Treviño), and *El Norte* (1983, Gregory Nava).

The second phenomenon, known as "Hispanic Hollywood," resulted from the greater participation of Latinos as producers and directors in Hollywood films beginning in the 1980s, which was believed to be a result of the pressure exerted on the studios by Hispanic civil rights organizations to open more jobs to Latinos. *La Bamba* (1987), *Born in East L.A.* (1987), *The Milagro Beanfield War* (1987), and *Stand and Deliver* (1988) were some or its most successful products.

The 1990s and 2000s saw a growing range of films marketed to Latino audiences, paralleling the growth in the United States' Latino population. However, lead roles for Latino actors in mainstream movies remained rare. Although Latino filmmakers achieved some success, it was also uncommon for directors, producers, screenwriters, and other Latino film professionals to reach the broader population. Change happened slowly, with a few films such as Gregory Nava's *My Family* (1995) highlighting Mexican Americans as complex characters and leading protagonists. The biopic *Selena* (1997), based on the life of Mexican American singer Selena, was a critical and commercial success, opening as the second-highest grossing film at the time. Actors such as Jennifer Lopez, Cameron Diaz, and Edward James Olmos became well known, shifting cultural perceptions and aiding acceptance of Latino media presence. Still, many actors continued to fight typecasting and many filmmakers struggled to find mainstream opportunities into the 2010s. A 2013 study from the University of California found that although Latinos made up the largest percentage of moviegoers, only 4 percent of all acting roles were played by Latinos.

PUERTO RICAN FILMS

After several failed attempts by private companies and the government to develop film production on the island, Viguié Film Productions, founded in 1951, and the Division of Community Education, established in 1949, began to turn out an ever-increasing number of films. In the 1970s and 1980s, the political climate spurred the production of documentaries, some of which were made by Puerto Rican filmmakers working in Boston, New York, and Philadelphia.

Among feature films, one of the finest is *Hangin' with the Home Boys* (1991), directed by Joseph B. Vásquez.

——*Graciela Bardallo-Vivero*

BIBLIOGRAPHY AND FURTHER READING

Berumen, Frank Javier Garcia. *Latino Image Makers in Hollywood: Performers, Filmmakers, and Films Since the 1960s.* Jefferson: McFarland, 2014. Keller, Gary D. *A Biographical Handbook of Hispanics and United States Film.* Tempe: Bilingual, 1997. Print.

Keller, Gary D. *Hispanics and United States Film: An Overview and Handbook.* Tempe: Bilingual, 1994. Print.

Puente, Henry. *The Promotion and Distribution of US Latino Films.* New York: Lang, 2011. Print.

Smith, Stacy L., Marc Choueiti, and Katherine Pieper. "Race/Ethnicity in 500 Popular Films: Is the Key to Diversifying Cinematic Content Held in Hand of the Black Director?" *Annenberg School for Communication and Journalism.* USC, 2013. Web. 28 Apr. 2015.

LATINOS: STEREOTYPES

To gain an understanding of the stereotyping of Latinos in the United States, one must consider issues of race and class inherent in the social structures of Latin American cultures as well as the multifaceted, often class-based biases held by various groups of Americans against persons of Hispanic origin. Historically, the roots of Latino stereotyping in the United States can be traced to early contact between Americans and Mexicans in what was to become the Southwest during the early nineteenth century. This initial interaction between cultures, frequently in the context of battle, left Anglo (non-Hispanic) Americans with both positive and negative images of the Spanish-speaking peoples they encountered: American settlers in Texas often characterized Mexicans as a backward people hampered by cowardice, laziness, and treachery, a perception that gained popular momentum during the Mexican-American War of 1846-1848; conversely, American explorers of modern-day California portrayed the Mexicans they encountered there as primitive, carefree, and romantic.

These early images of Mexican people endured through the twentieth century alongside modern stereotypes of Hispanics as illegal aliens with few interests or abilities other than unskilled labor, petty crime, gang violence, and the cultivation of large extended families. Much of this negative imagery can be attributed to generalized perceptions of non-white groups by a dominant white society (dominant group); nevertheless, stereotypes specific to Latinos and Latino culture (such as the assumption that most Latinos are illegal aliens) abound. These stereotypes were perpetuated over time by white fears of crime, illegal immigration, welfare statism, and erosion of white majority status. In addition, white fears of increased Hispanic presence in the United States, and consequently white stereotypes of Latinos, were projected upon other minority groups such as African Americans, exacerbating tensions already present between these groups because of cultural differences and competition for jobs and housing.

Popular American stereotypes of Latinos have influenced and have been influenced by the self-perceptions of Hispanic Americans. Ethnic prejudices within Latino communities, originating in colonial caste systems that favored colonials over indigenous peoples, have contributed to coopting of Anglo American stereotypes by Hispanic Americans seeking to elevate their status in a white-dominated society by distinguishing themselves from other Latinos. For example, Hispanic peoples from South America and the Caribbean have resisted association with Mexicans because of the latter's association with illegal immigration, and Latinos in general historically have emphasized their Spanish heritage to dissociate themselves from "inferior" native peoples. Similarly, many Hispanic Americans have rejected the terms "Hispanic" and "Latino," arguing that they inaccurately portray Spanish-speaking peoples as a single ethnic group and thus encourage blanket stereotyping.

Increased emphasis upon ethnic heritage and identity in the 1960's accelerated the trend toward cultural distinctiveness among Hispanic Americans, sparking a renewed interest among young Latinos in preserving and nurturing previously disdained cultural traits and ethnic labels. For example, Mexican American youth adopted the term "Chicano," as a manifestation of ethnic pride (Chicano movement). "Mexicano" often cultivated stereotypical portrayals of Mexicans as emotionally volatile, sexually aggressive, and given to excessive leisure. Ironically, the more redeeming traits of this cultural revival were often romanticized and exploited by white liberals, reviving paternalistic nineteenth century stereotypes of Latinos as "noble savages" best shielded from the "corrupting" influences of mainstream American society. In 2012 the *Huffington Post* printed a study by the University of Cincinnati that

reported on the effects of public attitudes toward immigrants in the United States. The study found that Latin American stereotypes have the biggest impact on public attitude regarding immigration— that is, Latin Americans, when compared against other immigrant groups, were rated unwilling to fit in with Americans. In 2014, a study by the Center for the Study of Ethnicity and Race at Columbia University said, "stories about Latinos constitute less than one percent of news media coverage, and the majority of these stories feature Latinos as lawbreakers."

——*Michael H. Burchett*

BIBLIOGRAPHY AND FURTHER READING

Cockcroft, James D. *Latinos in the Making of the United States.* New York: Watts, 1995. Print.

Fuller, Dawn. "UC Research Examines Stereotypes of Immigrants to the United States." *University of Cincinnati.* U of Cincinnati, 10 Aug. 2009. Web. 19 May 2015.

Gates, Sara. "Impact of Latino Stereotypes: Latin Americans Viewed Most Negatively in Immigrant Comparison Study." *Huffington Post,* TheHuffingtonPost.com, 21 Aug. 2012. Web. 20 May 2015.

Maciel, David, Isidro D. Ortiz, and María Herrer-Sobek. *Chicano Renaissance: Contemporary Cultural Trends.* Tucson: U of Arizona P, 2000. Print.

Negrón-Muntaner, Frances, Chelsea Abbas, Luis Figueroa, and Samuel Robson. "The Latino Media Gap: A Report on the State of Latinos in US Media." *Center for the Study of Ethnicity and Race.* New York: Columbia U, 2014. PDF file.

LATINOS: WOMEN (LATINAS)

The Latina population of the United States is a geographically, socially, culturally, and economically diverse one that is bound more than in any other way by commonality of language. The US Census Bureau lists "Hispanic or Latino" as a single ethnic category and estimates that the total Hispanic population of the United States was about 54.1 million, or about 17.1 percent of the population, in 2013. The category "Hispanic" comprises anyone whose ancestry includes

Spanish-speaking people residing in Mexico, the Caribbean, Central or South America, or Spain. The terms "Latino" and "Latina" also describe linguistic heritage and may also include speakers of Portuguese, such as from Brazil and Portugal, or francophone peoples from Caribbean islands (although these are not the foremost associations made with the terms).

Since the mid-1980s, which saw the emergence of an important and particularly strong literary

Sonia Sotomayor, Associate Justice of the Supreme Court of the United States. By Collection of the Supreme Court of the United States, Steve Petteway source.

movement by women of Hispanic heritage, the word "Latina" seems to have been deemed the most appropriate designation for women with such a background for two main reasons: because of its potential inclusion of several groups, and because it does not carry the burdensome, racially charged connotation of ethnic undesirability.

MEXICAN AMERICANS

In the United States, three groups of Latinos are dominant in the population. In the Southwest, Mexican Americans (Chicanos) make up a substantial portion of the demographic group; in California, 25 percent of the state's residents are Latino, the majority of these Chicano. Additionally, throughout the Southwest, in states such as Texas, New Mexico, Arizona, and even Colorado, the Chicano population constitutes the largest non-white demographic group. This figure serves as the legacy of the US annexation of these states from Mexico at the conclusion of the Mexican-American War (1846–48). Most Chicano residents of those regions did not actually immigrate to the United States, but rather were assumed into the country and suddenly became "foreigners" in the place of their birth. Resonance from this historic event echoed into the feminine experience recounted up to 140 years later, in short stories by Chicana writers who talk about linguistic and social assimilation that was particularly difficult for women whose role was mainly domestic.

CUBAN AMERICANS

Cuban émigrés living in Florida, and particularly Miami, make up a substantial percentage of the overall population of Cuban Americans. Miami is only 90 miles from the Cuban capital of Havana, and the city continues to receive waves of exiles from this Communist regime, which was formed after the takeover by Fidel Castro in 1959. The presence of Cubans in the United States is attributable principally to political circumstances in their homeland. Even under the circumstances of political exile, Cuban women in the United States for more than a generation begin to face the same issues that confront other ethnic groups on arrival to a new country. They must decide to what level of assimilation they are willing to aspire, a difficulty compounded by the traditional domestic role for women in this culture, which keeps them out of the economic, educational, and political spheres of life in their adopted country.

PUERTO RICANS

For Puerto Ricans, the decision to adopt a new homeland was, in a sense, made for them. When Spain lost the Spanish-American War of 1898, it ceded Cuba and Puerto Rico to the United States. Cuba became an independent state, but Puerto Rico was made into a "free associated state," that is, a colony of the United States. Beginning in the 1930s, Puerto Rican migration to the mainland has been a steady and ongoing process, with the result that in New York, the Puerto Rican community dominates the Spanish-speaking landscape, taking a substantial lead over immigrants from the Dominican Republic, who have also established a community within the city. In the Midwest, a number of immigrant groups of Hispanic origin have established thriving communities in cities such as Chicago and Milwaukee.

MARGINALIZATION OF LATINAS

Within this continually growing and dynamic establishment of Latin culture in North America, women had, until the 1960s, been relegated to a domestic role, as dictated by traditional practice. Such traditions developed under the influence of the Catholic church in Mexico and by Afro-Caribbean religion in Puerto Rico, Cuba, and the Dominican Republic, and they persisted in the new homeland. The Latina's role was that of wife and mother. Docile, self-abnegating, submissive, and subservient, she was expected to accept silently the confines of a patriarchal upbringing in preparation for a patriarchal marriage. When economic circumstance dictated, a woman was to work outside the home, but her primary responsibility was the wishes and demands of her husband and the service of her children. The women's movement in the United States in the 1970s gave Anglo women freedom and access to many institutions previously reserved only for men, but it fell short of opening those same doors for Latinas, whose culture was parallel to yet considerably different from that of their Anglo counterparts.

It is difficult to generalize about Hispanic culture in terms of social mores because of the rapidly evolving role of Latinas in society, both in Anglo-dominated North America and in Latin homelands, but some common features have been present among Latino groups. In 1976, a presentation to the Conference on Educational and Occupational Needs of Women discussed in detail the "cult of virginity" as a cornerstone of Latina upbringing. A young girl was reared to preserve and protect her chastity at all times. A woman who enjoyed sexuality was seen as "loose" or "modern," while one who adhered to the patriarchal prototype could be proud of her decorum and respect for traditional values and was considered a credit to her family and an honor to her household. The veneration of the Virgin Mary in the Catholic Church played no small part in promoting this restrictive, often-silent role for women both in and outside of the home. A Latina who did not choose early marriage to a dominant man, who was not a virgin on the day of her marriage, or who had a knowledge and enjoyment of her sexuality could not live up to the ideal that would elevate her to an almost holy status within the family.

Education of a woman was often a release from her dependence on a man—her father, husband, brother, or son—and deemed a potentially dangerous pursuit, primarily from within the Latin culture but also from the Anglo perspective, which deemed manual labor the appropriate occupation for the Hispanic community. Education is the primary step in the emancipation of any group of people, especially a group at the margin of a dominant culture. Because of linguistic gaps, however, the education of Latinos requires another commitment to their assimilation into Anglo culture. In the 1960s, the Civil Rights movement and the War on Poverty waged by the administration of Lyndon B. Johnson yielded bilingual education opportunities that allowed many Latinas to enter the educational mainstream during that decade and to emerge some twenty years later with a dynamic new literary voice that described the Latina experience in the United States.

——*Helena Antolin Cochrane*

BIBLIOGRAPHY AND FURTHER READING

Abalos, David T. *The Latino Family and the Politics of Transformation.* Westport: Praeger, 1993. Print.

Bejarano, Christina E. *The Latina Advantage: Gender, Race, and Political Success.* Austin: U of Texas P, 2013. Print.

Garcia, Lorena. *Respect Yourself, Protect Yourself: Latina Girls and Sexual Identity.* New York: New York UP, 2012. Print.

Gutiérrez, Gabriel. *Latinos and Latinas at Risk: Issues in Education, Health, Community and Justice.* Santa Barbara: Greenwood, 2015. Print.

Horno Delgado, Asunció. *Breaking Boundaries: Latina Writing and Critical Readings.* Amherst: U of Massachusetts P, 1989. Print.

Rodríguez-Seda de Laguna, Asela. *Images and Identities: The Puerto Rican in Two World Contexts.* New Brunswick: Transaction, 1987. Print.

Valdivia, Angharad N., and Isabel Molina. "Disciplining the Ethnic Body: Latinidad, Hybridized Bodies, and Transnational Identity." Governing the Female Body: Gender, Health, and Networks of Power. Ed. Lori Reed and Paula Saukko. Albany: State U of New York P, 2010. 206–32. Print.

Weyr, Thomas. *Hispanic USA: Breaking the Melting Pot.* New York: Harper, 1988. Print.

LAU V. NICHOLS

In 1954, the Supreme Court ruled in *Brown v. Board of Education* that the Fourteenth Amendment to the US Constitution forbade school systems from segregating students into separate schools for only whites or African Americans. The decision effectively overturned a previous Court ruling, in *Plessy v. Ferguson* (1896), that such facilities could be "separate but equal." Instead of desegregating, however, Southern school systems engaged in massive resistance to the Court's order during the next decade. Congress then passed the Civil Rights Act of 1964, which prohibits many types of discrimination. Title VI of the law bans discrimination by recipients of federal financial assistance, including school systems.

CHINESE-SPEAKING STUDENTS

In 1965, Congress adopted the Immigration and Nationality Act, under which larger numbers of Asian immigrants arrived in the United States than ever before. Their non-English-speaking children were enrolled in public schools. In the San Francisco Unified School District, students were required to attend school until sixteen years of age, but in 1967, 2,856 students could not adequately comprehend instruction in English. Although 433 students were given supplemental courses in English on a full-time basis and 633 on a part-time basis, the remaining 1,790 students received no additional language instruction. Nevertheless, the state of California required all students to graduate with proficiency in English and permitted school districts to provide bilingual education, if needed. Except for the 433 students in the full-time bilingual education program, Chinese-speaking students were integrated in the same classrooms with English-speaking students but lacked sufficient language ability to derive benefit from the instruction. Of the 1,066 students taking bilingual courses, only 260 had bilingual teachers.

Some parents of the Chinese-speaking children, concerned that their children would drop out of school and experience pressure to join criminal youth gangs, launched protests. Various organizations formed in the Chinese American community, which in turn made studies, issued proposals, circulated leaflets, and tried to negotiate with the San Francisco Board of Education. When the board refused to respond adequately, a suit was filed in federal district court in San Francisco on March 25, 1970. The plaintiffs were Kinney Kinmon Lau and eleven other non-English-speaking students, mostly US citizens born of Chinese parents. The defendants were Alan H. Nichols, president of the San Francisco Board of Education, the rest of the Board of Education, and the San Francisco Board of Supervisors.

FINDINGS AND RULINGS

On May 25, 1970, the Office for Civil Rights (OCR) of the US Department of Health, Education, and Welfare issued the following regulation pursuant to its responsibility to monitor Title VI compliance: "Where inability to speak and understand the English language excludes national-origin minority group children from effective participation in the educational program offered by a school district, the district must take affirmative steps to rectify the language deficiency in order to open its instructional program to these students." OCR had sided with the Chinese-speaking students.

One day later, the court ruled that the school system was violating neither Title VI nor the Fourteenth Amendment; instead, the plaintiffs were characterized as asking for "special rights above those granted other children." Lawyers representing the Chinese Americans then appealed, this time supported by a friend-of-the-court brief filed by the US Department of Justice. On January 8, 1973, the Court of Appeals also ruled adversely, stating that there was no duty "to rectify appellants' special deficiencies, as long as they provided these students with access to the same educational system made available to all other students." The appeals court claimed that the children's problems were "not the result of law enacted by the state... but the result of deficiency created by themselves in failing to learn the English language."

On June 12, 1973, the Supreme Court agreed to hear the case. Oral argument was heard on December 10, 1973. On January 21, 1974, the Supreme Court unanimously overturned the lower courts. Justice William O. Douglas delivered the majority opinion, which included the memorable statement that "There is no equality of treatment merely by providing students with the same facilities, textbooks, teachers, and curriculum; for students who do not understand English are effectively foreclosed from any meaningful education." The Court returned the case to the district court so that the school system could design a plan of language-needs assessments and programs for addressing those needs. In a concurring opinion, Chief Justice Warren E. Burger and Justice Harry A. Blackmun observed that the number of underserved non-English-speaking, particularly Chinese-speaking, students was substantial in this case, but they would not order bilingual education for "just a single child who speaks only German or Polish or Spanish or any language other than English."

The Supreme Court's decision in *Lau* ultimately resulted in changes to enable Chinese-speaking students to obtain equal educational opportunity in San Francisco's public schools, although it was more than a year before such changes began to be implemented. The greatest impact, however, has been among Spanish-speaking students, members of the largest language-minority group in the United States.

RECOGNITION OF BILINGUALISM

Subsequently, Congress passed the Equal Educational Opportunities Act in 1974, a provision of which superseded *Lau* by requiring "appropriate action to overcome language barriers that impede equal participation," which a federal district court later applied to the need for new methods to deal with speakers of "Black English" in *Martin Luther King, Jr., Elementary School Children v. Michigan Board of Education* (1979). Also in 1974, the Bilingual Education Act of 1968 was amended to provide more federal funds for second-language instruction so that school districts could be brought into compliance with *Lau*. Bilingualism was further recognized when Congress passed the Voting Rights Act of 1975, which established guidelines for providing ballots in the languages of certain minority groups.

In 1975, OCR established informal guidelines for four bilingual programs that would enable school districts to come into compliance with the Supreme Court ruling. The main requirement was first to test students to determine language proficiency. Students with no English proficiency at all were to be exposed to bilingual/bicultural programs or transitional bilingual education programs; secondary schools also had the option of providing "English as a second language" or "high intensive language training" programs. If a student had some familiarity with English,

these four programs would be required only if testing revealed that the student had low achievement test scores.

Because the OCR guidelines were not published in the *Federal Register* for public comment and later modification, they were challenged on September 29, 1978, in the federal district court of Alaska (*Northwest Arctic School District v. Califano*). The case was settled by a consent decree in 1980, when the federal agency agreed to publish a "Notice of Proposed Rulemaking"; however, soon after Ronald Reagan took office as president, that notice was withdrawn. By 1985, a manual to identify types of language discrimination was compiled to supersede the 1975 guidelines, but it also was not published in the *Federal Register* for public comment. Meanwhile, methods for educating limited-English-speaking students evolved beyond the OCR's original conceptions, and further litigation followed. In 1981, a US circuit court ruled in *Castañeda v. Pickard* that bilingual educational programs are lawful when they satisfy three tests: (1) the program is recognized by professionals as sound in educational theory; (2) the program is designed to implement that theory; and (3) the program actually results in overcoming language barriers.

During the presidency of Ronald Reagan, civil rights monitoring focused more on "reverse discrimination" than on violations of equal educational opportunities. Congressional hearings were held to goad OCR into action. Although in 1991 OCR's top priority was equal educational opportunities for national-origin minority and Native American students with limited-English proficiency (LEP) or non-English proficiency (NEP), results were difficult to discern, and a movement to make En-glish the official language of the United States (the "English-only" movement) threatened to overturn *Lau* and related legislation. Moreover, by the late 1990's the controversy over bilingual education had revived, as many teachers, parents, policymakers, and legislators—including a significant number of Latinos—acknowledged the disappointing results of bilingual programs and sought solutions through legislation. In 1998, for example, California voted to curtail bilingual education by passing Proposition 227. Such measures were perceived as appropriate means of forcing quick English-language acquisition by some, but as simplistic and counterproductive by others.

——Michael Haas

BIBLIOGRAPHY AND FURTHER READING

Hoang, Haivan V. *Writing against Racial Injury: The Politics of Asian American Student Rhetoric.* Pittsburgh: U of Pittsburgh P, 2015. Print.

McClain, Charles, ed. *Chinese Immigrants and the Law.* New York: Garland, 1994. Print.

Nakanishi, Don T., and T.Y Nishida, eds. *The Asian American Educational Experience: A Source Book.* New York: Routledge, 1995. Print.

LEAGUE OF UNITED LATIN AMERICAN CITIZENS

The League of United Latin American Citizens (LULAC) was formed in order to unite all Latin American organizations under one title. In 1927, the main Latin American groups were the Sons of America, the Knights of America, and the League of Latin American Citizens, and there were other less well-known groups. The Sons of America had councils in Sommerset, Pearsall, Corpus Christi, and San Antonio, Texas; the Knights of America had a council in San Antonio; the League of Latin American Citizens had councils in Harlingen, Brownsville, Laredo, Peñitas, La Grulla, McAllen, and Gulf, Texas.

As more Anglo-Americans moved into Texas in the early 1800's, persons of Spanish or Mexican descent experienced open discrimination and segregation that placed them in the position of second-class citizens. They had been under the rule of six different countries before Texas entered the Union in 1845. Most continued to live and work as they always had, without being assertive about their rights. As time progressed, many Hispanics found that prejudice and discrimination were becoming less tolerable. Groups began to form to give more impact to requests that these practices cease. The Sons of America Council No. 4 in Corpus Christi, led by Ben Garza, originated a unification plan, believing that if all Hispanic organizations would regroup into one strong, unified, and vocal organization, more attention would be brought to the plight of those who were being discriminated against.

On August 14, 1927, delegates from the Sons of America, the Knights of America, and smaller groups met in Harlingen, Texas, to form LULAC. The resolution that was presented was adopted by those in the meeting. It was expected that the leaders of the major groups—Alonso Perales, Luz Saenz, José Canales, and Juan Lozano of the Rio Grande Valley of south Texas—would be invited by the president general of the Sons of America to begin the unification process. In response to concerns about the merger expressed by some members, Council No. 4 of the Sons of America drafted an agreement between itself and the Knights of America to unite. These two groups waited a year for the merger to be completed. Perales, president general of the Latin American League, stayed in close contact with Garza to maintain interest in the merger among the three main groups. However, the president general of the Sons of America never called the convention. After the long wait, Council No. 4 withdrew from the Sons of America on February 7, 1929. Participants at this meeting again voted to have a general convention for the purpose of unification. On February 17, 1929, invitations were sent to all the groups to meet in Corpus Christi, Texas, to vote on the merger.

Along with interested members of the Hispanic groups, Douglas Weeks, a professor at the University of Texas, attended not only to study the merger but also to open the convention as a nonaligned attendee. Ben Garza was elected chairman pro tem. His popularity as an energetic and fair civic leader made him a good spokesperson for the new group. The assembly had to choose a chairman, plan a single constitution, and select a name that would encompass the goals of the previously separate groups. The committee chosen to select a name included Juan Solis and Mauro Machado of the Knights of America, Perales and Canales of the Latin American League, E. N. Marin and A. de Luna of Corpus Christi, and Fortunio Treviño of Alice, Texas. Machado, of the Knights of America, proposed "United Latin American Citizens." This was amended to read "League of United Latin American Citizens," which was seconded by Canales. On February 17, 1929,

LULAC formally came into being at Corpus Christi, Texas.

The naming committee undertook other proposals before coming back to the general convention. Canales proposed a motto, "All for One and One for All," as a reminder of their purpose in uniting and as a basis for their future activities. They set some basic rules to guide the league until the constitutional convention could be held. This meeting was called for May 18 and 19, 1929, with an executive committee made up of Garza, M. C. Gonzales as secretary, and Canales and Saenz as members at large. On May 18, the first meeting under the new title was called. The constitution proposed by Canales was adopted, and new officers were elected. The officers were Garza, president general; Gonzales, vice president general; de Luna, secretary general; and Louis C. Wilmot of Corpus Christi, treasurer general. George Washington's prayer was adopted from the ritual of the Sons of America, and the US flag was adopted as the group's official flag. Now, in union, the new group could work to remove the injustices that had been building for many years. LULAC was chartered in 1931 under the laws of the State of Texas and later in New Mexico, Arizona, California, and Colorado, as other councils were formed. LULAC began issuing *LULAC Notes*, but in August, 1931, the first issue of *LULAC News* was published. In the 1990's, this magazine carried the subtitle *The Magazine for Today's Latino*.

EVOLUTION

In the formative years, auxiliaries were started by women whose husbands were active LULAC members. In August, 1987, LULAC amended its constitution to admit women into the organization. Between 1937 and 1938, junior LULAC councils were formed under the sponsorship of adult councils. In 1940, LULAC councils peaked, but with the beginning of World War II, the councils weakened with the departure of the men to military service. In 1945 and 1946, LULAC began to make great strides as educated, trained men returned from the service. Prestigious positions were filled by Hispanics and discrimination lessened. Non-Hispanics were joining, and LULAC was moving toward its objectives.

When the Civil Rights movement of the 1960's began, other Hispanic groups with a more militant response to discrimination began to form. Leaders such as the charismatic preacher, Reies López Tijerina in New Mexico and Rodolfo Gonzales in Denver marched in protest of the treatment Hispanics were receiving. César Chávez led farm groups in California on peaceful marches, which frequently erupted into violent confrontations as the number of militant members rose. LULAC did not totally support all these movements. It preferred mediation to resolve serious disagreements and education for all Hispanics as better ways of blending peacefully into the US mainstream.

LULAC has evolved to stress education. Parents are encouraged to prepare their children well to enter school. English is encouraged as the primary language, Spanish as the second language. As students mature, they are encouraged to finish high school and enter college. For those who aspire to higher learning, LULAC sponsors many scholarships; it also offers other forms of financial aid and counseling. LULAC Education Centers are located in sixty cities in seventeen states to provide this help. With corporate and federal aid, these centers have made it possible for disadvantaged Hispanic American youth to become productive members of their American communities.

——*Norma Crews*

BIBLIOGRAPHY AND FURTHER READING

Latinos and the Political System (Notre Dame, Ind.: University of Notre Dame Press, 1988), edited by F. Chris Garcia, discusses some of the political problems that prompted the formation of organizations such as LULAC. Mario T. Garcia's *Mexican-Americans: Leadership, Ideology, and Identity 1930-1960* (New Haven, Conn.: Yale University Press, 1989) is a thorough treatise on Hispanic assimilation into the mainstream of US business and community. Earl Shorris's *Latinos: A Biography of the People* (New York: W. W. Norton, 1992) is a collection of information on Hispanics in the United States, and a general overview of those Hispanics who immigrated and settled during the 1900's.

THE LIBERATOR

The initial publication of white abolitionist William Lloyd Garrison's weekly newspaper, *The Liberator*, in Boston, on January 1, 1831, helped to transform the antislavery movement in the United States. It symbolized the beginning of a radical effort to abolish slavery and secure equal rights for African Americans throughout the country.

Garrison and his newspaper were products of the religious revival called the Second Great Awakening, which transformed Protestant theology in the United States. The Awakening engendered moral reform movements in New England and other parts of the North during the early decades of the nineteenth century. Unlike their Calvinist predecessors, those who engaged in moral reform assumed that human beings, by their actions, could create a perfect society and bring about the millennial return of Jesus Christ. In his perception of the sinfulness and criminality of slaveholding, which he believed deprived both slaves and masters of a chance for salvation, Garrison went beyond most of the other reformers of his time.

GARRISON'S BELIEFS
Garrison was born in Newburyport, Massachusetts, in 1805. Deserted by his seafaring father in 1808, Garrison was raised in poverty by his devout Baptist mother, who instilled in him her strict moral code. At thirteen years of age, he apprenticed with a printer at the *Newburyport Herald*, where he learned the newspaper business. By 1828, he was in Boston as the editor of *The National Philanthropist*, advocating the temperance movement. Garrison also supported what he and others perceived to be the antislavery efforts of the American Colonization Society (ACS), founded in 1817. As the dominant antislavery organization of the 1820s, the ACS advocated the gradual abolition of slavery, combined with the colonization of free black Americans in Africa.

It was Garrison's decision, later in 1828, to join Quaker abolitionist Benjamin Lundy in Baltimore as coeditor of Lundy's weekly newspaper, *The Genius of Universal Emancipation*, that led to *The Liberator* and a more radical antislavery movement. In Baltimore, Garrison observed slavery in practice. Influenced by members of Baltimore's African American community, Garrison came to believe that gradualism would never end the "peculiar institution." African American influences also led Garrison to conclude that the ACS perpetuated a racist assumption that blacks and whites could not live together as equals in the United States.

Garrison's increasing militancy made cooperation with the more conservative Lundy difficult. Garrison's radicalism also led to his imprisonment for libel in the Baltimore jail and to his decision to return to New England to begin his own antislavery newspaper.

GARRISON MAKES A STATEMENT
In the first issue of *The Liberator*, Garrison proclaimed his conversion to immediate abolitionism. Harshly condemning slaveholders as sinners and thieves, he pointed out that one did not ask sinners to stop sinning gradually or require that thieves gradually stop committing crimes. Christian morality and justice, he insisted, required that slaveholders immediately and unconditionally free their bondspeople.

Garrison was not the first to advocate immediate emancipation. What was significant was his rejection of moderation and his linkage of immediatism with a demand that the rights of the formerly enslaved be recognized in the United States. In his most famous statement, Garrison proclaimed, "I am in earnest—I will not equivocate—I will not excuse—I will not retreat a single inch—AND I WILL BE HEARD."

The initiation of *The Liberator* also is significant for its reflection of biracial cooperation in the antislavery movement. Although Garrison, like other white abolitionists, never entirely escaped the racial prejudices of his time, he and his newspaper enjoyed the strong support of African Americans. Wealthy black abolitionist James Forten of Philadelphia provided crucial financial support to *The Liberator* in its early years. During the same period, Garrison employed black subscription agents, and three-quarters of the newspaper's subscribers were black. In Boston, where white antiabolition sentiment could produce violent confrontations, Garrison enjoyed the physical protection of African Americans.

THE PAPER'S EFFECTS
Meanwhile, Garrison and *The Liberator* played an essential role in the formation of the American Anti-Slavery Society (AASS). Founded in December

1833, under the leadership of Garrison and New York City businessmen Arthur and Lewis Tappan, the AASS united immediate abolitionists in the United States during most of the 1830s. Reflecting the pacifistic views of Garrison, the Tappans, and others, the society pledged in its Declaration of Sentiments (modeled on the Declaration of Independence) to use peaceful means to bring about the immediate, uncompensated emancipation of all US slaves, without colonization. Promoted by *The Liberator*, dozens of other antislavery newspapers, and thousands of antislavery pamphlets, the AASS grew exponentially. By 1838, it had a membership in the North of approximately one-quarter million and as many as 1,350 local affiliates.

By the late 1830s, however, internal tensions were tearing the AASS apart. The essential problem was that Garrison and his closest New England associates, including Maria Weston Chapman, Wendell Phillips, and Henry C. Wright, had concluded that the spirit of slavery had so permeated the nation that the North—not just the South—had to be fundamentally changed.

Although other abolitionists were reaching similar conclusions in the late 1830s, many of them objected to the specific policies advocated in the columns of *The Liberator* to effect those changes. In particular, an increasingly unorthodox Garrison antagonized church-oriented abolitionists by his wholesale condemnation of organized religion. He also seemed to threaten traditional concepts of patriarchy by his championing of women's rights and, specifically, female equality within the AASS. He appeared to threaten government through his advocacy of nonresistance, the pacifist doctrine that physical force is never justified, even in self-defense or on behalf of law and order. He frustrated those who desired a separate abolitionist political party by condemning political parties as inherently corrupt.

As a result, the abolitionist movement splintered in 1840. Garrison, his New England associates, and a few others across the North retained control of the AASS, but the great majority of abolitionists left the organization. Lewis Tappan began the American and Foreign Anti-Slavery Society, which, until 1855, maintained a church-oriented antislavery campaign. Politically inclined abolitionists organized the Liberty Party. By the 1850s, a majority of non-Garrisonian abolitionists had come to support the Republican

Party, which advocated neither immediate abolition nor equal rights for African Americans.

In the 1840s and 1850s, Garrison, in *The Liberator* and elsewhere, continued to promote anticlericalism, women's rights, and nonresistance, as well as immediate emancipation and equal rights for African Americans. Although he and his former AASS colleagues remained in agreement on many points, there was also considerable mutual antagonism. Chances for reconciliation among them diminished in 1842, when Garrison began to call on the people of the North to dissolve the Union. He argued that it was Northern support that kept slavery in existence in the South, implying that, when the North withdrew its support through disunion, the slaves could free themselves. His abolitionist critics responded that disunion was tantamount to the North's exculpating itself from the slavery issue.

When the South, rather than the North, initiated disunion in 1860 and 1861, however, changing circumstances caused Garrison to draw back from some of his more radical positions. He compromised his pacifism and his opposition to party politics by supporting Republican president Abraham Lincoln's war to preserve the Union and free the slaves. When the war ended successfully for the North and slavery was formally abolished, Garrison, old, tired, and seeking vindication, announced that his work was done—although it was clear that black equality had not been achieved with the end of slavery. The last issue of *The Liberator* rolled off its press on December 29, 1865.

———*Stanley Harrold*

Bibliography and Further Reading

Abzug, Robert H. *Cosmos Crumbling: American Reform and the Religious Imagination.* New York: Oxford UP, 1994. Print.

Brennan, Denis. *The Making of an Abolitionist: William Lloyd Garrison's Path to Publishing* The Liberator. Jefferson: McFarland, 2014. Print.

Friedman, Lawrence J. *Gregarious Saints: Self and Community in American Abolitionism, 1830–1870.* New York: Cambridge UP, 1982. Print.

Kraditor, Aileen S. *Means and Ends in American Abolitionism: Garrison and His Critics on Strategy and Tactics, 1834–1850.* New York: Vintage, 1970. Print.

Stewart, James Brewer. *William Lloyd Garrison and the Challenge of Emancipation.* Arlington Heights: Harlan Davidson, 1992. Print.

Thomas, John L. *The Liberator: William Lloyd Garrison; A Biography.* Boston: Little, 1963. Print.

Williford, James. "The Agitator William Lloyd Garrison and the Abolitionists." *Humanities* 34.1 (2013): 24–27. Print.

Lincoln-Douglas debates

The most famous and consequential campaign debates in American history, the dialogue between Abraham Lincoln and Stephen A. Douglas, clarified how Democratic and Republican conceptions of justice differed and laid a foundation for a renewed national commitment to principles of freedom.

In 1858, Lincoln, a leader of Illinois' recently formed Republican Party and a former one-term member of the House of Representatives, ran for the Senate against incumbent Douglas. A national leader of the Democratic Party, Douglas based his campaign, and his future presidential ambitions, on "the great fundamental principle" of "self-government," or "popular sovereignty." People of the federal territories, he argued, had the right to vote for or against allowing slavery, as they saw fit, and no outsiders had a right to interfere with their decisions. To Douglas, no principle was more fundamental to American democracy than this right of self-government, even if it meant countenancing slavery.

Lincoln viewed Douglas's position as a repudiation of the principles of freedom enshrined in the Declaration of Independence, which, if they meant anything, meant that slavery was wrong. Slavery had existed in the nation since before it began, but Lincoln echoed Thomas Jefferson in recognizing that the founders had been keenly aware of its incompatibility with principles of freedom and that they hoped for its eventual end. For Lincoln and other Republican Party leaders, the issue of extending slavery into the territories—the dominant political controversy of the 1850's—demanded that the nation make a choice. It must either recommit itself to the principles of freedom by refusing to extend this odious institution to new areas or adopt a position of moral neutrality toward slavery, thereby allowing it to spread into the territories and eventually into the free states. At stake was not only the fate of African Americans but also the freedom of all Americans. If the American credo were to abandon the idea that "all men are created equal," tyranny of one form or other would surely follow.

These issues focused the seven debates that Lincoln and Douglas conducted throughout Illinois between August and October of 1858. In a format quite unlike modern political "debates," one man spoke for an hour, the other responded for an hour and a half, then the first finished with a half-hour rejoinder. They alternated speaking first.

Although Douglas was reelected to the Senate (the actual vote was by state legislators, who had pledged themselves to either Lincoln or Douglas in their own election campaigns), Lincoln's forceful defense of the antislavery position won him fame outside Illinois and greatly contributed to his election to the presidency in 1860. His elevation to the presidency, in turn, marked the political defeat of Douglas's position of moral indifference to slavery and led to a national reaffirmation that American justice would remain rooted in freedom and equality.

——*Joseph M. Bessette*

Literacy tests

In an election, a citizen is expected to be literate enough to read a printed ballot in order to cast a vote. It is unnecessary to exclude illiterates from voting, as their marks are likely to be random and therefore will not influence the outcome of an election.

After the Civil War (1861–65) and Reconstruction (1865–77), tests for literacy were adopted as voting requirements in many states. The aim was to exclude marginally literate persons from voting, in particular African Americans and recent immigrants. The way to exclude marginally literate persons was either to reject those applying to register to vote who had errors on their application forms or to ask such persons to explain esoteric provisions in the Constitution of the United States or other text to a voter registrar, who would turn down their application.

The Voting Rights Act of 1965 suspended all literacy tests in states in which less than 50 percent of the voting-age population had been registered or had voted in the 1964 election. The law had an immediate impact. By the end of 1965, a quarter of a million new black voters had been registered, one-third by federal examiners. In the Voting Rights Act of 1970, Congress prohibited the use of all literacy tests and similar tests as preconditions for voter registration.

——*Michael Haas*

LITTLE BIGHORN

The Treaty of Fort Laramie (1868) guaranteed the Sioux a permanent reservation that encompassed all of present South Dakota west of the Missouri River and from which encroaching white settlers were forbidden. The Sioux were also guaranteed the right to hunt in a larger unceded territory, also closed to whites. About three thousand free-roaming Sioux lived on these lands and despised the thought of reservation life. Crazy Horse and Sitting Bull were the most famous of these Sioux.

BACKGROUND TO THE BATTLE

The terms of the treaty, however, were blatantly violated. From 1871 to 1874, surveying parties with army escort trespassed on both the reservation and unceded territory, charting routes and finding gold in the sacred Black Hills. By mid-1875 hordes of white prospectors and adventurers were poised to invade Sioux territory, held back only by the army.

The government tried through persuasion and threats to induce the Sioux to sell the Black Hills but were unequivocally rebuffed. This led President Ulysses S. Grant to devise a plan to justify a war against the Sioux. Their defeat would remove the free-roaming Sioux from the unceded territory and place them on the reservation. The Black Hills and unceded territory would be opened for settlement and prospecting. The plan began with a decision not to enforce the ban on prospectors entering the Black Hills. Lies about Sioux misdeeds and crimes were publicly circulated. Then in December, 1875, the government gave an ultimatum to the free-roaming Northern Cheyenne and Sioux to surrender at their

agencies by January 31, 1876, or be forced there by military action.

The Indians bitterly resented this ultimatum. It violated the 1868 treaty, and the free-roaming groups were determined to maintain their traditional way of life and not go to reservations. Resentment was further fueled by a famine on the reservation caused largely by negligence and graft in the distribution of guaranteed rations. In addition, the sale of firearms to hunt needed food was prohibited. The Platte Sioux had been arbitrarily removed from their reservation to save on freight charges for their rations.

ANNIHILATION OF CUSTER'S FORCES

The Indians ignored the ultimatum, and the army was ordered to capture or disperse them. On June 24 the Seventh Cavalry, under the command of General George Armstrong Custer, found an Indian camp (predominantly Sioux but including some Northern Cheyenne and Arapaho) on the south bank of the Little Bighorn River. In the mid-afternoon of June 25, 1876, the Battle of the Little Bighorn commenced. Major Marcus Reno and his three companies of 175 soldiers and Indian scouts attacked the southern end of the camp. Reno aborted the attack, however, when he realized the number of Indians he would engage. He took cover in timber along the river but was forced to withdraw to a more defensible hilltop on the bluffs across the river when set upon by an overwhelming force of Indians. The withdrawal turned into a panic and a rout. Seven officers and 84 men made it to the hill. Forty were killed, 13 were wounded, and several were missing.

Custer observed Reno's charge from Weir Point, a high bluff. He searched for an opening that would permit him and his 210 troops to join the battle as soon as possible. Custer made contact with the Indians at around 3:45 PM, near the river. What then happened is not exactly clear, but Custer moved away from the river and ended up on Custer Hill, about four miles from Reno's hill. Almost 2,000 Indians attacked Custer's force and completely surrounded it. Within about an hour Custer and all his men were annihilated.

The third unit of Custer's force, 5 officers and 110 soldiers, was commanded by Captain Frederick Benteen. Benteen was under orders to search for hostiles to the left of Custer's force and then hurry back and join Custer. Benteen, however, contrary to orders, dawdled behind, probably in the belief that there were no Indian warriors in the area. Benteen did not get to the battlefield in time to help Custer. The fourth unit of Custer's force, the pack train carrying supplies, was manned by 2 officers and 134 soldiers. It languished in the rear and could not be of assistance when Custer was attacked.

When Benteen and the pack train arrived at the Little Bighorn they joined Reno on Reno Hill. This total force of 367 was able to withstand Indian attacks on the morning of June 26, with a loss of 7 men killed and 40 men wounded. The Indians were gone by June 27, and the battle was over. Total army casualties numbered 263 killed and 59 wounded.

The army's defeat was the result of several factors. Inadequate intelligence led Custer to underestimate the strength and temper of his foe: 2,000 battle-tested warriors resolved to defend their way of life against 597 cavalry. Custer's troops were divided into four units, only two of which fought, and then at different times and places and against overwhelming odds. Another factor was the strength of the Indians' leadership; Crazy Horse, Gall, and Rain-in-the-Face were all actively involved in the fighting.

The Indians' victory was short-lived. An angry American public, Congress, and military demanded revenge. The Indians were relentlessly pursued in 1877, and by the end of the 1870's nearly all Plains Indians had been killed or confined to reservations; the traditional Plains culture passed into history.

——*Laurence Miller*

BIBLIOGRAPHY AND FURTHER READING

Hatch, Tom. *The Last Days of George Armstrong Custer: The True Story of the Battle of Little Bighorn.* New York: St. Martin's, 2015. Print.

Lookingbill, Brad D., ed. *A Companion to Custer and Little Bighorn.* Hoboken: Wiley, 2015. Print.

Marshall, Joseph. *The Day the World Ended at Little Bighorn: A Lakota History.* New York: Viking, 2007. Print.

Stiles, T.J. *Custer's Trials: A Life on the Frontier of a New America.* New York: Knopf, 2015. Print.

LITTLE HAVANA

The term "Little Havana" was originally coined by the English-speaking community in Miami in the late 1920's and early 1930's to describe the small enclave of Cubans that lived in the Eighth Street and Flagler Avenue area. After the Cuban Revolution of 1959 led by Fidel Castro, a large number of Cuban refugees arrived in Miami. They, and more than a half million Cubans who arrived during the 1960's, settled in the Little Havana area of Miami. Though many Cuban immigrants have dispersed to other US cities, the enclave of Little Havana has remained.

Little Havana encompasses an area of about four square miles. It is located in the southwest portion of Miami, hence the Cuban name for the area, *Souwesera.*

Upon the arrival of the immigrants in the 1960's, the area took on a distinct Cuban flavor. Cuban businesses sprang up everywhere, especially on Eighth Street (also known as *Calle Ocho*). Most store signs were in Spanish; later signs reading "English spoken here" were placed in many storefronts in an attempt to avoid alienating other Miami residents. However, anyone living and doing business in Little Havana did not need to speak English.

The first wave of Cubans fleeing the 1959 revolution arrived with nothing except the clothes on their backs and nearly empty suitcases. Because they were often unfamiliar with the language or the culture, they tended to congregate with fellow Cuban

The cortadito is a famous espresso beverage popular all over Miami. The many cafeterías (window coffee shops) throughout Little Havana are popular gathering spots for locals, and quintessential of Little Havana (and Miami) culture. By cyclonebill from Copenhagen, Denmark.

Americans, much as the Irish, Swedish, Norwegians, and Italians had done during their mass migrations in the final third of the nineteenth century.

The Cubans accepted almost any employment they could find, which created racial conflict with other economically challenged groups in Miami, especially the African American community. The African American community felt that the Cuban refugees were taking many of the jobs and positions to which they aspired. Tensions ran high and finally boiled over with the Miami riots of 1980. Although these riots were the direct result of a Hispanic police officer being acquitted in the shooting of an African American, the underlying cause was all the years of tension between the two communities.

As time passed, many of the residents of Little Havana, some of whom had become prosperous, moved to suburbs such as Hialeah and Coral Gables and other Florida cities. Though this lessened the tensions between Cuban Americans and other ethnic and racial groups in Miami, it created problems between the Cuban Americans and the white, European American populace. The tensions were largely cultural: The white community resented the Cubans' use of Spanish, even among themselves, and attempted to legislate that they use only English. Though the "English only" proponents failed, they are likely to try again. Unlike other minorities or ethnic groups that migrated to the United States, the Cuban community has sought to preserve its cultural heritage more vigorously and openly. This in itself has created tensions with the US population as a whole.

——*Peter E. Carr*

BIBLIOGRAPHY AND FURTHER READING

Casavantes Bradford, Anita. *The Revolution Is for Children: The Politics of Childhood in Havana and Miami, 1959-1962.* Chapel Hill: U of North Carolina P, 2014. Print.

Lohmeier, Christine. *Cuban Americans and the Miami Media.* Jefferson: McFarland, 2014. Print.

Pérez Firmat, Gustavo. *Life on the Hyphen: The Cuban-American Way.* Austin: U of Texas P, 2012. Print.

Shell-Weiss, Melanie. *Coming to Miami: A Social History.* Gainesville: UP of Florida, 2009. Print.

LITTLE ITALIES

Millions of people from 1880 to 1930 came to the United States with the hope of finding a life better than the one they had left in their country of origin. The US census indicates that during this fifty-year period more than four million Italians (mostly from poor backgrounds) migrated to US cities such as New York, Boston, Philadelphia, and Chicago. In these cities, the Italian immigrants moved to areas that contained other Italians, specifically their *paesani*, or people from the same village in Italy. Italian communities known as Little Italies developed as an outcome of this migration.

The Italian Americans (1970), by Joseph Lopreato, indicates that Little Italies separated Italian immigrants from the mainstream American society and enabled them to maintain their ways of life, eating familiar foods, speaking their native language, and maintaining their close-knit family organization and religious practices. Lopreato demonstrates that the Little Italies shielded Italian immigrants from the ways and demands of American society. He points out that these immigrants, having distanced themselves from the old culture in Italy, needed a certain amount of time to understand and participate in the social organizations of the new society in the United States. The Little Italies acted as bridges between the old life in Italy and the new life in the United States.

Works such as *Italian Americans into the Twilight of Ethnicity* (1985), by Richard Alba, and *The Italians* (1976), by Patricia Snyder Weibust, Gennaro Capobianco, and Sally Innis Gould, describe the growth and decay that Little Italies have undergone in US cities. Between the 1880's and early 1940's, the Little Italies flourished, giving birth to many Italian American-owned businesses (including restaurants, bakeries, groceries, clothing shops, butcher shops, and pasta shops), Italian-language newspapers, and mutual benefit societies (organizations involved in helping Italian immigrants deal with sickness, death, and loneliness). Moreover, these communities were host to celebrations of *festa* (Italian religious festivals) and other religious activities. Before World War II, Little Italies reached their peak in development and activities. However, after the 1940's,

these communities began to shrink, partly because second- and third-generation Italian Americans were becoming wealthier and leaving the Little Italies for the suburbs. In addition, few Italians were immigrating to the United States. Since the 1970's, the bulk of Italian Americans have lived outside the Little Italies, where only a semblance remains of the old order. The number of Italian American-owned businesses, Italian-language newspapers, and mutual benefit societies in these communities has decreased tremendously. Certain activities, such as the *festas*, have continued to be held in Little Italies, some as simple appearances and others to keep the memories alive of an earlier time.

——Louis Gesualdi

BIBLIOGRAPHY AND FURTHER READING

Bove, Aldo, and Giuseppe Massara, eds. *'Merica: A Conference on the Culture and Literature of Italians of North America.* Stony Brook: Forum Italicum, 2006. Print.

Cinotto, Simone, ed. *Making Italian Americans: Consumer Culture and the Production of Ethnic Identities.* New York: Fordham UP, 2014. Print.

Harney, Robert F., and J. Vincenza Scarpaci, eds. *Little Italies in North America.* Toronto: Multicultural Historical Society, 1981. Print.

LITTLE ROCK SCHOOL DESEGREGATION

In the *Brown v. Board of Education* decision of 1954, the Supreme Court declared segregation unconstitutional, but its 1955 implementation order allowed the lower courts to develop plans to desegregate. It was the first time that the Court had not ordered immediate establishment of a constitutional right. In a state such as Arkansas, moderate and reluctantly willing to accept political and legal (though not social) equality, this approach seemed to suggest that a gradual process would be possible. Trouble seemed unlikely.

Little Rock school superintendent Virgil Blossom planned to start by enrolling a few black students at Central High School in 1957 and working down the grades year by year. The children, eventually pared

down to nine, were chosen for strong scholarship and character; they were from middle-class families. When school opened on September 3, however, these children met serious resistance.

Governor Orval Faubus had decided that his best bet for future political success—most immediately a third term—lay in making himself the leader of the lower-class white segregationist element in the state. Despite the fact that he had not previously been particularly (or at least overtly) racist, Faubus announced that he could not keep the peace and called out the National Guard to keep order.

Daisy Bates, head of the local chapter of the National Association for the Advancement of Colored People (NAACP), realized that families served by Central High School were predominantly lower class and were likely to be stirred to resistance by the governor's statements. She organized the students to arrive in a group. They were turned away at bayonet point. One student, Elizabeth Eckford, did not get the message and arrived alone to face a mob of angry whites. Blocked from the school by armed Guardsmen and cursed and reviled by the mob, she was rescued by a reporter from *The New York Times* and an older white woman. Such scenes as these were reported by the press and broadcast on television. The nation was forced for the first time to face the true ugliness of its prejudice.

President Dwight D. Eisenhower met with Faubus on September 14 and got what he thought was a promise to abide by the Supreme Court decision. When Faubus reneged, the president, on September 25, ordered elements of the 101st Airborne to Little Rock. The soldiers escorted the black children to school and protected them for several weeks. Then the state National Guard, placed under federal authority, took over. Despite continuing harassment by white students, all but one of the nine was graduated from Central High.

In Little Rock, the *Brown* decision had been enforced, but resistance to school integration continued in many areas of the South. Faubus, who continued to fight, won a total of six terms as governor. The Little Rock crisis was a vital first step in desegregation, but it was no more than that.

——*Fred R. van Hartesveldt*

BIBLIOGRAPHY AND FURTHER READING

Anderson, Karen. *Little Rock: Race and Resistance at Central High School.* Princeton: Princeton UP, 2010. Print.

Bowman, Kristi L. *The Pursuit of Racial Ethnic Equality in American Public Schools:* Mendez, Brown, *and* Beyond. East Lansing: Michigan State UP, 2015. Print.

Gordon, Noah. "The Little Rock Nine: How Far Has the Country Come?" *Atlantic.* Atlantic Monthly, 25 Sept. 2014. Web. 24 Apr. 2015.

Millhiser, Ian. "*Brown* Turns 60." *Nation* 2 June 2014: 7–8. Print.

Perry, Ravi K., and D. LaRouth Perry. *The Little Rock Crisis: What Desegregation Says about Us.* New York: Palgrave, 2015. Print.

LITTLE TOKYOS

In Los Angeles around 1885, Japanese immigrants gradually populated a small section of the city that became known as Little Tokyo. By 1910, Japanese shops, restaurants, language schools, and shrines were established, and Little Tokyo became the home of nearly 37,000 Japanese. Before World War II, Little Tokyos were also established in Seattle (almost 11,700 Japanese immigrants) and in San Francisco, where the Japanese ethnic community was the third largest in the United States, at about 5,000. Other Little Tokyos of more than 1,000 were in Sacramento and Stockton, California, Portland, Oregon, and New York City.

Although Japanese began immigrating as early as the mid-1850's, Little Tokyos were not established until the early twentieth century. They took much longer to be established than Chinatowns, probably because of the cultural differences between the two groups. The Japanese traditionally believed that

agriculture was the most virtuous occupation and that people who made their living as merchants were less respectable. As a result, the majority of the early Japanese immigrants gravitated to rural areas to be farmers, as opposed to the Chinese immigrants, who were usually merchants in the city.

In Canada, before World War II, more than 97 percent of Japanese immigrants resided in the province of British Columbia. By 1931, nearly one-third of the Japanese population (about 8,300) lived in Vancouver, and more than half of them were in the district known as Little Tokyo. This was the only Japanese ethnic community in Canada in those days. However, no physical structures or symbolic buildings such as shrines were built because of severe anti-Asian sentiment.

During World War II, Little Tokyos practically disappeared from North America following the incarceration of people of Japanese descent in internment camps. In the 1970's and 1980's, when the political and economic relationships between the United States and Japan flourished, Japanese Americans began to revitalize Little Tokyos. However, by then, Little Tokyos had become more tourist attractions than residential areas. Today new generations of Japanese Americans tend to live in all parts of the city and suburbs.

In Canada, after World War II, Japanese internees were not allowed to return to their homes in British Columbia. They had to choose between going to Japan or relocating to other provinces east of the Rocky Mountains. In 1949, Japanese Canadians were finally permitted to return to British Columbia. Some people returned and reestablished Little Tokyo in Vancouver. However, new generations of Japanese Canadians, like Japanese Americans, tend to live in the suburbs. Although Vancouver's Little Tokyo still maintains shops and restaurants along with cultural activities, people who work there do not live in that area.

Since the 1970's, Japanese corporations have sent many nationals to work in the United States and Canada. These workers are often encouraged to live among North Americans in order to become more proficient at speaking English and to avoid creating a threatening Japanese "ghetto." Japanese supermarkets, bookstores, and restaurants have sprung up in various cities where many Japanese nationals work, including Seattle, Portland, Chicago, New York, and Vancouver. These new "Little Tokyos," which are smaller in size than the prewar Little Tokyos and may not be as concentrated, are usually just shopping centers.

——*Nobuko Adachi*

BIBLIOGRAPHY AND FURTHER READING

Hayden, Dolores. *The Power of Place.* Cambridge: MIT P, 1997. Print.

Lyman, Stanford M. *Chinatown and Little Tokyo.* Millwood: Associated Faculty P, 1986. Print.

Murase, Ichiro Mike. *Little Tokyo.* Los Angeles: Visual Comm./Asian Am. Studies, 1983. Print.

LONE WOLF V. HITCHCOCK

Lone Wolf v. Hitchcock established the precedent that congressional plenary power over tribal property was virtually unlimited and that Indian treaties were subject to unilateral abrogation. Lone Wolf, a principal chief of the Kiowa Nation, sought a perpetual injunction against congressional ratification of a 1900 agreement that allotted tribal lands and led to a direct loss of more than two million acres of Indian territory. The tribes contended that the forced allotment of their lands violated Article Twelve of the 1867 Treaty of Medicine Lodge. This article explicitly stated that no cession of tribal lands would be valid without the consent of "three-fourths of all the adult male Indians."

In 1892 the Jerome Commission concluded an allotment agreement with certain representatives of the Kiowa, Comanche, and Apache (KCA) tribes. Although the commissioners secured a number of Indian signatures, the three-fourths provision was unfulfilled. Nevertheless, the agreement was rushed to Washington, D.C., for congressional ratification. Almost immediately upon hearing about the allotment agreement, more than three hundred KCA tribal members urged the Senate to disapprove the 1892 agreement because "misrepresentations, threats, and fraudulent" means had been used by the government's commissioners to secure Indian signatures. Tribal consent, in other words, had not been legitimately secured.

More important, as the 1892 agreement wound its way through the ratification process, Congress substantially revised the agreement. These revisions were never submitted to the KCA tribes for their approval. Nevertheless, on June 6, 1900, and despite the protestations of the tribes concerned, Congress ratified the amended agreement.

Justice Edward D. White wrote the opinion, which was, shortly after its pronouncement on January 5, 1903, called the "Dred Scott decision number two" because it inculcated the doctrine that Indian treaty rights, although the "supreme law of the land," could be disregarded with the passage of virtually any federal law. White stated that the 1867 treaty provision had been abrogated by the 1900 agreement even though the later statute contradicted the treaty provision and lacked tribal consent. This, White said, was in keeping with "perfect good faith" toward the Indians.

White inaccurately stated that Congress had exercised plenary authority over tribes "from the beginning" and that such power was "political" and therefore not subject to judicial review. These statements were legal rationalizations, yet they were also in line with the reigning policy view of Indians at the time held by the federal government: Indians were dependent wards, subject to their sovereign guardian—the United States.

Lone Wolf v. Hitchcock was a devastating blow to tribal sovereignty. The Court's brazen refusal to examine congressional acts that abrogated treaty-acknowledged property rights was particularly oppressive because the lion's share of tribal sovereign, political, and property rights was defined by the hundreds of ratified treaties and agreements tribes negotiated with the United States. Indian rights, in short, were not created by or included in the federal Constitution. As a result of this decision, treaties as legal contracts were no longer enforceable if Congress decided to act in a manner that violated their provisions.

——*David E. Wilkins*

Long Walk

In early March 1864, 1,443 Navajos (*Dineh,* meaning "the people," "men," or "earth people" in the Navajo language) began the Long Walk, as they described their journey, of 250 miles from their ancestral homes in northeastern Arizona and northwestern New Mexico to the Bosque Redondo reservation, located on New Mexico's eastern plains at Fort Sumner. Bosque Redondo, named by Spanish explorers for a round grove of cottonwood trees situated on the Pecos River, and adjacent Fort Sumner were viewed by the American military as appropriate locales for the forced assimilation into American life of the 8,354 Navajos and 405 Mescalero Apaches confined there by December 1864. Although most Navajos made the journey in 1864, smaller groups had made the journey the year before.

HISTORICAL BACKGROUND
Following the Mexican government's cession of 1.2 million square miles of territory to the United States by the Treaty of Guadalupe Hidalgo, February 2, 1848, relations between Americans and Navajos became increasingly tense as the United States government exerted control over the Southwest, land now under United States sovereignty. This increased tension characterized Colonel James Macrae Washington's expedition into *Dinetah* (Navajo land) in August 1849, an invasion which resulted in the death of a respected Navajo headman (*naataani*), Narbona, August 31, 1849. Narbona was "shot in four

or five places and scalped," according to an eyewitness. Ostensibly undertaken to assure Navajos of American "peaceful" intentions in constructing forts in and settling Navajo land, Washington's expedition had the opposite effect. Angered by Narbona's murder, his son-in-law, Manuelito, vowed to drive all white men from Navajo country. With the aid of another Navajo headman, Barboncito, on the night of April 29, 1860, Manuelito launched an offensive against Fort Defiance, built by Colonel Edwin Vose Sumner in 1851. Fort Defiance and its nearby canyon, Cañoncito Bonito (both adjacent to present-day Window Rock, Arizona, capital of the Navajo Nation), became central staging areas for the Long Walk.

CARLETON'S WAR, 1862–1864
Tensions with the Mescalero Apaches, evidenced in the murder of Nodnhi Apache chief Mangas Coloradus in January 1863, and the incursions of New Mexican raiding parties on Navajo land to purchase Navajo slaves resulted in a planned effort to exterminate both Mescalero Apaches and Navajos. Another impetus was Union brigadier general James H. Carleton's view that Apache and Navajo country contained gold and other minerals. Appointed commander of the New Mexico military department, Carleton reasoned that, following his successful 1862 recapture of Tucson for the Union, he could destroy Confederate designs on New Mexico by removing

American Indians from their ancestral homes and opening their lands to Anglo-American prospectors.

To realize this ambition, General Carleton's American Indian policy (approved by Mauhuache Ute agent Christopher "Kit" Carson; James L. Collins, Superintendent of American Indian Affairs in New Mexico; and New Mexico territory's new governor, Henry Connelly) called for his fifteen hundred California volunteers to force New Mexico's nonslave American Indians to surrender and to relocate at Bosque Redondo, situated on the alkaline Rio Pecos, 175 miles southeast of Santa Fe. There the Mescalero Apaches and Navajos would be taught agriculture and Christianity. Not without his misgivings about Carleton's policy, Kit Carson, now a colonel in the New Mexican territorial militia, waged war against the Mescalero Apaches and their chief, Cadete, during the 1862–1863 winter. By March 1863, more than four hundred Mescalero Apaches—men, women, and children—were confined to Bosque Redondo in an experiment in agricultural self-sufficiency from which they would flee in the autumn of 1865. Carson turned the attention of Carleton's California volunteers to the Navajos.

During the summer of 1863, General Carleton ordered a campaign of subjugation against the Navajos, an offensive begun August 5, 1863. From Forts Defiance and Wingate, Colonel Carson and his one thousand volunteers vied with Governor Connelly's companies of civilian volunteers to take Navajo captives. Connelly's civilians assumed that, if the Navajos surrendered to Carson, opportunity to profit from Navajo slavery was impossible. Carson urged his Ute guides to take Navajo captives, thus destroying the "collectiveness" of Navajo tribal interest.

CARSON'S WAR, 1863–1864

Navajos eluded capture by Carson's volunteers, headquartered at Fort Defiance (renamed Fort Canby by Carson in July, 1863). General Carleton reported to the federal government at the beginning of September 1863, that a mere 51 Navajos, including children and women, had been rounded up and sent to the Bosque Redondo reservation. Carleton ordered Carson to tell Navajo males: "Go to the Bosque Redondo, or we will pursue and destroy you." In the harsh 1863–1864 winter, Carson's pursuit of the impoverished Navajos, now scattered in small bands throughout Navajo country, was successful.

Carson's destruction of Navajo crops and livestock between Fort Canby and Canyon de Chelly resulted in the surrender of 188 Navajos and their Long Walk to Bosque Redondo in the autumn of 1863. The captured included Delgadito, a prominent Navajo headman, who agreed to Carleton's request to convince other headmen to relocate to the Bosque Redondo. Repeated American forays into the Navajo stronghold, Canyon de Chelly, resulted in the surrender of 1,200 Navajos at Fort Canby by mid-February 1864. Many of this group and the seven hundred Navajos surrendering to Fort Wingate authorities on Delgadito's advice formed the main part of the Long Walk of the Navajos to Fort Sumner and the Bosque Redondo in March 1864, accompanied by nearly five hundred horses and about three thousand sheep. Of the 1,443 Navajos on this trek, 10 died during the Long Walk and 3 children were kidnapped for use as slaves by New Mexican members of the soldier escort.

THE LONG WALK

In the mid-1860s approximately nine thousand Navajos were forced to live in imprisonment at Bosque Redondo. Navajo deaths among Long Walk participants were steep. On March 4, 1864, 2,400 Navajos, their numbers reduced by the deaths of 126 from dysentery the preceding week, left Fort Canby for the Bosque Redondo reservation. On reaching Fort Sumner, 197 remained behind, either dead or dying. The eight hundred Navajos leaving Fort Canby for their new home on March 20, 1864, experienced a four-day snowstorm, the kidnapping of many Navajo children, the loss of twenty-three wagons used to transport the infirm and elderly, and the loss of supplies at Los Pinos (south of Albuquerque). By the time the group reached Fort Sumner and Bosque Redondo on May 11, 1864, 110 had perished. By July 1864, some 5,900 Navajos were resettled at Bosque Redondo. General Carleton, guessing that only 2,000 Navajos remained in *Dinetah*, advised Kit Carson that Bosque Redondo could feed 7,500 Navajos.

Navajo leaders Barboncito and Ganado Blanco, son of Ganado Mucho, temporarily fled Bosque Redondo in July 1865. Their later return left two headmen, Ganado Mucho and Manuelito, remaining free in Navajo country. Manuelito had participated in the Long Walk but quickly returned home, informing a delegation of Navajo headmen sent by Carleton from Bosque Redondo that he would not return. On September 1, 1866, however, forty-eight-year-old Manuelito surrendered at Fort Wingate, arriving at Bosque Redondo one month later. In the autumn of 1865, Ganado Mucho and his band surrendered at Fort Wingate, New Mexico. Preceded on their Long Walk to Bosque Redondo by women and children, Ganado Mucho and the men of his band who herded his livestock learned in reaching Fort Sumner that Mucho's two daughters had been kidnapped near the Rio Grande. This tragedy was compounded by the tragedies of Navajo resettlement at Bosque Redondo.

END OF THE LONG WALK

Brigadier General Carleton's plan for the resettlement of Mescalero Apaches and Navajos at the Long Walk's terminus, Bosque Redondo, was not achieved. American Indian self-sufficiency in agrarian pursuits was overshadowed by traditional animosity between Mescalero Apaches and Navajos, corn crop failures caused by cutworm invasions, Comanche attacks, smallpox epidemics, and increased criticism of Carleton's policies from a number of quarters. Secretary of War Edwin M. Stanton removed Carleton from his command on September 19, 1866. The 7,304 Navajos living at Bosque Redondo were promised a return to a new 3.5-million-acre reservation on their homeland by the terms of a June 1, 1868, peace treaty signed by United States representatives William T. Sherman and Colonel Samuel F. Tappan and by 9 Navajo headmen. The US Congress appropriated $150,000 for Navajo travel expenses from Bosque Redondo. Escorted by four companies of US cavalry, they began their long walk home on June 18, 1868.

——*Malcolm B. Campbell*

BIBLIOGRAPHY AND FURTHER READING

Bender, Norman J. *"New Hope for the Indians": The Grant Peace Policy and the Navajos in the 1870's.* Albuquerque: U of New Mexico P, 1989. Print.

Denetdale, Jennifer. *The Long Walk: The Forced Navajo Exile.* New York: Chelsea, 2008. Print.

Iverson, Peter. *The Navajos.* New York: Chelsea, 1990. Print.

Iverson, Peter. *The Navajo Nation.* Albuquerque: U of New Mexico P, 1983. Print. Locke, Raymond Friday. *The Book of the Navajo.* Los Angeles: Mankind, 1976. Print.

Morales, Laurel. "Legacy of Forced March Still Haunts Navajo Nation." *Morning Edition.* NPR, 27 Jan. 2014. Web. 14 Apr. 2015.

Underhill, Ruth. *The Navajos.* Rev. ed. Norman: U of Oklahoma P, 1967. Print.

LONGEST WALK

The Longest Walk, one of the several major American Indian protest movements of the 1970s, was an attempt to persuade the US government to recognize and protect Indian treaty rights and tribal sovereignty. The protest was a five-month cross-country demonstration by Indian people to protest federal bills in Congress that were seen as destructive of the Indians' very existence. About two hundred Native Americans began the walk from the once Indian-occupied Alcatraz Island, in San Francisco Bay. Thousands of Indians participated along the way, ultimately arriving in Washington, DC, on July 15, 1978. One of the demonstrators was Russell Means of the American Indian Movement (AIM). The protesters set up a camp at the Mall, hoping to convince lawmakers not to pass the bills.

The pending legislation would have weakened Indian rights to land, resources, and self-government. For example, one bill proposed to limit Indian water rights, while others threatened to cancel Indian hunting and fishing rights and terminate all treaties between the United States and Indian tribes.

Congressional supporters and others assured the Indians that the anti-Indian bills would not pass. Nevertheless, they agreed with the Indian demonstrators that Congress and the American public should be aware that such legislation had been proposed. The Longest Walk was a symbolic victory for Indian people. It also demonstrated a solidarity among Indians from various tribes. A similar journey was held in 2008 to commemorate the original walk and to further promote Indian rights.

——*Raymond Wilson*

LOO MURDER

Asian Americans have been the victims of discrimination and violence throughout the course of US history. This was especially true during periods of significant Asian immigration and also during and after wars in which Asian nations were the United States' adversary.

One such instance of violence involved the murder of a Chinese American, Jim (Ming Hai) Loo, in Raleigh, North Carolina, in July, 1989. Two brothers, Robert and Lloyd Piche, who had lost relatives in the Vietnam War, mistakenly thought that Loo was Vietnamese and held him responsible for their relatives' deaths. They attacked Loo and killed him.

One of the killers, Robert Piche, was offered a plea bargain and a minimal sentence, but he opted for a trial. Although he expected an acquittal from a hometown jury, he was found guilty and sentenced to thirty-seven years in prison. His brother, Lloyd, was convicted of a misdemeanor and was sentenced to only six months in jail.

The media had reported on this case in a manner consistent with other murder trials; however, after Lloyd Piche's lenient sentence was handed down, the media joined Asian American civil rights organizations in urging the federal government to intercede and charge Lloyd with conspiracy to violate Loo's rights. An appeals court ordered a resentencing for Lloyd, and he was sent to prison for six years.

Loo's death clearly demonstrated the existing prejudice toward Asian Americans as exemplified by the expression, "They all look alike." Loo was killed not because he had done anything wrong but rather because he "looked" Vietnamese.

—*Stephen Schwartz*

LOS ANGELES RIOTS OF 1992

Before the Rodney King beating on March 3, 1991, many in the Los Angeles community believed that the Los Angeles Police Department (LAPD) had demonstrated a pattern of excessive force, particularly against minority groups. One significant example was Operation Hammer, begun in 1989, during which the LAPD allegedly rounded up African Americans and Hispanics without probable cause that they had committed a crime, simply because of the way the suspects looked and because the police wanted to avert the threat of gang violence. As a result, the chief of the LAPD, Daryl Gates, was despised by many in the African American community. The videotape of Rodney King's beating by members of the LAPD, therefore, came as no surprise to the African American community of Los Angeles. It merely confirmed what they already thought: that police brutality and use of excessive force against minorities was a common practice.

THE BEATING OF RODNEY KING

The videotape, recorded by private citizen George Holliday in the morning hours of March 3, 1991, contained eighty-one seconds of footage. The footage that was seen throughout the United States was of King, a six-foot, three-inch African American weighing 225 pounds, prone on the ground, sustaining blows to his head, neck, kidney area, and legs from four policemen, who were kicking and smashing at him with their truncheons. Not in full view on the videotape were nineteen other police officers surrounding the four who were administering the beating. Also not in view were the onlookers who were pleading that the beating stop. The police paid no attention to them. As a result of the beating, King sustained eleven fractures to his skull, a crushed cheekbone, a broken ankle, internal injuries, a burn on his chest, and some brain damage.

Television viewers also did not see what preceded the beating. During the evening, King had consumed the equivalent of a case of beer. His blood alcohol level was twice the legal limit. He was on parole at the time and ran the risk of landing back in jail if he were caught speeding. Police, led by Stacey Koon, started chasing King as he sped through the streets of Los Angeles. The chase escalated to one hundred miles per hour at one point, before the police were able to stop King and force him out of his car. Nor did television viewers see King fighting with the police, even standing up after being stunned twice with a Taser gun. People saw only the prone body of an African American man being assaulted repeatedly by white police officers.

The Trial

Four of the officers, including Koon, were charged with the beating at the end of March 1991, in Los Angeles. Their attorneys moved for a change of venue for the trial, which was granted. The trial was held in the spring of 1992 in Simi Valley, a suburban town an hour's drive north of Los Angeles. The town was the home for a large proportion of LAPD officers and retirees and was dominated by law-and-order conservatives. Six men and six women, none of whom was African American, made up the jury. According to those who were present, the prosecution presented a weak and diffuse case. The defense, however, was strong. It played the videotape in slow motion over and over until its effect became trivialized. The defense also emphasized how King presented a threat to the police. Koon testified about King's "hulk-like strength and how he groaned like a wounded animal," conjuring up for the jury the image of police representing the "thin blue line" that protects the forces of civilization from the savagery represented by King. To those who had likely settled in Simi Valley to get away from the alleged evils and crime of the inner city, the message resounded. After thirty-two hours of deliberation, on April 29, 1992, the jury acquitted the four officers. The verdict was announced on television at 2:50 P.M.

The Riots

At 4:00 P.M., in the South Central Los Angeles district near Florence and Normandie Boulevards, five African American gang members went to get some malt liquor at the Payless Liquor Store. They started to take it without paying, and the owner's son tried to stop them. One of the gang members smashed the son on the head with a bottle and allegedly said, "This is for Rodney King." Other gang members hurled the bottles they held through the store windows, while the owner pressed the alarm for the police. When two officers came, the suspects were not there.

At 5:30, at the corner of Florence and Normandie, eight black men wielding baseball bats started breaking the car windows of passing motorists.

Eighteen police cars and thirty-five officers from the LAPD sped to the area. They arrested three suspects but left at 5:45. In the next hour, the crowd attacking cars grew to two hundred people. One of the victims was Reginald Denny, a white truck driver, who was pulled from his truck and beaten by African Americans, including Damien Williams, with a fire extinguisher. The police from the 77th district of the LAPD still stayed away. Chief Gates had left police headquarters at 6:30 to attend a fund-raising event in the affluent suburb of Brentwood.

By 7:30, the crowd at Florence and Normandie had started lighting fires. An hour later, the LAPD finally returned to the area and began to disperse the crowd. By that time, the fires, rioting, and looting had spread to other parts of the city. The riots continued for two more days; local news coverage flooded the airwaves with helicopter views of hundreds of fires throughout the city and normally law-abiding citizens looting goods from stores. On Friday, May 1, 1992, Rodney King appeared on television with the plea, "Can't we all get along?" When the riots ended that day in Los Angeles, more than fifty people had died, more than twelve thousand people had been arrested, and the property damage was estimated to be $1 billion. Throughout the nation, uprisings had started in Atlanta, Las Vegas, Minneapolis, New York, Omaha, and Seattle.

The riots in Los Angeles following the King trial caused more damage and spread across a wider area than those of the 1960s. Gates subsequently was replaced by an African American chief of police, Koon and a fellow officer were convicted of violating King's civil rights in federal court, Williams was acquitted of most of the charges in the beating of Denny, and King won a civil suit against the city of Los Angeles. These actions reinforced the perception of many that the criminal justice system treats whites and African Americans differently, whereas others argued that the riots were less the result of racial tensions than of a widening gap between "haves" and "have-nots" in US society.

—*Jennifer Eastman*

Bibliography and Further Reading

Abu-Lughod, Janet L. *Race, Space, and Riots in Chicago, New York, and Los Angeles.* New York: Oxford UP, 2007. Print

Cannon, Lou. "Rodney King Remembered." *National Review* 9 July 2012: 22–25. Print.

King, Rodney, and Lawrence J. Spagnola. *The Riot Within: My Journey from Rebellion to Redemption.* New York: HarperOne, 2012. Print.

Monroe, Sylvester. "South Central: 20 Years Since . . ." *Ebony* May 2012: 132–40. Print.

Rissman, Rebecca. *Rodney King and the L. A. Riots.* Minneapolis: ABDO, 2014. Print.

LYNCHINGS IN AMERICAN HISTORY

Lynching, the deadliest form of vigilantism, has a long history in America. At the time of the American Revolution, lynchings were used to punish Tories or British sympathizers. Until the 1850's, lynchings were associated with nonlethal forms of punishment such as beatings and tarring and feathering. In the years immediately before the Civil War, lynching took on its fatal connotation as it was used to suppress slave insurrections. Although lynching is often associated with hanging someone, lynching includes all sorts of violent acts, including flogging, dismemberment, torture, burning, and shooting.

HISTORY OF LYNCHING

After the Civil War, lynching became more widespread as former slaves came to be viewed as a threat by their former masters. Accurate numbers on lynching are hard to come by, and it was not until 1872 that there was a systematic effort to obtain reliable data. Records kept by the Tuskegee Institute indicate that there were 4,743 lynchings in the United States between 1882 and 1968. Of those lynched, 3,446 (73 percent) were blacks and 1,297 (27 percent) were whites. Even these numbers underestimate what most scholars believe to be the actual number of lynchings. A more accurate estimate would be close to 6,000 lynchings.

Lynchings were most prevalent from the 1880's to the 1920's. During the last two decades of the nineteenth century, there was an average of 150 lynchings per year, with a high of 230 in 1892. Between 1901 and 1910 there was an average of 85 lynchings per year, and from 1911 to 1920 there was an average of 61 per year. Lynchings declined to an average of 28 per year during the 1920's, to 11 per year during the 1930's, and to 3 per year during the 1940's. From 1951 to 1985 a total of 10 lynchings were reported in the United States. Although almost every state experienced lynchings, 82 percent occurred in the South. Mississippi ranks first with 581, followed by Georgia with 530 and Texas with 493.

GROUNDS FOR LYNCHING

Although lynching was often justified as a method of protecting white women from black rapists, only 25 percent of lynching victims were suspected of rape or attempted rape. In most cases, lynching victims were summarily executed before receiving any trial. Their guilt was never established at all, let alone beyond a reasonable doubt. The justification for lynching in the cases of rape was to protect the white woman from the agony of testifying in court.

Approximately 40 percent of lynchings involved murder or attempted murder allegations. Nine percent involved assault or robbery charges, certainly not capital offenses, and 2 percent involved blacks insulting whites, particularly white women. The most famous example of a black who was lynched for insulting a white woman was Emmett Till . Till, a fourteen-year-old Chicago native, was visiting relatives in Mississippi in 1955. Prodded by some friends, Till asked a white woman for a date. The woman immediately rejected Till and went to get a pistol. Till walked out of the store saying, "Bye, baby," and "wolf whistled" at her. Till's actions violated one of the major cultural taboos in the South, and he would pay with his life. That same day, the woman's husband and her half-brother abducted Till from the home he was visiting. Three days later, Till's decomposing body was found floating in the Tallahatchie River. Till had been beaten and shot before his weighted-down body was thrown into the river. The two white men who abducted Till were charged with his murder, but it took an all-white jury less than one hour to acquit them.

THE CAMPAIGN AGAINST LYNCHING

Few individuals who participated in lynchings were ever prosecuted. Coroners' juries repeatedly concluded that the death had come "at the hands of parties unknown." Seldom was anything further from the truth. Often lynchings took on a festive air, and

Six African-American men lynched in Lee County, Georgia, on January 20, 1916.

Ames, one of the leading social reformers in the South, had forty thousand members in her organization within nine years of its establishment in 1930. When alerted about a possible lynching, Ames contacted women in the area who were members of her organization or sympathetic to its objectives.

One of the earliest objectives of the National Association for the Advancement of Colored People (NAACP) , a civil rights organization established in 1909, was to pressure the US Congress to pass a federal antilynching bill. On several occasions, the House of Representatives passed such legislation, but it was always filibustered by southern senators when it reached the Senate. In the late 1940's President Harry Truman appointed a President's Committee on Civil Rights (PCCR). The PCCR urged Congress to pass a federal antilynching law, but without success.

The NAACP met with greater success in attempting to mobilize public opinion against lynching. The NAACP investigated lynchings and often sent special investigators into areas where a lynching had occurred. The NAACP prepared written narratives of the lynchings, including photographs if available, and distributed them to any media outlet that would publicize the lynching. The effort was to try to shame the South into stopping this despicable practice.

———*Darryl Paulson*

local newspapers provided complete coverage, sometimes including photographs. In the event someone was arrested for the crime, such as the two white men accused of murdering Emmett Till, they would be found not guilty by all-white juries.

Leading the effort to abolish lynchings were the Commission on Interracial Cooperation, headed by Will Alexander, and Southern Women for the Prevention of Lynching, led by Jessie Daniel Ames.

BIBLIOGRAPHY AND FURTHER READING

Dray, Philip. *At the Hands of Persons Unknown: The Lynching of Black America*. New York: Modern Lib., 2003. Print.

Raper, Arthur. *The Tragedy of Lynching*. Rpt. Chapel Hill: U of North Carolina P, 2011. Print.

Rushdy, Ashraf H. A. *The End of American Lynching*. New Brunswick: Rutgers UP, 2012.

Thurston, Robert W. *Lynching : American Mob Murder in Global Perspective*. Farnham: Ashgate, 2011. Digital file.

White, Walter. *Rope and Faggot.* Notre Dame: U of Notre Dame P, 2002. Print.

Whitfield, Stephen. *A Death in the Delta: The Story of Emmett Till.* Baltimore: Johns Hopkins UP, 1991. Print.

LYNG V. NORTHWEST INDIAN CEMETERY PROTECTIVE ASSOCIATION

In 1982, the United States Forest Service (USFS) prepared an environmental impact report for construction of a paved road through federal lands in the Six Rivers National Forest in California. The study reported a section of this land was historically used for religious purposes by Yurok, Karok, and Tolowa Indians, and because the site was integral to the religious practices of these people, it recommended the road not be completed. That same year, despite its own report, the Forest Service decided to build the road. After exhausting administrative remedies, a coalition of Indian organizations filed suit in federal court, challenging the decision based on the right to free exercise of religion under the First Amendment and on similar guarantees in the American Indian Religious Freedom Act (1978).

In 1987, the US Supreme Court ruled against the Indian coalition even though the Court admitted the road would severely affect tribal religious practices. The Court declared that although the free exercise clause affords individual protections, it does not afford an individual right "to dictate the conduct of the government's internal procedures." Additionally, it ruled that the American Indian Religious Freedom Act has no enforcement mechanisms that could compel the government to halt construction on the road. This case severely reduced both the intent of the American Indian Religious Freedom Act and the protections it afforded Indian people, and it raised questions about basic protections afforded American Indian citizens of the United States.

———*Carole A. Barrett*

M

MACHINE POLITICS

In Ireland, several potato crops failed during the 1830's, resulting in a devastating famine that sent millions of immigrants to US shores. Like most of the refugees who came in the nineteenth century, the Irish expected to achieve fame and fortune—the American Dream. Instead, they found poverty and discrimination. One sign that appeared in the windows of many businesses read "Irish need not apply." Seeking a way out, many Irish Americans tried to climb the political ladder, thus creating an American phenomenon known as machine politics.

Early Irish bosses played an extremely important role in serving the immigrants' needs. In the days before Social Security, welfare, Medicare, and Medicaid, the bosses (or their agents) met the immigrant ships at the docks, helped the weary travelers find a place to live and a job and provided them with most of life's necessities. The urban machines served as a quasi-welfare agency. At Christmas, they delivered huge baskets of food to the poor who lived in the squalor of the slums. The machine provided patronage—jobs, housing, and other necessities—and in return, the immigrants supplied the votes to keep the machine in power.

It took a great deal of money to fuel these machines. Money came from profit-seeking businessmen and paycheck kickbacks from machine members. Irish bosses such as Daniel P. O'Connell of Albany, New York, James Michael Curley of Boston, and Patrick A. Nash and Edward J. Kelly of Chicago enraged middle-class, white Anglo-Saxon Protestant reformers by encouraging vote fraud, intimidation, graft, bribery, and many other forms of vice, sin, and corruption that sullied the image of US democracy.

Two of the most famous Irish bosses played an important role in electing a president. Harry S Truman emerged from the ranks of Thomas J. Pendergast's Kansas City, Missouri, organization. The Pendergast machine ran Kansas City with an iron hand from 1911 to 1938. The big boss provided the jobs and delivered the votes (many of them fraudulent) that sent Truman to the US Senate. Pendergast eventually received a prison sentence for income tax evasion.

Another boss, Chicago mayor Richard J. Daley, provided crucial support in shifting Illinois' electoral vote to John F. Kennedy during the 1960 presidential election. Daley, the last of the bosses, ran the "Windy City" from the 1950's to the 1970's and died while still in office in 1976. Before the mayor's death, he created the image of Chicago as a highly efficient city where the streetcars ran on time, garbage trucks routinely picked up the trash, and the police strictly maintained law and order.

For many years, white Anglo-Saxon Protestants viewed the Irish with distrust. Poverty in the Irish shanties seemed to produce myriad problems: juvenile delinquency, drug and alcohol abuse, unemployment, and other factors that led to the rise of the boss and his machine. Eventually, as the Irish moved up the socioeconomic ladder, they gained respectability. They gained acceptance from many segments of society, and the boss came to symbolize a stabilizing era in the history of the cities.

Eventually African American and Hispanic political leaders replaced the Irish bosses. Although the Irish machine tolerated or encouraged corruption, it played an important role in bringing order to the confusion and disorganization that characterized the American city in its formative stages.

—*J. Christopher Schnell*

MAFIA

Mafia is a general term referring to a handful of criminal organizations that have controlled illegal activities in America's cities during the last 100 years. The most powerful of these has been the Italian Mafia, also known as Cosa Nostra ("our thing"), which emerged at the beginning of the twentieth century as a rival to Irish and Jewish gangs in New York. Initially, it focused on protection rackets and robbery, but Prohibition changed all that, propelling the Italian Mafia to prominence through its bootlegging operations and making Mafiosi such as Al Capone household names.

Bloody wars among leading crime families over the control of bootlegging led to the creation, in 1931, of a Crime Commission comprising the heads of the New York and Chicago crime families and representing some twenty-five others across the country. A governing body of sorts, it was the brainchild of Lucky Luciano, who became known as "Father of the Italian Mafia." Ensuing peace enabled sizable expansion by establishing Italian crime families throughout the US Expansion brought new sources of income, such as gambling, prostitution, labor racketeering, extortion, blackmail, larceny, hijacking, money laundering, smuggling, drug trafficking, fraud, counterfeiting, and contract killings.

Despite their unparalleled notoriety as thugs and murderers, Italian Mafiosi have enjoyed an ironic popularity and fascination among the American public. Many have become pop-culture icons, inspiring films, television shows, and books and captivating a public that has come to view these unexpected protagonists as defenders of a kind of street justice the authorities are unable to provide. Treating Mafiosi as latter-day heroes is big business, but it does not sit well with most Italian-Americans. Groups like the Italian-American Civil Rights League have worked tirelessly to undermine stereotypes that equate Italian Americans with Mafiosi and to educate the public about Italian-Americans' contributions to American society and culture.

The Italian Mafia has deep roots, but it is not the oldest criminal organization in the US That distinction belongs to the Irish Mob (a.k.a. Irish Mafia). Concentrating mostly on contract murders, extortion, racketeering, hijacking, and drug trafficking and confined to a few northeastern cities plus Chicago, it has occasionally formed alliances with Italian crime families and, at other times, fought them. Another criminal organization with origins in turn-of-the-century New York is the Jewish Mafia. Unusually ambitious, it pioneered many of the lucrative criminal enterprises that became the mainstay of today's criminal organizations, including the Italian Mafia. Overlapping interests and similar tactics led to close collaboration between the Jewish and Italian Mafias. Like some of their Italian associates, Jewish Mafiosi like Meyer Lansky and Bugsy Siegel engendered unusual admiration among the public.

Federal prosecutors had little luck convicting Mafia leaders until the passage of the Racketeer Influenced and Corrupt Organizations Act (RICO) in 1970. RICO enabled US attorneys to try organized-crime figures not for any specific criminal act itself but as members of corrupt enterprises. Prosecution and conviction of Mafia bosses such as John Gotti and their underlings weakened the Italian Mafia considerably, reducing it to a mere shadow of itself by the early 1990s. Irish and Jewish Mafias, already in decline, fared no better.

Unfortunately, the government's success against these groups produced a power vacuum in America's cities that was filled by street gangs and Mafiosi from eastern and southern Europe. These "new" Mafias, are characterized by singular cruelty and indiscriminate violence and involved in international activities like human trafficking, narcotics, gunrunning, terrorism, contract killing and assassinations, securities fraud, and money laundering. With a long reach across a few continents, the Russian and Albanian Mafias have been especially deadly.

——*Tomislav Han*

BIBLIOGRAPHY AND FURTHER READING

Raab, Selwyn. *Five Families: The Rise, Decline, and Resurgence of America's Most Powerful Mafia Families.* New York, NY: Thomas Dunne Books, 2006.

Abadinsky, Howard. *Organized Crime*, 11th ed. Boston, MA: Cengage Learning, 2017.

Lyman, Michael D. *Criminal Investigation*, 2nd ed. New York, NY: Pearson, 2015.

Mainstreaming

The practice of mainstreaming began in the 1970s with national attention to the right of persons with physical and mental disabilities to attend the same public schools and be in the same classrooms as traditional students. For example, the Education for All Handicapped Children Act in 1975. In the area of race and ethnic relations, however, mainstreaming has come to mean something else.

Primarily, mainstreaming refers to the integration of ethnic minority students, mostly Spanish-speaking children, into traditional English-speaking classrooms. The Bilingual Education Act was passed in 1968 that provided an education for all students, regardless of their English language ability and included bilingual education as an approved way to educate students with limited English language skills. Since 1975, many Hispanic children have been taught through bilingual education. English as a Second Language (ESL) programs have been suggested as a way to transition students from bilingual education to an English-only school environment. In the 1990s, some efforts for legislation favoring ESL immersion succeeded in California (Proposition 227), and these developments appeared to be the leading edge of a national trend. In the landmark bilingual education case, *Lau v. Nichols*, the US Supreme Court mandated bilingual education in order to provide equal education opportunities for all students, which then produced the Equal Education Opportunity Act of 1974.

A fierce debate surrounds the various ways of achieving mainstreaming. Proponents argue that all public school instruction should be in English and that children who do not speak the language should be rapidly immersed in traditional classrooms. Critics argue that this is mere assimilationist rhetoric. They believe that children should have the opportunity to speak their own language while learning English and that cultural pluralism should be preserved in public schools.

——*Christopher Guillebeau*

BIBLIOGRAPHY AND FURTHER READING

Banks, James A., ed. *Encyclopedia of Diversity in Education.* Thousand Oaks: Sage, 2012. Print.
Sengstock, Mary C. *Voices of Diversity: Multi-Culturalism in America.* New York: Springer, 2009. Print.

Majority and minority

In general, the value placed on different racial and ethnic backgrounds is determined by the majority, those who hold power in a society. By establishing the values and norms of society, the majority consciously and unconsciously create a social structure that operates in their favor. Their positions of power allow them to enjoy certain privileges, including better housing, better schools, and higher incomes.

Because the resources and rewards found in society are limited, the privileged position of the majority is often gained at the expense of the opportunities available to minority groups within the society. Although the term minority often means less than half of the whole, when applied to people it does not necessarily refer to numerical proportion. Some minority groups, such as African Americans in some cities in the United States, have more members than the majority but receive fewer economic and political opportunities.

If a minority group has economic resources or a good education, its acceptance by the majority is typically easier. This is especially so in the United States, where class is largely defined by economic success. Although extreme economic and social inequalities continue to divide Americans into majority and minority groups, the divisions tend to be more a reflection of economic class than of ethnicity.

——*Alvin K. Benson*

BIBLIOGRAPHY AND FURTHER READING

Bailey, Eric J. *The New Face of America: How the Emerging Multiracial, Multiethnic Majority Is Changing the United States.* Santa Barbara: Praeger, 2013. Print.
Lewis, Daniel C. *Direct Democracy and Minority Rights: A Critical Assessment of the Tyranny of the Majority in the American States.* New York: Routledge, 2013. Print.
Wise, Tim J. *Dear White America: Letter to a New Minority.* San Francisco: City Lights, 2012. Print.

MANA (ORGANIZATION)

The Mexican American National Association (MANA) was founded in 1974 in Washington, DC, by Mexican American women. It began as a feminist organization associated with the women's movement of that era. Because other feminist groups were not addressing concerns of Mexican Americans, and because male-dominated Hispanic groups spoke for women in Congress, Mexican American women formed MANA. As membership in MANA grew and became more diversified, the group officially changed its name in 1994 to MANA, A Latina Organization and includes women of Mexican, Caribbean, Central American, South American, and Spanish decent. Dedicated to their cause, MANA members are expected to volunteer their services for ten to fifteen hours each month.

MANA has four national goals: to support and encourage Latinas to become community leaders, to create vibrant and dynamic Hispanic communities, to advocate for and change when necessary any public policies that promote equality and fairness for Latinas, and to grow and sustain the MANA organization. MANA has developed two primary programs that are aimed at achieving these goals. The AvanZamos Program is an adult leadership training program for Latinas, and the HERMANITAS Program is a national mentoring program for young adults. Education is a top priority for MANA, and it created HERMANITAS to encourage young Latinas to stay in school, pursue academic goals, and live healthy and safe lives. Hermanitas, which means "little sisters," helps junior high and high school Latinas with future career choices and guides them through the requirements needed for high school graduation and college.

MANA members have testified before Congress and have campaigned for the Equal Rights Amendment (ERA), the family leave act, and against sterilization abuse.

MANA has local chapters through the United States and on some college campuses. Many of its members are not Latinas but are concerned with the needs and issues that pertain to Latinas. the group's concerns have grown to include pay equity, teen pregnancy, and children in poverty. Information is transmitted to members through a quarterly newsletter, issue updates, and conventions. Through the group's efforts, many Latinas have broken through barriers to become leaders in their communities.

——*Marilyn Elizabeth Perry*

BIBLIOGRAPHY AND FURTHER READING

Rosen, Ruth. *The World Split Open: How the Modern Women's Movement Changed America.* New York: Penguin, 2007. Print.

MAQUILADORAS

Maquiladoras are the assembly plants, mainly foreign-owned, that have been operating in Mexico since 1965, mostly along the northern border with the United States. From Tijuana on the Pacific Coast to Matamoros on the Gulf of Mexico, these tariff-free plants experienced their biggest boom in the 1990s. Between 1994 and 1995, the maquiladoras created an additional 400,000 jobs.

The racial and gender dimensions of the maquiladora industry are complex. In some Mexican cities, Asian companies own the majority of the maquiladoras. In Mexicali, for example, many of the assembly plants are mainly owned by Taiwanese and Japanese investors. It took a long time for Asians to accept Mexican attitudes toward punctuality, company loyalty, and absenteeism, which run counter to those of the more disciplined Asian workforce. After several adjustments, Mexican laborers and Asian managers worked out compromises that were mutually acceptable.

In most factories, a large majority of the workers are women. These women have a median age of twenty-five and are more likely to possess a secondary education than other women their age. Most women working in maquiladoras are single and usually migrated to wherever they found employment. For the most part, these women are satisfied with their steady paychecks and health benefits, although many

A maquila in Mexico. By Guldhammer (Own work).

find that their jobs alienate them from family expectations. When they leave employment in the maquiladoras, it is normally because of family necessities, transportation problems, or disappointment with their jobs.

Many of these women undergo a transformation in their relationships with the men in their families. The fact that maquiladora workers contribute an average 40 percent to household budgets has a stressful impact on these women's relationships with men in the traditionally authoritarian Mexican family. However, it is usually a younger daughter who works in the factory, not the family's main provider. Many young women give their earnings to their mothers, keeping only a small amount for themselves.

Some women do become financially independent and therefore experience personal freedom; however, the family continues to maintain a substantial influence over them. Because interaction between men and women on the factory floor is limited, the large number of women has not significantly altered gender attitudes. Although most assembly-line supervisors are women, generally women do not seek out these positions. Accepting a supervisory role moves the women out of the work group and creates suspicion about their association with management.

Critics of maquiladoras have pointed out that the low wages paid to their employees constitute raw exploitation. Even with the numerous bonuses and benefits required by Mexican law, a large multinational maquiladora might pay its assembly-line workers a base of 50 to 60 cents per hour. With benefits, which include bonuses, social security, and health care, the total compensation rises to $1.50. The minimum wage in the United States in 1998 was well over $5.00 per hour.

Another controversy is the accusation that unless maquiladora wages rise substantially, the low-wage factories will constitute unfair competition and attract large numbers of US companies with a resultant loss of jobs in the United States. Nevertheless, manufacturers believe that higher wages could bite into the competitive edge that brought them to Mexico in the first place; maquiladora owners believe they are saving up to $25,000 per worker per year. Many American workers who lost their jobs have become bitter and resentful against Mexican policies that continue to lure manufacturers from the United States. The end result is that displaced white and African American workers sometimes regard Mexican immigrants as the problem, heightening racial as well as ethnic tensions within the United States.

——*Douglas W. Richmond*

BIBLIOGRAPHY AND FURTHER READING

Broughton, Chad. *Boom, Bust, and Exodus: The Rust Belt, the Maquilas, and a Tale of Two Cities.* New York: Oxford UP, 2015. Print.

Hampton, Elaine M, with Anay Palomeque de Carillo. *Anay's Way to Learn: A Woman's Education in the Shadows of the Maquiladoras.* Austin: U of Texas P, 2013. Print.

Lugo, Alejandro. *Fragmented Lives, Assembled Parts: Culture, Capitalism, and Conquest at the US-Mexico Border.* Austin: U of Texas P, 2008. Print.

MARIEL BOATLIFT

After Fidel Castro became dictator of Cuba in January, 1959, relations between the United States and Cuba steadily deteriorated, as Castro turned his country into a communist state allied with the Soviet Union, the United States' rival in the Cold War. Diplomatic relations with Cuba were broken, and an economic embargo was imposed upon the country.

The communization of Cuba alienated Cubans as well. From 1959 to 1962 (when Castro halted all further airplane flights from the island), about two hundred thousand Cubans fled their homeland, most of them settling in Miami. In late 1965, special freedom flights of refugees were organized with the cooperation of the Castro government; although registration for these flights was closed off in 1966, the flights themselves continued until 1973. The early refugees were disproportionately from Cuba's professional and white-collar classes; with extensive financial assistance from the US government, and their own hard work, they achieved a remarkable level of prosperity in the United States in a short time.

Hopes for rapprochement with Castro rose in 1977, when Jimmy Carter became president of the United States. A United States Interests section of the Swiss embassy was established in Havana, under a State Department official, Wayne Smith, to handle relations between Cuba and the United States. When Castro persisted in his military intervention in the African nation Angola, however, plans for lifting the US embargo were shelved indefinitely. In October, 1979, relations with Castro deteriorated when Washington, D.C., welcomed the hijacker of a Cuban boat as a freedom fighter.

Between January and March, 1979, Castro, to polish his image abroad and to gain badly needed foreign currency, allowed more than 115,000 Cuban Americans to visit their relatives in Cuba. The apparent prosperity of the Cuban Americans caused discontent among Cubans on the island because of the austerity and lack of consumer choices in the island's socialist economy.

MARIEL REFUGEES
On April 1, 1980, six Cubans commandeered a city bus and drove it through the gate of the Peruvian embassy, demanding asylum; in the ensuing melee, one Cuban guard was killed. Castro responded by removing the police guards from the embassy. By April 9, 1980, about ten thousand more Cubans had crowded into the embassy, demanding the right of

political asylum. On April 16, with Castro's permission, airplane flights began to take asylum-seekers to Costa Rica; on April 18, however, Castro, embarrassed by the blow to his image abroad, suddenly canceled these flights. On April 20, he opened the port of Mariel to all those who wished to leave the island and to anyone who wished to ferry discontented Cubans to Florida.

Persons sympathetic to the plight of the would-be emigrants chartered boats to sail to Mariel, pick up those who wanted to leave, and bring them to Key West, Florida. Once in Mariel, the boats' skippers were forced to accept everyone whom Cuban authorities wanted to be rid of, including criminals, the mentally ill, and homosexuals. Because some of the boats were not seaworthy, a tragic accident was always a possibility; and the US Coast Guard sometimes had to rescue refugees from boats in danger of sinking.

President Carter, distracted by the Iranian hostage crisis and the worsening of relations with the Soviet Union after the latter's occupation of Afghanistan, vacillated in regard to the boatlift. In a speech given on May 5, Carter urged the people of the United States to welcome the refugees with open arms. On May 14, however, he threatened criminal penalties for those who used boats to pick up Cubans, and ordered the Coast Guard to stop the boatlift by arresting and fining the skippers and seizing the boats. Without cooperation from Castro, this order was largely ineffective. It was not until September 25, after hard bargaining between Castro and State Department negotiators Wayne Smith and Peter Tarnoff, that Castro ended the boatlift; several hundred would-be refugees who had missed the boatlift were allowed to take air flights out of Cuba in November.

Between April and September, 1980, south Florida bore the brunt of the tidal wave of refugees, which is estimated to have reached as many as 125,000. In the Miami area, social services, health services, schools, and law enforcement authorities found their resources strained to the breaking point by the sudden influx. Housing was suddenly in short supply; quite a few Mariel refugees in Florida had to sleep in the Orange Bowl, underneath a highway overpass, or in tent cities. On May 6, Carter, in response to pleas from Florida governor Bob Graham, declared Florida a disaster area and authorized ten million dollars in relief for that state to help defray the cost of

the refugee influx; US Marines were sent to Florida to help process the refugees.

CAMPS AND DISCRIMINATION

In June, 1980, President Carter ordered all those refugees who had not found relatives or others willing to sponsor them placed in detention camps in Wisconsin, Pennsylvania, and Arkansas. In Pennsylvania and Arkansas, the refugees, bored and fearful about their future, rioted. By October, the majority of the Marielitos had been released into various communities, and the detention camps were closed.

News of the riots fueled a growing backlash in US public opinion against the Mariel refugees. The much-publicized presence of criminals among the refugees also helped generate a feeling of revulsion against the entire group: Marielitos were blamed for the upsurge in violent crime in Miami in 1981. In 1980, a year of economic downturn, many people in the United States feared that more Cuban refugees would mean higher unemployment.

Once released from custody, Marielitos faced a difficult adjustment. Unlike earlier Cuban refugees, the Marielitos did not arrive in the midst of general prosperity; they came when the twin plagues of inflation and recession were besetting a US economy still struggling to absorb refugees from Vietnam, Laos, and Cambodia. Hence, Marielitos did not receive as much financial assistance from the federal government as earlier Cuban refugees. In addition, more of the Marielitos were poorly educated people from blue-collar backgrounds; more of them were single men without family ties; and a larger percentage of them were black or mulatto. Marielitos of all colors faced prejudice and discrimination, not merely from Euro-Americans but also from longer-settled Cuban Americans, who saw the Marielitos as insufficiently hardworking and feared that popular US resentment of the Marielitos might rub off on them. In 1983, Marielitos in Miami had an unemployment rate of 27 percent; although the rate had been cut to 13 percent by 1986, they still lagged behind longer-settled Cuban Americans in employment and income.

Marielitos who ran afoul of the law quickly discovered that, however minor their offenses, they had fewer rights than native-born US criminals. Marielitos who had criminal records in Cuba or who committed crimes in the United States faced incarceration for an indefinite term in federal prisons. In 1985, President Ronald Reagan secured a promise from Castro to take back Marielito criminals; only a few hundred had been deported when Castro, enraged by US sponsorship of Radio Martí—an anti-Castro radio broadcast—canceled the agreement. In November, 1987, a new agreement provided for the deportation to Cuba of Marielito criminals in return for the acceptance by the United States of Cuban political prisoners; upon hearing of the agreement, Marielitos held in federal prisons in Oakdale, Louisiana, and Atlanta, Georgia, rioted, taking hostages. The riots ended only when the Reagan administration promised that no prisoner would be sent back to Cuba without individual consideration on his or her case, and that some of those whose offenses were relatively minor would be released into the community. In 1995, however, eighteen hundred Marielitos were still incarcerated in federal prisons.

THE AMERICAN REACTION

When the Mariel boatlift began, Islamic militants in Iran had already publicly humiliated the United States government by seizing and holding captive US diplomatic personnel. The seemingly uncontrollable Cuban refugee influx came to be seen as a symbol, not of the bankruptcy of Communism, but of Carter's alleged ineptitude in conducting US foreign policy. US voters' anger over the refugee influx, together with widespread frustration over economic recession and the Iranian hostage crisis, helped doom Carter's bid for reelection in November, 1980.

The Mariel boatlift of 1980 revived xenophobia among people in the United States. Until 1980, much of the US public had seen Cuban refugees as courageous freedom fighters, comparable to Czechs or Hungarians fleeing Soviet tanks rather than to Puerto Ricans or Mexicans fleeing poverty; the presence of

criminals and misfits among the Marielitos shattered the benign Cuban stereotype. After 1980, sentiment would build steadily for reducing the number of immigrants and refugees admitted into the United States. The ultimate consequence of the Mariel boatlift of 1980 was President Bill Clinton's decision in August, 1994, when faced with a new exodus from Cuba, to eliminate the privileged status of Cuban asylum-seekers.

——*Paul D. Mageli*

BIBLIOGRAPHY AND FURTHER READING

Mark S. Hamm's *The Abandoned Ones: The Imprisonment and Uprising of the Mariel Boat People* (Boston, Mass.: Northeastern University Press, 1995) is the best study of the Marielito prison riots of 1987; also contains much information on the 1980 boatlift. Alex Larzelere's *Castro's Ploy, America's Dilemma: The 1980 Cuban Boat Lift* (Washington, D.C.: National Defense University Press, 1988) is a detailed study on the boatlift, especially valuable for its look at the decision-making process within the Carter administration. Gil Loescher and John A. Scanlan's *Calculated Kindness: Refugees and America's Half-Open Door, 1945-Present* (New York: Free Press, 1986) examines the effect of the Mariel boatlift on the shaping of US refugee policy in general. Silvia Pedraza-Bailey's *Political and Economic Migrants in America: Cubans and Mexicans* (Austin: University of Texas Press, 1985) compares the demographic portrait of the Marielitos with that of earlier Cuban refugees. Alejandro Portes and Alex Stepick's *City on the Edge: The Transformation of Miami* (Berkeley: University of California Press, 1993) is one of the few deep studies of the Marielitos' adjustment problems.

MARITAL ASSIMILATION

In 1964, while attempting to analyze the general process of assimilation, sociologist Milton Gordon developed the notion of marital assimilation. He argued that marital assimilation has occurred in a society when intermarriage between two groups is widely accepted. Although this type of acceptance is likely to lead to a high level of intermarriage, the actual

rates of intermarriage are not the proper gauge of marital assimilation. Instead, marital assimilation is measured by the support the interracial or interethnic married couple receives from the rest of society. Gordon conceptualized marital assimilation as the third stage of a seven-step process by which minority groups eventually become assimilated into the culture of the dominant American society. He argued that marital assimilation can occur only after structural assimilation has taken place and that such assimilation precedes what he terms identification assimilation. Some scholars have argued that marital assimilation may also be the most critical stage of this process because if it lasts for an extended period of time and there are a high number of intergroup marriages, then both groups will begin not to think of themselves as separate groups. This may lead to the development of common values and shared identities.

——*George Yancey*

MARRANOS

As a result of the Spanish Inquisition, by 1492 all the Jews in Spain had either converted to Catholicism (about 100,000), had been murdered (about 30,000), or had been forced into exile (about 200,000). Expulsion or conversion was enforced in Portugal in 1497. As a result, Jews remaining in these nations subverted their religious beliefs but remained "secret Jews." Marranos were the secret Jews of Spain and Portugal. The word *marrano* generally is believed to be a derisive Spanish word meaning "swine" and is rejected by most descendants of secret Jews. In the 1990s, the term "Crypto Jews" was furthered by the Society for Crypto-Judaic Studies, which based its research primarily in the southwestern United States. *Anusim,* Hebrew for "forced one," also is a positive term that is often used. *Conversos* historically has referred to either sincere or insincere Jewish converts to Christianity, and "New Christians" has differentiated Jewish converts to Catholicism from Old Christians (Spanish Catholics).

Brazil had the largest number of secret Jews in the Americas, and a few overt and secret Jews escaped the Inquisition there to begin the first Jewish settlement in the United States in 1654 in New Amsterdam (later New York City). The Dutch governor of New Amsterdam applied restrictions that were rapidly removed because of pressure from the Jewish community in Holland.

Small numbers of descendants of secret Jews who settled in Protestant areas in the eastern United States usually were openly Jewish and relatively accepted. However, most secret Jews in North America were in Mexico, where the Inquisition also existed. They mostly moved into isolated parts of present-day New Mexico and other Mexican territories in order to minimize threats from the Inquisition's headquarters in Mexico City. Frequently they remained secretly Jewish but openly practiced Catholicism because of fears of the Inquisition, Spanish Catholicism's generally negative attitude toward Jews, and the pervasiveness of Catholicism. Over several centuries, most became Catholics in belief as well as practice; however, specific Jewish rituals sometimes remained. Some practitioners knew that the customs were Jewish, and others continued these practices but over time lost knowledge of their Jewish meaning. In the southwestern United States, beginning in the 1980's, a noticeable number of descendants of Crypto Jews began returning to Judaism. In many cases, they were strongly criticized by members of their families because of strong Catholic family identities, family fears of stigmatization, or anti-Semitism.

Traditional (Orthodox) Judaism has rigid rules requiring that a person's mother be Jewish or that an Orthodox conversion take place before an individual is considered Jewish. Therefore, descendants of the Crypto Jews are not accepted as Jewish unless they undergo an Orthodox conversion. Conservative Judaism and Reform Judaism have some religious flexibility, but most North American Jews have backgrounds in Eastern Europe (Ashkenazim) and know little about Crypto Jewish history and survival. This lack of knowledge, a tendency to define Jewishness (customs, foods, language, and so on) in Eastern European terms, and some traditional religious objections have hindered understanding of and acceptance of descendants of Crypto Jews who have returned openly to Judaism. Sephardim (Jews descended from the Jews of Spain and Portugal) are more knowledgeable about Crypto Jewish history and practices, but traditional religious beliefs have prevented full acceptance of Crypto Jews. A few rabbis in the southwestern United States accept

Crypto Jewish descendants as Jews without conversions, viewing them as returning Jews.

———*Abraham D. Lavender*

BIBLIOGRAPHY AND FURTHER READING

Bejarano, Margalit. "The Sephardic Communities of Latin America." *Contemporary Sephardic Identity in the Americas: An Interdisciplinary Approach* (2012): 3–30. Print.

Kamen, Henry. "The Other Within: The Marranos, Split Identity, and Emerging Modernity." *Common Knowledge* 19.1 (2013): 146–47. Print.

Kaplan, Debra. "Jews in Early Modern Europe: The Sixteenth and Seventeenth Centuries." *History Compass* 10.2 (2012): 191–206. Print.

Kunin, Seth Daniel. *Juggling Identities: Identity and Authenticity among the Crypto-Jews.* New York: Columbia UP, 2009. Print.

Wexler, Paul. *The Non-Jewish Origins of the Sephardic Jews.* Albany: SUNY P, 2012. Print.

MARXIST MODELS

There are two models of race relations that are held by interpreters within the Marxist tradition. The first and oldest view is quite similar to the social class theory of race relations proposed by the sociologist Oliver Cox in *Race Relations: Elements and Social Dynamics* (1976) and by the historian Herbert Aptheker, in works such as *American Slave Revolts* (1943). This interpretation sees racism as part of the method used by the wealthy, ruling class to divide the working class. If African American and white workers hate each other because of their skin color, they are less likely to join together to challenge the capitalist system. Racial consciousness is another aspect of "false consciousness," which for Marxists refers to the totally false and misleading view of how the world works that is presented to the victims of exploitation by the ruling elite. This false consciousness, which says that African Americans are biologically and culturally inferior to whites, prevents workers from seeing their common interest, which is the destruction of capitalism.

A newer Marxist perspective does not deny the earlier interpretation but adds a significant new factor to it. The best explanation of this view is found in the work of historian Eugene Genovese, especially in *Roll, Jordan, Roll: The World the Slaves Made* (1974). The new factor is the creation of a racial consciousness among the exploited population that challenges the supremacist ideas of the ruling class. This spirit of nationalism among the victims of racist thought helps them create a sense of purpose and dignity. These values help them eventually come together to challenge the economic and political power of the dominating elite.

Both Marxist views describe black-white relations within the context of a capitalist economy. Capitalist society is already divided into social classes that have unequal power, so the division of the lowest class, the workers, into racially hostile camps makes the task of organizing a revolution just that much more difficult. For Marxists, a revolution led by workers is the only way to eliminate inequality. Racism, like low wages and child labor, is another form of inequality. The question is how attitudes based on white supremacy can be overcome.

One proposal calls for all workers to unite in a colorless, raceless, revolutionary struggle simply by recognizing the absurdity of racist pronouncements. The other model for change calls for workers to discover the contradictory nature of racism. They need to understand that racism is a source of oppression and division that prevents workers from joining together in the fight for equality. However, at the same time, the horrors of white society's racist past have stimulated an ideology of liberation and unity among the people most severely injured by that past. Eventually that new spirit of revolt (black nationalism) will help lead the way toward the destruction of capitalist society itself. Marxists generally believe that once economic exploitation is ended, racism, too, will disappear, because there will no longer be a need for it. More recent Marxian scholars are more skeptical of that view and less sanguine about any end to economic exploitation.

———*Leslie V. Tischauser*

BIBLIOGRAPHY AND FURTHER READING

"Marxism, Racism and the Construction of 'Race' as a Social and Political Relation: An Interview with Professor Robert Miles." Interview by Brendan F. McGeever and Stephen D. Ashe. *Ethnic and Racial Studies* 12 (2011): 2009+. Print.

Mills, Charles W. *From Class to Race: Essays in White Marxism and Black Radicalism.* Lanham: Rowman, 2003. Print.

Spencer, Stephen. *Race and Ethnicity : Culture, Identity and Representation.* Hoboken: Routledge, 2014. Print.

Waymer, Damion. *Culture, Social Class, and Race in Public Relations: Perspectives and Applications.* Lanham: Lexington, 2012. Print.

MASS INCARCERATION OF AFRICAN AMERICANS AND OTHER ETHNIC MINORITIES

America's prison population has grown enormously since the 1970s. Scholars cite several reasons for this expansion. Crime rates had grown during the previous decade and, coupled with the fear of public disorder that accompanied the civil rights and anti-war movements, a "war on crime" promised to stem such disruption. Politicians across the ideological spectrum determined that "law and order" and being "tough on crime" were popular positions. Meanwhile sweeping global economic changes led to high levels of unemployment among unskilled workers. Such changes hit young black men in inner cities especially hard. This group became a symbol of social disorder and a target for social control. Media attention to high-profile crimes and sympathetic victims helped to promote a victims' rights movement. States and the federal government invested heavily in prison construction as both a job creator and a solution to a social problem. Finally, a generally conservative political ethos supported the idea that those who committed crimes did so by their own free choice and therefore deserved punishment rather than rehabilitation. These trends together led to a huge growth in incarceration, a growth that had a disproportionate negative effect on minority groups.

FACTS OF MASS INCARCERATION

Numbers released by the Bureau of Justice Statistics reveal the extraordinary expansion of America's prison population during the last decades of the twentieth century and the beginning of the twenty-first century. In 2003, more than 5.6 million Americans had served time in prison. More than one-fifth of all the people incarcerated in the world were in the United States, as the US had the highest incarceration rate of any nation. Between 1980 and 2010 the number of prisoners increased by 373 percent, from 319,598 to 1,543,206. At the same time, if one also included those in jails and under probation or parole supervision in the community, the numbers increased from less than 2 million to more than 7 million. The average cost of incarcerating a person was $29,000 per year, more than ten time what it would cost for community supervision. The numbers alone paint a picture of a system of incarceration that experienced exponential growth.

The reasons for this expansion can be correlated with several policy trends. On the one hand, the "War on Drugs" saw both states and the federal government opt for longer sentences for a variety of drug-related offenses. At the same time, most state legislatures in the 1990s chose to abolish parole—a policy that resulted in inmates serving out their full sentences, rather than having an option for an earlier release. Both state and federal judges lost some of their sentencing discretion, as more jurisdictions adopted mandatory minimum requirements for many crimes. In addition, during the late twentieth century, "three strikes" laws aimed at repeat offenders could mean a sentence of twenty-five years to life, even for some fairly minor crimes. Finally, many inmates were sent back to prison after release because of "technical violations," not for a new crime but for such infractions as failing to meet with a probation officer. Although the vast number of people in prison included many violent criminals who belonged behind bars for reasons of public safety, they were not the bulk of those in prison. More than two-thirds of those incarcerated annually were convicted of nonviolent crimes—drug offenses in particular. Imprisonment rates tended to be highest in the south, lower in the northern and midwestern states.

The impact of the mass incarceration movement has fallen disproportionately on members of minority groups. While African Americans and Latinos made up 30 percent of the general population in 2013, they accounted for 58 percent of prison inmates. Incarceration rates for black men are five times as high as for white men. One in eight African American men in their late twenties is currently serving time, and one in five black men can anticipate a prison sentence at some point in his life.

Some scholars have argued that the disparate effect of mass incarceration on minority groups is a foreseeable result of deliberate policy choices. Certainly much of the "War on Drugs" was carried out in ways that targeted racial minorities. Perhaps the most notorious example is the federal law that established sentence differentials for crack cocaine (associated with African Americans) and powdered cocaine (associated with whites). Although the drugs are essentially similar, the penalty for crack distribution was 100 times the penalty for distributing powdered cocaine. After decades, Congress finally addressed this issue by lowering the penalty ratio to 18:1. It is also widely recognized that law enforcement agencies have often chosen to fight the drug war on the streets of the inner city rather than on college campuses or in more affluent areas. Given the decision to target such "hot spots," it is not surprising that minorities are more likely to be apprehended. Aside from drug-related arrests, policies such as "stop and frisk," used by the New York City police, led to detaining millions of citizens, disproportionately African Americans and Hispanics. Once brought into the criminal justice system and charged with a crime, minorities are more likely to be denied bail, to receive inadequate legal representation, and to receive longer sentences due to prior offending. It is the cumulative effects of all of these factors that contribute to longer sentences, not necessarily based on overt racial bias but with a foreseeable negative impact.

COLLATERAL DAMAGE

It may be argued that mass incarceration has created a new mechanism of social control that locks many racial and ethnic minorities into a life-long inferior status. People who have served a prison sentence are likely to be permanently stigmatized and marginalized. They will have problems reintegrating into society as finding employment will be difficult, especially for the unskilled. Laws enacted during the most punitive era of the 1980s and 1990s frequently prohibit ex-offenders from welfare eligibility, educational or housing opportunities, and, in many states, from voting or enjoying the full benefits of citizenship. Likewise, the damage for families and neighborhoods from the disproportionate imprisonment of African American men extends into future generations.

——*Mary Welek Atwell*

BIBLIOGRAPHY AND FURTHER READING

Alexander, Michelle. *The New Jim Crow: Mass Incarceration in the Age of Colorblindness*. New York: New Press, 2010. Print.

Clear, Todd and Natasha A. Frost. *The Punishment Imperative: The Rise and Failure of Mass Incarceration in America*. New York: New York UP, 2014. Print.

Ingle, Joseph B. *Slouching Toward Tyranny: Mass Incarceration, Death Sentences, and Racism*. New York: Algora Publishing, 2015. Print.

Simon, Jonathan. *Mass Incarceration on Trial: A Remarkable Court Decision and the Future of Prisons in America*. New York: New Press, 2014. Print.

Spohn, Cassia. "Race, Crime, and Punishment in the Twentieth and Twenty-first Century." *Crime and Justice* 44.1 (2015). Web. 14 March 2017.

MASSACHUSETTS "BODY OF LIBERTIES"

From its outset, the Massachusetts Bay Colony endorsed the idea of unfree labor. One hundred eighty indentured servants arrived with the original colonists. Food shortages led to the surviving servants' being set free in 1830. Unfree labor, however, continued on a private basis, and some white criminals were made slaves of court-appointed masters. Captives from the Pequot War of 1636–1637 were given over into slavery. Some of these captives were subsequently transported to a Puritan enclave off the coast of Nicaragua, and black slaves were introduced from there to the Massachusetts colony. The colony, however, remained without a formal endorsement of slavery until the promulgation of the Body of Liberties in 1641.

THE CREATION OF THE DOCUMENT

The Body of Liberties evolved out of the gradually weakening authority of Governor John Winthrop and his first Board of Assistants, and the emergence of the General Court as a representative body of freemen. In 1635, the General Court had appointed a committee to draw up a body of laws for the rights and duties of the colonists. This committee stalled over the church-state conflict, and another committee was impaneled in 1636. John Cotton sat on this committee. Cotton was a devout churchman who drafted a document that derived much of its authority from scripture. Cotton did, however, believe in limitations on authority and resisted adopting biblical statutes wholesale. Winthrop, who was lukewarm to the entire idea, called Cotton's code, "Moses his Judicialls."

Cotton's counterpart in drawing up the code was Nathaniel Ward. Ward was a Puritan with a sense of humor and a literary bent. Like most Puritans, he was a friend to strict discipline, but he also was a foe to arbitrary authority. He agreed with Winthrop and Cotton that all law was the law of God, but he insisted that the code be based on English common law rather than on the Bible. He became the chief architect and intellectual godfather of the Body of Liberties. The Pequot War slowed deliberations, but by 1639, the committee had created a document that combined Cotton's and Ward's work. The final document was adopted in November, 1641.

THE SLAVERY ISSUE

In many ways, the Body of Liberties was an enlightened document and certainly remarkable by seventeenth century standards. A compilation of one hundred laws, the Body of Liberties allowed for wide judicial discretion and for each case to be judged on its merits. It also effectively barred the legal profession from defending anyone for pay, and it protected married women from assault. It addressed the liberties of servants in humanitarian terms for those times, limiting the number of lashes given to servants to forty. The capital laws were more lenient than those of England. The one problem, however, was slavery. This bold document addressed the slavery issue thus:

There shall never be any bond slaverie, villainage or captivitie amongst us unles it be lawfull captive, taken in just warres, and such strangers as willingly selle themselves or are sold to us. And these shall have all the liberties and Christian usages which the law of God established in Israell concerning such persons doeth morally require. This exempts none from servitude who shall be judged thereto by authoritie.

Although not a ringing endorsement of slavery, the Body of Liberties nevertheless admits of it, opening the way for the official sanction of slavery. Later and stricter codes would formalize the institution in New England on a colony-by-colony basis, largely because trading in slaves was profitable. Yankee traders found that slaves were more valuable as cargo to be sold to the plantation colonies or in the West Indies than as laborers in the northern economy.

By 1680, Governor Simon Bradstreet estimated the number of "blacks or slaves" in the Massachusetts colony at one hundred to two hundred. The equation of race ("blacks") with slavery here is important. Some special laws were passed restricting the movement of African Americans in white society, but the Puritans encouraged Christian conversion and honored marriages between blacks. The conditions of slavery were not as harsh as in the plantation colonies. Slaves needed to read and write to do their jobs. Although there were occasional isolated rebellions, the slaves benefited from the New England love for learning and the strong Puritan emphasis on marriage and family.

Slavery gradually faded away in Massachusetts, perhaps because of its vague legal status. In the aftermath of the American Revolution, a national clamor for a Bill of Rights led individual colonies to adopt their own. While none expressly forbade slavery, the institution seemed at odds with the rhetoric. By 1776, the white population of Massachusetts was 343,845 and the black population was 5,249. The census of 1790 showed Massachusetts as the only state in which no slaves were listed.

Despite the legalization of slavery in the Body of Liberties, slavery was never popular in Massachusetts except as incidental to trade—and the slave trade was an accepted practice by seventeenth century European standards. The Puritans themselves were products of a rigorous, harsh, isolated experience. They were humanists and intellectuals with contradictions. They prized sincerity and truthfulness, yet practiced repression and inhibition to steel themselves against life's ills. They had a strong element of individualism in their creed, believing that each person must face his maker alone. Puritan humanism therefore never squared with the institution of slavery.

———*Brian G. Tobin*

BIBLIOGRAPHY AND FURTHER READING

Bailey, Richard A. Race and Redemption in Puritan New England. New York: Oxford UP, 2011. Print.

McManus, Edgar J. Black Bondage in the North. Syracuse: Syracuse UP, 1973. Print.

Hardesty, Jared Ross. Unfreedom: Slavery and Dependence in Eighteenth Century Boston. New York: New York UP, 2016. Print.

White, Deborah Gray, Mia Bay, and Waldo E. Martin, Jr. Freedom on My Mind: A History of African Americans, with Documents. Boston: Macmillan, 2012. Print.

Winch, Julie. Between Slavery and Freedom: Free People of Color in America from Settlement to the Civil War. Lanham: Rowman, 2014. Print.

MASSIE CASE

One evening in 1931, Thalia Massie, wife of naval lieutenant Thomas Massie, walked home from a nightclub in Waikiki, Honolulu, Hawaii. Arriving home with her face bruised and her lips swollen, she claimed that she had been raped by dark-skinned local men. After police arrested five young men who were having an altercation with a couple in another car, they took the five men to her hospital room, where she identified the five as her rapists but only after police brought them into her hospital room four or five times. The evidence was so slim that a jury of local residents refused to bring in a verdict in *Hawaii v. Ahakuelo* (1931).

Incensed that justice had not prevailed, the Massies sought revenge. With the aid of two subordinate naval officers, the Massies arranged to abduct one of the defendants, who was tortured and accidentally shot. In *Hawaii v. Massie* (1932), the conspirators were convicted of murder despite an eloquent defense by their attorney, Clarence Darrow. After sentence was passed, Governor Lawrence Judd commuted the sentence to one hour of detention in the office of the governor. For Asian Americans and native Hawaiians, the Massie case became the symbol of white misrule over nonwhites.

———*Michael Haas*

BIBLIOGRAPHY AND FURTHER READING

Leverenz, David. *Honor Bound: Race and Shame in America.* New Brunswick: Rutgers UP, 2012. Print.

Rosa, John P. *Local Story: The Massie-Kahahawai Case and the Culture of History.* Honolulu: U of Hawaii P, 2014. Print.

McCLESKEY V. KEMP

In *McCleskey v. Kemp*, the Supreme Court on April 22, 1987, rejected a death row inmate's claim that Georgia's system of sentencing people to death was unconstitutional because it discriminated on the basis of race.

In 1978, Warren McCleskey, a black man, was convicted of killing a white police officer during an armed robbery of a store in Atlanta, Georgia. McCleskey's jury—which consisted of eleven whites and one black—sentenced him to die in Georgia's electric chair. McCleskey sought a writ of *habeas corpus*, arguing, among other things, that the Georgia capital sentencing process was administered in a racially discriminatory manner and violated the United States

Constitution. According to McCleskey, the jury's decision to execute him violated the Eighth Amendment because racial bias rendered the decision arbitrary and capricious. Also, the equal protection clause of the Fourteenth Amendment was violated because McCleskey, a black man, was treated differently from white defendants in the same position.

To support his claim of racial discrimination, McCleskey offered as evidence a sophisticated statistical study performed by Professor David B. Baldus and his colleagues at the University of Iowa (the Baldus study). The Baldus study showed that race played a dual role in deciding whether convicted murderers in Georgia would be sentenced to death. First, the race of the murder victim played a large role in whether a defendant would be sentenced to die. According to the study, defendants charged with killing whites received the death penalty in 11 percent of the cases. Defendants charged with killing blacks received the death penalty in only 1 percent of the cases. After taking account of thirty-nine variables that could have explained the disparities on nonracial grounds, the Baldus study concluded that, in Georgia, defendants charged with killing white victims were 4.3 times as likely to receive a death sentence as defendants charged with killing blacks.

Second, the race of the defendant played an important role during capital sentencing. According to the Baldus study, black defendants were 1.1 times as likely to receive a death sentence as other defendants. Thus, the study showed that black defendants such as McCleskey who had killed white victims had the greatest likelihood of receiving the death penalty.

By a 5 to 4 vote, the Supreme Court ruled against McCleskey. The Supreme Court accepted the validity of the Baldus study but held that McCleskey failed to prove "that decisionmakers in his case acted with discriminatory purpose." In other words, McCleskey failed to show that his constitutional rights were violated because he did not prove that anyone involved in his particular case intentionally discriminated against him based on his race. Justice Lewis Powell's opinion for the majority expressed special concern that if the Court accepted McCleskey's argument—that racial bias impermissibly tainted capital sentencing proceedings—all criminal sentences would be subject to attack based on allegations of racial discrimination. The *McCleskey* decision is a landmark ruling in the modern era of capital punishment.

Warren McCleskey died in Georgia's electric chair on September 25, 1991. That same year Justice Powell, whose 5 to 4 majority opinion had sealed Warren McCleskey's fate, told a biographer that he would change his vote in that case (thus sparing McCleskey's life) if he could. Also, although executions had resumed in the United States in 1977, 1991 marked the first time in the modern era of American capital punishment that a white defendant (Donald "Pee Wee" Gaskins) was executed for killing a black person.

——Randall Coyne

MEECH LAKE ACCORD

Fears that Quebec might break away from the rest of Canada led Canadian prime minister Brian Mulroney and the ten provincial premiers in 1987 to propose a set of amendments to the 1982 Constitution Act. The proposal, known as the Meech Lake Accord after the site of the meeting, recognized French-speaking Quebec as one of the founding nations of Canada and as a distinct society with its own language and culture. The accord, however, granted no such courtesy to the aboriginal peoples of Canada. In order for the accord to become law, it required ratification by all ten provinces before June 23, 1990.

An additional provision of the Meech Lake Accord dealt with admission of a new province to the Confederation. That provision required the unanimous consent of the ten existing provinces in order to establish a new province. Since many of the provinces have territorial desires to extend their borders north, this virtually ensured that the Yukon and Northwest territories, as well as the proposed Nunavut Territory, would be precluded from ever achieving provincial status. Unlike the rest of Canada, the two regions have overwhelmingly native populations.

Native organizations fought bitterly against ratification of the accord. Their leaders insisted that native cultures were no less distinct than Quebec's and that aboriginal rights also deserved formal recognition in the body of the constitution. Since the courts had held that despite the addition of the Charter of Rights and Freedoms to the constitution, aboriginal rights were not assured, the natives' concerns were well justified. The leaders further demanded guarantees that they would be given a role in all future First Ministers' conferences affecting natives. George Erasmus, national chief of the Assembly of First Nations, was especially vocal.

Thinking that a looming deadline would help assure passage, Prime Minister Mulroney delayed pushing for ratification of the accord until the very end of the ratification period. That delay proved fatal to the proposal. It allowed Elijah Harper, Manitoba's only native legislator, to prevent consideration of the Meech Lake Accord by the Manitoba Legislative Assembly. Supported by native organizations, Harper exploited a procedural error made by Manitoba Premier Gary Filmon. Manitoba law required unanimous consent of the legislators to begin public hearings on any issue with less than a forty-eight-hour notice. Harper withheld his consent, and the deadline for ratification passed without the Meech Lake Accord ever being considered by the Manitoba Legislative Assembly.

——*Richard G. Condon and Pamela R. Stern*

MELTING POT THEORY

At the beginning of the twentieth century, the playwright Israel Zangwill described the United States as a society in which cultural, ethnic, and racial differences would disappear, and people would become amalgamated. His vision was of people from many different racial and ethnic groups socializing freely with one another, sharing customs and values, intermarrying, and creating one uniquely American culture. This vision was called the "melting pot ideal."

Many Americans share a melting pot ideal, but some ethnic groups have "blended in" far more easily than others. Immigrant ancestors of some white ethnic groups, including the Irish and Jews, experienced much prejudice and discrimination. Over time, however, whites have been better able to gain access to the power structure than nonwhites, enabling them to blend in and shape the dominant American culture. White Americans whose families have been in the United States for many generations usually are not viewed as "hyphenated" Americans—Swedish Americans or German Americans—and major cultural distinctions among descendants of most white ethnic groups have "melted" away over time. These groups have intermarried, have learned the English language, have worked to achieve higher socioeconomic standing, and have become acculturated. Most whites, therefore, epitomize the melting pot ideal.

Discrimination and poverty, however, have prevented many members of nonwhite ethnic groups

The image of the United States as a melting pot was popularized by the 1908 play The Melting Pot.

from blending in with the rest of the society. Only with the passage of civil rights legislation in the 1960's were many nonwhites even allowed to vote. For example, black slaves and most of their descendants were denied opportunities to achieve higher education, obtain jobs, enter the middle class, live in white neighborhoods, gain access to power structures, and be recognized for personal achievements and their contributions to the United States. One consequence is that almost one-third of African Americans live below the poverty line, compared with one-tenth of whites. African Americans, historically, have been one of the least successful groups at blending into the great melting pot of mostly middle-class Americans.

In the second half of the twentieth century, immigrants have been far more likely to come from a variety of Latin American and Asian countries rather than European nations. Many find it difficult to assimilate because of anti-immigrant attitudes among some long-established Americans who sometimes claim that immigration means fewer jobs and more taxation for themselves. Welfare stereotypes have also contributed to xenophobia, or hatred of foreigners. As a result, some politicians have proposed public policies that deny immigrants and their children access to schools, jobs, citizenship, and basic social services. Even when those proposals do not become law, a hostile climate for nonwhite ethnic groups develops, making a true melting pot impossible.

Moreover, not all Americans wish to completely blend into the dominant culture, believing that the United States is enriched by celebrating diverse cultural traditions, and not by asking or forcing people to completely assimilate. Proponents of this position prefer the metaphor of the mixed salad bowl, in which each ingredient (ethnic group), makes a unique and important contribution to the taste of the entire "salad." It is further argued that idealizing the United States as a melting pot merely provides justification for members of the power structure to impose their cultural values on others—for example, with English-only initiatives. Still others argue that more "melting" must take place among the ethnic groups before a true sense of unity can be attained among all Americans.

——*Grace Maria Marvin*

BIBLIOGRAPHY AND FURTHER READING

Orosco, José-Antonio. *Toppling the Melting Pot: Immigration and Multiculturalism in American Pragmatism*. Bloomington: Indiana UP, 2016. Print.

Sollers, Werner, ed. *Theories of Ethnicity: A Classical Reader.* New York: New York UP, 1996. Print.

Wilson, Sarah. *Melting Pot Modernism*. Ithaca: Cornell UP, 2010. Print.

MERITOCRACY MYTH

The myth of meritocracy assumes that those at the pinnacle of society's institutions have achieved their status solely through merit. Many elites possess meritorious criteria: intelligence, prestigious degrees, and high scores on "objective" tests. Therefore, proponents of meritocracy argue that stratification is the legitimate result of talented, hardworking individuals besting lackluster or lazy ones. Some even argue that those who fail to achieve are either genetically or culturally inferior. Critics of meritocracy ask whether racial and ethnic minorities have an equal chance to compete—that is, whether there is equality of opportunity in the United States. They point out that social circumstances, from the onset of life to its end, are profoundly unequal. Some children are born into

families through which they inherit privileges and advantages. Familial advantages are augmented by institutional discrimination, such as in education in the United States. Critics argue that as a myth, or moral fiction, meritocracy justifies racial and ethnic (and class and gender) stratification and masks power and privilege; moreover, opponents submit that the measures of merit (for example, intelligence tests) are culturally biased. One policy question since 1965 (affirmative action) has been debated by those who, opposing the myth, want to implement more inclusive, multicultural standards, and merit fundamentalists who contend that merit is untainted and should prevail as the undiluted justification of status.

——*Gil Richard Musolf*

BIBLIOGRAPHY AND FURTHER READING

Lippert-Rasmussen, Kasper. *Born Free and Equal?: A Philosophical Inquiry into the Nature of Discrimination.* New York: Oxford UP, 2014. Print.

McNamee, Stephen J., and Robert K. Miller. *The Meritocracy Myth.* Lanham: Rowman, 2013. Print.

MESTIZO

"Mestizo" is a Spanish word that comes from the Latin *mixtus*, meaning mixed, and it refers to any person of mixed ancestry. The term always implies that the mestizo speaks either Spanish or Portuguese fluently, and there have also been implications of biological superiority and inferiority associated with the term. In Latin America, the definition of "mestizo" varies from country to country, and it must be understood in its cultural context. In Central and South America, it designates a person of combined Indian and European extraction. In Mexico, the word was originally used to indicate any person of mixed Indian and white ancestry, but the definition has become so vague and variable that it is no longer used in census reports in Mexico. The upper-class people of mixed ancestry in Mexico are now called Creole or *cruzado* rather than mestizo. In some countries, particularly Ecuador, mestizo has taken on social and cultural connotations, referring to pure-blooded Indians who have adopted European dress and customs. In Brazil, a person who speaks Portuguese, lives as a storekeeper or trader in the backwoods, and deals with the Indians is typically referred to as a mestizo. However, in the Philippines, the term denotes any person of mixed foreign and native ancestry.

——*Alvin K. Benson*

MÉTIS

In the broadest sense, *métis* (pronounced mehTEE), with a small *m*, refers to people of a dual North American Indian and white ancestry. *Métis*, with a capital *M*, indicates a distinctive ethnic group with a particular sociocultural heritage and/or political or legal category. In Canada, Métis usually refers to people who are descendants of Scottish or French fur traders who married Cree or Ojibwa women. The French traders operated along the St. Lawrence River in Acadia (part of New France) and the British in the Hudson Bay region, creating two groups of Métis, those with French ancestry along the Ottawa River and Upper Great Lakes and those of Scottish ancestry in the Hudson Bay region from the Rupert River to Churchill.

FRENCH MÉTIS

The French contingent of the Métis is older and more populous than its Scottish counterpart. Initially, French officials supported intermarriage, hoping to forge trading and kinship ties, encourage conversion to Christianity, and populate New France. In the 1600's, Métis families and communities developed from Acadia to Labrador. The union was usually between a French man and a native woman. During this period, Métis were used as interpreters, intermediaries, and distributors of gifts from French officials.

By the eighteenth century, partly because of the increased presence of white women, policy and opinion shifted against mixed marriages, especially those not sanctioned by the church. The official policy of discouraging mixed unions was probably one of several factors that led to the formation of distinct Métis communities in New France. Numerous American and Canadian communities around the Great Lakes originated as biracial communities, namely Detroit and Michilimackinac in Michigan; Sault Sainte Marie in Ontario; Chicago and Peoria in Illinois; Milwaukee, Green Bay, and Prairie du Chien in Wisconsin.

These communities developed a culture of their own, which included an attenuated form of French Catholicism. Family and daily life was largely based on the norms of Indian society. Métis worked as

MÉTIS, NON-ABORIGINAL, AND OVERALL POPULATION IN CANADA, BY SEX, 2006

	Métis	Non-Aboriginal	Total Population
Both sexes	389,780	30,068,240	31,241,030
Male	193,500	14,754,175	15,326,270
Female	196,285	15,314,065	15,914,760

Source: Statistics Canada, 2006.

MÉTIS AND NON-ABORIGINAL POPULATION IN CANADA BY AGE GROUPS, 2011

	Métis	Non-Aboriginal
0–4 years	34,860	1,737,585
5–9 years	32,845	1,677,585
10–14 years	36,710	1,785,520
15–24 years	80,035	4,069,550
25–64 years	237,705	17,712,545
65 years and older	29,635	4,468,850

Source: Statistics Canada, National Household Survey, 2011.

guides, interpreters, voyagers, or suppliers to the forts. The region was rich in game, fish, wild rice, and maple sugar, and the climate and environment were conducive to a slash-and-burn style of farming. In essence, the Métis of French ancestry followed the Indian way of life. An Indian woman was indispensable, because in that society, a man lost position and respect if he did any tasks considered women's work, such as cooking or sewing.

SCOTTISH MÉTIS

The Métis of Scottish ancestry developed quite differently. After the Treaty of Utrecht in 1713, Hudson's Bay Company posts were established north of the Great Lakes watershed, the region draining into Hudson Bay. Enclaves of Cree Indians formed around the trading posts, and the Indians became provisioners who were crucial for the survival and success of the company. To consolidate trade and ensure a lasting friendship, the Crees offered women as wives to the Europeans. No white women were at the trading posts, but the Hudson's Bay Company had strict rules prohibiting its employees from marrying Indians. The company believed it necessary to prohibit white-Indian unions because it wanted to maximize security, minimize expenses (such as those incurred by dependents of the employees), and decrease friction with the Indians. Despite the prohibition, unions occurred. By 1810, the company began to take responsibility for educating the progeny of its trading post employees; however, it also discouraged the formation of communities dependent on the trading post by removing from the Hudson Bay region all retired and dismissed employees and encouraging the Indians to disperse to their hunting grounds each winter. Except for a few children who became servants for the company, mixed-race offspring were absorbed by the Crees.

ESTABLISHING A MÉTIS IDENTITY

With the British conquest of New France in 1760, a sense of separateness began developing among the Métis. Francophones were relegated to lower ranks, and in the United States, after the Canadian-United States boundary was established in 1794, American white settlers and governments displaced numerous

Métis communities in the lower Great Lakes region. These refugees migrated northwest to Manitoba and Minnesota.

In the northwest, the Métis evolved a distinct way of life that was neither Indian nor European but uniquely Métis. When conflict erupted in the region, the North West Company argued that the Métis were defending an identity and interest of their own. The company policy had the side effect of helping the Métis develop a sense of unity. Catholic missionaries encouraged the Métis to maintain their French language and Catholic faith. Group identity was further fostered when a large group of Métis settled at Red River, attracted by the mission of Bishop Joseph Provencher and led by Cuthbert Grant, who was of mixed ancestry. However, it was the buffalo hunt that brought the Métis together. The excitement of hunting buffalo and profits from selling pemmican and buffalo meat were preferred over the dullness and low profitability of agriculture. Hunting for buffalo and working on boat brigades to St. Paul encouraged Métis to remain nomadic.

DECLINE OF THE MÉTIS

Change for the Métis came fast when Canada began annexing the northwest. The buffalo hunt was ending, and railroads were replacing boats and carts. An attempt by the Canadian government to survey the Red River without respecting the land held by the Métis resulted in the Riel Rebellion of 1869–70 (also known as the Red River Rebellion). The Métis, led by Louis Riel Jr., set up a provisional government to fight for their collective rights. Negotiations that followed promised a land base for the Métis, but the promises were not kept, and European Canadian settlers and troops who arrived in the area from 1870 on were hostile to the Métis. Although some Métis went south to the United States and others went north, most went west to the Catholic mission near Fort Edmonton. While the government was negotiating treaties with the Indians and land rights with the railroads, the Métis sought clear land titles but were ignored. In frustration, the Saskatchewan Métis took up arms under Riel and Gabriel Dumont in the Second Riel Rebellion of 1885 (also known as the Northwest Rebellion). They were defeated at Batoche, Riel was executed, and the Métis dispersed, particularly to Alberta, weakened politically and cohesively.

From 1885 to the mid-1900's, the Métis were impoverished and demoralized. Some lived on reservations with the Indians, but others did not identify as strongly with this part of their heritage. During this time, they formed some associations, including the Union Nationale Métisse St. Joseph de Manitoba, which collected documents and testimony that led to A. H. de Trémaudan's *Hold High Your Heads: History of the Métis Nation in Western Canada*. In addition, new leaders, such as Patrick "Jim" Brady and Malcolm Norris, emerged to build a political base to defend Métis interests. Provincial organizations then developed, and the Métis eventually were successful in obtaining some land for their group and passage of the Métis Population Betterment Act of 1938.

MODERN MÉTIS CULTURE

Of the 451,795 self-identified Métis in Canada in 2011, nearly 85 percent resided in the western provinces or Ontario. The Métis have a distinct culture, often combining Indian and Euro-Canadian culture. For example, "jigging," a form of Métis dance, combines the reels of Scotland and France with the chicken dance of the Crees. The Métis language combines English, French, and Cree words and is spoken in addition to English. Most in the settlements retain Indian spiritual beliefs and customs. The Métis are working to make schools in their region more responsive to their culture.

The economy is dominated by ranching, logging, farming, and energy products. The Métis have developed a mixed plan that combines traditional economic activities with industrial and other commercial ventures. Also, efforts to grant land titles to the Métis began in the mid-1980s.

——Arthur W. Helweg

BIBLIOGRAPHY AND FURTHER READING

"Aboriginal Peoples in Canada: First Nations People, Métis and Inuit." *Statistics Canada.* Government of Canada, 28 Mar. 2014. Web. 1 Apr. 2015.

"Aboriginal Peoples Highlight Tables, 2006 Census." *Statistics Canada.* Government of Canada, 15 Jan. 2008. Web. 1 Apr. 2015.

Gadacz, René R. "Métis Settlements." *Canadian Encyclopedia.* Historica Canada, 27 Oct. 2014. Web. 7 Apr. 2015

Sealely, D. Bruce, and Antoine Lussier. *The Metis: Canada's Forgotten People.* Winnipeg: Pemmican, 1981. Print.

Zeilig, Ken, and Victoria Zeilig. *Ste. Madeleine: Community without a Town.* Winnipeg: Pemmican, 1987. Print.

MEXICAN AMERICANS AND MEXICAN IMMIGRANTS

Although Mexican immigration and the status of many Mexican Americans have become political flashpoints in recent decades, how Mexican Americans have been culturally included/excluded has been an issue in the United States at least since the end of the Mexican-American War. During the last twenty years, there have continually been more than one million people in Mexico on the waiting list for legal immigration to the United States, with about 65,000 per year being admitted in the past decade.

HISTORICAL PERSPECTIVE

Although Mexico did not exist as a country until 1821, people from the colony of New Spain lived in what would eventually become territory within the United States for centuries prior to that date. With the American victory in the Mexican-American War in 1848, the territorial gain created substantial numbers of new Mexican Americans. While these individuals were legally full citizens of the United States, they generally were not treated as equals by those coming from the Eastern states. With the exception of the 1930 census, Americans who came, or whose ancestors came, from Mexico were normally categorized as white. Only with the 1970 census did the nonracial category of Hispanic begin to be used on some forms. However, the fact that most immigrants from Mexico were legally considered white by the federal government did not mean they were recognized as such by all states, or that there was not discrimination in some settings.

Early in the twentieth century, large numbers of Mexican migrant agricultural workers were recruited. Being exempt from the Immigration Act of 1924, this continued until the Depression. Beginning with the World War II labor shortage, temporary Mexican immigrants were sought in large numbers, again with some social animosity directed toward them by people from other racial/ethnic groups. Many of these 1940s immigrants eventually became permanent residents,

or citizens. However, in the early 1950s, the overall number of legal immigrants was greatly reduced. Thus, more Mexicans desired to work in the United States than were able to get proper documentation. Even with these restrictions, except for the decade after World War II when Germany surpassed Mexico as the largest source of immigrants, more Mexicans have legally moved to the United States than from any other country. People from Mexico also have continually comprised the largest group of illegal immigrants in the post–World War II era.

Immigration reform in 1965 established a more complex system (previously it was a national origins quota system), with the plan that new immigrants have the skills needed by American businesses. However, there was no net change in immigration from Mexico, as it remained the largest source of legal immigrants to the United States due to the continued need for agricultural workers and to families being divided by the border. It should be noted that under the new system, more immigrants from Mexico worked in white-collar jobs and executive positions than had previously been the case. However, the majority of people still filled agricultural and manual labor positions. Prior to 1965, many temporary visa programs allowed only men into the country, but this gradually changed with the emergence of greater equality for women. Because the demand for farm-workers in the Southwest far surpassed the legal number of Mexican immigrants, many were "unofficially" allowed to overstay their visas, since farm owners were willing to hire workers who lacked the proper documentation. This pattern of high demand, and a low supply of legal workers, has caused many employers to ignore the law since the 1950s.

The Immigration Reform and Control Act of 1986 was supposed to penalize employers for hiring undocumented workers, but the measure was generally seen as a complete failure in terms of stopping illegal immigration, although more illegal immigrants had to purchase forged documents. Both categories of Mexican Americans, legal and undocumented, continued to increase until the opening years of the present century. Of the Hispanics in the United States, about 64 percent have their roots in Mexico. They tend to be concentrated in the two states—California and Texas—that have traditionally provided the most agricultural jobs for them although they have moved to virtually all areas where there is a high demand for semi-skilled agricultural workers or for people willing to undertake common manual labor. This also resulted in Mexican immigrants being, on average, ten years younger than all other immigrants during the period of 1960 through 1990. According to a Pew Research Center study, 28 percent of all immigrants (legal and illegal) came from Mexico during the period of 1965 to 2015.

RECENT SITUATION

The 1970 census recorded the lowest percentage of foreign-born residents/citizens ever in the United States, due to the strict laws which had been in place (1924 and 1952 laws). According to census data, foreign-born residents/citizens was generally about 13 percent from the mid-nineteenth century to 1920, then slowly dropping to less than 5 percent in 1970, before continually rising to return to 13 percent in 2010. Mexican Americans, as the most numerous group in this total (about 28 percent of all foreign born residents/citizens), became the group which was targeted by those desiring to decrease the number of foreign-born residents/citizens in the United States. (In 2013, Mexico was the largest source of immigrants in thirty-three of the fifty states.)

In addition, after attempts to control illegal immigration with major new laws in 1986 and 1990 failed, the number of undocumented immigrants became a political issue, with major divisions between the Democratic and Republican parties. In 2012, it was estimated that over 26 percent of foreign-born individuals in the United States were here illegally, with about 52 percent of those being Mexican. In more recent years, the issue of Mexican immigration, legal and illegal, has mixed with the larger issues of nationalism and racism in the United States. When discussed at the national level, Democrats tend to support "pathways to citizenship" for those who are in the country illegally (especially those who came as children, brought by their parents), while Republicans hold the opposite position.

The continual increase in the number of Mexican Americans, since World War II, ended by 2005. Since that time, more Mexican Americans have moved back to Mexico than the number of Mexicans coming to the United States. However, even with this outflow of Mexicans, in early 2017, the Mexico's share of the 11 million undocumented aliens had increased to about two thirds of the total.

As economic immigrants, Mexican Americans have an average income which is three times as high as the average income in Mexico. However, it is low for the United States, as the general population averaged $51,400 (2014) in income, while Mexican Americans averaged only $38,000. This reflects the fact that, in 2010, nationally, about 40 percent of workers were in management, professional, or related occupations, while only about 18 percent of Mexican Americans fell into this category. In addition, although the rate of homeownership is higher for Mexican Americans than for Hispanics in general, the average savings, home equity, and other economic resources, is, for Hispanics, less than 20 percent of the national average for all residents in, or citizens of, the United States.

2016 PRESIDENTIAL ELECTION AND BEYOND

In the 2016 presidential campaign, the Republican candidate, Donald J. Trump, featured a pledge that he would "Build a Wall" along the border with Mexico. This morphed into one of the most popular chants at his rallies. Most voters supporting the Republican candidate did not realize that President Obama had been deporting more people back to Mexico than had his predecessors. As president, Trump has had federal agents take dramatic steps toward increasing deportation further. Trump has also asked for proposals from companies desiring to build a wall, although there has been no progress toward his promise of making Mexico pay for the wall. Whatever the eventual outcome, the popularity of this promise demonstrated that there was strong anti-Mexican immigrant sentiment in the United States. Although the wall, if built, would only affect the flow of illegal immigrants, many of Trump's supporters seemed to lump all Mexican immigrants together as a threat to American culture and the stability of the nation. This belief has created a divide within the nation, as agricultural interests, among others, still depend on Mexican labor (in addition to Mexican Americans) to produce their crops. Also, more of the immigrants have become involved in animal husbandry; many dairy farms in western states would have to close without these workers. While many US citizens want to decrease, or eliminate, workers coming from Mexico, the companies that employ Mexican and Mexican American workers do not have a ready pool of applicants willing to replace them. This is the key factor to immigration from Mexico. If the legal, and even more so the illegal immigrants, were not offered employment, the incentive for them to cross the border would virtually disappear. As long as those already in the United States are unwilling to perform tasks required in the jobs generally filled by Mexicans and Mexican Americans, there will be an incentive for continued border crossings.

Cultural Influences

Since the acquisition of what is now the southwestern United States, the influence of Mexican culture has been very strong in that region. The regional architectural style, cuisine, religious observances, language (Spanish), and other cultural activities reflect the significant number of people of Mexican ancestry. Prior to the 1980s, outside this region these influences were limited to isolated pockets among the general population. However, with the increasing number of Mexicans moving throughout the United States, as well as interest by the general population, Mexican (or Mexican-inspired) cuisine has become commonplace throughout the nation. The only other Mexican tradition that has translated to the United States (albeit in a hybridized manner) has been the celebration of Cinco de Mayo, even though in Mexico it was never a major holiday. In part, the lack of cultural influence within the broader American population has been due to the fact that most Mexicans are labor immigrants, not cultural migrants or middle-class émigrés. In addition, Spanish as a primary or secondary language has limited some

cultural interchange, although use of the language has become so widespread that businesses, as well as governmental entities, have introduced programs/services to meet the needs of their customers/clients who prefer to use Spanish. (A 2010 survey indicated that 64 percent of Mexican Americans spoke English proficiently.) However, it seemed that for many Americans, this latter shift pushed many into a more anti-Mexican, anti-immigrant, stance. Even though most previous immigrant groups who did not speak English took a few generations to fully assimilate into the English language culture, probably because Mexican immigration has been ongoing, rather than just a short burst of migration, the kind of breathing space allowed previous generations does not seem to have been given to recent Mexican immigrants.

—Donald A. Watt

Bibliography and Further Reading

Gonzales, Manuel G. *Mexicanos, Second Edition: A History of Mexicans in the United States.* Bloomington: Indiana UP, 2009. Print.

Gutiérrez, David G. *Walls and Mirrors: Mexican Americans, Mexican Immigrants, and the Politics of Ethnicity.* Berkeley: U of California P, 1995. Print.

Library of Congress. "Immigration . . . Mexican." *Library of Congress: Classroom Materials.* Washington: Library of Congress, 2017. Web. 13 March 2017.

Pew Research Center. "Modern Immigration Wave Brings 59 Million to U.S., Driving Population Growth and Change Through 2065: Views of Immigration's Impact on U.S. Society Mixed." Washington, D.C.: Pew Research Center, September, 2015. Web. 11 March 2017.

Preston, Julia. "The Truth About Mexican-Americans." *The New York Review of Books,* Dec. 3, 2015. Web. 13 March 2017.

Vasquez, Jessica M. *Mexican Americans Across Generations: Immigrant Families, Racial Realities.* New York: New York UP, 2011. Print.

Miami riots of 1980

On December 17, 1979, Arthur McDuffie, a thirty-three-year-old African American insurance agent with no criminal record, was riding along the

highway on his motorcycle when several officers of the Public Safety Department of Dade County ordered him to stop. When he refused to do so, he was pursued; when captured, he was beaten severely with nightsticks and heavy flashlights. McDuffie died a few days later from the injuries he had sustained at the hands of the police. This was the last of several incidents of alleged police brutality in the county in 1979: These included the shooting death of a teenager in Hialeah; the alleged sexual abuse of a prepubescent African American girl by a white police officer; and the severe beating administered by police to a black schoolteacher, after the police had raided his house in search of illegal drugs.

THE TRIAL AND AFTERMATH

The state attorney for Dade County, Janet Reno, prepared a case against four Dade County police officers who had beaten McDuffie. The case was brought to trial on March 31, 1980, in the town of Tampa, on the state's gulf coast; it was believed that the officers could not get a fair trial in Miami. Because of peremptory challenges by the defense attorney, the jury before which the case was tried was all white. The jury's decision, handed down on Saturday afternoon, May 17, 1980, shocked Miami's African American community: The police officers were acquitted of all charges.

In the early evening hours of May 17, the anger of the black Miamians boiled over into violence; rocks began to fly, and mobs began to attack individuals. Later that evening, after a mob attempt to set fire to the Metro Justice Building was barely repulsed, the governor of Florida, Bob Graham, ordered the National Guard to Miami; it did not arrive in full force, however, until Tuesday. It was not until May 23 that the situation was returned to normal. As a result of the riots, eighteen people died and hundreds were injured. There was eighty million dollars' worth of property damage and 1,100 people were arrested. Many Miami businesses were burned: African American, Cuban, and native-born white business owners all suffered.

Major arteries of traffic, used by motorists of all races and ethnic backgrounds, ran through Liberty City, a black area near Miami. In the evening hours of May 17, several white motorists, presumably unaware of the verdict, drove through that neighborhood, where they encountered maddened crowds, composed mostly of young people, bent on revenge. About 250 whites were injured that night in attacks

by rioters; seven whites died as a result of the injuries sustained. Of those who died, one middle-aged woman perished from severe burns when her car was set afire; a young sales clerk, a teenager, and a sixty-three-year-old Cuban refugee butcher died as the result of severe beatings. The reign of terror that night was mitigated only by the willingness of some courageous African Americans to rescue persons threatened by the mobs. The deliberate attacks on whites distinguished the Miami riot from the urban riots of the late 1960s, in which most deaths had occurred by accident.

In the days following that bloody Saturday, African Americans were riot victims as well. Some of those killed were rioters; others were law-abiding individuals mistaken for rioters by the police; still others appear to have been random shooting victims of unknown white assailants. Most Miami-area African Americans were neither rioters nor heroes nor victims; they simply waited for the disturbances to end.

For the United States, the Miami riot of 1980 ended twelve years of freedom from major urban riots. Riots broke out again in Miami's African American ghetto in December 1982; in January 1989 (when a Hispanic police officer, William Lozano, shot and killed an African American motorcyclist); and in July 1995. The later riots, however, were not as costly in lives or property as the 1980 outburst. In May 1993, Lozano's acquittal by a jury in Orlando was not followed by violence.

The Miami riot of 1980 was an alarm bell, warning the United States of the sharp tensions between the races that still persisted a decade and a half after the legislative victories of the Civil Rights movement, and of the combustible possibilities that existed wherever African Americans, native-born whites, and Hispanic immigrants lived side by side. The triggering of the Miami riot by an unpopular jury verdict rather than by immediate actions by the police foreshadowed the trajectory of the disastrous riot of April 29–May 1, 1992, in Los Angeles, California.

——*Paul D. Mageli*

BIBLIOGRAPHY AND FURTHER READING

Anderson, Paul. *Janet Reno: Doing the Right Thing*. New York: Wiley, 1994. Print.

Mohl, Raymond A. "On the Edge: Blacks and Hispanics in Metropolitan Miami Since 1959." *Florida Historical Quarterly* 69 (1990). Print.

Porter, Bruce, and Marvin Dunn. *The Miami Riot of 1980: Crossing the Bounds.* Lexington: Heath, 1984. Print.

Portes, Alejandro, and Alex Stepick. *City on the Edge: The Transformation of Miami.* Berkeley: U of California P, 1993. Print.

Skolnick, Jerome H., and James J. Fyfe. *Above the Law: Police and the Excessive Use of Force.* New York: Free, 1993. Print.

MIDDLEMAN MINORITIES

"Middleman" minorities, or middle minorities, are groups that, in a number of societies around the world, act as intermediaries between producers and consumers. This intermediary position frequently causes conflict with dominant and subordinate groups and includes (primarily) such functions as moneylending, trading, and shopkeeping. Historically, many groups have occupied this niche. They include Jews, the "overseas Chinese," Indians in East Africa, the Lebanese in West Africa, and Armenians in Ethiopia. The fact that such diverse groups, operating in very different societies, exhibit similar traits has led to much theorizing about middleman minorities. According to sociologist Robin Ward, these theories seek to answer three key questions: why particular groups become middleman minorities, why these groups enter into the specific occupations characteristic of middleman minorities, and what causes hostility toward them?

REASONS FOR BECOMING MIDDLEMEN

The first question is, in fact, two questions, because social scientists must not only account for why particular groups become middleman minorities but also explain why others do not. Answers to the first part of this question fall into two broad categories: structural factors and cultural attributes. Structural factors refer to the economic opportunities that unfold before certain groups, thereby enabling them to become traders, moneylenders, or any of the other occupations characteristic of middleman minorities. For example, in "The Koreans: Small Business in an Urban Frontier" (1987), sociologist Ilsoo Kim argues that as Jewish and Italian small business owners have retreated from inner cities, Korean immigrants, using readily available cash, have bought their stores. This option is attractive because, though many are highly educated, their difficulties with English hinder advancement in the professions. Moreover, the Korean community possesses a variety of institutions, both religious and social, that facilitate the immigrants' transition into American life. To these structural factors must be added such cultural traits as frugality (which includes hiring relatives at low wages), clannishness, and hard work. Thus, Koreans' success as small-business owners has resulted from a combination of structural and cultural factors. The same is true of other groups, such as the Chinese and Japanese.

In the United States, the success of these groups in small business has been contrasted to the relative lack of success by African Americans. This difference is heightened because African Americans have a much longer history in the United States and because many Asian (especially Korean) small businesses operate in black enclaves of the larger American cities. The answer appears to lie in a combination of structural and cultural barriers. Historically, racial discrimination in obtaining start-up capital has been the chief structural barrier faced by would-be African American businesspeople. Yet, as sociologist Ivan Light argued in *Ethnic Enterprise in America* (1972), this explanation by itself is inadequate, since black West Indian immigrants have played the role of middleman minorities in Harlem. He attributes success in this role to West Indians' continuation of the African cultural tradition of rotating credit associations, which allowed them to generate start-up capital within the immigrant community, thereby partially bypassing discriminatory treatment by banks. In contrast, this practice has died out among African Americans; consequently, they have had fewer non-discriminatory resources on which to draw to start small businesses.

OCCUPATIONAL CHOICE

There are a variety of reasons why middleman minorities enter into particular occupations, some of which have already been discussed. For the sake of convenience, these may be placed into three categories: economic, historical, and sociocultural. Economic factors include situations (as noted for Koreans in the United States) in which groups find that a demand exists in certain areas of society and take advantage of it. This suggests a certain element of chance. As sociologist Donald L. Horowitz has shown in *Ethnic Groups in Conflict* (1985), however, colonial policy in some developing countries steered some groups into particular occupations. Over time, a pattern of ethnic recruitment occurred, and folk beliefs justifying why some groups are more "suitable" to certain occupations arose. Examples include Chinese traders in Malaysia and Sikh artisans in India. In these examples, historical and sociocultural factors overlap to create middleman minorities.

VIOLENCE AND MIDDLEMAN MINORITIES

A third key question with respect to middleman minorities is why they are so often the victims of deliberate violence. The reasons for this violence are many, and violence toward middleman minorities originates from both the dominant and subordinated groups in society. Economist Thomas Sowell argues that a general reason for this violence is the view that, despite their usefulness, middleman minority occupations are inherently degraded. Hence, different groups performing the same role in different societies will face similar criticisms. A second reason is that middleman minority occupations become identified with all members of the group regardless of the actual occupations of individual members. This ethnocentric response identifies and intertwines despised minorities with despised roles. Sowell notes that a third reason for conflict is the ability of middleman minorities to achieve success in the professions. They come to be seen as formidable competitors and are resented, especially by subordinated minorities who view this success as coming at their expense. Political manipulation of latent antimiddleman minority sentiments is yet another reason for violence against middleman minorities. Horowitz shows that this occurs, for example, where subordinated minority groups, seeking to start businesses but finding middleman minorities as competitors, stir up trouble in an attempt to gain a competitive advantage.

HISTORICAL CONTEXT

The middleman minority concept has had a long history, rooted in the similar experiences of a number of groups around the world. Particularly important is the experience of Jews in Europe, for as social scientist Walter P. Zenner has pointed out, many of the theories of middleman minorities originated as attempts to explain anti-Semitism. Historically, European Jews have closely matched the profile of the middleman minority. They stood as intermediaries between nobles and serfs, performing such occupations as moneylending and merchandising. They tended to be frugal, hardworking, clannish, and highly educated. The result was economic success but at the cost of great hostility from their non-Jewish neighbors. A variety of negative stereotypes about Jews developed. These included charges of disloyalty (for refusing to assimilate), deviousness, and dishonesty in business. Additionally—and significantly, in societies dominated by Catholicism—they were accused of being anti-Christian. Stereotypes such as these resulted in the ghettoization of Jews and repeated pogroms, culminating in the Holocaust of World War II. Thus, both Jewish economic success and the persecution of Jews in Europe were intimately tied to their peculiar status as middleman minorities.

The historical experiences of Jews closely match those of a number of other such groups, which points to the need for a concept to tie a minority group's experiences to its economic function relative to dominant and subjugated groups. For example, sociologist D. Stanley Eitzen has shown the existence of close historical similarities between the Jewish experience and that of the Chinese in the Philippines. As is the case with the Jews in Europe, Chinese contact with the Philippines dates back hundreds of years. By the time the Spanish took control of the Philippines in 1571, the Chinese had already established themselves as craftsmen, merchants, and moneylenders. Initially welcomed by the Spanish for their useful economic function, they soon experienced ghettoization and mass killings (by the Spanish) because of their new economic power. This hostility has lasted through the period of American occupation (from 1898 to 1946) to the present. In the post-1946 independence period, nationalistic fervor combined with anti-Chinese sentiment to limit opportunities for the Chinese in the Philippines. For example, the Filipino government has made it difficult for Chinese to become citizens, limited their ownership of land, and prevented their entrance into certain industries.

The historical similarities between groups are the result of the economic roles they occupy in society rather than of who they are. It seems that a particular combination of brokering occupations and values that enhance economic success in these occupations always leads to hostility. The historical evidence suggests that as long as some groups exist in this mode they will to some degree remain outsiders to the societies in which they live and will suffer success mixed with persecution.

——*Milton D. Vickerman*

BIBLIOGRAPHY AND FURTHER READING

Edna Bonacich's "A Theory of Middleman Minorities" (*American Sociological Review* 38, October, 1973) attributes middleman minorities' occupational choices and values (for example, clannishness) to their "sojourner" status. Donald L. Horowitz's *Ethnic Groups in Conflict* (Berkeley: University of California Press, 1985) downplays the idea that middleman minority occupations cause conflict. Illsoo Kim's "The Koreans: Small Business in an Urban Frontier," in *New Immigrants in New York* (New York: Columbia University Press, 1987), edited by Nancy Foner, argues that a combination of economic opportunity, fiscal preparedness, education, community organization, and values have helped Koreans achieve success in the United States. Ivan Light's *Ethnic Enterprise in America* (Berkeley: University of California Press, 1972) investigates the factors making for success—or the lack of it—among minorities. Thomas Sowell's "Middleman Minorities" (*The American Enterprise* 4, May/June, 1993) argues that the possession of certain values is the central characteristic of middleman minorities.

MIGRANT DETENTION CENTERS

The United States detains approximately 41,000 migrants daily (as of January 2017), and a total of almost 450,000 per year, to constitute the largest migrant detention system in the world. Detainees are held in over 200 facilities around the country, in a mix of government-owned detention centers, state- and county-owned prisons, and contract detention facilities run by private companies, at a cost of about $2.3 billion per year. Migrant detention in the United States has always been connected to scapegoating immigrants in times of economic anxiety, and nativist efforts to define American identity according to race-based markers. Massive expansion in migrant detention in recent years is also tied to the belief that it deters future migrants, and the involvement of private companies.

HISTORY AND LEGAL FRAMEWORK
While migrants have been detained throughout US history, the legal framework for detention in place today began to take shape in the late 1800s and early 1900s. The federal government passed a series of laws now known as Chinese Exclusion that blocked new Asian immigration, targeted already-present Chinese for deportation, and established a framework for pre-deportation detention. The government also began to detain immigrants for pre-entry inspection on the US-Mexico border, as well as at Ellis Island outside New York City and Angel Island near San Francisco.

From the 1920s to the early 1950s, when deportation was used to deport labor and anarchist leaders often of eastern and southern European origin), the government detained immigrants in local jails and prisons pursuant to deportation. The first large-scale detention project was the World War II internment of over 33,000 "enemy aliens": primarily people of Japanese descent (including US citizens), from 1942 to 1946. In the three decades after Japanese internment, overall detention numbers generally remained low. A notable exception was Operation Wetback in 1954, which resulted in the deportation of about one million Mexicans, and often entailed detention prior to deportation.

In the 1980s, major changes in immigration policy initiated the current era of mass migrant detention. In the late 1970s and early 1980s, anxiety about growing numbers of immigrants and asylum-seekers from Central America combined with Cold War–era security concerns to create strong anti-immigrant feelings. The new Reagan administration embraced the belief that detention works as a deterrent to future immigration (an unsubstantiated assumption that continues to dominate immigration policymaking today), and in 1981 mandated detention for most asylum-seekers. When existing migrant detention facilities filled, the Immigration and Naturalization Service (INS) contracted with private prison operators and local governments to increase capacity. The United States also detained Cubans and Haitians interdicted at sea, in transit countries and US-held Guantanamo, to prevent them from accessing rights to which migrants on US territory are entitled. Additional changes throughout that decade, under Reagan and then George H.W. Bush, continued to increase migrant detention numbers.

The use of detention intensified with the deepening anti-immigrant climate of the 1990s. New laws in 1996 produced another jump in detention use by, among other provisions, broadening the list of deportable offenses, making detention mandatory for more immigrants, and curtailing immigrants' rights to fight deportation. Detention skyrocketed. In 1994, the United States detained 5,532 migrants. In 1997, this number tripled to 16,000, and by 2000 it had grown to 188,000 detainees per year.

The terrorist attacks of September 11, 2001, sharply heightened anti-immigrant sentiments and the criminalization of non-white immigrants, spurring more detention. Under President George W. Bush, the new Department of Homeland Security (DHS) replaced INS with Immigration and Customs Enforcement (ICE), with a bigger budget, more personnel, and a new goal of deporting all "removable" immigrants. Together DHS and Congress again expanded immigration officials' power to detain and deport, and eroded tools available to detainees to contest deportation. In 2004, Congress provided for 8,000 new detention "beds" each year between 2006 and 2010. In addition to the continued emphasis on deterrence and the use of contracting to increase capacity, another important characteristic of the post-9/11 era was increasing cooperation between federal immigration officials and state and local law enforcement officers. Such cooperation makes more immigrants, especially in the US interior, vulnerable to detention and deportation.

While immigrants and advocates had hoped that President Barack Obama would reverse course on detention and deportation policies, his administration instead brought deportation rates to historic highs, reaching a peak of almost 410,000 in 2012 alone, and deporting a total of over 2.5 million people during his presidency. Expanding detention capacity was central to these increases. In 2009, Congress put in place the "detention bed mandate" that drove a new expansion in detention capacity by requiring DHS to keep a certain number—currently 34,000—of detention beds filled at all times. After a "surge" beginning in 2014 of women and children, including unaccompanied minors, fleeing extreme violence and poverty in Central America, DHS contracted with private companies and local governments to raise family detention capacity to approximately 3,500 per day. In 2016, total detention capacity was further expanded in response to a general jump in migrants attempting to cross the US-Mexico border, to 41,000 per day.

As of this writing (March 2017), the new administration of Donald Trump has outlined a range of policy changes to do with immigration, including the detention of every apprehended undocumented immigrant. If fully executed, the changes will entail exponential expansion in migrant detention.

CHARACTERISTICS OF MIGRANT DETENTION

Today, most migrant detention centers are operated with the goal of making a profit. Per single adult detained, ICE pays facility operators an average of approximately $125 per day, and $340 per person in family detention. In addition to prison companies and local governments leasing jail space, there are many kinds of companies and individuals who make money from migrant detention, such as phone companies, food service providers, and transportation companies. An example of how companies and local governments make money off of detention beyond what ICE pays is the "Voluntary Work Programs" offered in many detention centers. Detainees perform low-skilled jobs, such as cleaning, food preparation, dishwashing, laundry, and maintenance. In exchange for an eight-hour shift, detainees receive one dollar, which they typically use to pay for phone calls or buy extra food in facility commissaries, also operated for profit. Entities that profit from detention have been very influential in the shaping of contemporary immigration policy.

All migrant detention facilities are required to follow ICE's Performance Based National Detention Standards. While these standards should guarantee detainees' rights are observed and that they receive appropriate care, there is little oversight or enforcement. Numerous reports document a range of complaints and abuses.

Being detained critically limits migrants' access to support networks and resources, and curtails efforts to fight deportation. Detainees typically feel isolated and disoriented, due to limited access to phones (and now in some facilities, email) as well as the cost of calls; most phone systems are contracted out to private companies that inflate rates. In addition, detained migrants are often transferred multiple times between facilities, and they may be detained for extended periods of time, from months to years in the case of those waiting to see an immigration judge. Detainees often suffer from hunger due to insufficient or inedible food. There are also problems with inadequate medical care, and there have been nearly 170 deaths in immigration detention since 2003. Some detainees complain of being held in uncomfortably cold rooms without sufficient clothing. Some violations pertain specifically to family detention, such as inadequate schooling, inappropriate nutrition for children, and threats of separating parents and children as punishment.

The overwhelming majority of detained immigrants are people of color. While this partly has to do with the countries of origin of many undocumented immigrants, it is also due to racialized immigration enforcement practices that target non-white immigrants.

——*Nancy Hiemstra*

BIBLIOGRAPHY AND FURTHER READING

Conlon, D., and N. Hiemstra. "Examining the everyday micro-economies of immigrant detention in the United States." *Geographica Helvetica* 69, 2014: 335-344. Web. 14 March 2017.

Detention Watch Network. "Immigration Detention 101." 2017. Web 14 March 2017.

Doty, R. L., and E. S. Wheatley. "Private Detention and the Immigration Industrial Complex." *International Political Sociology* 7, 2013: 426-443. Print.

Dow, M. *American Gulag: Inside U.S. Immigration Prisons.* Berkeley: U of California P, 2004. Print.

Golash-Boza, T. *Immigration Nation: Raids, Detentions, and Deportations in Post-9/11 America.* Boulder: Paradigm, 2012. Print.

Hernández, D. M. "Pursuant to Deportation: Latinos and Immigrant Detention." *Latino Studies* 6, 2008: 35-63. Print.

Kanstroom, D. *Deportation Nation: Outsiders in American History.* Cambridge: Harvard UP, 2007. Print.

Welch, M. *Detained: Immigration Laws and the Expanding I.N.S. Jail Complex.* Philadelphia: Temple UP, 2002. Print.

MIGRANT SUPERORDINATION

Migrant superordination refers to the process whereby an immigrant group of "foreigners" subdues the native people of a territory. The classical form of this relationship is colonization, in which the migrant group uses force to dispossess the indigenous group of land, resources, or work. The resulting superordinate/subordinate relationship can take economic, political, and cultural forms. This relationship is characterized by the institutionalization of dominant-minority relations in which the migrants enjoy disproportionate power, resources, and prestige. The power relationship is then justified by a system of beliefs that rationalizes the superiority of the immigrant group in relation to the indigenous people. Reactions on the part of the indigenous people range from resistance and rebellion to accommodation and assimilation. Examples of migrant superordination include the European conquest of Native Americans in the Western Hemisphere and of Africans in South Africa.

——*M. Bahati Kuumba*

MILITARY AND RACIAL/ETHNIC RELATIONS

The regular service of minorities, especially African Americans, in the US military is a relatively recent phenomenon. Before the Civil War (1861-1865), the US military tradition was one of erratic militia-based service and sanctioned prejudice. Therefore, minorities played very little role in US military life (African Americans in the Civil War). The Civil War saw the first real attempt to incorporate blacks into the service, strangely enough, on both sides of that conflict. However, they were largely used in noncombat roles, especially in the South, and their use, though playing a marginally important part in the Union's victory, was hotly debated and carefully segregated. This segregation continued well into the twentieth century through two world wars.

The years immediately after World War II saw the first impetus for change. Various segregated black units and a few individual black servicemen (such as Dorrie Miller, a Navy hero at Pearl Harbor) had distinguished themselves in battle, and this opened the debate on the Military desegregation of the armed forces. President Harry S Truman initiated new policies on race relations in the military, and the services were mostly integrated by the start of the Korean War in 1950. The US Navy, previously the most conservative branch, actually took the early lead in promoting equality within the ranks. Gradually, African Americans began gaining some ground, a few even rising to officer status. During the Vietnam War (1957-1975), a multitude of problems arose, many of which concerned black troops.

FROM CONSCRIPTION TO THE ALL-VOLUNTEER FORCE

The United States' modern wars, from the Civil War to the Vietnam War, were largely fought by conscripts or draftees. In the two world wars, conscription and segregation went hand in hand. The wars in Korea and Vietnam, especially the latter, were the United States' first experience with draftees fighting in an integrated service. Although conscription was designed to promote equitable social and ethnic representation in the services, it was often alleged that blacks were overly represented and burdened with the risks of combat during the Vietnam War. Indeed, the poor and minorities appear to have suffered from the inequities of the draft, in large part because middle-class and more affluent people could more easily be excused from service or obtain deferments. This discrepancy was also caused by the war's increasing unpopularity. As the combat effectiveness of conscripts declined in the later years of the Vietnam War, the debate ensued as to the desirability of having an all-volunteer force (AVF).

Initially, opposition to ending the draft arose from many quarters. This opposition was based on notions that a large, all-volunteer force (all-volunteer army overview) would be mercenary, ineffective, socially unrepresentative, and costly. Nevertheless, in 1970, a presidential task force known as the Gates Commission forwarded recommendations that an AVF was possible if military pay and benefits were raised to meet civilian standards. By 1973, the AVF was in place as the last US troops left Vietnam. This AVF seemed to function well at first, but problems arose that led to a decline in quality of personnel for the next decade. The 1980's, however, saw two important changes occur: the onset of serious effort and spending to upgrade the AVF and the implementation of solid racial policies in the US military.

THE AVF AND RACE RELATIONS

The 1980's saw a marked improvement in the overall effectiveness of the AVF. Higher pay, better benefits, and more effective advertising have been cited as the cause. Enlistment eligibility requirements were raised considerably during this time. The number of blacks enlisting in the service continued to rise, reaching 22 percent in 1989. The greatest increase in black recruits occurred in the US Navy, where enlistment doubled. Because of the higher eligibility standards, the educational and aptitude levels of all recruits, including minorities, continued to rise into the 1990's. With this higher-quality recruit came a concerted effort at improving race relations and the advancement prospects of minorities in the services. In some respects, an outward attempt was made to make the AVF not only combat effective but also an ideal model in the areas of cost-efficiency, team effort, and race relations. Efforts to improve recruits' sensitivity to race began as early as 1973, but the US military consistently added policies throughout the years that have achieved a remarkable level of color-blind professionalism. Racial incidents underwent a steady decline and have been dealt with sternly. The military maintains a complex system of grievance procedures and racial protocol. Indeed, the US military's record on race is, by most accounts, far better than its record on gender and other issues.

The issue of race and social representation is also a factor in both vocational placement and promotion through the ranks. For active-duty personnel, there appears to be equal representation in combat roles, while blacks occupy larger numbers of clerical, administrative, and logistical positions. A few experts have even suggested capping minority recruitment in some areas, although this would revive the issue of discrimination. The US military boasts the largest percentage of minorities in command roles in its entire history, and an African American officer, General Colin Powell, served as chairman of the Joint Chiefs of Staff during the critical period of the Persian Gulf War. When that conflict erupted in early 1991, it was seen as a major test of the effectiveness of the AVF. Powell later served as US Secretary of State between 2001 and 2005. Smart bombs and other high-tech weaponry may have garnered the attention of most viewers, but professional military men were quick to point out the readiness and steady professionalism of the men and women of the all-volunteer force that handily won the Gulf War—even if subsequent conflicts have been less definitive in terms of strategic victories and/or failures.

——*Gene Redding Wynne, Jr.*

BIBLIOGRAPHY AND FURTHER READING

Bailey, Beth L. *America's Army: Making the All-volunteer Force.* Cambridge: Harvard UP, 2009. Print.

Bogart, Leo. *Project Clear: Social Research and the Desegregation of the United States Army.* New Brunswick: Transaction, 1992. Print.

Bowman, William, Roger Little, and G. Thomas Sicilla. *The All-Volunteer Force After a Decade.* Washington, DC: Pergamon-Brassey's, 1986. Print.

Segal, David R. *Recruiting for Uncle Sam.* Lawrence: UP of Kansas, 1989. Print.

Stouffer, S. A. *The American Soldier.* Princeton: Princeton UP, 1949. Print.

MILITARY DESEGREGATION

On July 26, 1948, President Harry S. Truman established a major precedent in the history of equal opportunity for all races when he issued two executive orders. The first, 9980, allowed governmental employees to appeal discriminatory employment procedures to the Fair Employment Board, a subdivision of the Civil Service Commission. The second, 9981, potentially revolutionized race relations in the United States by integrating the armed forces of the United States.

The president's military desegregation order exhibited a characteristic bluntness that came to symbolize his presidency. "It is hereby declared," he commanded, "to be the policy of the president that there shall be equality of treatment and opportunity for all persons in the armed services without regard to race, color, religion, or national origin."

Critics immediately lambasted the order. The *Baltimore Sun* accused Truman of trying to win African American votes. There may have been some merit to this charge: African American leader A. Philip Randolph quickly announced the cancellation of a civil disobedience campaign planned for August 18, 1948. However, when General Omar Bradley insisted that the US Army would not participate until "the nation as a whole" joined the effort, Truman struck back. He would not equivocate on this issue; he would not retreat a single inch. The military was to obey. Unlike other presidents who tried but failed to protect civil rights in the military, Truman personally ensured the end of racial discrimination and segregation in the armed forces.

By January 1950, Executive Order 9981 effectively integrated most of the military. For example, African Americans and whites were working together in the US Air Force, and some black officers now commanded white enlisted airmen. Changes in the Air Force did not attract much attention, however, since only 351 African American officers served in the corps, constituting less than 1 percent of the entire branch.

Similar advances, despite stubborn resistance by some officers, occurred in the US Navy. By December 22, 1949, all black US Marines experienced integrated basic training. The Navy also increased its promotional campaign to recruit more African Americans into its Reserve Officer Training Corps. African Americans previously relegated to the lowly rank of steward now found themselves being promoted to petty officer.

In the Army, however, integration proceeded at a slower pace. On June 7, 1949, Secretary of the Army Louis Johnson ordered the tempo increased. When that failed, African American newspapers called upon the president to intervene. Truman, however, allowed the process to develop at a natural rate, and the Army adhered to a 10 percent quota of African American troops until the beginning of the Korean War. As part of the war effort, the quota was removed, and African American enlistments dramatically increased, prompting Army commanders to desegregate basic training camps. African Americans increased to 11.4 percent of the Army within sixty days after North Korean troops invaded South Korea in June 1950.

By the time Truman left office in January 1953, he had reached his goal of nearly total integration of the US military. Although his personal popularity with the US public reached new lows in presidential polls, African American voters remained loyal to the Democratic Party. Executive Order 9981 no doubt played a major role in this significant development.

——*J. Christopher Schnell*

BIBLIOGRAPHY AND FURTHER READING

Geselbracht, Raymond H., ed. *The Civil Rights Legacy of Harry S. Truman.* Kirksville: Truman State UP, 2007. Print.

Goethals, George R. *Presidential Leadership and African Americans: "An American Dilemma" from Slavery to the White House.* New York: Routledge, 2015. Print.

Goldfield, David. "Border Men: Truman, Eisenhower, Johnson, and Civil Rights." *Journal of Southern History* 80.1 (2014): 7–38. Print.

Kruse, Kevin M., and Stephen Tuck, eds. *Fog of War: The Second World War and the Civil Rights Movement.* New York: Oxford UP, 2012. Print.

Taylor, Jon E. *Freedom to Serve: Truman, Civil Rights, and Executive Order 9981.* New York: Routledge, 2013. Print.

MILLIKEN V. BRADLEY

In *Milliken v. Bradley* (1974), the US Supreme Court decided that courts did not have the authority to order school desegregation plans that required moving schoolchildren across school district lines unless it could be shown that school district lines had been constructed in a manner designed to preserve segregation.

By the early 1970's, many urban school districts continued to operate schools with a majority black population because of the dearth of white students in those school districts. In 1971, the US Supreme Court in *Swann v. Charlotte-Mecklenburg Board of Education* had held that urban school boards could be required to engage in extensive school busing to integrate their schools. The *Swann* decision, however, did not address the issue of how to integrate urban school districts that had few white students.

In the early 1970's, a group of black parents, with the assistance of the National Association for the Advancement of Colored People Legal Defense and Educational Fund, brought suit seeking to desegregate the Detroit school system. In 1972, federal district court judge Stephen Roth ruled that the Detroit schools were in fact illegally segregated and ordered a multidistrict desegregation plan involving the Detroit city school district along with fifty-three surrounding suburban school districts. One year later, the US Court of Appeals for the Sixth Circuit affirmed, holding that the Detroit schools could not be adequately desegregated without such a multidistrict plan. Shortly thereafter, the US Supreme Court agreed to hear the case.

In 1973, the Supreme Court had considered a similar multidistrict desegregation plan involving the Richmond, Virginia, schools. In that case, the Court had divided 4 to 4, with Justice Lewis Powell recusing himself because of his prior membership on the Richmond School Board. The Court took the Detroit case to decide the question of whether multidistrict desegregation plans were required when inner-city school districts could not otherwise be desegregated. In the meantime, the specter of multidistrict desegregation prompted a firestorm of activity in Congress, as many members of Congress backed both legislation and amendments to the Constitution restricting the ability of federal courts to order extensive desegregation plans.

The Supreme Court held in the *Milliken v. Bradley* decision, with a 5-4 vote, that a district court should not order an interdistrict remedy unless it could be shown that the school district lines had been constructed in a manner to preserve segregation or unless state government officials had taken other

action that contributed to the interdistrict segregation. This was a burden of proof that would prove difficult to meet. The *Milliken* decision marked the first time that the Supreme Court had declined to refine existing school desegregation jurisprudence to further integrationist goals.

In the wake of the *Milliken* decision a few metropolitan areas did adopt interdistrict desegregation remedies, but, for the most part, the decision undermined desegregation efforts in America's cities. Unable to utilize an assignment plan that included children from surrounding suburban school districts, inner-city school boards were greatly restricted in their efforts to desegregate their schools.

——*Davison M. Douglas*

MILLION MAN MARCH

On October 16, 1995, more than a million men of African descent converged on Washington, D.C. They came from all over the United States. The majority were poor and working class, a sizable number were middle class, and some were affluent. They all came with the intention of becoming better men once they returned to their homes. The event was known as the Million Man March, and it was one of the major media stories of 1995.

Led by the controversial Nation of Islam leader, Louis Farrakhan, and a former National Association for the Advancement of Colored People (NAACP) leader, Benjamin Chavis, the march generated an ample amount of positive and negative publicity. Farrakhan is well known for his virulent anti-Semitic remarks, and Chavis was voted out of his position as NAACP president after it was disclosed that he had paid $332,400 in organizational funds to his former mistress. Farrakhan, by addressing the deepest concerns of many African Americans at a time when many other black politicians were alarmingly silent, managed to insert himself into the center of what was (and still is) an ongoing racial debate in the United States. Because of the march's success, many mainstream media pundits conceded that Farrakhan was a force to be acknowledged. Ted Koppel, on ABC's *Nightline,* stated that Farrakhan could be called "one of the most influential leaders in black America." During the march, Farrakhan advocated pride, love, and black self-reliance.

Aerial view of the march. By The Library of Congress.

DISSENTERS

From the outset, the event was mired in controversy. Many leaders, black and white, questioned the ability and/or sagacity of Farrakhan and Chavis to cosponsor a march that called for equality and brotherhood. Critics of Farrakhan pointed to his virulent anti-Semitic attacks on Jews and other minorities; critics of Chavis noted his larceny and infidelity. Both men were chided by many women and women's rights organizations for their deeply ingrained sexism.

Mary Francis Berry, chairperson of the US Commission on Civil Rights, wrote a letter in the October, 1995, issue of *The Washington Post* in which she stated, "I do not trust Louis Farrakhan or Benjamin Chavis to lead us to the Promised Land." More than a few African Americans endorsed Berry's sentiments. A *US News & World Report* poll taken in 1995 found that 31 percent (almost a third) of African Americans harbored an unfavorable impression of Farrakhan. Such disdain was echoed by many Jewish leaders as well. On September 19, 1995, the Anti-Defamation League of B'nai B'rith (a Jewish civil rights organization) took out a full-page advertisement in *The New York Times* aggressively denouncing Farrakhan. The advertisement stated, "This march will be led by the most mainstream anti-Semite in recent American history." Alvin Poussaint, a leading black psychiatrist at Harvard University Medical School, said that Farrakhan had to confront his controversial racist past. Poussaint argued that Farrakhan could not continue to speak out of both sides of his mouth and fail to take into account how his own remarks were interpreted.

The Million Man March also exposed the tension that existed between men and women in the African American community. Syndicated columnist Julianne Malveaux; Gloria Watkins, distinguished professor of English at City College in New York; and other prominent African American women denounced the event because of what they saw as the endemic paternalism and sexist message that the march promoted. Other African American women raised similar arguments. With the exception of poet Maya Angelou and the late Betty Shabazz (widow of Malcolm X), virtually no African American women were present at the march.

Supporters of the "no women allowed" policy argued that by prohibiting African American women from attending the march, African American men would be able to concentrate on themselves as individuals and their responsibilities as men, and would not be distracted. Opponents of excluding women from the march argued that such a decision demonstrated the lack of sensitivity that has always been a part of the Nation of Islam regarding women. By engaging in such an act, Farrakhan and his supporters had ignored the crucial role that African American women have played in the struggle for freedom. By relegating African American women to a secondary role, Farrakhan demonstrated either his historical ignorance or gross insensitivity toward his female brethren.

ECONOMIC CLASS

Other supporters of the march participated out of a spirit of defiance. Although a sizable number of middle-class men attended the march, the majority of the men came from working-class backgrounds. These were men who had seen their economic prospects falter and had become increasingly distrustful of many successful people, white or black. This was also the group within the African American community that has most recently responded to the message of manhood, greater family responsibility, and black pride.

Farrakhan provided hope for many working-class blacks, who used the march to demonstrate their rage against and resentment of many mainstream Americans, black and white, who argued that African Americans should stay away from the march and that Farrakhan and Chavis were nothing more than two racist and sexist hatemongers who epitomized everything that was negative about black nationalism. On the contrary, for many blacks in this socioeconomic class, these two men embodied all that was absent in their lives. Farrakhan and Chavis were able to tap into the hopelessness, despair, and uncertainty that many of these men felt. Despite opposition, even the Million Man March's detractors conceded that the event was a success. The march put the spotlight on African American men and gave Farrakhan a renewed sense of visibility and importance.

——*Elwood David Watson*

BIBLIOGRAPHY AND FURTHER READING

Alex-Assensoh, Yvette M., and Lawrence J. Hanks, eds. *Black and Multiracial Politics in America*. New York: New York UP, 2000. Print.

Gibson, Dawn-Marie. *The Nation of Islam, Louis Farrakhan, and the Men Who Follow Him.* New York: Palgrave Macmillan, 2016. Print.

Newton, Judith. *From Panthers to Promise Keepers: Rethinking the Men's Movement.* Lanham: Rowman and Littlefield, 2005. Print.

MILLION WOMAN MARCH

The Million Woman March took place in Philadelphia, Pennsylvania, on October 25, 1997, and provided African American women the opportunity to discuss some key racial issues. The streets were filled with women pushing baby strollers, beating drums, and walking with the determination to be counted among the several hundred thousand women who attended the historic gathering. Participants carried the red, black, and green flag of the national African American movement and banners that showed the many areas from which they had traveled. The event was organized by activist and bookstore owner Phile Chionesu and was attended by many African American celebrities, including actors Blair Underwood, Margaret Avery, and Jada Pinkett, as well as Winnie Mandela, former wife of South African president Nelson Mandela.

The women marched to draw strength from one another and to focus on their common problems. The event provided a forum to address many issues that are not typically dealt with by women's groups. Some of the main issues discussed were human rights abuses against African Americans, the start of independent African American schools, and a demand for an investigation into allegations of Central Intelligence Agency involvement in selling crack cocaine in African American neighborhoods. Most of the women left inspired to make changes in their communities, and Chionesu planned to hold a second Million Woman March.

A second, more impromptu mass women's march took place on January 21, 2017, the day after the inauguration of Donald Trump as president. Angela Davis, Jonelle Monet, America Ferrera, Van Jones, Ashley Judd, Gloria Steinem, and Madonna, among many others, spoke to the estimated 500,000 attendees about women's rights and racial and ethnic injustice. Comparable marches took place in numerous other cities throughout the United States and in cities in Europe and elsewhere, the result being that over a million women across the globe were mobilized against Trump and his incoming administration.

——*Alvin K. Benson, updated by Michael Shally-Jensen*

BIBLIOGRAPHY AND FURTHER READING

Faulkner, Carol, and Alison M. Parker. *Interconnections: Gender and Race in American History.* Rochester: U of Rochester P, 2012. Print.
Stavrianos, Cynthia. *The Political Uses of Motherhood in America.* New York: Routledge, 2015. Print.

MINORITY AND MAJORITY GROUPS

"Minority group" and "majority group" are complementary concepts (one implies the other) that denote a hierarchical relationship of dominance and subjugation between groups. The terms carry much emotional and political baggage because of their association with two related concepts, "race" and "ethnicity." To understand minority and majority groups, one needs to distinguish between the sociological viewpoint just outlined and the meanings attributed to the terms by the ordinary person in the street. Sociologists tend to define the concepts strictly, whereas nonacademics define them loosely. This lack of precision lends itself to misconceptions, but it is also true that the sociological viewpoint has inherent problems.

SCHOLARLY V. POPULAR DEFINITIONS

Anthropologists Charles Wagley and Marvin Harris put forward a widely accepted definition of the term "minority group." In *Minorities in the New World: Six Case Studies* (1958), they argued that five characteristics identify these groups. First, they are relatively powerless compared with members of the dominant group. Second, they share distinctive cultural and/or physical characteristics that distinguish them from the dominant group. This fact, along with their powerlessness, exposes them to unequal treatment. Third, their distinctive traits cause minority groups to become self-conscious social units. Fourth, an established rule of descent exists for transmitting membership in minority groups across generations. Fifth, members of minority groups tend to marry within their groups.

Most social scientists agree that these criteria are not equally important. They view minority groups' relative powerlessness as the most important criterion distinguishing them from majority groups. For example, in *Majority and Minority: The Dynamics of Race and Ethnicity in American Life* (1991), sociologist Norman Yetman argues that "minority group" is synonymous with the term "subordinate," and "majority group" is synonymous with "dominant." The main implication of this viewpoint is that, contrary to what one might assume, members of minority groups can constitute a numerical majority in their society, and majority group members might be a numerical minority. The classic example of this is South Africa, where African Americans, although they constitute approximately 75 percent of the population, were powerless under apartheid, while whites, constituting approximately 14 percent of the population, were dominant.

Sociologists distinguish between racial, ethnic, religious, and gender groups, on one hand, and minority and majority groups on the other. They view the latter twin concepts as subsuming the others. That is, majority groups and minority groups may consist of distinct races, ethnic groups, religious groups, and gender groups. These various types of majority/minority groups differ from each other symbolically. Thus, racial majority/minority groups are set apart by physical features, ethnic majority/minority groups by their unique cultural attributes, religious majority/minority groups by unique spiritual beliefs, and gender majority/minority groups by societal expectations of sex-linked characteristics. A minority and majority group might display a number of these characteristics simultaneously. An example of an overdetermined minority group would be black, Haitian, female Catholics.

Nonacademics often adopt a loose definition of minority and majority groups. They tend to ignore the latter concept and focus on the former. In this focus, "minority group" becomes synonymous with specific racial and/or ethnic groups, and the term "minority" is often used to refer to individuals belonging to these groups. Thus, in the United States, the term "minorities" is often understood to mean African Americans and/or Hispanics. This is controversial, because such usage often occurs in a pejorative context and may be viewed as a way of attacking those two groups. Used in this way, the term "minority" can become a weapon in intergroup conflict.

PROBLEMS WITH DEFINITIONS

Adopting the sociological viewpoint on majority/minority groups leaves less room for confusion. Nevertheless, this viewpoint also has problems. To begin with, it seems counterintuitive to suggest that numerical majorities can be, in fact, "minorities." This is not a problem when a group—for example, African Americans—is both numerically smaller and less powerful than the dominant group. As the authors of the *Dictionary of Race and Ethnic Relations* (2016) have suggested, however, colonial subjects who vastly outnumber their colonial rulers might take umbrage at the notion that they constitute a "minority." The problem is that the commonsense understanding of "minority" conflicts with sociological usage; therefore, the potential for confusion exists.

One of the *Dictionary*'s original authors, Peter Van den Berghe, has argued that this confusion is deliberate, since it serves useful political purposes. In pluralistic societies—such as the United States—that have instituted affirmative action programs to aid historically disadvantaged groups, being identified as a "minority group" can prove beneficial in some instances. The problem lies in deciding which groups are minority groups. African Americans and Hispanics are uncontroversial choices, but whether Jews, Japanese Americans, and Chinese Americans should be considered minority groups is more problematic and controversial. These groups, though numerical minorities, enjoy a level of socioeconomic success which far outstrips that of African Americans and Hispanics. Thus, the term "minority group," with its connotation of powerlessness and relative deprivation, seems somewhat inappropriate. A fuzzy definition of "minority group," however, would give these economically successful groups a firmer claim to minority status and, with it, even greater access to societal resources. Van den Berghe suggests that similar confusion over the term "majority group" allows the tiny elite who exercise hegemony over the United States to cloud their identity and escape criticism by being lumped into a larger category—white Anglo-Saxon Protestants—who are perceived, mistakenly, as the dominant group.

USE OF THE CONCEPT
The concept of minority groups has long been used in Europe to describe national groups who, for whatever reason (for example, through conquest by another group), have come to form small enclaves in societies dominated by other groups. Early in the twentieth century, the concept was adopted by American sociologists seeking a comprehensive term to describe the multifaceted intergroup conflict that has been a recurring theme in American history. With respect to African Americans, American Indians, the Chinese, and the Japanese, the conflict seemed to be racial; with respect to groups such as Eastern European Jews, the Irish, and Italians, the conflict seemed to revolve around religious and cultural differences. As noted above, the unifying thread was domination by one group (native whites) of these various other groups. This suggested to sociologists such as Donald Young the need for a word to encapsulate all these various conflicts. In *American Minority Peoples* (1932), he suggested that the term "minority groups" be used to describe the distinctive groups who found themselves in conflict with the white majority.

Since the time of Young's proposal, the minority group/majority group concept has gained widespread acceptance because of the universality of intergroup conflict following European decolonialization. This process created new states such as India and Pakistan, but it also led to widespread racial, ethnic, religious, and nationalistic conflicts. Not all of these can be described as minority group/majority group situations, but many are. Examples include the Rodiya and Sinhalese in Sri Lanka, the Hutu and Tutsi in Burundi, and the Osu and Ibo in Nigeria. In *Ethnic Groups in Conflict* (2000), Donald Horowitz gives numerous examples of such conflict occurring in formerly colonized areas.

The more industrially developed areas of the world are also the scene of numerous minority group/majority group conflicts. The conflict between African Americans and whites in the United States is perhaps the best known, but to this could be added French Canadians and English-speaking Canadians, aboriginal Canadians and white Canadians, Australian aboriginals and white Australians, white New Zealanders and Maoris, and nonwhite immigrants and whites in the United Kingdom. Even more pressing examples are to be found in Eastern Europe, where the breakup of the former Soviet Union has allowed long-standing racial, ethnic, religious, and nationalistic hatreds to flare into open warfare. This breakup has combined with economic recession in Western Europe to reawaken antiminority fervor. Thus, in West Germany, Eastern European, Turkish, Vietnamese, and African immigrants have been repeatedly attacked by neo-Nazi groups. In France, agitation against Arab and African immigrants led the government to pass laws making it easier to track the movement of these immigrants. Even traditionally tolerant countries such as Denmark have experienced anti-immigrant sentiment. The prevalence of this type of conflict illustrates why the twin minority/majority group concept is likely to retain its utility.

——*Milton D. Vickerman*

BIBLIOGRAPHY AND FURTHER READING
Cashmore, Ellis, et al. *Dictionary of Race and Ethnic Relations,* 4th ed. New York: Routledge, 2016. Print.
Horowitz, Donald. *Ethnic Groups in Conflict,* 2d ed. Berkeley: U of California P, 2000. Print.
Rose, Peter I. *They and We: Racial and Ethnic Relations in the United States and Beyond.* 7th ed. Boulder: Paradigm, 2014. Print.
Simpson, George Eaton, and J. Milton Yinger. *Racial and Cultural Minorities.* 5th ed. New York: Plenum, 1985. Print.
Soen, Dan, Mally Shechory, and Sarah Ben David, eds. *Minority Groups: Coercion, Discrimination, Exclusion, Deviance and the Quest for Equality.* Hauppage: Nova Science, 2012. Print.
Yetman, Norman, ed. *Majority and Minority: The Dynamics of Race and Ethnicity in American Life.* 6th ed. Boston: Allyn, 1999. Print.
Young, Donald. *American Minority Peoples.* New York: Harper, 1932. Print.

MINORITY VOTING DISTRICTS

The 1965 Voting Rights Act prohibited limiting the rights of all people to vote and called on the federal government to examine suspect elections. Specifically, it addressed efforts by whites in the American South to keep African Americans from voting. The act was successful in eradicating exclusionary practices and resulted in substantial increases in the numbers of African Americans who voted, but minority political disfranchisement still existed. Minorities remained proportionally underrepresented in elected offices nationwide.

The 1982 amendment mandated the creation of "majority-minority" voting districts in states with a history of racial disfranchisement. Such districts contain populations of minorities large enough to constitute a majority or elect a candidate of their preference. This is achieved through reapportionment, or redistricting, a process whereby districts are periodically redrawn by state legislatures, typically following the decennial US census. Reapportionment ideally reflects the changes in population occurring since the last census count. However, districts were gerrymandered during reapportionment to preclude the election of minorities by dividing minority populations across districts. Such gerrymandering for political self-interest is commonplace and was named after Massachusetts governor Elbridge Gerry, who, in 1812, advocated a salamander-shaped voting district.

Redistricting to create minority voting districts has been successful if measured by the numbers of minorities elected to office in such districts. However, minority districts face constitutional challenges.

——*Robert P. Watson and Claudia A. Pavone Watson*

BIBLIOGRAPHY AND FURTHER READING

Behr, Joshua G. *Race, Ethnicity, and the Politics of City Redistricting: Minority-Opportunity Districts and the Election of Hispanics and Blacks to City Councils.* New York: State U of New York P, 2004. Print.

Bullock, Charles S., and Ronald Keith Gaddie. *The Triumph of Voting Rights in the South.* Norman: U of Oklahoma P, 2009. Print.

Miller, William J., and Jeremy D. Walling, eds. *The Political Battle over Congressional Redistricting.* Lanham: Lexington, 2013. Print.

MISCEGENATION LAWS IN THE US

State miscegenation laws were examples of explicit racial discrimination in US statutory law; they criminalized and penalized the unions of persons of differing racial heritages and denied legal legitimacy to mixed-race children born to such interracial couples.

Thirty-eight US states at one time had miscegenation laws in force; seven of those thirty-eight repealed their laws before 1900. All southern states (not including the District of Columbia) had miscegenation statutes. Many western states (including Arizona, California, Montana, Nevada, Oregon, Utah, and Wyoming), in addition to forbidding intermarriage between blacks and whites, also specifically prohibited unions between whites and American Indians or whites and Asian Americans. Penalties upon conviction varied from a maximum imprisonment of more than two years in most of the South and some other states (ten years in Florida, Indiana, Maryland, Mississippi, and North Carolina) to sentences ranging between a few months and two years in other states. Enforcement of the laws was random and irregular.

The key case in ending miscegenation laws was *Loving v. Virginia* (1967). At the time that the US Supreme Court heard the *Loving* case, sixteen states still had miscegenation laws in force. Virginia's laws dealing with racial intermarriage were among the nation's oldest. They stemmed from statutes formulated in the colonial period (1691) and had been strengthened by more stringent miscegenation legislation passed in the mid-1920's in which whiteness was very narrowly defined. The codes that became law in 1924 were aimed primarily at discriminating against people of mixed African American and white heritage and/or of American Indian background.

In the *Loving* case, Richard Perry Loving, who was white, had married Mildred Delores Jester, who was African American, in Washington, D.C., in June, 1958. The Lovings made their home between Fredericksburg and Richmond in Caroline County,

Virginia. They were issued warrants of arrest in July, 1958, and in January, 1959, they were convicted before the Caroline County court of violating Virginia's antimiscegenation statute. Their minimum sentences (of one year imprisonment each) were suspended on agreement that they would leave the state. They moved to Washington, D.C., until 1963, when they returned to their farm in Virginia and worked with attorneys Bernard Cohen and Philip Hirschkop of the American Civil Liberties Union (ACLU), who placed their case under appeal. The miscegenation law and the Lovings' convictions were upheld by the Virginia Supreme Court of Appeals in March, 1966, but in June, 1967, the US Supreme Court overruled the appellate finding. The Supreme Court ruled that use of race as a basis for prohibiting marriage rights was unconstitutional under the Fourteenth Amendment's equal protection and due process provisions. The ruling nullified all remaining laws forbidding interracial marriage. Previous to the unanimous 1967 ruling, the US Supreme Court had taken a conservative approach to this civil rights issue. It had repeatedly avoided reviewing lower court convictions based on state antimiscegenation laws (*Jackson v. Alabama*, 1954; *Naim v. Naim*, 1955; *McLaughlin v. Florida*, 1964).

———*Barbara Bair*

BIBLIOGRAPHY AND FURTHER READING

Kenley, David L. "Antimiscegenation Laws." *Asian American History and Culture: An Encyclopedia.* Ed. Allan W. Austin and Huping Ling. Armonk: Routledge, 2014. 18–20. Print.

"Loving v. Virginia." *Legal Information Institute.* Cornell U Law School, n.d. Web. 30 Apr. 2015

Maillard, Kevin Noble, and Rose Cuison Villazor. *Loving vs. Virginia in a Post-Racial World: Rethinking Race, Sex, and Marriage.* New York: Cambridge UP, 2012. Print.

MISSIONS, MISSIONARIES, AND AMERICAN INDIANS

From the 1500s, when Spanish and French explorers brought Roman Catholic priests to North America, until the 1950s, missionaries influenced both American Indians and US policy toward Indians. Missionaries taught English, built schools and churches, and created pantribal connections. They also, however, spread disease and forced assimilation and Christianization on Indians. Most missionaries were well-meaning, but their efforts were often misguided. Some were so convinced of the correctness and superiority of their own culture and belief system that they tried to suppress and destroy those of the Indians. Missionary work supported by various denominations continues today, but since the 1950s, missionaries have been more sensitive than their predecessors to Indian culture. Missionaries and their missions remain controversial in most American Indian communities today.

SIXTEENTH CENTURY THROUGH EIGHTEENTH CENTURY

Missionaries first entered North America through the Spanish Empire in Mexico and through French trading posts in Quebec. The Spanish viewed Christianization as their holy duty to God and used it to rationalize conquest. State-sponsored Catholic missionaries developed missions in New Mexico, Texas, Arizona, and California. They provided protection, food, and shelter to the weaker tribes, such as the Pueblo Indians, while being constantly threatened by the stronger tribes, such as the Apaches and the Navajos. This system suffered a setback in the 1680 Pueblo Revolt (also known as Pope's Revolt), when tribes rose up and chased the missionaries and the Spanish settlers out of New Mexico. The Spanish reestablished the missions within fifteen years.

The French allowed Catholic missionaries into their territory, but they were not state-sponsored as they were in the Spanish Empire. Jesuits attempted to Christianize the Hurons, but instead they brought smallpox, which decimated the tribe. This upset the tribal balance of power, and the Iroquois attacked and killed off most of the Hurons. The Jesuits retreated and simply kept missions at trading posts until the 1790's.

The English Protestants also saw Christianization of the Indians as part of their role in North America. In the seventeenth century, John Eliot of Massachusetts established praying villages where Indians lived "as white men": They wore English clothes, learned farming techniques, and became Christians. As disease decimated many of the Northern Woodlands tribes, the remaining members joined the praying villages for survival. The villages appeared to be successful at attracting converts. Though many of the Indian residents did convert, most died from diseases spread by the whites within the praying villages.

David Brainerd, an Eliot student, began a mission among the Cherokee in Tennessee. The Cherokee used the mission to learn English and to learn about white culture. The high attendance rate made the school appear to be a success, which inspired other Protestant groups to send missionaries among the Indians. All these early missionaries—Spanish, French, and English—believed in the power of Christianity, the importance of sedentary farming, and the necessity of extinguishing Indian culture.

NINETEENTH CENTURY

Mission work exploded with the development of large missionary societies between 1830 and 1850. Presbyterian, Methodist, Baptist, and Catholic societies sponsored hundreds of missionaries, both male and female, to work with Indians. Missionaries built schools and churches to attract Indians to Christianity and white civilization. They expected Indians to convert in large numbers and to support their own missions financially (as the natives of India and Africa had done). Despite these efforts, the Indians showed little interest in converting to Christianity.

In the 1850s, the missionary societies grew impatient with the lack of progress. They accepted money from the American government to help support their missions. In return, the government demanded that the missionaries increase their efforts to Christianize and "civilize" the Indians. Money was supplied to help assimilate all Indian groups to sedentary farming and Christianity. This method was a general failure, perhaps most conspicuously with Plains and Northwest Coast groups.

By the 1870s, missionary societies lost patience with the lack of success and cut off funding for missionaries. Individual missionaries became responsible for their own financial support. Many entered into agreements with the US government that tied them to conversion quotas. The government wanted a certain number of "pacified" Indians in exchange for its invested dollars. Additionally, missionaries wrote pamphlets and books about the "wretched condition" of specific Indian groups. These writings influenced public views of the condition of the American Indian. Many of these missionary works formed the basis for anthropological studies of the Sioux, the Cheyenne, the Navajo, the Salish, and other native groups.

Despite their funding problems, missionaries continued their program of assimilation, agrarianism, and cultural extermination. The height of this policy occurred during the 1870s when the government's "peace policy" allowed missionaries to administrate the Bureau of Indian Affairs (BIA). At this time, residential schools became popular. Missionaries removed Indian children from their parents and sent them away to be acculturated into white society. Missionaries forbade the children to speak their own language, wear their own clothes, or practice any aspect of their own culture. At this point, missionary and government policy coalesced into one united front against Indian culture. By the end of the nineteenth century, missionaries had fallen out of favor with the government, which saw their attempts at fostering assimilation as failures. Few Indians had converted to Christianity; most had developed a resentment of missionaries and saw them as agents of cultural genocide.

Missionaries remained part of Indian policy through the 1950s. They ran schools, wrote reports, and continued to act as agents and intermediaries for the government.

POSITIVE CONTRIBUTIONS

Though missionaries generally attempted to destroy Indian cultures and societies in their efforts to help Indians, they made some positive contributions. First, education and acculturation provided Indian groups with a common language—English. Second, the residential school system provided a common experience for native leaders and gave them the opportunity to meet people from different tribal groups. Finally, education created bicultural natives who understood their own culture and white culture.

This development helped many tribal groups in their legal battles against white governments.

——*C. L. Higham*

BIBLIOGRAPHY AND FURTHER READING

Beaver, Robert Pierce. *Church, State, and the American Indians.* St. Louis: Concordia, 1966. Print.

Berkhofer, Robert. *Salvation and the Savage: An Analysis of Protestant Missions and American Indian Response, 1787–1862.* Lexington: UP of Kentucky, 2014. Print.

Devens, Carol. *Countering Colonization: Native American Women and Great Lakes Missions, 1630–1900.* Berkeley: U of California P, 1992. Print.

Grant, John Webster. *Moon of Wintertime: Missionaries and the Indians of Canada in Encounter Since 1543.* Toronto: U of Toronto P, 1984. Print.

Kelley, Robert. *American Protestantism and United States Indian Policy.* Lincoln: U of Nebraska P, 1983. Print.

Reyhner, Jon, and Jeanne Eder. *American Indian Education: A History.* U of Oklahoma P, 2015. Print.

MISSISSIPPI FREEDOM DEMOCRATIC PARTY

The Mississippi Freedom Democratic Party (MFDP) was founded to bring attention to the lack of political freedom in Mississippi (Voting Rights Act of 1965). The Freedom Summer project had registered only sixteen hundred voters in Mississippi in 1964, and the ruling Democratic Party barred civil rights activists from attending party conventions. The Council of Federated Organizations (COFO) therefore created a new party and selected sixty-eight delegates and alternates to attend the Democratic Party's national convention in Atlantic City, New Jersey. Their mission was to contest the seats held by Mississippi's all-white delegation, arguing that the MFDP was the only truly democratic party in the state.

Civil rights workers testified before the national Democratic Party's Credentials Committee about conditions in Mississippi. Fannie Lou Hamer, a sharecropper's daughter, delivered a riveting account of being threatened and beaten for attempting to register to vote. President Lyndon B. Johnson feared losing the support of white Democrats and tried to arrange a compromise that would allow the Mississippi Freedom Democractic Party token representation. Even though white liberals and moderate civil rights leaders such as Martin Luther King, Jr., were willing to accept this compromise, a majority of the MFPD's members were not. This disagreement solidified the split in the Civil Rights movement between integrationist moderates and separationist radicals.

——*Robert E. McFarland*

MISSOURI COMPROMISE

Between 1818 and 1819 both the territories of Missouri and Maine petitioned the US Congress to be admitted as new states. The Missouri Territory had been created from the Louisiana Purchase (1803) and was promised constitutional protection. However, Congress could not decide if the right of property applied to the institution of slavery. Should it be allowed in Missouri and the rest of the Louisiana Purchase, or did Congress have the moral responsibility to rectify the issue of slavery that had been avoided since the Constitutional Convention of 1787?

It would take three sessions of Congress between 1818 and 1821 before Missouri was fully admitted as a state. The issue of slavery sparked by the ensuing debate spread throughout the country and threatened to cause disunion between the northern and southern regions.

THE ISSUE OF SLAVERY

At the time that Missouri and Maine applied for statehood, the United States consisted of eleven free states and eleven slave states. This political balance had been achieved since 1789 by admitting a slave state and then a free state determined by geographical location and each region's past history with regard to slavery. This arrangement supplied each section with an equal number of senators (two per state) and attempted to equalize representation in the House of Representatives through the three-fifths clause.

The three-fifths compromise, added to the final draft of the Constitution, allowed slave states to count each slave as three-fifths of a person to balance their representative power against that of the more densely populated North. Nevertheless, the North had a majority of representatives in Congress (105 to 81). Missouri's admission as a free or slave state therefore became an important issue in the very body that would resolve it. Missouri threatened to extend the influence of the industrial free North in the Senate or provide the majority to the agrarian slaveholding South.

In 1818, Missouri's boundaries were approximately the same as those of today, and the territory was estimated to have 2,000 to 3,000 slaves. Slavery was a historical by-product of prior French and Spanish colonial policies. Missouri reasoned that slavery should be allowed to continue as it had in other territories that had been granted statehood since 1789.

In February, 1819, the House of Representatives responded to this debate by adopting the Tallmadge amendment. Representative James Tallmadge of New York proposed an amendment to the bill allowing Missouri to frame a state constitution. The two clauses in the amendment would restrict the further introduction of slavery into Missouri and provide that all children born to slaves would be free at age twenty-five. Both clauses passed the House. Southern senators were shocked by the bitterness of the debate in the House and the ability of the North to muster votes. They saw the Tallmadge amendment as the first step in eliminating the expansion of slavery. Voting along sectional lines, the Senate rejected both clauses.

Congress adjourned session until December 6, 1819. During this interim, Maine formed a constitution and applied for admission as a free state. Maine had been incorporated into the Massachusetts Bay Colony in 1691 but had started to agitate for separate statehood during and after the War of 1812. Its application for statehood as a free state seemed to provide a possible solution to the Missouri debate

that threatened the stability of the young nation. On February 18, 1820, the Senate Judiciary Committee joined the two measures and the Senate passed Maine's and Missouri's applications for statehood but without mentioning slavery. This infuriated Maine, which had, as part of Massachusetts, outlawed slavery in 1780. What should have been a routine confirmation of new states became part of the most explosive issue to face the country. Maine would be allowed to separate from Massachusetts and gain statehood as long as Congress approved it by March 4, 1820, or the nine counties would revert back to Massachusetts. Even so, many of Maine's constituency urged that Maine's application fail so that slavery would not spread into Missouri.

SECTIONAL POLARIZATION

Senator J. B. Thomas of Illinois offered a compromise amendment to the Senate bill that would admit Missouri as a slave state with the proviso that the remaining territories in the Louisiana Purchase above 36°30', Missouri's southern border, would be free of slavery. The Northern-controlled House responded by rejecting this Thomas amendment and passed a proviso prohibiting the further introduction of slavery anywhere. The result was polarization along sectional lines. In turn, the Senate struck out the antislavery provision and added the Thomas amendment. Thus began the final debate over whether slavery would be allowed to expand.

Senator Rufus King of New York continued the debate by stating that Congress, under Article IV, section 3 of the Constitution, was empowered to exclude slavery from the territory and to make slavery an issue for statehood. "New states *may be* admitted by the Congress into this Union." A precedent had been established under Article IV, section 3 of the Constitution which forbade slavery in lands above the Ohio River in the Northwest Ordinance of 1787. Therefore, in the minds of many of the northern congressmen, they should take this opportunity to eliminate slavery from any point west of the Mississippi. In response, Senator William Pickering of Maryland stated that the United States was composed of an equal number of slave states and free states; Missouri should be allowed to determine its own fate.

Missouri responded with anger and frustration, asserting that the issue was not about slavery but rather the issue of state sovereignty. Congress had delayed its admission for years. Missouri, like other states, had the right to choose its property laws. In Missouri as well as the rest of the South, the issue swung from one dealing with slavery to one dealing with property rights and the equality of states within the United States. These issues captured the attention of citizens throughout the country and led to heated debates on all levels. For the first time, slavery was being justified and defended as a good way of life by not only southern politicians but also the southern clergy. Would the country be influenced by restrictionists who sought to control this institution, or would states' rights be preserved?

The Compromise

A compromise between the two houses was eventually reached in a conference formed to break the deadlock. Speaker of the House Henry Clay of Kentucky stated that he would not support Maine's admission unless Missouri was admitted with no restrictions. The Senate took the House bill and inserted the Thomas amendment. The House under Henry Clay's leadership voted to admit Maine as a free state and Missouri as a slave state and restricted slavery north of 36°30 . It is interesting to note that seven of Maine's nine representatives in the Massachusetts delegation voted against Maine's admission so that their state would not be used to provide a solution to the slavery issue.

Missouri continued to be an issue when it presented a state constitution in November, 1820. As if to get the final word, the Missouri Constitutional Convention had incorporated into its constitution a provision excluding free blacks and mulattoes from the state. This provision incited the antislavery factions in the Senate and House and threatened to destroy the fragile compromise. A "Second Missouri Compromise" was needed which stated that Missouri would not gain admission as a state unless its legislature assured Congress that it would not seek to abridge the rights of citizens. The Missouri legislature agreed to this in June, 1821. On August 10, 1821, President James Monroe admitted Missouri as the twenty-fourth state. After waiting a short time, Missouri's state congress sought to have the last say when it approved statutes forbidding free blacks from entering the state.

The Missouri Compromise would stand for the next three decades. During that time it served to mark a clear delineation between the growing regional and sectional problems of the North and South and made states' rights the rallying cry for the South until the Civil War.

——*Vincent Michael Thur*

Bibliography and Further Reading

Richard H. Brown's *The Missouri Compromise: Political Statesmanship or Unwise Evasion?* (Boston: D.C. Heath, 1964) contains primary source material showing views of contemporary leaders and varying perspectives of historians. R. Douglas Hurt's *Agriculture and Slavery in Missouri's Little Dixie* (Columbia: University of Missouri Press, 1992) is a study of the political and legal impact of the Missouri Compromise in a seven-county area along the Missouri River. Glover Moore's *The Missouri Controversy, 1819-1821* (Gloucester, Mass.: Peter Smith, 1967) is a significant monograph on the political compromise that signaled nineteenth century sectional controversies during the antebellum era.

"Model" minorities

The concept of the "model" minority has been studied and debated since the 1960s when the term first appeared. Its validity has been both defended and attacked, and the possible harmful effects of the concept as an accepted and unquestioned stereotype have been argued. Another particularly contentious issue is that the suggestion that certain minorities are "model" implicitly contains the opposite idea: Other minorities are less than "model" and are perhaps even deficient in some way.

Definition and History of the Term

A "model" minority is any minority group (typically of non-European background) that does well despite having faced discrimination. The criteria by which a minority group is judged as doing well or not doing well vary, but they have included average family income; success in entrepreneurship; children's educational achievement (for recently settled groups); and extent of symptoms of deviance or social pathology. The higher the first three, and the lower the last one, the likelier a group is to be considered a model minority. Since every ethnic or minority group in the United States has produced at least a few high achievers and at least a few failures and criminals, social scientists' judgments of ethnic group success or failure are always statements of averages; they are often based on census data.

The term first appeared in an article in the January 9, 1966, *New York Times Magazine.* It was titled "Success Story, Japanese-American Style" and was written by white American sociologist William Petersen. Before World War II, Petersen points out, those Japanese Americans born in Japan could neither own land in California nor become naturalized American citizens; their American-born children (the Nisei) were barred from many types of employment. During World War II, Japanese Americans living in the Pacific coast states were herded into internment camps. Yet in the two decades after World War II, Japanese Americans achieved a level of education higher than that of white Americans; a level of family income at least equal to that of whites, and a level of social pathology (such as juvenile delinquency) lower than that of whites. Hence, Petersen calls Japanese Americans "our model minority."

In *Japanese Americans: The Evolution of a Subculture* (1969), Harry L. Kitano, a Japanese American sociologist, also uses the term "model minority," acknowledging its origin with Petersen. Kitano expresses ambivalence about the term, which he regards as an ethnocentric white majority's view of a racial minority. Yet, like Petersen, Kitano ascribes the economic success of Japanese Americans after World War II to ethnic Japanese cultural values.

MODEL GROUPS

Japanese Americans are not the only Asian American ethnic group that has been noted by social scientists for its level of achievement since the 1960s. Chinese and Korean Americans have also been so identified. The business success of Chinese, Korean, and Japanese Americans has been attributed by some sociologists and historians to ethnic cultural values, as exemplified by the rotating credit systems that

immigrants established to help provide one another with funds to start businesses. Korean business success has been similarly explained. The academic success of Indochinese refugee schoolchildren has been ascribed to the congruence of the refugees' Confucian ethic with the ethic of the American middle class. Louis Winnick, a scholarly expert on urban neighborhoods, went so far as to lump all Asian Americans together as a model minority.

Some non-Asian groups have also been viewed as model minorities as well. In the early 1970s, post–1959 Cuban refugees were praised in the mass media for having overcome adversity quickly. Thomas Sowell, a black conservative intellectual, asserts that British West Indian immigrants (who are mainly black) outperform native-born black Americans economically and educationally. Similarly, Ivan Light argued in 1972 that British West Indian immigrants do better in small business than native-born black Americans; they do so, he said, because of their rotating credit system. Writing in 1993, two journalists (white New Yorker Joe Klein and Haitian émigré Joel Dreyfuss) contended that Haitian immigrants exhibit fewer social pathologies and more signs of economic and educational advance than native-born black Americans. Social scientist Kofi Apraku has described post–1965 African immigrants (such as refugees from Ethiopia) as above average in occupational and entrepreneurial attainment.

SOCIOLOGICAL VIEWPOINT

Sociologists who employ or support the model minority concept usually adhere to the assimilation model of interethnic relations. According to this theoretical model, the ultimate destiny of any American ethnic or minority group is to climb upward into the broad middle class. Such thinkers tend to see the progress of any ethnic or minority group as a function of its cultural values rather than of the extent of the discrimination it suffers. The relative slowness of any particular group to overcome poverty and win the acceptance of the majority is ascribed, at least in part, to that group's cultural values; hence, one can regard some minorities as "model" and others as less exemplary.

Such structural theorists as sociologist Stephen Steinberg, by contrast, argue that it is not cultural deficiencies that retard minorities' progress but discriminatory barriers erected by the majority. These barriers can be far more widespread and insidious than is first apparent. Such theorists also contend that the seemingly miraculous progress of some model minorities can be explained by the social class background of the immigrants and by the opportunity structure that they found upon arrival rather than by any alleged superiority of those minorities' cultural values.

IMPLICATIONS

The model minority concept has most often been applied in discussions of the relative success of certain Asian ethnic immigrant groups in the United States. The term has engendered much debate because of its implicit criticism of other groups—if these "model" groups could succeed, it suggests, then others should be able to as well. This implication then leads to the question: If certain groups cannot succeed as well as others in American society, where does the problem lie—with discrimination, with the attitudes of the dominant culture, or with the cultural attributes and attitudes of the minority groups themselves?

The model minority concept has surfaced repeatedly in debates over the status of African Americans, the minority group that has been in the United States the longest but that has arguably assimilated least effectively. In the late 1950s and the 1960s, many white Americans felt anxieties about the Civil Rights movement; the urban unrest of the late 1960s exacerbated fears and uncertainties about the future of race relations. Then, in the late 1970s and 1980s, white resentment of affirmative action programs, which primarily benefited African Americans, grew. At the same time, there was some bewilderment that inner-city black poverty persisted despite affirmative action. The model minority concept, with its evidence of Asian American success, seemed to suggest that such programs might be, or should be, unnecessary.

Hence, from 1966 onward, the notion of Asian Americans as a model minority found receptive ears among conservative white Americans. By the middle and late 1980s, it was being purveyed in a speech by President Ronald Reagan (in 1984), in magazine articles, and on television news programs (which placed special emphasis on the scholastic achievements of Asian American youth). Although most blacks in the 1980s resented being compared unfavorably with Asian Americans, some conservative black intellectuals, Thomas Sowell, Walter E. Williams, and Shelby Steele among them, defended the concept and pointed to Asian American success as an example for blacks to follow.

CONTROVERSY AND CHALLENGES

Because of its use in arguments over public policy, the model minority thesis is hotly disputed. Thus a laudatory report on Indochinese refugee schoolchildren by Caplan, Whitmore, and Choy was criticized by sociologist Rubén Rumbaut for having covered only the Vietnamese, Sino-Vietnamese, and Lao, omitting data on the less successful refugees, the Hmong and the Cambodians. The overall high Asian American average in income and education, Asian American scholars Ronald Takaki, Deborah Woo, Peter Kwong, and Arthur Hu point out, hides a bipolar distribution: Chinese immigrants, for example, include both sweatshop laborers and scientists. Many of the Asian American youth who excel in school, it is emphasized, are children of well-educated immigrants who either hold professional jobs in the United States or did so in Asia; Asian immigrant teenagers from poorer, less well-educated families are not always high achievers, and they are sometimes members of urban juvenile gangs. Asian American immigrant family incomes, it is conceded, may equal or surpass those of whites, but only because of a larger number of earners per family. Per capita income is less than that of whites; moreover, Asian Americans tend to live in areas with a higher than average cost of living, such as Hawaii, New York, and California. Also, Asian Americans statistically must achieve higher education levels than white Americans to equal their incomes.

Sowell's portrait of British West Indian immigrants to the United States as an ethnic success story has also been challenged. These immigrants, economist Thomas Boston argues in *Race, Class, and Conservatism* (1988), exceed both the average British West Indian and the average native-born black American in educational level; hence, the superior West Indian economic performance in the United States is no simple rags-to-riches story. Sociologist Suzanne Model, using census data, asserts that any West Indian socioeconomic lead over American-born blacks had disappeared by 1990.

If the "model" part of "model minority" has been criticized, so has the "minority" part, at least regarding Asian Americans. Although everyone agrees that certain Asian American groups have been unjustly persecuted, some scholars, such as political scientist Lawrence Fuchs, argue that no Asian American group was ever discriminated against as consistently, or for as long a time, as black Americans were.

Some view the Asian American model minority stereotype as potentially harmful to Asian Americans themselves. Writing in the late 1980s, Ronald Takaki warned that widespread acceptance of the stereotype might lead to governmental indifference to the plight of those Asian Americans who are poor and to neglect of programs that would help Asian immigrants learn English and find jobs. Takaki, worried about the loss of legitimate minority status, points to examples of low-income Asian American university students being denied aid under educational opportunity programs. He also thinks that the envy generated among black and white Americans by the model minority stereotype partially explains the violent anti-Asian incidents of the 1980s.

——*Paul D. Mageli*

BIBLIOGRAPHY AND FURTHER READING

Barringer, Herbert R., Robert W. Gardner, and Michael J. Levin. *Asian and Pacific Islanders in the United States.* New York: Russell Sage, 1993. Print.

Gibson, Margaret A. *Accommodation without Assimilation: Sikh Immigrants in an American High School.* Ithaca: Cornell UP, 1988. Print.

Hartlep, Nicholas Daniel. *The Model Minority Stereotype: Demystifying Asian American Success.* IAP, 2013.

Hsu, Madeline Y. *The Good Immigrants: How the Yellow Peril became the Model Minority.* Princeton: Princeton UP, 2015. Print.

Pang, V. O., and J. D. Palmer. "Model Minorities and the Model Minorities Myth." *Encyclopedia of Diversity in Education.* Thousand Oaks: Sage, 2012. 1518. Print.

Takaki, Ronald. "Breaking Silences." *Strangers from a Different Shore: A History of Asian Americans.* Boston: Little, Brown, 1989. Print.

MOLLY MAGUIRES

The Molly Maguires were an Irish and Irish diaspora secret society active in Ireland, England (mainly Liverpool), and the United States in the nineteenth century. They are most well known for their operations in the anthracite coal region of eastern Pennsylvania from 1854 to 1877. The Molly Maguires of America adopted their name from one of the Ribbon societies of Ireland that had waged a campaign of intimidation and attacks against landlords and process servers between 1835 and 1855. The Pennsylvania Molly Maguires consisted of similarly disfranchised Irishmen, but there was no direct connection between the two organizations. The American organization was associated with the Ancient Order of Hibernians, a benevolent society having branches throughout North America and Great Britain. Membership in the order required a person to be of Irish birth or descent and a Roman Catholic with Roman Catholic parents. Despite its links to Catholicism, the Order of Hibernians was a secret society and thus under official ban of the Catholic Church.

In the eastern mining district of Pennsylvania, the Order of Hibernians eventually came under control of militants who created an inner order of Molly Maguires, with the intention of improving living and working conditions in the mining industry. To achieve their goals, the Mollies waged a violent terror campaign, harassing, intimidating, and murdering mine owners and supervisors, mine-owner-dominated police officers and judges, and miners of non-Irish descent. By plan, violent acts of arson, thuggery, and assassination were carried out in one district by Mollies from another district so the crimes were always perpetrated by non-locals, making criminal identification more difficult.

The Molly Maguires grew in strength during the Civil War when the increased demand for coal caused an influx of Welsh, English, and German miners to eastern Pennsylvania, displacing Irish American miners. During the war, the Mollies opposed enlistment in the Union Army and harassed federal recruitment officers. During the postwar years, between 1865 and 1875, the Molly Maguires' violent activities increased as wages and living conditions deteriorated for mining families in eastern Pennsylvania. During this time, the group organized a union and initiated several coal strikes. Eventually, members of the group ran for public office to advance mine workers' interests.

In 1873, after repeated efforts to bring the Molly Maguires to justice had failed, and the ongoing threat of the group became intolerable to mine owners, Franklin B. Gowen, president of the Philadelphia and Reading Railroad and its affiliated Coal and Iron Company hired the Pinkerton Detective Agency to eradicate the group. James McParland (or McParlan), an Irishman and Pinkerton detective, infiltrated the Molly Maguires and for more than two years was a member of the Shenandoah division, one of the most violent of the Molly Maguire lodges. McParland collected enough evidence to break the organization through a series of murder trials lasting from 1875 through 1878. McParland's evidence and testimony aided in convicting twelve of the nineteen Mollies eventually found guilty and hanged. Of historical and legal interest is the fact that the destruction of the Molly Maguires was initiated by a private corporation with the aid of a private police force, and the defendants on trial were prosecuted by mining company attorneys, then executed: All of this took place outside the confines of the US judicial system.

——*Randall L. Milstein*

BIBLIOGRAPHY AND FURTHER READING

Bulik, Mark. *The Sons of Molly Maguire: The Irish Roots of America's First Labor War.* New York: Fordham UP, 2015. Print.

Kenny, Kevin. *Making Sense of the Molly Maguires.* New York: Oxford UP, 1998. Print.

Linder, Douglas, O. "The Molly Maguires Trials: An Account." *Famous Trials.* U of Missouri-Kansas City School of Law, 2010. Web. 8 Apr. 2015

Riffenburgh, Beau. *Pinkerton's Greatest Detective: The Rough-and-Tumble Career of James McParland, America's Sherlock Holmes.* New York: Penguin, 2014.

Weisman, Peter A. "The Molly Maguires." *Lehigh.edu.* Lehigh U, 1999. Web. 8 Apr. 2015.

MONGRELIZATION

The term "mongrelization" was adopted by racist proponents of immigration restriction in the early decades of the twentieth century to dramatize their fear of the consequences of permitting unlimited immigration into the United States. A leading exponent of these ideas was Madison Grant, a distinguished naturalist who was a founder and president of the New York Zoological Society. In *The Passing of the Great Race* (1916), he classified national and ethnic groups as "races" and arranged them in an evolutionary order, with the "Nordic" peoples of northern and western Europe considered the most highly evolved, and the peoples of eastern and southern Europe, especially Jews, Italians, and Slavs, ranked as markedly inferior. Grant believed that it had been scientifically established that mental as well physical traits were genetically determined and could not be significantly altered by the environment. He also believed that in any mixture, inferior genes would triumph and "produce many amazing racial hybrids and some ethnic horrors that will be beyond the powers of future anthropologists to unravel." Grant was sure that "the surviving traits will be determined by competition between the lowest and most primitive elements and the specialized traits of Nordic man; his stature... and his splendid fighting and moral qualities, will have little part in the resultant mixture."

——*Milton Berman*

MONTGOMERY BUS BOYCOTT

When the Supreme Court issued its decision in *Brown v. Board of Education* in May, 1954, ruling that racial segregation in public schools was unconstitutional, it marked the beginning of a period of dramatic change in the relationships between African Americans and whites. Until the mid-1960's, that change was hastened by the organized nonviolent resistance by many African Americans to laws and conditions that they regarded as discriminatory. The first occasion in which such tactics proved successful

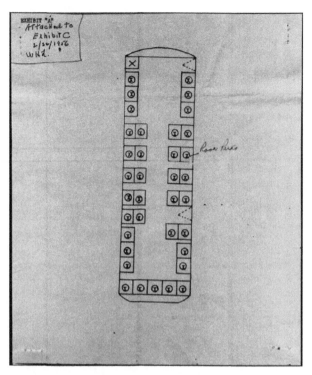

A diagram showing the location where Rosa Parks sat which was in the unreserved section at the time of her arrest.

was a boycott of public buses in Montgomery, Alabama.

Although African Americans had achieved some hard-fought successes before 1954—most notably the desegregation of the armed forces—in many respects they remained a separate community, enjoying fewer rights and opportunities and less legal protection than whites. This was especially true in the Deep South, where the doctrine of "separate but equal" was held to apply to most areas of daily life and was used to justify a decidedly unequal segregation. Hundreds of laws, many of them passed in the late nineteenth century, restricted the rights of black southerners to eat, travel, study, or worship with whites.

The school desegregation ruling brought no immediate change to race relations in Montgomery. Once the capital of the Confederacy, this city of about 130,000 people—50,000 of whom were African American—continued resolutely in the old pattern of racial separation. The African American community of Montgomery had undertaken initial steps to challenge certain local segregation practices that were particularly offensive. E. D. Nixon of Montgomery

headed the National Association for the Advancement of Colored People (NAACP) in Alabama. Because he worked as a sleeping-car porter, a unionized profession, he was less susceptible to attempts by the white establishment to control his behavior by threatening his job. Jo Ann Robinson helped lead the African American clubwomen in Montgomery, who provided a powerful organizational backbone among the small African American middle class in Montgomery. This nascent movement still lacked both a unified structure and a single issue to mobilize the African American community to push for civil rights.

Rosa Parks's Arrest

The issue came to a head on December 1, 1955, when Rosa Parks, a seamstress at a Montgomery department store and formerly the secretary of the local NAACP chapter, refused to give up her seat to maintain a row of vacant seats between white and black riders on the public bus system in Montgomery, as required by law. She was arrested and charged with violating the segregation ordinance. Parks's action was in part spontaneous—she had not boarded the bus with the intent to violate any segregation ordinance. Yet she had attended the Highlander Folk School in Tennessee, where members of the community learned to become more effective, and a lifetime of enduring racial indignities had made her acutely aware of the evil nature of segregation.

Immediately, Montgomery's African American community sprang into action. Fred Gray, one of but four black lawyers in Alabama, contacted Clifford Durr, a liberal white attorney, to post bail for Parks. Nixon brought together two ministers, Ralph David Abernathy and Martin Luther King, Jr., with Jo Ann Robinson to plan for a massive boycott of Montgomery public buses, a majority of whose riders were African American. It would be necessary to arrange for transportation for scores of African Americans who did not own cars. To coordinate the massive undertaking, Montgomery's African American leaders created the Montgomery Improvement Association (MIA), presided over by King, the twenty-six-year-old pastor of Dexter Avenue Baptist Church. The boycott began on December 5, 1955.

The Response to the Boycott
At first, whites reacted with indifference or amusement, until the bus company's revenues dropped

by 75 percent. A series of meetings between the city commissioners, representatives of the bus company, and the MIA failed to produce any agreement on the African Americans' demands—courteous treatment by bus drivers; a first-come, first-served seating arrangement, with blacks filling the rear and whites the front of the bus; and the employment of African American drivers on routes that served predominantly African American neighborhoods of Montgomery. Instead, the city police department began to harass the carpools that had been set up by the MIA to provide alternative transportation, and they arrested some of the drivers. Police officers arrested King himself for speeding, and on January 30, persons unknown blasted King's house with dynamite. The houses of two other boycott leaders met a similar fate.

These acts of violence and intimidation affected the course of events in several ways. First, they united the African Americans in Montgomery, inspiring them to continue the boycott for more than a year. The violence also attracted national attention to Montgomery and led to substantial outside support for the boycott, assistance vital to its success. Finally, the violence served as a foil for the rhetoric of nonviolent resistance that King so eloquently articulated. In one mass meeting after another, he urged his followers to ignore hostile provocations, to confront their persecutors passively, and to refuse to fight back, relying on the moral authority of their actions to sway the hearts and minds of their antagonists.

While the boycott continued, the legal issues it raised were argued in federal courts. On February 1, 1956, five Montgomery women filed suit to have the Court strike down the city bus seating ordinance. The case was heard on May 11, by which time eighty-nine MIA members faced local charges for conspiracy to interfere with normal business. In November, city officials obtained an injunction against the MIA officials for running a carpool, which nearly brought the boycott to a halt. Nevertheless, the federal suit received a favorable hearing and was affirmed by the Supreme Court in *Browder v. Gayle* in November, and the Court ordered the seating on Montgomery buses desegregated on December 17,

1956. Four days later, King, Abernathy, and Nixon rode the bus downtown and were able to sit wherever they wanted.

RESULTS OF THE BOYCOTT

The boycott succeeded for a number of reasons, not the least of which was the timely court ruling. It also benefited from fissures in the white community across gender, age, and economic lines. White, middle-class women often transported their black maids to and from work, unwittingly aiding the boycott. Within the Chamber of Commerce, a coalition of young businessmen called the Men of Montgomery demanded that the city fathers end the boycott because the city's tarnished image made it difficult to attract outside businesses.

Successful in its immediate objective, the boycott established a precedent for other economic protests over the next decade. Because of his role in the boycott, Martin Luther King, Jr., emerged as the most important spokesperson for African Americans. His tactics of nonviolent passive resistance remained the major tool of the Civil Rights movement until the mid-1960's. Shortly after the boycott's conclusion, King was instrumental in founding the Southern Christian Leadership Conference, which applied the Montgomery formula to other southern cities. African American leaders tried nonviolent resistance and economic protests in Birmingham, Alabama, and Albany, Georgia. The Montgomery bus boycott was an important harbinger of the most profound social changes in the United States during the 1960's, in that it marked a change in the attitudes and strategies of African Americans to confront racial indignity.

——*Courtney B. Ross, updated by Edward R. Crowther*

BIBLIOGRAPHY AND FURTHER READING

Branch, Taylor. *The King Years: Historic Moments in the Civil Rights Movement*. New York: Simon and Schuster, 2013. Print.

King, Martin Luther, Jr. *Stride Toward Freedom: The Montgomery Story*. 1964. Boston: Beacon, 2010. Print.

Theoharis, Jeanne. *The Rebellious Life of Mrs. Rosa Parks*. Boston: Beacon, 2013. Print.

MOOSE LODGE NO. 107 V. IRVIS

In *Moose Lodge No. 107 v. Irvis*, the Supreme Court on June 12, 1972, ruled that a state did not deny the equal protection of the law when it granted a license to serve alcohol to a racially discriminatory private club.

Moose Lodge No. 107 was a private club in Harrisburg, Pennsylvania, that served both food and alcohol, the latter under a license granted by the Pennsylvania Liquor Control Board. The club was often used by members of the state legislature for lunch breaks and after-hours relaxation. A white member of the lodge brought an African American fellow legislator, K. Leroy Irvis, into the club's dining room and bar, where the pair were refused service on the grounds of Irvis's race.

The Fourteenth Amendment to the Constitution forbids state action in furtherance of racial discrimination. Since the lodge's refusal to serve Irvis amounted to racial discrimination, the Supreme Court was asked to determine whether Pennsylvania's granting of a liquor license constituted state action in furtherance of that discrimination.

The Court ruled in a 6–3 vote that mere state licensing of a private club on private land did not make every action of the club an action of the state. The majority noted that the impetus for discrimination did not have to originate with the state in order for there to be state action, so long as the state was involved in enforcing private discrimination in a significant way. If the lodge had been a tenant in a state-owned building and had opened its facilities to all members of the public except African Americans, the state would have been engaged in a joint venture with the club, and the club's discrimination would have been state action. In this case, however, the building was privately owned, it rested on privately owned land, and its facilities were open not to the public in general, but to members only. The Court observed that the state provided many services, among them water, electricity, licensing, and police and fire protection. The mere provision of such services was not enough to convert every action of the beneficiary into state action.

The dissenters argued that there was state action, since the liquor regulatory scheme was pervasive, regulating "virtually every detail of the operation of the licensee's business." They also observed that since the quota for liquor licenses had been exceeded in Harrisburg, the state's renewal of the Moose Lodge's license prevented a different facility with nondiscriminatory policies from opening.

This important case limited the reach of the Fourteenth Amendment by defining state action narrowly. It remained possible for victims of discrimination to find recourse in federal and state antidiscrimination statutes. Leroy Irvis was able to do just that when he brought suit against Moose Lodge No. 107 under Pennsylvania's public accommodations law. He eventually gained admission to the club's facilities and was later elected speaker of the Pennsylvania House of Representatives.

——*William H. Coogan*

BIBLIOGRAPHY AND FURTHER READING

Kull, Andrew. *The Color-Blind Constitution.* Cambridge: Harvard UP, 1994. Print.

Omi, Michael, and Howard Winant. *Racial Formation in the United States.* New York, Routledge, 2014. Print.

Purcell, Richard. *Race, Ralph Ellison and American Cold War Intellectual Culture.* New York: Palgrave Macmillan, 2013. Print.

Reskin, Barbara. "The Race Discrimination System." *Annual Review of Sociology* 38 (2012): 17–35. Print.

MORMONS

Mormonism is the only faith that can claim to be completely American. Not even the Shakers, Amish, or Pentecostals can say as much. With roots in New York state during the 1820s, ninety-five percent of its members belong to the Church of Jesus Christ of Latter-day Saints (LDS). One of the leading proselytizing religions, approximately 60 percent of its 14 million members live outside the US, with a presence in Latin America, Asia, Europe and to a lesser extent Canada, Africa, and Oceania. Its 5.5 million members in the US constitute 1.7 percent of the population, roughly equal to the proportion of Jews and twice that of Muslims and Buddhists. Utah, whose population is almost 60 percent Mormon, is home to the largest number, comprising 12 percent of the US total. Small in membership, fundamentalist sects are scattered in isolated parts of Utah, Nevada, Arizona, and New Mexico.

The Mormon Church was founded by Joseph Smith, whose translation of sacred writings engraved on golden plates revealed to him by the angel Moroni became the *Book of Mormon: Another Testament of Jesus Christ*. Containing the teachings of ancient prophets of North America and centered on the belief that Jesus Christ had visited this continent following his resurrection, the *Book of Mormon* became a central text of the new religion. In search of a home for his growing congregation, Smith led them to Ohio, Missouri, and finally Illinois before being killed by an angry mob that felt threatened by his political power and apparent fanaticism. The Mormons encountered hostility, ostracism, and violence in all three states, motivating their new leader, Brigham Young, to find a more hospitable home. They settled in a sparsely populated frontier, which became the Utah Territory a few years after their arrival.

Over the years, much of the prejudice against Mormons has dissipated. Mormons have gained prominence in politics, business, and even sports beyond their actual numbers, and their missionary work has spread throughout the world. Young single men devote at least two years of service to communities in the US and elsewhere that need spiritual guidance and material aid, while young women and married couples help in any way they can. Nonetheless, the Mormon Church still attracts opposition from those devoted to discrediting the faith. Polygamy, which the mainstream church renounced as a condition of Utah's statehood but is still practiced by

LDS fundamentalists, was an early stain on its reputation that time has not fully removed. Claims that Mormonism is the "only true religion on earth" and that Scripture is flawed are considered blasphemy by some Christians, as are doctrines that question the Holy Trinity.

A culture that is supposedly sexist has elicited undeserved scorn from critics who do not understand its institutional practices and familial relationships. The situation is not helped by the existence of fundamentalist groups and radicals like the convicted child-abuser Warren Jeffs, who have benefited from sensationalized media coverage and endless fascination by a public that gets much of its information about Mormons through reality television. Some critics have highlighted the fact that more than 85 percent of Mormons are white, while no more than three percent are African-American and seven percent Hispanic. Even otherwise laudable characteristics, such as the prohibition of tea, coffee, tobacco, and alcohol and the effort to limit the consumption of meat have come under fire. Despite the existence of critics who wish to undermine an institution that has contributed to the nation's social, economic, and political wellbeing, the Mormon Church has been unusually resilient and adaptable since its founding.

——*Tomislav Han*

BIBLIOGRAPHY AND FURTHER READING

Bushman, Richard Lyman. *Mormonism: A Very Short Introduction.* New York, NY: Oxford University Press, 2008.

Grant, Hardy. *Understanding the Book of Mormon: A Reader's Guide.* New York, NY: Oxford University Press, 2010.

McKeever, Bill and Eric Johnson. *Mormonism 101: Examining the Religion of the Latter-day Saints.* Grand Rapids, MI: Baker Books, 2015.

MORRILL LAND GRANT ACT OF 1890

In 1862, the United States Congress passed the first Morrill Land Grant Act to authorize the establishment of a land-grant university in each state to educate citizens in agriculture, mechanic arts, home economics, and other practical professions. Because of the emphasis on agriculture and mechanic arts, these institutions were referred to as A&M colleges. Because of the legal separation of the races in the South, African Americans were not permitted to attend these original land-grant institutions. This situation was rectified in 1890, when Congress passed the second Morrill Land Grant Act, expanding the 1862 system of land-grant colleges to provide support for the establishment of African American institutions of higher learning in states that lacked such facilities.

Each of the southern states that did not have an African American college by 1890 established one or more under the second Morrill Land Grant Act. The 1890 institutions evolved into a major educational resource for the United States. For years these institutions provided the principal means of access to higher education for African Americans, particularly in the Jim Crow South, until the civil rights movement opened other educational opportunities. Many historically black colleges and universities (HBCUs) continue to be respected institutions of higher learning, not only for black students but for students of all races.

——*Alvin K. Benson*

BIBLIOGRAPHY AND FURTHER READING

Geiger, Roger L., and Nathan M. Sorber. *The Land-Grant Colleges and the Reshaping of American Higher Education.* New Brunswick: Transaction, 2013. Print.

Sternberg, Robert J. *The Modern Land-Grant University.* West Lafayette: Purdue UP, 2014. Print.

MOTOWN RECORDS

Named after Detroit, Michigan, the "Motor City," Motown Record Company was founded in 1959 by Berry Gordy, Jr. His record company brought African American performers and music to mainstream popular music charts by fusing gospel and popular music into an appealing, melodic sound. This style of popular soul music would become known as the Motown Sound and became highly influential throughout the music industry. Motown Records brought great pride to the African American community by demonstrating that blacks could become superstars and perform worldwide. Some of Motown's greatest artists and groups were Smokey Robinson and the Miracles, Gladys Knight and the Pips, the Four Tops, Martha and the Vandellas, Stevie Wonder, Marvin Gaye, Diana Ross and the Supremes, the Temptations, and the Jackson Five.

As a successful and high-profile African American–owned company during the civil rights era, Motown Records was an inspiration for generations of African Americans to have hope for a better economic future. The popularity of the company's African American stars also helped to shape a positive public image of African Americans during a time of suspicion and mistrust. To many people, not just African Americans, the music of Motown holds uplifting, identifiable messages that translate into working-class dance music. By generating love, soul, and inspiration through their music, Motown entertainers became heroes and heroines to thousands of people, and the Motown style and messages crossed race barriers, providing a common bond between blacks and whites.

——*Alvin K. Benson*

BIBLIOGRAPHY AND FURTHER READING

Aronson, Virginia. *The History of Motown.* New York: Chelsea House, 2001. Print.

Smith, Suzanne E. *Dancing in the Street: Motown and the Cultural Politics of Detroit.* Cambridge: Harvard UP, 2003. Print.

"The Story of Motown Records." *Classic Motown.* Universal Music, 2014. Web. 10 Apr. 2015.

MOYNIHAN REPORT

One explanation for high levels of impoverishment in black communities was published in *The Negro Family* (1965), by Daniel Patrick Moynihan, a white social scientist of Irish descent who later became a US senator. By postulating that "the family structure of the lower-class Negroes is highly unstable," the Moynihan Report argued that family deterioration was at the heart of high unemployment, welfare dependency, low achievement, and crime. In Moynihan's view, black communities were enmeshed in a "tangle of pathology." The report relied heavily on earlier observations by E. Franklin Frazier (1932), who conceptualized lower-class culture as disorganized and pathological. This thesis has since been used by others who contend that disadvantaged poor and minority groups encourage cultural practices that fuel their continued poverty.

Reaction to the Moynihan Report was generally negative on the part of leaders of the Civil Rights movement—especially clear when the report's conclusions were dismissed by those participating in the November 1965, meeting of the White House Conference on Civil Rights. The idea that poverty is caused by subcultural patterns has implications for public policy. Instead of focusing on federal efforts to ensure good jobs, housing, education, health care, and income maintenance, those who hold this view focus on improving the character of individuals and families. Critics of the report said that this culture-of-poverty theory was a form of victim blaming that ignored societal and institutional structures—such as unequal access to jobs, segregated education, and unaffordable, deteriorating housing—that make groups who are discriminated against more susceptible to poverty and the problems it causes for families and communities. Poor and minority people have the same values as those in more advantaged sectors of society, but their barriers to achievement are much greater.

This perspective continues to offend and enrage many people, including African Americans, civil rights workers, and progressive community and government activists.

—Eleanor A. LaPointe

BIBLIOGRAPHY AND FURTHER READING

Geary, Daniel. *Beyond Civil Rights: The Moynihan Report and Its Legacy.* Philadelphia: U of Pennsylvania P, 2015. Print.

Greenbaum, Susan D. *Blaming the Poor: The Long Shadow of the Moynihan Report on Cruel Images about Poverty.* New Brunswick: Rutgers UP, 2015. Print.

McLanahan, Sara, and Christopher Jencks. "Was Moynihan Right?" *Education Next* 15.2 (2015): 14–20. Print.

MULATTOES

Before the Civil Rights movement of the 1950's and 1960's, white supremacy was a prevalent concept in US society. White supremacists held that whites were better than people of other races. Under slavery, mulattoes (people of mixed white and black ancestry) were often accorded greater privileges than other enslaved people. The US Census Bureau counted blacks and mulattoes separately on censuses between 1850 and 1920, due to pseudoscientific research that suggested there were mental or physical handicaps in mixed-race individuals, who were increasingly seen as a threat to white society following emancipation.

Laws passed by white legislators usually discriminated equally against mulattoes and people of unmixed African ancestry. However, over time, white leaders were generally more willing to interact with mulattoes than with darker-skinned African Americans. Consequently, blacks and whites alike saw having light skin as an asset; most African American leaders were mulattoes.

This began to change, however, during the Civil Rights movement. African Americans began to exhibit an increased sense of positive self-worth—black pride—and to emphasize their African culture in their hairstyles, manner of dress, language, and artistic expression. Many African Americans thought that mulattoes should be discriminated against because their physical characteristics were not more obviously African.

In time, as white supremacy diminished in US society, African Americans began to view mulattoes as simply African Americans with light skin. (More frequent media portrayals of African Americans with lighter skin have continued to perpetuate that feature as a beauty ideal, however.) Consequently, the word "mulatto" has lost both its legal and social significance and slipped from general usage in the United States. "Mulatto," which also had a similar but distinct history in Latin America, is still used as a self-designation by some Latinos of African descent.

——*Roger D. Hardaway*

BIBLIOGRAPHY AND FURTHER READING

Alvaré, Bretton T. "Mulatto/a." *Latino History and Culture: An Encyclopedia*. Ed. Carmen R. Lugo-Lugo and David J. Leonard. Armonk: Routledge, 2014. 360–61. Print.

Brown, Kevin D. *Color Matters: Skin Tone Bias and the Myth of a Postracial America*. Ed. Kimberly Jade Norwood. New York: Routledge, 2014. Print.

Davis, F. James. "Who Is Black? One Nation's Definition." *Frontline*. WGBH Educational Foundation, 2014. Web. 30 Apr. 2015

MULTICULTURALISM

The word "multicultural" first emerged after World War II; its derivative, "multiculturalism," came into use during the Civil Rights movement and gained currency in the 1980s. Whereas "multicultural" is a descriptive term referring to the presence of many cultures in a multiethnic and multiracial society such as the United States, "multiculturalism" is a prescriptive concept that entails attitudes, value judgments, public policies, and controversies with regard to the diverse cultures present, especially as to how such cultures are to be identified and represented. Although differences in race, ethnicity, gender, age, ability, and sexuality are subsumed under the term "multicultural," multiculturalism has often been seen in particular as the antithesis of Western civilization or the culture of the white Anglo-Saxon Protestant (WASP) male. Encoded as the identity politics of ethnic minorities, women, and gays and lesbians, in the 1990s it became the major issue of the "culture wars"—the struggle to control the symbols and interpretations of American culture—and hence the definition of the national identity and the exercise of political power.

THE US REALITY

In the United States, Americans contemplating the history and reality of their country as well as their own identities must come to terms with the fact that their nation was shaped not only by the settlement of Europeans but also by other circumstances, including the deprivation of indigenous tribes, the slavery of Africans, the conquest of the Southwest (which once was a Mexican territory), the colonization of other countries (Puerto Rico, Hawaii, and the Philippines prior to its independence), military interventions in the politics of other regions (Korea, Vietnam, the Middle East, and South America), the immigration of peoples from all over the world, the contribution of American women from all races, and the global contexts of American politics and economy. This fundamentally multicultural fact, which is reflected in the nation's motto, *e pluribus unum* (out of many, one), has been either suppressed (as in segregation and discrimination) or recognized at different historical junctures, usually after political conflicts of varying magnitudes ranging from the Civil War to racial riots and civil rights demonstrations. On the legal level, such recognition came in the form of constitutional amendments, Supreme Court decisions, and civil rights legislation. The counterpart of such recognition in the domain of culture production, ideological discourse, and education is multiculturalism.

As a loosely defined set of principles meant to orient the social behavior of Americans, multiculturalism is closely related to the concept of "cultural pluralism," a doctrine that encourages the recognition and coexistence of differences. What sets multiculturalism apart from the assimilation and integration of ethnic minorities into the mainstream is its explicit criticism of the dominant culture as a kind of ethnocentricity, xenophobia, and oppression—hence the rejection of the melting pot model of acculturation in favor of the promotion of difference, self-esteem, and ethnic pride. As the cultural extension of the Civil Rights movement, multiculturalism became a celebrated cause in itself. Gaining support from educators, cultural workers, and various agencies across the nation, it was gradually implemented in the curricula of schools and colleges. The cultural sector, especially publishers, also began to respond to the needs of multiculturalism; results of this include the emergence of ethnic writers and artists, the sensitive portrayal of minorities in the mass media, and the reassessment of historical events such as the arrival of Christopher Columbus in the "New" World.

MULTICULTURALISM AND EDUCATION

Multiculturalism at the school level is often seen to be instrumental in the successful education of an increasingly diverse student population in terms of their scholastic proficiencies, civic aptitudes, and comprehensive preparation for the global economy of the twenty-first century. Important themes and issues in multicultural education and include the cultural heritages of different ethnic groups, bilingual education, cultural sensitivity, tolerance of difference, overcoming prejudice and racism, heroes from other cultures, self-esteem, and the strength of diversity. Some educators suggest that by means of multicultural education, an individual should be transformed intellectually and emotionally into a person who is capable of seeing things from another's perspective, committed to the unity and equality of the human race, and ultimately ready to take action in bringing about social justice.

In higher education, the adoption of multiculturalism is reflected in the curriculum, especially the creation of programs and departments, the transformation of core requirements, the diversification of course offerings, and the incorporation of texts addressing the history and culture of African Americans, Latinos, Asian Americans, American Indians, women, gay men and lesbians, and other identifiable groups. Initially, curricular expansions of this kind were sometimes accomplished through the activism of minority students, but gradually they have been institutionalized. One important result of this curricular reform in the humanities is the revision of the "canon"—that is, the inclusion of previously silenced or ignored texts (usually by women, minorities, and non-Western authors) and their displacement of certain other privileged classics (books by European male authors). Another effect is the critical rereading of canonized texts from the perspectives of race, ethnicity, gender, and sexual orientation.

As publicized—sometimes sensationalized—in national magazines, at the height of the multicultural movement (late 1980s to early 1990s), its advocates began to draw the critical attention of the public. Some critics were alarmed at the erosion of Americans' "cultural literacy" (E. D. Hirsch, Jr.), "the closing of the American mind" (Allan Bloom), and the "disuniting of America" (Arthur M. Schlesinger, Jr.) as a result of multiculturalism. The "victims' revolution" (Dinesh D'Souza) behind the politics of multiculturalism was also questioned. Complicating such controversies are certain policies regulating the multicultural reality of college campuses, for example, affirmative action admissions and hirings, the distribution of scholarships and funds, the treatment of ethnic student bodies, and sexual conduct. One particular controversy that captured the public's imagination was related to codes of proper behavior and speech with regard to women, minorities, and people with disabilities. Ridiculed as "politically correct" (PC), such codes have come to be seen as an extremist form of multiculturalism that reproduces rather than ameliorates the tensions of the multiracial, multiethnic, and multicultural society at large. On a further radicalized front, the dangers of the co-optation and institutionalization of multiculturalism have also been called into question as the debate continues.

——*Balance Chow*

BIBLIOGRAPHY AND FURTHER READING

Berry, J. W. "Living Together in Culturally-plural Societies: Understanding and Managing Acculturation And Multiculturalism." *Foresight* (2013). Print.

D'Souza, Dinesh. *Illiberal Education: The Politics of Race and Sex on Campus.* New York: Vintage, 1992. Print.

Fryberg, Stephanie A., and Ernesto Javier Martínez. *The Truly Diverse Faculty: New Dialogues in American Higher Education.* New York: Palgrave Macmillan, 2014. Print.

Hirsch, E. D. Jr. *Cultural Literacy: What Every American Needs to Know.* Boston: Houghton, 1987. Print.

Kalantzis, Mary. "The Cultural Deconstruction of Racism: Education And Multiculturalism." *Sydney Studies in Society and Culture* 4 (2013). Print.

Modood, Tariq. *Multiculturalism: A Civic Idea.* 2nd ed. Malden: Wiley, 2013. Print.

Schlesinger, Arthur M. Jr. *The Disuniting of America.* New York: Norton, 1992. Print.

Shohat, Ella, and Robert Stam. *Unthinking Eurocentrism: Multiculturalism and the Media.* New York: Routledge, 2014. Print.

MULTICULTURALISM ACT

On October 8, 1971, Prime Minister Pierre Trudeau established multiculturalism as the official social policy of Canada, making the nation the first and only one to have such a policy. On July 21, 1988, Canada passed a national multiculturalism law, which made multiculturalism a fundamental component of Canadian society and gave it an integral place in the decision-making process of the federal government. The core of multiculturalism is the idea that differing cultural or ethnic groups can coexist harmoniously in a pluralistic society. Canada has made multiculturalism its official doctrine and instituted corresponding policies that formally promote and incorporate ethnic and racial differences as integral components of the political, social, and symbolic order. Whereas American society has been compared to a melting pot, promoting conformity to a particular norm, Canadian society is likened to a patchwork quilt where ethnic boundaries are encouraged and supported by government policies and monetary resources. Just as the patches of a quilt determine its unique pattern, the different cultures in Canada determine its unique character.

For a policy of multiculturalism to work, a nation's policies and ideologies must promote minority rights to social equality and cultural identity within a pluralistic environment. Although Canada was initially oriented toward Anglo-conformity, diversity was a part of some of its laws and given some consideration. Aboriginal people had a special status, and the French and English were established as charter groups. Also, to encourage settlement of the prairie before World War I, the Canadian government promised to protect the immigrants' languages and cultures. The Citizenship Act of 1947 gave immigrants and native-born people similar status and rights in Canadian society.

During the 1960s, Canada's aboriginals became more assertive, the Québécois resented exclusion from central political institutions, and other ethnic minorities feared losing their culture and becoming second-class citizens. It was in this context that the policy of multiculturalism was implemented, allowing all Canadian citizens to choose to live according to their preferred culture while respecting the rights of others. The multiculturalism law of 1988 focused equally on cultural maintenance and social integration within a framework of equal opportunity.

The Multiculturalism Act has affected many aspects of Canadian society. Schools developed programs to accommodate more than sixty language groups and seventy ethnocultural communities and implemented multicultural and antiracism programs. Media have also experienced growth. Toronto has more than one hundred non-English newspapers, and more than forty cultures are represented in Canada's ethnic press. Ethnic radio and television programs are thriving. Programs have been developed on the community level, and at the federal level, supportive laws and policies have been instituted to help create additional multicultural and ethnic heritage programs.

Critics of multiculturalism argue that it is divisive, creates social and cultural ghettos, and in the long run inhibits opportunities for minorities. Others see antiracism and multiculturalism as being incompatible. However, multiculturalism appears, for the most part, to be working in Canada.

——Arthur W. Helweg

BIBLIOGRAPHY AND FURTHER READING

Berry, John W. "Research on Multiculturalism in Canada." *Multiculturalism, Beyond Ethnocultural Diversity and Contestations.* Spec. issue of *Intl. Jour. of Intercultural Relations* 37 (2013): 663–675. Print.

Foster, Cecil. *Genuine Multiculturalism: The Tragedy and Comedy of Diversity.* Montreal: MQUP, 2013. *eBook Collection (EBSCOhost).* Web. 5 May. 2015

Haque, Eve. *Multiculturalism within a Bilingual Framework: Language, Race, and Belonging in Canada.* Toronto: U of Toronto P, 2012. *eBook Collection (EBSCOhost).* Web. 5 May. 2015.

Winter, Elke. "Rethinking Multiculturalism after Its 'Retreat': Lessons from Canada." *Amer. Behavioral Scientist* 59.6 (2015): 637–657. *Publisher Provided Full Text Searching File.* Web. 5 May 2015.

Winter, Elke. "Us, Them, and Others: Reflections on Canadian Multiculturalism and National Identity at the Turn of the Twenty-First Century." *Canadian Rev. of Sociology* 51.2 (2014): 128–151. *SocINDEX with Full Text.* Web. 5 May. 2015.

MULTICULTURALISM IN CANADA

The idea behind multiculturalism, a term that developed in the 1960s, is to find unity in diversity, to enable immigrants to assimilate linguistically, politically, and into the labor force while retaining some affinity with their countries of origin via public endorsement and funding of their cultural and linguistic heritage. Multiculturalism has frequently been contrasted with the melting pot concept more prevalent in the United States, whereby some groups have assimilated into the dominant culture in about two or three generations following immigration. The aim of Canadian multiculturalism is to build a rich social tapestry of different traditions that combine to create a unique Canadian identity. Ideally, being "Canadian" would imply identification with many cultural systems, loyalty to an individual's own roots, tolerance for different peoples, and mutual respect. In reality, multiculturalism is a work in progress with as many setbacks as advances.

Head Tax Receipt - The head tax was introduced in 1885, as a means of controlling Chinese immigration. By User Bourquie on en.wikipedia.

Multiculturalism was perhaps inevitable given that when Canada became a confederacy in 1867, the country already contained three distinctive societies, dominated by British immigrants (60 percent), French immigrants(30 percent), and indigenous peoples. By the early 1990s, nearly 42 percent of the population of Canada had an ethnic origin that was neither British nor French.

GOVERNMENT POLICY

In October, 1971, the government of Canada announced its ethnocultural policy with the objectives of (1) assisting groups to retain an identity based on origin; (2) enabling ethnic minorities to participate as equals within Canadian society; (3) encouraging cultural exchanges within the country; and (4) helping immigrants learn one of the two official languages. The policy was funded with an initial grant of $200 million (Canadian) for a decade. The establishment of a Multicultural Directorate (1972) expanded the mandate to assist minorities with human rights problems and to promote freedom from racial discrimination. In 1973, multiculturalism acquired its own ministry within the federal bureaucracy, and linkages were encouraged with a variety of ethnic associations.

The "institutionalization" of multiculturalism continued when the concept was enshrined in the Canadian Charter of Rights and Freedoms (1982). Section 27 of the charter directs that its interpretation shall be consistent with the preservation and enhancement of Canada's multicultural heritage. The charter also guarantees equality before the law regardless of national or ethnic origin.

Of considerable significance was the passage by Parliament of the Multiculturalism Act in 1988, because Canada became the first country to convert this concept into a national law. The act provided for full participation in all aspects of Canadian society but recognized the right of every Canadian to choose and identify with the individual's cultural heritage. The legislation concentrated on the need to end racism (especially systemic racism), to eradicate discrimination in Canadian society, and to promote minority involvement in Canada's institutions.

The short-lived Department of Multiculturalism and Citizenship (1989) undertook the task of implementing the act with community involvement in a variety of programs to enhance appreciation and acceptance of the growing diversity of Canada's population. Although the department was disbanded in 1993, the objectives of seeking fairness and participation for all minorities were incorporated in new programs headed by a secretary of state for multiculturalism.

PERCEPTIONS OF MULTICULTURALISM

There are probably as many opinions on multiculturalism as there are ethnic groups in Canada. This is because Canadians are not certain about the precise meaning or application of multiculturalism or the cost of being part of a multicultural society. A 1991 Angus Reid poll showed that 78 percent of Canadians supported the concept. The majority anglophone population (people whose mother tongue is English), while espousing multiculturalism in principle, found practical difficulty in reconciling diverse cultures into the Canadian mainstream. Researchers have found the strongest support for multiculturalism among well-educated, young Canadians.

The francophone population of Quebec (those whose mother tongue is French) is so focused on its own distinct identity that it often fears an erosion of its French influence if so many cultures are given recognition within Canadian society. There has been consistent criticism of multiculturalism for diluting Canadian identity from its original British/French cultural orientation, for encouraging minorities to reject assimilation into the prevailing cultural mainstream, for fostering division rather than unity, and for diverting Canadian attention from more pressing considerations such as the economy and the national debt.

The reaction of allophones (those whose mother tongue is something other than English or French) in Canada is varied. While applauding the verbal and written guarantees of racial equality, they point to the all-too-frequent problems encountered by visible minorities in crucial areas such as employment, housing, and education as a sign that multiculturalism has progressed institutionally and bureaucratically as a notion but has a long way to go with respect to effective implementation in Canadian society. The policy's inability to stem racism has provoked much of the criticism from visible minorities.

Other allophones are skeptical of the whole process, which provides funding for ethnic festivals complete with food and dancing in colorful costumes while visible minorities continue to be grossly underrepresented in federal and provincial civil service positions and still encounter racism in numerous cities and towns in Canada. Critics also suggest that fostering diversity encourages a psychology of separateness and isolation among immigrants and that this imperils the already threatened political unity of Canada. Interestingly, multiculturalism has made Canada a far more popular tourist destination, and this has generated considerable revenue.

The concept of multiculturalism has been a positive ideal for a nation composed largely of immigrants from a variety of backgrounds. Canada's contribution has been in enshrining this concept within its constitution, in giving it the force of law, and in promoting, to a limited extent, its implementation. The many setbacks to the creation of Canada as a tolerant society free of racial discrimination cannot obscure the fact that the constitutional and legal guarantees provide a direction and a guide for all Canadians to follow. Although it has been extensively criticized by politicians, journalists, academics, and writers, multiculturalism continues to be one path to forging a more harmonious Canadian identity.

——Ranee K. L. Panjabi

BIBLIOGRAPHY AND FURTHER READING

Fleras, Augie. *Racisms in a Multicultural Canada: Paradoxes, Politics, and Resistance.* Waterloo: Wilfrid Laurier UP, 2014. Print.

Haque, Eve. *Multiculturalism Within a Bilingual Framework: Language, Race, and Belonging in Canada.* Toronto: U of Toronto P, 2012. Print.

Samuels, Barbara. *Multiculturalism in Early Canada.* Calgary: Weigl Educational, 2011. Print.

Tierney, Stephen, ed. *Multiculturalism and the Canadian Constitution.* Vancouver: UBC P, 2007. Print.

MULTIRACIAL IDENTITY

The growth in the multiracial population can be traced back to changes that took place since the dismantling of Jim Crow laws—particularly the 1967 removal of the last laws against miscegenation in *Loving v. Virginia*—and the implementation of civil rights legislation during the 1950s and 1960s. The comparatively more fluid intergroup relations led to increased interracial marriage. Census data indicate that the number of children born of interracial marriages grew from less than 500,000 in 1970 to about 2 million in 1990. The majority of these children have one parent who is European American. Interracial couples have used various terms to describe their offspring, including "rainbow," "brown," "melange," "blended," "mixed," "mixed-race," "biracial," "interracial," and "multiracial." The 2010 US Census showed that between 2000 and 2010 the multiracial population in the United States grew from about 6.8 million to 9.0 million people. During the same time period, the multiracial population growth rate was 32.0 percent, while the growth rate of the single-race population was 9.2 percent.

Also in 2010, according to the Census, there were 5.4 million interracial or interethnic households involving married couples. That figure represents 9.5 percent of all married couples and an increase from 2000, when 7.4 percent of married-couple households were interracial or interethnic. Table 1 shows the racial/ethnic combinations tallied—at least for the more common household types.

TABLE 1. 2010 CENSUS, PERCENTAGE OF INTERRACIAL/INTERETHNIC HOUSEHOLDS.

White and Hispanic (any race)	37.6
White and Black	7.9
White and American Indian/Alaska native	5.2
White and Asian	13.7
One partner of multiple races	15.6
Both partners of multiple races	6.4
Hispanic and non-Hispanic (non-white)	7.3

Source: US Census Bureau, 2010 Census. "Mapping Interracial/Interethnic Married-Couple Households in the United States: 2010."

THE MULTIRACIAL IDENTITY PARADIGM

A multiracial identity is not, however, indicative of someone who simply acknowledges the presence of various ancestries in his or her background. This identity, therefore, differs from that of other racial groups that may have multiple racial backgrounds but have monoracial identities, such as African Americans and Latino Americans. Multiracial individuals seek to replace these one-dimensional identities with multidimensional configurations. A multiracial identity is similar to, yet not synonymous with, an identity that is multiethnic in nature. A multiethnic identity is displayed by individuals who consider themselves to be members of several groups that are thought to be racially similar but culturally different, for example, individuals who are English and German American or Chinese and Japanese American. Social inequality in the United States has been determined more by notions of racial difference than by differences that are cultural in nature.

A multiracial (or multiethnic) identity is not the same as a multicultural identity. A multicultural identity is applicable to any individual who, irrespective of genealogy or ancestry, displays a general temperamental openness and sensitivity to racial and cultural differences. These individuals have an affinity with the values, beliefs, and customs of more than one racial or cultural group because of exposure to multiple racial and cultural groups. Multiethnic individuals feel a sense of kinship with several groups in direct response to the multiple cultural backgrounds in their genealogy. Similarly, multiracial individuals feel a sense of kinship with those groups directly in response to the multiple racial backgrounds in their genealogy. Exposure to these backgrounds enhances this feeling of kinship. Simple awareness of those backgrounds, however, can also bring about this sentiment. A lack of contact does not prevent it from being present.

IMPACT ON THEORIES OF MARGINALITY

Because of the multidimensional nature of their identity, multiracial individuals operate on the margins of several racial groups. However, this marginality, or sense of being "betwixt and between," does not necessarily result in the personal alienation traditionally ascribed to this phenomenon. Those traditional frameworks (particularly misinterpretations of sociologist Robert Ezra Park's theories) were formulated before the 1970s. They argued that marginality itself is necessarily pathological and the source of lifelong personal conflict. Consequently, multiracial individuals supposedly felt divided and ambivalent about their group loyalties. This interpretation is largely a result of the mutually exclusive nature of United States racial identities and a society that historically has been hostile to the idea of a multiracial identity. These theorists paid little attention to the sociological forces that made psychological functioning difficult for multiracial individuals and instead characterized them as "psychologically dysfunctional" because this image was acceptable to then current beliefs that sought to discourage miscegenation. These theorists thus distorted, or at least misinterpreted, Park's theory of marginality. They also overshadowed other contemporary theorists who argued that marginality could provide individuals with a broader vision and wider range of sympathies because of their ability to identify with more than one racial or cultural group.

The traditional theories of marginality were further challenged by data collected beginning in the 1980s. A consensus was developing that multiracial-identified individuals, in their journey to reach racial and cultural wholeness, may experience various ambiguities, strains, and conflicts. These phenomena come "naturally" with marginality in a society that views racial identities as mutually exclusive categories of experience. However, the negative feelings associated with marginality can be counterbalanced by an increased sensitivity to commonalities and appreciation of racial and cultural differences in interpersonal and intergroup situations.

IMPACT ON INTERGROUP RELATIONS

The models of multiracial identity that have emerged since the dismantling of segregation laws in the 1950s and 1960s challenge traditional US racial boundaries and categories in much the same way that their historical predecessors did. These historical manifestations of multiracial identity include integration through "passing" for a white person and the formation of rural enclaves and pluralistic urban elites, such as

blue-vein societies and Louisiana Creoles of color. However, those identities were motivated by the legal system of segregation, which sought to control the potential "threat" to white dominance posed by individuals of color. Consequently, they were not so much a response to the forced denial of European ancestry or cultural orientation as they were a reaction to being subordinated and to being denied the privileges that these criteria implied. These traditional identities also maintained the hierarchical value attached to racial differences by the larger society. Such attitudes were the products of Eurocentrism and were responsible for colorism among Americans of color. Colorism involves the preferential treatment of individuals who more closely approximate whites in terms of consciousness, behavior, and phenotype within the various communities of color as well as the larger society.

The "new" multiracial identity is not premised on the desire to gain privileges that would be precluded by identifying as a person of color and therefore is not synonymous with the psychosocial pathology of colorism. This identity instead contests the mutually exclusive nature of American racial boundaries and challenges the hierarchical valuation of racial (and cultural) differences. A multiracial identity thus recognizes the commonalities among various communities (integration) and, at the same time, appreciates the differences (pluralism). More important, this identity is premised on an egalitarian dynamic between pluralism and integration, which are viewed as relative, rather than absolute extremes, on a continuum of grays.

——G. Reginald Daniel

BIBLIOGRAPHY AND FURTHER READING

Bailey, Eric. *The New Face of America: How the Emerging Multiracial, Multiethnic Majority Is Changing the United States.* Santa Barbara: Praeger, 2013. Print.

Jones, Nicholas, and Jungmiwha Bullock. "The Two or More Races Population: 2010." *2010 Census Briefs.* Washington, DC: US Census Bureau, 2012. *US Census Bureau.* Web. 14 May. 2015

Kennedy, Randall. *Interracial Intimacies: Sex, Marriage, Identity, and Adoption.* New York: Vintage, 2004. Print.

Mahtani, Minelle. *Mixed Race Amnesia: Resisting the Romanticization of Multiraciality.* Victoria: U of British Columbia P, 2015. Print.

Maly, Michael. *Beyond Segregation: Multiracial and Multiethnic Neighborhoods.* Philadelphia: Temple UP, 2005. Print.

Spickard, Paul R. *Mixed Blood: Intermarriage and Ethnic Identity in Twentieth-Century America.* Madison: U of Wisconsin P, 1989. Print.

United States. US Census Bureau. "2010 Census Shows Multiple-Race Population Grew Faster Than Single-Race Population." *US Census Bureau.* Dept. of Commerce, 27 Sept. 2012. Web. 14 May. 2015.

MULTIRACIAL MOVEMENT

In 1979, interracial couples in Berkeley, California, founded I-Pride (Interracial/Intercultural Pride) in order to provide general support for interracial families. However, its specific goal was to get the Berkeley public schools to reflect the identity of their offspring accurately by including a multiracial designator on school forms. During 1979–80, the Berkeley public schools added "interracial" to school forms, the first time such a classification had been used in modern United States history. By the 1990s, I-Pride had become part of a coalition of more than fifty grassroots organizations that had come into existence since the 1970s. The coalition began pressuring for the addition of a multiracial identifier to the decennial census. These organizations included groups such as Multiracial Americans of Southern California in Los Angeles (MASC), the Biracial Family Network in Chicago (BFN), the Interracial Family Alliance in Atlanta (IFA), the Interracial Family Circle in Washington, D.C. (IFC), and a national umbrella organization called the Association of Multiethnic Americans (AMEA). This coalition also included A Place for Us/National, which is a national nondenominational religious support network for interracial families, organizations such as the Georgia-based activist, informational, and educational Project RACE (Reclassify All Children Equally), and *Interracial Voice,* an advocacy journal on the Internet that provides a public forum for the discussion of issues related to multiracial-identified and interracially married individuals.

This network of organizations encompasses individuals from various racial backgrounds; however, it has attracted a significant number of black and white couples and their children, largely because of the one-drop rule of hypodescent, which designates everyone of African descent as black. The network also has attracted a smaller number of "multigenerational" individuals who have backgrounds that have been blended for several generations. Although they have been socially designated as members of the various traditional United States racial groups (European American, African American, Native American, Latino American, and so on), they have resisted identifying solely with those socially assigned communities.

THE 1990 CENSUS

The controversy over the issue of multiracial identity became intense in 1988. On January 20 of that year, the Office of Management and Budget (OMB), the branch of the government responsible for implementing changes in federal statistical surveys, published in the *Federal Register* a notice soliciting public comment on potential revisions in Directive No. 15. This directive was implemented in May 1978 as the government-wide guide for conducting racial/ethnic surveys. The revisions would permit individuals to identify themselves as "other" if they believed they did not fall into one of the four basic official racial categories—black, white, Asian/Pacific Islander, American Indian and Alaska Native—or in the so-called "ethnic" category, Hispanic. Heretofore, the OMB advised that the category that most closely reflected how the individual was recognized by the larger community should be used in cases where there was any uncertainty. (Although an "other" category has not been used on all statistical surveys, it has been provided on each census since 1910 to increase the response rate to the race question. However, write-in responses in the "other" category are reassigned to one of the traditional racial categories.)

Many interracial couples and multiracial-identified individuals requested that a multiracial or biracial identifier, instead of "other," be added to the five categories. (On the 1970 census, multiracial offspring were classified in terms of the father's racial identity; in 1980, the US Census Bureau shifted

US CENSUS BUREAU ASSIGNMENT OF MULTIRACIAL RESPONSES IN THE OTHER CATEGORY: 1990 (1990 CENSUS, TEN MOST FREQUENTLY USED RESPONSES)

Response	Assigned Category	Total
Black and white	Black	47,835
Mixed, multiracial (or multiethnic)	Other	32,505
Mulatto (or quadroon, octoroon)	Other	31,848
White and black	White	27,926
Eurasian	Asian	19,190
Amerasian	Asian	18,545
Biracial (or interracial)	Other	17,202
White and Japanese	White	9,329
White and Filipino	White	7,081
Creole	Other	6,244

Notes: In 1990, Amerasian and Eurasian were reassigned from the other category to the Asian category. That same year, Creole was reassigned to the other category although in 1980 it had been recoded as black. Also, individuals who used terms such as mulatto, quadroon, or octoroon remained in the other category; previously they had been reassigned to the black category. Those individuals who listed themselves as two or more racial groups were reassigned to the first racial group listed.

Source: Data are from the US Bureau of Census. 1990 Census.

to a formula relying on the identity of the mother. However, a "biracial" or "multiracial" designation was not permitted.) The OMB received overwhelmingly negative responses from the public to the proposed changes to Directive No. 15, particularly the addition of a multiracial identifier. This included some federal agencies, such as the Civil Rights Division of the Department of Justice, the Department of Health and Human Services, the Equal Employment Opportunity Commission, the Office of Personnel Management, and several large corporations. Some of this opposition was based on logistical and financial concerns about the increase in data collection, paperwork, changes in the format of forms and computer programs for data analysis, and data burden on respondents.

Various African American leaders and organizations in particular voiced their opposition to the change. They argued that most, if not all African Americans, have some European, and in many cases, Native American ancestry (although most identify solely with the black community). Consequently,

they feared that many individuals would designate themselves as "multiracial" rather than black in order to escape the continuing negative social stigma associated with African Americans. Similar concerns were expressed by individuals and organizations representing other traditional communities of color, including Latinos, Native Americans, and Asian Americans. In addition, opponents argued that the rule of hypodescent, if originally oppressive, has also been a means of mobilizing communities of color in the struggle against white racial privilege. More important, this mechanism has prevented a reduction in the number of individuals who would be counted as members of the traditional communities of color. These numbers were needed to enforce and support civil rights legislation and claims aimed at tracking historical and contemporary patterns of discrimination. They were particularly important in arriving at goals for achieving social and economic equity in the manner of affirmative action.

On November 12, 1988, the AMEA was formed in Berkeley to serve as a national network for the various independent support groups. Its overall goal was to promote healthy images of interracial couples and multiracial individuals. More specifically, its purpose was to increase public awareness about the importance of adding a multiracial identifier to the decennial census. A flurry of telephone calls and correspondence between officials at the OMB and the Census Bureau and various individual groups affiliated with the AMEA ultimately resulted in some clarity as to how multiracial individuals might be accommodated on the 1990 census. Officials said they would specifically code write-in responses in the "other" category as "biracial," "multiracial," or some other designation that clearly indicated a blended identity. This would help determine what, if any, changes should be made on the year 2000 census. This was a departure from policy on previous censuses. However, none of the approximately 253,000 multiracial responses in the other category on the 1990 census can be used as a accurate estimate of the actual number of individuals who identify as multiracial. Also, vast numbers of individuals followed the tradition of circling one box because they were unaware of any other alternative.

THE YEAR 2000 CENSUS

Efforts to get the US Census Bureau to make "multiracial" an acceptable means of self-identification were unsuccessful for the 1990 census. Nevertheless, forms for the Operation Desert Shield/Storm Deployment Survey included a multiracial designator for the offspring of returning intermarried veterans. Under the guidance of Project RACE, several states included "multiracial" as an acceptable official means of self-identification. Georgia, Ohio, Illinois, Michigan, Indiana, and Maryland made this option available on all official state forms. Florida and North Carolina included a multiracial identifier on all school forms. A 1994 survey of eight hundred public school districts, conducted by the Education Office for Civil Rights, found that approximately 30 percent of the school districts use a special separate category. Other districts simply use the mother's racial designation; some use the father's. The American College Test (ACT), which is the alternative to the Scholastic Aptitude Test (SAT) college entrance exam, included "multiracial" as an acceptable means of identification. Most universities were resistant to any changes in the collection of racial data; however, Williams College in Williamstown, Massachusetts,

included a multiracial identifier on its official forms. Beginning in 1989, reports prepared by the Center for Assessment and Demographic Studies at Gallaudet University in Washington, D.C., counted individuals who indicated identification with a multiracial background. Nevertheless, these data were reassigned at the federal level to one of the four official racial categories (along with the Hispanic identifier, when it was given as an option) or added into the figures for each of the racial groups with which multiracial individuals identified. This second method is especially useful when trying to track those whose background includes historically underrepresented groups of color for the purposes of affirmative action.

"Multiracial" was not accepted as a means of self-identification on federal forms during the early 1990s. However, the OMB began a comprehensive review process in 1993 to discuss possible changes in this direction on the year 2000 census. After extensive cognitive research and field testing of sample households, the OMB on October 30, 1997, approved changes that would allow multiracial individuals to identify themselves as such on official forms. (The key findings based on the comprehensive review were that between 1 percent and 1.5 percent of the public would select a multiracial identifier when offered an opportunity to do so.)

Most activists had hoped for a combined format that would include a separate multiracial box but would also allow individuals to check the other boxes representing the various components of their background. The OMB proposed a format that read: "What is this person's race? Mark[X] one or more races to indicate what this person considers herself/himself to be." This format was chosen partially in response to the unanimous support it received from the various federal agencies that require data on race and ethnicity. These agencies argued that the mark-one-or-more alternative—unlike the combined format—would require fewer changes in formatting on existing forms and allow for data continuity. More important, the data could be counted in each of the existing official racial categories with which multiracial individuals identified, thus including the historically underrepresented racial components in their background. This would be especially important for the purposes of the continued enforcement of civil rights legislation and in meeting affirmative action guidelines. This format is similar to the one that appears on the Canadian census. Since the 1980s, Canada has allowed individuals to check more than one box on the census race/ethnic ancestry question. In addition, Canadian census data have been used for the purposes of achieving "job equity" in a manner similar to affirmative action and other civil rights mandates in the United States.

The mark-one-or-more format also received strong support from traditional civil rights organizations such as the National Association for the Advancement of Colored People (NAACP), the National Urban League, the Congressional Black Caucus, and the Mexican American Legal Defense and Education Fund (MALDEF). These groups argued that a standalone multiracial identifier would lead to a decline in their numbers. (It should be noted, however, that the combined format would have prevented this loss. In addition, that format would have had the advantage of making it possible to count the data in each of the racial groups with which multiracial individuals identify as well as specifically acknowledging the identity of multiracial individuals.) Furthermore, the traditional communities of color expressed concerns about the potential divisiveness of even the appearance of a multiracial box, whether as a stand-alone identifier or in combination with checking multiple boxes. These concerns were very influential in prompting the OMB officials to chose the mark-one-or-more format. In addition, various representatives from traditional communities of color expressed concerns about how the data would actually be tabulated even though they supported the mark-one-or-more format. The OMB officials indicated that they would make recommendations and provide additional guidance with respect to this question before the year 2000 census after consulting with officials from various federal agencies, interested groups, demographers, planners, and social scientists. The year 2000 census forms used the mark-one-or-more format without a standalone multiracial identifier.

THE YEAR 2010 CENSUS

Like the year 2000 census form, the year 2010 census form used the mark-one-or-more format without a standalone multiracial identifier. The 2010 census also included examples of self-identified races respondents could fill in for "Other Asian" and "Other Pacific Islander," although respondents were not limited to these options. The examples for "Other Asian" are Hmong, Laotian, Thai, Pakistani, and Cambodian. The examples for "Other Pacific Islander" are Fijian and Tongan. Although forms for both years provided separate questions about Hispanic origin and race, and instructed respondents to answer both questions, the year 2010 form specified that the census did not consider Hispanic origins to be races.

——G. Reginald Daniel

BIBLIOGRAPHY AND FURTHER READING

Root, Maria P. P., ed. *The Multiracial Experience: Racial Borders as the New Frontier.* Thousand Oaks: Sage, 1996. Print.

Root, Maria P. P., ed. *Racially Mixed People in America.* Thousand Oaks: Sage, 1992. Print.

Spencer, Jon Michael. *The New Colored People: The Mixed-Race Movement in America.* New York: NYUP, 1997. Print.

United States Census Bureau. *United States Census 2010.* Washington, DC: US Census Bureau, US Dept. of Commerce, 2010. Digital file. Zack, Naomi, ed. *American Mixed Race: The Culture of Microdiversity.* Lanham: Rowman, 1995. Print.

MUSLIM HOLIDAYS AND CELEBRATIONS

The following Muslim holidays and celebrations are a chance for Muslims to celebrate their faith and perform their devotion to Allah. The faith of Islam includes many sects that often follow differing practices. The events listed here are common to all—or, at the very least, to the majority—of Muslim sects.

The list, therefore, is far from comprehensive, but it does detail the major holy events of the Islamic calendar and bears witness to the vibrancy of the Muslim faith.

The prophet Muhammad's Higra—his arrival at Medina from Mecca—occurred on July 16, 622 and marks the beginning of the Islamic calendar. The Islamic year follows a lunar calendar with twelve months. The Qur'an prohibits the use of an intercalary month to align this calendar with the common solar calendar. Therefore, Muslim holidays and celebrations fall on a different day of the common solar calendar each year and are denoted here with their Islamic month and date.

RAMADAN

The entire month of Ramadan, the ninth month of the Islamic calendar, is considered holy. Throughout the month, Muslims fast from dawn to dusk. The practice dates back to the prophet Muhammad who commonly fasted during the day. The obligatory fasting during Ramadan—sawm or siyam in Arabic—comprises one of the five pillars of the Islamic faith. Commonly, Muslims enjoy a predawn meal as well as a fast-breaking meal immediately after sundown. Prepubescent children and the elderly are exempt from this practice, as are those with medical conditions which preclude them from participating. Those traveling or sick during Ramadan can break their fast; however, they are usually expected to make up for their missed fasts after the month ends. Given the holiness of the period, Muslims attempt to abstain from swearing, anger, and the like throughout month. It also stands as a time for particular giving to the poor, another of the five pillars of Islam.

The holy month commemorates when the prophet Muhammad first began putting the Qur'an into writing. A time for prayer follows the post-sunset, fast-breaking meal, and many Muslims may gather at their local mosques for both the meal and prayer session. The entire month is celebrated; however, Laylat al-Qadr, or The Night of Power, marks the exact night when Muhammad began penning the Qur'an. This night is commonly observed on the twenty-seventh of Ramadan, but the prophet Muhammad himself proclaimed only that the day falls in the final third of the month and that his followers should strive to discern it's occurrence on their own. Laylat al-Qadr is a day of mercy when practitioners engage in prayer, discussion, self-examination, and the seeking of forgiveness.

ID AL-FITR

Immediately following Ramadan, Id al-Fitr, or the Feast of Fast-Breaking, falls on the first three days of the tenth month of the Islamic calendar, Shawwal.

Although the festival lasts for three days, the first day stands as the most important. After fasting from sunset to sunrise for all thirty days of Ramadan, Muslims celebrate their first daytime meal on the first of Shawwal. They gather in the morning at the mosque or in the open air for a communal prayer and/or a sermon from the local imam. The feast, the central part of the holiday, follows. It is a time to visit with friends and extended family; some Muslim communities have even adopted the practice of gift giving. Many Muslim majority countries issue a national holiday for the first or the first two days of Id al-Fitr. The festival is an opportunity to celebrate community, renewal, and the mercy of Allah.

HAJJ

The Hajj, or the annual pilgrimage to Mecca, occurs on the eighth, ninth, and tenth of the Islamic month of Dhu al-Hijjah. Every Muslim man must fulfill this pilgrimage, one of the five pillars of Islam, once in their lifetime, provided that they are able. Many women also complete the pilgrimage, but they must be accompanied by a close male relative. The journey includes several distinct phases. These begin with the announcement to their home community and spiritual preparation for the journey. Near Mecca, pilgrims gather outside of the sacred land and the men put on white robes made from a single cloth. Other phases include, reenacting Hagar's search for water for Ismail, reenacting Muhammad's Farewell Pilgrimage, and gathering forty-nine small stones to throw at three pillars where Satan appeared to Ibrahim. The entire festival lasts for three days, and afterwards participants are considered Hajji.

Islam places itself as an heir to Judaism and Christianity; both its inheritance of Jewish belief and its own uniqueness are represented in the celebration of the Hajj. The pilgrimage celebrates three events: the forgiveness and reunion of Adam and Eve, Ibrahim's willingness to sacrifice his son Ismail, and Muhammad's obedience to Allah. Ibrahim is believed to have constructed the Kaaba and to have made annual pilgrimages to Mecca before he died and the city lapsed into paganism. The prophet Muhammad smashed the idols and restored the Kaaba to the center of worship. Though most of the events of the Hajj are distinctly Islamic, some, such as the circling of the Kaaba, have been adapted from preIslamic Meccan practices.

ID AL-ADHA

The celebration of Id al-Adha begins on the final day of the Hajj and lasts for four days in the Islamic month of Dhu al-Hijjah (Dhu al-Hijjah 10-13). These four days are held to be the holiest in the Islamic calendar. Unlike the Hajj which is centered in the city of Mecca, Id al-Adha—or Days of Sacrifice— is celebrated by Muslims across the globe. Similar to the Hajj, Muslims utilize Id al-Adha to celebrate Ibrahim's obedience to Allah witnessed in his willingness to sacrifice his son Ismail. Muslims have inherited this story from Judaism; however, they have modified it. For example, they focus on Ibrahim's son Ismail instead of his son Isaac. Since Allah offered a ram in the stead of Ismail, Muslims celebrate Id al-Adha with prayers at the local mosque and the sacrifice of an animal for consumption. Traditionally, they then give a third of the meat to the poor, share a third of the meat with friends and family, and retain the final third of meat for their own feast. The word Islam means submission and this holiest of holidays is a chance for Muslims to celebrate Ibrahim's submission and for them to perform their own.

LAYLAT AL-MIRAJ

On the twenty-seventh of the Islamic month of Rajab, many Muslims celebrate Laylat al-Miraj, or the Night of the Journey and Ascension. Towards the end of his human life, Muhammad is believed to have traveled to Jerusalem from Mecca and from there to have ascended to heaven in the year 620. While there, he met the previous prophets and received the words of the daily prayers directly from Allah. Muslims celebrate his ascension on Laylat al-Miraj. Many do so by attending their local mosque for prayer, self-examination, and a reading of the Qur'an.

——*Anthony Vivian*

BIBLIOGRAPHY AND FURTHER READING

Council on Islamic Education (U.S.). *Muslim Holidays: Teacher's Guide and Student Resources.* Fountain Valley, CA: Council on Islamic Education, 1997. Print.

Gulevich, Tanya. *Understanding Islam and Muslim traditions.* Detroit, MI: Omnigraphics, 2004. Print.

Kelly, Aidan A., Peter D Dresser, and Linda M Ross. *Religious Holidays and Calendars: an Encyclopaedic Handbook.* Detroit, MI: Omnigraphics, 1993. Print.

Melton, J. Gordon, ed. *Religious Celebrations: An Encyclopedia of Holidays, Festivals, Solemn Observances, and Spiritual Commemorations: Volumes I-II.* Santa Barbara: ABC-CLIO, 2011. Print.

Sakr, Ahmad Huessein. *Feast, Festivities and Holidays.* Lombard, IL: Foundation for Islamic Knowledge, 1999. Print.

MUSLIMS IN NORTH AMERICA

By the late 1900's, Muslim American communities of significant size and number had developed in the United States and Canada. However, some people felt threatened by the rise of Islam in North America.

MUSLIMS IN THE UNITED STATES

Muslim American immigrants are one of the country's more recent immigrant groups: according to a 2011 survey by the Pew Research Center, a full 71 percent of foreign-born Muslims arrived after 1990. Nevertheless, the number of Muslim Americans is large and still growing. In 2016, Pew Research Center updated their estimates and said that there were approximately 3.3 million Muslims living in American in 2015. Growth in the population is due both to an increase of Muslim immigrants and to Americans who are converting to Islam. Exact figures are difficult to obtain as the US Census does not cover religion, but the Muslim American population was estimated to be at least 2.7 million people in 2014. Other estimates have placed the number as high as 7 million. While the Pew Research Center has projected some estimates based on their 2011 survey, no new survey had been taken as of early 2016.

According to the Pew survey, 63 percent of Muslim Americans are first-generation immigrants, though 70 percent of these are naturalized citizens, a higher proportion than in most immigrant groups. Although the majority of the world's Muslims live in South Asia, the survey found that 41 percent of the foreign-born US Muslim population came from the Middle East and North Africa, while only 26 percent came from

South Asia. Islam has also had a significant presence in the African American community since the 1930s, when the Nation of Islam was founded. In 2011, 40 percent of the US-born Muslim population identified as black. The Muslim American population was 55 percent male and 45 percent female, due partly to single Muslim men being more likely to immigrate than single Muslim women and partly to American men being more likely than women to convert to Islam.

Many children of Muslim immigrants are adopting mainstream American ways. Muslim women have active mosque and professional roles, and some young people are dreaming of becoming Muslim American politicians. However, many retain a strong sense of Muslim identity—according to the Pew survey, nearly half think of themselves as Muslim first, American second, and nearly 70 percent say that their religion is very important in their lives. The community is also fairly close-knit, with the majority of adult Muslim Americans living in entirely Muslim households (though this is less true of African American Muslims).

Following the September 11, 2001, terrorist attacks and the United States' subsequent prosecution of war in Iraq and Afghanistan, many Muslim Americans began to experience increased discrimination due to a growing public perception of Islam as a violent religion. Systemic discrimination also increased, with those whose names or manner of dress suggested that they might be Muslim receiving greater scrutiny from police and security personnel, especially when boarding airplanes. However, Muslim Americans are not as economically disadvantaged as many minority groups; the median income of Muslim Americans and the percentage of Muslim Americans with college degrees were still very close to those of the general population as of 2011.

Another wave of anti-Muslim sentiment arose during the 2016 presidential election, when Donald J. Trump drove the issue to the forefront during his campaign. Trump sparred publicly with the Muslim American father of a soldier who was killed in the Iraq War, and spoke of the need to impose a "total ban" on Muslim immigration in order to prevent the entry of foreign "radical Islamic terrorists." (This, even though no such persons had been involved in any domestic threat or attack since the 9/11 events; the violent incidents that had taken place prior to

the November 2016 election were carried out by "homegrown" radicalized individuals.) Once in office, Trump indeed imposed a temporary Muslim ban through executive order, but the measure was declared unconstitutional by a federal district court. Despite opposition, a legally less fraught version of the ban was rolled out subsequently, thereby casting a shadow over the issue of Muslim–non-Muslim relations in the United States.

MUSLIMS IN CANADA

Canada, which does cover religion in its census, had an estimated Muslim population that makes up 2.8 percent of the nation's population. Islam is the country's fastest-growing religion, although Muslim Canadians often encounter similar suspicion and hostility to their American counterparts. As in the United States, they are relative newcomers; although there have been Arab Canadian immigrants since the late nineteenth century, the majority of these earlier immigrants were Christians. Muslim, Hindu, Sikh, and Buddhist immigrants together made up only 2.9 percent of immigrants prior to 1971, whereas they accounted for 33 percent of immigrants between 2001 and 2011. Unlike the US Muslim population, however, the majority of the Muslim immigrant population in Canada comes from South Asia, particularly Pakistan. Muslim Canadians tend to gather in metropolitan areas, with two-thirds of the population residing in Canada's three largest cities, Toronto, Montreal, and Vancouver. The Muslim population is predicted to grow, as the country took in six thousand Syrian refugees (displaced the Syrian Civil War) in 2015 and was anticipated to meet its promised quota of ten thousand for 2015 in the first months of 2016. The population of Muslims living in Canada is estimated to grow to 2.7 million in 2030. In the wake of the 2017 Trump Muslim ban in the United States, Canadian officials stated that they would welcome increased immigration to the country by migrants from Muslim-majority countries in the Middle East, including Syria, where over a million refugees were seeking to escape the ravages of a grim civil war.

PRACTICAL PROBLEMS

Being a practicing Muslim is not easy in the United States and Canada. Muslims do not eat pork or pork products or consume alcohol and often find it hard to obtain meat butchered according to

Islamic tradition. Required to pray five times per day, Muslims sometimes find it difficult to fit their prayers into schedules designed for non-Muslims. Schools and businesses generally do not recognize Islamic holidays, and not every community has a mosque. The practical problems that are experienced by devout Muslims are in many respects similar to those experienced by Orthodox Jews.

During Ramadan (the ninth month of the Islamic calendar, which is a lunar calendar and means that Ramadan shifts each year), Muslims and their families fast during the day. This makes it difficult for Muslims to entertain non-Muslim business clients and social guests. During their holiest month, observant Muslims suffer from heightened isolation.

In addition, with the Trump administration's ban of Muslim immigration from selected countries in the Middle East, and its general hostility toward Islam and Muslims generally, an atmosphere of increased fear and tension has been created. In a politically divided country, Muslim citizens/residents face increased scrutiny in many regions, even as they continue to be welcomed in others.

FUTURE PROJECTIONS

The Muslim population in North America is increasing, although recent US immigration measures have temporarily slowed down entry into that country from outside. Muslim Americans could outnumber Jewish Americans within the first quarter of the twenty-first century, and the Muslim Canadian population is also growing rapidly. Therefore, both Muslims and the larger society have a strong interest in Muslim participation in interfaith relations. In addition, religious scholars are beginning to document changes in Islam among North American practitioners to illustrate the impact of democracy

and multiculturalism on a nearly fourteen-hundred-year-old religious tradition. Still, a wave of anti-Muslim sentiment has been fomented by President Trump and his administration, so the future of good relations in the country remains something of a question.

——*Susan A. Stussy, updated by Michael Shally-Jensen*

BIBLIOGRAPHY AND FURTHER READING

Alsultany, Evelyn. *Arabs and Muslims in the Media: Race and Representation after 9/11*. New York: New York UP, 2012. Print.

Aslan, Reza, and Aaron J. Hahn Tapper, eds. *Muslims and Jews in America: Commonalities, Contentions, and Complexities*. New York: Palgrave, 2011. Print.

"Canada's Muslim Population Rapidly Expanding." *Immigration.ca*. Canadian Citizenship & Immigration Resource Center, 2015. Web. 11 Jan. 2016

Kazemipur, Abdolmohammad. *The Muslim Question in Canada: A Story of Segmented Integration*. Vancouver: UBC, 2014. Print.

Lipka, Michael. "Muslims and Islam: Key Findings in the U.S. and Around the World." *Pew Research Center*. Pew Research Center, 7 Dec. 2015. Web. 11 Jan. 2016

Nimer, Mohamed. *The North American Muslim Resource Guide: Muslim Community Life in the United States and Canada*. New York: Routledge, 2002. Print.

Yasmeen, Samina, and Nina Marcovi, eds. *Muslim Citizens in the West: Spaces and Agents of Inclusion and Exclusion*. Burlington: Ashgate, 2014. Print.

Zine, Jasmin, ed. *Islam in the Hinterlands: Muslim Cultural Politics in Canada*. Vancouver: UBC, 2012. Print.

N

NAÏVETÉ EXPLANATION OF RACISM

Paul Sniderman, professor of political science at Stanford University, concluded that most white Americans are not racists. Although Americans may sometimes express a simple-minded, naïve, prejudiced view of black people, this disappears when researchers delve more deeply into their true beliefs concerning equality. Sniderman's views are found in *Reaching beyond Race* (1997), which he cowrote with Edward G. Carmines. Sniderman discovered that about as many white Americans believe in equality for African Americans as are opposed to the concept. His surveys led him to conclude that modern conflicts over racial policies are driven as much by a white person's view of what the government should try to do as by any deep prejudice or racial hatred of African Americans. Sniderman found that many Americans, white and black, share the basic values of liberalism: a belief in the equality of all human beings, a belief that government can be a positive force for social change, and a deep commitment to help those in society who are not well off. His surveys show that it is a mistake to believe that before equality can be achieved white values, based on prejudice, must be changed. It is not the prejudice of whites that prevents change, he argues, because many whites no longer express or hold racist views of black inferiority. Sniderman believes that the overall impact of racial prejudice on political choices made by whites is very "modest."

Instead, Sniderman concludes, the programs advocated by civil rights groups are the biggest obstacles to equality because they seem to be opposed to another basic American value: fairness. Programs dedicated to creating equal opportunity, such as affirmative action, are seen as condoning unequal treatment under the law. Race-conscious policies aimed at overcoming prejudice blame people living now for crimes committed many years and generations ago. Many white Americans who are not prejudiced against African Americans see this as unfair. Similarly, laws outlawing hate speech bother many white Americans who see them as preventing free discussion and free speech.

Surveys of racial attitudes conducted by Sniderman show an increase, even since 1993, in the number of whites who bear goodwill toward black people. He finds two forces at work in white America: a diminishing core of citizens who hate blacks fully and completely and a growing number who wish to see improvement in the quality of lives led by African Americans.

Sniderman suggests that it is no longer necessary to change the "hearts and minds" of white Americans to bring about full equality. What should be done is to change the terms of the debate. Political leaders who support programs aimed at helping impoverished black families should broaden their views to include help for all poor families. They should base their appeals for help on the moral principle of fairness, that all people who need help should get it, regardless of race. According to Sniderman, a platform calling for social justice, rather than racial justice, would end racial divisions in the United States and bring about a true biracial coalition that would change the nation forever.

——*Leslie V. Tischauser*

BIBLIOGRAPHY AND FURTHER READING

Hunt, Matthew O., and George Wilson, eds. *Race, Racial Attitudes, and Stratification Beliefs*. Thousand Oaks: Sage, 2011. Print.

Kivisto, Peter, and Paul R. Croll. *Race and Ethnicity: The Basics*. New York: Routledge, 2012. Print.

Schuman, Howard. Rev. of *Reaching beyond Race*, by Paul M. Sniderman and Edward G. Carmines. *Public Opinion Quarterly* 62.1 (1998): 121–23. Print.

Schuman, Howard, et al. *Racial Attitudes in America: Trends and Interpretations.* Rev. ed. Cambridge: Harvard UP, 1997. Print.

Sniderman, Paul M., and Edward G. Carmines. *Reaching beyond Race.* Cambridge: Harvard UP, 1997. Print.

NATION OF ISLAM

The Nation of Islam (NOI) is a religious organization that has successfully melded orthodox Islam, black nationalism, and a set of social and economic principles to produce a highly structured way of life for its African American membership. Founded in 1930 in Detroit, Michigan, the NOI crystallized around three leaders: W. D. Fard, Elijah Muhammad, and Malcolm X.

BELIEFS

The Nation of Islam embraces the essential teachings of orthodox Islam. Both groups stress cleanliness and a strict moral code, and shun alcohol, drug abuse, and eating pork. Early NOI leaders, however, expanded orthodox Islam because of the historic oppression of African Americans. The Nation of Islam is orthodox Islam customized for the African American experience, with solidarity and racial pride being key added features. Black Muslims are required to drop their European last names, associated with enslavement, and adopt the "X" until they earn an Islamic surname. Additional elements, such as advocating a separate nation for its members and teaching about the racist deeds of the "white man," were the source of much outside criticism and prevented the NOI's acceptance into the official fold of orthodox Islam.

HISTORY

In the midst of Great Depression woes and the past specter of slavery, many African Americans were disillusioned and susceptible to philosophies and leaders who promised improvements. Consequently, a number of nationalistic and religious movements developed. In 1930, W. D. Fard formed the Nation of Islam, which espoused the political nationalism of Jamaican-born Marcus Garvey, who amassed thousands of followers in the United States from 1916 until his imprisonment in 1923 and subsequent deportation. Garvey advocated a separate African American nation, economic and political solidarity, and racial pride.

Fard, the first prophet of the Nation of Islam, is shrouded in mystery. Although believed to be from Mecca, his national origins, his real name, and the circumstances of his 1934 disappearance are not known. Fard's achievements, however, are well documented. In four years during the Great Depression, Fard established the church's basic philosophy, created a security force known as the Fruit of Islam, opened the University of Islam, built its first temple, and amassed about eight thousand followers. Many of his followers, including Elijah Muhammad, thought Fard to be an incarnation of Allah. After Fard's sudden disappearance Elijah Muhammad became the group's leader.

Elijah Muhammad was born Elijah Poole in Sandersville, Georgia. His parents had been slaves and sharecroppers. He married Clara Evans in 1919, and during the 1920's he and his family migrated to Detroit, where he met Fard and became one of his most devoted converts. He was rewarded by being chosen as Fard's successor, and he transformed Fard's sincere project into a thriving organization.

ELIJAH MUHAMMAD

After Fard's disappearance, rivalry caused some factionalism and a sharp decrease in NOI membership. Muhammad, often the victim of harassment and death threats, was imprisoned. Consequently, he moved the NOI headquarters from Detroit to Chicago, where he was able to rebuild and strengthen the organization. When Muhammad died in 1975, the Nation of Islam had temples and schools from coast to coast; owned a string of restaurants, apartments, and other businesses and real estate; operated a major printing press; and had a membership of more than one hundred thousand. Much of Muhammad's success, however, can be attributed to one of his ministers, Malcolm X.

MALCOLM X

Malcolm X was born Malcolm Little in Omaha, Nebraska. His parents, Earle and Louise Little, were organizers for Marcus Garvey's Universal Negro Improvement Association. Because of their views, the Littles were forced to move. They eventually settled in East Lansing, Michigan, where Earle apparently was murdered and Louise had a breakdown. Malcolm wandered between odd jobs and engaged in petty crime. He was imprisoned from 1946 to 1952, and he married Betty Shabazz in 1958. He was murdered in New York on February 21, 1965.

In prison, Malcolm became self-educated and converted to Islam. After his release, he met Elijah Muhammad, received his X, and trained for the NOI ministry. He headed temples in several cities before becoming the primary spokesperson for the Nation of Islam. His frank speeches and numerous public appearances catapulted the NOI into the national forefront. Membership swelled due to Malcolm's visibility, but his enemies increased also. For unauthorized remarks made about President John F. Kennedy's assassination, Malcolm was suspended from the NOI. Around that time, he changed his name to El Hajj Malik El-Shabazz. He left the NOI in March, 1964, and formed two new organizations, which were curtailed by his death.

After Elijah Muhammad's death, his son, Warith, also known as Wallace, became the NOI leader. Warith's changes forced another NOI split, spearheaded by Louis Farrakhan. The NOI expanded under Farrakhan, a controversial figure for some of his adamant and at times incendiary statements. His nondenominational Million Man March in October, 1995, immensely added to his visibility and to some extent mitigated his controversial image.

——*Linda Rochell Lane*

Bibliography and Further Reading

Carson, Clayborne. *Malcolm X: The FBI Files.* New York: Carroll & Graff, 1991. Print. Clark, John Henrick. *Malcolm X: The Man and His Times.* Trenton: African World P, 1990. Print.

Curtis, Edward E. *Black Muslim Religion in the Nation of Islam, 1960-1975.* Chapel Hill: U of North Carolina P, 2006. Print.

Gibson, Dawn-Marie. *The Nation of Islam, Louis Farrakhan, and the Men Who Follow Him.* New York: Palgrave Macmillan, 2016.

Gibson, Dawn-Marie. *Women of the Nation: Between Black Protest and Sunni Islam.* New York: New York UP, 2014. Print.

Muhammad, Elija. *The Supreme Wisdom.* Brooklyn: Temple of Islam, 1957. Print.

National Advisory Commission on Civil Disorders

The National Advisory Commission on Civil Disorders was created by executive order in 1967 with Governor Otto Kerner of Illinois as chairman and Mayor John V. Lindsay of New York City as vice chairman. The commission, also known as the Kerner Commission, had eleven members, including four members of Congress as well as labor, civil rights, and law enforcement leaders. Other public officials and private citizens participated on advisory panels studying such things as private enterprise and insurance in riot-affected areas.

Racial violence had escalated with the riots in Watts in 1965 and, by the summer of 1967, was spreading to other American cities. After extensive study, the commission recommended new and expanded employment and educational opportunity programs, national standards for welfare programs, and increased access to housing. The commission's report stated that the United States was becoming "two societies, one black, one white—separate and unequal." It was the first major study to place the blame for creating black ghettos on white society.

The commission studied the major race riots, identified patterns in the violence, developed profiles of participants, and analyzed the conditions prior to and following the disorders. Despite concern among some officials that the violence was being encouraged by radical groups, the commission determined that the principal causes were widespread discrimination and segregation and the increasing concentration of the black population in inner-city ghettos offering little opportunity. These conditions, according to the Kerner Commission's report, led to pervasive frustration, the acceptance of violence as a means of retaliation, and growing feelings of power-lessness. A spark was all that was necessary to ignite violence, and the police often provided it.

The commission recommended new federal programs to address the problems of poverty, unemployment, education, and housing and the expansion of existing urban programs, such as the Model Cities Program, to provide economic opportunity to residents of the inner city. Guidance was also offered to state and local officials for identifying potentially violent conditions, reducing the likelihood of violence, providing training to police to lessen tensions in minority communities, and organizing emergency operations in response to escalating violence.

BIBLIOGRAPHY AND FURTHER READING

Cobb, Jelani. "Crimes and Commissions." *New Yorker* 8 Dec. 2014: 27. *Academic Search Completed.* Web. 5 May. 2015.

Davis, E. E., and Margret Fine. "The Effects on the Findings of the US National Advisory Commission on Civil Disorders: An Experimental Study of Attitude Change." *Human Relations* 28.3 (1975): 209–227. *Education Source.* Web. 5 May. 2015.

Feighery, Glen. "Two Visions of Responsibility: How National Commissions Contributed to Journalism Ethics, 1963–1975." *Journalism & Communication Monographs* 11.2 (2009): 167–210. *Academic Search Complete.* Web. 5 May. 2015.

Light, R. J., and R. L. Green. "Report Analysis: National Advisory Commission on Civil Disorders." *Harvard Educational Review* 38 (1968): 756–771. *Education Source.* Web. 5 May. 2015.

Newkirk, Pamela. "The Kerner Legacy." *Media Studies Journal* 12.3 (1998): 58+. *Academic Search Complete.* Web. 5 May. 2015.

United States. Natl. Advisory Comm. on Civil Disorders. *Report on the National Advisory Commission on Civil Disorders.* Intro by Tom Wicker. New York: Bantam, 1968. Print.

NATIONAL ASSOCIATION FOR THE ADVANCEMENT OF COLORED PEOPLE

The Niagara Movement, founded in 1905, was the forerunner to the National Association for the Advancement of Colored People (NAACP). A group of African American leaders headed by W. E. B. Du Bois and William Monroe Trotter met at Niagara Falls, Canada. Their chief purpose was to develop an aggressive campaign for the full citizenship of African Americans. They were dissatisfied with the approach of Booker T. Washington, who advocated black achievement while submitting to the injustice of segregation. Race riots, in which a number of African Americans were shot, beaten, burned, or hanged by lynch mobs in the early twentieth century, served as the backdrop for the meeting. Among the primary goals of the Niagara Movement were erasing all distinctions based on race, gaining respect for all working men, and attaining black suffrage. The Niagara Movement was the first attempt to organize African Americans after the Reconstruction Era (1863-1877).

Open-minded whites, moved to action by the race riots, called for a national conference on Lincoln's birthday in 1909 and invited Niagara Movement members. The NAACP was formally founded in May of 1910, and the Niagara Movement was incorporated into it. Most charter members were white rather than people of color. They had a wide range of expertise and resources. One of its most notable African American members was W. E. B. Du Bois, the great African American leader and scholar. The new organization vowed to fight de jure (legal) segregation and to work for equal education for white and black children, complete suffrage for African Americans, and the enforcement of the Fourteenth and Fifteenth Amendments. During its first year, the NAACP established programs for blacks in economic development and job opportunities. It pushed for more police protection in the South and for anti-lynching and lawlessness initiatives in the nation. *The Crisis*, the official publication of the NAACP, served as the "cutting edge" of critical thought regarding the "race question," publicizing injustices against African Americans. Du Bois served as editor.

CIVIL RIGHTS OR ECONOMIC ADVANCEMENT?

Early tension within the NAACP centered on the question of whether the budding organization should focus primarily on civil rights or should tackle economic issues as well. Noneconomic liberalism became the guiding light for the organization, since a consensus could not be reached over the importance of economic issues. The liberal white who served as president starting in 1930, Joel E. Spingarn, believed that once the racial issue in the United States had been resolved, African Americans would be able to compete on an equal footing in the economic and educational arenas. Future leaders of the NAACP would include Walter White, Roy Wilkins, Benjamin Hooks, and Benjamin Chavis.

There was considerable debate over whether African Americans should pursue a social agenda of equality and civil rights as opposed to economic development and independence. In its most acute form, this involved public debate between W. E. B. Du Bois and Booker T. Washington. Washington was renowned as the founder and president of Tuskegee Institute (now University) in Alabama. He was often consulted by presidents and invited to the White House. Washington argued that African Americans should focus on vocational education and training. He viewed politics as secondary and social equality for blacks as less important—a philosophy that pleased white southerners and presidents. Civil rights, to his way of thinking, would gradually evolve as African Americans developed their own business enterprises. Until then, African Americans should not be too pushy, for fear of alienating whites. In short, blacks should remain subservient to whites and, particularly in the South, reconcile with the prevalent racism.

Du Bois, on the other hand, argued that Washington's approach was inadequate and asked African Americans to give up too much. Du Bois held that African Americans needed higher education. He held that a "talented tenth," meaning those with higher education, would be in the position to lead the masses and working class. Unlike Washington, Du Bois maintained that economic progress was irrelevant without political participation and political power. To his way of thinking, political power would nurture economic development, not vice versa.

The failure of noneconomic liberalism can be seen in the results of the Great Depression. While the NAACP focused on social status and targeted race and racism, African Americans were devastated by the Depression. Already on the bottom of the economic ladder, many African Americans began to migrate to northern industrial cities in search of job opportunities and an improved standard of living relative to that in the South. The timing of their migration, however, collided with the Great Depression. African Americans in the South still survived at a subsistence level, trying to make a living as sharecroppers in an agricultural economy. The arrival on the political stage of Marcus Garvey in the early 1920's stirred the black masses. Preaching black nationalism and economic independence, Garvey urged African Americans to return to the Mother Country (Africa), emphasizing self-determination and independence. Garvey developed a large following in a short period of time between 1919 and 1925. Du Bois realized that the Garvey phenomenon, combined with the effects of the Depression of the 1930's, revealed a critical flaw in the thinking and philosophy of the NAACP. In 1934 Du Bois challenged the NAACP to question its organizational philosophy of noneconomic liberalism and to stress economic development and issues. The organization, still with Spingarn and a board of directors dominated by whites, failed to heed the call. Their agenda remained centered on racial equality. It was at this point that Du Bois broke with the NAACP.

ROLE IN JUSTICE AND EQUALITY

A black and white team of lawyers of the NAACP, constituting its legal committee, won three significant legal cases during the first fifteen years of the NAACP's existence. In *Guinn v. United States* (1915) the Supreme Court invalidated the grandfather clause in Maryland and Oklahoma, ruling that it was unconstitutional under the Fifteenth Amendment. Two years later, in the case of *Buchanan v. Warley* (1917), the Court voided a Louisville ordinance requiring African Americans to live in certain sections of the city. In the case of *Moore v. Dempsey* (1923), the Court ordered a new trial in a case in which an African American had been convicted of murder in Arkansas. The poverty-stricken defendant had been tried before an all-white jury. As a result of these early victories, the NAACP soon realized that the court system could be a valuable ally in the fight against racial injustice and the struggle for equality.

In addition, the NAACP supported or provided the legal expertise in a number of cases that successfully challenged aspects of the "separate but equal" doctrine of racial segregation established in *Plessy v. Ferguson* (1896). This doctrine was premised on the notion that it was legal to have separate facilities for blacks and whites as long as those facilities were equal. Successful challenges included restrictive covenants in the case of *Corrigan v. Buckley* (1926) and the legality of the white primary in *Nixon v. Condon* (1927, 1932). In the wake of *Smith v. Allwright* (1944), which finally sounded the death knell for the white primary, the NAACP began to organize local voter leagues in the South. Repression from local governments and the White Citizens' Council, however, led to the decrease of the NAACP's influence in the South in the 1950's, to be replaced by younger organizations such as the Southern Christian Leadership Conference.

The 1954 US Supreme Court case of *Brown v. Board of Education* gained the greatest attention for the NAACP and its sister organization, the NAACP Legal Defense and Educational Fund. Thurgood Marshall argued this landmark case. In its decision, the Court ruled that the pernicious "separate but equal" doctrine of racial segregation in the public schools was unconstitutional, stating that separate schools for whites and blacks were inherently unequal. The *Brown* case served as the defining moment for the NAACP and the Civil Rights movement in the 1950's.

LEGAL DEFENSE AND EDUCATIONAL FUND

The NAACP Legal Defense and Educational Fund (LDEF) was founded in 1939. It was designed to be the chief legal arm of the NAACP. It claimed to be a nonprofit entity, yet it had an interlocking membership with the NAACP. As a result of objections by the Internal Revenue Service in 1957, the legal and educational arm formally separated from the NAACP. Thus, the NAACP Legal Defense and Educational Fund developed its own staff, board of directors, budget, and policies. Thurgood Marshall became the first director-counsel until 1961, followed by Jack Greenberg, who served in this capacity until 1984, when Julius L. Chambers took over. The LDEF had represented thousands of cases in education, employment, prisoners' rights, housing, health care, voting rights, and other areas by the end of the 1980's.

The NAACP continued to push for civil rights and racial integration in the 1950's and 1960's as the Civil Rights movement intensified its efforts to overcome racial segregation in every phase of American society. Like other civil rights organizations of the time, the NAACP engaged in a number of nonviolent activities. The NAACP, along with a number of other organizations, was partly responsible for the Civil Rights Act of 1964. The NAACP, and the Civil Rights movement as a whole, reached its zenith in this decade, as the 1964 Civil Rights Act, the 1965 Voting Rights Act and the 1968 Civil Rights Act were passed. In the 1970's and 1980's, the organization became increasingly irrelevant, since constitutional civil rights guarantees were in place and had been upheld by the courts. At the same time, the social movement in African American communities switched increasingly toward community control, black nationalism, and separatism, which were diametrically opposed to the organizational goals of the NAACP. In the 1980's, as the federal government and the Reagan administration was less supportive of civil rights and previous black gains, the NAACP Legal Defense and Educational Fund continued to play an important role in the legal arena.

By the 1990s, the NAACP had broadened its agenda to address such issues as police misconduct, the status of black foreign refugees, and questions of economic equality and community growth. These and other issues, including environmental justice, voting rights, and health equity, continued to draw energy in the 2000s and 2010s.

——*Mfanya D. Tryman*

BIBLIOGRAPHY AND FURTHER READING

Anderson, Carol. *Bourgeois Radicals: The NAACP and the Struggle for Colonial Liberation, 1941-1960*. New York: Cambridge UP, 2015. Print.

Brown-Marshall, Gloria J. *The Voting Rights Wars: The NAACP and the Ongoing Struggle for Social Justice*. Lanham: Rowman and Littlefield, 2016. Print.

Bynum, Thomas L. *NAACP Youth and the Fight for Black Freedom, 1936-1965*. Knoxville: U of Tennessee P, 2013. Print.

Verney, Kevern, and Lee Sartain, eds. *Long Is the Way and Hard: One Hundred Years of the National Association for the Advancement of Colored People*. Fayetteville: U of Arkansas P, 2009. Print.

Woodley, Jenny. *Art for Equality: The NAACP's Cultural Campaign for Civil Rights*. Lexington: UP of Kentucky, 2014. Print.

NATIONAL ASSOCIATION FOR THE ADVANCEMENT OF COLORED PEOPLE LEGAL DEFENSE AND EDUCATIONAL FUND

The National Association for the Advancement of Colored People Legal Defense and Educational Fund (LDF or LDEF) was established in 1939–1940 as a tax-exempt corporation by the National Association for the Advancement of Colored People. Its charter was handwritten in March 1940 by Thurgood Marshall, who stated the new organization's dual purpose: to provide legal aid to African Americans "suffering legal injustices by reason of race or color" and to create education opportunities for African Americans that had been denied them by reason of race or color.

The LDF was founded to carry on litigation in the spirit of the social change agenda already established by the actions of NAACP attorneys in the American courts. It provides or supports legal representation on behalf of African Americans and other people of color in defending their legal and constitutional rights against discrimination in education, employment, land use, recreation, transportation, housing, voting, health care, and other areas. It has successfully argued against grandfather clauses, restrictive housing covenants in city ordinances, white primaries, white juries, capital punishment, and segregation of public facilities.

Since the 1950s the LDF has operated independently from its parent organization, which maintains its own legal department, and at times the relationship between the LDF and NAACP has involved some conflict. The LDF both represents individuals and brings suit on behalf of civil rights groups. It has been based in New York City since its formation and also maintains a center in Washington, DC.

——*Barbara Bair*

BIBLIOGRAPHY AND FURTHER READING

Greenberg, Jack. "War Stories: Reflections on Thirty-Five Years with the NAACP Legal Defense Fund." *St. Louis U Law Jour.* 38.3 (1994): 587–603. Print.

Natl. Assn. for the Advancement of Colored People Legal Defense and Educational Fund. *NAACPLDF.org.* NAACP Legal Defense and Educational Fund, n.d. Web. 12 May. 2015.

NATIONAL ASSOCIATION OF COLORED WOMEN

Near the end of the eighteenth century, grave concerns about African Americans being treated as second-class citizens compelled a group of African American women to move beyond their local and state associations to devise plans for the formation of a national body that would systematically and professionally address the problems that they believed threatened the very survival of African Americans. Economic disparities, political disfranchisement, and social ostracism presented the greatest threats to African American aspirations for freedom and inclusion in the American system of democracy. Meeting at the Nineteenth Street Baptist Church in Washington, DC, in July 1896, the National Federation of Afro-American Women and the National League of Colored Women joined forces to form a national organization known as the National Association of Colored Women (NACW). Mary Church Terrell served as the organization's first president.

Operating through a series of departments and a strong executive cabinet, the NACW became an umbrella group for African American women's organizations at both state and local levels. The organization's official publication, *National Notes*, served as an instrument to unite the women and to educate them in the concepts and techniques of reform, advocating racial uplift, improved race relations, and protection of women. From its inception, the NACW has worked to improve the lives of African American people in the United States and to help them achieve full citizenship rights.

——*Alvin K. Benson*

NATIONAL BLACK WOMEN'S POLITICAL LEADERSHIP CAUCUS

Founded in 1971 by Democratic Michigan state representative Neilis James Saunders, the National Black Women's Leadership Political Caucus was committed to helping African American women work toward equality and increase their knowledge of the role of women in the political process. The organization had its headquarters in Washington, DC, but it also had groups in three regions and thirty-three states throughout the United States. Aside from its primary members, the caucus had an auxiliary membership that included men, senior citizens, and youth. The organization encouraged African American women and youth to participate in the country's economic and political systems. In addition, the caucus enabled women to familiarize themselves with the functions of city, state, and federal government. The group was also involved in research, conducting studies in the areas of African American families, politics, and economics. A variety of other services were provided, such as training in public speaking; federal, state, and local legislative workshops; children's services; charitable programs; awards for humanitarianism; and placement services. A split in the organization's leadership occurred in 1984 when Congresswoman Shirley Chisholm and others formed another group, the National Black Women's Political Caucus, which later became the National Congress of Black Women and overshadowed the political leadership caucus.

———K. Sue Jewell

NATIONAL COALITION OF BLACKS FOR REPARATIONS IN AMERICA (N'COBRA)

The National Coalition of Blacks for Reparations in America (N'COBRA) is a coalition of organizations across the United States that support reparations for African Americans. African Americans were supposed to receive "forty acres and a mule" from the US government upon emancipation in reparation for the time they spent in slavery, but this order issued January 1965 by Union General William T. Sherman was overturned by President Andrew Jackson fall of 1965. The newly freed African Americans lacked property, capital, education, and job experience, giving them a severely disadvantaged start. In addition, not long after slavery was made illegal, a system of segregation known as Jim Crow took effect. Segregation blocked equal access to home ownership, which is the main source of capital for most Americans, and this government-sanctioned inequality can be seen as the root cause of the wealth gap between black and white Americans in modern times, according to Melvin Oliver and Thomas Shapiro in *Black Wealth/White Wealth* (1995). N'COBRA supports and lobbies for HR 40, a congressional bill introduced every year since 1989 by John Conyers, a Democratic representative from Illinois, that demands reparations for African Americans not unlike those received by American Indians for land seized by the government and by Japanese Americans for time spent in internment camps during World War II.

———Eileen O'Brien

BIBLIOGRAPHY AND FURTHER READING

Brennan, Fernne, and John Packer, eds. *Colonialism, Slavery, Reparations and Trade : Remedying the Past?* New York: Routledge, 2012. Print.

Coates, Ta-Nehisi. "The Case for Reparations." *Atlantic* June 2014: 54–71. Print.

Feagin, Joe R. *Racist America: Roots, Current Realities, and Future Reparations.* 3rd ed. New York: Routledge, 2014. Print.

Myers, Barton. "Sherman's Field Order No. 15." *History & Archaeology.* New Georgia Encyclopedia. 3 Aug. 2016. Web. 9 Mar. 2017.

McCarthy, Thomas. "Repairing Past Injustice: Remarks on the Politics of Reparations for Slavery in the United States." *Global Dialogue* 14.2 (2012): 111–26. Print.

Wemmers, Jo-Anne M. *Reparation for Victims of Crimes against Humanity: The Healing Role of Reparation.* New York: Routledge, 2014. Print.

NATIONAL COALITION ON RACISM IN SPORTS AND MEDIA

Formed in October 1989, the National Coalition on Racism in Sports and Media (NCRSM) seeks to dispel racism, racist messages, and racist images from sports and media. They also serve as an educational entitiy, to help the public understand the effects persistent racist images in sports and media have on individuals and stereotyped groups.

The foundation and their mission is supported by the American Psychological Association and the American Sociology Association. The Golden State Warriors (a National Basketball Association team) is just one of over 1400 teams throughout high school, collegiate, and professional leagues that has changed or altered its derogatory names or mascots.

Charlene Teters appears before the Senate Committee on Indian Affairs during a May 5, 2011 hearing. By US government employee at May 5, 2011 hearing of Senate Committee on Indian Affairs.

MILESTONES IN COLLEGIATE MASCOT NAME CHANGES

Year	Event	Impact
1963	National Indian Youth Council is formed.	Initiatives are made to remove "Indian" sports stereotypes.
1968	National Congress of American Indians organizes national campaign to end use of "Indian" references in sports.	
1970	University of Oklahoma retires use of "Little Red" mascot.	UO is the first school to stop use of "Indian" sports stereotypes. This begins a trend with schools changing mascots every year for the next five years.
1978-2001	Colleges and universities continue to change/alter the names and images of their mascots.	
2003	The Native American Journalists Association issues the report asking the news media to recognize the racism prevalent in team nicknames and mascots.	
2005	National Collegiate Athletic Association (NCAA) bans use of American Indian mascots during postseason tournament.	
2013	A statewide ballot initiative to keep the University of North Dakota mascot name "Fighting Sioux" was defeated by a two-thirds 'no' vote.	The general public's understanding of the consequences on the group psyche of the stereotyped is expanded and more readily accepted.

The most notable battle over a name change is with the National Football League (NFL) team Washington Redskins. Despite urging from civic groups, local government, media, and President Barack Obama for a name change, Dan Snyder, team owner, asserts that there will never be a name change.

The NCRSM contends that this is a dogma set forth by the original owner George Preston Marshall, a known segregationist (in 1962, the team became the last of all NFL teams to integrate with African American layers).

—Sagirah Jones

NATIONAL CONGRESS OF AMERICAN INDIANS (NCAI)

The National Congress of American Indians (NCAI), organized in 1944, is a coalition of sovereign nations recognized by the United States through treaty and executive agreement. Its purpose is to protect the rights of American Indians as citizens of nations and tribes within the boundaries of the United States. It is supported through annual membership dues and special fund-raising endeavors. It is organized as a congress, with American Indian governments voting to participate and selecting delegates and alternates to represent them in the NCAI convention and executive council, where they have blocks of votes.

American Indian delegates representing fifty tribes with homes in twenty-seven western states met in Denver, Colorado, in 1944. The NCAI's initial stated goals included pursuit of American Indian rights within the United States, expansion and improvement of Indian education, preservation of Indian values, and equitable settlement of Indian claims. During the 1950s, it aided in the struggle against termination and relocation. More recently, it has been in the forefront of the struggle for Native American cultural rights legislation, which has brought on more reasonable approaches to repatriation of Indian remains and artifacts.

—Howard Meredith

BIBLIOGRAPHY AND FURTHER READING

Natl. Congress of Amer. Indians. *NCAI.org.* Natl. Congress of Amer. Indians, 2001–2015. Web. 12 May. 2015.
Wunder, John R. "The National Congress of American Indians: The Founding Years." *Amer. Historical Rev.* 106.2 (2001): 600–602. Web. 12 May. 2015.

NATIONAL COUNCIL OF AMERICAN INDIANS

In the early part of the twentieth century, a movement known as the Red Progressive movement called for American Indians to assimilate to the general American lifestyle. It was led by Indians who were well educated and had achieved success in mainstream American society. Among its leaders were Henry Roe Cloud, Thomas L. Sloan, Arthur C. Parker, physicians Charles Eastman and Carlos Montezuma, and Gertrude Simmons Bonnin, a Sioux writer and musician who became known as Zitkala-Sa or Red Bird.

The Red Progressives united at first under the Society of American Indians (SAI), but by the early 1920s that organization had split into several rancorous factions. A number of new organizations appeared, including the National Council of American Indians, founded in 1926 by Gertrude Bonnin and her husband. The organization was closely aligned with the General Federation of Women's Clubs, a mostly white and black organization of successful women. Bonnin had served as secretary of the Society of American Indians and in 1924 had coauthored *Oklahoma's Poor Rich Indians: An Orgy of Graft and Exploitation of the Five Civilized Tribes—Legalized Robbery,* a muckraking exposé of graft and greed involving Oklahoma lawyers, judges, and politicians.

The slogan of the National Council of American Indians was "Help the Indians Help Themselves in Protecting Their Rights and Properties." Its major early emphasis was promoting voting and participation in politics after the passage of the Indian Citizenship Act in 1924. It was most successful in these efforts in Oklahoma and South Dakota. The organization also advocated banning peyote use and the Native American Church; it took a moderate stance toward the Bureau of Indian Affairs.

In January, 1934, representatives of several organizations were called together in Washington, DC, to confer with President Franklin Roosevelt's commissioner of Indian affairs, John Collier, on reforms needed to ameliorate the living conditions of Indians. The Bonnins represented both the National Council of American Indians and the General Federation of Women's Clubs. They strongly supported the Indian Reorganization Act, which was adopted by Congress the same year. The council successfully pushed for a requirement for majority rule elections for tribal offices.

The National Council of American Indians, like its predecessors, was torn by factionalism; the Bonnins were its major support. With the coming of World War II, the council faded from existence, but it left behind a strong heritage of Indian political participation.

——*Fred S. Rolater*

BIBLIOGRAPHY AND FURTHER READING

Hafen, P. Jane. "'Help Indians Help Themselves': Gertrude Bonnin, the SAI, and the NCAI." *Amer. Indian Quarterly* 37.3 (2013): 198–218. Web. 12 May. 2015.

Iverson, Peter, and Frederick E. Hoxie. *Indians in American History.* Hoboken: Wiley, 2014. 2nd ed. Print.

Littleton, Steven A., and James E. Seelye. *Voices of the American Indian Experience.* Santa Barbara: Greenwood, 2013. Print.

Wilkins, David E. *American Indian Politics and the American Political System.* Lanham: Rowman, 2011. Print.

NATIONAL COUNCIL OF COLORED PEOPLE

On July 6, 1853, more than one hundred delegates from around the country assembled in Rochester, New York, for a three-day convention to form the National Council of Colored People. This organization was an outgrowth of the Negro Convention movement, which had begun during a meeting on September 20-24, 1830, in Philadelphia. Richard Allen formed the convention with the intention of improving the lives of African Americans by raising their social status through education and, possibly, emigration. The convention met many times in many cities, discussing plans for improvement, and the group thrived on the increasing solidarity among its members. It was at one of the convention meetings, in Rochester, New York, that the plan for the National Council of Colored People was adopted. The meeting in Rochester drew many prominent African American leaders, including Frederick Douglass, James McCune Smith, and James Pennington.

FORMATION OF THE COUNCIL

At the meeting in 1853, a constitution was drawn up for the new organization, and a president and several vice presidents were chosen. The group discussed the rampant racial oppression of the African American people. Members of both the convention and the newly formed National Council of Colored People believed that, in order to increase the rate of improvement of the social status of African Americans, it was necessary to create a new institution for the education of African American youth. The new institution would be an industrial school that concentrated on agriculture and the mechanical arts. On the second day of the convention, the council elected to withdraw the proposed school plan because of the exclusive nature of the school. In the final hours of the last day of the convention, the council endorsed two seminaries as places for the education of African Americans—McGrawville College and Allegheny City College.

On November 15, 1853, elections were held in several cities to elect delegates for the formation of new state councils that would act in accordance with the National Council of Colored People. The leading delegates would attend the national council meetings as well as their own state council meetings. The first meeting of the National Council of Colored People was held November 23, 1853, in New York. At least one council member each from the states of New York, Connecticut, Rhode Island, and Ohio was missing, but because of the great distance the other council members had traveled, the meeting continued. After proceeding with the meeting, one delegate from Ohio appeared and demanded that all prior proceedings be nullified. This caused great distress among the council members and created a somewhat hostile working environment, which contributed to the short life of the council. Despite the bleak beginnings of the national council, the state councils operated much more smoothly and with enthusiasm.

DISAGREEMENTS CONTINUE

In both the national and state councils, the idea of an African American school was revisited. Frederick Douglass defended the school plan unsuccessfully for two years. The country was experiencing an economic depression, which made it hard to fund the school. There also was still concern over the exclusive nature of an African American school. The idea of a separate African American school brought many emotions to the forefront. Integrationists were wary of accepting such a school plan because of the isolation of the school and its students, yet even they saw benefits in an all African American school. Emigrationists considered the proposal and were much more willing to begin work on construction. Amid much opposition, in October, 1855, the convention elected to discontinue plans for the proposed school. The other committees set up by the first national convention and their ambitious plans to assist African Americans in business pursuits and the creation of a library and museum seemed to have stopped on paper.

The second meeting of the National Council of Colored People was scheduled for May 24, 1854, in Cleveland, but it was postponed in order to accommodate more delegates. Eventually, only a few delegates were able to attend. Among the members attending, a debate developed over the recognition of Ohio at the national level, creating a deadlock. A suggestion was made to dissolve the organization, but after a close vote, the National Council of Colored People continued to operate. Ohio, however, withdrew its participation.

At the meeting of May 8, 1855, nearly all the delegates were from New York, as most others had declined to participate. The issue of an African American school again was discussed and once again defeated. Another issue was discussed for the first time—emigration to Canada. Although most delegates at the convention were willing to remain in the United States, they expressed trepidation on the matter of the United States Constitution and the issue of slavery. The issue of emigration was the last to be discussed before the close of the final meeting of the National Council of Colored People. The state councils continued to operate and pursue social equality for African Americans for a few years longer, with councils in some states surviving longer than others.

——*Jeri Kurtzleben*

BIBLIOGRAPHY AND FURTHER READING

Bell, Howard Holman. *A Survey of the Negro Convention Movement, 1830–1861.* New York: Arno, 1969. Print.

Blassingame, John W., and John R. McKivigan, eds. *Frederick Douglass Papers.* Vols. 2–4. New Haven: Yale UP, 1991.

Harmer, H. J. P. *Longman Companion to Slavery, Emancipation and Civil Rights.* London: Routledge, 2014. Print.

Ploski, Harry A., and James Williams, eds. *The Negro Almanac: A Reference Work on the African American.* Detroit: Gale, 1989. Print.

NATIONAL COUNCIL OF LA RAZA

The National Council of La Raza, a nonprofit organization formed in 1968, was founded as a nationwide civil rights and advocacy organization for the Latino community. It has since grown to include three hundred affiliates in thirty-seven states, as well as Puerto Rico and the District of Columbia, to represent and assist Hispanics in civic, economic, educational, and social matters important to the community.

The organization receives condemnation because of the use of the term "la raza." In Spanish, "la raza" literally translates to "the race." Critics of the group point to this translation as evidence that the group is a type of supremacist organization. However, defenders state that the term was originated by Mexican scholar Jose Vasconcelos as a way to encompass the expansive heritage and culture of Hispanics. Thus, the term was used to refer broadly to "the people."

In 2016, the group received backlash from political conservatives because they believed it to be a racist hate group, when then presidential candidate Donald Trump incorrectly invoked their name in association with US District Court Judge Gonzalo Curiel. Judge Curiel is actually affiliated with the California La Raza Lawyers Association. Donald Trump intimated that an association with La Raza by Judge Curiel would bias the judge in his proceedings over a class action lawsuit against Trump's defunct Trump University.

——*Sagirah Jones*

NATIONAL COUNCIL OF NEGRO WOMEN

The National Council of Negro Women (NCNW), founded in 1935, seeks to facilitate cooperation among women and act as an advocate for women's issues nationally and internationally. Founded by Mary McLeod Bethune (1875-1955), an African American educator and presidential adviser, the organization is composed of a coalition of thirty-one national organizations and individuals. It has local chapters throughout the United States, the Women's Center for Education and Career Advancement in New York City, and offices in western and southern Africa. The NCNW maintains a clearinghouse in which information that will improve the socioeconomic status of African American women and other women of color is compiled and disseminated. The organization also publishes *Black Woman's Voice*, a periodical, and *Sister's Magazine*, a quarterly. In addition, the council is responsible for an archive for black women's history and the Bethune Museum. One of the primary goals of the council is to assist women in developing leadership skills to be used on community, national, and international levels. One of its international projects is to improve social and economic conditions for rural women in Third World countries.

——*K. Sue Jewell*

NATIONAL INDIAN ASSOCIATION

After the Civil War (1861–1865), a series of groups devoted to Indian "reform" arose in the eastern United States. The events of 1876–1878, including General George Custer's defeat in the Battle of the Little Bighorn in 1876, the Nez Perce escape attempt of 1877, and the Bannock War and the tragic Cheyenne escape attempt in 1878, led to the establishment of several influential organizations. Five of these became the core of the Friends of the Indian movement. One was the US government's Board of Indian Commissioners, founded in 1869 and consisting of private citizens who served without pay. Two others, established in 1879, were the Boston Indian Citizenship Commission and the National Indian Association (also known as the Women's National Indian Association), established by a group of Protestant churchwomen in Philadelphia. The Indian Rights Association and the National Indian Defense Association followed in the early 1880s.

Between 1879 and 1886, the National Indian Association established eighty-three branches in cities across the nation. It published a monthly periodical, *The Indian's Friend*, often presented petitions to Congress and the president protesting the mistreatment of Indians, stridently pushed for reform of the Bureau of Indian Affairs, and demanded that the US government follow the provisions of its treaties with Indians with "scrupulous fidelity." Its other major issues included improving education for Indians (with regard to the number and quality of schools), extending citizenship to all Indians, and dividing Indian lands into private homesteads for each family.

The association participated yearly in the Lake Mohonk Conference of the Friends of the Indian and the annual meeting of the Board of Indian Commissioners. These agencies shared responsibility for helping persuade the government to pass the General Allotment Act (Dawes Severalty Act), enacted in 1887, which subdivided the majority of Indian

reservations into individual allotments. This act was ultimately disastrous for Indians, as the National Indian Defense Association had feared. The National Indian Association was successful in increasing the number of schools available to Indians. The association failed to influence the government's honoring of treaties.

——*Fred S. Rolater*

BIBLIOGRAPHY AND FURTHER READING

Genetin-Pilawa, C. Joseph. *Crooked Paths to Allotment: The Fight over Federal Indian Policy after the Civil War.* Chapel Hill: U of North Carolina P, 2012. Print.

Mathes, Valerie Sherer. *Divinely Guided: The California Work of the Women's National Indian Association.* Lubbock: Texas Tech UP, 2012. Print.

Mathes, Valerie Sherer. "Nineteenth Century Women and Reform: The Women's National Indian Association." *Amer. Indian Quarterly* 14.1 (1990): 1–18. Web. 12 May. 2015.

Mathes, Valerie Sherer, ed., and Project Muse. *The Women's National Indian Association: A History.* Albuquerque: U of New Mexico P, 2015. Print.

NATIONAL INDIAN YOUTH COUNCIL

Ten Native American college students gathered to form the National Indian Youth Council (NIYC) in August 1961 at Gallup, New Mexico. Two months earlier, these students had met at the National Congress of American Indians (NCAI) conference at the University of Chicago. After hearing the discussions encouraging self-determination and denouncing termination, the students decided to start their own group.

The foundation for the NIYC had been laid in 1953 when Herbert Blatchford (Navajo) initiated the first intertribal student group, the Kiva Club, at the University of New Mexico. Blatchford was also the founding director of the NIYC. At the August meeting, Mel Thom (Paiute) was elected the chairperson; Clyde Warrior (Ponca), president; and Shirley Witt (Mohawk), vice president. The NIYC's founding members came from different tribes and interests, but they had a common bond: a spirit to recover native rights and respect. Differing from the

NCAI, the NIYC focused on the voices of the youth and employed strategies that were more aggressive and activist.

During its first decade, NIYC targeted problems with Native American education and discrimination. Members editorialized their opinions through NIYC's first publication, *American Aborigine*, edited by Blatchford. In 1963, the NIYC began publishing its long-running newspaper, *ABC: Americans Before Columbus*. The following year, the NIYC went to Washington State to hold a series of fish-ins. Members defied state law by fishing in rivers that had been closed to native fishing even though treaty language had reserved for the tribes permanent fishing rights. Other activist groups banded together to assist NIYC's "Washington Project."

With national support, NIYC members stepped into the political arena. Thom encouraged a 1964 Washington, DC, audience to stand up for self-determination. At a Memphis, Tennessee, poverty conference in 1967, Warrior delivered his passionate speech, "We Are Not Free." When Warrior died the following year, the NIYC initiated the education-based Clyde Warrior Institute in American Indian Studies. A 1967 Carnegie Foundation program researched educational methodology and addressed acculturation. With this growth, the NIYC in 1970 had opened chapters on several college campuses and reservations to serve more than two thousand members.

The NIYC also undertook lawsuits against irresponsible mining companies on reservation lands and instituted native employment and training programs. Other NIYC projects range from conducting voting surveys to creating an all-native film company, Circle Film. To help preserve native sacred lands and to protect native rituals, the group appealed to the United Nations and was granted recognition as an "official and non-governmental organization."

From its headquarters in Albuquerque, and field offices in Albuquerque, Farmington, and Gallup New Mexico, the NIYC hosts international native conferences that create strong networks of indigenous views. With its broadened vision, NIYC's nationwide membership stood at about fifteen thousand in 2009.

——*Tanya M. Backinger*

BIBLIOGRAPHY AND FURTHER READING

McKenzie-Jones, Paul. *Clyde Warrior: Tradition, Community, and Red Power.* Norman: U of Oklahoma P, 2015. Print.

McKenzie-Jones, Paul. "Evolving Voices of Dissent: The Workshops on American Indian Affairs, 1956–1972." *Amer. Indian Quarterly* 2 (2014): 207. Print.

Shreve, Bradley Glenn. *Red Power Rising: The National Indian Youth Council and the Origins of Native Activism.* Norman: U of Oklahoma P, 2011. Print.

NATIONAL URBAN LEAGUE (NUL)

The National Urban League was founded in 1910 as the National League on Urban Conditions Among Negroes, an organization that helped black migrants coming from the rural South in the Great Northern Migration to find work and make transitions to living in northern cities. The league merged in 1911 with the Association for the Protection of Colored Women and the Committee for Improving the Industrial Conditions of Negroes in New York, both groups founded in 1906 to aid urban migrants, and adopted its shorter title by 1920. The emphasis of the organization has shifted over the years from serving black workers in northern cities to assisting the rural and urban poor in all regions of the country, and from an educational, service, and investigational association to one involved in political action.

A nonmembership organization, the National Urban League has a centralized structure, with a main headquarters in New York and local units in major cities; the local units have their own boards and budgets and adapt national policies to local needs. The league maintains regional bureaus in Washington, DC; Akron, Ohio; St. Louis, Missouri; and Atlanta, Georgia. The national governing board is, according to organization bylaws, interracial. As of 2013 25 percent of its members were under the age of thirty.

From 1923 until 1948 the National Urban League published the influential magazine *Opportunity*, which, along with the National Association for the Advancement of Colored People's *Crisis*, also based in New York, was a voice for black intellectuals, writers, and social reformers. From 1910 through the 1930s Depression, the league focused on services to those seeking jobs and housing, and lobbied to end discrimination in federal policies and the labor movement. The league grew in size and influence during World War II, when many thousands of blacks moved to northern industrial cities to do war-related work. The organization was conservative in its approach until the 1960s, when the severity of the problems of segregated housing, ghetto conditions, and inferior education called for more activist policies.

The league emerged as a major advocate for civil rights under the leadership of Whitney M. Young, Jr., who became its executive director in 1961. Under the influence of the Civil Rights and Black Power movements, Young and the National Urban League pursued active protest politics, including a sponsorship role in the 1963 March on Washington. Young's successors, Vernon E. Jordan, Jr., and John Jacob, established several community-based improvement programs. These include street academies to aid high school dropouts in finishing school; job training and placement services in computer skills, law enforcement, and the construction industry; voter registration drives; a Business Development Program for black businesspersons; and a National Consumer Health Education Program to supply health workers to local neighborhoods.

In 2003 the National Urban League appointed Marc H. Morial, a former mayor of New Orleans, as its president and chief executive officer. He oversaw a revitalization effort for the organization,

including its flagship annual report, the *State of Black America.*

————*Barbara Bair*

BIBLIOGRAPHY AND FURTHER READING

Moore, Jesse Thomas. *A Search for Equality: The National Urban League, 1910–1961.* University Park: Pennsylvania State UP, 1981. Print.

National Urban League. *Martin Luther King, Jr. and the Global Freedom Struggle.* Martin Luther King, Jr. Research and Education Institute, n.d. Web. 24 Apr. 2015

National Urban League. "Mission and History." National Urban League, 2015. Web. 24 Apr. 2015

Weiss, Nancy J. *The National Urban League, 1910–1940.* New York: Oxford UP, 1974.

Wormser, Richard. "Urban League." *Rise and Fall of Jim Crow.* PBS, WGBH, 2002. Web. 24 Apr. 2015.

NATIVE AMERICAN

The term "Native American" is commonly used to refer to the many peoples of North America whose cultures existed on the continent when Europeans first arrived. It does not eliminate the possibility of their foreign origin in an earlier era. The term was coined as a collective name for the native peoples of the Americas that would not carry the obvious falseness and the historically racist overtones of such terms as "American Indian" and "Indian." Yet, as is the case with virtually any collective term suggested, there are problems inherent in the term; for example, literally speaking, anyone of any ethnicity born in the Americas could be considered a "native American."

Beginning in the 1970s, the term Native American lost favor among activist groups and many others concerned with American Indian politics. Nevertheless, the term is still widely used, and some still prefer it to American Indian (although by the 1990s, the latter had become more common). Some American Indians find the offensiveness of all such collective terms to be about the same. All are generalizations that deny the unique, tribal-specific cultural heritage and political legacy of the many discrete nations and bands ("tribes") that inhabited the Americas.

————*M. W. Simpson*

NATIVE AMERICAN CHURCH

The collection of teachings that became the doctrine of the Native American Church had their beginnings in the 1880's, probably among the Kiowas and Comanches living in Oklahoma. The church emphasizes the brotherhood of all American Indians. Among the main themes of the church's ethical code are mutual aid among members, a

strong family, self-reliance, and the avoidance of alcohol.

The Native American Church was chartered as a Christian church in 1918. At that time, American Indians of every tribe were still reeling from the devastating effects of three centuries of contact with European American culture. Indians had been subjected to slaughter, enslavement, forced labor, the destruction of food supplies, the confiscation of land, forced dispersal, catastrophic depopulation, and forced religious conversion. Yet American Indians in the late nineteenth and early twentieth centuries created a monotheistic church with discernible and complex doctrines, ethics, and rituals; a strong sense of morality; a body of symbolically rich origin legends; and an individualistic approach that emphasized profound original spiritual experiences.

The ceremony that was to become central to the Native American Church was first described by anthropologist James Mooney in 1892. Its form was similar to that of present-day meetings. After 1900 the ceremony spread rapidly throughout tribal North America. Opposition to its spread came from traditional tribalists, Christian missionaries, and Indian agencies. Wherever the church entered a tribe, it rejected both significant belief aspects of that tribe and the dominant white culture. In 1918, it was chartered as a legal church. Anthropologists helped write the articles of incorporation and appeared before judicial and legislative bodies in defense of the church, shrewdly aided by insightful Indians who included Christian elements to make the chartering process more amenable to legislatures.

The ingestion of peyote is part of the ritual of the church (the church has sometimes been called the Peyote Church). Peyote produces an altered state of consciousness. To members of the Native American Church, peyote is both a teacher and a healer. The use of peyote is strictly limited to the church's ceremonies, and other use is vigorously opposed. Nevertheless, the use of peyote has at times made the church controversial among Indian leaders and organizations. Jesus is seen as a deified spirit with whom church members can communicate. Today church members find the universalism of Christian ideology acceptable, but it is rare to find Christian symbols in the ceremony. Some songs still appeal to Jesus for health and help. Christian sin, judgment, and redemption are not found in Native American Church doctrine.

By 1947 the Native American Church was widely prevalent among the Indians of the United States and had assumed the proportions of an intertribal religion. In 1960, the church was believed to have about 200,000 members, or half the population of adult Indians. By the early years of the 21st century, membership was estimated to be 250,000. Because US law classifies peyote as a psychotropic drug and prohibits non-Indian participation, non-Indian participation is minimal. The Native American Church continues to exist as an important pan-Indian movement uniting diverse cultures in common goals.

——*Glenn J. Schiffman*

BIBLIOGRAPHY AND FURTHER READING

Calabrese, Joseph D. *A Different Medicine: Post-Colonial Healing in the Native American Church.* New York: Oxford UP, 2013. Print.

Kahan, F.H. *A Culture's Catalyst: Historical Encounters with Peyote and the Native American Church in Canada.* Winnipeg: U of Manitoba P, 2016. Print.

Maroukis, Thomas Constantine. *The Peyote Road: Religious Freedom and the Native American Church.* Norman: U of Oklahoma P, 2010. Print.

Treat, James, ed. *Native and Christian: Indigenous Voices on Religious Identity in the United States and Canada.* New York: Routledge, 1996. Print.

NATIVE AMERICAN CHURCH v. NAVAJO TRIBAL COUNCIL

In 1958, the Navajo Tribal Council, in an effort to limit activities of the Native American Church on its reservation, enacted an ordinance making it illegal to bring peyote onto the Navajo Reservation. Navajo members of the Native American Church filed a suit against the tribe in federal court charging the ordinance violated their First and Fourteenth Amendment rights. They claimed their rights to freedom of religion and to protection against arbitrary and oppressive ordinances were totally disregarded.

In 1959, the United States Court of Appeals heard the case and sided with the Navajo tribe, ruling that tribal councils existed prior to the establishment of the United States and so were not bound to uphold the United States Constitution unless "they have expressly been required to surrender [their sovereign powers] by the superior sovereign, the United States." The decision upheld tribal sovereignty and the right of tribes to manage their own internal affairs without interference. However, the decision also caused many in Congress to perceive a need to lessen tribal authority and extend certain basic constitutional protections to individuals living under tribal governments. *Native American Church v. Navajo Tribal Council* influenced passage of the American Indian Civil Rights Act (1968) by Congress, which, in part, requires tribes to guarantee an individual's freedom of religion when living under tribal governance.

—*Carole A. Barrett*

NATIVE AMERICAN GAMING AND GAMBLING

During the late twentieth century, commercial gambling became a major source of income on reservations across the United States. While many Native American cultures practiced forms of gambling (such as the Iroquois peachstone game), there was no prior large-scale experience with gambling as a commercial enterprise. The arrival of gaming has brought dividends to some American Indians, but it has brought controversy culminating in firefights and death to others.

DEVELOPMENT OF RESERVATION GAMBLING

The history of reservation gambling begins in 1979, when the Seminoles became the first Indian tribe to enter the bingo industry. By early 1985, seventy-five to eighty of the federally recognized Indian tribes in the United States were conducting some sort of organized game of chance. By the fall of 1988, the Congressional Research Service estimated that more than one hundred Indian tribes participated in some form of gambling, which grossed about $255 million a year. In October of 1988, Congress passed the Indian Gaming Regulatory Act, which officially allowed legalized gambling on reservations. The act also established the National Indian Gaming Commission to oversee gaming activities. By 1991, 150 native reservations recognized by non-Indian governmental bodies had some form of gambling. According to the US Department of the Interior, gross revenue from such operations passed $1 billion that year.

Individual prizes in some reservation bingo games were reported to be as high as $100,000, while bingo stakes in surrounding areas under state jurisdiction were sometimes limited to $100. Marion Blank Horn, principal deputy solicitor of the Department of the Interior, described the fertile ground gambling enterprises had found in Indian country:

The reasons for growth in gambling on Indian land are readily apparent. The Indian tribal governments see an opportunity for income that can make a substantial improvement in the tribe's [economic] conditions. The lack of any state regulation results in a competitive advantage over gambling regulated by the states. These advantages include no state-imposed limits on the size of pots or prizes, no restrictions by the states on days or hours of operations, no costs for licenses or compliance with state requirements, and no state taxes on gambling operations.

By the early 1990's, gambling had provided a small galaxy of material benefits for some formerly impoverished native peoples. A half-hour's drive from Minnesota's Twin Cities, blackjack players crowded forty-one tables, while 450 other players stared into video slot machines inside the tipi-shaped Little Six Casino, operated by the 103 members of the Shakopee Mdewakanton Sioux. By 1991, each member of the tribe was getting monthly dividend checks averaging $2,000 as shareholders in the casino. In addition to monthly dividends, members became eligible for homes (if they lacked them), were guaranteed jobs (if they were unemployed), and were offered full college scholarships. The tribe had taken out health insurance policies for everyone on the reservation and established day care for children of working parents. The largest casino in North America, the Foxwoods Resort Casino, opened in 1992 in Ledyard, Connecticut. By 2008 Foxwoods, run by the Mashantucket Pequot Tribe, was earning more than $9 billion per year.

DEATH AT AKWESASNE

While gambling has brought benefits to some Native American communities, it brought violence to the Akwesasne Mohawks of St. Regis in upstate New York. As many as seven casinos had opened illegally along the reservation's main highway; the area became a crossroads for the illicit smuggling of drugs, including cocaine, and tax-free liquor and cigarettes.

Tension escalated after early protests against gambling in the late 1980's (including the vandalizing of one casino and the burning of another) were met by brutal attempts by gambling supporters to suppress this resistance. Residents blockaded the reservation to keep the casinos' customers out, prompting the violent destruction of the blockades by gambling supporters in late April, 1990. By that time, brutal beatings of antigambling activists, drive-by shootings,

and night-long firefights had culminated in two Mohawk deaths during the early morning of May 1, 1990 and Determined Residents United for Mohawk Sovereignty were beginning to talk of blocking the route. Intervention of several police agencies from the United States and Canada followed the two deaths; outside police presence continued for years afterward.

——*Bruce E. Johansen*

BIBLIOGRAPHY AND FURTHER READING

Lane, Ambrose I., Sr. *Return of the Buffalo: The Story Behind American's Indian Gaming Explosion.* Westport: Bergin, 1995. Print.

Walke, Roger. *Gambling on Indian Reservations.* Washington, DC: Library of Congress, 1989. Print.

NATIVE AMERICAN MASCOT CONTROVERSY

Syracuse University was one of the first to use Native Americans as a symbol of their sports team with an Indian mascot who was said to represent "noble savagery." Subsequently, the tradition of using Native Americans as mascots for sports teams would spread throughout the sporting world. High schools, universities, and professional sporting organizations have taken on aspects of the Native American culture through mascots, slogans, logos, dances, and chants. Team names such as the Redskins, Warriors, and Chiefs are commonly used, and symbols like the tomahawk and traditional headdress are popularly used as team images and logos. While some people believe this tradition honors Native American culture by celebrating the bravery and fighting talents of American Indians, others feel this practice perpetuates the kind of stereotypes that work to keep an already marginalized population down.

Native American images as mascots continue being used despite pleas from activists and organizations to stop the practice. These groups believe the use of these mascots propagates negative stereotypes about American Indians, which contributes to racism and oppression of the Native American population. The concern goes beyond whether or not people are offended by the mascots and extends to profound

impacts on the Native American community. The propagation of negative stereotypes significantly impacts the self-esteem of younger American Indians, with this group seeing disproportionately high school drop-out and suicide rates. Furthermore, these stereotypes contribute to the institutionalized racism contributing to things like high poverty rates and less access to quality educational opportunities within the Native American community. The false imagery used by sporting teams encourages a hostile environment in which American Indians feel marginalized.

While the fight to end the use of Native American-based team mascots has been ongoing since the 1960s, it has only been in recent times that significant action has been taken to cease this practice. In 2001 the US Commission on Civil Rights issued a declaration calling for non-Native schools to end the use of Native American images and team names. The National Collegiate Athletic Association (NCAA) decided in 2005 it would no longer allow the display of Native American mascots or imagery during any NCAA-sponsored events. Those who violated the provision would be ineligible to host NCAA championships in the future. In 2014 the US Trademark and Patent Office Trademark Trial Appeal Board issued a ruling in the case of Blackhorse v. Pro Football, Inc.

voiding all trademarks regarding the Washington, D.C. National Football League Franchise, the Washington Redskins. While these decisions have been met with criticism from sports fans, college alumni, and team owners, supporters of these actions believed this is a good start to addressing this problematic issue. While there is certainly more work to be done, as there has not been anything said or done to completely end the practice of using Native American stereotypes as team symbols, progress has been made.

——*Amber R. Dickinson*

BIBLIOGRAPHY AND FURTHER READING

Deloria Jr, Vine, and Vine Deloria. "Foreword," in *Team Spirits: The Native American Mascots Controversy.*
Edited by Richard C. King and Charles Fruehling Springwood. Lincoln: U of Nebraska P, 2001. Print.

King, Richard C., ed. *The Native American Mascot Controversy: A Handbook.* Lanham: Rowman and Littlefield, 2010. Print.

Spindel, Carol. *Dancing at Halftime: Sports and the Controversy over American Indian Mascots.* New York: New York UP, 2002. Print.

Staurowsky, E. J. ""You know, we are all Indian": Exploring White Power and Privilege in Reactions to the NCAA Native American Mascot Policy." *Journal of Sport & Social Issues*, vol. 31, no. 1, 1 Feb. 2007, pp. 61–76. Web, 17 Feb. 2017.

NATIVE AMERICAN RIGHTS FUND

The Native American Rights Fund (NARF) is a nonprofit, public-interest legal organization that was founded in 1970. It was established to represent tribal clients in litigation in state and federal courts and to strengthen tribal governments. Operations are supported by federal funds as well as by private and corporate contributions. Its attorneys are mostly Native Americans; the group's headquarters is in Boulder, Colorado, with satellite offices in Washington, DC, and Anchorage, Alaska. One of the organization's primary activities is to handle cases involving "federally recognized tribes" that cannot afford the full financial burden of litigation in US courts. The organization is led by a board of directors composed of thirteen volunteer Native Americans from various tribes, while the staff of sixteen attorneys handles more than fifty cases at any given time. NARF also acts as a consultant in the drafting of federal Indian policy.

NARF's objectives include preservation of tribal existence and independence, protection of tribal resources, promotion of human rights such as education and the equitable treatment of Indian prisoners, and development of Indian law to improve tribal legal resources. The Indian Law Support Center and the Carnegie-sponsored National Indian Law Library are components of NARF, working in conjunction with its Legal Services Corporation. The law library houses a collection of more than six hundred tribal codes.

The Native American Rights Fund has taken on a number of well-known cases involving tribal land and water interests. The group gained national notice and respect for its handling of the 1982 land rights case brought by the Penobscot and Passamaquoddy against the state of Maine. The tribes were awarded $27,000 plus the money to purchase 300,000 acres of land. (An important footnote is that, although the case was regarded as a success story, the money did not go very far for some recipients. In addition, many such cases, even when legally successful, become bogged down by governmental bureaucracy.) NARF has been involved in litigation to strengthen aspects of the 1978 American Indian Religious Freedom Act dealing with the repatriation of ancestral bones and archaeological artifacts. NARF also assists non-federally recognized tribes in attempts to gain official tribal recognition, which may involve the restoration of at least some tribal homelands. It has litigated successfully for the Menominee of Wisconsin and the Siletz of Oregon.

NARF has not been without its critics. Some have argued that, because the organization is not self-sufficient and must rely on federal funding, it cannot truly be an effective advocacy group. From this perspective it may appear to be an extension of the federal system. Another criticism leveled against the group is that it has never attempted to challenge the European American legal paradigm by insisting on complete internal sovereignty for a client; rather, its negotiations seek negotiation, consensus, and settlement.

——*M. A. Jaimes*

BIBLIOGRAPHY AND FURTHER READING

"About Us." *Native American Rights Fund.* NARF, n.d. Web. 13 May. 2015.

"Native American Rights." *Indians.org.* Indians.org, 2015. Web. 13 May. 2015.

Native American Rights Fund." *Encyclopedia of the Great Plains.* U of Nebraska-Lincoln, 2011. Web. 13 May. 2015.

Native American Rights Fund. *Native American Rights Fund: 25 Years of Justice.* Boulder: NARF, 1995. Print.

NATIVE AMERICAN STUDIES

Since the late 1960s, American Indian studies (or Native American studies) programs have served as the most important scholarly approach to knowing and understanding American Indian culture. Traditional teachings of tribal and village elders remain the solid foundation of American Indian and Native American studies. These culture bearers provide the understanding essential to the legitimate study of the native peoples of the Americas.

ESTABLISHMENT OF PROGRAMS

Dependence upon European American (notably Anglo-American) source materials has made for distortion in scholarly studies of American Indians. As professor Henrietta Whiteman has stated, "Cheyenne history, and by extension Indian history, in all probability will never be incorporated into American history, because it is holistic, human, personal, and sacred. Though it is equally as valid as Anglo-American history it is destined to remain complementary to white secular American history." This specific difficulty led in large part to the creation of American Indian studies programs in existing institutions of higher learning. Despite limited funds, Native American programs began to emerge as interdisciplinary curricula. Most American Indian studies programs focus on long-term goals involved with cultural preservation, unlike Western academic disciplines such as history and ethnology, which attempt to take a more objective, social-scientific approach. American Indian studies use teaching, research, and service to cross cultural boundaries and create an atmosphere for understanding. In many instances, the American Indian studies degree programs are the only non-Western courses of study on a given campus.

American Indian or Native American studies programs vary considerably in method and subject matter. These also represent different degrees of institutional support, budget size, and quality of program leadership. In the late 1960s and early 1970s, various programs began to emerge at the University of California, Berkeley, and the University of California, Los Angeles. Other programs developed in the California State University system on campuses at Long Beach, Fullerton, and Northridge. At that time, California had the largest Native American population in the United States. Oklahoma had the second-largest native population. Two degree programs were created in Oklahoma in the early 1970s, one at Northeastern State University at Tahlequah, the capital of the Cherokee Nation, and one at the University of Science and Arts of Oklahoma in Chickasha. The Native American studies degree program at the University of Oklahoma was accepted by the higher regents in 1993. Other American Indian studies degree programs were created at the University of Minnesota, the University of Washington, Evergreen State College, Washington State University, the University of Arizona, the University of Illinois (Chicago), Dartmouth College, the University of North Dakota, Montana State University, the University of New Mexico, and Cornell University, among others. By the mid-1980s, eighteen programs offered a major leading to a bachelor's degree. Of these, six programs also offered a master's degree.

TRIBALLY CONTROLLED COLLEGES

Tribally controlled colleges added new energy to American Indian studies. In 1968, the Navajo Nation created the first tribally controlled institution of higher learning. Navajo Community College was a success and led to the passage of the Tribally Controlled Community College Act of 1978. This act provides for some federal support for tribally controlled colleges initiated by tribes in the western United States. Initially, this helped support thirteen tribally controlled colleges. Since the act's passage, at least nine additional colleges have been initiated. Colleges that followed the creation of Navajo Community College include Sinte Gleska University, Standing Rock College, Blackfeet Community College, Dull Knife Memorial College, Salish Kootenai College, Little Bighorn College, and Stone Child College, among others. Lummi College of Aquaculture in Washington has expanded to become the Northwest Indian College. Sinte Gleska University on the Rosebud Sioux Reservation in South Dakota has grown to become the first fully accredited tribally controlled four-year institution of higher learning.

In all these examples, the tribally based community colleges have not only aided the education of individual Indian young people but also improved the development of the tribal communities that they serve. Of primary importance is that Indian people are now controlling institutions that directly affect them. The tribally controlled colleges are far outstripping the state-supported and private colleges and universities in retention of American Indian students. The tribally controlled colleges have become important centers of research. These colleges have proved to be well suited to the needs of American Indian students and communities. The tribally controlled colleges offer hope to tribes that have, all too often, survived in a climate of despair.

ISSUES AND CONCERNS

Today (2016), as often in the past, American Indian studies is marked by a healthy debate regarding methods and practices concerning spirit, philosophy, structures, roles, contexts, and intent. The quest for meaning and value appears in many guises. The interest in the emotional component of community life, the expansion of traditional approaches to knowledge and wisdom, the acceptance of grammar and logic stemming from native languages, and the hope of differentiating Western-based interpretation from traditional knowledge all reflect the aim of uncovering purpose, meaning, and perspectives on truth in presentation. There is occasional anxiety that the individual is being submerged in community. There is additional attention being given to the way people feel as well as the way they behave. There is also a movement in American Indian studies toward narrative storytelling in the literature. American Indian studies places human beings and the comprehensible societies in which they live into the story. These are real stories, however, not dry and forbidding pieces of analysis. Increasingly, the natural environment becomes part of the story.

The quest for meaning only multiplies the pluralism of current research and teaching. The very process of recovering deeper motivations and attitudes, dragging the latent out of the manifest, requires such personal feats of imagination and use of language that questions about plausibility and proof are bound to arise. Senior faculty at one state-supported university in Oklahoma challenged the continuation of a bachelor's degree in American Indian studies, stating, "While the program is inessential to a liberal arts education, it is not inconsistent with one." This type of Euro-American bias makes it difficult to pursue knowledge and wisdom in an atmosphere with freedom of thought and feeling.

The obverse of the quest for meaning is an uneasiness with the material conditions of life that until recently seemed so compelling. A clear, single idea emerges from the doubts that have been expressed about the power of economic development. As American Indian studies turns to more emotional content, the demand is for a more elusive process of comprehension. Analytical and technical research is increasingly limited, as mental patterns, attitudes, and symbolic acts become more prominent.

Questions of the use of quantification arise because of the almost exclusive use of United States and Western social science data. What is at stake is a profound epistemological question, not just a disagreement over collection of data. American Indian studies many times are very personal and intuitive. The insights are justified within a specific tribal context with powerful rhetorical and imaginative methods. They appeal to an interest in behavior that is very different from Anglo-American intellectual concerns, but never claim to be definitive.

The establishment of an agenda for American Indian studies, of a set of methods or purposes indigenous to the Americas, or of a special task for its practitioners, hardly seems plausible. American Indian studies is united in its respect for tribal traditions. There is observation of certain fundamental rules for using evidence so as to be intelligible across cultural boundaries. None of these skills is difficult to learn; neither is the telling of a sustained story, which is a special mark of scholars and teachers in American Indian studies. The one form of synthesis used most often by those in American Indian studies blends the disparate methods of current research in examinations of tribally specific localities. This synthesis convincingly links physical conditions, economic and demographic developments, social arrangements, intellectual and cultural assumptions, and political behavior, with mythic patterns and images.

ARCHIVES AND TRIBAL RECORDS

The most important repository of American Indian knowledge remains with the tribal elders. There is no substitute for this significant information. This knowledge and wisdom can be gained only with real commitment over a significant period of time. Tribal elders have become wary of "instant experts," whether Indian or non-Indian. All scholarship must access this wisdom and knowledge to reflect tribal tradition and history.

Once removed from this vital core of information are the tribal archives and records. These are held in a variety of ways. For example, the Wichita and Affiliated Tribes maintain their tribal archives as a part of the Wichita Memory Exhibit Museum at the tribal complex on reserve land north of Anadarko, Oklahoma. A second example is that of the Navajo Nation, which collects and preserves its records as a part of the Navajo Tribal Council Reference Library in Window Rock. A third example is that of the Cherokee Nation, which maintains a portion of its records in the Archives of the Cherokee National Historical Society in Tahlequah, while the records of the Cherokee Nation from 1839 through 1906 are held in the Indian Archives of the Oklahoma Historical Society, which functions as a trustee for the United States government. These records were placed in trust in 1906, just before Oklahoma statehood, before the National Archives of the United States was created. Each tribe maintains its records in

an individual way. Contact with the tribes is the best means to understand their respective record-keeping systems.

US NATIONAL ARCHIVES

Large numbers of records about American Indian peoples are held by the National Archives of the United States. These are housed in the Washington National Records Center, Suitland, Maryland, and in eleven regional Federal Archives and Records Centers throughout the United States. Additional records holdings concerning American Indian peoples are contained at the presidential libraries administered by the National Archives and Records Service. The papers of the presidents and many of those of other high officials, including the files of individual members of Congress, are regarded as their personal property. These personal papers are collected in large part by state-supported university manuscripts collections.

The basic organizational unit in the National Archives collections is the record group. This refers to the records of a single agency, such as the Bureau of Indian Affairs and its predecessors. The National Archives endeavors to keep records in the order in which they were maintained by the respective agency.

Additional materials concerning Indian-white relations are contained in the United States Supreme Court decisions, the research that was used in the Indian Land Claims Act of 1946, and in the manuscript collections of major universities throughout the United States.

American Indian studies has long been limited in perspective because of the heavy dependence upon documents generated by Euro-American policymakers, businesspersons, and military personnel. Scholarly works accepted many of the assumptions of those who produced these sources. American Indian people were perceived either negatively as an enemy or romantically as part of the environment. In the last decade, scholarship in American Indian studies has changed significantly from this approach. More balanced efforts are being made by American Indian scholars utilizing native languages and tribal sources. All American culture and society is being shown in a new light as a result of the creative images and ideas of American Indian studies.

——*Howard Meredith*

BIBLIOGRAPHY AND FURTHER READING

Aguilera-Black Bear, Dorothy, and John W. Tippeconnic III, eds. *Voices of Resistance and Renewal: Indigenous Leadership in Education.* Norman: U of Oklahoma P, 2015. Print.

Boyer, Paul. *Capturing Education: Envisioning the Building of the First Tribal Colleges.* Pablo: Salish Kootenai College P, 2015. Print.

Kidwell, Clara Sue, and Alan Velie. *Native American Studies.* Lincoln: U of Nebraska P, 2005. Print.

Morrison, Dane, ed. *American Indian Studies: An Interdisciplinary Approach to Contemporary Issues.* New York: Lang, 1997. Print.

Simpson, Audra, and Andrea Smith. *Theorizing Native Studies.* Durham: Duke UP, 2014. Print.

NATIVISM

As a nation of immigrants, the United States has always exhibited a certain ambivalence toward immigrants. On one hand, immigrants have been welcomed as a necessary addition to the labor force and as a source of economic growth. On the other hand, they have been feared and resented because of their alien ways and their competition for jobs and political power. Nativists, the most outspoken critics of immigration, feared that the American way of life, and even the republic itself, was in danger from the constant stream of newcomers. They developed an ideology of nativism that comprised three identifiable strains: anti-Catholic nativism; racial nativism; and antiradical nativism. These three strains often overlapped in the various nativist organizations that emerged in the nineteenth and twentieth centuries.

ANTI-CATHOLIC NATIVISM

Anti-Catholic nativism had its roots in the religious views of the earliest English settlers in the American colonies. As products of the Protestant Reformation in Europe, the early colonists viewed the pope as a foreign monarch who exercised dangerous influence through the Roman Catholic Church. The large influx of Irish Catholic immigrants in the early nineteenth century fueled an upsurge of anti-Catholic propaganda, which alleged that Irish Catholics were agents of the pope intent on undermining republican institutions. In the 1830's, inventor Samuel F. B. Morse's tract, *Foreign Conspiracy Against the Liberties of the United States* (1834), which called for the formation of the Anti-Popery Union to resist the papal plot, became required reading in many Protestant Sunday schools. In 1834, an anti-Catholic mob burned the Ursuline Convent in Charlestown, Massachusetts. Ten years later, riots erupted in Philadelphia when

NOT WANTED

Heroes of the Fiery Cross 1928, published by the Pillar of Fire Church. .

Irish Catholics opposed the use of the Protestant King James version of the Bible in public schools.

The American Protective Association (APA), organized in 1887, was the most visible manifestation of anti-Catholic nativism in the late nineteenth century. Its members swore never to vote for Catholic candidates, employ Catholic workers over Protestants, or join with Catholic strikers. The APA drew strong support from workers in the midwestern and Rocky Mountain states who feared competition from cheap Irish labor. By the late 1890's, however, as Irish and German Catholics became an important part of the electorate, the more extreme anti-Catholic sentiment dissipated. The APA itself disappeared in the 1890's.

RACIAL NATIVISM
In the later nineteenth century, a racial strain of nativism, cultivated by the self-professed guardians of Anglo-Saxon culture and apparently supported by scientific research, began to be directed against immigrant groups. Ever since colonial times, white settlers had viewed themselves as culturally and physically different from, and superior to, Native Americans and African Americans. Some intellectuals adapted the biological research of Charles Darwin to argue that certain races would inevitably triumph over others because of their inherent superiority. English and American intellectuals confidently trumpeted the superiority of the Anglo-Saxon "race" and its institutions, and researchers set out to "prove" their cultural assumptions by measuring the cranial volumes of skulls from members of various ethnic groups and devising crude intelligence tests. As a new wave of immigrants from Asia and southern and eastern Europe began to arrive, these newcomers were quickly labeled racially inferior.

Racial nativism reached its zenith in the early twentieth century. Influenced by the European eugenics movement, with its emphasis on breeding the right racial groups, American nativists expressed alarm over the impact of the new immigrants. Madison Grant's widely read *The Passing of the Great Race* (1916) summarized many of the racial nativist arguments. He argued that the superior Nordic "race" was being destroyed by the influx of southern and eastern Europeans, and warned that race mixing would result in an inferior hybrid race and the destruction of Anglo-Saxon civilization. Jewish and Italian immigrants, in particular, were often singled out for criticism in nativist publications because of their alleged racial inferiority.

ANTIRADICAL NATIVISM
Immigrants also came under attack for political reasons in the late nineteenth century. Nativist writers worried that most immigrants came from nondemocratic societies, harbored socialist or anarchist sympathies, and would foment revolution in the United States. The participation of some immigrants in the labor agitation of the period seemed to confirm these fears of alien radicalism. Antiradical nativism intensified following the 1917 Bolshevik Revolution in Russia and the onset of an economic crisis in the United States. Although most immigrants were not socialists, immigrants nevertheless constituted a majority of the membership of the American Socialist Party. During the Red Scare of 1919-1920, when many Americans feared that a communist revolution was imminent, immigrants and radicalism became synonymous in the public mind.

IMPACT ON PUBLIC POLICY
Nativism had its most significant impact on public policy in the area of immigration restrictions designed to discriminate against Asians and southern and eastern Europeans. In 1882, the Chinese Exclusion Act cut off further immigration by Chinese laborers. During World War I, Congress overrode a presidential veto to enact literacy tests for all immigrants, which discriminated against southern and eastern Europeans who had less access to basic education. In the 1920's, the United States adopted a system of quotas based on national origins for European immigration, imposing a maximum annual limit of 150,000 and allocating most of the slots to northern and western European countries. The national origins quota system formed the basis of immigration law until it was abolished in 1965.

A resurgence of nativism accompanied the election of Donald Trump as president in 2016. Trump had run on a platform of "America First!" and on promises to expel undocumented immigrants and ban or severely restrict entry by Muslims from the Middle East. These were all extreme positions by American historical standards, and yet they won a sufficient following among the population of white, non–college educated voters (the bulk of Trump's supporters) to deliver the presidency to Trump and raise the banner of nativism throughout the land. Trump's election, one of the most controversial in US history, also brought with it waves of protest by those opposing his strident views.

——*Richard V. Damms, updated*
by Michael Shally-Jensen

BIBLIOGRAPHY AND FURTHER READING

Behad, Ali. *A Forgetful Nation: On Immigration and Cultural Identity in the United States.* Durham: Duke UP, 2005. Print.

Bennett, David H. *The Party of Fear: From Nativist Movements to the New Right in American History.* Chapel Hill: U of North Carolina P, 1988. Print.

Higham, John. *Strangers in the Land: Patterns of American Nativism, 1860-1925.* 1955. New Brunswick: Rutgers UP, 2002. Print.

Knoble, Dale T. *America for the Americans: The Nativist Movement in the United States.* New York: Twayne, 1996. Print.

Perea, Juan F., ed. *Immigrants Out! The New Nativism and the Anti-Immigrant Impulse in the United States.* New York: New York UP, 1996.

Schrag, Peter. *Not Fit for Our Society: Nativism and Immigration.* Berkeley: U of California P, 2010. Print.

NATURALIZATION ACT OF 1790

Naturalization is the legal process by which a state or country confers its nationality or its citizenship to a person after birth. In most cases, the primary beneficiaries of naturalization are immigrants.

After the American colonies gained their independence from Britain in 1787, each state adopted different rules for conferring US citizenship upon its residents. President George Washington suggested that a uniform naturalization act at the federal level was needed.

Article I, section 8 of the US Constitution empowers Congress to pass uniform laws for naturalization. Congress exercised this power, for the first time, when it passed "An act to establish an uniform Rule of Naturalization" on March 26, 1790. This act granted "all free white persons" with two years of residence the right of citizenship. In addition, the act stated that "the children of citizens of the US that may be born beyond sea, or out of limits of the US, shall be considered as natural born citizens."

In effect, the act created two separate classes of people: free and white citizens, able to hold political office and entitled to the rights and privileges of citizenship, and nonwhite persons, ineligible for membership in the US community. The act further reinforced the part of the Constitution that limits membership in Congress to citizens who meet stipulated residence requirements and the presidency to natural-born citizens. The Naturalization Act was repealed five years later.

——*Stephen Schwartz*

NAVAJO REHABILITATION ACT

The Navajo-Hopi Long Range Rehabilitation Act of 1950 (Public Law 81-474) was passed by Congress to construct basic facilities on the Navajo and Hopi reservations. Passed in response to more than twenty years of deteriorating economic conditions on the Navajo Reservation, the act authorized funding for school construction, roads, and other projects.

In the 1930s the federal government had initiated a range-management program on the Navajo and Hopi reservations. Central to the program was reducing the amount of livestock on the range. This devastated the Navajo sheep-based pastoral economy. The full effects of stock reduction were partially obscured during World War II, when thousands of Navajos joined the service or worked in war-related industries. When these people returned home, however, livestock regulations and insufficient resources prevented a renewal of the pastoral economy.

Unusually harsh winters added to the distress and drew national attention to the impoverished conditions among the more than sixty thousand Navajos residing in Navajo country.

Reservation schools could accommodate only about 25 percent of the student-age population. All-weather roads were practically nonexistent on the reservations. Inadequate roads contributed to health, education, and economic problems. Infant mortality was high and school enrollment low. After passing minor emergency relief measures, Congress considered a more comprehensive approach.

A 1949 bill to fund improvements on the Navajo and Hopi reservations, reflecting a resurgent congressional interest in limiting tribal sovereignty, also included a provision which extended the jurisdiction of state law over the two reservations. Citing this provision, President Harry S. Truman vetoed the bill.

In 1950, the president signed the Navajo Rehabilitation Act, which emerged from Congress without the offending jurisdictional provision. This version also provided expanded opportunities for Hopi participation in projects. The act appropriated $88,570,000. The largest portion, $25 million, was for school construction, followed by $20 million for roads and $19 million for rangelands and irrigation projects. Lesser amounts were appropriated for health and water facilities, industrial development, and other projects. More than $9 million was allocated for relocating and resettling individuals away from the two reservations. There were also provisions for loans and leases. Finally, one provision (ignored for more than thirty years) authorized the Navajo tribe to adopt a tribal constitution.

In 1958, Public Law 85-740 provided an additional $20 million to complete road construction. By 1962, more than 80 percent of the total appropriation had been expended, including nearly all the money targeted for roads and schools.

The major benefit of the act was the substantial improvement in roads and schools on the reservation. All-weather roads have provided greater access to job locations and markets. School attendance increased dramatically through the 1950s and 1960s, as did the overall educational attainment of the population.

——*Eric Henderson*

BIBLIOGRAPHY AND FURTHER READING

Bailey, Garrick Alan, and Roberta Glenn Bailey. *A History of the Navajos: The Reservation Years.* Santa Fe: School of American Research, 1999. Print.

DeJong, David H. *Promises of the Past: A History of Indian Education in the United States.* Golden: North American, 1993. Print.

Iverson, Peter, and Monty Roessel. *Diné: A History of the Navajos.* Albuquerque: U of New Mexico P, 2003. Print.

Wilkins, David E. *The Navajo Political Experience.* 4th ed. Lanham: Rowman, 2013. Print.

NAVAJO WAR

Disputed grazing lands near Fort Defiance were a major factor leading to the 1863–1866 Navajo War. The site was favored for rendezvous by Navajo medicine men who collected herbs there. For generations, these lands were also used as pasture for Navajo livestock. Shortly after the establishment of Fort Defiance on September 18, 1851, soldiers who wanted to pasture their horses on these lands shot the Navajo-owned horses. Revenge was swift: Navajos raided army herds to replace their losses.

Through the decade, the raids continued and the army retaliated until, in 1859, army troops attacked and destroyed the home, crops, and livestock of the Navajo clan leader, Manuelito. In 1860, Manuelito—aided by leaders of other clans—assaulted Fort Defiance and nearly captured it, but was driven back. The army pursued the attackers into the Chuska mountains but was demoralized by the hit-and-run tactics of the Navajos. In January of 1861, the Navajos met with army representatives and agreed to work for peace. The uneasy truce was broken when, in September of 1861, a riot broke out over a horse race. Artillery was used to quell the disturbance, killing ten Navajos.

Raids for plunder and revenge increased, and the army responded. On September 6, 1863, Colonel Christopher "Kit" Carson was chosen to lead a campaign of "pacification." In the following months,

Carson's scorched-earth offensive burned Navajo corn fields, orchards, and hogans; livestock was confiscated and destroyed. Tribes unfriendly to the Navajos were encouraged to attack and harass them. Navajo tribe members surrendered or were rounded up and relocated to Bosque Redondo (Round Forest) in the barren plains of eastern New Mexico. Some clan leaders and their followers held out as long as possible, but by the end of 1864 about eight thousand half-starving Navajos surrendered and were marched to Bosque Redondo. Some two hundred people died on the grueling three-hundred-mile march known as the Long Walk. Manuelito and twenty-six followers surrendered in September of 1866. When another clan leader, Barboncito, surrendered in November of 1866 with twenty-one followers, the Navajo War of 1863–1866 was over.

——*Moises Roizen*

BIBLIOGRAPHY AND FURTHER READING

Denetdale, Jennifer. *The Long Walk: The Forced Navajo Exile.* New York: Chelsea, 2008. Print.

Morales, Laurel. "Legacy of Forced March Still Haunts Navajo Nation." *Morning Edition.* NPR, 27 Jan. 2014. Web. 14 Apr. 2015.

Trafzer, Clifford E. *The Kit Carson Campaign: The Last Great Navajo War.* Norman: U of Oklahoma P, 1982. Print.

NAVAJO-HOPI LAND SETTLEMENT ACT

The Navajo-Hopi Land Settlement Act was enacted by Congress on December 22, 1974, primarily to clarify rights of the Navajo and Hopi tribes in the 1882 "Executive Order Reservation" established by President Chester A. Arthur. This executive order set aside 2,472,095 acres "for the use and occupancy of the Moqui [Hopi] and such other Indians as the Secretary of the Interior may see fit to settle thereon." At the time, both Hopis and Navajos were living in the set-aside area. Disputes increased as the Navajo population in the area expanded.

In 1934 Congress consolidated the boundaries of the Navajo Reservation without altering the 1882 Executive Order Reservation. The Bureau of Indian Affairs (BIA) then established grazing districts on both reservations. District 6, exclusively for Hopi use, consisted of about 25 percent of the 1882 reservation. The remainder was occupied largely by Navajo stock raisers. Disputes between members of the two tribes continued.

In 1958 Congress authorized a lawsuit to settle conflicting claims to the 1882 reservation. In 1962 a federal court, in *Healing v. Jones*, held that for the area outside District 6, the Hopi and Navajo had "joint, undivided and equal interests." Because the Navajos occupied most of the area, however, they controlled the most surface resources in the Joint Use Area (JUA).

Negotiations between the two tribes concerning management of the JUA were unsuccessful. In the early 1970s the Hopis sought and obtained a court order for livestock reduction in the area. The continuing controversy stimulated congressional interest, and the Navajo-Hopi Land Settlement Act was enacted in 1974.

The act was comprehensive. It directed that a mediator make recommendations to the district court, which would then partition the surface rights of the JUA. In 1977, each tribe received half of the JUA. Money was appropriated for livestock reduction and boundary fencing. The act, and a 1980 amendment, allowed for the transfer of some federal lands to the Navajos to help offset lost JUA land. In 1983 about 370,000 acres of "new lands" along the southern edge of the Navajo Reservation were selected.

The act required the removal of members of one tribe living on lands transferred to the other tribe. This involved a relatively small number of Hopis but thousands of Navajos. An independent commission was created to administer the relocation program, but it was inept, contributing to the hardships of relocatees. The $52,000,000 initial appropriation was inadequate. Congress belatedly responded in the 1980s, amending the act to restructure the commission and authorizing hundreds of millions of additional dollars for relocation.

As a final touch of irony, one section of this legislation, designed to resolve controversy over the 1882 reservation, allowed the tribes the right to sue to settle rights in lands within the 1934 Navajo Reservation. In 1992, a federal district court decided that the Hopis and San Juan Southern Paiutes (who had intervened in the lawsuit) had rights in portions of the Navajo Reservation long used by tribal members.

————*Eric Henderson*

BIBLIOGRAPHY AND FURTHER READING

Bailey, Garrick Alan, and Roberta Glenn Bailey. *A History of the Navajos: The Reservation Years*. Santa Fe: School of American Research, 1999. Print.

Benedek, Emily. *The Wind Won't Know Me: A History of the Navajo-Hope Land Dispute*. Norman: U of Oklahoma P, 1999. Print.

Johansen, Bruce E., and Barry M. Pritzker. *Encyclopedia of American Indian History*. Santa Barbara: ABC-CLIO, 2008. Print.

NAZISM

A German political movement that advocated racial nationalism (including anti-Semitism), dictatorial government, and expansion into eastern Europe by means of war, Nazism, a contraction of the term "National Socialism," was a German political movement that emerged in the aftermath of World War I with Adolf Hitler as its leader. From the very start, it espoused ideas that rejected Western values of humanitarianism, rationalism, liberalism, democracy, and socialism in favor of extreme nationalism, racism, and a political system of single-party dictatorship. Nazi policies and practices violated human and civil rights, first in Germany and later in conquered Europe, and resorted to violent power politics in international affairs.

BEGINNINGS

The forerunner of Nazism as a political party was the German Workers' Party, which was organized in Munich early in 1919. Adolf Hitler, a lower-middle-class Austrian by birth and a corporal in the German army during World War I, joined the German Workers' Party later in the year. It soon was renamed the National Socialist German Workers' Party, and Hitler, showing oratorical and organizational talent, became its undisputed leader in 1921.

The main tenets of Nazism were drawn from the party program of 1920, Hitler's speeches and writings (especially his ponderous two-volume *Mein Kampf*, published in 1925 and 1926, and other Nazi publications. They attacked liberalism and parliamentarianism, including democracy, as inherently weak political systems and branded the early leaders of the Weimar Republic, liberals, socialists, and Jews as "November criminals" of 1918, who had overthrown the imperial government. In place of the failed parliamentary democracy, Nazism offered authoritarian rule rooted in a solid hierarchical system of leaders and followers. At the head would be a führer, or "leader," who, with the support of the Nazi Party, would exercise total control over the society and mobilize it for the achievement of the political and social goals that he postulated.

WHITE SUPREMACY

Nazism, above all, extolled racial nationalism, which was derived from the nineteenth-century racial theories of the Frenchman Joseph-Arthur de Gobineau, the Germanized Englishman Houston Chamberlain, and the German Paul de Lagarde. Proponents of Nazism contended that human races were divided into culture-creating and culture-destroying groups, which were engaged in a Social Darwinian struggle of survival of the fittest. At the top of the culture-creating races stood the Nordic-Aryan-Germanic group, the "master race," which was destined to dominate inferior races. At Hitler's instigation, Nazism singled out the Jews as the greatest threat to the pure Aryans because the Jews, the leading culture-destroying race, were conspiring to gain domination over the world. In Nazi foreign policy, the idea of the primacy of the Aryan race was combined with a Great German nationalism or imperialism, whose aim it was to create a Great German empire far beyond the borders of the German nation. Such an expansion was to give the German people the *Lebensraum*, or "living space," that it needed to ensure its security and economic independence.

German American Bund parade on East 86th St., New York City, October 30, 1939. By New York World-Telegram and the Sun staff photographer.

The Nazis did not conceal that, although they would attain power legally, once in office they would destroy the constitutional system. Within one month after Hitler was appointed chancellor early in 1933, he had communists and many socialists confined to quickly established concentration camps and suspended civil rights. Through cajolery, pressure, and terror, he prevailed upon the Reichstag (parliament) to give him dictatorial powers, which he used to eliminate trade unions and all political parties except the Nazi Party. In 1934, he murdered the top leadership of the Storm Troopers, or SA, and some non-Nazis, when he felt threatened by a rival from within his own ranks. He justified these acts of criminality by declaring: "I was responsible for the fate of the German people and thereby I became the Supreme Judge of the German people."

The Nazi practices of eliminating opponents by sending them to concentration camps or murdering them, persecuting Jews purely on racial grounds, maintaining a police state, and pursuing an aggressive foreign policy left no room for the observance of ethical principles in politics. It is important to realize, however, that liberal democratic governments also generally do not feel bound by ethical constraints if the national interest is at stake. Though idealists among philosophers and scholars argue that, for example, foreign policy must be based on prudence and ethical principle, realists (and they are a majority) maintain that in world politics moral or ethical concerns must be subordinated to national interest. Given the absence of accepted international standards of morality and effective bodies of enforcement when violations occur, each government, being concerned with military security, the integrity of its political life, and the well-being of its citizens, must act on its own to protect its national interests. Implied in this stance, however, is a sense of moderation and responsibility when pursuing the national interest in international relations.

WORLD WAR II AND THE HOLOCAUST

The Nazi regime under Hitler's direction defined national interest in the most expansive terms. Hitler once characterized Germany's foreign policy by declaring: "Germany will become a world power or it will not exist at all." In the early years of Nazi dictatorship, he and his associates constantly proclaimed the German Reich's "sincere desire for peace," while unilaterally abrogating the restrictions of the Treaty of Versailles, rearming Germany, and then, in 1938, annexing Austria and the German-speaking Sudetenland of Czechoslovakia. In 1939, Nazi Germany unleashed World War II through aggression against Poland, followed by campaigns into France and other European countries in 1940. One year later, Hitler attacked the Soviet Union, waging a brutal ideological war in the quest for *Lebensraum* in the East.

While worldwide violence was raging as a result of war, the Nazi regime also prepared for the elimination of "racially inferior" populaces and "those of lesser value" in society. The persecution of German Jews culminated in the violence against Jewish property and people of the *Kristallnacht* of 1938. With the outbreak of the war in 1939, a euthanasia program was begun, resulting in the killing by injection or by gassing of almost one hundred thousand mentally and physically handicapped persons, most of whom were German. Finally, the plan to liquidate all European Jews in Nazi hands—the "final solution"—was implemented by Hitler and some of his immediate associates in 1941. Known as the Holocaust, it claimed the lives of almost six million people. In addition, Nazi actions led to the murder of millions of Gypsies, Slavs, homosexuals, and other racial and political "enemies." This unprecedented mechanized genocide was only stopped by the defeat of Nazi Germany and the suicide of Hitler in 1945.

After the total defeat of Germany and the inglorious death of the führer, Nazism never revived as a significant force. Following the establishment of the Federal Republic of Germany in 1949, its Federal Constitutional Court outlawed the noisy but unimportant Socialist Reich Party in 1952 as a neo-Nazi organization. In the 1960s and 1980s, two right-wing parties were formed: the National Democratic Party and the Republicans. Both have shown some neo-Nazi features but have achieved little influence. More noteworthy have been a number of small neo-Nazi groups formed since the 1970s, whose racist hate propaganda and violence, directed not primarily against Jews but against foreigners, especially Turks and other immigrants from the Middle Ease, have aroused consternation since the unification of Germany in 1990. These groups cannot, however, be viewed as the forerunners of an organized neo-Nazi movement.

——*George P. Blum*

BIBLIOGRAPHY AND FURTHER READING

Evans, Richard J. *The Third Reich in History and Memory*. New York: Oxford UP, 2015. Print.

Fleming, Gerald. *Hitler and the Final Solution*. Berkeley: U of California P, 1984. Print.

Spielvogel, Jackson J., and David Redles. *Hitler and Nazi Germany: A History*. 7th ed. Upper Saddle River: Pearson, 2014. Print.

NEGRO CONVENTIONS

Mass conventions were a popular means of protest among African Americans of the nineteenth century. Rooted in constitutional principles of free assembly and petition, these conventions were a product of the group consciousness that emerged among free blacks in northern urban areas following the American Revolution and were a reaction to a burgeoning institutional racism that legitimized slavery and stripped free African Americans of basic civil rights during the post-revolutionary period. The first great national Negro convention, held at Philadelphia in August, 1817, produced resolutions opposing slavery and denouncing a plan proposed by the United States Congress to colonize black Americans in Africa. Although largely symbolic, the convention of 1817 inspired the Negro Convention movement of the 1830s, which was to provide a forum for expressions of militancy and nationalism among the growing population of free blacks in the North.

The Negro Convention movement of the 1830s was aided by the emergence of black leaders with national status and varied agendas. Although dominated by antislavery societies, the six national Negro Conventions held between 1830 and 1835 addressed a variety of issues, including the organization of economic boycotts and mass protests, the observance of national days of prayer and fasting, and the establishment of temperance societies and African missionary groups. The conventions exerted a considerable influence upon local black communities, chiefly through the encouragement of verbal agitation; yet the movement was cut short in mid-decade by white abolitionists who, fearing that the black separatism often advocated by convention delegates would damage the antislavery movement, infiltrated the conventions and split their leadership. The Negro Convention movement was briefly revived in the early 1840s, when young black militants in New York and Philadelphia called a convention of black leaders to protest slavery and racial inequality. However, this convention, which failed by one vote to endorse slave insurrection, proved a militant exception to a new spirit of gradualism among black abolitionists. The last notable antebellum Negro Convention, held in Cleveland, Ohio, in 1854, yielded compromise proposals for the repatriation of African Americans that early conventions had so vehemently opposed.

The end of the Civil War and the beginning of Reconstruction sparked a revival of Negro Conventions in the 1870s and 1880s, as southern freedmen and northern agitators sought vehicles to petition the government for civil rights and protection from mob violence. These conventions were chiefly local and regional in nature, designed to facilitate political organization and to appeal directly to legislators and state governors. Nevertheless, national conventions continued, the most notable being the National Colored Convention held in Louisville, Kentucky, in 1883, in which the delegates called for an end to economic peonage in the South, equal rights and suffrage for African Americans, and integration of schools and the military.

The Negro Convention movement died out in the 1890s as Jim Crow laws and mob violence swept the South and accommodationism replaced agitation and protest as a political strategy for black leaders. However, the tradition of assembly and militancy brought about by the convention movement survived in the black conferences of the early twentieth century (for example, the Niagara Movement of 1909, which spawned the National Association for the Advancement of Colored People), in the mass protest marches of the Civil Rights movement during the 1960s, and in the Million Man and Million Woman Marches of the 1990s.

——Michael H. Burchett

BIBLIOGRAPHY AND FURTHER READING

Basker, James G., ed. *American Antislavery Writings: Colonial Beginnings to Emancipation.* New York: Lib. of America, 2012. Print.

Cromwell, John Wesley. *The Early Negro Convention Movement.* New York: Arno, 1969. Print.

"National Negro Convention Movement." *Africans in America.* WGBH, PBS, 1999. Web. 14 May. 2015.

Rael, Patrick. African-American Activism Before the Civil War: The Freedom Struggle in the Antebellum North. New York: Routledge, 2008. Print.

Yee, Shirley. "National Negro Convention Movement." (1831–1864)." *BlackPast.org.* BlackPast.org, 2015. Web. 14 May. 2015.

Neo-Nazism

Neo-Nazism is a white-supremacist movement motivated by the racist beliefs of Adolf Hitler and the genocidal policies of the German Third Reich. After the Second World War, former Nazi officials living in South America sought to establish an underground network dedicated to the resurrection of Nazi power in postwar Germany. This new Nazi, or Neo-Nazi, movement quickly attracted sympathizers throughout the Western hemisphere, the United States included. Armed with conspiracy theories about Jewish exploitation of the US economy and financial institutions, the loss of white-American jobs to immigrants and minorities, and the surrender of US economic and military power to non-Caucasian countries, their message has been dangerously attractive to white Americans who have felt betrayed by their government and society. Neo-Nazism's initial effort to intimidate, segregate, disenfranchise, and even assault black Americans and Jews soon expanded to immigrants, homosexuals, all non-Anglo-European Americans, non-Christians, and many others.

Although Neo-Nazism did not formally emerge in the US prior to the 1950s, it has a long ancestry, especially, but not exclusively, in the American South. Racism against blacks justified the existence of slavery and later supported the emergence of the Ku Klux Klan, a white-supremacist

organization still in existence today and currently devoted to the suppression of almost all non-Caucasians and immigrants. The Ku Klux Klan may be independent of the Neo-Nazis in name, as is the Aryan Brotherhood, a Neo-Nazi prison gang, but their aims are almost identical. Still, those who call themselves Neo-Nazis have a unique symbolism and culture that evokes memories of the German Reich and Nazi intolerance. Appointed with fascist insignia such as the swastika, Nazi flag, and German-inspired paramilitary uniforms and denying the existence of the Holocaust, their allegiance to a shameful past and their white-supremacist agenda are never in doubt.

——*Tomislav Han*

Bibliography and Further Reading

Ezekiel, Raphael S. *The Racist Mind: Portraits of American Neo-Nazis and Klansmen.* New York, NY: Penguin Books, 1996.

Langer, Elinor. *A Hundred Little Hitlers: The Death of a Black Man, the Trial of a White Racist, and the Rise of the Neo-Nazi Movement in America.* New York, NY: Metropolitan Books, 2003.

Strum, Philippa. *When the Nazis Came to Skokie.* Lawrence, KS: University Press of Kansas, 1999.

New York City Slave Revolt

The New York City Slave Revolt of 1712 calls attention to the fact that slavery had become more firmly established in colonial New York than in any other British province north of Chesapeake Bay. Slaves were already an integral part of the labor force when England conquered Dutch New Netherland in 1664. As European immigration lagged, slave labor became increasingly important. Between 1703 and 1723, New York's total population almost doubled, increasing from 20,540 to 40,564, but its black population (slaves and free blacks were always lumped together and listed in the census as Negroes) almost tripled, jumping from 2,253 to 6,171.

Background

As the number of bondsmen increased, so did the anxiety level of white New Yorkers. In 1708, following the grizzly murder of a Long Island planter and his family, four slaves were tried, convicted, and executed "with all the torment possible for a terror to others." Shortly thereafter, the provincial assembly passed An Act for Preventing the Conspiracy of Slaves, which defined the judicial proceedings and made death the penalty for any slave found guilty of murder or attempted murder. Fear of slave conspiracy led whites to look with ambivalence upon Anglican catechist Elias Neau's teaching among New York City blacks and Native Americans.

Small-scale slave owning prevailed in New York. Few white families owned more than a slave or two, so slave husbands, wives, and children might be scattered among several households. Regulations restricting their freedom of movement were bitterly resented by slaves, because they interfered with their domestic life. Such restrictions often were more apparent than real, because slavery in New York City and surrounding villages, where slaves were most heavily concentrated, was tied to a developing urban economy that demanded a flexible, if not free, labor supply. Slaves in New York City and Albany often hired themselves out, splitting the pay with their respective owners, but otherwise lived separately from their masters. The hustle and bustle of the urban economic scene afforded slaves considerable opportunity to meet, socialize, and discuss common grievances, despite the best efforts of whites to keep them under surveillance.

The slave uprising of 1712 apparently began as a conspiracy on March 25, then celebrated as New Year's Day. The ringleaders reportedly were of the Cormantine and Pawpaw peoples, Africans who had not been long in New York; a few Spanish Indian slaves; and at least one free black, a practitioner of African medicine and magic who reportedly supplied special powder to protect the rebels from the white man's weapons. Their motivation, according to both Governor Robert Hunter and Chaplain John Sharpe, was revenge for ill treatment at the hands of their respective masters. Their goal was freedom, which, claimed Hunter and Sharpe, was to be achieved by burning New York City and killing the white people on Manhattan.

THE REVOLT

During the early morning hours of Sunday, April 6, 1712, about two dozen conspirators, armed with guns, swords, knives, and clubs, gathered in an orchard in the East Ward on the northeast edge of New York City. They set fire to several outbuildings and waited in ambush for the whites who came to put out the blaze, killing nine and wounding seven. Soldiers were dispatched from the fort, but when they arrived, the rebels had dispersed, taking refuge in the woods surrounding the town. The next day, local militiamen systematically searched Manhattan Island for the rebellious blacks. Rather than surrender, six slaves killed themselves, several cutting their own throats.

White New Yorkers were in full panic. "We have about 70 Negro's in Custody," read a dispatch from New York, dated April 14 but published in the *Boston News-Letter* on April 21, but it was "fear'd that most of the Negro's here (who are very numerous) knew of the Late Conspiracy to murder the Christians." Fear of another uprising drove the judicial proceedings. On April 9, a coroner's jury implicated thirty-eight slaves, identifying fourteen of them as murderers. In accordance with the 1708 Conspiracy Act, the coroner's findings were turned over to the Court of Quarter Sessions of the Peace, which convened on April 11. Attorney General May Bickley handled the prosecution, moving the trials on from the Quarter Sessions to the State Supreme Court on June 3.

THE TRIALS

Forty-two slaves and one free black were indicted and tried. Crucial to both the indictments and trials was the testimony of two slaves, Cuffee, who belonged to baker Peter Vantilborough, and Dick, a boy slave owned by Harmanus Burger, a blacksmith. The coroner's jury had found Cuffee and Dick guilty of at least two murders, but Attorney General Bickley apparently promised them immunity, and they became the Crown's prime witnesses. Some whites, including such substantial citizens as former mayor David Provost, coroner Henry Wileman, and lawyers Jacob Regnier and David Jamison, testified for a few of the defendants. However, the general adequacy of defense counsel may well be doubted. Many of the convictions hinged upon the dubious testimony of Cuffee and young Dick, both of whom were manipulated by Attorney General Bickley, described by Governor Hunter as "a busy waspish man." Bickley also demonstrated considerable bias against certain slave defendants, depending upon who owned them. For example, Mars, belonging to Jacob Regnier, a rival attorney with whom Brickley had a private quarrel, was tried twice and acquitted before being found guilty in the third trial and sentenced to be hanged.

Most of the trials were over by early June. Twenty-three slaves were convicted of murder; fifteen slaves were acquitted, along with one free black. Two slaves were found guilty of assault with intent to kill, and two were acquitted of that charge. The twenty-five who were convicted were sentenced to death. Twenty were to be hanged; three were burned alive, one in a slow fire for eight to ten hours until consumed to ashes. Another was broken upon the wheel and left to die, and one was hung in chains and "so to continue without sustenance until death." Eleven were "executed at once," including those burned, broken at the wheel, and chained without food or water. These barbaric executions were defended by Governor Hunter as "the most exemplary that could be possibly thought of."

Yet even Hunter doubted the justice of it all. He postponed the execution of six slaves, including two Spanish American Indians taken during Queen Anne's War (1702-1713) and sold as slaves despite their claim of being free men, a pregnant slave woman, and the much tried and finally convicted Mars. At Hunter's request, the queen pardoned several of them, and perhaps all of those he had reprieved (the record is rather vague), despite the efforts of Bickley in New York and Lord Cornbury, a former governor of New York, in London to obstruct the pardons.

IMPACT OF THE REVOLT

There were other ramifications of the slave uprising. The provincial government passed laws making it impossible to free slaves without putting up a two-hundred-pound bond and paying the freed slave twenty pounds per year for life. Africans, American Indians, and mulattoes were prohibited from inheriting or otherwise owning property. Finally, due process rights were weakened for slaves accused of murder or conspiracy. In the wake of the revolt, Elias Neau, the preacher and catechist of Trinity Church, found it difficult to continue his school for blacks and Indians. Only two of his many pupils were implicated

in the conspiracy, and Chaplain John Sharpe doubted that either was involved in the violence.

After the rebellion, New Yorkers were reluctant to import slaves directly from Africa or to purchase Spanish Indians as slaves. Black slaves from the West Indies were preferred over the other two groups. Yet slavery remained a primary source of labor for both the province and city of New York, slaves constituting about 15 percent of the population. In 1730, other regulations were added to the slave code because "many Mischiefs had been Occasioned by the two great Liberty allowed to Negro and other Slaves." In 1741, white paranoia and slave discontent provoked a so-called slave conspiracy in which 150 slaves and 25 whites were jailed. Of that number, 18 slaves and 4 whites were hanged, 13 blacks burned alive, and 70 were sold and sent to the West Indies.

——*Ronald W. Howard*

BIBLIOGRAPHY AND FURTHER READING

Goodfriend, Joyce D. *Before the Melting Pot: Society and Culture in Colonial New York City, 1664-1730.* Princeton: Princeton UP, 1992. Print.

Kammen, Michael. *Colonial New York: A History.* New York: Scribner's, 1975. Print.

Lustig, Mary Lou. *Robert Hunter, 1666-1734.* Syracuse: Syracuse UP, 1983.

Rucker, Walter C. *The River Flows On: Black Resistance, Culture, and Identity Formation in Early America.* Baton Rouge: Louisiana State UP, 2006. Print.

Woods, Peter. "Slave Resistance," in *Encyclopedia of the North American Colonies*, vol. 2. New York: Scribner's, 1993. Print.

NEWARK RACE RIOTS

Race relations, already tense in much of the United States in 1967 and prompting riots in other cities, were especially poor in Newark, New Jersey. In addition to high unemployment, African Americans were angry about a proposal to relocate inner-city residents from their neighborhoods in order to build a medical and dental college. On July 12, 1967, rumors spread through the city that police had beaten an African American during an arrest. Protesters throwing bottles and shouting insults soon surrounded the

police station, but the crowd dispersed in the early morning hours. The following night, a full-scale riot erupted, and the governor called out the National Guard. Despite the presence of troops, the rioting continued for several days. Twenty-three people died, and more than fifteen hundred people were injured. Police reported more than sixteen hundred arrests. Damage to buildings and property was estimated at more than ten million dollars. Although the Newark riot evidenced the frustration that many

African Americans felt concerning the slow pace of economic and social change in the United States, the violence shocked many white Americans and diminished enthusiasm for continued government efforts in the area of civil rights.

——*Thomas Clarkin*

BIBLIOGRAPHY AND FURTHER READING

Curvin, Robert. *Inside Newark: Decline, Rebellion, and the Search for Transformation.* New Brunswick: Rutgers UP, 2014. Print.

Herman, Max Arthur. *Summer of Rage: An Oral History of the 1967 Newark and Detroit Riots.* New York: Lang, 2013. Print.

Mumford, Kevin J. *Newark: A History of Race, Rights, and Riots in America.* New York: New York UP, 2007. Print.

NEWBERRY V. UNITED STATES

In 1918, Truman H. Newberry, Republican candidate for the US Senate, was tried in Michigan, along with more than one hundred associates, for conspiring to violate the Federal Corrupt Practices Act of 1910. The statute violated had set a limit on campaign financing, and the indictment claimed that Newberry had exceeded this limit in primary and general election expenditures. Newberry and his associates were found guilty in the US District Court for the Western District of Michigan.

The US Supreme Court reversed the conviction and sent the case back to the lower court, finding that the statute on which Newberry's conviction rested had no constitutional authority. The Court argued that prior to the Seventeenth Amendment, the only part of the Constitution empowering Congress to regulate the election process was to be found in Article I, section 4, which pertained only to the time, place, and manner of holding general elections and failed to address such matters as party primaries and conventions, additions to the election process unforeseen by the framers of the Constitution. Consequently, the Court ruled that in the relevant section of the Corrupt Practices Act, Congress had exceeded its authority. The Court also maintained that because the statute antedated the ratification of the Seventeenth Amendment, which extended congressional authority, it was invalid at the time of its enactment. The Court held that a power later acquired could not, *ex proprio*, validate a law that was unconstitutional at the time of its passing. The Court did not question a state's right to regulate primaries and campaign financing, claiming that "the state may suppress whatever evils may be incident to primary or convention."

The *Newberry* ruling imposed an important barrier to the enfranchisement of black Americans in the single-party South. Although the Court would strike down laws expressly prohibiting African Americans from voting in primaries, as late as 1935, in *Grovey v. Townsend,* it upheld legal measures taken in Texas to bar blacks from participating in the state Democratic convention, arguing that such "private" discrimination did not come under constitutional purview. *Grovey* and *Newberry* were finally successfully challenged in *United States v. Classic* (1941), which held that Congress had the authority to regulate both primary and general elections for federal offices.

Three years later a final legal blow to de jure disfranchisement of African Americans was dealt in *Smith v. Allwright* (1944), which held that laws governing all elections—local, state, and federal—could be invalidated if they violated Article I, section 4 of the Constitution. Sponsored by the National Association for the Advancement of Colored People, the plaintiff argued that Texas Democratic Party officials had denied him a primary ballot because of his race. The Supreme Court concurred, noting that state laws regulated both primary and general elections and were therefore responsible for barriers to the ballot box erected on racial grounds.

——*John W. Fiero*

NEWS MEDIA AND RACIAL/ ETHNIC RELATIONS

News media form an integral part of a society's power structure. Media exercise power by setting agendas, framing issues, portraying groups and individuals in particular ways, controlling the direction of discourses, and shaping public opinion. The power of the media to "manufacture consent" has been studied by Edward S. Herman and Noam Chomsky, among others, and it has been shown that news and entertainment programs also serve as propaganda vehicles. Through its portrayal and framing of racial and ethnic minorities, news media also influence race and ethnic relations.

MEDIA REPRESENTATIONS OF RACIAL/ETHNIC GROUPS

Media produce news for consumption by the majority population or the "in-group" of a society. Often, racial and ethnic minorities constitute an "out-group" about whom stories are constructed—by selecting items that highlight their otherness. Racial and ethnic groups represent an internal Third World, as it were, replete with conditions of poverty, corruption, discord, and criminality. In particular, crime reports that involve ethnic and racial minorities serve as cautionary tales for the in-group, warning them to be watchful about the troubled groups/communities in their midst.

Crime news constitutes a large portion of TV and newspaper reports, and sociologists who have analyzed such reports have noted that they heighten the readers' moral sensibilities and sense of righteousness, making them think that they, unlike those about whom they are reading/hearing, are not criminals or even like criminals. In most cases, crime reports provide information about the racial or ethnic identity of the perpetrator, if that person belongs to a minority group. When, however, the offender is white, there is typically little or no information given about that person's race, ethnicity, or national origin. For example, the gunman in the 2007 Virginia Tech mass shooting that killed twenty-seven students and five faculty members was identified by CNN as follows: "Seung-Hui Cho was a senior at Virginia Tech, majoring in English. He was born in South Korea in 1984 and became a permanent US resident in 1992." By making such an explicit

reference to his foreignness, a false impression was created that there was a link of some sort between his being born in Korea and the horrific crime he committed. In contrast, in a report by CNN released on December 16, 2016 under the title, "Charleston Church Shooting: Who is Dylann Roof?," which described the mass shooter who killed nine people at the Emanuel African Methodist Episcopal Church in South Carolina in 2015, there was no mention at all of his race or ethnic background. Associating a crime with a person's racial or ethnic identity serves to "otherize" not only the individual but also the racial or ethnic group to which that individual belongs. Associating a crime with the perpetrator's immigration status is also a common practice in news reporting, although immigrants are no more likely than citizens to commit crimes. This practice implies some linkage between immigration and crime, triggering moral outrage and reinforcing biases against immigrants. Studies have shown that media often conflate ethnic with foreign, even in cases where the offender is a citizen by birth or naturalization.

A 2014 research report, "Race and Punishment: Racial Perceptions of Crime and Support for Punitive Policies," produced by the Sentencing Project, synthesizes the findings of two decades of research, noting that racial perceptions of crime are skewed: White Americans overestimate the amount of crime committed by people of color. By overrepresenting racial minorities as crime suspects and white Americans as crime victims, the report states, television news and newspapers "fuel racial perceptions of crime."

Perhaps no other racial minority has been as much disadvantaged by being labeled as criminals as African Americans. African Americans have been portrayed in the news media as criminals ever since the end of the Civil War. As the 2016 documentary *13*[th] highlights, the Thirteenth Amendment to the US Constitution, which ironically re-instituted slavery by defining imprisoned persons as slaves of the state, has been exploited by southern states to incarcerate, even for minor offenses, large numbers of African Americans for the purpose of forcing them to do slave labor. The disproportionate incarceration rates of African Americans, which have continued to this day, have influenced the news media and the public to view members of that community through the lens of crime, activating and reinforcing the historical association of race and crime. In daily crime reports African Americans are portrayed as violent, aggressive, and dangerous, ignoring the fact that they have also been victims of horrific violence perpetrated against them by whites, including lynching, murder, and rape.

Although they comprise only about 13 percent of the US population, African Americans constitute 35 percent of jail inmates and 37 percent of prison inmates. Researchers have noted that the high arrest and incarceration rates for African Americans do not accurately reflect their differential criminal involvement, but rather betray built-in structural biases in the criminal justice system. At every stage of the justice process the unfairness of the system is on display. Many who are innocent are forced to admit guilt through the plea bargaining process, which has been described as a perversion of justice. Their high incarceration rates, which destroy families and communities, are reported in the mainstream news media not as a matter of concern, but as confirmation of the public perception that African Americans are inherently criminal. The fact that they are victims of crime at a higher rate than whites is rarely mentioned in the mainstream media.

A 2001 study titled "Media Representations & Impact on the Lives of Black Men and Boys," conducted by the *Opportunity Agenda* Studies, shows that media present a distorted view of African American men and boys in many ways. For instance, they are underrepresented as positive role models; their unemployment or poverty is exaggerated; their positive qualities are limited to sports, physical prowess, and virility. Such skewed reporting has contributed to public antagonism toward young African American men and support for harsh punitive measures.

Constituting over 17 percent of the US population, the largest minority group in the United States is Latinos. Because the growth of the Latino population has far outpaced that of any other group (from 6.5 percent in 1980 to the current 17 percent), and because the highest percentage of the foreign-born population is Latino (37 percent of the total foreign-born), there is considerable anxiety among the white "in-group" populace generally about continued immigration from Mexico and other Latin American countries. According to a survey conducted by the

National Hispanic Coalition in 2012, a sizable number of non-Latinos (about 30 percent of those surveyed) believe that at least half of the Hispanics are illegal immigrants—which is false. The survey also found that news and entertainment programs have helped create negative perceptions about Latinos, such as: "They don't keep up their homes"; "They take jobs from Americans"; "[They have] too many children"; "[They] refuse to learn English"; and "[They are] less educated and welfare recipients." In movies and television programs, Latinos are frequently cast in such roles as criminal, gardener, or maid. Studies have found that those who are exposed to negative media portrayals of the Latinos hold more negative views about them, as compared to those who have had direct contacts. It has also been found that those who rely on conservative news media outlets are more likely to hold negative views about Latinos than those who get their information from liberal sources.

Generalizations about news reports involving Asian Americans are difficult to make because of the large diversity among Asian Americans. Asian Americans represent fifty-one different countries and belong to thousands of ethnic groups, even though together they form only about 5.6 percent of the total US population. News reports about them are generally positive, but they tend to exaggerate their positive attributes such as hardworking, polite, academically talented, and upwardly mobile. Negative stereotypes are also found in the representation of Asian Americans in the news media, such as being ill-adapted to American culture, sly, ill-mannered, and manipulative. With China's rising economic and military power, Asia is now treated as almost synonymous with China and news coverage of other Asian countries – except perhaps the major ones such as India, Japan, and Korea – is sparse.

Arab Americans have always been viewed through the lens of the old European images about them, which were popularized during the middle Ages. Reflecting and reinforcing those old stereotypical images, the news media depict them, through words and photographs, as wealthy but uncultured, dishonest, corrupt, backward, prone to violence, barbarous, fanatical, women abusers, and terrorists. Although Arabs are a very diverse group of people belonging to a variety of religions, most news reports give the impression that they are all Muslims. The pervasive negative portrayals of Arabs have become even more negative after the events of September 11, 2001. Reports of the sporadic acts of terror committed by persons of Middle Eastern origin in recent years have only helped to reinforce those stereotypes.

SOURCES OF BIAS

The structural factors that contribute to distorted news reporting about racial and ethnic minorities are many. The mainstream media reflect the segregation and stratification of American society itself, to which the media both belong and act to define. Most of the owners and managers of the mainstream media, and the journalists who work for them, are whites with limited contacts with minority populations. According to a survey conducted in 2015 by the Radio Television Digital News Association, minorities are underrepresented in the news business at all levels.

Another factor is known as the sourcing bias. Experts and government officials chosen by media professionals for interviews on social issues are most often white. According to a Pew Research survey published in 2016, whites are more likely than non-whites to be interviewed by journalists. The voices of minority persons are rarely heard, or their views rarely quoted, in news reports. Furthermore, corporate news media select and frame news in ways that please their consumers, shareholders, and advertisers, and use news to couch their preferred political views.

Media's ability to accurately report news has come under intense scrutiny in recent years, and they are under attack from all sides. A 2016 Gallup Poll showed that trust in mass media has fallen steadily since the 1990s and that most adults, particularly young adults, report having little trust in the mainstream media. Minorities' distrust of the mainstream media is even more widespread. According to a survey conducted in 2014 by the Media Insight Project, 75 percent of blacks and 66 percent of Hispanics express distrust in the mainstream media. Such widespread distrust has prompted all groups to seek alternative sources of news, and minorities have turned to ethnically aligned news media for a more sympathetic and meaningful reporting of the issues affecting them.

——*Mathew Kanjirathinkal*

BIBLIOGRAPHY AND FURTHER READING

Bjornstrom, Ellen E.S., et al. "Race and Ethnic Representations of Lawbreakers and Victims in Crime News: A National Study of Television Coverage." *Social Problems* 57 (2), 2010: 269-293. Print.

Chuang, Angie. "Representations of Foreign Versus (Asian) American Identity in a Mass-Shooting Case: Newspaper Coverage of the 2009 Binghamton Masscre." *Journalism and Communication Quarterly*, 89 (2), 2012: 244-260. Print.

Dixon, Travis L. and Christina Azocar L. "Priming Crime and Activating Blackness: Understanding the Psychological Impact of the Overrepresenation of Blacks as Lawbreakers on Television News." *Journal of Communication* 57(2), 2007: 229-253. Print.

Gallup. "Americans' Trust in Mass Media Sinks to New Low." Web.

Juan González, Juan and Joseph Torres. *News for All the People: The Epic Story of Race and the American Media.* London and New York: Verso, 2012. Print.

Libby, Lewis. *The Myth of Post Racialism in Television News.* New York: Routledge, 2016. Print.

Parker, Cherie. "Before and After 9/11: The Portrayal of Arab Americans in US Newspapers." Thesis, U of South Florida, 2008. Web.

Piquero, Alex R. and Robert W. Brame. "Assessing the Race–Crime and Ethnicity–Crime Relationship in a Sample of Serious Adolescent Delinquents." *Crime and Delinquency* 54(3), 2009: 390-422. Web.

Sentencing Project. "Race and Punishment: Racial Perceptions of Crime and Support for Punitive measures." 2010. Web.

Sung-Yeon Park, et al. "Race in Media Coverage of School Shootings: A Parellel Application of Framing Theory and Attribute Agenda Setting." *Journalism and Mass Communication Quarterly*, 89 (3), 2012: 475-494. Print.

Tung, Ling-hsuan L. "Images of Asians and Asian Americans: The Under-representation and Misrepresentation of Asians and Asian-Americans on American Television. *Intercultural Communication Studies* XV (1), 2006: 87 – 93. Print.

NEZ PERCE EXILE

During the nineteenth century, the Nez Perce tribes occupied various areas of the Northwest, including Washington, Idaho, and Oregon. There were five separate groups, each under the leadership of an autonomous chief. One group occupied Oregon territory in the Imnaha and Wallowa Valleys and was under the leadership of Joseph the Elder, or Old Chief Joseph. In 1855, the governor of the Oregon Territory signed a celebrated treaty with him and numerous other Nez Perce leaders, allowing the tribe ownership of all the land in the Imnaha and Wallowa Valleys. The treaty was ratified by the United States Senate.

The treaty of 1855 proved short-lived, however: The Civil War and the discovery of gold at Orofino, Idaho, in 1860, led to an ever-increasing surge of immigration of white settlers into the valleys and territories claimed by the Nez Perce. Because of increasing tensions between the whites and the natives, in 1863 a new treaty was negotiated. The new terms excluded the Imnaha and Wallowa Valleys and other vast areas of land that had been dedicated to the Nez Perce in 1855. The revised treaty was signed by James Reuben and Chief Lawyer, but Chiefs Old Joseph, White Bird, and Looking Glass refused to ratify it. Thus, the treaty was recognized as having treaty Nez Perce and nontreaty Nez Perce.

THE ACCESSION OF CHIEF JOSEPH

In 1871, Old Chief Joseph died, leaving the leadership of the Wallamwatkins to his son, the new Chief Joseph , or Joseph the Younger. The continuing influx of white immigrants into the Nez Perce lands caused increasing problems between the Nez Perce and whites. In 1876, a commission was appointed to investigate complaints, and it was decided that the nontreaty Nez Perces had no standing and that all groups should go onto designated reservations. In 1877, the US Department of the Interior issued instructions to carry out the commission's recommendations. Preparing for the transition, a council of tribal leaders and US government officials was set to meet on May 3, 1877. Chief Joseph and his brother, Alokut, represented the Nez Perce, while General Oliver O. Howard represented the US government. The final understanding was that the nontreaty Indians would be on the designated reservations by June 14, 1877.

On June 15, 1877, word was received at Fort Lapwai, Idaho, that the Wallamwatkins had attacked and killed several settlers around Mount Idaho, Idaho. US Army troops were sent from Fort Lapwai to counterattack. On June 17, troops headed into Whitebird Canyon and engaged in a bitter encounter with the Wallamwatkins. The US Army lost thirty-four troops and numerous horses; the Nez Perce, numbering only seventy warriors, had only four wounded in the battle. On July 1, regular troops and Idaho volunteers under Captain Stephen C. Whipple attacked Looking Glass's village. The troops shot, destroyed property, and looted at random. As a result, Looking Glass joined the war effort with Chief Joseph.

RETREAT

By July 13, after numerous skirmishes with General Howard's troops and other soldiers, Chief Joseph led approximately four hundred of his people eastward toward the Lolo Trail in the Bitterroot Mountains. On July 15, Looking Glass urged escape to Montana and proposed joining with the Crow of the plains. Chief Joseph agreed, Looking Glass became supreme war leader, and on July 16, the nontreaty Nez Perces summarily left their homeland.

Chief Joseph and Looking Glass kept track of Howard's position and were able to stall and otherwise frustrate Howard's advance. As a result, the chiefs led the Wallamwatkins through Lolo Trail and into the Missoula area. General Howard subsequently contacted Colonel John Gibbon at Fort Shaw, Montana, and instructed him to take up the pursuit. Gibbon was able to muster 146 men of the Seventh Infantry and thirty-four civilians.

Chief Joseph and Looking Glass crossed the Continental Divide and encamped their weary followers in the Big Hole Valley, unaware of Colonel Gibbon's pursuit and position. On August 9, Colonel Gibbon's troops made a surprise attack on the Wallamwatkins' camp and engaged in a long and difficult battle. Many Nez Perce lives—mostly of women and children—were lost in the initial confrontation. Chief Joseph and White Bird outflanked Gibbon's troops and led the families to safety, while the warriors under Alokut and Looking Glass split Gibbon's forces. After holding the Army in siege for several days, the warriors eventually broke off the engagement, and the Nez Perce continued their retreat through the Montana territory.

THE BEAR PAWS BATTLE

By August 27, Chief Joseph had led the Wallamwatkins into Yellowstone Park, with General Howard and his troops in continuing pursuit. By September 6, Chief Joseph and Looking Glass had made their retreat through the northeast corner of Yellowstone Park. Continuing north, Chief Joseph led his people up through the Snowy Mountains and finally into the northern foothills of the Bear Paw Mountains, an easy day's ride from the Canadian border. Unknown to Chief Joseph, Colonel Nelson A. Miles had been notified by General Howard and was in pursuit from Fort Keogh paralleling Chief Joseph's trail from the north. On September 30, Colonel Miles's troops made a surprise attack on the Wallamwatkins' camp. The fighting during the Bear Paws Battle was intense. The army lost fifty-three men and the Nez Perce lost eighteen warriors, including Alokut, Tulhulhutsut, and Poker Joe. On the night of October 4, General Howard rode into Miles's camp and provided the reinforcements that would ensure a final surrender from Chief Joseph. On October 5, General Howard sent terms of surrender to the Nez Perce. A brief skirmish evolved, and Looking Glass was fired on and killed. Colonel Miles assured Chief Joseph that he and his tribe would be allowed to return home to the Northwest in peace. Feeling that he could do so with honor, Chief Joseph offered one of the most famous surrendering speeches ever documented. Turning to the interpreter, Chief Joseph said:

Tell General Howard I know what is in his heart. What he told me before, I have in my heart. I am tired of fighting. Our chiefs are killed. Looking Glass is dead. Tulhulhutsut is dead. The old men are all dead. It is the young men who say yes or no. He [Alokut] who led on the young men is dead. My people, some of them, have run away to the hills and have no blankets, no food; no one knows where they are—perhaps freezing to death. I want to have time to look for my children and see how many of them I can find. Maybe I shall find them among the dead. Hear me, my chiefs. I am tired; my heart is sick and sad. From where the sun now stands I will fight no more, forever.

Thus ended the Nez Perce War, one of the most remarkable American Indian war campaigns of US history.

EXILE

Chief Joseph surrendered with 86 men, 148 women and 147 children. The Nez Perces were transported to Fort Keogh for temporary holding. On November 1, despite Colonel Miles's assurances that the tribe would be allowed to return to the Northwest, he was ordered to take his prisoners farther south, to Fort Lincoln, near Bismarck, North Dakota. On November 27, Chief Joseph and his people were moved again (by train) to Fort Leavenworth, Kansas. Kept in unsanitary conditions, plagued by disease and twenty deaths, in July 1878, Chief Joseph and his people were again moved to the Quapaw Reservation in Kansas territory. By the end of the year, nearly fifty more tribe members had died from disease.

After repeated requests to return to the Northwest, in 1885, eight years after their surrender, the 268 survivors of the nontreaty bands taken into captivity were allowed to return to the Northwest. About half of them were housed at Lapwai, Idaho, and Chief Joseph's Wallowa band was housed at Nespelem on the Colville Reservation in eastern Washington. From the time of his return to the Northwest until his death, September 21, 1904, Chief Joseph attempted in vain to gain permission to return his people to his homeland in the Wallowa Valley in eastern Oregon.

——*John L. Farbo*

BIBLIOGRAPHY AND FURTHER READING

Beal, Merrill D. *I Will Fight No More Forever: Chief Joseph and the Nez Perce War.* Seattle: U of Washington P, 1963. Print.

Carson, Kevin. *The Long Journey of the Nez Perce: A Battle History from Cottonwood to the Bear Paw.* Yardley: Westholme, 2011. Print.

Gidley, Mick. *Kopet: A Documentary Narrative of Chief Joseph's Last Years.* Seattle: U of Washington P, 1981. Print.

Tonkovich, Nicole. *The Allotment Plot: Alice C. Fletcher, E. Jane Gay, and Nez Perce Survivance.* Lincoln: U of Nebraska P, 2012. Print.

NIAGARA MOVEMENT

In the early years of the twentieth century, two major approaches to achieving African American progress were separated by their differing philosophies: Booker T. Washington was a pragmatist who acknowledged current policies toward blacks and wanted to make the lives of African Americans as easy as possible within that framework. Washington held that "it is important and right that all privileges of law be ours, but it is vastly more important that we be prepared for the exercise of those privileges." He assumed that as African Americans became productive workers who were not troublemakers, they would be seen as valuable assets to US society. Then they would slowly but surely move up the economic and political ladder.

BEGINNINGS

The leaders of what came to be known as the Niagara Movement, by contrast, asserted that Washington's programs would keep African Americans at the bottom of the political, economic, and social ladder. One of the Niagara Movement's major leaders was W. E. B. Du Bois, a professor at Atlanta University at the beginning of the movement. Du Bois maintained that it was important for African Americans to press for the immediate implementation of their civil rights: "We want full manhood suffrage and we want it now. . . . We want the Constitution of the country enforced. . . . We want our children educated. . . . And we shall win!" The leaders of the Niagara Movement were convinced that as long as African Americans were not protected by law, economic and social advances would never come. They believed that the structures of United States society were developed in such a way that, without the force of law, other advances would never occur. These two different views of how to achieve progress for African Americans not only separated Washington and Du Bois throughout their lives but would remain at the heart of discord over how best to achieve freedom and progress for African Americans in the United States.

The Niagara Movement was formed on July 11, 1905, when twenty-nine radical African American intellectuals, headed by Du Bois, met at Niagara Falls, in Ontario, Canada. (Even though some organizational activities were held in Buffalo, New York,

on the other side of the US-Canadian border, most meetings were held in Canada because of the difficulty of finding places in the United States that would accommodate African Americans.) On nearly every issue, the Niagara Movement stood in direct contrast to Washington's approach. In sharp language, in a policy statement entitled the Negro Declaration of Independence, movement leaders placed full responsibility for the race problem on whites, denouncing the inequities of segregation and disfranchisement laws; they maintained that economic progress was not possible in a democratic society without the protection afforded by the ballot; and they insisted, above all, that African Americans could gain their rights only by agitation. Members of the Niagara Movement spoke out against an accommodationist approach at a time when almost all white and African American leaders believed that such policies were critical if blacks were to achieve equality in US society and politics.

About five years after it had been established, the Niagara Movement had approximately four hundred members. Most were Northern, urban, upper-class college graduates. The movement never developed the wide following it wanted. Some assert that the movement did not reach a broad enough spectrum in the African American community, let alone create an appeal to the broader society of which it was part. At first women were excluded from the Niagara Movement, both as members and as a focus of emancipation. Some of the movement's organizers reasoned that fighting for women's rights along with rights for African American males would result in defeat of the movement's policies and goals. Du Bois, however, argued that African American civil rights would not be complete without women as well as men tasting the fruits of freedom. He argued that to obtain male suffrage on the backs of women was immoral and not in keeping with the solidarity that African Americans must maintain in the face of the hostility of the dominant white society. Du Bois's position finally prevailed.

THE NAACP

During its existence, the Niagara Movement held conferences in 1906, at Harpers Ferry, West Virginia; in 1907, at Boston, Massachusetts; and in 1908, at

Oberlin, Ohio. Civil rights protests in cities across the nation were organized by the Niagara Movement, which gained a reputation for demanding recognition of the equality of all human beings through social protest and demonstrations. In the wake of a race riot in Springfield, Illinois, in 1908, the movement began to dissolve as members turned their attention to a new organization. On February 12, 1909, the ideas on which the Niagara Movement was founded were absorbed into the framework of the National Association for the Advancement of Colored People (NAACP), which not only developed a wider following but also addressed the broader issues of equality and civil rights that the Niagara Movement was not able to address effectively. Important members of the Niagara Movement, such as Du Bois, became instrumental in the NAACP as well. Du Bois, however, decided that even the NAACP was not forceful enough in addressing issues such as lynching, rape, and voting rights. He would end his life in exile in Africa.

Although the Niagara Movement survived only five years—formally disbanding in 1910—it had served as the foundation upon which later movements were built. It can be seen as both a negative reaction to Washington's accommodationist approach to African American equality and the progenitor of such later groups as the Student Nonviolent Coordinating Committee (SNCC), the Congress of Racial Equality (CORE), and the Black Panthers.

——*Paul Barton-Kriese*

BIBLIOGRAPHY AND FURTHER READING

Burns, W. Haywood. *The Voices of Negro Protest in America.* Westport: Greenwood, 1980. Print.

Christensen, Stephanie. "Niagara Movement (1905–1909)." *BlackPast.org.* BlackPast.org, 2015. Web. 14 May. 2015.

Jones, Angela. *African American Civil Rights: Early Activism and the Niagara Movement.* Santa Barbara: Praeger, 2011. Print.

Niagara Movement: Black Protest Reborn. Washington, DC: Assn. for the Study of African-American Life and History, 2005. Print.

Wormser, Richard. "Niagara Movement (1905–10)." *The Rise and Fall of Jim Crow.* WGBH, PBS, 2002. Web. 14 May. 2015.

NISGA'A AGREEMENT IN PRINCIPLE

The Nisga'a Agreement in Principle, published in February, 1996, attempted to lead to the "full and final settlement of Nisga'a aboriginal title, rights, and interests." This agreement, dealing with an aboriginal group from the Pacific coast of Canada, covered many areas, including land and reserves, access to the land, fisheries, wildlife, environmental assessment and protection, Nisga'a government, fiscal matters including taxation, and cultural heritage protection.

Under the agreement, the Nisga'a were defined as an aboriginal people under the constitution with all the charter rights, benefits, and obligations of other Canadians; they did not by this agreement acquire any special rights or privileges. The criminal code of Canada continued to govern them, and they continued to pay taxes. In time, the tax-exempt status for Nisga'a citizens was to be eliminated as the Nisga'a began to assume more power for taxation.

The agreement stipulated that the Nisga'a govern themselves in a democratic manner with four village governments and an overall Nisga'a government with its own constitution. This government was empowered to make laws governing cultural, linguistic, social, educational, vocational, environmental, and related matters. In addition, this government, with provincial approval, administered justice through provision of police services and a Nisga'a court with jurisdiction over its own lands. The agreement made the Nisga'a the owners of about nineteen hundred square kilometers of land in the area of the lower Nass River, including the four villages of New Aiyansh, Canyon City, Greenville, and Kincolith. These lands, however, were to remain accessible to the general public for recreation, hunting, and fishing. All existing legal interests on the lands were to be maintained, and the roads in them were to be governed and maintained by the province.

The agreement stipulated that a financial transfer of $190 million, in addition to $11.5 million for the purchase of commercial fishing vessels and licenses, was to be paid over a period of years. The Nisga'a would receive an annual quota of salmon and other fish to be caught and were expected to conserve the stocks. Overall management was shared between the Nisga'a and the federal and provincial governments. The Nisga'a received permission to hunt wildlife subject to existing restrictions and laws of conservation. The Nisga'a were made responsible for overall environmental protection and were required to meet or exceed existing federal and provincial requirements.

The agreement was finalized through the Nisga'a Final Agreement, which was approved and ratified in 2000. The formation of the Nisga'a Lisims Government ended the jurisdiction of the Indian Act over the Nisga'a people.

—Gregory Walters

BIBLIOGRAPHY AND FURTHER READING

"About: Accomplishments and Benefits of Nisga'a Treaty." *Nisga'a Lisims Government.* Nisga'a Lisims Government, 2015. Web. 14 May. 2015.

Foster, Hamar. "The Nisga'a Agreement in Principle." *Torch* 15.2 (1996): n.p. *U of Victoria.* Web. 14 May. 2015.

"History of the Negotiations with the Nisga'a Tribunal Council." *Aboriginal Affairs and Northern Development Canada.* Government of Canada, 15 Sept. 2010.

Web. 14 May. 2015. Ponting, J. Rick. *The Nisga'a Treaty: Polling Dynamics and Political Communication in Comparative Context.* Peterborough: Broadview, 2006. Print.

Wood, Chris. "Nisga'a Land Treaty." *Canadian Encyclopedia.* Historica Canada, 16 Dec. 2013. Web. 14 May. 2015.

9/11 ATTACKS AND RACIAL/ETHNIC RELATIONS

Racial and ethnic relations in the United States reflect what has been termed the "racializing actions" and structures that shaped the nation and the course of its racial history from the very beginning. Racializing actions are those that precipitate the establishment of laws, policies, and structures that target those who are considered the "other." The other—those who are deemed strange, hostile, or inferior—require surveillance, containment, repression, segregation, expulsion, or exclusion. The establishment of European settlements by driving the natives out of their lands and the importation of African slaves to work on plantations were the foundational racializing actions in US history, which still play out in the nation's social and political life. The racializing actions that followed include wars for territorial expansion, codification of slavery, and denial of citizenship to people of non-European origin, laws that stopped or suspended immigration from China, and South Asia, and the internment of the Japanese during World War II. Prejudice and discrimination toward a particular minority group changes in intensity and texture in response to a particular racializing event that might occur periodically such as a terroristic act (except white or Christian terrorism that rarely gets named as a terrorist act), war, illegal immigration, or economic threats.

9/11 AS RACIALIZING EVENT

The horrific terroristic acts committed by young Muslim men from the Middle East on September 11, 2001, destroying the Twin Towers in New York along with approximately 3,000 lives, followed by the prolonged global war that the United States launched in response, constituted the major racializing events at the start of the twenty-first century. Those events radically and abruptly changed racial and ethnic relations within the United States and Europe, impacting not only Muslims but also brown people from the Middle East and South Asia. Groups that look like Muslims, such as the Sikhs, also became victims of racial hate.

The massive military response of Western nations to the events of September 11, 2001, led by the United States, resulting in the invasion of

Afghanistan and Iraq, accentuated and threw into sharp relief the racializing impact of those events in unforeseen ways. The unending and universal war on terror declared by the United States immediately after September 11, 2001, quickly expanded to include many more countries of Asia and Africa, leading to the toppling of the government of Libya, the fomenting of a prolonged and horrific civil war in Syria and Yemen, and the destabilization of Pakistan. Added to these actions is the sharpening of the hostility toward Iran, a country that is accused of supporting terrorism and pursuing nuclear weapons. Because the targeted countries are Muslim-majority countries, Muslims in the United States are viewed with suspicion, causing strained relationships between them and the mainstream groups. Disparaging cartoons of Muhammad were published in Sweden and France, under the pretext of defending and celebrating the freedoms the Western world enjoys.

During the 2016 US presidential campaign, anti-Muslim rhetoric reached a high pitch and after the election the new president imposed travel bans against persons from seven predominantly Muslim countries located in the Middle East and Africa. Thus, the end result of 9/11 and its aftermath has been an exacerbation of the perception that Muslims are led by an ideology of violence and hate and, therefore, are to be closely watched or excluded.

This perception ignores the fact that, except for the commonality of their religious identity, Muslims in the United States are a very heterogeneous group racially, ethnically, and politically. Not all of them hail from the Middle East, North Africa, or South Asia. Approximately a third of the Muslim population in the United States is comprised of African Americans who converted to Islam. Others come from as many as seventy-seven different countries, including the countries of Europe. Racially, they identify themselves very differently as White, Black, Hispanic, Asian or Mixed. Despite their high social visibility due to the negative attention they receive, they comprise just about 1 percent of the total US population. Approximately 70 percent of them are US citizens, either by birth or through naturalization. Easily forgotten too is the fact that nearly 60 percent of the immigrants from the Middle East are Christians, despite the general tendency to equate people of Middle Eastern descent with Muslims.

Worthy of note as well is the fact that the media portrayals and public discourse around 9/11 generally ignore the historical and political contexts by posing the seemingly innocent question, "Why do they hate us?" By framing 9/11 as an act of hate against the freedom, culture, and lifestyle of the Christian democratic West and the United States, the media have effectively transformed a politically motivated crime into a racializing event, an attack by the uncivilized world on the civilized world.

9/11 AND REACTION

Immediately after September 11, 2001, the US government targeted Muslims within the United States regardless of their citizenship status for racializing actions. Those actions included interrogation of large numbers of Arabs and Muslims, arrests and indefinite detention of some, deportation of thousands of Muslims on any legal ground that was available, and fingerprinting and registration procedures targeting people from selected countries. All such measures led to the stigmatization of Muslims as a dangerous and hostile group. Those actions and the continuous media coverage flashing horrifying images of the terrorist attacks, which lasted for weeks following September 11, created an atmosphere that helped deepen Islamophobia.

The speeches of the US President following the 9/11 terrorist attacks drew sharp contrasts between the civilized and uncivilized, "us and them," *our* freedom and *their* oppressive culture, and our civility and their barbarity, lending credence to the perception that Muslims everywhere were a dangerous and backward people. Intellectual discourse located the root cause of terrorism in a clash of civilizations. Academics and pundits contributed to this narrative by revisiting the thesis, advanced by Samuel Huntington, a Harvard professor, nearly a decade earlier, that there has been and continues to be a clash of civilizations at play, affirming his conclusion that Western and non-Western civilizations are fundamentally irreconcilable. This kind of narrative trope foreclosed the possibility of dialogue and reconciliation in the aftermath of the tragedy.

Following 9/11, many Muslims have suffered serious personal harm from being stigmatized as potential terrorists, from being 'otherized' for having a Muslim-sounding name, for speaking a Middle Eastern language, or for wearing a hijab or head cover. People of Middle Eastern and South Asian origin have been subjected to racial profiling by the aviation industry and the federal transportation security personnel—the phenomenon has been described as "flying while brown." Passengers continue to be "selected" for heightened screening, subjected to degrading, hostile, and humiliating interrogation practices prior to boarding, or being removed from the aircraft in front of other passengers for interrogation and detention without due process for no reason other than that they fit a particular profile. Numerous Muslims report suffering discrimination in employment, housing, and education due to their religion. Surveys show that the majority of Americans support racial profiling for people of Arab or South Asian descent, indicating the strained racial and ethnic relations in the nation. Another indication that September 11 and its aftermath have caused harm to individuals and communities is a spike in hate crimes against Muslims and people who are mistaken for Muslims.

The psychological impact of the negative societal and official reactions on Arabs and South Asians are not yet fully recognized. There is evidence to believe that these communities have become more inward-looking as they turn to each other for support. The long-term impact of this isolation is unknown. One measure of this isolation may be how Arabs now self-identify racially. In the US Census people of North African and Middles Eastern origins are officially classified as white despite the wide variation in their skin color.

Such classification occurred due to the historical fact that at one time only whites were eligible to be citizens (other than freed slaves), and therefore Syrians, the first immigrants from the Middle East, argued that they were white because they were Christians. A series of court cases that include *George Dow v. United States* established that Syrians were white. Racial identification of a population as white is a measure of that group's acceptance and acculturation into the US culture. Interestingly, researchers have pointed out that after September 11 there has been a tendency for people from the Middles East not to self-identify as white, indicating their alienation and feeling of isolation. One might also interpret this tendency broadly as reflective of a growing social distance between the brown and the rest. In the aftermath of September 11, that is, the color of terror has become brown.

——*Mathew Kanjirathinkal*

BIBLIOGRAPHY AND FURTHER READING

Collet, Tanja. "Civilization and Civilized in post-9/11 US Presidential Speeches." *Discourse and Society* 20 (4), 2009, pp. 456–475.

Jamal, Amaney, and Nadine Naber, eds. *Race and Arab Americans Before and After 9/11: From Invisible Citizens to Visible Subjects.* Syracuse: Syracuse UP, 2008.

Khan, Mussarat, and Kathryn Ecklund. "Attitude Towards Muslim Americans Post 9/11." *Journal of Muslim Mental Health,* 7 (1), 2012, 1-16.

Morey, Peter, and Amina Yaqin. *Framing Muslims.* Cambride, MA: Havard UP, 2011.

Peek, Lori. *Behind the Backlash: Muslim Americans After 9/11.* Philadelphia: Temple UP, 2011.

NIXON V. HERNDON

In 1921, the US Supreme Court ruled in *Newberry v. United States* that Congress lacked authority to regulate primary elections. Southern state legislatures immediately took advantage of this decision to prohibit black participation in state primary elections. "White primaries" were quickly adopted throughout the South.

Texas, during the first half of the twentieth entury, was part of the Democrat-dominated South. The only competition that mattered was within the Democratic Party, so if blacks were not allowed to participate in the Democratic primary they would effectively be denied any meaningful choice in the electoral process.

In 1924, the Texas legislature passed a law barring blacks from voting in the Democratic primary. L. A. Nixon, a black resident of El Paso, attempted to vote in the primary and was refused by Herndon, an election judge. Nixon and the National Association for the Advancement of Colored People (NAACP) claimed that the Texas law violated the Fourteenth and Fifteenth Amendments. The Supreme Court did not deal with the issue of the Fifteenth Amendment, but a unanimous Court found that the Texas white primary law violated the equal protection clause of the Fourteenth Amendment.

The NAACP won the battle but temporarily lost the war. Texas responded to the Court's decision by engaging in the strategy of "legislate and litigate." By passing a different white primary law after their defeat in *Nixon v. Herndon*, the Texas legislature forced the NAACP to institute another attack on the white primary. When the second law was declared unconstitutional in *Nixon v. Condon* in 1932, Texas came up with a third variation of the white primary. This time, in *Grovey v. Townsend* (1935), the US Supreme Court upheld the Texas white primary, arguing that no state discrimination was present. According to the Court, the Texas Democratic Party, a private voluntary association, decided to exclude blacks from voting in the primary elections. It was not until *Smith v. Allwright* (1944) that a unanimous Supreme Court declared that the Fifteenth Amendment could be used as a shield to protect the right to vote in primary elections.

From the passage of the first white primary law in 1924 until the final abolition of white primaries in the *Smith* case in 1944, blacks were denied the right to vote in Democratic Party primaries, the only election of significance at that time. The white primary cases illustrate one of the dilemmas in using the federal courts—the fact that justice delayed is justice denied.

————*Darryl Paulson*

NONVIOLENT RESISTANCE (RACIAL RELATIONS)

Although the term "nonviolent resistance" is a twentieth-century concept based on analysis of the strategies and conditions necessary for successful nonviolent action, its practice is deeply rooted in United States history. Religious groups from Europe such as the Amish and the Society of Friends (Quakers), who practiced a literal understanding of Jesus's teachings forbidding the use of violence, fled to North America to escape persecution. Their continued witness to principles of pacifism has influenced a tradition and philosophy of nonviolent protest. Additionally, the early colonists engaged in nonviolent resistance against British rule. In 1766, Britain passed an import tax, the Stamp Act. American merchants organized a boycott of goods, causing the repeal of the act. This action marked the first organized resistance to British rule and led to the establishment of the First Continental Congress in 1774. The legal basis for nonviolent action was established in the First Amendment to the Constitution, which protects the rights of persons to "freedom of speech," peaceful assembly, and petitioning the government "for a redress of grievances." The United States has a long history of expression of such rights.

VARIOUS APPLICATIONS

In 1845, Henry David Thoreau was jailed for refusing to pay a poll tax in protest of the Mexican-American War. In his essay "Civil Disobedience," Thoreau proclaimed the moral necessity of resistance in the face of immoral government action. Nonviolent protest has accompanied every war in which the United States has engaged, and it was so widespread during the Vietnam War that it became a central reason the United States withdrew from Vietnam in 1974. Nonviolent protest has also been central to various movements seeking to ban and limit nuclear weapons and in war tax resistance movements, in which members refuse to pay taxes to support the military budget. Strategies of nonviolent resistance were also employed by the women's rights movement, which culminated in the right to vote (1920) and in greater social and economic equality for women. The labor movement has used nonviolent tactics in the form of strikes, labor slowdowns, and boycotts to force improvement of working conditions and income. Despite strong, often violent responses by corporate owners, the Wagner Act, passed by Congress in 1935, recognized the legal right of workers to organize and use such methods. César Chávez effectively used consumer boycotts in the 1970s and 1980s to win better conditions for farmworkers. Nonviolent strategies have been used by environmental groups to block construction of nuclear power plants, stop the cutting of forests, or alter policies considered to be ecologically hazardous. They have also been employed since the 1980s by antiabortion groups attempting to close abortion clinics.

RACE RELATIONS

The most prolonged, successful use of nonviolent resistance, however, came in the Civil Rights movement led by Martin Luther King, Jr., in the 1950s and 1960s. Drawing on the work of Mahatma (Mohandas) Gandhi, the movement used marches, sit-ins, and boycotts to force an end to legal racial segregation in the South and informal (de facto) segregation in the North. This campaign demonstrated the ambiguity of governmental response to such tactics. Often participants were arrested and convicted under local statutes, only to have such laws ruled invalid by higher courts; this occurred during the Montgomery bus boycott. On the other hand, King and his followers were under constant surveillance by the Federal Bureau of Investigation and were considered threats to political stability by many government officials. The debate has also focused on what constitutes "freedom of expression" and "peaceful assembly." The "plowshares eight," in 1980, protesting nuclear weapons, entered a General Electric plant in Pennsylvania and dented the nose cone of a warhead. They were sentenced to prison on grounds of trespass and destruction of private property.

The use of nonviolent resistance has continued to flourish in the 21st century. On February 26, 2012, a man named George Zimmerman fatally shot an unarmed seventeen-year-old named Trayvon Martin. On July 13, 2013, a jury acquitted Zimmerman of second-degree murder. In the aftermath of the acquittal, the hashtag #BlackLivesMatter first appeared and began trending on Twitter. The

BLM movement has since grown significantly and often spearheads non-violent demonstrations, particularly after police shootings of unarmed African Americans. Despite the the nonviolent stance of the movement, critics, particularly some white critics, sometimes accuse Black Lives Matter of advocating violence. Similar sentiments were voiced about the nonviolent movements of the 1960s.

Say Her Name is a nonviolent movement that spreads awareness of police and anti-black violence against African American women. Indeed, the string of police killings of unarmed African American citizens has sparked individuals not affiliated with any activist organization into action. Nonviolent demonstrations of all sorts have been taken up, including "die-ins," in which demonstrators lie down feigning death en masse. Sometimes, nonviolent resistance comes in the form of celebrities shining a light on issues dear to them. Beyonce's music videos *Lemonade* and *Formation* both bring attention to the plight of African Americans. Colin Kaepernick, a quarterback for the San Francisco 49ers, began a practice of kneeling during the singing of the National Anthem at sports events to protest injustices committed against the African American community.

Nonviolent resistance's relationship with race expands beyond African Americans. Latinos and others have employed nonviolent resistance to combat the inhumane treatment of undocumented immigrants. Native Americans have spearheaded nonviolent resistance at such places as the Dakota Access Pipeline, which infringes on their water rights and sacred spaces. (The US Army Corps of Engineers refused to grant an easement that the pipeline needed to advance construction. However, shortly after taking office, President Donald Trump signed an executive order advancing the pipeline.)

THEORY AND STRATEGY

Nonviolent resistance has two distinct traditions. The religious tradition centers on the moral claim that it is always wrong to harm another and that only love of the "enemy" can transform persons and societies. Violence and hatred cannot solve social problems or end social conflict, for each act of violence generates new resentments. This spiral of violence can be ended only if some group absorbs the violence and returns only nonviolence and love. Central to this vision is a commitment to justice that requires adherents to engage injustice actively wherever they find it.

The political tradition focuses on strategies for organizing political and social power to force another, usually a political authority, to change policies. As Gene Sharp, a leading analyst, notes, government requires the consent of its citizens. In nonviolent resistance, dissenters organize forms of power including economic power, labor power, and the power of public opinion in order to undermine consent and force authorities to change policies.

The use of these theories and techniques remains important in stable, democratic societies as a way of resolving conflict, generating social change, and challenging power structures, especially on behalf of the powerless, whose rights are often ignored. Without the legal sanctions which permit such protest, the only recourse becomes open societal violence and conflict, even to the point of civil war.

——*Charles L. Kammer, updated by Anthony Vivian*

BIBLIOGRAPHY AND FURTHER READING

Ackerman, Peter, and Jack Duvall. *A Force More Powerful: A Century of Non-Violent Conflict.* New York: St. Martin's, 2001. Print.

Barash, David P., and Charles P. Webel. *Peace and Conflict Studies,* 3d ed. Thousand Oaks: Sage, 2013. Print.

King, Martin Luther, Jr. *A Testament of Hope: The Essential Writings and Speeches of Martin Luther King, Jr.* Ed. James M. Washington. San Francisco: Harper, 1991. Print.

May, Todd. *Nonviolent Resistance: A Philosophical Introduction.* Malden: Polity, 2015. Print.

Sharp, Gene. *How Nonviolent Struggle Works.* Boston: Albert Einstein Institute, 2013. Print.

NORDIC "RACE"

This term was one of three pseudo-racial categories employed beginning in the late nineteenth century to classify the population of Europe; the other categories were Alpine and Mediterranean. Nordic people were thought to come from northern Europe, especially Scandinavia. Physically, the Nordic race was characterized as tall, often blond, blue-eyed, and dolichocephalic (having a comparatively long head). Members of the Nordic race were reputed to be superior, naturally individualistic, self-reliant, freedom-loving, and gifted in terms of state organization.

The use of the concept of the Nordic race was popular during the 1920's when "scientific" theories of race were propounded to explain the development of civilization. Significant achievements of humankind were traced to members of the Nordic race. These racist theories were associated with exclusionary immigration and antimiscegenation laws in the United States. Nazi Germany also used this rationale to support its race-cleansing policies.

As Thomas F. Gossett points out in *Race: The History of an Idea in America* (1963), the argument that the important elements of Western civilization are due in large measure to the Nordic race is closely related to earlier racist theories of Aryan and Teutonic origins. According to the latter view, Anglo-Saxons were primarily responsible for the development of democratic institutions, from the town-hall meeting to national systems of representative government.

——*Gary A. Cretser*

BIBLIOGRAPHY AND FURTHER READING

Baum, Bruce. "Racialized Nationalism and the Partial Eclipse of the 'Caucasian Race,' ca. 1840–1935." *The Rise and Fall of the Caucasian Race: A Political History of Racial Identity.* New York: New York UP, 2006. 118–61. Print.

Brøndal, Jørn. "'The Fairest among the So-Called White Races': Portrayals of Scandinavian Americans in the Filiopietistic and Nativist Literature of the Late Nineteenth and Early Twentieth Centuries." *Journal of American Ethnic History* 33.3 (2014): 5–36. PDF file.

Jackson, John P., Jr., and Nadine M. Weidman. "The Hardening of Scientific Racism, 1900–1945."

Race, Racism, and Science: Social Impact and Interaction. Santa Barbara: ABC-CLIO, 2004. 97–128. Print.

Sussman, Robert Wald. *The Myth of Race: The Troubling Persistence of an Unscientific Idea.* Cambridge: Harvard UP, 2014. Print.

THE NORTH STAR

When the first issue of *The North Star* appeared on December 3, 1847, critics and readers discovered a newspaper that blended sardonic humor with moral urgency, written in a polished style. Some readers, however, were skeptical of editor Frederick Douglass's sophistication. Fathered by a white man and born to the slave Harriet Bailey in Talbot County, Maryland, Frederick Bailey had worked in bondage as a slave for Thomas Auld, witnessing the horrors of slavery, the brutal beatings, and even murder. In his teens, he had taught himself to read and write from a discarded speller and copybook, and learned public speaking by imitating orations appearing in *The Columbian Orator*, an abolitionist publication. *The Columbian Orator* led to his awareness of the abolitionist movement and influenced his writing style when he later published *The North Star*. Clashing with his master in 1838, Frederick escaped from Baltimore to New York with Anna Murray, a free African American domestic servant. Once married, they settled in New Bedford, Massachusetts, which offered sanctuary. To prevent recapture, Frederick changed his surname to Douglass, in honor of a character in Sir Walter Scott's poem *Lady of the Lake*.

DOUGLASS AND GARRISON

Douglass became active in local abolitionist gatherings, discovering his gift as a compelling speaker who provided firsthand examples of barbaric slavery. He became a favorite on the lecture circuit during the early 1840s; his autobiography, *Narrative of the Life of Frederick Douglass* (1845), sold more than thirty thousand copies over the next five years. Douglass came under the tutelage of the leading abolitionist of the times, a white man named William Lloyd Garrison. From Garrison's abolitionist newspaper, *The Liberator*, Douglass no doubt learned much about newspaper operations.

As Douglass's fame increased, so did his risk of capture as an escaped slave. In 1845, he sailed for England, then on to Scotland and Ireland, where he passionately lectured on the inhumane treatment of slaves. His newfound friends, moved by his personal plight, arranged to purchase Douglass's freedom for $711.66. Before returning to the United States in 1847, he also received $2,175 to bankroll his own antislavery newspaper.

When Garrison objected to Douglass's projected newspaper, the two close friends became estranged, then bitter enemies. Douglass believed that the white abolitionists thought him a child to be led. African Americans, he insisted, must lead to gain respect. He held that his newspaper could create that leadership and help increase self-respect among African Americans. Douglass knew of the hazards in starting an African American newspaper, because about one hundred such papers already existed in the United States, the first having been started in 1827. He located in Rochester, New York, because of the area's strong antislavery sentiments and because publishing there reduced the competition with *The Liberator* in Boston and the *National Anti-Slavery Standard* in New York City.

On December 3, 1847, the first issue of *The North Star* appeared—a four-page weekly with a subscription cost of two dollars per year, circulation of two to three thousand, and publishing costs of eighty dollars per week at the first print shop owned by an African American. Douglass chose journalist Martin Delaney as coeditor, but the two soon clashed over the issue of "colonization," by which freed slaves would seek a separate homeland in Africa rather than integrate within the United States white society. When a disgusted Delaney left in 1848 to found a colony in the Niger Valley, in Africa, Douglass became sole editor, vigorously espousing the principles of integration, as he did throughout his life.

June 2, 1848 issue. By Frederick Douglass.

ADVOCACY FOR ALL

In the first issue of *The North Star*, Douglass urged African Americans to become politically active and pledged that his newspaper would aggressively attack slavery, work to free Southern slaves, and promote African American morality and progress. The lead article recounted the convention of "colored people" of 1847, with its primary objectives of abolishing slavery and elevating free African Americans. In subsequent years, *The North Star* dealt with a plethora of burning issues: injustice, inequality, racism, the avoidance of drink and dissipation, the benefits of integrated school systems, the elimination of segregated hotels and railroads, the folly of war and capital punishment, the worth of laborers, the imperative need for racial unity among African Americans, and the unfair voting practices leveled against African Americans in northern states. *The North Star* came to the defense not only of persecuted African Americans but also of American Indians, the Irish, and other immigrant groups.

From its beginnings, *The North Star* lived up to its masthead: "Right Is Of No Sex—Truth Is Of No Color—God Is The Father Of Us All, and All We Are Brethren." Douglass vigorously supported the women's rights movement, linking enslaved women to the abolition movement itself. At the Seneca Falls Convention in 1848, Douglass was the only one of the thirty-two men attending to speak and vote in favor of Elizabeth Cady Stanton's Declaration of Sentiments, which demanded equality for women. He effectively used *The North Star* to promote Stanton's feminist cause.

SUBSEQUENT PAPERS

Financially, *The North Star* foundered after six months. Douglass mortgaged his house and used his lecture fees to keep the paper going. From time to time, he received financial gifts from Gerrit Smith, a philanthropist, reformer, and wealthy New York landowner. In 1851, the two men agreed to merge the financially troubled *North Star* with Smith's struggling *Liberty Party Paper*. Douglass maintained editorial control over the paper while including political news of the Liberty Party; he broadened his readership to four thousand; and he accepted a comfortable subsidy from Smith. The new effort, *Frederick Douglass' Paper*, appeared in June, 1851, and lasted until 1859. The paper continued Douglass's efforts in regard to

abolition, equality, and women's rights. Douglass also dabbled in the Liberty Party campaigns, endorsing Smith and helping him win a seat in Congress. In 1852, Douglass himself became the first African American nominated for vice president on the Equal Rights Party ticket of 1852.

Recurring financial problems forced Douglass to reduce the size and frequency of his paper in 1859. His third effort, *Douglass' Monthly*, circulating in England as well as in the United States, lasted until the middle of the Civil War, 1863. Like the other two papers, *Douglass' Monthly* remained a magnet for African American writers and reformers and framed Douglass's own inimitable style and wit as well. He actively recruited African American soldiers for the war. He viewed Abraham Lincoln as the best hope for his race, pressing for the Emancipation Proclamation that Lincoln delivered in 1863. He proposed land reform, federally financed education, and a national association for African Americans. He believed that interracial marriages would someday eliminate racial hatred.

After the Civil War, Douglass moved to Washington, DC. There he published the *New National Era*, focusing on the interests of the newly freed African Americans. During that paper's existence (1870–1873), Douglass editorialized on Reconstruction, the rise of mob lynchings in the South, race relations, politics, labor, and education. From 1873 until his death in 1895, Douglass continued to be heard on the lecture circuit and in leading newspapers. A self-made man, rising against great odds from slavery to publisher, race leader, prominent abolitionist, social reformer, and political activist, Douglass is one of the most important African Americans of the nineteenth century and became a powerful symbol in the Civil Rights movement throughout the twentieth century.

——*Richard Whitworth*

BIBLIOGRAPHY AND FURTHER READING

Douglass, Frederick. *The Frederick Douglass Papers*. Three series. New Haven: Yale UP, 1979–2012. Print.

Huggins, Nathan I., and Oscar Handlin. *Slave and Citizen: The Life of Frederick Douglass*. New York: Longman, 2001. Print.

Martin, Waldo E. *The Mind of Frederick Douglass*. Chapel Hill: U North Carolina P, 1984. Print.

Rogers, William B. *"We Are All Together Now": Frederick Douglass, William Lloyd Garrison, and the Prophetic Tradition.* New York: Garland, 1995. Print.

Voss, Frederick S. *Majestic in His Wrath: A Pictorial Life of Frederick Douglass.* Washington, DC: Smithsonian Inst., 1995. Print.

NORTHWEST ORDINANCE

By the Peace of Paris with Britain (1783), the United States acquired a vast inland empire bounded by the Appalachians, the Mississippi River, the Great Lakes, and the Gulf of Mexico. The task of disposing of this territory fell to the government as it was organized under the Articles of Confederation (1781-1789). Conflicting claims of states, settlers, land companies, and American Indians confused the issue. Lands south of the Ohio River were settled separately from those north of it. The Old Northwest, including the present-day states of Ohio, Indiana, Illinois, Michigan, and Wisconsin, was claimed by Virginia, Connecticut, and Massachusetts. Thomas Jefferson chaired a committee that in 1784 proposed to Congress the creation of a temporary government for the Northwest and the area's eventual division into sovereign states eligible to join the Confederation on terms equal to those enjoyed by the original members. Though the plan was not enacted, it did provide a model for the Northwest Ordinance and facilitated the cession of western lands by Virginia (in 1784), Massachusetts (1784-1785), and Connecticut (1784-1786) to the national government.

If state claims were resolved, those of Native Americans were refused. Under British rule, by the Proclamation of 1763, the entire West had been set aside as Indian Country, starting at the Appalachian Divide. The pressure for white settlement of the region had been a contributing cause of the American Revolution, a lesson the Confederation had learned. As settlers from New England, Pennsylvania, and the South pressed toward the Ohio Country, Indian claims were extinguished. By the Treaty of Fort Stanwix (1784) the Iroquois, exhausted by war, surrendered their claims to western New York and Pennsylvania. The next year, major Ohio tribes relinquished their claims to most of the future state, with the exception of the southwest shores of Lake Erie. Formal concession came within a decade in the Treaty of Fort Greenville (1795), when, for a ten-thousand-dollar annuity, twelve tribes relinquished the southwest portion of the Old Northwest (Ohio and Indiana).

Utilizing Jefferson's plan, the Congress of the Confederation (1787), even as the Constitutional Convention was meeting, established the Northwest Ordinance, by which those lands would be organized as a territory, with a nationally appointed governor, secretary, and judges. It stated that when five thousand free white males resided there, a bicameral legislature was to be created. Eventually three to five states were to be formed (with a minimum of sixty thousand free white inhabitants needed for statehood), each to be admitted to the United States and to be equal in standing to the original states. Freedom of religion, the right to jury trial, public support of education, and the prohibition of slavery were to prevail. While this legislation is traditionally regarded as the greatest achievement of the Confederation Congress, it set a tragic precedent by riding roughshod over the rights of Native Americans.

——C. George Fry

NUNAVUT TERRITORY

In 1993, the Nunavut Land Claims Agreement was signed with Canada's federal government. It stated that, on April 1, 1999, the Northwest Territories would be divided and the eastern region would become Nunavut Territory. "Nunavut" comes from the Inuit language Inuktitut and means "our land."

The Inuit have inhabited these lands for thousands of years, and they made up 80 percent of the population in the late 1990's. The Inuit have long desired a territory of their own, and the agreement gave the Inuit control over more than 350,000 square kilometers of land, mineral rights, and financial aid. This

Captive iceberg in Resolute Bay. By Arctichistorian01 (Own work).

agreement is designed to give the Inuit people control over their own education, health, social services, and many other provincial-type responsibilities.

The government of the territory is to be democratically elected to represent all residents of the territory: about twenty-two thousand people, seventeen thousand of whom are Inuit. The agreement placed the seat of government in Iqualuit and described the territory as containing twenty-eight villages or communities, including Iqualuit, which is located on Baffin Island.

——*Gregory Walters*

O

OBAMA, BARACK, FIRST AFRICAN-AMERICAN US PRESIDENT

Barack Hussein Obama, elected as America's forty-fourth president, was the first African-American to occupy the White House. Obama rode a wave of enthusiasm and hope in the 2008 election and offered voters an ambitious domestic and diplomatic agenda. The combination of his young age, promise, and optimism reminded many voters of John F. Kennedy and inspired the Nobel Committee to award him the Peace Prize in 2009. Obama had a penchant for public service from an early age and entered politics a few years after earning his J.D. from Harvard Law School. He won a seat in the Illinois state Senate in 1996, displaying, among other things, an interest in health-care reform that would stay with him until his presidency. After an unsuccessful run for the US House of Representatives in 2000, Obama ran for the US Senate in 2004 and won in a landslide over Alan Keyes, an African-American talk radio host and conservative political activist.

A Chicagoan by choice, Obama was born in Honolulu in 1961 to a white mother and a Kenyan father. Raised mostly by his maternal grandmother, he first encountered prejudice, despite his biracial heritage, while attending an elite nearly all-white preparatory school. Like many African-American youth, though under different circumstances, Barack grew up without the presence of a father, who left while his son was still an infant. It was an experience that influenced his development as a public figure and led to a certain kinship with inner-city African-Americans. Obama's emotional ties to the African-American community would reassure and encourage black voters eager for a president sympathetic to their needs and priorities, although he could at times be emotionally aloof and overly intellectual. His marriage to Michelle Robinson, a down-to-earth Chicago native and a formidable public servant herself, solidified his bona fides among African-Americans.

A powerful and skillful speaker, Obama captured the attention of American voters at the 2004 Democratic National Convention with a performance that many rank alongside Ted Kennedy's and Jesse Jackson's in 1980 and 1988 as the greatest convention speeches of the television era. His abilities as an orator served him well on the campaign trail in 2008 and 2012, attracting record numbers of African-American and young voters. In 2008, he had a tough fight in the primaries but ultimately prevailed over Hillary Clinton, who appeared out of touch with both constituencies. John McCain and Mitt Romney, the Republican nominees in the 2008 and 2102 general elections, had the same problem. Still, Obama was unable to silence some of his most fervent critics, who impugned him both as an American and a politician.

Opponents on the far right, who gained tacit support from hardliners in rural and southern states, made race an implied issue against Obama. So-called Birthers claimed that Obama had forged his birth certificate to hide his actual citizenship, which was reportedly Kenyan or Indonesian. Others, citing his name and supposed religious activities during his youth, accused him of being a closet Muslim. Obama's association with controversial pastor Jeremiah Wright and Michelle Obama's comment at a Milwaukee campaign rally that, for the first time in her life, she was proud to be an American convinced his political enemies that he harbored anti-American beliefs and could not be trusted as commander-in-chief. Evidence to the contrary never mollified those on the far right, but they did far more harm to themselves than to the President. During his two terms in office, race became decreasingly relevant, with many Americans viewing Obama not so much as the first

African-American president as a president that was also African-American.

———*Tomislav Han and Lori Cox Han*

BIBLIOGRAPHY AND FURTHER READING

D'Antonio, Michael. *A Consequential President: The Legacy of Barack Obama*. New York: St. Martin's Press, 2016.

Maraniss, David. *Barack Obama: The Story*. New York: Simon & Schuster, 2012.

Obama, Barack. *Dreams from My Father: A Story of Race and Inheritance*. New York: Three Rivers Press, 1995.

OBERGEFELL V. HODGES

Four separate same-sex marriage cases in four states were consolidated in *Obergefell v. Hodges*. The states were Ohio, Kentucky, Michigan, and Tennessee. Each state had enacted a statute or statutes that banned same-sex marriage within their jurisdiction or refused to recognize same-sex marriages that had been performed in other states that allowed for such marriages. In each state the plaintiffs argued that the statutes violated the Equal Protection Clause and the Due Process Clause of the Fourteenth Amendment. In one state the plaintiffs also filed a claim under the Civil Rights Act.

The trial court in each case had found for the plaintiffs. The United States Court of Appeals for the Sixth Circuit reversed those decisions, holding that the plaintiffs' rights to due process and equal protection under the law were not violated by the states' bans on same-sex marriage and refusal to recognize same-sex marriages performed in other states.

When the Supreme Court of the United States took up the case, it was picking up an issue that had not been addressed in a related 2013 case, *United States v. Windsor*. In *Windsor*, the Supreme Court had ruled that part of HR 3396—Defense of Marriage Act (DOMA) was unconstitutional, but it had not addressed the issue of same-sex marriage as a constitutional right.

Windsor had resulted in many states legalizing same-sex marriage, which in turn made *Obergefell v. Hodges* inevitable at some point. When the Supreme Court struck down part of DOMA, it ruled that the Constitution guarantees that same-sex couples must receive equal treatment under federal law. This meant that federal benefits that were available to opposite-sex married couples were also extended to same-sex married couples. But the Court did not rule on the constitutionality of same-sex marriage itself.

In agreeing to hear the case, the Court asked two questions: Does the Fourteenth Amendment require a state to license a marriage between two people of the same sex? and Does the Fourteenth Amendment require a state to recognize a marriage between two people of the same sex that was legally licensed and performed in another state? The Court heard oral arguments in April of 2015 and handed down a split decision in June of 2015.

OPINION OF THE COURT

The Supreme Court was narrowly divided on both of the questions, but a 5–4 majority reversed the ruling of the Court of Appeals for the Sixth Circuit and held that the right to marry is guaranteed by the Fourteenth Amendment. The Court asserted that the right to marry is a fundamental liberty protected in the Constitution and that the right applies equally to same-sex and opposite-sex couples. Since same-sex marriage is a protected right, state statutes prohibiting it were struck down, and all states are required to recognize same-sex marriages that are performed in other states.

Justice Anthony Kennedy wrote the majority opinion. He was joined in his opinion by Justices Sonia Sotomayor, Ruth Bader Ginsberg, Stephen Breyer, and Elena Kagan. Chief Justice John Roberts and Justices Antonin Scalia, Clarence Thomas, and Samuel Alito each authored a dissent.

Justice Kennedy's opinion noted that judicial precedent established the concept that the right to marry is a fundamental liberty. He identified four "principles and traditions" that provided the precedent under the Due Process Clause. First, personal choice in marriage "is inherent in the concept of individual autonomy." Second, marriage "is fundamental because it supports a two-person union unlike any other in its importance to the committed individuals." Third, it "safeguards children and families and thus draws meaning from related rights of importance to the committed individuals." Fourth, it is "a keystone of [our] social order." He concluded that there "is no difference between same- and opposite-sex couples with respect to this principle."

Kennedy also invoked the Equal Protection Clause of the Fourteenth Amendment in his opinion. He referenced a famous interracial marriage case, *Loving v. Commonwealth of Virginia,* and noted that new views within society can uncover "unjustified inequality within our most fundamental institutions that once passed unnoticed and unchallenged." His conclusion was succinct:

> It would misunderstand these men and women to say they disrespect the idea of marriage. Their plea is that they do respect it, respect it so deeply that they seek to find its fulfillment for themselves. Their hope is not to be condemned to live in loneliness, excluded from one of civilization's oldest institutions. They ask for equal dignity in the eyes of the law. The Constitution grants them that right.

Chief Justice John Roberts' dissent argued that the Constitution does not address same-sex marriage, and therefore the Court had no business deciding whether or not states have to recognize such unions. He felt the issue should have been left to state legislatures. He also felt that the majority opinion depended on a too-expansive a reading of the Due Process and Equal Protection Clauses of the Fourteenth Amendment. Justices Antonin Scalia, Samuel Alito, and Clarence Thomas joined the dissent and wrote separate dissents as well. They wrote that the Court was overstepping its authority, acting within the purview of the legislative branch, and infringing on religious rights.

IMPACT

The Court returned its rulings on June 26, 2015, triggering furious and overjoyed reactions from different sides of the political divide. The immediate consequence was that James Obergefell, the named plaintiff from Ohio who wanted to put his name on his husband's death certificate as surviving spouse, was able to do so. Thousands of same-sex couples immediately applied for marriage licenses across the country.

In opposition, Texas attorney general Ken Paxton called the decision a "lawless ruling." He offered free legal defense to state workers who refused on religious grounds to marry same-sex couples. Many religious organizations and publications expressed concern that the ruling conflicted with religious liberty. Many county clerks and other officers of courts refused to issue marriage licenses to or perform nuptial services for same-sex couples. But by the end of 2015, less than one-tenth of a percent of United States citizens lived in counties that refused to issue marriage licenses to same-sex couples.

——John K. Manos

BIBLIOGRAPHY AND FURTHER READING

Chemerinsky, Erwin. *Constitutional Law: 2015 Case Supplement.* New York: Kluwer Law & Business, 2015. Print.

Kennedy, Anthony M. *The United States Supreme Court Decision on Marriage Equality As Delivered by Justice Anthony Kennedy.* Brooklyn: Melville House, 2015. Electronic.

"LGBT Rights on the Docket: *Obergefell v. Hodges.*" *ACLU.* American Civil Liberties Union of Ohio, n.d. Web. 3 Jan 2016.

Neubauer, David W., and Stephen S. Meinhold. *Judicial Process: Law, Courts, and Politics in the United States.* 7th ed. Boston: Cengage Learning, 2017.

"Obergefell v. Hodges." *US Supreme Court.* US Supreme Court, 26 June 2015. Web. 7 Feb. 2016.

OCTOBER CRISIS

The October crisis of 1970 was a tragic period in Quebec's history, marked by kidnapping, murder, and the suspension of civil liberties. It followed a decade of profound change and intellectual turbulence, not simply in the province of Quebec but throughout the world. Decolonization was in vogue, wars of liberation were being fought in several countries, and youth were questioning the values of their parents and the capitalist system. During the 1960's, Quebec society, once rural and religious, had undergone rapid transformation and was well on the way to becoming a modern, secular, progressive society.

THE SEPARATIST MOVEMENT

Increasingly self-confident and assertive French-speaking Quebecers (Québécois) were no longer willing to accept passively the Anglo-Canadian domination of previous centuries. In addition, they feared for the future of the French language and Québécois culture. This led many to join the ranks of the so-called separatist, or sovereignist, movement, which advocated political sovereignty or even outright independence for Quebec.

While these sovereignists followed a democratic path, others were not so patient. The Front de Libération du Québec (FLQ) was an underground revolutionary movement dedicated to creating a socialist, independent Quebec. Officially founded in 1963, it was composed primarily of French Canadian youth, often college or university students, willing to accept political violence as a means to liberate Quebec and destroy capitalism. They drew intellectual inspiration from the popular left-wing cult figures of this epoch, including Herbert Marcuse, Karl Marx, Mao Zedong, and Ernesto "Che" Guevara. They were also deeply influenced by recent historical events, especially the successful wars of national liberation that had been waged in Algeria and Cuba. The FLQ perceived itself as part of a worldwide movement fighting for liberation and decolonization, which included such groups as the Weathermen and Black Panthers in the United States, the Palestine Liberation Organization in the Middle East, Roman Catholics in Northern Ireland, and the Viet Cong engaged in bitter conflict with the United States in Vietnam.

The FLQ never had a large membership; it was limited, at any one time, to perhaps fewer than one hundred activists. Nor was it highly organized: There was no mastermind or central committee that operated on a strict hierarchical basis. The FLQ was composed of cells, each one knowing little or nothing about the other, which made it difficult for police to penetrate. Five or ten young zealots would form a cell

and then commit acts of violence or publish revolutionary tracts under the FLQ banner.

The FLQ began operations in 1963, planting bombs in post office boxes located in the affluent English-speaking section of Westmount in Montreal. Eventually, other targets were selected, including armories, federal buildings, the provincial Department of Labor building, and the Montreal Stock Exchange, at which a particularly bloody bombing in 1969 injured twenty-five people. FLQ members also robbed banks for funds and stole explosives from construction sites. Occasionally, the police were successful in destroying cells, but there were always new ones to take their place. It was estimated that the FLQ was responsible for some two hundred bombings, seven deaths, dozens wounded, and millions of dollars in property damage between 1963 and 1970. Although their propaganda was crude and unsophisticated, it resonated with many Québécois who could understand the forces that propelled young people to lash out against the injustices of society.

OCTOBER VIOLENCE

This violence, at first directed mainly against property, took a deadly turn in 1970. On October 5, one cell kidnapped the British trade commissioner in Montreal, James Cross. The kidnappers' ransom demands included receiving $500,000 in gold, the release of twenty-three political prisoners, and broadcasting the FLQ manifesto. The federal and provincial authorities allowed the broadcast but rejected the other demands, although they did offer to fly the kidnappers out of the country if they released their hostage. On October 10, another FLQ cell kidnapped Pierre Laporte, the provincial minister of labor and immigration.

The immediate result was confusion and chaos. In Montreal, Mayor Jean Drapeau believed his city was close to panic. Police forces throughout Quebec appeared stymied and incapable of protecting property or individuals. No one knew if this was the work of a few individuals or whether the province was facing the prospect of a large, well-organized left-wing insurrection. Quebec's premier, Robert Bourassa, was inexperienced, only thirty-seven years of age, and in office for only five months. His cabinet was divided as to whether to negotiate with the kidnappers or take a tough line. Police pushed for more legal powers to combat terrorism, while Laporte's friends and wife pressed the cabinet to negotiate.

RESPONSES

The federal government in Ottawa was in no mood for compromise. The Canadian prime minister, Pierre Trudeau, a Quebecer, was pushing authorities in Quebec to take a stiff line, and John Turner, the federal minister of justice, feared an erosion of will on the part of the Quebec government. Gérard Pelletier, the Canadian secretary of state for external affairs, privately was alarmed at what he thought was too much sympathy for the FLQ on the part of many students, intellectuals, and sovereignists within Quebec. Eventually, the Quebec government formally requested that the Canadian Army be sent into the province and that the War Measures Act be invoked. On October 12, the army moved into Quebec in order to guard public buildings and protect government officials, and on October 16, the War Measures Act was proclaimed. Public opinion polls showed that Canadians and Quebecers overwhelmingly approved of these federal actions.

Nevertheless, implementation of the War Measures Act eventually caused much controversy. This act permitted the government to suspend normal civil liberties and empowered authorities to use a variety of weapons—including censorship, arrest, detention, deportation, and control of transportation—to fight a state of apprehended insurrection. Many civil libertarians believed this proclamation was heavy-handed and unnecessary. Even Trudeau, who advocated a tough stance, was not enthusiastic about using this legal tool, but he deferred to the judgment of authorities on the scene in Quebec. More than 465 people were detained, but no charges were filed and most of those arrested were innocent of any criminal wrongdoing. It appears that the authorities considered almost anyone who was a sovereignist or embraced left-wing views to be a potential insurrectionist. Civil libertarians later pointed out that when the kidnappers were apprehended, it was due to routine police work and not to the special legal powers granted to the authorities.

On October 18, Laporte was found dead in the trunk of an automobile, having been strangled by his captors the previous day. In early December, the police located the hideout at which Cross was detained. After negotiations, Cross was released unharmed and the kidnappers allowed to fly to Cuba. Later that month, police finally apprehended the men responsible for the kidnapping and death of Laporte. Paul Rose and Francis Simard were found guilty of murder and sentenced to life imprisonment, although neither served more than twelve years before being paroled. In January, 1971, the army withdrew from Quebec, although the state of emergency legislation remained in effect until April 30, 1971.

After these events, the Front de Libération du Québec went into a period of steep decline. The organization had completely alienated public opinion in Quebec, including leftists and sovereignists. Moreover, the increasing popularity of the Parti Québécois, founded in 1968 to fight for sovereignty, was convincing many people that there was a viable alternative to violence and revolution. The memory of the October Crisis remained firmly imprinted upon the Québécois psyche, one of the darkest moments in their modern history.

——*David C. Lukowitz*

BIBLIOGRAPHY AND FURTHER READING

Quebec, Canada and the October Crisis (Montreal: Black Rose Books, 1973), edited by Dan Daniels, is a collection of the revolutionary literature of the period, including documents, pamphlets, and poetry. Louis Fournier's *F.L.Q.: The Anatomy of an Underground Movement* (Toronto: NC Press, 1984), translated by Edward Baxter, is a detailed, sympathetic account of the organization, placing it and the October crisis within the context of national and global events. In Gérard Pelletier's *The October Crisis* (Montreal: McClelland and Stewart, 1971), translated by Joyce Marshall, the Canadian secretary of state at the time justifies his agonizing decision to support the use of the War Measures Act. *Power Corrupted: The October Crisis and the Repression of Quebec* (Toronto: New Press, 1971), edited by Abraham Rotstein, collects essays by Anglo-Canadians highly critical of the suppression of civil liberties in Quebec. In Pierre Elliott Trudeau's *Memoirs* (Toronto: McClelland and Stewart, 1993), the Canadian prime minister justifies his actions in a relatively brief section dealing with the events of 1970, but leaves many questions unanswered.

OFFICIAL LANGUAGES ACT

The implementation of the Official Languages Act of 1969 was a crucial element of Prime Minister Pierre Elliott Trudeau's policy of maintaining a united Canada. It also was a major step in developing a policy enabling French, English, and immigrant and aboriginal communities to maintain their ethnicities and languages. To maintain national unity while promoting cultural diversity, Canada assumed that a workable language policy was crucial. Canada was unique, in that it attempted to implement a language policy designed to influence language usage in ways to serve the interests of the Canadian people—a mutable policy developed without establishing linguistic territoriality. The Official Languages Act of 1969 became the foundation to this process.

ORIGINS OF THE LANGUAGE CONFLICT

The language issue in Canada was not new. The conflict between the two major colonizing powers in North America, the French and the English, set the stage for ongoing contention. When the French territory was ceded to the British, the French were allowed to practice their Roman Catholic religion, and the French language continued to assert itself. Since then, a two-language and two-culture policy has been in effect. The Constitutional Act of 1791 divided the colony of Quebec into two units, Upper Canada and Lower Canada, where the majority of the Parliamentarians were francophones. Although challenged in practice, administratively and legislatively, the French language remained vigorous. The Constitution of 1867, from which Canada claims its origins, institutionalized the use of French in the Quebec legislature and in some federal and Quebec courts. The constitution seemed to enable the French language and culture to spread. In addition to the right to use French in Quebec, Francophones were led to believe that as French settlers moved west, they would find adequate guarantees of linguistic rights elsewhere. Also, the French viewed the constitution as an agreement between two "founding people."

The next fifty years proved disastrous for the use of French. In 1890, Manitoba abrogated the use of French (which was not restored until 1985); Ontario abolished French schools in 1912; and limitations were imposed on instruction in French in other provinces. Francophones became increasingly confined

to Quebec, with Montreal becoming an anglophone area. It was only the high birth rate of the French in Quebec that compensated for the large French emigration from Quebec to the United States and English-speaking immigrants flocking into Montreal. In spite of accommodations to allow French in the courts, military, and other official bodies, it was clear that English was ascending over French and any other language. As a result of the majority rule principle and the decline of French language usage, the two peoples became cut off from each other. Many French Canadians had to separate themselves or they would, under majority rule, lose to the English speakers and risk extinction.

By the 1960s, the language issue required serious attention. The French language was in rapid decline outside Quebec and, although less rapidly, inside the province as well. Within Quebec, the birthrate of the French had declined to one of the lowest in the world. It was becoming apparent that English was not only the language of North America but also the international language. Even Francophones were learning and using English.

THE B & B COMMISSION

This situation resulted in civil unrest and a movement to have Quebec separate from Canada. In 1963, Prime Minister Lester Pearson created the Royal Commission on Bilingualism and Biculturalism (the B & B Commission) to examine the relationship between English and French Canada. More specifically, the commission was asked to review and assess Canadian language policy. The primary concern was to promote a federal-provincial response to the crisis in English-French relations. The commission also had to consider the increasing number of Canadians who had no inborn allegiance to either French or English.

In its report, the commission rejected territorial solutions. It found, however, that the use of French had fallen behind English, for example, in public service, to a politically and socially unacceptable level. It urged that a new charter, founded on the concept of "equal partnership," be implemented at both the federal and provincial levels. It was in response to the commission's recommendations that the Official Languages Act of 1969 was created.

The B & B Commission endorsed the value of linguistic diversity as an "inestimable enrichment that

Canadians cannot afford to lose. . . . Linguistic variety is unquestionably an advantage and its beneficial effects on the country are priceless." What happened eventually was the establishment of the "official languages," English and French, and the "heritage languages," recognized languages of other ethnic communities. Initially, the issue of heritage languages was not supported, but after pressure from other communities, three types of programs for teaching heritage languages were in place by the 1990s: instruction incorporated into the school curriculum, after-hours instruction in the school system, and instruction that used school resources but was not part of the school program.

In the meantime, Canadian nationalism was rising, especially against US policies concerning Vietnam. Outside economic and cultural influence on Canada was resented, especially in 1971, when Canada's economic dependency on the United States was made manifest—the United States could not buy enough of Canada's products, and Europe provided no help. In Quebec, the decline of French was becoming a prominent issue. In Montreal, riots promoting Quebec's nationalism became endemic. One particular disturbance was in 1968, when rioting had broken out at the Saint-Jean Baptiste Day parade, and Trudeau faced a bottle-throwing crowd. The maintenance of a united Canada was a central issue for Trudeau. Dismissing the "two nations" vision of Canada, he argued that Canada must be a truly federal state with equality for all provinces, yet also a homeland for both French and English culture. The Official Languages Act became the key to this policy.

The Official Languages Act of 1969 was supported by the opposition as well as the party in power. Based on the findings of the B & B Commission, the act named French and English as the official languages and guaranteed official-language minorities in the country certain basic rights in dealing with the federal government and its various agencies. It was, however, the francophone minority outside Quebec that needed such guarantees of bilingualism in Canada. The act also set forth a number of measures to provide the francophone community with the same guarantees outside Quebec that the English enjoyed within Quebec. Parliament's intention was to place French on an equal footing with English as far as the federal government was concerned. The federal government improved its capacity to deal with

Canadians in the official language of their choice and to allow public servants to use either language at work, in certain areas. Some provinces, such as Ontario and New Brunswick, provided government services in both languages and tried to implement their own language policies, particularly in regard to minority and second-language education.

As a result of the act, a commissioner of official languages was created and appointed—a linguistics ombudsman to report annually on the progress of implementing various provisions of the act. However, the commissioner had to devote much time to persuading Canadians that the reforms were necessary and just.

The act created a great deal of controversy. Some anglophones complained that the act forced French on them. The act was also criticized for giving French a position it no longer merited, especially in areas where speakers of languages other than English outnumbered francophones. In spite of the controversy, principles of the Official Languages Act were incorporated into the 1982 Canadian Constitution through its Canadian Charter of Rights and Freedoms. The British Parliament renounced any future legislative role in amending the Constitution, and on April 17, 1982, Queen Elizabeth II proclaimed the Constitution effective. Quebec, headed by René Lévesque of the Parti Québécois, did not agree to the Constitution and refused to sign it, charging that it did not go far enough in protecting Quebec's unique place in Canada.

——Arthur W. Helweg

BIBLIOGRAPHY AND FURTHER READING

Conrick, Maeve, and Vera Regan. *French in Canada: Language Issues.* New York: Lang, 2007. Print.

Haque, Eve. *Multiculturalism Within a Bilingual Framework: Language, Race, and Belonging in Canada.* Toronto: U of Toronto P, 2012. Print.

Jedwab, Jack, and Rodrigue Landry, eds. *Life After Forty: Official Languages Policy in Canada.* Kingston: School of Policy Studies, Queen's U, 2011. Print.

Morris, Michael A. *Canadian Language Policies in Comparative Perspective.* Ithaca: McGill-Queen's UP, 2010. Print.

"Understanding Your Language Rights." *Office of the Commissioner of Official Languages.* Commissioner of Official Languages, 19 Mar. 2015. Web. 28 Apr. 2015.

OKA CRISIS

The conflict that erupted in early July, 1990, at Oka in Quebec was the result of long-standing problems both within the Mohawk community in Canada and between that community and various other—mainly governmental—bodies. It was brought on in large measure by disputes regarding the ownership of the relevant lands at Oka that dated back to the early eighteenth century.

The lands at Oka do not fit the usual pattern of disputed territory, and for this reason, a 1975 land claim presented to the Canadian government was rejected outright. The Mohawk community nonetheless continued to make a claim based on territorial sovereignty, treaty rights, the Royal Proclamation of 1763, unextinguished aboriginal title under common law, and land rights from obligations imposed by order of the King of France in the eighteenth century.

Later origins of the conflict date back to 1987 and pertain both to internal conflicts in the Mohawk community over issues of governance and legitimacy of leadership in the community and to external conflicts with various governments, chiefly local, about disputed land known as "the Pines." By the late 1980s, the Municipality of Oka had proposed to allow expansion of a local golf course onto the disputed lands and followed the lead of the federal government in refusing to consider a Mohawk land claim against the "the Pines." Mohawk protest ensued in the form of barricades, which the Municipality asked the Sûreté du Québec police force to dispense with in restoring law and order. It was this move on July 11, 1990, by the Sûreté du Québec that brought about the armed conflict and resulted in the death of a Sûreté officer. As the report of the Parliamentary Standing Committee on Aboriginal Affairs stated, "Eventually the controversy over land use in the Pines became symbolic of Mohawk land rights in general. This pattern of escalating conflict continued until the shaky state of peace that managed to hold from 1987 was completely shattered by the events of July 11, 1990."

Those events would unite the previously fractured Mohawk community and would galvanize public opinion in general in favor of a solution to the land claim problem provided violence was not again used. This public support prompted the standing committee, in its fifth report, *The Summer of 1990*, to set forth several recommendations. The committee did not explore all the historical and other details of the

Members of the Seton Lake Indian Band blockade the BC Rail line in support of Oka, while a Royal Canadian Mounted Police officer looks on. Later in the day, several of the elders protesting were arrested and a confrontation with the band community ensued as Mounties marched the squad cars holding those arrested through the reserve en route to Lillooet.

conflict but concluded its report with a series of recommendations to resolve aboriginal issues in general and the Mohawk-Oka conflict in particular. Those recommendations included the formation of a royal commission; a review of the National Defense Act, under which Quebec was able to ask and receive from the federal government the use and support of the army in resisting the Mohawk standoff; and a better process for federal land claims and dispute resolution. More specifically, they proposed that there be an independent inquiry into Quebec's handling of native issues and of the Sûreté in responding at Oka; the appointment of a mediator to resolve the conflict around land claims; and a process of healing and compensation begun in order to build a better future for all concerned.

——*Gregory Walters*

BIBLIOGRAPHY AND FURTHER READING

Belanger, Yale Deron, and P. Whitney Lackenbauer. *Blockades or Breakthroughs? Aboriginal Peoples Confront the Canadian State.* Montreal: McGill-Queen's UP, 2014. Print.

Ladner, Kiera L., and Leanne Simpson, eds. *This is an Honour Song: Twenty Years Since the Blockades.* Winnipeg, Arbeiter Ring, 2010. Print.

Marshall, Tabitha. "Oka Crisis." *Canadian Encyclopedia.* Historica Canada, 15 July 2014. Web. 28 Apr. 2015. "Standoff at Oka." *Demand to Be Counted.* CBC, 2001. Web. 28 Apr. 2015. Swain, Harry. *Oka: A Political Crisis and Its Legacy.* Vancouver: Douglas, 2010. Print.

OKLAHOMA INDIAN WELFARE ACT OF 1936

A major reform of US policy toward American Indians resulted in the Indian Reorganization Act (IRA, or Wheeler-Howard Act), enacted by Congress on June 18, 1934. With this act, further allotment of tribal lands to individual Indians was prohibited, purchase of additional lands for Indians by the secretary of the interior was authorized, and a fund (the Revolving Loan Fund for Indians) was established that could be used for tribal enterprises. The IRA allowed and encouraged the tribes or groups to adopt written constitutions allowing for self-government, gave Indians applying for positions in the Bureau of Indian Affairs (BIA) preference over other applicants, and called for very strict conservation practices on Indian lands. Oklahoma, however, was excluded from the IRA because the IRA was essentially a system of reservation government, and it was deemed inappropriate for Oklahoma because, at the time of statehood, the Five Civilized Tribes had given up their autonomy.

In 1936, the benefits of the IRA were extended to Oklahoma by way of a separate statute, the Oklahoma Indian Welfare Act. This act authorized the secretary of the interior to purchase, at his discretion, good agricultural and grazing land, from within or without reservations, to hold in trust for the tribe, band, group, or individual Indian for whose benefit the land was acquired. Title to all lands was to be taken in the name of the United States and held by the United States. All land was exempt from any and all federal taxes, but the state of Oklahoma could levy and collect a gross production tax upon all oil and gas produced from the land. The secretary of the interior was responsible for overseeing the payment of these taxes to Oklahoma. Any tribe or band in the state of Oklahoma was given the right to organize for its common welfare and could adopt a constitution and bylaws; these had to follow the rules and regulations set forth by the secretary of the interior. Any ten or more Indians, as determined by the official tribe rolls, or Indian descendants of such enrolled members, in convenient proximity to each other, could be chartered as a local cooperative association for the following purposes: credit administration, production, marketing, consumers' protection, or land management. Funds from the Revolving Loan Fund for Indians could be used to provide interest-free loans to these groups.

——*Lynn M. Mason*

BIBLIOGRAPHY AND FURTHER READING

Blackman, Jon S. *Oklahoma's Indian New Deal.* Norman: U of Oklahoma P, 2013. Print.

Fixico, Donald Lee. *Indian Resilience and Rebuilding: Indigenous Nations in the Modern American West.* Tucson: U of Arizona P, 2013. Print.

"Oklahoma Indian Welfare Act: 1936." *Chickasaw History & Culture.* Chickasaw.tv, n.d. Web. 28 Apr. 2010.

Rader, Brian F. "Oklahoma Indian Welfare Act." *Encyclopedia of Oklahoma History and Culture.* Oklahoma History Center, 2009. Web. 28 Apr. 2015.

Rusco, Elmer R. *A Fateful Time: The Background and Legislative History of the Indian Reorganization Act.* Reno: U of Nevada P, 2002. Print.

OLE MISS DESEGREGATION

In January, 1961, James Meredith, a native Mississippian and an Air Force veteran attending Jackson State College, one of Mississippi's all-black colleges, decided to transfer to the University of Mississippi, affectionately called "Ole Miss." His application was rejected because, Ole Miss officials maintained, Jackson State was not an approved Southern Association Secondary School and because Meredith did not furnish letters of recommendation from University of Mississippi alumni. On May 31, 1961, he filed a lawsuit against the university, charging that he had been denied admission because of his race. In its 114-year history, the University of Mississippi had never admitted an African American student.

MEREDITH'S LEGAL VICTORY

A federal district court judge dismissed Meredith's suit, but in June, 1962, a US court of appeals ruled that Meredith had been rejected from Ole Miss "solely because he was a Negro," a ruling based on the *Brown v. Board of Education* school desegregation case of 1954. The court ordered the university to admit Meredith, and the ruling was upheld by Justice Hugo L. Black of the United States Supreme Court. On September 13, Mississippi governor Ross Barnett delivered a televised speech and stated, "No school will be integrated in Mississippi while I'm governor." A week later, the board of trustees of Ole Miss appointed Governor Barnett as the university's registrar, and he personally blocked Meredith from registering for courses that same day.

Throughout Meredith's court appeals, the US Department of Justice had been monitoring the case. Attorney General Robert F. Kennedy, the brother of President John F. Kennedy, made more than a dozen phone calls to Governor Barnett, hoping to persuade him to allow Meredith to matriculate and thereby avoid a confrontation between the state of Mississippi and the federal government. The attorney general had provided Meredith with federal marshals to protect him as he attempted to register.

On September 24, the court of appeals that initially had heard Meredith's case again ordered the Board of Higher Education of Mississippi to allow Meredith to register. The following day, Meredith reported to the registrar's office in the university's Lyceum Building, but again Governor Barnett was there to block his registration. During a phone conversation with Attorney General Kennedy that same day, Barnett declared that he would never agree to allow Meredith to attend the University of Mississippi. When Kennedy reminded Barnett that he was openly defying a court order and could be subject to penalty, Barnett told Kennedy that he would rather spend the rest of his life in prison than allow Meredith to enroll. On September 26, Meredith again tried to register for courses, and for the third time, Governor Barnett turned him away. Two days later, the court of appeals warned Barnett that if he continued to block Meredith's admission to Ole Miss, the governor would be found in contempt of court, arrested, and fined ten thousand dollars per day. On Saturday, September 29, Governor Barnett appeared at an Ole Miss football game and proudly announced, "I love Mississippi, I love her people, her customs! And I love and respect her heritage. Ask us what we say, it's to hell with Bobby K!"

That evening, President Kennedy called Governor Barnett and told him that the federal government would continue to back Meredith until Ole Miss admitted him. Under direct pressure from the president, Barnett began to reconsider. Finally, he agreed to allow Meredith to register on Sunday, September 30, when, the governor surmised, few students and news reporters would be milling around the campus. On Sunday evening, Meredith arrived at the Lyceum Building protected by three hundred marshals, armed in riot gear and equipped with tear gas.

As Meredith and his escorts approached the campus, a group of twenty-five hundred students and other agitators attempted to block their passage. The crowd began to shout and throw bricks and bottles at the federal marshals, who retaliated with tear gas. Some of the protesters were armed with guns and began firing random shots. One federal marshal was seriously wounded by a bullet in the throat. Two onlookers, Paul Guihard, a French journalist, and Roy Gunter, a jukebox repairman, were shot and killed by rioters.

KENNEDY'S NATIONAL ADDRESS

On Sunday evening, while Mississippians rioted on the Ole Miss campus, President Kennedy addressed the nation on television. The Meredith crisis had captured the country's and news media's attention, and the president attempted to show Mississippians and other US citizens that his administration's commitment to Civil Rights movement was serious and unwavering. He reminded his audience that "Americans are free . . . to disagree with the law but not to disobey it. For in a government of laws and not of men, no man, however prominent or powerful, and no mob, however unruly or boisterous, is entitled to defy a court of law." He told Mississippians, "The eyes of the nation and all the world are upon you and upon all of us. And the honor of your university—and state—are in the balance."

The situation at the University of Mississippi was deteriorating. The federal marshals, low on tear gas, requested additional help to control the unruly mob. President Kennedy federalized Mississippi National Guardsmen and ordered them to Oxford. At dawn on Monday morning, the first of five thousand troops began arriving at Oxford to restore order. During the evening's rioting, more than one hundred people were injured and about two hundred were arrested, only twenty-four of whom were Ole Miss students.

On Monday morning, October 1, at 8:30 AM, Meredith again presented himself at the Lyceum Building to register. He was closely guarded by federal marshals, and National Guardsmen continued patrolling the Ole Miss campus and Oxford's streets. Meredith, dressed impeccably in a business suit, registered for classes and began his matriculation at the University of Mississippi. "I am intent on seeing that every citizen has an opportunity of being a first-class citizen," Meredith told a reporter the next day. "I am also intent on seeing that citizens have a right to be something if they work hard enough."

During his tenure at Ole Miss, Meredith was often the target of insults and threats. Federal marshals remained with him during his entire time at the university. On August 18, 1963, Meredith graduated from the University of Mississippi with a bachelor of arts degree in political science. After a year of study in Africa, Meredith enrolled at Columbia University of Law. In 1966, the year before he completed his law degree, Meredith was wounded by a sniper's gunshot during a voter registration march from Tennessee to Mississippi.

MEREDITH'S IMPACT

As a result of his successful effort to desegregate Ole Miss, Meredith became one of the heroes of the Civil Rights movement. In his "Letter from Birmingham Jail" (1963), Martin Luther King, Jr., states that "One day the South will recognize its real heroes. They will be the James Merediths, courageously and with a majestic sense of purpose facing jeering and hostile mobs and the agonizing loneliness that characterizes the life of the pioneer."

Meredith's victory at the University of Mississippi was a key triumph for the Civil Rights movement during the 1960's. Within two years, the University of Alabama, the University of Georgia, and other Southern colleges and universities that had prevented African Americans from enrolling were also desegregated public schools, as the era of overt segregation in US institutions of higher learning came to an end.

The Meredith case also convincingly demonstrated that the federal government would use its power to end racial segregation in the South. Despite Governor Barnett's defiance, President Kennedy and his attorney general were able to force the state of Mississippi to comply with a federal court order, signaling that the South would be unable to block the subsequent wave of federal legislation designed to void the region's segregation laws.

——*James Tackach*

BIBLIOGRAPHY AND FURTHER READING

Barrett, Russell. *Integration at Ole Miss*. Chicago: Quadrangle, 1965. Print.

Meredith, James H. *Three Years in Mississippi*. Bloomington: Indiana UP, 1966. Print.

Schlesinger, Arthur M. *Robert Kennedy and His Times*. Boston: Houghton, 1978. Print.

Wexler, Sanford. *The Civil Rights Movement: An Eyewitness History*. New York: Facts on File, 1993. Print.

OLIPHANT V. SUQUAMISH INDIAN TRIBE

On March 6, 1978, the United States Supreme Court in the case of *Oliphant v. Suquamish Indian Tribe* decided that tribes do not have jurisdiction over non-Indians who commit crimes on reservations. In 1978, during a tribal celebration, two non-Indian residents of the Port Madison Reservation of the Suquamish Tribe in Washington violated tribal laws. Mark Oliphant was arrested for assaulting tribal police officers and resisting arrest, and Dan Belgarde was arrested for hitting a tribal police car in a high-speed chase. The two argued the Suquamish tribe had no criminal jurisdiction over non-Indians, and they took their case to federal court.

The Supreme Court agreed with them and determined that non-Indians, even those residing on a reservation and charged with a crime, are not subject to the jurisdiction of tribal courts. This ruling dealt a major blow to tribal sovereignty and the authority of tribal courts because it determined that tribes lack the power to enforce laws against all who come within its borders. This ruling created serious and important law-and-order problems on reservations. Some tribes have approached the problem by cross-deputization with local and county police or by arranging for non-Indians on the reservation to submit voluntarily to tribal authority. Tribal authority was somewhat expanded with the 2010 Tribal Law and Order Act as well as the Violence Against Women Reauthorization Act of 2013, with the latter specifically providing tribal jurisdiction over non-Indian men accused of assault against Indian women.

——*Carole A. Barrett*

BIBLIOGRAPHY AND FURTHER READING

Champagne, Duane. "Oliphant Decision Led to Jurisdictional Issues on Indian Reservations." *Indian Country Today Media Network.com.* Indian Country Today Media Network, 7 Jan. 2012. Web. 28 Apr. 2015.

Fixico, Donald Lee. *Treaties with American Indians: An Encyclopedia of Rights, Conflicts, and Sovereignty.* Santa Barbara: ABC-CLIO, 2008. Print.

Fletcher, Matthew L. M. "DOJ Takes Step Toward Addressing Violent Crime Against American Indian Women." *American Constitution Society for Law and Policy.* ACS, 4 Aug. 2011. Web. 28 Apr. 2015.

Knowles, F. E., Jr. *The Indian Law Legacy of Thurgood Marshall.* Basingstoke: Palgrave: 2014. Print.

"Oliphant v. Suquamish Indian Tribe." *Oyez.* Oyez, IIT Chicago-Kent College of Law, 2014. Web. 28 Apr. 2015.

ONE-DROP RULE

The one-drop rule is a definition of race that says that a person with any known amount of black ancestry is to be legally and socially classified as black. Although there is no "pure" race, some people believe otherwise and want to keep the dominant group racially "pure" and delegate all "impure" people to the subordinate or stigmatized group.

The one-drop rule originated in the southern United States before the Civil War (1861–1865) but had not been rigidly conceptualized, and a few black-white mixed-race individuals (who physically appeared white) were accepted as white by the dominant white culture. White attitudes became more rigid at the time of the Civil War, and the one-drop rule became strictly enforced and largely accepted throughout the United States. In 1896, the United States Supreme Court (in *Plessy v. Ferguson*) approved the one-drop rule as a legal definition by defining it as "common knowledge." Although state laws against mixed-race marriages (miscegenation) were declared illegal by the Supreme Court in 1967, the one-drop rule still applies in some states. Socially, some whites support the rule to maintain "white racial purity," and some blacks support it to keep from losing members of their group to the dominant white group. The one-drop rule is unique to the United States.

——*Abraham D. Lavender*

BIBLIOGRAPHY AND FURTHER READING

Bradt, Steve. "'One-Drop Rule' Persists." *Harvard Gazette*. President and Fellows of Harvard College, 9 Dec. 2010. Web. 28 Apr. 2015.

Davis, F James. *Who Is Black? One Nation's Definition.* 10th anniversary ed. University Park: Pennsylvania State UP, 2005. Print.

Lee, Jennifer, and Frank D. Bean. *The Diversity Paradox: Immigration and the Color Line in Twenty-First Century America.* New York: Russell Sage Foundation, 2012. Print.

fcSweet, Frank W. *Legal History of the Color Line: The Rise and Triumph of the One-Drop Rule.* Palm Coast: Backintyme, 2005. Print.

OPERATION BOOTSTRAP

Operation Bootstrap was a program instituted by the United States and Puerto Rican governments in 1947 for the purpose of transforming the island of Puerto Rico—a US territory lacking natural resources whose economy was based largely on the exportation of agricultural products—into a modern urban-industrial economy. This goal was to be accomplished by attracting industrial investment from the US mainland. Incentives offered included freedom from island taxes, cash grants for operational costs, and assistance with site location. In addition, new companies would benefit from the island's federal income tax exemption, and exports to the mainland would be free of tariffs.

This program was part of a comprehensive plan not only to modernize industry but also to improve the health and education of the population, relieve unemployment, elevate living standards, and improve the island's infrastructure. The endeavor was initiated by the Popular Democratic Party (PPD), led by Senator (later Governor) Luis Muñoz Marín, which had gained legislative control of the island government in 1940. In 1942, the government established several industries that manufactured products previously imported. It was hoped that these enterprises would stimulate private-sector economic initiatives. In 1947, as a result of several factors (including limited available capital), these were sold to private island interests and the new policy, Operation Bootstrap, was instituted.

In 1950, legislation established the Puerto Rico Economic Development Administration (PREDA) and its subsidiary the Puerto Rico Industrial Development Company (PRIDCO, known as FOMENTO in Spanish). This agency established offices in major mainland cities, conducted research, and devised programs to attract new industry. By 1958, five hundred new factories had located on the island, adding tens of thousands of new jobs. From 1940 to 1955, island production increased 120 percent, averaging more than 6 percent annual growth. During this same period, per-capita income increased 300 percent. Accompanying these economic dividends were significant improvements in the life expectancy and literacy of the Puerto Rican population.

The establishment in Puerto Rico of facilities by more than five hundred mainland corporations contributed to the diffusion of US Anglo culture throughout the island. The resulting familiarity with mainland culture and products, in combination with high island unemployment, a booming post-World War II economy on the continent, and inexpensive transportation, resulted in a massive migration from Puerto Rico to the mainland United States, primarily through New York City. The number of Puerto Rican immigrants residing on the mainland increased from fewer than 70,000 in 1940 to more than 615,000 in 1960.

——*Edward V. Mednick*

BIBLIOGRAPHY AND FURTHER READING

Ayala, César J., and Rafael Bernabe. *Puerto Rico in the American Century: A History Since 1898.* Chapel Hill: U of North Carolina P, 2009. Print.

Dietz, James L. *Puerto Pico: Negotiating Development and Change.* Boulder: Rienner, 2003. Print.

Flores, Lisa Pierce. *The History of Puerto Rico.* Santa Barbara: Greenwood, 2010. Print.

Korrol, Virginia Sanchez. "The Story of US Puerto Ricans: Part Four." *Center for Puerto Rican Studies.* Hunter College, 2010. Web. 28 Apr. 2015.

"Operation Bootstrap." *Dept. of Latin American and Puerto Rican Studies.* Lehman College, n.d. Web. 28 Apr. 2015.

OPERATION WETBACK

A fact of life for the nation of Mexico is the existence of a highly prosperous colossus to the north, the United States. While there has long been a tendency for Mexican workers to seek to enter the more prosperous United States to work, the government of Mexico took a number of steps in the 1940's and 1950's to provide good jobs to keep workers at home. These steps included the building of irrigation projects and factories. Most of these projects were located in northern Mexico and had the effect of drawing a large number of workers to the border area. Jobs were not available for all who came, and many chose to make the short trip across the border into the United States to find work. The average annual income of workers in the United States was more than ten times that of Mexican workers—a strong enticement for Mexican laborers to emigrate to the United States, legally or illegally, temporarily or on a permanent basis.

Mexican laborers who crossed the border into the United States in the early twentieth century most often found seasonal agricultural jobs. Starting about 1930, however, the Great Depression meant that many now-unemployed US workers were willing to do back-breaking work in the fields for low pay. Accordingly, job opportunities for Mexicans evaporated, and those who did not leave voluntarily often were deported. Then, in 1941, war raised levels of employment in the United States, and as US farmworkers departed to enter the military or to work in war factories, Mexican workers again began to enter the US to do agricultural work. Most of the jobs they found were in California, Arizona, and Texas.

THE BRACERO PROGRAM

The US and Mexican governments worked together to start a formal system called the bracero program. The program involved recruitment of Mexican laborers, the signing of contracts, and the temporary entry of Mexicans into the United States to do farm work or other labor. The Mexican government favored the bracero program primarily because the use of contracts was expected to guarantee that Mexican citizens would be fairly treated and would receive certain minimum levels of pay and benefits. The US government favored this formal system because it wanted to control the numbers of Mexicans coming into the United States and hoped the use of contracts would make it easier to ensure that the workers left when the seasonal work was completed. Labor unions in the United States supported the program because bracero workers could be recruited only after certification that no US citizens were available to do the work.

The bracero program worked with some success from 1942 until its discontinuation in 1964. In some years, however, and in certain localities, the use of illegal, non-bracero workers from Mexico continued. Some US employers found too much red tape in the process of securing bracero laborers, and they also noted that bracero wage levels were much higher than the wages that could be paid to illegal immigrants. Many Mexicans crossed the border illegally, because not nearly enough jobs were available through the bracero program. When the US economy stumbled in 1953 and 1954, many US citizens began to speak out against the presence of illegal aliens. They complained that illegal immigrants were a drain on US charities and government programs. They also claimed that the immigrants took jobs at substandard wages that should go to US citizens at higher wages.

When reporters first asked President Dwight D. Eisenhower and Attorney General Herbert Brownell if they intended to enforce vigorously the immigration laws, both men seemed uninterested in the issue. As popular agitation increased, however, the Eisenhower administration began to develop plans for Operation Wetback. The operation was designed to round up illegal aliens and deport them, while forcing large farming operations to use the limited and controlled bracero labor instead of uncontrolled and illegal alien labor. Operation Wetback was under the overall control of the Immigration and Naturalization Service (INS), directed by Joseph Swing, while day-to-day operations were supervised by an official of the Border Patrol, Harlon B. Carter.

OPERATION WETBACK BEGINS

Operation Wetback took its name from a slang term first used in the southwestern United States to refer to Mexican immigrants who swam the Rio Grande or otherwise crossed into the US illegally, seeking economic opportunities. The INS and its Border Patrol launched the operation in California on June 10, 1954, relying heavily on favorable press coverage to secure the support and cooperation of the general public. INS officials greatly exaggerated the number of agents they had in the field and the number of illegal aliens who had left or had been deported. Press coverage in California was generally quite favorable to Operation Wetback, praising the professional attitude of Border Patrol and INS agents. On the first day, more than a thousand persons were sent out of California on buses chartered by the INS. For several weeks, the number of daily deportations hovered around two thousand. The deportees were handed over to Mexican authorities at border towns like Nogales in Sonora, and the Mexican government sent them farther south by rail, hoping to prevent any quick reentry into the United States.

By July 15, the main phase of Operation Wetback in California was complete. On that day, Border Patrol agents began their work in Texas. There, they met stiff local opposition from powerful farm interests, who were quite content to hire illegal aliens and pay them only half the prevalent wage earned by US or bracero workers. Agents met a hostile press as well, and in some cases had trouble securing a meal or lodging. Still, the operation resulted in the deportation by bus of tens of thousands of illegal workers from Texas. The INS conducted smaller phases of Operation Wetback in Arizona, Illinois, Missouri, Arkansas, Tennessee, and other states. Most of the illegals picked up nationwide were farmworkers, but some industrial workers were apprehended in cities from San Francisco to Chicago.

During the operation, some complaints were registered about the conduct of Border Patrol officers. The officers sometimes were characterized as harsh and hateful in their actions, and they were regularly accused of harassing US citizens of Mexican ancestry. Some of these complaints seem to have been without

foundation, particularly in Texas, where the powerful farm interests opposed the entire operation. On the other hand, there were a number of documented cases of US citizens who had darker skin or Hispanic surnames being apprehended and deported to Mexico. Many of the aliens who were detained were kept in camps behind barbed wire pending their deportation. Some Mexicans and Mexican Americans spent several months hiding in terror, having quit their jobs to prevent their being apprehended at work. Deportees had to pay for their bus passage back to Mexico, to the dismay of human rights activists, who pointed out the unfairness of making someone pay for a trip he was being forced to take. The INS responded that the deportees should agree that paying for a bus trip back to Mexico was preferable to prosecution under the immigration laws and a possible jail sentence.

STEREOTYPES AND NATIVISM

Operation Wetback opened the door to stereotypes of Mexicans in the non-Hispanic community: Some press reports implied that the aliens were ignorant, disease-ridden union busters. As for the effectiveness of the operation in meeting its goals, nearly one hundred thousand illegal immigrants were returned to Mexico in the space of about three months. On the other hand, INS claimed that more than one million illegal immigrants fled to Mexico on their own rather than face arrest were grossly exaggerated. Moreover, the boost to the bracero program given by Operation Wetback was only temporary; many employers returned to the use of illegal workers before the end of the 1950's. Operation Wetback, while effective in the short term, provided no long-term solutions to the needs of Mexican workers, US employers, or those who clamored for a more restricted US border.

The operation was recalled favorably by presidential candidate Donald J. Trump during his successful run, on an anti-immigrant nativist platform, for the White House in 2016. Trump claimed that he would use the program as a model in rounding up and deporting undocumented migrants. His critics objected to the inhumanity of such an operation and to the impact it would have on the US economy, which relies, in part, on low-wage work done by migrants.

——*Stephen Cresswell, updated by Michael Shally-Jensen*

BIBLIOGRAPHY AND FURTHER READING

García, Juan Ramon. *Operation Wetback: The Mass Deportation of Mexican Undocumented Workers in 1954.* Westport: Greenwood, 1980. Print.

Mitchell, Don. *They Saved the Crops: Labor, Landscape, and the Struggle over Industrial Farming in Bracero-Era California.* Athens: U of Georgia P, 2012. Print.

Mize, Ronald L., and Alicia S.C. Swords. *Consuming Mexican Labor: From the Bracero Program to NAFTA.* Toronto: U of Toronto P, 2011. Print.

Norquest, Carrol. *Rio Grande Wetbacks: Migrant Mexican Workers.* Albuquerque: University of New Mexico Press, 1972. Print.

OPPOSITIONAL CULTURE

Oppositional culture refers to a system of beliefs and practices that challenge the dominant way of life. Also referred to as "cultures of resistance," these systems counter hegemonic and dominating ways of life experienced by subjugated groups. They often include aspects of a traditional culture that have been devalued or partially destroyed. Thus, they serve to enhance the survival of social groupings under the conditions of colonialism, enslavement, and other forms of racial or ethnic oppression. In their study of racial and ethnic groups in the United States, sociologists Bonnie Mitchell and Joe Feagin found oppositional culture to be a powerful survival tool for groups blocked from formal avenues of power and influence. They found that these practices temper the negative effects of sociocultural dominance, reaffirm a sense of peoplehood, and distinguish the practicing group from the dominant culture. The development of an oppositional culture can be an important strategy for survival and contestation for subordinated racial/ethnic groups.

——*M. Bahati Kuumba*

OPPRESSION MENTALITY

The Jewish ethnicity is one of the oldest ethnic groups in the world, tracing their history back about eighteen centuries before the beginning of the Christian era. Jewish identity involves national, religious, and genetic aspects. A long and diverse history of anti-Semitism has accompanied Jewish history. As a people whose small nation was conquered by larger nations and who for much of their history were forced to live in other countries far from their Middle Eastern homeland, Jews have frequently suffered from religious or genetic ("racial") oppression. Jews have struggled to maintain their distinctive identity within larger societies that were different both culturally and religiously. Often, the dominant group reacted with hostility and even persecution.

In Christian countries especially, Jews have been oppressed not only because of their distinctiveness but also because of the Christian teaching that held Jews responsible for the death of Jesus and the Christian belief that Christianity is the only true religion. Major examples of oppression of Jews in Christian countries include the Crusades in the early Middle Ages, the Spanish Inquisition in the 1400's, the pogroms in Eastern Europe in the few centuries leading up to the twentieth century, and the Holocaust in Nazi Germany in the 1930's and 1940's, in which six million Jews (almost 40 percent of the world's Jewish population at the time) were killed. Islamic countries also have oppressed Jews, although usually not nearly as severely as Christian countries. Some communist countries have oppressed Jews because of the Jewish refusal to give up religious identity. Opposition to contemporary Israel by Arab countries basically has been based on disputes over land, but frequently anti-Semitic stereotypes have been used against Israel. This history of oppression has led to a belief by some Jews that their existence is precarious, and that oppression is eventually to be expected everywhere.

In the United States, Jews frequently suffered from restrictive quotas in college admissions and discrimination in housing, jobs, and other areas until shortly after World War II, when conditions slowly began to improve. Shock at the magnitude of the Holocaust somewhat modified negative attitudes toward Jews. Moreover, the increasing ethnic diversity of the United States has made Jews stand out less as a minority group. US Jews thus face a dilemma. They live in a society where anti-Semitism is widespread but persecution is not.

Nevertheless, the Holocaust, the treatment of Jews in the former Soviet Union, the rise of neo-Nazism in Germany, and other events point out the continuing threat to Jews. Regardless of the reasons for the conflicts between Jews and Arabs, one major reason for American Jews' strong support for Israel is the belief that there must be one safe place in case there is renewed major oppression in the future.

Some American Jews, especially those who are acculturated or assimilated, emphasize the advances Jews have made and deny any possibility of oppression. Other Jewish Americans emphasize the history of oppression, current world events, and fear of history repeating itself. They are labeled paranoid by the acculturated, while they label the acculturated as deniers or naïve. Most American Jews fall between these two extremes.

——*Abraham D. Lavender*

BIBLIOGRAPHY AND FURTHER READING

Cohen, Robert Z. *Jewish Resistance Against the Holocaust.* New York: Rosen, 2015. Print.

Kerenji, Emil. *Jewish Responses to Persecution.* Lanham: Rowman, 2015. Print.

Marcus, Kenneth L. *Jewish Identity and Civil Rights in America.* New York: Cambridge UP, 2011. 49—64 Print.

Medoff, Rafael. *Jewish Americans.* Pasadena: Salem, 2011. Print.

Yancey, George A. *Neither New nor Gentile: Exploring Issues of Racial Diversity on Protestant College Campuses.* New York: Oxford UP, 2010. Print.

ORANGEBURG MASSACRE

On Thursday night, February 8, 1968, three African Americans (two male college students and the teenage son of a college employee) were killed by police gunfire on the campus of almost entirely black South Carolina State College in Orangeburg. Twenty-seven other students were injured. Nearly all were shot in the back or side as they attempted to flee an unannounced fusillade of police gunfire. One police officer had been seriously injured by an object thrown at the police, but despite uncorrected false reports in the media, the students were unarmed. African American students had started protesting three nights earlier because the only bowling alley in Orangeburg continued to exclude African Americans despite pleas from local white and black leaders and students.

The Orangeburg massacre was the first incident of US college students being killed by police because of protesting, but the killings received almost no national attention, largely because many white Americans had developed negative attitudes toward black protesters following a series of urban riots in 1967. Twenty-seven months later, the killing of four white students at Kent State University in Ohio during a Vietnam War protest received international publicity. A campus monument memorializes Henry Smith, Samuel Hammond, Jr., and Delano Middleton, whose lives were taken "in pursuit of human justice."

——*Abraham D. Lavender*

BIBLIOGRAPHY AND FURTHER READING

Cohen, Robert, and David J. Snyder, eds. *Rebellion in Black and White: Southern Student Activism in the 1960s.* Baltimore: Johns Hopkins UP, 2013. Print.

Eversley, Melanie. "Orangeburg Massacre Stirs Debate 44 Years Later." *USA Today.* USA Today, 21 Sept. 2012. Web. 24 Apr. 2015.

Levy, Peter B. *The Civil Rights Movement in America: From Black Nationalism to the Women's Political Council.* Santa Barbara: Greenwood, 2015. Print.

Shuler, Jack. *Blood and Bone: Truth and Reconciliation in a Southern Town.* Columbia: U of South Carolina P, 2012. Print.

Turner, Jeffrey A. *Sitting In and Speaking Out: Student Movements in the American South, 1960–1970.* Athens: U of Georgia P, 2010. Print.

ORIENTALISM

According to Edward Said's 1978 study, Orientalism is a Eurocentric perspective that reflects the domination of the West (the Occident) over the East (the Orient) from the early expansion of capitalism and imperialism to the present. It is a racist construction of Eastern societies as stagnant, militaristic, irrational, and despotic in contrast to Western societies as progressive, civil, rational, and individualistic. By extension, this approach also portrays the peoples of Asia as intrinsically inferior to Europeans. Hence, Orientalism is an ideology that justifies the oppression and colonization of Asians in Asia and North America.

Increasingly, Orientalism also refers to an overgeneralized and stereotypical way of thinking about all Asian Americans as physically and culturally identical. This style of thought or misconception is very common among white Americans as well as other non-Asians. Chinese Americans and Vietnamese Americans are often mistaken for Japanese Americans, who may in turn be mistaken for Korean Americans. Non-Asian Americans, because of what they perceive as Asian Americans' indistinguishable non-European appearance, frequently view Asian Americans as "foreigners" regardless of their nativity, generation, nationality, and citizenship status. The misconceived Asian cultural homogeneity breeds cultural insensitivity. Furthermore, the misconception of Asian similitude from time to time results in anti-Asian violence based on "mistaken identities." In 1982, Chinese American Vincent Chin was "mistaken" for a Japanese and murdered; in 1989, Chinese American Jim Ming Hai Loo was murdered by people who thought he was Vietnamese.

——*Philip Q. Yang*

BIBLIOGRAPHY AND FURTHER READING

Attwell, David, Anna Bernard, and Ziad Elmarsafy. *Debating Orientalism.* New York: Palgrave, 2013. Print.

Rudolph Valentino and Agnes Ayres in The Sheik, 1921. By Guil2027.

Kennedy, Valerie. *Edward Said: A Critical Introduction.* Cambridge: Wiley, 2000. Print.

Macfie, Alexander Lyon. *Orientalism.* Hoboken: Routledge, 2014. Print.

Said, Edward W. *Orientalism.* 1978. New York: Knopf, 2014. Print.

"OTHER" THEORY AND RACIAL AND ETHNIC RELATIONS

The "other" theory has been advanced by sociologists and cultural critics of racial and ethnic relations, including Winthrop Jordan. In this theory, the "other" represents the totality of difference, the race that is apart from the self and therefore can be exoticized, appropriated, and dominated. Because white people have historically been the dominant group socially, politically, and economically in North America, the other refers to nonwhite people. "Otherness" is a psychological and social construct that assumes various forms. The three most typical expressions of the other theory are seen in fashion, sexual imagining, and projected images of aggression.

On the level of fashion and style, white identification with the other is represented by what scholar Cornel West calls "the Afro-Americanization of white youth": young men who sport dreadlocks, baggy jeans, and backward baseball caps. For young women, the markers of this identification include corn-rowed hair and big gold earrings, though these markers are less distinct in the popular imagination.

Fashion is a benign form of "otherizing," or fetishizing, and may or may not lead to a more sexual imagining of the other, referred to by cultural critic bell hooks as "eating the other." In this instance, the salient experience in the confrontation with the other is the desire for sexual pleasure and domination. Difference is seductive not only because of historical myths about the more primitive, sensual, and sexually uninhibited nature of black people but also because, as some scholars describe it, "the other is coded as having the capacity to be more alive, as holding the secret that will allow those who venture and dare to break with the [incapacity for happiness] and experience sensual and spiritual renewal" (bell hooks, *Black Looks*, Boston: South End Press, 1992). Once otherness and whiteness converge, physically and spiritually, in the white imagination, the abhorrent history of subjugation and exploitation of dark others by white people is magically obviated. Whites can not only experience the other, they can become the other.

In the midst of this racial transcendence, how does the creation of the other in the white imagination lead to racism and racial violence? Encounters with the other invite both a vicarious engagement with primitive desires and a further psychological distancing between the white person and the dark other. When an individual from the dominant group believes that an individual from a minority group is so different from himself or herself that the minority group member's humanity is unrecognizable (a central justification for slavery was that Africans were not human), then fantasies have free rein. For while the other is perceived as having liberating, primitive qualities, the repugnant side of racial mythmaking, fed by images in popular culture of the black male "thug," is the notion of the dark other as more aggressive and violent. Historically, the dominant group has responded to the perceived threat of violence with swift, preemptive violence.

——*Chalis Holton*

BIBLIOGRAPHY AND FURTHER READING

Cots, Montserrat, et al, eds. *Interrogating Gazes: Comparative Critical Views on the Representation of Foreignness and Otherness.* Bern: P. Lang, 2014. Print.

Fernandez Ulloa, Teresa. *Otherness in Hispanic Culture.* Newcastle upon Tyne: Cambridge Scholars Pub., 2014. Print.

Freidenreich, David M. *Foreigners and Their Food: Constructing Otherness in Jewish, Christian, and Islamic Law.* Berkeley: U of California P, 2011. Print.

Hartelius, E. Johanna, ed. *The Rhetorics of US Immigration: Identity, Community, Otherness.* University Park: Pennsylvania State UP, 2015. Print.

Picard, David, and Michael A. Di Giovine, eds. *Tourism and the Power of Otherness.* Toronto: Channel View, 2014. Print.

OUT-GROUP

An out-group is a group to which a person does not belong. People differentiate between the groups to which they belong (in-groups) and the groups to which they do not belong (out-groups). Out-group membership can be based on ethnicity, gender, geographic location, class, team membership, or any other feature that people use to differentiate themselves from others.

Out-group categorization affects how people are perceived and often how they perceive themselves. For example, people categorized as out-group members are more likely to be viewed according to unfavorable stereotypes. A by-product of such categorization is stereotype threat, whereby out-group members feel pressured by the potential for a negative stereotype to be confirmed by that member's performance.

Stereotypes are also perpetuated in literature. Out-group members also are seen as very similar to one another, a phenomenon called out-group homogeneity. Many people have an in-group bias and more readily perceive negative behaviors in out-group members than in-group members. In-group members often exaggerate differences between themselves and the out-group on traits that the in-group members regard as superior. People in Eastern (collectivist) societies tend to differentiate between in-groups and out-groups more than people in Western (individualistic) societies. One way to reduce prejudice toward out-group members is to recategorize them as in-group members.

———*Lyn M. Van Swol*

OZAWA V. UNITED STATES

In the early twentieth century, naturalization was under the effective control of local and state authorities. In California and other Pacific states, fears of the "yellow peril" or "silent invasion" of Asian immigrants were deeply entrenched and politically exploited. In such states, citizenship had been repeatedly denied to both Chinese and more recent Japanese settlers, although there were some rare exceptions. The prevailing belief among the nativist majority was that such settlers should be ineligible for US citizenship.

BACKGROUND
Partly to test the Alien Land Act—a California law passed in 1913 that barred non-citizens from owning land in that state—Takao Ozawa sought US citizenship in defiance of a 1906 law (US Revised Statute, section 2169) that limited naturalization to "free white persons," "aliens of African nativity," and "persons of African descent." Although born in Japan, Ozawa had been educated in the United States. He

was graduated from high school in Berkeley and for three years attended the University of California. He was aware that some Issei (first-generation Japanese immigrants) had been naturalized, even in California. Specifically, Ozawa may have known of Iwao Yoshikawa, the first Japanese immigrant to be naturalized in California. Yoshikawa had arrived in San Francisco from Japan in 1887. A law clerk in his homeland, he had studied US law in his adopted country and served as a court translator. In 1889 he began the naturalization process, which, presumably, was completed five years later, although there is no extant record of his naturalization. His case was publicized because it broached such issues as mandatory citizenship renunciation and the legality of dual citizenship.

Regardless of Ozawa's knowledge of Yoshikawa, on October 16, 1914, Ozawa applied for US citizenship before the district court for the Territory of Hawaii. He argued that he had resided in the United

States and its territory of Hawaii for a total of twenty years, had adopted the culture and language of his host country, had reared his children as Americans in heart and mind, and was, by character and education, wholly qualified for naturalization.

The district court ruled against Ozawa on the grounds that his Japanese ethnicity denied him access to naturalization. Ozawa then took his case to the Ninth Circuit Court of Appeals, which passed it to the US Supreme Court for instruction. In turn, the Supreme Court upheld the laws that in effect declared Ozawa ineligible for citizenship.

Rather than question the justice of the racial restrictions on naturalization, the opinion limited its focus to clarifying the meaning of the term "white persons" and distinguishing between "Caucasian" and "white person," determining that the latter, while a more inclusive term than the former, is not so inclusive as to include persons of Asian extraction. It concluded that "a person of the Japanese race is not a free white person, within the meaning of US Rev. Stat. § 2169[the 1906 law], limiting the provisions of the title on naturalization to aliens being free white persons, and to aliens of African nativity, and to persons of African descent, and therefore such Japanese is not eligible to naturalization as a United States citizen.…"

In tracing the history of the naturalization laws, the Court attempted to demonstrate that all statutes preceding the 1906 act contested by Ozawa had the same intent: the selective admission to citizenship based on the interpretation of "white," not as a racial appellation but as a reflection of character. It argued that the words "free white persons" did not indicate persons of a particular race or origin, but rather that they describe "personalities" and "persons fit for citizenship and of the kind admitted to citizenship by the policy of the United States." According to that doctrine, any non-African alien, if desired by Congress, might be deemed "white." Thus, the Court reasoned, "when the long-looked-for Martian immigrants reach this part of the earth, and in due course a man from Mars applies to be naturalized, he may be recognized as white within the meaning of the act of Congress, and admitted to citizenship, although he may not be a Caucasian."

Regardless of this race disclaimer, however, the Court, in reasoning through its arguments, distinguished between "whites" (all Europeans, for example) and "nonwhites" (such as the Chinese) on ethnic grounds pure and simple. The decision throughout sanctioned racial biases that assumed that an individual's character was in some way delimited by his or her racial heritage. For example, at one point it provided a formulaic approach to determining citizenship eligibility for persons of mixed blood, supporting the idea, widely observed, that in order to be construed as white, a person must be "of more than half white blood." Clearly, the decision upheld the seriously flawed assumption that character and racial heritage were inextricably interrelated.

NATIVIST SENTIMENT

The Supreme Court's ruling reflected the prevailing nativist bias against Asian immigrants, an attitude that was reflected in both law and policy through the first half of the twentieth century. In fact, no more formidable barriers to citizenship were erected than those facing the Issei (first-generation Japanese), Chinese, and other Asian immigrants. In 1924, an isolationist Congress enacted an immigration act placing numerical restrictions on immigrants allowed into the United States based on national origin. One provision of the Immigration Act of 1924, known as the Johnson Act, excluded immigrants ineligible for naturalization. Its obvious aim—to bar entry of Japanese aliens—quickly led to a deterioration in the diplomatic relations between Japan and the United States.

The plight of Japanese already in the United States also worsened in the anti-Asian climate. In separate rulings, the Supreme Court went so far as to revoke citizenship that had been granted to some Issei. In 1925, it even denied that service in the armed forces made Issei eligible for naturalization, overturning a policy that had previously been in effect. Not only were Issei barred from naturalization; in many states, "alien land laws" prohibited them from owning land and even entering some professions.

That codified prejudice partly accounts for but does not justify the terrible treatment of Japanese Americans during World War II, when 112,000 of them, including 70,000 Nisei (persons of Japanese descent born in the United States), were rounded up and incarcerated in detention centers that bore some grim similarities to the concentration camps of Europe. It was not until the passage of the

Immigration and Nationality Act of 1952 that the long-standing racial barriers to naturalization finally came down.

——*John W. Fiero*

BIBLIOGRAPHY AND FURTHER READING

Curran, Thomas J. *Xenophobia and Immigration, 1820-1930.* Boston: Twayne, 1975. Print.

O'Brien, David J., and Stephen Fugita. *The Japanese American Experience.* Bloomington: Indiana UP, 1991. Print.

Takaki, Ronald. *Strangers from a Different Shore: A History of Asian Americans.* Boston: Little, Brown, 1989. Print.

Vile, John R., ed. *American Immigration and Citizenship: A Documentary History.* Lanham: Rowman and Littlefield, 2016. Print.

P

PADILLA V. COMMONWEALTH OF KENTUCKY

José Padilla, a Honduras national, was a permanent resident of the United States, having lived in the country for about forty years. He had served in the US military during the Vietnam War. Padilla worked as a truck driver. In September 2001 he was arrested in Kentucky after a police officer conducted a document check on Padilla's truck, and with Padilla's permission, searched his vehicle and found nearly two dozen boxes that contained altogether about a half ton of marijuana. Padilla was later indicted by a Kentucky grand jury on counts of trafficking more than five pounds of marijuana, possession of marijuana, possession of drug paraphernalia, and operating a tractor/trailer without a weight and distance tax number. Based on Kentucky law, if convicted, Padilla could receive a sentence of five to ten years in prison because the weight of the marijuana that was discovered in his possession made it a Class C felony.

Padilla was given a state-funded attorney. In 2002, he pleaded guilty to the first three counts, which his lawyer advised, as long as the last charge was dismissed. As part of the plea, he would serve five years in prison and be on probation for another five years. Padilla's lawyer told him that Padilla did not need to be concerned with deportation because of his legal status as a permanent resident and the length of his residency in the United States.

Under federal law, the charges against Padilla could have led to his deportation. Because he feared being deported, in August 2004, Padilla filed a motion that his lawyer misadvised him and that he only pleaded guilty because of the reassurance by his counsel that he would not be deported. He filed this motion because he worried that he would be deported. Padilla explained that he would have never pleaded guilty had he known that the charges against him could lead to his deportation. The Kentucky Court of Appeals reversed Padilla's conviction and remanded the case. In 2008, the Kentucky Supreme Court reversed this decision, stating that even if an attorney fails to tell a client that about "collateral consequences" (any additional civil state penalties that are attached to criminal convictions) or misadvises a client about collateral consequences that is not grounds for changing or lightening the conviction. Padilla then petitioned the US Supreme Court. The two questions posted before the Court in March 2012 were: (1) Is the mandatory deportation that results from a guilty plea to trafficking marijuana a collateral consequence that releases counsel from having to advise his or her client based on the rights outlined in the Sixth Amendment; and (2) if deportation is a collateral consequence, can counsel's lack of advice about such deportation serve as grounds for putting aside a guilty plea that was entered by a client based upon that advice?

OPINION OF THE COURT

In a 7–2 decision, the Supreme Court ruled that Padilla's Sixth Amendment rights (i.e., a criminal defendant is entitled to effective assistance when deciding whether to plead guilty) were violated when Padilla's counsel did not disclose to him—a noncitizen—that a guilty plea could lead to his deportation. Further, counsel should inform a noncitizen of collateral consequences that would lead to the noncitizen's deportation. Justices John Paul Stevens, Anthony Kennedy, Ruth Bader Ginsburg, Stephen Breyer, and Sonia Sotomayor concurred. As Justice Stevens wrote:

The importance of accurate legal advice for non-citizens accused of crimes has never been more important. These changes confirm our view, that as a matter of federal law, deportation is an integral part—indeed, sometimes the most important part—of the penalty that may be imposed on noncitizen defendants who plead guilty to specific crimes.

Justice Samuel Alito, who was joined by Justice John Roberts, wrote a concurring opinion. Alito expressed that the Court cannot expect that a criminal defense attorney be versed in all of our country's immigration laws and that an alien (noncitizen) should consult an immigration attorney about matters relating to immigration consequences.

Justice Antonin Scalia, who was joined by Clarence Thomas, wrote the dissenting opinion. Scalia said that the Court was expanding and going beyond the text of the Sixth Amendment, which outlines that counsel must provide good advice about the collateral consequences of the conviction.

IMPACT

In a day and age when there has been a plethora of immigration laws passed that make some criminal convictions grounds for deportation, the Court's decision in *Padilla v. Commonwealth of Kentucky* had significant implications. First, it gave noncitizens, especially Latinos, more faith in the US legal system, especially as it makes counsel, which in many cases can be state-funded and appointed, accountable for his or her advice in plea bargains. Second, the Court's decision in *Padilla* brought to light that citizenship takes a key place in the process of criminal cases. Deportation is a real threat to many immigrants in the United States, especially Latinos. As immigration reform continues to be a hot topic among political parties and platforms, many immigrants are concerned they could be deported and their families broken apart. Many hold the perception that there is a general feeling among the American public on immigration reform and the need to limit immigration.

Consequently, not long after the *Padilla* decision, Senior Counsel and founder of the Immigrant

Defense Project (IDP), Manuel D. Vargas, compiled an advisory and a number of resources for practitioners to aid them in the evaluation of consequences that are added to criminal convictions

———*Amy Weber*

BIBLIOGRAPHY AND FURTHER READING

Arnold, Kathryn R. *Contemporary Immigration in America: A State-by-State Encyclopedia.* Santa Barbara: ABC-CLIO, 2015. Print.

Kurbin, Charis E., Marjorie S. Zatz, and Ramiro Martinez, eds. *Punishing Immigrants: Policy, Politics, and Injustice* (New Perspectives in Crime, Deviance, and Law). New York: New York UP, 2012. Print.

Love, Margaret Colgate. "Collateral Consequences after *Padilla v. Kentucky*: From Punishment to Regulation." *Saint Louis University Public Law Review* (2011): 87–128. Web. 2 Feb. 2016

Luna, Erik, and Marianne Wade. *The Prosecutor in Transnational Perspective.* New York: Oxford UP, 2012. Print.

Murphy, Kara B. "Representing Noncitizens in Criminal Proceedings: Resolving Unanswered Questions in *Padilla v. Kentucky*." *Journal of Criminal Law and Criminology* 101.4 (2011). Web. 2 Feb. 2016.

"Padilla v. Commonwealth of Kentucky." *Supreme Court of the United States.* Supreme Court of the US, 2011. Web. 2 Feb. 2016.

Rosenberg, Joanna. "A Game Changer? The Impact of *Padilla v. Kentucky* on the Collateral Consequences Rule and Ineffective Assistance of Counsel Claims." *Fordham Law Review* 3.7 (2013). Web. 2 Feb. 2016.

"Supreme Court of the United States Jose Padilla, Petitioner v. Kentucky." *Legal Information Institute.* Cornell University Law School, n.d. Web. 2 Feb. 2016.

PAGE LAW

On February 10, 1875, California congressman Horace F. Page introduced federal legislation designed to prohibit the immigration of Asian female prostitutes into the United States. Officially titled "An Act Supplementary to the Acts in Relation to

Immigration," the Page law evolved into a restriction against vast numbers of Chinese immigrants into the country regardless of whether they were prostitutes. Any person convicted of importing Chinese prostitutes was subject to a maximum prison term of five years and a fine of not more than five thousand dollars. An amendment to the law prohibited individuals from engaging in the "coolie trade," or the importation of Chinese contract laborers. Punishment for this type of violation, however, was much less severe and was much more difficult to effect, given the large numbers of Asian male immigrants at the time. As a consequence of this division of penalties, the law was applied in a most gender-specific manner, effectively deterring the immigration of Asian females into the United States. Within seven years following the implementation of the law, the average number of Chinese female immigrants dropped to one-third of its previous level.

Enforcement and Implementation

An elaborate bureaucratic network established to carry out the Page law's gender-specific exclusions was a catalyst for the decline in Chinese immigration rates. American consulate officials supported by American, Chinese, and British commercial, political, and medical services made up the law's implementation structure. Through intelligence gathering, interrogation, and physical examinations of applicants, the consulate hierarchy ferreted out undesirable applicants for emigration and those suspected of engaging in illegal human trafficking.

This investigative activity evolved well beyond the original intent of the law's authors. Any characteristic or activity that could be linked, even in the most remote sense, to prostitution became grounds for denial to emigrate. Most applications to emigrate came from women from the lower economic strata of society; low economic status therefore became a reason for immigration exclusion. The procedure was a complicated one. Many roadblocks were placed in the way of prospective immigrants. Acquiring permission to emigrate took much time and effort. Passing stringent physical examinations performed by biased health care officials was often impossible. Navigating language barriers through official interviews aimed at evaluating personal character often produced an atmosphere of rigid interrogation, bringing subsequent denial of the right to emigrate. Such a complex system aimed at uncovering fraudulent immigrants placed a hardship upon those wishing to leave China.

Because Hong Kong was the main point of departure for Chinese emigrating to the United States, all required examinations were performed there with a hierarchy of American consulate officials determining immigrant eligibility. In a sense, the Page law actually expanded consulate authority beyond any previous level.

Corruption Charges

Such increased power of the consular general in implementing the law provided an opportunity for possible abuses of power. In 1878, the US consul general in Hong Kong, John Mosby, accused his predecessors of corruption and bribery. According to Mosby, David Bailey and H. Sheldon Loring were guilty of embezzlement. Both men were accused of setting up such an intricate system to process immigration application that bribery soon became the natural way to obtain the necessary permission to do so. Mosby went on to charge that Bailey had amassed thousands of dollars of extra income by regularly charging additional examination fees regardless of whether an exam was performed. Mosby also accused Bailey of falsifying test results and encouraging medical personnel to interrogate applicants in order to deny immigration permission to otherwise legal immigrants.

Most of the allegations of corruption surrounded the fact that monies allotted by the federal government for implementation of the Page law were far below the amount Bailey required to run his administration of it. Given this scenario, the US government scrutinized Bailey's conduct. No indictments came from the official investigation, however, and Bailey, who had previously been promoted to vice consul general in Shanghai, remained in that position. Further examination of Bailey's tenure in Hong Kong has suggested that, if anything, he was an overly aggressive official who made emigration of Chinese women to the United States a priority issue of his tenure there rather than an opportunity for profit.

Bailey was replaced in Hong Kong by H. Sheldon Loring. Unlike his predecessor, Loring did not enforce the Page law with as much vigor, allowing a slight yet insignificant increase in the annual numbers of Chinese immigrants. Nevertheless, Loring did enforce the law in an efficient manner, publicly suggesting that any ship owner who engaged in the illegal transport of women would be dealt with to the fullest extent of the law. Even so, Loring was accused of sharing Bailey's enthusiasm for the unofficial expensive design of the immigration procedure.

During Loring's tenure, questions about his character began to surface mostly on account of his past relationships with individuals who engaged in questionable business practices in Asia. By the time that Mosby replaced him, such questions had become more than a nuisance. The new US consul to Hong Kong began to describe his predecessor as a dishonest taker of bribes. Once again, the official dynamics of such charges brought forth an official inquiry from Washington. Like the previous investigation of Bailey, however, this investigation produced no official indictment against Loring. The only blemish concerned an additional fee that Loring had instituted for the procuring of an official landing certificate. As there was precedent for such a fee, Loring, like his predecessor, was exonerated of all charges.

Having decided that his predecessors were indeed corrupt, yet unable to prove it, Mosby pursued enforcement of the Page law with relentless occupation. Keeping a posture that was above accusations of corruption, Mosby personally interviewed each applicant for emigration, oversaw the activities between the consulate and the health examiners, and eliminated the additional charges for the landing permits. In the end, the numbers of Chinese immigrants remained similar to those of Loring and below those of Bailey, with the numbers of Chinese female immigrants continuing to decline. Aside from being free from charges of corruption, Mosby's tenure in office was as authoritative as those of his predecessors.

Regardless of the personalities of the consulate officials in charge of implementing the Page law, the results were the same: The number of Chinese who emigrated to the United States decreased dramatically between the 1875 enactment of the law and the enactment of its successor, the Chinese Exclusion Act of 1882. Furthermore, the law's specific application to Chinese women ensured a large imbalance between numbers of male and female immigrants during the period under consideration. In the long run that imbalance negatively affected Asian American families who had settled in the United States. The barriers that the Page law helped to erect against female Chinese immigrants made a strong nuclear family structure within the Asian American community an immigrant dream rather than a reality.

——*Thomas J. Edward Walker and Cynthia Gwynne Yaudes*

BIBLIOGRAPHY AND FURTHER READING

Abrams, Kerry. "Polygamy, Prostitution, and the Federalization of Immigration Law." *Columbia Law Review* 105.3 (2005): 641–716. Web.

Cheng, Lucie, and Edna Bonacich. *Labor Immigration Under Capitalism.* Berkeley: U of California P, 1984. Print.

Foner, Philip, and Daniel Rosenberg. *Racism, Dissent, and Asian Americans from 1850 to the Present.* Westport: Greenwood, 1993. Print.

Luibhéid, Eithne. "A Blueprint for Exclusion: The Page Law, Prostitution, and Discrimination against Chinese Women." *Sex, Gender, and Sexuality: The New Basics: An Anthology.* 2nd ed. New York: Oxford UP, 2013. 276–291. Web. 12 May 2015. Peffer, George Anthony. "Forbidden Families: Emigration Experience of Chinese Women Under the Page Law, 1875–1882" *Journal of American Ethnic History* 6 (1986). Print.

PAN-AFRICANISM

A broad movement aimed at the political unification of Africa through the destruction of European colonialism, Pan-Africanism includes the political independence and freedom of all peoples of African descent who live in the West Indies, the Americas, and other concentrated areas. Pan-African Congresses provide the forum at which movement members can disseminate ideas. The first Congress was held in London during the summer of 1990. W. E. B. Du Bois, credited as the father of the concept, and George Padmore, a West Indian intellectual, were both prolific advocates and key theoreticians of the Pan-African ideology.

Early post-colonial nation-states' leaders—such as Kwame Nkrumah (Ghana), Eric Williams (Trinidad/Tobago), Norman Manley (Jamaica), Gamal Abdel Nasser (Egypt), and Jomo Kenyatta (Kenya)—were significantly influenced by Pan-Africanist philosophy and espoused and utilized its concepts in forming their own organizations to advance the liberation of peoples of African descent. Marcus Garvey's Back-to-Africa social movement in the 1920s was the largest and best approximation of this movement in the United States. Finally, this movement can also be regarded as the theoretical precursor to the black nationalism movement that swept the United States in the 1960s.

——*Aubrey W. Bonnett*

BIBLIOGRAPHY AND FURTHER READING

Falola, Toyin, and Kwame Essien, eds. *Pan-Africanism and the Politics of African Citizenship and Identity.* New York: Routledge, 2014. Print.

James, Leslie. *George Padmore and Decolonization from Below: Pan-Africanims, the Cold War, and the End of Empire.* New York: Palgrave, 2014. Print.

Sherwood, Marika. *Origins of Pan-Africanism: Henry Sylvester Williams, Africa, and the African Diaspora.* New York: Routledge, 2011. Print.

PANETHNICITY

Panethnicity (or macroethnicity) refers to inclusive group identities formed through the merger of smaller national, regional, or tribal groups. For example, the Hispanic or Latino American panethnicity encompasses such ethnicities as Puerto Rican, Mexican American, and Cuban American. Some major panethnic groups are Hispanic Americans, Euro-Americans, Jewish Americans, Asian Americans, Native Americans, Arab Americans, West Indians, and African Americans (if the term is applied to all peoples of the African diaspora).

For individuals, panethnic affiliations represent one choice among multiple layers of ethnic identity. Depending on the context, a person could present himself or herself as, for example, Afro-American, West Indian, or Jamaican—the more specific

identities being especially meaningful within the panethnic group. As a social phenomenon, panethnicity reflects the social construction and variable nature of ethnic identities. Although early discussions of panethnicity emphasized the importance of cultural similarity, recent works have focused upon the role of structural forces. In *Asian-American Panethnicity: Bridging Institutions and Identities* (1992), Yen Le Espiritu observed that the creation of panethnic groups involves both the active building of political coalitions among smaller groups and the imposition of labels by external groups, such as racial categories employed by the US government. Consequently, panethnic identities are constantly undergoing change.

——*Ashley W. Doane, Jr.*

PAN-INDIANISM

Since the 1960s American Indians have become increasingly politicized and reform-minded. This mobilization has occurred along three lines: tribal, pantribal, and pan-Indian. Tribal activity focuses on organizations or actions by and for members of a specific tribe. This type of movement usually concentrates on the protection or expansion of a single tribe's rights or opportunities. Pantribalism occurs when two or more tribal entities unite in pursuit of a mutually beneficial goal. The Council of Energy Resource Tribes (CERT) is an example of such activity. Tribal and pantribal mobilizations are distinct from the pan-Indian movement, which promotes the universality of the Indian experience and

emphasizes ethnic identification rather than tribal affiliations. According to Vine Deloria, Jr., a nationally recognized authority on Indian rights, in his work *The Nations Within: The Past and Future of American Indian Sovereignty* (1984), "the tribes are concerned with the substance of Indian life while the ethnics [pan-Indianists] look to the process."

HISTORICAL BACKGROUND

The pan-Indian movement had its inception during the opening decades of the nineteenth century. The first definable pan-Indian action occurred during the War of 1812 at the instigation of the Shawnee chief Tecumseh and his brother, a revivalist religious leader named Tenskwatawa (the Shawnee Prophet). Urging the various tribes at the frontier to put aside their differences and to oppose the encroachment of the US government, Tecumseh proclaimed in 1810, "The only way to stop the evil is for the red men to unite in claiming a common and equal right in the land, as it was at first and should be now—for it was never divided but belonged to all." The pan-Indian activity during the remainder of the nineteenth century focused on a combination of strategies and objectives guided largely by religious inspiration. The most notable of these mobilizations remains the Ghost Dance revivals of the Great Plains fostered by the Paiute spiritual leader Wovoka.

At the beginning of the twentieth century, this movement acquired different direction and form. The focal point shifted from religious revival toward political and civil equity and more formal organization. In 1912, for example, a group of Indians drawn together by common experience founded the Society of American Indians. This group continues its commitment to collective action and its promotion of a variety of pan-Indian and pantribal activities. One such organization was the National Congress of American Indians, founded in 1944 by the Indian employees of the Bureau of Indian Affairs. Its primary purpose remains the lobbying for American Indian causes and rights.

DEVELOPMENTS SINCE WORLD WAR II

During the last half of the twentieth century, distinctions between pantribal and pan-Indian mobilizations became more pronounced. Government programs and policies aimed at termination of tribal status gave the movements greater impetus. The general atmosphere of protest and reform during the 1960s and early 1970s radicalized the behavior of Indian reformers. An early indicator of the growing schism and changes in tactics was the founding of the National Indian Youth Council in 1961. Frustrated by the "poetic" responses of the older, more established pan-Indian organizations, a group of younger, more radical leaders led by Clyde Warrior, a Ponca, and Mel Thom, a Paiute, formed a new organization. They urged their audiences to come to grips with the continued paternalism of the federal government and its failure to correct dire social and economic conditions confronting Indians everywhere. Their cause, according to Thom, was "a Greater Indian

America." This action also foreshadowed the development of the Red Power mobilizations of the 1970s and the constituency within which they would find their base. This movement attracted the interest of urban Indians whose identification was ethnic rather than tribal in nature.

Among the most important and visible organizations of the next generation of organizations was the American Indian Movement (AIM), founded in 1968 in Minneapolis by Dennis Banks, George Mitchell, and Clyde Bellecourt of the Chippewa (Ojibwa), and Russell Means, a Sioux. This group advocated a much broader range of tactics to accomplish their purpose. In addition to legal recourse, they employed protest demonstrations, sit-ins and occupations, and occasional violence to promote their causes. Two of the most memorable of these activities were the occupation of Alcatraz Island in 1969 and the violent stand-off at Wounded Knee in 1973. The founding of the International Indian Treaty Council and the Women of All Red Nations represents institutional outgrowths of the AIM mobilization.

During the 1970s and into the 1980s, this movement has also discovered some limitations, especially with regard to goal setting and continued competition with traditional tribal organizations. The strongest supporters of the pan-Indian mobilization remain urban Indians whose tribal affiliations have eroded. In large and often hostile cities, Indians of various tribes find it easier to identify with one another than with the larger communities that surround them. They acknowledge a common ethnic origin and welcome partnerships across tribal lines. This tendency places them at odds with many tribalists who are more traditional in their approach and perceive this blending as a dilution of their identities. Pan-Indianists have also realized that defining themselves, their ideals, and their objectives in the abstract is much simpler than developing specific plans of action. All but the broadest of their objectives involve groups too specific to be truly considered pan-Indian in nature.

——*Martha I. Pallante*

BIBLIOGRAPHY AND FURTHER READING

Lawson, Russell M., ed. *Encyclopedia of American Indian Issues Today.* Santa Barbara: ABC-CLIO, 2013. Print.

McGlennen, Molly. *Creative Alliances: The Transnational Designs of Indigenous Women's Poetry.* Norman: U of Oklahoma P, 2014. Print.

McPherson, Dennis H., and J. Douglas Rabb. *Indian from the Inside: Native American Philosophy and Cultural Renewal.* 2nd ed. Jefferson: McFarland, 2011. Print.

Shreve, Bradley G. *Red Power Rising: The National Indian Youth Council and the Origins of Native Activism.* Norman: U of Oklahoma P, 2011. Print.

Pasadena City Board of Education v. Spangler

In 1968, several students and their parents filed suit against the Pasadena Unified School District in California, alleging that the district's schools were segregated as a result of official action on the part of the district. In 1970, the federal district court found for these plaintiffs, concluding that the district had engaged in segregation and ordering the district to adopt a plan to cure the racial imbalances in its schools. The federal court's order provided that no school was to have a majority of minority students. The district thereafter presented the court with a plan to eliminate segregation in the Pasadena schools; the court approved the plan, and the district subsequently implemented it.

Approximately four years later, the Pasadena Unified School District asked the district court to modify its original order and eliminate the requirement that no school have a majority of minority students. The district contended that though it had abandoned its racially segregative practices, changing racial demographics had created new racial imbalances in the district's schools. The federal district court refused to modify its original order, however, and the Ninth Circuit Court of Appeals upheld the district court's ruling.

Reviewing this decision, Justice William H. Rehnquist, joined by five other justices, concluded that the district court had abused its authority in refusing to remove the requirement that no district school have a majority of minority students. According to the Supreme Court, there had been no showing that changes in the racial mix of the Pasadena schools had been caused by the school district's policies. Since the school district had implemented a racially neutral attendance policy, the federal district court was not entitled to require a continual reshuffling of attendance zones to maintain an optimal racial mix. Justices Thurgood Marshall and William Brennan dissented from this holding, emphasizing the breadth of discretion normally allotted to federal district courts to remedy school segregation once a constitutional violation had been shown.

The majority's decision signaled that the broad discretion with which the Court previously had seemed to have invested federal district courts was not without limits. It had been widely thought that once officially sanctioned or de jure segregation had been shown, a federal court had great latitude in eliminating not only such de jure segregation but also de facto segregation—that is, segregation not necessarily tied to official conduct. The majority's decision in this case, however, signified otherwise.

——Timothy L. Hall

Passing and race relations

Passing is the concealment of one's racial identity or ethnicity to gain access to another racial or ethnic group, usually to obtain social and economic benefits. Passing has been used by African Americans, Asian Americans, and Latino Americans as a means of transcending racial stigmatization and marginalization, especially during the period of de jure segregation. Most commonly, individuals of biracial or multiracial descent who had certain characteristics associated with whiteness broke from their minority heritage and lived within the dominant white community. These characteristics included a light skin tone, "European" facial features, and a high level of acculturation to white society. Because the differences in skin tone and facial features are typically less dramatic, Asian Americans and Latino Americans generally had an easier time passing for white than did African Americans. Asian Americans and Latino Americans who wished to pass as white and have the necessary physical characteristics might only have had to anglicize their names or adopt white surnames. African Americans unable to pass as white often passed as Asian Americans or Native Americans to achieve a slightly higher status in society.

Passing could be temporary or permanent. It was a largely urban phenomenon, since individuals in rural areas were more likely to be recognized and hence were less able to escape their racial identities. The most common form of passing involved a temporary leave from one's racial identity, possibly to enter a white establishment or to hold a job; cases of individuals who permanently left their racial identities to assume lives within white society were probably less common.

There were drawbacks associated with both temporary and permanent acts of passing. For example, those who passed temporarily in order to hold jobs were faced with the constant pressure of operating in two different and antagonistic worlds while keeping their two identities separate. Those who chose to pass for white permanently were generally forced to leave behind their families and friends, and they lived with the constant fear that someone might learn their secret. Because of the secretive nature of the phenomenon, it is impossible to assess with any accuracy the number of individuals who have engaged in passing. It is also difficult to know whether passing has actually decreased in the era of desegregation, though the greater access that racial minorities have to all realms of society has probably removed the immediate impetus behind the act of passing.

The concept of passing is based on ideas of racial purity and the drawing of rigid racial boundaries by which individuals of biracial or multiracial descent are considered part of the minority group. An example of this is the "one-drop rule," which stipulated that any individual with even one drop of black blood was black. The idea of passing thus has meaning only within a society that defines race as mutually exclusive categories. Two important works that deal with the issue of passing are Paul R. Spickard's *Mixed Blood: Intermarriage and Ethnic Identity in Twentieth-Century America* (1989) and Maria P. P. Root's *Racially Mixed People in America* (1992).

——*Erica Childs*

BIBLIOGRAPHY AND FURTHER READING

Davis, F. James. "Who Is Black? One Nation's Definition." *Frontline.* WGBH Educational Foundation, 2014. Web. 30 Apr. 2015.

Guterl, Matthew Pratt. "Passing." *Seeing Race In Modern America.* Chapel Hill: U of North Carolina P, 2013. Print.

Hobbs, Allyson. *A Chosen Exile: A History of Racial Passing in American Life.* Cambridge: Harvard U, 2014. Print.

Mahtani, Minelle. *Mixed Race Amnesia: Resisting The Romanticization of Multiraciality.* Vancouver: U of British Columbia P, 2014. Print.

Norwood, Kimberly Jade, ed. *Color Matters: Skin Tone Bias and the Myth of a Postracial America.* New York: Routledge, 2014. Print.

Puente, Henry. "Racial Passing: Images of Mulattos, Mestizos, and Eurasians." *Images That Injure: Pictorial Stereotypes in the Media.* Ed. Paul Martin Lester and Susan Dente Ross. Santa Barbara: Praeger, 2011. 121–32. Print.

PATRIARCHAL SYSTEM

"Patriarchy" is defined as institutionalized power relationships that give men power over women. Motherhood, according to feminist poet Adrienne Rich, is also a social institution. In American society, motherhood is characterized by its isolation; it is difficult, tedious, and often frustrating work. The experience of motherhood is a mixture of satisfaction and

pleasure plus anger, frustration, and bitterness; it is also a role exclusively reserved for women.

Patriarchal systems, in which men dominate the social institutions of society by creating, developing, and managing those institutions, are maintained when women are designated as the primary child rearers. By ensuring that the weight of the responsibility for child rearing falls on women's shoulders, men win for themselves the right of "paternal neglect" (throwing themselves into their work, which ensures their primary role as economic provider). When women carry the primary responsibility for child rearing, their opportunities for professional success are necessarily limited, and as a result their economic dependence on their husbands is maintained. Alternative arrangements for rearing children and for balancing work and family commitments are not pressing concerns for men; the structural relegation of women to domestic service suits men's interests very well. Simply put, women's responsibility for children in the context of the nuclear family is an important buttress for a male-dominated society. It helps keep women out of the running for economic and political power.

——*Rochelle L. Dalla*

PELTIER CASE

On June 26, 1975, two agents of the Federal Bureau of Investigation (FBI) were killed in a shootout on the Lakota Indian Reservation in Pine Ridge, South Dakota. Leonard Peltier, a member of the American Indian Movement (AIM), was found guilty of the killings. Peltier declared himself innocent. Peltier appealed his conviction many times. During the appeals, the court found that the government had acted improperly in arresting and trying him. Federal authorities admitted to falsifying affidavits used to extradite Peltier from Canada. Witnesses in the original trial had been coerced, and evidence supporting Peltier's claims was suppressed. In spite of these irregularities, the courts refused to overturn Peltier's conviction. Peltier's case became known throughout the world. Many people believed that, even if he were guilty, he had not been granted a fair trial. Amnesty International declared him a political prisoner, and important religious leaders spoke out on his behalf. A book and three films were made about the case. In 2004, the Supreme Court rejected Peltier's appeal of a lower-court denial of parole. The following year, Bob Robideau, another AIM activist whose self-defense plea had led to his acquittal, confessed to the killings. Peltier's being denied parole again in 2009, his supporters continue to hope that they can win his release.

——*Cynthia A. Bily*

BIBLIOGRAPHY AND FURTHER READING

Johansen, Bruce E. "Peltier, Leonard." *Encyclopedia of the American Indian Movement.* Santa Barbara: Greenwood, 2013. 211–17. Print.

"Leonard Peltier." *Amnesty International.* Amnesty International USA, 2015. Web. 27 Apr. 2015.

Matthiessen, Peter. "The Tragedy of Leonard Peltier vs. the US." *New York Review of Books* 19 Nov. 2009: n. pag. Web. 27 Apr. 2015.

Peltier, Leonard. *Prison Writings: My Life Is My Sun Dance.* Ed. Harvey Arden. New York: St. Martin's, 1999. Print.

PENNSYLVANIA SOCIETY FOR THE ABOLITION OF SLAVERY

On April 14, 1775, a group of men gathered at the Sun Tavern on Second Street in Philadelphia to establish the first antislavery society in America. After electing John Baldwin their president and adopting a constitution, they named their organization the Society for the Relief of Free Negroes Unlawfully Held in Bondage. Sixteen of the twenty-four founders were members of the Society of Friends, or Quakers. The creation of this antislavery society was instigated when Philadelphia Quakers Israel Pemberton and Thomas Harrison aided Native American Dinah Neville and her children, who were being detained in Philadelphia pending their shipment to the West Indies to be sold as slaves.

Harrison was fined in a Philadelphia court for giving protection to the Neville family. When this incident gained notoriety, members of the Quaker Philadelphia Meeting mobilized to form the antislavery society. At its first meeting, the antislavery society enlisted legal counsel to help the Nevilles and five other victims illegally held in bondage and to form a standing committee to investigate any conditions of slavery in the Philadelphia area.

The Revolutionary War interrupted regular meetings until 1784. At this time, Quaker abolitionist Anthony Benezet revived the antislavery society as members learned that two African Americans had committed suicide rather than be illegally enslaved. Benezet increased the membership to forty, including Benjamin Franklin, James Pemberton, and Dr. Benjamin Rush. The society renamed itself the Pennsylvania Society for Promoting the Abolition of Slavery, for the Relief of Free Negroes Unlawfully Held in Bondage, and for Improving the Condition of the African Race. Since the majority of the members were Friends, the group developed directly from Quaker religious beliefs and within the Quaker social structure. To explore the founding of the Pennsylvania Society for the Abolition of Slavery, it is critical to trace events and movements within the Society of Friends in seventeenth century colonial Pennsylvania.

QUAKER BEGINNINGS

One of the basic principles espoused by Quaker founder George Fox was that all people are created equal. On a visit to the colonies in 1671, Fox spoke at Friends' meetings and encouraged Quaker slaveholders to free their slaves after a specified period of service. In 1676, Quaker William Edmundson, an associate of Fox, published the first antislavery literature in Rhode Island. While Quakers were formulating an antislavery position early in their movement, German Mennonites migrating to America had vowed that they would not own slaves. Several members of the Mennonite community and Dutch Pietists adopted Quakerism and became members of the Friends' Germantown Meeting. These German Quakers, their minister Pastorius, and other Friends of the Germantown Meeting delivered a petition to the Philadelphia Meeting in 1688 demanding that slavery and the slave trade be abolished. The protest addressed to slave owners of the Philadelphia

Monthly Meeting challenged these Friends to explain why they had slaves and how such a practice could exist in a colony founded on the principles of liberty and equality.

Representing the radical leadership of Philadelphia Friends, George Keith published a tract entitled *An Exhortation and Caution to Friends Concerning Buying or Keeping of Negroes*. He gave several directives: that Friends should not purchase African slaves except for the express purpose of setting them free, that those already purchased should be set free after a time of reasonable service, and that, while in service, slaves should be given a Christian education and taught how to read.

During the early eighteenth century, the conservative, wealthy membership of the Philadelphia Meeting took a somewhat confusing position on slavery. Their inconsistent policies included a separate meeting for African Americans, a request that Quakers in the West Indies stop shipping slaves to Philadelphia, and disciplinary measures for members of the meeting who were engaged in antislavery activity. Many prominent Quakers, such as James Logan, Jonathan Dickinson, and Isaac Norris, continued to purchase and own slaves.

The customary procedure of resolving issues at Friends' meetings was to achieve a consensus. Thus, the Quaker drift toward an antislavery sentiment gained momentum with the efforts of a few radicals but achieved success only when the majority bowed to the principles of Quaker conscience.

Unpopular radical member Benjamin Lay was unwelcome at the Philadelphia Meeting because of his unorthodox promotion of the antislavery cause. For example, Lay once had kidnapped a Quaker youth in order to illustrate the tragedy of abduction of African children for the slave trade. In 1738, at the Philadelphia Yearly Meeting, he wore a military uniform to emphasize the connection between slavery and war and concealed under his cloak an animal bladder that he had filled with red juice. Delivering an inflamed speech on the evils of slavery, he concluded by saying that slavery took the very lifeblood out of the slave, simultaneously piercing the bladder and splashing the horrified audience with simulated blood.

By the 1730s, the effects of the antislavery movement were evident among Quakers as more Friends provided for the manumission of their slaves in their wills. In addition, the increased immigration of Germans in need of work eliminated the demand for slave labor in the Middle Colonies.

John Woolman

Much of the credit for the success of the antislavery movement among Quakers must be given to New Jersey Quaker John Woolman. Known for his gentle, persuasive approach as a Quaker minister, he began a series of visitations to Quaker slaveholders in New England, the Middle Colonies, and the South in 1743. In 1754, he published *Some Considerations on the Keeping of Negroes*, which proclaimed the evils of slavery and the absolute necessity for Friends to free their slaves. Meetings throughout the colonies and England effectively used his visitations to pressure Quakers to free their slaves. By 1774, Quaker meetings in England, New England, and Pennsylvania had adopted sanctions to disown any member for buying slaves or for serving as executor of an estate that included slaves. It also required slaveholders to treat their slaves humanely and to emancipate them as soon as possible.

Some have argued that Quakers were willing to emancipate their slaves because slavery was not profitable in Pennsylvania in the absence of labor-intensive agriculture. Others claim that Quaker sensitivity to antislavery was aroused not by their own religious ideals but rather by eighteenth century Enlightenment philosophy, which held that liberty is a natural human right. These may be considered arguments; nevertheless, it was the Quakers who first championed the antislavery cause and who organized the first antislavery group in America.

Spread of the Antislavery Movement

The Pennsylvania Society for the Abolition of Slavery served as a model for other antislavery groups. As early as 1794, other states that had formed antislavery societies were asked to send representatives to Philadelphia for annual meetings. As new associations were formed, Friends constituted a majority of the membership. Statesmen such as Franklin, Rush, Alexander Hamilton, John Jay, and Thomas Paine believed that the institution of slavery contradicted the ideals of the Declaration of Independence and joined in support of the Friends' antislavery campaign.

——*Emily Teipe*

Bibliography and Further Reading

Davis, David Brion. *The Problem of Slavery in the Age of Revolution, 1770–1823*. Ithaca: Cornell UP, 1975. Print.

Frost, J. William. *The Quaker Origins of Antislavery*. Norwood: Norwood, 1980. Print.

James, Sydney V. *A People Among Peoples: Quaker Benevolence in Eighteenth Century America*. Cambridge: Harvard UP, 1963. Print.

Nash, Gary B. *Quakers and Politics: Pennsylvania 1681–1726*. Princeton: Princeton UP, 1968. Print.

Soderlund, Jean R. *Quakers and Slavery: A Divided Spirit*. Princeton: Princeton UP, 1985. Print.

People of color

This term refers to nonwhite, non-Anglo ethnic minorities who historically have been the victims of discrimination by the dominant majority group. The concept is inclusive of all people whose skin color or other physical features are not commonly perceived as white. The term specifically includes African Americans, Asian Americans, American Indians, and Mexican Americans and other Latino people such as Puerto Ricans and Central and South Americans (even though many of them self-identify as "white"). The term "people of color" is neither politically loaded nor derogatory; in fact, it is both neutral and respectful in referring to the combination of these ethnic and racial groups.

The term is often broken down to "men of color" and "women of color" to refer to groups of men or women, respectively, who are from the ethnic and racial groups noted above. The experiences of both of these groups, although they overlap with the experiences of the general population, are different in several important ways from those of whites as well as from each other. Women of color, for example, often experience the discriminatory consequences of both ethnicity and gender.

——*Celestino Fernández*

BIBLIOGRAPHY AND FURTHER READING

Malesky, Kee. "The Journey from 'Colored' to 'Minorities' to 'People of Color.'" *NPR.* NPR, 30 Mar. 2014. Web. 15 May. 2015.

Ratts, Manivong J., and Paul B. Pedersen. "Using Appropriate Terminology." *Counseling for Multiculturalism and Social Justice: Integration, Theory, and Application.* 4th ed. Alexandria: Amer. Counseling Assn., 2014. 85–88. Print.

Sen, Rinku. "Minorities? Try 'People of Color.'" *CNN.* CNN, 18 May 2012. Web. 15 May. 2015.

PEOPLE V. GEORGE HALL

In *People v. George Hall* (1854), the California Supreme Court ruled that a Chinese person could not testify against a white person in a California court. The court overturned the murder conviction of a white man by invalidating the testimony of Chinese witnesses for the prosecution based on a state law prohibiting "black or mulatto person(s), or Indian(s)" from giving testimony against whites in court. Writing for the majority, Chief Justice Hugh C. Murray argued that the term "Indian" was meant to include Asians, whom he characterized as a genetically inferior people largely "incapable of progress" and unfit to participate in determining the fate of white Californians. *People v. George Hall* provides a striking example of how the philosophy of white supremacy dominated the political and social structures of the antebellum United States. In addition, the case demonstrates the pervasiveness of anti-Asian sentiments in the nineteenth century American West and illustrates how state officials in California legalized the classification of Asian Americans as second-class citizens during the nineteenth and early twentieth centuries. The California Supreme Court upheld the *Hall* decision eighteen years later in *People v. McGuire* (1872), but legislation that overturned state laws restricting the legal testimony of Chinese Americans took effect in January, 1873, nullifying court decisions upholding the restrictive statutes.

——*Michael H. Burchett*

PEYOTE RELIGION

To the American Indians who practice peyotism, peyote is considered a spiritual being. This is a concept that defies accurate definition in Western terms. Adherents describe peyote iconically and refer to it as "medicine"; it is used as a sacrament. The ritualistic use of peyote in a religious setting to communicate with and be instructed by "spirit" is an accepted way to "return to the source."

Peyote itself comes from a type of cactus with the scientific name *Lophophora williamsii*, a small, spineless cactus with a rounded top. The parts of the cactus that contain peyote are referred to as "buttons." A peyote button contains more than fifty alkaloids, one of which, mescaline, induces a state of consciousness that its users liken to a healing or religious experience.

PEYOTE RELIGION

The religion, often called peyotism or the peyote cult, is at the center of a pan-Indian movement. The religion has doctrine, an ethical code, unique rituals, and origin legends. Fire, water, the medicine, the eagle, and a drum are the central symbols. Precise rituals involve long, extensive prayer meetings and require knowledge of many songs with repetitive, chanted musical bridges. The peyote religion, referred to formally as the Native American Church of North America (NAC), is pan-Indian, both geographically and tribally. It appeared suddenly after 1880 and spread rapidly.

The origin of the peyote religion as practiced in North America is unknown. In *The Peyote Religion* (1956), James Slotkin describes twenty-nine different traditions of origin. The ritual of the modern Native American Church is very different from how pre-Columbian and indigenous Mexican peoples used peyote. Peyote reveals itself as a transformer that is integrable and renewing. After 1880, tribal religious traditions, devastated by the relentless encroachments

Peyote ceremony tipi. By Haiduc (Own work).

developed, leading to various forms referred to as Kiowa-Apache, Southern Plains, and Oklahoma Fireplace. A number of elements, however, are consistent at every meeting since James Mooney's description of a peyote ceremony in 1892. At all the fireplaces the door opens east, and the roadman, or church leader, sits opposite the door. The meeting opens with the placing of the Chief Peyote on the altar and closes with the Chief's removal. The most common form for the altar is a crescent or half-moon shape. There are five officers, or roadcrew, who have various formal functions in the ceremony: roadman, drummer, cedarman, fireman, and dawn woman. Each one at some point during the meeting will offer a "prayer smoke," rolling tobacco in a corn husk and praying with this smoke communicant.

All movement during the meeting is clockwise. The drum is a water drum made from a six-quart metal pot into which are placed water and four coals from the fire. The vessel is then covered with a hide, usually deerskin, and tied with a long rope. The rope wraps around seven stones pocketed in the hide, making a seven-pointed star, seen as the morning star, around the bottom of the vessel. The fireman, in addition to keeping a ritually constructed fire going through the night, maintains a poker or burning stick from which all prayer smokes are lit. Other ritual paraphernalia invariably found at meetings are a bone whistle, gourd rattles, a beaded staff, sage, feather fans, and corn husks and tobacco used in making the hand-rolled prayer smokes. There are always four stages to each meeting: opening, midnight, morning, and closing ceremonies. Particular songs are sung in conjunction with these stages no matter which tribe or fireplace is holding the ceremony, because these particular songs were given through the origin story. Four foods—meat, berries, corn, and water—are also always a part of the ceremony.

Some details of the four stages vary with each roadman. The reason is that peyote teaches a roadman his way; this is a mark of the church's and the religion's vitality. These variations come from

of European Americans, opened to the inevitability of profound change. The church origin legends reflect the devastation suffered by the old ways and depict the need for transformation in the Indian psyche.

Origin legends and doctrinal formulations are of secondary importance to practitioners, who are more concerned with original religious experiences. If there is doctrine, it is the belief that God put humankind on Earth for a purpose, and it is up to humans to learn that purpose directly from God on "the peyote road," the mediation of peyote, prayer, and focus or awareness. As outlined by Slotkin, the peyote road consists of four main tenets: brotherly love (that is, "members should be honest, truthful, friendly and helpful to one another"), care of family ("married people . . . should cherish and care for one another, and their children"), self-reliance ("members should work steadily and reliably at their jobs, and earn their own living"), and avoidance of alcohol ("there is a maxim, 'Peyote and alcohol don't mix'").

CHURCH RITUAL

Church members describe their religion and ritual as uniquely Indian. Some standards seem to have prayer, searching, and the medicine. A roadman's ceremony is called his Fireplace.

Meetings usually last a minimum of twelve hours, and the roadman is in control and aware of the psychological state of every member of the meeting throughout. For each of the participants, the ceremony often has aspects of a long, soul-searching journey through the night. It is understood to be a prayer meeting from beginning to end. Church members come to a sacred area, concentrate on its transcendental center or source, and sit with their peers in community to receive healing and instruction.

——*Glenn J. Schiffman*

BIBLIOGRAPHY AND FURTHER READING

Maroukis, Thomas C. *The Peyote Road: Religious Freedom and the Native American Church.* Norman: U of Oklahoma P, 2010. Print.

Slotkin, James S. *The Peyote Religion: A Study in Indian-White Relations.* Glencoe: Free, 1956. Print.

Stewart, Omer C. *Peyote Religion: A History.* Norman: U of Oklahoma P, 1987. Print.

Wiedman, Dennis. "Upholding Indigenous Freedoms of Religion and Medicine: Peyotists at the 1906–1908 Oklahoma Constitutional Convention and First Legislature." *American Indian Quarterly* 36.2 (2012): 215–46. Print.

PHILADELPHIA RIOTS

Rapid population growth, industrialization, and cultural conflict characterized urban America in the 1840s and helped produce bloody anti-Irish riots in Philadelphia's industrial suburbs of Kensington and Southwark in the summer of 1844. Already the second largest US city in 1840, Philadelphia grew by more than one-third in the 1840s, from twenty-five thousand people to thirty-six thousand. Irish immigrants, hard-pressed by the Great Famine that had decimated the potato crops in their homeland, stimulated this growth and made up 10 percent of Philadelphia's population in 1844. Prior to commuter railroads and automobiles, most people lived near their workplaces and cities were densely populated. Low-income newcomers such as the Irish resided in cheap, substandard housing and symbolized the ill effects of disorderly urban growth to longtime Philadelphians.

NATIVIST SENTIMENT

Lacking in job skills and capital, Irish immigrants filled the bottom rungs in the emerging industrial order's occupational ladder. As its population grew, Philadelphia expanded its involvement in large-scale manufacturing. By 1840, half of Philadelphia's sixteen thousand working adults labored in manufacturing, and 89 percent of the workers in Kensington toiled in industrial trades. American-born whites predominated in such well-paying craft occupations as ship carpenter and ironmaker, leaving low-paying jobs requiring less skill, such as weaving, for

Irish newcomers. Perceiving immigrants and African Americans as competitors, many white American workers used violence to drive them from trades and neighborhoods.

In the 1830s, Philadelphia, like other major cities, hosted a strong working-class trade union and political movement. At its height, the General Trades Union (GTU) of Philadelphia City and County included more than ten thousand workers representing more than fifty different trades. Collective action in an 1835 general strike for a ten-hour day succeeded in winning shorter hours and wage hikes in numerous workplaces. GTU activists voted against conservative Whigs opposed to strikes and Catholic immigrants. The Panic of 1837 weakened the GTU and undermined the solidarity of its culturally and occupationally diverse constituency.

In the 1840s, native-born Protestant skilled workers fought for a dwindling supply of jobs and received little help from the financially weakened GTU. Evangelical Protestants from all social classes joined moral reform campaigns for temperance and strict observance of the Sabbath. Temperance and Sabbatarianism symbolized American-born white workers' efforts to survive hard times through personal discipline. Workers made up the majority of temperance societies in industrial suburbs such as Kensington and Southwark. Moral reforms often attacked immigrant cultural institutions, such as the Roman Catholic church and Sunday tavern visits. Economic contraction and moral reform eroded the

GTU's bonds of working-class solidarity, which might have prevented ethnic conflict in 1844.

The American Republican Party, dedicated to eliminating the influence of Catholic immigrants in public life, best exploited the anxieties of native-born workers. The party flourished briefly in eastern cities in the mid-1840s, drawing support from American-born workers and middle-class professionals such as Philadelphia's Lewis Levin, a struggling lawyer and aspiring politician from South Carolina. In the spring of 1844, American Republicans campaigned against Catholic voters' attempts to protect their children from Protestant religious instruction in the public schools. Protestant-dominated Philadelphia schools used the King James version of the Bible as a classroom textbook. Objecting that the King James version was not authoritative, Catholics preferred the Douay Bible, which included annotations written by the Vatican. Philadelphia's Catholic bishop, Francis Kenrick, wanted public schools to allow Catholic students to bring their Bibles to class or be exempted from Protestant religious instruction. American Republicans accused Philadelphia Catholics of plotting to remove the Bible from the schools entirely and to have priests take over classrooms.

In April 1844, American Republicans staged rallies across the city to whip up support for their nativist program. Violence between the Irish and nativists broke out when nativists gathered near Irish neighborhoods. American Republicans scheduled a mass meeting for May 6 in Kensington's third ward, a neighborhood composed mainly of Irish weavers. On May 6, rain drove hundreds of nativists who traveled to the third ward rally to seek cover at the Nanny Goat Market, a covered lot of market stalls. Approximately thirty Irish waited at the market, and one yelled, "Keep the damned natives out of the market house; it don't belong to them. This ground is ours!" Samuel Kramer, editor of the pro-American Republican *Native American* newspaper (named for Anglo-American nativists, not American Indians), tried to finish his speech against the Catholic proposals for the Douay Bible, but Irish hecklers drowned him out. A shoving match escalated into fistfights and gunfire as nativists and Irish battled for control of the market house. Police arrived at dusk and temporarily restored order. Four men died, three of them nativists, and many more were wounded in the fighting.

The next day, nativists massed in Kensington for revenge. The *Native American* ran the headline: "Let Every Man Come Prepared to Defend Himself!" A parade of nativists marched through Kensington under a US flag and a banner declaring, "This is the flag that was trampled underfoot by Irish Papists." Nativist mobs rampaged through Kensington for two more days, burning homes and invading two Catholic churches, where rioters defaced religious objects and looted valuables. Although Sheriff Morton McMichael tried to calm public disorder, police were too few in number to stop the violence. Needing reinforcements, McMichael called on General George Cadwalader, commander of the First Brigade of Pennsylvania state militia, stationed in Philadelphia. On May 10, state troops brought peace to the city and kept it under martial law for a week.

Tension prevailed in June, amid criticism of city officials and militia commanders for failing to prevent violence. American Republicans still had public support, and Catholics worried about more violence. Catholics feared that nativists would use July 4 patriotic celebrations as a pretext to riot. Parishioners at St. Philip's Church in Southwark, just south of Philadelphia, hoarded weapons inside the church in order to defend it. Hearing of the arms cache, on July 5, Levin led thousands of nativists, including volunteer militia with cannons, to St. Philip's to demand the weapons. Stung by earlier criticism, Cadwalader's militia promptly seized the church and ordered nativists away. When the mob refused to move, Cadwalader opened fire and a pitched battle involving cannon and rifle fire ensued for a day and a half. The militia, helped by city police, prevailed in fighting that left two rioters dead and dozens of state troops and civilians wounded.

CONSEQUENCES

The American Republican Party campaigned on the riots by attacking reigning politicians as the allies of Irish Catholics and making martyrs of the nativists killed in the riots. In October, Levin and another American Republican won election to the US House of Representatives, and nativists captured several county offices, mostly on the strength of votes from working-class Kensington and Southwark. The American Republicans faded in the late 1840s, but nativists returned in the 1850s under the aegis of the American, or Know-Nothing, Party.

The riots forced Irish Philadelphians to band together as an ethnic group. The most prominent Irish opponent of the mobs was Hugh Clark, a master weaver and ward politician worth more than thirty thousand dollars in 1850. Clark had stridently opposed striking Irish journeymen weavers prior to 1844. Master weavers, some of them Irishmen like Clark, cut journeymen's wages in the wake of the Kensington riot, confident that few non-Irish workers would protest the cuts. Bishop Kenrick urged conciliation and softened his public position on the Bible controversy. American Republican anger at police and militia actions temporarily stalled police reform, but in the 1850s, Philadelphia and other cities established professional police departments to prevent more riots like those of 1844.

——*Frank Towers*

BIBLIOGRAPHY AND FURTHER READING

Davis, Susan G. *Parades and Power: Street Theatre in Nineteenth-Century Philadelphia.* Philadelphia: Temple UP, 1986. Print.

Feldberg, Michael. *The Philadelphia Riots of 1844: A Study of Ethnic Conflict.* Westport: Greenwood, 1975. Print.

Knobel, Dale T. *Paddy and the Republic: Ethnicity and Nationality in Antebellum America.* Middletown: Wesleyan UP, 1986. Print.

Lannie, Vincent P., and Bernard C. Diethorn. "For the Honor and Glory of God: The Philadelphia Bible Riots of 1844." *History of Education Quarterly* 8 (1968). Print.

Laurie, Bruce. *Working People of Philadelphia, 1800-1850.* Philadelphia: Temple UP, 1980. Print.

Montgomery, David. "The Shuttle and the Cross: Weavers and Artisans in the Kensington Riots of 1844." *Journal of Social History* 5 (1972). Print.

Warner, Sam Bass, Jr. *The Private City: Philadelphia in Three Periods of Its Growth.* Philadelphia: U of Pennsylvania P, 1968. Print.

PHILIPPINE INSURRECTION

United States involvement in the Philippines began during the Spanish-American War of 1898. US naval strategists already had a plan for attacking the Spanish fleet at Manila Bay in the event of war with Spain. As relations between the United States and Spain worsened in 1897, Commodore George Dewey, commander of the United States Navy's Asiatic Squadron, was ordered to move his fleet to Hong Kong, with instructions to attack Manila Bay in case of war. War was declared on April 24, 1898. On the morning of May 1, Dewey's fleet steamed into Manila Bay. By noon, his ships had sunk or disabled every Spanish ship.

Washington was slow to react to the victorious news. The quick defeat of the Spanish fleet was unexpected, and President William McKinley had not planned what to do with the Philippines once the war was ended. McKinley considered either taking the entire archipelago, establishing a naval base, or returning the islands to Spain. Complete independence for the islands was never seriously considered. While McKinley contemplated the fate of

the Philippines, relations between the US military occupation force at Manila Bay and the Filipino population deteriorated. At first, the Filipinos welcomed Dewey's forces as liberators. The Filipinos soon realized that the Americans intended to control the islands at least until the end of the war, perhaps longer. In early May, McKinley dispatched an expeditionary force, under the command of General Arthur MacArthur, to Manila Bay. MacArthur arrived just in time to accept the Spanish garrison's surrender at the end of the war, an honor Filipino forces had assumed would be theirs.

FILIPINO INSURGENCY

Filipino insurgents had been fighting the Spanish since early 1896. Spanish efforts to destroy the infant revolution had failed; rebel leaders fled to the jungled hills of the islands to hide out and organize bases for guerrilla warfare against the Spanish. In 1897, both sides, weary of the increasingly bloody war, agreed to a cease-fire to discuss peace. The Spanish authorities refused to consider independence, forcing the

Filipino insurgents to continue their rebellion. Under the military leadership of Emilio Aguinaldo and the intellectual direction of Apolinario Mabini, rebel leaders established a base of operations at Hong Kong, where they could easily purchase supplies and arms. It was at this time that the Spanish-American War began, bringing an unexpected opportunity for the rebels.

Filipino leaders first believed that the United States would assist them in expelling the Spanish and establishing an independent Philippine state. Aguinaldo accepted anticolonial statements by US consular officers at face value. The Filipinos soon found, however, that Dewey was more cautious, speaking only of military cooperation to defeat Spain and saying nothing of independence. Aguinaldo organized an army of thirty thousand men and won notable victories; nevertheless, the United States held supreme authority, accepting the surrender of Manila Bay and refusing to allow Filipino forces into the city without permission. When the Spanish flag came down, the Stars and Stripes, not the Filipino revolutionary flag, replaced it.

Faced with the realization that the United States was going to annex the islands, Aguinaldo moved to organize a new government. On June 12, 1898, he proclaimed independence for the Philippines. In September, a constituent assembly was convened, and on November 29, a constitution was adopted. The United States largely ignored this move toward independence. The McKinley administration, mainly because of racial prejudice, arbitrarily decided that the Filipinos were not ready for self-government. In addition, there was a fear that an independent Philippines might fall easy prey to an ambitious European power, such as Germany or Great Britain. Therefore, the United States proceeded to obtain full control by a provision for annexation of the Philippines in the peace treaty ending the war with Spain.

ARMED CONFLICT

While the United States Senate debated ratification of the peace treaty, a series of clashes between US and Filipino forces beginning on February 4, 1899, soon escalated into large-scale fighting. The Philippine insurrection against US rule had begun. The United States, because of its decision to assume responsibility for "civilizing" the Filipinos, was forced to wage a bitter war, which would cost much more money and take many more human lives than the war with Spain.

The Philippine insurrection was, in many ways, a prototype of modern guerrilla warfare. Filipino revolutionary leaders quickly lost the support of conservative Filipinos who accepted US rule. As a result, Aguinaldo and his forces retreated to fight the US troops in the jungles, as they had done earlier against Spanish forces. In early 1899, United States forces moved into central Luzon, where they captured and burned Malolos, the rebel capital. Rebel forces, however, escaped into the hills, where they were supplied by sympathetic villagers until spring rains forced US troops to withdraw.

US commanders finally admitted that Aguinaldo had extensive popular support and that total war was necessary to pacify the islands. Washington responded by sending reinforcements, bringing the number of US troops in the Philippines to seventy-four thousand. As the scale of the fighting rose, vicious tactics and brutality on both sides also increased. Both sides committed atrocities involving soldiers and civilians. US forces systematically burned villages and took hostages in an effort to deny popular assistance to rebel forces. Gradually, the overwhelming strength of the United States prevailed, as US forces took rebel strongholds in the hills and rural regions. By 1901, 639 US garrisons dotted the islands, breaking Filipino resistance.

The insurrection finally collapsed with Aguinaldo's capture in March, 1901. He was seized by Colonel Frederick Funston and three other US officers pretending to be the prisoners of a group of Filipino defectors, who led the officers directly to Aguinaldo's headquarters in northeastern Luzon. After his capture, Aguinaldo reluctantly took an oath of allegiance to the United States. By July 4, 1901, civil government, under United States auspices, was instituted everywhere in the Philippines, except in southern Mindanao and the Sulu Islands, where Moro tribesmen continued resistance.

On July 4, 1902, the Philippine insurrection was formally declared over. The United States issued a proclamation of general peace and amnesty. As a result of the struggle, the United States suffered forty-two hundred dead and twenty-eight hundred wounded. While close to twenty thousand rebels were killed in the war, another two hundred thousand

Filipinos died from disease, famine, and other war-related causes.

William Howard Taft served as the first US governor of the Philippines. Taft continued to be heavily involved in the administration of the islands as secretary of war and president of the United States. It was Taft who coined the phrase "little brown brothers," which referred to his hope that the United States could somehow "Americanize" these native peoples. This phrase remained a strong racial force in US relations with the states in the Pacific and Latin America. The Philippine Islands remained under US jurisdiction until 1934, when Congress passed the Tydings-McDuffie Act, granting independence to the Philippines. World War II delayed complete independence for the islands until 1946.

——*Theodore A. Wilson, updated by William Allison*

BIBLIOGRAPHY AND FURTHER READING

Brands, H.W. *Bound to Empire: The United States and the Philippines.* New York: Oxford UP, 1992. Print.

Burleigh, Michael. *Small Wars, Faraway Places: Global Insurrection and the Making of the Modern World, 1945-1965.* New York: Viking, 2013. Print.

Jones, Gregg R. *Honor in the Dust: Theodore Roosevelt, War in the Philippines, and the Rise and Fall of America's Imperial Dream.* New York: New American Library, 2012. Print.

Karnov, Stanley. *In Our Image: America's Empire in the Philippines.* New York: Random House, 1989. Print.

Miller, Stuart Creighton. *Benevolent Assimilation: The American Conquest of the Philippines, 1899-1903.* New Haven: Yale UP, 1982. Print.

PINE RIDGE SHOOTOUT

In 1973, members and supporters of the American Indian Movement (AIM) occupied the town of Wounded Knee, South Dakota, on the Pine Ridge Reservation. The activists were demonstrating against what they considered to be autocratic and sometimes corrupt practices of the Oglala Sioux tribal political leaders, especially Richard Wilson, the tribal chair. Wilson, an aggressive opponent of AIM, along with local officials of the Bureau of Indian Affairs (BIA), requested federal support in removing the activists. The occupation evolved into a state of siege lasting seventy-one days and leaving two native people dead. AIM leaders were indicted, but the case was dismissed after a federal judge accused the Federal Bureau of Investigation (FBI) of gross misconduct.

Discontent and strong opposition to the Pine Ridge Reservation tribal government and the chair continued. On June 25, 1975, violence erupted again when a BIA police officer killed a young Oglala man. The following day, in an exchange of gunfire, two FBI agents were slain outside a house about fifteen miles from the town of Pine Ridge. Although the occupants of the house fled, two Oglala men were ultimately apprehended and charged with the murders; they were acquitted. Leonard Peltier, another suspect, was arrested in Canada, extradited to the United States, and sent to prison after a controversial trial in which he was sentenced to two consecutive life terms. After Peltier's imprisonment, Indian rights activists lobbied for his release, and he was considered to be a political prisoner by Amnesty International. Other victims of the 1975 violence included Leonard Crow Dog, an Oglala medicine man and spiritual leader of the movement who was arrested at his home on the neighboring Rosebud Reservation, and AIM supporter Anna Mae Aquash, a Micmac Indian woman, believed by the FBI to be a witness to the killing of the two agents. Aquash was found murdered in 1976.

——*Lucy Ganje*

BIBLIOGRAPHY AND FURTHER READING

"American Indian Movement." *American Countercultures: An Encyclopedia of Nonconformists, Alternative Lifestyles, and Radical Ideas in US History.* Ed. Gina Misiroglu. New York: Taylor, 2015. Print.

Hendricks, Steve. *The Unquiet Grave: The FBI and the Struggle for the Soul of Indian Country.* New York: Avalon, 2006. Print.

Johansen, Bruce E. "The Federal Bureau of Investigation." *Encyclopedia of the American Indian Movement.* Santa Barbara: Greenwood, 2013. 1075–83. Print.

Lee, Jacob F. "Wounded Knee II (1973)." *Revolts, Protests, Demonstrations, and Rebellions in American History: An Encyclopedia.* Ed. Steven Danver. Santa Barbara: ABC-CLIO, 2011. Print.

Matthiessen, Peter. *In the Spirit of Crazy Horse.* 1983. New York: Random House, 1992. Print.

PLATT AMENDMENT

In 1895, Cuban revolutionaries initiated what was ultimately to become a successful revolt against Spanish colonial domination. The break from Spain was brought about by a variety of factors, the two most critical being the repressive nature of the colonial rule of Spain and a change in US tariff policy as a result of the recessions and depressions in the United States during the 1890's. The Wilson-Gorman Tariff of 1894 imposed a duty on Cuban sugar arriving in the United States, which previously had entered duty-free. With the economy of Cuba reeling from dwindling Cuban-United States trade because of the new tariff, Cuban dissidents, who had been waiting for an opportunity to act, launched a revolution.

Led by José Martí, who had strong ties to the United States, the rebels who called for Cuban independence began a guerrilla war against the Spanish. Even after the death of Martí during the first year of fighting, the ranks of the Cuban rebel forces continued to increase. Spanish authorities responded to the groundswell of domestic support for the rebels by attempting to separate the rebels from their supporters in rural areas. Under a new policy known as reconcentration, more than a quarter-million Cubans were interred in concentration camps guarded by Spanish soldiers. Thousands of Cubans died in the unfit camps, which served as breeding grounds for disease. US sympathy for the Cuban rebels was stimulated by reports of atrocities occurring as a result of the new Spanish policy, and people in the United States began to call for an end to the conflict through reconciliation. The mysterious sinking of the battleship *Maine* in Havana harbor on February 15, 1898, ended all hope of a peaceful resolution to the conflict.

THE SPANISH-AMERICAN WAR

The sinking of the US battleship, which had been ordered to Cuba in an effort to display US concern for events unfolding on the island and to protect US citizens, drew the United States further into the conflict. Naval investigators concluded that a Spanish mine had caused the explosion. US president William McKinley responded to events by demanding that Spain grant Cuban independence. Finding the Spanish response unsatisfactory, McKinley requested on April 11, 1898, that Congress grant him authorization to stop the war in Cuba by force, if necessary. Following some debate, on April 19 Congress declared that Cuba was and should be independent, demanded an immediate withdrawal of Spain from Cuba, authorized the use of force to accomplish that withdrawal, and vowed not to annex the island. Known as the Teller Amendment, the vow not to annex Cuba was perhaps the most controversial of the issues debated.

Despite the Teller Amendment, the entrance of the United States into the conflict initiated the beginning of an exploitive relationship between the United States and Cuba, which was dictated by the former. As the war drew to an end and Spanish withdrawal began to be realized, the United States downplayed the role of the Cuban rebels in the success of the military campaign. The Treaty of Paris, which halted the conflict, required Spain to surrender all claims to Cuba, but the McKinley administration refused to recognize the former Cuban rebels as a legitimate government or the Cuban people as being capable of self-rule. For two years, the US military performed the functions of government. Although the US military made substantial improvements in the infrastructure of Cuba and generally improved the quality of life on the island, Cubans resented the US occupation. Many Cubans felt that they had traded one colonial master for another.

In 1900, Cubans were allowed to draft a constitution and hold elections. The United States refused to withdraw its troops, however, until provisions were made for the continuation of Cuban-United States relations. Elihu Root, the US secretary of war, proposed such provisions, which ultimately were included in a bill sponsored by Senator Orville H.

Platt. Platt, a Republican from Connecticut, attached a rider to the Army Appropriations Bill of 1901 that essentially made Cuba a US protectorate.

The Platt Amendment, as the provisions would come to be known, severely restricted Cuba's ability to make treaties and its right to contract public debt. The United States also declared its right to intervene in Cuban affairs in order to preserve Cuban independence and maintain order. Cuba also was expected to give the United States the right to maintain naval bases and coaling stations on the island. The Cuban government reluctantly appended the provisions of the Platt Amendment to the Cuban constitution. The last US forces finally withdrew from Havana in 1902. The Platt Amendment became a formal part of a US-Cuba treaty on May 22, 1903.

The Platt Amendment formed the basis for United States-Cuban relations for the next sixty years, until Fidel Castro emerged as the leader of Cuba. Forced to submit to the will of the United States, Cuba was soon inundated with US investment. Foreign investors controlled and manipulated Cuban politics and the economy. US troops reoccupied Cuba from 1906 to 1909, under the authority of the Platt Amendment, following an uprising that protested, among other things, US involvement in Cuban affairs.

THE ROOSEVELT ADMINISTRATION
The election of Franklin D. Roosevelt as US president in 1933 initially brought little change in US-Cuban relations, despite his "good neighbor policy," which was based on the belief that no state had the right to intervene in Latin America. Roosevelt was forced to deal with a Cuba in turmoil. President Gerardo "the Butcher" Machado y Morales, who had dominated Cuban politics for a decade, was forced to resign in 1933 because of popular opposition and US pressure. His successor, Ramón Grau San Martín, was no more acceptable to the Roosevelt administration. Viewed as too radical by Roosevelt, the government

of Grau was never recognized as legitimate by the US administration.

It was not until Fulgencio Batista y Zaldívar led a coup and installed a government acceptable to the United States that the Roosevelt administration agreed to discuss revoking the Platt Amendment. The second Treaty of Relations, as it came to be known, eliminated the limitations on Cuban sovereignty imposed by the Platt Amendment. The new treaty did allow the United States to retain its naval base at Guantanamo Bay, which could be revoked only by mutual consent of both states.

Despite the formal end of US involvement in Cuba, the new Cuba, which was controlled by Batista, was no less tied to the United States financially or politically. Batista was viewed by many international observers as a puppet for the US government. Cuba attracted more US investment under Batista than ever before. Many Cubans argued that despite the end of the Platt Amendment, Cuba was still a US dependency. It was this sense of frustration over their inability to achieve a true sense of sovereignty that served as a catalyst for Fidel Castro's successful coup in 1959.

————*Donald C. Simmons, Jr.*

BIBLIOGRAPHY AND FURTHER READING
Langley, Lester D. *The Cuban Policy of the United States.* New York: Wiley, 1968. Print. Perez, Louis A., Jr. *Cuba: Between Reform and Revolution.* New York: Oxford UP, 1988. Print.

Perez, Louis A., Jr. *Cuba Under the Platt Amendment: 1902-1934.* Pittsburgh: U of Pittsburgh P, 1986. Print.

Suchlicki, Jaime. *Cuba: From Columbus to Castro and Beyond.* Washington, DC: Brassey's, 2002. Print.

Thomas, Hugh, *Cuba: Or, The Pursuit of Freedom.* New York: Harper & Row, 1971. Print.

PLESSY V. FERGUSON

On July 10, 1890, the Louisiana General Assembly, over the objection of its eighteen African American members, enacted a law which read, in part:

> ...all railway companies carrying passengers in their coaches in this state shall provide equal but separate

accommodations for the white and colored races, by providing two or more passenger coaches for each passenger train, or by dividing the passenger coaches by a partition so as to secure separate accommodations.

The law empowered train officials to assign passengers to cars; passengers insisting on going into a car set aside for the other race were liable to a twenty-five-dollar fine and twenty days' imprisonment. In addition, the company could refuse to carry an obstreperous passenger and, if it were sued for doing so, was immune from damages in state courts. A third section outlined the penalties for noncomplying railroads and provided that "nothing in this act shall be construed as applying to nurses attending children of the other race."

OPPOSITION TO THE LAW

The prominent black community of New Orleans organized to mount a legal attack on the new law. A group calling itself the Citizens' Committee to Test the Constitutionality of the Separate Car Law, led by Louis Martinet and Alexander A. Mary, organized to handle the litigation and enlisted the services of Albion W. Tourgée. Tourgée was to serve as chief counsel and devote his considerable talents to rallying public opposition to the Jim Crow system typified by the Louisiana law. Martinet engaged James Walker to assist in handling the Louisiana phase of the controversy. Before the first test of the Louisiana law (also featuring an African American who could "pass for white") could be settled, the Louisiana Supreme Court decided that the 1890 law could not be applied to interstate travelers since it was an unconstitutional regulation of interstate commerce (*State ex rel. Abbot v. Hicks*, 11 So. 74 in 1892). The *Plessy* case, then, relitigated the question raised in the 1890 Mississippi railroad case, but as a problem in the constitutional law of civil liberties rather than one of interstate commerce.

The person recruited to test the segregation law was Homer Adolph Plessy, a person of seven-eighths Caucasian and one-eighth African ancestry, in whom "the mixture of colored blood was not discernible." On June 7, 1892, holding a first-class ticket entitling him to travel on the East Louisiana Railway from New Orleans to Covington, Louisiana, Plessy took a seat in the car reserved for whites. The conductor, assisted by a policeman, forcibly removed Plessy and, charging him with violating the segregation law, placed him in the parish jail. The state prosecuted Plessy in the Orleans Parish criminal district court before Judge John H. Ferguson. Plessy's plea that the law was unconstitutional was overruled by Ferguson,

who directed the defense to address itself to the questions of fact. Having no defense in the facts, Tourgée and Walker appealed Ferguson's ruling on the law's constitutionality to the Louisiana Supreme Court by asking that court to issue a writ of prohibition which in effect would have directed Ferguson to reverse his ruling on the constitutional question.

On December 19, 1892, Associate Judge Charles E. Fenner of the Louisiana Supreme Court ruled the law constitutional in an opinion which served as a model for that written later by Justice Henry Billings Brown of the US Supreme Court. After a delay of almost four years—a delay that Tourgée encouraged on the grounds that it gave the opponents of segregation needed time—the United States Supreme Court heard the arguments in Plessy's case on April 13, 1896. On May 18, 1896, Justice Brown handed down the majority opinion, supported by six other justices (Justice David Brewer did not participate, and Justice John Marshall Harlan dissented).

Justice Brown first disposed of Tourgée's argument that the segregation law was a "badge of servitude," a vestige of slavery prohibited by the Thirteenth Amendment (1865). Decisions in 1873 (*Slaughterhouse* cases) and 1883 (*Civil Rights* cases), wrote Brown, indicated that it was because the Thirteenth Amendment barred only outright slavery and not laws merely imposing "onerous disabilities and burdens" that the movement for the Fourteenth Amendment was successful.

Brown in his opinion delivered a famous statement on the relationship between law, prejudice, and equality:

> The [plaintiff's] argument also assumes that social prejudice may be overcome by legislation, and that equal rights cannot be secured to the negro except by an enforced commingling of the two races. We cannot accept this proposition. If the two races are to meet on terms of social equality, it must be the result of natural affinities, a mutual appreciation of each other's merits and a voluntary consent of individuals.

The law in question, however, specifically interfered with the "voluntary consent of individuals."

EFFECTS OF THE DECISION

The Court thus sanctioned Jim Crowism. What comfort blacks derived from the case had to be found in the strong dissenting opinion of Justice Harlan, who once again proved himself to be a staunch champion of a broad interpretation of the Reconstruction amendments. Harlan construed the ban on slavery to cover segregation laws; he insisted on Tourgée's thesis that a railroad was a public highway and that under the Fourteenth Amendment government could make no racial distinctions whether one considered the case under the privileges and immunities, due process, or equal protection clauses of that amendment. Harlan attacked the Court's reliance on pre-Fourteenth Amendment precedents; his most memorable language appeared in connection with his charge that the majority usurped constitutional power by assuming authority to decide on the "reasonableness" of state social legislation:

> The white race deems itself to be the dominant race in this country. And so it is, in prestige, in achievements, in education, in wealth, and in power. So, I doubt not that it will continue to be for all time, if it remains true to its great heritage and holds fast to the principles of constitutional liberty. But in view of the Constitution, in the eye of the law, there is in this country no superior, dominant, ruling class of citizens. There is no caste here. Our Constitution is color-blind, and neither knows nor tolerates classes among citizens. In respect of civil rights, all citizens are equal before the law.

Harlan turned out to be a competent soothsayer:

> The destinies of the two races in this country are indissolubly linked together, and the interests of both require that the common government of all shall not permit the seeds of race hate to be planted under the sanction of law.

It would, however, take the general public and the justices of the Supreme Court decades to adopt Harlan's views and interpretation of the Constitution. *Plessy's* strong sanction of segregation in transportation lasted formally until 1950 *(Henderson v. United States)* and in education until 1954 *(Brown v. Board of Education)*. Antimiscegenation laws were not outlawed until 1967 *(Loving v. Virginia)*.

——*James J. Bolner, updated by Brian L. Fife*

BIBLIOGRAPHY AND FURTHER READING

Davis, Thomas J. *Plessy v. Ferguson*. Santa Barbara: Greenwood, 2012. Print.

Hoffer, Williamjames Hull. *Plessy v. Ferguson: Race and Inequality in Jim Crow America*. Lawrence: UP of Kansas, 2012. Print.

Lofgren, Charles A. *The Plessy Case: A Legal-Historical Interpretation*. New York: Oxford UP, 1987. Print.

Woodward, C. Vann. *American Counterpoint: Slavery and Racism in the North-South Dialogue*. Boston: Little, Brown, 1971. Print.

PLURALISM V. ASSIMILATION

The Great Seal of the United States and several American coins carry the Latin motto *E pluribus unum*, or "One composed of many"—a social paradox that lies at the heart of the controversy over pluralism and assimilation.

These two terms represent contrasting views on the question of whether American society should perpetuate its diverse cultural and ethnic patterns or, rather, should blend homogeneously into a single culture with a common set of social practices. Those who favor pluralism want the distinctive features of the multiple social subgroups to flourish; those who favor assimilation think that all subgroups should move toward merging with the United States' traditional culture, which uses the English language and historically has been most heavily influenced by European—particularly British—social patterns.

Pluralists fear that assimilation leads to a crushing social conformity, while assimilationists fear that pluralism leads to the social disintegration of the nation.

The terms used in this debate have many variants. Approximate synonyms for pluralism include "multiculturalism" and "cultural pluralism." The term "segregation," though it carries many negative connotations because separateness was once legally enforced on African Americans, also describes extreme pluralism, since absolute pluralism would keep ethnic identities separate and intact. Hardly any theoretical academicians favor this extreme. However, some members of racial and ethnic subgroups fiercely defend their own social patterns and unique attributes, effectively accepting self-segregation as an ideal. The idea that blacks, for example, comprise a "separate nation" follows the teachings of the Nation of Islam.

ASSIMILATION

Assimilation—also sometimes called "depluralization," "amalgamation," "acculturation," and "Americanization"—is nearly synonymous with what in the 1960s was promoted as social integration. This was a process by which minorities (especially African Americans) could move into the dominant culture and enjoy its socioeconomic advantages. The civil rights movement of the 1950s and 1960s, led by leaders such as Martin Luther King, Jr., advocated assimilation as a means to achieve a just society that deemphasized ethnic differences and removed class and racial barriers to progress. Most white liberals and social planners supported social integration. Yet by 1990 the various experiments (and many failures) at making it work—notably compulsory busing as a means of achieving educational assimilation—had created widespread skepticism that social unity could be achieved. Some observers had come to doubt that a single society with common customs was even a worthy goal. Meanwhile, the economic gap between middle-class white Americans and the poorer classes—containing high percentages of black and Hispanic people—had widened.

Through most of the nation's history, Americans have viewed their country as a cultural "melting pot," and a pattern of cultural assimilation has been taken for granted. Second-generation immigrants—often white Europeans—generally drifted away from their cultural heritages, learned English, and moved into the social and economic mainstream. The myth grew that the United States had an amalgamated culture.

RISE OF PLURALISM

Beginning in the late 1960s and early 1970s, however, vocal minorities launched the "new ethnicity" movement to gain respect for their native cultures and ethnic identities and to question the traditional patterns of assimilation. Hispanic Americans joined in, as that group grew numerically in the Southwest and in many American cities. American Indians found leaders to voice their protests against the cultural majority. The black ethnocentrism of the 1970s had rediscovered the African heritage and promoted black pride. In 1977, Alex Haley's immensely popular book *Roots: An American Saga* (1976) was turned into a television miniseries; the book and series helped give African Americans a sense of collective identity— a shared story of suffering and survival to replace old cultural insecurities and negative images. By the late 1970s, many subgroups of Americans were vocal about expressing their own unique identities as well as their own grievances and political demands.

The traditional American ethos of the melting pot came under fire from feminists, lesbian and gay people, and other groups, including people with disabilities. They claimed that the dominant American culture had discriminated against them and had never let them assimilate; therefore, the way to meet their goals was to emphasize their differences. Increasing attention was paid to the idea that the American melting pot, rather than creating a unique society by melting many cultures into a new, synthesized culture, actually forced other cultures to acculturate to the ways of the dominant culture, which was largely of Anglo descent. The term white Anglo-Saxon Protestant (WASP) became an increasingly pejorative tag. Among the political ramifications of this perception was the fact that the US Congress was increasingly seen as a club of privileged white males who did not represent the American people. President Bill Clinton, after his 1992 election, vowed to make his administration "look like America," thereby acknowledging the popular appeal of social pluralism.

One clear irony of the movement toward pluralism in the late 1980s and 1990s was that, in the 1960s, assimilation had been essentially a liberal movement aimed at social reform. Yet by the early 1990s, the idea seemed conservative and, to many liberals, an outmoded idea. The new liberal position was to accept and respect ethnic and cultural diversity.

CONTEXT

Except for American Indians, the United States is a "nation of immigrants," so every American has a "first" culture demanding some degree of recognition. Thus, despite the "melting pot" myth, pluralism was not really new in 1970. African Americans had always been mostly segregated, because of white racist policies as well as immigration patterns, and maintained their own social patterns. Forced onto reservations in the eighteenth and nineteenth centuries, American Indians had also held on to vestiges of their heritages. Neither of these groups had been able to participate in the American dream of upward mobility. American Jews, though often economically successful, had also faced discrimination and traditionally maintained a social separateness. Every large American city had its "Little Italy" or "Chinatown"; ethnic sections and suburbs had always existed, proliferating as new groups of immigrants such as Middle Easterners and Asian Indians settled in the country. Separate religious sects such as the Mennonites and the Amish had also refused assimilation. Though many other Americans paid only lip service to the "hyphenated" part of their self-definitions, a widespread sense of heritage persisted among large numbers of individuals.

The 2010 US census showed a mosaic of racial and ethnic groups in the United States, with African Americans comprising 12.6 percent of the population; Hispanics, 16.3 percent; Asian Americans, 4.8 percent; and American Indians and Alaska Natives, 0.9 percent. The projection is that by 2050, racial and ethnic subgroups will make up nearly half of the country's population. It appears that "managing" pluralism so as to take full advantage of diverse cultural strengths while avoiding ethnic splintering of the country will be the greatest social challenge of the twenty-first century.

——*Roy Neil Graves*

BIBLIOGRAPHY AND FURTHER READING

Fuchs, Lawrence H. *The American Kaleidoscope: Race, Ethnicity, and the Civic Culture.* Hanover: Wesleyan UP, 1995. Print.

Hing, Bill Ong. *To Be an American: Cultural Pluralism and the Rhetoric of Assimilation.* New York: New York UP, 1997. Print.

Humes, Karen R., Nicholas A. Jones, and Roberto R. Ramirez; United States Census Bureau. "Overview of Race and Hispanic Origin: 2010." *2010 Census Briefs.* Washington, DC: US Census Bureau, March 2011. Digital file.

Lambert, Wallace E., and Donald M. Taylor. *Coping with Cultural and Racial Diversity in Urban America.* New York: Praeger, 1990. Print.

Morgan, Gordon D. *America without Ethnicity.* Port Washington: Kennikat, 1981. Print.

PLURALISM V. PARTICULARISM

These terms describe the ways that groups and individuals of differing ethnic, religious, cultural, racial, national, or other characteristics relate to one another and to society at large. Pluralism does not have a single meaning. Generally, it refers to the fact that modern society, at least in the West, is characterized by a diversity of fundamental philosophical, religious, and sociopolitical ideas or beliefs.

The early twentieth century educator and philosopher Horace Kallen originated the concept of cultural pluralism to represent an ideal society where ethnic groups would live in cooperation, harmony, and mutual respect, a democracy of nationalities free to cultivate difference while sharing loyalty to the nation. Kallen's view contrasted with assimilationist positions of his day, which sought to homogenize immigrant groups into a new American nationality.

Pluralism signifies conditions that encourage group diversity and the maintenance of group boundaries. Sociologist Milton Gordon theorized that various groups, each with a psychological sense of its own historical peoplehood, maintain some structural separation from each other in intimate primary group relationships and in certain aspects of institutional life. This separation creates the possibility of maintaining cultural patterns that are different from those of other groups and from the larger society.

In his textbook *Race and Ethnic Relations: American and Global Perspectives* (1985), Martin N. Marger identified several dimensions of pluralism. Cultural pluralism denotes the existence of distinct but coexisting groups within a common economic and political system, each preserving its own tradition and culture but loyal to the national unity. Structural pluralism entails the existence in some degree of segregated ethnic communities within which much of social life occurs for group members. Equalitarian pluralism occurs when groups maintain cultural and structural integrity and autonomy and remain relatively equal in power, participating freely and equally within common political and economic institutions. Inequalitarian pluralism results where groups maintain structural segregation and cultural distinctiveness but are unequal in political and economic power. Finally, in some nations, corporate pluralism arises where structural and cultural differences are protected by the state, and provisions are made to create an ethnically proportionate distribution of political and economic power.

Particularism implies the undivided adherence or devotion to one particular party, system, or interest. Sociologist Talcott Parsons paired particularism with universalism and termed them a pattern variable, a basic pattern of decision making and action for individuals and groups. Particularism, in contradistinction to universalism, depicts an orientation in which the values and criteria used to organize action and to make choices are internal to the person or group, without any reference to values or criteria beyond themselves.

A stance of particularism encourages people to identify only with their own ethnoracial category. Taking pluralism to the extreme, particularistic arguments deny that any common culture is possible or desirable. Extreme forms of particularism result in attitudes of ethnocentrism, cultural superiority, and separatism.

New multicultural models of pluralism emerged in the 1990s, seeking to redress the racial and economic inequalities of American society.

Multiculturalists insisted on promoting cultural equality rather than mere mutual respect and tied equality to empowerment and the equalization of power relations. This development sparked intense controversy among scholars and extended the ongoing debate on how a nation embraces human diversity and simultaneously promotes a commitment to a common culture.

——*Eric M. Levine*

BIBLIOGRAPHY AND FURTHER READING

Marger, Martin N. *Race and Ethnic Relations: American and Global Perspectives.* Belmont: Thomson, 2006. Print.

Murphy, Michael. *Multiculturalism : A Critical Introduction.* Milton Park: Routledge, 2012. *eBook Collection (EBSCOhost).* Web. 14 May 2015.

Qirko, Hector N. "Current Trends in Cultural Particularism: The Problem Does Seem to Lie with Anthropology." *Topics in Cognitive Science* 6.1 (2014): 155–156. *MEDLINE with Full Text.* Web. 14 May 2015.

Rodríguez-García, Dan. "Beyond Assimilation and Multiculturalism: A Critical Review of the Debate on Managing Diversity." *Journal of International Migration & Integration* 11.3 (2010): 251–271. *SocINDEX with Full Text.* Web. 14 May 2015.

Toffolo, Cris E. *Emancipating Cultural Pluralism.* Albany: State U of New York P, 2003. *eBook Collection (EBSCOhost).* Web. 14 May 2015.

PLYLER V. DOE

In May of 1973, the Texas legislature amended its education laws to require that persons who were illegally in the United States and in the state of Texas pay a modest tuition charge for attending the public schools. In passing the amendments, the Texas legislature noted that the federal government denied the benefits of at least eight federal programs, including the food stamp program and Supplemental Security Income (SSI), to illegal aliens. According to the state, the purpose of the amendment was to "prevent undue depletion of its limited revenues available for education, and to preserve the fiscal integrity of the state's school-financing system against an ever-increasing flood of illegal aliens." It further claimed that it did not have the same responsibility to provide free benefits at taxpayer expense to those people illegally within the state as to its own citizens.

A bare majority of five Supreme Court justices disagreed, on the grounds that a policy of charging illegal aliens a modest tuition fee was not a rational means of furthering the state's legitimate fiscal ends.

The majority conceded both that public education is not a fundamental right granted by the Constitution and that illegal aliens cannot be treated as a suspect class since they are in violation of federal law. The Court declined, however, to accept any suggestion that "illegal immigrants impose any significant burden" on the economy and therefore concluded that the policy, which provided free tuition to lawful citizens but declined free benefits to unlawful ones, failed to further a substantial state interest and therefore violated the equal protection clause of the Constitution.

The minority view, expressed by Chief Justice Warren Burger, argued that the legislative policy was clearly related to the legitimate state purposes of preserving the fiscal integrity of the state school system and not placing the burden of educating foreign nationals illegally in the state on its own tax-paying citizens: "It is simply not 'irrational,' " Burger concluded, for a state to determine that "it does not have the same responsibility to provide benefits for persons whose very presence… is illegal as it does to provide for persons lawfully present." Noting that Congress itself had denied certain benefits to illegals, the dissent was of the view that "by definition, illegal aliens have no right whatever to be here, and the state may reasonably, and constitutionally, elect

not to provide them with governmental service at the expense of those who are lawfully within the state."

This case was cited in an injunction against the implementation of Proposition 187, passed by the California electorate in 1994, which sought to deny certain benefits to illegal aliens in California. *Plyler v. Doe* has been a focal point in the debate over immigration policy and the problems in providing services to illegal immigrants. It should be noted that the Court in this case found only that Texas had failed to put forward sufficient evidence of the state's legitimate purpose in enacting the statute. This left open the possibility that future litigation on this issue may turn on the ability of a state to provide more complete evidence in the record of the state's objective and interest in such policies.

——*Robert M. Hardaway*

POGROM

Originally a Russian word meaning "destruction" or "devastation," as an international term, "pogrom" was applied to coordinated mob attacks by Russians against the lives and property of Jews, and to the systematic persecution of Jews living under the Nazis. A pogrom is an expression of religious and racial hatred that is directed toward an easily identified powerless minority and is either approved or condoned by authorities.

In modern Russian history, pogrom-like attacks were initially leveled against the Armenians, Tatars, and the Russian intelligentsia. As it is employed in many languages specifically to describe the pillage, murder, and rape of Russian Jews, however, the term "pogrom" denotes three large-scale waves of devastation between 1881 and 1921. Each of these pogroms surpassed the preceding one in scope and savagery

and occurred during periods of severe social and political upheaval in Russia. For example, the first pogroms of the 1880s followed the assassination of Czar Alexander II as a result of false rumors about widespread Jewish involvement in the plot. Mobs from more than two hundred towns, inspired by local leaders acting with official support, took part. Pogroms greatly influenced Russian Jewry and history. In their wake, the Russian government adopted systematic policies of discrimination, harassment, and persecution of the Jews. The murder of innocent individuals and whole families was commonplace. This led numerous European anti-Semites to conclude that violence was legitimate and thus helped to pave the way for pogroms to be carried out later in Poland and Germany.

——*Andrew C. Skinner*

POLICE BRUTALITY

Police brutality includes the excessive use of force to compel a citizen to obey police orders or to arrest someone, the excessive use of force to compel an assembly of people to disperse, the physical maltreatment of someone who has

already been taken into police custody (often for purposes of extracting a confession), and the use of deadly force against a fleeing suspect unless it is necessary to save the officer's own life or the lives of others.

Protest march in response to the Philando Castile shooting, St. Paul, Minnesota, July 7, 2016. By Fibonacci Blue from Minnesota, USA.

easily be second-guessed at leisure, often must be made with great speed, and it is often difficult to know exactly how much force is "excessive" in any particular instance. The main protection that police officers believe they possess is the respect and fear that others have of them; if they encounter signs of defiance or disrespect on the part of a citizen, they may feel compelled to arrest the person—and to use force if the person resists. The possibility of death and maiming at the hands of criminals is, moreover, a hazard of the job. The trust that police officers must place in one another in order to survive sometimes produces an "us versus them" attitude of distrust of citizens. When the public at large demands that police crack down on crime at all costs, police officers are tempted to violate individual rights in order to get results. Moreover, police officers' need to make split-second decisions tempts them to stereotype citizens by age, sex, and race; hence, decisions regarding whom to stop and when to use force may be made, or seem to be made, in a discriminatory manner.

URBAN RACIAL CHANGE AND POLICE BRUTALITY

From 1940 to 1990, the major cities of the northern and western United States, once overwhelmingly white, witnessed dramatic increases in their African American and Hispanic populations. Until the 1970's, however, the ranks of police officers consisted overwhelmingly of non-Hispanic whites. The tendency of big-city police officers, as time went on, to live in predominantly white suburbs further alienated them from many of those they policed, as did the replacement of foot patrols by two-person patrol cars. High unemployment among young urban blacks promoted petty crime and disorderly conduct, thereby making police-citizen confrontations more likely. The high physical identifiability of most African Americans, and the tendency of white Americans to stereotype them as potential criminals, made police brutality an issue with resonance for middle-class as well as poor blacks. In New York City, Chicago, Denver, and Los Angeles, complaints

Because of the stresses inherent in their work, some tendency toward brutality has probably always existed among police officers. In the second half of the twentieth century, however, the changing racial makeup of large cities has made the American public (and that of some other countries) more sensitive to the problem than ever before. Although urban riots triggered by allegations of police brutality made headlines in the 1960's, 1980's, early 1990's, and 2010's, a less well publicized, peaceful struggle against police brutality has proceeded throughout the United States along several fronts: the push for civilian complaint review boards, civil suits and criminal prosecutions, Supreme Court decisions, and reforms within the police departments themselves.

POLICE SUBCULTURE AND POLICE BRUTALITY

To do their job, police officers must be able to use physical force as a last resort to compel obedience, and they inevitably must be granted a certain amount of leeway, or discretion, as to when such force is to be used. The decision to use force, although it can about police brutality frequently arose among Hispanics as well as blacks.

Although most controversial incidents of police use of force have elicited only peaceful protests, minority group anger over alleged police brutality has sometimes exploded into violence. For example, riots erupted in New York City in July, 1964 (after a police officer killed a black youth); in Los Angeles in 1965; in cities throughout the United States in 1967; in Miami in May, 1980 (after the police officers who had beaten to death a black motorcyclist were acquitted); in Miami again in January, 1989 (after a black motorcyclist was shot to death by a police officer); in Los Angeles on April 29-May 1, 1992 (after the acquittal of police officers involved in the video-taped beating of black motorist Rodney King); and in Ferguson, Missouri, on August 9, 2014 (after a white police officer killed an unarmed black teenager).

POLICE BRUTALITY AND PUBLIC ASSEMBLY
Excessive use of force against people demonstrating publicly for particular causes was a common complaint in the 1960's, a decade of unusual political ferment in the United States; even after that era ended, such incidents sometimes occurred. Examples include the use of police dogs against blacks demanding desegregation in southern cities in the early 1960's, the clubbing of youthful (and mostly white) demonstrators against the Vietnam War in Chicago in August, 1968, and the use, in 1989, of painful restraint devices against predominantly white antiabortion demonstrators in Los Angeles.

CIVILIAN POLICE REVIEW BOARDS
Handling citizen complaints about police brutality was the exclusive concern of police department internal affairs units until the late 1950's and early 1960's, when the American Civil Liberties Union joined minority civil rights activists in demanding the establishment of civilian review boards (bodies with at least half their members from outside the police department) to hear such complaints. A civilian review board was instituted in New York City in 1966 but was abolished after a referendum; it was not reestablished until 1993. By 1990, about half of the fifty largest American cities had some form of civilian oversight over the police.

Police officers who opposed civilian review boards feared that such bodies would be dominated by militant antipolice activists; on the other hand, it was also argued that civilian arbiters would accept excuses for brutality that would never pass muster with professional police officers. By the early 1990's, scholarly advocates of civilian review boards, while conceding their imperfections, viewed them as a necessary (although inefficient) way to assure citizens that complaints of brutality would be treated fairly.

FIGHTING POLICE BRUTALITY THROUGH THE COURTS
Even though the beating of Rodney King by members of the Los Angeles Police Department on March 3, 1991, was recorded on videotape, the four officers who had beaten him were acquitted in their first jury trial, before a state court, on April 29, 1992. For a number of reasons, many police officers suspected of acts of brutality are never brought to trial at all. District attorneys, who need willing police cooperation to try cases, are usually reluctant to prosecute police; police officers are usually unwilling to testify against other officers; it is widely understood that jurors often sympathize with police officers; and victims of police brutality are not always entirely blameless individuals. One of the few cases in which a police officer was both prosecuted and convicted of brutality in a state criminal trial was that of New York City patrolman Thomas Ryan, sentenced in 1977 to four years in prison by a Bronx jury for beating Israel Rodriguez to death in 1975. Another was the sentencing of two white Detroit police officers to stiff prison terms in 1993 for the 1992 death of a black man, Malice Green.

Police officers can also be tried on federal criminal charges of having violated the brutality victim's civil rights. In April, 1993, two of the four officers who had beaten Rodney King were convicted of such charges. In *Monroe v. Pape* (1961), the Supreme Court laid the basis for such legal action by holding that the Civil Rights Acts of 1871 (originally passed to protect African Americans in the South) applied to abuses of power by local police officers anywhere in the country. As of the early 1990's, however, federal trials of local police officers were rare. The Department of Justice lacked the personnel to check up on police abuses throughout the country.

Two milestones made civil suits a more effective means of obtaining redress: the Supreme Court decision (unconnected with police brutality) in *Monell v. New York City Department of Social Services* (1978), holding local governments financially liable for the transgressions of their employees, and a 1976 act of Congress permitting judges to award attorneys' fees to a plaintiff if the plaintiff wins the case. In April, 1994, Rodney King was awarded $3.8 million in damages from the city of Los Angeles; other American cities have also paid out considerable sums. Brutality lawsuits have the best chance of success when the victim has suffered obvious physical harm. In 2015 and 2016, the families of Eric Garner and Tamir Rice received $5.9 and $6 million, respectively, as part of out-of-court settlements. The police officers involved were never indicted for these events.

THE SUPREME COURT AND POLICE BRUTALITY

In the decisions *Brown v. Mississippi* (1936) and *Rochin v. California* (1952), the Supreme Court voided criminal convictions based on confessions extracted by torture. Under Chief Justice Earl Warren (whose term lasted from 1953 to 1968), the Supreme Court increasingly imposed on state and local police forces the restrictions of the Bill of Rights, which had been formerly imposed only on federal authorities. In *Mapp v. Ohio* (1961), the Court ordered local police to obey the Fourth Amendment's ban on searches without warrant; in *Miranda v. Arizona* (1966), it ordered the police to inform those in custody of their rights to remain silent and to have legal counsel. The Court provided no guidelines for disciplining erring officers; it only stated that evidence obtained through torture or illegal searches could not be used in a trial.

After Warren's retirement, the Supreme Court no longer led the way in the fight against police brutality. In *Rizzo v. Goode* (1976), the justices, in a 5-4 decision, declined to interfere in the operations of the Philadelphia police department, which had been accused of systematic brutality toward minorities. In *Lyons v. Los Angeles* (1982), the Court refused to outlaw the use of chokeholds by the Los Angeles Police Department. In two cases decided in 1984, the Court allowed certain exceptions to the rules established in *Mapp* and *Miranda*. In 1985, in *Tennessee v. Garner*, the justices decreed that the police should no longer automatically have the right to shoot at a fleeing felony suspect, but this doctrine had already been adopted by many local police departments before the Supreme Court ratified it.

POLICE CHIEFS' AND THE DOJ'S EFFORTS AT REFORM

In the 1960's, critics of the police accused police chiefs of automatically defending any officer accused of brutality. During the 1970's and 1980's, however, chiefs of police in many American cities took measures to discipline officers guilty of brutality and to reduce the number of incidents in the future. Black and Hispanic police chiefs, becoming more common by the 1980's, made special efforts in this regard. In 1972, New York City police commissioner Patrick V. Murphy instituted strict new rules governing the use of deadly force; in 1985, New York City police commissioner Benjamin Ward punished officers who had used stun guns against suspects in their custody. In 1990, Kansas City police chief Steven Bishop summarily dismissed officers who had severely beaten a suspect involved in a high-speed car chase. Police departments in Oakland, California, and Miami, Florida, aided by social scientists, instituted programs to teach officers how to defuse potentially violent police-citizen confrontations. Some departments brought back foot patrols to enable officers to get to know people in minority neighborhoods better. Even in Los Angeles, where real reform began only after the 1992 riot and the subsequent retirement of police chief Daryl Gates, widespread public outcry in the early 1980's ended the use of chokeholds. After unrest in Ferguson, Missouri, in the summer of 2014, the practice of employing military-grade equipment has come under greater scrutiny. In the 2010's, many police departments adapted the use of body cameras to strive for greater transparency.

Due to the civil unrest following the spate of unarmed citizens killed by police officers in the 2010's, the US Department of Justice decided to track police shootings and other violent encounters. Meanwhile, the Justice Department under Attorney General Loretta Lynch took a more aggressive approach to oversight of individual city police departments having histories of police brutality and discrimination, such as Baltimore, Ferguson, and Chicago. Their findings from Ferguson, for example, did not support civil rights charges against Darren Wilson, the officer who shot Michael Brown on August 9, 2014; however, they did find a pattern of systemic racism, stating that "the Ferguson Police Department (FPD) engaged in a pattern or practice of conduct that violates the First, Fourth, and 14th Amendments of the Constitution."

Such oversight can help hold police departments accountable. On the other hand, Lynch's successor, Jeff Sessions, dismissed the findings of the reports on Ferguson and Chicago without ever reading them. Thus, the positive steps overseen by Lynch might very well prove fleeting.

MINORITY RECRUITMENT AND POLICE BRUTALITY

Affirmative action has increased the percentage of minority officers in police departments and reduced somewhat the level of prejudice-motivated brutality, but it has not worked miracles. Minority police officers are sometimes guilty of brutality themselves. In 1994, in Detroit, Michigan, and Compton, California, black police officers were accused by Hispanic activists of brutality against Hispanics. The Miami police officer who shot to death a black motorcyclist in 1989 was Hispanic.

ATTEMPTS AT CONTROLLING BRUTALITY

Although considerable progress in decreasing police brutality was made in the 1980's, the Rodney King beating brought home the fact that brutality was still a problem in the 1990's. Three examples of events that engendered protests from 1994 and 1995 illustrate the continued existence of the problem. Protests arose in New York City in April, 1994, after a black man died in police custody; in Paterson, New Jersey, in February, 1995, after police shot a black teenager; and in Cincinnati, Ohio, in April, 1995, after a white police officer was videotaped beating an eighteen-year-old black youth.

In spite of such examples, however, some scholars saw a general trend toward stricter regulation of the police use of force. They view the actions and attitudes (and what was described by an investigative commission as the "siege mentality") of the pre-1992 Los Angeles Police Department, for example, as an exception rather than the rule. Although in 1990 civil libertarians in Chicago accused the police of torturing alleged police-killer Andrew Wilson while he was in custody, torture of suspects by the police was almost certainly much less common by the mid-1990's than it had been in 1931, when the federally appointed Wickersham Commission found such "third-degree" tactics to be widespread. Between 1970 and 1984, shooting deaths of fleeing suspects, although not completely eliminated, decreased in

number, and the once yawning gap in police shooting deaths between blacks and whites had appreciably narrowed.

Just as the Rodney King beating did in the 1990's, a string of police killings in the 2010's belied the perception of progress. On July 17, 2013, Eric Garner was killed by Daniel Pantaleo, an NYPD officer, performing a choke hold on him–a tactic that is prohibited by the NYPD. On August 9, 2014, Ferguson police officer Darren Wilson shot Michael Brown, who was unarmed at the time. On November 22, 2014, Cleveland police officer Timothy Loehmann killed twelve-year-old Tamir Rice; the child had a toy gun on him. Video evidence shows Loehmann shooting Rice within two seconds of his arrival on the scene police also failed to administer first aid to the dying child for over four minutes and put his fourteen-year-old sister in handcuffs for trying to help her brother. On April 4, 2015, North Charleston police officer Michael Slager shot Walter Scott, who was unarmed and running away away from the officer. Slager then attempted to plant his own taser on Scott's body. In all of these instances, the victim was black and the officer was white. These events—and others like them—occurred amid increasing public attention and calls for police reform. Some advocates point to many police departments' implementation of body cameras as a silver-lining to these tragedies; however, they mostly stand as a stark reminder of the progress that remains to be made.

——*Paul D. Mageli, updated by Anthony Vivian*

BIBLIOGRAPHY AND FURTHER READING

Balko, Radley. *Rise of the Warrior Cop: The Militarization of America's Police Forces.* Washington, DC: PublicAffairs, 2014. Print.

Bornstein, Jerry. *Police Brutality: A National Debate.* Hillside: Enslow, 1993. Print.

Nelson, Jill, ed. *Police Brutality: An Anthology.* New York: Norton, 2001. Print.

Skolnick, Jerome H. *Justice Without Trial: Law Enforcement in Democratic Society,* 4th ed. New Orleans: Quid Pro, 2011. Print.

Spence, Gerry. *Police State: How America's Cops Get Away with Murder.* New York: St. Martin's, 2015. Print.

Walker, Samuel, and Charles Katz. *The Police in America: An Introduction,* 8th ed. New York: McGraw-Hill Education, 2013. Print.

POLISH AMERICANS

Polish Americans (White ethnics) are generally defined as those whose heritage was connected to the Polish language, culture, and Roman Catholicism. Polish Americans who arrived between 1608 and 1800 came for personal reasons, and those emigrating from 1800 to 1860 came to escape foreign control over their homeland. The third and largest wave of 2.5 million immigrants between 1870 and 1924, sought to escape the economic hardships of their homeland. After World War II, a fourth wave of Polish came to the United States as displaced persons or political refugees fleeing the communist government.

INTERGROUP RELATIONS

The relatively small number of Polish arriving during the first two immigration periods meant that intergroup relations were rather limited. The settlers who arrived from 1608 to 1800 did not establish communities, and relations with others in the United States were almost exclusively on an individual basis. However, Polish Americans who served during the American Revolutionary War were regarded positively, and the political refugees, who made up the bulk of the next wave, gained the respect of Americans for their dedication to independence, nationalism, and liberalism. The large group of Polish arriving during the 1870-1924 wave interacted as a group with established American society, with earlier immigrants, and with other eastern and southern European immigrants.

Because most Polish immigrants came to the United States to work as unskilled laborers in urban-industrial areas, established Americans viewed them as essential but not necessarily welcome additions. The vast differences in language and customs and the formation of distinct ethnic communities caused many people to question whether Polish could ever adapt to American society. Established Americans also mistrusted Polish because of their support of labor unions and their use of alcoholic beverages, which were contrary to Protestant ethics of individualism and sobriety.

Relations between Polish Americans and earlier immigrants were often strained. The Polish resented the English, Welsh, Scottish, and Irish immigrants who constituted the skilled laborers and bosses in the mines, mills, and factories. The Polish reacted against Irish American control of the Roman Catholic hierarchy by forming their own ethnic national parishes. This desire for a separate Polish Catholic identity became so strong that a schism with Roman Catholicism occurred when the Reverend Francis Hodur founded the Polish National Church in 1904.

Although this group of Polish faced circumstances similar to those faced by other immigrants from southern and eastern Europe, relations between these groups were not always the best. The Polish held stereotypical views of and harbored resentments against other Slavs, and many had come to the United States with a tradition of anti-Semitism. When the Polish and Lithuanians shared churches, the result was less than harmonious, and splits were usually the result. Although direct confrontations with Italians were not common, each group often accepted the prevalent stereotypes about the other.

However, Polish American businesspeople often had solid working relationships with people of various ethnic backgrounds. Many young Polish immigrant women served as domestics in the homes of Euro-Americans or Jewish Americans and built a warm relationship with their employers. Despite the remnants of Old World anti-Semitism, Polish laborers and Jewish shopkeepers developed respectful and trusting business dealings. The Polish cooperated with other immigrants from eastern and southern Europe to form labor unions. Their success in this venue played an important role in the establishment of unions as a powerful force in the United States.

ASSIMILATION AND INTERGROUP RELATIONS

By the 1920's, the passage of time and restrictive immigration laws hastened the assimilation process. Although Polish Americans were becoming more Americanized, new social structures were being established, altering intergroup relations. During the latter part of the twentieth century, Polish American intergroup relations involved the relations of the more elderly urban blue-collar workers, the white-collar professionals, and the new associations of refugees from Poland.

Many urban blue-collar workers came of age during the Great Depression and World War II. They endured a life of sacrifice and want but were able to gain social and economic mobility in the postwar boom years. However, by the 1970's, economic decline had hit the major employers of many Polish Americans, and an increasing number of African Americans and Hispanics had moved into traditionally Polish neighborhoods. Although most Polish Americans had adequate financial resources to sustain them into retirement, the combination of their weakened economic situation and the loss of their ethnic communities often resulted in resentment toward the newer residents. Although violent conflict was rare, tensions were high between urban Polish Americans and their new neighbors, the African Americans and Hispanics. Polish white-collar professionals, who often married non-Polish, tended to identify less with the ethnic group and more with the concerns of their socioeconomic class. At times, this caused them to become estranged from the older Polish Americans. The refugees from communism, relatively small in number, tended to affiliate with their socioeconomic and employment peers.

Despite the differences in class and status, Polish Americans still face a certain degree of discrimination. Stereotypes that depict Polish Americans as lacking intelligence have been especially hurtful.

Polish American acceptance of such humor has perhaps, contributed to this prejudice. Although Polish Americans increasingly identify with middle-class values, some of these traditional patterns of intergroup dynamics persist.

——*Paul J. Zbiek*

BIBLIOGRAPHY AND FURTHER READING

Bukowczyk, John J. *Polish Americans and Their History: Community, Culture, and Politics.* Pittsburgh: U of Pittsburgh P, 2006. Print.

Gatush, William John. *For More than Bread: Community and Identity in American Polonia, 1880-1940.* Boulder: East European Monographs, 2006. Print.

Jaroszynska-Kirchmann, Anna D. *The Exile Mission: The Polish Political Diaspora and Polish Americans, 1939-1956.* Athens: Ohio UP, 2004. Print.

Lopata, Helena Z. *Polish Americans,* 2d ed. New Brunswick: Transaction, 1994. Print.

Pula, James S., ed. *The Polish American Encyclopedia.* Jefferson: McFarland, 2011. Print.

Silverman, Deborah Anders. *Polish American Folklore.* Urbana: U of Illinois P, 2000. Print.

POLITICAL CARTOONS AND ISLAM: AN OVERVIEW

In September 2005, the Danish newspaper *Jyllands-Posten* published twelve cartoons, many depicting caricatures of the Islamic prophet Muhammad. In many Islamic traditions, it is strictly forbidden to depict Muhammad. Furthermore, many of the cartoons associated Muhammad with Islamic fundamentalism and terrorist acts. For many Muslims in Denmark and abroad, the images were deeply offensive and constituted an act of blasphemy. Strong reactions from local Muslim organizations drew international attention to the cartoons, leading newspapers and magazines around the world to subsequently republish them. Protests erupted throughout the Muslim world in reaction to the widespread republication of the cartoons.

The publication of the Danish cartoons and the passionate response from Muslims and other critics of the images generated an international debate over multiculturalism, religious tolerance, the limits of free speech, and self-censorship. Critics decried the Danish cartoons as insensitive, Islamophobic, and racist. Others argued that the publication of such cartoons is expression of free speech, and contributes to an ongoing dialogue over Islam and the threat of Islamic fundamentalism.

While the Danish cartoons drew a significant amount of international attention, they are not an isolated incident. The animated television show *South Park* has further deepened this controversy by depicting Muhammad in several episodes, three of which were censored by television networks. And the controversial 'Everybody Draw Muhammad Day,' in 2010, was organised in defiance of threats against the Danish cartoonists and the producers of *South Park. Charlie Hebdo,* a satirical French magazine, has also published controversial cartoons depicting Muhammad, which resulted in terrorist attacks against the organization in 2011 and 2015. The depictions of Muhammad in cartoons and animation are meant, in part, to celebrate the right to free speech in democratic countries. They have also led to continued protests and criticism from those who see such cartoons as acts of blasphemy or prejudice against Islamic peoples.

HISTORY

During various periods in the history of Judaism, Christianity, and Islam, the depiction of religious figures or icons was expressly prohibited. In Judaism and Christianity, the second commandment forbids the fashioning and worship of idols. Some early Christian sects were wary of depicting any religious image other than the cross, and some Christian groups today still question whether it is appropriate to depict religious figures such as saints. Such prohibitions exist to prevent people from worshiping an image of something rather than what the image represents.

Although the Qur'an, the central religious text of Islam, does not forbid the depiction of Muhammad, later Islamic writings forbid the practice. Today, the acceptability of depicting Muhammad is a topic of debate within Muslim societies. Typically, Sunni Muslims believe that the depiction of the prophets should be forbidden, especially those of Muhammad. Many Shia Muslims, though, accept or tolerate respectful depictions of Muhammad.

In 2005, Danish author Kåre Bluitgen set out to write a children's book on the life of Muhammad. Bluitgen had difficulty finding an illustrator for the book, with many authors fearing that depicting Muhammad would make them a target of violence from fundamentalist Muslims. The difficulty in finding an illustrator, combined with recent incidents of fundamentalist violence in Europe, led to a debate over self-censorship and the public criticism of Islam. On September 17, 2005, the Danish newspaper *Politiken* published an article entitled, 'The profound anxiety about the criticism of Islam', which discussed artists who avoided the subject of Islam for fear of violent retaliation.

On September 30, 2005, in response to the debate over self-censorship, the Danish newspaper *Jyllands-Posten* published twelve politically motivated cartoons, the majority of which depict Muhammad. Along with the cartoons was a brief editorial text arguing that Islam should not be immune to criticism and ridicule. The cartoons accompanying the

text were particularly critical of fundamentalist Islam, with some of them portraying Muhammad as a terrorist. One of the most controversial cartoons depicted Muhammad with a bomb in his turban.

The publication of the cartoons roused an immediate response from local Muslim organizations that condemned the cartoons. The Danish government refused to intervene in the emerging controversy, so Muslim organizations decided to mount a legal challenge to the publication of the cartoons, claiming that the cartoons violated Danish laws against blasphemy and racial prejudice. Under the Danish legal system, it is illegal to disrupt public order by publically disrespecting any religious group; it is also illegal to publically attack citizens based on their race, ethnicity, or sexual orientation. The case was dropped after a prosecutor argued that there was insufficient evidence that the cartoons violated the law.

The legal challenge to the cartoons attracted an international response. In covering the story, many newspapers and magazines throughout the world reprinted the cartoons, increasing exposure to the images. The vast international republication of the cartoons prompted a wave of protests throughout the Muslim world and inspired harsh criticisms. Some of the protests turned violent, resulting in acts of vandalism and stampedes. (In fact, six were killed during protests in Afghanistan, Somalia, and Lebanon in February 2006.) Danish Muslim leaders toured the Middle East, decrying the publication of the cartoons and calling for greater recognition of and respect for the Muslim faith. Several death threats were made against the cartoonists and those responsible for publishing them, and consumers in many Muslim countries organised a boycott of all Danish goods.

Other critics came out against the publication of the cartoons. Various Muslim and non-Muslim organizations denounced the cartoons as insensitive, racist, and Islamophobic. Some argued that the cartoons unfairly associated Muhammad and Islam with fundamentalism and terrorism, reducing the religion to its most extreme forms. After republishing the cartoons, the Danish newspaper *Politiken* apologised for any offense they might have caused. While supporting the Danish newspaper's right to freedom of speech and freedom of the press, the United States government condemned the cartoons for inciting ethnic and religious strife. And in 2009, Yale University Press exercised self-censorship by removing the cartoons from the book *The Cartoons that Shook the World*, by Jytte Klausen, which was written about the scandal.

In response to the political and economic fallout, many came out in support of the cartoonists, arguing that the cartoons were an expression of freedom of speech. Others argued that the true motivation behind not publishing images of Islamic or any religious figure was a result not of sensitivity or tolerance, but of fear of reprisal. Newspapers, journalists, artists, and writers in Denmark and around the world supported the right of journalists and cartoonists to freely express their views on religion.

In the years following the publication of the cartoons, controversy, provocation, and violence continued. On the anniversary of the cartoons' publication, a video was issued showing members of the Danish People's Party, a right-wing political party, participating in a contest to see who could draw the most insulting cartoon of Muhammad. The video reignited debate over the cartoons. Death threats, which had begun immediately after the 2005 publication of the cartoons, from various Muslim organizations continued against the cartoonists, and in October 2008, Qari Yousuf Ahmadi, a spokesperson for the Taliban, stated that Danish troops in Afghanistan would be targeted specifically because of the cartoons.

In defiance of threats of violence against cartoonists and the censorship of *South Park* cartoons depicting Muhammad, cartoonist Molly Norris organised the controversial "Everybody Draw Muhammad Day." The idea spread through the social networking site Facebook, gathering a number of supporters while instigating further criticism and protests. Consequently, another group, "Against 'Everybody Draw Muhammad Day'," was also established on the social networking site.

POLITICAL CARTOONS & ISLAM TODAY

The controversy over the *Jyllands-Posten* cartoons prompted a surge of Muslim animosity towards the West, erupting in protests throughout the Muslim world and threats of violence from extremists. The publication of the cartoons also symbolised an act of freedom of speech, a core value of many Western democracies. Supporters of the cartoons argued that although the expression of freedom of speech might not always be respectful, it is a fundamental aspect of any democratic society. They stated that the

cartoons were a political intervention into the dialogue over freedom of speech and self-censorship. To supporters, the cartoons were published, in part, as a way of expressing that Islam should not be exempted from public criticism and ridicule. It was also contended that the cartoons were published as an act of defiance against possible threats of violence. In contrast, critics of the cartoons found them disrespectful, blasphemous, and intentionally provocative.

The controversy was deepened because of the growing Muslim presence in European countries. There are between 1.3 and 1.8 billion Muslims worldwide in the early twenty-first century; obviously, consensus among such a large (and geographically disseminated) group is nearly impossible to attain. Some Muslims were wary of the publication of cartoons not because of religious doctrine, but because of the backlash they anticipated from other Muslim groups, as well as the worldwide response to that backlash. This backlash ranged from civilised–protests and boycotts of Danish goods–to fanatical–death threats and attempted murder. (Kurt Westergaard, the artist who drew the image of Muhammad in a bomb/turban, was attacked in 2010, five years after the cartoon's publication, by a twenty-eight year-old Muslim man from Somali, and two years prior, was the subject of an assassination plot conspired by three Muslim men, two of whom were from Tunisia and the other from Morocco.) The moderate Islamic community was understandably concerned about the provocation of its radical factions, as their response can contribute to the vicious cycle of increased secular scrutiny and provocation of potentially violent fundamentalists, and subsequent anti-Muslim sentiment.

Jytte Klausen, the author of *The Cartoons that Shook the World*, argues that rather than being an issue of culture, the controversy over the cartoons was the product of competing political interests. Within Denmark, different political groups and organizations used the controversy as a means to express and advance their own platforms, whether for greater recognition of the Danish Muslim community, or to stir anti-Islamic sentiment. Fundamentalist groups used the publication of the cartoons as a way of rousing public anger against the West and mobilised protests aimed at destabilizing governments in the Muslim world, particularly in Pakistan, Lebanon, Libya, and Nigeria.

Although both Australia and New Zealand republished the cartoons in local news publications, the two countries have so far avoided the same level of controversy as European and Middle Eastern countries. In particular, then-New Zealand Prime Minister Helen Clark and former opposition leader (of the National Party) Don Brash, both condemned the cartoons while stating that it was up to news publications to decide whether to republish the cartoons. New Zealand Muslim groups also expressed discontent over the cartoons and their republication in New Zealand, but insisted that Muslim communities not boycott Danish goods.

In 2012, an anti-Islam film produced in the United States and posted on YouTube drew worldwide outrage within the Muslim community over. Titled *The Innocence of Muslims,* the movie—for which two fourteen-minute "trailers" were posted on YouTube—depicts Muhammad as a degenerate. Protests over the film erupted in the Middle East, as well as several European nations, and Australia. In Sydney, protests on September 15 turned violent when police and protestors clashed outside the US Consulate. The incident resulted in the arrest of several protestors, and drew condemnations from then-prime minister Julia Gillard, and a group of the country's Muslim leaders. In 2015, terrorists attacked the offices of *Charlie Hebdo,* a satirical French magazine that published what many considered to be derogatory images of Muhammad. Twelve people were killed in the attack, which sparked both outrage in France and other countries around the world and debate about the limits of free speech. Australians and New Zealanders generally supported the magazine's right to publish, but some journalists noted that such cartoons would likely be deemed illegal in Australia under section 18C of the Racial Discrimination Act.

——*Alexandra Neame*

BIBLIOGRAPHY AND FURTHER READING

Hull, G. *Muhammad: The "Banned" Images,* Gilbert: Voltaire, 2009. Print.

Klausen, J. *The Cartoons That Shook the World.* New Haven: Yale UP, 2009. Print.

Reports & Periodicals

Agius, Christine. "Performing Identity: The Danish Cartoon Crisis and Discourses of Identity and Security." *Security Dialogue* 44.3 (2013): 241–58. Print.

Bjorner, S. 'Mohammad Cartoons: The Online History of an International Controversy', *Searcher* 16.8 (2008): 55–59. Print.

"Fears Cartoons Depicting Mohammed in French Magazine Charlie Hebdo May Fan Islamic Anger." *Australian.* Australian, 19 Sept. 2012. Web. 23 Sept. 2012.

Glyn, Justin. "Free Speech beyond the Pale." *Eureka Street* 19 Oct. 2012: 47–48. Print.

Kessler, Clive S. "Islamophobia as a Moral Bludgeon." *Australian.* Australian, 20 Sept. 2012. Web. 23 Sept. 2014.

Levey, G, and Modood, T. 'The Muhammad Cartoons and Multicultural Democracies'. *Ethnicities,* 9.3 (2009): 427–447. Print.

Soage, A. B. 'The Danish Caricatures Seen from the Arab World', *Totalitarian Movements and Political Religions* 7.3 (2006): 362–369. Print.

West, Andrew. "Islamophobia: Reality or Myth?" *ABC.* ABC, 26 Sept. 2012. Web. 23 Sept. 2014.

POLITICAL CORRECTNESS

Political correctness, or PC, although reputed to be a form of censorship, can justly claim that it has made a positive contribution to improving race relations. It is an ideology based on the principle that in a truly democratic, egalitarian, and multicultural society, there must be a sympathetic understanding of the needs and rights of all people, without regard for race, sex, nationality, age, physical condition, or even sexual orientation. Fundamental to PC is the belief that racially and other negatively charged words must be purged from discourse, including both blatantly offensive terms and those that have been interpreted as carrying subtler or hidden slurs. The movement has thus helped sensitize people to the fact that language and certain types of seemingly innocent behavior can mask, among other things, racial stereotyping and bias. For example, a "flesh-colored" bandage is colored so that it matches the skin tones of whites, not African Americans or Asian Americans. Calling someone an "Indian giver" perpetuates a usage based on an old stereotype of Native Americans.

Although the term "political correctness" was coined in 1975 by the president of the National Organization for Women, Karen DeCrow, it was not widely used until the late 1980s, when opponents employed the term in critical attacks on the ideology's adherents and their aims. Detractors argued that the movement to divest the English language of derogatory terms and grammatical usage had gone to irrational lengths—finding, for example, racial and gender insults in perfectly innocent expressions. The term thus carries the implication of an excessive, witch-hunting effort to control both language and thought, and it has become the object of condemnation that has at times seemed justified.

PC and the Disadvantaged
Whatever its excesses, PC has promoted a multicultural sensitivity working in tandem with the civil and human rights movements. It is not, of course, limited strictly to language or racial concerns. For example, the visuals in media programming have also been scrutinized for offensive, stereotypical images that carry negative messages about various groups, including African Americans, women, the elderly, gays, religious minorities, and the handicapped. Politically, PC has been identified with the Left, largely because it has advocated changes that undermine the status quo; therefore, from a conservative perspective, it is seen as an insidious tool of political liberals, particularly dangerous because of its influence on schools and their curricula.

PC and Education
Although many advocates of curriculum revision in public schools argue that there is really no such thing as political correctness, since the early 1980's a continuing effort has been made to select books and develop lesson plans and courses that reflect a new multicultural awareness and tolerance for others who do not have a stake in the heterosexual male, Euro-American heritage that has dominated traditional schoolbooks and much course content

in the humanities. Opponents of these changes have used political correctness as a tarring brush, claiming that proposed revisions have been politically motivated by special-interest groups less interested in learning than in advancing their own interests and political agendas. In higher education, critics complain, history is being badly distorted and the literary canon attacked, not by consideration of merit but by the political ends of underrepresented writers, including African Americans. According to detractors, the revamping of the canon has forced the exclusion of deserving works simply because they were written by "dead white males." Thus it is that academia remains the principal battleground for PC advocates and those who support a return to "the three R's" (the fundamentals: reading, writing, and arithmetic).

Political Incorrectness
In the 1990s, it became fashionable to be politically *incorrect*, not by using offensive language but by mocking the flagrant extremes to which adherents of PC have sometimes gone in efforts to rid language of hurtful words and phrases. No educated, rational person would promote the use of racially offensive or demeaning words in public debate or discourse. However, some PC advocates have made the ideology susceptible to ridicule through their extreme efforts to make language agreeable to all. They have tried to replace simple and direct words with neutral but colorless words, awkward circumlocutions, and ridiculous neologisms, whereby, for example, short people become "the vertically challenged" and the unemployed become "the involuntarily idled." Some, in their excesses, have made the job of the parodist easy, as in the efforts of radical feminists to expunge the word "man" from the English language, replacing, for example, "manhole" with "femhole." Such substitutions are easy to mock and attack as examples of reverse discrimination. They give fuel to those who believe that the true agenda of PC is to replace the dominant cultural values of the United States and Canada with those of minority and special-interest groups without regard to truth or fact. The harshest critics claim that the movement is a new sort of tyranny imposed from the political Left and warn that reactions to it could result, not in improving, but in deteriorating racial and ethnic relations. The 2016 presidential campaign of Donald Trump was

propelled, in part, by the candidate's open disregard for political correctness.

THE NEED FOR PC

Political correctness remains a theoretical lodestone for improving the lot of society's disadvantaged. It accepts as a fundamental concept what linguists and social psychologists have argued for years—that language does more than simply reflect social values; it both facilitates and empowers the biases of those who shape and control it. Its advocates must be cautious, however. Little is gained if one sort of intolerance is replaced by another, if, for example, one group is demonized in an effort to facilitate the political agenda of another.

——*John W. Fiero*

BIBLIOGRAPHY AND FURTHER READING

Berstein, Richard. *Dictatorship of Virtue: Multiculturalism and the Battle for America's Future* (New York: Knopf, 1994. Print.

Collini, Stefan. *That's Offensive! Criticism, Identity, Respect.* New York: Seagull, 2010. Print.

D'Souza, Dinesh. *Illiberal Education: The Politics of Race and Sex on Campus.* New York: Free Press, 1991. Print.

Fox, Claire. *"I Find That Offensive!"* London: Biteback, 2016. Print.

Hentoff, Nat. *Free Speech for Me—but Not for Thee.* New York: HarperCollins, 1992. Print.

Hughes, Geoffrey. *Political Correctness: A History of Semantics and Culture.* Malden: Wiley-Blackwell, 2010. Print.